The Law of Debtors
and Creditors

11 U.S.C. §547(c)(1)

Published by Wolters Kluwer in New York.

Wolters Kluwer Legal & Regulatory U.S. serves customers worldwide with CCH, Aspen Publishers, and Kluwer Law International products. (www.WKLegaledu.com)

To contact Customer Service, e-mail customer.service@wolterskluwer.com, call 1-800-234-1660, fax 1-800-901-9075, or mail correspondence to:

> Wolters Kluwer
> Attn: Order Department
> PO Box 990
> Frederick, MD 21705

Printed in the United States of America.

2 3 4 5 6 7 8 9 0

ISBN 978-1-4548-9351-6 (Casebound)

Library of Congress Cataloging-in-Publication Data

Names: Warren, Elizabeth, author. | Westbrook, Jay Lawrence, author. |
   Porter, Katherine (Katherine M.) author. | Pottow, John A. E., author.
Title: The law of debtors and creditors : text, cases, and problems /
   Elizabeth Warren, Leo Gottlieb Professor of Law Emeritus, Harvard
   University; Jay Lawrence Westbrook, Benno C. Schmidt Chair of Business
   Law, University of Texas; Katherine Porter, Professor of Law (On Leave),
   University of California, Irvine; John A. E. Pottow, John Philip Dawson
   Collegiate Professor of Law, University of Michigan.
Description: Eighth edition. | New York : Wolters Kluwer, [2021] | Series:
   Aspen casebook series | Includes bibliographical references and index. |
   Summary: "This is a casebook intended for use in an upper level
   bankruptcy or debtor/creditor course" —Provided by publisher.
Identifiers: LCCN 2020035442 (print) | LCCN 2020035443 (ebook) | ISBN
   9781454893516 (casebound) | ISBN 9781543823479 (ebook)
Subjects: LCSH: Debtor and creditor—United States. | LCGFT: Casebooks
   (Law)
Classification: LCC KF1501 .W37 2021 (print) | LCC KF1501 (ebook) | DDC
   346.7307/7—dc23
LC record available at https://lccn.loc.gov/2020035442
LC ebook record available at https://lccn.loc.gov/2020035443

Certified Chain of Custody
Promoting Sustainable Forestry
www.sfiprogram.org
SFI-01681

SFI label applies to the text stock.

ASPEN CASEBOOK SERIES

THE LAW OF DEBTORS AND CREDITORS

Text, Cases, and Problems

Eighth Edition

ELIZABETH WARREN
Leo Gottlieb Professor of Law Emeritus
Harvard University

JAY LAWRENCE WESTBROOK
Benno C. Schmidt Chair of Business Law
University of Texas

KATHERINE PORTER
Professor of Law (On Leave)
University of California, Irvine

JOHN A. E. POTTOW
John Philip Dawson Collegiate Professor of Law
University of Michigan

About Wolters Kluwer Legal & Regulatory U.S.

Wolters Kluwer Legal & Regulatory U.S. delivers expert content and solutions in the areas of law, corporate compliance, health compliance, reimbursement, and legal education. Its practical solutions help customers successfully navigate the demands of a changing environment to drive their daily activities, enhance decision quality and inspire confident outcomes.

Serving customers worldwide, its legal and regulatory portfolio includes products under the Aspen Publishers, CCH Incorporated, Kluwer Law International, ftwilliam.com and MediRegs names. They are regarded as exceptional and trusted resources for general legal and practice-specific knowledge, compliance and risk management, dynamic workflow solutions, and expert commentary.

SUMMARY OF CONTENTS

CONTENTS

═══════════════════════ ASSIGNMENT 11 ═══════════════════════

UNSECURED CREDITORS IN CHAPTER 13   219

SECTION 4: THE CONSUMER BANKRUPTCY SYSTEM   *241*

═══════════════════════ ASSIGNMENT 12 ═══════════════════════

THE MEANS TEST   243

PREFACE

We start by making a statement that we have repeated since the first edition: we love to teach. This book is a product of the delight we have found in introducing students to a part of the law that is as filled with human drama as it is with intellectual complexity and social importance.

This preface is a little like the owner's manual that comes with a new car, albeit in abbreviated form. It tells you, the students who will be using this book, how it works and points out some special features. Like all owner's manuals, the preface reflects our efforts to see that everyone uses this book to best advantage. It also reflects our fervent hope that students will have as much fun using the book as we had writing it.

The book's primary objective is to make learning debtor-creditor law lively, interesting, and intellectually challenging. You will confront the Bankruptcy Code as the primary law, as interpreted and applied in cases ranging from unpublished orders to Supreme Court decisions. Bankruptcy law tends to pop up many times in nearly everyone's practice (few of us will escape dealing with financially distressed individuals or floundering businesses). Thus, this is a good place to learn not only black letter bankruptcy law, but also the process of problem-solving that is central to every area of practice.

At the same time, bankruptcy law is a complex, niche field to master. This specialized aspect is evidenced by the existence of dedicated bankruptcy courts, a unique system of appeals, certification programs for legal experts, and many trade organizations. Together these features and institutions help create a tightly woven "system" of bankruptcy law that transcends the written law itself. It is the actors (attorneys, judges, debtors, creditors, trustees, debt collectors, and others) giving effect to the formal law and relying on informal practices that jointly produce this system. Our goal in the book is to teach you not just the Bankruptcy Code, but also the operation of a legal system—both marvelous and flawed.

Organization of Material

The fundamental organizing principle of *The Law of Debtors and Creditors* is the division between consumer and business bankruptcy. This approach is distinct from the Bankruptcy Code and many leading treatises, which use an organization that often lumps together doctrinal issues without regard to factual context. Our experience as lawyers and our empirical research suggest that both social policy questions and the realities of the functional practice of law are quite different in consumer and business cases. We have also found that many students find the material more accessible and interesting when consumer bankruptcy is presented first. You can master basic principles and see how they interrelate in this more familiar setting before tackling the twists of bankruptcy law in a complex business reorganization.

The Law of Debtors and Creditors is organized into five parts: Introduction to Debtor-Creditor Law, Consumer Bankruptcy, Business Bankruptcy: Foundations, Business Bankruptcy: Plans and Beyond, and Functions and Boundaries. The parts are of neither equal size nor importance, and your teacher may not assign them equally. But we think seeing the structure of the book is useful to you in considering how individual topics fit into the big picture and in organizing your intellectual task for the course.

Part I covers the key points of debt enforcement outside bankruptcy, giving the view from 10,000 feet of state and federal nonbankruptcy law. It sets the stage for seeing the advantages and innovations of bankruptcy. Complementing this is Appendix B, which is a primer on secured credit for those who have not taken a class in that subject yet. The substance of bankruptcy law in Parts II, III, and IV is covered in much more detail. Part II, consumer bankruptcy, begins with generally applicable bankruptcy principles, then covers consumer liquidation cases (chapter 7 of the Code) and payout cases (chapter 13). It concludes with a study of how the two types of cases fit together and operate within a "system" that includes attorney counseling, ethics, policy, and theory. Parts III, IV, and V largely repeat this structure but in the business setting. Part III covers basic elements of bankruptcy and liquidation (chapter 7) for businesses as well as the fundamentals of reorganization for businesses (the world-famous chapter 11); Part IV focuses on chapter 11 plans, both in their traditional and more modern, sales-focused iterations; and Part V explores more advanced topics, such as domestic and international jurisdiction and bankruptcy theory. These final subjects implicate the boundaries and limits of the bankruptcy system, which you are prepared to address critically after learning much about law and practice.

Problem Method of Learning

This book is designed to be taught primarily through the problems. We offer ample explanatory text to permit you to understand the law and legal system, coupled with realistic problems to test and expand that understanding. The text uses cases selectively to demonstrate principles of law and to illustrate the factual context in which legal problems arise. You should read this book alongside the Bankruptcy Code, studying the statutes as they are mentioned in the cases and referenced in the problems. We eschew assigning the Code as formal reading because we think bankruptcy law is a contact sport. We want you to be participants, not spectators (especially since your eyes may glaze over at certain parts of the Code—ours sure do). Working the problems requires you to analyze and apply the law to specific facts and are the best and most fun approach we have found in years of teaching this material.

The problems are typically of three types: (1) statute readers and case extension problems, which help you examine key legal provisions; (2) theoretical and policy problems, which require you to engage in the social and policy implications of the law; and (3) transactional problems, which encourage you to think about planning and counseling (reversing the litigation orientation of much of legal education). As students learn the law, problem-solving increasingly becomes a function of putting pieces together and selecting the right legal tool to achieve a certain result or to analyze a policy choice. One of your main tasks as a student is to synthesize the class discussions and your "answers" to the problems with this textbook and the Code. This integration and review may be difficult, especially at first, but we believe you will find it very helpful when it all comes together at exam time (and in real life). While some of the problems have "correct" answers (and unfortunately for you, a wrong answer is always possible), other problems defy a concrete, definitive resolution. Each year, we learn from students and professors who give us new ideas to confront difficult issues.

It is our intention to make every problem "real," that is, realistic in operation and designed to teach the context as well as the law. The problems, even with the biggest business issues, are also intended to have a human face—to be the kind of problem a student might actually confront after graduation. In addition to assigning the obvious role of counsel to a debtor or creditor, the problems sometimes put the student in the role of bankruptcy trustee, judge, legislative aide, judicial clerk, or empirical researcher. Problems raising ethical issues are interwoven with other substantive topics because that is how they arise in practice (although they are given special attention at the end of both the consumer and business coverage). Together, the problems give a combination of perspectives. We hope to help you appreciate issues beyond the mechanics of the Code, and we think that the complex realities revealed in the problems produce more interesting insights than do neoclassical ruminations. Enjoy!

Our Perspectives

These materials reflect our premises (or prejudices) about the modern role of bankruptcy law and bankruptcy lawyers, so we should declare upfront those that are most important to us:

1. We believe that several factors have combined to make bankruptcy commonplace in contemporary U.S. life. One important factor has been the enormous growth in international trade competition and the creation of world markets. The consequence has been, and will continue to be, accelerating economic instability and change domestically, sometimes with one industrial or geographic sector booming while another is in sharp recession. Bankruptcy is a central part of the painful process through which families and businesses adjust to the effects of rapidly changing world markets.

2. We believe that bankruptcy will be in the mainstream of law and practice for the foreseeable future. It is therefore critical that it be understood by every lawyer and every policymaker concerned with the functioning of our economic system. Bankruptcy law is a core business law subject. Every deal or contract carries with it the risk of failure or nonperformance; bankruptcy is the backstop to capitalism.

3. We believe that bankruptcy law is public interest law. Legal aid intake reflects the harsh truth that generally, the biggest problem that poor

people have is that they are poor. We say this with all due respect to our colleagues counseling public interest lawyers to take rights-based courses. Increasingly, lawyers working under a large umbrella of "cause lawyering," including labor law, women's issues, community development, racial justice, and asset building, have found bankruptcy a locus for social reform. Bankruptcy, like tax law and retirement law, reflects Congress's efforts at public policy. Lawyers who care about our society, as well as our economy, find bankruptcy an important tool.

4. Finally, we believe that debtor-creditor law has been dominated too long by easy stereotypes and untested assumptions. Sneers at deadbeats, or disdain for Wall Street, reflect an over-simplified view of the complexities of financial relationships. Too often these emotional attachments or political positions serve as substitutes for detached analysis and careful research. One of the most important things we want to do for our students is to teach against their prejudices and, harder still, our own.

Why We Love Bankruptcy

Charles Warren began his 1935 history of American bankruptcy law with the words: "Bankruptcy is a gloomy and depressing subject." We reject that proposition. The economic pathology that leads to bankruptcy may indeed be depressing, but bankruptcy itself is the process of healing and restoration. Bankruptcy is an integral part of a free market system that permits individuals and businesses to fail; a strong bankruptcy system undergirds a market-based economy. Bankruptcy lawyers and judges help individuals and businesses pick up the pieces, right the wrongs, and begin anew when old approaches have failed. Bankruptcy is about the future. It is the search for economic healing: a treatment of financial wounds that is less painful and more permanent. It is good work, the work of the healer, and there is much of it to be done.

Warren, Westbrook, Porter & Pottow
Professors, Former Professors, and
Sometimes Professors of Law.

Ann Arbor, Michigan
Austin, Texas
Washington, DC (doubly)
November 2020

PREFACE TO THE EIGHTH EDITION: A NOTE TO TEACHERS

You will be relieved to hear the Eighth Edition was not nearly so substantial as the rewrite we did last time. You're welcome. But it would offer false hope to say all we did was update some cases. True, the major structure has stayed the same—39 assignments of same topics—but some have gone through heavy overhaul. Even in the overhauled assignments, we have tried to preserve the structure as much as possible, substituting in new cases and links as necessary. One stylistic change that should receive student cheers: a rarely exceeded cap of 25 pages per assignment, which required lots of triage on the advanced topics like jurisdiction and transnational bankruptcies. We also added an Appendix that provides students who have not taken a course in commercial law a background "primer" in secured credit. It is formally an Appendix to Assignment 2 but could probably be read before class begins for those who want.

In the intervening time since the Seventh Edition, we've had the Supreme Court come mess with bankruptcy jurisdiction some more, wade into consumer debt collection, and blow the whistle on the privatization of chapter 11, all of which we have addressed. But perhaps the most significant development—with real potential to be a sea change—is the Small Business Restructuring Act (SBRA), which kicked into effect in 2020, and then was immediately amended by the CARES Act in response to COVID-19. It seems to have arrived just in time (effective February 1, 2020), almost perfectly coincident with the pandemic and its enormous economic shock. Various changes in the Bankruptcy Code are being discussed in Congress but further changes on either the consumer or the business side are yet to emerge. Most of the discussions we have heard, moreover, are firmly based on the concepts and approaches in the current Code. We have incorporated the SBRA developments throughout the quartet of assignments focusing on traditional chapter 11, Assignments 27-30. In this edition, we also continue to devote two assignments to chapter 11 liquidations ("363 sales"). Our latest empirical work shows chapter 11 liquidations slowly increasing, but overall these data suggest cases may remain closely divided between sales and traditional reorganizations, so the jury may still be out as to the ultimate import of sales.

We repeat here what we have consistently said in prior editions. The Preface provides an overall description of how this book approaches the law of debtors and creditors. Generations of students have found it helpful, and we continue to recommend that you assign it. We also recommend that you address the problem approach directly with your class, perhaps on the first day, and then maybe again a few weeks later. While this pedagogy has become much more common since the first edition pioneered it (and we did not patent it), many students continue to rely unduly on the cases at the expense of reading the Code and applying it to the facts of the problems. Students also will appreciate your explaining that the problems are not merely homework; they are the primary learning vehicle for developing mastery—both for the exam and for a life in the law. Students will need guidance and affirmation about techniques for preparing the problems and reading the statutes. Here, we are thinking of things like drawing timelines of key dates and events, paying special attention to whether a statute is disjunctive or conjunctive, and being aware of defined (or undefined) terms. One of the great delights for us in using this book is seeing our students develop translatable legal skills to complement their familiarity with the Code.

As always, while we have made every effort to ensure that this edition is current and reflects the most pressing issues, the book is not a treatise expounding each minute wrinkle and clever twist of a statutory provision. We have chosen not to include extensive citations to the majority rule, the minority rule, and the Virginia exception as recently amended. Instead, we devote our pages to explaining difficult concepts and central provisions of the Code as clearly and accurately as we can. We leave the details to the hornbooks and the practitioner services.

This edition also continues to refer extensively to empirical studies, but as before, we limit our citations to those that we think are especially accessible and helpful to students trying to understand the bankruptcy system, rather than provide a greatest hits list based on some academic hierarchy. One slight change: while our case selection continues to depend much more on the teaching value of a case than on the prominence it might be given in a law review article, the Supreme Court's insistence on sticking its nose into bankruptcy is making it harder to avoid. We adhere to our core commitment that this book be a vehicle for learning by students, not a vehicle to demonstrate academic acumen; we have kept it, as best we can, from turning into a Fed Courts text.

A final thought we always like include in this note. We see our job as teachers as similar to our students' task as explained in the Preface—to study (again) the Code (where we promise you'll see something new every year), to read the cases (where we promise some fact pattern will simply leave you stunned at the richness of real life), and to play with the problems (where we promise that the students will join with you in searching for solutions, ideas, and tools). Bankruptcy can be a complex and sometimes daunting subject, even with a book that aims to be as student-friendly as this. Indeed, two of us can attest to that, having been students reared on prior editions of this book. The other two feign shock that this book did not assuage all angst. We have tried hard to incorporate our own experiences as students—and of course, as teachers—in this revision. We recognize, however, that we are just four people. We eagerly anticipate your suggestions and feedback about our mutual work in progress.

—Elizabeth, Jay, Katie & Pottow.

ACKNOWLEDGMENTS

This section is the most fun to write because as we write it we know we are finished. It is also fun to write because it causes us to reflect on how much this book is the product of wonderful students, helpful colleagues, tireless research assistants, tolerant spouses, enthusiastic friends, and patient children. For all the help and support, we are grateful.

Some people deserve special thanks for their extraordinary help. For the Eighth Edition, we especially shout out the following colleagues who gave us comments: Leif Clark, Allan Gropper, Ted Janger, Dan Keating, Chris Klein, Jason Kilborn, Jonathan Lipson, Stephen Lubben, Chris Redmond, and Stephen Ware, but especially Angie Littwin and Bob Lawless, who went above and beyond to give us problems, power points, and useful grief.

These wonderful collaborators have built upon the work of previous friends and colleagues, whom we continue to thank here: Laura Bartell, Evelyn Biery, Jeff Bohm, Samuel Bufford, Jon Eddy, Jaime Dodge, Jessica Gabel, Jackie Gardina, Melissa Jacoby, Dalié Jiménez, Kenneth Kettering, Stephen Kropp, Jennie Latta, Adam Levitin, Keith Lundin, Stephen Lubben, Dick McQueen, Bruce Markell, Nathalie Martin, Gary Neustadter, Ray Nimmer, Rafael Pardo, Paul Razor, Marie Reilly, Steve Rhodes, William Rochelle, Karl Rysted, Mark Scarberry, Tara Twomey, George Van Cleve, Eugene Wedoff, William Woodward, and Timothy Zinneck. We also thank Jean Braucher, Dov Cohen, and Robert Lawless for allowing us to use materials in the Teacher's Manual on chapter choice, and Rich Leonard for pointing us to the John Paul Smith hearing. Lynn LoPucki, Douglas Whaley, and Ronald Mann were especially generous with their tough comments in earlier editions, going back to the first wrinkled notes from when we started.

Speaking of old timers, we owe a special debt to Alan Axelrod who taught one of us bankruptcy law, and then read and commented on early outlines and sample chapters. Barry Cass has been a special friend, teaching our classes—and us—a great deal about the tax implications in business bankruptcy. Teresa Sullivan, one of our favorite sociologists, helped us develop a view of bankruptcy that looks beyond legal doctrine to difficult social and policy implementation issues. Debb Thorne, another favorite sociologist, continued this important role. Our colleague and friend Doug Laycock has given the best kind of support—always willing to argue a point, challenge a premise, and enjoy a new insight.

We have been blessed with intelligent and dedicated research assistants. The Eighth Edition would not have been possible without Conor McNamara (Michigan 2018), Rebecca Marston, Matthew Thornburg, and Eric Wendorf (all Michigan 2020), Angelika Glogowski and David Sheinfeld (both Michigan 2021), and Chris Wawro and Chris Weil (both Texas 2020). This fantastic team built upon the work of their Seventh Edition predecessors: Amy Bowles and Hannah Hyon (both UC Irvine 2015), Suzanne Lawson (UC Irvine 2013); Sarah Coleman and Jennifer Johnson (both Texas 2014), Matthew Driscoll and Jaaron Sanderson (both Texas 2013), Dr. Sarah Reed (Texas); Joshua Clark, Hyung Seok Kang, Meredith Morgan (all Michigan 2013), Emily Iversen, Daniel Nadal, Pete Osornio, and Katharine Roller (all Michigan 2014). They, in turn, built upon the work of many cohorts of predecessors now too lengthy to list here.

The students in our classes, some of who are now valued colleagues or accomplished bankruptcy lawyers, have remained unfailingly cheerful—even enthusiastic—about helping us with the book, and many of the successful problems and comments in the following pages stem from interesting discussions with them, right down to the emails they have forwarded us. Although their number has become too great to name each of them, we remember them fondly and gratefully. (Warren and Westbrook have special memories of Catherine Nicholson and Kimberly Winick, who were there at the start.)

We also give a special thanks to outstanding staff who have worked on this project, including Rebecca Chelberg at Michigan, who has managed the remarkable feat of stepping into the shoes of the remarkable Margaret Klocinski, who sailed off into the Floridian sunset of a well-deserved and granddaughter-beckoning retirement.

Finally, thanks to our friends and families who patiently listened to alternative versions of how to teach section 1111(b) elections and the merits of learning voidable preferences in a business rather than a consumer context. We are richly blessed.

Warren, Westbrook, Porter & Pottow
Professors, Former Professors, and
Sometimes Professors of Law.

Ann Arbor, Michigan
Austin, Texas
Washington, DC (doubly)
November 2020

We also thank the following authors and copyright holders for permission to use their materials:

Baird, Douglas G., Bankruptcy's Uncontested Axioms, 1080 *Yale L.J.* 573 (1998).

Baird, Douglas G., and Robert K. Rasmussen, Chapter 11 at Twilight, 56 *Stan. L. Rev.* 673, 673-77 (2003). Reprinted with permission.

Baird, Douglas G., and Robert K. Rasmussen, The End of Bankruptcy, 55 *Stan. L. Rev.* 751, 751-55, 777-78, 787 (2002). Reprinted by permission.

Betker, Brian, Stephen Ferris, and Robert Lawless, Warm with Sunny Skies: Disclosure Statement Forecasts, 73 *Am. Bankr. L.J.* 809 (1999).

Church, Steven and Dawn McCarty, Wanxiang Wins Fisker Asset Auction With $149 Million Bid., Bloomberg News 2/15/2014. http://www.bloomberg .com/news/2014-02-14/wanxiang-s-149-million-fisker-bid-tops-hybrid -tech-in-auction.html. Used with permission of Bloomberg L.P. Copyright © 2014.

Clement, Zack A. and R. Andrew Black, How City Finances can be Restructured: Bankruptcy Debt Discharge and Contract Impairment Cases Follow a Similar Approach, 88 *Am. Bankr. L.J.* 41 (2014).

Collection Agency Headed by "Thugs" Helps Merchants, *Daily Iowan*, Apr. 12, 1982, at 8B. United Press International, Inc.

Deadbeat Dad Who Owed Nearly $700k Is Off to Prison, Copyright © 2008 by wftv.com.

Drennan, John, Insolvency applicants who can get bus won't be allowed a car, *Sunday Independent*, March 24, 2013.

Feibelman, Adam, Defining the Social Insurance Function of Consumer Bankruptcy, *American Bankruptcy Institute Law Review* 129 (2005).

Gross, Karen, Failure and Forgiveness: Rebalancing the Bankruptcy System, Yale University Press, 1999.

Hall, Carla, More Hoopla at Simpson Home Auction, *Los Angeles Times*, July 15, 1997. Copyright © 1997. *Los Angeles Times*. Reprinted with permission.

"It Was 1961," Cartoon from *Punch*, Mar. 30, 1983. Published with permission of Punch Cartoon Library/TopFoto.

Jacoby, Melissa, The Detroit Bankruptcy, Pre- Eligibility, 41 *Fordham Urb. L.J.* 849 (2014).

Jones, Edith H., and Todd J. Zywicki, Time for Means-Testing, 1999 *BYU L. Rev.* 177 (1999).

Kale, W., Dressed for Success Davenport, IA. *Chicago Tribune*, April 20, 1982. Photograph published by permission of the *Chicago Tribune*.

"Ladies and gentlemen. . . .", Leo Cullum. Cartoon from The New Yorker, Mar. 3, 1991. Published with permission from Cartoon Collections.

Lawyer's Methods, Debtors' Nightmare, *Philadelphia Inquirer*, June 12, 1994, at Al and A8. Reprinted with permission from the Philadelphia Inquirer Copyright © 2014.

LoPucki, Lynn M., Contract Bankruptcy: A Reply to Alan Schwartz, 109 *Yale L.J.* 317 (1999). Reprinted with permission.

LoPucki, Lynn M., The Debtor's Lawyer as Trojan Horse, Debtor Creditor Game (Player's Manual 2d ed. 1986). Reprinted with permission of the author.

LoPucki, Lynn M., and Joseph W. Doherty, Bankruptcy Fire Sales, 106 *Mich. L. Rev.* 1 (2007). Reprinted with permission of the author.

Lubben, Stephen, No Big Deal: The GM and Chrysler Cases in Context, 83 *Am. Bankr. L.J.* 531, 536-42, 545-46 (2009). Reprinted with permission of the author.

Lupica, Lois, Credit Slips, March 29, 2011, www.creditslips.org.

Mayer, Caroline E., Bankrupt and Swamped with Credit Offers, *Washington Post*, April 15, 2005.

McKnight, Protection of the Family Home from Seizure by Creditors: The Sources and Evolution of a Legal Principle, 86 *Sw. Hist. Q.* 364 (1983).

Moor, Tom, Repo man relies on timing, skills, *South Bend Tribune*, Oct. 31, 2008.

Norris, Floyd, Basking in Islands of Legalisms, *The New York Times*; Jan. 22, 2010. © 2010 The New York Times Company. All rights reserved. Used under license.

Porter, Katherine, The Pretend Solution: An Empirical Study of Bankruptcy Outcomes, 90 *Tex. L. Rev.* 103 (2011-12).

Rao, John, Debt Buyers Rewriting of Rule 3001: Taking the "Proof" out the Claims Process, 23-6 *ABI J.* 16 (July/August 2004).

Rasmussen, Robert K., Debtor's Choice: A Menu Approach to Corporate Bankruptcy, 71 *Tex. L. Rev.* 51 (1992).

Roe, Mark J., and David Skeel, Assessing the Chrysler Bankruptcy, 108 *Mich. L. Rev.* 727 (2010). Reprinted with permission of the authors.

Schwarcz, Steven L., Rethinking Freedom of Contract: A Bankruptcy Paradigm, 77 *Tex. L. Rev.* 515 (1999). Reprinted with permission of the author.

Schwartz, Alan, Bankruptcy Contracting Reviewed, 109 *Yale L.J.* 344 (1999). Reprinted with permission.

Strasser, Annie-Rose, Hostess Blames Union for Bankruptcy After Tripling CEO's Pay, *ThinkProgress* (Nov. 16, 2012).

Texas Insurance Code Annotated §1108.051, §1108.053. Westlaw 2019. Courtesy of Thomson Reuters.

Texas Property Code §41.001, §41.002, §41.003, §42.001, §42.002, §42.005. Westlaw 2019. Courtesy of Thomson Reuters.

Warren, Elizabeth, A Theory of Absolute Priority, 1991 *Ann. Survey Am. L.* 9, 13.

Warren, Elizabeth, Bankruptcy Policy, 54 *U. Chi. L. Rev.* 775 (1987).

Warren, Elizabeth, Bankruptcy Policymaking in an Imperfect World, 92 *Mich L. Rev.* 336 (1993).

White, James J., Bankruptcy Noir, 106 *Mich. L. Rev.* 691 (2008). Reprinted with permission of the author.

White, James J., Death and Resurrection of Secured Credit, 12 *Am. Bankr. Inst. L. Rev.* 139 (2004).

Wolfe, Tom, excerpts from *A Man in Full*. Copyright © 1998 by Tom Wolfe. Reprinted by permission of Farrar, Straus and Giroux. All rights reserved.

Wyoming Statutes Annotated. Westlaw 2019. Courtesy of Thomson Reuters.

SPECIAL NOTICE

We have edited cases and articles for the sake of smoother reading. Citations and footnotes have been deleted without indication. Sometimes we use ellipses to designate omissions. Footnotes that were not eliminated retain their original numbers; asterisks indicate editors' footnotes.

The Bankruptcy Code is referred to as "the Code," and citations to it are by section number only. "The Act" refers to the Bankruptcy Act of 1898.

Citations to other federal law are usually to the United States Code. Some references to consumer laws are to the public law sections because this conforms to popular usage.

The problems in this book are filled with debtors, creditors, lawyers, trustees, and others who are the products of our imaginations. Any resemblance to any real person, solvent or insolvent, is purely coincidental.

The Law of Debtors
and Creditors

PART I

INTRODUCTION TO DEBTOR-CREDITOR LAW

A rapid glance at history is enough to show the subversive role consistently played, ever since money existed, by the phenomenon of debt. The cancellation of debts was the principal feature of reforms of both Solon and Lycurgus. And later on, the small Greek cities were more than once shattered by movements in favor of another cancellation. The revolt by which the Roman plebeians won the institution of the tribuneship had its origin in a widespread insolvency, which was reducing more and more debtors to the condition of slavery; and even if there had been no revolt, a partial cancellation of debts had become imperative, because with every plebeian reduced to a slave, Rome lost a soldier.

The payment of debts is necessary for social order. The nonpayment of debts is quite equally necessary for social order. For centuries humanity has oscillated, serenely unaware, between these two contradictory necessities. Unfortunately, the second of them violates a great many seemingly legitimate interests and it has difficulty in securing recognition without disturbance and a measure of violence.

Simone Weil, Esquisse d'une apologie de la banqueroute
("On bankruptcy"), (1937)

FIGHTING OVER MONEY

This is a book about debtors and creditors. It deals with the laws governing debtor and creditor behavior, laws that prescribe when obligations must be paid, how unpaid obligations can be collected, and how bankruptcy law can change those legal obligations. Not surprisingly, this is a book laden with rules, regulations, common law doctrines, state codes, federal statutes, and enough other "law" to challenge even the most diligent student.

Although there is much law in this book, there is also much that relies on bookkeepers, accountants, and actuaries. For unlike most courses you have taken so far in law school, where you read cases with facts not in dispute but with complex analysis of what those facts mean to an evolving common law (e.g., whether a collection of undisputed facts give rise to a lack of reasonable care), here you will find parties fighting frequently and heatedly over specific, plain-old facts, such as the value of an asset. So upping the intellectual ante, we will have to consider both complex law *and* disputed facts. (Stop checking the drop-add deadline: *lean in!*)

But it would be a mistake to think you will find here a musty cupboard filled with rules and numbers. Bankruptcy law is ultimately about human conduct in the charged context of financial distress. It is one thing to fight hard to win a lawsuit; when there is not enough money to go around, people fight even harder. *"And may the odds be ever in your favor!"* This text is thus equally filled with stories of tragic circumstances and shrewd uses of leverage. It is sometimes about people who wear pin-striped suits and live without passion, but it is also about rugged self-help and self-defense in a very tough world. Don't believe us? Take a look at this story; we couldn't have made this up had we tried.

Son Can't Pay, So Father's Body Is Returned

Richmond, Tex.—The body of a man who died Friday was dumped on his son's doorstep by a funeral home on Monday evening because the son had been unable to pay the full price of cremation. [(AP) *New York Times*, October 14, 1992, at A16, col. 1.]

According to this newspaper article (and the subsequent one), Larry Bojarski only paid $299 of the $683 cremation cost of his father, George, who had passed away at age 66 of esophageal cancer. Evans Mortuary decided to encourage payment by threatening bringing George back home—a threat apparently made good on when a sheet-covered cadaver greeted Larry at his apartment doorstep on a pallet three days after the death. (A neighboring undertaker, Hernandez Funeral Home, donated free cremation services, saying they had never heard of anything like that in "50 years" in the business.)

Thus, there is an almost infinite array of possible collection techniques creditors will try informally. Of course, these informal forms of repayment persuasion tend to encourage informal responses.

Dead Man's Son, Mortuary Worker Gets into Fistfight

RICHMOND, Texas—A man whose father's corpse was left on his doorstep and a funeral home worker who helped unload the body have accused each other of assault.

. . .

Larry Bojarski, 37, said he suffered a broken thumb and nose and needed six stitches to close up his forehead after a Tuesday night fight with Allen Evans [33, nephew of Evans Mortuary proprietor, Newell Evans, and who apparently lived in the same apartment complex!—Eds.], who said his elbow and hand were swollen after the fight.

. . .

Richmond Police Lt. George Paruch said the district attorney's office will decide about charges. [UPI Archives, Oct. 15, 1992.]

Beyond stark tales like this one are larger questions about the role of debt in society. Debt lies at the heart of every modern economy. Many agree that the invention of a permanent national debt through the "gilt" bonds of the Bank of England in the eighteenth century was the foundation for the Industrial Revolution. If any cultural tool deserves a comparison with fire, it is debt: essential, yet dangerous.

In American society, and increasingly in every country around the world, the bankruptcy process lies at the heart of the evolving role of debt in both the global economy and lives of ordinary people. At the macro level, the central place of debt is epitomized by the bankruptcy of Lehman Brothers in 2008. At $600 billion, it was not just the largest bankruptcy in the history of the galaxy, it was part of a financial collapse of interconnected debt instruments that was a major precipitating cause of the Great Recession. At the micro level, debt's prevalence has been seen in the numerous studies documenting how widespread consumer debt financing has become: we now know that more adults have major consumer debt than go to church, have college degrees, or vote in major elections.

A.   THE STRUCTURE OF DEBTOR-CREDITOR LAW

The law in the United States relating to debts can sometimes be framed as a series of dichotomies: debtors and creditors; state and federal law; secured and unsecured credit; in-court and out-of-court resolution; liquidation vs. payout; and more. Perhaps the most fundamental distinction as a matter of practical social policy is the one between the debts that arise from the daily lives of consumers and those that are created by the operation of a business. A human who is broke raises many similar concerns to a corporation that is floundering, but there are even more differences. A second major distinction is the one between collection of a specific debt by a single creditor (for example, by that creditor's seizure of the debtor's wages) and the resolution of all debts in a collective proceeding, such as a bankruptcy petition. One creditor's pursuit of a debtor for recovery on a debt raises different concerns from ten creditors' pursuit of ten debts in a single proceeding.

In this book, we first divide the materials between consumer debtors and business debtors. Then we divide each section between single-debt enforcement and the collective-debt enforcement of bankruptcy. Finally, we divide the bankruptcy materials between liquidation ("sellout") and reorganization ("payout"). Although we do not spend equal time on each area, we use this analytical framework to underscore how bankruptcy is an *overlay* upon a rich fabric of pre-existing collections law. We start the consumer section with a creditor's attempt to collect a single debt, sampling the jungle warfare of debt collectors, credit reports, and repossessions that are the main enforcement mechanisms against consumers. Then we turn to consumer bankruptcy with its policy pendulum swinging between enforcing an individual's promises to repay on the one hand and providing cancellation of debts as a "fresh start" for the debtor on the other.

The business section is also divided into collection of single debts and a collective resolution in bankruptcy. It starts with the ancient writs commanding a sheriff to seize the debtor's property and contrasts them with the modern use of secured creditor repossessions under Article 9 of the Uniform Commercial Code. The business section then moves on to the fascinating world of chapter 11 where some contenders, like Lehman, simply collapse into liquidation but others, like all the major airlines, seem to fly through in (relative) health. Sometimes success means forgiveness of parts of debts or extensions of repayment terms by lenders, sometimes success means merging into a strategically similar former rival (like those airlines), and sometimes success can mean a combination of the two.

The basic consumer-business distinction is not a sharp line. A large empirical study of bankruptcy has shown that many individuals who file for bankruptcy do so as their small businesses collapse. Elizabeth Warren & Jay L. Westbrook, Financial Characteristics of Businesses in Bankruptcy, 73 Am. Bankr. L.J. 499 (1999) (hereafter cited as *Financial Characteristics*); see also Robert Lawless & Elizabeth Warren, The Myth of the Disappearing Business Bankruptcy, 93 Cal. L. Rev. 745 (2005); Douglas G. Baird & Edward R. Morrison, Serial Entrepreneurs and Small Business Bankruptcies, 105 Colum. L. Rev. 2310 (2005). That said, the great majority of cases are clearly either business or nonbusiness, and a grasp of the two distinct operating systems and their differences is necessary.

B.   A BRIEF INTRODUCTION TO BANKRUPTCY THEORY (AND DATA)

If the field of bankruptcy had produced a generally accepted Grand Theory, with perhaps some details disputed, it might make sense to begin with that so a student could analyze each part of the material through the appropriate lens of the theory and gauge its fit. Alas, it has not. On the contrary, bankruptcy law has sprouted a spirited theoretical discourse that we will explore a bit, in time. It also occurs to us that a student has little basis for critique and comparison at the start of a course, especially one such as bankruptcy that has many moving parts. Thus, we intentionally postpone a full-blown discussion of bankruptcy theory until the last assignment in this book.

In lieu of a full discussion at the outset, we present a quick sketch showing some of the different theories—sometimes just arguments—of what bankruptcy law should be. As you move through the book and find yourself mired in the complexities of the statute, this summary of bankruptcy theory may help you hear the music behind the madness.

In the consumer realm, it is fair to say that many if not most American theorists accept, albeit with varying degrees of enthusiasm, that bankruptcy is largely about a "fresh start" for individual debtors. See, e.g., Local Loan Co. v. Hunt, 292 U.S. 234 (1934). It would be hard to argue otherwise in a country whose central myths are captured in Ellis Island and in the Conestoga wagon setting out across the plains to a new life. Comparatively, the United States has always been, and remains, more committed to the fresh start idea for consumers who file bankruptcy than any other country in the world.

Some theorists explain the fresh start in economic terms, noting the insurance-like function of bankruptcy's discharge. See, e.g., Barry E. Adler, Bankruptcy Primitives, 12 Am. Bankr. Inst. L. Rev. 219 (2004). Others look to more morality-based grounds of the discharge, noting the deep-seated norm of forgiveness in many Western cultures. Heidi M. Hurd & Ralph Brubaker, Debts and the Demands of Conscience: The Virtue of Bankruptcy (Oxford Univ. Press, forthcoming). We can therefore say as a high-level theoretical matter that most believe consumer bankruptcy is about a fresh start, but then we quickly dissolve into disagreement about just why a fresh start is important. Similarly, when critiquing legislative policy, these different theoretical approaches lead to different arguments. Take, for example, the intermittent cries for less generous relief to consumers (i.e., restricting the fresh start). They are sometimes grounded in considerations of ethics ("Easy discharge is more proof that we are going to heck in a handbasket!"), but are sometimes grounded by economic concerns ("Easy discharge drives up the price of unsecured consumer credit!"). Moreover, both of these theoretically based arguments themselves contain implicit empirical suppositions. *Are* we going to heck in a handbasket? *Does* ease of bankruptcy discharge affect the price of consumer credit? If so, how much? (They also raise what philosophers would call epistemic questions: *how do we know* whether we are going to heck in a handbasket?)

Thus, in addition to theoretical debates about how to think about the consumer bankruptcy system, on which scholars have not reached consensus, we also have rich second-order debates on empirical matters. Whether and to what extent bankruptcy law affects the cost of consumer credit is hotly debated by hard-working scholars and policymakers on all sides, but that empirical debate is of greater interest to those who are grounded in an economic theory of justification of the fresh start. And just to make your head truly spin, sometimes people of the same theoretical orientation toward bankruptcy law arrive at opposite conclusions of what the law should be. Take a moral philosopher's approach to bankruptcy. One might say that easy bankruptcy discharge results in laxity that is undesirable for our collective conception of the good and so the discharge should be constrained. Or . . . one might say that an eroding social safety net requires, on the contrary, that the bankruptcy discharge be loosened up just to preserve the moral status quo, lest members of our society fall into greater indignity. So philosophers might fight with each other—but at least agree that economists are looking at this question the wrong way.

Business bankruptcy, at least from a creditor's perspective, addresses the problem of the "common pool," which is the difficulty of acting collectively and cooperatively to maximize the value of a debtor's assets (and thus the creditors' aggregate return). Think of it this way: individually, each creditor faces an incentive to break one of the debtor's fingers to encourage him to pay up and redouble his efforts at earning income. If ten creditors, however, each break a finger, then the debtor may not be able to work *at all* for a bit, and so there will be less wage income than if the creditors had just done nothing. (Taken to an extreme of course, a dead debtor can't pay anything; in fact, worse than that, a dead debtor actually incurs burial costs, which economists might bemoan as deadweight loss.) One prominent theory suggests that a huge collective action problem means bankruptcy law rests upon a "Creditors' Bargain," which means bankruptcy law should be built around what creditors would theoretically put into a hypothetical contract they would all agree to upfront to achieve the best collective result for creditors. (Hat tip, John Rawls.)

The Creditors' Bargain approach assumes, however, that only creditors' interests matter in bankruptcy, not those of the owners of the business or its employees. In response, a number of scholars have argued that bankruptcy law reflects an enormous complex of conflicting social and economic goals that cannot be over-simplified. Elizabeth Warren, Bankruptcy Policymaking in an Imperfect World, 92 Mich. L. Rev. 336 (1993). This "complex policies" crowd also notes that bankruptcy law, in reallocating assets in circumstances of scarcity, serves a necessarily distributive function, which often makes the "just-solve-collective-action" types want to curl up into a ball and cry. While there has been spirited debate between these two constituencies, at a certain point matters reduce to axiomatic first principles of what one believes bankruptcy law *should* be about— principled differences that may be irreconcilable. Douglas G. Baird, Bankruptcy's Uncontested Axioms, 108 Yale L.J. 573 (1998).

A related and significantly correlated theoretical dichotomy divides "contractualists," who believe the best way to decide these hypothetical bargains of creditors is to allow them actually to sit down and decide with the debtor what their bankruptcy law should be, case-by-case, subject to some state-enforced ground rules, versus "collectivists," who believe that a mandatory bankruptcy code protects the interests of non-participating third parties and more efficiently tracks the likely outcome obtained by such envisioned negotiations without wasting all the time and expense.

One point is conceded by all: a major goal of bankruptcy is to preserve value. Bankruptcy preserves economic value, even in liquidation. The collective approach to orderly liquidation of assets is more value-preserving than the often chaotic process of seizure and sale by a host of competing creditors. Second, reorganization bankruptcy preserves the "going concern" value of a continuing business, reflecting the simple economic fact that businesses, like people, are often worth more alive than dead. Bankruptcy helps to preserve social values as well. Bankruptcy liquidation is an orderly and efficient way to bury a failed business, while bankruptcy reorganization offers the hope of saving jobs and the communities that depend on them, as well as ameliorating the inevitable social pain of business failure.

When you go through the business materials, keep these theoretical debates in your head, just as you should think about the fresh start issues on the consumer side.

For our part, we will defer jumping into these theoretical skirmishes for now, but we do want you to think about the empirical suppositions that are behind many policy recommendations purportedly flowing from these theories, and sometimes immanent in the theories themselves. Accordingly, throughout the book we reference studies that present data on how the bankruptcy system actually works as a *descriptive* matter, because only then can we engage, at least in our opinion, in an intelligent discussion of where the law should evolve as a *normative* matter.

The most comprehensive empirical studies are the five iterations of the Consumer Bankruptcy Project, in some or all of which each of us joined as investigators. The data collections for these studies occurred in 1981, 1991, 2001, 2007, and on an ongoing basis since 2013, providing the foundation of over a hundred published works. Consumer Bankruptcy Project, http://www.consumerbankruptcyproject.org/. Some of the key work includes: Teresa A. Sullivan, Elizabeth Warren & Jay L. Westbrook, As We Forgive Our Debtors: Bankruptcy and Consumer Credit in America (Oxford 1989) (hereafter cited as *As We Forgive*); Teresa A. Sullivan, Elizabeth Warren & Jay L. Westbrook, The Fragile Middle Class: Americans in Debt (Yale 2000) (hereafter cited as *Fragile Middle Class*); Robert M. Lawless, Angela K. Littwin, Katherine M. Porter, John A.E. Pottow, Deborah K. Thorne & Elizabeth Warren, Did Bankruptcy Reform Fail?: An Empirical Study of Consumer Debtors, 82 Am. Bankr. L.J. 349 (2008) (hereafter cited as *Reform*); and Katherine Porter (Ed.), Broke: How Debt Bankrupts the Middle Class (Stanford University Press, 2012) (hereafter cited as *Broke*). The American Bankruptcy Institute (ABI) also has studied consumer bankruptcy and recommended changes to the bankruptcy system. The commission's report covered topics ranging from chapter 7 trustee compensation to racial justice in bankruptcy. American Bankruptcy Institute Commission on Consumer Bankruptcy, Final Report and Recommendations (2019) (available for download at https://consumercommission.abi.org/commission-report).

Empirical studies of business bankruptcy encompass examinations of both large, public companies and small businesses and individual entrepreneurs. A comprehensive look at the entirety of business cases can be found in *Financial Characteristics*, as well as updates in Elizabeth Warren & Jay L. Westbrook, Contracting Out of Bankruptcy: An Empirical Intervention, 118 Harv. L. Rev. 1197 (2005); and Elizabeth Warren & Jay L. Westbrook, The Success of Chapter 11: A Challenge to the Critics, 107 Mich. L. Rev. 603 (2009). Just as it did in the consumer context, the ABI also formed a commission to study and recommend reforms to the commercial bankruptcy system. Among other suggestions, the ABI commission recommended creating an alternative restructuring scheme for small- and medium-sized enterprises to better address their needs, reasoning that mom-and-pop shops do not have the same resources (and problems) as the

Fortune 500. American Bankruptcy Institute Commission to Study the Reform of Chapter 11, Final Report and Recommendations (2014) (available for download at http://commission.abi.org/final-report).

A number of more discrete studies, both consumer- and business-oriented, have also added important insights, and we point to those data at relevant places in the book, too. We also draw on data from the Administrative Office of the Courts and other sources of national data on credit and finance. Today, there are opportunities for students to dip their toes into the empirical bankruptcy seas using a handy website. The UCLA-LoPucki Bankruptcy Research Database, available at no cost to all researchers, contains data on public company bankruptcies with large assets. It is available at http://lopucki.law.ucla.edu/index.htm.

C.   A *VERY* BRIEF HISTORY OF U.S. BANKRUPTCY LAW

Although ancient civilizations had laws regulating the treatment of defaulting and insolvent debtors, those antecedents are murky and their connection with modern bankruptcy law is more proclaimed than demonstrated. It is said that in Roman times the creditors did not merely divide the debtor's possessions, but took the debtor to the plaza and divided him. Theodor C. Albert, The Insolvency Law of Ancient Rome, 28 Cal. Bankr. J. 365, 368 (2006). Whether or not it was so (and whether or not "bankruptcy" derives from the Italian "banca rotta" or "broken [merchant's] table"), the clearest origins of United States bankruptcy law are to be found in England.

From the original English bankruptcy statute, adopted in the reign of the first Elizabeth, until the time of the American Revolution, "bankruptcy" was an involuntary creditor's collection device—a sort of super-attachment of all the debtor's property for equal division among creditors. Generally, it could be used only against traders or merchants. The benefit to bankrupts was release from the unpaid portion of their debts, the "discharge." A separate and later development was "insolvency" law, designed for the relief of debtors. Insolvency was always voluntary. Debtors who placed all their property in the hands of their creditors and the court were "discharged" from debtors' prison but not released from their debts in the modern sense of the word. Their obligations to pay remained, and creditors could still use collection devices other than imprisonment. See generally Emily Kadens, The Last Bankrupt Hanged: Balancing Incentives in the Development of Bankruptcy Law, 59 Duke L.J. 1229, 1236 (2010) (joylessly exposing cutting-debtor-up lore as likely myth).

In the United States, combining bankruptcy and insolvency elements into a unified debtor-creditor statute was a difficult process marked by various unsuccessful attempts. Notwithstanding specific constitutional recognition that a uniform national bankruptcy law was vital to national interests, U.S. Const. art. I, § 8, cl. 4, more than a century passed before our legal ancestors could fashion a permanent federal bankruptcy statute acceptable to competing constituencies. For history buffs and students of social class, Bruce H. Mann's book, A Republic of Debtors, provides an outstanding analysis of bankruptcy, morality, and the economy in early America. It methodically shows how the most basic questions about the morality of bankruptcy relief and about the economic consequences of discharge provoked sharp debates in our government—debates that echo still today.

Throughout the nineteenth century, there were periodic struggles between mercantile and borrower interests over enactment of "bankruptcy" or "insolvency" laws. The farmers of the South and West detested the idea of involuntary bankruptcy, while the Northern and Eastern merchants wanted a discharge to be contingent on creditor agreement by specified majorities. Many believed that the two bodies of law, insolvency and bankruptcy, could not stand together ("a bill to serve God and Mammon"). As we said, the debates were sharp. The intensity of feeling generated by what is regarded by many as a dry and technical subject was quite remarkable:

> [The proposed bankruptcy law] comes from the class of men who are grinding the face of the poor . . . [and from] the same spirit that hung [sic] and killed and drew and quartered women for witchery.

31 Cong. Rec. S2362-408 (daily ed. March 2-3, 1898) (statements of Senator Stewart, Nev.).

Insolvency and bankruptcy were brought together only fleetingly, in a series of short-lived acts. See generally David A. Skeel, The Genius of the 1898 Bankruptcy Act, 15 Bankr. Dev. J. 321 (1999) (presaging his later book on bankruptcy history). The bankruptcy "system" for the first 109 years after the adoption of the federalization of bankruptcy in the Constitution was thus little more than a series of brief legislative fiats, alternately pro-creditor or pro-debtor, accompanied by a growing awareness that a uniform compromise law would better serve everyone. In the meantime, various states enacted their own insolvency laws, which were permitted to stand in the absence of congressional legislation.

The interests of "God and Mammon" were at last accommodated in the Bankruptcy Act of 1898 (the "Act"), in the aftermath of an economic panic. The panic jolted both creditors and debtors into compromise, realizing their needs for legal order in financial failure, and so both constituencies gave more ground than they had in the past. The benefit to debtors of this compromise was obvious, providing debt relief through discharge, a concept that creditors had repeatedly fought. Creditors for their part accepted that a workable bankruptcy system, providing orderliness to the collection process and encouraging debtors to make at least some payments, was worth the cost of permitting debtors a discharge. The legislation enacted in 1898 thus represented a series of fine compromises on a host of difficult issues. With its passage, the first enduring American bankruptcy law took shape.

The Act was amended a number of times in the following years, but it was not revised extensively until the 1930s, following the greatest economic collapse of them all, the Great Depression. The Chandler Act, encompassing the most extensive of these changes, was adopted in 1938. From a modern perspective, the two most important innovations of the Chandler Act were the adoption of new procedures for the reorganization of businesses and the scheduled payment of debt over time by financially troubled wage-earners. The details of the evolution of reorganization (today's chapter 11) are discussed later in the section on business bankruptcy. The wage-earner's scheduled payment plan (today's chapter 13) provided a way to reorganize a family's finances in much the same way a business could reorganize its obligations. It effectively introduced into federal bankruptcy the debt compositions (reductions) and extensions of state law, but more importantly it added the federal law power of a discharge of remaining debt upon payment plan completion (a power that states could only exercise in limited circumstances thanks to the pesky constraints of the Constitution).

Bankruptcy law enjoyed a quiet period for several decades thereafter. By the early 1970s, however, Congress decided the bankruptcy laws were badly out of date. It created a National Bankruptcy Commission to propose reforms. Its report to Congress in 1973 offered recommendations for both consumer and business bankruptcy that were the foundations of the Bankruptcy Code adopted in 1978. That law, while subject to some important revisions, is still basically the law today. The bankruptcy community often refers to this law as the "Code," and contrasts it with old precedents decided under the "Act." The Code also retained the famous "chapter" system of bankruptcy, including liquidation procedures in chapter 7 for businesses and consumers, reorganization for businesses in chapter 11, and repayment bankruptcy for individuals in chapter 13. (If you ever see Roman numerals in a bankruptcy case—such as Chapter XIII—the reference relates to the Act; we use some important old precedents, so look at the date of the case you are reading.)

In the 25 years after 1978, Congress enacted modest amendments, most of which responded to pressures of interest groups or specific concerns. In 1984, for example, Congress added sections benefiting grain farmers and shopping center landlords, among others. In 1986, Congress added a new type of bankruptcy, chapter 12, especially for family farmers. It also created a new U.S. Trustee's office in the executive branch of government to provide assistance to the courts and to serve various administrative functions.

The consumer credit industry, which grew tremendously with deregulation in the 1980s and 1990s, began to press Congress for bigger changes to consumer bankruptcy law. A new National Bankruptcy Review Commission was convened and issued a report in 1997 that contained a large and comprehensive set of proposals for changes to consumer and business bankruptcy law. There were strong dissents on a number of issues, primarily on whether the existing consumer system was unduly generous.

Unhappy with the Commission Report, the credit industry took its case to Congress, drafting the basics of a bill to reform the consumer bankruptcy system in a manner more to its liking. The amendments came close to passing several times between 1998 and 2005, when Congress finally enacted the Bankruptcy Abuse Prevention and Consumer Protection Act ("BAPCPA"). With respect to consumer bankruptcy, these 2005 Amendments contained the most far-reaching changes since the adoption of the Code. The amendments reflect a view that bankruptcy law needed to be rebalanced in favor of creditors because it was too often being abused by debtors. Most bankruptcy specialists believe that the basic premise of

BAPCPA is wrong (and its name Orwellian), because most debtors who file for bankruptcy do so in the aftermath of a serious economic shock such as a job loss or medical problem, and that a change in the laws will not change the underlying economic realities facing people in serious financial trouble. Although the system is still adjusting to the new law—and equilibrium is tough to gauge given the foreclosure crisis that began in 2007—it seems that fundamental components of the prior system still survive.

D.   BANKRUPTCY COURT ORGANIZATION

No introduction to bankruptcy would be complete without a discussion of procedure. (You thought you left procedure behind in the first year? Quelle naïveté!) Bankruptcy cases are filed in special federal courts. This is more the exception rather than the rule if we look at other systems, and so many a foreign lawyer is confused about these special tribunals when working on cross-border disputes. The legal basis of these courts' jurisdiction, putting matters delicately, is complex and uncertain. That topic is covered in detail in the assignment on jurisdiction. At this early point, however, understanding the practical operation of the courts is important.

Again, a little history will help. Before 1978, there were no specialized bankruptcy judges. But even under the nineteenth century bankruptcy statutes, federal district judges usually had specialized help with bankruptcies. Full-time or part-time officials handled much of the work in such cases. Under the Act, these officials were called "referees," and they made many of the everyday decisions in bankruptcy matters. Their position was roughly equivalent to that of a specialized "master" who served on a regular basis. The referees were appointed by the district judges.

One of the principal reforms of the Code in 1978 was to expand greatly the bankruptcy jurisdiction of the district courts (and hence, indirectly, the power of these judicial helpers, who by this point were being called, although not without controversy, "bankruptcy judges"). This expanded jurisdiction was to be exercised primarily by the bankruptcy judges as part of the district court organization. The new bankruptcy judges were non-Article III judges, appointed for 14 years, unlike their Article III counterparts on the federal bench. The Supreme Court took the wind out of these jurisdictional sails by declaring the new system unconstitutional, albeit in a fractured decision with no clear majority. See Northern Pipeline Construction Co. v. Marathon Pipe Line Co., 458 U.S. 50 (1982). Moreover, the Court subsequently held unconstitutional related but lesser aspects of the Code's jurisdictional provisions (pertaining to jury trial rights).

Congress responded to *Marathon* in 1984 with a crazy quilt of jurisdictional provisions that make the bankruptcy court now a "unit" of each district court under the supervision of the district judges. The courts of appeals were given the responsibility of appointing bankruptcy judges to solve other constitutional problems raised by *Marathon*, but the job of overseeing the functioning of the bankruptcy court was given largely to the district courts. The biggest post-*Marathon* change to buttress the constitutionality of the bankruptcy courts was to divide the universe of bankruptcy matters into "core" and "noncore" proceedings, with different jurisdictional treatment of each. Congress delegated jurisdiction over "core" proceedings in bankruptcy to the bankruptcy judges directly (subject to district court discretion); their decisions are final judgments by a court of law. With regard to "noncore" proceedings, a bankruptcy judge can hear them only as a master who submits *proposed* findings to the district court (unless the parties involved consent to a binding decision by the bankruptcy judge); these are not final judgments and can be reviewed *de novo* by the district court upon timely party objection. The noncore system is similar to that of magistrate judges.

Under this congressional scheme, therefore, bankruptcy judges' decisions on matters within their core jurisdiction can be appealed to the district court, which reviews their factual findings on a "clearly erroneous" basis. If a party is dissatisfied with the district court's resolution of an appeal, it may appeal further to the court of appeals, as with any other district court decision. The Code also permits any of the circuit courts to adopt a special appellate procedure whereby the first appeal from a bankruptcy court decision is to a panel of bankruptcy judges instead of to a district judge. Code § 158(c). These alternatives to the district courts are called "BAPs," referring to their statutory names: Bankruptcy Appellate Panels. While an appeal to a BAP sidesteps the district court, panel jurisdiction is consensual; any party can insist that the appeal be heard by the district court. Parties disgruntled with the bankruptcy court's proposed findings of fact and conclusions of law in a *noncore* proceeding simply object and the district court is required to conduct a *de novo* review (with further appeal as usual to the circuit).

Since 1984, the Supreme Court has twice pronounced these provisions constitutionally tainted, although with twists and caveats that left the situation increasingly confused. In the spring of 2011, the Supreme Court achieved the apogee of its confusion in deciding Stern v. Marshall, 564 U.S. 462 (2011). The case was the usual boring technical problem in a bankruptcy case, a dispute over many millions of dollars between a famous Playmate (Anna Nicole Smith), and the children of her deceased billionaire husband—more suitable for reality TV than the lofty chambers of the Supreme Court (at least until the inevitable reality TV show about the Supreme Court). There was brisk, sometimes frantic debate whether this decision threatens the entire jurisdictional structure of the Code, because *Stern* has left in its wake great confusion over the powers of the approximately 350 bankruptcy judges who preside each year over hundreds of thousands of consumer cases and business cases involving billions of dollars, but the Supreme Court soothed some of those fears in its follow-on decision of Wellness Int'l Network, Ltd. v. Sharif, 575 U.S. 665 (2015), which held that constitutional defects in a bankruptcy judge's authority can be cured by the consent of the parties to proceed before the judge in noncore matters. But few are comfortable that the constitutional storm has fully blown over. Stay tuned.

Incidentally, the Supreme Court also has a more pedestrian job, promulgating the Federal Rules of Bankruptcy Procedure, in much the same way it does the Federal Rules of Civil Procedure. The rules must defer to any controlling provision of the Code. In general, these rules, and the accompanying official forms, prescribe the procedures for administration of the bankruptcy estate, the filing of claims by creditors, the forms and schedules to be completed by each petitioning debtor, and the like.

The taxonomy of disputes in the Rules is noteworthy, particularly for understanding the posture of many cases included in this book. Part VII of the Rules governs "adversary proceedings," which are defined in Rule 7001. Such proceedings include, for example, actions to invalidate a lien on the debtor's property and actions that have been removed to bankruptcy court from state court. Adversary proceedings are full-blown federal lawsuits within the larger bankruptcy case, so they typically carry two captions: the "In re" bankruptcy caption of the broader case and the more familiar "A v. B" caption of the specific dispute. So in Warren v. Westbrook (In re Pottow), you are reading a case in which Warren (say, the trustee) filed the adversary complaint against Westbrook (say, a creditor) within the overall proceeding of Pottow's bankruptcy. Part VII of the Bankruptcy Rules virtually incorporates the Federal Rules of Civil Procedure. The Federal Rules of Evidence are also applicable to adversary proceedings. Disputes other than adversary proceedings, such as objecting to a claim as improper, are denominated "contested matters" and are subject to the less elaborate procedures described in Rule 9014. Those that are reported will appear as motion decisions with only the "In re" caption.

E. A SPECIFIC INTRODUCTION TO THE CODE

Title 11 of the U.S. Code is devoted wholly to the Bankruptcy Code. It is divided into "chapters." For historical reasons, all but one of the chapters are odd-numbered: 1, 3, 5, 7, 9, 11, 12, 13, and 15. Chapters 1, 3, and 5 are general provisions that are applicable in all proceedings in bankruptcy unless explicitly made inapplicable in a specific context. Chapters 7, 9, 11, 12, 13, and 15 each govern a different type of bankruptcy proceeding. Except for certain situations in chapter 15 (which covers multinational bankruptcies), a debtor can be in only one of these chapters at any given time.

Chapter 1 is devoted to structural subjects such as definitions, rules of construction, general powers of the bankruptcy court, and the debtor eligibility requirements for each of the types of proceedings available. Chapter 3 governs case administration, including appointment and compensation of someone called "the trustee," whom we will discuss soon, and of other professional persons such as attorneys and accountants. It also contains the provisions governing the operation of a bankruptcy estate. Chapter 5 provisions include regulation of the claims and distribution process, discharges, and special bankruptcy-specific powers to trump certain pre-existing legal rights.

The next chapters house the specific rules for each type of bankruptcy. Chapter 7 governs the classic "straight" bankruptcy liquidation for both consumers and businesses. Chapter 9 has the special provisions for the bankruptcy of a municipality or other governmental unit. Chapter 11 is the chapter most often used by reorganizing businesses. Chapter 12 governs reorganization bankruptcies filed by family farmers or fishermen. Chapter 13, which excludes corporations, is the reorganization procedure discussed above that allows consumers to make payments to their creditors over time without having to relinquish their assets. A chapter 15 case is a special "ancillary" proceeding in which the United States court assists a foreign court that has primary bankruptcy jurisdiction over a foreign debtor.

The jurisdictional and procedural provisions governing bankruptcy are found in Title 28 of the U.S. Code. The criminal provisions, which define and establish sanctions for offenses such as bankruptcy fraud, are in Title 18 of the U.S. Code.

Certain provisions of Title 11 are not covered in depth in these materials. For example, there will be only a summary discussion of chapter 9 municipal bankruptcies, such as the bankruptcy filed by Jefferson County (Birmingham) Alabama amidst the stench of the financial maneuvers used to finance its new sewer system. There is also no coverage of Subchapters III and IV of chapter 7, which provide special rules for the bankruptcies of stockbrokers and commodity dealers, respectively. These are highly specialized and technical areas of an already-technical law.

F.   BEYOND LAW: WHY BANKRUPTCY?

Filing bankruptcy is a wrenching decision for virtually all the people and businesses that seek relief. The motivations vary, but perhaps two forces prevail above all others. One is the debtor's need for relief, and indeed, the filing of a bankruptcy petition triggers something not ironically called the "order for relief." § 301. Debtors from exhaustion or other reasons feel the need to halt once and for all the collection activity that is grinding away at them to gain some control over their lives or the operation of their business. We discuss these pressures more in the next assignment, in the consumer context, and later on, in the business context. The second motivation for filing is a desire to preserve one's assets. For consumers, this sometimes is as much sentimental as financial, such as trying to hold on to a home with a mortgage the debtor is struggling to pay. For businesses, the calculus is more likely to be purely economic. Haste makes waste, and allowing a creditor to seize and sell assets at a forced sale is nearly always a loss of value. As with so many of life's important lessons, O.J. Simpson illustrates the point with verve.

More Hoopla at Simpson Home Auction

The traveling circus that is the O.J. Simpson affair loaded up its wagons and made one more spectacular pass through L.A. County—this time in a modest, glamour-free swatch of suburbia.

Simpson's fabled Brentwood estate was put on the auction block Monday—it's estimated he owed well over $100,000 in back mortgage payments—on the steps of the county courthouse in Norwalk. At last,

Norwalk citizens had their own moment to bask in the reflected glare of television cameras, as the bank that has held title to the home turned in the winning bid of about $2.6 million.

"It's the only O.J. event on the Eastside—and it took 'em three years to get here," said Dick Whitrock, who left his South Whittier home to observe.

As rudimentary public auctions of property in foreclosure go, this one set a standard for excitement. The action unfolded before a sprawling array of a hundred-some reporters, television cameras from around the world and another couple hundred curious onlookers. The bidding itself was done in a matter of minutes.

. . .

"We've been filmed before—but it's usually because someone is going to sue us," said Renee Patrick, vice president of Trustee's Assistance Corp., which set up the auction on behalf of winning bidder Hawthorne Savings, the bank holding the trust to the house.

The mere fact that the auction was so open and ritualized gave it a certain riveting rawness—kind of like a flogging in a town square.

Dutifully, an official polled those cordoned behind police tape in the courtyard, calling out several times for bidders. "Any other qualified bidders? Please, please come forward," said Patrick Dobiesz, the gray-suited, bespectacled head of the company that took care of the foreclosure proceedings for the bank. Without blinking—or laughing—he uttered this to a crowd mostly composed of tense reporters and curious members of the public, some in shorts and T-shirts drinking coffee, munching cookies and looking more in the market for groceries than multimillion-dollar Brentwood property.

"Melrose" Larry Green, the perpetual call-in hound to the Howard Stern radio show, signaled the official that he wanted to bid, producing a financial statement showing a balance of $933,799.26 in an investment account he said was his. But that wasn't good enough, and he was turned away.

In fact, nothing less than a cashier's check for $2,531,259—or the cool cash itself—would have gotten you a chance to bid in the bright sunlight. That's the amount owed to the bank.

Auctioneer Garth Russell opened the bidding at $1.875 million, but within minutes the house was sold at $2,631,259. To the bank. There were two other qualified bidders. One never opened his mouth and slipped out in the post-auction pandemonium.

The other bidding party consisted of Glendale investor Steve Whitlock and Pasadena investor John Hall, who routinely buy properties at auction and turn around and sell them. But they quickly discovered there was nothing routine about their bid Monday.

. . .

"STEVE Whitlock, the LOSING bidder . . .," intoned a television reporter corralling Whitlock into a stand-up interview.

A tall, lanky gray-haired man in a plaid shirt and dark green slacks, Whitlock shrugged off the attention.

"It just looked like a good deal," he said. "The fact that it was O.J.'s house—we're here three times a week bidding on property."

Neither Whitlock nor Hall had any intention of moving into the house. "We'd have sold it fast," said Whitlock, who figures the residence could fetch $4 million.

Whitlock bid one dollar over the full sum that Simpson owed the bank and brought several checks to cover various potential bid amounts. "I would have gone to $2.6 million," he said. The winning bid was only about $31,000 more than that, and the two investors were peppered with inquiries about why they didn't try to top the bank's last offer.

"You set the amount you're willing to pay," Whitlock said. "If it goes over that, you move on to the next thing."

Now that the bank has bought the house, it essentially pays itself back the $2.5 million it is owed by Simpson. (Hawthorne Savings initiated foreclosure proceedings in late March, when Simpson had fallen $86,000 in arrears in mortgage payments.) It will pay the extra $100,000 to one or more of the many lien holders on the property.

Now that the bank has the property, it can turn around and try to sell the house for a handsome profit.

"They'll probably do what you and I would do if we wanted to sell our houses," said Dobiesz, whose T.D. Service Co. took care of the foreclosure proceedings and represented the bank at the auction. "They might hire brokers."

Dobiesz also figured the bank wouldn't be standing on Simpson's lawn that afternoon to throw him out. "I think they'll turn it over to their attorneys and let them go through the proper procedures," he said, estimating that would take two to three months. [*Los Angeles Times*, July 15, 1997.]

If one believes arms-length auctions as the best arbiters of value, it would appear the Simpson house was worth $2.63 million in July 2017.

O.J.'s House for Sale (Again): Only $3.95 Million

For Sale: 6,400-square-foot home on gated Brentwood estate, seven bedrooms, seven and a half baths, pool with waterfall. Freeway close. Heisman Trophy and grand piano not included: $3.95 million.

That's not the *real* ad for O.J. Simpson's Brentwood mansion, which was listed Monday with Fred Sands Estates, one of the nation's largest real-estate firms, but then again, as O.J.-trial watchers know, anything could happen. [Apparently the listing agent, Fred Sands Realty, was anxious to make sure only real bidders were interested and not just gawkers; it required proof of a 25% down payment ability, or $1 million, before showings. We have no evidence that "Melrose" Larry Green came back with his financial statement.—Eds.] [Ken Neville, https://www.eonline.com/news/34967/o-j-s-house-for-sale-again-only-s3-95-million (Aug. 5, 1997).]

As a final twist, the person who finally bought the house for almost $4 million bulldozed it and built a new one. Why would a house that sold at a creditor's sale for only $2.6M be put on the market a month later for $3.9M? One element might be the rule that permits the bank lender to Simpson to "credit bid," which means that it can "bid" its debt and has to put up cash only for the $31,000 that it bid in excess of what it is owed. The Supreme Court has held that the statute gives a creditor a right to credit bid in most cases. RadLAX Gateway Hotel, LLC v. Amalgamated Bank, 566 U.S. 639 (2012). The Juice's next home in Miami-area Florida also fell into foreclosure—and was also sold by the bank for profit—when he finally went to jail for nominally unrelated reasons to the forgoing notariety. As of current writing, he is spending his parole in a 5,000-foot Las Vegas golf course home estimated to be worth almost $2 million. Much of the $33 million civil judgment entered against him remains unpaid.

This acquisition allowed the bank to pocket a quick million-plus by getting the house at a forced sale and then being able to sell it at its leisure. Yet Messrs. Whitlock and Hall were also there, willing to bid a similar amount to—but not much more than—the outstanding debts on the property, and Whitlock predicted the ultimate sale price almost exactly. So what kept them from bidding more? Maybe this profit was not such a sure thing for the bank or maybe bidders at forced sales are only interested in a great bargain.

A central purpose of modern bankruptcy law is to preserve value and eliminate, or at least mitigate, the fact that forced sales destroy value. To improve the results at forced sales, or better still, avoid them, is a goal upon which almost all scholars agree. More importantly, consumers and businesses alike recognize that bankruptcy has the potential to prevent the loss of value.

G.   CONCLUSION

More households file for bankruptcy each year than any other form of litigation. The vast majority of these cases are either under chapter 7 or chapter 13. Who are these people? Perhaps not who you might think, which brings us to some empirical data. Research shows that when measured by enduring social criteria—education, occupation, homeownership—these families in bankruptcy represent a broad cross-section of the middle class, from doctors and lawyers to salesclerks and fast-food workers. Elizabeth Warren & Deborah Thorne, A Vulnerable Middle Class: Bankruptcy and Class Status, in *Broke*. Although many of them have poverty-level incomes when they file for bankruptcy, few of them are from the long-term poor. They may be down at the moment of filing, but the debtors are solidly in the middle of American society. Along with these families, who share many characteristics with our neighbors and co-workers, is a star-studded cast that has included Stephen Baldwin, Kim Basinger, Boris Becker, Nicholas Cage, 50 Cent, Marvin Gaye, M.C. Hammer, Larry King, Tom Petty, Burt Reynolds, Mike Tyson, Michael Vick, Dionne Warwick, and the group TLC.

The corporate list has its own stars, including megabusts and culturally significant downfalls (and sometimes rebirths) of such commercial icons as Ascena (parent to Ann Taylor, Lane Bryant, etc.), Barney's, Blockbuster, Borders Books, Boston Market, Boy Scouts of America, Brooks Brothers, California Pizza Kitchen, Chrysler, Chuck E. Cheese, Circuit City, Cirque du Soleil, Claire's, Einstein's Bagels, Enron, Forever 21 [well, apparently not—Eds.], Frederick's of Hollywood, General Motors, GNC, Gold's Gym, Hertz, Interstate Bakeries (Twinkies), J.C. Penney, J. Crew, Kmart, Kodak, Lehman Brothers, Lord & Taylor, Marvel Entertainment, Muzak (of elevator fame), Nieman Marcus, Pacific Gas & Electric (twice), Payless Shoes, Pier 1 Imports, Popeye's, Radio Shack, Sears, Tailored Brands (parent of Men's Wearhouse and JoS. A. Bank), Toys "R" Us, Trump Casinos, Worldcom (MCI), two major league ball clubs (the Texas Rangers and the L.A. Dodgers), and, perhaps most sadly for some, a number of law firms. In some industries, bankruptcy verges on a rite of passage. (Can you name the major airline carrier that has *not* filed bankruptcy? Hint: LUV.) Other companies land in bankruptcy when their entire industry collapses, with bankruptcy becoming the graveyard to bury the former industry leaders; the subprime mortgage industry is a somewhat recent example.

Still other companies look to bankruptcy to solve specific problems, such as tort liability for asbestos exposure. The management of most companies file chapter 11 to try to reorganize themselves as a going concern—who wants to admit defeat at the start?—but a good chunk of these companies will eventually wind up liquidating.

At the intersection of the statutes, the doctrine, the cases, the empirical data, and a host of normative convictions lies a system that powerfully affects the lives of hundreds of thousands of our fellow citizens and the economic futures of thousands of businesses each year. As you go through the materials in this book, feel free to flip back to this introduction, both for its explanatory "cheat notes" on, for example, the different chapters in the Code as well as for its theoretical overview of what this important legal system is trying to do.

Problem Set 1

1.1. After graduation from law school you spent two years in a big firm doing SEC securities registration statements. You began to feel catatonic and so decided that there had to be more variety and interest to the practice of law. You and two old classmates (one who had hibernated in the library for a litigation department and one who had taken rich people to lunch for a trusts and estates department) opened up a general practice firm.

The firm has been in existence for over a year now, and it is becoming solidly established. Over lunch one day, you and your partners reflect on the nature of your practice. It seems that the bulk of your clients are not disputing whether money is owed (ah, those lovely contract and tort hypos you mastered in law school); instead they are engaged in either trying to make someone pay money or trying to avoid paying money themselves. You recognize that much of your time is spent guiding clients in coercing or avoiding payment.

Chatting over lunch today, the three of you are once again exchanging horror stories (as all lawyers do) about what the client didn't tell you and how terrible your legal advice turned out to be because of the key fact the client didn't reveal. You tell of hearing in a deposition for the first time that your debtor-client had a huge asset his creditors could grab or that your creditor-client was about to push a debtor into a bankruptcy, not realizing bankruptcy would invalidate an important security interest your client held in one of the debtor's assets.

This conversation leads you and your partners to revise your standard interview form. Your current form includes a typical question asking debtors to list assets and liabilities. You believe your clients really intend to make a full disclosure to you, but you find that many people do not recognize immediately where they may owe money or where they may have unrealized assets. You conclude that a more particularized list might trigger more complete information from your clients, so you and your partners decide to compile checklists of potential debts and assets for both consumer and business clients. What is on each list?

1.2. You work for a major firm in a large city. One of the firm's most important clients is Security Bank. Security is having trouble with collection of an unsecured loan of $183,366 from a local physician, Janille Talis.

The firm has asked you to help the bank determine the wisest course of action with Dr. Talis.

Talis is a pathologist employed by Community Hospital. Her take-home salary is $12,500 per month. She owes $1,200 per month to your client. She spends about $1,800 on food, utilities, dry cleaning, and other day-to-day essential expenses. Her other monthly payments are listed below. Her credit report has no late payments, except to Security Bank.

Central Bank, home mortgage	$4,200
USA Savings, car loan	$650
Young Professionals Fitness Centre (two-year contract)	$450
Amon Kwart (dentist)	$675
Robbie Reich, co-worker	$150
Farmington Country Club, Initiation Fee	$300
MasterCard & Visa	$1,050
Fancy Nancy's Boutique Clothing Store	$850
John South, alimony payment	$2,325

Before exploring possible legal actions you try to evaluate Security's leverage as it compares with other creditors' positions. Of the creditors on this list, who is Talis most likely to pay? Why? How can Security try to improve its relative position?

1.3. Kim Sung-joo owns a home that he bought in 2005 for $205,000. He paid $15,000 down and signed a mortgage obligation for $190,000, which he has now paid down to $160,000. His salary as a convention planner was ample to cover the monthly payments, but he was laid off last year and has now missed three payments. His current job as a sales clerk ("only temporary, of course") will not support the mortgage payments. He has talked to the mortgage servicer, a bank in another city, about waiting just a little longer until the upturn in the local economy gets him his old job back. The servicer has so far been vague about what it could or would do, but said it might consider foreclosure.

A similar house in a nearby subdivision sold three months ago for about $180,000, after being put on the retail market for two or three months and listed with a real estate broker, who charged a 6% commission. A similar house sold in a foreclosure sale last month for $129,428. It was bought by the creditor for whom the sale was being held for exactly the amount of the debt owed the creditor. The creditor was the only one who showed up at the sale. A lawyer friend told Mr. Sung-joo he will owe personally any shortfall on the mortgage debt above the money received at a sale.

Should Mr. Sung-joo ask the bank to employ a broker to sell the house? Try to sell the house himself (with or without a broker)? Should the bank foreclose now or wait a few months more? If winning price at such a fore-closure sale is less than $160,000, what happens to Kim?

If you were the county tax appraiser, what would you list as the value of this home?

COLLECTING FROM CONSUMER DEBTORS

Consumer debt collection has formal legal procedures, both in-court for unsecured creditors and out-of-court for secured creditors. But equally if not more important are the informal collection efforts creditors undertake to encourage debtors to repay. That informal world also is regulated by laws. Some directly set the divide between permissible and impermissible persuasion; others exert indirect effects by regulating areas likely to be of interest to creditors and debtors jockeying for leverage.

A. LEVERAGE

1. Competing Concerns

As we saw with Dr. Talis (Assignment 1), the debtor-creditor payment process can best be viewed as a constant balancing. A debtor who has bills to pay makes a series of decisions about the costs and benefits of paying each bill. The process may be explicit or unarticulated, but either way debtors decide when to pay, which bills to pay first, or whether to pay at all.

Creditors engage in another balancing process. A creditor tries to determine how, at the lowest cost, to make it more attractive for the debtor to pay the money owed. The creditor looks for means to enhance its leverage in convincing the debtor to pay the obligation.

Collection Agency Headed by "Thugs" Helps Merchants

Davenport, IA. (UPI)—Quad Cities' businessmen, burdened with bundles of bad checks by the faltering economy, are turning to an unconventional collection agency with a pair of tough-looking hombres at the helm.

Dressed in leather jackets over Harley-Davidson T-shirts, Kenneth Fitzpatrick and Maurice Holst don't look like modern entrepreneurs.

But just let someone dare to not pay up on a rubber check. That's when Fitzpatrick, better known as Doc, pushes back the bandanna tied around his head, reaches into his jacket and whips out a worn copy of the Iowa Code.

While he explains the state's penalties for passing bad checks, Holst, who prefers to be called Trammp, scowls and looks menacing. A person might easily get the impression that they'll knock the garbage cans over on the way out.

But they don't. They may look like "Easy Riders," but they never use violence or threatening language. Folks seem to be scared of them anyway and cough up the requested money.

"One person even ran next door to borrow the money to make good on a check," Trammp said.

Local businessmen have welcomed the crusty, street-smart pair with open arms. In less than two months, 2 Outlaws Check Collecting Service has grown into a thriving business.

Photo Credit: Walter Kale/Chicago Tribune

"They're happy to see us," Doc said of the clients. "They say we're just what they're looking for. It's a crazy world out there where people are scared to collect money for themselves."

"They have to manage their business," Trammp said. "They don't have time for collecting bad checks."

Doc got the idea for the business while working for a liquor store in California, where he made a little extra money collecting the store's bad checks.

Then when he moved to Iowa and ran into money problems with a broken leg, he bounced a few checks of his own.

"I noticed that all these people (collection agencies) do is call you," he said. "That didn't scare me."

Doc and Trammp decided they could do better. After checking the legalities of such an enterprise, the pair registered their trade name with the Scott County Recorder's Office, printed up business cards and went to work.

"We gave one business card to an alderman and I guess he was pretty shook up about it," Trammp said, describing the reaction of Davenport councilman Larry d'Autremont, who runs a medical supply store.

"They didn't do anything to me," d'Autremont confided. "But they scared the hell out of me."

Doc said the pair started out collecting a $5 check for a local restaurant, but since then, "things started to snowball." About 10 friends have joined the business, which blossomed into rent collection and unpaid charge accounts.

"We work in pairs," Doc said. "That protects us as well. We don't want anybody saying we threatened them."

The collectors begin with a courteous telephone call.

"Most of the time the people say they'll pay up and send a check in the mail," he said. "Maybe 15 to 20 percent will pay just on a phone call. But sometimes you have to investigate them, if they've skipped town or something."

If a phone call doesn't work, Doc and Trammp show up on the offender's doorstep for a personal visit. Sometimes it takes more than one visit, or more than two people.

If that fails, they may institute legal action by filing a suit in small claims court or—if there is a large amount of money involved—talk the county prosecutor into filing criminal charges.

For their services, 2 Outlaws receives half of whatever they collect, whether it is a $5 check or a $1,000 charge account.

"Most people are happy to give it to us," Trammp said. "Half is better than nothing." . . . [*Daily Iowan*, Apr. 12, 1982, at p. 8B.]

If the 2 Outlaws are not available, creditors must turn to other tools to increase the odds of repayment. Harassing phone calls or including the debtor's name and picture in a "Deadbeat of the Month" advertisement in the local paper might be an inexpensive—but effective—means of encouraging debtor repayment. Of course, debtors can try to discourage creditor collection efforts. Keeping a pack of large dogs, having an unlisted phone number, or even moving every few weeks might deter certain collection activities. At a certain point, creditors give up.

Leverage is thus important both to debtors and creditors. Yet the exercise of this leverage is cabined by legal and social constraints. Legally, there is both restriction (no assault, regardless of debt amount) and channeling (court orders are required for garnishment). Socially, a debtor may have emotional motivations, such as loyalty in paying back a family member who stood by with financial support during tough times or fear that a doctor who is not repaid may withhold future service. There is also baseline variation in moral beliefs whether debts "should" be repaid driven by cultural norms and plain old personal preference. The content of law and norms affects leverage.

2. The Role of Law

Most money owed is repaid without resort to any legal process. Even when there is a dispute whether a debt is payable, or when a debtor is unable to repay on time, resort to legal devices to coerce (or avoid) payment is rare. Formal proceedings are a sizeable fraction of state and federal court cases, but they still are a tiny fraction of the universe of potential debt collection "events."

Professor William Whitford explains in an empirical study that one reason for this infrequent resort to formal law is that many creditors are unlikely to use courts because they see litigation as loaded with unnecessary costs and risks:

> A risk inherent in almost all litigation is that one party will net nothing by losing the case entirely. For the creditor in consumer credit collection, this risk takes the form either that the debtor will be judgment proof or that the creditor will be judged not to own a valid debt. The creditor can avoid the risk that the debt may be declared invalid by obtaining voluntary debtor payment. Moreover, when the debtor is judgment proof, it does not usually mean that he or she is assetless, but rather that available assets are exempt [from collection] or encumbered [with a security interest]. Nothing in the exemption laws, however, prevents the debtor from making a voluntary payment from otherwise exempt assets. Alternatively, a judgment proof debtor can attempt to borrow from a friend or relative, or to obtain a consolidation loan from a finance company, in order to settle a debt. These sources of payment cannot be reached directly by a creditor through coercive execution, of course, and hence create additional incentives to the creditor for voluntary settlement.

Whitford, A Critique of the Consumer Credit Collection System, 1979 Wis. L. Rev. 1047, 1055.

You might conclude that you can close up this book right now because mastery of the legal system is therefore irrelevant. Nice try. The most obvious point, of course, is that there is still the other one-third of pre-bankruptcy cases, and attorneys are frequently called to aid in resolving those disputes. A lawyer who is unfamiliar with the rules of debtor-creditor law is not in a position to provide effective help. The less obvious point is that formal law matters for bankruptcy debtors who have not been the targets of legal actions for two reasons. First, the formal rules of collection and their associated costs provide the backdrop against which parties reach informal, negotiated agreements. Second, as mentioned above, the legal system also sets ground rules for what parties can do in those informal negotiations, even though not all creditors and debtors follow the law (indeed, many do not).

B.   INFORMAL REMEDIES FOR NONPAYMENT OF DEBT

Laws create negotiating endowments for informal debtor-creditor negotiations. The universe of laws that could affect these negotiations is vast. Some laws do so intentionally, either by expressly setting rules on what counts as permissible persuasion, such as the Fair Debt Collection Practices Act, or by implicitly affecting the process by regulating areas likely to have a profound effect on these repayment negotiations, such as the Fair Credit Reporting Act. Still other laws are a step removed from regulating the negotiating world but nevertheless have an equally important effect on leverage: if you can't get your driver's license renewed until you pay your child support, your ex-spouse has strong leverage as your creditor, even though the driving certification laws ostensibly have nothing to do with debtor-creditor law. We examine each of these types of laws in turn.

1.   The Rules of the Game: Fair Debt Collection Practices

One of the oldest restrictions on collection was blunt and direct: usury laws. If a creditor charged more than a specified rate of interest, the loan would be deemed usurious. This meant the interest, and under some statutes the principal itself, would be deemed uncollectible and sometimes the creditor's conduct deemed criminal. Usury laws regulate the debt itself and thus sit at the core of debtor-creditor law. While usury has ancient foundations, and remains in use in most nations, it has limited applicability in the United States. A series of Supreme Court cases and statutes has effectively "deregulated" interest rates for most common consumer transactions, such as credit cards and mortgages, allowing creditors to shop for favorable state law. See Marquette National Bank v. First Omaha Service Corp., 439 U.S. 299 (1978).

Freed from interest rate restrictions, lenders charged higher rates and fees and lent to riskier customers. These practices, along with the usual bumps in the economy such as recessions, led to a burgeoning debt collection industry. Technological advances, such as automated phone dialing, and social changes, such as an increased proclivity to post identifying information on the Internet, have concomitantly lowered collection costs. Other new technologies, however, such as mobile phones and caller ID, have hampered debt collection, so the net technology effect remains unclear. The law struggles to keep up with the inventiveness of the parties, especially the repeat-player debt collectors. In the 1970s, Congress adopted the Fair Debt Collection Practices Act ("FDCPA"). The statute provides a federal remedy for debt collection abuses. Even with the FDCPA firmly in place, however, some debt collectors continue the quest for innovation.

Lawyer's Methods, Debtors' Nightmare

Edwina Rizzo vividly remembers the day her husband was on life support waiting for a heart transplant and Steven B. Zats called demanding payment of an overdue cable television bill.

Rizzo, of Havertown, says she explained her husband's critical condition and the bill collector replied: "Hey, people get sick and die every day. That's not my problem."

Zats told her in another conversation, she says, to bring payment to his office without delay. "You crawl, you walk, you get a bus," Rizzo remembers him saying, "you do whatever you can to get here."

And that, according to many who have dealt with him, is vintage Steven Zats.

A slender man who dresses in sneakers, blue jeans and T-shirts, Zats, 33, is perhaps the most aggressive—and some say the most unmerciful—small debt collector in the Philadelphia region.

Many of the debtors Zats pursues are poor, unemployed or disabled. Their debts often involve a single unpaid bill—usually a disputed payment for medical services. Most of his 600 clients are doctors, dentists or health-care firms.

Zats, a lawyer, routinely obtains judgments against them, freezes their bank accounts, and adds his own fees to their debts, driving up costs hundreds of dollars. . . .

"I was gullible, all right?" says Viola Hartman, of Kensington [a Legal Services client]. "They called and said it was a survey on banks and all this."

Hartman is 63 and a widow. She works as a part-time housekeeper in a Philadelphia public school.

She owed $1,500 for a laser surgery bill which she believed her insurance was supposed to pay.

It didn't.

Zats sued to collect.

When someone from [Zats' corporation] called earlier this year [posing as a telephone survey company], Hartman disclosed that she banked at CoreStates Bank.

In February, Zats froze her account there and cleaned it out.

Hartman bounced checks for her water and telephone bills.

"I didn't even know that they could do such a thing to you," she said. "I'm two months behind on everything now because of it. I'm behind in my mortgage, my gas bill. . . ." [*The Philadelphia Inquirer*, June 12, 1994, at pp. A1 and A8.]

Mr. Zats declined to be interviewed for this story, but *The Philadelphia Inquirer* reported the contents of a letter from Mr. Zats to his debtors that said: "My goal in business is to please my clients, not to please the debtors. Debtors don't like to have their bank accounts frozen and their personal belongings sold to satisfy the debts. Since the debtors have not been concerned with paying the bill . . . my office cannot be concerned if the debtors can't pay their rent because of a frozen bank account."

Debt collection abuses are not rare. One reason is that many Americans are in debt trouble. A 2007 poll found that one in seven Americans was contacted by a debt collector in the preceding year, and that was in good financial times. For many years, the Federal Trade Commission has received hundreds of thousands of complaints about debt collectors, although the number of complaints has decreased in recent years. The FTC has obtained civil fines of $1 million in each recent year for widespread collection abuses. See Federal Trade Commission, Consumer Sentinel Network Data Book for January-December 2019 (Jan. 2020), *available at* https://www.ftc .gov/reports/consumer-sentinel-network-data-book-2019.

Large effort and frequent abuses both arise from the fact that collecting relatively small debts can be immensely profitable. Much of the debt in the collection process has been written off by the original creditor and bought for pennies on the dollar by collectors. As one author explains about a debt-buyer named Aaron, "If he could buy debts with 'face values' of $15,000 for $15—and if his agencies could collect just 10 percent of what was owed—he could make a fortune." Jake Halpern, Bad Paper: Chasing Debt from Wall Street to the Underworld (2014).

The FDCPA imposes a number of restrictions on debt collectors, but does not cover creditors collecting for their own account ("originators"). It forbids misrepresentation in debt collection and includes a requirement that collection agencies verify the accuracy of debt information. The statute bars harassing tactics and includes specific examples, such as using obscenities or calling past 10:00 P.M. Another provision forbids unfair practices like getting postdated checks as a method to threaten criminal prosecution. Like much long-in-the-tooth regulation, it also proscribes conduct we might consider outdated (no post cards mailed to work!). The Act provides for both administrative and private enforcement, with recovery for violations of actual damages, costs, and $1,000 in statutory damages. The relatively new Consumer Financial Protection Bureau has authority to enforce the FDCPA, along with a slew of other consumer protection and financial regulations. Its online complaint process handles millions of disputes annually. Go visit it: https://www.consumerfinance.gov/about-us/blog/how-we-keep-you-safe-consumer-financial-marketplace/. Because many statutory supplements do not include the FDCPA, we include excerpts in Appendix A to this book, along with excerpts from some other federal statutes that regulate consumer credit. (We tried to excerpt only the "juicy" stuff of most interest to law students.)

The prohibitions in the FDCPA did not come out of thin air: Congress was responding to documented abuses. But collectors' business models may now have one-upped the law.

HENSON v. SANTANDER CONSUMER USA, INC.
137 S. Ct. 1718 (2017)

GORSUCH, J., delivered [his first—Eds.] opinion for a unanimous Court.

Disruptive dinnertime calls, downright deceit, and more besides drew Congress's eye to the debt collection industry. From that scrutiny emerged the Fair Debt Collection Practices Act, a statute that authorizes private lawsuits and weighty fines designed to deter wayward collection practices. So perhaps it comes as little surprise that we now face a question about who exactly qualifies as a "debt collector" subject to the Act's rigors. Everyone agrees that the term embraces the repo man—someone hired by a creditor to collect an outstanding debt. But what if you purchase a debt and then try to collect it for yourself—does that make you a "debt collector" too? That's the nub of the dispute now before us.

The parties approach the question from common ground. The complaint alleges that CitiFinancial Auto loaned money to petitioners seeking to buy cars; that petitioners defaulted on those loans; that respondent Santander then purchased the defaulted loans from CitiFinancial; and that Santander sought to collect in ways petitioners believe troublesome under the Act. The parties agree, too, that in deciding whether Santander's conduct falls within the Act's ambit we should look to statutory language defining the term "debt collector" to embrace anyone who "regularly collects or attempts to collect . . . debts owed or due . . . another."

Even when it comes to that question, the parties agree on at least part of an answer. Both sides accept that third party debt collection agents generally qualify as "debt collectors" under the relevant statutory language, while those who seek only to collect for themselves loans they originated generally do not. These results follow, the parties tell us, because debt collection agents seek to collect debts "owed . . . another," while loan originators acting on their own account aim only to collect debts owed to themselves. All that remains in dispute is how to classify individuals and entities who regularly purchase debts originated by someone else and then seek to collect those debts for their own account. Does the Act treat the debt purchaser in that scenario more like the repo man or the loan originator?

For their part, the district court and Fourth Circuit sided with Santander. . . .

[P]etitioners suggest that Santander can qualify as a debt collector not only because it regularly seeks to collect for its own account debts that it has purchased, but also because it regularly acts as a third party collection agent for debts owed to others. Petitioners did not, however, raise the latter theory in their petition for certiorari and neither did we agree to review it. Second, the parties briefly allude to another statutory definition of the term "debt collector"—one that encompasses those engaged "in any business the principal purpose of which is the collection of any debts." § 1692a(6). But the parties haven't much litigated that alternative definition and in granting certiorari we didn't agree to address it either.

With these [important, possibly dispositive—Eds.] preliminaries by the board, we can turn to the much narrowed question properly before us. In doing so, we begin, as we must, with a careful examination of the statutory text. And there we find it hard to disagree with the Fourth Circuit's interpretive handiwork. After all, the Act defines debt collectors to include those who regularly seek to collect debts "owed . . . another." And by its plain terms this language seems to focus our attention on third party collection agents working for a debt owner—not on a debt owner seeking to collect debts for itself. Neither does this language appear to suggest that we should care how a debt owner came to be a debt owner—whether the owner originated the debt or came by it only through a later purchase. All that matters is whether the target of the lawsuit regularly seeks to collect debts for its own account or does so for "another." . . .

Petitioners reply that this seemingly straightforward reading overlooks an important question of tense. They observe that the word "owed" is the *past* participle of the verb "to owe." And this, they suggest, means the statute's definition of debt collector captures anyone who regularly seeks to collect debts *previously* "owed . . . another." So it is that, on petitioners' account, the statute excludes from its compass loan originators (for they never seek to collect debts previously owed someone else) but embraces many debt purchasers like Santander (for in collecting purchased debts they necessarily seek to collect debts previously owed another). If Congress wanted to exempt all present debt owners from its debt collector definition, petitioners submit, it would have used the *present* participle "owing." That would have better sufficed to do the job—to make clear that you must collect debts *currently* "owing . . . another" before implicating the Act.

But this much doesn't follow even as a matter of good grammar, let alone ordinary meaning. Past participles like "owed" are routinely used as adjectives to describe the present state of a thing—so, for example, *burnt* toast is inedible, a *fallen* branch blocks the path, and (equally) a debt *owed* to a current owner may be collected by him or her. . . . Widening our view to take in the statutory phrase in which the word "owed" appears—"owed or due . . . another"—serves to underscore the point. Petitioners acknowledge that the word "due" describes a debt *currently* due at the time of collection and not a debt that *was* due only in some previous period. So to rule for them we would have to suppose Congress set two words cheek by jowl in the same phrase but meant them to speak to entirely different periods of time. All without leaving any clue. . . .

. . . Congress never had the chance to consider what should be done about those in the business of purchasing defaulted debt [when drafting the statute]. That's because, petitioners tell us, the "advent" of the market for defaulted debt represents "'one of the most significant changes'" to the debt market generally since the Act's passage in 1977. Brief for Petitioners 8 (quoting Consumer Financial Protection Bureau, Fair Debt Collection Practices Act: CFPB Annual Report 2014, p. 7 (2014)). Had Congress known this new industry would blossom, they say, it surely would have judged defaulted debt purchasers more like (and in need of the same special rules as) independent debt collectors. Indeed, petitioners contend that no other result would be consistent with the overarching congressional goal of deterring untoward debt collection practices.

All this seems to us quite a lot of speculation. . . .

In the end, reasonable people can disagree with how Congress balanced the various social costs and benefits in this area. We have no difficulty imagining, for example, a statute that applies the Act's demands to anyone collecting any debts, anyone collecting debts originated by another, or to some other class of persons still. Neither do we doubt that the evolution of the debt collection business might invite reasonable disagreements on whether Congress should reenter the field and alter the judgments it made in the past. After all, it's hardly unknown for new business models to emerge in response to regulation, and for regulation in turn to address new business models. Constant competition between constable and quarry, regulator and regulated, can come as no surprise in our changing world. But neither should the proper role of the judiciary in that process—to apply, not amend, the work of the People's representatives.

The judgment of the Court of Appeals is
Affirmed.

═══════════════

As mentioned by the Court, the statute contains another definition of "debt collector" that turns on whether debt collection is the debtor's primary business. The Court's decision to ignore this definition leaves its grammatical fate unresolved. As things stand, however, it is hard to know which will prevail: the debt enforcers changing their business models to the purchaser form or congressional amendments to expand the application of the statute. But it may not matter (unless someone brings a preemption challenge). Many state statutes encompass more entities than the FDCPA's list and provide for larger penalties and longer statutes of limitation.

Ironically, left untouched by *Henson* is the application of the statute to lawyers, a group that was astounded when it felt the Act's restraining hand in Heintz v. Jenkins, 514 U.S. 291 (1995). Although Congress did later agree to exempt formal pleadings, § 1692e(11), see also Obduskey v. McCarthy & Holthus LLP, 139 S. Ct. 1029 (2019) (filing of nonjudicial real estate foreclosure not debt collection under the Act). When lawyers do get into the collection business, they find themselves with no special immunity.

McCOLLOUGH v. JOHNSON, RODENBURG & LAUINGER
637 F.3d 939 (9th Cir. 2011)

THOMAS, Circuit Judge

. . .

Tim McCollough, a former school custodian, opened a credit card account with Chemical Bank sometime around 1990. Chemical Bank merged with the Chase Manhattan Bank ("Chase Manhattan") in 1996 and continued business under the Chase Manhattan name. McCollough continued to make purchases on the account.

McCollough and his wife fell behind on their credit card bills after he allegedly suffered a brain injury at work and she underwent surgery. When McCollough made his last payment on the Chase Manhattan account in 1999, an unpaid balance of approximately $3,000 remained. In 2000, Chase Manhattan "charged off" the account on its books.

Collect America, Ltd. ("Collect America"), through its subsidiary, CACV of Colorado, Ltd. ("CACV"), is a purchaser of bad debt portfolios — typically, debts that have been charged off by the primary lender. CACV purchases the debts; Collect America attempts collection.

In 2001, CACV purchased McCollough's delinquent account from Chase Manhattan. CACV sued McCollough in 2005 for $3,816.80 in state court to collect the debt. Acting pro se, McCollough replied that the "statute of limitations is up." Two weeks later, CACV dismissed the case. CACV documented service of the complaint and McCollough's response in its electronic files.

In 2006, Collect America retained JRL [Johnson, Rodenburg & Lauinger], a law firm specializing in debt collection, to pursue collection of McCollough's outstanding debt. . . . Charles Dendy was the JRL attorney who handled the law firm's collection cases for Montana. During the period from January 2007 through July 2008, JRL filed 2,700 collection lawsuits in Montana. On an average day, JRL filed five lawsuits in the state; on one day, JRL filed 40 lawsuits. JRL attorney Lisa Lauinger testified that approximately 90% of the collection lawsuits resulted in a default judgment.

The contract between JRL and Collect America contained the following disclaimer: "Collect America makes no warranty as to the accuracy or validity of data provided." In addition, the contract expressly made JRL "responsible to determine [its] legal and ethical ability to collect these accounts." CACV transmitted information about McCollough's account to JRL using debt collection software. CACV also sent the law firm the electronic file.

The law firm's screening procedures flagged a statute of limitations problem with McCollough's debt. On January 4, 2007, JRL account manager Grace Lauinger wrote to CACV: "It appears that the Statute of Limitations has expired on this file as of August 21, 2005. If you can provide us with an instrument in writing to extend the Statute of Limitations." The next day, JRL recorded in the electronic file that "* * * NO DEMAND HAS GONE OUT ON THIS FILE * * * THIS IS THE COLLECT AMERICA BATCH THAT WE ARE HAVING PROBLEMS W[ITH]."

. . .

On April 17, 2007, JRL filed a collection complaint signed by JRL attorney Charles Dendy against McCollough in Montana state court. The complaint sought judgment for an account balance of $3,816.80, interest of $5,536.81, attorney's fees of $481.68, and court costs of $120.00.

. . .

On June 13, 2007, McCollough filed a pro se answer to the complaint, asserting a statute of limitations defense:

> FORGIVE MY SPELLING I HAVE A HEAD INJURY AND WRITING DOSE NOT COME EASY
>
> (1) THE STACUT OF LIMITACION'S IS UP, I HAVE NOT HAD ANY DEALINGS WITH ANY CREDITED CARD IN WELL OVER 8 1/2 YEARS
> (2) I AM DISABLED I GET 736.00 A MONTH S.S.I. . . .
> (3) WHEN WORKERS COMP STOPED PAYING I RAN OUT OF MONEY, CHASE WOULD NOT WORK WITH ME, THEY PASSED IT ON TO COLLECTOR'S. . . .
> (4) THIS IS THE THIRED TIME THEY HAVE BROUGHT ME TO COURT ON THIS ACCOUNT, . . . WHEN WILL IT STOP DO I HAVE TO SUE THEM SO I CAN LIVE QUIETLY IN PAIN

One month later, McCollough also telephoned Dendy and left a message indicating that he would be seeking summary judgment on the basis of the statute of limitations. . . .

In October 2007, Dendy served on McCollough a list of twenty-two requests for admission that included the following: [All statements in the Complaint are true and correct. Defendant McCollough made a payment on the Chase credit card on or about June 30, 2004 in the amount of $75.00.].

On December 7, 2007, Dendy sent to CACV an email marked "URGENT." The email read:

> An attorney has appeared in this action and has served discovery requests. . . . The attorney is one who is anti purchased debt and who attempts to run up costs in an attempt to secure a large cost award against plaintiff. . . . Please provide me with copies of everything you can get for documentation as soon as possible. . . .

. . . CACV instructed Dendy to dismiss the suit "asap" because of the "SOL problem." JRL then moved for dismissal with prejudice and the state court dismissed the action.

McCollough sued JRL in federal district court alleging violations of the FDCPA. . . .

The case was then tried to a jury over the course of three days. At trial, lay witnesses Keri Henan and Ken Lucero testified about their experiences being sued by JRL. Michael Eakin, a consumer law attorney with Montana Legal Services, testified about the rapid growth of debt-collection lawsuits in Montana and about JRL's role in that trend; he also testified that "a vast majority" of JRL's lawsuits against debtors result in default judgments because JRL tries its cases without consideration for the pro se status of most of its defendant-debtors. James Patten, a Montana collection lawyer, described the importance of reasonable pre-suit investigation and testified that it was JRL's "factory" approach of "mass producing default judgments," rather than any mistake, that caused JRL to prosecute the time-barred debt. . . .

The jury found in favor of McCollough . . . and awarded him the $1,000 statutory maximum for violations of the FDCPA; $250,000 for emotional distress; and $60,000 in punitive damages.

. . .

II.

The district court properly granted summary judgment against JRL on the FDCPA claims. The FDCPA prohibits debt collectors from engaging in various abusive and unfair practices. See Heintz v. Jenkins, 514 U.S. 291 (1995). The statute was enacted to eliminate abusive debt collection practices; to ensure that debt collectors who abstain from such practices are not competitively disadvantaged; and to promote consistent state action to protect consumers. 15 U.S.C. § 1692(e). The statute defines a "debt collector" as one who "regularly collects . . . debts owed or due or asserted to be owed or due another," 15 U.S.C. § 1692a(6), and covers lawyers who regularly collect debts through litigation, Heintz, 514 U.S. at 293-94, 115 S. Ct. 1489.

A.

Although the FDCPA is a strict liability statute, it excepts from liability those debt collectors who satisfy the "narrow" bona fide error defense. Reichert v. Nat'l Credit Sys., Inc., 531 F.3d 1002, 1005 (9th Cir. 2008) (quotation omitted). . . .

The district court correctly concluded that JRL's bona fide error defense failed as a matter of law. JRL argues that it maintained adequate preventive procedures by utilizing a system to flag potential statute of limitations problems. However, the procedures that support a valid bona fide error defense must be " 'reasonably adapted' to avoid the specific error at issue." Reichert, 531 F.3d at 1006 (quoting Johnson v. Riddle, 443 F.3d 723, 729 (10th Cir. 2006)). JRL's error in this case was not its failure to catch time-barred cases; indeed, JRL initially spotted the limitations period problem and sent a letter to CACV requesting "an instrument in writing to extend" the limitations period. Instead, JRL erred by relying without verification on CACV's representation and by overlooking contrary information in its electronic file. JRL thus presented no evidence of procedures designed to avoid the specific errors that led to its filing and maintenance of a time-barred collection suit against McCollough.

. . .

The undisputed evidence established that JRL's reliance on CACV's email was unreasonable as a matter of law. First, Collect America's contract with JRL expressly disclaimed "the accuracy or validity of data provided" and instructed that JRL was "responsible to determine [its] legal and ethical ability to collect" the account. Second, the electronic file confirmed that the event that took place on June 30, 2004, was the return of "unused costs" rather than a partial payment. Third, the electronic file also indicated that McCollough had asserted a statute of limitations defense to a collection action filed against him in 2005 over the same debt. Finally, McCollough informed JRL that the debt fell outside the limitations period both in his answer to JRL's complaint and in a phone call. . . .

[With respect to the request for admissions,] JRL contends that the FDCPA should not be read to cover discovery procedures such as requests for admission, although JRL concedes that the FDCPA covers both the filing of complaints and the service of settlement letters during the course of litigation, Our precedents do not support such a distinction. Rather, the FDCPA "applies to the litigating activities of lawyers." *Heintz*, 514 U.S. at 294, 115 S. Ct. 1489. . . .

The district court correctly held that JRL's service of false requests for admission violated the FDCPA as a matter of law. . . .

JRL's requests for admission asked McCollough to admit facts that were not true: that he had never disputed the debt, that he had no defense, that every statement in JRL's complaint was true, and that he had actually made a payment on or about June 30, 2004. JRL had information in its possession that demonstrated the untruthfulness of the requested admissions.

The requests for admission did not include an explanation that, under Montana Rule of Civil Procedure 36(a), the requests would be deemed admitted if McCollough did not respond within thirty days. Because we consider the debt collector's conduct from the standpoint of the least sophisticated debtor, we must conclude that the service of requests for admission containing false information upon a pro se defendant without an explanation that the requests would be deemed admitted after thirty days constitutes "unfair or unconscionable" or "false, deceptive, or misleading" means to collect a debt. Here, JRL effectively requested that McCollough admit JRL's entire case against him and concede all defenses. The least sophisticated debtor cannot be expected to anticipate that a response within thirty days was required to prevent the court from deeming the requests admitted. The district court properly granted summary judgment on this claim. . . .

Affirmed.

2.   *Playing the Game: The Credit Reporting System*

A primary source of leverage is the power to refuse new credit to debtors who did not repay prior debts. The problem, of course, is that debtors may find it easy to walk away from a single creditor. Creditors know that their leverage will be stronger if there is nowhere else for the debtor to walk. In other words, if a creditor can influence *other* providers of goods and services (and credit) to withhold future credit from a deadbeat debtor, the unpaid creditor gains much greater leverage in encouraging repayment.

To maximize this leverage effect, creditors need an inexpensive, fairly accurate method of tracking and reporting debtors' payment behavior. Well-established credit reporting agencies in the United States do the trick. The three largest entities are Experian, Equifax, and TransUnion. Creditors participate in two ways with the bureaus. They are both "furnishers," because they provide information on their borrowers, and "users," who access bureau data to evaluate applicants' creditworthiness (and also to obtain names for credit card solicitations).

The credit reporting companies gather extensive information. Such information nearly always includes things such as the number of credit accounts the debtor has, the credit limits for each account, the timeliness and amounts of the debtor's payments, and the number of times a debtor has been delinquent in repayments. It also includes information from public records, such as foreclosures and other lawsuits, and most relevant to this book, whether a person has filed bankruptcy. Although their data are extensive, credit reporting agencies sometimes have been criticized for not collecting some information, such as income, employment history, and payment records for rent or utilities. This skew in collected data ironically gives those who eschew credit cards and other traditional forms of credit a thin file, which is interpreted adversely.

Information in a credit report is also used to calculate a "credit score," a numerical estimate of a consumer's credit risk. The most well-known is the FICO score, whose acronym comes from the industry leader in such scores, the Fair Isaac Company. Five data categories make the following relative contributions to a FICO score: payment history: 35%; amounts owed: 30%; length of credit history: 15%; recent credit use: 10%; types of credit in use: 10%. The credit agencies, and many creditors, have different proprietary algorithms for creating their own scores, but the FICO score is frequent shorthand. Experian and VISA even have a "BankruptcyPredict" score that purports to gauge the likelihood of a future bankruptcy filing. The inputs into these scores and the formulas are tightly guarded proprietary secrets.

The information in credit reports is refreshed on a daily basis. Each month the consumer reporting agencies enter an estimated 4.5 billion pieces of information into their databases. Creditors make widespread use of credit reporting, asking bureaus to pull about three million files every day.

The system, however, is far from perfect. A 2012 study by the Federal Trade Commission found that one in five credit reports contained errors, and that one in twenty contained errors big enough to deny consumers credit or increase their cost of borrowing. Errors can go in either direction, positive or negative. Errors of omission are a particular concern for consumers trying to improve a score. A 2002 Consumer Federation study found that 78% of files were missing a revolving account that was in good standing, and 31% of files were missing a mortgage account that had never been delinquent. These errors are troubling, because as one Congressman explains, "A poor credit history is the 'Scarlet Letter' of 20th century America." 136 Cong. Rec. H5325-02 (daily ed. July 23, 1990 (statement of Rep. Annunzio)).

Why all the errors? On the one hand, creditors should care about data accuracy because they are users of credit reports. On the other hand, as furnishers, creditors may care less about updating files on customers who are current, which incurs direct creditor costs for diffuse benefits, than they do about tattling on delinquent debtors, which generates creditor leverage. (It is no accident that the collections script starts "Protect Your Credit Rating.")

The Fair Credit Reporting Act, 15 U.S.C. § 1681 et seq., provides procedures to which a reporting agency must adhere when the accuracy of a creditor's report is questioned. (See Appendix A.) The agency cannot defend itself by blaming the creditors for any misinformation; both are responsible, and both often find themselves as co-defendants when something goes awry. The remedies are quite limited, however, and as with much of consumer law, the substantive law is hollow without enforcement.

Both consumers and businesses are rated as credit risks and threats to credit ratings are an important part of collecting unsecured debt in the United States. The ratings have grown in power as they are more and more often used not only for granting credit, but also for employment and housing and increasingly for insurance purposes. They have even become weapons in abusive relationships. Angela Littwin, Escaping Battered Credit: A Proposal for Repairing Credit Reports Damaged by Domestic Violence, 161 U. Pa. L. Rev. 363 (2013). You should not be surprised at the allure of incentivizing human behavior through "scoring," although you may be surprised at how far it is being taken in some places.

China's New Tool for Social Control: A Credit Rating for Everything

Beijing wants to give every citizen a score based on behavior such as spending habits, turnstile violations and filial piety, which can blacklist citizens from loans, jobs, air travel.

HANGZHOU, China—Swiping her son's half-fare student card through the turnstile here one Monday after noon, Chen Li earned herself a $6 fine and a reprimand from a subway-station inspector for not paying the adult fare. A notice on a post nearby suggested more-dire consequences. It warned that infractors could be docked points in the city's "personal credit information system." A decline in Ms. Chen's credit score, according to official pronouncements, could affect her daily life, including securing loans, jobs and her son's school admission. . . . In time, Beijing expects to draw on bigger, combined data pools, including a person's internet activity. . . . The national social-credit system's aim . . . according to a slogan repeated in planning documents, is to "allow the trustworthy to roam everywhere under heaven while making it hard for the discredited to take a single step. . . ." China's judiciary already has already created a blacklisting system that would tie into the national social-credit operation. Zhuang Daohe, a Hangzhou legal scholar, cites the example of a client, part-owner of a travel company, who now can't buy tickets for planes or high-speed trains because a Hangzhou court put him on a blacklist after he lost a dispute with a landlord. [*Wall Street Journal*, Nov. 28, 2016.]

3.   All Part of the Game: Other Laws Affecting Leverage

While creditors can sue when a debtor has not paid, the process is expensive and fraught with the possibility of mistake. Creditors are delighted to offload this risk to the government.

Deadbeat Dad Who Owed Nearly $700k Is Off to Prison

For the first time in Central Florida, a deadbeat parent has been sentenced to prison for not paying child support. Robert Abraham owed $697,000. His children and ex-wife have been trying to collect for the last 17 years.

Abraham was handcuffed, fingerprinted and carted off to state prison, Tuesday. He'll spend two years behind bars. "It wasn't only money they were cheated out of," said his ex-wife Sandi Pinkham. "He cheated them out of being a father and not once did he ever say, 'Sorry.'"

Pinkham has spent years in courtrooms fighting her ex-husband for the money he owes. In March, Abraham pleaded guilty to being a deadbeat dad. Today, he told the judge he had no money.

"I was in jail for six months," said Abraham. "If I had the money don't you think I would've purged myself out. I got a staph infection, got sick, I almost died. Don't you think I would've gotten out if I could?"

But prosecutors pointed out that Abraham bought expensive watches, took trips to Europe and at one time owned two homes. His son testified against him.

"He didn't live the way we did," said his son Reed Abraham. "I can't tell you how many times we'd have mac and cheese for dinner and my mom wouldn't eat."

Because Abraham has continuously ignored court orders for 17 years, the judge said leniency was not an option.

As he was being taken out of the courtroom, Abraham looked at his ex-wife and son, frowned, and shook his head. After prison, he will have three years of community control and probation. And, he'll have to account for every dollar earned and every dime spent.

Abraham is the first man in Central Florida to face third degree felony charges for non-payment of child support. Usually, the state comes up with other ways to make deadbeat parents pay. That can include suspending driver's licenses, taking tax refunds or lottery winnings. The state can even file liens against homes owned by the deadbeat parents. [Copyright 2008 by wftv.com. All rights reserved.]

The Florida statute that brought down Father Abraham was clearly intended to coerce payment, but other laws may achieve that incentive more obliquely. For example, a bank that has not been repaid may report the debtor to the IRS for "income" from the forgiveness of debt. (If a creditor forgives a debt—that is, releases the debtor from the obligation to pay—tax law treats that release as the functional equivalent of receiving income, on which, of course, tax is due. 26 U.S.C. § 61(a)(12). "Cancellation of debt" income is conceptually logical, but the results can be awkward, to say the least.)

Dozens of similar provisions in the state and federal laws indirectly reallocate the leverage between debtors and creditors. Few would show up in an index of debtor-creditor laws, but many have powerful effects on the leverage a party can exercise in collecting a debt.

C.   FORMAL REMEDIES FOR NONPAYMENT OF DEBT

Some debtors do not pay in response to the usual tools of persuasion. At this point, creditors can invoke formal legal remedies. The classic process is a lawsuit to obtain a judgment, but some creditors enjoy self-help rights or can intervene in relationships the debtor has with third parties to collect. We cover these topics only briefly because collection, apart from the constraints of the FDCPA, is generally governed by state law, meaning that there are local twists and terminologies. These are crucial for the practitioner but overwhelming for the student. You're welcome. The most important thing to know is whether the debt is secured. If it is, the creditor has statutory self-help remedies (usually modeled on Article 9 of the Uniform Commercial Code) that have no analogue for unsecured creditors. *If you have not taken a background course in secured credit, you should review Appendix B, in which we offer a brief primer on secured debt collection.*

1.   Collection Without Suit: Repossession (*Secured Creditors Only)

Secured creditors have very special collection remedies against consumers under Article 9 of the Uniform Commercial Code, of which the most important is self-help repossession, which provides fast and relatively cheap relief (no lawyer required in most cases). The threat of it also provides unrivaled leverage to secured creditors and often is the precipitating event for a consumer bankruptcy.

Tradesfolk specializing in repossession are a colorful lot called "Repo Men," the subject of the near-eponymous 1984 film.

Repo Man Relies on Timing, Skills

MISHAWAKA—Ron Brunkel has seen the great lengths people will go to avoid having their cars repossessed. He's seen guns on the front seat as a warning to stay away . . . dogs chained to the bumpers . . . vehicles parked in the neighbor's garage. Not to mention verbal—sometimes even physical— confrontations. "We get threatened all the time," said Brunkel, vice president of Mishawaka-based SS Recovery. "But when we get that threat, we either leave the car or talk the person out of it. We get training on what to say, and on what not to say." Brunkel said some of his employees have had guns pulled on them, while others have been assaulted. A 23-year-old Mishawaka man was taken to Memorial Hospital Oct. 24 after he was

assaulted while attempting to repossess a car in the 1800 block of East
Randolph Street in South Bend. While the man and a co-worker were preparing to remove the vehicle, a man at the address jumped in the car and
started driving away. The man drove the vehicle into the repo worker, who
flew across the hood and struck his head on the windshield, cracking the
glass, the co-worker told police. The worker clung to the vehicle for two
blocks before he slipped off near the intersection of Randolph and Sampson
streets. . . . "We try and keep our average up to 95 percent when it comes
to avoiding any altercations," Brunkel said. "We do that based upon good
timing and actual training. We do a little bit of background work to see if
this person has been in trouble before. So basically we profile the person
we're going to get the car from." Workers often will confiscate the car in the
middle of the night to avoid disputes; they do not knock on doors to alert
the person they are taking a car. "We try and outsmart them," Brunkel said.
[*South Bend Tribune*, Oct. 31, 2008.]

The availability of bankruptcy to the consumer lowers the risk of violence in debt collection, an illustration of bankruptcy's appeal in every
context as an orderly, controlled, and peaceful method of resolving highly
emotional and potentially explosive disputes.

A secured creditor will rarely invoke bankruptcy for reasons we will
study, but if it wants to avoid the brusquerie of repo, it can invoke the
formal legal process by using its secured status to seek a writ of replevin
or sequestration, which ends with the sheriff taking the property. Resort
to formal legal process is more likely in the real estate realm, where about
half of all states require a mortgagee to file a lawsuit to foreclose a mortgage. Secured creditors' remedies are cumulative: they have the neat repo
trick, but if that is dangerous or daunting, they can follow the lesser route
of their unsecured cousins and sue on the debt, a process to which we
now turn.

2.   *Suing the Debtor: Judgment and Execution*

Unsecured creditors (or secured creditors opting for this route) can sue to
collect from a debtor that refuses to pay. When a creditor pursues judicial
collection, the first step is to establish in court that the debt is owed. This
may involve a complex trial, rich with factual disputes and legal questions
of contract, tort, and the like, or it may be the more banal and abbreviated
suit under Article 3 of the UCC on a check or other like instrument. Even
quicker, and more common in the consumer context, the court process
may be nothing more than the entry of a default judgment following the
debtor's failure to appear. Default judgments sometimes occur because the
debtor has no defense to the debt, but even with a valid defense, cash-
strapped consumers who are not paying their debts can ill afford to hire
an attorney or miss work to go to court. The procedural requirements of
defending a lawsuit, even in a small claims process, may overwhelm them,
or they may have been the victims of so-called "sewer service" and not
even realize a lawsuit is occurring. Furthermore, many consumer contracts
require arbitration of debt disputes, so many court judgments are really
just summary entries of arbitration orders.

Still, the paradigm is the civil trial, and attorneys (at least in the popular mind) exult in the litigation process. Yet those same attorneys, once victorious in litigation, may have no idea what to do in real life if the losing defendant fails to write out a check for the judgment. Defendants who pay as they are leaving the courthouse after an unfavorable verdict are unheard of; let us know if you encounter one in practice. The judgment gives the successful plaintiff no priority in any of the debtor's property or income. Without further action, it is a piece of paper suitable only for framing. The victorious plaintiff, now a *judgment creditor*, is still just a plain old unsecured creditor, one who has now incurred legal fees to boot. It is the attorney's next job — arguably the one the client cares more about — to translate that paper judgment into paper money, usually a check or cash.

The postjudgment collection process begins with procuring a writ, which is simply a court order. The most basic writ for debt collection is variously called a writ of *execution* or *attachment* or even *fi. fa.* (pronounced "fi fay," from *fieri facias*). (The terms are arcane, vary from state to state, and sometimes are used interchangeably.) The clerk of court will issue such writs as a routine matter upon request of the judgment creditor showing a copy of the judgment.

The writ directs the sheriff or marshal to look for non-exempt property of the judgment debtor, seize it, sell it, and pay the proceeds to the judgment creditor until the judgment is fully paid. Physically hunting for the debtor's property can be a tough job. In practice, the lawyer for the judgment creditor will often tell the sheriff where to look and may even go along. Ordinarily, the sheriff will take physical possession of any property found (e.g., a stereo or some tools) and lock it up back at the courthouse. If personal property cannot be seized immediately (e.g., because it is too big for sheriff's pickup), the sheriff may tag it with a notice of seizure. Since real property can never be physically hauled off, it is always seized by posting notice of seizure and sale or some similar method. The entire process of seizure is often called a *levy*, and what the sheriff does is "levy upon" the property. The whole process, from writ issuance to seizure, is often called an *execution*.

Once the sheriff has levied upon a specific piece of the debtor's property, a lien attaches (and is perfected simultaneously) by operation of law, rendering the judgment creditor a *judicial lien creditor* ("lien creditor" for short). A judicial lien is just as valid and as helpful as a voluntarily created secured interest, but it takes much longer to create, as this cumbersome procedure reveals. There are two other drawbacks. First, in part because the lien creditor has a non-consensual property interest, it must sell its property via a formal procedure. It cannot just retain the property in satisfaction of the debt or sell it using a commercially reasonable procedure, both options available to Article 9 secured creditors. Instead, the sheriff will advertise the property for public sale and sell it to the highest bidder, remitting the proceeds (after fees) to the judicial lien creditor. (Any remaining proceeds will be paid back to the judgment debtor, unless some subsequent judgment creditor levied symbolically upon the property while it was stored at the courthouse.) After sale and distribution, an entry is made in the judgment record noting the partial or complete satisfaction of the judgment. If the proceeds are insufficient to pay the judgment in full, then the sheriff will be commanded to look for more of the debtor's property to seize, and the process will start over.

Second, each state has laws exempting certain types of property from creditor execution. These *exemption* laws vary widely across states and will be studied in more detail in Assignments 4 and 5. What is important to note for now is that these exemptions only protect against sheriff levy, i.e., involuntary seizure by an unsecured creditor. A secured creditor, by contrast, can have a debtor grant it a voluntary lien against property that would otherwise be exempt from levy. If the debtor defaults on such a secured loan, in most cases nothing in the state's exemption laws prevents the collateral's seizure.

3.   Suing Third Parties: Garnishment

Law generally follows practical necessity, and nowhere is that more evident than in the law of collections. Not all property is physically in the hands of the true owner. (Think of the coin collection in a safety deposit box at the bank or even a dented car sitting overnight at an auto shop.) In addition, some property exists only in the abstract. The most common example is a debt owed to the debtor by a third party. (Think of wages in the period after the employee has done the work but before the employer has issued a paycheck or think about an account receivable for goods already delivered.) The law has developed a means by which creditors can direct these third parties to turn over the debtor's property or to divert payments that otherwise would go to the debtor in satisfaction of intangible property like an account receivable.

To seize property held by a third party or intangible property requires writs that are different from the standard execution ones. The most common is a writ of *garnishment*, which, despite its name, does not involve adorning the judgment with a sprig of parsley. Instead, a garnishment writ is typically used to attach debts owed to the debtor for the benefit of the debtor's judgment creditor. A creditor may garnish a debtor's wages by obtaining a writ directing the employer to pay the wages to the creditor rather than to the employee. Similarly, a creditor might garnish a bank to obtain funds in a checking account or the contents of a safety deposit box.

The garnishment writ has two parts: (1) a set of questions designed to determine whether the party served with the writ—the "garnishee," e.g., the employer or the bank—owes any money to the debtor or has any property belonging to the debtor, and (2) a command to the garnishee to withhold payment or return of the debtor's property pending further order of the court. If the garnishee answers the questions falsely or disobeys the command to withhold payment or delivery, it may be liable to the judgment creditor. For example, the employer who pays wages to the debtor after service of the writ of garnishment (which would violate the writ's command) may owe the judgment creditor an amount equal to the wages wrongly paid. The same may be true of the bank that honors the debtor's checks after service of the writ.

As a procedural matter, a garnishment is an ancillary lawsuit against the third-party garnishee. If, for example, the third party denies owing anything to the debtor (e.g., the debtor missed the last two weeks of work), a trial may be held on that issue. It more often happens that the garnishee asserts a defense to the writ in the form of some superior right in the debtor's property (e.g., the employer has a right of setoff against a salary advance the debtor had previously drawn). The judgment debtor receives notice of this process and may well participate in it. If the garnishee is found to owe money to the debtor or to have the debtor's property without any superior rights therein, a judgment will be entered against the garnishee. This judgment is satisfied when the garnishee delivers the debtor's property or pays the debt to the judgment creditor. The delivery or payment simultaneously satisfies the garnishee's obligation to the debtor.

While garnishment procedures vary widely, in most states the garnishing creditor gets a temporal "net"—the time between service of the garnishment writ and the garnishee's answer—during which the creditor gets to "catch" obligations arising in favor of the debtor. Thus garnishment of a bank account will let a creditor obtain not only the amount on deposit on the date the writ was served, but also funds deposited thereafter up until the time that the answer to the garnishment writ is due. By contrast, a few states use a "spear" approach, where a writ only catches whatever is available at the moment of service.

Wage garnishments present a special issue of concern about abusive practices. If a garnishing judgment creditor could seize the entire salary or wages that an employer owed to a judgment debtor, a person's ability to survive might be seriously jeopardized. Surely the debtor's incentive to work would be sharply reduced, resulting in hardship to the debtor's family and increased social costs. Moreover, such garnishment power would give the creditor excessive leverage to strike a new bargain with a defaulting debtor. A debtor facing garnishment of all wages might well offer the creditor property that the law protects from seizure as exempt or promise to pay a much higher interest rate on the debt. In response to such concerns, Congress limited the amount of wages that creditors may garnish. 15 U.S.C. § 1671 et seq. One impetus for the federal law is the enormous variation that existed among states. Some states prohibit garnishments altogether (with the frequent exception of efforts to collect family support obligations), while other states have no restrictions. Many states are scattered between these extremes. The federal garnishment restrictions act as a floor, creating a minimum protection.

UNITED STATES v. ASHCRAFT
732 F.3d 860 (8th Cir. 2013)

MELLOY, Circuit Judge.

Joyce Ashcraft appeals the district court's order denying her objection to the garnishment of her disability payments. The district court ruled Ashcraft's disability payments were not "earnings" within the meaning of the Consumer Credit Protection Act (the "Act"), which limits garnishment of "earnings." We reverse and hold Ashcraft's disability payments are "earnings" within the meaning of the Act. . . .

I.

In 2004, Ashcraft pleaded guilty to several criminal charges. She was sentenced to a term of imprisonment and to restitution. She was released from custody in November 2012. At some time prior to her incarceration, she worked for Amana Refrigeration. Amana provided long-term disability insurance to its employees through Principal Life Insurance Company ("PLIC"). Ashcraft's employment with Amana aggravated a medical condition, rendering her unable to work; as a result, Ashcraft receives disability payments from PLIC. Those payments will continue until she reaches the age of sixty-five in November 2016. The government does not dispute that the disability insurance providing Ashcraft's current disability payments was provided by Amana in the course of Ashcraft's employment.

In February 2012, the government sought to garnish Ashcraft's disability payments pursuant to her restitution sentence. Ashcraft objected. Ashcraft argued her disability payments are "earnings" within the meaning of the Act and are thus subject to the Act's limitations on garnishment.

The district court ruled Ashcraft's disability payments are not "earnings" within the meaning of the Act and overruled her objection to garnishment. Ashcraft appealed. . . . The government argues that Ashcraft's disability payments are not "compensation paid or payable for personal services" as the Act requires and that the Act does not expressly include disability payments within the definition of "earnings."*

II.

. . .

The Act states, in relevant part:

(a) The term "earnings" means compensation paid or payable for personal services, whether denominated as wages, salary, commission, bonus, or otherwise, and includes periodic payments pursuant to a pension or retirement program.

(b) The term "disposable earnings" means that part of the earnings of any individual remaining after the deduction from those earnings of any amounts required by law to be withheld. . . .

15 U.S.C. § 1672.

(a) [T]he maximum part of the aggregate disposable earnings of an individual for any workweek which is subjected to garnishment may not exceed

---

*The government argues we must decide whether Ashcraft's disability payments are "earnings" under the Act or "property" under the Federal Debt Collection Practices Act, while Ashcraft argues that the categories of "earnings" and "property" are not mutually exclusive. For purposes of this appeal, we need only determine whether Ashcraft's disability payments are "earnings"; we do not determine whether they are or may also be "property."

(1) 25 per centum of his disposable earnings for that week, or

(2) the amount by which his disposable earnings for that week exceed thirty times the Federal minimum hourly wage . . . in effect at the time the earnings are payable, whichever is less.

15 U.S.C. § 1673.

Whether disability payments are "earnings" within the meaning of the Act is an issue of first impression for our court, and neither party points to a case from any of our sister circuits offering a ruling on the present issue. While several courts have previously interpreted the meaning of "earnings" under the Act, most of those courts considered whether pension payments and retirement savings constitute "earnings"[3]; they did not address the Act's applicability to disability payments. However, two prior cases are particularly relevant, and we introduce those cases before moving to our analysis.

First, courts interpreting the Act's definition of "earnings" rely heavily on Kokoszka v. Belford, 417 U.S. 642, 94 S. Ct. 2431, 41 L. Ed. 2d 374 (1974). In *Kokoszka*, the Supreme Court analyzed both the Act and the Bankruptcy Act and determined that income tax refunds did not constitute "earnings." Quoting with approval the Second Circuit's holding that "earnings" did not include "every asset that is traceable in some way to such compensation," the *Kokoszka* Court stated:

> [T]he Consumer Credit Protection Act sought to prevent consumers from entering bankruptcy in the first place. . . . There is every indication that Congress, in an effort to avoid the necessity of bankruptcy, sought to regulate garnishment in its usual sense as a levy on periodic payments of compensation needed to support the wage earner and his family on a week-to-week, month-to-month basis.

Id. at 651.

. . . Based on the Act's plain language, Ashcraft's disability payments constitute "earnings." By defining "earnings" as "compensation paid or payable for personal services, *whether denominated as* wages, salary, commission, bonus, or otherwise," the Act prioritizes the character of the payment over its label. Thus, although Ashcraft's evidence that the IRS lists her disability payments as wages may support her claim, whether or not the disability payments are labeled as wages is not the central issue; the central issue is whether the disability payments are "compensation paid or payable for personal services." We hold they are.

Ashcraft receives the disability payments through her former employer. They are payments designed to function as wage substitutes; they are not merely "traceable in some way" to Ashcraft's compensation, but are themselves a direct component of the compensation Amana provided to Ashcraft in return for the personal services Ashcraft rendered to Amana. . . .

---

[3]Although the Act expressly includes payments pursuant to a pension or retirement program, "district courts around the country have divided over whether monthly pension-benefit payments constitute 'earnings' under the [Act]." . . .

III.

For the reasons stated above, we conclude Ashcraft's disability payments are "earnings" within the plain meaning of the Act and are therefore subject to the Act's limitations on garnishment.

A bank account is often the target of a garnishing creditor. The law regards the account as a debt the bank owes to the depositor, so garnishment is the way to reach the asset. The account, with its ready liquidity, is attractive to the judgment creditor as an easy way to satisfy the judgment debt. But banks often have multiple relationships with their depositors. It is not uncommon for a business or individual to maintain a checking account with the same bank where one or more loans are outstanding. The customer then becomes the bank's creditor for the deposit account and bank's debtor on the loan accounts. When the deposit account is garnished, the bank rapidly switches hats, agreeing as account debtor that the money is owed to the customer but arguing that as loan creditor it is owed offsetting amounts that must be settled before any garnishor is paid. The bank then offers to satisfy the writ only the net amount—if any—left in the account after the bank's own *setoff*. Of course, there is often a dispute between the judgment creditor and the bank on whose debt has priority, with the creditor claiming that its writ was served and a lien attached before the bank had properly accelerated and offset the debtor's obligation to it, and the bank claiming the converse. For the moment, it is enough to say that the bank almost always wins.

Problem Set 2

2.1. Renee Black has come to see you about the attempts to collect by the new owner of the mortgage on her family's home. The mortgage holder has threatened to foreclose but has held off so far. When you look at the documents she has given you, you see that the original bank lender on the $150,000 home mortgage had sold its mortgage to the Comstock Financial Company as part of the sale of millions of dollars of its mortgage portfolio to Comstock. After notice of the sale, the Blacks had sent their monthly payments to Comstock as directed, but they were returned uncashed. In June, they got a letter from Comstock saying they were in default and owed almost $4,000 in arrearages and fees, which they should pay immediately together with their usual monthly payments of $510. Several times the Blacks asked for ordinary statements of principal and interest, along with details of alleged arrearages and fees. The mortgage agreement refers to a formula for calculating interest rates and fees, but you cannot see how the formula relates to the amounts Comstock is demanding.

A series of phone calls and letters from Comstock demanded escalating amounts due, without explanation, starting at $3,900 and culminating in a demand for $29,000 for reinstating the loan. When Renee called Comstock, its senior manager Al Jenkins made statements like these:

"We're foreclosing. We're foreclosing."

"You don't deserve statements. You don't deserve statements. We're foreclosing."

"I don't care about your family."

"Your house is mine. Your house is ours. We're taking your house. There is nothing you can do. You can't do anything."

"You don't need to know [how the amount due was calculated]. That's our business. You didn't pay. You owe."

"I'm going to take your house. Your house is mine."

At that point, Renee decided to seek your advice. Putting to one side other state and federal laws, does the FDCPA offer possible relief? See § 1692e(2)(A), 1692e(10).

2.2. You decided to forsake the lure of the big firm and go with a small practice in Columbus. You like the eight partners in the firm and are eager to make yourself useful. The firm has carved out a niche in what the partners call "Main Street" law—real estate closings, car accidents, contract disputes, unpaid bills for local businesses, etc.

Last month you received an assignment for Condoleezza Chalmers, who owns a small rental house. She is upset that a tenant moved out and left about $2,000 worth of damages beyond the security deposit. You reviewed the case and sent out one of the firm's standard form letters outlining the damages claimed by the client, demanding a quick resolution, and indicating that you will take immediate legal action, including a lawsuit, if the outstanding amount isn't paid promptly. You were shocked to receive a letter this morning from the former tenant claiming violations of the FDCPA and agreeing to settle the matter if Ms. Chalmers will drop all claims. You do a little investigating and discover that the former tenant is a third-year law student. (It now occurs to you why no one wanted to rent to you when you were in law school.) Advice?

2.3. Bruno Holtry is one of your company's best repossession agents. He's quick at his work, which limits the potential for violent responses from debtors. Bruno just called you to report on his last job of the night. He says that he was headed to the employer of Isabel Fury to repossess her 2000 Honda Accord when she passed him headed home from work. He followed her. She stopped the car in front of a modest ranch house and went to the door. He verified that the address was not her home based on your records but figured since it was a few blocks away that he would repo the car and let her walk home. The job was easy, he reported, because Isabel left the keys in the car and the windows rolled down. He heard her yelling and chasing after him when he was a half-block away, but he knew better than to stop and invite trouble.

At this point, you are wondering why you got the call when Bruno says that he better call you back "because a helicopter's landing out back." You are nonplussed but can't put the pieces together. Waiting for Bruno to call you back, you flip on the office TV. Across the bottom of the screen is an "Amber Alert" for a missing two-year old, Jermaine Fury. When the telephone rings back, it is a police detective, who explains that when Bruno took the car, Jermaine was asleep in his car seat. Apparently, Bruno did not notice him, but Isabel called 911 to report a stolen child. After launching an intense missing child protocol, the police called Bruno and had him check the car. When the police and Isabel arrived on the scene, Bruno was giving the toddler his first root beer. Is your company in legal trouble based on the day's events? Is Bruno? Is Isabel? Is Jermaine? See UCC § 9-609.

2.4. Mark Watkins has had continuing difficulties with credit charges on his account at Highland Department Store. Apparently, Highland transposed two numbers in recording monthly charges sometime last spring, and it billed Watkins for $4,000 in goods Watkins did not purchase. Watkins notified a call center representative of the error, but Highland continued to issue bills. After three months and two letters, Watkins decided he had done all he could do, tossing all subsequent bills.

Watkins recently decided to purchase a condominium and hired you to handle the transaction. When he applied for a mortgage, however, he was turned down. The mortgage company sent him a form letter explaining that he was not "within the range of applicants" to whom the mortgagee made loans. Having a good job and timely bill payments, he is outraged and thinks Highland is to blame. How can he confirm his suspicions? See Fair Credit Reporting Act (§ 1681b, i, m, n, o). Would it matter if Watkins's dispute were for $40 instead?

2.5. Cash2U, Inc. makes small-dollar, unsecured consumer loans. It obtained a $6,000 judgment against one of its borrowers, Wayne Smettles. On February 1, Cash2U delivered a writ of garnishment to the sheriff for service on Amos State Bank, where Wayne has his checking account. On that date the account was overdrawn by $10. On February 5, Wayne's employer direct deposited his $5,000 paycheck into the account. The sheriff served the writ of garnishment on the bank on February 9. Ignorant of the writ, Wayne wrote a check for $400 to the telephone company on February 9, which the bank paid on February 10. The bank answered the writ on February 15, the day before Wayne's direct deposit workplace expense reimbursement of $300 arrived, and five days before the writ's answer was due. You are the bank's junior counsel. Who gets what?

PART II

CONSUMER BANKRUPTCY

"What is a bankrupt, father?" asked Eugenie.

"A bankrupt," replied her father, "is guilty of the most dishonourable action that can dishonour a man."

"It must be a very great sin," said Mme Grandet, "and our brother will perhaps be eternally lost."

"There you are with your preachments," her husband retorted, shrugging his shoulders. "A bankrupt, Eugenie," her father continued, "is a thief whom the law unfortunately takes under its protection. People trusted Guillaume Grandet with their goods, confiding in his character for fair dealing and honesty; he has taken all they have, and left them nothing but their eyes to weep with. A bankrupt is worse than a highwayman; a highwayman sets upon you, and you have a chance to defend yourself; he risks his life besides, while the other—Charles is disgraced in fact."

The words filled the poor girl's heart; they weighed upon her with all their weight; she herself was so scrupulously conscientious; no flower in the depths of the forest had grown more delicately free from spot or stain; she knew none of the maxims of worldly wisdom, and nothing of its quibbles and its sophistries. So she accepted her father's cruel definition and sweeping statements as to bankrupts; he drew no distinction between a fraudulent bankruptcy and a failure from unavoidable causes, and how should she?

Honoré de Balzac, Eugénie Grandet 108 (1833)

Section 1

The Beginning

Collecting from consumer debtors at state law is a cumbersome and atomistic legal process. Unsecured creditors have to obtain a judgment, hunt down assets of the debtor, cajole a sheriff to take action, and hope for the best. Secured creditors have a somewhat better lot because they can engage in self-help repossession and conduct a private sale of the collateral, but they, too, face risks: collateral may disappear or dissipate in value, a rankled debtor may breach the peace to halt repossession, etc. All this occurs while dunning letters, calls, and emails bombard the debtor.

Federal bankruptcy law presents an alternative for both creditors and debtors. Its chief contrasting feature from the creditor's perspective is a collectivization that corrals all stakeholders—and all assets—into one legal proceeding. From the debtor's perspective, federal bankruptcy law offers two rewards unknown and unavailable at state law: an automatic *stay* that halts the scrum of collection and the ability to pursue a *discharge* from unpaid debts. Bankruptcy also imposes burdens on creditors and debtors, but on the whole, many parties stand a better chance at a better recovery under the orderly collective process.

Most consumers file one of two basic proceedings: a liquidation under chapter 7 or a repayment under chapter 13 of the Bankruptcy Code. The upcoming materials delve into chapter 7 and chapter 13 in that order because chapter 7 is the primal form of bankruptcy against which chapter 13 developed. Each type of consumer bankruptcy is the subject of several assignments. Despite being a procedure for ordinary people, the law is extraordinary in its complexity. The consumer bankruptcy part concludes with a section on the interaction between the two chapters and a look at how the system as a whole functions.

We start, appropriately, in this single-assignment introductory section, called "The Beginning." Do not be misled by its brevity. Although it is a single assignment, the content is fundamental to a bankruptcy under any chapter. The two foundational pillars of any bankruptcy are the creation of something called "the estate," into which all of a debtor's property is deposited, and the imposition of something called "the automatic stay," which halts all creditor collection activity against the debtor, shunting it into one venue.

THE BANKRUPTCY ESTATE AND THE AUTOMATIC STAY

A. INTRODUCTION

Bankruptcy is technically an *in rem* proceeding, meaning that it affects property. We say "technically" because its main practical consequence is to discharge a consumer from all ongoing obligations, which sounds pretty personal to us—as we suspect it does to the creditors who kiss their obligations goodbye. § 524. Nevertheless, as good lawyers, we acknowledge the formalism of the bankruptcy process and note that bankruptcy's *in rem* proceeding starts with something called the bankruptcy *estate*.

Remember first year property law (and you thought it was just Civ Pro you would have to remember)? Remember when a rich uncle wants to give his spendthrift nephew some property (like cash or Blackacre) but does not want him to get full control of it for fear he will blow it all fast and foolishly? The solution was to create a *trust*, into which uncle (settlor) would put the property (*res*). Legal title and control would go to a trusted friend (trustee), who would shepherd the property for the benefit of nephew (beneficiary). Although nephew enjoyed the *benefits* of the property and perhaps got periodic disbursements from the trustee, he could never demand money out of the trust because he did not *own* the property. Nor could uncle, because once he divested himself of ownership of property to the trustee, he could not change his mind and take it back; the trustee was now in control: legal owner of the trust property, for the benefit of nephew.

Filing bankruptcy creates a similar trust—albeit a poor man's trust—with all the same elements. Here, upon filing the bankruptcy petition, the trust is created as a matter of law, the *res* of which is called "the estate." The trust's beneficiaries are all the debtor's creditors. Who gets to be the trustee? Appropriately enough, someone the Bankruptcy Code calls "the trustee." Just as the anxious nephew cannot access any property without the trustee's permission, so too anxious creditors of a debtor can do nothing on their own; the trustee is in control of the estate. And just as the rich uncle cannot take property back from the trust, so too do debtors lose all control of what was formerly their property. The trustee runs the show. To reinforce this control, the trustee is assisted by a legal *stay* (injunction) that arises automatically upon filing bankruptcy. The stay enjoins any creditor from trying to seize estate property or otherwise pursue collection against the debtor. This automatic stay gives most debtors their first relief from months of creditor dunning, a welcome price to pay to cede control to a trustee.

The trustee, sometimes called the "trustee-in-bankruptcy" ("TIB") or "panel trustee," is usually a local lawyer (picked from a "panel" of certified practitioners). The selection of a trustee depends on the chapter of bankruptcy at issue, and in some instances, on the creditors' level of participation in the case. The trustees in a particular case are different from the federal employees called "U.S. Trustees," apparently to confuse bankruptcy students. You should not conflate the two. The U.S. Trustees work for the U.S. Department of Justice and largely do oversight and administration (including empaneling regular trustees). Their tasks are quite different from the rank-and-file lawyers who serve as the trustees who control the hundreds of thousands of consumer bankruptcy cases each year. The vast majority of debtors are so broke they have no distributable assets with which to create their estates. See David T. Stanley & Marjorie Girth, Bankruptcy: Problem, Process, Reform 87 (1971); Herbert & Pacitti, Down and Out in Richmond, Virginia: The Distribution of Assets in Chapter 7 Bankruptcy Proceedings Closed in 1984-1987, 22 U. Rich. L. Rev. 303 (1988); Pamela Foohey, Robert M. Lawless, Katherine M. Porter & Deborah Thorne, "No Money Down" Bankruptcy, 90 S. Cal. L. Rev. 1055 (2017). This makes the job of trustee hardly a glamorous one, but yeoman's service in the trustee ranks helps chances for appointment when a high-ticket, fee-generating liquidation finally rolls into the district.

The trustee administers the debtor's estate by gathering all the estate assets. In a liquidation case, the trustee sells them; in a reorganization case, the trustee administers the proceeding. The trustee has a special obligation (by custom and common law) to unsecured, general creditors, see e.g., In re Dinh, 80 B.R. 819, 822 (Bankr. S.D. Miss. 1987) ("[I]t is a fundamental concept in bankruptcy that a trustee's primary duty is to the unsecured creditors rather than to the secured creditors. The secured creditors, for the most part, should be able to look to their collateral for satisfaction of their claims."), and is especially charged with scrutinizing the debtor's reports to locate any concealed property or to discover any wrongdoing that might result in a failure to get a discharge, § 704(a)(4), (6). The trustee is also careful to be sure that no one creditor tries to take more than its share and thus challenges security interests or claims to special priority treatment. Trustees are thus both the creditors' friend and nemesis. They stand for the proposition that equity is equality. That maxim means that unless a creditor can clearly demonstrate that it deserves some priority in the bankruptcy payout, the trustee will assume all creditors are equal and try to maximize the pot for that collective. Also, the trustee fees are calculated in part as a percentage of the funds distributed and that distribution is primarily to unsecured creditors. §§ 326, 330.

These two features of a bankruptcy case filing—(1) the creation of an estate and concomitant vesting of all control over that estate in a trustee, and (2) the automatic imposition of a stay against all creditor action—are critical to the bankruptcy system, and so we examine each in more detail below. Before we proceed, we flag four other case-initiation issues worth noting.

First, nearly all bankruptcy cases start voluntarily, with a debtor filing a *petition* to commence the case. Petitions are often filed when a debtor is fed up with being hounded by creditors ranging from anxious to belligerent. The petition is the basic request for bankruptcy relief and is signed by the debtor, on penalty of perjury, as certification that all the information contained in the filing is true. The completed petition and required fee are filed with the clerk of court and date-stamped with the minute, hour, and day of filing. In a voluntary case, this is the instant at which the bankruptcy estate is created and the automatic stay on all collection actions arises. The mere filing of that petition thus has the effect of the entry of a judicial order and so is called the *order for relief*. § 301.

Second, filing a bankruptcy case requires a ton of initial paperwork, which is why even cash-strapped debtors frequently have lawyers. A bankruptcy debtor must pull together copious information on assets, debts, and income to complete the bankruptcy petition's *schedules*. Even a diligent lawyer with a fairly well-organized client may get some of the pieces wrong, and Heaven help the lawyer with a client whose recordkeeping is spotty. Current bankruptcy law puts significant pressure on lawyers, who must sign the petition, to verify the accuracy of the debtor's records. In consumer cases, attorney signature certifies the completion of a "reasonable investigation" into that accuracy and the absence of knowledge that the information in the schedules is incorrect. § 707(b)(4)(C), (D). A lawyer who fails to do that may forfeit fees in the case, or, even worse, become subject to sanctions. §§ 526, 707(b). *Pro se* debtors flounder under the paperwork requirements, even those who can juggle octuplets. See Order and Notice of Dismissal, In re Suleman, No. 8:12-bk-15375-CB (Bankr. C.D. Cal. May 15, 2012). Cases filed without the assistance of an attorney are several times more likely to be dismissed for paperwork problems or other technical reasons than those filed by lawyers. See Angela K. Littwin, The Do-It-Yourself Mirage, in *Broke* (noting also most debtors do have lawyers).

Third, the debtor doesn't just get to file the petition and quietly await the benefits of the order for relief without ever confronting creditors. All debtors must attend a meeting of creditors, often called the *341 meeting*, in reference to the Code section that mandates it, within 40 days of the petition. Think of it as the Confrontation Clause of bankruptcy, to enable examination of the debtor by the trustee and any interested creditors. But other than that, in the absence of motions practice or some other litigation fight, a debtor can generally avoid court (and creditors) altogether.

The fourth and final note is the most significant. A consumer debtor will generally have to decide whether to seek relief under chapter 7 or chapter 13, an important decision with serious effects on debtors and their creditors. We defer scrutinizing the mechanics and consequences of that crucial choice until those chapters have been studied. We note simply that the commencement of a case involves not just busywork, but important legal and strategic choices.

B.   THE ESTATE

At the instant of filing the bankruptcy petition, all the property owned by the debtor becomes "property of the estate," § 541(a), a deliberately expansive concept, with only a few specific exceptions set forth in § 541(b) of the Code. Some of those few exceptions are policy-based, such as § 541(b)(7) for employee contributions to retirement accounts, while some appear more lobbying-based (Anyone wish to explain the special treatment of liquid or gaseous hydrocarbons under § 541(b)(4)?). But on the whole, § 541(a)'s reach is broad.

The most important exception to this expansive scope is for "services performed by an individual debtor after the commencement of the case." § 541(a)(6). This means that consumers' wages, commissions, and the like earned after the petition is filed do not become property of the estate and do not have to be surrendered to creditors. This is the first benefit of the "fresh start."

This naturally raises questions about what is the debtor's old, pre-commencement property (and hence the estate's) and what is new, post-commencement property (and hence the debtor's). If the debtor gets a present from a friend three days after filing bankruptcy, that sounds like new property. If the same friend pays back an old I.O.U. three days after the bankruptcy, that sounds like monetization of old property, because the I.O.U. note would be property that went into the estate, and the cash from the friend's payment would be traceable back to that pre-commencement property. While it is easy to say the estate contains "all property" of the debtor, courts still struggle with these relation-back sorts of issues.

PROCHNOW v. APEX PROPERTIES, INC. (d/b/a REMAX)
467 B.R. 656 (C.D. Ill. 2012)

MYERSCOUGH, District Judge.

STATEMENT OF FACTS

Prochnow was at all relevant times a duly licensed salesperson—also referred to as a realtor or realtor associate—[of] Apex Properties Inc., d/b/a Remax Choice of Bloomington, Illinois (ReMax) [and] was at all relevant times a duly licensed real estate broker. In August 2006, Prochnow and ReMax, through its predecessor, entered into a Broker-Realtor-Associate Contract (Associate Contract). The compensation paid to Prochnow and other realtor-associates licensed with ReMax was arranged on a commission basis.

On August 3, 2009, Prochnow filed his Chapter 7 bankruptcy petition. Prochnow was at that time still a realtor-associate with ReMax and continued in that capacity until January 8, 2010. On his Schedule B, Prochnow affirmatively represented that he had no accounts receivable, no liquidated debts owed to him, and no contingent or unliquidated claims of any nature. On January 8, 2010, Prochnow ceased working as a realtor-associate with ReMax. On February 23, 2010, Prochnow's bankruptcy case was closed. On June 16, 2010, Prochnow, represented by new counsel, filed a Motion to Reopen Case. In the Motion, Prochnow alleged that he became entitled to the payment of compensation from ReMax for real estate commissions from [certain] closings occurring after August 3, 2009, the date Prochnow filed his bankruptcy petition. . . .

The bankruptcy court granted ReMax's Motion for Summary Judgment. . . . First, the bankruptcy court found that Prochnow had earned the . . . contract commission pre-petition and that it was part of the bankruptcy estate. Because Prochnow failed to disclose his interest in a share of the . . . contract commission on his schedules, the bankruptcy court [also] found he was judicially estopped from claiming an interest in those funds. This appeal followed.

ANALYSIS

Prochnow argues . . . said commission was earned post-petition and was not an asset of the bankruptcy estate. . . . Prochnow asserts the commission was earned post-petition, when the real estate closing occurred. In support thereof, Prochnow relies on the language of the Associate Contract which specifically provides: "No commissions shall be considered earned or payable to Realtor-Associate until the transaction has been completed and the commission has been collected by the Broker." . . .

1. The Commission Was Part of the Bankruptcy Estate

The bankruptcy court found that the . . . contract commission was part of the bankruptcy estate. "Whether property is included in the bankruptcy estate is a question of law." In re Parsons, 280 F.3d 1185, 1188 (8th Cir. 2002). "To determine the nature of a debtor's interest in property, we look to state law; to determine whether that interest counts as property of the debtor's estate, we look to federal bankruptcy law." In re Krueger, 192 F.3d 733, 737 (7th Cir. 1999). Section 541(a) of the Bankruptcy Code defines "property of the estate" to include "all legal or equitable interests of the debtor in the property as of the commencement of the case." 11 U.S.C. § 541(a)(1). This definition of property of the estate is broad — "including interests of all types and degrees of contingency" — but is generally limited to interests in existence at the time of the commencement of the case. In re Taronji, 174 B.R. 964, 967 (Bankr. N.D. Ill. 1994). "Section 541(a)(6) expands this basic definition of property of the estate to include certain property interests that are acquired after the commencement of the case." Id. "However, Section 541(a)(6) contains an express exception, exempting earnings from services performed by an individual debtor after the commencement of the case." In re Jokiel, 447 B.R. 868, 871 (Bankr. N.D. Ill. 2001) (quoting 11 U.S.C. § 541(a)(6)).

On appeal, Prochnow essentially argues that he earned the commission post-petition because the Associate Contract provided that commissions were not earned until the transaction (*i.e.* the closing on the property) had been completed and the commission was collected by ReMax. This Court first notes that the provision in the Associate Contract merely made Prochnow's interest contingent. Under Illinois law, a broker (which in this case would be ReMax), is entitled to a commission for the sale of real estate when he procures a buyer who is ready, willing, and able to purchase the real estate on the terms prescribed by the seller. As the bankruptcy court noted, "once the Hudson [c]ontract was signed and the financing contingency set forth in the contract was met, ReMax, as the broker in the transaction, had earned its commission." In re Prochnow, [474 B.R. at 607]. . . .

"A debtor's contingent interest in future income has consistently been found to be property of the bankruptcy estate." In re Yonikus, 996 F.2d 866, 869 (7th Cir. 1993). In fact, "[a] contingency is no bar to [a] property interest becoming property of the bankruptcy estate, even if the contingency requires additional postpetition services, and even if the right to enjoyment of the property may be defeated." In re Allen, 226 B.R. 857, 865 (Bankr. N.D. Ill. 1998). Moreover, the test for determining whether post-petition income is property of the bankruptcy estate depends on whether the income accrues from pre-petition or post-petition services. *See* In re Laflamme, 397 B.R. 194, 199 (Bankr. D.N.H. 2008) (commissions received postpetition are property of the estate if "all acts of the debtor necessary to earn it are rooted in the pre-bankruptcy past") (internal quotation marks omitted). As stated by the Seventh Circuit, in a case involving a tax refund, "[t]he background rule under the old Bankruptcy Act, to which courts still refer in the era of the Bankruptcy Code, defines the bankruptcy estate to include property that is 'sufficiently rooted in the pre-bankruptcy past and so little entangled with the bankrupts' ability to make an unencumbered fresh start.'" In re Meyers, 616 F.3d 626, 628 (7th Cir. 2010) (quoting Segal v. Rochelle, 382 U.S. 375, 380, 86 S. Ct. 511, 15 L. Ed. 2d 428 (1966)).

Although Prochnow's right to the commission may have vested post-petition, the payment was actually for pre-petition services. *See* In re Jokiel, 447 B.R. at 872 (noting that the key issue to determining whether a post-petition severance payment was property of the bankruptcy estate was "whether the severance payment was rooted in pre- or post-petition services"). When Prochnow filed his petition for bankruptcy, the amount of the commission was clearly established. In addition, Prochnow had done all he needed to do to receive the commission even though the commission was contingent on the transaction actually being completed. *See, e.g.,* In re Dzielak, 435 B.R. 538, 546 (Bankr. N.D. Ill. 2010) (finding that the debtor's potential interest in a 401(k) plan was property of the estate even though the divorce court had not yet issued an order distributing an interest in the property; the debtor had "a claim for, or a contingent interest in, all or part of the retirement account"). Prochnow has not identified any services performed post-petition which would suggest the need to allocate the commission between pre- and post-petition services. *See, e.g.,* In re Bagen, 186 B.R. 824, 829 (Bankr. S.D.N.Y. 1995) (finding that the debtor's "pre[-]petition contingent contractual rights to postpetition property is property of the estate" but allocating the sum between pre- and postpetition services), *aff'd* 201 B.R. 642 (S.D.N.Y. 1996). Therefore, this Court finds that the bankruptcy court properly found that Prochnow's portion of the commission for the Hudson contract was property of the bankruptcy estate. . . .

Prochnow is [in the alternative] judicially estopped from pursuing the commission. *See* Cannon–Stokes v. Potter, 453 F.3d 446, 448 (7th Cir. 2006) (noting that "[j]udicial estoppel is an equitable doctrine, and it is not equitable to employ it to injure creditors who are themselves victims of the debtor's deceit"). . . . Prochnow was required to disclose any assets on his schedule when he filed his bankruptcy petition. *See* 11 U.S.C. 521(a)(1)(B)(i) (requiring that a debtor file a schedule of assets); 11 U.S.C. § 101(5)(A) (defining a claim to include a "right to payment, whether or not such right is reduced to judgment, liquidated, unliquidated, fixed, contingent, matured, unmatured, disputed, undisputed, legal, equitable, secured, or unsecured"). . . .

The Seventh Circuit has held that "a debtor in bankruptcy who denies owning an asset, including a chose in action or other legal claim, cannot realize on that concealed asset after the bankruptcy ends." Cannon-Stokes, 453 F.3d at 448 (citing cases). That is precisely what Prochnow is attempting to do here. The bankruptcy court did not therefore abuse its discretion by finding Prochnow was judicially estopped from pursuing the commission.

THEREFORE, the decision of the Bankruptcy Court is AFFIRMED.

Do you think this was a close case, given the contract's language saying the commission was not earned until closing? If so, does the fact the court was inclined to estop Prochnow from claiming the funds (for being sneaky in his bankruptcy filings) predetermine how it was going to rule? Sneaky debtors make poor test cases. For another arguably closer case that went the other way (with a less sneaky debtor), consider Sharp v. Dery, 253 B.R. 204 (E.D. Mich. 2000) (reversing bankruptcy court and holding that debtor's annual bonus for the fiscal year completed prepetition—but issued two months into the next year—was *not* property of the estate because the debtor had to remain employed "in good standing" to be entitled to the prior year-end bonus).

Conceptually, disputes about the inclusion of certain expectancies in "property of the estate" under § 541 can be divided into three main categories: future interests, restrictions on transfer, and degree of legal entitlement. The first, illustrated by *Prochnow* and *Sharp*, involves timing: legal interests that are not enforceable at the date of bankruptcy but may be enforceable at a future time. The question is whether they are sufficiently matured and certain to be included in the estate. Knowing in your heart of hearts you had a great year at work does not give you a legally enforceable right to demand a bonus from your boss. Nor does her saying, "What a great year you've had!" at the office Christmas party. Sidestepping estoppel doctrines, mere expectations or hopes are not property. These "ripening" disputes also raise ancillary questions of allocation when some but not all rights are enforceable. For example, the *Sharp* court declined an interesting argument to try to prorate the bonus as without legal basis. But see Stoebner v. Wick (In re Wick), 276 F.3d 412 (8th Cir. 2002) (prorating, between trustee and debtor based on pre- and postpetition labor of the debtor, the value of stock options that were unvested at time of bankruptcy filing).

The second type of dispute involves restrictions on transfer. Suppose the debtor owns a small family cottage, but the deed contains a restriction that it cannot be sold to someone outside the debtor's family. The cottage is surely the debtor's property, but if the restriction were valid in bankruptcy, then it could not pass to the trustee (a trustee related to the debtor would be disqualified) and hence to the bankruptcy estate, leaving the debtor's creditors out in the cold. For that reason, such restrictions are not generally favored in bankruptcy as a policy matter, and provisions such as § 541(c)(1) make most of them unenforceable. Congress has allowed only a few exceptions, the most important is the § 541(c)(2) protection of bona fide spendthrift trusts validly created under applicable law. As the case below shows, however, that exception is construed narrowly.

In re CHAMBERS

451 B.R. 621 (Bankr. N.D. Ga. 2011)

MULLINS, Bankruptcy Judge.

The issue before the Court is whether campaign contributions made to a candidate for public office ("campaign funds"), who files bankruptcy without incorporating the campaign, are property of the bankruptcy estate. Debtor alleged that a garnishment order froze certain bank accounts, including her State Representative Campaign Account (a Wachovia government checking account) containing the subject campaign funds, in violation of section 362 of the Bankruptcy Code. The Court held an expedited hearing on October 26, 2010, and thereafter entered an Interim Order requiring the campaign funds be held in trust by the Chapter 13 Trustee [pending this opinion on the merits].

FACTUAL BACKGROUND

On October 6, 2010, the Debtor filed a chapter 13 petition. At the time of filing, the Debtor was running a campaign for re-election as a Georgia State Representative. The Debtor did not incorporate her campaign. Prior to the bankruptcy filing, Miami Circle filed a garnishment order on Wachovia Bank, which froze Debtor's bank accounts, including her campaign funds account. The Debtor filed chapter 13 in an attempt to free the campaign funds from garnishment, make them available to her campaign, and shield them from the reach of her personal creditors, including Miami Circle.

CONCLUSIONS OF LAW

The scope of section 541(a) of the Bankruptcy Code is intentionally broad. It not only includes property in which a debtor has an equity interest, it includes all property in which a debtor has *any* interest. 11 U.S.C. § 541(a); United States v. Whiting Pools, Inc., 462 U.S. 198, 103 S. Ct. 2309,

76 L. Ed. 2d 515 (1983). The United States Supreme Court stated that section 541(a) sweeps in, as property of the estate, even a debtor's equitable right of redemption. *Whiting Pools*, 462 U.S. at 204-05, 103 S. Ct. 2309. Following this decision, *Whiting Pools* has had a talismanic presence in bankruptcy law, affecting a wide range of subject matter and guiding courts in nearly all circuits. Although the scope of section 541(a) is broad, it is limited to the rights debtor had prepetition. Section 541(a) cannot alter the pre-petition interest a debtor had in the property; the estate merely steps into a debtor's prepetition shoes. *Whiting Pools*, 462 U.S. at 205, 103 S. Ct. 2309.

This attribute is commonly seen in the context of security interests. For example, if there are liens attached to account funds prepetition, the inclusion of the funds as property of the estate does not destroy the liens; the secured creditors would be entitled to adequate protection of their interest. *See* Butner v. United States, 440 U.S. 48, 55, 99 S. Ct. 914, 59 L. Ed. 2d 136 (1979) ("Property interests are created and defined by state law. Unless some federal interest requires a different result, there is no reason why such interests should be analyzed differently simply because an interested party is involved in a bankruptcy proceeding."). Section 541(a) does nothing other than characterize property of the estate. It does not determine which creditors are entitled to the estate property.

The breadth of the concept of property of the estate is reinforced by section 541(c)(1)(A) which states, "an interest of the debtor in property becomes property of the estate under section (a)(1) . . . notwithstanding any provision in . . . applicable nonbankruptcy law . . . that restricts or conditions transfer of such interest by the debtor." 11 U.S.C. § 541(c)(1)(A). Section 541(c)(1)(A) is commonly referred to as the "anti-alienation provision."

An exception to the anti-alienation provision is found in section 541(c)(2) of the Bankruptcy Code which excludes from the bankruptcy estate a debtor's interest in a spendthrift trust. 11 U.S.C. § 541(c)(2); Patterson v. Shumate, 504 U.S. 753, 758, 112 S. Ct. 2242, 119 L. Ed. 2d 519 (1992). Section 541(c)(2) states, "a restriction on the transfer of a beneficial interest of the debtor in a trust that is enforceable under applicable nonbankruptcy law is enforceable in a case under this title." 11 U.S.C. § 541(c)(2). Applying the canon of statutory construction that the express mention of one thing excludes all others (*expressio unius est exclusio alterius*) to an integrated reading of sections 541(a), (c)(1)(A), and (c)(2), leads to the conclusion that creating a spendthrift trust is the only state law property transfer restriction that allows a debtor's interest in property to escape the reach of section 541(a).

Legal Analysis

The issue before the Court is a matter of first impression. Application of section 541 to the facts directs the Court to conclude that the campaign funds are property of the estate.

The Debtor has a property interest, however restricted by state law, in the campaign funds. Therefore, per section 541(a) and *Whiting Pools*, the campaign funds constitute property of the estate. 11 U.S.C. § 541(a)(1).

Nothing more []or less than the Debtor's prepetition interest in the campaign funds becomes property of the estate. *Whiting Pools*, 462 U.S. at 205 n.8, 103 S. Ct. 2309 ("§ 541(a)(1) does not expand the rights of the debtor in the hands of the estate . . ."). All section 541(a) does is define the estate and what the estate is comprised of; it does not address which creditors have rights to estate property. Because section 541(a) does nothing more than characterize what constitutes property of the estate, the Court does not reach the issue of whether certain creditors (e.g. campaign creditors) have priority claims with respect to the campaign funds. Section 541(a) including the campaign funds as property of the estate is comparable to the funds being held in the hands of a fiduciary.

Section 541(c)(1) provides further support for this inclusion by affirmatively invalidating any use restriction state law places on the campaign funds. [Georgia elections law] limits what campaign funds may be spent on:

> Contributions to a candidate, a campaign committee, or a public officer holding elective office and any proceeds from investing such contributions shall be utilized only to defray ordinary and necessary expenses.

[This law] describes how a candidate may *not* treat the campaign funds: "[c]ontributions and interest thereon, if any, shall not constitute personal assets of such candidate or such public officer." Although [the state law] restricts use of the campaign funds, the anti-alienation provision prevents the state law from excluding the funds from becoming property of the estate. Additionally, the spendthrift trust exception to the anti-alienation provision does not apply here because the campaign funds are not held in a spendthrift trust under Georgia law. There is no evidence of a writing creating an express trust, let alone an express trust containing a valid spendthrift provision. *See* O.C.G.A. § 53-12-80(a); In re Hipple, 225 B.R. 808 (Bankr. N.D. Ga. 1996) (Cotton, J.). Even if the campaign funds were held in a trust, the writing creating that trust would have to unequivocally state the spendthrift provision and the Debtor would have to lack access to the funds. In *Hipple*, Judge Cotton noted, ". . . the purpose of a . . . spendthrift trust is to protect the beneficiary from himself and his creditors . . . such a trust fails when the beneficiary exercises 'absolute dominion' over trust property." In re Hipple, 225 B.R. at 814. The Debtor presented no evidence of her lack of access to the campaign funds, because Georgia's campaign finance law does not restrict *access*. In contrast to a spendthrift trust, Georgia's campaign finance law theoretically allows candidates to be lavish and irresponsible in spending their campaign funds, it simply restricts the *kinds* of expenses that can be paid from the campaign funds.

Without a valid trust, the spendthrift trust exception to the anti-alienation provision does not apply.

CONCLUSION

The campaign funds are property of the estate pursuant to section 541 of the Bankruptcy Code and *Whiting Pools* and its progeny. If this outcome has political implications, they are simply a derivative, necessary consequence of the Court's adherence to the Bankruptcy Code and controlling case law.

IT IS ORDERED.

─────────────

Introducing a third law school course you took earlier—constitutional law—note that the Supremacy Clause makes clear § 541(c)(1) brushes aside Georgia elections law. One wonders how the Republican campaign supporters of Representative Chambers would feel knowing their contributions are helping satisfy the debts of a credit card company whose chairman runs a Democratic Super-PAC (hypothetically, of course). This gives a flavor of the difficult policy balances—more precisely, policy overrides—presented by the broad-reaching scope of the Bankruptcy Code. (Sadly, Jill Chambers (R-Atlanta) did not succeed in her quest for reelection. Local pundits made much of the fact that she was the financial watchdog of the Atlanta public transit system while her own financial chaos led to bankruptcy.)

The third and final type of dispute regarding "property of the estate" involves entitlement. It raises the tricky question whether certain legal prerogatives are sufficiently (in)alienable to qualify as private *property*. (The distinction between a "property" right and a mere "license" right of contract is analogous to the constitutional distinction between a "right" and a mere "privilege.") The problem often arises as to new kinds of property, such as a license to broadcast over the television airwaves. These more ethereal issues arise predominately in the business context, so we defer fuller exploration until then.

C.   THE AUTOMATIC STAY

Filing a bankruptcy petition not only creates a new estate, it also triggers an automatic stay that prohibits any creditor's attempt to continue to collect from the debtor or the debtor's property. The automatic stay is often likened to "closing the windows and locking the doors" to prevent any property from leaving the newly formed estate. Eventually, the court will oversee the gathering and distribution of the assets, but until that time or until the stay is lifted, creditors are generally stopped in their tracks. Section 362(a) details the prohibitions of the stay, while § 362(b) provides exceptions that permit certain types of actions to continue.

In many respects, bankruptcy law is about control, a point that we will explore in more depth in the business section. For now, it is enough to emphasize that it is the automatic stay that puts the court in full control of the debtor's assets instantly, all over the United States (and, to some extent, all over the world). The automatic stay is also the first intrusion of federal bankruptcy laws into the state actions for creditors discussed in Assignment 2. As the following cases illustrate, the power of the automatic stay is broad and the consequence of flouting it, severe.

===== In re GREEN =====

2011 WL 5902502 (Bankr. E.D.N.C. Oct. 20, 2011)

Doub, Bankruptcy Judge.

The Debtor filed a voluntary petition for relief under Chapter 7 of the Bankruptcy Code on August 10, 2009.

BACKGROUND

The Debtor attended ECU [East Carolina University] for a number of semesters including the Fall of 2007. The evidence presented at the hearing shows that the Debtor received grants and scholarships from various sources to fund her education. In the Fall of 2007, one of these sources was a Federal Perkins Loan in the amount of $750.00. Federal Perkins Loans are managed by the Office of Student Loans at ECU. The letters and invoices ECU sent the Debtor regarding payment of the Perkins Loan are the subject of the alleged willful violations of the automatic stay the Debtor asserts against ECU.

Another source of the Debtor's financial aid was a North Carolina Department of Health and Human Services, Division of Services for the Blind grant, which paid the remainder of any unpaid tuition not covered by other sources of financial aid, such as federal grants and loans, or institutional grants and loans. [An administrative error resulted in an overpayment by the Division of Services for the Blind of approximately $1,949.83 that ECU was required to refund. As such, the Debtor became liable to ECU for $1,949.83 plus interest because ECU repaid the Division of Services for the Blind on her behalf.]

Subsequent to the petition date, the Debtor continued attending ECU. Specifically, Debtor attended two Summer Sessions at ECU in the Summer of 2010. The Debtor withdrew from school during one of these sessions, causing her to become ineligible for some of her financial aid. As such, a portion of the financial aid for which the Debtor had not earned by finishing the session was returned to its originator by ECU. This resulted in the Debtor owing ECU $3,212.00. After the Debtor's discharge was entered, ECU began billing the Debtor for the unpaid $3,212.00 and the $1,949.83 overpayment from the Fall of 2007 plus interest totaling $5,344.50. . . .

The Debtor appeared pro se at the September 29, 2011 hearing. The Debtor introduced evidence tending to show ECU attempted to collect on an outstanding pre-petition debt while the automatic stay was in place. More specifically, the Debtor proffered letters and invoices sent by the ECU Office of Student Loans in an attempt to collect on the $750.00 debt that were mailed after the automatic stay was in effect and after ECU received notice of the filing of the bankruptcy petition.

. . .

In the Response, ECU asserts that it did not engage in any actions that warrant the imposition of sanctions. At the hearing, ECU stipulated to the previously mentioned invoices and letters sent by the Office of Student Loans. However, ECU argued at the hearing that the collection attempts were not willful violations of the automatic stay because they were inadvertently sent to the Debtor as a result of a lack of communication between the various departments at ECU. ECU presented evidence through the testimony of Debra Bailey. . . . Ms. Bailey further explained that the letters and invoices were printed and mailed through an automated process on a thirty-sixty-ninety day interval. Therefore, any mailing of them was not an intentional act but an error produced because the Office of Student Loans was not informed of the bankruptcy petition. Furthermore, Ms. Bailey testified that ECU has since taken steps to institute a procedure whereby the different departments within the university are required to check a software system to ensure no student has filed a bankruptcy petition prior to attempting to collect on a debt.

DISCUSSION

Section 362(a) of the Bankruptcy Code imposes a stay on "any act to collect, assess, or recover a claim against the debtor that arose before the commencement of a case under" title 11. 11 U.S.C. § 362(a)(6). The Bankruptcy Code also provides that any "individual injured by any willful violation of a stay provided by this section shall recover actual damages . . . and in appropriate circumstances, may recover punitive damages." 11 U.S.C. § 362(k)(1). This Court has held that "willfulness does not refer to the intent to violate the automatic stay, but the intent to commit the act which violates the automatic stay." Lofton v. Carolina Fin. LLC (In re Lofton), 385 B.R. 133, 140 (Bankr. E.D. N.C. 2008) (citing Citizens Bank v. Strumpf, 37 F.3d 155 (4th Cir. 1994), overruled on other grounds 516 U.S. 16, 11 (1995)). . . .

[B]ecause the Office of Student Loans caused the letters and invoices to be sent and such actions were a violation of the automatic stay, ECU willfully violated the automatic stay.

. . .

In the Debtor's case, ECU has stipulated that violations of the stay occurred and has recognized the significance of the automatic stay by correcting internal practices to allow for notification of any bankruptcy petition between departments. However, ECU is a large state supported university with a Cashier's Office and Office of Student Loans. The collection of tuition, fees, and loans is big business involving millions of dollars. ECU is to be commended for curing its deficiencies in collection procedures, but should have done so long before 2010. For having failed to do so prior to 2010, the imposition of punitive damages is merited. No actual damages were proven by the Debtor.

Based on the foregoing, the Court finds that ECU's willful acts of sending four letters or invoices to the Debtor after receiving notice of the bankruptcy were in willful violation of the automatic stay. The Debtor is entitled to recover sanctions in the amount of $500.00 per violation of the automatic stay, totaling sanctions of $2,000.00.

Therefore, the Motion for Sanctions is GRANTED. . . .

Green nicely illustrates the power and the breadth of the automatic stay barring any attempt to collect a debt, as well as the court's unwillingness to permit a large organization to plead bureaucracy as a defense, even when it has prospectively cleaned up its act. The next case, which features a bureaucracy defense that stretches credulity, adds in the question of just what counts as "an act to collect" in violation of the stay.

NISSAN MOTOR ACCEPTANCE CORP. v. BAKER

239 B.R. 484 (N.D. Tex. 1999)

KENDALL, District Judge.

This is an appeal from a judgment entered by the United States Bankruptcy Court for the Northern District of Texas, Dallas Division, on February 6, 1996. The Bankruptcy Court held that various actions of Appellant-Creditor Nissan Motor Acceptance Corporation ("Appellant") violated the terms of the automatic stay provided by 11 U.S.C.A. § 362(a) (West 1998). The Bankruptcy Court awarded actual and punitive damages for Appellees Debtors ("Appellees") in the amount of $23,000, and reasonable attorneys' fees and expenses in the amount of $4,981.75. The Bankruptcy Court granted Appellant the option of satisfying the actual and punitive damages portion of the judgment by delivering to Appellees a new 1996 Nissan Pickup Truck B, Model SE, together with its title free and clear of any liens. For the reasons stated below, the judgment of the Bankruptcy Court is affirmed.

I. FACTUAL BACKGROUND

Appellees filed a Chapter 7 bankruptcy petition on December 30, 1993. At the time of filing, Appellees listed their 1991 Nissan Pickup ("Vehicle"), for which Appellees were in arrears to Appellant by more than two monthly payments. In their Statement of Intentions submitted with their petition, Appellees stated an intent to reaffirm the debt to Appellant for the Vehicle. On January 4, 1994, Appellant, without knowledge of Appellees' bankruptcy, repossessed the Vehicle. Both sides admit that Appellees' counsel contacted Appellant following the repossession to inform Appellant of Appellees' bankruptcy. Appellant disputes Appellees' assertion that they requested the return of the Vehicle. Nonetheless, the Bankruptcy Court found that as of January 4, 1994, Nissan had notice of Appellees' bankruptcy.

Appellant did not turn over the Vehicle upon notice of Appellees' bankruptcy, but retained possession of the Vehicle. On February 23, 1994, almost two months after the bankruptcy was filed and over six weeks after Appellant received notice of the bankruptcy, Appellant filed its motion for relief from stay, or, in the alternative, adequate protection [a motion seeking bankruptcy relief for secured creditors whose collateral is depreciating (see Assignment 10). However, while this motion was pending before the Bankruptcy Court, Appellant sold the Vehicle on March 16, 1994. The Bankruptcy Court, which did not know of the sale of the Vehicle, eventually granted Appellant's motion on June 1, 1994.

In November 1994, Appellees filed the adversary proceeding subject to this appeal seeking damages for violation of the automatic stay provided by § 362. . . .

II. ANALYSIS

The bankruptcy court's findings are reviewed under the clearly erroneous standard, and its legal conclusions are reviewed de novo. See Fed. R. Bankr. P. 8013.

Nissan's first assertion on appeal is that the Bankruptcy Court erred in holding that Appellant's exercise of control over the Vehicle after notice of the automatic stay was a willful violation of the stay. Interwoven in Nissan's argument is the issue of adequate protection—whether a secured creditor is required to turn over its collateral, which is property of the estate, without first receiving adequate protection. . . .

At particular issue here is § 362(a)(3), which states that the automatic stay prohibits "any act to obtain possession of property of the estate or of property from the estate or to exercise control over property of the estate." Numerous cases have held that a creditor's continued retention of estate property after notice of a bankruptcy filing constitutes an "exercise of control" over property of the estate in violation of the automatic stay [just as some others have held that it does not, a dispute the Supreme Court will sort out just in time to miss this book's press deadline. See City of Chicago v. Fulton, 926 F.3d 916 (7th Cir. 2019), *cert. granted*, 140 S. Ct. 680 (2019).—Eds.]

There is nothing in § 363(e) that grants a creditor like Appellant the authority to engage in self-help to retain estate property as adequate protection, which is exactly what Appellant did in this case. Moreover, contrary to Appellant's argument, § 542(a) provides that a creditor like Appellant "*shall* deliver to the trustee, and account for, [estate] property or the value of such property" (emphasis added). Section 542(a) has been construed to establish an affirmative obligation on the creditor to return estate property unless it is of inconsequential value to the estate, and nothing in § 542(a) requires the debtor to provide the creditor with adequate protection as a condition precedent to turnover. Appellant's action is a violation of its obligation under § 542(a) to turn over estate property, and subverts the authority of the Bankruptcy Court as specified in § 363(e) to order adequate protection when the Bankruptcy Court, not the creditor, deems such protection necessary.

Appellant's second issue on appeal is whether Appellant's sale of the Vehicle was a willful violation of the stay. . . . Appellant knew that the stay was in effect when it filed its motion on February 23, 1994. Appellant cannot "play dumb" and rely on its "records," which inexplicably indicated to Appellant that the stay had lifted on March 5, 1994, when there was no order from the Bankruptcy Court relating to Appellant's motion until June 1, 1994. Appellant's disregard of the Bankruptcy Court's authority is inexcusable, and the Bankruptcy Court did not err in finding that Appellant's sale of the Vehicle was a willful violation of the stay. . . .

Appellant's fourth issue on appeal is whether there was sufficient evidence to award actual damages. . . . Appellant ignores the ample testimony offered by Appellees on their actual damages. In addition to Appellees' testimony that they paid their daughter-in-law to drive them when necessary, Appellees testified that the Vehicle was the only reliable source of transportation that they had, that Appellee Baker's daily commute to and from his work was ninety miles, that Appellees struggled to secure reliable transportation after the Vehicle was repossessed by Appellant, and that Appellees had to purchase and finance a used Honda Civic in May 1994, as a replacement for the Vehicle. This evidence belies Appellant's contention that there was no other proof of actual damages. Thus, the Bankruptcy Court's award of actual damages was not clearly erroneous.

Appellant's fifth issue on appeal is whether the Bankruptcy Court erred and abused its discretion in awarding punitive damages. . . . In light of Appellant's willful violation of the stay by exercising self-help to possess and sell estate property, the Bankruptcy Court did not err, nor did it abuse its discretion, in awarding punitive damages. . . .

Finally, Appellant's seventh issue on appeal is whether there is sufficient evidence to support the Bankruptcy Court's award of "excessive" attorneys' fees under § 362(h). . . . Under the facts and circumstances of this case, the Court finds that the Bankruptcy Court's award of $4,860.00 in attorneys' fees per § 362(h) is not clearly erroneous.

III. CONCLUSION

For the reasons stated above, the judgment of the bankruptcy court . . . is AFFIRMED.

Notice that the court was willing to "lift" the stay, which we will talk about in greater detail in subsequent assignments. This means that Nissan could have gotten the car if it had asked the court to lift the stay. But when Nissan acted on its own without approval from the bankruptcy court, it ran up nearly $30,000 in damages. There's a message here, and it is not a subtle one.

This ability to lift the stay also shows that bankruptcy is not just about debtor relief. While a debtor's life may be greatly improved at the moment the bankruptcy petition is filed by the breathing room accorded by the automatic stay, that respite may be short-lived. Some creditors may be entitled to relief from the stay, and an even greater number will claim that they are entitled to relief (or at least posture so).

Nissan also showed a court angry enough to impose punitive damages. Does that "egregious" conduct happen a lot? We have no empirical data, but in one rare case, the debtor actually kept a diary of her mortgage lender's repeated, relentless foreclosure conduct in the face of unambiguous notice of the stay, resulting in suicide attempts and serious medical problems in a former competitive athlete. Judge Klein's 107-page opinion documenting Bank of America's "[K]afkaesque" treatment of homeowners (who at one point requested a modification of their mortgage, were told they had to default first before the bank would consider it, and then, upon default, had their home foreclosed upon, even after they filed bankruptcy to stay the foreclosure) culminated in a nice, round punitive damages award of $45 million that could "not be laughed off in the board room as petty cash or 'chump change.'" Sundquist v. Bank of America N.A. (In re Sundquist), 566 B.R. 563 (E.D. Cal. 2017). This decision was later vacated in part by In re Sundquist, 580 B.R. 536 (E.D. Cal. 2018), in which Bank of America sought to pay the homeowners several million dollars more than their awarded damages in exchange for the court's dismissal of the adversary proceeding and withdrawal of its earlier opinion. While the court said "no dice" to "eras[ing] the record," it did agree to vacate the damages judgment against Bank of America and close the adversary proceeding without formal resolution so long as the settlement agreement reached between the parties was honored.

Finally, pause to reflect how many different actions can violate the automatic stay. In *Nissan*, merely "doing nothing" but holding onto the car violated the stay. In a case likely to be of interest to students, Andrews University v. Merchant (In re Merchant), 958 F.2d 738 (6th Cir. 1992), the court held refusal to turn over a foreign-national alumnus's transcript—as required for his U.S. naturalization petition—due to unpaid tuition was a four-square violation.

Problem Set 3

3.1. You have just been appointed trustee for the estate of Donald Lapman, whose flaky other-worldliness has long charmed his friends and has now brought him into chapter 7 bankruptcy. Donald had some connection with the following property on the day he filed his bankruptcy petition:

(a)   his parakeet, Toto;
(b)   a 2017 Ford Focus he bought used, which is still subject to a purchase-money security interest in an amount exceeding its value;
(c)   candid snapshots of hundreds of his friends, some of them quite intimate;
(d)   two tickets to an upcoming Björk concert;
(e)   household furniture, including dishes, pans, chairs, a couch, and the like;
(f)   25 shares of Monumental, Inc. left to him by his Uncle Rufus;
(g)   an undivided 3/48ths interest in a big-game hunting preserve, also left by Rufus;
(h)   3,214 bubble gum baseball cards, some dating back to 1948;
(i)   an arrangement with his younger brother: when Donald left home for college years ago, he lent his brother his catcher's mitt, with the understanding Donald could get it back whenever he wanted it;

(j) a bank account on which Donald is the named trustee for the benefit of his little niece Sherry, in the amount of $2,750;

(k) his salary for the month prior to the petition, which he received just hours after filing;

(l) his retirement account, which he cannot touch until he retires;

(m) his interest in the Lovey Lapman Irrevocable Trust, the corpus of which is presently $450,000, which entitles him as sole beneficiary of this non-assignable trust to a monthly distribution of $2,500 until Lovey, his mother, dies, at which point he gets the remainder.

A month after the petition was filed, the parakeet unexpectedly laid two eggs, which have since become two little parakeets. A month later, Donald received from Monumental an annual dividend in the amount of $225. In addition, in the two months since the petition was filed Donald continued working and was paid his salary; his employer also made a contribution to his retirement fund. Lovey is quite ill. The doctors say she might last six months, but definitely not a year.

Which of the above items are "property of the estate" under § 541?

3.2. On March 1 a local farmer, Frances Alleta, contracted to sell her winter wheat crop of 10,000 bushels to a local grain warehouse for the market price prevailing on July 1. Unable to make it financially, Frances filed a bankruptcy petition April 1. The immature wheat had no market value at that moment. On March 1 the market price for wheat was $10 a bushel, but a severe drought in Argentina raised world prices so that it was worth $15 a bushel on April 1 and $20 a bushel on July 1, when Frances harvested it. When the buyer pays the $200,000, who gets what?

3.3. Sydney Leavens has done her best to pay her bills, but the combination of medical problems and a cutback at work has left her in a deep financial hole. On Monday, Advanta Bank seized her car. She was desperate to get it back, so she cashed out the money in her retirement account, and she wrote a check to Advanta to pay off the car loan. The company said they would return the car when the check cleared. Recognizing that she was in a financial mess, Sydney decided on Tuesday to see a bankruptcy lawyer, who filed a petition that afternoon. On Wednesday, Advanta deposited Sydney's check. On Thursday, the check cleared, but Advanta has called you for advice before they return the car. What do you tell them? See §§ 362(a), (h), 521(a)(2).

3.4. Joe Weiner has come to see you about getting some help with his staggering debt burden. Joe makes about $34,000 per year as a meat cutter, but he hurt his arm last year and was out of work for nearly eight months. His current wages are reduced by $100 per week because they have been garnished in an action by a finance company. Joe owes about $68,000 in unsecured debt, including credit cards, medical bills, credit union loans, finance company loans, past due alimony and child support, store charge cards, and overdue utility bills. He also owes $4,500 on his car loan and another $750 to an auto repair garage. Joe adds that he has been receiving dunning letters and phone calls, his doctor's collection agency has threatened legal action if he doesn't come up with some money by tomorrow, the utility company has sent a notice that service will be discontinued at midnight, and both the car lender and the garage have threatened repossession.

To try to hold things together, Joe takes each paycheck and makes small payments to each creditor. When the car lender threatened to repossess his car, Joe wrote him a check for the balance due even though he had only $44.12 in the bank. He has just received a summons from the district attorney to appear in court tomorrow morning on a bad check charge. Joe is late on his rent again, and his landlord has threatened to evict him if he doesn't pay his past-due rent by Friday. His credit counselor has run out of suggestions.

Joe's assets consist of his car, clothing, kitchen utensils, and small pieces of furniture. He will get paid tomorrow morning for the two-week pay period that ended yesterday. He has filled out all the necessary paperwork and produced the required documentation. You have satisfied yourself that he is qualified for a chapter 7, which he has asked you to file later today. Joe wants to know what he can expect to happen in the next few weeks. He especially wants to know if he will get his full paycheck, undiminished by the garnishment, tomorrow and every two weeks thereafter. See §§ 362(a), (b)(2), (b)(22), (b)(23), 366.

3.5. Puja Seam arrives in your office in tears. She shows you a notice that her house has been posted for sale by foreclosure at noon tomorrow. She explains that she has been in the middle of a divorce, and that her ex-husband claimed that he was making mortgage payments when he was not. She had called him about the earlier notices, but he had said that the notices were "mistakes" and he would "straighten them out." For the past month she has been unable to find him, and she fears he has fled the state. She tried calling the mortgage company, but her loan modification efforts keep ending in lost paperwork and disconnected phone calls. Now the sheriff's department says the sale is going forward. You know that if it does, she and her children will lose their home.

Puja has filled out all the schedules in your conference room today, but she did not know to bring paycheck stubs, tax returns, or any other paperwork with her; nor has she sought credit counseling. She lives an hour away and isn't sure where all that paperwork is at home. What can you do for her today? Make a list of what you need from Puja and how you can get it. See 11 U.S.C. §§ 521(a), (b), (i), 101(12A), 109(h), 526, 707(b)(4)(C), (D). When your paralegal points silently to the value listed for the car ($250), does that raise an issue beyond asking her if she is sure of it?

Section 2

Chapter 7 Liquidation

The primal form of bankruptcy is liquidation. It resides in chapter 7 of the Code. The basic structure is straightforward: decide on what is owed, decide on what assets are available, and then sell off those assets for the benefit of the creditors. The most unusual part of the Code, historically and comparatively, is the immediate discharge of debt that follows liquidation. The discharge effectuates the main policy goal of consumer bankruptcy: giving consumers a "fresh start." The concepts and rules of chapter 7 form the core of all bankruptcy procedures.

While chapter 7 is widely used by both businesses and individuals, the latter dwarf the former in number. Indeed, an individual chapter 7 is one of the most common civil proceedings in the United States, taking its place alongside divorce, probate, benefits denials, and similar bread-and-butter actions that make up the non-glamorous bulk of the nation's legal dockets.

This section begins by looking at what assets are available for creditors in a chapter 7. It then explores how creditors make and calculate claims against those assets, examining the rules that give some creditors special priority for their claims. Finally, it turns to the discharge: how it works, what is covered, and why debtors still have ongoing creditor relations even after its invocation.

PROPERTY EXEMPT FROM SEIZURE

A. INTRODUCTION

If you have ever seen a cartoon of a skinny little guy who is broke and wearing only a barrel, you may have wondered why the creditors left the barrel. The law in every state makes at least some property exempt from execution and other legal process so that no debtor can be reduced to absolute destitution. The policy reasons include a desire to avoid results so draconian as to threaten the social fabric of the community, which for similar reasons precludes the pledging of a pound of flesh as collateral. In addition, exemption policies also express a healthy dose of self-interest by non-debtors. The concern that a creditor not leave the debtor with so little property that the debtor and the debtor's family will become a charge on the community means that exemption laws are often directed toward making certain that every debtor retains enough basic property to have a chance to get out of the hole and make a fresh start. (Applicants cannot go to most job interviews naked.) Still another policy reason for some property exemptions is that certain items of personal property, such as clothes, have little monetary value for the creditor but are crucial to the debtor. Although the line between the two can be fuzzy, the law attempts to distinguish between seizing property to satisfy a debt and seizing property solely to inflict pain.

Recall that "exempt" property under state law means exempt from seizure by writ through the formal collections law. When the debtor waives that exemption, by granting a voluntary security interest with a home mortgage or car lien, the exemption protection falls by the wayside. This results in a neat divide among creditor groups: secured lenders like home mortgage companies, car lenders, and pawnbrokers for the most part care little about the scope of an exemption law, while credit card issuers, health care providers, tort victims, and others who cannot get a security agreement in advance feel the statute's teeth.

In bankruptcy, all property not listed as exempt is denominated non-exempt and will be sold by the trustee so that the proceeds can be distributed to the creditors. This may be the general unsecured creditor's last chance to get paid. Having said that, it is important to remember that most consumer debtors have so little unencumbered property it is not worthwhile for a trustee or creditor to bother objecting to their exemption claims.

B.   FEDERALISM IN EXEMPTION LAWS

Every state has exemption laws, although the amount of protection varies widely. Once a debtor files for bankruptcy, federal law preempts state collection efforts with the automatic stay, but the question about which property is exempt becomes even sharper. After all, the deal in chapter 7 is that the debtor will give up all non-exempt property to get a debt discharge. The federal bankruptcy process must have rules about what the debtor must give up.

The 1898 Bankruptcy Act deferred to the states on the exemption issue. This meant, for example, that a Texas debtor in bankruptcy could protect whatever a Texas debtor outside bankruptcy could protect, while a Wyoming debtor in or out of bankruptcy could protect whatever property Wyoming exempted. The fact that Texas and Wyoming protected very different items or values was irrelevant, even though bankruptcy law is federal.

When the bankruptcy laws were modernized in 1978, many experts believed that it was time to develop uniform national exemptions. That proposal drew fire from two opposing camps: those in Congress who represented states with much smaller exemptions who thought the uniform proposals were too generous and (you guessed it) those in Congress who represented states with far more generous exemptions who thought the federal exemptions were too stingy. A compromise that only lawyers could love was born: the Code would establish uniform federal exemptions, *but* states would be permitted to "opt out" of those exemptions, forbidding their own citizens the ability to claim them upon bankruptcy. 11 U.S.C. § 522(b)(2). That's a pretty big "but"— and we cannot lie—of which 35 states have availed themselves. The constitutionality of opting-out has been challenged, upheld, and has ceased to be widely disputed. See, e.g., In re Lauch, 16 B.R. 162 (Bankr. M.D. Fla. 1981).

1.   State Exemptions

We reproduce illustrative excerpts from two states' exemption laws. The first is from Texas, and the second is from Wyoming. (Several specific exemptions from each state are omitted, notably extensive provisions exempting most retirement plans regulated by the Internal Revenue Code.)

===== TEXAS EXEMPTION STATUTES =====

Texas Property Code Annotated (Westlaw 2019)

§ 41.001. Interests in Land Exempt from Seizure

(a) A homestead and one or more lots used for a place of burial of the dead are exempt from seizure for the claims of creditors except for encumbrances properly fixed on homestead property.

(b) Encumbrances may be properly fixed on homestead property for

(1) purchase money;
(2) taxes on the property;
(3) work and material used in constructing improvements on the property if contracted for in writing. . . .

(c) The homestead claimant's proceeds of a sale of a homestead are not subject to seizure for a creditor's claim for six months after the date of sale.

§ 41.002. DEFINITION OF HOMESTEAD

(a) If used for the purposes of an urban home or as both an urban home and a place to exercise a calling or business, the homestead of a family or a single, adult person, not otherwise entitled to a homestead, shall consist of not more than 10 acres of land which may be in one or more contiguous lots, together with any improvements thereon.

(b) If used for the purposes of a rural home, the homestead shall consist of

(1) for a family, not more than 200 acres, which may be in one or more parcels, with the improvements thereon; or
(2) for a single, adult person, not otherwise entitled to a homestead, not more than 100 acres, which may be in one or more parcels, with the improvements thereon.

(c) A homestead is considered to be urban if, at the time the designation is made, the property is

(1) located within the limits of a municipality or its extraterritorial jurisdiction or a platted subdivision; and
(2) served by police protection, paid or volunteer fire protection, and at least three of the following services provided by a municipality or under contract to a municipality
(A) electric;
(B) natural gas;
(C) sewer;
(D) storm sewer; and
(E) water.

(d) The definition of a homestead as provided in this section applies to all homesteads in this state whenever created.

§ 41.003. TEMPORARY RENTING OF A HOMESTEAD

Temporary renting of a homestead does not change its homestead character if the homestead claimant has not acquired another homestead.

§ 42.001. Personal Property Exemption

(a) Personal property, as described in Section 42.002, is exempt from garnishment, attachment, execution, or other seizure if

(1) the property is provided for a family and has an aggregate fair market value of not more than $100,000, exclusive of the amount of any liens, security interests, or other charges encumbering the property; or

(2) the property is owned by a single adult, who is not a member of a family, and has an aggregate fair market value of not more than $50,000, exclusive of the amount of any liens, security interests, or other charges encumbering the property.

(b) The following personal property is exempt from seizure and is not included in the aggregate limitations prescribed by Subsection (a)

(1) current wages for personal services, except for the enforcement of court-ordered child support payments;

(2) professionally prescribed health aids of a debtor or a dependent of a debtor; and

(3) alimony, support, or separate maintenance received or to be received by the debtor for the support of the debtor or a dependent of the debtor.

(4) a religious bible or other book containing sacred writings of a religion that is seized by a creditor other than a lessor of real property who is exercising the lessor's contractual or statutory right to seize personal property after a tenant breaches a lease agreement for or abandons the real property.

(c) Except as provided by Subsection (b)(4), this section does not prevent seizure by a secured creditor with a contractual landlord's lien or other security in the property to be seized.

(d) Unpaid commissions for personal services not to exceed 25 percent of the aggregate limitations prescribed by Subsection (a) are exempt from seizure and are included in the aggregate.

(e) A religious bible or other book described by Subsection (b)(4) that is seized by a lessor of real property in the exercise of the lessor's contractual or statutory right to seize personal property after a tenant breaches a lease agreement for the real property or abandons the real property may not be included in the aggregate limitations prescribed by Subsection (a).

§ 42.002. Personal Property

(a) The following personal property is exempt under Section 42.001(a)

(1) home furnishings, including family heirlooms;

(2) provisions for consumption;

(3) farming or ranching vehicles and implements;

(4) tools, equipment, books, and apparatus, including boats and motor vehicles used in a trade or profession;

(5) wearing apparel;

(6) jewelry not to exceed 25 percent of the aggregate limitations prescribed by Section 42.001(a);

(7) two firearms;

(8) athletic and sporting equipment, including bicycles;

(9) a two-wheeled, three-wheeled, or four-wheeled motor vehicle for each member of a family or single adult who holds a driver's license or who does not hold a driver's license but who relies on another person to operate the vehicle for the benefit of the nonlicensed person;

(10) the following animals and forage on hand for their consumption

(A) two horses, mules, or donkeys and a saddle, blanket, and bridle for each;

(B) 12 head of cattle;

(C) 60 head of other types of livestock; and

(D) 120 fowl; and

(11) household pets.

(b) Personal property, unless precluded from being encumbered by other law, may be encumbered by a security interest under Subchapter B, Chapter 9, Business & Commerce Code, or Subchapter F, Chapter 501, Transportation Code, or by a lien fixed by other law, and the security interest or lien may not be avoided on the ground that the property is exempt under this chapter.

§ 42.005. Child Support Liens

(a) Except as provided by Subsection (b), Sections 42.001, 42.002, and 42.0021 do not apply to a child support lien established under Subchapter G, Chapter 157, Family Code.

(b) The exemption from attachment, execution, and seizure for the satisfaction of debts provided under Section 42.0021 for a plan or account described by Section 42.0021(a)(8), (9), or (10) applies to a child support lien established under Subchapter G, Chapter 157, Family Code.

——— TEXAS INSURANCE EXEMPTION ——— STATUTES
Texas Insurance Code Annotated (Westlaw 2019)

§ 1108.051. Exemptions for Certain Insurance and Annuity Benefits

(a) Except as provided by Section 1108.053, this section applies to any benefits, including the cash value and proceeds of an insurance policy, to be provided to an insured or beneficiary under:

(1) an insurance policy or annuity contract issued by a life, health, or accident insurance company, including a mutual company or fraternal benefit society; or

(2) an annuity or benefit plan used by an employer or individual.

(b) Notwithstanding any other provision of this code, insurance or annuity benefits described by Subsection (a):

(1) inure exclusively to the benefit of the person for whose use and benefit the insurance or annuity is designated in the policy or contract; and

(2) are fully exempt from:

(A) garnishment, attachment, execution, or other seizure;

(B) seizure, appropriation, or application by any legal or equitable process or by operation of law to pay a debt or other liability of an insured or of a beneficiary, either before or after the benefits are provided; and

(C) a demand in a bankruptcy proceeding of the insured or beneficiary.

§ 1108.053. Exceptions to Exemptions

The exemptions provided by Section 1108.051 do not apply to:

(1) a premium payment made in fraud of a creditor, subject to the applicable statute of limitations for recovering the payment;

(2) a debt of the insured or beneficiary secured by a pledge of the insurance policy or the proceeds of the policy; or

(3) a child support lien or levy under Chapter 157, Family Code.

═══════ WYOMING EXEMPTION STATUTES ═══════
Wyo. Const., Art. 19 § 9. Exemption of Homestead

A homestead as provided by law shall be exempt from forced sale under any process of law, and shall not be alienated without the joint consent of husband and wife, when that relation exists; but no property shall be exempt from sale for taxes, or for the payment of obligations contracted for the purchase of said premises, or for the erection of improvements thereon.

Wyoming Statutes Annotated (Westlaw 2019)

§ 1-15-511. Limitation on Continuing Garnishment

(a) The maximum portion of the aggregate disposable earnings of a judgment debtor which are subject to continuing garnishment under this article is the lesser of:

(i) Twenty-five percent (25%) of the judgment debtor's disposable earnings for that week; or

(ii) The amount by which the judgment debtor's aggregate disposable earnings computed for that week exceeds thirty (30) times the federal minimum hourly wage prescribed by the Fair Labor Standards Act of 1938, 29 U.S.C. 206(a)(1), in effect at the time the earnings are payable, or, in case of earnings for any pay period other than a week, any equivalent multiple thereof prescribed by the administrator of the Wyoming Uniform Consumer Credit Code in the manner provided by W.S. 40-14-505(b)(iii).

§ 1-20-101. Homestead Exemption; Right and Amount

Every resident of the state is entitled to a homestead not exceeding twenty thousand dollars ($20,000.00) in value, exempt from execution and attachment arising from any debt, contract or civil obligation entered into or incurred.

§ 1-20-102. Homestead Exemption; When Operative

(a) The homestead is only exempt as provided in W.S. 1-20-101 while occupied as such by the owner or the person entitled thereto, or his or her family.

(b) When two (2) or more persons jointly own and occupy the same residence, each shall be entitled to the homestead exemption.

§ 1-20-104. Homestead Exemption; Composition

The homestead may consist of a house on a lot or lots or other lands of any number of acres, or a house trailer or other movable home on a lot or lots, whether or not the house trailer or other movable home is equipped with wheels or resting upon immovable support.

§ 1-20-105. Wearing Apparel

The necessary wearing apparel of every person not exceeding two thousand dollars ($2,000.00) in value, determined in the manner provided in W.S. 1-20-106 is exempt from levy or sale upon execution, writ of attachment or any process issuing out of any court in this state. Necessary wearing apparel shall not include jewelry of any type other than wedding rings.

§ 1-20-106. Exemption of Other Personal Property; Personalty Used in Livelihood; Appraisement

(a) The following property, when owned by any person, is exempt from levy or sale upon execution, writ of attachment or any process issuing out of any court in this state and shall continue to be exempt while the person or the family of the person is moving from one (1) place of residence to another in this state:

(i) The family bible, pictures and school books;

(ii) A lot in any cemetery or burial ground;

(iii) Furniture, bedding, provisions and other household articles of any kind or character as the debtor may select, not exceeding in all the value of four thousand dollars ($4,000.00). When two (2) or more persons occupy the same residence, each shall be entitled to a separate exemption;

(iv) A motor vehicle not exceeding in value of five thousand dollars ($5,000.00).

(v) Not more than three (3) firearms not exceeding in all the value of three thousand dollars ($3,000.00) and their associated ammunition not to exceed one thousand (1,000) rounds per firearm.

(b) The tools, team, implements or stock in trade of any person, used and kept for the purpose of carrying on his trade or business, not exceeding in value of four thousand dollars ($4,000.00), or the library, instruments and implements of any professional person, not exceeding in value of four thousand dollars ($4,000.00), are exempt from levy or sale upon execution, writ of attachment or any process out of any court in this state.

§ 1-20-108. EXCEPTION; RESIDENCY REQUIRED

(a) No property claimed as exempt under W.S. 1-20-101 through 1-20-106 is exempt from attachment or sale upon execution for the purchase money of the property.

(b) Any person claiming these exemptions shall be a bona fide resident of this state.

§ 26-15-129. EXEMPTION OF PROCEEDS; LIFE INSURANCE

(a) If a policy of insurance is executed by any person on his own life or on another life, in favor of a person other than himself, or except in cases of transfer with intent to defraud creditors, if a policy of life insurance is assigned or in any way made payable to that person, the lawful beneficiary or assignee thereof, other than the insured or the person executing insurance or executors or administrators of such insured or the person executing the insurance, are entitled to its proceeds, including death benefits, cash surrender and loan values, premiums waived and dividends, whether used in reduction of premiums or otherwise, excepting only where the debtor, subsequent to issuance of the policy, has actually elected to receive the dividends in cash, against the creditors and representatives of the insured and of the person executing the policy, and are not liable to be applied by any legal or equitable process to pay any debt or liability of the insured individual or his beneficiary or of any other person having a right under the policy, whether or not:

(i) The right to change the beneficiary is reserved or permitted; and

(ii) The policy is made payable to the person whose life is insured if the beneficiary or assignee predeceases that person, and the proceeds are exempt from all liability for any debt of the beneficiary existing at the time the policy is made available for his use.

(b) However, subject to the statute of limitations, the amount of any premiums paid for insurance with intent to defraud creditors, with interest thereon shall inure to their benefit from the policy proceeds. . . .

§ 26-15-132. Exemption of Proceeds; Annuity Contracts; Assignability of Rights

(a) The benefits, rights, privileges and options which under any annuity contract issued are due or prospectively due the annuitant, are not subject to execution nor is the annuitant compelled to exercise any such rights, powers or options. Creditors are not allowed to interfere with or terminate the contract, except:

(i) As to amounts paid for or as premium on the annuity with intent to defraud creditors with interest thereon, and of which the creditor gives the insurer written notice at its home office prior to the making of the payment to the annuitant out of which the creditor seeks to recover, which notice shall specify:

(A) The amount claimed or facts to enable the ascertainment of the amount; and

(B) Facts to enable the insurer to ascertain the annuity contract, the annuitant and the payment sought to be avoided on the ground of fraud.

(ii) The total exemption of benefits presently due and payable to any annuitant periodically or at stated times under all annuity contracts under which he is an annuitant shall not at any time exceed three hundred fifty dollars ($350.00) per month for the length of time represented by the installments, and any periodic payments in excess of three hundred fifty dollars ($350.00) per month are subject to garnishee execution to the same extent as are wages and salaries;

(iii) If the total benefits presently due and payable to any annuitant under any annuity contracts at any time exceed three hundred fifty dollars ($350.00) per month, the court may order the annuitant to pay to a judgment creditor or apply on the judgment, in installments, that portion of the excess benefits as to the court appear just and proper, after regard for the reasonable requirements of the judgment debtor and his family, if dependent upon him, as well as any payments required to be made by the annuitant to other creditors under prior court order.

(b) If the contract provides, the benefits, rights, privileges or options accruing under that contract to a beneficiary or assignee are not transferable nor subject to commutation, and if the benefits are payable periodically or at stated times, the same exemptions and exceptions contained in this section for the annuitant, apply to the beneficiary or assignee.

═══════════

The opt-out provision offers yet another place for irony. Texas, with its generous exemptions, did not opt out, leaving a Texan free to choose between an unlimited homestead and $50,000 in value in other property or a federal homestead exemption of $25,150 and about $23,000 or so in other property under the Code. § 522(d). While Texas lets its citizens choose between federal and state exemptions, Wyoming says no. Wyoming opted out.

A number of states have bifurcated their exemptions by giving debtors struggling in the state court system one set of exemptions but by having another set of exemptions for those who have filed bankruptcy. Among the states enacting these various "bankruptcy-specific" exemptions are Delaware, Georgia, Indiana, Iowa, Kentucky, Michigan, New York, Ohio, and West Virginia. In some of these states, the bankrupt debtor will be limited to smaller exemptions than the generally applicable state exemptions, and in some cases a bankruptcy filing will entitle the debtor to greater values of property or more kinds of property.

Changing exemptions when a debtor files bankruptcy might mean that the state has impermissibly encroached on the federal bankruptcy power, on the theory that the Code allows for opt-out *vel non*. The contrary position is the greater federal power conferring the opt-out decision to the states surely includes the lesser power of "limited opt-out," which is what a bankruptcy-specific exemption really is. There is a sharp split among the federal courts on this question. See, e.g., In re Schafer, 455 B.R. 590 (B.A.P. 6th Cir. 2011) (reviewing split in holding Michigan provision unconstitutional under the Bankruptcy Clause), *rev'd* 689 F.3d 601 (6th Cir. 2012) (upholding statute but implying as one basis the fact that the bankruptcy-specific exemptions were more generous than the general state ones).

All states (and the federal government) must wrestle with the same set of issues about what a debtor can keep and what a creditor can demand that the debtor give up to satisfy unpaid debts. It is unsurprising that exemption amounts may range from non-existent to unlimited. The policy questions can be sliced razor-thin. For example, some states have age-contingent exemptions that allow senior debtors to exempt more than others; others have proposed treating debtors with certain causes of financial distress (e.g., medical problems) more generously. See John A.E. Pottow, The Rise in Elder Bankruptcy Filings and the Failure of U.S. Bankruptcy Law, 19 Elder L.J. 119, 155 (2011) (canvassing existent laws and proposals).

Nowhere are these disparities more evident (or hotly debated) than with homesteads. The Texas statute cited above limits a homestead in terms of acreage. So long as the home is on less than ten acres in a city or 200 acres in the country, the debtor is entitled to exempt that property from attachment, regardless of its dollar value. Near the other end of the spectrum is Wyoming, which limits the homestead exemption to $40,000 for a married couple and only $20,000 for a single person.

Homestead exemptions are the sorts of laws likely to be important only for the subset of debtors who (a) own homes, and (b) have enough equity in their homes to have exemptible amounts. But the flipside is they are likely to be *very* important to those debtors; homestead equity is precisely what gets wiped out (more accurately, transferred from the debtor to the creditor) in foreclosure sale where the winning bid is usually the foreclosing creditor's exact mortgage amount and not a cent more. Other exemption types carry a similarly disproportionate punch. An office worker with no tools of the trade couldn't care less about that exemption category, but a plumber trying to make a living depends on it—and the cap may look very low. Can laws be updated rapidly enough to reflect changing market conditions? A casual stroll through exemption laws reveals more protections for church pews than for smart phones. And even those church pews may produce windfalls their long-dead drafters did not foresee. See In re Robinson, 811 F.3d 267 (7th Cir. 2016) (184-year-old first edition Book of Mormon exempt under statutory provision covering "necessary wearing apparel, bible, school books, and family pictures").

2.   *Federal Exemptions*

The federal exemptions range from crime reparation payments to unmatured life insurance policies. To the extent that exemptions are limited to specific dollar amounts, such as the $4,000 exemption in a car, those amounts are adjusted every three years for inflation. § 104(b). In its most recent amendments, Congress expanded the federal exemption for retirement funds and flexed a bit of Supremacy Clause might (perhaps in response to the rise of bankruptcy-specific state exemptions), protecting retirement funds *regardless* whether the debtor lives in an opt-out state. § 522(b)(3)(C), (d)(12). In fact, it took most retirement funds out of the estate altogether, adding a belt to the suspenders, § 541(b)(7), or possibly even another set of pants to the belt and suspenders given that many pension plans are already structured as trusts. § 541(c). Phew for the generous pension plan enjoyed by members of Congress, we suppose, but little comfort to the median (and modal) debtor in our empirical studies, whose pension assets upon filing are *zero*.

As generous as they are, the Texas exemptions add no special protection for renters to match the protection available to homeowners. By comparison, § 522(d) gives a special boost to renters. Anyone who does not claim a homestead exemption under (d)(1) is permitted to claim about half the value of the unclaimed homestead exemption in any property at all under (d)(5). Why half? It looks like another atheoretical but pragmatic compromise—halfway between those who believe only homes should be protected and those who believe renters should have the same chance to protect value, whether it is in a home or checking account.

Recall that both Texas and Wyoming, like most states, make the exemption laws unavailable for property being pursued for various domestic support obligations and liens. There are other "exceptions from exemptions" (try saying that phrase five times quickly). The big, federal elephant in the room—a stampeding, angry elephant—is the IRS. Nothing precludes Congress from preempting state exemption laws (subject to the Due Process Clause), and it has done so with federal tax collection statutes. If you don't pay your federal taxes in Texas, the IRS comes after your home, and nothing in Texas law can stop it.

C. CLASSIFICATION OF PROPERTY

Because exemption statutes are often written to exempt only listed types of property, disputes between debtors and creditors frequently center on classification issues. Debtors argue that the property they intend to keep fits within the statutory classifications, and judgment creditors argue the reverse. Ironically, federal bankruptcy judges are thus often called upon to determine the meaning of state exemption laws more frequently than state judges themselves. See, e.g., In re Johnson, 14 B.R. 14 (Bankr. W.D. Ky. 1981) (upholding exemption of 1969 60-seat Dodge bus under statutory automobile exemption for "one motor vehicle and its necessary accessories, including one spare tire") ("Is a Moped a motor vehicle?. . . . What would Gertrude Stein have to say about what a motor vehicle is? . . . We are bold to say that a bus is a motor vehicle, . . . [a]bundantly confident that this opinion will find its way alongside *Marbury v. Madison* and *McCulloch v. Maryland* in the lasting library of legal logic[.]"). These category cases are not in short supply in the bankruptcy courts.

═══════════════ In re WILKINSON, [M.D.] ═══════════════
402 B.R. 756 (Bankr. W.D. Tex. 2009)

CLARK, Bankruptcy Judge.
The debtors claimed an exemption in firearms. The Trustee objected. This decision explains why the court sustains the objection to exemption.

FACTUAL AND PROCEDURAL BACKGROUND

On August 26, 2008, the debtors filed amended schedules in which they claimed state law exemptions in the following items:

- MP .45 rifle, .380 pistol, two .22 caliber pistols, .30-.30 rifle and a .45 caliber pistol (collectively, the "Firearms") under Texas Property Code §§ 42.001(a), 42.002(a)(8) (sporting goods and equipment).
- 17 antique handguns and 1 dummy gun (the "Collection") under Texas Property Code §§ 42.001(a), 42.002(a)(1) (home furnishings, including heirlooms).

On November 5, 2008, the chapter 7 trustee (the "Trustee") filed an objection to the debtors' claim of exemption to the Firearms and the Collection [Docket No. 184]. The Trustee argues that, pursuant to Texas

Property Code § 42.002(7), "[t]he Debtors must select only two firearms eligible for exemption." . . .

After the Objection was filed, on November 14, 2008, the debtors amended Schedule C [Docket No. 196], so that they now claim as exempt the following firearms:

- a Sharps cavalry carbine circa 1863; a Sharps new model rifle, .52 caliber c. 1860; a Spencer repeating rifle, .52 caliber c. 1860; an English Blunderbuss saddle gun, silver, c. 1845; a Burnside cavalry carbine, c. 1863; an English blunderbuss, flintlock, with bayonet; and an English blunderbuss, flintlock, c. 1750.

. . .

The debtors assert that those Guns that are not replicas saw action in wars that took place prior to 1898 and are each "affixed to a wooden plaque bearing a brass plate which describes the weapon . . . [and] adorn the walls of the Debtors' rural home." Response, ¶15 at 4. Due to the age of the Guns, the debtors argue, they are no longer considered firearms under the Texas Property Code. Although the debtors cannot point to any specific provision of the Texas Property Code to support this contention (since none exists), the debtors rely by analogy on § 46.01 of the Texas Penal Code, which criminalizes possession of a firearm by certain persons (felons). That statute excludes from its definition of "firearm" any gun that is "(A) an antique or curio firearm manufactured before 1899." . . . [T]he debtors argue that the court should overrule the Trustee's objection to the debtors' exemption claim with respect to the Guns and allow the debtors to claim them as exempt home furnishings under § 42.002(a)(1) of the Texas Property Code.

. . .

In the context of both statutes' use of the term "firearm," the Texas Property Code and the Texas Penal Code do not have a similar object or purpose. One governs the relationship between debtors and creditors, limiting the latters' rights in order to assure debtors are permitted to keep a certain modicum of property regardless of how much they owe their creditors. Firearms happen to be one of a number of specifically described items or categories of property deemed to be appropriate for debtors in this state to have, free of the demands of their creditors. The Penal Code, meanwhile criminalizes ownership of certain types of firearms by certain kinds of individuals in Texas, to wit, convicted felons, in the interests of protecting the peace and safety of the rest of the citizenry of Texas. One statute focuses on what all Texans should be allowed to keep (at least relative to the claims of their creditors),[1] while the other statute focuses on what certain Texans

---

[1] Here is how this court described the function and purpose of Texas' exemption law in an earlier opinion:

[E]xemptions represent a statement of public policy regarding what the citizens of this state believe all persons are entitled to retain, no matter how much they (convicted felons) are not allowed to keep, for reasons having nothing to do with their creditors. One statute regulates commercial activity. One is a health and safety regulation.

. . .

Thus, whether a convicted felon may carry an antique firearm—apparently deemed by the legislature not to be a threat to public safety due to its age—does not have much to do at all with whether a creditor may reach that same antique gun for purposes of getting repaid. It is certainly not a threat to public safety for a debtor to repay his debts by the sale of an antique gun.

. . .

THE TEXAS PROPERTY CODE

Up to a cap of $60,000 per family, or $30,000 per single person, the current iteration of the Texas Property Code allows a debtor to exempt certain categories of personal property from the reach of creditors, including two firearms. Another permitted category of personal property available for exemption is "home furnishings, including family heirlooms." Because the Texas Property Code does not define "firearm," the court must look to other interpretive aids, the first of which is to consult the term's ordinary meaning.

Black's Law Dictionary says that a firearm is "[a] weapon that expels a projectile (such as a bullet or pellets) by the combustion of gunpowder or other explosive." Black's Law Dictionary 666 (8th Ed. 2004). . . .

One way to test a word's meaning is to examine how it is ordinarily used. In that regard, common usage gives a word meaning when it can be said that one person using a given word will be easily understood to mean the same thing as the user intended the word to convey. See Ludwig Wittgenstein, Philosophical Investigations, at 43 (G.E.M. Anscombe, transl.) (Oxford Press 1953) ("[T]he meaning of a word is its use in the language."). In ordinary usage, the fact that a firearm or gun is antique would not preclude one from referring to it as a firearm. One visiting the Wilkinsons' home could well comment, "[T]hat's a very nice firearm you have mounted up there on the wall," and no one would wonder what he or she was talking about. By the same token, one would be surprised if, in response to the query, "[W]hat's that firearm[?]" Wilkinson were to reply, "[T]hat's not a firearm, that's a home furnishing."

. . .

might owe to their creditors. Some exemptions are preserved primarily because they truly are necessary to the very survival of the family as an independent economic unit not on the public dole. Others, such as jewelry, are allowed not so much to assure mere survival as to assure survival with a modicum of dignity. . . . The purpose underlying exemption legislation is securing to the unfortunate debtor the means to support himself and his family, the protection of the family being the main consideration.

Even if the term were thought to be ambiguous, however, the court would still arrive at the same conclusion regarding its intended scope in the Texas Property Code. Although Texas, as early as 1866, listed specific items of personal property as qualified for exemption, guns or firearms did not specifically show up on the list until the Act of 1870, at which point "one gun" was, for the first time, explicitly protected from forced sale for debts. Acts 1870, 12th Leg., p.127, Ch. LXXVI, § 2 reprinted in Tex. Rev. Civ. Stat. Ann., art. 2335 (repealed) (1879). It is no stretch to believe that guns were vital to a Texan's survival in 1870, perhaps explaining their being included on the list of property qualified for exemption. The court was unable to locate either legislative reports or testimony to glean the legislature's intent in exempting a gun in 1870, but a Texas Supreme Court case from 1857 perhaps sheds some light on what might have been on the Legislature's mind just over a decade later. In Choate v. Redding, 18 Tex. 579 (1857), the Texas Supreme Court rather reluctantly denied a debtor's request that his rifle gun be exempt from his creditor's reach. . . . The court lamented that it was "extraordinary" that there was not a Texas statute exempting the gun from execution. The court colorfully explained its frustration thusly:

> It has been comparatively but a few years since the first settlements of Americans were made in Texas. The whole country was then infested by savages. Subsequently there were hostilities with Mexicans, and the frontiers are still exposed to the incursions of Indians. The country has been settled, and still is settling, by, in a great measure, force of arms. The people of Texas are now, and ever have been, emphatically an armed population.

Id. at 581. [The more we change, the more we stay the same?—Eds.] The court added that the right to bear arms was protected in both the Constitutions of the United States and Texas for the purpose of securing a free state through a well-armed militia. (Indeed, the court dryly observed that, if militia laws were enforced, were a man to show up to the "muster ground" without his gun, he could be fined.) Said the court—with evident chagrin—although "the right to keep and bear arms cannot be infringed by legislation, yet, strange as it may be, it must succumb to the power of a creditor." *Id.* Based upon the court's analysis, it would not be a stretch to infer that the Texas Legislature, in adding "one gun" to the list of personal property eligible for exemption . . . to provide Texans with the ability to defend their home[s] and provide for their family, and perhaps to be able, regardless their financial circumstances, to answer the call to arms should the militia be called up.[2]

. . .

Obviously, by 1973, Texas was no longer the frontier it had been when the Texas Supreme Court discussed the vital role guns played in everyday life in 1857. . . . However, "the [gun] exemption survived . . . [as] a witness

---

[2] This early authority also suggests that the only firearms that it made sense for a debtor to even claim as exempt were working firearms—creditors could have the firearms that didn't work, as they would be of no use against "savages" or in the Texas Militia.

to the Texas ethos that still cherishes the frontier spirit, and celebrates it every hunting season." In re Schwarzbach, 1989 WL 360742, at *4. In fact, because in 1973 the statute required that personal property be reasonably necessary to the debtor, the specific allowance of two guns could be read as a nod to "[t]he typical hunter serious about his or her sport [since he or she] will have a shotgun for birds and a rifle for other game." *Id*. As it turned out, the debtor in *Schwarzbach*, an avid hunter, was not allowed to exempt more than two of his guns, on the theory that the additional guns could qualify as athletic and sporting equipment.

. . .

As this court stated in In re Mitchell, 103 B.R. 819, 823 (Bankr. W.D. Tex. 1989), the Texas Property Code, subject to the cap in § 42.001(a), provides Texans with an explicit, approved list of items that the legislature has decided debtors should be allowed to keep regardless of what they owe their creditors. "Exemptions are in fact a limit on a creditor's right to satisfaction of its claim out of the debtor's assets. The limitations are imposed for reasons of public policy. There is no *public* policy served in preserving the lifestyles of the rich and bankrupt." *Id*. at n.7 (emphasis original).

Doctor Wilkinson might be a stereotypical "rich and bankrupt" debtor given his valuable collection of antiques (most other debtors' older property would carry less flattering labels), but he had a colorable argument based on the statute that his collection fit within the exemption. This raises the serious question of the importance of classifying property. Is fighting over whether a Texan's thirteenth cow is a pet (or heirloom, or provision for consumption, or [future] wearing apparel) the absurd but inescapable consequence of laws based on categories? See, e.g., In re Hall, 169 B.R. 732 (Bankr. N.D. Okla. 1994) (rejecting debtor's claim that tractor-lawnmower is "household furniture" in Oklahoma). If so, should the approach be jettisoned? And if not, how flexibly should courts read these statutes that are likely designed with a "typical" family in mind? If there is ambiguity, do lenity concerns suggest ties should go to the debtor? See A. Mechele Dickerson, Race Matters in Bankruptcy Reform, 71 Mo. L. Rev. 919 (2006).

D.   PARTIALLY EXEMPT PROPERTY

If there is a dollar limit on an exempt category, does property of a greater value cease to be exempt? Yes and no. We call this property "partially exempt," and in most cases the property can be levied on and sold. The exemption does attach, up to its dollar limit, but to the net proceeds after sheriff sale, rather than the property itself. If there are extra proceeds after the debtor's exemption has been paid off, they go to the seizing judgment creditor (at state law) or the trustee (in bankruptcy). A few examples help illustrate. A debtor in a state with a $1,000 automobile exemption who owns a car, free and clear of any liens, worth $800 will be able to protect that car from creditor attachment, period. Another debtor who owns a car worth $2,800 free and clear in the same state will be subject to having the car sold for the benefit of creditors. If a creditor is owed $3,000, the car brings its full $2,800 at sale, and there are $100 in sales costs, the proceeds will go as follows: Sale costs, $100; Debtor, $1,000; Creditor, $1,700. Once again, the importance of valuation is apparent, and here most strikingly; it makes or breaks the difference between the debtor keeping the exempt property on the one hand and having it involuntarily sold on the other (with the consolation prize of a portion of the proceeds equaling the exemption amount). Thus property may have a "retention value" for the debtor beyond its market value or the exemption amount.

E.   PROCEEDS AND TRACING

Exemptions are typically by category of property—wages, tools of the trade, motor vehicles, etc.—but property is not static in nature. Wages may be deposited in checking accounts, and checking accounts may be withdrawn as cash on hand. Property may be sold, and contract obligations may be satisfied. Whenever the form of property changes, issues arise about *proceeds*—that is, whether the property's "former" or "current" state is relevant for exemption purposes.

In re KING

508 B.R. 71 (Bankr. N.D. Ind. 2014)

KLINGBERGER, Bankruptcy Judge.

This Chapter 7 case was initiated by a voluntary petition filed by the debtor Margaret Naomi King ("King") on March 22, 2013. On June 3, 2013, Kenneth A. Manning, as Trustee of the Chapter 7 bankruptcy estate of Margaret Naomi King ("Trustee") filed an objection to the debtor's exemptions [record # 20] . . . that this entire amount could be traced back as the earned income credit ("EIC") portion of a tax refund that was previously deposited into her bank account. It is these funds that are the source of the dispute between the parties and the issue is to what extent, if any, King can exempt the $3,138.63 as an earned income credit.

. . .

3.   The IRS tax return claimed and asserted a tax refund of $8,548, consisting of:

W-2 withholdings of $1,010
Earned Income Credit of $5,891
Additional Child Tax Credit of $1,647

4.   The IRS return was filed by and through the H & R Block Tax Group.

5. Prior to receipt of any tax refund, Margaret Naomi King fully assigned all her right, title, and interest in the claimed $8,548 tax refund to H & R Block Tax Group, pursuant to the agreement with H & R Block, for the specific purpose of the Refund Anticipation Check.

6. H & R Block filed Margaret Naomi King's taxes, and received her refund check by deposit into the Refund Anticipation Check account created specifically for Debtor.

7. The refund check was deposited into a bank account which was opened for Margaret Naomi King by H & R Block, with H & R holding exclusive control over the account, for the benefit of Debtor.

8. H & R Block withdrew the amount Margaret Naomi King owed them for preparing her taxes from this account plus other service charges, then direct deposited the remaining funds into Debtor's 1st Midwest account.

9. On February 8, 2013, the sum of $8,196.55 was deposited in Margaret Naomi King's personal checking account at 1st Midwest Bank by H & R Block.

10. On February 8, 2013, Margaret Naomi King withdrew the sum of $3,000 from her 1st Midwest Bank Account.

11. On February 13, 2013, the sum of $3,138.63 was debit memo (i.e. frozen) from the 1st Midwest Bank Account; this was the result of a garnishment by Margaret Naomi King's judgment creditor Credit Acceptance Corporation.

. . .

CONTENTIONS OF LAW

1. The Trustee contends that the $3,138.63 released by Credit Acceptance Corporation now in possession of Debtor is non-EIC funds, property of the Estate, and must be turned over to the Trustee.

2. Debtor contends the $3,138.63 released by Credit Acceptance Corporation is EIC credit proceeds, exempt property of the estate, and should not be turned over to the Trustee.

3. Trustee contends that the nature of the funds changed when they were deposited into a bank account opened and controlled exclusively by a third party (H & R Block), and then later transferred to the Debtor.

4. Debtor contends that funds were deposited into a bank account opened by a third party (H & R Block), for the specific purpose of depositing her tax refund in order to pay preparation and various other fees, thereby creating an account holding funds in trust for Debtor's benefit.

5. The Trustee contends that by assigning the entire amount of her tax refund to H & R Block and that third party receiving the Debtor's refund; the funds became a refund to Debtor by

        H & R Block of amounts overpaid and not due under the Refund
        Anticipation Check agreement between Debtor and H & R Block.
6. Debtor contends that after the H & R Block account was created
    for her benefit; she retained an interest in the account consistent
    with the documents creating the account; and said tax refunds
    were not commingled with other funds and therefore specifically
    traceable back to Debtor's tax refund.
7. The Trustee contends that under the Refund Anticipation Check
    contract, the funds Debtor received from H & R Block were char-
    acterized not as tax refund funds but rather "Refund Anticipation
    Check" funds, which changes the nature of the funds by agree-
    ment of the parties.
8. The Trustee contends that Debtor made no objection or claim
    of exemption of the funds in the state court proceeding, thereby
    waiving her claim of exemption under I.C. 34-55-10-6 and I.C.
    34-55-10-12.
9. Debtor contends that she did not waive her claim of exemption
    under I.C. 34-55-10-6 and I.C. 34-55-10-12. . . .

The earned income credit exemption is provided by I.C. § 34-55-10-2(c)(11) and states as follows:

(c) the following property of a debtor domiciled in Indiana is exempt:

    (11) The debtor's interest in a refund or a credit received or to be received under the following:
    (A) Section 32 of the Internal Revenue Code of 1986 (the federal earned income tax credit),
    (B) IC 6-3.1-21-6 (the Indiana earned income tax credit)

    The scope of a statutory exemption is to be interpreted liberally in favor of the debtor. . . .

    The plain language of I.C. § 34-55-10-2(c)(11) is extremely broad and exempts the *"debtor's interest in a refund or a credit received or to be received"* under Section 32 of the Internal Revenue Code. In the case of In re: Shashunte Jameca Norwood, Case No. 08-20259, the court found that when an earned income credit has been received by a debtor and deposited into a bank account pre-petition, the amount deposited retains its exempt status under I.C. 34-55-10-2(c)(11) as long as it is traceable.

    In the case at bar, the Trustee's arguments mainly focus on the nature of the transaction underlying the refund anticipation check, i.e. the deposit of the refund into H & R Block's bank account. The Trustee first posits that the tax refund became something other than a tax refund between the time it was deposited into H & R Block's account, which King had no control over, and subsequently re-deposited into King's account at 1st Midwest . . . :

    The bank account was created so H & R had a place to deposit the Debtor's tax refund, withdraw whatever amounts they deemed necessary for their fees, cover any preexisting debts of the Debtor, and then refund any remaining monies to the Debtor. Any amount sent back to the debtor was an overpayment of preparation fees, costs, and so on, from non-exempt funds which had been assigned to H & R Block.

The Trustee cites no *legal* authority whatsoever in support of this theory. Just because the refund was initially deposited into H & R Block's bank account, before being distributed back to King, does not mean that it somehow became something other than easily traceable funds in which King had a property interest. Remember, the refund was deposited into the H & R Block account for the *benefit* of the debtor. The entire point of the transaction was so that King could ultimately *receive* her refund. It would fly in the face of the broad nature of the exemption provided by I.C. § 34-55-10-2(c)(11) if the court held that King no longer had an interest in a refund "to be received" under Title 32 of the Internal Revenue Code simply because the refund passed through H & R Block's bank account on its way to the debtor.

Also in support of this theory, the Trustee argues that through the agreement between the parties the nature of the funds "changed":

> Under the Refund Anticipation Check contract, the funds Debtor received from H & R Block were characterized not as tax refund funds but rather "Refund Anticipation Check" funds, which changes the nature of the funds by agreement of the parties.

The Trustee points to other instances where he contends that the wording of the agreement somehow morphed the tax refund into something that was no longer a tax refund. But based upon the contract and disclosures concerning the transaction which were submitted with the Stipulation, the court finds that this is not the case. . . .

The Trustee's next argument is that once exempt funds are commingled with nonexempt funds, the exemption is lost. . . . More importantly, in two prior decisions, the court has decided that commingling of an earned income credit refund with other funds does not affect the ability to claim the statutory earned income credit exemption.

The court finds that the earned income portion of King's tax refund can be readily determined and traced. . . .

Pursuant to the Stipulation, the tax refund of $8,548 consisted of:

W-2 withholdings of $1,010.00
Earned Income Credit of $5,891.00
Additional Child Tax Credit of $1,647.00

68.92% of the total refund was earned income credit ($5,891.00/ $8,548.00), so obviously 68.92% of every dollar spent is EIC. [The court deducted H & R Block fees, and some debtor checks, deposits, and withdrawals—Eds.]

Knowing that 68.92% of the total refund was EIC, we apply that percentage to the $2,271.26 which was what was left of the refund. . . . $1,565.35 is an exempt asset of King's bankruptcy estate. . . .

All these rules raise the possibility of "exemption planning" by the clever, discussed in the next assignment, but there are equally pitfalls for the less clever. For example, in a feat of financial planning that may give some clue as to why he ended up in bankruptcy, Kenneth Dasher cashed out every last nickel in his exempt retirement account to buy a non-exempt pickup truck. In re Dasher, 2002 U.S. Dist. LEXIS 10563 (Neb. 2002). His schedules claimed his new pickup as exempt, pointing out that it was just his retirement account invested in a tangible portfolio. The court said no, carefully distinguishing "retirement account" from "pickup truck." If Mr. Dasher had just waited to cash in his retirement account until after his bankruptcy case was closed a few weeks later, presumably he would have discharged his debts and owned the pickup outright instead of losing it to the trustee. But sometimes a man can't wait.

F.   SECURITY INTERESTS IN EXEMPT PROPERTY

When exempt property is encumbered by a valid security interest, the secured party moves ahead of both the debtor and the levying creditor (at state law) and the trustee (in bankruptcy). If the car mentioned above were worth $1,000, but the secured creditor's debt was for $2,000, the secured party would take the car, and the state's $1,000 exemption would be irrelevant. The debtor would have no equity in the car to claim as exempt. In bankruptcy, the car is thus useless to the trustee, although as Nissan learned the hard way in the case reproduced in Assignment 3, the car is still property of the estate until the trustee abandons it. § 554.

If the car were worth $3,000, however, then the car would be sold, sale expenses paid, and the secured party would take the first $2,000 of the net proceeds (the full amount of its debt); the debtor would receive the remaining money under the exemption. Only when the value of the car is so great that it exceeds the sum of the sales costs, the secured creditor's debt, and the debtor's exemption would the trustee in bankruptcy (or levying creditor at state law) get any money. Many otherwise exemptible consumer items subject to liens, especially PMSIs, are abandoned by bankruptcy trustees for this very reason. Their bankruptcy sale value is dwarfed either by liens or by the costs of sale. Sometimes debtors move to compel abandonment to clarify that property will not be sold by a trustee; other times trustees are eager to abandon property.

G.   AVOIDING JUDICIAL LIENS AND NON-PMSI LIENS

In addition to exemptions, Congress fashioned another protection to improve the economic position of debtors after bankruptcy. Section 522(f)(1) permits the avoidance of certain kinds of liens on certain categories of exempt property. Two kinds of liens are made avoidable: *judicial* liens, which are liens imposed by a court after a judgment has been rendered, property has been levied, and a defendant has not paid, § 522(f)(1)(A), and *"nonpossessory, nonpurchase-money"* consensual security interests in certain consumer goods, § 522(f)(1)(B). This cumbersome second category refers to non-PMSI liens, i.e., loans made on the debtor's existing consumer goods. It also excludes pawnbrokers, whose security interests, while non-PMSI, are still possessory (they hold physical possession of the collateral). A nonpossessory, nonpurchase-money loan would be when a debtor pledges a car as collateral for a title loan. Section (f)(1)(B) only covers low-ticket exemptions, like household furniture and clothes. The statute contains some very specific restrictions, which was drafted at a time when VCRs were of interest as collateral. § 522(f)(4)(A)(vi).

Lien avoidance on the denominated exempt property allows the debtor to "reclaim" an exemption by bumping the lienholder back into the general unsecured creditor pile to the extent the lien impedes the exemption. With judicial liens, this is not a big deal; federal law can invalidate or trump judicial liens under the Supremacy Clause and Bankruptcy Clause. The lien avoidance power of consensually granted security interests is more controversial. After all, the liens at issue are security interests, in which the debtor fully and freely waived exemptions. So why the freebie in bankruptcy on this property? Congress reviewed several studies documenting creditors' practices of taking security interests in all of a debtor's clothing, in children's toys, in family photographs, etc. Critics pointed out that these security interests were not taken to provide alternative resources to satisfy the loan if the debtor should become unable to pay. (Do you buy used underwear from the sheriff? *But cf.* Bernie Madoff Auction (£120 for 14 pairs of boxers).) Instead, the security interests were taken for their "hostage value," the likelihood that threatened repossession would cause the debtor to make any sacrifice to find a way to pay and keep the property. Section (f)(1)(B) was adopted in 1978 to defeat these practices. The FTC soon followed suit by imposing similar restraints on creditors outside bankruptcy, making it an unfair practice for a company to take a nonpossessory, nonpurchase-money security interest in certain listed goods. FTC Trade Regulation Rule on Credit Practices, 16 C.F.R. § 444.1 (1985). The rule was adopted in part to limit consumers from needing to file bankruptcy solely to guard against these non-possessory, non-PMSI security interests in household goods and the like.

Can Congress just rub consensual liens off property? Isn't that an unconstitutional taking? Six Justices of the Supreme Court opined in dictum yes, while three believed no, but the majority used the avoidance doctrine to duck the question by interpreting § 522(f) to apply prospectively—only to security interests created after its enactment, which everyone agreed was fine. United States v. Security Indus. Bank, 459 U.S. 70 (1982). The larger point—to what extent can Congress use the bankruptcy power to affect established property rights—has arisen many times but has thus far eluded definitive resolution.

Perhaps in response to the *Security Bank* opinion, or a concern that § 522(f)(1)(B) was frustrating the expectations of the "high-yield" lending market, Congress passed § 522(f)(3). It seems to say that if the debtor takes the state-law exemptions in an opt-out state (or one that allows the debtor to waive the federal exemptions, a power we think is likely either redundant or unconstitutional) *and* those exemptions are *either* really generous (unlimited in amount) *or* really strict (cannot be invalidated under state law), then for a *limited subset* of otherwise lien-erasable property, the debtor may not strip off *at least part* of the lien under § 522(f)(1)(B). For fun, see if you can figure it out. If you can, please tell us. (Perhaps this is the note topic you've been searching for!) In parsing the statute, do be sure to give full effect to the plain meaning, and if that doesn't help, just try to further the goal Congress was trying to achieve with the provision, which is, umm, let us get back to you.

Problem Set 4

4.1. Harv and Lois Hughes live in an apartment in Houston, Texas. They are unable to pay several of their debts and are worried about which of their assets may be vulnerable to creditor attachment. Their largest creditor is their credit union, to whom they owe about $5,000. They list their assets as follows:

Item	Value
Household furniture and appliances	$ 8,000
Clothing	$ 2,000
Lois's law books	$ 2,400
Lois's moped	$ 800
Harv's 1970 convertible (left over from high school, now up on blocks)	$ 500
Cash value on Lois's insurance	$ 2,000
Lois's wedding ring	$ 1,000
Lois's computer	$ 1,200
100 shares Disney Co. (Lois's dad knew Walt)	$ 5,000
Joint checking account	$ 400
Harv's customized computer set-up	$ 7,500
1804 French one-pounder cannon	$ 6,000
Harv's motorized wheelchair	$18,000
Fluffy (Persian cat, nasty temper but very beautiful)	$ 200
Soccer ball	$ 2
Anticipated tax refund (estimated to arrive in three weeks)	$ 1,000

Harv, who is a computer programmer, was injured last year when his car was struck by a train. He has been rated at a 40 percent disability as a result. His lawyer says he can likely settle with the railroad for about $250,000. (There were some serious contributory negligence issues.) Both are very reluctant to file for bankruptcy. Absent bankruptcy, what can Harv and Lois protect as the creditors begin to move in? What if they filed a chapter 7? What could they protect if they lived in Cheyenne, Wyoming?

4.2. Harv's cousin, Suzan Hughes Berttus, ran away from home at 17, married a partner of the Dusty R Bar in Running Springs, Wyoming at 18, and is now a widow at 21. Her financial affairs are a mess, plagued by high credit card bills, delinquent car loans, and her debts as a co-signer for her husband's business loans. The bank has repossessed the bar, and she is ready to walk away from the old double-wide trailer and start her life again. Suzan's grief is lessened a little bit by the fact that Mr. B had a $1 million insurance policy. If Suzan decides to declare bankruptcy, what can she keep? If Suzan and Mr. B had been living in Odessa, Texas, would the outcome be the same?

4.3. **A.** Lynh Tran has a 2014 Chevy Malibu. Jingle Lending loaned her $2,000 unsecured, but she believes that the loan was usurious and wouldn't repay unless Jingle agreed to accept in full payment the amount she would owe at a reasonable interest rate. Jingle has now sued her and she realizes she can't afford a lawyer or the time off work to defend the case. The Bluebook value of the car is $5,000, although hers is in better shape than most. At the last auto auction in her county, a 2014 Malibu with some dents brought $1,000. If Jingle gets a default judgment and serves a writ for seizure and sale of the car, what can Lynh hope to salvage from the proceeds, given that her state offers a $1,500 exemption for one car? Consider foreclosure sale returns (after sheriff's costs) of $1,000, $2,000, or $5,000.

B. Suppose Lynh still had $2,000 left to pay on the car, secured by a purchase money lien on it? How would returns of $1,000, $2,000, or $5,000 be distributed? Do you think a higher sale price could be achieved in bankruptcy by the trustee?

4.4. Charley Wilson has worked for 12 years on construction sites, most recently as a crane operator. When the local construction industry crashed, Charley decided to go into business by himself. His new business has not been very successful, and Charley filed for bankruptcy two months after opening, although he was still trying to make a go of the business. Charley filed bankruptcy because a creditor from the business got a default judgment for $8,500 and got the sheriff to seize the truck, which is worth $10,000 and owned free and clear by Charley. Charley has taken the federal exemptions using his full home exemption and "wildcard" for other property.

A. Can he keep the truck? What if he backed his truck into a tree at a construction site and now the truck is worth only $5,000 (or maybe even $2,000)? See § 522(f).

B. What if his new business was called "Charley's Trash Hauling and Light Deliveries" and he has used his pickup as collateral from a secured loan from Jingle Finance, a company specializing in high-interest loans from people with cars, to get $8,500 in debt (instead of the judgment creditor)? See § 522(d) and (f).

PROPERTY EXEMPTIONS II

You have learned the basics about exemptions as they affect most debtors. Because the great majority of debtors have few assets of any value, apart from a heavily mortgaged home, exemptions are important to them only at the "barrel" level—that is, enough protection to cover their clothes, basic household goods, unfancy vehicles to get to work, and the like. Exemptions beyond a very basic floor thus just don't matter to most bankruptcy debtors. The process of disclosing assets and trying to fit everything into a protected category adds expense and complexity, but most debtors only dream of having to worry about such issues.

Exemptions do matter, however, to a small minority of more affluent debtors, including personal proprietorships. These people need sophisticated legal advice if they are going to hang onto their stuff. Exemptions that are capped serve as a check on affluent debtors who might exploit laws that are too forgiving. The fear of bankruptcy abuse drives a rigorous and ongoing debate about unlimited exemptions, which many states have for homesteads. Part of that debate—as with any debate—is likely driven by high-salience public events: well publicized instances of famous people escaping their debts by manipulating luxury property, while their creditors, including sometimes fraud victims or worse, get left in the cold. Thus, the debate about bankruptcy exemptions has a curious skew. The barrel-level exemptions affect the vast majority of debtors, and in a significant way, but not even the most heartless churl begrudges them (okay, maybe there is some economist out there that has an argument, but we aren't persuaded). The policy action is over that sliver of the debtor population for whom exemptions are important to retain assets of high value and who have the capacity to maximize legal protections.

This assignment addresses the issues surrounding that small minority. And it is not just about exemption laws. The other way more affluent debtors protect assets from creditors is by excluding certain assets from their estates altogether. Exclusions may be built directly into the Bankruptcy Code (e.g., § 541's exclusion of most retirement funds requires little planning on the debtor's part other than sound pension investments). Other property requires a little more work and requires the debtor to structure holdings in specifically advantageous ways (e.g., holding marital property in the entirety). The most significant of these "structured exclusions" is holding property in trusts, which you will recall are excluded under

§ 541(c)(2). Either route—exemptions or exclusion—parks the debtor's assets beyond the reach of unpaid creditors. We start with a focus on homesteads, due to their significance in value and prevalence.

A. HOMESTEADS

1. Homestead History: Why Homesteads?

The struggle over what property debtors may or may not keep has deep social and economic implications, and this tension comes to a head with the family home. The homestead is the most important type of exempt property for many debtors, which is typically the real property they occupy as a residence. Financially, homes are the most significant assets owned by most Americans. Even after several years of a sorry homeownership market, primary residences accounted for 29.5% of total family assets in 2010 (Federal Reserve Board, 2010 Survey of Consumer Finance). Homeownership is a cumulative phenomenon, with about 64% of households being owner-occupied, and even higher ownership rates among couples and older Americans (Federal Reserve Board, 2016 Survey of Consumer Finance). Homeownership is particularly popular among wealthier families; over 90% of the top quartile of households by income own the homes they live in. For many families, a home represents not only a valuable asset but is also a visible marker of middle-class status (or beyond). Empirical research has shown that more than half of debtors own their homes and that many of them file bankruptcy specifically to attempt to save their homes. It is not surprising that protection for the home has been woven into our legal culture for a long time:

> In popular as well as legal parlance, homestead means not only family home but property that is accorded particular protection because it is the family home. From one American state to another, and elsewhere as well, the most significant protection of the home is that which is accorded it against seizure by the owner's creditors for payment of general, private debts. The term homestead was also once used to refer to a sovereign grant of western lands where the frontiersman and his family made their home. But it is in the sense of a home protected from creditors that the concept of homestead is one of the most significant later contributions to family jurisprudence. Legal tradition has long acknowledged that this notion of homestead emerged on the Mexican-Texan frontier.

Joseph McKnight, Protection of the Family Home from Seizure by Creditors: The Sources and Evolution of a Legal Principle, 86 S.W. Hist. L.Q. 369, 369 (1983).

Professor McKnight bases his analysis on the continuing political concerns of the independent government of Coahuila y Texas to protect resident debtors—and attract new settlers:

> Moving West was a frequent early nineteenth-century response to the series of economic crises in the new American nation. A move to Texas where land was cheap was particularly attractive to venturous spirits in the

southern United States. The Texas colonists were by no means generally insolvent, but there were some who came to Texas with the hope of leaving debts permanently behind them, and those debts were sometimes large. By the mid-1820s Texas had achieved the reputation as a haven for debtors. First in 1826 and again in 1828 the United States Congress directed questions to the president concerning the obvious irritant to American creditors whose debtors had removed themselves to Mexican territory. The perception of Texas as a refuge for debtors was a consequence of several factors: Texas's primitive judicial system, the difficulty of finding debtors there, and, most particularly, the reluctance of local judges to enforce foreign debts against fellow colonists.

The American financial crisis of 1837, which precipitated the movement of so many distressed debtors into Texas, was a likely catalyst to the 1839 Texas enactment.

Id. at 375, 393.

The Texas enactment in 1839 was the predecessor of generous homestead and family property exemptions that followed and reflected a blending of legal cultures:

> The Hispanic and Anglo-American traditions of exempt property thus interacted to produce the lasting concept of protecting the family home and certain movables from the claims of creditors. These ideas came to full flower in the formulation of the homestead and chattel-exemption provision of the Texas Constitution of 1845. Forceful minds, well versed in the Hispanic concepts of exempt property and their further development in the decree of 1829, composed and passed the constitutional provision that would publish the expanded concept of exempt property in louder tones to the rest of the United States. The idea had already spread, on the apparent inspiration of the 1839 act, to Mississippi, Georgia, and Florida; within a few years more, similar provisions were enacted in a number of other states and were added to some state constitutions. Well before the end of the century the family home had been extended protection from creditors in almost every American state.

Id. at 396.

Homestead exemptions are now available in a large number of jurisdictions. Even so, not every homeowner is protected. Typically, a homestead is exempt only up to a given dollar amount. Thirteen states protect less than $25,000 equity in a homestead, at least for some debtors. But seven states and the District of Columbia now offer homestead protection based on area or some other test. For example, Iowa protects homesteads up to a half-acre in a city and 40 acres in the country. Iowa Code § 561.2. Some states offer differing exemptions based on debtor attributes; California, for instance, has a greater exemption for low-income homeowners who are over age 55, and for older residents who are disabled. Cal. Civ. Proc. Code § 704.710.730. These specialty exemptions statutes are often well intentioned, but every act of legislative kindness adds complexity and creates transactional incentives.

Some states, such as Pennsylvania, only offer homestead protection through a property doctrine known as "tenancy by the entirety" rather than by a separate homestead provision. The rule prohibits a creditor of only one spouse from foreclosing on a homestead held by the entirety—that is, jointly owned by the married couple. See, e.g., Patterson v. Hopkins, 371 A.2d 1378 (Pa. 1977). This effectively stops a general unsecured creditor from forcing a sale of a home to satisfy a debt if the creditor is owed an obligation by only one spouse, regardless of the value of the home. It does not, of course, have any restraining effect if the creditor was careful to have both husband and wife sign for the debt, as you can bet most Pennsylvanian mortgage lenders do. Nor does it help the single debtor, an outcome we find romantically regressive.

Recall the Code allows debtors picking the federal exemptions to claim a homestead of $25,150. § 522(d)(1). It can be doubled by a couple filing a joint bankruptcy petition, allowing for the protection of what might strike law students on their way to be first-time homebuyers as a lot of equity. But most bankruptcy debtors are well into their middle age, and even after years of plummeting (or at best, stagnant) home prices, the median home-owning American family has a home valued at $185,000 (Federal Reserve Board, 2016 Survey of Consumer Finance). If that family made a 20% down payment at purchase, it would be nip-tuck to protect all its equity. Then again, perhaps the lesson of the last decade is that few families put down 20%, or if they did, cash-out refinancing eliminated all or most of their equity.

At the legislative level, policy debates continue over how generous exemptions should be and what classes of debtor should find favor. One loud debate is in Florida, where a homestead of unlimited value can be protected, a circumstance that is said to have attracted several noteworthy personages. The other states with unlimited homestead exemptions evidently have not been so attractive to those fleeing their creditors. The explanation in some states, such as Iowa, is that the homestead exemption only halts creditors trying to recover on debts that became owed after the debtor purchased the homestead. Iowa Code § 561.21. Or it could be the meteorological handicap most unlimited homestead states, such as South Dakota, suffer compared to the Sunshine State.

2. Homestead Planning: Reallocating Assets into the Homestead

In states like Florida and Texas with unlimited homestead exemptions, the debtor has the opportunity to do some careful planning.

===================== In re REED =====================

12 B.R. 41 (Bankr. N.D. Tex. 1981)

Brister, Bankruptcy Judge.

The debtors filed petition for order for relief under Chapter 7 of Title 11, United States Code, on December 21, 1979. During the two week period preceding the filing of the petition the debtors, obviously engaging in prebankruptcy planning, sold nonexempt personal property for approximately 50% of the value which they had assigned to those properties and applied the proceeds of $34,500.00 towards liquidation of liens against their residence homestead. The trustee filed a complaint challenging entitlement to the exemptions. The following summary constitutes the findings of fact contemplated by Rule 752 after nonjury trial.

Since his childhood Hugh D. Reed had collected approximately 35 guns, some of them commemorative guns or otherwise having collector's value. On a financial statement dated April 1, 1979, he had valued the gun collection at $20,000.00. On December 11, 1979, ten days prior to filing the petition in bankruptcy, he sold the entire gun collection to a friend, Steve Gallagher, for $5,000.00 cash.

Reed had been an antique collector, also. On the April 1, 1979, financial statement he had valued his antiques at $3,000.00. Three months later, in August, 1979, he purchased additional antiques from an estate for $11,000.00. In late November, 1979, he sold three items from the antique collection to an acquaintance, Charles Tharpe, for $3,500.00, applying the proceeds to payment of a note to Bank of the West. On December 11, 1979, he sold the remaining antiques to the friend, Steve Gallagher, for $5,000.00 cash.

In November 1979, approximately one month prior to the commencement of the bankruptcy proceedings, he purchased for $15,000.00 an interest in a corporation with the intriguing name of Triple BS Corporation. He sold that interest to the friend, Steve Gallagher, on December 11, 1979, for $5,000.00 cash.

In three separate transactions between October 5, 1979, and November 13, 1979, Reed had purchased gold coins—Krugerrands and Mexican Pesos—for the total sum of $22,115.00. On or about December 10, 1979, he sold those coins for $19,500.00 cash.

Thus, ten days prior to bankruptcy debtors sold nonexempt assets with aggregate value of $68,500.00 (according to their financial statements or based upon the amount actually paid by them on recent purchases), receiving as proceeds the sum of $34,500.00. They received market value for the gold and when that transaction is not considered they received less than 20% of the apparent value of the guns, the antiques and the interest in Triple BS Corporation.

In October 1978, the debtors had executed a note and mechanic's lien to a lending institution in the sum of $20,000.00 to pay for improvements to their residence, consisting of a sun-deck room, swimming pool and pool facilities. On December 11, 1979, $19,892.00 from the proceeds of sale of nonexempt assets were applied to pay off that improvement loan. The balance of $15,000.00 was applied by the debtors towards the vendor's lien note against the residence, reducing the balance of that note to approximately $28,000.00.

The scope of this memorandum is narrow. The trustee insists that the homestead exemption on the residence should be avoided, because of the flagrant prebankruptcy planning in which they engaged. As evidence of fraudulent intent, the trustee contends that the debtors received less than a reasonably equivalent value for the nonexempt assets. [As will be explored later in Assignments 23 & 24, transfers of the debtor's property for less than "reasonably equivalent value"—a standard Reed likely flunked on his transactions with his willing friend, Steve Gallagher—are voidable in bankruptcy, which allows the trustee to claw that property back into the estate per § 548.—Eds.] Mr. Reed very candidly testified that had he received more money for the nonexempt assets he would have applied those additional monies to the homestead liens.

The issue as to whether the homestead exemptions may be set aside under those facts is clearly drawn.

The debtor, in support of his contention that he could properly pay the liens with proceeds of nonexempt property, and thus engage in obvious exemption planning, cites a comment in the legislative history following § 522(b):

> As under current law, the debtor will be permitted to convert nonexempted property into exempt property before filing a bankruptcy petition. See Hearings, pt. 3, at 1355-58. The practice is not fraudulent as to creditors, and permits the debtor to make full use of the exemptions to which he is entitled under the law.

While that language may express the law in some jurisdictions, it is not universally true. Certainly it is not an accurate expression of Texas law because Texas law specifically prohibits the retention of an exemption in personal property so acquired with proceeds of nonexempt property where there was intent to defraud, delay or hinder a creditor or other interested persons.

In this case, however, there was no proof that the debtors had applied the proceeds to acquisition of exempt personal property. All of the evidence indicates that the entire proceeds of $34,500.00 were applied on the real estate liens. The Texas legislature, at the time it adopted V.A.T.S. Article 3836(b), [predecessor to § 42.004, supra—Eds.] had the opportunity to include the same language in V.A.T.S. Article 3833, [predecessor to § 41.002, supra—Eds.] which provides the homestead exemption in real estate. It failed to do so, and had it included that type of language it is doubtful that it would have passed constitutional muster. Historically Texas law has jealously protected the homestead from forced sale except under very limited conditions. Article 16, § 50 of the Texas Constitution prohibits forced sale for any purpose except for purchase money liens, improvement liens, or taxes.

That provision in the Texas constitution prohibits the granting of the relief sought by the trustee in this case and the challenge to the homestead exemption in the residence is denied.

But Mr. Reed was not, dare we say, "home free." His trip to bankruptcy court was to discharge all his debt but keep his (dramatically deleveraged) exempt property, a strategy upon which the bankruptcy court frowned. On appeal, the Fifth Circuit took a hard look at Mr. Reed and the Triple BS Corporation and was not amused.

In re REED

700 F.2d 986 (5th Cir. 1983)

RUBIN, Circuit Judge.

We hold that a debtor who converts nonexempt assets to an exempt homestead immediately before bankruptcy, with intent to defraud his creimtors, must be denied a discharge in bankruptcy because of the provisions of Section 727 of the Bankruptcy Code, 11 U.S.C.A. § 727 (West 1979), and, therefore, we affirm the decision of the district court.

I

Hugh D. Reed, as sole proprietor, opened a shop using the trade name, Reed's Men's Wear, in Lubbock, Texas. He financed the venture in part by obtaining from the Texas Bank & Trust Company a $150,000 loan which was guaranteed by the Small Business Administration (SBA). Three months later, the bank gave Reed a $50,000 line of credit, and the SBA agreed that the original loan would be subordinated to the line of credit. The store showed a profit for the first nine months of operation in 1977, but began to lose money in 1978.

By February 1979, Reed knew that his business was insolvent. After meeting with the bank, the SBA, and his major trade creditors, he signed an agreement to turn over management of the store to a consulting firm for the year 1979. In turn, Reed's trade creditors agreed to postpone collection efforts and Reed promised to resume payments in January 1980. Despite management by the consultant, the business continued to fail, and on December 15, 1979, Reed and his wife, Sharon Marcus Reed, signed a foreclosure agreement surrendering the store to the bank. Six days later, the Reeds filed voluntary petitions for bankruptcy.

. . .

Reed had catholic interests and much energy. He found time to collect antiques, gold coins, and guns, and to make other investments. In a financial statement provided to the bank and to the SBA on April 1, 1979, Reed valued his gun collection at $20,000 and his antiques collection at $3,000. In the four months prior to bankruptcy, Reed augmented each of his collections. He caused Reyata [Corporation, which Reed owned] to borrow $11,000, which he used to purchase more antiques. In three separate transactions during October and November, Reed accumulated, at a cost of $22,115, a collection of Krugerrands and Mexican fifty-peso pieces. One month before filing for bankruptcy, Reed purchased, for $15,000, a one-third interest in a business known as Triple BS Corporation.[1]

Two months before bankruptcy, Reed opened an account at the Bank of the West without the knowledge of his creditors. From that time until the store closed in mid-December, he deposited the daily receipts from Reed's Men's Wear in this separate account. From this account, in late November Reed repaid the loan Reyata made to purchase the antiques.

Reed began selling his personal assets in late November. He first sold three items from his antiques collection to an acquaintance, Charles Tharpe, for $3,500. He sold the remainder of his antiques on December 11 to a friend, Steve Gallagher, for $5,000. Whether this represented their fair market value was not established, but the total realized on the antiques was $8,500, while the original value plus the cost of recent purchases was

---

[1] The significance of the initials is not elucidated in the record.

$14,000. On December 10, he sold his gold coins through a broker for $19,500 cash, their approximate market value. The next day, on December 11, Reed sold to Gallagher for $5,000 each both his gun collection and his Triple BS stock. Whether or not Gallagher paid fair market value for the items was not established, but the stock had been purchased only one month earlier for $15,000.

Reed applied all of the proceeds to reduce the mortgages on his family residence, which was exempt from creditor's claims under Texas law, with the objective, the bankruptcy court found, of reducing the value of his non-exempt assets and increasing the value of his homestead exemption prior to bankruptcy. Thus he raised about $35,000, applying about $30,000 [should read "$20,000" — Eds.] to wipe out a second mortgage home improvement loan and applying the balance of approximately $15,000 to reduce the first mortgage on his home to about $28,000.

Reed cavalierly justified his sale of assets for what appeared to be less than their fair market value. This was of no concern to his creditors, he testified, because, if he had received more for the assets, he would have simply applied the additional sum to reduce the mortgage on his homestead. No matter how much he got, there would be nothing for his creditors.

Reed also failed to account for the disposition of $19,586.83 in cash during the year preceding filing. Reed attempted to explain the "unaccounted for" cash by testifying that he habitually carried huge sums of money in cash on his person and frequently made purchases and payments in cash without obtaining receipts. He argued that the amount of "unaccounted for" cash represents only a small percentage of the amount of money which went through his hands in 1979.

The bankruptcy judge found that Reed had effected transfers designed to convert nonexempt property into exempt property less than two weeks before bankruptcy with the intent to hinder, delay, or defraud creditors. 11 U.S.C.A. § 727(a)(2) (West 1979). He found that, regardless of the amount of money that might have passed through Reed's accounts, $19,586.83 is a significant sum, and that Reed had failed satisfactorily to explain its loss. This constituted an additional basis for denying discharge. 11 U.S.C.A. § 727(a)(5) (West 1979).

The district court affirmed the judgment.

II

The Bankruptcy Code provides that a debtor may be denied discharge if he has transferred property "with intent to hinder, delay, or defraud a creditor," 11 U.S.C.A. § 727(a)(2) (West 1979), or has "failed to explain satisfactorily . . . any loss of assets. . . ." 11 U.S.C.A. § 727(a)(5) (West 1979), Reed was denied discharge on both bases. Though either would suffice, we review the grounds seriatim.

In considering the effect of Reed's transfers of assets, we distinguish, as did the careful opinion of the bankruptcy court, the debtor's entitlement to the exemption of property from the claims of his creditors and his right to a discharge from his debts. The Bankruptcy Code allows a debtor to retain property exempt either (1) under the provisions of the Bankruptcy

Code, if not forbidden by state law, 11 U.S.C.A. § 522(b) and (d) (West 1979), or (2) under the provisions of state law and federal law other than the minimum allowances in the Bankruptcy Code, 11 U.S.C.A. § 522(b)(2) (West 1979).

Under the Bankruptcy Act of 1898, most courts, applying state exemption laws, had held property that would otherwise have been exempt to be deprived of its immunity if there was evidence other than the simple act of conversion showing that the debtor had acquired it with the intention of defrauding his creditors. If intent to defraud was not proved, however, and it was shown only that granting the exemption would defeat the creditor's claim, the exemption was granted. As stated in 3 Collier on Bankruptcy, ¶522.08[4] (15th ed. 1982): "Under the Act, the mere conversion of nonexempt property into exempt property on the eve of bankruptcy was not of itself such fraud as will [sic] deprive the bankrupt *of his right to exemptions.*" (Emphasis supplied.)

Before the Bankruptcy Code was adopted in 1978, it had been urged that property obtained in such last-minute conversions be ineligible for exemption. *Id.* The Code, however, adopts the position that the conversion of nonexempt to exempt property, without more, will not deprive the debtor of the exemption to which he would otherwise be entitled. 3 Collier, supra, ¶522.08[4]. Thus, both the House and Senate Reports state:

> As under current law, the debtor will be permitted to convert nonexempt property into exempt property before filing a bankruptcy petition. The practice is not fraudulent as to creditors, and permits the debtor to make full use of the exemptions to which he is entitled under the law.

H.R. Rep. No. 595, 95th Cong., 1st Sess. 361 (1977), reprinted in 1978 U.S. Code Cong. & Ad. News 5963, 6317; S. Rep. No. 989, 95th Cong., 2d Sess. 76, reprinted in 1978 U.S. Code Cong. & Ad. News 5787, 5862. The rationale behind this congressional decision is summed up at 3 Collier, *supra,* ¶522.08[4]: "The result which would obtain if debtors were not allowed to convert property into allowable exempt property would be extremely harsh, especially in those jurisdictions where the exemption allowance is minimal." Nonetheless, the phrase, "[a]s under current law," qualifies the apparently blanket approval of conversion, since as noted above, courts denied exemptions under the Act if there was extrinsic evidence of actual intent to defraud (and if the state law permitted disallowance of the exemption for fraud).

Reed elected to claim his exemptions under state law. The bankruptcy judge, therefore, referred to Texas law to determine both what property was exempt and whether the exemption was defeated by the eleventh-hour conversion. Texas constitutional and statutory protection of the homestead is absolute, and the bankruptcy judge interpreted Texas law to allow the exemption in full regardless of Reed's intent.

While the Code requires that, when the debtor claims a state-created exemption, the scope of the claim is determined by state law, it sets separate standards for determining whether the debtor shall be denied a discharge. The debtor's entitlement to a discharge must, therefore, be determined by federal, not state, law. In this respect, 11 U.S.C. § 727(a)(2) is absolute: the discharge shall be denied a debtor who has transferred property with intent to defraud his creditors. The legislative history of the exemption section, as noted above, does not mean that conversion is never fraudulent as to creditors, but simply that, as under prior law, mere conversion is not to be considered fraudulent unless other evidence proves actual intent to defraud creditors. While pre-bankruptcy conversion of nonexempt into exempt assets is frequently motivated by the intent to put those assets beyond the reach of creditors, which is, after all, the function of an exemption, evidence of actual intent to defraud creditors is required to support a finding sufficient to deny a discharge. For example, evidence that the debtor, on the eve of bankruptcy, borrowed money that was then converted into exempt assets would suffice to support a finding of actual intent to defraud. Only if such a finding is made may a discharge be denied.

The evidence amply supports the bankruptcy court's finding that Reed had an actual intent to defraud. Reed's whole pattern of conduct evinces that intent. *Cf.* Farmers Co-op. Assn. v. Strunk, 671 F.2d 391, 395 (10th Cir. 1982) ("Fraudulent intent of course may be established by circumstantial evidence, or by inferences drawn from a course of conduct"). His rapid conversion of nonexempt assets to extinguish one home mortgage and to reduce another four months before bankruptcy, after arranging with his creditors to be free of payment obligations until the following year, speaks for itself as a transfer of property in fraud of creditors. His diversion of the daily receipts of Reed's Men's Wear into an account unknown to his creditors and management consultant and his subsequent use of the receipts to repay a loan that had been a vehicle for this conversion confirm his fraudulent motivation. . . .

The fact findings of the bankruptcy judge, affirmed by the district court, are to be credited by us unless clearly erroneous. . . . [T]he finding of actual intent to defraud, based on evidence other than the fact of the conversion, patently was not permeated with error. The denial of a discharge on this ground alone was appropriate. It would constitute a perversion of the purposes of the Bankruptcy Code to permit a debtor earning $180,000 a year to convert every one of his major nonexempt assets into sheltered property on the eve of bankruptcy with actual intent to defraud his creditors and then emerge washed clean of future obligation by carefully concocted immersion in bankruptcy waters.

Reed asserts that denial of a discharge makes the exemption meaningless. This is but fulmination. Reed may retain his home, mortgages substantially reduced, free of claims by his creditors. In light of the ample evidence, aside from the conversion itself, that Reed had an actual intent to defraud his creditors, he simply is not entitled to a discharge despite the fact that a generous state law may protect his exemption.

The argument that we should reject the other ground for denying discharge gets but the short shrift it deserves. . . .

III

The district court found that Sharon Marcus Reed benefited from the "prohibited activities" and possibly had knowledge of them but that she did not participate in them. Accordingly, he granted her discharge. The evidence showed that Sharon Reed made out the daily reports of the sales receipts of Reed's Men's Wear during the time that Reed was surreptitiously diverting those receipts to a bank account unknown to his creditors and management consultant. From this, it would have been possible to infer that Sharon Reed shared her husband's fraudulent intent, but the bankruptcy judge's findings to the contrary are not clearly erroneous. . . .

The double *Reed* opinions show how the courts have tried to negotiate a line that provides protection for debtors and yet does not permit them to take undue advantage. It also illustrates how courts may see themselves bound by the legislature that created exemptions, or how they can read extremely open-ended language to craft what they believe is a more sensible solution, albeit one that defies precise definition.

Mr. Reed elicits many reactions, few of them sympathetic. When Congress clamped down on bankruptcy abuse, it tried to go after the Reeds of this world by adding a tool the bankruptcy court did not have: invalidating the actual exemption on the property. The Code now includes a provision that reduces the dollar value of the homestead protection by any amount that is attributable to otherwise non-exempt property that the debtor disposed of with intent to hinder, delay, or defraud a creditor. § 522(o). To catch even long-time planners, the provision has a ten-year reach-back period. So now debtors will have to come up with better plans than Mr. Reed and Triple BS—or start their planning a lot further in advance.

But even Congress is aware of a sticky problem. Surely many debtors convert assets from non-exempt to exempt before bankruptcy all the time. Think of paying your monthly car loan out of your non-exempt checking account. Haven't you just converted a non-exempt asset (cash) into an exempt one (car equity)? Have you become the next Reed? What will you tell your parents? Don't panic. That's why Congress has added the requirement that the conversion be with the intent to hinder, delay, or defraud your creditors (a standard we shall see later when studying fraudulent conveyances). Courts interpreting § 522(o) have indeed looked to those fraud cases for guidance of how to find intent, see, e.g., In re Crabtree, 562 B.R. 749 (B.A.P. 8th Cir. 2017), appreciating that few fraudsters are as candid as Mr. Reed in testifying regarding their intentions to stymie creditors or as colorful in signaling their intent as the incorporators of Triple BS. *Cf.* In re Enron Corp. Sec., Derivative & ERISA Litig., 235 F. Supp. 2d 549 (S.D. Tex. 2002) (uncovering scheme with corporate entities named "JEDI" and "Chewco"). So we have easy poles: your monthly car bill on one end and Triple BS on the other. Somewhere in the vast, more complex middle is a debtor who asks a bankruptcy attorney if it's better to use the remainder of a Christmas bonus in that account to pay down a car loan early or save it up for a condo down payment. When does active exemption planning and maximizing statutory entitlements lose the virtue of prudence and acquire the tinge of intent to defraud? When does tax planning become tax avoidance? It is said bankruptcy courts are courts of equity, and so perhaps precise definition in some instances is neither possible nor desirable.

3. Homestead Hunting: Moving to Better Homesteads

Section 522(o) is fairly weak tea. It would appear Congress's zeal for cracking down on poorer consumer debtors does not carry over to laws that might affect their more elite donors. Indeed, when the BAPCPA debates turned to millionaires exploiting unlimited homesteads, a proposal to have a hard federal cap of a quarter-million dollars on homestead exemptions in bankruptcy, pre-empting contrary state law, was quickly and forcefully killed by a contingent including the Texas delegation. Congress did add one hard homestead cap on securities fraud perpetrators, § 522(q), to appease post-Enron bloodlust, but if you work through its requirements, that stronger tea may not have many drinkers. The real consolation prize for those upset by mansion-owners staring down from their parapets on discharged creditors was a crackdown on debtors who try to move to better exemptions when storm clouds gather, evidently deciding the bucolic settlement era chronicled by Professor McKnight has come to an end. For a time after relocation, a debtor's exemptions must be determined by an earlier place of residence.

According to § 522(b)(3), the applicable exemptions are those of the state where the debtor resided for 730 days (two years in the parlance of ordinary speakers of English) before the bankruptcy filing. In other words, it takes a full two years of residence to take advantage of your new home state's exemptions. Surely that is long enough for an angry creditor to find the debtor and begin the collection process.

What if the debtor did not have only one home state during the two-year period before bankruptcy, say because of an earlier move or peripatetic lifestyle? Then go back and look at where the debtor resided during the 180 days that preceded the 730 days to see where the debtor resided for the majority of the time *then*. So the exemption laws that apply to your bankruptcy may require a multi-stage legal treasure hunt.

Few state exemption laws were written anticipating these new twists and turns of federal bankruptcy law. Many laws protect only a homestead "in the jurisdiction." Consider Edward and Cecilia Tate. They left Texas for Oregon, bought a home, and by the time of their bankruptcy, had $60,000 in equity. Because they had not lived in Oregon for the requisite 730 days, however, the court determined that Texas exemptions applied. Unfortunately for the Tates (and fortunately for their creditors), the bankruptcy court decided that Texas homestead law did not cover an "extra-territorial" home in Oregon. In re Tate, 2007 Bankr. LEXIS 98 (Bankr. D. Or. 2007). Trying to fix this, the Code says that if the debtors are not eligible for any state exemption, they can take the federal exemptions, even if their state has opted out. § 522(b)(3). The Tates did so.

The consequences of § 522(b)(3) keep everyone on their toes, as the players in an otherwise ordinary consumer bankruptcy case filed in the Middle District of Tennessee must suddenly learn to interpret the state exemption laws for Alaska merely because the debtor moved to Nashville from Anchorage a year and a half ago. Better-off debtors are more likely to get attorneys who are thinking about exemption planning and they are more likely to have the resources to wait out the various time period restrictions in the Code's exemption laws.

These rules affect all exemptions (not just homesteads). But given the particular significance of homesteads, Congress passed an additional

BAPCPA rule dissuading debtor flight. The "mansion loophole" amendment imposes a hard cap of about $170,350 for anyone moving across state lines within the 1,215 days preceding bankruptcy. § 522(p). (We don't know where they come up with these numbers and what important policy interest underlies the distinction between 1,215 days and 730 days; these numbers sound like the compromise of sausage-making.) The statute also seeks to nab people who stay put in their home states during the lookback period, but plow money into their homes—like good old Mr. Reed. The statute says the debtor "may not exempt any amount of interest [in property] that was acquired by the debtor during the 1,215-day period preceding the filing of the petition that exceeds in the aggregate $170,350 in value in real or personal property that the debtor . . . uses as a residence." § 522(p)(1)(A). The million-dollar homestead is available only for those who bought a fancy place at least 3.33 years ago. The newly rich need to find somewhere else to protect their wealth besides their home—and moving to another "where" won't help.

That outcome may seem fair enough to some, but what does it mean to acquire an interest in property? Buying a home, sure. How about paying down its mortgage? Isn't that "acquiring" more equity in your home, and isn't equity an "interest" in property? Courts split on mortgage paydown. Compare In re Anderson, 374 B.R. 848, 858 (Bankr. D. Kan. 2007) (not acquiring an interest, but could try to show actual intent under § 522(o)), with In re Rasmussen, 349 B.R. 747 (Bankr. M.D. Fla. 2006) (yes, in dicta, paydown is acquiring an interest, but passive appreciation due to inflation/housing market is not acquisition). If you believe legislative history is important and Congress was battling exemption hunters, should it matter whether the payment is a monthly mortgage payment (with some principal amortization) due in the ordinary course or a lump-sum paydown? Mr. Anderson plonked down $240,000 in Kansas (unlimited homestead exemption), but the court held fast, saying that "acquiring an interest in property" is not the same as deleveraging debt on a property. In a later hearing on actual intent to defraud under § 522(o), the court concluded "that the debtor here did nothing more than take advantage of an exemption to which he is entitled." In re Anderson, 386 B.R. 315, 331 (Bankr. D. Kan. 2008). Thus, once again, all roads go back to Mr. Reed and how to prove intent to do something bad when the actual conduct itself is not necessarily bad and is indeed approved in the legislative history.

B. BEYOND HOMESTEADS

It would be a mistake to think that homesteads are the only vehicles for asset planning.

1. *Personal Property Exemptions*

The sound and fury over homestead exemptions overshadows unlimited exemptions in personal property, but those exemptions raise the same concerns of justice and fairness as homestead exemptions, especially the lightening rod of when "planning" becomes "intent to hinder."

One example came out of Minnesota. Dr. Tveten, a physician who dabbled in more than the healing arts, managed to amass $19 million in debts in a real estate deal that went south. He consulted his attorney, who had two pieces of advice: Convert your assets to protect as much as you can and then file for bankruptcy. The good doctor took the advice, using 17 transfers to sell off his land and liquidate his non-exempt life insurance and retirement accounts. All the transactions were for fair value. Dr. T put the money into about $700,000 of life insurance and annuity contracts with the Lutheran Brotherhood, a fraternal benefit association. Under Minnesota law, these are exempt. Best of all, the exemption has no dollar limit.

Dr. T conceded that the purpose of these transfers was to shield his assets from creditors. He wasn't trying to cheat anyone, he said. He was just trying to meet the legal requirements of how he should best hold his assets. When Dr. T came up for a discharge in bankruptcy court, the bank that had financed the real estate deal and obtained his unsecured guarantee objected to his discharge. Norwest Bank Nebraska, N.A. v. Tveten, 848 F.2d 871 (8th Cir. 1988). The bankruptcy judge, following the analysis of the Fifth Circuit in *Reed*, denied the discharge and both was affirmed on district and circuit appeal.

But there was a stinging dissent by Judge Richard Arnold:

> The Court reaches a result that appeals to one's general sense of righteousness. I believe, however, that it is contrary to clearly established law, and I therefore respectfully dissent.
>
> Dr. Tveten has never made any bones about what he is doing, or trying to do, in this case. He deliberately set out to convert as much property as possible into a form exempt from attachment by creditors under Minnesota law. Such a design necessarily involves an attempt to delay or hinder creditors, in the ordinary, non-legal sense of those words, but, under long-standing principles embodied both in judicial decisions and in statute, such a purpose is not unlawful. The governing authority in this Court is Forsberg v. Security State Bank, 15 F.2d 499 (8th Cir. 1926). There we said:
>
> > It is well settled that it is not a fraudulent act by an individual who knows he is insolvent to convert a part of his property which is not exempt into property which is exempt, for the purpose of claiming his exemptions therein, and of thereby placing it out of the reach of his creditors.
>
> Id. at 501. Thus, under the controlling law of this Circuit, someone who is insolvent may convert property into exempt form for the very purpose of placing that property beyond the reach of his creditors. . . . The same principle was confirmed by Congress when it enacted the Bankruptcy Code of 1978. The report of the House Judiciary Committee states as follows:
>
> > As under current law, the debtor will be permitted to convert nonexempt property into exempt property before filing a bankruptcy petition. See Hearings, Pt. Ill, at 1355-58. The practice is not fraudulent as to creditors, and permits the debtor to make full use of the exemptions to which he is entitled under the law.

In re Tveten, 848 F.2d at 877 (Arnold, J., dissenting).

What made the *Tveten* case particularly noteworthy was that on the very day that it was announced the same court also announced the unanimous opinion in Hanson v. First Nat'l Bank in Brookings, 848 F.2d 866 (8th Cir. 1988). The Hansons were South Dakota farmers who, on similar advice of counsel, sold all their non-exempt property, two vans, a car, a motor home, and all their household goods to family members. On agreement with the purchasers, the Hansons retained possession of many of the goods. They received the market value of the goods, $27,115, which they promptly used to pay down their mortgage and to buy exempt life insurance policies. Their lender bank objected to the Hansons' exemptions, wanting to reach the assets they had secreted away. The court explored the same questions about whether the debtors had engaged in fraudulent conduct. The bankruptcy judge said the Hansons got their discharge and kept their newly exempt property. Both the district court and the Eighth Circuit affirmed.

Judge Arnold sided with the majority in the *Hanson*, but he used that decision to sharpen his outrage about the result in *Tveten*:

> The Court is entirely correct in holding that there is no extrinsic fraud [in *Hanson*]. The money placed into exempt property was not borrowed, the cash received from the sales was accounted for, and the property was sold for fair market value. The fact that the sale was to family members, "standing on its own, does not establish extrinsic evidence of fraud." Ante, at 869.
>
> With all of this I agree completely, but exactly the same statements can be made, just as accurately, with respect to Dr. Tveten's case. So far as I can tell, there are only three differences between Dr. Tveten and the Hansons, and all of them are legally irrelevant: (1) Dr. Tveten is a physician, and the Hansons are farmers; (2) Dr. Tveten attempted to claim exempt status for about $700,000 worth of property, while the Hansons are claiming it for about $31,000 worth of property; and (3) the Minnesota exemption statute whose shelter Dr. Tveten sought had no dollar limit, while the South Dakota statute exempting the proceeds of life-insurance policies, is limited to $20,000. The first of these three differences—the occupation of the parties—is plainly immaterial, and no one contends otherwise. The second—the amounts of money involved—is also irrelevant, in my view, because the relevant statute contains no dollar limit, and for judges to set one involves essentially a legislative decision not suitable for the judicial branch. The relevant statute for present purposes is 11 U.S.C. § 522(b)(2)(A), which authorizes debtors to claim exemptions available under "State or local law," and says nothing about any dollar limitations, by contrast to 11 U.S.C. § 522(d), the federal schedule of exemptions, which contains a number of dollar limitations. The third difference—that between the Minnesota and South Dakota statutes—is also legally immaterial, and for a closely related reason. The federal exemption statute, just referred to, simply incorporates state and local exemption laws without regard to whether those laws contain dollar limitations of their own. . . . If there ought to be a dollar limit, and I am inclined to think that there should be, and if practices such as those engaged in by the debtor here can become abusive, and I admit that they can, the problem is simply not one susceptible of a judicial solution according to manageable objective standard.

Hanson, 848 F.2d at 870-71 (Arnold, J., concurring).

This pair of cases is notable for another feature that does not play a prominent part in the opinion: both states let people squirrel away cash—that most precious of resource for the financially troubled debtor—in a Fraternal Benefit Association fund. Fraternal Benefit Associations? They sound so, um, *pokey*, but some lawyers have seen real potential in the idea of using them to stash a client's assets so that they cannot be reached by creditors—whether the debtor eventually files for bankruptcy or not. According to the Collier bankruptcy treatise, 42 states, the District of Columbia, and Puerto Rico all permit such unlimited exemptions in beneficiary associations—even as they slap hard caps on cars and homesteads.

Homesteads at least had a rich legal and cultural history. But insurance accounts?! Perhaps this is a lobbying story. Do large cash balances in insurance investments strike you to be prevalent assets of the working class? (*But cf.* Hanson.) We've come a long way from the skinny guy's barrel.

2.   *Asset Exclusions*

The fancier way to hide assets (and the one most heavily advertised in certain circles) is called an asset protection trust. The operation is fairly simple. For example, Ryan Spear transfers a big batch of his property to the Ryan Spear Trust, names himself both trustee and beneficiary, then sits back and smiles. Ryan keeps right on using the property—driving the car, sailing the boat, dropping in on the winter place in Aspen and the summer place in Maine. If Ryan runs over someone with his Hummer or lets his attention wander during open-heart surgery the tort victim might sue him and, worse for Ryan, win. But when it comes time to collect by seizing the cars/boats/condos, Ryan can smile and say, "Sorry, Sheriff, but those aren't mine. They are the property of the Ryan Spear Trust. The trustee lets me use them sometimes."

The idea of a self-settled trust (self-settled because Ryan gave assets to a trust for which he was the beneficiary) was anathema to trust law. Anything like this looked like a plain old fraud on the creditors. And that remains the law in most places. Most. A few years back, Alaska made self-settled asset protection trusts legal. Never one to pass up something that might generate legal fees, Delaware immediately jumped in and made them legal as well. The race was afoot. "Asset protection" is now a competitive legal field, with a newcomer every year or two joining the club. There are now at least 13 states that permit asset protection trusts. Best of all, many of these states make the trusts available to out-of-state residents. Unlike the Texas or Florida homesteads, the asset protection trusts are available without ever leaving home. Are those debtors sweating through Florida summers unfashionably using yesterday's solution?

As an Internet ad proclaims,

Domestic asset protection trusts reflect the willingness of elected representatives to make sure wealthy people can dodge creditors, at least if the debtors plan in advance. But the race is not limited to the domestic venue.

Basking in Islands of Legalisms

The Cook Islands have a smaller population—about 20,000—than one apartment complex in Manhattan, and an economy with little to offer except tourism and pearl exports. The country contracts out its national defense to New Zealand, which is four hours away by plane.

But sand and sun are not the attractions for some Americans who have sent their money to the Cook Islands. Under Cook Islands law, foreign court orders are generally disregarded, which is helpful for someone trying to keep assets away from creditors.

In fact, getting an American court order can make it harder to get money out of the Cook Islands. If someone who stashed funds in a Cook Islands trust asks for the money back because a court ordered him to do so, Cook Islands law says that person is acting under duress, and the local trustee can refuse to return the money.

Over the years, a number of less-than-upstanding Americans have found the islands attractive for that reason. . . .

The latest to use that tactic is the wife of Jamie L. Solow, a former broker in Florida who evidently has a silver tongue and certainly has a lot of angry former customers. In one year, he earned more than $3 million in commissions selling a form of collateralized debt obligations known as "inverse floaters." . . .

The investments proved to be disastrous, and the Securities and Exchange Commission persuaded a jury in West Palm Beach, Fla., that he had committed securities fraud. Now a federal judge has ordered Mr. Solow to go to prison on Monday for civil contempt for failing to come up with a large part of the $6 million he was ordered to pay in disgorgement, interest and penalties.

Mr. Solow claimed he had virtually no assets, since his wife owned everything in the family and had put most of it in a Cook Islands trust. . . .

Mr. Solow did sell all the assets he acknowledged owning—an old pickup truck and some office furniture—and sent $2,639 to the court. The family Rolls Royce was also sold, for $205,000, but the Solows say it was actually owned by Mrs. Solow, even though her husband had put up the money to buy it and signed the sale documents.

This week, Mr. Solow asked that his incarceration be delayed, on the grounds that he and his wife were now willing to ask the Cook Islands trustee to return the money. They have not actually made that request, and in the past, Cook Islands trustees have refused to honor such requests. In ordering Mr. Solow to prison, Judge Donald M. Middlebrooks, of the United States District Court for the Southern District of Florida, said his inability to pay was self-created, and thus no excuse. . . .

In setting up the trust, Mr. Solow's wife, Gina, followed a blueprint laid out in a 2005 article in an accounting publication, written by Howard D. Rosen, a lawyer in Florida whom she hired a few days after the jury verdict in early 2008.

The Solows own a waterfront home in Hillsboro Beach, Fla., which they view as their permanent residence even though they have not lived in it for several years because of hurricane damage. . . .

The house was already encumbered by $2.4 million in mortgages, but a Cook Islands bank lent $5.2 million more secured by the house. The money from that was immediately placed in a Cook Islands trust to benefit only Mrs. Solow.

The judge noted that the mortgage could not have been taken out without Mr. Solow's consent.

The house is now listed for sale for $6.1 million, far less than the combined mortgages, but the bank in the Cook Islands was taking no real risk. The proceeds from the mortgage were deposited in the Cook Islands, and the interest earned is used to pay the interest on the mortgage.

. . .

In a telephone interview, Mr. Rosen, who had testified in the case on behalf of Mr. Solow, told me that Judge Middlebrooks "simply does not understand the laws of the United States" and voiced confidence that an appeals court would overturn the ruling.

In an e-mail message, he compared the use of an offshore trust to a company's decision to incorporate in Delaware rather than some other state. "Establishing a trust in the Cook Islands or other suitable asset protection jurisdiction in order to gain a protective advantage is no different," he wrote. "It is a choice-of-law matter." [*New York Times*, Jan. 22, 2010, at B10]

How much value is tucked away in these accounts? In fact, how many of them are there? Hard numbers are hard to come by. A few years ago, the marketing was clearly to a select demographic. There were glossy brochures to take cruises and learn about asset protection trusts (presumably the cruise ships were well stocked with fast talkers ready to take your money to set up a trust on the spot). Now anyone can click on Nexis and search for "asset protection trusts" and turn up more than 2.5 million hits, including one like the following:

Call Today for a Free 20 Minute Consultation! 1-800-800-xxxx
We specialize in protecting Personal and Business and Professional assets from claims and creditors. We help you preserve your wealth from credators, liitigation, divorce and estate taxation.

Asset protection maybe, spelling no.

What happens to asset protection trusts in bankruptcy? If they are structured correctly, including a spendthrift provision, and for good measure an automatic appointment of a third party as trustee if the trustee-debtor is sued, they are excluded from the estate outright. Remember § 541(c)(2)? It's back. The trust is statutorily excluded from property of the estate. The reference to state law seems to give the trusts full protection, at least in 13 states if the trust is a domestic one. No need to worry anymore about exemptions!

As far as we can tell, asset protection plans seem to work well from the debtor's perspective. The Asset Protection Society, a tradegroup, boasts that "simply put, to date there has **never** been a situation where an offshore asset protection trust has been broken and where the money in such a trust has been forced to return to the U.S. and returned to a creditor." Ryan Spear, keep smiling and counting your cash (sorry, *the trust's* cash).

The linchpin, of course, is a cadre of professionals willing to do the good work of keeping the world safe from creditors. If, for 100% protection, you need to turn control of your trust over to a faraway professional, you're really putting the "trust" into trust. They know this and advertise accordingly.

The Harris Organisation About the Founder

Marc M. Harris graduated from North Carolina Wesleyan College with a 4.0 average at the age of 18. Shortly thereafter, while still only 18, he passed his Certified Public Accountant (CPA) examination and is believed to be the youngest person in the United States to accomplish this. He went on to Columbia University for his MBA with a concentration in Investment Finance. . . .

After substantial changes in the American tax law in 1986, Mr. Harris refocused the firm's strategy in favor of international tax planning and legitimate methods for Americans to take advantage of offshore tax havens. In order to better service his growing international clientele, he relocated the center of operations to Panama. Today, with over 150 employees, The Firm of Marc M. Harris, Inc. has become the largest independent provider of . . . financial services in Latin America and the Caribbean.

Mr. Harris . . . has personally received many awards which include the key to the city of Miami Beach and Most Distinguished Alumni at North Carolina Wesleyan College. He has established a personal foundation that contributes to Panamanian society by funding nutritional project. . . . [He] has assisted in drafting new financial services legislation for several Latin American countries and is a contributor to various financial journals and newsletters on a regular basis.

. . .

The Marc M. Harris Advantage

The Firm of Marc M. Harris, Inc. is run by Americans, for Americans, specializing in American needs. All work is done by The Firm's experienced in-house accountants, attorneys, investment advisors, investment bankers, brokers and administrators. Panama is a jurisdiction that imposes severe civil and criminal penalties for disclosure of confidential information. . . . The timing in asset protection and financial planning is everything. You can't purchase fire insurance while the building is on fire. An attack on your assets can come from any direction at any time, i.e., law suits, tax increases, currency crashes, etc. . . . We will only advise and complete transactions that are completely legal. . . .

You may contact us by e-mail at globalinvesting@marc-harris.com. Initial contact by telephone is not recommended. . . .

Is Marc Harris just a guy making a buck within the law or a bottom-feeder (top-feeder?) who should be ashamed of himself? And now, this: https://www.tax-news.com/news/Marc_Harris_Faces_17_Year_Jail _Sentence____16197.html (2004). (The $26 million fine appears never to have been paid, suggesting he still has a trick or two up his sleeve.)

Can creditors do anything about debtors who opt their assets out of bankruptcy? Asset protection trusts and their fraternal order cousins in exemption law can always be set aside by the approach taken in *In re Reed* by the Fifth Circuit: even if the trust works at state law, the debtor will be denied the protection of a discharge in bankruptcy. And BAPCPA's § 522(o) is supposed to help, but as *Anderson* reveals, that's a high hurdle to clear.

Indeed, as the *Reed-Anderson* dichotomy demonstrates, one man's hindering is another man's prudence; there is a lot of room for debtors to litigate over intent. BAPCPA's addition of § 548(e) is unlikely to change much: that invalidation of asset protection trusts created within the past ten years once again turns on the trustee carrying the burden of showing actual intent to hinder, delay, or defraud creditors. Indeed, a court's reach may be even more circumscribed than before the amendment because the language in § 548(e)(2) describes such transfers as including those made "in anticipation of any money judgment" or to escape "judgments in connection with securities fraud" (but not "murdering your ex-spouse while wearing ill-fitting gloves"). Does the inclusion of specific examples mean textually that transfers for *other* reasons would otherwise *not* indicate a fraudulent intent? We won't hold our breath for Congress. While some complain these legal shams need to be purged for fairness to creditors, others are busy exhorting their states to join the club where they are legally sanctioned.

C.   WHO CARES ABOUT EXEMPTIONS?

We began our study of exemptions with the guy in the barrel, thinking about why he might get to keep his clothes. We end the section with a Congress not willing to prevent multimillionaires from protecting unlimited assets. The policy grounds for this result for some may be elusive.

In light of the difficulty of designing exemptions, what is at stake in setting the exemption level too low or too high? What is the real world effect of a given set of exemption laws? The studies are sparse and inconclusive. Michelle White, Professor of Economics at the University of California at San Diego, studied state exemptions and entrepreneurial start-ups. She concluded that the likelihood of a homeowner owning a business was 35% higher in states with unlimited homestead exemptions. Michelle White, Bankruptcy and Small Business, Regulation (Summer 2001, p.18). She concluded that changing bankruptcy laws and narrowing exemptions would "discourage many entrepreneurs from going into business and some of the discouraged businesses would inevitably involve innovative new ideas that would have generated jobs and economic growth." More recent research shows just how complex these issues are. The presence and size of homestead exemptions may also have effects on mortgage behavior. One study suggests that more generous homestead exemptions encourage borrowers to buy more housing and take out larger mortgages on a loan-to-value basis, but when controlling for house value, more generous homestead exemptions discourage mortgage borrowing, resulting in more homeowner equity. Qianqian Cao, Bankruptcy Exemption, Home Equity and Mortgage Credit, 42 Real Est. Econ. 938 (2014). Homestead exemption levels may even have impacts on mortgage repayment activity. Another study finds that in jurisdictions with large homestead exemptions, there are significantly lower mortgage default and foreclosure rates than in low homestead exemption states. This effect is most pronounced in the riskiest market segments. Chintal A. Desai, Gregory Ellihausen & Jevgenijs Steinbuks, Effects of Bankruptcy Exemptions and Foreclosure Laws on Mortgage Default and Foreclosure Rates, 47 J. Real Est. Fin. & Econ. 391 (2013).

What does this mean for unsecured creditors? In theory, they should recover less in high-exemption states than low-exemption ones. Is this true? And, if so, should those creditors charge Texans higher interest than they charge folks in Wyoming? One study claims that creditors charge higher rates to borrowers in states with larger exemptions, though their method compared the rates on secured car loans (that aren't likely to be much affected by exemption levels). See Reint Gropp, John Karl Scholz & Michelle J. White, Personal Bankruptcy and Credit Supply and Demand, 112 Q.J. Econ. 217-51 (February 1997). Sure, we understand that there could be some spillover effects on secured creditors from the exemptions (they might have less opportunity to collect deficiency judgments). But that takes attenuated analysis and stylized factual assumptions (that deficiencies occur with regularity, that car lenders in turn go after them, and that the payoff has an upfront pricing effect in lending). Besides, if car lenders were worried about deficiencies, wouldn't credit card companies, who are unsecured, be far more affected? Yet they show no sensitivity in either the terms of their loans or the amount of credit they offer. Indeed, shouldn't secured lenders like *higher* exemptions, which protect debtors from unsecured creditors, leaving more breathing room to pay the secureds? We confess that the Gropp et al. study based on secured car loans leaves us scratching our heads.

In his dissertation at MIT, economist Fredrick Link examined the cost and availability of general unsecured credit (the debt that should have been affected by exemption levels) in states with high exemptions and those with low exemptions. He determined that the differences among the states were statistically indistinguishable. Fredrick Link, The Economics of Personal Bankruptcy (MIT June 2004). He also found that homestead exemptions were negatively correlated with homeownership, suggesting that state protection seems to yield fewer, not more, homeowners. Link's findings should caution against making easy assumptions on the effect exemptions have on credit.

Finally, what about the other side of the exemption debate? Unlimited homestead exemptions and the unsavory characters who hide in mansions to evade creditors is a sexy press topic. Yet the less glamorous, but surely more important, stingy homestead exemptions that will cost people their homes in low- or no-exemption states draw little press interest. During the debates over BAPCPA, Senator Russell Feingold, D-WI, proposed a floor on homestead protection for older Americans: anyone 65 or older could protect equity in a homestead up to $125,000 in value, regardless of state exemption laws or state opt-outs. The amendment was defeated. Cook Islands 1, AARP 0.

Problem Set 5

5.1. Kevin LoVecchio is battling a host of angry former partners in a real estate business scheme, who last week won a $10 million judgment against him for breach of contract.

Kevin, a law school grad who never wanted to settle down and practice law ("too boring"), owns a gorgeous penthouse condo in Chicago and not much else ("temporary slump"). He has lived in the condo for five years, except for about two-and-a-half years ago when he rented an apartment in Florida for 91 days ("moved there for business, couldn't stand the heat") and a period last year when he moved to Wisconsin for a couple of months ("thought I could commute to Chicago, but it was too far"). In both Florida and Wisconsin he applied for a driver's license, registered to vote, and changed the address for his *Financial Times* subscription. Kevin came to see you yesterday to ask that you file his chapter 7 petition. Can he keep his condo? (Illinois is an opt-out state that permits a debtor to protect a $15,000 homestead.) Does he face any other obvious problems? See § 522(b)(3)(A).

5.2. Woody Woodward ran a stock scam that was so tangled that it took years for his investors to figure it out. The SEC still can't explain it well enough to get an indictment, but a civil jury just awarded some of the victims $25 million. Woody and his fourth wife, Ingrid, just bought a home in Pennsylvania Dutch Country, a beautiful estate on 16 acres, for $10 million cash. Woody and Ingrid are current on all their bills, and Woody is ready to file for bankruptcy to deal with the big judgment. He tells you with cool confidence, "We plan to keep the house." Can he do that? See § 522(b)(3)(B).

5.3. A. On their wedding day, Emily and Ryan Morrissey closed on what they describe as a "nice, normal house" in Texas. They paid $1 million cash for the purchase price and have spent the last several years filling up the six bedrooms with children. About three years ago, they purchased the adjoining five-acre empty lot and added bedrooms to their house to accommodate the nanny, the tutor, and the housekeeper, all of whom help care for their brace of children. These home improvements cost another million, including a second pool and a backyard guest house for Grandma when she visits. Famous neighbors, mostly retired Texas Rangers, have moved nearby, adding to their home's worth; they estimate it at $4 million.

The Morrisseys are in serious financial trouble because of medical bills relating to their new children, triplets who were born prematurely. Despite both being licensed physicians, the Morrisseys had no medical insurance, figuring they didn't need it because they could care for each other. The medical creditors—including the hospital where they work—hound them about the unpaid bills, and they are at their breaking point with the stress. They know bankruptcy will let them discharge their medical debts but they want to make sure they can protect the house too. What do you tell them? See § 522(b)(3) and (p)(1).

B. The Morrisseys' less affluent cousins, Frank and Leslie Shankly, have their own problems. Mr. Shankly, now 62, was transferred by his employer just over two years ago from Las Vegas to Providence. Although their grown children live in Nevada, they decided they couldn't afford retirement for another six years, so reluctantly accepted the transfer rather than look for work in a rough market. When they sold their Nevada home, they netted $350,000. In Rhode Island they downsized to a three-bedroom condo that cost $200,000. The other $150,000 from the sale of the home went into their retirement account, accelerating their retirement plans by two years. The bad news is Frank co-signed his brother Jim's $500,000 business loan, which has been reduced to judgment after default. (Jim was last seen in the presence of a cocktail waitress named Ali in Northern Canada.) The worse news is Leslie just passed away.

Frankly, Mr. Shankly is a sickening wreck. Still adjusting to being a widower, he wants the anguish of the judgment and its threat of collection to be behind him. Nevada has a $550,000 homestead exemption; Rhode Island's is $300,000. Retirement accounts are exempt under Rhode Island law. How will the Shankly assets fare in bankruptcy? Assuming the condo and retirement accounts are the only major assets, what should Mr. Shankly do?

5.4. Your long-time tennis partner, Dr. Panoply, is an ob-gyn who is known and beloved throughout your community as a fine doctor and a community leader who always has time for charities. He knows you are a tort litigator and has always joked that he's always been proud that he's never needed your services for malpractice defense. He came to your office last week, and said, "I've heard so many frightening things, and the malpractice premiums have become so extraordinary, I think I should try an asset-protection plan, like the kind my friends have." He wants to set up a trust to hold all his investments safe from juries "who apparently don't understand that medicine is an art, not a science." What sort of state remedies should he fear, and how will your advice help? Are there collection remedies that might threaten him regardless of advice?

After you discuss things with him awhile, he says, "I have to admit, it's not just the malpractice thing. I have been in this terrible dispute with Stock, Lock, and Barrel, the well-known brokerage firm, and it's in arbitration, and I am afraid they may win, to the tune of a million dollars." Does this fact change your advice? Or your interest in representing him?

5.5. You are the new legislative aide to Virginia Bethania Herring, the ranking member of the Judiciary Committee. Two proposals for amending the Bankruptcy Code have just been dropped in the hopper, and she asks you to give her a preliminary assessment on each.

- Drop the categories in § 522(d) and simply put in a dollar amount. Debtors can protect any value up to that amount, regardless of what type of asset.
- Remove the ability of debtors to choose exemptions and require them to take only the federal exemptions.

What do you tell her? Be prepared to begin your discussion with a clear position on whether she should defend the existing system or adopt one of the two alternatives above.

CLAIMS AND DISTRIBUTIONS

Once it is clear what property belongs in the debtor's estate and what property the debtor may properly exempt, the trustee begins to assemble any non-exempt property for sale. In order to give each creditor the appropriate share of those sale proceeds, the trustee's attention turns from the debtor to the creditors. We thus now examine the process of asserting, calculating, and disputing creditors' claims, as well as to look at some insights into the modern consumer debt market that that process accords.

A. FILING CLAIMS

Ordinarily, a creditor will receive and complete a straightforward *proof of claim* form (Official Form No. 410) with the notice of the bankruptcy. Its completion and filing are governed by Rules 3001-3008. In chapter 7 and chapter 13 cases, a proof of claim must be filed within 90 days after the 341 meeting, with certain exceptions. Bankr. R. 3002. In chapter 11 cases, the court fixes a *bar date* before which claims must be filed. Bankr. R. 3003. In chapter 7 or 13 cases, a creditor must file a claim in order to receive a dividend, even if the creditor was listed on the debtor's schedules; in chapter 11, a creditor who is scheduled is not so required. Bankr. R. 3002, 3003.

Practitioners report that some creditors simply fail to file claims in consumer cases. In chapter 7 cases, the habit of non-filing might be understandable since few cases involve non-exempt assets available for distribution. A U.S. Trustee report from 2002 pegs around 96% of chapter 7 cases as no-asset, a percentage that has not varied much in decades. In chapter 13 cases, in which there is typically some payout for all creditors, the failure to file a proof of claim is more surprising. Perhaps most unsecured creditors just do not bother to distinguish between chapter 7 and chapter 13 cases in their collection practices, and there are more than twice as many chapter 7s as 13s. Still, identifying the debts that will produce payment in bankruptcy can be a lucrative business. Investment bank Bear Stearns owned a debt buying business devoted to purchasing consumer bankruptcy debts at a steep discount. It *did* file proofs of claim and got checks from trustees that aggregated to millions each year. Of course, its subprime mortgage business worked out, shall we say, less well for it. Irony?

If no objection is filed by the trustee (or if that objection is overruled), the claim becomes an *allowed claim*. § 502(a). Contrast how efficient and rapid this process is to the cumbersome obtaining and enforcing of judgments at state law that was introduced back in Assignment 2. Most claims are so resolved without objection and paid a pro rata dividend of the bankruptcy estate's proceeds. It is worth a moment's reflection to note this remarkable occurrence: claims are satisfied, through a court, without any state or federal adjudication that the money is owed. The parties simply agree on claims, and the trustee, representing the interests of all the creditors, ratifies them. This speed illustrates the efforts taken in bankruptcy to spend the available money on distribution to the creditors rather than on litigation about which creditors are entitled to collect.

We don't want to suggest, however, that the claims process is a free pass. There are *some* rules. One notable requirement is that a claim based on a writing must have a copy of the writing attached. Bankr. R. 3001. In the case that follows, there was shoddy documentation—not enough to kill the claim, but enough to enrage the judge sufficiently to resolve ambiguities adversely.

In re LANZA

51 B.R. 125 (Bankr. E.D. Pa. 1985)

GOLDHABER, Bankruptcy Judge.

The pivotal inquiry . . . is whether the evidence supports a bank's entitlement to the . . . claim[] at issue, notwithstanding its apparent gross deviations from standard banking practice. After carefully weighing the evidence, we will reduce the amount of the . . . first claim. . . . First Peoples National Bank ("the Bank") filed three proofs of claim. In support of the first proof of claim (No. 15) it appears that the debtors conveyed a mortgage on a parcel of real estate to the Bank in exchange for a construction loan with which to improve the subject property. This mortgage was executed for a denominated indebtedness of $200,000.00, although only $125,000.00 was advanced at settlement. The Bank later advanced $170,000.00 to the debtors through a series of unsecured loans, none of which, the Bank concedes, were charged against the original mortgage. Apparently, after some criticism of these advances from its auditors, the Bank convinced the debtors to grant another mortgage for $350,000.00 using the now improved property as collateral and allocating $125,000.00 of the proceeds to satisfy the original mortgage and $177,520.00 to discharge the unsecured indebtedness and interest. The mortgage was then properly filed and recorded. At the hearing the Bank presented conflicting testimony on the outstanding balance remaining on the mortgage and, weighing this discrepancy against the bank, we adopt the lowest figure presented by the Bank—namely, $300,000.00.

. . .

. . . The examples of so-called bookkeeping for a public financial institution that were presented to us as evidence could easily warrant for a half-dozen or so loan officers an other-worldly judgment[3] of perdition, forever condemning them to scramble about the floor of Pandemonium, each looking for the missing beads of his shattered abacus.

. . .

On the . . . claim, the debtors argued that the lack of supporting documents and mismanagement of the file should invalidate the Bank's claim. However, as stated above, the burden of proof is not on the Bank to substantiate its claim with extensive documentation, the onus is on the debtor to overcome the presumption of validity. . . . However, because of conflicting statements by the Bank's own employees on the balance of the indebtedness, we adopt the Bank's lowest figure of $300,000.00. The Bank should rightfully bear the burden of the ambiguity in light of its abysmal bookkeeping.

Ironically, the rise of technology has been making matters worse. E-commerce has facilitated a debt-trading market, and loans now change hands faster than you can say, "housing market collapse." (Recall the Bear Stearns consumer-debt buying subsidiary.) As a result:

> Th[e] growth of the [multibillion-dollar] debt buying industry has transformed the bankruptcy claims process. Driven by the economics of the assignment process, debt buyers in particular have given short shrift to the Bankruptcy Rules. Rather than attaching card member agreements, promissory notes and account statements to proofs of claim, and providing itemized statements of interest and additional charges, debt buyers have been attaching to the claim form a one-page "Accounting Summary" that provides the debtor's name and account number and merely restates the balance owed listed in paragraph 4 on Official Form 10. Proofs of claim are filed in this manner without any actual review of loan documents or account statements because the supporting documents required by Rule 3001 are not provided to debt buyers.

John Rao, Debt Buyers Rewriting of Rule 3001: Taking the "Proof" out of the Claims Process, 23-6 ABI J. 16 (July/August 2004) (footnotes omitted). In 2011, the Bankruptcy Rules were amended to address concerns about the accuracy of consumer claims. Some changes are arguably just clarifications, but the amendments allow sanctions if a proof of claim fails to meet the requirements. A court can preclude the offending creditor from presenting as evidence any information that should have been included that was not and/or award other relief, including reasonable attorneys' fees for the additional proceedings required due to noncompliance. One unavailable weapon—the FDCPA. The Supreme Court has held that it is not a violation of the FDCPA to file bankruptcy claims that are unenforceable at state

---

[3] We of the bankruptcy court could enter no such final judgment, the subject matter not being a core proceeding since that power is justifiably reserved to a higher "judicial" authority.

law (e.g., time-barred by statute of limitations), even if the creditor knows full well they cannot be enforced. Apparently, the Court believes there is value to keeping trustees on their toes for illegitimate claims. Midland Funding, LLC v. Johnson, 137 S. Ct. 1407 (2017).

B. CALCULATING CLAIMS

1. Unsecured Claims

a. The Claim

While § 501 lays out the procedure for filing a claim, § 502 explains the mechanics of calculating it. All claims, whether secured or unsecured, begin with a § 502 calculation. This section is the beginning point for claims against the debtor.

Let's work through an example. Sarina has a charge account with Sears. The terms are cash in full within 30 days or interest thereafter at an annual rate of 12% (unrealistic, but it keeps the calculations easy). Sears is also entitled under the agreement to attorneys' fees and costs of collection equal to 20% of the debt if it has to take legal action to collect (a standard clause in credit agreements). At the date of bankruptcy Sarina had made one charge for $1,000, was three months late in paying, and Sears had begun collection efforts. Under these facts, Sears would file a proof of claim for $1,000, plus $30 interest for three months before bankruptcy (simple interest, not compounded, which is also unrealistic, but again it keeps the calculations easy). For clarity, this $30 is called "prepetition" interest because it accrued before Sarina filed her bankruptcy petition. Sears would also claim the $200 it spent on prepetition collection costs, for a total of $1,230. Under § 502, Sears is entitled to assert the full amount as an *allowed claim* because all of the amounts are treated as having accrued before bankruptcy and are therefore permissible prepetition claims. Because Sears has no security, it has an *unsecured claim*.

After the non-exempt assets have been sold, if the proceeds equal 10% of the total value of all allowed unsecured claims, the trustee will send Sears a check for $123, i.e., "ten cents on the dollar," as its pro rata share. The shortfall between what Sears will be allowed as its unsecured claim—the same amount as it would in a nonbankruptcy lawsuit—and what it will receive as its dividend from the trustee upon liquidating Sarina's estate is "lost" to Sears; at the conclusion of the case, all debts, including this unrecovered portion, are *discharged* (a subject to which we turn in Assignment 8). In this example, Sears only got $123 on its allowed unsecured claim of $1,230, and so $1,107 was discharged.

b. Interest on the Claim

It will probably take some time for Sarina's estate to be liquidated and Sears to get paid. If five months elapse between the bankruptcy filing and the distribution, does Sears get another $50 in *postpetition* interest? If Sears is an unsecured creditor, the answer is no. Assuming someone objects, Sears will be denied the opportunity to collect interest on its unsecured claim after the filing while the bankruptcy is pending. § 502(b)(2). In the terms of the statute, this interest, while contractually obligated, is "unmatured" on the filing date. Admittedly, "unmatured interest" is like "unfallen rain"—a concept only a lawyer could love. It refers to interest in which the right to payment has not yet vested. Does that just mean not yet due? No. Interest can be vested but not yet due. Consider a loan that provides for a lump-sum payment of interest all at the end rather than interest calculated and payable over time in installments. Even though none of the interest is yet due, if a filing occurs midway through its term, a bankruptcy court would reanalyze which portion of the interest was "matured," and hence could be added to the claim, and which was not.

There is no doubt that the delay in distribution is costly to Sears. It loses the time value of money, and yet it can make no claim for this interest after the bankruptcy is filed. That may seem unfair, but think of it from the perspective of Sarina's other creditors. The prohibition on unmatured interest is an extension of the pro rata distribution among unsecured creditors in bankruptcy: everyone rides in the same boat and shares together in proportion to allowed claims. Because the amount available for distribution doesn't increase, any postpetition interest tacked onto Sears' claim—unless the same interest rate is applied to every other creditor's claim—will increase Sears' relative recovery, giving it a larger slice of the pie than other creditors.

There are only three ways to deal with postpetition interest soundly: (1) no unsecured creditors collect interest, period; (2) every unsecured creditor collects interest, at the same rate (perhaps a statutory one); or (3) every unsecured creditor collects interest, at whatever rate, if any, its contract, if any, allows. The Code takes approach (1). It rejects option (2) presumably on the theory that to add interest to claims of an already bankrupt debtor will not increase the collective recovery; on the contrary, it'll just add more debt to be discharged. It rejects option (3) for the reasons of equity discussed above. Some creditors will have high interest rates by contract and others will have low or no interest running. The Code should not incentivize the higher-interest creditors to languish and the lower ones to rush in to bankruptcy. Remember, many creditors may not have negotiated for an interest rate at all (think tort victim). By treating all unsecured creditors the same—that is, for all to collect a pro rata share of whatever is available for distribution, without postpetition interest—bankruptcy reinforces the goal of equality among these unsecured creditors. (For those who feel bad, consider never-employed § 726(a)(5).)

c. Complications with the Claim: Acceleration

Unmatured interest is not allowed, but what about unmatured principal? Because bankruptcy means all of the debtor's obligations are about to be resolved in a single forum, once and forever, there exists a need to accelerate all prepetition debts whether they have matured or not. Otherwise, long-term creditors whose loans were not in default (and therefore would have no immediate claim) could not recover from the estates of debtors about to discharge all their debts. A *statutory acceleration* of claims (to be differentiated from a *contractual acceleration* clause that makes the entire balance of a loan fall due upon default) derives from the broad definition of "claim," § 101(5)(A), which you will note includes "unmatured" rights to payment. It has few parallels outside bankruptcy law. As a result, sometimes the claims process can involve difficult esoteric questions. A debtor who has guaranteed a loan before the bankruptcy filing, for example, has an undisputed prepetition obligation. But the debtor may never have to pay anything on the guaranty, and any amount that might have to be paid will change depending on how many payments the primary obligor makes before defaulting. Figuring out how to value such a guaranty claim can be hard. Or perhaps the debtor has polluted, and both the pollution and its effects remain unknown. Or perhaps the debtor has engaged in conduct alleged to be in restraint of trade, for which it is not sure whether it is liable (and if so, what damages it might face). These valuation questions all end up in the lap of the bankruptcy judge to be sorted out. We flag the issue now but will address it in more detail in a later assignment.

d.   Postpetition Claims

We can anticipate a distinction that will be important in the next section. Suppose the trustee decided to repaint some of Sarina's non-exempt furniture before selling it (in order to get a better price) and the paint was coincidentally purchased at Sears on credit. Sears would have another claim to be paid by the estate, but it would be a *postpetition* claim and therefore made under § 503—"expenses of administration"—not § 502. Ordinarily, Sears would be paid in full on its § 503 claim; administrative claims are usually paid first before all other unsecured claims. § 507(a)(1)-(2). (Do you see why? That furniture's not going to paint itself.) We will explore priority claims in the next assignment when we discuss distribution.

2.   *Secured Claims*

a.   The Claim

If Sears has a secured claim, the first part of the calculation remains the same. Sears shows what it is owed pre-bankruptcy through the calculation of a § 502 claim. But as creditors line up for payment from the trustee, bankruptcy newbies rapidly find that the oft-repeated maxim "equity is equality" takes on unexpected meanings. The largest differentiation among creditors is the distinction between the treatment afforded creditors with valid security interests and that given to their unsecured counterparts. Section 502(b) governs the permissible nature and extent of an allowed prepetition claim, but § 506 adds special postpetition and collection rights of secured creditors.

Section 506(a) grants a secured creditor an *allowed secured claim* up to the value of its collateral. If the total claim is less than or equal to the value of that collateral, then the entire claim is secured, or in the parlance of the trade, "fully secured." If the claim is greater than the value of the collateral, then the claim is only "partially secured." (You may have heard the more colloquial term "underwater," which we guess means by analogy a fully secured creditor could be considered "overwater.") For partially secured claims, the portion that exceeds the value of the collateral is still allowed, but only as an unsecured claim against the estate.

The typical treatment of a secured creditor is illustrated by another Sarina purchase from Sears. Let's assume she bought a top-of-the-line riding lawnmower in which Sears took a security interest and consider two scenarios. First, say Sarina made substantial payments so that at the time of filing, Sears is still owed $5,000, but the lawnmower is worth $6,500. This gives Sears an allowed secured claim of $5,000 against the estate under § 506(a). If the trustee sells the lawnmower, the costs of sale come first from the proceeds, § 506(c), and then Sears will get paid in full on its claim. The remaining proceeds go to the trustee for distribution to the unsecured creditors (or in a rare case, back to the debtor as exempt).

If, however, in a second scenario, the lawnmower had been ridden hard and poorly maintained, it might be worth $3,500 and an unsecured claim for $1,500 (the difference between the § 502 claim and the allowed secured claim under § 506). Sears will get all proceeds from the sale (after sales costs, § 506(c)) with nothing left for the trustee. If the costs of sale were, say $500, Sears would get $3,000 from the sale and have to add another $500 to its allowed unsecured claim (bringing it to $2,000). If we continue the assumption from earlier that this is a "ten cents on the dollar" case, Sears will get another $200 for its allowed unsecured claim, resulting in a grand total recovery of $3,200. In effect an *undersecured* creditor gets a bifurcated claim under § 506: a secured claim equal to the value of the collateral and an unsecured claim for the deficiency. The jingle is that the allowed secured claim equals the amount of the debt or the value of the collateral, whichever is less. This isn't nearly as good as if Sears had been fully secured and collected the full $5,000, but it isn't nearly as bad as if the whole claim were unsecured and Sears had collected only $500 (the ten cents on the dollar all other unsecured claims got).

b. Interest on the Claim

Another important difference between secured and unsecured creditors is in their entitlement to interest for the period following the filing of the bankruptcy petition. As we saw, both secured and unsecured creditors are entitled to prepetition interest, assuming that their agreements with the debtor so provide, but an unsecured creditor cannot claim any interest for the period following bankruptcy. Not so with secured creditors. The rich get richer, and some secured creditors can receive postpetition interest under § 506(b), whose explicit grant of postpetition interest trumps the general ban on unmatured interest in § 502(b)(2). Specifically, if the secured creditor is *oversecured*, i.e., if the value of its collateral exceeds the full pre-bankruptcy debt (including pre-bankruptcy interest), then it can receive post-bankruptcy interest, generally at its contract rate, until the value of the collateral is exhausted.

In the scenarios above, Sears could have collected interest in the first but not in the second. In the first, where the net value of the lawnmower ($6,000) exceeded the allowed claim ($5,000), Sears would have had an allowed secured claim for $5,000 and it would have collected postpetition interest on that amount during the pending bankruptcy (sometimes called *pendency* interest). As the bankruptcy wore on, Sears could have its allowed interest grow and augment its secured claim until it reached a total claim amount that matched the collateral's net value. In our example, Sears could get up to another $1,000 in postpetition interest. If the bankruptcy dragged on after that point, it would then be in the same interest-deprived boat as unsecured creditors. In the second scenario, in which the claim exceeded the value of the collateral, Sears could not have collected any postpetition interest. This point emphasizes that being a secured creditor is not an abstract status but an entitlement to a priority claim on the value of a certain asset.

c.   Complications with the Claim: Attorneys' Fees

Not only do the rich get richer under § 506, they get positively spoiled. Attorneys' fees incurred prior to the bankruptcy filing are treated the same as prepetition interest: if a creditor, secured or unsecured, is entitled to prepetition attorneys' fees by contract or state law at the moment of bankruptcy, then the fees are part of the creditor's allowed (secured or unsecured) claim. Secured creditors who are oversecured, however, are also entitled to *postpetition* attorneys' fees, similar to postpetition interest, until the total claim exceeds the remaining value of the collateral. § 506(b). Even so, those fees must still be provided for by the contract and reasonable.

JONES v. WELLS FARGO BANK, N.A. (In re JONES)
366 B.R. 584 (Bankr. E.D. La. 2007)

MAGNER, Bankruptcy Judge.

. . .

4. ASSESSMENT OF POSTPETITION FEES AND CHARGES . . .

b. Post-Confirmation Fees and Charges

Therefore, a creditor's right to assess postpetition attorney's fees and charges is prescribed by state law and the terms of its contract with Debtor. Unless allowed under state law and Wells Fargo's documents, no fee or charge may be assessed. The postpetition . . . charges and fees assessed by Wells Fargo are itemized as: 1) attorney's fees, 2) statutory expenses, and 3) inspection charges. Under the terms of the Wells Fargo Note and mortgage, Wells Fargo was entitled to charge Debtor's account for attorney's fees and inspection charges incurred in connection with the loan.

Beyond the actual right to charge the amounts requested, the Wells Fargo documents also require that the assessments be reasonable. *See,* Exh. 2, Mortgage of Wells Fargo, page 8, ¶7 (Lender or its agent may make reasonable inspections of the property), page 8, ¶9 (if borrower fails to perform or if there is a significant proceeding that may affect lender's rights such as bankruptcy, lender may do *whatever is reasonable* to protect its interests in the property and borrower will be obligated to reimburse lender for said expenses, including reasonable attorney's fees); Wells Fargo Note, ¶9 (borrower commits to reimburse lender for costs of collection including *reasonable* attorney's fees) (emphasis supplied).

Under Louisiana law, the creditor bears the burden of establishing its debt. Additionally, the fees and charges must be reasonable. The right to seek reimbursement for a charge is not the equivalent of an unfettered right to assess the charge against the loan. For example, Louisiana law provides that attorney's fees and charges may be contractually authorized, but even if contractually allowed, their assessment must be reasonable. Thus, both under the terms of the Wells Fargo Note and mortgage and Louisiana law, this Court reviews the charges and fees assessed for reasonableness.

At trial, Wells Fargo offered no evidence as to the nature of the attorney's fees imposed post confirmation or their reasonableness. It neglected to produce invoices identifying the counsel who performed the services or any description regarding the services performed, time spent, or amounts charged. As a result, the Court cannot determine the reasonableness of the fees incurred because the Court was given no evidence as to what services were performed, much less why they were necessary. Wells Fargo simply failed to meet its burden of proof on this issue. Therefore, the attorney's fees . . . are denied.

At trial, Wells Fargo offered no explanation or evidence to support its "statutory charge" of $106.58. Therefore, it is also disallowed.

Following the institution of this case, Wells Fargo ordered sixteen (16) inspections against Debtor's property during the twenty-nine (29) months the case was pending and Wells Fargo's debt remained outstanding. Wells Fargo testified that, upon default, the employee in charge of administering the loan had discretion to order an inspection as often as he or she deemed advisable. . . . Throughout this period, the reports reflect that the property was generally in good condition. In fact, there is little to no change in the property's condition from month to month reflected in the reporting. Under questioning by Debtor's counsel, Wells Fargo's representative could not list a single reason why an inspection would have been ordered post-petition. . . . The inspection reports change little from month to month, and nothing in them gives cause for concern. Thus, nothing in the reports justified continued monitoring. Given Wells Fargo's failure to explain the necessity of the services or their reasonableness, the charges may not be assessed against Debtor's account. Exhibit "C" to this Opinion reflects the post-filing loan history for this debt after taking into account the above findings. All postpetition charges not previously approved by the Court and denied as set forth in this Opinion have been removed from the history.

The entitlement of *undersecured* creditors to postpetition attorneys' fees is less clear. In our view, which is widely but by no means universally shared, undersecured creditors (like unsecured creditors) cannot claim postpetition attorneys' fees. The reason is that postpetition claims are governed by § 503 of the Code, which only allows attorneys' fees under specific circumstances. (Recall § 502 deals with the calculation of regular prepetition claims against the estate.) Our conclusion is supported by § 506(b), which explicitly grants postpetition attorneys' fees to oversecured creditors, thus showing that Congress knows how to grant postpetition fees when it so desires. There is no analog to § 506(b) for undersecured (or unsecured) creditors. Notwithstanding what we believe to be a fairly clear statement in the Code, the case law is somewhat confused. Cases holding to the contrary hang on the specific disallowance of unmatured (e.g., postpetition) interest in § 502(b)(2). These cases observe that there is no proscription of unmatured attorneys' fees in § 502(b)'s disallowance list.

Unfortunately, this situation became more muddled after the Supreme Court's decision in Travelers Casualty & Ins. Co. v. Pacific Gas & Electric Co., 549 U.S. 443 (2007). The Court upheld postpetition attorneys' fees in an unsecured claim, but in a bizarre procedural posture, in which it admitted it did not address § 506(b)'s textual relevance (whoops!), but explained somewhat defensively it was only because the parties forgot to plead it in time. (Civ Pro 1, Bankruptcy 0.) For a careful analysis, see Mark S. Scarberry, Interpreting Bankruptcy Code Sections 502 and 506: Post-Petition Attorneys' Fees in a Post-Travelers World, 15 Am. Bankr. Inst. L. Rev. 611 (2007). Incredibly, two circuits have tried to "follow" *Travelers* and cheerfully held postpetition fees are recoverable by unsecured creditors. See Ogle v. Fidelity & Deposit Company of Maryland, 586 F.3d 143 (2d Cir. 2009) (postpetition attorney's fees allowed to unsecured creditor because "deemed" to arise prepetition); In re SNTL Corp., 571 F.3d 826 (9th Cir. 2009) (permissibility of postpetition fees depends on *state* law). Sigh.

d. Postpetition Claims

Can the trustee grant liens to secure debts postpetition, thus creating a *postpetition* secured claim (i.e., can the trustee buy that paint at Sears and grant a security interest in it)? The answer is yes, but under very constrained circumstances (and complex enough to warrant their own assignment, which we provide later on in the business section).

C. DISPUTING CLAIMS

The most frequent challenge by a debtor or trustee is that there was no valid debt under state law or that the amount of the debt was lower than claimed, either through calculation error or setoff (e.g., the lawnmower Sears sold was defective). But challenges are rare. In a study of mortgage claims in chapter 13 cases filed by homeowners—where high stakes would suggest closer scrutiny—one of us found only 4% of claims drew objections, despite facial defects in paperwork and other failures in rule compliance. Katherine Porter, Misbehavior and Mistake in Bankruptcy Mortgage Claims, 87 Tex. L. Rev. 168 (2008) (*Misbehavior*). The rarity of objections is likely because lawyers aren't free. Similarly, once a debtor has filed for bankruptcy, if the claim is to be discharged anyway, the debtor may have little incentive to spend money fighting rather than settling a claim. Of course, the debtor's loss of interest in whether he is going to discharge $2,859 or $2,589 in unsecured credit card debt—he's too busy doing a little discharge dance—is precisely why the trustee must review the claims; accepting the larger amount means a bigger piece of the pie for the claiming creditor but a smaller piece for the others, and the trustee keeps things fair.

In the rare case of objection, the dispute is resolved as a "contested matter" by motion under Rule 9014. In the event of a dispute, fact-finding and dispute resolution is quick. Courts usually consider the papers filed by the parties and schedule an hour or two to hear evidence. Occasionally, the objection involves the sort of demand that bumps it up to the more formalized "adversary proceeding" under Rule 7001, which creates a full federal lawsuit within the bankruptcy (an "adversary proceeding") beginning with service of a complaint and all the rest.

As mentioned above, claims disputes are actually increasing in the brave new world of debt trading. We believe this has been especially fueled by *securitization*, especially in the residential mortgage market and the commercial leveraged loan market (of which more later). What's securitization? Simply: selling stakes in loans. More complexly: it starts with a lender making a loan to a homeowner for a home mortgage. The thought of that lender keeping that loan while the debtor repays for decades is now, in many circles, charmingly quaint. Instead, the lender packages up its loans and sells them, just as a manufacturer boxes up radios from an assembly line for sale. The buyers are entities, who in turn sell shares of the bundle of loans they bought. Technically, the loan bundles are often put into a trust, which then sells ownership interests (securities) to investors.

The investors don't bear equal risk of nonpayment. Rather, the trust is sliced into tranches, with the lowest-risk (and most expensive) securities taking the first set of mortgage payments that come in for the month, and the riskiest (and cheapest) taking the last payments (or no payments if the riskiest debtors default). These securitization trusts work the same way investors in corporations with different risk appetites might buy bonds, preferred, or common stock. When the underlying loans in the trust are secured debts, the securities issued by the trust are *asset-backed securities*, of which *mortgage-backed securities* are a specific type. For more detail on securitization, see generally Steven Schwarcz, Bruce Markell & Lisa Broome, Securitization, Structured Finance and Capital Markets (2001).

Securitization is so complicated, the trusts even need specialists whose sole job is to keep track of all the underlying debtors and process their monthly payments, making sure they go to the right place. These *servicers* are the ones who interact with the homeowner on the phone and by mail, but they as servicers actually have no ownership of the underlying mortgages and so have limited investment in the fate of the debtor. This is a *simplified* version of a securitization chart:

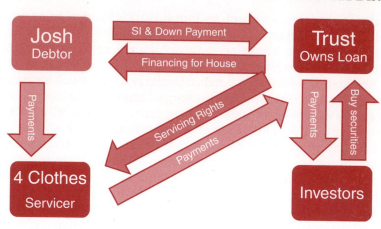

As one court candidly observes:

> The securitization of home mortgage loans has divorced the lending community from borrowers. Not only are the new holders of the mortgage notes nontraditional lenders, but a mortgage service provider is a buffer in the relationship between lender and borrower. The holders of notes do not see themselves as lenders, but investors in an asset. They have little interest in the relationship between lender and borrower except as it might affect their return on investment.
>
> Mortgage service providers administer notes for a fee. The terms of their agreements with investors, as well as the guidelines the investors set for administration of the loan, have ramifications for the borrower. Most servicing agreements allow the service provider to charge a flat fee, usually stated as a percentage of the portfolio under administration. All principal and interest payments collected are paid to the note holder. Usually, fees are additional income to the service provider while costs are simply a pass through, or reimbursable items. In addition, servicers invest the "float," or funds held on deposit, and retain earnings on that investment. Therefore, amounts held in escrow or in debtor suspense are an additional source of revenue for the servicer. While a mortgage service provider and note holder's interests are closely aligned, they are not perfectly aligned. It is in a mortgage service provider's interest to collect fees and hold funds, both of which generate additional income for its account. Conversely, a note holder or investor is interested in the collection and application of payments to principal and interest.

In re Stewart, 391 B.R. 327, 335-36 (Bankr. E.D. La. 2008), 2009 WL 2448054 (E.D. La. Aug. 7, 2009), *vacated in part, appeal dismissed in part*, 647 F.3d 553 (5th Cir. 2011).

Servicers are thus more likely to drive homeowners into foreclosure given their divergent incentives than the actual loan owners. Fees, delay, and miscommunication create problems. This is because the sheer complexity of the securitization process provides both increased risk of genuine error (lots of changing of hands so chances to mistype numbers, likely compounded by the need to rely on rote automation) as well as an incentive to cut corners or even to defraud (lots of paperwork to hide behind in byzantine file systems). This in turn means more disputes in bankruptcy that will come to a head in the claims process. In the great mortgage crisis of 2007-2010, for example, it is not surprising some of the first problems became exposed in the bankruptcy courts, which play an important watch-guard role for consumer protection.

Mr. Jones, whom we have seen struggling with the chaos created by his mortgage lender, Wells Fargo, had only begun to suffer. In the next episode, midway through his chapter 13 bankruptcy plan, he tried to refinance his mortgage. The payoff statement that Wells Fargo sent to close out the prior loan stated a balance he thought was suspiciously high. When Jones called Wells Fargo, it stalled and gave answers that he found to be evasive. He brought an action in bankruptcy court to obtain a correct accounting. Even that proved near-impenetrable, which the court said "resulted in such a tangled mess that neither Debtor, who is a certified public accountant, nor Wells Fargo's own representative could fully understand or explain the accounting offered."

======= In re JONES (cont'd) =======

I. FACTUAL FINDINGS

Debtor filed a voluntary petition for relief under Chapter 13 of the Bankruptcy Code on August 26, 2003. At the time of his filing, Debtor was obligated to Wells Fargo on a debt secured by his residence. Prior to the institution of this case, Wells Fargo had filed a foreclosure action against Debtor in State Court. . . . It also filed a proof of claim setting forth the amounts owed by Debtor as of the petition date. The proof of claim contained a schedule reflecting the following prepetition amounts as due:

1. Eight (8) mortgage payments totaling $18,796.19
2. Accrued late charges $823.04
3. Foreclosure fees $750.00
4. Court costs $1,283.87
5. Inspection fees $60.00
6. Escrow shortage $111.59
7. Broker's price opinion charges $435.00
     Total $22,259.69.

Attached to the proof of claim was a copy of an adjustable rate note dated April 4, 2001, evidencing the Wells Fargo debt ("Wells Fargo Note").

Debtor's plan of reorganization provided for payments to the Chapter 13 Trustee ("Trustee") of $2,105.35 per month for thirty-six months followed by a final payment of $625.97. From these payments, Wells Fargo was to be repaid on the prepetition arrearage represented by Wells Fargo's proof of claim. . . . [The debtor was also paying his ongoing regular monthly mortgage payments in addition to the payments on arrearages.—Eds.]

II. LAW AND ANALYSIS

A. Calculation of Amounts Due Under the Wells Fargo Note

The indebtedness due to Wells Fargo is represented by an adjustable rate note dated April 4, 2001. The interest rate on the Wells Fargo Note is based on a published financial index plus 8.25%. . . .

1. Prepetition Debt Calculation

A review of Wells Fargo's accounting from the date of the loan's inception until the petition date reveals several accounting errors. These errors can be generally described as: 1) simple mathematical errors and 2) mistakes in the amount Wells Fargo reported were incurred. There do not appear to be any errors caused by an improper calculation of interest as the loan's effective interest rate was constant through the date the last prepetition payment was received in December of 2002. The first mistake in the calculation of the prepetition arrearage involved Wells Fargo's representations as to the amount of foreclosure costs it incurred. . . . [The court made several adjustments due to errors in the way the claim calculated the amount owed for escrow, which are payments made for taxes, insurance, and the like, as well as foreclosure costs and other prepetition charges.—Eds.] The end result is that as of January 4, 2006, Wells Fargo was owed a prepetition past due balance of $2,251.21.

2. Assessment of Additional Prepetition Charges

Wells Fargo has also added to its prepetition arrearage, without amendment to its proof of claim or disclosure to the Trustee or Court, additional prepetition charges. [These charges included recoupment of commissions charged by the sheriff. Wells Fargo was later embarrassed by the sheriff's testimony that the sheriff does not charge these commissions if the debtor is in bankruptcy per longstanding and well-known protocol.—Eds.]

3. Calculation of Postpetition Debt

Starting on August 26, 2003, Debtor's loan was current. From that date forward, Debtor's past due account was "zeroed out" because the arrearage was payable through the plan. Therefore, Debtor's postpetition balance consisted of only principal, or $213,949.06, and Debtor's next installment was due for September 1, 2003.

Initially, Debtor's case did not go well. Because Debtor suffered a heart attack in November 2003, he immediately fell behind in his direct payments to Wells Fargo. These payments were aggregated into the Consent Order Sum, once again bringing Debtor's account current by agreement.

Wells Fargo's subsequent actions, however, caused Debtor to pay almost $13,000.00 in additional interest charges over the life of the plan. Throughout the succeeding years, Debtor made his payments in the amounts directed by Wells Fargo. However, rather than apply the amounts received to the postpetition installments for which they were intended, Wells Fargo applied them to prepetition installments, prepetition costs or fees, and postpetition charges not authorized or disclosed to Debtor, the Court, or the Trustee. . . .

The result was the addition of significant interest charges not really due and a loan balance out of sync with the actual amounts owed.

4. Assessment of Postpetition Fees and Charges

POSTPETITION, PRECONFIRMATION FEES

Postpetition charges incurred prior to confirmation may be included in the debts necessary to cure a default under a plan. Therefore, they must be disclosed and are subject to review by the bankruptcy court for reasonableness. . . . [Several were not disclosed.—Eds.]

VIOLATIONS OF THE STAY

Wells Fargo charged Debtor's account with unreasonable fees and costs; failed to notify Debtor that any of these postpetition charges were being added to his account; failed to seek Court approval for same; and paid itself out of estate funds delivered to it for the payment of other debt. All of this was accomplished without notifying anyone, Debtor, the Trustee, or the Court, that Wells Fargo was assessing postpetition charges and diverting estate funds for their satisfaction. . . .

IV. Conclusion

For the above stated reasons, this Court determines that the amount owed by Debtor on the loan as of January 4, 2006, was $207,013.32 and that the collection of $231,463.97 from Debtor at the closing of his refinancing was substantially in excess of the sums due. As a result, Wells Fargo owed Debtor the full sum of $24,450.65 as of January 4, 2006. Since $7,598.64 was returned on April 20, 2006, a remaining balance of $16,852.01 is still outstanding and due to Debtor. For the reasons set forth above, Wells Fargo will be ordered to return the sum of $16,852.01 in accordance with this Opinion. The amounts due will bear interest at the legal rate from date of judicial demand until paid in full.

Debtor's request for damages incurred as a loss of personal time are denied because he did not prove at trial that he suffered any monetary loss as a result of the time he spent working. Although Debtor testified that he spent nights and weekends working on this matter, there was no testimony that he missed work or incurred a loss of income due to the time he spent. [A hearing on sanctions for violation of the automatic stay was held, and the judge entered an order compelling Wells Fargo to clean up its accounting procedures in lieu of sanctions.—Eds.]

It took a diligent court quite some time to untangle a mess that Wells Fargo itself could not explain. Had the debtor not been a CPA refinancing his home, and represented by counsel, would he have even known in the first place to challenge a payoff statement that was off by tens of thousands of dollars? Do we have systemic dysfunction, or is Wells Fargo just the one bad apple? One study reports:

Using original data from 1,700 recent Chapter 13 bankruptcy cases, I conclude that mortgage companies frequently do not comply with bankruptcy law. A majority of mortgage claims are missing one or more of the required pieces of documentation for a bankruptcy claim. Furthermore, fees and charges on claims often are poorly identified, making it impossible to verify if such fees are legally permissible or accurate. In nearly all cases, debtors and mortgage companies disagree on the amount of outstanding mortgage debt.

Porter, *Misbehavior*, at 121.

D.   THE INSTITUTIONAL FUNCTION OF THE CLAIMS PROCESS

This assignment began with an analysis of the claims filing and calculation process. It may appear to be a dry and technical area of bankruptcy law, crawling with numbers and percent signs, but that should not mask an important socio-legal truth: bankruptcy is a public proceeding (sometimes a spectacle) in a court of law. While many debtors are mortified to see the details of their financial lives splashed across the pages of the bankruptcy reporters, lenders too find themselves coming under open scrutiny. Wells Fargo's curious "statutory charge"—we would guess charged on the account of any homeowner who files bankruptcy—and unnecessary inspections and sheriff's commissions left the *Jones* court nonplussed; its hidden charges on the postpetition workout plan—incurred seemingly out of thin air and with no notice to the debtor, trustee, or court—made the court irate. And this is the tip of the iceberg. Some of what has come to light in bankruptcy courts and in state courts processing mortgage foreclosure suits has been shocking to even the most jaded observers of commercial law.

Now more from the folks at Wells Fargo, who were doubtless delighted to face Judge Magner once again.

In re STEWART
391 B.R. 327 (Bankr. E.D. La. 2008)

MAGNER, Bankruptcy Judge.

LAW AND ANALYSIS

Damages and Sanctions Accounting and Administrative Abuses

. . .

The reconciliation of Debtor's account took Wells Fargo four months to research and three hearings before this Court to explain. An account history was not produced until two months after the filing of the Objection. An additional two months were spent obtaining the necessary information to explain or establish the substantial charges, costs, and fees reflected on the account.

In the end, Wells Fargo charged nine (9) BPOs [Broker Price Opinions—Eds.] to Debtor's account but could only produce two corresponding reports. At least three sets of BPOs were duplicative of each other; two BPOs were probably never performed due to the closure of Jefferson parish following Hurricane Katrina; and all contained hidden fees for Wells Fargo disguised as costs. Only two BPOs were ultimately accepted as validly performed.

Wells Fargo charged Debtor with forty-four (44) inspections; the Court allowed one (1). Wells Fargo also charged Debtor forty-nine (49) late charges; only ten (10) of which were approved. Almost every disallowed inspection and late fee was imposed while Debtor was making regular monthly payments [in the bankruptcy], was assessed under circumstances contrary to Wells Fargo's stated policies or the Note's terms, and was unreasonable under the circumstances. Substantial legal fees were also claimed without over $1,800.00 in credits being posted.

The calculation of Debtor's monthly escrow was almost incomprehensible and virtually incorrect in every instance. This caused Wells Fargo to demand substantially erroneous and increased payments from Debtor. But one of the most troubling problems with the accounting delivered by Wells Fargo was the preference for the payment of fees and charges over escrow, principal, and interest payments in contravention of the Note and Mortgage's clear terms. . . .

Improper Conduct in Connection with Bankruptcy Filings

Although Wells Fargo was specifically asked to reconcile the amounts reflected on its prior proofs of claim with the amounts claimed on its account history, it did not. A review by the Court revealed why: the proofs of claim filed in the 2004 and 2007 Bankruptcies were so significantly erroneous that a reconciliation was not possible. Charges for NSF [nonsufficient funds—Eds.] fees, tax searches, property preservation fees, and unapproved bankruptcy fees appeared on the proofs of claim filed in this and previous cases without explanation or substantiation. Further, these charges never appeared as entries on the account history. . . .

. . .

The Court finds that Wells Fargo was negligent in its practices and took insufficient remedial action following this Court's rulings in *Jones v. Wells Fargo* to remedy problems with its accounting. . . . In order to rectify this problem in the future, the Court orders Wells Fargo to audit every proof of claim it has filed in this District in any case pending on or filed after April 13, 2007, and to provide a complete loan history on every account. For every debtor with a case still pending in the District, the loan histories shall be filed into the claims register and Wells Fargo is ordered to amend, where necessary, the proofs of claim already on file to comply with the principles established in this case and *Jones.* For closed cases, Wells Fargo is ordered to deliver to Debtor, Debtor's counsel and Trustee a copy of the accounting.

The Court will enter an administrative order for the review of these accountings and proofs of claim. The Court reserves the right, if warranted after an initial review of the accountings, proofs of claim and any amended claims filed of record, to appoint experts, at Wells Fargo's expense, to review each accounting and submit recommendations to the Court for further adjustments based on the principles set forth in this Memorandum Opinion and *Jones.*

Wells Fargo seemed to have dodged a bullet, with a clearly exasperated judge (once again) only ordering an accounting slap on the wrist in lieu of sanctions. Incredibly, *it appealed*—to protest the constitutional indignity of having a non-life-tenured bankruptcy judge issue such creative relief. The Fifth Circuit ultimately agreed and vacated the order. This meant the *Jones* decision, still pending on appeal with its similar injunction, was vacated too. Thus, thanks to a like-minded Court of Appeals panel and a tireless litigation strategy, Wells Fargo got just what it asked for.

JONES v. WELLS FARGO HOME MORTGAGE INC. (In re JONES)

2012 WL 1155715 (Bankr. E.D. La. Apr. 5, 2012)

MAGNER, Bankruptcy Judge.

This matter is on remand from the United States Court of Appeals for the Fifth Circuit ("Fifth Circuit"). . . . The mandate required reconsideration of monetary sanctions in light of *In re Stewart.*

. . .

II. PROCEDURAL BACKGROUND

. . .

This Court previously found that Wells Fargo willfully violated the automatic stay imposed by 11 U.S.C. § 362. That ruling is not at issue. The only issue before the Court is the appropriate relief available. In light of the Fifth Circuit's ruling in *Stewart*, the application of the Accounting Procedures to all debtors in the district would be an improper exercise of authority beyond the bounds of this case. Because this relief was ordered *in lieu* of punitive sanctions, the mandate on remand directs that monetary relief be considered. . . .

A. *Degree of Reprehensibility*

. . .

The net effect of Wells Fargo's actions was an overcharge in excess of $24,000.00. When Jones questioned the amounts owed, Wells Fargo refused to explain its calculations or provide an amortization schedule. When Jones sued Wells Fargo, it again failed to properly account for its calculations. After judgment was awarded, Wells Fargo fought the compensatory portion of the award despite never challenging the calculations of the overpayment. In fact, Wells Fargo's initial legal position both before this Court and in its first appeal denied any responsibility to refund payments demanded in error! The cost to Jones was hundreds of thousands of dollars in legal fees and five (5) years of litigation. . . .

Wells Fargo has taken the position that every debtor in the district should be made to challenge, by separate suit, the proofs of claim or motions for relief from the automatic stay it files. It has steadfastly refused to audit its pleadings or proofs of claim for errors and has refused to voluntarily correct any errors that come to light except through threat of litigation. Although its own representatives have admitted that it routinely misapplied payments on loans and improperly charged fees, they have refused to correct past errors. They stubbornly insist on limiting any change in their conduct prospectively, even as they seek to collect on loans in other cases for amounts owed in error.

Wells Fargo's conduct is clandestine. Rather than provide Jones with a complete history of his debt on an ongoing basis, Wells Fargo simply stopped communicating with Jones once it deemed him in default. At that point in time, fees and costs were assessed against his account and satisfied with postpetition payments intended for other debt without notice. Only through litigation was this practice discovered. Wells Fargo admitted to the same practices for all other loans in bankruptcy or default. As a result, it is unlikely that most debtors will be able to discern problems with their accounts without extensive discovery.

Unfortunately, the threat of future litigation is a poor motivator for honesty in practice. Because litigation with Wells Fargo has already cost this and other plaintiffs considerable time and expense, the Court can only assume that others who challenge Wells Fargo's claims will meet a similar fate.

Over eighty percent (80%) of the chapter 13 debtors in this district have incomes of less than $40,000.00 per year. The burden of extensive discovery and delay is particularly overwhelming. In this Court's experience, it takes four (4) to six (6) months for Wells Fargo to produce a simple accounting of a loan's history and over four (4) court hearings. Most debtors simply do not have the personal resources to demand the production of a simple accounting for their loans, much less verify its accuracy, through a litigation process.

Wells Fargo has taken advantage of borrowers who rely on it to accurately apply payments and calculate the amounts owed. But perhaps more disturbing is Wells Fargo's refusal to voluntarily correct its errors. It prefers to rely on the ignorance of borrowers or their inability to fund a challenge to its demands, rather than voluntarily relinquish gains obtained through improper accounting methods. Wells Fargo's conduct was a breach of its contractual obligations to its borrowers. More importantly, when exposed, it revealed its true corporate character by denying any obligation to correct its past transgressions and mounting a legal assault ensured it never had to. . . .

VI. CONCLUSION

Wells Fargo's actions were not only highly reprehensible, but its subsequent reaction on their exposure has been less than satisfactory. . . . [T]he Court finds that a punitive damage award of $3,171,154.00 is warranted to deter Wells Fargo from similar conduct in the future. This Court hopes that the relief granted will finally motivate Wells Fargo to rectify its practices and comply with the terms of court orders, plans and the automatic stay.

——————————————

Drinks on Jones and Stewart! Incidentally, how expensive would it have been to reprogram the "proprietary software" that Wells Fargo pointed to in explaining its procedures in bankruptcy cases? If less than $3 million, Wells Fargo goofed. Apparently not a company to change strategies lightly, Wells Fargo appealed the sanction award. The decision was upheld. Jones v. Wells Fargo Home Mortgage, 489 B.R. 645 (E.D. La. 2013).

For all its problems, Wells Fargo is only one mortgage servicer. But the problems with de-linked lending and mass processing of debts have extended across much of the industry and many of its practices. Another illustration of these problems lies in the apparently simple process of transferring the consumer's note from each originating bank to the securitization trust. That process creates a chain of title showing who actually owns what interest in each note. Because an actual human being has to execute those transfer documents, curious developments have arisen. To wit, some banks hired minimum-wage "robo-signers" to sign the name of purported corporate officers hundreds of times per hour in soulless monotony. One company, DOCX, specialized in the logistics of these mortgage transfers (and foreclosure affidavits, which require a sworn signature), had the absurdity of its forgeries exposed when it was discovered that someone named "Linda Green" had apparently executed a considerable percentage of all mortgage transfer documents in the entire United States. For an excellent report, see the expose at *60 Minutes: The Next Housing Shock* (CBS television broadcast Aug. 7, 2011), *available at* https://www.cbsnews.com/news/mortgage-paperwork-mess-next-housing-shock-07-08-2011/, which includes tracking down the actual Ms. Linda Green, a mail room clerk, whose name was apparently chosen for its brevity and ease in remembering by robo-signers.

When the mortgage default rate skyrocketed in the Great Recession and homeowners found themselves in state court foreclosure and federal bankruptcy proceedings, these brazen legal violations were finally discovered. (Warren Buffett says that it is only when the tide goes out that we discover who was swimming nude.) We end by letting these pictures speak a thousand words for themselves about the high-volume world of consumer collection that the bankruptcy claims process helps reveal.

Problem Set 6

6.1. Corinne Zeppo lost her job last month and filed a chapter 7 bankruptcy last week. One creditor, Miller Plumbing Co., claimed $3,000, plus (a) $200 in past-due interest accrued prior to bankruptcy; and (b) another $100 in interest accrued since the bankruptcy began. Interest was calculated for the pre-bankruptcy period according to the contract between Zeppo and Miller Plumbing and according to the state law judgment rate for the post-bankruptcy period. Miller Plumbing, however, has no security interest in any of Corinne's property. What is the amount of Miller's allowed unsecured claim in bankruptcy? See § 502(a), (b).

6.2. Corinne had only two non-exempt assets: her car, worth $10,000, and 1,000 shares of MacroSoft stock, worth $15,000. At the time of filing, she owed her bank $8,000 on the car, and the bank had a valid and enforceable security interest in the car to secure its loan. In addition to the $8,000 principal, the bank claimed (a) past-due interest that accrued prior to bankruptcy of $500; (b) interest since the bankruptcy was filed of $400; and (c) attorneys' fees of $1,000 expended in trying to collect. The bank was entitled to collect all these amounts under its loan and security agreement and under state law. What is the amount of the bank's allowed secured claim in bankruptcy? See §§ 502(b), 506(a), (b).

6.3. If, contrary to the pre-sale estimates, the car had brought only $5,000 when it was sold, how would the bank stand? See §§ 502(b), 506 (a), (b).

6.4. Ten other unsecured creditors of Corinne are owed a total of $20,000, but none of them is claiming any interest. If you were appointed trustee and collected $5,000 for the car and $15,000 for the stock, how should you distribute the money (ignoring costs, including your own fee as trustee)?

6.5. Josh Clark has missed four months of mortgage payments and received default notices from Four Clothes Loan Servicing, which services the mortgage for a securitization trust. The house was bought a few years ago for $150,000 and Josh's balance is now down to $140,000. But the property values in the area have fallen sharply since Josh purchased the home.

You are in charge of Default Servicing at Four Clothes, and upon reviewing Josh's file, your interest is piqued by several things: that a Default Relationship Manager made several calls to Josh around 10:00 p.m. to encourage him to make a payment, that the debtor has recently sent in several amounts constituting partial payments that are sitting in a suspense account rather than having been applied to the loan balance, and that inspections have been ordered weekly, pursuant to standard operating procedure. The mortgage agreement allows Josh to be billed "reasonable fees" should Josh's mortgage ever go into default, and the servicing agreement allows the servicer to agree to "reasonable" financial workouts and to bill the investors for its "reasonable" time in doing so. It gets a fixed fee (generally higher) if it has to initiate a foreclosure. State law forbids deficiency judgments against homeowners after foreclosure sales.

Josh's lawyer, Garth Ceia, just called to say that Josh has gotten a better job. He proposes a repayment plan: all penalty charges and interest will be waived, and Josh can complete "catch-up" payments over 12 months in addition to resumption of his regular monthly payments. He needs to know by the day after tomorrow, though, because Josh will file for bankruptcy if he can't get his mortgage situation worked out, as he also faces the threat of an overdue credit card lender garnishing his wages unless he starts making payments on the judgment immediately—something he can't do without a reduced mortgage payment. What do you think? What if it will take you a week to order Josh's original mortgage loan documents from archives?

PRIORITY AMONG UNSECURED CREDITORS

Although secured creditors have priority only in their collateral, their security interests often swallow virtually all the value in an estate, making secured credit the highest priority of them all. If there is value remaining, however, the trustee distributes that value to the unsecured creditors. The secured creditors who were undersecured because the sale of their collateral did not satisfy their allowed secured claims also receive distributions in this process.

Because many unsecured creditors have not received priority by contract as the secured creditors have, Congress in § 507 determines the appropriate order and amount of the payout to them. The creditors again find that "equity is equality" is not strictly the rule. Some unsecured creditors are, by congressional preference, paid ahead of other unsecured creditors. In creating this priority scheme, does Congress (a) simply solve a collective action problem among private parties who cannot contract for priority among themselves; (b) serve broader public interests; (c) simply respond to various political pressures; or (d) some of each? Consider these possible justifications as you read the priority rules in § 507.

In the great majority of liquidation cases, only priority creditors even have a shot at getting a distribution or *dividend* from the estate under § 726, and often they don't get anything. In the minority of cases in which there is enough value left, creditors may be willing to litigate, if necessary, to get paid in the order and amount to which they believe the law entitles them. Note too that this priority scheme applies indirectly in large chapter 11 cases, where there is plenty to fight over.

Problem Set 7

Harold Smith declared chapter 7 bankruptcy on April 7, 2020. His non-exempt assets consisted of his vacation condo in Kitty Hawk, which the trustee sold for $400,000 but which was subject to a $360,000 mortgage, and miscellaneous personal property that sold for $25,000 after expenses of sale. All his other property was exempt. The claims filed in bankruptcy court were the following:

1. John Nelson, a private duty nurse whom Harold hired while his father was seriously ill: $16,000.
2. Social Security Administration, Social Security deducted from John's earlier paychecks: $1,600.
3. City of Eden, property taxes: $3,000 per year for the last three years, plus $500 penalties per year for the three years—the standard fee for any delay in paying.
4. George Nartowski, down payment against a tractor lawnmower Harold had agreed to sell to George but had not yet given him: $300.
5. State Department of Revenue and IRS, income taxes: state $4,000, federal $14,000.
6. Telephone, utility, and other regular bills following bankruptcy: $3,000.
7. Sara Fleet, Harold's attorney: $1,750 in fees ($500 for a will; $1,250 for preparing this bankruptcy filing).
8. Sue Smith, Harold's ex-wife, negotiable note: $25,000.
9. First Bank of Seminole, deficiency on Harold's car loan after the car was sold prior to bankruptcy: $2,200.
10. Trustee's fee for administering estate and performing legal work for it: $4,000.
11. Insurance premiums for insurance on the non-exempt personal property prior to its sale by the trustee: $750.
12. Costs of sale of Harold's non-exempt real estate, including advertising: $2,800.
13. Harold missed a stop sign, but didn't miss the pedestrian crossing the street. The jury verdict against him was $10,000.
14. Other unsecured claims: $7,000.

Who will get what under §§ 507 and 726(a)(4), (b)?

DISCHARGE

A. THE POST-DISCHARGE INJUNCTION

As the debtor's non-exempt assets are liquidated by the trustee and the creditors receive their dividends (if any), the debtor gets a discharge. The discharge enjoins most, but not all, creditor conduct after bankruptcy, the same way as the automatic stay enjoins creditor conduct during bankruptcy. Technically, the judge grants the debtor the discharge to trigger the § 524 injunction. § 727; *cf.* §§ 944, 1141, 1228, 1328 (parallel provisions).

The post-discharge injunction is not simply "Automatic Stay, the Sequel." Once again, the differential treatment of unsecured and secured creditors is stark, as the case below explains. Chapter 7 enjoins all further action by unsecured creditors, but secured creditors can spring back to action with respect to collateral because a lien is typically unaffected by the bankruptcy.

In re HENRY
266 B.R. 457 (Bankr. C.D. Cal. 2001)

BUFFORD, Bankruptcy Judge.

. . .

B. DISCHARGE INJUNCTION VIOLATIONS — § 524(a)(2)

The automatic stay in a bankruptcy case does not last indefinitely. In a chapter 7 case for an individual, the automatic stay terminates when a discharge is granted or denied. In this case the discharge was granted on March 9, 1998. Upon the grant of a discharge, the automatic stay is replaced with the discharge injunction provided by § 524(a).

The discharge injunction provision relevant to this case is § 524(a)(2), which provides that a bankruptcy discharge "operates as an injunction against an act, to collect, recover or offset any such debt as a personal liability of the debtor, whether or not discharge of such debt is waived." See Molloy v. Primus Automotive Fin. Servs., 247 B.R. 804, 815 (C.D. Cal. 2000).

The discharge injunction is permanent. It survives the bankruptcy case and applies forever with respect to every debt that is discharged. [T]he Senate Report explains the impact of the injunction:

> The injunction is to give complete effect to the discharge and to eliminate any doubt concerning the effect of the discharge as a total prohibition on debt collection efforts. This paragraph cover[s] any act to collect, such as dunning by telephone or letter, or indirectly through friends, relatives, or employers, harassment, threats of repossession and the like.

S. Rep. No. 95-989, at 182-83 (1979). The permanency of the discharge injunction contrasts with the temporary character of the automatic stay.

At the same time, the discharge injunction is narrower than the automatic stay in a material way. . . . While the automatic stay prohibits essentially all creditor collection activities absent court order, the discharge injunction is more selective.

Although the discharge eliminates a debt as a personal liability, it does not affect a lien that provides security for the debt. See § 522(c)(2). Indeed, the law has been settled since 1886 that a discharge in a liquidation bankruptcy case (a chapter 7 case under present law) does not discharge a lien against real or personal property: liens survive or pass through bankruptcy unaffected. See, e.g., Johnson v. Home State Bank, 501 U.S. 78, 83, (1991); Long v. Bullard, 117 U.S. 617, 620 (1886). The Supreme Court expressed the principle as follows in Johnson: "Notwithstanding the discharge, the [secured creditor]'s right to proceed against [the debtor] in rem survived the Chapter 7 liquidation." 501 U.S. at 80. . . .

Johnson dealt with the question of whether a debtor can reorganize a secured debt under chapter 13 after having discharged it in a chapter 7 case. As a prelude to answering this question, the Supreme Court described the nature of the security interest that survives a chapter 7 liquidation as follows:

> A mortgage is an interest in real property that secures a creditor's right to repayment. But unless the debtor and creditor have provided otherwise, the creditor ordinarily is not limited to foreclosure on the mortgaged property throughout the United States, Ch. 176, § 20, 14 Stat. 517 (1867) (repealed 1878). While under Bankruptcy Code § 101(5) a secured claim can now be made, the principle remains valid should the debtor default on his obligation; rather, the creditor may in addition sue to establish the debtor's in personam liability for any deficiency on the debt and may enforce any judgment against the debtor's assets generally. A defaulting debtor can protect himself from personal liability by obtaining a discharge in a Chapter 7 liquidation. However, such a discharge extinguishes only the personal liability of the debtor. Codifying the rule of Long v. Bullard, the Code provides that a creditor's right to foreclose on the mortgage survives or passes through the bankruptcy.

Id. at 83 . . . (citations omitted). . . .

A chapter 7 discharge extinguishes only one mode of enforcing a claim, an action in personam against the debtor. It leaves intact the right to proceed in rem against the property. *Johnson*, 501 U.S. at 84, 111 S. Ct. 2150.

This difference is reflected in the statutory scope of the automatic stay and the discharge injunction. While the automatic stay prohibits any act to enforce a lien against property of the estate, there is no comparable provision in the discharge injunction. Thus the bankruptcy discharge eliminates the personal liability of the debtors on the debt, and converts the loan into a non-recourse loan. See id. at 86-87, 111 S. Ct. 2150. However, the lien on the property remains, and the creditor may proceed to enforce the lien, to the extent authorized by state law, once the automatic stay terminates (whether by operation of law or by order of the court).

In the jargon of the trade (not the Code, as usual), after discharge the debt becomes "nonrecourse," in that the personal liability of the debtor is erased and there can be no suit for a deficiency, but the debt is still secured by the collateral, which the creditor is free to repossess.*

Procedurally, the discharge in chapter 7 lacks pomp. In those courts that still require the debtor to attend, the debtor appears at a hearing before a judge, who will review the bankruptcy file, sign the papers declaring the debtor discharged from all listed debts, and close the case. Such hearings are usually mass affairs, with the judge making a few remarks to dozens of debtors gathered for the occasion. Nearly all courts now dispense with the hearing, instead mailing the discharge papers to the debtor on the theory that requiring a struggling debtor to lose a day's pay to attend a discharge ceremony is wasteful.

---

*We generally loathe footnotes, but serious confusion in the courts requires it here. Saying "the lien stays on" the collateral after discharge leaves open the question just how much that lien is for. To answer that, we start with the bifurcation of undersecured claims into secured and unsecured portions under § 506(a)'s definition of "allowed secured claim." That means, for example, a wholly underwater undersecured creditor (say, a second mortgage holder behind an already undersecured first) has an allowed secured claim of precisely zero. (Is that even a secured claim?) Now look at § 506(d)(2), which seems to say that any lien beyond the allowed secured claim is void. That surely leads to the conclusion that a wholly underwater second mortgage is stripped off the collateral by operation of § 506. Enter the Supreme Court, which held in two baffling chapter 7 decisions that "allowed secured claim" in § 506(d)(2) means something different from how the term is defined three paragraphs north in § 506(a)(1). The result of this "§ 506(d)(2)-only" definition of allowed secured claim is that the lien is not avoided, period, and remains on the collateral after bankruptcy to secure the *full value of the debt*. Quite the opposite result of how you might read the statute. See Bank of Am. NA v. Caulkett, 575 U.S. 790 (2015); Dewsnup v. Timm, 502 U.S. 410 (1992). For various reasons, the full extent of those holdings are unclear, especially its application to chapter 13. You do not need to know more about these cases for now, other than to note that *Caulkett*'s author added a footnote for six Justices suggesting that this line of reasoning was shaky and should probably be overruled (but not overruling it because the debtor did not request it).

B. EXCEPTIONS TO DISCHARGE

Discharge is not a right but a privilege. That said, the overall discharge will be granted unless it is challenged. The trustee or creditors may object to the debtor's discharge of particular debts under § 523 or of all debts under § 727. It is important to see the distinction between a § 523 denial of discharge and one made under § 727. The former renders only one debt nondischargeable (a "rifle shot"), while a denial of discharge under § 727 renders all of the debts nondischargeable (a "shotgun blast"). Global denial of discharge under § 727 leaves a debtor who has turned assets over to the trustee for sale and distribution with no relief from debt other than the actual payments made. Even a rifle shot denial leaves the debtor without complete relief; if the excepted debt was substantial, it may leave the debtor in almost as bad shape as before.

For a creditor, of course, prevention of a discharge is usually the creditor's last remaining hope to receive any payment on the debt. As a result, when the grounds for denial of discharge arise, they are often more hotly disputed than other points of potential conflict in consumer bankruptcies.

The list of nondischargeable debts or the events for which a debtor can be denied any discharge at all continues to grow. In some cases, the growth has come in response to unanticipated abuses that Congress wants to stop. In other cases, special interest groups have lobbied for an exception to the bankruptcy discharge. The categories of specific nondischargeable debts in § 523 presently number 19, a panoply that now includes debts obtained by lying on a credit application, debts for luxury goods worth more than $725 obtained within 90 days of bankruptcy, fraud by a fiduciary, alimony and child support, and judgments resulting from drunk driving (or drunk boating) accidents. The grounds for total denial of a discharge now number 12, starting with the declaration that corporations do not receive discharges in chapter 7 and continuing with denials of any discharge for debtors who have lied or filed false documents in connection with the bankruptcy case or failed to complete a personal finance course. Reading them all is worthwhile. They are stern reminders of the edges of forgiveness in the bankruptcy system.

The following cases reflect a sampling of the grounds for denial of discharge and a flavor of the courts' analyses. First, a case involving a global challenge to the discharge.

In re McNAMARA
310 B.R. 664 (Bankr. D. Conn. 2004)

SHIFF, Bankruptcy Judge.

. . .

BACKGROUND

The debtor was the only witness at the trial. He testified that he had $150,000 in a briefcase as a result of numerous withdrawals from bank accounts during the summer of 1998 and that immediately after he was ordered to deposit the money in an escrow account, he gambled $130,000 in a winner-take-all stud poker game at a private residence in Brooklyn, New York. He was not able to provide any further details about the poker game except that someone, who no longer lives in the country, drove him there. In an effort to explain his failure to remember details, the debtor claimed that he was under the influence of alcohol and medication for severe depression. He further stated that he had just lost his job and had been taken to a hospital in New York with what he initially thought was a second heart attack. He did not, however, produce any evidence to corroborate that claim, such as medical or hospital records or the testimony of anyone who witnessed his condition. The debtor testified that he reserved enough money to pay for a Caribbean vacation, which was supported by receipts from that trip. He denied that he deposited any money into off-shore bank accounts.

Apart from his difficulty to recall the details of the poker game, the debtor's credibility was also challenged by an unlikely difficulty recalling the details of significant bank account deposits and withdrawals prior to and concurrent with the alleged gambling losses. For example, he was unable to remember the source of an October 14, 1998 deposit of $44,247.87. He speculated that it was either from life insurance policies, despite testimony that other deposits were from those policies, or from his salary, even though it was a single large deposit, and he claims to have lost his job more than a month earlier. The debtor was also unable to credibly testify how he spent over $200,000 between June 1998 [and] February 1999. For example, he claimed that he spent a part of that money on renovations to his former marital residence, but the trustee reminded him that the property was sold in May 1998.

The evidence justified the trustee's suspicion that the debtor's claimed gambling loss i[s] a fictional attempt to hide money that he considered to be his and not subject to his former wife's claims. He testified that he had an agreement with her that they would separate for five years rather than get divorced, so that he could maintain his health insurance through her employment. That issue was prompted by the debtor's claim that he was told he would require a heart transplant in the future. In return for her agreement, he claims to have agreed to give her custody of the children and repair the marital residence. The debtor testified that after she repudiated the agreement, he believed he was entitled to the $150,000:

> I told her that if that was the case, that if she would not change her mind and go along with the agreement, that I would be forced to sell the house, take the $150,000 that I felt was mine. . . .
>
>   . . .
>
> I told her that I would take my monies—if she would not go along [with his plan to set up a trust] . . ., that I would be forced to sell the home, take the $150,000 that I felt . . . was my part. . . .

(Tr. of 11/8/00 at 56).

I had taken my 150 that I thought was mine.

(Tr. of 11/8/00 at 60).

DISCUSSION

11 U.S.C. § 727(a)(5)

11 U.S.C. § 727(a)(5) provides that the debtor shall be granted a discharge unless "the debtor has failed to explain satisfactorily, before determination of denial of discharge under this paragraph, any loss of assets or deficiency of assets to meet the debtor's liabilities."

> The plaintiff has the burden of introducing evidence of the disappearance of assets or of unusual transactions. The burden then shifts to the defendant to satisfactorily explain the loss or deficiency of assets. The test under this subsection relates to the credibility of the proffered explanation, not the propriety of the disposition. An explanation is not satisfactory if it is not offered in good faith or if it is vague, indefinite and uncorroborated. In re Maletta, 159 B.R. 108, 116 (Bankr. D. Conn. 1993) (citations omitted).

The standard of proof is a preponderance of the evidence. Id. at 111.

The trustee satisfied her burden by her effective cross-examination of the debtor, which demonstrated that he could not recall any details to support his claim that he lost $130,000 in a winner-take-all stud poker game. A person who loses $130,000 in a poker game would be expected to have some recollection of the details of the event which could be corroborated, or at least a credible explanation for why he did not.

For the same reasons that the trustee has satisfied her burden of proof, the debtor has not. Although the debtor attempted to excuse his inability to recall any details on the claim that he was suffering from depression, he did not provide a scintilla of evidence to support that claim, such as a medical report or a witness testifying that he was in poor health. Apparently, his alleged condition did not interfere with his decision to reserve at least $11,000 for a Caribbean vacation, which supports the trustee's suspicion that he deposited money in offshore banks. The fact that the debtor withdrew the money over a period of months further supports the conclusion that he was formulating a plan to hide it from his wife.

. . .

The debtor's schedules listed his former wife as a creditor, with a debt that is nearly all of his total liabilities. The parties agree that the alleged gambling occurred within one year of the bankruptcy filing.

[T]he debtor's testimony demonstrated he was angered by his former wife for breaking an alleged agreement not to divorce him, and he believed he was entitled to the $150,000. So, he took money he had been ordered to turn over to a state court escrow fund . . . and lost it in a poker game. In the best light, it was his intention to take a chance on either increasing the money, which would enable him to satisfy the court order and still keep the original amount, or lose it all. He cavalierly explained that his plan "didn't work out":

> [A friend] told me about this gambling situation. I went to try to double the money so that I would have money for my medical and pay them off [his former wife and/or the court ordered escrow] before the 25th. It didn't work out. I lost. I then went on that vacation for ten grand or whatever it was.

(Tr. of 11/8/00 at 78). The debtor's testimony demonstrated he did not care that he lost the money because he believed it was his to lose and that his wife had no right to it.

Bankruptcy is a privilege, not a right.

. . .

For the foregoing reasons, IT IS ORDERED that the debtor's discharge is denied under 11 U.S.C. § 727(a)(2)(A) & (5).

The rapper 50 Cent, whose real name is Curtis J. Jackson III, went to court in Connecticut this week to explain to a judge that he used fake prop money in Instagram photos of him lounging amid bundles of cash.

CNN Money, Mar. 9, 2016

As with the cases discussed earlier in the homestead section of the previous assignment, these discharge cases involve a great deal of judgment and discretion. In a case in Texas involving an elderly couple, the court in a thoughtful opinion accepted their explanation for the disappearance of large amounts of cash on the basis that South Texas ranchers often carry around a lot of cash to hire day laborers for work on the land. The fact that the debtors had disclosed everything was a major factor in the decision. In re Lee, 309 B.R. 468 (Bankr. W.D. Tex. 2004). In the opinion the court quoted a famous test to be applied to the phrase "explain satisfactorily" in § 727(a)(5):

> The word "satisfactorily" . . . may mean reasonable, or it may mean that the court, after having heard the excuse, the explanation, has that mental attitude which finds contentment in saying that he believes the explanation—he believes what the bankrupts say with reference to the disappearance or shortage. He is satisfied. He no longer wonders. He is contented.

In re Shapiro & Ornish, 37 F.2d 403, 406 (N.D. Tex. 1929).

Very different from a global denial is denial of discharge of just one debt. For certain kinds of rifle-shot denials under § 523(a), the creditor must object to discharge in bankruptcy court or the debt will be discharged automatically. § 523(c).

====== In re SHARPE ======
351 B.R. 409 (Bankr. N.D. Tex. 2006)

JERNIGAN, Bankruptcy Judge.

I.

. . .

The matter before the court is essentially a dispute between two parties, former friends, regarding various loans in the aggregate sum of $150,000 made by Ms. Baker to Mr. Sharpe in 2005. It was the undisputed testimony of the parties that Ms. Baker and Mr. Sharpe met sometime in December of 2004, shortly after Ms. Baker's divorce had become final, and that they became fast friends. Both parties, in fact, agreed that at one point their relationship could be fairly characterized as that of "best friends." During the period of their friendship, Ms. Baker and Mr. Sharpe spent a large amount of time together and spoke to each other most every day on the telephone.

In 2005, Mr. Sharpe and Ms. Baker were both involved in a business known as UltimateMatch.com. . . . During the first part of 2005, Ms. Baker made two loans to Mr. Sharpe evidenced by promissory notes, and made several other loans not so documented. All of such loans, the parties agree, aggregate to $150,000. The loans were made starting late 2004 through August or September of 2005. Mr. Sharpe does not dispute that he took such loans and, in fact, scheduled Ms. Baker as an unsecured creditor in the amount of $175,000 describing the nature of her debt as a "personal loan." . . .

There was . . . testimony that Mr. Sharpe had, for some months, been preparing to file for bankruptcy protection. Mr. Sharpe's former office assistant, Eileen Wolkowitz, testified that Mr. Sharpe maintained a file into which bills were placed, which at her deposition she had referred to as a "bankruptcy file."

The parties agree that Mr. Sharpe dressed expensively at the time the loans were made, wearing custom-made suits and designer label clothes and accessories, and that he continues to so clothe himself today. Mr. Sharpe characterized his manner of dress as "dressing for success." Ms. Baker testified that Mr. Sharpe's manner of dress led her to believe that he was a wealthy man. She also testified that based upon his demeanor and appearance she thought he had money. Ms. Wolkowitz also testified that Mr. Sharpe led a lifestyle that led her to believe that he was a successful, wealthy person and that she believed Mr. Sharpe intended to lead people to believe that he was a wealthy person. There was testimony that Mr. Sharpe utilized an American Express card, which had his name on it, but was to an account belonging to a Johnny Vaughn, a friend of Mr. Sharpe, to make many extravagant purchases. Mr. Sharpe stipulated to the fact that high-dollar charges reflected on an American Express bill, Plaintiff's Exhibit 7, were his charges.

Next, Ms. Wolkowitz testified that, over the 11 years that she has known Mr. Sharpe, she has known him to make a lot of money and to have lost a lot of money. She also testified that his disposition is such that he often attempts and genuinely desires to do more than he is financially capable of doing. And, indeed, what is remarkable about Mr. Sharpe's testimony throughout the trial, though convoluted and often confused, is the sense of a desperate, "pie-in-the-sky" optimism on his part that maybe, someday things will work out his way and he will be as rich as he aspires to be.

The parties also agree that, in addition to dressing extravagantly, Mr. Sharpe lived extravagantly, flying on a business associate's Lear jet, dining in expensive restaurants (often with Ms. Baker in tow), drinking expensive wines, and shopping in designer boutiques and expensive stores, such as Cartier. . . . Finally, there was also undisputed testimony that Mr. Sharpe described himself on MySpace.com, at some point during 2006, as "Funny guy with killer body and money to burn seeks classy woman who doesn't believe everything she reads!" Ms. Baker emphasizes the phrase "money to burn"; Mr. Sharpe emphasizes the phrase "doesn't believe everything she reads!"

Ms. Baker also recounted, as evidence of Mr. Sharpe's extravagant bent, a particular evening out with Mr. Sharpe and other friends or associates at one of the Dallas/Fort Worth area's finer steakhouses, Del Frisco's Double Eagle Steak House (Del Frisco's). Ms. Baker testified that she became familiar with Mr. Sharpe's spending habits by watching him spend money and that she knew that he would spend hundreds and hundreds of dollars on his frequent trips to Del Frisco's. Indeed, during the evening in question, Ms. Baker testified that Mr. Sharpe had ordered the most expensive bottle of wine the restaurant offered, a bottle priced at $15,000, and that Ms. Baker took it upon herself to approach the owner or manager of the restaurant to request that a less expensive bottle of wine be served instead. Upon Ms. Baker's request, a $5,000 bottle of wine was delivered for the evening's consumption. . . .

Further to the allegations of false representations on the part of Mr. Sharpe is Ms. Baker's testimony that Mr. Sharpe had represented to her at the time the loans were made that he was able to repay the loans because he was essentially hiding assets from his second wife, Jennifer Sharpe, in order to prevent her from obtaining her share of those assets as part of the then-pending divorce settlement. . . . Mr. Sharpe absolutely disputes Ms. Baker's assertion. . . .

The court finds Ms. Baker's testimony concerning the proposed plan to repay the loans to be the most credible. The court finds it difficult to fathom that repayment of Ms. Baker's loans would be out of income from Ultimate Match.com to which Ms. Baker would be legally entitled in any event. Moreover, Mr. Sharpe's alternative testimony that Ms. Baker made the loans based upon his own future earning potential was directly contradicted by Ms. Baker and the court finds her to be a more credible witness, if for no other reason but that she has but one, consistent story regarding why the loans were made and how they were to be repaid. . . .

III. Conclusions of Law

A. Do the trappings of wealth, demeanor and an extravagant lifestyle, together with an oral representation by the Debtor that he has sufficient funds to repay a debt, rise to the level of false pretenses, false representation or actual fraud such that the debt is nondischargeable pursuant to 11 U.S.C. § 523(a)(2)(A)?

"A discharge under section 727 . . . of this title does not discharge an individual debtor from any debt for money, property, services, or an extension, renewal, or refinancing of credit, to the extent obtained by false pretenses, a false representation, or actual fraud, other than a statement respecting the debtor's or an insider's financial condition." 11 U.S.C. § 523(a)(2)(A). Ms. Baker is hamstrung by the last clause of this provision, which—when read in conjunction with section 523(a)(2)(B)—requires that a statement respecting the debtor's financial condition be in writing in order to result in nondischargeability. Ms. Baker, by her own admission, relied upon Mr. Sharpe's *oral* representations that he had hidden away funds which were sufficient to repay Ms. Baker upon his divorce from Jennifer Sharpe. Ms. Baker, therefore, could not move under section 523(a)(2)(B) to seek nondischargeability of her debt. . . .

B. Mr. Sharpe made oral verbal and nonverbal misrepresentations concerning his financial condition to Ms. Baker.

This court finds that, during 2005, Mr. Sharpe lived a lifestyle and put forth a demeanor that suggested wealth. The expensive clothes, the expensive dinners, the extravagant spending, and all the rest were calculated by Mr. Sharpe to portray himself as a successful man of means. Mr. Sharpe characterizes this as "dressing for success"—and the court, having spent many years in private legal practice, certainly understands this maxim well. Ms. Baker sees a more sinister motive, one designed to dupe her (and, one presumes, others like her) into giving him large sums of money. The court also finds that Mr. Sharpe's concealment of his dire financial condition during 2005, and his, at least, vague intention to file bankruptcy—as reflected by the so-called "bankruptcy file"—are also misrepresentations of his financial wherewithal to repay the loans to Ms. Baker. But there is a problem with Ms. Baker's argument: the clothes, food, spending habits, *et cetera* are all false representations concerning Mr. Sharpe's financial condition. Patently, these do not fall within the ambit of section 523(a)(2)(A), which specifically excludes from it statements concerning a debtor's financial condition.[1]

---

[1] Indeed, Ms. Baker—or at least her attorney—knew there was this very large flaw in her argument, for in the Plaintiff's Brief in Support of Non-Dischargeability of Indebtedness Under 11 U.S.C. § 523(a)(2)(A) and (a)(6) filed with this court in advance of trial, the Plaintiff

These representations pale, however, in comparison to the admitted linchpin representation to Ms. Baker: in obtaining from Ms. Baker, at least, the two large loans aggregating $95,000 in principal, Mr. Sharpe represented to her that he had the funds available to repay her hidden away pending his divorce from Jennifer Sharpe. . . . Ms. Baker's unequivocal testimony is that the key inducement to her making the loans was Mr. Sharpe's oral representations to her that he had the funds to repay her and that he would repay her from such funds.

Every representation made by Mr. Sharpe to Ms. Baker in inducement of the loans was either explicitly or implicitly a representation concerning his financial condition. As such, they cannot form the basis of a cause of action under section 523(a)(2)(A). Section 523(a)(2)(A) excepts from it the broad category of "statements respecting the debtor's . . . financial condition," and does not require that such statements be formalized financial statements. The Tenth Circuit has set forth succinctly the policy behind requiring that statements concerning a debtor's financial condition be in writing:

> [G]iving a statement of financial condition is a solemn part of significant credit transactions; therefore, it is only natural that solemnity be sanctified by a document which the debtor either prepares or sees and adopts. . . .
>
> A creditor who forsakes that protection, abandoning caution and sound business practices in the name of convenience, may find itself without protection.

Bellco First Federal Credit Union v. Kaspar (In re Kaspar), 125 F.3d 1358, 1361 (10th Cir. 1997).

For these reasons, the court concludes that it cannot provide relief to Ms. Baker under section 523(a)(2)(A). Mr. Sharpe's representations, though false, all concerned his financial condition, which fall under section 523(a)(2)(B), and which requires a writing to accord relief. . . .

IV. Conclusion

For the foregoing reasons, Plaintiff's $150,000 debt is found to be dischargeable. . . .

―――――――

The next case involves a popular form of loan in the pre-crash housing industry: the "stated income" loan, so called because the applicant's statement of income did not have to be verified by pay stubs, income tax returns, or the like. They were widely available, often over the Internet. Because of the lack of the usual verification, in some quarters they were called "liar

―――――――

quoted section 523(a)(2)(A), but left out, with the convenient use of an ellipsis, the critical phrase "other than a statement respecting the debtor's or an insider's financial condition." Thankfully, the court has several copies of the Bankruptcy Code handy so it could consult the entire statutory provision in addressing this question.

loans." With a nickname like that, satisfying the formal requirements for a financial statement may not be enough.

In re HILL

2008 WL 2227359 (Bankr. N.D. Cal. May 23, 2008)

Tchaikovsky, Bankruptcy Judge.

In this adversary proceeding, plaintiff National City Bank (the "Bank"), a foreclosed out former junior deed of trust holder, seeks to except its approximately $250,000 claim from the above-captioned debtors' (the "Debtors") chapter 7 discharge pursuant to 11 U.S.C. § 523(a)(2)(B). For the reasons stated below, the Court will enter judgment in favor of the Debtors.

Summary of Facts

This adversary proceeding is a poster child for some of the practices that have led to the current crisis in our housing market.

The Debtors bought their home in El Sobrante, California (the "House") nearly 20 years ago for $220,000. They filed for chapter 7 bankruptcy in April 2007. After purchasing the House, as the value of the House increased, the Debtors refinanced the original first deed of trust to obtain additional cash. They also obtained a junior deed of trust, which they refinanced several times. At the time they filed their bankruptcy petition, the Debtors scheduled the debt secured by the House as totaling approximately $683,000.

The Debtors' income was modest. Mr. Hill was a parts manager at Auto Wholesaling, earning an annual salary of up to $39,000, depending on overtime. Mrs. Hill was self-employed, using a dba of C Ann H Distributing, distributing free periodicals for various companies. Her income also fluctuated, depending on how many companies were employing her for this purpose. According to the Debtors' Statement of Financial Affairs, filed in their bankruptcy case, in 2006, Mrs. Hill's annual gross income was between $25,000 and $26,000. It appears doubtful that the Debtors' combined annual gross income was ever greater than $65,000.

In April 2006, Mrs. Hill contacted a mortgage broker, Winston Ellerback ("Ellerback"), seeking to refinance the Debtors' existing second deed of trust debt. Ellerback, who testified at trial, stated that he had acted as the Debtors' loan broker on five prior occasions. At that time, the second deed of trust was held by someone other than the Bank. The debt secured by the second deed of trust had a balance of approximately $100,000. The Debtors sought and obtained from Bank an equity line of credit for $200,000, thereby obtaining approximately $60,000 in cash after paying the cost of the refinance and other consumer obligations. They used the cash to pay off their consumer debt and to "fix up" the House.

In the loan application submitted to obtain this loan (the "April Loan Application"), Mr. Hill's monthly income was listed as $8,176 (i.e., $98,112 on an annual basis) and Mrs. Hill's [monthly] income was listed as $3,967 (i.e., $47,604 on an annual basis) for a combined [monthly] income of approximately $12,143 (i.e., $145,716 on an annual basis). Ellerback stated that he obtained this income information from Mrs. Hill over the phone, inputted it into the application form, and sent the application to the Debtors for their signature.[1]

In October 2006, the Debtors were in need of more cash. The Bank permitted them to increase their equity line of credit to $250,000. This time, instead of contacting Ellerback to handle the transaction, Mrs. Hill dealt with the Bank directly. . . .

[A bank manager] noted that both this loan and the loan obtained by the Debtors in April 2006 were "stated income" loans which did not require verification of income. Eubanks testified that the loans were generated for the purposes of sale and that certain guidelines (the "Guidelines") had to be followed to render them acceptable for that purpose. . . .

According to the Guidelines, for a borrower who was self-employed, the Bank could choose one of three types of verification: (1) a copy of the borrower's business license, (2) a copy of the most recent month's bank statement reflecting liquidity at least equal to one-tenth of the borrower's annual income, or (3) a CPA letter verifying the existence and ownership of the business. . . . A copy of a letter verifying the existence and ownership of Mrs. Hill's business was introduced into evidence. The letter was written on the letterhead of a CPA, but was signed by someone other than the CPA whose name was on the letterhead. . . .

In April 2006, the House had been appraised at $785,000. In October 2006, the House was appraised at $856,000. Shortly after the Debtors filed for bankruptcy in April 2007, the first deed of trust holder purchased the House at its foreclosure sale pursuant to a credit bid based on a secured debt of approximately $450,000, no one having submitted an overbid.

DISCUSSION

A. Applicable Law

A creditor seeking to establish a debt as nondischargeable under § 523(a)(2)(B) must demonstrate that: (1) The debtor made a written representation . . . respecting the debtor's financial condition; (2) the representation was material; (3) the debtor knew at the time the representation was made that it was false; (4) the representation was made with the intent to deceive the creditor; (5) the creditor relied on the representation; (6) the reliance was reasonable; and (7) the damage suffered by the creditor proximately resulted from the representation. . . .

---

[1] Mrs. Hill denied having told Ellerback that her and her husband's incomes were in the amounts set forth on the loan application. She and her husband both testified that they had not read the loan application before signing it and that moreover they had never read a loan application in their lives. The Bank presented evidence that called into question the credibility of this testimony. In April 2006, together with the loan application, Ellerback sent the Debtors an estimated closing statement for their signatures. He had inadvertently checked a box on the second page of the document in a section dealing with pre-payment penalties. Mrs. Hill called Ellerback and told him about the error. He told her to cross it out and initial the change. She did so.

B. Decision

As set forth above, the Ninth Circuit has identified seven elements to a claim under § 523(a)(2)(B). The creditor seeking to except its debt from the debtor's discharge must prove each of these elements by a preponderance of the evidence.

The first two elements of the Bank's claim were not in dispute: i.e., that the Debtors made a false representation to the Bank in writing concerning their financial condition and that the misrepresentation was material. The Debtors admitted that they submitted the October Loan Application and that the figures listed for their incomes were significantly overstated. Those representations concerned their financial condition and were false. Thus, the first element of the Bank's claim is established. If their true incomes had been disclosed, the Debtors would not have qualified for the loan. Their debt to income ratio would have exceeded the maximum permitted by the Guidelines. Thus, the false representation was material, thereby establishing the second element of the Bank's claim.

The Court concludes that the Bank met its burden of proof with respect to the second and third elements of its claim: i.e., that the Debtors knew that the representation was false at the time it was made and that they made the representation with the intent to deceive the Bank. The Debtors testified that they did not supply the false figures regarding their income and did not read the October Loan Application before they signed it. As a result, they contended, the Bank failed to establish either their knowledge or the falsity of the representation or their intent to deceive the Bank. The Court did not find their testimony credible.

In large part, this conclusion is drawn from the evidence presented with respect to the April 2006 loan. . . .

Ellerback testified that Mrs. Hill provided him with the income information. He also testified that, before signing and submitting the April Loan Application, Mrs. Hill caught a mistake he had made in one of the loan documents and called it to his attention. The Court found Ellerback to be a more credible witness than Mrs. Hill. The Debtors' lack of credibility concerning the April 2006 loan transaction undermines the credibility of their testimony concerning the October 2006 loan transaction.[5]

Moreover, the Hills, while not highly educated, were not unsophisticated. They had obtained numerous home and car loans and were familiar with the loan application process. . . .

However, the Bank's suit fails due to its failure to prove the sixth element of its claim: i.e., the reasonableness of its reliance. As stated above, the reasonableness of a creditor's reliance is judged by an objective standard. In general, a lender's reliance is reasonable if it followed its normal business practices. However, this may not be enough if those practices deviate from industry standards or if the creditor ignored a "red flag." Here, it is highly questionable whether the industry standards—as those standards are reflected by the Guidelines—were objectively reasonable. However,

---

[5] The Court also found it likely that Mrs. Hill avoided using Ellerback to obtain the October 2006 loan for fear that he would have questioned her concerning the changes in their income figures as compared to six months earlier.

even if they were, the Bank clearly deviated to some extent from those standards. In addition, the Bank ignored a "red flag" that should have called for more investigation concerning the accuracy of the income figures.

As noted above, the Guidelines required an evaluation of the reasonableness of the salary listed by an employed borrower based on job type and geographical area, among other things. No evidence was provided by the Bank that this evaluation was done. Additionally, with respect to a self-employed individual, the Guidelines required a letter from a CPA verifying the existence and ownership of the business. While the letter relied upon by the Bank verifying the existence and ownership of Mrs. Hill's business was on the letterhead of a CPA, whose existence was itself independently verified by the Bank, the letter was not signed by the CPA. The person signing the letter did not identify himself as a CPA and may not even have been an employee of the CPA on whose letterhead the letter was written.

More important, the Bank ignored the "red flag" established by the variation in the incomes set forth on the April Loan Application as compared to the incomes set forth on the October Loan Application. The Bank employee handling the loan transaction in October 2006 knew that the Bank had made a loan to the Debtors just six months earlier and that they were now attempting to increase the amount of the loan. The employee necessarily had at her disposal the file with respect to the earlier loan. Not only were the total income figures on the October 2006 Loan Application substantially higher than the figures on the [April] 2006 Loan Application, the income figures for the spouses were switched. The total annual income listed for the Debtors on the April 2006 Loan Application was $145,716. On the October Loan Application, it was $190,000. On the April Loan Application, Mr. Hill's annual income was listed as $98,112 and Mrs. Hill's as $47,604. On the October Loan Application, Mr. Hill's annual income was listed as $67,200 and Mrs. Hill's as $123,600.

Based on the foregoing, the Court concludes that either the Bank did not rely on the Debtors' representations concerning their income or that its reliance was not reasonable based on an objective standard. In fact, the minimal verification required by an "income stated" loan, as established by the Guidelines, suggests that this type of loan is essentially an "asset based" loan. In other words, the Court surmises that the Bank made the loan principally in reliance on the value of the collateral: i.e., the House. If so, the Bank obtained the appraisal upon which it principally relied in making the loan. Subsequent events strongly suggest that the appraisal was inflated. However, under these circumstances, the Debtors cannot be blamed for the Bank's loss, and the Bank's claim should be discharged.

CONCLUSION

While the Court finds and concludes that the Debtors made a material false representation concerning their financial condition to the Bank in October 2006, with knowledge of its falsity and the intent to deceive the Bank, the Court finds and concludes that the Bank's nondischargeability claim under § 523(a)(2)(B) must fail. The Bank failed to prove that it reasonably relied on the Debtors' false representation concerning their income, as set forth in the October Loan Application. As a result, the Bank's claim has been discharged.

═══════════════

One particular debt that has been singled out for special protection against discharge in bankruptcy is the student loan. While some people may fear soon-to-be-rich doctors and lawyers waltzing into bankruptcy to discharge huge loans incurred in college and grad school, many people are struggling with student loans used to acquire skills that do not pay nearly so well, a topic gaining greater significance as scrutiny of for-profit schools intensifies. Andrew Delbanco, College: What It Was, Is, and Should Be (Princeton University Press, 2012).

In 2007, one-quarter of consumer bankruptcy debtors owed student loans. Among this group, 30% had dropped out of their educational program, adding further fuel to a heated debate about student loans in bankruptcy. Katherine Porter, *Broke*, 85, 93.

THOMAS v. DEPARTMENT OF EDUCATION
931 F.3d 449 (5th Cir. 2019)

EDITH H. JONES, Circuit Judge.

Appellant Thomas challenges the bankruptcy court's denial of discharge of her student loan debt pursuant to 11 U.S.C. § 523(a)(8). . . . Finding no error, we AFFIRM.

I. FACTUAL BACKGROUND

Vera Frances Thomas, the Appellant, is over 60 years old and had to file a Chapter 7 bankruptcy case in 2017. Ms. Thomas suffers from diabetic neuropathy, a degenerative condition that causes pain in her lower extremities. Ms. Thomas is now unemployed and subsists on a combination of public assistance and private charity. In February 2012, however, she had worked for eight years at a call center in Southeastern Virginia and was earning $11.40 per hour with benefits. That year, Ms. Thomas decided to enroll at a local community college to improve her career prospects (she had a high school diploma, but no higher education credits). She obtained two $3,500 loans through the Department of Education, the first on February 14, 2012 and the second on September 21, 2012 to finance her first two semesters of courses. Ms. Thomas did not return for a third semester, and her loans went into repayment in December 2013. In spring 2014, she made payments of $41.24 and $41.61 on the loans.

Ms. Thomas's health began to decline significantly in 2014 when she was diagnosed with diabetic neuropathy. The condition, which often reduces circulation in patients' lower extremities, caused muscle weakness, numbness, and pain in her legs and feet after prolonged standing. Ms. Thomas frequently took unpaid leave from work at the call center to manage her symptoms and incurred significant medical expenses. In 2016, her employer was acquired by another company, and the new employer fired her for violating company policies. Because she was terminated for cause, Ms. Thomas was ineligible for unemployment benefits.

To defray costs, Ms. Thomas moved to Texas to live with her then-boyfriend. She obtained work with Perfumania, then Whataburger, and finally UPS. But each job required her to be on her feet, and she could not maintain these positions. Since quitting UPS in 2017, Ms. Thomas has not obtained employment that comports with her need for sedentary work.

Unable to make payments on her student loans and other significant debts, Ms. Thomas filed Chapter 7 bankruptcy in Dallas and received a general discharge of her debts. Seeking a discharge of her student loan debt as well, Ms. Thomas initiated an adversary complaint in bankruptcy court against the Department of Education.

II. Procedural Background

To discharge student loan debt under the Bankruptcy Code, a debtor must show that the debt would impose an "undue hardship" on the debtor if it is not discharged. 11 U.S.C. § 523(a)(8).[2] In In re Gerhardt, 348 F.3d 89 (5th Cir. 2003), this court adopted the three-prong test for evaluating "undue hardship" claims established by the Second Circuit in Brunner v. New York State Higher Education Services Corp., 831 F.2d 395 (2d Cir. 1987).

. . .

The bankruptcy court held a trial to review Ms. Thomas's complaint, applied *Gerhardt*, and determined that "Ms. Thomas has not met her burden of showing undue hardship under the controlling standard in the Fifth Circuit...." The bankruptcy court concluded that she had satisfied the first prong of *Brunner*—showing an inability to maintain a minimal standard of living if forced to repay the loan—because her monthly expenses ($640) exceeded her monthly income ($194). Ms. Thomas failed to pass *Brunner*'s second standard, however, because she "conceded that she is unable to show she is completely incapable of employment now or in the future"; she admitted that she could not establish that her present state of affairs would persist for a significant portion of the loans' repayment period.

The bankruptcy court noted that the exceptionally demanding second prong of *Brunner* requires more than a showing of dire financial straits because the debtor must show that circumstances out of her control have resulted in a "total incapacity" to repay the debt now and in the future (quoting *Gerhardt*, 348 F.3d at 92). Moreover, the court observed that such

---

[2] This provision states: "A discharge under section 727 . . . of this title does not discharge an individual debtor from any debt . . . unless excepting such debt from discharge under this paragraph would impose an undue hardship on the debtor and the debtor's dependents, for—[enumerated government-backed and other student loans]." 11 U.S.C. § 523(a)(8).

situations are so rare that "in fifteen years on the bench, the undersigned judge has never discharged a student loan over the objection of the lender." Having concluded that Ms. Thomas could not satisfy the second *Brunner* prong, the court did not reach a conclusion regarding the third prong.

Ms. Thomas appealed the bankruptcy court's decision to the federal district court, which affirmed essentially for the reasons stated by the bankruptcy court. Despite ruling that her student loans were non-dischargeable, both courts indicated sympathy for Ms. Thomas and their discomfort with the demanding nature of the *Brunner/Gerhardt* test. Ms. Thomas has appealed to this court.

. . .

Ms. Thomas principally contends that the *Brunner/Gerhardt* test is inconsistent with the plain meaning of the term "undue hardship" in § 523(a)(8) and urges this court to adopt a "totality of the circumstances" test instead. As she concedes, this court is bound by *Gerhardt* until an en banc panel of this court or the Supreme Court opts to alter our interpretation of § 523(a)(8).

. . .

The government does not challenge the bankruptcy court's finding that Ms. Thomas satisfied the first prong of the *Brunner* test because she cannot maintain a minimal living standard if forced to repay the student loans. We accept that finding for present purposes. Nor need we opine, despite the government's urging, on the third *Brunner* prong, which evaluates Ms. Thomas's good faith efforts to repay the loan.[3] Thus, the controlling inquiry here is whether Ms. Thomas demonstrated that due to external circumstances beyond her control, *i.e.*, her deteriorating diabetic conditions and the costs associated with it, she is unable to maintain employment and is unlikely to ever be able to repay the debt. Phrased in terms of *Brunner/Gerhardt*, the question is whether because of external factors, her present inability to pay her student loans and maintain a minimal standard of living will persist throughout a significant portion of the loan repayment period.

The answer to this question must be negative. Ms. Thomas's argument that she meets the second *Brunner* prong is contradicted by the record. Foremost, she is, by her own admission, capable of employment in sedentary work environments. Second, her actual employment experience demonstrates that after losing the call center job, she was hired by three different employers, although she quit when they were unable to accommodate her need to remain sedentary for periods of time during her shifts. Finally, she lost her job at the call center not because of physical problems beyond her control but for a violation of company policies.

---

[3] The government's position is based on various avenues by which a student loan debtor may seek reduction of payments, modifications of the terms, and in some instances outright cancellation of all or part of the debts. Ms. Thomas availed herself of none of these alternatives. The lower courts, however, did not make findings or conclusions based on this prong of the *Brunner/Gerhardt* test.

In sum, there is no evidence that Ms. Thomas's present circumstances, difficult as they are, are likely to persist throughout a significant portion of the loans' repayment period. . . .

IV. CRITIQUES OF *BRUNNER* AND *GERHARDT*

Although the lower courts' decision must be affirmed in light of our governing authority, Ms. Thomas, along with an amicus, expends much of her briefing on an extended critique of *Brunner/Gerhardt* and a plea that these decisions be reevaluated. She argues that *Brunner* is no longer good law because the court failed to engage in the close textual analysis that, accurately conducted, would have substantially ameliorated the debtor's burden to show "undue hardship." . . . These critiques are unconvincing in view of both the text of § 523(a)(8) and the context in which the provision was created and amended. Congress has amended federal bankruptcy law on several occasions, increasing the threshold for student loan discharges each time, before finally settling on an "undue hardship" standard. . . . *See, e.g.,* In re Pelkowski, 990 F.2d 737, 742-43 (3d Cir. 1993) ("It is undisputed that section 523(a)(8) was enacted in response to the belief that students were taking advantage of the loan program," and the provision's passage "focused on the twin goals of rescuing the student loan program from fiscal doom and preventing abuse of the bankruptcy process by undeserving debtors").

In 1990, Congress changed the law again, extending the required repayment period from five years to seven years prior to discharge. . . . Congress's series of amendments clearly evinces an intent to limit bankruptcy's use as a means of offloading student loan debt except in the most compelling circumstances. . . . The plain meaning of the words chosen by Congress is that student loans are not to be discharged unless requiring repayment would impose intolerable difficulties on the debtor. The threshold by definition must be greater than the ordinary circumstances that might force one to seek bankruptcy relief.

It is difficult to overstate the contentiousness of student loan discharge exception. Even when there is agreement on the correct test, opinions diverge sharply on application. Consider the Eighth Circuit panel in In re Jesperson, 571 F.3d 775 (8th Cir. 2009), which produced three separate opinions on whether a lawyer in his mid-40s was required to continue sleeping on his brother's basement couch to avoid undue hardship (2-1 reversal of lower courts; no discharge). Among the facts that court wrestled with: Attorney Jesperson drove a pickup with over 200,000 miles on it, which he used in part to attend AA meetings; he quit one of his jobs because his supervisor drank at work; he tried to set up his own legal practice but only garnered two clients, one of whom was a relative. But he also just couldn't seem to keep his stuff together: according to the bankruptcy court, Jesperson's "record of work experience is besmirched by a patent lack of ambition, cooperation and commitment." For entertainment analogies, those of a certain generation might see him as a down-on-his-luck Francis Garvin, but more cynical folks of a younger generation might just see him as the next Barry Zuckerkorn. The divided panel in *Jesperson* may herald a counter-movement. The Chief Judge of the Southern District of New York Bankruptcy Court, Cecilia Morris, handed down a scathing opinion in In re Rosenberg, 2020 Bankr. LEXIS 73 (Bankr. S.D.N.Y. 2020). In it, she maintained that *Brunner* (the seminal case discussed above in *Thomas*) had been entirely misread:

> The harsh results that often are associated with *Brunner* are actually the result of cases interpreting *Brunner*. . . . These retributive dicta were then applied and reapplied so often . . . they have subsumed the actual language of the *Brunner* test. They have become a quasi-standard of mythic proportions so much so that most people . . . believe it is impossible to discharge student loans.

Id. at 6-7.

The court returned to the words of the test stated in *Brunner*, finding that the debtor's stated negative income ($2,456 monthly income less $4,005 expenses) was undisputed and therefore he could not pay and maintain a minimal standard of living. In addition, his debt had been accelerated and was due in full. Given that he was not currently eligible for a repayment plan, he could not now pay in full and he was not required to seek out a possible payment plan as a condition of discharge. The court also found he had in the past at various times made good faith efforts to pay, although in relatively small amounts. The result was that the debtor was not required to show the lack of a possible ability to pay in the future.

On the broader question why student loans are nondischargeable in the first place, one of us has subjected various proffered rationales to scrutiny and found them theoretically wanting. See John A.E. Pottow, The Nondischargeability of Student Loans in Personal Bankruptcy Proceedings: The Search for a Theory, 44 Can. Bus. L.J. 245 (2006).

C.   TAX PRIORITIES AND DISCHARGE

The protected position for tax obligations raises important policy questions for both the debtor and the other creditors.

The kinds of taxes specified in § 507(a)(8)(A)-(G) are not only given priority in payment, but any unpaid portion of those taxes is exempted from discharge by § 523(a)(1)(A). If the estate generates any money, the tax payment will receive a priority distribution, and the debtor remains personally liable for any unpaid portion post-discharge.

Prepetition interest on § 507(a)(8) priority claims shares the priority of the claims themselves and enjoys their nondischargeable status. Collier on Bankruptcy § 523.07[7] (16th ed. 2009). Postpetition interest does not accrue on unsecured tax claims against the trustee and the property of the estate, § 502(b), but postpetition interest does accrue against the debtor as to any unpaid, undischarged tax debts that survive discharge. Id. In other words, the part the debtor will have to pay after bankruptcy is growing larger by the day, even during the course of the bankruptcy. The Taxman Cometh.

Penalties on nondischargeable taxes are also nondischargeable, § 523(a)(7), regardless whether entitled to priority by virtue of their relation to pecuniary loss, § 507(a)(8)(G).

It gets worse for the debtor. Not only are these tax debts nondischargeable, but the Internal Revenue Service has the right to satisfy them by seizing property that is otherwise exempt under state law. See United States v. Rodgers, 461 U.S. 677 (1983). State Exemptions 0, Supremacy Clause 1. Strapped debtors are frequently advised by counsel to pay their tax debts above all else.

D. WORSE THAN NO DISCHARGE—BANKRUPTCY CRIMES

In the basic course on bankruptcy there is insufficient time to deal with bankruptcy crimes. Nonetheless, it is important to note that the acts that trigger denial of discharge may also put the debtor in jeopardy for criminal prosecution. Concealment of assets, false oaths, false claims, fee fixing, and a number of other bankruptcy specific actions are made federal crimes in 18 U.S.C. §§ 151-155.

This case is a tale of a mendacious lawyer who discovers poetic justice.

UNITED STATES v. CLUCK
143 F.3d 174 (5th Cir. 1998)

Jolly, Circuit Judge.

Elwood "Jack" Cluck appeals his conviction and sentence for committing bankruptcy fraud in violation of 18 U.S.C. § 152(1) & (3). Finding no merit in any of Cluck's multitudinous and niggling points of error, we affirm. . . .

A.

Before the events in this case, Cluck was an attorney who specialized, by his own admission, in the legal avoidance of income, estate, and gift taxes.[1] His practice was, by all accounts, quite successful, allowing Cluck to enjoy many of the finer things in life. In his case, the finer things ranged from an assortment of properties located throughout the state of Texas, to his own Beechcraft Bonanza airplane, to a collection of classic Jaguar automobiles.

---

[1] An undoubtedly satisfying profession that we do not disparage. See Estate of McLendon v. Commissioner of Internal Revenue, 135 F.3d 1017, 1025 n.16 (5th Cir. 1998).

Smooth travel sometimes comes to an abrupt halt, however, and so it was in the case of Cluck. In October 1989, the road ahead worsened considerably when a state court rendered judgment against him in the staggering amount of $2.9 million.[2] Although Cluck had high hopes that an appellate detour would shortly return him to his golden highway,[3] he soon found that the detour itself would require a steep toll of 10 percent in the form of the supersedeas bond necessary to forestall execution. Short of funds and in need of a cul de sac in which to safely park his troubled vehicle for a while, Cluck turned to the refuge of the bankruptcy court, as many a similarly threatened sojourner had done before him.

Unlike these other voyagers, however, Cluck apparently concluded that his resources would need more protection than the bankruptcy court could provide until his appellate travels had reached their final destination. Thus, before invoking the power of Title 11, he perceived that it might be useful to keep some Jaguars in reserve, some money within easy access, and, maybe, just for good measure, a few of his favorite things beyond the reach of his creditors and the bankruptcy court. To this end, on March 26, 1990, Cluck returned a note for $50,000 to its grantor, Perfect Union Lodge. Perfect Union was one of Cluck's clients, and the note had been originally tendered in payment of certain legal services. Three days later, on March 29, Cluck pawned three Jaguars, a 1983 Chevrolet truck, his airplane, a Lone Star boat, and a Winnebago camper shell ("the Jaguars, etc.") to a used car dealer for $32,000,[4] retaining for himself and his designee a right to reacquire at a set price[5] within thirty to ninety days of the sale.

B.

His affairs now in preliminary order, on March 30, Cluck filed his petition for Chapter 7 liquidation in the United States Bankruptcy Court for the Western District of Texas. As part of the standard Chapter 7 procedure, Cluck was required to file a Schedule of Assets and a Statement of Financial Affairs. These documents required, among other things, disclosure of all accounts receivable, rights of acquisition, and asset transfers during the prior year. On his forms, Cluck made no mention of the assets recently pawned to the used car dealer or of his right to reacquire. He also did not disclose his return of the $50,000 note or the corresponding account receivable from Perfect Union Lodge. In addition, Cluck failed to list a transfer of 351 acres of land in McMullen County, Texas, that he had made on June 21, 1989. Finally, and significantly for this appeal, Cluck also neglected to include a further $150,000 in pre-petition accounts receivable from another of his clients, the O.D. Dooley Estate.

---

[2] The suit was based on alleged fraudulent conduct by Cluck in his handling of the estate of Booney M. Moore, one of his tax planning clients. It was brought pursuant to Texas's Deceptive Trade Practices Act, whose punitive damage provisions gave rise to the large award.

[3] As well he should have. The judgment entered on the jury's verdict was reversed. . . .

[4] A price that was, needless to say, significantly below the assets' fair market value.

[5] About $38,000.

On July 31, Cluck's bankruptcy came to its first purported close, and the bankruptcy court entered an order discharging him from all dischargeable debts. Thinking his plan to have succeeded, on November 9, Cluck collected $48,000 from the O.D. Dooley Estate in partial payment of that client's aforementioned pre-petition account receivable. On November 16, the remaining $102,000 followed. About seven months later, on June 28, 1991, Cluck collected $35,000 from Perfect Union in settlement of its still-outstanding $50,000 account receivable. Of these funds, a portion was deposited into the account of First Capitol Mortgage, a Nevada corporation owned by Cluck's wife, Kristine. By this time, First Capitol had also reacquired all of the assets that had been pawned to the used car dealer. As might be suspected, neither the receipt of the money nor the reacquisition of the assets was revealed to the bankruptcy trustee. . . .

II.

The bankruptcy court's finding of intentional concealment apparently aroused the interest of the U.S. Attorney, and on March 27, 1995, Cluck was charged with eight counts of bankruptcy fraud in violation of 18 U.S.C. § 152(1) & (3). The counts were essentially as follows:

[False statements and fraudulent concealment.]

On January 16, 1997, a jury found Cluck guilty on counts one, three, four, five, six, seven, and eight, and not guilty on count two. On May 22, 1997, Cluck was sentenced to concurrent terms of twenty-four months imprisonment on each count, and ordered to pay restitution in the amount of $185,000. Cluck appeals his conviction, sentence, and restitution order on multiple grounds. . . .

C.

Cluck next attempts to persuade us that the evidence was insufficient on all the counts of his indictment with respect to intent. Under § 152(1) & (3), the prosecution must show that the concealment or false statement was made "knowingly and fraudulently." Cluck argues, essentially, that the evidence showed only that he was careless in providing information to his bankruptcy attorney, not that he committed intentional fraud. . . .

. . . It is well established that "'[c]ircumstances altogether inconclusive, if separately considered, may, by their number and joint operation, especially when corroborated by moral coincidences, be sufficient to constitute conclusive proof.'" United States v. Ayala, 887 F.2d 62, 67 (5th Cir. 1989) (quoting The Slavers (Reindeer), 69 U.S. (2 Wall.) 383, 401, 17 L. Ed. 911 (1864)).

In this case, it is manifestly clear that Cluck's repeated omissions and history of coincidental and questionable transfers formed just the sort of "circumstances" that the Supreme Court had in mind in the *Reindeer* case. Based on our review of the record, we are convinced that a rational jury could have inferred the existence of an intentional plan to defraud from the bare facts of Cluck's systematic concealment and false statements. We therefore find no merit to his argument that the evidence was insufficient on this point. . . .

Having found no merit in any of Cluck's numerous points of error, for the foregoing reasons, the judgment of the district court is AFFIRMED.

━━━━━━━━━━
━━━━━━━━━━

Denial of discharge is one form of discipline, and prison is another. While our consumer bankruptcy laws may fairly be characterized as generous to troubled debtors, it is important that the debtors be fair with the system. The threat of jail is useful in keeping the system in balance, and many other countries' bankruptcy systems are far more punitive on debtors. Unfortunately, not many U.S. attorneys are prepared to invest resources in this kind of prosecution. In the *Cluck* case, it may be that the spectacle of a fellow lawyer behaving as he did was enough to produce action. Attorney Cluck's fraud-gauntlet thrown down was apparently picked up more recently by Russell Louis Geyer, who fled the state, falsely claimed two types of cancer, swindled his wife of $70,000, stole the identity of an attorney, and ultimately faked his own death. Rachel Olding, Virginia Man Faked His Own Death in Ridiculously Elaborate Plot to Avoid Bankruptcy, Daily Beast (May 07, 2020), https://www.thedailybeast.com/virginia-man -russell-geyer-faked-his-own-death-in-ridiculously-elaborate-plot-to-avoid -bankruptcy. Truth is stranger than fiction.

Problem Set 8

8.1. Wallace Laymon has held a variety of jobs during the past ten years. He is restless and has some difficulty getting along with co-workers. He sometimes walks off jobs, gets fired, abruptly moves, or just "gets tired." Laymon's financial records are a complete disaster. He has no checking statements, no bill receipts, and no clear record of any of his financial dealings except a handful of bills and dunning notices that have arrived in the past two months. Nor is he even remotely computer literate. Does Laymon face any difficulties in bankruptcy? Should he? Was he required by any law to keep better financial records? See § 727.

8.2. Gordon Gram was in serious financial difficulty for several months before he sought your advice. During this time he gave a financial statement to his principal creditor, Dina Chapman, to persuade her to hold off on enforcing the judgment she had gotten against him. The statement falsely stated that he owned 1,000 shares of AT&T stock, which he promised he would deliver to Dina as security for the debt. In the meantime, he also fraudulently conveyed his only significant asset, a ski chalet, to his daughter. When the stock was not forthcoming, Dina started searching for property to grab. After she found out about the chalet scam, she initiated execution on the judgment and a levy but before she could collect, Gram filed for chapter 7. Ignoring the question whether her judgment lien survives in bankruptcy, and assuming respectful compliance with the automatic stay, will Dina be able to continue her quest after Gram's bankruptcy? See §§ 523, 727. If Dina has an option, under which provision should she file her objection?

8.3. Chickie Narduchi makes his living through "creative debt collection services." Chickie has been very successful, but recently he has encountered a series of financial reversals that have forced him into bankruptcy. Among Chickie's creditors is a tort claimant who had owed money to one of Chickie's clients. The claimant has an $800,000 judgment against Chickie for breaking four of his fingers, a favorite kneecap, and his big toe. Will the judgment creditor be discharged in bankruptcy? (Keep in mind that you might later discover that Chickie secretly owns 5% of the Forbidden Pleasures Casino, so he is not without assets worth pursuing.) See § 523(a).

8.4. Shortly after Reynaldo and Maria Lujan were married, having watched a lot of HGTV, they purchased a rambling old home advertised as a "handyman's special." While they had visions of creating a quaint and charming nest, the home sucked up virtually all their cash. During the next three years, they worked constantly on the house and added such decorator touches as replacing the septic tank and rewiring the entire second floor. During that time, they carried maximum amounts on their credit cards, using the cards to support purchases for their house and to meet as many personal needs as they could finance through extended credit. Four months ago Maria was laid off and Reynaldo's income could not support the house and all the credit cards. Unfortunately, during that time their reliance on credit cards increased rather than decreased, so that their cards now represent $16,000 in unsecured debt.

Reynaldo and Maria have filed for chapter 7 bankruptcy and sold the house, which brought just enough to pay off all the mortgages and home improvement loans and leave them with a small amount of exempt cash. As their attorney, you have looked over their credit card charges, and you see purchases of wallpaper ($450), plane tickets ($1,200), and clothes from a nice men's store ($400) within the three months preceding the filing. The card issuers have filed exceptions to discharge. What will you do at the hearing? See § 523(a).

8.5. You are a young but up-and-coming consumer bankruptcy practitioner in Topeka, Kansas. You've acquired a reputation for honesty with clients and level-headed decision making. You chalk up much of your success to the bankruptcy text your class used in law school and your keeping up-to-date on the latest research. This morning you read a study that found that student loans are discharged in bankruptcy about 40% of the time. This was contrary to what all your mentors had taught you but surely the numbers don't lie. Later that day, 32-year-old Jamarah Harris came to see you about her financial problems, primary of which is $23,700 in defaulted student loans from six years ago when she attended an accredited, online graphic design school. She has never worked as a graphic designer and has struggled with lupus, diagnosed while she was in school. She is a single mother to four young children and would have to scrape hard to pay your fee for a chapter 7 case. She asks you, point blank, what are my odds of discharging these student loans? What do you tell her? Do you have any thoughts on what you can do to improve those odds?

THE DEBTOR'S POSITION AFTER BANKRUPTCY

You learned in the previous assignment that the discharge injunction forbids any attempt to collect a dischargeable debt. Like the automatic stay, it has potentially unlimited penalties and is enforced summarily by contempt, although the Supreme Court has whittled away that protection by decreeing that a creditor enjoys immunity from contempt if there is an "objectively reasonable basis for concluding that the creditor's conduct might be lawful." *Taggart v. Lorenzen*, 139 S. Ct. 1795, 1799 (2019). (Good news for creditors facing unresolved circuit splits!) While discharge is the capstone of a bankruptcy case, however, it often is merely the beginning of an elaborate end game in which disappointed creditors may retaliate and shrewd ones may maneuver. This means that despite the language of financial rebirth and fresh start so pervasive in bankruptcy literature, post-bankruptcy debtors are not like new babies unstained by past events. Instead, families exit bankruptcy with many of the same underlying challenges—illness, job problems, or low incomes—that led them to seek relief in the first place. Also, in some instances, the same debt that sank these families the first time around can remain a burden, even after discharge. We turn to this post-discharge world.

A. SECURED DEBTS: KEEPING COLLATERAL

Many debtors file bankruptcy in an effort to hang onto their homes, cars, and other property. Chapter 13 bankruptcy, covered in the upcoming two assignments, has some special tools to help families keep property. What happens to chapter 7 debtors' property? As we have already said, exempt property is kept and non-exempt property lost. But what about exempt property that is collateral for a secured creditor's lien? The Code suggests a tidy list of three options (surrender, redeem, or reaffirm); the reality is a messy scramble of strategic choices.

While unsecured debt is mostly discharged, secured debt plays a huge role in the post-bankruptcy financial lives of debtors. The 2007 Consumer Bankruptcy Project found that 74% of the debtors had loans secured by their cars, their furniture, their appliances, and other personal property. These debtors owed secured debts that were, on average, equal to nearly

85% of their total assets. Secured debt, and the collateral that backs it, is important in the lives of bankruptcy debtors.

As we noted in the prior assignment's *Henry* case, a lien remains attached to its collateral and can be enforced against that property after bankruptcy. The post-discharge injunction only protects the debtor from in personam suit for the deficiency, § 524(a)(2) (forbidding only an attempt to collect "as a personal liability"); it in no way halts actions against the collateral in rem. As we also saw in *Henry* (at least if we were reading it carefully), there is no specific statutory provision commanding this result. Rather, it is a principle cobbled together from Supreme Court case law, a generalized belief that "everybody knows it," and perhaps an inverse statutory construction of § 524(a)(2) (and § 506(d), which voids certain liens on collateral). The same is true for exempt property: the lien survives. § 522(c)(2). If the liens stay on all property, why do we need § 522(c)(2) to confirm that the lien stays on exempt property? It could be simple congressional clarification that nothing magical about property exemptions saves them from liens. Or it could be that the generalized assumption that the lien survives bankruptcy is actually wrong, but that would suggest more liens on post-bankruptcy exempt property than non-exempt property, a result that would be somewhere between weird and absurd and, worse, suggest the Supreme Court is wrong. So let's not rock that boat. Instead, let's just note that collection by seizure of collateral after the bankruptcy is over is not only permissible but often anticipated.

Hence, we get the tidy list of three options referenced above. Individuals who file chapter 7 are required to file a "Statement of Intention" (Official Bankruptcy Form B 108) with respect to collateral. This form must be filed within 30 days of the first date set for the 341 meeting described back in Assignment 3. Formally, this duty applies to all debts secured by property: consumer or nonconsumer, real or personal property, etc. See § 521(a)(2). Practically, however, these intentions only matter for exempt or abandoned property, because if it is not exempt or abandoned by the trustee, the debtor's intentions regarding property are quite beside the point: the trustee is selling it off to pay creditors (or if it is fully lien-encumbered, abandoning it back the secured creditor, § 554).

The Statement of Intention lists three primary options: (1) surrender it to the creditor; (2) redeem it under § 722; or (3) negotiate a reaffirmation agreement with the creditor under § 524(c). Case law has created a fourth option, which is usually called ride-through, or sometimes known as retention. (The form cryptically (begrudgingly?) offers "Other" as an option, which former versions of the form explicitly suggested would be for lien avoidance based on specific laws.)

The first alternative, surrender, sounds simple. Debtors let creditors know they do not want to keep the collateral, and creditors go get it. In most instances, it works just like that. The down real-estate market after the Great Recession created an interesting twist: creditors who decline this gracious invitation to reclaim the collateral promptly—and debtors who try to force them to. Consider § 523(a)(16) of the Code, which bizarrely excepts from discharge postpetition condo fees. One court described the problem: "In the case of a chapter 7 debtor who has surrendered her home in bankruptcy and been relieved of any personal liability on the mortgage, she cannot truly be given a fresh start because HOA [Home Owners Association] fees are still accumulating until a lender chooses to foreclose. If the lender never forecloses, that homeowner's liability for the HOA fees continues in perpetuity . . . [which] deprives the debtor of a fresh start, and thwarts the goals of the entire Bankruptcy Code." In re Pigg, 453 B.R. 728, 733 (Bankr. M.D. Tenn. 2011). Similar problems can occur with taxes, tort liability, or blight violations if a lender does not foreclose after a debtor surrenders the property; these problems are quite a reversal of the stories about debtor's strategically filing bankruptcy merely to stall foreclosure.

The debtor's calculation on whether to surrender exempt collateral or to try to use what we call bankruptcy's "3Rs" (Redemption, Reaffirmation, or Ride-through) depends both on the applicable law and on the economics of the situation. Say Jane Debtor owns a car worth $5,000 and the loan is $7,500. If it is a spare vehicle, surrender is the easy answer. Bankruptcy discharges the remaining $2,500 on the loan, and she reduces her carbon footprint. But Jane may want—or need—to keep the car. The reasons are myriad, ranging from the unassailable (only way to get to work) to the sentimental (vintage model she lovingly restored). The considerations Jane would think about include whether and how easily she can afford the monthly payments on the loan, whether she believes she would have trouble getting credit to buy a new car after bankruptcy, and whether the property is replaceable. Each of the 3R choices requires Jane to meet certain conditions—and pay a certain price—to keep the car. We examine each in turn.

1.   Redemption

Redemption allows the debtor to keep certain types of exempt or abandoned collateral by paying the creditor the full loan or the full value of the collateral in cash, whichever is less. § 722. This option is a big benefit of bankruptcy over state law. Under Article 9 of the UCC, a debtor is allowed to redeem collateral after default only by paying the full amount owed, including late charges and other costs. UCC § 9-623. The leverage created by permitting the creditor to demand more than the value of the collateral ($7,500 for a car worth $5,000, for example) was too much for Congress to sanction in consumer bankruptcy cases, so bankruptcy redemption allows the debtor to keep the collateral by paying the amount of the allowed secured claim, i.e., the value of the collateral. In the previous example, Jane could redeem the $5,000 car by paying $5,000 in cash, with the remaining amount owed on the loan being treated as an unsecured and dischargeable claim. This outcome may seem to disadvantage creditors unfairly in bankruptcy but note that it leaves the creditor in the same economic position it would have been in had Jane surrendered the car and the lender repossessed and sold it post-bankruptcy. Any benefit to the debtor from redemption is coming from the discharge of unsecured obligations. Creditors should theoretically be indifferent between redemption and surrender, but we suspect, assuming the collateral is fairly valued, that most prefer having hard cash in hand to a car that has to be tracked down and sold, while carry costs are mounting.

The rub in the real world is that the debtor does not have $5,000 cash to realize this marked-to-market buyout. For most debtors, § 722 might as well base redemption on the debtor successfully running a three-minute mile. Perhaps the most practical possibility for a few debtors is a loan from a friend or relative, in which case the debtor emerges from bankruptcy still greatly encumbered by debt. A business aptly named 722 Redemption has popped up in some states, offering to lend money to debtors, at a hefty rate, so that they can redeem their cars. The math is simple. Any debtor who is better off with the terms offered by 722 Redemption now has an alternative to reaffirming with the original creditor: refinancing the loan on 722 Redemption's terms and electing to redeem under the statute. Even 722 Redemption has underwriting standards, however—we asked—and most debtors have financial problems serious enough that even a bankruptcy specialist will be selective.

2.   *Reaffirmation*

The Code provides the alternative of reaffirmation for debtors who want to negotiate to keep their collateral but don't have that cash. In reaffirmation, the debtors sign a legally binding, totally new agreement "reaffirming" their secured debt, which means they waive their discharge and resurrect their deficiency liability by contract (albeit with some oversight). § 524(c), (k).

As a contract, reaffirmation thus requires a willing creditor to accept the proposal. The reaffirmation process reflects a negotiating tension between the debtor and the creditor—what each wants with respect to the collateral—and the procedural hurdles both must clear to create an enforceable agreement. In many instances, the creditor will insist the debtor agree that certain amounts be included in the reaffirmation agreements that were never in the original contract. For example, the creditor in one oft-cited case required as a condition of reaffirmation that the debtors pay $250 in attorneys' fees to cover the costs of negotiating and preparing the reaffirmation agreement. The debtors objected, but the court explained the leverage in these situations:

> Debtors fail to recognize that the reaffirmation process involves [contractual] negotiation. Even if debtors were correct in their assertions respecting the lack of a clause providing for attorney's fees in their original contracts, Leader Federal is nonetheless not prohibited from negotiating a provision for the payment of attorney's fees in its reaffirmation agreements. Likewise, the debtors are not prohibited from endeavoring to negotiate reaffirmation agreements with terms differing from those contained in their original contracts.
>
> Clearly, as in any negotiation process, give and take will be required. It appears to the court that, under circumstances involving reaffirmation, a debtor has considerable bargaining power. In the first place, the creditor must recognize that in the absence of reaffirmation its debt will be discharged leaving recourse against its collateral as its sole remedy. Secondly, the creditor must consider reaffirmation in terms of expenses associated with repossession and foreclosure. It must also consider the resale value of its collateral.

Merchants and secured lenders are in business to make a profit. They recognize the impact of bankruptcy and realize the advantage of negotiating a reaffirmation agreement which maintains an existing security interest, retains personal liability on the debtor and continues an uninterrupted stream of payments. Foreclosing a security interest in property whose value is generally speculative would, in this court's opinion, be a creditor's least desirable option.

In re Pendlebury, 94 B.R. 120 (Bankr. E.D. Pa. 1988).

The debtor's negotiating leverage "power" predicted by the court led to an additional $250 promise to pay over and above the original debt. Hmm. Still, as the court notes, collateral retention through reaffirmation is not a right but a free-market activity. While the statute requires certain disclosures and affidavits, the price is always up for grabs.

Does something worry you about reaffirmation's "undischarge"? Should the Code protect these debtors from improvidence? Before the 1978 Code, the statute did not address the enforceability of a promise to pay a debt discharged in bankruptcy. This bounced the question back to the common law of contracts, which remains quite clear: such debts would be enforced. See Restatement of Contracts (Second), § 83 (1981); Zavelo v. Reeves, 227 U.S. 625, 629 (1913) ("It is settled, however, that a discharge, while releasing the bankrupt from legal liability to pay a debt that was provable in the bankruptcy, leaves him under a moral obligation that is sufficient to support a new promise to pay the debt."). The 1970s era of consumer protection deemed this result unacceptable, and the 1973 Report of the Bankruptcy Commission recommended a complete ban on reaffirmations. The credit industry objected, and the result in the 1978 Code was a requirement that the court make an independent inquiry into whether a reaffirmation was in the "debtor's best interests" before approving the agreement.

Unsurprisingly, this cut the number of reaffirmations dramatically. (Nothing is worse than a reform that works.) The credit industry didn't like this, so it came back in 1984 with a Code amendment that substituted the debtor's lawyer for the courts as the signing-off entity, with courts as backup for *pro se* debtors. As the authors of an important empirical study of reaffirmation noted, "The new reaffirmation routine placed debtors' attorneys in a difficult position. They were to be decision-makers for, rather than advisors to, their clients." Marianne B. Culhane & Michaela M. White, Debt After Discharge: An Empirical Study of Reaffirmation, 73 Am. Bankr. L.J. 709, 716 (1999). Sometimes this puts lawyers in an impossible position.

═══════════ In re HUSAIN ═══════════

364 B.R. 211 (Bankr. E.D. Va. 2007)

HUENNEKENS, Bankruptcy Judge.

Now before the Court are two reaffirmation agreements submitted for approval by the Debtors, Akhter and Farah Husain (the "Debtors"). For reasons set forth below, the Court finds that the agreements are not in the best interests of the Debtors, and therefore, the Court declines to approve the two reaffirmation agreements.

FACTUAL BACKGROUND

The Debtors filed their joint chapter 7 bankruptcy case on October 24, 2006. Throughout these proceedings, the Debtors have been ably represented by competent bankruptcy counsel. The meeting of creditors pursuant to § 341 of the Bankruptcy Code was held on November 20, 2006. On December 8, 2006, the chapter 7 trustee filed a report of no distribution based upon her determination that there were no assets to administer for the benefit of unsecured creditors.

The Debtors' schedules and statement of affairs initially indicated that they intended to redeem their two vehicles. However, the Debtors instead promptly undertook action to reaffirm their obligations with respect to the two vehicles. . . . [O]n January 2, 2007, Debtor Akhter Husain filed with the Court a reaffirmation agreement with Toyota Motor Credit Corporation ("the Toyota Agreement") and a motion for approval of that agreement. In the Toyota Agreement, Debtor Akhter Husain agreed to reaffirm debt to Toyota Motor Credit Corporation in the amount of $15,438.92, at a simple interest rate of 15.6%. Securing this debt was a 2003 Toyota Avalon automobile, originally purchased for $26,617.90 and valued upon the Debtors' schedules at $8,415.00. Under the Toyota Agreement, Debtor Akhter Husain agreed to make 61 monthly payments in the amount of $388.15 each.

Although the Debtors were represented by counsel throughout their bankruptcy case, neither [agreement] filed with the Court contained a certification by the attorney for the Debtors in accordance with 11 U.S.C.A. § 524(c)(3) that the Agreement(s) did not impose an undue hardship on the Debtors. In Part D of each Agreement, Debtor Akhter Husain represented to the Court as follows:

> I believe that this reaffirmation agreement will not impose an undue hardship on my dependents or me. I can afford to make the payments on the reaffirmed debt because my monthly income (take home pay plus any other income received) is $3,145.83 and my actual current monthly expenses including monthly payments on post-bankruptcy debt and other reaffirmation agreements total $7,148.87, leaving $[4,003.04] to make the required payments on this reaffirmed debt. I understand that if my income less my monthly expenses does not leave enough to make the payments, this reaffirmation agreement is presumed to be an undue hardship on me and must be reviewed by the court. However, this presumption may be overcome if I explain to the satisfaction of the court how I can afford to make the payments here. I expect to close the gap between my income and expenses with an expected raise and through working more hours.

The Bankruptcy Code contemplates that counsel's failure to certify a reaffirmation agreement terminates further consideration of the client's ability to reaffirm the debt. Undeterred, the Debtors proceeded on the assumption that their counsel's refusal to execute the certification contained in Part C of the Agreement(s) rendered the Debtors "not represented by an attorney during the course of negotiating" the Agreement(s), and they requested the Court to approve the Agreement(s) under 11 U.S.C.A. § 524(c)(6) absent their counsel's certification. On January 31, 2007, the Court conducted a hearing pursuant to 11 U.S.C.A. § 524(d) on the Debtors' request that the Agreements be approved (the "Hearing").

CONCLUSIONS OF LAW

Section 524 of the Bankruptcy Code allows a debtor to enter into an agreement to reaffirm a debt that would be otherwise dischargeable in the debtor's bankruptcy case. In order to enter into such a reaffirmation, the debtor and the creditor must comply with a prescribed procedure which is designed to ensure that the debtor is well informed and is willingly assuming an obligation that would otherwise have been discharged. The debtor's attorney is required to certify, as part of that procedure, that the agreement does not impose an undue hardship on the debtor and that the debtor has been fully advised of the legal effect and consequences of the agreement. 11 U.S.C.A. § 524(c)(3). If the debtor is not represented by an attorney, then the debtor must certify to the court that the agreement does not impose an undue hardship and that the agreement is in the debtor's best interest. The court then may approve the agreement. 11 U.S.C.A. § 524(c)(6)(A).

Strict compliance with the provisions of § 524 of the Bankruptcy Code has always been a prerequisite to enforce a reaffirmation agreement. Reaffirmation agreements that fail to comply fully have been held void and unenforceable. See, e.g., In re Hovestadt, 193 B.R. 382, 386 (Bankr. D. Mass. 1996). Strict compliance was designed to protect the honest but unfortunate debtor's fresh start. In re Vargas, 257 B.R. 157, 166 n.12 (Bankr. D.N.J. 2001).

For a reaffirmation agreement to be enforceable following enactment of BAPCPA, more is required than just an executed agreement coupled with counsel's certification that the debtor understands the agreement and that it does not impose an undue hardship. The Debtor must now be provided with the detailed disclosures that are set forth in 11 U.S.C.A. § 524(k). The addition of § 524(k) into the Bankruptcy Code is considered one of the primary protections that Congress afforded to chapter 7 debtors when it enacted BAPCPA. The addition was designed to provide an extra measure of consumer protection over and above that previously provided in the Bankruptcy Code.

Section 524(m) of the Bankruptcy Code conditions even further the debtor's ability to enter into a binding reaffirmation agreement by establishing a presumption that any reaffirmation agreement imposes an undue hardship on the debtor "if the debtor's monthly income . . . less the debtor's monthly expenses is less than the scheduled payments on the reaffirmed debt." The debtor may overcome the presumption by submitting to the court, in writing, an explanation of the source of the additional funds that will be needed to comply with the terms of the proposed reaffirmation agreement. 11 U.S.C.A. § 524(m). If the court is satisfied that the debtor is able to overcome the presumption of undue hardship, it may then approve the reaffirmation agreement. Id.

Congress did not anticipate the factual scenario presented in the case at bar when it enacted the statutory framework for enforcement of reaffirmation agreements. The new provisions of BAPCPA contemplate that either (1) a debtor presenting a reaffirmation agreement to the court was represented by counsel throughout the negotiation of the agreement, or (2) the debtor was totally unrepresented by counsel throughout the negotiation.

In this case, however, the Debtors were represented by counsel who found himself in a situation where he was unable to certify to the Court in good conscience that an "undue hardship presumption" did not apply to his clients. This obviously placed Debtors' counsel in an extremely awkward situation.[5] Counsel was forced to choose between the roles of advocate and advisor. Counsel ultimately was not able to abandon his clients and their sincere wishes to reaffirm their debt in spite of the "undue hardship" their decision would impose upon them. Yet, counsel could not agree with his clients that the hardship did not exist.

The Court is cognizant that often, as is the case here, debtors desperately desire to retain their vehicles and that they will continue making their regular payments because transportation is such a crucial element in their search for a "fresh start." If a reaffirmation agreement is approved, however, the debtors will be exposed to a potential deficiency judgment which would be avoided if the reaffirmation agreement were not enforceable.

Counsel resolved the dilemma by declining to execute Part C of the Agreements but by advocating, nevertheless, at the hearing the Debtors' desire that the Agreements be approved as enforceable for the sole reason that the Debtors needed to be able to keep their cars. This position places the Court in a quandary. Is counsel's decision to not execute the Part C certification of the Agreement(s) equivalent to the Debtors' not being represented by an attorney during the course of negotiating the Agreement(s), thus permitting the Court to conduct a hearing pursuant to the provisions of 11 U.S.C.A. § 524(d) and (c)(6)? Or on the other hand, does counsel's refusal to sign the "No undue hardship" certification put an end to any further inquiry and, in and of itself, terminate the reaffirmation process?

Even if counsel had executed Part C of the Agreements, § 524(m) of the Bankruptcy Code, as noted above, would have required further Court scrutiny. That section raises a rebuttable presumption that a reaffirmation agreement imposes an undue hardship on the debtor if the debtor's monthly income, less the debtor's monthly expenses as shown on the debtor's completed and signed statement in support of the agreement, as required by § 524(k)(6)(A) of the Bankruptcy Code, is less than the scheduled payments on the reaffirmed debt. 11 U.S.C.A. § 524(m). Here, the Debtors' income after expenses is not adequate to make the monthly payments required by

---

[5]At the hearing on the reaffirmation Agreements, the Court asked counsel for Debtors whether he thought reaffirmation would constitute an undue hardship for Debtors. Debtors' counsel asked the Court to permit him to simply stand by the fact that he had not signed the Part C certification without requiring him to further weigh in on the subject. The Court granted this request.

the Agreements.[6] Thus, the presumption of undue hardship applies in this case. Section 524(m) requires that the presumption "shall be reviewed by the court." As § 524(m) further provides that the presumption of undue hardship may be rebutted "to the satisfaction of the court," this Court has the discretion to look beyond the raw numbers in determining whether the reaffirmation agreement should be approved.

In this case, the Debtors can rebut the presumption (i) by providing an explanation that identifies additional sources of funds to make the payments as agreed upon under the terms of the reaffirmation Agreements (ii) by demonstrating that the value of the asset exceeds the amount of the debt to be assumed, or (iii) by proving to the satisfaction of the Court that the Debtors' need for the vehicles outweighs the Court's consideration of the sources for those additional funds or the undersecured nature of the obligation the Debtors desire to assume.

The evidence advanced by the Debtors to rebut the presumption on the first point included the statement of Debtor Akhter Husain that "I expect to close the gap between my income and expenses with an expected raise and through working more hours." Counsel for the Debtors proffered the testimony of the Debtors (who were both present at the Hearing) that Mr. Husain was slated to begin a job in February of 2007 which the Debtors expected would bring in an additional $1,000.00 per month in monthly net income. As this projected additional income would still leave the Debtors with a deficit of expenses over income of approximately $3,000.00 per month, the Court finds that it is insufficient to overcome the § 524(m) presumption of undue hardship. [Motion to reaffirm denied; a separate order shall issue.]

Was the Husains' lawyer's solution a Solomonic compromise or a violation of the rules of professional conduct? Some courts frown when lawyers try to wiggle with "limited representation" that disavows an attorney-client relationship (leaving the debtor *pro se*) when the discrete issue of reaffirmation arises: "[T]he decision to reaffirm an otherwise dischargeable debt plays a critical role in the bankruptcy process—so critical, that assistance with the decision must be counted among the necessary services that make up competent representation of a Chapter 7 debtor." In re Minardi, 399 B.R. 841, 848 (Bankr. N.D. Okla. 2009). This court also refused to relieve counsel of responsibility for addressing a client's desire to reaffirm a debt because the Code itself put such a responsibility "at the feet of debtor's counsel." Id. The ABI Commission confronted this ethical division among courts toward allowing limited representation and was bold to conclude: "The Commission has not taken a position on the specific question of whether attorneys can properly unbundle services related to reaffirmation agreements from other bankruptcy services." ABI Report § 3.02.

---

[6] The Debtors' schedules I and J filed in this case and their statement of income included in Part D of the reaffirmation Agreements each indicate that their monthly income is exceeded by their monthly expenses (including the scheduled payments on the subject debts to be reaffirmed) by $4,003.04.

Few lawyers relished being required to attest that the objective numbers showing facial unaffordability of the reaffirmation contract ought nonetheless be ignored (in the best interests of the debtor, no less). Continuing legal education programs are filled with lamentations by attorneys that are not certified financial planners or accredited credit counselors—or generally their client's keepers. Yet lawyers often give business advice to their commercial clients, so are they protesting too much? While the consumer lawyer is not a financial counselor, the lawyer may have more experience that bears on these decisions than anyone otherwise available to a consumer debtor.

Nonetheless, the fundamental point for many lawyers is that they traditionally are their clients' advocates, not the arbiters of their decisions. No question could cut closer to the lawyerly bone than a debtor who has been refused the lawyer's signature on a reaffirmation agreement and asks "Whose side are you on, anyway?" The National Consumer Law Center sums up the recommended position in response to the 2005 amendments and case law interpreting them.

> Attorneys should be extremely cautious in negotiating and validating reaffirmation agreements. There are serious problems of possible malpractice liability if such an agreement later causes harm to the debtor, for example through the debtor's loss of property if the debtor does not later pay the reaffirmed debt. . . . Thus, it is usually better practice to avoid reaffirmations if at all possible.

Consumer Bankruptcy Law and Practice, § 15.5.3.

As a future lawyer, you should like the sound of avoiding malpractice liability, but wonder exactly how to "avoid" reaffirmations. Many lawyers, if locally forbidden to carve out reaffirmations from their representation, do have a blanket policy of refusing to approve them, particularly when the debtor lacks equity in the property. As one firm explains in its website, the result of no reaffirmation in such a situation is that "Certainly you will have to find another vehicle. This takes some effort but it can be done." We wonder if the retention agreement for these attorneys now includes in its package of service the cost of an attorney negotiating a new car loan for the debtor at a buy-here, pay-here car dealer. Ken Bensinger, A Vicious Cycle in the Used-Car Business, *L.A. Times*, Oct. 30, 2011. We also hope that a lawyer who reserves the right not to approve a reaffirmation discloses that position before representing a client who indicates a powerful desire to reaffirm.

As if reaffirmation weren't complicated enough with all the above considerations, there are special rules for credit unions. This impressive bit of political maneuvering resulted from credit card companies trying to keep the credit unions on board with BAPCPA. Now a credit union can get a reaffirmation agreement, even if the budget numbers show that the debtor cannot pay for it so long as the debtor says it's all good. § 524(m)(2), (k)(6)(B). As a bonus, the debtor's attorney only has to certify that there is no undue hardship, but is excused from having to attest to the debtor's actual ability to pay when the creditor is a credit union, further enabling this fuzzy math. § 524(k)(5)(C). It might seem an odd position for the consumer-friendly credit unions to take, pressing for special rights to squeeze their members for demonstrably unpayable debts, but credit unions have taken the position that making people stick to their promises is a good lesson in financial literacy and "responsibility." Does that mean the fresh start of the bankruptcy discharge promotes illiteracy and irresponsibility?

One last note on reaffirmation. Nothing in the Code differentiates secured debt from unsecured debt. That means a debtor could, if inclined, reaffirm a wholly unsecured and thus completely dischargeable debt that can't imperil any of the debtor's property. We explore this later in the assignment, but note here that the concerns about protecting debtors from improvident decisions and the discomfort of lawyers are even sharper with unsecured debts.

3.   *Ride-through*

The third of the 3Rs for keeping property is ride-through or retention. You will search the Code in vain for mention of this option because it results from case law, not statute. The basic idea is simple—the debtor just keeps on keepin' on, making the contractual payments without signing any new agreements, and the creditor cashes those payments while letting the collateral stay put with the debtor. Keeping the collateral by continuing to make the pre-bankruptcy payments, without redeeming or reaffirming—but discharging any personal liability on the debt—sounds like the best of all worlds for the debtor. If the collateral is damaged or destroyed, the debtor can simply walk away from it, bearing no responsibility for any deficiency. But the creditor might make out better too. If the debtor keeps paying, the creditor will be repaid in full notwithstanding the debtor's bankruptcy, a much greater return than if the debtor cashed out the creditor with a redemption, paying only the market value of the collateral and taking a pass on the rest of the loan amount. Crucially, to ride through, the debtor must not be in default at the time of bankruptcy; otherwise there would be a default that likely authorizes repossession once the stay is lifted when the case is over.

Because the Code made no specific reference to ride-through, the issue of whether a debtor could even make such a move reached the courts of appeals, with a number of decisions each way. Congress appears to have tried to eliminate ride-through in BAPCPA, which courts have generally held for the most part worked, at least for personal property. Daimler Chrysler Fin. Servs. Am., LLC v. Jones (In re Jones), 591 F.3d 308 (4th Cir. 2010). But the twists and turns of the law on ride-through are now incredibly complex, making what used to be one of the simplest ideas in bankruptcy—I keep paying you and you let me keep the collateral—into a real puzzler. At the heart of the confusion are multiple Code provisions that provide room for inconsistent readings. The starting point is § 521(a)(2) (largely echoed by § 521(a)(6)), which commands debtors to state an intention to do one of three things, § 521(a)(2)(A), and then to do them, § 521(a)(2)(B): surrender the property, reaffirm the contract with the secured party, or redeem pursuant to § 722. Creditors enjoy three separate Code sections that help enforce these obligations: §§ 362(h), 521(a)(6), and 521(d). The first section simply removes the collateral from the estate and lifts the stay unless the debtor takes the stated action. There is an exception if the debtor tries to reaffirm on the loan's original terms and the creditor refuses to agree (a small shake of the congressional finger at the *Pendlebury* court?). The second is similar, without the *Pendlebury* exception, but appears to apply only to PMSIs. The third resurrects certain contract clauses halted by bankruptcy's automatic stay if the debtor flouts § 521.

Notwithstanding these remedies, ride-through is alive and well in practice, albeit in fewer circumstances than before and with major splits of judicial opinion.

In re SCHWASS
378 B.R. 859 (Bankr. S.D. Cal. 2007)

Bowie, Chief Judge.

. . .

On July 2, 2007, Mary Catherine Schwass (Debtor) filed a petition commencing this chapter 7 case. Prior to the filing Debtor had borrowed money from Pacific Capital Bancorp dba Santa Barbara Bank & Trust (Movant) to purchase a 2001 Ford Explorer (Vehicle). Debtor granted Movant a security interest in the Vehicle to secured repayment of the loan.

With her petition Debtor filed a Statement of Intention which indicated that she intended to reaffirm her obligation to Movant. Counsel for Movant wrote to Debtor's counsel requesting that he prepare the reaffirmation agreement. Debtor's counsel replied that Debtor had no obligation to prepare the agreement, but that he would do so for a fee payable by Movant. Movant replied that it was Debtor's responsibility, thus completing the stalemate. Thirty days elapsed from the date set for the first meeting of creditors with no reaffirmation agreement having been filed. Thereafter, Movant moved for relief from stay on the ground that Debtor did not timely follow through with her intention to reaffirm. A hearing was held and the Court took the matter under submission.

DISCUSSION

Section 521(a)(2)(A) requires that the statement of intention be filed within 30 days of the petition. As noted, Debtor included with her petition a statement of intention to reaffirm her debt to Movant, thus complying with subsection (A).

Section 521(a)(2)(B) provides that a debtor must perform her stated intention within 30 days after the first date set for the § 341(a) meeting of creditors. In this case the meeting was set for August 9, 2007. Thus, under § 521(a)(2)(B) Debtor was required to "perform" on her statement of intention to reaffirm on or before September 8, 2007. It is undisputed that no reaffirmation agreement has been filed in this case. Thus, the issue is whether performance under § 521(b)(2)(B) requires a debtor to prepare and file the reaffirmation agreement, or whether it is sufficient that a debtor state her intent to reaffirm and stand by ready to execute a reaffirmation agreement prepared by the secured creditor—in this case Movant.

Reaffirmation of debts and the agreements and disclosures required therefor is governed by 11 U.S.C. § 524(c) and (k). The Court is aware of no express provision or court decision dictating that one party or the other shall prepare the reaffirmation agreement. However, it appears clear to the Court from a review of the requirements of § 524(c) and (k) that the responsibility for preparing the agreement falls on the secured creditor.

Section 524(c)(2) provides that a reaffirmed debt is excepted from discharge only if "the debtor received the disclosures described in subsection (k) at or before the time at which the debtor signed the agreement. . . ." If the debtor is to receive the disclosures under subsection (k), it makes sense that the disclosures come from the secured party—it would be nonsensical to have a debtor receive the disclosures from herself. It is of course possible for a debtor to receive the disclosures from her own counsel. However, debtors acting pro se are also able to reaffirm debts. See subsection 524(k)(5)(A) ("Certification of Debtor's Attorney (If Any) . . .").

Subsection (k) is even more convincing. First, the disclosure statement required under subsection (c) must contain the total amount of the debt to be reaffirmed including fees and costs incurred as of the date of the disclosure statement. See subsection 524(k)(3)(C). Obviously, this is information most readily supplied by the secured creditor. Second, the disclosure statement is replete with phrases such as "may obligate you," "you have agreed," "your loan," "if you have questions," and "if you want to reaffirm." This is clearly language directed to the debtor. It would make no sense for a debtor to prepare such a disclosure statement with such disclosures to herself. Finally, the reaffirmation agreement as described in subsection (4) begins with the required phrase "I (we) agree to reaffirm" which clearly refers to the debtor(s). There is also a requirement for certification by debtor's attorney. Again, these are apparent indications that the reaffirmation agreement, along with the disclosure statement, are designed to be directed to, as opposed to prepared by, the debtor. Since the only other party to the agreement is the secured creditor whose debt is to [be] reaffirmed, it follows that the responsibility to prepare the documents falls on such secured creditor.

The Court is comfortable with this arrangement, since it is the secured creditor who stands to benefit from the reaffirmation of the debt. Further, under § 524(c) the reaffirmation agreement is enforceable only if, among other things, the debtor receives the prescribed disclosures on or before the time the debtor signs the agreement.

So ride-through survives, at least in some circumstances. But ride-through may or may not bring repossession risk. Wait, how can a creditor repossess if the debtor is current on the loan, a precondition of ride-through, and hence not in default? Slick lenders contractually make the grounds for default much more capacious than simply missing a payment. They make, e.g., the mere filing of bankruptcy itself, ipso facto, a ground of default. Think it through: if merely filing bankruptcy is a default, then after the bankruptcy case is over and the stay is lifted, the lender could immediately seize the collateral for this default, as few debtors have time machines to go back and undo a default of merely filing. Concerned by this technicality, many courts invalidated such ipso facto default clauses under a combination of policy, the structure of the Bankruptcy Code, and specific provisions you will learn about later like § 365(e). These courts may be right: it seems strange to say bankruptcy gives debtors a fresh start but the debtors can be held in default and lose their property immediately upon filing for bankruptcy. Riggs Nat'l Bank v. Perry, 729 F.2d 982 (4th Cir. 1984).

As part of BAPCPA's clamp-down on ride-through, Congress provided the aforementioned third remedy, § 521(d), that enforces the § 521(a)(2), (6) obligations. Section 521(d) resurrects the enforceability of ipso facto default clauses (legislatively overruling the contrary cases that invalidate them) when debtors flunk the § 521 and § 362(h) requirements. Clever lawyers and courts, however, have found ways to overcome even these provisions, giving us the wonderful idea of a "back door" ride-through.

In re WILSON

2012 WL 2411918 (Bankr. N.D. W. Va. June 26, 2012)

FLATLEY, Bankruptcy Judge.

Pending before the court is a motion by Johnnie W. Wilson ("Debtor") to approve a reaffirmation agreement ("Reaffirmation Agreement") with CSC Logic. The Debtor and his wife, Linda L. Wilson, filed their joint chapter 7 bankruptcy petition on February 15, 2012. On that same date, the Debtor filed a statement of intention, seeking to reaffirm a debt secured by his 2001 Dodge Caravan ("Vehicle"). On March 19, 2012, the Debtor filed his Reaffirmation Agreement and a Motion for Approval of Reaffirmation Agreement. The Clerk set a reaffirmation hearing because his motion indicated that he was not represented by an attorney during the negotiation of the Reaffirmation Agreement. 11 U.S.C. §§ 524(c)(6)(A)-524(d); see 11 U.S.C. § 524(m).

During the reaffirmation hearing on April 20, 2012, Debtor's counsel appeared and explicitly noted on the record that he did not approve of the Reaffirmation Agreement.[3] He urged this court, however, to permit a "ride-through" because the Debtor complied with the strictures of 11 U.S.C. §§ 524(c) and 521(a) and has "made the payments every time" on the Vehicle; he further emphasized that retention of the Vehicle was necessary

---

[3]The court differentiates between Debtor and his counsel to illustrate that although the Debtor was not represented by counsel during the course of negotiating the Reaffirmation Agreement, Debtor's counsel attended the reaffirmation hearing to argue in the alternative: if the Motion for Approval of Reaffirmation Agreement was denied, the court should consider a "ride-through." It is not uncommon that attorneys find themselves in just such an awkward position. See generally In re Husain, 364 B.R. 211, 216 (Bankr. E.D. Va. 2007); Lisa A. Napoli, *Reaffirmation After the Bankruptcy Abuse Prevention and Consumer Protection Act of 2005: Many Questions, Some Answers*, 81 Am. Bankr. L.J. 259, 271-72 (2007) ("BAPCPA has left debtor's counsel in a quandary as to what to do about the Attorney Certification.").

for the Debtor to transport his wife to Morgantown, West Virginia for medical appointments. . . .

A presumption of undue hardship arises under § 524(m) if the debtor's declaration indicates a budget that is insufficient to make payments on the reaffirmed debt. § 524(m) (stating that a reaffirmation agreement "shall be presumed" an undue hardship "if the debtor's monthly income less the debtor's monthly expenses . . . is less than the schedule payments on the reaffirmed debt."). A debtor may rebut this presumption by submitting a written explanation to the court that specifies how additional funds will be obtained to comply with the terms of the proposed reaffirmation agreement. Id.; see Fed. R. Bankr. P. 4008(b).

Here, the presumption of undue hardship arises because the Debtor's income after expenses is insufficient to make the monthly payments as required by the proposed Reaffirmation Agreement. § 524(m). According to the Debtor's Schedules I and J and statement of income and expenses included in the Reaffirmation Agreement, his monthly expenses exceed his income by $158.00. The Debtor explained in Part II.C of the Reaffirmation Agreement that he can afford the payments on the reaffirmed debt because his son helps him make the payments. At the hearing on April 20, 2012, the Debtor said his son helps him make the payments because he mows his lawn. The Debtor, however, provided no evidence regarding the son's continuing ability to pay for his services. . . . The court finds that the Debtor failed to rebut the presumption of undue hardship; accordingly, the court disapproves of the Reaffirmation Agreement.

In the alternative, the Debtor argues that this court should permit him to retain the Vehicle and have it "pass-through" the bankruptcy case unaffected. The option the Debtor requests, commonly known as a "back door ride-through" or "pay and drive" in bankruptcy jargon, is an issue of first impression for this court; however, not novel to sister bankruptcy courts within the Fourth Circuit. This court agrees with the holdings of In re Chim, 381 B.R. 191 (Bankr. D. Md. 2008) and In re Husain, 364 B.R. 211 (Bankr. E.D. Va. 2007) that the back door ride-through remains viable after BAPCPA for personal property. . . .

The Debtor in this case fully performed his duties under §§ 521(a) and 362(h). . . . Consequently, the Debtor has avoided the implications of § 521(d); namely, any ipso facto clause contained in the loan agreement becoming operative. § 521(d) ("If the debtor fails timely to take the action specified in . . . [§ 521(a)(6), § 362(h)(1), or § 362(h)(2)], with respect to property which . . . a creditor holds a security interest . . . , nothing in this title shall prevent or limit the operation" of an ipso facto clause in the underlying agreement).

Conclusion

At the reaffirmation hearing, the Debtor said that he is current on Vehicle payments; the automatic stay and discharge injunction will continue provided that the Debtor remains current on his payments due under the Reaffirmation Agreement. In re Husain, 364 B.R. at 219 ("Once the discharge is granted, the creditors may not repossess the vehicles [e.g., on account of ipso facto default] without violating the discharge injunction unless there is a subsequent payment or insurance default."). CSC Logic may continue to accept payments under § 524(l)(1). In re Stevens, 365 B.R. 610, 612 (Bankr. E.D. Va. 2007). And because the Debtor has complied with §§ 521(a) and 362(h), CSC Logic cannot exercise the relief provisions of §§ 362(h), 521(a)(6), and 521(d). A separate order will be entered pursuant to Fed. R. Bankr. P. 9021.

———————————

This chaos of back doors and workarounds suggests that ride-through just won't die, which suggests economic forces out of step with formal law. The reality is that many debtors desperately need to keep collateral subject to a security interest, such as, in many regions, a car that is the near-indispensable means of getting to work. Blithely asserting reaffirmation is the solution makes no sense when debtors are deeply underwater on the property, which is surely why lawyers are pushing back. Because redemption under § 722 requires an oft-unaffordable lump-sum payment, ride-through seems necessary to fill a void in chapter 7. It also explains the need many debtors have to file chapter 13 when they want to hold onto critical collateral, such as that car.

B.   UNSECURED DEBTS: FUTURE OBLIGATIONS

While courts may question the wisdom of reaffirmations, debtors continue to file such agreements at a steady clip. The Administrative Office of the U.S. Courts reports that there was at least one reaffirmation agreement filed in 22% of chapter 7 cases closed in 2018. Unfortunately, no reliable data exist on how many of these agreements pertain to secured versus unsecured debts, let alone the approval rate by courts or attorneys.

Of course, a debtor can always repay a creditor voluntarily after bankruptcy. § 524(f). A properly obtained reaffirmation agreement, however, goes much further than voluntary repayment; its effect is to revive the debt and make it fully enforceable in a court of law. The concerns about the potential drag that reaffirmations can place on the debtor's financial recovery after bankruptcy are even more acute for unsecured debts, when the debtor cannot offer the justification of reaffirming to keep collateral that applies to secured debt. Creditors do have leverage to persuade debtors to reaffirm unsecured debts. For example, a creditor may be willing to drop or eschew filing an objection to discharge if a debtor reaffirms an obligation. Or a debtor might reaffirm to prevent a creditor from pursuing a co-signer on the debt, especially when the co-signer is a family member. In re Paglia, 302 B.R. 162 (Bankr. W.D. Pa. 2003). The case below explores a creditor's other major leverage point: the opportunity to engage in future borrowing.

In re DUKE
79 F.3d 43 (7th Cir. 1996)

WOOD, Circuit Judge.

Although bankruptcy is normally viewed as a process through which a debtor obtains relief from pre-petition obligations and gets a fresh start in life (financially, at least), things are not always that simple. This case presents a wrinkle that occurs when, during the bankruptcy proceeding, a creditor makes an offer to a debtor to reaffirm a pre-petition debt, in exchange for certain benefits. The debtor's lawyer here believes that the creditor was too heavy-handed in its tactics, and thus ran afoul of the automatic stay rule of 11 U.S.C. § 362(a). The district court disagreed and ruled that the creditor had played by the rules. We affirm.

On September 23, 1994, William Duke filed a Chapter 7 bankruptcy petition in which he listed Sears, Roebuck & Co. (Sears) as one of his creditors. Duke's filing triggered the automatic stay provision of the Bankruptcy Code, 11 U.S.C. § 362(a)(6), which prohibits a creditor from engaging in "any act to collect, assess, or recover a claim against the debtor that arose before commencement of the case under this title." After it received notice of the automatic stay, Sears sent the following letter to Duke's attorney, with a copy to Duke himself "for information purposes":

Dear Robert L. Adams:

We have been notified that you are representing our customer in Chapter 7 bankruptcy proceedings.

There is a balance of $317.10 on this account.

Should your client elect to reaffirm the Sears account upon liquidation of the outstanding balance in accordance with the Reaffirmation Agreement, charge privileges will be reinstated with a line of credit in the amount of $500.00.

Enclosed are copies of the proposed Reaffirmation Agreement. Your courtesy and cooperation in this matter are greatly appreciated. Please let me know if we may be of further assistance.

Very truly yours,
K. Jaggers
Bankruptcy Representative
cc: Debtor (For information purposes only)

First before the bankruptcy court, then in the district court, and now here, Duke claimed that this letter amounted to an impermissible attempt to "collect, assess, or recover a claim" in violation of § 362(a)(6).

In essence, this case presents a question about the relation between the automatic stay of § 362(a)(6) and reaffirmation agreements, which are authorized and regulated by 11 U.S.C. § 524. A reaffirmation agreement is one in which the debtor agrees to repay all or part of a dischargeable debt after a bankruptcy petition has been filed. As one bankruptcy court explained it, "a reaffirmation agreement has the effect of reaffirming a debtor's preexisting in personam liability on the underlying obligations giving rise to the debt." In re Walker, 180 B.R. 834, 846 (Bankr. W.D. La. 1995). See also In re Grabinski, 150 B.R. 427, 430 (Bankr. N.D. Ill. 1993). The debtor choice to reaffirm creates a voluntary exception to the "fresh start" that bankruptcy otherwise confers. For that reason, the Bankruptcy Code contains various safeguards designed to assure that reaffirmations are genuine and that they are not the product of abusive creditor practices. See 11 U.S.C. § 524(d); . . . [s]ee also In re Edwards, 901 F.2d 1383, 1386 (7th Cir. 1990) (reaffirmation is a fully voluntary negotiation on both sides).

The automatic stay provision of § 362, as noted above, generally prohibits the creditor from taking "any act" to collect pre-petition debts. Its purpose, as this Court explained in Matthews v. Rosene, 739 F.2d 249, 251 (7th Cir. 1984), is "to benefit a debtor by preventing harassment and frustration of rehabilitation efforts through pursuit by creditors in individual actions." Taken to its logical extreme, § 362 could be construed to prohibit all contact between creditors and debtors after a petition has been filed, with respect to dischargeable debts. The courts have not pushed it that far, however, not least because to do so would create significant tension with the right to reaffirm. Instead, they have focussed on the anti-harassment purpose of § 362. . . .

This Court has not yet had the occasion to decide whether a creditor violates § 362(a)(6) when it sends a letter to a debtor offering to reaffirm a pre-petition debt. A majority of the bankruptcy courts have found that these actions do not violate § 362(a)(6) as long as the letter is nonthreatening and non-coercive. See, e.g., In re Hazzard, 1995 WL 110588 (Bankr. N.D. Ill. 1995); In re Jefferson, 144 B.R. 620, 623 (Bankr. D.R.I. 1992) (citing additional cases); see also In re Epperson, 189 B.R. 195, 198 (E.D. Mo. 1995). Duke can prevail here only if we accept one of two propositions: (1) that all creditor-initiated offers to reaffirm debts violate § 362(a)(6); or (2) that offers to reaffirm in general are permissible if they are not threatening or coercive, but this one falls within the prohibited group.

As we note above, other courts have rejected the extreme reading of § 362(a)(6) that the first of these propositions would require, and we think rightly so. The option of reaffirming would be empty if creditors were forbidden to engage in any communication whatsoever with debtors who have pre-petition obligations. If that were the rule, it is also hard to see what purpose the detailed rules governing enforceability of reaffirmation agreements contained in § 524(c) would serve. By requiring a right to rescind, filing with the court, and an attorney's affidavit attesting that the debtor was fully informed, acted voluntarily, and that the agreement does not impose an undue hardship on the debtor, § 524(c) addresses the fairness of a completed reaffirmation agreement. The assumption behind these provisions is that debtors will be agreeing to enter into some reaffirmation agreements, and that it is important to have in place certain institutional protections to guard against creditor overreaching. See Collier on Bankruptcy, para. 524.04 & n.2 (15th ed. 1995).

There is no reason to believe that reaffirmation agreements inevitably disadvantage debtors, and thus that the automatic stay should be used to protect debtors against this type of creditor effort to collect a pre-petition debt. Debtors might find the idea of a new credit relationship attractive, since this too can be part of a fresh financial start after bankruptcy. A line of credit can be a convenience for larger purchases, as the habits of millions of Americans so richly attest. . . . Creditors, obviously, like the idea that bankruptcy may not result in a complete write-off of amounts due to them. Under both the rule that ensures that creditor offers to reaffirm are not coercive or threatening and the statutory protections of § 524(c), both parties can enjoy the legitimate benefits of reaffirmations, and the debtor is protected from abuse of the system. . . .

Duke does not argue that this particular letter was threatening or coercive in its contents. It is true that the letter extends the "carrot" of the $500 line of credit for Duke if he decides to reaffirm the $317.10 debt and he pays it off. It is also true that the line between withholding of a benefit and imposition of a penalty can be elusive at times. Nevertheless, this letter is as bare-bones and straightforward as one can get. There is not a hint of unfavorable action that would be taken against Duke if he does not reaffirm. It does not even say that his chances of re-establishing credit with Sears would be prejudiced if he chooses not to reaffirm and then later seeks new credit after his discharge in bankruptcy. Under the circumstances, Duke was wise not to rely on this line of argument.

That leaves the possibility that it is inherently coercive to send a copy of a letter to an attorney directly to the debtor-client, for information purposes only (as the letter stated). The record is not clear as to whether "K. Jaggers, Bankruptcy Representative," was acting as an attorney for Sears or as an employee of the Sears collection department. If K. Jaggers was acting as an attorney or under the direction of an attorney, the Sears practice of "cc'ing" represented consumer debtors raises questions under the rules of professional conduct for attorneys. Illinois Rule of Professional Conduct 4.2 states generally that a lawyer should not communicate or cause another to communicate with a represented person unless the first lawyer obtains the prior consent of the second lawyer, "or as may otherwise be authorized by law." If K. Jaggers was acting purely as a debt collector, the practice Sears has adopted raises questions under the Fair Debt Collection Practices Act. 15 U.S.C. §§ 1692 et seq. Under § 1692c(a)(2), a debt collector may not communicate with a consumer, without the consumer's permission, "if the debt collector knows the consumer is represented by an attorney with respect to such debt and has knowledge of, or can readily ascertain such attorney's name and address." In either case, there is no dispute that Sears knew that Duke was represented, and it knew the name and address of Duke's attorney. Duke, however, did not raise these points either in the lower courts or before this Court, and they are therefore not before us.

We conclude that the letter Sears sent to Duke did not violate the automatic stay provisions of § 362, nor does the Bankruptcy Code require as a matter of law that the creditor refrain from copying the debtor on correspondence to the debtor's attorney. We therefore AFFIRM the judgment of the district court.

Note the economics of the deal presented to Mr. Duke. Sears offered him $500.00 in credit in return for committing to repay $317.10. This is not the same as offering him a "net" $182.90 in new credit, however, because he has to pay interest on the full outstanding balance. In essence, Duke has to draw 63% of his new credit line upfront and start the interest clock ticking if he wants to keep a Sears account. Ouch. One year after the *Duke* decision, another court took a hard look at Sears' reaffirmation process and did not like what it saw. See In re Lantanowich, 207 B.R. 326 (Bankr. D. Mass. 1997) (Sears' massive practice of "rogue" reaffirmations out of compliance with § 524's rules required $300-500 million in sanctions [which some academics later estimated was a fraction of their annual reaffirmation business]).

Some research suggests that all the debate and lawmaking about reaffirmations may be missing the larger problem that hinders financial recovery: some people simply do not earn enough to pay their ongoing bills, even with a discharge of past debt. Consider this finding. One year after receiving a discharge, one-third of chapter 7 debtors reported to researchers that their financial situation was the same or worse than when they filed bankruptcy. See Katherine Porter & Deborah Thorne, The Failure of Bankruptcy's Fresh Start, 92 Cornell L. Rev. 67, 87 (2006). Reaffirmations did not seem to be a factor. Id. at 98-99. Instead, ongoing income problems from things like weak employment situations or chronic illness that prevented full-time work held families back from recovering their financial footing. Id. at 94.

Empirical research has also opened a window into how bankruptcy affects access to credit. One of us found that not only was it possible for debtors to borrow after bankruptcy but that creditors aggressively market to those they lament to Congress as "deadbeats." Katherine Porter, Bankrupt Profits: The Credit Industry's Business Model for Postbankruptcy Lending, 93 Iowa L. Rev. 1369 (2008) (reporting that 87% of households said they had received credit offers specifically mentioning their bankruptcies); see also Song Han & Geng Li, Household Borrowing After Personal Bankruptcy, 43 J. Money, Credit & Banking 491 (2011). Freed from old debts, these families are attractive borrowers because new creditors will not have to compete with dozens of other lenders for repayment and the borrower cannot get another chapter 7 bankruptcy discharge for eight years. § 727(a)(8). But there's a catch: people who have filed bankruptcy do pay higher rates than nonbankrupts for credit, even secured credit, notwithstanding the hungry lenders.

Despite this widespread credit availability, many debtors eschew borrowing or sharply curb prior habits, particularly with respect to credit cards. Katherine Porter, Life After Debt: Understanding the Credit Restraint of Bankruptcy Debtors, 18 Am. Bank. L. Rev. 1, 9 (2010) (finding that 75% of debtors who filed chapter 7 in 2001 had not accepted new credit in the first year after bankruptcy). The law also gives chapter 7 debtors a powerful incentive to steer clear of debt in the years after a discharge: the eight-year ban on another chapter 7 discharge. A debtor given a chapter 13 discharge in the prior six years is similarly prohibited from getting a chapter 7 discharge.

C. NONDISCRIMINATION AND CREDIT SCORING

In addition to worrying about creditors that try to avoid the effects of the discharge, debtors seeking a fresh start also face the risk that employers or government agencies will look askance at someone who has been bankrupt and will refuse a job, a license, or a permit crucial to the debtor's livelihood or well-being. Conscious of that risk, Congress included § 525 in the Code, which forbids that sort of discrimination. This supplants the prohibition on firing employees for having a garnishment order (but apparently not two garnishment orders). 15 U.S.C. § 1674(a). On the whole, however, the reported cases find the courts interpreting these provisions narrowly. It appears more debtors have lost than won.

Bankruptcy can stay on your credit score for ten years under the FCRA, 15 U.S.C. § 1681c(a)(1), but the major credit bureaus have policies of removing bankruptcies after seven years. People who file bankruptcy may find their fresh start in life encumbered by the double dings to their credit score: the late payments and defaults that typically preceded the bankruptcy, and the act of filing for bankruptcy relief itself. Deborah Thorne, Personal Bankruptcy and the Credit Report: Conflicting Mechanisms of Social Mobility, 11 J. Poverty, no. 4, 2008, at 23 (noting ironic confluence of policies that substantially undermine bankruptcy's fresh start through negative social consequences of reduced credit scores that saddle debtors for years). See Jay L. Zagorsky & Lois R. Lupica, A Study of Consumers' Post-Discharge Finances: Struggle, Stasis, or Fresh-Start?, 16 Am. Bankr. Inst. L. Rev. 283 (2008). That may not be the note on which you were hoping to end this assignment, but the data are what the data are.

Problem Set 9

9.1. The Muscle Mart is the only complete bodybuilding gym in Missoula, Montana. It charges a monthly membership and adds assessments for use of the sauna and items ordered at the juice bar. MM has a firm policy (would they have flabby policies?): if two months of dues or sauna fees are left unpaid, the membership is revoked, and the former member is not permitted to use any of the equipment until the unpaid balance is paid in full.

Peter Lanier has just filed for a chapter 7 bankruptcy, discharging among his other debts two months' worth of MM dues. MM has revoked Peter's membership, and Peter is frantic to get back to his workouts. He has offered to pay a month in advance, but MM refuses. What would you advise Peter? See § 524(a), (c).

9.2. Two months ago, you handled a routine chapter 7 bankruptcy for Kevin James. Kevin is a gentle soul, and the bankruptcy has been bothering him. Last week, he was in a local hardware store when the owner (a former creditor) made a remark about "stiffing your friends." Kevin said he felt terrible and offered to repay the debt. The owner, an enterprising fellow, got this promise in writing. Now Kevin fears this was not very smart. He is struggling with his current obligations and is not sure he can pay the hardware store. He calls you to ask if that written agreement is enforceable. What do you tell him? See § 524(c).

9.3. Bob "Bull" Horne supports his wife and five children at a marginal level with his job as a janitor at a local bar. Bull lives for weekends in the mountains at his home-away-from-home, "Carnage Cabin." Bull hunts from dawn to dusk and often invites friends to join him. He uses much of the meat, including venison, to feed his family, but you got the impression from his wife that she would rather have him helping with the kids. The cabin is subject to a $10,000 mortgage, with $100 monthly payments. Bull says the cabin is "priceless," pointing out he built it with his own hands, but you suspect its market value is close to $5,000. Bull has a few exempt assets, including a retirement account worth $25,000, but his family lives pretty much hand-to-mouth on its budget. The creditor on the cabin loan is a national bank; you've called counsel several times with no response yet and you aren't waiting by the phone for it to ring. Bull has forcefully told you that he wants to keep the cabin and that he thinks it's your job to make that happen. Consider all options for Bull in chapter 7 bankruptcy. See §§ 524(c), 722.

9.4. Christine Johnson is a single mother of two children who until recently has managed to keep the family in reasonable shape after her husband's death in a car–train accident. Her skills as a die etcher in the local microchip plant produced a decent income until a year ago, when the plant headed for somewhere in Asia. She held out for a technical job for quite a while, running up substantial bills, but she has been waiting tables and working a night-shift cleaning job to keep food on the table. Her big worry is holding on to her house and her car. The credit union has the mortgage. You've dealt with them before and know their policy: They'll happily agree to a reaff on the mortgage, but only if Christine also reaffirms in full all her other debts to the credit union, which include a car loan and a credit card. The car is a four-year-old Honda the couple bought used almost three years ago. She owes $7,300 on it, although its Bluebook value is $5,900. She is desperate to keep it, because it works pretty well (her husband was a mechanic and knew cars). If she had to buy a new one, "they could sell me trash and I wouldn't know it." Without a car, she couldn't get to either job. The house is her dream home, and Christine says she'd work three jobs to keep it. What do you advise her and what will you do? See § 524(c), (m).

9.5. Your firm represents Peoples State Bank, which does a substantial amount of consumer lending. Because your firm has taken care of PSB's legal work for years, you know that PSB has a very protective lending agreement that includes a provision that the debtor's declaration of bankruptcy is an automatic default under the contract. PSB brings a case to you: The debtor, Jason Jansen, has gone into bankruptcy owing PSB $7,899. The loan is at slightly better than average market rates. The loan is secured by a valid PMSI on a car worth $6,000. It would cost PSB about $500 to repossess and resell the car. Jansen is not in default, has a good job, and the car is depreciating at an ordinary rate.

PSB has three questions, two specific and one general: (1) can it get the car back in this situation after bankruptcy, if it wants to; (2) if Jansen keeps the car, what portion of the amount owed will be repaid; and (3) what is your overall advice about how to handle this sort of problem? Keep in mind as you deal with PSB that they want you to develop some generalized principles that they can give to a loan officer so the loan officer can deal with bankrupt debtors without having to call you for expensive individualized analyses each time.

9.6. A new client, Edwin Peraza, contacted you for advice about an employment matter. Edwin interviewed with Buster Accounting, an industry leader, for a position as a mid-level accountant. Linda Townsend, the supervisor who interviewed Edwin, called him immediately after the interview saying he was the most impressive applicant and offered him the job on the spot, but said it was contingent upon Edwin's successful completion of the firm's standard background and credit report check. Edwin accepted and completed the hiring paperwork. A week later, Linda called Edwin to inform him that the firm was rescinding its offer of employment for reasons as a policy matter they do not discuss but wishing him well. Edwin tells you that he believes the firm refused to hire him due to his chapter 7 bankruptcy case, which was a routine matter with a discharge entered a few months after filing. Will Edwin succeed in an action against Buster Accounting? He also asks you for any tips you have on his job search in light of Buster Accounting's actions. What would you advise? See 11 U.S.C. § 525.

Section 3

Chapter 13 Repayment

For individuals, the major alternative to chapter 7 is chapter 13. Compared to liquidation, chapter 13 bankruptcy has more of everything: it takes longer, it has higher attorneys' fees, it offers the potential for a broader discharge, it allows the opportunity for greater creditor recoveries, and it is just in general more complex. The centerpiece of chapter 13 is the debtor's retention of assets—the same assets that must be sold off in a chapter 7. In exchange for keeping those assets, the debtor does not get an immediate discharge. Instead, debtors must pledge future income to their creditors for a period of generally three to five years. Only once they survive that regimen, do they get their discharge. The specific amounts to be paid are proposed as a "plan" that the debtor offers the creditors, albeit with statutory provisions on minimum plan requirements and other creditor protections.

As in chapter 7, secured creditors and unsecured creditors are treated differently. The two assignments that make up this section on chapter 13 consider the rights of each in turn.

SECURED CREDITORS IN CHAPTER 13

A. ELEMENTS OF AN ACCEPTABLE PLAN

1. Overview of Chapter 13

In the preceding assignments, we have taken a consumer debtor through the steps of a chapter 7 bankruptcy. The Bankruptcy Code provides an alternative for consumer debtors in financial trouble called a chapter 13 adjustment of debts or "wage-earner's plan," as it was once known, to which we now turn. This section of the book has two main purposes. The first is to provide an overview of the chapter 13 process and the key elements of a chapter 13 plan. The second is to discuss creditor entitlements in chapter 13, with a specific emphasis on what goes by the term "cramdown," another piece of bankruptcy jargon that everyone uses but that is nowhere in the Code. "Cramdown" is the minimum amount a debtor can pay to a creditor and still have the repayment plan confirmed over creditor objection—evocatively, the plan is crammed down such creditors' throats. As with much of the Code, this requirement is different for secured and unsecured creditors, and so the next two assignments proceed accordingly.

Although chapter 7 and chapter 13 have much in common, including the creation of an estate consisting of all the debtor's property and an automatic stay that freezes collection efforts, the chapter 13 repayment option differs significantly from chapter 7 liquidation. In chapter 7, debtors effectively freeze their assets and debts at the moment they file for bankruptcy. Their non-exempt *assets* (if any) are the source of paying claims. In return, the debtor is relieved of any future obligations to pay dischargeable, prepetition debts, and all the debtor's subsequent earnings are free from the reach of these former creditors.

By contrast, chapter 13 focuses on using *future earnings*, rather than accumulated assets, to pay creditors. This means chapter 13 lets the debtor keep all assets—even if not exempt—in exchange for an agreement to relinquish future income for the benefit of creditors for a minimum of three years. Secured creditors must receive certain minimum payments for the debtor to retain collateral, while unsecured creditors must be paid what remains of the debtor's disposable income. The trustee takes a percentage of the debtor's income for each pay period, deducts a part to cover administrative expenses, and then distributes the remainder to the creditors according to a court-approved plan. When the debtor has completed the agreed payout, the debtor's remaining obligations are discharged. If the debtor fails to complete the repayment plan, the case is dismissed, and the debtor gets no discharge (although the debtor may be able to convert to chapter 7 or refile bankruptcy).

As a result, every debtor who is eligible for both chapter 7 and chapter 13 must make a fundamental choice: seek an immediate discharge in chapter 7 but lose non-exempt assets, or try to pay some or all debts in installments under a chapter 13 plan and get to keep assets. The debtor who chooses chapter 13 must prepare a plan detailing the amounts to be repaid and the terms of repayment in accord with certain statutory requirements. As we will see in a later assignment, there are a number of provisions in chapter 7, including § 707(b), that may bar a debtor from that chapter, leaving a "choice" for some debtors between chapter 13 and no bankruptcy relief at all.

From a creditor's standpoint, the difference between chapter 7 and chapter 13 is the prospect of payment obtained by selling the debtor's assets versus payment from the debtor's future income. In light of most debtors' circumstances, this usually boils down to no payment (chapter 7) versus waiting for some payment—or at least the prospect of some payment (chapter 13). From the debtor's viewpoint, chapter 13 is a much more involved, long-term process than chapter 7. Court supervision lasts from the day of filing until plan payments are completed, a period of three to five years. No discharge from debt will be granted until the debtor makes the very last payment on the plan. This is a marked contrast to the chapter 7 debtor who is usually discharged within six months of filing. The timing of the chapter 13 discharge also differs from a discharge in a corporate chapter 11, under which the court approval of a plan generates an immediate discharge even before the payments begin. For debtors, chapter 13 means a long wait until discharge, although the debtor is protected by the automatic stay during the course of the case.

The chapter 13 trustee has a different role from that of the chapter 7 trustee. The debtor, not the trustee, retains control of property of the estate in chapter 13 cases, § 1303, and that estate is broader than in chapter 7, specifically including the postpetition wages, which makes sense given those wages fund plan payments. § 1306. Thus, the chapter 13 trustee does not have the function of collecting, preserving, and selling the property of the estate as in chapter 7. § 1302(b)(1). The debtor retains property and proposes the repayment plan.

The chapter 13 trustee does have several important responsibilities. The trustee makes a recommendation to the court on plan confirmation. § 1302(b)(2)(B). Ordinarily, the plan provides that debtors will make a lump-sum monthly payment to the trustee for distribution, although some secured creditors may be paid directly (a procedure known as payment "outside the plan"). Trustees often use wage attachment orders to collect payments; these divert a portion of the debtor's wages directly to the trustee for plan payments. Because the attachment is made pursuant to federal bankruptcy law, state restrictions on wage garnishment are inapplicable. If the debtor's payments fall behind, it is usually the trustee who files to dismiss the debtor's case for nonpayment. The trustee is responsible for ensuring that the debtor gives up the required amount of income. The trustee, like creditors, can object to the debtor's discharge. The trustee also is charged with objecting to improper creditor claims, and making distributions to creditors. § 1326. At the same time the trustee has a duty to assist the debtor in the performance of the debtor's duties. § 1302(b)(1), (4). In short, the trustee scrutinizes everyone connected with the case—debtor and creditors—to make sure that they are following the Code.

Chapter 13 administration is complex. Many districts have a "standing" chapter 13 trustee to perform this task for all cases, rather than an individual from a panel appointed anew in each case. § 1302(a); 28 U.S.C. § 586(b). In those districts, especially populous urban ones, the position of standing trustee is not just a full-time job but an active business relying on a highly sophisticated, computerized system of receipts and disbursements. Fees are fixed by regulation subject to a statutory maximum. Id. § 586(e). Billions of debtor dollars flow through this processing system each year.

Chapter 13 collection also means Big Business for speculators. Collection of sixteen cents on the dollar on debt for which a debt purchaser may have paid the original creditor eight cents produces a 100% profit. Making this a multimillion-dollar venture, of course, means investing major money. Enter Wall Street. An article in *Forbes Magazine* written prior to BAPCPA was headlined "Uncle Sam Is My Collection Agent." It explained that the investment bankers at Bear Stearns were making big bucks from "the growing multibillion dollar trade in personal debt" by buying chapter 13 debt at steep discount and then collecting the trustee's monthly disbursements, enjoying the subsidized public collection system the standing trustee provides. These bankers also anxiously awaited what would become BAPCPA, knowing the new law would increase their collections (and thus profits) still more. We mentioned earlier the ironic collapse of Bear Stearns despite the success of this part of their business.

The financial and policy questions surrounding chapter 13 deserve attention, but first we will focus on how it works, starting with the required elements of a plan. The Code provisions that tell us what may or must be in a chapter 13 plan seem to be arbitrarily distributed between §§ 1322 and 1325. Section 1322(a)(2) gives the debtor the power to use a plan to modify the rights of creditors, both secured and unsecured. This power includes, for example, paying a reduced amount of the obligation and stretching out the period of time over which payment can be made. Other provisions in the two sections then substantially constrain that broad power, especially with regard to secured creditors.

2.   *Payments to Secured Creditors*

One of the most common reasons for choosing a chapter 13 bankruptcy is the debtor's desire to keep property that is subject to a security interest. When a significant asset, such as a car or furniture, is subject to a valid security interest, the chapter 13 plan is often built around satisfying the legal requirements for retaining that property and structuring a new payment schedule.

Just as secured creditors in chapter 7 enjoy enhanced status compared to unsecured creditors, so too the secured creditor in chapter 13 enjoys better protection. If a debtor proposes in a chapter 13 plan to retain collateral, the secured party will sometimes object, declaring the debtor in default and demanding the collateral. Whether the creditor can exercise its right to repossession and sale, realizing the value of the collateral and terminating its contract with the debtor, will depend on whether the debtor can comply with the provisions of chapter 13 that protect secured creditors. Because the collateral is property of the estate, albeit in the control of the debtor, the creditor still must ask the court for relief from the stay.

Courts must thus solve two separate but related issues when a secured creditor wants to repossess and sell the collateral. The first issue is *protection* of the secured party's interest in the collateral while the case is going on. Because the debtor proposes to keep the property, the secured party is naturally concerned about the risk that the collateral will lose its value during the three to five years of chapter 13 (think about whether you'd rather repossess a car now or after five more years of the debtor's driving). If the debtor defaults later on, the secured party could be left with collateral worth considerably less than when bankruptcy was originally filed. This problem is usually cast in terms of providing "adequate protection" for the secured party under § 362(d). The two principal types of risks that concern the secured creditor are a loss of the collateral (e.g., by fire, theft, or simple neglect) and a decline in its value (such as depreciation over time).

The second issue is adequate *payment* to the secured party if the debtor chooses to modify the debt (without a rule setting the payment terms, some debtors would surely modify the debt down to zero). There is a statutory formula, discussed below, that calculates the minimum amount the debtor must pay in order to keep collateral over the objection of the secured creditor. In the typical elegance of bankruptcy terminology, the process is called "cramdown."

In chapter 11 business cases the two issues are fairly distinct, with the first, adequate protection, focusing on immediate payments even while the plan negotiations are proceeding and the second, minimum payments, ensuring that the long-term payments will compensate the secured creditor on the obligation. Chapter 11 plans are often proposed months or years after filing, so the protection issue must be dealt with quickly, while the payment issue can await the battle over plan confirmation. In a chapter 13, by contrast, the debtor's plan is frequently filed alongside the petition and confirmed within a month or two; the result of this condensed timeline is that the two issues often collapse into joint consideration. Because they are analytically distinct, however, we consider each in turn.

a.   Adequate Protection

As we learned earlier, a creditor can move to lift the automatic stay by arguing under § 362(d) that its interest in the collateral is not adequately protected. In chapter 7, because an immediate liquidation is anticipated, adequate protection is rarely an issue. In chapter 13, by contrast, the debtor proposes to retain the collateral and make payments over a long period of time, often on quite different terms from the original loan. Creditors may argue that the debtor's proposed actions insufficiently protect their rights.

In the following case, creditor GMAC had already repossessed the debtor's car before the bankruptcy filing, and it wanted to retain and sell the car to pay off its outstanding loan balance. With the automatic stay in place, GMAC could not proceed with a sale, so it moved to lift the stay, arguing the application of both § 362(d)(1) and (2). Because GMAC had possession of the car, the debtor made two arguments in response: one against the lifting of the stay, to prevent GMAC from selling the car immediately, and the other for return of the car to the debtor, as custodian of estate property under chapter 13 and an avid fan of driving to work. (Note the second argument invoked the trustee's "turnover" power of § 542, which the chapter 13 debtor, *qua* trustee, gets to use, because the debtor retains control of the estate's property.)

In re RADDEN

35 B.R. 821 (Bankr. E.D. Va. 1983)

SHELLEY, Bankruptcy Judge.

These matters involve the proper disposition of a 1979 Ford Mustang automobile (the "property"). The debtor, along with Priscilla Coe, purchased the property from Hechler Chevrolet, Inc. ("Hechler") on October 17, 1981. The property was titled in the debtor's name alone. Hechler financed this purchase by a retail installment sales contract secured by the vehicle. This installment sales agreement was assigned to GMAC pursuant to its agreement with Hechler entered July 3, 1980. . . .

The debtor failed to make the contractually required payments to GMAC for the month of June, 1983. This constituted the first default under the assigned installment sales contract. The debtor did not cure the default and also failed to make the required monthly payment in July, 1983. [Apparently, GMAC lawfully repossessed the car prior to bankruptcy.—Eds.] GMAC notified the debtor and the cobuyer, Priscilla Coe, of their right to redeem the property and of a proposed sale of the property on August 12, 1983, if they did not redeem the property prior thereto.

On August 10, 1983, the debtor filed for relief under Chapter 13 of the Bankruptcy Code. In his Chapter 13 plan the debtor lists the value of the property as $2,700.00 and the balance due on the contract as $4,400.30. The Chapter 13 plan proposes to pay, through the standing Chapter 13 trustee, GMAC in full to the extent of the value of the collateral plus interest thereon at the rate of 5 percent per annum in deferred monthly cash payments of $89.68 over a period of 36 months. To the extent that the amount on the contract exceeds the value of the collateral, the obligation owing to GMAC is treated as an unsecured claim. Under the plan, unsecured claims are to receive seventy cents on the dollar.

The debtor lives about a mile and a half from his place of employment and about three blocks from a food store. He has been able to get groceries without difficulty since the time GMAC obtained possession of the property. He has gotten to and from work either by obtaining rides from friends, by using his mother's automobile, or by walking. The debtor testified that (1) he is presently working from 3:00 until 11:00 and that a friend with an automobile in the same apartment complex works the same shift; (2) that he has missed very little work in the past five years at Western Electric, except that on at least one occasion he was absent because of inability to get to work; (3) that when he must walk home he does so on a street that is busy with traffic, is not lighted, and does not have a sidewalk; (4) that he has not yet been required to walk home from work in cold weather; (5) that he seeks a turnover of the property to enable him to get to and from work; (6) that although the property is not presently insured by him for collision and liability, he would re-obtain insurance on the property; (7) that he has the present finances to procure such insurance; and (8) that he has presently a valid driver's license.

Conclusions of Law

GMAC here seeks relief based both on the lack of adequate protection, id. § 362(d)(1), and on the grounds that the debtor does not have any equity in the property and that such property is not necessary for the debtor's effective reorganization. Id. § 362(d)(2).

As to the latter basis for obtaining relief from the stay, this Court needs to find only that the property is necessary for an effective reorganization to deny GMAC relief pursuant to § 362(d)(2). The debtor admits in his Chapter 13 plan and his memorandum in support of his adversary proceeding and in opposition to GMAC's adversary proceeding that he lacks equity in the property. Therefore, if the property questioned here is not necessary for the debtor's effective reorganization, the creditor is entitled to relief from stay.

The debtor bears the burden of proving that the property is necessary for his effective reorganization. § 362(g). This Court is satisfied that an automobile is necessary for an individual's effective reorganization in today's society. As the debtor testified, he needs the property to get to and from his place of employment. Moreover, individuals need transportation to obtain medical as well as other necessary services. Having found that the property is necessary for an effective reorganization, this Court will not grant GMAC relief from the stay pursuant to § 362(d)(2).

As an alternate basis for obtaining relief from the stay, GMAC alleges that it has an interest in property that is not adequately protected. Lack of adequate protection is sufficient "cause" pursuant to § 362(d)(1) for a court to grant a creditor relief from the automatic stay. The resolution of GMAC's claim in this regard turns on the issue of what is GMAC's "interest in property. . . ."

The Court notes initially that the property in which GMAC has an interest is currently in GMAC's possession, therefore, GMAC is in the best position to protect its interest in the property from the likelihood of theft, vandalism, or destruction by natural cause.

Second, under the provisions of the debtor's plan, GMAC will retain their lien on the collateral and receive the amount of their allowed secured claim with interest and, therefore, its interest in property will be adequately protected if the plan is effectively consummated. GMAC has not demonstrated that the debtor's chances of rehabilitation are remote. To the contrary, the debtor has established that he has a stable employment record and that he is capable of meeting the payments to the standing trustee under the plan. The debtor has a reasonable likelihood of having his plan confirmed and consummated and, therefore, GMAC will likely receive the allowed amount of their secured claim through deferred cash payments. Recognizing this likelihood, GMAC's interest in property is adequately protected under the Chapter 13 plan and, therefore, GMAC requires no relief from the automatic stay to protect said interest. . . .

Finally, this Court now addresses the issue of the debtor's turnover complaint. The debtor seeks to recover the property that was returned voluntarily to GMAC prior to the filing of bankruptcy. The debtor seeks this turnover pursuant to § 542. . . .

The debtor here has filed a petition pursuant to Chapter 13 of the Bankruptcy Code. Section 1303 provides the debtor with the rights and powers that a trustee would have under Chapter 7 or the debtor in possession would have under Chapter 11. Consequently the debtor is a proper party to seek turnover pursuant to § 542(a) because the property that the debtor seeks to have turned over is property that he as debtor may use in the ordinary course of business. See § 363.

Having found that the debtor is the proper party to bring a § 542 turnover complaint, this Court notes the elements of § 542 include (1) an entity has possession, custody, or control of property (2) that the debtor may use the property pursuant to § 363 and (3) that the property has value or benefit to the estate. . . .

For the reasons discussed above, this Court should and will order that GMAC return possession of the property to the debtor. The Court will not, however, order such turnover without providing adequate protection to the creditor of his interest in the property. The debtor's "use of the vehicle pursuant to § 363(b) will presumably cause the value of the vehicle to decline." In re Williams, 6 B.R. at 792. This Court is satisfied, however, that if the debtor (1) procures adequate insurance on the property at the time of recovering possession and (2) makes monthly payments under the contract with GMAC until the time that a plan is confirmed, GMAC's interest in the subject property will be adequately protected and, therefore, the requirements of § 361 and [§ 362(d)] will be satisfied.

For Mr. Radden, chapter 13 became an extraordinarily powerful tool. He was able to restructure his loan payments and to reclaim a car from a creditor that had lawfully repossessed it after default. Once Radden filed for bankruptcy, GMAC could not sell the duly repossessed car and realize its value until the court granted its motion under § 362(d). With a lift-stay motion denied, GMAC was off down the path of the three- to five-year chapter 13 payout to recover on its debt.

Note that GMAC lost on both § 362(d) arguments. The court rejected application of § 362(d)(2). While conceding the debtor had no equity in the property, it concluded that the property was necessary for an effective reorganization. Did this strike you as a generous conclusion in light of the evidence that the debtor had little difficulty getting to work and nearby shopping? Concluding that an item of collateral is "necessary for an effective reorganization" can blur into a value judgment in the consumer context, but it usually has real bite in chapter 11 business cases, which use the exact same Code provisions on stay relief.

In its second argument, GMAC argued that the stay should be lifted because its interest in the car was not adequately protected as required in § 362(d)(1). The debtor would have possession of the car if the stay continued to restrain GMAC from selling the car due to the turnover action. Thus a real possibility existed that the car would decline in value or even be destroyed. The *Radden* court found that the debtor's payments and agreement to arrange for sufficient insurance addressed those risks such that GMAC was adequately protected.

b.   Adequate Payment

For the secured creditor that does not succeed in a lift stay motion, which would effectively let it bypass chapter 13 and liquidate the collateral, the next battle is fighting for maximum payment under the chapter 13 plan. Unless the debtor and the secured creditor make a deal, a plan will be crammed down on the secured creditor if the debtor promises to pay a certain amount. A court must make two factual determinations to establish the minimum amount that a debtor must pay to a secured creditor to present a permissible chapter 13 plan:

1.   the amount of the allowed secured claim under § 506(a); and
2.   the present value of the allowed secured claim under § 1325(a)(5)(B)(ii).

The general rule about required payments to secured creditors is contained in § 1325(a)(5), which contains two requirements: a secured creditor must be paid its full, allowed secured claim *and* it must be paid interest on that claim (i.e., must be paid the "value" of that claim, § 1325(a)(5)(B)(ii)) because the debtor in chapter 13 spreads the payment over time. Of the minimum payment dividend, think of the first requirement as a principal component and the second as an interest component. The debtor's plan must satisfy both components.

i.   Value of the Claim

We discussed previously the calculation of an allowed secured claim in Assignment 6 and saw that an undersecured debt is bifurcated by § 506(a) to yield two claims: a secured claim equal to the value of the collateral and an unsecured claim for the deficiency. Under the general rule of § 1325(a)(5), the cramdown section, the debtor promises to pay the allowed secured claim (i.e., the value of the collateral) in full, while treating the unsecured portion of the debt like any other unsecured claim under the plan, which often can be paid only in part.

The key factual question is therefore the value of the collateral; that figure will determine the amount of the allowed secured claim that must be paid in full. The Supreme Court addressed the issue in Associates Commercial Corp. v. Rash, 520 U.S. 952 (1997). The case was not about methods of valuation, which we will address in the business section, but rather about what definition of "value" should be used for chapter 13 cramdown: liquidation value or replacement value. That issue had split six circuits at least three ways, proving once again that this stuff is hard for everyone.

The Rashes were a couple that had purchased a truck for freight-hauling. They still owed $41,000, about 60% of the purchase price, when they filed for chapter 13, but they alleged that the truck would bring only $28,500 in a liquidation sale. On that basis, their chapter 13 plan proposed to cram down the lender with a promise to pay $28,500 over 58 months of their plan. The creditor replied that it would cost the Rashes around $41,000 to buy a similar truck and that amount should be considered the value for purposes of determining if § 1325 is satisfied. Such a definition of value would have required the Rashes to pay the entire debt, $41,000, over the course of the plan if they wanted to keep the truck.

The Court's opinion turned on § 506(a), which refers to "the value of the creditor's interest in the estate's interest in [the collateral]." The Rashes reasoned that focus on the creditor's entitlement means that the creditor should get what it would get in a UCC (Uniform Commercial Code) Article 9 sale if it exercised its legal rights: liquidation value. Replacement value would give the creditor a bankruptcy windfall compared to its state-law entitlement. The Court, per Justice Ginsburg, disagreed in an 8-1 decision, pointing to § 506(a)'s next sentence, which directs that valuation be determined "in light of the proposed use of the property." Since the Rashes proposed to keep the truck, she concluded that what it would cost them to buy an equivalent truck was the proper measure of its value for the purposes of a chapter 13 plan. (The Court also specifically rejected a third approach, which split the difference between the replacement and liquidation values.) The Court's opinion had some qualifying footnotes too, including infamous footnote 6 that implies that deductions from replacement value can be made for marketing and other costs. While Rash clarified that at the very least, liquidation value was incorrect, its effort to define replacement value was pretty fuzzy. Many people read Rash to require the use of what you might think of as "adjusted replacement value," leaving fighting in the trenches about the adjustments—and of course, the method of valuation used to come up with the starting replacement value.

BAPCPA both codified and revised Rash by adding a new paragraph (2) to § 506(a). Look carefully at its restrictions as to which sorts of property it applies. It generally adopts a replacement value approach but does not appear to allow the deductions from the Rash footnote. It also makes clear that replacement value means used value, not new. Yet disputes persist. The textual reference to "retail value" for some specific property implies to some that the proper measure for replacement for non-specified property might be wholesale value. As a practical matter, we think that many courts continue to split the difference between wholesale and retail prices as a rough-justice measure of value for cramdown purposes. In the context of cars, this is often the midpoint between the published retail and wholesale prices for any given used vehicle. This approach likely results from confusion on how to apply *Rash* and its footnotes and from the fact that the economics of consumer bankruptcy will not support an elaborate hearing, complete with experts, for each vehicle to be valued. "Adjustments" to replacement value, indeed.

ii.   *Interest on the Claim*

Once the allowed secured claim is determined, the court can establish a payment schedule that permits the creditor to recover the present value of the claim. The concept of "present value" (in statutory terms, "value, as of the effective date of the Plan," § 1325(a)(5)(B)(ii)), reflects the elementary proposition that a dollar due to be paid a year from now is worth less than a dollar paid now. Absent bankruptcy, the secured creditor would be allowed to repossess and sell the collateral today and invest its proceeds; chapter 13 requires a three-to-five-year wait. Because of this deferral, the Code gives the creditor the right to receive interest on its allowed secured claim. The total to be received by the creditor over time must equal the present value of the collateral at the time of plan confirmation.

For the mathletes, a number of formulas can be used to calculate present value. One is given here:

$$\mathrm{PV_a} = \left[\frac{1 - 1/(1+i)^n}{i}\right] \times (a)$$

where a = a dollar amount of installment payment
i = a current annual interest rate
n = the number of annual payments

Computations for other than annual payments require corresponding adjustment of the i variable; e.g., monthly payments use $i/12$. But perhaps that is a bit much. Before you conclude that present value is simple in theory but hopelessly complex to compute, be reassured that "there's an app for that," and for the Luddites, there are published tables to calculate present value.

Any formula requires the insertion of values, and in chapter 13, both value (as discussed in the prior section) and interest rate are up for grabs. Equally important to someone contemplating monthly payments for multiple years is the required interest rate. Chapter 13's requirement that the creditor receive the present value of its allowed secured claim depends on *current* interest rates, not the rate in the loan contract signed by the debtor possibly years ago, which may be higher or lower. This is another instance of a debtor modifying its loan contract via chapter 13. Not surprisingly, this maneuver tends to disappoint creditors when interest rates have gone down. To give certainty to the chapter 13 plan process, some courts held that when the debt is contractual and there was an interest rate specified for the loan, that rate should be rebuttably presumed to be the market rate a debtor must pay under the plan. The Supreme Court in a 4-1-4 opinion, said no. See Till v. SCS Credit Corporation, 541 U.S. 465 (2004). The interest rate for cramdown should be the current prime rate "adjusted" for the riskiness of the debt. It declined to tell the bankruptcy courts just how to make that adjustment, noting that it will vary from case to case, but did cite a collection of cases suggesting that it will usually be between 1-3% (empirical basis unspecified).

The cramdown power to mark-to-market a consumer loan to the current value of its collateral and to reset the interest rate is one of the processes by which a debtor can keep its collateral over creditor protest. Another, which we have already seen, is redemption under § 722. Chapter 13 has a great advantage over redemption, however, because it allows the debtor to make those collateral-preserving payments over a multiple-year plan. Chapter 13 can thus be thought of as a "redemption by installment" regime.

3. Treatment of Liens Generally

Recall in chapter 7 that after bankruptcy, a secured creditor's lien remains on collateral; once the stay is over, the creditor can go after that property *in rem* to redress default because the discharge is only of personal liability. But in chapter 13, the debtor's broad "modification" power of § 1322 includes the right to remove the lien altogether, at least after the plan is concluded. §§ 1325(a)(5)(B)(i)(I)(bb), 1327(c). This accords the debtor the power to *strip* a lien off encumbered property upon successful completion of a chapter 13 plan.

As an example, consider a couple who granted a security interest for a loan on their office equipment, then, two years later, filed for bankruptcy. At the time of filing, the loan was $10,000 but the collateral was worth only $4,000. Assuming they have promised to pay 50% of the amount of unsecured claims under the chapter 13 plan, they would pay the undersecured creditor $4,000 (secured claim for value of collateral, with interest to account for present value) and $3,000 (50% of the $6,000 unsecured claim). If the debtors complete the plan, they will discharge the remaining debt. For $7,000 total plus a little present-value interest, they keep the equipment during and after bankruptcy for less than the amount of the loan.

This treatment of an undersecured claim upon plan completion is often called "lienstripping." Because it can be imposed over the secured creditor's objection, it is a form of cramdown. (Contrast the power dynamic with reaffirming secured debt to keep collateral after chapter 7.) If the debtors fail to complete the plan, they will still remain saddled with liens. Their debts will not be discharged, and after bankruptcy the secured creditor will once again be able to enforce its security interest with regard to all the unpaid debt. § 1325(a)(5)(B)(i). But if they complete the plan, the unpaid, unsecured amount of the debt is discharged *and* the lien is eliminated by the completed payment on the secured claim. Chapter 13 therefore accords great leverage to debtors: they don't just keep, they *unencumber* their collateral upon plan completion. What a contrast from chapter 7, where the debtor gets a respite from the secured creditor during the case, but the creditor gets to come back for the collateral (but not the debtor) post-discharge.

4.   *Special Rules for Purchase Money Liens and Mortgages*

The lienstripping rules have never applied to mortgages on a debtor's principal residence. § 1322(b)(2). In 2005, Congress added another lienstripping carveout at the end of § 1325(a) that covers certain purchase money liens on personal property. We discuss them in reverse order.

a.   **Purchase Money Liens**

Because the new language exempting certain purchase money security interests was added as an unnumbered textual coda to pre-existing subsections, it is commonly referred to as the "hanging" paragraph; the best citation we've seen used is 11 U.S.C. § 1325(a)(*). Although the language is inartful, to say the least, these additional exemptions seem to forbid lienstripping certain purchase money security interests on collateral acquired during specified periods before bankruptcy. If the secured creditor objects to the plan, a debtor who wants to keep the collateral must promise to pay the purchase-money debt in full. Ignoring nuance, the "allowed secured claim" the debtor must pay for cramdown is the *full debt*, regardless of the collateral's value.

The first purchase money security interest exempted from lienstripping is one granted within the year before bankruptcy, regardless of the nature of the collateral. Second, for one specially favored secured creditor—the holder of a purchase money security interest in a motor vehicle—the time period is rolled further back to exempt in a similar fashion the stripping of security interests granted within two and a half years (910 days) before the petition. This is a big change. For many people, keeping a car is critical, and many car loans are undersecured, for three typical reasons: because the debtor financed 100%, and the value of an automobile drops sharply upon leaving the dealer's lot; because the debtor overpaid in the first place; or because fees, penalty interest rates, and penalties that were added when the debtor missed payments have caused the debt to swell. One of the biggest attractions of chapter 13 used to be the ability to keep the car by paying only its replacement value (plus interest to present value the claim). BAPCPA protects car dealers and their finance companies from the consequences of their undersecured loans to the annual tune of many millions of dollars.

Yet, as always in bankruptcy, things are not as simple as they seem. The courts have had to confront the Zen specter of "negative equity."

══════════ FORD MOTOR CREDIT CO. v. DALE ══════════
582 F.3d 568 (5th Cir. 2009)

HAYNES, Circuit Judge.

This appeal involves the proper construction of the "hanging paragraph" in 11 U.S.C. § 1325(a), which was added to the Bankruptcy Code (Code) by the Bankruptcy Abuse Prevention and Consumer Protection Act of 2005 (BAPCPA). Under the Code, a lien creditor generally holds a secured claim only to the extent of the present value of the collateral that the lien encumbers. If the amount of the secured claim exceeds the present value of the collateral, the Code treats the excess amount as a separate, unsecured claim. This process is known as bifurcation or "stripping down" the secured claim to the value of the collateral. The hanging paragraph is an exception to this general rule, preventing bifurcation of a claim when the creditor has a "purchase-money security interest" (securing the claimed debt) in a motor vehicle acquired for the debtor's personal use within 910 days of the debtor's bankruptcy filing. The issue here is whether the purchase-money security interest exception contained in the hanging paragraph applies to those portions of a claim attributable to the pay-off of negative equity in a trade-in vehicle, gap insurance, and an extended warranty. The district court found that it does. We AFFIRM.

I. FACTS

The facts of this case are undisputed. Debtor Rebecca Ann Dale purchased a 2006 Ford F150 pick-up truck from Gullo Ford Mercury of Conroe, Texas. The vehicle was for her personal use and had a cash price of $38,291.42. Ford Motor Credit Company, LLC (Ford) financed the sale under a retail sales contract (Sales Contract) and retained a security interest in the vehicle to secure the unpaid balance of the total sale price.

As part of the transaction, Dale traded in a 2003 Ford Expedition. That vehicle had a negative equity, with Dale owing $4,760 more on the vehicle than its then-market value. As required by Texas law, Ford paid off this negative equity before accepting Dale's trade-in and included the sum in the new vehicle's total sale price.[1] The total sale price also included a gap insurance premium of $576.84; taxes not included in the cash price totaling $1,450.03; fees totaling $162.73; and an extended warranty charge of $3,030. Dale financed this entire amount totaling $48,271.02 through Ford at 0% interest.

Dale filed for bankruptcy less than one year later and submitted a Chapter 13 reorganization plan. Of the $41,834.94 still owed under the Sales Contract, Dale's Chapter 13 plan proposed to pay Ford $23,900

---

[1] Under Texas law, it is a felony for a dealer to accept a trade-in without discharging the existing lien on the vehicle. Tex. Penal Code § 32.34.

over 37 months at 10.25% interest. Under Dale's proposal, the remaining amount owed to Ford would be paid pro-rata with other unsecured claims. Ford objected to this plan and filed a proof of claim in the amount of $41,834.94, secured by the 2006 F150. . . . The [bankruptcy] court ruled that Ford's purchase-money security interest did not extend to those portions of the vehicle loan attributable to the pay-off of negative equity, the gap insurance premium, and the extended warranty charge. The court deemed these portions of the loan unsecured.

[T]he district court reversed. The court held that Ford had a purchase-money security interest in the entire Sales Contract, including those portions attributable to negative equity, gap insurance, and the extended warranty. Dale challenges that conclusion in this appeal.

II. Discussion

The proper scope of the hanging paragraph presents a legal question, which we review de novo. We must decide whether the Code's hanging paragraph applies to the portion of a secured claim attributable to the pay-off of a trade-in vehicle's negative equity, gap insurance, and an extended warranty.

While bankruptcy courts across the country have divided on this issue, see In re Graupner, 537 F.3d 1295, 1300 (11th Cir. 2008) (collecting cases), three circuit courts and a state's highest court on certified questions have recently weighed in on the debate, uniformly holding that the hanging paragraph prevents bifurcation of vehicle loans, including those portions attributable to negative equity pay-off. . . .

We adopt this emerging majority position for the reasons explained below.

1. Statutory Scheme

The hanging paragraph was enacted as part of the BAPCPA. Prior to the enactment of the BAPCPA, the Code allowed a Chapter 13 debtor to modify the rights of a secured creditor with a purchase-money security interest in a vehicle by bifurcating the claim into secured and unsecured portions based on the vehicle's then-market value. 11 U.S.C. §§ 506(a)(1), 1325(a)(5).

Under this provision, a creditor with a $15,000 claim secured by a vehicle with a present market value of $10,000 would have a secured claim of $10,000 and an unsecured claim of $5,000. Under a Chapter 13 plan, the $10,000 secured claim would be paid in full with interest, while the $5,000 unsecured claim would be paid pro-rata with other unsecured claims. Use of § 506 in this manner is known as "bifurcation and cramdown" because the secured claim is reduced to the present value of the collateral, while the remainder of the debt becomes unsecured, forcing the secured creditor to accept less than the full value of its claim. Before the enactment of the BAPCPA, this cramdown provision had a pernicious effect on car dealers: it forced them to sustain a deficiency loss on the unsecured portion of the claim, while also forcing them to wait for payout on a now-reduced loan balance, with all the attendant risks of default that accompanied the original loan.

In apparent response to the undesirable effects of this cramdown on car dealers, Congress enacted the hanging paragraph as part of the BAPCPA. That provision eliminates bifurcation and cramdown in value if the vehicle was purchased within 910 days of the filing of the bankruptcy petition, and "if the creditor has a purchase-money security interest securing the debt that is the subject of the claim." . . .

Under the hanging paragraph, a creditor with a $15,000 claim secured by a vehicle with a present market value of $10,000 would avoid bifurcation and cramdown under § 506 and instead retain a secured claim in the entire purchase price of the vehicle.

2. Proper Scope of the Hanging Paragraph

In this case, it is undisputed that Dale incurred her debt within 910 days of filing for bankruptcy, that this debt was secured by a motor vehicle, and that Dale acquired this vehicle for her personal use. Thus, the sole issue is whether Ford has a "purchase-money security interest" securing that portion of the debt attributable to negative equity, gap insurance, and the extended warranty.

Ford urges, and the district court held, that the "plain and unambiguous" meaning of "purchase-money security interest" coupled with the hanging paragraph's pertinent legislative history is sufficient to resolve this issue. Statutory construction, of course, begins with the plain language of the statute. But the phrase "purchase-money security interest" does not have an ordinary or generally understood meaning; rather, it is a term of art. The phrase is used in only one other place in the Code, see 11 U.S.C. § 522(f), and the Code itself does not provide a definition. In short, the plain text of the hanging paragraph is insufficient to resolve this appeal.

Because the Code does not define "purchase-money security interest" and that term does not have a common ordinary meaning, we agree with the great majority of courts to address this issue that state UCC law must be used to define the hanging paragraph's phrase "purchase-money security interest." It is common in the bankruptcy context to look to state law to define security interests created under state law. . . .

The parties agree that the relevant state law is that of Texas. In Texas, a "purchase-money security interest" in goods is defined as a security interest in goods that are "purchase-money collateral," and "purchase-money collateral" is in turn defined as goods that secure a "purchase-money obligation." Tex. Bus. & Com. Code § 9.103. Texas defines "purchase-money obligation" as "an obligation . . . incurred as all or part of the price of the collateral or for value given to enable the debtor to acquire rights in or the use of the collateral if the value is in fact so used." Id. The definition of "purchase-money obligation" thus contains two prongs: (i) the price of the collateral, and (ii) value given to enable the debtor to acquire rights in or use of the collateral. . . .

Official Comment 3 to the UCC elaborates on the scope of these prongs. That Comment provides:

> As used in subsection (a)(2), the definition of "purchase-money obligation," the "price" of collateral or the "value given to enable" includes obligations for expenses incurred in connection with acquiring rights in the collateral, sales taxes, duties, finance charges, interest, freight charges, costs of storage in transit, demurrage, administrative charges, expenses of collection and enforcement, attorney's fees, and other similar obligations.

Tex. Bus. & Com. Code § 9.103, Official Comment 3. As we have recognized, Official UCC Comments are "by far the most useful aids to interpretation and construction." Weathersby v. Gore, 556 F.2d 1247, 1256 (5th Cir. 1977).

Examining the language of the statute and the Comment, we conclude that "price" and "value given to enable" include certain expenses that might not otherwise come within the common understanding of "price," such as "freight charges," "demurrage," "administrative charges," "expenses of collection and enforcement," and "attorney's fees." Inclusion of these expenses dispels any notion that "price" and "value given" are limited to the price tag of the vehicle standing alone.

The Comment's language "and other similar obligations" demonstrates that the enumerated expenses are merely examples and do not constitute an exhaustive list of eligible expenses. . . .

Negative equity and related expenses fit perfectly within the "value given to enable" prong of § 9.103. That prong states that a "purchase-money obligation" can consist of "value given to enable the debtor to acquire rights in or the use of the collateral if the value is in fact so used." . . .

Dale also argues that negative equity is antecedent debt, and thus cannot be considered value given to enable. This is not so. Ford extended new credit to pay off the negative equity on the trade-in vehicle, which enabled Dale to purchase the new F150. The discharge of the amount owed on the old vehicle was directly related to Dale's acquisition of the new car. The funds used to pay off Dale's negative equity are thus properly considered "value given to enable."

Based on this analysis, we conclude that negative equity, gap insurance, and extended warranties constitute "purchase-money obligations" under Texas law, meaning Ford has a "purchase-money security interest" in the debt associated with those items. As such, the Code's hanging paragraph operates to prevent bifurcation of this debt. . . .

═══════════

While most courts have agreed with *Dale*, there is a circuit split. In re Penrod, 611 F.3d 1158 (9th Cir. 2010) (holding that negative equity is not included in a purchase money security obligation). Because the underlying issue is state law, there is also the possibility that any particular state's law could be held to differ from that examined in the opinions to date.

b.   Home Mortgages

A home is the single biggest asset of more than half the debtors who file chapter 13. We mentioned earlier that one type of security interest has always been exempted from the modification of secured debt: the home mortgage. Yet chapter 13 can help debtors keep their homes, primarily by enabling them to catch up on the arrears in their mortgage payments. The typical homeowner in a chapter 13 case owes an arrearage to their mortgage company that is equal to six months in payments. Missed regular payments, as well as default fees, contribute to this arrearage. Katherine Porter, Arrears and Default Costs of Homeowners, 22 NACTT Q. 15 (2010). For such debtors, the automatic stay of chapter 13, combined with its tools to address secured debt may be the best way to save a home that is at risk of foreclosure.

As to the mortgage itself, the general rule is that a mortgage on the debtor's principal residence must be paid in full. § 1322(b)(2) (prohibiting modification of liens "secured only by a security interest in real property that is the debtor's principal residence"). The Supreme Court in Nobelman v. American Savings Bank, 508 U.S. 324 (1993) suggested as a corollary that if a second (or third) mortgage is wholly underwater, then it may no longer be a claim "secured" by the primary residence due to the absence of any collateral available to satisfy the lien, in which case the modification bar may not be triggered. Under this analysis, lien-stripping such valueless liens would be fair game in chapter 13. That window, however, may have been shut by the logic of Bank of America, N.A. v. Caulkett, 575 U.S. 790 (2015). If so, the only relief in chapter 13 for home mortgages is to "cure and maintain," catching up on the past-due arrearages (cure) while making current payments on the mortgage as they come due (maintain). § 1322(b)(5).

Because homes don't depreciate as fast as vehicles and homes are necessary for a family to reorganize, adequate protection fights are rare. Disputes in chapter 13 cases are more likely to involve two other problems: (1) in the short term, saving the home from foreclosure sale by defending a relief from stay motion, and (2) in the long term, proposing a cure-and-maintain plan to comply with the strict provisions of chapter 13 that protect the rights of mortgage lenders. In the following case, however, the debtors find that they have a different opinion from that of their lender regarding the scope of their power to "cure" a default in chapter 13.

═══════════════ ANDERSON v. HANCOCK ═══════════════

820 F.3d 670 (4th Cir. 2016)

Wilkinson, Circuit Judge.

In a case where the rate of interest on the debtors' residential mortgage loan was increased upon default, we consider whether a "cure" under § 1322(b) of the Bankruptcy Code allows their bankruptcy plan to bring post-petition payments back down to the initial rate of interest. We hold that the statute does not allow this, as a change to the interest rate on a residential mortgage loan is a "modification" barred by the terms of § 1322(b)(2).

I.

On September 1, 2011, William Robert Anderson, Jr. and Danni Sue Jernigan purchased a home in Raleigh, North Carolina, from Wayne and Tina Hancock. The purchase was financed via a $255,000 loan from the Hancocks. In exchange for the loan, Anderson and Jernigan granted the Hancocks a deed of trust on the property and executed a promissory note requiring monthly payments in the amount of $1,368.90 based on an interest rate of five percent over a term of thirty years.

The note provided, however, that

> In the event borrower has not paid their monthly obligation within 30 days of the due date, then borrower shall be in default. Upon that occurrence, the borrower's interest rate shall increase to Seven percent (7%) for the remaining term of the loan until paid in full. The increase in interest rate shall result in a new payment amount of $1696.52, which shall be due and payable monthly according to the terms stated herein, save and except the increase in rate and payment.

. . .

On April 1, 2013, Anderson and Jernigan failed to make their monthly payment. On May 4th, 2013, after continuing to receive no payment, the Hancocks notified Anderson and Jernigan that they were in default and that future payments should reflect the increased seven percent rate of interest provided for in the note. . . .

On August 30th, having continued to receive no payments, the Hancocks initiated foreclosure proceedings. Anderson and Jernigan in turn filed a Chapter 13 bankruptcy petition in the Eastern District of North Carolina on September 16, 2013, invoking bankruptcy's automatic stay and halting foreclosure proceedings. They also filed a proposed bankruptcy plan contemporaneous with their bankruptcy petition. Aspects of that plan are at issue here.

The bankruptcy plan proposed to pay off prepetition arrears on the Hancock loan over a period of sixty months. Arrears were calculated using a five percent interest rate. The plan also reinstated the original maturity date of the loan, and proposed that the debtors again make post-petition payments at a five percent interest rate.

The Hancocks objected, contending that post-petition payments should continue to reflect the seven percent default rate of interest provided for in the promissory note. They also argued that arrears to be paid off over the life of the plan should be calculated using a rate of seven percent interest beginning in June, 2013. . . .

Evaluating Anderson and Jernigan's claim requires us to examine the language of the § 1322(b). Section 1322(b)(2) provides that a bankruptcy plan may "modify the rights of holders of secured claims, other than a claim secured only by a security interest in real property that is the debtor's principal residence." . . . Plans may also "provide for the curing or waiving of any default. . . ."

The question is therefore whether the plan's proposed change to the debtors' rate of interest is part of a "cure" permissible under § 1322(b)(3) and (5), or alternatively, is a "modification" forbidden by the terms of paragraph (2).

The loan is secured by the debtors' princip[al] residence, and so Section 1322(b)(2) forbids "modification" of the Hancocks' "rights." While "[t]he term 'rights' is nowhere defined in the Bankruptcy Code," the Supreme Court has held that it includes those rights that are "bargained for by the mortgagor and the mortgagee" and enforceable under state law. Nobelman v. Am. Sav. Bank, 508 U.S. 324, 329, 113 S. Ct. 2106, 124 L. Ed. 2d 228 (1993). Courts have accordingly "interpreted the no-modification provision of § 1322(b)(2) to prohibit any fundamental alteration in a debtor's obligations, e.g., lowering monthly payments, converting a variable interest rate to a fixed interest rate, or extending the repayment term of a note." In re Litton, 330 F.3d 636, 643 (4th Cir. 2003). . . .

One authoritative treatise, in its section explaining the purpose of § 1322(b)(5), comments that

> Section 1322(b)(5) is concerned with relatively long-term debt, such as a security interest or mortgage debt on the residence of the debtor. It permits the debtor to take advantage of a contract repayment period which is longer than the chapter 13 extension period, which may not exceed five years under any circumstances, and may be essential if the debtor cannot pay the full allowed secured claim over the term of the plan.
>
> The debtor may maintain the contract payments during the course of the plan, without acceleration based upon a prepetition default, by proposing to cure the default within a reasonable time.

8-1322 Collier on Bankruptcy P 1322.09 (15th 2015). The meaning of "cure" thus focuses on the ability of a debtor to decelerate and continue paying a loan, thereby avoiding foreclosure.

The context of § 1322(b)'s enactment confirms this understanding. . . . The Senate subsequently amended (b)(2), which in its prior version would have allowed modification of any secured claim, to exclude modifications of claims "wholly secured by mortgages on real property," and later, after reconciliation with the House, claims "secured only by a security interest in real property that is the debtor's principal residence." Id. at 245-46. This language survives today. The implication, then, is that while Congress meant to allow debtors to decelerate and get a second chance at paying their loans, "home-mortgagor lenders, performing a valuable social service through their loans, needed special protection against modification," including modifications that would "reduc[e] installment payments." Id. at 246.

Congress has thus drawn a clear distinction between plans that merely cure defaults and those that modify the terms of residential mortgage loans. Understanding that the meaning of "cure" focuses upon the "maintenance" of pre-existing payments, see 11 U.S.C. § 1322(b)(5), we therefore hold that turning away from the debtors' contractually agreed upon default rate of interest would effect an impermissible modification of the terms of their promissory note. See 11 U.S.C. § 1322(b)(2).

Anderson and Jernigan object, citing one of our cases for the proposition that a cure is anything that "reinstates a debt to its pre-default position, or [] returns the debtor and creditor to their respective positions before the default." Appellants' Br. at 10-11 (quoting *Litton*, 330 F.3d at 644). In the debtors' view, a cure thus unravels every consequence of default, and "[r]eturning to pre-default conditions for an increased interest rate requires decreasing the interest rate back to its pre-default amount." Appellants' Br. at 16.

But *Litton*'s invocation of "pre-default conditions" again contemplates the deceleration of otherwise accelerated debt. It speaks of a cure as a reinstatement of "the original pre-bankruptcy agreement of the parties," or "a regime where debtors reinstate defaulted debt contracts in accordance with the conditions of their contracts." *Litton*, 330 F.3d at 644. And "the original pre-bankruptcy agreement of the parties" here specified a higher, default rate of interest upon missing a payment.

. . .

Litton and other cases' rejection of plans that tamper with residential mortgage interest rates is altogether sound. The interest rate of a mortgage loan is tied up with the "payments" that a legitimate cure requires must be "maintain[ed]." 11 U.S.C. § 1322(b)(5). Absent foreclosure and bankruptcy, the debtors would have been required to make payments totaling $1,696.52 per month based on a seven percent interest rate. Reducing the interest rate to five percent would lower this monthly amount to $1,368.90. That would "hardly constitute[] 'maintenance of payments.'" In re McGregor, 172 B.R. 718, 721 (Bankr. D. Mass. 1994). "The phrase connotes an absence of change." Id. In order to cure and maintain payments, the debtors must, as the district court put it, "mak[e] the same principal and interest payments as provided in the note." J.A. 70 (quoting In re Martin, 444 B.R. 538, 544 (Bankr. M.D.N.C. 2011)).

We therefore reject the debtors' attempt to modify the terms of their residential mortgage loan. It is contrary to Congress's prescription in § 1322(b)(2). The post-petition payments here should reflect the parties' agreed upon default rate of interest — seven percent.

Problem Set 10

10.1. Fran Belinsky is a graphic artist with an income in excess of $52,000 per year. Last year she guaranteed a large business loan for her brother. Her brother skipped town, and now Fran is left to pay the loan. She has filed a chapter 13 and plans to make a substantial repayment in a five-year plan.

Fran's only asset of significant value is a one-year-old computer setup with high-end peripherals that is subject to a valid $4,600 purchase money security interest from InterNet CompFinance (IC). She testified at her section 341 meeting that the setup is worth about $5,000. The IC people think that value is about right for now, but IC can predict that new technology will render the setup obsolete and almost valueless in three years. IC asks for your help in repossessing. What can you do? See §§ 361, 362(d).

10.2. George Grey has suffered a series of financial reversals. He was laid off for 17 months from his job as a steel worker, he has incurred medical bills of over $90,000 for his younger daughter, and his son just wrecked the car. But things may be looking up for George now. He has been rehired and is working nearly 20 hours per week overtime. Recognizing that he needs some protection from his creditors, he is prepared to file a chapter 13.

His chief concern at this point is his fishing cabin. Before he was laid off, he had bought the land from LeisureLand, Inc. for no money down and a $40,000 five-year note. During the time he was unemployed, he went out to the site almost every day. He cleared the land and built a one-room cabin with the materials he found on hand. It has no plumbing or electricity, but George cherishes the cabin. He even uses some of the timber from there to sell as firewood to supplement his income. Now he is afraid he will lose it.

George made only four payments on the land; the principal balance owed is $39,980. In addition, LeisureLand claims $12,300 in past-due interest, penalties, and attorneys' fees provided for under the contract. They have begun foreclosure proceedings, and the land is scheduled for sale next week. The contract interest rate is now running at 14% on the principal balance and 21% on all accumulated past-due payments and penalties. Because the area where George lives is in a serious economic slump, even with George's improvements vacation land would not sell for more than $41,000. What can LeisureLand demand in a chapter 13? See §§ 506, 1322(b)(2), 1325(a)(5)(B)(ii).

10.3. Donnie Rhodes bought a house seven years ago and took out a 30-year mortgage to finance the purchase. The home is now valued at $55,000, and the outstanding mortgage is $62,000. Rhodes is required to make monthly payments of $250. Rhodes sells farm machinery and as the farming industry took a nosedive, so did his sales. He went for eight months with no income, but now things have picked up and he is back to his regular earnings. He has decided to go into chapter 13 to restructure his debts, but he remains worried about his home. After seven years of regular mortgage payments, Rhodes missed six in a row and now has racked up $500 in penalties and costs under the contract. What must his plan provide? See § 1322(b)(2), (b)(5).

10.4. Carlos Esposito had a successful dive shop in Key West, but it sank in a recent downturn. Although he has a lot of unsecured debt, he is mainly worried about his personal car, a 2018 Acura that he bought two years ago. His credit union has a lien on the Acura for the $18,000 balance of the purchase price and for some $15,000 of Visa charges that he owed when he bought the car. The credit union "loan facilitator" told him the Visa balance looked bad for his credit rating, but that the credit union would be glad to pay it off for him and add it to his car loan. Otherwise, the facilitator was unsure the loan committee would approve the loan. Carlos agreed. Now he is having trouble making the payments on the $33,000 balance and complains that "the car has been banged up somewhat so it can't be worth more than $12,000." He is ready to file for chapter 13. How much will he have to promise to pay under his plan in order to keep the car?

10.5. Jewel Snitz has filed a chapter 13 bankruptcy. She owns a Ford Explorer she bought about a year ago to haul around her real estate clients and to take to the beach on weekends. The outstanding loan balance, together with accumulated interest and penalty payments, is $30,000. During the period between filing the chapter 13 and the confirmation of the plan, another $250 in interest will accumulate. The local bankruptcy court has settled on 10% as a market interest rate for car loans in chapter 13.

The Dealer's Bluebook lists the retail value of the car as $32,100 and the wholesale value as $28,400. At a liquidation sale the car would probably bring $26,300. Through a private Craigslist ad it would likely sell for $33,300. How much will Jewel have to pay for her car in a chapter 13 bankruptcy? If the car has some unusual scratches, chipped paint, and a funny little knock in the engine, who will want to point that out? See §§ 506(a), 1325(a).

UNSECURED CREDITORS IN CHAPTER 13

The requirements for secured creditors in chapter 13 are only one of myriad of requirements that a chapter 13 plan must meet for confirmation. The Bankruptcy Code prescribes treatment for unsecured creditors as well as directing judges to evaluate the chapter 13 plan against other benchmarks. These requirements burden debtors and their counsel, and they increase the amount of litigation and negotiation in chapter 13, especially as compared to the typical chapter 7 case. The final decision rests with the court at a confirmation hearing. § 1324. In chapter 13—unlike the chapter 11 system covered later in the book—creditors do not cast ballots on the plan, but any creditor, the chapter 13 trustee, or the U.S. Trustee can file an *objection* to confirmation. The judge is accorded wide latitude in whether to sustain or deny most of these objections, which in turn leads to wide divergences in outcomes that creditors and debtors achieve in chapter 13. In this assignment, we focus on the entitlements of unsecured creditors in chapter 13 by studying the grounds on which they can object to plan confirmation.

A. UNSECURED CREDITORS' PROTECTIONS GENERALLY

A chapter 13 case involves a debtor's proposal of a plan to the creditors. To deal with the secured creditors and prevent repossession of the debtor's property subject to the security interests, the debtor must make payments that satisfy the statutory requirements for the present value of each allowed secured claim. If the plan so provides, a secured creditor's objection will be denied. See § 1325(a)(5). The general unsecured creditors do not have similarly individualized protection for their claims. Instead, they are pooled together for pro rata treatment. (Priority unsecured creditors still get priority, of course, which we will discuss below.) Think of the debtor as paying into a pot a certain amount of money over the life of the plan. An unsecured creditor's objection boils down to, "We want a bigger pot." Because of the free-rider potential (who wants to pay the lawyer to file this objection on behalf of all unsecured creditors?), the trustee is often the objecting party.

The Code's protection of unsecured creditors in chapter 13 is a minimum floor on what the debtor *must* pay into this pot over the course of the plan. Unsecured creditors can of course accept less than this floor, but if the debtor meets the statutory minimum plan contributions, any objection to the plan by an unsecured creditor who wants more money will be denied. Creditors have more diffuse protections, such as the requirement that chapter 13 plans be filed in good faith, § 1325(a)(3), as we will see in one of the cases below, just as they are entitled to equal treatment, § 1322(a)(3), but for now we focus on the most important safeguards.

The floor for unsecured creditors is found in three provisions of § 1325. Each creates a minimum payment requirement for a chapter 13 plan, assuming the trustee or a creditor objects to less favorable treatment. The first provision is that debtors must pay priority creditors in full, although without interest. The second provision, the "best interests" test, requires that each creditor receive at least as much as that creditor would have received if the debtor had gone into chapter 7. § 1325(a)(4). The theory presumably is that if the creditor is better off in chapter 13 than it would be if the debtor chose chapter 7, it should just shut up. The third is that debtors must devote all their projected "disposable income" to funding the pot for unsecured creditor payments over the life of the chapter 13 plan. § 1325(b).

The practical effect of these tests differs given the realities of most consumers' situations. The priority-creditor provision has some teeth, although not all debtors have priority claims. The best interests test is not likely to prove a constraint in many chapter 13s. After all, most chapter 7s involve debtors with no unencumbered, non-exempt assets, which means the ordinary chapter 7 dividend for a general unsecured creditor is zero; requiring a chapter 13 plan to pay at least zero over the life of the plan daunts few debtors. (Best interests matters in chapter 11, as we shall learn later.) The real bite in chapter 13 is the disposable income test.

B.   PRIORITY CREDITORS AND THE "FULL PAYMENT" REQUIREMENT

Secured creditors are ensured minimum payments based on the value of their collateral. Unsecured creditors are ensured minimum payments based on pro rata distribution from the debtors' monthly disposable income (the "pot"). The payment rule for priority creditors takes a third approach. Creditors with claims that would receive a priority under § 507(a) are entitled to payment in "full" in chapter 13 over the course of the plan. § 1322(a)(2). Priority claims, however — unlike allowed secured claims — are not paid in present value dollars. Instead, the debtor is required to pay only the nominal amount of the claim, without interest. The language in § 1325(a)(5) (emphasis added) requires payment to secured creditors based on "the *value*, as of the effective date of the plan," which the courts uniformly understand to mean present value and hence requiring interest payments to compensate for the multi-year duration of a plan. See also § 1325(a)(4) (same, best interests test). But the priority-debt language in § 1322(a)(2) (emphasis added) refers only to "*full* payment, in deferred cash payments," conspicuously different text. Courts say this means no interest required for multi-year plans. See, e.g., In re Pitt, 240 B.R. 908 (N.D. Cal. 1999) (discussing Bruning v. United States, 376 U.S. 358 (1964)); In re Pardee, 218 B.R. 916 (B.A.P. 9th Cir. 1998). The simple sum of the payments made to a priority creditor must equal the amount of its filed priority claim. So, the good news for a priority creditor is that it will be paid in full; the bad news is the present value of that payment is often much less than the filed claim.

Because repayment in full of all priority debts is a requirement for confirmation of the plan, priority creditors are no longer placed in the competitive position they sometimes suffer in chapter 7. Unless the party entitled to repayment waives this right, each and every priority debt must be paid in full—whether it is a first priority or a fifteenth priority debt. This may be one reason why a debtor chooses a longer than three-year plan: the plan cannot be confirmed unless it proposes to pay the priority creditors 100% of their claims, with rare exceptions. § 1322(a)(4). If those debts are big enough, some families are effectively blocked from chapter 13. Let's look at the most common categories of these priority claims that can complicate a chapter 13.

1. Administrative Expenses

Some debtors pay § 507(a) administrative expenses in their chapter 13 plans. A debtor who did not have enough cash to pay the filing fee, for example, may pay the filing fee as a priority repayment in chapter 13. (Under Bankruptcy Rule 1006(b), the filing fee must be paid within 120 days of filing, which means that the filing fee is to be paid in installments in the first four post-filing payments.) Also, most debtors pay at least a portion of their attorneys' fees in chapter 13, although the amount of the fee, and the fraction of it that is typically paid prepetition, varies.

Under § 330(a)(4)(B), services necessary for representing the debtor in connection with a bankruptcy case are compensable; this rule applies only to individuals in chapter 12 or 13 cases (typically to be an administrative expense a benefit must inure to the *estate*, as opposed to the *debtor*, and so § 330(a)(4)(B)'s provision for payment to the debtor's individual lawyer might be considered anomalous—perhaps a congressional carrot to encourage choosing chapter 13?

2. Domestic Support Obligations

Some debtors owe alimony or child support, both back amounts and going-forward obligations. Because domestic support obligations are entitled to priority repayment in § 507(a)(1), they also enjoy full repayment priority in chapter 13. § 1322(a)(2). Indeed, many chapter 13 trustees point with pride to an unexpected benefit of having an ex-spouse in bankruptcy: the trustee will take over the function of collecting domestic support and distributing it to the intended recipients.

The bankrupt ex-spouse who owes support obligations may face a different set of incentives after a bankruptcy filing. To get a plan confirmed, the debtor must show he or she is current on all domestic support obligations that became due after filing. § 1325(a)(8). After confirmation, the failure to make plan payments will involve potential dismissal of the chapter 13 case, § 1307(c)(11), which can mean repo of a car or resumption of various other creditor unpleasantries. So much for stiffing the ex while paying everyone else. That said, the Code does not condemn debtors to servitude when they are behind on family payments. If they are *really* behind, government agencies often intervene and take over the payments to the beneficiary, subrogating to the claim against the delinquent debtor. Those government claims get priority, § 507(a)(1)(B), but get discharged if the debtor sweats out a full five-year plan. § 1322(a)(4). The theory must be that the government can spread this loss and the debtor needs a fresh start.

3.   Tax Claims

In addition to administrative and support claims, some consumer debtors face substantial tax debts. If the debtor gets into bankruptcy before the IRS files a lien, the tax claims will be unsecured. And even if the IRS does get a lien, the tax claims can still be partially unsecured, such as when the tax debt exceeds the value of the collateral bearing the lien, or when the lien secures some but not all taxes. The automatic stay will prevent the IRS from taking any further collection actions, including securing a new lien on the debtor's property. As we saw in the earlier assignment on § 507, this unsecured tax claim will often get priority.

Once a priority tax claim is determined by reference to § 507(a)(8), the debtor can then propose a plan to pay the amount of the tax claim in nominal dollars over the length of the repayment plan. This means that when the interest payments on tax debts stop at the time of filing, they really stop; note the contrast with secured claims, where stretched-out payment over time requires paying interest to ensure the claim's present value is satisfied.

Recall that because taxes are nondischargeable under § 523(a)(1), a debtor with a tax problem rarely receives much direct relief in his dealings with the taxing authorities from a chapter 7 filing. As such, chapter 13 offers three advantages: (1) letting the debtor pay the taxes over a time that can be as long as five years, with the automatic stay holding off the IRS throughout—remember the stay lasts until discharge, which in chapter 13 isn't until the plan is completed, § 362(c)(2)(C); (2) denying postpetition interest on unsecured claims, which will lock the tax claim at its value as of the date of the bankruptcy filing, § 502(b)(2); and (3) allowing that (locked) claim to be paid in nominal, not real, dollars over the length of the plan, which is especially helpful to the debtor in inflationary times. The chance to pay off back taxes over time without interest makes chapter 13 a valuable tool for taxpayers; savvy accountants often suggest a bankruptcy consultation if IRS negotiations stall—and are sure to let the IRS know about it (although if it has not liened the debtor's property, it may be moved to do so if it knows about the bankruptcy consultation).

As a reminder, taxes, like most domestic support obligations, are both priority claims and nondischargeable. But the overlap is not perfect. The smart lawyer must plan for both.

C. UNSECURED CREDITORS AND THE "DISPOSABLE INCOME" REQUIREMENT

The robust unsecured creditor protection is the requirement that the debtor must pay all "disposable income" for the length of the chapter 13 plan. § 1325(b)(1)(B). This requirement embodies both legal and factual complexities. While of course the minimum payment requirements only arise if the trustee or an unsecured creditor objects to the plan, as a practical matter such an objection to plan confirmation will nearly always be filed unless the chapter 13 trustee is satisfied that the debtor is paying all disposable income to unsecured creditors. An exception is if the unsecured creditors are receiving 100% payment. In such a situation, disposable income does not come into play as the unsecured creditors are deemed to have accepted the plan. § 1325(b)(1)(A).

Note at the outset we say the debtor's disposable income must be paid over "the course of the plan," language that is not used in the Code. Instead, it eschews common English and says the debtor's disposable income must be devoted to the pot for the "applicable commitment period," § 1325(b)(4)(A); although we prefer thinking of "plan length." But how long is that plan (the "applicable commitment period")? For most debtors, namely, those with below-median income, the plan must be a minimum of three years and a maximum of five years (with an exception for cases paying 100% of claims, which can be shorter than three years. § 1325(b)(4)(B)). The rest of debtors (above-median-income) have different rules that will be discussed below in Section C.3 (*spoilers*: five years). Why on earth does median income matter for chapter 13 rules? The short answer is BAPCPA says it does.

The idea of a minimum length is intuitive; if the debtor gets to earn a discharge *and* keep non-exempt property under chapter 13, then the unsecured creditors need some minimum amount of repayment effort to fund their pot; otherwise debtors would propose four-day plans and go home. But why a maximum? Isn't longer paying into the pot better for the creditors? Perhaps Congress doesn't want individuals under the supervision of the bankruptcy courts for too long, or perhaps it thinks eventually enough is enough, even if the debtor wants to keep going. Or maybe it is difficult enough to project income and expenses over five years, and after that point, nothing stops voluntary repayment post-discharge. Thus, plans can generally vary between three and five years in length, with that length often determined by the debtor's factual situation—e.g., what is the amount of mortgage arrearage and how long does the debtor need to stretch such payments out to find enough money in the monthly budget to "cure" it? Indeed, some debtors *want* to make longer plans than the three-year minimum because there are certain carrots within the Code (e.g., debtors paying more than 70% of their unsecured debts are not barred from refiling bankruptcy for a certain interval of time, § 727(a)(9)).

1.   Permissible Expenses

Whatever the length of the plan, the debtor must devote all "disposable income" to the unsecured creditors' pot. For the below-median debtor, "disposable income" is defined in the Code as all income "less amounts reasonably necessary to be expended . . . for the maintenance or support of the debtor or a dependent of the debtor. . . ." § 1325(b)(2)(A)(i). *Reasonably necessary?* That sounds like a squishy standard, doesn't it? Well, that's what bankruptcy judges are for (creditors, too, in an adversarial system).

In the Matter of WYANT
217 B.R. 585 (Bankr. D. Neb. 1998)

MINAHAN, Bankruptcy Judge.

This case is before the court to consider confirmation of the debtor's Amended Plan, Debtor's Counsel's Application for Attorney Fees, and the Resistance by the Chapter 13 Trustee. The plan is not confirmed; the debtor shall file an amended plan within 21 days hereof.

The amended plan is not confirmed because the debtor does not propose to pay disposable income to the trustee as required by § 1325(b)(1)(B). [§ 1325(b)(2) in post-2005 Code.—Eds.]

[The court reviewed various expenses, commenting critically on the debtor's "pre-bankruptcy planning," before turning to the last item.]

I further conclude that the debtor's proposed expenditures on veterinary expenses and livestock feed are unreasonable. The debtor is in the unfortunate position of owning several horses and dogs, which are elderly and which require extraordinary veterinary expenses. It is commendable that the debtor is willing to care for these animals and to attend to their feed and medical needs. On the other hand, this is a bankruptcy case in which the debtor is seeking to be discharged from his obligations to pay creditors. As between the debtor's elderly horses and dogs and his creditors, I think that the creditors should be paid first. The proposed expenditures on these animals are excessive, unreasonable, and not necessary for the maintenance or support of the debtor or his dependents.

On the other hand, the debtor should be encouraged to proceed in Chapter 13 in order that his creditors will receive payments over time. The disposable income analysis should not be so strict as to deprive the debtor of all discretionary income. Accordingly, I conclude that it is appropriate for the debtor to expend $100.00 per month for feed and veterinary expenses. This means that the proposed payments under the plan shall be increased and that for the 36 months of the plan, the debtor shall pay the trustee $1,300.00 per month. This sum represents proposed payments of $850.00 a month, plus disallowed expenses of $450.00 ($375.00 plus $75.00). . . .

By separate order, the proposed Amended Plan is not confirmed, the Chapter 13 Trustee's Objection to Confirmation is sustained, and the Application for Attorney Fees is denied.

Was confirmation at the Pet Cemetery? Did the Visa representative volunteer to waive payment in favor of Rover? Is Mr. Wyant a cynical manipulator or a man struggling as he loses the core pieces of his life? Judges are forced into intensely personal moral decisions by a provision that appears merely financial. How about one's commitment to religion?

In re CLEARY

357 B.R. 369 (Bankr. D.S.C. 2006)

DUNCAN, Bankruptcy Judge.

The chapter 13 trustee objects to confirmation on the basis that expenditures for private school tuition are not reasonable and necessary expenses and thus that the plan does not provide "that all of the debtor's projected disposable income to be received in the applicable commitment period . . . will be applied to make payments to unsecured creditors under the plan." 11 U.S.C § 1325(b)(1)(B).

FINDINGS OF FACT

1. Kevin Paul Cleary ("Debtor") filed a voluntary petition for relief under chapter 13 of the Bankruptcy Code on July 31, 2006.

2. Debtor is married, although his spouse did not join in the petition. Mr. and Mrs. Cleary have six children, the youngest age 7.

3. Debtor is employed as a driver for a nationwide parcel delivery service, and has been so employed for 21 years. His current net monthly take home pay, after deduction for taxes, union dues, and a 401k contribution, is $4,522.00.

4. Mrs. Cleary was not employed outside the home for approximately 15 years of the marriage. She has been employed as a teacher's aide at a parochial school for the past 2 years. Her net take home pay, after taxes and a small 401k contribution, is $918.50. An additional $813.00 is deducted from her pay check for tuition for three of the couple's children who attend the school. Mrs. Cleary's actual take home pay is $105.50.

5. The family's gross annual income is reported on Form B22C in the amount of $86,283.60.

6. The applicable median income for a South Carolina family of 8 is $86,918.00.

7. The family currently spends $1,165.00 for the mortgage payment, including taxes, insurance and home maintenance; $265.00 for utilities; $1,500.00 for food; $85.00 for automobile taxes and insurance; $465.00 for miscellaneous expenses (clothing, laundry, medical, recreation and

personal); and $100.00 for transportation. The family spends $1,513.00 for private school (elementary and secondary) tuition each month.

8. Five of the six children attend private school. The sixth child attended private school until the current school year when he asked to attend public school for the experience. The testimony was that the sixth child would like to return to private school next year. Mr. and Mrs. Cleary receive assistance from the private high school in the form of reduced tuition because of their income and family size.

9. Mr. and Mrs. Cleary own an "$150,000" 3-bedroom ranch style home and modest furnishings. They also own three vehicles; a late model van, under lien, and two older cars. The home is subject to two mortgages and has little equity if Debtor's statements of the current market value and mortgage balances are correct.

10. In addition to the mortgages and automobile loan the Debtor has two purchase money furniture accounts, two loans secured by avoidable liens on household goods, and less than $18,000 in unsecured debt, mostly from credit cards.

[Conclusions of Law]

For a below median income debtor, as we have here, the amounts reasonably necessary to be expended for the maintenance or support of the debtor or a dependent of the debtor are determined in the context of the estimated average monthly expenses reported on Schedule J.

These expenses must undergo judicial analysis, in the face of an objection, as to reasonableness and necessity; or as some might say, "the old fashion[ed] way." This Court considers Schedules I and J in the confirmation process for both above and below median income debtors. *See* In re Edmunds, 350 B.R. 636 (Bankr. D.S.C. 2006). . . .

The debtor bears the burden of showing that an expense is reasonable for confirmation purposes. In re Watson, 403 F.3d 1 (1st Cir. 2005); Lynch v. Tate (In re Lynch), 299 B.R. 776, 779 (W.D.N.C. 2003). . . . The majority of the cases reject private school tuition as a reasonable and necessary expense; at least in the absence of educational necessity or special needs. Earlier decisions expressed the "view that a debtor's creditors should not pay tuition for the debtor's children." In re McNulty, 142 B.R. 106 (Bankr. D.N.J. 1992); *See also* In re Jones, 55 B.R. 462 (Bankr. D. Minn. 1985) (Expressing the view, no longer held in many circles, that the public education was of high quality[]). The fulcrum was to balance "creditor's rights against the appropriate basic needs of the debtors and their dependents." *Watson* at 8. . . .

While the Debtor is retaining real estate, paying a 1% dividend to general unsecured creditors, and the children have no special education needs other than the fact that they are bright and need to be challenged; these factors are outweighed by others. The Debtor and his family have shown long term enrollment at parochial schools. All of the children attend private school, save one—who plans to return to private school next year. The Debtor's wife attended private school. The Debtor and his wife have strongly held religious convictions. The Debtor's wife would not work outside the home (and did not do so for many years) except to provide additional income to pay for private school tuition. In fact, Mrs. Cleary's pay check is reduced by the amount of tuition for the couple's children who attend the elementary school where she works.

The family's sacrifice of other basic expenses to fund private school tuition is noteworthy and, in this case, the deciding factor for the Court in approving the necessity and reasonableness of the expense for private school tuition. *See* In re Grawey, 2001 WL 34076376 (Bankr. C.D. Ill. 2001) (private school tuition and belt-tightening in the context of the dischargeability of student loans—sacrifices other basic necessities such as health care insurance). Debtor, if his testimony and schedules are truthful, could file a chapter 7 petition and it is very likely that he would lose no assets to administration for creditors. He is curing a small arrearage on his home loan through the chapter 13 plan, but the amount is *de minimis.* Debtor is giving up furniture secured by purchase money loans. For these reasons the Court finds that private school tuition is a reasonable and necessary expense of the debtor.

This aspect of the decision is limited very narrowly to the facts of this case. Mrs. Cleary is not a co-debtor. Her income would likely not be available if the children withdrew from private school because she would not work outside the home. It is only because of her religious convictions that she works outside the home and sends her children to private school. Debtor and his family sacrifice significantly in the purchase of food and clothing and in the areas of recreation and transportation expense. The expense of $1,513.00 for private school tuition is a reasonable and necessary expense.

The objection of the trustee is overruled. The plan will be confirmed by separate order.

━━━━━━━━━━
━━━━━━━━━━

For reasons we will see in the next assignment, a plausible argument that school fees are more entitled to statutory protection can be made post-BAPCPA, and so maybe the law has changed. For an "old school" perspective on an old school case, consider Univest-Coppel Village, Ltd. v. Nelson, 204 B.R. 497 (E.D. Tex. 1996). Mr. and Mrs. Nelson paid $395 a month to keep their 15-year-old daughter in Liberty Christian School. When they filed for chapter 13, one of their creditors objected to the expense, saying that this money should be counted as disposable income. Dad pointed out that the girl was "adamant" about not changing schools, and, in what he thought would be the clincher argument, he noted that she was the "only freshman to make the cheerleading squad." The bankruptcy court allowed the expense, but the district court said no, send the kid to public school. ("Gimme a B! Gimme an O! Gimme an O!")

The disposable income test for below-median debtors has thus been fraught with arguments to judges over various expenses, some of which serve as a reminder that people live varied lives—even if they are bankrupt. Over time, chapter 13 trustees and local lawyers develop a sense of what is likely to be acceptable to the judges in the district. The shorthand rules are often repeated, "Don't drive a car nicer than the judge" or "Cut the cord; the judge doesn't watch cable." Flexibility sounds grand, but it puts the judge's values right in the middle of the choices.

2.   *Available Income*

OK, so maybe "reasonably necessary . . . for maintenance and support" is a squishy standard that puts the debtor at the mercy of a bankruptcy judge for which expenses can be deducted from the monthly budget in determining "disposable income," but at least the first half of the calculation—income—sounds pretty straightforward. Just look at the debtor's W2, right? Were only it so. This is the Bankruptcy Code we're talking about.

In re WAECHTER
439 B.R. 253 (Bankr. D. Mass. 2010)

HOFFMAN, Bankruptcy Judge.

This matter came before me for hearing on the objection of Denise M. Pappalardo, the standing Chapter 13 Trustee, to confirmation of the Debtor's amended Chapter 13 plan. The Trustee argues that the amended plan fails to provide for the unsecured creditors to receive the Debtor's entire projected disposable income and that in any event the plan is not proposed in good faith. The Debtor disagrees.

The parties' dispute stems from a premarital agreement entered into on April 7, 2008 by the Debtor and her then fiancé, Joao Da Silva, in which the couple agreed to keep their property and financial obligations entirely separate throughout their marriage. Subsequently, on November 2, 2009, the Debtor, but not her now husband Mr. Da Silva, filed a voluntary petition for relief under Chapter 13 of the Bankruptcy Code. . . . [T]he Debtor lists combined monthly income after payroll deductions for herself and Mr. Da Silva of $7,453.46, which includes Mr. Da Silva's net income of $1,348. . . . [T]he Debtor lists her monthly expenses including a line item of $1,309.46 described as "Spouse's prerogative, pursuant to premarital agreement, not to share income." This expense has the practical effect of offsetting all but $38.57 of Mr. Da Silva's income . . . thus leaving the Debtor with only $119 per month in disposable income to fund her Chapter 13 plan. The plan provides no dividend to general unsecured creditors.

Bankruptcy Code § 1325(b)(1)(B) provides that if a trustee objects to plan confirmation the court may not confirm the plan unless the plan provides for all of the debtor's projected disposable income received during the life of the plan to be applied to make payments to unsecured creditors under the plan. The Trustee argues that the disposable income figure which is the basis for the Debtor's proposed plan payment is significantly understated, and thus violative of Section 1325(b)(1)(B), because while the Debtor includes her husband's income in Schedule I, she backs virtually all of it out in Schedule J, effectively giving her husband a free ride on all marital living expenses.

To rule on the Trustee's objection that the Debtor fails to dedicate her true projected disposable income to her plan, I turn first to the Bankruptcy Code, which defines "disposable income" as the "current monthly income received by the debtor . . . less amounts reasonably necessary to be expended" for the maintenance or support of the debtor or a dependent of the debtor, charitable contributions, and other items. Bankruptcy Code § 1325(b)(2). "Current monthly income" is defined as "the average monthly income from all sources that the debtor *receives* . . . without regard to whether such income is taxable income . . ." (emphasis added). Bankruptcy Code § 101(10A). Courts are generally in agreement that in order to be considered part of the debtor's current monthly income, and, therefore, included in the disposable income calculation, income from a non-filing spouse to help cover household expenses must actually be received by the debtor. *See, e.g.,* In re Quarterman, 342 B.R. 647 (Bankr. M.D. Fla. 2006).

In a typical case where spouses pool some or all of their income to pay for joint household expenses, courts look at the amount of pooled household expenses and assume that the non-filing spouse contributed a proportional amount of his or her income to the debtor for paying such expenses. *See, e.g.,* In re Mathenia, 220 B.R. 427, 431 (Bankr. W.D. Okla. 1998). In the present case, however, the Debtor concedes that her husband does not contribute anything to the household expenses. Accordingly, since the Debtor does not actually receive any income from Mr. Da Silva, her plan satisfies the requirements of § 1325(b)(1)(B).

The inquiry does not end there, however, and as the Trustee correctly points out, the Debtor must still satisfy the separate good faith requirement of Bankruptcy Code § 1325(a)(3). The majority of courts in this circuit apply a "totality of the circumstances" test in evaluating whether a plan is proposed in good faith. In re Torres Martinez, 397 B.R. 158, 166 (1st Cir. BAP 2008).

Where questions of good faith arise with respect to a non-filing spouse's contribution, or lack thereof, to a debtor's disposable income in Chapter 13 cases, some courts have investigated the lifestyle choices of the non-filing spouse. Thus, for example, if the debtor received income towards household expenses from her non-filing spouse while at the same time enjoying the benefits of excessive luxury household expenses paid for exclusively by the spouse, courts have denied plan confirmation on the basis of bad faith. *See* In re McNichols, 254 B.R. 422, 430 (Bankr. N.D. Ill. 2000). On the other hand, if it is clear that the non-filing spouse is using his surplus income substantially to pay his own obligations, and is not otherwise subsidizing the debtor's luxury lifestyle while the debtor's creditors take it on the chin, then courts will find the debtor's plan to be filed in good faith. *See* In re Nahat, 278 B.R. 108 (Bankr. N.D. Tex. 2002).

Section 1 of the premarital agreement provides that each party will pay his or her own debts and that neither party is to be held liable for the debts of the other in any way. Given this restriction, the Debtor may in good faith propose a plan in which she is solely responsible for the mortgage payment on the marital home, title to which remains solely in the Debtor's name. This analysis, however, does not extend to a plan in which the Debtor purports to pay all other joint household expenses while her husband pays nothing.

Unlike the Debtor's mortgage payment, nothing in the premarital agreement requires that the couple not share general household expenses of the marital home. While the agreement clearly requires that the couple not share their income, it does not address how they will divide the joint day-to-day expenses of their married life. Therefore, the Debtor may not rely on the premarital agreement as justification for taking full responsibility for paying household expenses, effectively subsidizing her husband's [wealth] at the expense of her creditors.

According to Schedule J, the Debtor pays a total of $520 per month for utilities, water, sewer, cable, telephone and internet expenses. As the co-occupant of the marital home, Mr. Da Silva benefits from each of these expenses. In addition, the Debtor pays $649 per month for home maintenance and food, further benefitting Mr. Da Silva. In order to interpret Schedule J in a manner most favorable to the Debtor, I will assume that the Debtor's expenses for an additional telephone (presumably a mobile phone), clothing, transportation and health care costs, are solely for her benefit. This results in monthly household expenses which benefit both spouses of $1,169. If Mr. Da Silva were to contribute a proportional share of his income towards these expenses from which he benefits, the Debtor's projected disposable income would increase to $330 per month. If he were to contribute a full 50% share of these expenses, the Debtor's disposable income would jump to $703.50. In either circumstance, the Debtor could propose a plan providing for a significant dividend to her general unsecured creditors.

While I do not have the authority to order Mr. Da Silva to pay his share of the marital expenses, I can, and do, find that based on the totality of the circumstances, the Debtor's plan, in which she proposes to pay a disproportionate amount of the couple's shared household expenses, is not proposed in good faith. I will sustain the Trustee's objection to confirmation of the plan.

———

Another ambiguity about the scope of income for bankruptcy purposes concerns the exclusion in § 101(10A)(B) for "benefits received under the Social Security Act." Unemployment compensation has its legal basis in that law, but the majority of courts has concluded that such benefits must be counted as income—and paid out to creditors. See In re Washington, 438 B.R. 348 (M.D. Ala. 2010) (collecting cases on both sides of issue).

Taken together, this case law of permissible expenses and available income provides judges with a basis for determining a below-median debtor's "disposable income" that must be committed to the pot for unsecured creditors over the plan's "applicable commitment period." If an unsecured creditor does not believe the debtor is paying this amount, it is a basis for objecting to plan confirmation. But remember that chapter 13 is not income-generating. That is, if a debtor's monthly mortgage bill, car payment, food, and all other reasonable expenses *exceed* monthly income, the debtor does not find a sympathetic ear in chapter 13. On the contrary, this means that the debtor will be unable to confirm a plan and hence have the case dismissed. § 1325(a)(6) (requiring that "the debtor will be able to make all payments under the plan and to comply with the plan"). Thus, some debtors may have such financial distress that they cannot proceed in chapter 13 with a plan of repayment, even if they want to do so. Because their expenses are already reasonable and necessary, debtors may have difficulty downsizing further (although perhaps a cheaper car or house is an option), or, if they are eligible, filing for chapter 7. Why might debtors propose such "unpayable" chapter 13 plans? Sunny optimism, to be sure, but more often because they want relief that only chapter 13 can bring, such as ability to cure a home mortgage default. Consider what Judge Yun said about these debtors:

> Chapter 13 plans premised on contributions from family and friends are much too common before the court and are often proposed by debtors in their impractical and often futile attempts to save their homes that are overencumbered by secured debts. Many of these chapter 13 plans not only fail to meet the requirements for confirmation under § 1325 but also defeat the primary purpose of bankruptcy for individuals—a fresh start.

In re Deutsch, 529 B.R. 308 (Bankr. C.D. Cal. 2015) (denying confirmation and converting case to chapter 7 notwithstanding declaration from debtor's "new boyfriend" that he would contribute $700 per month to the plan "for as long as he could").

Do you think this decision hindered or helped the budding romance?

3.   *Special Rules for Above-Median-Income Debtors*

Under BAPCPA, Congress decided to graft two important additional requirements onto chapter 13 plans regarding the disposable income test for certain higher-income debtors. Its conception of higher income—merely being above the pertinent state median income—takes what might be considered an expansive view toward identifying a high roller (a 51%-er?). The first requirement, as mentioned above, is that these above-median-income debtors have a minimum "applicable commitment period" of five years for their chapter 13 plans. § 1325(b)(4). The idea is that unless a debtor is paying 100% of unsecured creditors' claims, the plan must be five years in duration.

The second and more complicated add-on for above-median-income debtors in chapter 13 is that Congress decided to pre-specify, by statute, just what these debtors would be allowed as their "reasonable and necessary expenses" in calculating the disposable income test. This was a congressional repudiation of the case-by-case adjudication of the bankruptcy judge's exercise of discretion, which continues to be the sole determination of income for below-median-income debtors. But for those above-median folks, Congress substituted multiple pages of dense statutory text on what may be deducted from income as a permissible expense. Confusingly, this statutory budget for repayment plans is not in chapter 13. Instead, it is found in § 707(b), which has to do with eligibility to file chapter 7. § 1325(b)(3).

It is difficult to overstate how complicated Congress made this, so let's unpack it. Chapter 13 confirmation requires payment of the debtor's "projected disposable income [over the] applicable commitment period," § 1325(b)(1)(B), and the Code in the next subparagraph specifies a definition of "disposable income" that turns on "reasonably necessary" expenses, § 1325(b)(2). Then the subparagraph after that provides yet another definition, this time of "reasonably necessary," but the definition is contingent and applies only to above-median-income debtors, and that is the definition that invokes the means test budget, § 1325(b)(3).

Because the entire upcoming assignment looks at § 707(b)—often called "the means test"—we will defer exploring the statutory budget that applies to above-median-income chapter 13 debtors. Just recognize that for any chapter 13 filer with above-median income, "reasonable and necessary" is not nearly so free-wheeling as it sounds; it is in fact quite the opposite. You may wonder since above-median-income debtors have to endure five-year plans and calculate their minimum contributions to the unsecured creditor pot using a statutory budget that may not resemble their actual expenses, why they would file chapter 13. The simple answer is sometimes they want the advantage of legal tools unavailable in chapter 7—such as the ability to de-accelerate and cure a defaulted home mortgage. The more complicated answer is that sometimes they are *forced* to choose chapter 13; that's what soon-to-be-explored § 707(b) is about.

Before you get carried away thinking this above-median statutory budget is going to apply to half of debtors—after all, above-median means everyone above the 50th percentile—remember that people who go bankrupt tend to have much lower incomes than the general population when they file (although often they had higher incomes at some time in the past when they incurred their current debts). Indeed, median income for debtors in chapter 13 was only about $35,700 in the national sample of the 2007 Consumer Bankruptcy Project. Two-thirds of chapter 13 filers had income below the applicable median for their households and will only need to satisfy the traditional disposable income test. They never have to worry about the statutory budget explained in more detail in Assignment 12.

D.   MODIFICATION OF CHAPTER 13 PLANS

A chapter 7 involves only the liquidation of already-acquired assets. By contrast, a chapter 13 plan relies on payment out of future income. Often debtors in chapter 13 bankruptcies already have had significant financial disruptions, and projections of income and expenses frequently are not borne out. In short, "disposable income" can change. If so, the debtor, the trustee, or a creditor may move to have the plan modified. § 1329(a). Most often, the debtor seeks modification because of decreased income or increased expenses that have made payment of the originally promised amounts much more difficult.

An obvious limit on modification is whether the debtor has any disposable income at all; the more nuanced problem is whether the debtor's income at the time of modification will permit the debtor to continue making payments on secured debts. Modification can reduce payments to unsecured creditors but it doesn't change the statutory minimums owed to secured and priority creditors.

Modification is constrained by the statutory limit on plan length at five years. § 1322(d)(1). When a plan is modified, it must still meet all the chapter 13 requirements, including this five-year limit. Most debtors, however, are already in a five-year plan. 2007 Consumer Bankruptcy Project; see also Scott F. Norberg & Andrew J. Velkey, Debtor Discharge and Creditor Repayment in Chapter 13, 39 Creighton L. Rev. 473, 526 & Tbl. 36 (2006) (reporting that 60% of cases proposed five-year plans). This wipes out significant flexibility in reworking a plan if a debtor falls behind, even for those below-median-income debtors whose plans do not have an "applicable commitment period" of five years. This means the debtor has to find a way somehow to make up for the missed payments, despite an income from which all spare change has already been fully committed.

Sometimes trustees work around this by waiting a couple of months before filing a motion to dismiss for missing plan payments as an informal "grace period" for struggling debtors. By that point, some debtors have resumed payments, and the trustee and court simply tack on the non-payment months to the end. Indeed, one trustee reports that most successfully completed plans are now 62 or 63 months in length, an outcome that one will find explicitly contemplated nowhere in the Code with its cap on chapter 13 plans at 60 months—and yet the world still spins.

Of course, modification goes both ways. That is, some debtors will get a raise, work a little overtime, or have a kid get a job and move out of the basement. This good news may be short-lived for the debtor. Creditors or the trustee may trumpet the debtor's changed circumstances and argue that the plan should be modified to permit higher payments. This monetary joy that has touched the debtor's life is even better news for the creditors, who can ask to take it all. Because the debtor is already in "disposable income" territory, any new income would seem to flow directly to them.

In re DREW

325 B.R. 765 (Bankr. N.D. Ill. 2005)

Squires, Bankruptcy Judge.

[B]oth matters involve a common issue: whether the Debtors' confirmed plans can be amended under § 1329 to increase the dividends payable to the pre-petition unsecured creditors as a result of the Debtors refinancing their respective real properties and receiving lump sum cash payments as part of the refinancing. . . . The Trustee contends that the cash payments should be added to the total pot that the Debtors should be required to pay under the terms of their confirmed plans.

The Drews filed their Chapter 13 petition on December 16, 2002. On March 12, 2003, their plan was confirmed. Pursuant to the plan, the Drews were to pay $350.00 per month to the Trustee for a minimum term of thirty-six months (totaling $12,600.00) in order for unsecured creditors' allowed claims to receive a minimum ten percent dividend. The order confirming the plan provided that if the unsecured creditors would receive one hundred percent of their allowed claims, they could pay less than the aggregate sum of $12,600.00. At the time the Trustee's motion was filed, January 24, 2005, the Drews had not made thirty-six months of payments under the confirmed plan. Rather, they paid a total of $9,380.00. In January 19, 2005, the Court granted the Debtors' motions to obtain credit in order to refinance their properties. In the Drews' case, the Trustee alleges that at the time of confirmation, their real estate was valued at $90,000.00, and they refinanced it for $105,000.00.

In the Debtors' responses, they concede the valuations of the subject properties that were scheduled at the time of confirmation, but assert that the Trustee is now estopped from challenging those valuations at this point. They contend that the higher valuations, for refinancing purposes, show that the real properties have appreciated over the passage of time since confirmation. The Debtors argue that they should be able to keep the surplus equity and should not be required to pay those funds to the unsecured creditors and increase their dividends. The Debtors contend that granting the Trustee's motions would effectively discourage other debtors from seeking relief under Chapter 13. . . . According to the Trustee, the motions to modify the plans satisfy the requirements of § 1329(b)(1), § 1325(a)(1), § 1325(b)(1) and § 1325(a)(3).

The debtor, the trustee or any holder of an allowed unsecured claim has standing to seek modification of a plan after confirmation. *See* 11 U.S.C. § 1329(a). Section 1329(a)(1) expressly permits post-confirmation plan modifications to increase the amount of payments on claims of a particular class. The Trustee has standing under § 1329 to seek post-confirmation modification of the plans in order to increase the dividends to the unsecured claim holders. . . .

[The] specific issue at bar [is] whether the Court can modify the confirmed plans to increase the dividends payable to the unsecured creditors as a result of the Debtors receiving lump sum cash payments from the refinancing of their real properties. It is undisputed that the Debtors have appropriately sought and received approval to refinance the mortgages on their homes that they are attempting to keep and save in the context of their confirmed Chapter 13 plans. . . .

The interplay of 11 U.S.C. § 1327(c), § 541 and § 1306(a)(1) deals with and provides an interesting interaction with the expanded definition of property of the estate in a Chapter 13 case. This is because § 541 broadly defines property of the estate to include "all legal or equitable interests of the debtor in property as of the commencement of the case." 11 U.S.C. § 541(a)(1). In addition, § 1306(a)(1) includes "all property of the kind specified in [§ 541] that the debtor acquires after the commencement of the case but before the case is closed, dismissed or converted. . . ." 11 U.S.C. § 1306(a)(1). Thus, property that a Chapter 13 debtor acquires post-petition, like the refinancing proceeds the Debtors received in the cases at bar, becomes property of the estate pursuant to § 1306, in contrast to the post-petition acquisitions that do not become part of a Chapter 7 or Chapter 11 estate. Accordingly, it has been held that a Chapter 13 estate can include gifts, inheritances and windfalls that are acquired by the debtor post-petition. *See, e.g.,* In re Euerle, 70 B.R. 72 (Bankr. N.H. 1987) (inheritance); In re Koonce 54 B.R. 643 (Bankr. D.S.C. 1985) (lottery winnings); Doane v. Appalachian Power Co. (In re

Doane), 19 B.R. 1007 (W.D. Va. 1982) (money loaned to the debtor by a relative).

There exists a statutory tension between § 1306(a)(1) and the vesting provisions of § 1327(c). Although § 1327(c) notes that property vesting in the debtor includes all property acquired after the petition is "free and clear of any claim or interest of any creditor provided for by the plan," some courts have left room for the re-creation of the Chapter 13 estate after confirmation and hold that the estate continues and can be refilled with property acquired after confirmation. *See, e.g.,* In re Nott, 269 B.R. 250 (Bankr. M.D. Fla. 2000) (although property of the estate at confirmation vested in debtor pursuant to § 1327(b), a $300,000.00 inheritance one year after confirmation is property of the estate pursuant to § 1306(a)).

The Seventh Circuit has stated that § 1306(a)(2) provides that upon confirmation, the plan returns so much of the estate to the debtor's control as is not necessary for the fulfillment of the plan. Black v. United States Postal Serv. (In re Heath), 115 F.3d 521, 524 (7th Cir. 1997). Under that dictum, the portions of the refinancing proceeds intended by the Debtors to be paid to complete their confirmed plans are part of the continuing estates under § 541 and § 1306(a)(1).

Thus, the Court holds that the refinancing proceeds are part of the Debtors' bankruptcy estates post-confirmation because those proceeds were acquired by the Debtors for use in making payments under their confirmed plans. . . .

Section 1329(a)(1) can be invoked by trustees or unsecured creditors who timely move to increase a debtor's payments under a confirmed plan where the debtor's financial situation has improved. In his treatise, Judge Lundin aptly stated that:

> There is obvious fairness to requiring debtors to share good fortune with creditors. This is the same fairness that permits Chapter 13 debtors to reduce payments to creditors when circumstances disable the debtor from completing the original plan. . . . It is of more than academic interest that were the debtor to convert to Chapter 7 after winning a lottery or realizing new income, the postpetition assets and income belong to the debtor and would not be available for distribution to creditors in the Chapter 7 case. Perhaps the sharing of postpetition good fortune is seen by some courts as the cost of the Chapter 13 discharge. . . . [C]ases support the proposition that an allowed unsecured claim holder [or the trustee] can force the debtor with improved financial condition to a choice: accept an increase in payments to creditors or get out of Chapter 13.

3 Lundin, § 266.1 at 266-14 (footnotes omitted). *See also id.* at 266-1-5 (collecting cases for the proposition that courts have aggressively allowed trustees and unsecured claim holders to modify plans to increase payments—often over the strong opposition of debtors). It is "not the design of the Bankruptcy laws to allow the Debtor to lead the life of Riley while his creditors suffer on his behalf." In re Bryant, 47 B.R. 21, 26 (Bankr. W.D.N.C. 1984). . . .

Although the refinancing by the Debtors in these cases involved new debt incurred by them, the refinancing transactions were not necessarily "washes" where the increased values of the subject properties were completely offset by the new loans. The record here is not at all comprehensive, but the Court doubts that the new loans made to these Debtors were at a one hundred percent loan to value ratio. Indeed, most real estate lenders in this District lend at a much lower loan to value ratio to provide some residual cushion in the event of subsequent default by the debtor with resultant foreclosure of the new mortgage. Thus, although the record is not at all clear, it is probable that each property's value has increased substantially more than the amounts loaned. Hence, there is likely additional equity in each property that the Debtors enjoy and will retain because the properties are not being sold. The Trustee's motions effectively seek to compel the Debtors to contribute so much of that equity to the unsecured creditors' dividends as the Debtors are cashing out via the refinancing. Section 1329 permits this result. . . .

Section 1329 provides a mechanism for the Trustee to "up the ante" for the benefit of the unsecured creditors if she so moves in time, just as the statute is more frequently invoked by debtors whose situations have worsened post-confirmation and appropriately seek to effectively reduce the unsecured dividends. The statute can work either way. . . .

There has been no evidence proffered to support the speculative argument that increasing the dividends to unsecured creditors will somehow discourage debtors from either filing Chapter 13 petitions or serve as a disincentive for debtors to seek to exit the system sooner. . . . [T]he possibility of relief under § 1329 only occurs after a Chapter 13 debtor's plan has achieved the major hurdle of being confirmed in the first instance, and many Chapter 13 cases never get to that point. Moreover, of those that do, the Court has anecdotally observed over the past seventeen years that the vast majority of § 1329 motions are brought by debtors who seek to lower the dividend to unsecured creditors because of their subsequent adverse circumstances. . . .

———————————————

Although the Code now permits judges or any party in interest to request annual financial updates, § 521(f)(4), the common practice is to scrutinize the tax returns each year instead. This is likely the only practical means for creditors to learn of positive changes to a debtor's financial situation. When these matters do get to litigation, some courts have held that a putatively modifying creditor must show a "substantial and unanticipated post-confirmation change," whereas others see no such requirement in the Code. See, e.g., In re Eckert, 485 B.R. 77 (Bankr. M.D. Pa. 2013) (discussing cases) (denying modification to 59-year-old debtor whose new job had mandatory overtime where debtor testified "I'm hoping to get away from overtime, 50 hours a week on my feet is a lot for me").

E.   STATUTORY BARS ON CHAPTER 13 ELIGIBILITY

We close our general discussion of chapter 13 with a caution that this repayment option, even with its hefty requirements, is not open to everyone. Section 109(e) restricts who can use chapter 13. A filer must be an individual. This means no entities, even if they are affiliated with the human debtor. As a practical matter, this does not mean that businesses do not get help in chapter 13. Many self-employed people run businesses but are not incorporated or otherwise organized as legal entities. Much of these folks' business debt creates personal liability, for example, because it is charged to a credit card used for both personal and business expenses or because of a personal guarantee or home mortgage to secure a business line of credit. See Robert M. Lawless & Elizabeth Warren, The Myth of the Disappearing Business Bankruptcy, 93 Cal. L. Rev. 3 (2005).

Another bar to chapter 13 is the requirement of regular income, which comes from the history of chapter 13 being a "wage-earner's plan." By moving from wage-earners to regular income, Congress was trying to expand the relief available (to housewives, contractors, trust fund babies, etc.), so the lingering effect today of this clause as a restriction is minimal: blocking those with no income from chapter 13 and shunting them to chapter 7 or out of the bankruptcy system altogether. Courts have broadly interpreted the provision, and so today, litigation is infrequent. For a discussion from the nation's top expert on chapter 13, see Judge Lundin's opinion in In re Murphy, 226 B.R. 601 (Bankr. M.D. Tenn. 1998) (stay-at-home stepmother eligible for chapter 13; had regular income even though not married to children's father who paid bills such as debtor's car payment). Some courts stretch, suggesting debtors with insufficient income to meet expenses lack "enough" income for chapter 13, but that seems a stretch of "regular" and raises concerns better reserved for feasibility analysis.

A third restriction—secured and unsecured caps on noncontingent, liquidated debt—has more bite. § 109(e). It seems designed to keep "the rich" from chapter 13 (they can file for an individual's plan in chapter 11 as we will see later on), consistent with chapter 13's populist origins. It's an odd tool to do so, however, because it focuses on debts not income. Poor people can have loads of debt; they tend to lack income.

In a world of home mortgages, it's easy to see why the secured debt cap is higher than the unsecured one. The debt caps do a lot more work in jurisdictions with high-cost housing, such as coastal California, or urban centers. Setting these caps at the "correct" level, however, is hard, and Congress really hasn't tried. The numbers were set back in 1978 and were not adjusted for decades thereafter. Post-2005, the debt limits adjust every three years, as with many other figures in the Code. 11 U.S.C. § 104(b).

The conjunctive requirements of noncontingency and liquidation are conceptually difficult. Examples may help. A *noncontingent* debt is one that is not dependent on future events. For example, if I run over your foot and you claim I owe you two million dollars for my negligence, I may counter that your wearing black clothes and lying in the middle of the road at nighttime was contributory. Even if you think you have a winner, your claim against me is contingent because liability has not been determined. This contingent debt does not count against the chapter 13 debt limit. Or think of your parents, who may have guaranteed your student loans. If they file for bankruptcy, those obligations, while real, are contingent, as you may never default.

Liquidated means we know what the actual amount is. If I admit negligence in the car vs. foot hypo but claim there is no way—*No. Way.*—a broken foot is worth two million dollars, then we have to go to court to liquidate my negligence debt. Imagine also a losing defendant who has just been found to have violated the antitrust laws: noncontingent liability, but no idea what amount of damages will be awarded. Many debts can be both contingent *and* unliquidated: car manufacturers' warranty claims are a good example. The cars may never be defective (contingent), and if they are, the amount of the repair claims is unknown (unliquidated). These characteristics of the claims don't make them any less real—the creditors line up and file their bankruptcy claims—it just means they don't count against the chapter 13 eligibility cap.

Assuming that chapter 13 should be limited to middle class debtors and that a debt restriction is a sensible way to do so (both arguable propositions), debt limits are confined to noncontingent, liquidated ones for good reason. Consider what happens if a specious debt is alleged by an angry creditor: wouldn't you be troubled if that could block you as a debtor from chapter 13 relief? Compare Fountain v. Deutsche Bank Nat'l Tr. Co. (In re Fountain), 612 B.R. 743, 749 (B.A.P. 9th Cir. 2020) ("A dispute over liability of a claim does not make the debt contingent.") with Ho v. Dowell (In re Ho), 274 B.R. 867 (B.A.P. 9th Cir. 2002) (unknown basis and degree of liability—minority shareholder of corporate litigation defendant—renders debt unliquidated).

Problem Set 11

11.1. You are filing your first chapter 13 case since entering practice. In your jurisdiction, judges are randomly assigned as cases are filed. The three bankruptcy judges seem to have rather different views about the requirements for confirmation of a chapter 13 plan—two are very strict and one is quite lenient. All three permit the debtor to propose an amended plan if the initial plan is not confirmed. Your client, Maria Jackson, is a single parent who supports herself and three children on the $23,000 annual salary she earns as a department store clerk in Atlanta. She is left with $60 per week after she has paid her rent, utilities, insurance, food, and gas. This amount would give her creditors about 50 percent of their outstanding debt over three years or 80 percent over five years, but it would also leave her without any cushion of any kind. Giving $60 to the trustee would also require termination of piano lessons for one child and prevent another child from starting much-needed orthodontic treatment. What kind of a plan do you propose for her? Does your malpractice insurer have an opinion on what you should do? See §§ 1322, 1325, 1329.

11.2. Christoph Paulus lives in a nice apartment in Milwaukee with his girlfriend Manuela, who works as a physical therapist and shares the rent and other household expenses. When he first got out of college he went a little nuts with his credit cards, so he now has $40,000 in credit card debt. He has settled down now, and, until recently, he was steadily reducing the debt by living frugally, driving the old family car his parents gave him, eating at home, shopping at Costco, and so on. Unfortunately, his elderly dad got very ill and even with Medicare coverage had substantial out-of-pocket medical expenses. Chris co-signed for the necessary charges the day his dad died and now finds himself with $60,000 in medical debt in addition to the credit cards, so he is contemplating some form of bankruptcy filing.

In the last year, Chris earned a total of about $24,000 as a temporary and contract worker, but the work has been a bit up and down and hard to predict from month to month. He recently finished his part-time MBA program and has been offered a job selling financial packages to executives. The salary would be about what he made last year, but he thinks that if he worked very hard he could make a great deal more. He values his easy-going life, but is worried about his debts and can't decide whether to take the sales job or not. Chris wants to know what his options are and what a chapter 13 plan would look like. What can you tell him? See §§ 1322, 1325.

11.3. Myrtle Tundra owes over $120,000 to banks, credit card issuers, and stores, and she has a $250,000 mortgage on her house. She has about $50,000 in non-exempt personal property. Her legal practice is doing well, and she makes about $150,000 a year. Myrtle has come to see you as a bankruptcy expert because she is nervous about a debt that she guaranteed.

The debt was the mortgage on the small office building that her old law firm owned and in which it maintained its office. Her former partner, John Ice, kept the building as part of their agreed wind-up of the firm's affairs. The mortgage is presently about $775,000, payable over 18 more years. The building is currently worth about $600,000, but it is in a rapidly developing area. A reliable real estate agent has told Myrtle that when a nearby freeway and shopping center are completed in about six months, the property will easily be worth $900,000.

John is having some trouble making the payments and may have missed this month's payment already. The mortgage is held by Loraine Ice, John's former wife, who hates both John and Myrtle for reasons Myrtle does not wish to discuss. Myrtle says Loraine would viciously exploit any default in an effort to hurt John and Myrtle. What is your advice? See § 109(e).

11.4. You are completing preparation of a chapter 13 plan for Justin D'Angelis. He wants to file but his wife, who is not employed outside the home, does not. Their income is $45,000. After you have computed his expenses, it appears that he will have about $425 a month that would be available for distribution to his creditors. Mr. D is very reluctant to pay anyone, and he keeps asking if he can't claim some more expenses. Finally, he looks at the expense list and says, "I want to make contributions to my church." You ask the amount, and he says, "$425 a month." You ask if he has made regular contributions in the past, and he says, "No, but I'm turning over a new leaf." Can Mr. D confirm a plan that pays nothing to his unsecured creditors? What do you advise him? See § 1325(b)(2)(A).

11.5. Last year you represented Doris Frankel in her chapter 13 bankruptcy. When you met Doris she was a recently widowed, middle-aged woman who had never worked outside the home. At her husband's death, she was left with huge bills from his final illness and a load of debts from his business for which she was jointly liable. After she used all the insurance and sold the business, she was still $120,000 in debt. Doris took a job as a clerk at the local Mega-Lo-Mart, and she asked for your help with her creditors, including her husband's hostile business partners. You took her into a chapter 13, and she insisted on a 25 percent repayment of her unsecured debt. You thought that amount was too high and that she would have nothing left over, but she said it was important to her self-esteem, so you got the plan confirmed.

Today, Doris is back in your office. She hardly looks like the same woman. While she worked at the Mega-Lo-Mart and another part-time, evening job, she began real estate classes. She has passed her exams, quit her other jobs, and has been selling commercial real estate for four months. Last night she got a call from a well-known real estate developer. It seems that he had met Doris and liked her quiet, sincere style. He checked her background and decided she was just the woman he wanted to be in charge of the completion and leasing of his latest office building. She recognizes the enormous work that she will have to do. She must supervise all finishing work, find tenants, negotiate leasing arrangements and customizing work, all of which will require substantial overtime. But if she can pull it off, the bonuses for 95-percent leasing in the first year could be as much as $50,000. You are delighted for her, but do you have any free advice? See § 1329.

Section 4

The Consumer Bankruptcy System

Now that you understand the provisions of chapter 7 and chapter 13 of the Code, this final consumer section of the textbook puts it all together. It starts with the all-important decision about the chapter under which to file the debtor's petition and then proceeds to consider the theoretical and policy issues underlying the consumer bankruptcy system that judges, scholars, lawyers, and law students should all think about in analyzing the Code. The myriad factors to consider in choosing the best chapter of the Code under which to file a consumer petition was already a complicated affair before Congress jumped in and passed BAPCPA; after BAPCPA, it is enough to test one's sanity. To make things digestible, we break out chapter choice into two assignments: the first on the BAPCPA means test—which acts as an eligibility bar to chapter 7, the same way § 109(e) acts as an eligibility bar to chapter 13. This means test is the central tool Congress has adopted to identify the debtors who could (or should) pay their debts and force them into chapter 13, where they will face a statutory budget immune from judicial intermeddling. The second part of this section discusses the other statutory and extra-statutory considerations that influence chapter choice once eligibility has been established. The exploration of theory and policy constitutes the third assignment and concludes our study of consumer bankruptcy.

THE MEANS TEST

In passing BAPCPA, Congress accepted the position that too many debtors were walking away from their debts through the perceived easy discharge of bankruptcy. To rectify this, it designed what is called the "means test" as a statutory bar to filing a chapter 7 petition, forcing those caught by its screen to face a series of less palatable options. ("Means test" is, once again, a term found nowhere in the Code and used everywhere in the bankruptcy world.) Barred consumer debtors would have to (1) file under chapter 13, where now mandatory five-year plans and statutory budgets await higher-income debtors, (2) file under some other chapter of the Code, such as chapter 11, which is a weird outcome for consumer debtors as that chapter is traditionally for business-based reorganizations, or (3) give up on a federal bankruptcy discharge and have to face their creditors with state exemptions but little more.

Courts and Congress have always been concerned about abusive use of the Bankruptcy Code, and so the means test was just the latest and most dramatic step in a long history of debtor policing. (Bankruptcy courts are often called courts of equity and so fairness considerations are intrinsic. Adam Levitin, Toward a Federal Common Law of Bankruptcy: Judicial Lawmaking in a Statutory Regime, 80 Am. Bankr. L.J. 1 (2006).) We start this assignment with the historical provisions for controlling debtor abuse to situate properly the means test's radical transformation of the Bankruptcy Code, then confront the means test in all its glory, and finally close with a discussion of its operation in chapter 13. Fasten your seatbelts.

A. THE HISTORICAL BAR TO CHAPTER 7: DISCRETIONARY DISMISSAL FOR SUBSTANTIAL ABUSE

There is no right to bankruptcy. Indeed, chapter 7 has always had some statutory bar or another, even before chapter 13 came along, and so the initial eligibility bars were complete exclusions from the system. For example, the first bankruptcy laws were available only to traders, an early recognition that debt relief was essential to encouraging entrepreneurial undertakings. By the mid-nineteenth century, bankruptcy laws accommodated both troubled businesses and families in financial distress. When Congress enacted the 1978 Bankruptcy Code, it kept broad access to chapter 7 with only the smallest exceptions. Indeed, the Code does not even require a showing of debtor insolvency as a precondition of filing, a requirement of many other legal systems. See, e.g., Insolvency Act, 1986, c. 45, § 272 (U.K.) Bankruptcy and Insolvency Act, R.S.C., 1985, c. B-3, s. 2 ("insolvent person") (Austl.).

On the other hand, Congress has since the 1978 Code evinced a policy of wanting more people in financial distress to use chapter 13. The pro-13 policy could stem from a number of factors, ranging from Protestant work ethic sensibilities to a belief that creditors get higher returns in chapter 13 than in chapter 7. Today's restrictions on chapter 7, therefore, are less bars to bankruptcy than "encouragements" for debtors to file in chapter 13. The 1978 Code used carrots, such as a (now-diminished) super-discharge for certain debts that weren't dischargeable in chapter 7, and perhaps more importantly, a right to cure a defaulted home mortgage. Some might say these statutory carrots worked, but we suspect that a massive campaign to educate lawyers and judges to use a "new and improved" chapter had an equal if not greater effect. See Katherine Porter, The Pretend Solution, An Empirical Study of Bankruptcy Outcomes, 90 Tex. L. Rev. 103 (2011). By the mid-1980s, about one-third of all families in bankruptcy filed chapter 13 cases.

In the eyes of some, however, two problems then emerged with the consumer bankruptcy system. The first was that Congress overshot the mark in making bankruptcy relief more available resulting in "too many" people filing for bankruptcy, and the second was that not enough of these bankrupt people were choosing chapter 13, whose uptake rate stabilized during the 1980s and 1990s at around one-third (albeit with wide variation among judicial districts). In response to these concerns, the credit industry lobbied to tighten bankruptcy relief.

In 1984, Congress gave bankruptcy judges the discretion to dismiss chapter 7 cases if the filing involved "substantial abuse." § 707(b) (1984). Judges responded by dismissing the cases of debtors who had committed bad acts, criminal activities, or otherwise irked a sense of fair play, even though the technical eligibility requirements for bankruptcy had been met. Case law developed the contours of "substantial abuse" and came to cover, at least in some districts, debtors who had the ability with a modest amount of sacrifice to repay their creditors but were filing in chapter 7 instead of chapter 13. Circuit court precedents abounded, see, e.g., In re Green, 934 F.2d 568 (4th Cir. 1991), and so bankruptcy judges became the primary gatekeepers of chapter 7 eligibility, leaving the dismissed debtors typically with a "choice" of chapter 13 or remaining outside the bankruptcy system.

Ironically, many courts deciding a § 707(b) motion for substantial abuse in a chapter 7 case undertook the same sort of consideration that underlies the scrutiny of a chapter 13 debtor's proposed budget: is the debtor scrimping enough to earn the privilege of a discharge? But as Green and other precedents made clear, "substantial abuse" was intended for the rogue outlier—a sort of safety valve to preserve system integrity. Indeed, a procedural presumption in § 707(b) clarified that the debtor enjoyed a presumption of *non-abuse*. Dismissal of chapter 7 was reserved for egregious exceptions rather than routine sorting. The case below illustrates the discretionary, judicially administered bar on chapter 7 that operated before 2005.

═══════════════ In re SHAW ═══════════════

311 B.R. 180 (Bankr. M.D.N.C. 2003)

CARRUTHERS, Bankruptcy Judge.

The Debtors are a married couple in their early 50s with two grown children, ages 21 and 24. . . . The Debtors have been continuously employed for at least the past five years. The Debtors' 2001 Federal tax return shows adjusted gross income of $138,554.00, with an increase in 2002 to $157,024.00.

Despite their consistent income during the last several years, the Debtors have been unable to make a dent in the repayment of their debts and have consistently spent more money than they were able to earn. The Debtors contend that they need a fresh start in a Chapter 7 so that they can retain their home and three vehicles [while discharging $130,000 in unsecured credit card debt—Eds.].

The Debtors' proposed [monthly] family budget as listed on Schedule J in the amount of $6,312.52 is excessive and unreasonable. First, the Debtors' mortgage payment expense is clearly unwarranted. The Debtors purchased the home in 1993. At the hearing, the Debtors explained that they needed a large [half-million dollar—Eds.] home so that there would be sufficient space for Mrs. Shaw's mother to live with them and yet not interrupt their children's lives. Mrs. Shaw's mother passed away in 1998. The Debtors currently pay $3,349.28 to maintain a home with approximately 3200 square feet as well as a finished basement. The Debtors' children are now grown, however, their 24-year-old son lives at home and contributes nothing to the monthly housing payment. If the Debtors wish to take advantage of the protections afforded by the Bankruptcy Code, they simply must obtain less expensive housing.

In addition, the court finds that the vehicle lease payments of $349.00 per month and college expenses of $520.00 per month for the Debtors' daughter are not reasonable and necessary expenses under these circumstances. While supporting a daughter in college is an admirable goal, the Debtors propose to do so at the expense of their creditors. Therefore, the Debtors' budget can be further reduced by $869.00 per month. Further reductions can be made by trimming the Debtors' telephone expenses for two home lines and two cell phones and by eliminating the ongoing expenses for the swimming pool. The court finds that the transportation cost, exclusive of car payments and insurance, is unreasonable and excessive. With just these adjustments alone, the Debtors could be able to contribute approximately $2,000.00 per month to a Chapter 13 plan. The Chapter 13 Trustee estimates a dividend of 29% over 36 months [and obviously much higher under a five-year plan—Eds.].

The Debtors admit that their bankruptcy was not the result of a sudden illness, calamity, disability, or unemployment. . . . While the Debtors have experienced some short period of unemployment, their road to financial distress was the result of lifestyle choices they made. . . . The Shaws have been living beyond their means for years. The Debtors made purchases in anticipation of future bonuses and were unable to pay off those purchases when bonuses were not received or were smaller than expected. For example, Mrs. Shaw testified that she purchased a bedroom suite less than two years ago for approximately $4,000.00 with the expectation that Mr. Shaw would get an anniversary bonus. Mr. Shaw did not receive that bonus.

The Debtors contend that they have never incurred debt maliciously or with an intent not to pay, and that their enormous debt has accumulated over a period of years. The fact that these debts accumulated over a long period of time makes it all the more difficult for the court to understand why the Debtors did not change their spending behavior years ago. According to the Debtors' testimony, they have been struggling to make payments on their debts for years, and yet continued to make expensive decisions, such as purchasing a 2002 Oldsmobile Bravado and a 2001 Oldsmobile Alero, and a $4,000.00 bedroom suite and contributing over $1,000.00 per month towards their daughter's college expenses. Thus, the Debtors have clearly been aware of their inability to pay their ever-increasing debt for years, and continued to incur cash advances and consumer purchases beyond their ability to pay.

The Debtors elected to file a Chapter 7 petition to maintain their present lifestyle. They have the ability to repay a substantial portion of the debt with their high income. The Debtors incurred cash advances and made consumer purchases far in excess of their ability to repay and their proposed family budget is both excessive and unreasonable given their current circumstances.

The court concludes that based upon the totality of the circumstances these debtors do not satisfy the criteria to be Chapter 7 debtors. To allow such would be a substantial abuse of the bankruptcy system and goals; and therefore, this Chapter 7 case should be dismissed under 11 U.S.C. § 707(b) of the Bankruptcy Code.

═══════════════

Despite the courts' willingness to crack down in cases such as *Shaw*, most debtors didn't have high incomes and big discretionary expenses to cut back on. Empirical studies, including our own, showed that most people filed for bankruptcy following job losses, serious medical problems, and family break-ups, and that very few of them could repay any meaningful amount to their creditors. Good studies, however, may not trump good lobbying, and creditors continued to point to a "problem" with consumer bankruptcies. In 2005, nine years after a bill drafted by the credit industry was first introduced, Congress passed BAPCPA, which made bankruptcy less accessible for all individuals. The centerpiece of these amendments was a new statutory screen, the means test, to determine who could file chapter 7.

B.   THE CURRENT BAR TO CHAPTER 7: MANDATORY DISMISSAL UNDER THE MEANS TEST

1.   The Overview

Perhaps blaming bankruptcy judges for the continuing rise in filings, Congress in BAPCPA removed them as the primary gatekeepers of chapter 7 access. Instead, it imbedded a fixed statutory formula to determine "abuse" and hence who can remain in chapter 7. This test runs several single-spaced pages of text, and frankly is difficult for anyone, much less students, to read. The overview below gives you a reader's guide to the statute, but there is no substitute for your working through it yourself. Technically, the heart of the means test is § 707(b)(2), but the broad structure of 707 is crucial to seeing how § 707(b)(2) does its work. Section 707(a) allows courts to dismiss cases generally for "cause," including the reasons specifically stated therein. Section 707(b) adds an additional dismissal screen on *consumer debtors*, presumably in the belief that they might be especially prone to abuse the bankruptcy system.

BAPCPA renumbered the substantial abuse section that was § 707(b) in 1984 (the one discussed in *Shaw*) as new § 707(b)(1), and made two modifications. First, it deleted "substantial" before "abuse," presumably to signal that courts should now be able to throw debtors out of chapter 7 for mere garden-variety abuse without it rising to the level of being substantial. Second, it deleted the important procedural presumption of non-abuse previously enjoyed by the debtor. These were important changes, to be sure, but nothing radical; they are extensions of the approach of prior amendments.

The actual "means test" of paragraph (2) of § 707(b), however, was radical. The key point of the multi-page paragraph is to create a "presumption" of abuse if the debtor can repay more than a certain minimum amount to creditors based on a complex statutory calculation. The presumption can nominally be "rebutted," but only by showing "special circumstances" that can meet the further test of § 707(b)(2)(B)(i). (For everyone else, the presumption is irrebuttable.) Finally, paragraph (3) allows additional grounds on which the court *may* dismiss a consumer debtor's petition for abuse beyond the mandatory grounds for which dismissal *shall* be ordered under paragraph (2)'s means test. We turn to paragraph (3) in the next assignment; paragraph (2)'s means test will keep us busy enough for now.

For newcomers, it is hard to discern the degree to which BAPCPA was a transformative event in the bankruptcy system's evolution. When chapter 13 was rolled out in the 1930s and thereafter in various districts, debtors were offered free choice between chapter 7 and chapter 13. Then in the 1978 Code, carrots were added to encourage debtors toward 13. In 1984, judge-administered sticks were added to underscore that encouragement. Now there is an extremely detailed formula that screens each and every debtor to determine whether chapter 7 is or is not an "abuse," the outcome of which relegates judges to the sidelines.

This judge-supplanting statutory screen on eligibility is called a "means test" because it depends upon the debtor's means, which is measured by a particularized definition of income. Other federal statutes, such as Medicaid, have means-based eligibility screens, so this is not unheard of; it was just unprecedented in the United States to evaluate people to make sure they were "poor enough" to be bankrupt. The numerical test of § 707(b) uses two approaches to measure a debtor's income: *gross* and *net* (these are our terms; you will find them nowhere in the statute). Debtors can pass either way; some have gross incomes so low they never have to undergo all the scrutiny of expenses involved in the net income screen. Higher-income filers must endure intense scrutiny of their expenses to confirm their net income is not so high as to make their chapter 7 case a presumed abuse. Not surprisingly, given the workload of bankruptcy judges, the primary party to use the means test is the U.S. Trustee. Thus, BAPCPA has the effect of giving a big boost in responsibility to this administrative branch of the federal government, while signaling reduced confidence in the bankruptcy courts to police access to chapter 7.

2.   The Gross Income Bypass

In what surely makes the short list for worst statutory drafting ever, buried away in paragraph (7) of § 707(b) is what looks like a dry standing rule. It is actually a bypass of the means test. In fact, it serves to exempt more than 90% of filers. Rephrased in English, § 707(b)(7) says that if the debtor's "current monthly income" is less than the applicable median state income, nobody can raise the means test presumption.* Functionally, an unraisable means test is a passed means test. Of course, this bypass doesn't stop the debtor from having to file a complicated means test calculation worksheet, see Form B 122A-2, but it does mean that the means test is just another piece of paperwork for most families. The U.S. Trustee Program's data show the great majority of chapter 7 debtors are below the median. (Median income, as a reminder, is the same measure used to trigger a mandatory five-year plan and statutory budget in chapter 13.)

Section 101(10A)'s definition of "current monthly income" has little at all to do with current monthly income. Instead, it uses a six-month retrospective approach. It includes income from all sources, not just wages, such as interest on checking accounts, unemployment compensation, income tax refunds, or, in the case of a debtor who runs a small business, revenues and possibly accounts receivable (depending on accounting practices). It also includes amounts paid by others toward household expenses, § 101(10A)(B). Out of the gates, we see the Code has nothing to

---

*Paragraphs six and seven read together are daunting. On first view, they seem to say the same thing, but on closer inspection, paragraph six is a standing rule that allows only judges and trustees—not individual creditors—to raise objections against below-median-income debtors on non-means test grounds (e.g., the discretionary dismissal power of paragraph (3)), whereas paragraph seven is a categorical bar on anyone—judges, trustees, the whole lot—from bringing a means test objection (i.e., paragraph (2)) against below-median-income debtors.

do with what the IRS might think about as income, where we bet at least some of you were hoping to look for interpretative guidance. Sorry.

Making matters worse, neither does the Census Bureau give us any help. You might assume that because the Code directs comparison of the debtor's current monthly income with the state median income measured by the Census, those two measures of income would be comparable. Nope. The Census approach to determining income does not include sources such as capital gains; money received from the sale of property (unless the recipient was engaged in the business of selling such property); the value of income "in kind" as in food stamps; tax refunds; exchange of money between relatives living in the same household; gifts and inheritances; insurance payments; and other types of lump-sum receipts, many (if not all) of which fall under § 101(10A)'s broad sweep. So what remains is a special bankruptcy definition of "income" unmoored from Census or IRS metrics. Note too that this disconnect between Bankruptcy Code income and Census Bureau income goes both ways. Recall the explicit exclusion of Social Security benefits from current monthly income (credit lobby scared by the AARP?). The Census Bureau *does* include this in its income measure, rendering the median income comparison of § 707(b)(7) all the more arbitrary.

The absurdity of measuring *current* monthly income with a *retrospective* test makes some people's heads spin—including the Justices of the Supreme Court. This absurdity boiled over in chapter 13, in which you will recall above-median-income debtors must use these means test calculations to determine their projected disposable income for a five-year repayment plan. § 1325(b)(3). So that means for above-median-income debtors, *future* income, projected over five years, is, as a matter of law, *past* income for the previous six months! This doublespeak was too much for the Court, which held, 8–1, that the modifier "projected" before "disposable income" in § 1325(b)(1)(B) allows some textual fudging, such that changes in income for chapter 13 debtors "known or virtually certain to occur" can be incorporated into an above-median-income debtor's plan, notwithstanding the explicit definition of "disposable income" in § 1325(b)(2) and (3) commanding use of the retrospective means test. Hamilton v. Lanning, 560 U.S. 505 (2010) (above-median-income debtor's one-time employment buyout properly excluded from her chapter 13 disposable income notwithstanding its capture in the means test's six-month-retrospective statutory definition of income). If you guessed that the dissenting Justice's name was Scalia, you win. Prying apart some of the textual certainty of BAPCPA has now led lower courts to confusion. For example, is *Lanning* limited to chapter 13, or could its logic be carried over to chapter 7 cases as well, where there is no difficulty in guessing what will happen five years hence? See, e.g., Danielson v. Flores, 692 F.3d 1021 (9th Cir. 2012) (holding *Lanning* inapplicable to chapter 7 and noting circuit split) (divided opinion), *reversed by* 735 F.3d 855 (9th Cir. 2013) (en banc). It seems everyone finds these issues hard. (As you will see below, lower courts are still struggling with this question.)

The second challenge with the Code's gross income test is to find the right household size for purposes of identifying the comparison figure from the Census. The debtor's household size matters because usually (although not always) larger households in the general population have higher median incomes. But even with all the legislative ink spilled on the means test, Congress declined to define "household."

===== JOHNSON v. ZIMMER =====
686 F.3d 224 (4th Cir. 2012)

AGEE, Circuit Judge.

In this direct appeal from the United States Bankruptcy Court for the Eastern District of North Carolina, we address . . . how[] the "household" size of a debtor seeking bankruptcy relief to be calculated[.] Upon receiving notice of the Debtor's motion for confirmation of a plan, the Debtor's ex-husband, William H. Zimmer ("the Creditor"), objected. The basis for the Creditor's objection was that the proposed plan overstated the Debtor's household size.

[T]he parties stipulated to the following facts: the Debtor and Creditor share joint custody of their two minor sons. Neither party pays child support; they share "expenses for clothing, school supplies, and other incidental expenses for their sons based on where the sons live when an expense is necessary." Out-of-pocket medical expenses are divided equally. By oral agreement, the Debtor's sons reside with her and are in her care and custody for 204 days each year. The Debtor's current husband has joint custody of three children from his previous marriage: two minor sons and a nineteen-year-old daughter. The Debtor's step-children reside with her and her husband approximately 180 days per year.

The Debtor . . . claimed a household of seven members, counting individually each person who resided in her home for any period of time within the past six months (i.e., the Debtor, her husband, her two children, and her three step-children). The Creditor asserted that the Debtor did not actually have seven members of her household because the five children and step-children did not live at her residence full-time. He contended that rather than simply counting the number of "heads on the bed" to determine household size, the Debtor's plan should use a method that better approximated the actual economic impact of each individual on the Debtor's expenses.

In examining the parties' dispute, the bankruptcy court observed that the Code does not define "household," there was no binding precedent on point, and that other bankruptcy courts followed three different approaches to define that term. As described in greater detail below, those three approaches are: the "heads-on-beds" approach that follows the Census Bureau's broad definition of a household as "all the people who occupy a housing unit," without regard to relationship, financial contributions, or financial dependency; the "income tax dependent" method derived from the Internal Revenue Manual's ("IRM") definition that examines which individuals either are or could be "included on the debtor's tax return as dependents"; and the "economic unit" approach that "assesses the number of individuals in the household who act as a single economic unit by including those who are financially dependent on the debtor, those who financially support the debtor, and those whose income and expenses are intermingled with the debtor's."

The bankruptcy court adopted a variation of the "economic unit" approach, first assessing the number of individuals whose income and expenses are intermingled with the Debtor's, and then calculating how much time any part-time residents were members of the Debtor's household. In adopting the "economic unit" approach, the bankruptcy court noted that the other two definitions were inconsistent with the purpose of the Code and were the least flexible in terms of adapting to an individual debtor's circumstances. In deciding that part-time residents should count as part-time members of the Debtor's "household," the bankruptcy court acknowledged that "[d]ividing children into fractions is not ideal," but concluded that this additional step in applying the economic unit approach best "capture[d] the nuances of familial support and bonds" and enabled the court to "account for dependents who reside with the debtor on a part-time basis . . . in calculating variable costs such as food, utilities, and out-of-pocket health care expenses." Accordingly, the court relied on the parties' stipulated facts to determine that each of the Debtor's two sons constituted .56 members of the Debtor's household (residing with her 204 days out of a possible 365), and that each of the Debtor's three step-children constituted .49 members of her household (residing with her 180 days out of a possible 365).

Implementing this fractional economic unit approach thus resulted in the Debtor having a total of 2.59 children in her household full-time, which the court then rounded up to three children. Thus, the Debtor, her husband, and the deemed three children yielded a "household" of five persons.

Despite the centrality of the term to the requisite analysis, the Code does not state how the size of a debtor's "household" . . . is to be calculated for determining his or her disposable income.

[W]ords that are not defined in the relevant statutory provisions are typically "interpreted as taking their ordinary, contemporary, common meaning." United States v. Lehman, 225 F.3d 426, 428 (4th Cir. 2000) (quoting Perrin v. United States, 444 U.S. 37, 42, 100 S. Ct. 311, 62 L. Ed. 2d 199 (1979)). The Court "customarily turn[s] to dictionaries for help in determining whether a word in a statute has a plain or common meaning." Nat. Coalition for Students v. Allen, 152 F.3d 283, 289 (4th Cir. 1998). In this instance, however, reviewing the dictionary definition of "household" does not resolve the matter because this term has multiple definitions of varying scope and consequence. For example, *Black's* defines the noun "household" as "1. A family living together. 2. A group of people who dwell under the same roof." *Black's Law Dictionary* 744 (7th ed. 1999).

Context provides some guidance in this case, but ultimately does not resolve the fundamental uncertainty of what Congress intended "household" to mean. On the one hand, Congress used the word "household" as opposed to "family," "dependent child," or "dependent," all of which are used elsewhere in the surrounding and cross-referenced Code provisions. Consistent with the principle that "[t]he use of different terms within related statutes generally implies that different meanings were intended," this would often mean that Congress intended the term "household" to mean something other than what those terms mean. *See* Cunningham v. Scibana, 259 F.3d 303, 308 (4th Cir. 2001) (quoting 2A Norman J. Singer, *Sutherland's Statutes and Statutory Construction*, § 46.06, at 195 (6th ed. 2000)). On the other hand, as set forth above, the dictionary definitions of "household" overlap with each of these terms to varying degrees, as "household" may or may not be defined to include the concept of familial connection or domestic interconnectedness.

[Section] 707(b) also refers to a debtor's "dependents" as opposed to his or her "household." Congress' use of "dependents" . . . would tend to suggest that although Congress used "dependent" and "household" at different points, they may nonetheless have related meanings. However, none of these approaches is directly required by the statutory language and is consequently based on inference and implication to one degree or another.

These are the hallmarks of statutory language that is anything but plain. Because the term "household" "lends itself to more than one reasonable interpretation," it is ambiguous. Accordingly, "our obligation is to find that interpretation which can most fairly be said to be imbedded in the statute, in the sense of being most harmonious with its scheme and the general purposes that Congress manifested." Id. Put differently, where statutory language is ambiguous, we "turn to other evidence to interpret the meaning of the provision," interpreting provisions harmoniously, where possible, or by reference to the legislative history, and always with the goal of ascertaining congressional intent. *See* New Cingular Wireless PCS, LLC v. Finley, 674 F.3d 225, 249 (4th Cir. 2012).

A handful of bankruptcy courts have adopted the heads-on-beds approach, using the Census Bureau definition of "household," although they use different—and in some cases no—reasons to explain why. Some bankruptcy courts have stated that this definition of "household" is simply its plain meaning. We are not persuaded that Congress intended for "household" to be so broadly defined. At the outset, nothing in § 1325(b) directly or indirectly incorporates the Census Bureau's definition of "household." Although there is a cross-reference to the Census Bureau's median income tables, that is not sufficient to demonstrate a congressional intent to adopt the usage utilized by the Census Bureau in its wholly separate sphere of government work. Moreover, while the use of "household" as opposed to "family" or "dependents" (terms used elsewhere in [the Code] would indicate that the term means something different from those words, that does not automatically indicate that Congress intended for the term "household" to be synonymous with the Census Bureau's definition and refer to *any* person living in a particular residence. . . .

[Its definition of "all of the people, related an unrelated, who occupy a housing unit"] serves the Census Bureau's need to compile demographic information identifying the number of people in a particular geographic region. It is wholly unrelated to any bankruptcy purpose and does not serve the Code's objective of identifying a debtor's deductible monthly expenses and, ultimately, his or her disposable income. The calculation of a debtor's monthly income and expenses is aimed at ensuring that debtors pay the amount they can reasonably afford to pay to creditors. It makes little sense to allow debtors to broadly define their "households" so as to include individuals who have no actual financial impact on the debtor's expenses. This result would be entirely at odds with the stated purpose of the BAPCPA: "The heart of the bill's consumer bankruptcy reforms consists of the implementation of an income/expense screening mechanism ('needs-based bankruptcy relief' or 'means testing'), which is intended to ensure that debtors repay creditors the maximum they can afford." H.R. Rep. No. 109-31(I), *89.

Next, we consider whether the bankruptcy court erred in using the "economic unit" approach. The approach is flexible because it recognizes that a debtor's "household" may include non-family members and individuals who could not be claimed as dependents on the debtor's federal income tax return, but who nonetheless directly impact the debtor's financial situation. Thus, the entire purpose of identifying a debtor's household size is to use that number to determine his or her financial obligations and ability to pay. A definition of "household" that is also tailored to reflect a debtor's financial situation focuses directly upon the ultimate purpose of the Code.

The foregoing analysis does not end our inquiry, however, because the bankruptcy court opted to further refine the economic unit approach to account for the part-time members of the Debtor's "household." The Debtor contends that even if the bankruptcy court did not err in using an economic unit analysis to determine her household size, it nonetheless erred in dividing individuals (the Debtor's children and stepchildren) into "fractions and percentages" of her "household" when the Code "only speak[s] in terms of whole 'person[s]' and 'individuals.'" She points to the majority of courts that have used the economic unit approach to contend that the bankruptcy court relied [an] outlier case . . . to "carve[ ] children into fractions" and thus lead to "a contrived result."

We find no error in the bankruptcy court's method of applying the economic unit approach in a manner that accounted for part-time members of the Debtor's household. We recognize . . . that dividing individuals into fractional members of a household is less than ideal. At the same time, we recognize that the Debtor's situation is increasingly common in modern American life, and that the number of individuals with a financial relationship to a debtor may well vary depending on the day of the week and other circumstances. . . . Nor did the bankruptcy court err in exercising its discretion to accommodate this reality in the debtor's situation by representing the individuals as fractional full-time members of the household and then rounding to a whole number.

Because Congress' intent will most often be best implemented through a definition of "household" that is based on whether individuals operate as a single economic unit and are financially interdependent, we conclude the bankruptcy court did not err in applying this method to determine the Debtor's "household" size. Accordingly, we affirm the order of the bankruptcy court.

WILKINSON, Circuit Judge, dissenting.

While there is much in the majority's thoughtful opinion with which I agree, I cannot approve the bankruptcy court's decision to break a debtor's children into fractions. . . . That approach contravenes statutory text, allows judges to unilaterally update the Bankruptcy Code, and subjects debtors to needlessly intrusive and litigious proceedings. The bankruptcy court's approach embraces the startling conclusion that the meaning of the terms "individuals" and "dependents" in these provisions can encompass fractional human beings.

A textual rendering of statutes may seem inconvenient and even incorrect at times, but it has the long-term benefit of pushing Congress to precision and courts to observance of enacted law. The approach below may seem to reflect the economic realities of modern domestic life where children split time between parents, but it is hardly the only approach capable of doing so. Indeed, as the majority acknowledges, bankruptcy courts have a variety of other options available that may suit the circumstances of the case without so grievous an assault upon the statutory text.

The fact that Congress did not define "household," "individuals," or "dependents" in a definitions section does not entitle bankruptcy courts to take liberties with those terms. On the contrary, "[w]hen terms used in a statute are undefined, we give them their ordinary meaning," Hamilton v. Lanning, [560] U.S. [505], 130 S. Ct. 2464, 2471, 177 L. Ed. 2d 23 (2010) (internal quotation marks and citation omitted), and the common meaning of the words "individual" and "dependent" does not include partial people. As the Supreme Court recently observed, the word "'individual' ordinarily means '[a] human being, a person.'" Mohamad v. Palestinian Auth., [566] U.S. ___, 132 S. Ct. 1702, 1707, 182 L. Ed. 2d 720 (2012) (quoting 7 Oxford English Dictionary 880 (2d ed. 1989)).

My disagreement with the lower court's approach does not end with its lack of textual support. I also object to its decision to update the Bankruptcy Code to address the increase in split custody arrangements. From the start, the bankruptcy court made clear that its interpretation would be guided by the need to "address[ ] the growing number of debtors with blended families and joint custody obligations without ignoring the economic realities of a debtor's living situation." It consequently chose to employ fractional units not because of any textual analysis, but out of a belief that this approach was "the best method the court can employ to 'adapt to dynamic economic change including various types of family structures regardless of size, shape, or composition.'"

These may be laudable goals, but in our legal system, we leave the updating of statutes to Congress. . . . Thus, while it may be true that many modern "households look increasingly different from the outmoded images of the 'traditional' family," In re Robinson, 449 B.R. 473, 482 (Bankr. E.D. Va. 2011), it is not our job to amend the Bankruptcy Code to account for these social changes.

Finally, by allowing judges to treat dependents as fractions, today's decision will require courts to conduct more intrusive and more litigious proceedings. . . . Assigning dependents precise percentages will almost always demand a more searching examination of a debtor's circumstances than an approach that treats them as whole beings.

In this case, for instance, the bankruptcy court divided the number of days of the year Johnson's sons and stepsons lived with her by 365 and then rounded off the results to two decimal places. Calculations involving this degree of precision are unlikely to be simple affairs. For while the parties in this case stipulated to the number of days Johnson's sons and stepsons reside with her each year, that will not always be the case. One can easily envision estranged parents disputing the details of their custody arrangements in bankruptcy court, especially when those details were not settled in or vary from a state court order. To be sure, treating children in joint custody arrangements as whole individuals may lead to some inaccuracies redounding to the benefit of either debtors or creditors, depending on the particular case. But that problem "is the inevitable result of a standardized formula like the means test." Ransom v. FIA Card Servs., 131 S. Ct. 716, 729 (2011). The same inaccuracy would occur, for example, if a debtor bore all the costs of child support while remaining frugal, as the means test would allow him to claim standardized expenses greater than his actual costs. *Kops*, 2012 WL 438623, at *5 n.18. In the interest of administrability, "Congress chose to tolerate the occasional peculiarity that a brighter-line test produces." *Ransom*, 131 S. Ct. at 729. We have no authority to rework that formula today.

I recognize that bankruptcy courts have a degree of discretion in applying the Code, and I do not seek to needlessly constrain their flexibility. But that discretion is not unlimited. "Bankruptcy courts lack authority to . . . depart from [rules] in the Code . . . to implement their own views of wise policy," In re A.G. Fin. Serv. Ctr., Inc., 395 F.3d 410, 413-14 (7th Cir. 2005), and dividing a debtor's dependents into fractions falls outside those statutory bounds. Nor is such an approach even necessary to preserve flexibility in administering the Code. Eliminating the option of carving up children for purposes of the means test does not prevent bankruptcy courts from choosing from among multiple ways to calculate a debtor's household size or from taking the economic circumstances of a debtor into account. Judges can get along just fine in this area without embracing interpretations that co-opt the legislative function. With all respect for my friends who see this matter differently, I would reverse the judgment.

And the gross income bypass is the *easy* part of the means test! But we can be satisfied, at least, that after we have worked through the gross income test we have made the most important determination: is the debtor above or below median? Those who are below median—which is the great majority of all consumer filers according to the 2007 CBP data—may now bid a relieved farewell to § 707(b); they are free to file in chapter 7, and if they choose chapter 13, they can be done in three years of paying their "reasonable and necessary" expenses. The above-median debtors, however, must continue their descent into the depths of § 707(b)(2).

3.   *The Net Income Determination*

The policy behind exempting debtors under a certain gross income from the means test is clear: they presumably earn so little that their case is not likely to be abusive. But to find whether a debtor "needs" to file chapter 7 based on a statutory calculation ought not to rest on gross income alone. Few would contend that a debtor with $1 more than the state's applicable median income who uses the lion's share of that money to pay for a drug regimen of cancer treatment is similarly situated to a debtor with the identical income but whose expenses consist of weekly facials, restaurant dinners, and expensive wine collections. Some people have more expenses than others, but it's the nature of those expenses even more than their size that should matter for abuse. Accordingly, § 707(b) analyzes debtors' *net incomes*, after allowable expenses are deducted, to gauge eligibility for chapter 7 relief. Those expenses are found in § 707(b)(2)(A)(ii). Only a small number of chapter 7 filers—those who do not escape under the gross income bypass—must run this gauntlet. Its central characteristic is that it is mechanical, designed to ensure that softy judges will not permit can-pay debtors into chapter 7.

What is a debtor's true net income? That depends on what expenses we think a debtor *must* incur versus those we think a debtor *wants* to incur. Food yes, yachts no. Even food is open to debate: bread yes, caviar no. "Creditors should not be expected to pay for steak, when hamburger would do." In re Felske, 385 B.R. 649, 657 (Bankr. N.D. Ohio 2008). To be sure, this is what judges do all the time in chapter 13 plans when looking at challenges to debtors' proposed budgets of "reasonable and necessary" expenses. The pickle is that the means test was premised upon creditors' dissatisfaction with how the bankruptcy judges were doing in weeding out purportedly abusive chapter 7 filers under old § 707(b). To kill two birds with one stone by scrutinizing debtors' expenses *and* cabining bankruptcy judges, Congress designed a mechanical, statutory budget that is immune from interference by sentient jurists. While many federal programs deploy net income measures and while government data reveal what families actually expend on household expenses, Congress took a curious but revealing approach for what to put in this budget of permissible expenses. It turned to the IRS.

For years the IRS has negotiated with people who fail to pay their taxes. Instead of simply prosecuting and putting these people in jail or seizing their homes via tax liens, the IRS sometimes offers a repayment plan. If the tax delinquent pays a certain monthly amount toward past-due taxes, the IRS defers asset seizure and prosecution. Since even tax deadbeats need to eat, the IRS has to determine permissible expenses to calculate net income available for tax repayment. The Service developed guidelines to inform field offices engaged in these colorful negotiations, and these guidelines include various lists of expense allowances. The IRS calls some "National Standards," for those imposed uniformly across the country, and others "Local Standards," for those that vary with the debtor's residence. The Standards sometimes use sliding scales; for example, one person is allowed $386 a month for food, while a four-person household is allowed $958. (The IRS evidently believes that there are important economies of scale in meal preparation.) The Code's means test expressly defers to these IRS Guidelines for most expenses under § 707(b)(2). Whether Congress chose a budget for tax cheats for bankruptcy debtors to send an expressive message remains an open question.*

The U.S. Trustee Program's website reproduces the IRS expenses. https://www.justice.gov/ust/means-testing. Although derivative of the IRS, the site goes further, for example, by breaking out mortgage costs from home operating costs, because this is required for the official bankruptcy form for the means test, Form B 122A-2.

The means test does confer some discretion on judges, albeit modest and residual. For example, § 707(b)(2)(A)(ii)(I)'s final sentence allows judges to round up the National Standard's food and clothing allowance by up to 5% upon the debtor's showing such actual expenses are reasonable and necessary. And some deductions are allowed that are not even in the National Standards. See § 707(b)(2)(A)(ii)(II) (elder care), (IV) (private schools). All these deductions are included on Form B 122A-2.

As the court in *Zimmer* noted above, the means test is hyper-rigid and seems to allow the applicable IRS expenses without regard to whether the debtor *actually* incurs them. Suppose a frugal debtor regularly spends only $250 per month on food, an amount the debtor would disclose in their budget of reasonable and necessary expenses on Official Form 106J (the monthly expense form, which existed before the means test and continues to be required). The means test per the National Standards provides as of this writing for a fixed deduction of over $386 for a single individual. Is that a loophole for the skinny?

================ In re SCOTT ================

457 B.R. 740 (Bankr. S.D. Ill. 2011)

GRANDY, Bankruptcy Judge.

Can a debtor whose secured debt payment on a car is less than the I.R.S. Standard receive the benefit of the full deduction? . . .

---

*The sources for and strictures of the National Standards are not entirely clear. The IRS website explains that the numbers are based on the Bureau of Labor Statistics and Consumer Expenditure Survey, but that it has flexibility on how much the families can deduct in the various categories. As one court explains:

The IRM first sets "Expectations," and in paragraph 6 of section 5.15.1.1, states:

The standard amounts set forth in the national and local guidelines are designed to account for basic living expenses. *In some cases, based on a taxpayer's individual fact's [sic] and circumstances, it may be appropriate to deviate from the standard amount when failure to do so will cause the taxpayer economic hardship.* (emphasis added). . . .

In re Kimbro, 389 B.R. 518, 528 (B.A.P. 6th Cir. 2008), *rev'd and remanded on other grounds*, 409 Fed. App'x 930 (6th Cir. 2011). Ironically, the bankruptcy courts do not enjoy the same discretion—at least not within the structure of § 707(b)(2)(A)(ii), which directs a uniform bright-line use of the IRS "Guidelines." If this isn't bizarre enough, the IRS has tried to avoid institutional responsibility for the use of its Guidelines in bankruptcy by posting a disclaimer on its site that the Guidelines are *not* for bankruptcy use!

The local standard for a "transportation ownership/lease expense" is found at lines 28 (vehicle 1) and 29 (vehicle 2) [of Form B 122A]. The I.R.S. Standard for such an expense in this district is $496.00 per vehicle. The debtors maintain that they are entitled to claim the entire I.R.S. Standard for each of their two vehicles based on a plain language interpretation of § 707(b)(2)(A)(ii)(I). Specifically, the debtors focus on the portion of the statute that provides that "the debtor's monthly expenses *shall be* the debtor's applicable monthly expense amounts *specified under the National and Local Standards.* . . ." 11 U.S.C. § 707(b)(2)(A)(ii)(I) (emphasis added). As car payments are listed under the local standards on Form [B 122C] and not as an "Other Necessary Expense[]" (which, under the statute, is limited to a debtor's *actual* monthly expense), debtors argue that they are entitled to claim the specified standard amount, despite the fact that their actual monthly vehicle payment is less. Under the debtors' interpretation, there is no room for equivocation concerning expenses: they *shall be* the national and local standards on certain 'applicable' expenses. . . .

[T]his Court believes that allowing the debtors to take the full I.R.S. Standard likewise gives meaning and distinction to the different categories of expenses in § 707(b)(2)(A)(ii)(I). Once the debtors can show that they have a secured car ownership expense, they are entitled to claim the I.R.S. Standard because that is the "applicable" expense. Had Congress intended to limit the car ownership expense to actual cost, it could have said so. . . . Under the express language of § 707(b)(2)(A)(ii)(I), only "the categories specified as Other Necessary Expenses" are to use actual expenses. There is no provision in § 707(b)(2)(A)(ii)(I) for "reducing the specified amounts to the debtor's actual expenses. . . ." In re Barrett, 371 B.R. 855, 858 (Bankr. S.D. Ill. 2007). Congress did not tell us to use actual expenses for the categories subject to the national and local standards, although it clearly knew how, had it chosen to do so. . . .

The Trustee's other . . . argument is that the debtors' approach frustrates BAPCPA's "overall purpose of ensuring that the debtors repay creditors to the extent that they can." Adopting the Trustee's position in the cases at bar would provide a greater return to unsecured creditors, as in each case, the debtors' disposable income would be increased by more than $100.00 per month. He argues that the I.R.S. Standard is not "reasonably necessary" as the term is used in § 1325(b)(2) when the actual expense is less because that would not maximize the return to unsecured creditors.

Certainly, maximizing repayment to creditors was a primary goal in enacting BAPCPA. However, this Court believes that Congress intended to advance other policy objectives through BAPCPA as well. One such objective was the removal of judicial discretion in determining disposable income. As this Court previously stated in In re Nance:

> [F]ocusing on repayment to creditors as Congress' ultimate goal . . . ignore[s] other potential competing goals of Congress under BAPCPA, particularly the desire to eliminate judicial discretion. It is clear from the Chapter 7 means test, the adoption of standardized expense calculations for above-median debtors, and the calculation methods for determining "projected disposable income" that a major goal of Congress was to replace judicial discretion with specific statutory standards and formulas.

371 B.R. 358, 366 (Bankr. S.D. Ill. 2007). *See also* In re Rudler, 388 B.R. 433, 439 (1st Cir. BAP 2008) ("Congress' intent in adding the means test was to create a more objective standard for establishing a presumption of abuse and to reduce judicial discretion in the process."); Musselman v. eCast Settlement Corp., 394 B.R. 801, 812 (E.D.N.C. 2008) ("In enacting BAPCPA, Congress had more than one policy goal in mind. Beyond ensuring greater payouts by Chapter 13 debtors to their creditors, Congress, in its amendments to § 1325(b) also sought to impose objective standards on Chapter 13 determination, thereby removing a degree of judicial flexibility in bankruptcy proceedings."); In re Cutler, 2009 WL 2044378 (Bankr. S.D. Ind. 2009) ("repayment to creditors may have been one of the goals behind BAPCPA, but Congress' intent in creating the means test under § 707(b)(2) was to eliminate judicial discretion and replace it with a mathematical formula to determine abuse in Chapter 7 cases."). Permitting debtors to take the I.R.S. Standard furthers this goal by reducing judicial involvement. This Court recognizes that, by using a standardized approach to determining disposable income, anomalous results may occur. . . . The approach adopted by this Court still advances the goal of maximizing the return to creditors—it simply does so *within the framework prescribed by Congress and Form [B 122C]* [which] tells us to measure the maximum return by using the applicable I.R.S. Standard—not actual.

Adopting the Trustee's approach would essentially bring this Court back to the pre-BAPCPA practice of evaluating disposable income based on the debtors' Schedules I and J, a practice that was eliminated by Congress with the enactment of BAPCPA and creation of Form [B 122C].

One way to think of *Scott*'s holding is that if the debtor's frugality allows her to incur lower food expenses than the IRS allows tax delinquents, that frugality should inure to her benefit and not perversely be used as evidence of abuse in declaring bankruptcy. (Was BAPCPA really worried about the frugal?) Certainly a contrary holding would create gluttonous incentives. The corollary is that even if a debtor regularly and honestly spends $400 each month on food, and even if a bankruptcy judge were to consider such an amount "reasonable and necessary," the means test doesn't care. Congress says buy in bulk, skip the organic produce, or just slim down.

This harshness of the means test's ambivalence toward a debtor's actual expenses—in contrast to chapter 13's treatment of below-median debtors (for whom reasonable necessity suffices to permit an expense)—is softened somewhat by provisions such as § 707(b)(2)(A)(ii)(V), which augments the IRS's Local Standards for housing and utility expenses by allowing deductions for the debtor's *actual* documented reasonable heating costs, even if higher than the guidelines. *But cf.* In re Trimarchi, 421 B.R. 914, 923 (Bankr. N.D. Ill. 2010) ("The Court finds a swimming pool is not a basic need required by the average American family or this family. . . . Here, the Debtor does not need [$250 monthly] to heat the pool.").

But just how far are we willing to take the mechanical nature of a means test that flies in the face of reality for the sake of standardization?

Perhaps the limiting case is zero, at least for the Supreme Court. In Ransom v. FIA Card Services, N.A., 562 U.S. 61 (2011), the Court held that an above-median-income debtor forced to use the means test budget in chapter 13 could not take the IRS standard deduction for motor vehicle ownership expenses (the IRS breaks out the *ownership* expenses, which is for lease or loan payments, from *operating* expenses, which is for gas, maintenance, etc.) when the debtor owned the car free and clear and hence had neither loan nor lease expenses. Presumably indifferent to the economic ravages of depreciation, the 8–1 majority decided that whatever the statutory rigidity of the means test, it was too much to let the debtor get away with this ownership expense deduction, even though it is included in the means test. As a textual hook (some might say fig leaf), the Court pointed to the means test's instruction to take the *applicable* deductions under the IRS test, and if someone has no expenses whatsoever of a given category, the deduction would not be "applicable," namely, "appropriate, relevant, suitable, or fit." Id. at 69-70. You will sadly get no extra points on your exam for guessing who the lone dissenting Justice was, but we will tell you he had some thoughts to share about whether the Court should defer to Congress's decision to favor bright-line standardization on statutes it enacts, even if that sometimes means giving a seeming boondoggle to a debtor.

You may have noticed that § 707(b)(2)(A)(ii)(I) specifically prohibits monthly payments on debts to be included in the means test budget; "credit card bills" is not a permissible monthly expense. This makes some sense because part of the test is to see how much money is left over to pay creditors, and it would be oddly recursive accounting to include payments to those creditors in calculating that surplus. But apparently not that odd! When it adopted the means test, Congress seemed concerned that the application of the strict IRS guidelines for transportation might require many debtors to give up their cars—to the great dissatisfaction of the car lenders. (Without the support of the car lenders, the proposed amendments would likely have never made it into law. See William C. Whitford, A History of the Automobile Lender Provisions of BAPCPA, 2007 U. Ill. L. Rev. 143.)

Congress responded by making secured debt an additional permitted deduction category under the means test, resulting in the odd insistence of no deductions for debts in one breath under § 707(b)(2)(A)(ii)(I) but the explicit allowance of their deduction for secured debts in the next under § 707(b)(2)(A)(iii). Note the omission of the "reasonable and necessary" qualifier so prevalent in the rest of the means test when it comes to the debtor's car. Well lobbied, Detroit. Home mortgage lenders also jumped aboard this gravy train (gravy car?). See id. The kicker is that § 707(b)(2) (A)(iii) allows deductions for payments "scheduled as contractually due," which suggests the whole secured debt contractual payments are allowed, not just the amount necessary to pay off the allowed secured claim.

4.   The Actual Test: "Presumption" of Abuse

Now the actual means test: once the debtor's net income under § 707(b)(2)(A)(ii) has been calculated, the debtor compares it to the formula in § 707(b)(2)(A)(i). The means test is flunked and abuse is presumed if the debtor's net income is greater than a certain amount, which, maddeningly, is contingent upon the debtor's total unsecured nonpriority debt.

Here is the test for whether the debtor passes: First, take the debtor's monthly net income and multiply it by sixty months (five years), which we call the debtor's "five-year payback" (because it assumes all net income goes toward paying unsecured creditors for the maximum length of a chapter 13 plan). Abuse is presumed if the five-year payback equals or exceeds the *lower* of two figures: (1) $13,650; *or* (2) 25% of the debtor's total unsecured nonpriority debt (down to a floor of $8,175).

Let's unpack what's going on. It helps to start at the end and calculate (2) from above: 25% of the total unsecured debt. Congress thinks if your five-year payback is more than this number—a quarter of what you owe your unsecured creditors—it's abusive for you to be in chapter 7 instead of chapter 13 and tough it out. Regarding number (1), it also thinks you're abusing the system if your five-year payback is $13,650, period. The thinking there seems to be that's just a lot of money to pay in the abstract, even if it's only a fraction of what you owe your creditors.

But don't forget the floor of $8,175 to (2), from above. Think of that floor as a safety valve. Congress seems to think that if that's really all you can scrounge up to pay over five years after you've taken all the means test deductions—a paltry $1,635 per year—you're just not doing that well and so can't be abusing the system by filing for chapter 7 (even if that small amount is more than 25% of your total unsecured debt). Now when you look at § 707(b)(2)(A)(i) you will see how this all falls into place. (You're welcome.)

Another way to understand this tangle is to think of means test debtors as falling into three categories: the Happy—debtors whose monthly net income is less than $136 (five-year payback of only $8,175)—who all pass the test automatically; the Sad—debtors whose monthly net income is more than $227 (five-year payback of $13,650)—who all fail the screen automatically; and the Uncertain Middle—debtors falling between these two poles—who pass *only if* their five-year payback is less than 25% of unsecured, nonpriority debt. For example, if a debtor owed $32,000 unsecured and had means-test monthly net income of $141.67 (five-year payback of $8,500), the presumption of abuse would arise. This is because the five-year payback of $8,500, even though well under $13,650, is $500 greater than $8,000 (i.e., 25% of the total unsecured debt of $32,000) and is $325 greater than the floor of $8,174. Off to chapter 13 for this abuser—unless she can "rebut" the presumption.

Speaking of which, just how *does* one rebut the presumption? If the net income test shows merely a *presumption* of abuse, then perhaps it can be rebutted by introducing evidence showing a non-abusive, legitimate reason to file for bankruptcy, such as perhaps years of struggling with debts and the incursion of those liabilities through non-extravagant means? Nope. Although nominally captioned a "rebuttal" of the means test, § 707(b)(2)(B)(i) clarifies the *only* way to rebut it is to show "special circumstances, such as a serious medical condition or a call or order to active duty in the Armed Forces . . . that justify additional expenses or adjustments of current monthly income."

The "rebuttal" thus works *only* if the debtor can prove documentable changes in income or expenses that allow the debtor to pass the means test. See § 707(b)(2)(B)(iv). In other words, it's just an additional category of discretionary inputs into the means test; it is not a way of escaping the eligibility bar that is the output of the formula. Evidence of virtuous work ethic and sterling character is irrelevant to the presumption of abuse. As one of us puts it:

> The operation of the means test enables the debtors to challenge the metric, but not the merits, of their surplus income. Professors at law schools . . . that strip faculty of jurisdiction to change grades after submission to the registrar but provide an exception for mistabulated grades should find this framework familiar. . . . To say that it creates a "rebuttable presumption" that the submitted grade is the final grade when the only way of rebutting the presumption is to show that the grade was added up incorrectly is doublespeak of the highest order. It is not a *presumption*, let alone a rebuttable one, that submitted grades are final. It is a *rule* that submitted grades are final, absent calculation error.

John A.E. Pottow, The Totality of the Circumstances of the Debtor's Financial Situation in a Post-Means Test World, 71 Mo. L. Rev. 1053, 1059-60. Perhaps pushing back against this straightjacket, courts have been flexible in finding "special circumstances," such as extra housing expenses for special needs children, high commuting costs, student loan payments, and repaying a 401(k) loan. Compare In re Cribbs, 387 B.R. 324 (Bankr. S.D. Ga. 2008) (special circumstances for loan taken out to repay creditors in attempt to avoid bankruptcy), with In re Egebjerg, 574 F.3d 1045 (9th Cir. 2009) (pension loans are not special circumstances). Compare also In re Brown, 500 B.R. 255 (Bankr. S.D. Ga. 2013) (private school tuition for child diagnosed with ADHD, speech, and auditory difficulties constituted special circumstances), with In re Maura, 491 B.R. 493 (Bankr. E.D. Mich. 2013) (no special circumstances when debtors failed to demonstrate lack of reasonable alternatives to Catholic school).

Whew! What a lot of work to shake money out of the pockets of the people who want to file bankruptcy. With more than a million consumer filings annually, attorneys and courts have routinized and computerized much of the undertaking. Nearly all attorneys use software that is programmed with the IRS expenses and spits out a red or green light on the means test (it works much like tax preparation software). But with substantial variations around the country due both to the many open legal issues arising under the law and to the factual variation of each debtor's individual expenses, challenges still abound.

This complexity burden is not borne solely by the debtor; the U.S. Trustee's office is required to look at every case filed by an individual debtor to see if the presumption of abuse is triggered and to file a statement reporting its finding that is sent to every creditor. § 704(b)(1). If the debtor is above median income, the office either files a motion to dismiss or convert the case if presumptive abuse is present or a statement explaining why it has not done so. § 704(b)(2). These "declination" statements and the required review are not cheap. They subsume a substantial amount of resources of the U.S. Trustee Program.

C.   CHAPTER 13 IN A MEANS TEST WORLD

Although the means test's location in § 707(b) suggests its primary function is as the eligibility screen to chapter 7, do not forget its second major role in the Code: the statutory budget for above-median-income debtors in chapter 13. § 1325(b)(3). Congress has determined that the surplus amount that remains from such above-median debtors' incomes after the means test expenses are deducted must be paid each month to their repayment plans, period.

Oddly, the Code dictates this compulsory means test budget is for *all* above-median chapter 13 filers, regardless of whether they passed or flunked the means test for chapter 7. In other words, the statutory budget applies to even those above-median debtors who chose to file chapter 13 voluntarily after having passed the means test and been eligible for chapter 7. It is hard to see why a Congress that wanted to see fewer chapter 7 cases and more chapter 13 cases would impose tougher rules on above-median-income chapter 13 volunteers, creating a marginal incentive on them to choose chapter 7, but that's what the Code says. § 1325(b)(4)(A)(ii). Does this seemingly clear text create "absurd" results?

Subject perhaps to this last point, the means test thus does double service to implement the intent of Congress in BAPCPA. First of all, it is used as a screen to force some people into chapter 13, and it is then secondarily used as a forced budget on those conscripts to dictate what will be allowed as their permissible expenses during their five-year stay. In fact, given the data already discussed that the overwhelmingly majority of chapter 7 debtors have income under the applicable median (the gross income bypass that renders the means test irrelevant), the means test's role as a chapter 7 eligibility bar is much less relevant in actual case outcomes than its role as the required chapter 13 budget for above-median-income debtors (a group that makes up more than one-third of chapter 13 filers). To see how it all fits together, the following diagram may be of some help.

Figure 1. Consumer Bankruptcy: Chapter 7, Traditional Chapter 13 or the New Chapter 13?

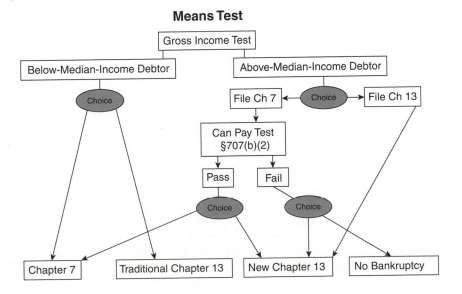

We close on a note about reality. Above-median-income debtors must live on the statutory budget for five full years (their applicable commitment period), regardless of what their current monthly expenses actually are. For some, that may require some belt-tightening or relocating to different housing. For others, it may simply mean they can't make it through chapter 13, and they will convert into chapter 7 if means-test eligible. For families who can't make it on the budget in chapter 13 and who are statutorily barred from chapter 7, that may mean no relief from creditors under the federal Bankruptcy Code.

Indeed, the bizarreness of using a six-month retrospective figure for "current" monthly income and using fixed categories unrelated to actual expenses under the IRS National Guidelines in dictating a debtor's five-year budget likely explains the impulse of the Supreme Court cases, like *Lanning* and *Ransom*, to fudge BAPCPA's strict text. Both of those, it is no coincidence, were chapter 13 cases, in which the divergence of statutory budget from reality proved too much for the Court. As the *Flores* court notes, these means-test precedents may or may not apply when that mechanical and discretion-stripping test is used as the screen in chapter 7. In the next assignment, we turn to the other parts of the Code that courts and litigants use to reinsert flexibility and judgment into the system and the strategic choices that debtors face as a result.

Problem Set 12

12.1. On June 30, 2020, Marissa Allegretti comes into your office in Detroit to see you about filing for bankruptcy. She explains that when the accounting firm she worked for closed, she scraped by on $650 a month unemployment for nearly six months, running up a pile of bills. Four months ago, she found a good job. Her base pay is $4,100 a month, but she has worked every weekend and as many late nights as she could since she joined the company, bringing in overtime that adds another $2,000 each month. She is putting everything she can into catching up on her mortgage payments, and she is making good progress. Even so, she says that she is struggling with her credit cards, with those debts multiplying at 29.99% interest.

You ask about her personal circumstances, and Marissa explains that she and her ex-husband, Tommy, share custody of their son Jamal. At the divorce five years ago, Marissa was granted $1,000 a month in child support. Her ex never paid, but he buys clothes for the boy and he has been paying $6,000 each semester for tuition at the local Catholic school, so Marissa hasn't pushed the point.

Is Marissa eligible for chapter 7? See §§ 101(10A), 707(b)(6), (b)(7). What advice do you give her at this point? Marissa can barely scrape together your standard $900 fee; how aggressive can she afford for you to be?

12.2. Eduardo and Sydney came to see you today, May 1, 2020, about filing for bankruptcy. They live near your office in Montgomery County, a suburb of Philadelphia. Both are in their mid-30s. Over the past six months, Eduardo's earnings averaged $6,600 a month as an auto mechanic, and Sydney's job as a fourth-grade teacher at the nearby primary school averaged $5,400 per month (gross). They have two children, a kindergartener and an

18-month-old baby. The younger child was born with a serious heart problem. He has had three major surgeries and now lives on a regimen of drugs and monitoring. Even though they have health insurance, the expenses for the baby have left them about $100,000 in debt. Some of it is medical co-pays and services, supplies, and drugs that weren't covered, and some was credit card debt they ran up when Sydney took a seven-month leave from her job last year during the surgeries and recuperations and Eduardo too missed a lot of time from work. By skipping other payments and falling behind on everything else, Eduardo and Sydney have been paying about $600 a month on these bills, but that doesn't even cover the interest on the credit cards. Every month, the pile of bills gets higher.

Sydney and Eduardo live in a small three-bedroom house on a busy street. Their monthly payments are high because they had no money for a down payment, so they financed 100% of the purchase price. With their already-damaged credit, that gave them a high interest rate and a high payment. But they are proud of the fact that they have remained current on their mortgage.

You ask Eduardo and Sydney to work with your paralegal to come up with a list of their monthly expenses. They are sure about some parts, like income and taxes, because those are on their paystubs, but they are less sure about expenses. Here's what they identify:

Expenses	Amount
Home mortgage (principal, interest, taxes, & insurance)	$2,450
Utilities (water, gas, sewage, landline phone)	$190
Internet	$35
Satellite television	$75
Cell phone (basic service phones for Sydney and Eduardo)	$30
Honda Odyssey minivan (principal, interest, required insurance)	$650
Gas and maintenance for minivan	$190
Food	$1,000
Cleaning supplies	$20
Personal care (haircuts, etc.)	$25
Clothing	$500
Laundry and dry cleaning	$10
Miscellaneous (newspapers, dog food, etc.)	$50
Lunch money for Sydney, Eduardo, kindergartener	$100
Daycare for baby, after school care for kindergartener	$1,200
Drugs, other health care supplies for baby	$250
Health insurance	$940
Social Security and income taxes	$3,394
Life insurance, Sydney and Eduardo	$200
TOTAL	$11,309

Are Eduardo and Sydney eligible for chapter 7? Do you have any additional questions or advice for them? If they rented the house next-door for the same monthly payment, would it make a difference? See § 707(b)(2). Use Form B 122A-2 to complete the problem, but skip line 36.

12.3. You have worked through the means test numbers for Michael Negron, a competitive skateboarder who seems to have run up $30,000 in general unsecured debt after he broke his leg last year. He rents a modest apartment and he drives an old clunker. His income over the past six months puts him above the median for a one-earner family in his state, and after allowable expenses, Michael seems to have available about $150 a month. His income has been very erratic as he tries to make a comeback, and he's not even sure if the leg is OK or will ever be. He is very reluctant to commit to a chapter 13 plan. Do you have any advice to make him eligible for chapter 7? See §§ 707(b)(2)(B)(iv), 707(b)(2)(A)(iii), 707(b)(1), 101(12A), 526(a)(4).

12.4. Emily Iversen and Katharine Roller met in law school and stayed together as a couple for seven years. Their finances were kind of a mess, partially commingled, partially separate. They are discussing how to divide their property as they go their separate ways. Both cars (the Subaru and the Jeep Wrangler) are in Katharine's name; Emily has agreed she will take over the car payments of the Subaru she regularly drives but will leave title in Katharine's name to save money on the state transfer and registration fees. That's fine with Katharine, especially since they both know the Subaru is worth less than the loan on the car. The discussions are all quite amicable.

Katharine is getting ready to file chapter 13 because of credit card debts. Katharine would pass the means test despite having above-median income, but chapter 7 is out because of some precious and sentimental non-exempt jewelry she wants to keep. Recognizing she is above-median, she is OK with doing a five-year plan and with making the payments the means test requires as her budget. As Katharine waves goodbye to Emily, do you see her chapter 13 as easy-peasy or will the car situation create grief? See §§ 1325(b)(3), 707(b)(2)(A)(iii), 1329.

12.5. Ken Lyarre was a phenomenally successful CEO, twice featured on the cover of *Business Week*. The first time was when his privately owned string of diet centers took the health and fitness market by storm, and the second when he lost a class-action lawsuit against him for violations of state consumer protection laws and the jury returned a verdict of a nice, round $1 billion. Ken's lawyers are planning an appeal, but they can't seem to make eye contact with him when they discuss his chances.

Ken thinks he has a better strategy: chapter 7 liquidation. He has about $1 million in assets lying around loose; the rest of his portfolio is in various spendthrift and offshore trusts, and he says he is glad to give that $1 million to deal with the verdict. His future income, drawn from the trusts, will be about $2 million annually. Is Ken eligible for chapter 7? See § 707(a), (b)(1), (b)(2). *Cf.* § 523(a)(2)(A), (4).

CHAPTER CHOICE

Nothing is more central to a debtor's fate than choice of the chapter under which to file a petition. That choice determines what relief the debtor can seek in bankruptcy. It also greatly affects the creditors' claims and what, if anything, the creditors can do to protect themselves. The means test of the prior assignment is a complex statutory maze, but it is only one of the puzzles that debtors and their attorneys must solve in making that all-important chapter choice.

Section 109(e) and the means test are statutory bars to eligibility to chapter 13 and chapter 7 respectively that operate on the "front end," blocking debtors from proceeding. Yet there are also "back end" statutory constraints on relief that a debtor must consider in choosing chapters. These provisions operate much more discretionarily and hence present a trickier moving target for the attorney to gauge up front. Compounding this challenge are extra-legal concerns that bear on chapter choice, such as attorneys' fees, client counseling practices, and even local legal culture. In this assignment we turn first to these back-end statutory restrictions and then consider the strategic choices and risk-benefit analyses of chapter choice.

A.   STATUTORY CONSIDERATIONS

We begin with a look at the explicit statutory constraints on chapter choice.

1.   Discretionary Dismissal from Chapter 7: Bad Faith and Totality of the Circumstances

Even if the putative chapter 7 filer survives the means test screen, there is always the risk of discretionary dismissal under § 707(b)(3). This resid-ual standard covers all consumer debt filers, not just the above-medians. Subparagraph (A) seems straightforward, if undefined; "bad faith" is never welcome from those seeking a federal discharge of their debts. But what about (B)? This "totality of the circumstances" language seems to invite broad consideration of equitable factors, perhaps similar to the ones used to gauge "substantial abuse" in the pre-means test world. (Think back to the Shaws from last assignment and their new bedroom suite.)

This seemingly flexible, multi-prong "totality" standard must apply, however, in a straightjacketed, post-means test world. So are the old cases under former § 707(b) still good law on what constitutes "abuse" of chapter 7, or does the addition of the means test now eliminate some of the issues that courts previously got to police with the totality test? Suppose a judge thinks the means test is just too darned generous (particularly when the debtor's actual expenditures are below the IRS limits) and faces a debtor with a monthly net income of only $100, who thus passes the means test formula. Can the judge boot that debtor out of chapter 7 because $100, in that judge's mind, is a lot of money that could go toward repaying creditors and it is "abusive" for the debtor not to be making payments in chapter 13? After all, it is harder to imagine a broader swath of discretion than the "totality of the circumstances." Is such a dismissal a savvy use of statutorily conferred discretion or a judicial arrogation of power?

In re DEUTSCHER

419 B.R. 42 (Bankr. N.D. Ill. 2009)

BARBOSA, Bankruptcy Judge.

The Debtors filed a voluntary petition for relief under Chapter 7 of the Bankruptcy Code with the Court on November 6, 2008. According to the Debtors' schedules, they have $336,752 in secured debt, $2,220 in unsecured priority debt, and $61,817 in unsecured nonpriority debt. The Debtors have admitted that their obligations are primarily consumer debts. Over half of their secured debt, or $177,782, is from a loan used to purchase a 42-foot Silverton yacht, purchased by the Debtors in September 2007. Another $11,000 is from the purchase in August 2008 of a 2006 15-foot Sea Doo Sportsliner boat, and $30,000 is from the purchase of a 2008 MKZ Lincoln SUV in June 2008. . . . The Debtors do not need the boats for work. . . . Although the Debtors' income is above the median for an Illinois household of two, there is no presumption of abuse under 11 U.S.C. §§ 707(a) and 707(b)(2) (the "means test"), largely because of the large secured debt payments.

As the Seventh Circuit Court of Appeals has stated, failing the means test simply means that the debtor's petition is not presumed abusive. . . . [T]he UST can still request dismissal . . . under section 707(b)(3), either for bad faith or based on the totality of circumstances (which can take into consideration a debtor's actual income and expenses). Ross-Tousey v. Neary (In re Ross-Tousey), 549 F.3d 1148, 1161-62 (7th Cir. 2008). Under the totality of the circumstances test, "a debtor's ability to pay may be the most relevant factor, but the Court must also consider: (1) whether the bankruptcy petition was filed because of sudden illness, calamity, disability or unemployment; (2) whether the debtor incurred cash advances and made consumer purchases far in excess of his ability to pay; (3) whether the debtor's proposed family budget is excessive or unreasonable; and (4) whether the debtor's schedules and statement of current income and expenses reasonably and accurately reflect the true financial condition." In re Cutler, 2009 WL 2044378, at *3 (Bankr. S.D. Ind. July 9, 2009) (citing In re Green, 934 F.2d 568, 572 (4th Cir. 1991)).

The focus of the means test under Section 707(b)(2) is on whether debtors have sufficient income to repay a substantial portion of their debt, see, e.g., Eugene R. Wedoff, *Judicial Discretion to Find Abuse Under Section 707(b)(3)*, 71 Mo. L. Rev. 1035, 1036 (2006). Because this is also a factor under the totality of circumstances test, courts have struggled to define the intersection between Sections 707(b)(2) and (3). Some courts have expressed concern that a court might simply use Section 707(b)(3) to substitute its own test for the means test. See, e.g., In re Nockerts, 357 B.R. 497, 506 (Bankr. E.D. Wis. 2006) ("To apply the means test, dislike the result, and then examine the debtor's ability to fund a chapter 13 plan under § 707(b)(3), renders the means test 'surplusage.'"). When addressing ability to pay under section 707(b)(3), a court must therefore be attentive to the policy choices made by Congress in drafting the means test, including the fact that it gave preferred treatment to secured creditors by allowing scheduled payments of secured debt to be listed as deductions without limitation. See, e.g., In re Le Roy, 2009 WL 357923, at *3 (Bankr. E.D. Wis. Feb. 12, 2009) ("[T]he U.S. Trustee sought to reclassify the debtors' secured debt payments as income available to pay creditors. The court determined that the Code expressly permits the deduction of secured debt payments under the Means Test, thereby providing an advantage to secured creditors over unsecured creditors. To ignore the Code's mandate and disallow secured debt expenses allowed by the Means Test would violate Congressional policy.")

. . . [W]hile a desire to reaffirm secured debt is not in itself abuse, a court can find abuse under the totality of circumstances when there is "evidence that the Debtor has manipulated the means test, purchased luxuries on credit on the eve of bankruptcy, altered his expenses in his Schedules, accrued significant debt prior to the petition, or that his budget is excessive or unreasonable." *Le Roy*, 2009 WL 357923, at *4.

[T]he vehicles can be characterized as luxury items, [and] the purchases seem to demonstrate a pattern of living beyond the Debtors' means. This lifestyle also seems to have been one of the main factors contributing to their financial difficulties. The Debtors have admitted that their financial situation was not caused by a "sudden illness, calamity or disability." Although much of the cause might have been the economic downturn and its impact on Mr. Deutscher's painting business, these large purchases, which took place during a period Mr. Deutscher claims to have been unemployed, clearly exacerbated the situation. Instead of learning from their mistakes, the Debtors appear to want to continue this lifestyle even after seeking a bankruptcy discharge by reaffirming their debt on these luxury items rather than follow the expectation that "when seeking bankruptcy relief, debtors may be expected to do some belt tightening, including, where necessary, foregoing the reaffirmation of those secured debts which are not reasonably necessary for the maintenance and support of the debtor and his family." In re Harter, 397 B.R. 860, 864 (Bankr. N.D. Ohio 2008). [Motion to Dismiss granted.]

========================

Is any § 707(b)(3) decision involving a yacht likely to end well for the debtor? *But cf.* Matter of Booker, 753 F. App'x 316 (5th Cir. 2019) (holding bankruptcy court clearly erred in finding debtors' chapter 13 plan not proposed in good faith simply because debtors proposed retaining fishing boat). Yet we remain skeptical about the propriety of imposing a "judicially administered Alternative Minimum Means Test." John A.E. Pottow, The Totality of the Circumstances of the Debtor's Financial Situation in a Post-Means Test World, 71 Mo. L. Rev. 1053, 1061 (2006).

A bitter critic might say that the purpose of BAPCPA was to restrict bankruptcy relief and so any discretion exercised to dismiss one more debtor's petition is not judicial impertinence but welcome support of Congress. But the policy analysis is more complex. Consider the role of secured creditors: they don't find it remotely abusive to have debtors budget to pay secured debts in chapter 7, as Congress chose to allow with the means test; in fact, they cheer clearing the brush of unsecured debt that impedes a debtor's ability to afford secured debt payments. Secured creditors would thus claim that the "implicit policy" of the Code is to protect secured credit and judges who undermine the means test's protections are rogues. Some "totality" cases have taken just that view; the debtors who filed In re Jensen, 407 B.R. 378 (Bankr. C.D. Cal. 2009), were paying their secured creditors around $5,600 a month from about $8,600 in monthly income, including a boat payment of $760 a month. Refusing to dismiss for abuse, the court summarized the pro-secured-debt position as follows:

> Courts and commentators have struggled to define the interaction between §§ 707(b)(2) and (b)(3). . . . This Court certainly shares the discomfort other courts have felt at the prospect of permitting debtors to retain luxury goods in defiance of their unsecured creditors. However, the Bankruptcy Code seeks to further policies other than making unsecured creditors whole, especially in situations where unsecured creditors can be made whole only at the expense of secured creditors. Chief among these policies is advancing the availability of secured credit. See, e.g., In re Proalert, LLC, 314 B.R. 436, 441 (9th Cir. BAP 2004) ("Embodied in the Bankruptcy Code is a policy decision to protect secured credit practices."). . . . Therefore, refusing to permit debtors to retain secured-debt property does more than punish the debtors—it also reallocates the balance of risk between secured and unsecured creditors. As one commentator has observed, in the zero-sum battle between secured and unsecured creditors, "the secured creditor's advantage is the unsecured creditor's disadvantage." Homer Kripke, Law and Economics: Measuring the Economic Efficiency of Commercial Law in a Vacuum of Fact, 133 U. Pa. L. Rev. 929, 949 (1985).

Jensen, 407 B.R. at 383-88.

Another perspective on BAPCPA—advanced forcefully by the consumer debtor bar—is that the legislative intent of the means test was to promote uniformity and guidance to the parties. To advance these objectives, the means test should be read to limit the ability of a court or creditor to revisit any expense deemed acceptable under the means test deductions. Revisiting a debtor's food budget under the totality standard, for example, judicially undermines that desired clarity.

Judges, scholars, and lawyers all continue to struggle with identifying the boundaries of § 707(b)(3). Discretionary dismissal remains on the books, yet almost certainly has a different function—if not statutory meaning—after the means test (can the plain meaning of a statute be altered by *ex post* insertion of a preceding non-referential paragraph?). Perhaps the only generalizable trend is that case outcomes seem to track "conventional sensibilities." Compare, e.g., In re Rivers, 466 B.R. 558 (Bankr. M.D. Fla. 2012) (no abuse by debtor with endometriosis surgery and two kids with severe food allergies), with, e.g., In re Roppo, 442 B.R. 888, 895 (Bankr. N.D. Ill. 2010) (finding abuse and remarking on the debtor's luxurious lifestyle: "It is baffling why the Debtor's wife acquired a Mercedes automobile the year following her [own] Chapter 7 case"). Some courts try hard to establish guidelines.

In re DURCZYNSKI

405 B.R. 880 (Bankr. N.D. Ohio 2009)

SPEER, Bankruptcy Judge.

As previously noted by the Court, bankruptcy is "meant to provide a debtor a fresh start, but not a head start. Thus, when seeking bankruptcy relief, debtors may be expected to do some belt tightening, including, where necessary, foregoing the reaffirmation of those secured debts which are not reasonably necessary for the maintenance and support of the debtor and his family." In re Wadsworth, 383 B.R. 330 (Bankr. N.D. Ohio 2007) (internal citations omitted). In this matter, the Debtors devote a significant amount of their income to maintain their home. To service the necessary obligations attendant with their home, the Debtors must allocate $2,187.21 from their monthly budget. This figure constitutes approximately 40% percent of the Debtors' net monthly income of $5,585.35. It is also 2½ times the amount that is allowed under the "means test" formulation of § 707(b)(2). At the time the Debtors filed their bankruptcy petition, the allowable monthly mortgage expense for a family of five when applying the "means test" of § 707(b)(2) was $888.00. While the "means test" of § 707(b)(2) is not strictly applicable in this case, its standards do serve to show that a significant portion of the expenses associated with the Debtors' residence are not necessary for their basic living needs, but instead constitute a "lifestyle" choice.

The purchase of a home is a highly personal choice and is one which requires debtors to assess not only the present needs of their family, but also their long-term needs. In re Kitson, 65 B.R. 615, 620-21 (Bankr. E.D.N.C. 1986). Debtors may, therefore, be afforded some latitude in their choice of a home which as opposed to a purely financial decision—for example, whether to purchase cable television—involves a moral and value based judgment on the part of the debtor. Notwithstanding, assessing a debtor's ability to pay for purposes of § 707(b)(3) still requires that a court scrutinize a debtor's expenses. It, thus, cannot be avoided that an "ability to pay" inquiry under § 707(b)(3) may encroach on the highly personal choices that all individuals make about how to prioritize their expenses and, on a more basic level, how to live their lives. In re Fauntleroy, 311 B.R. 730, 736 (Bankr. E.D.N.C. 2004).

Within this context, it is fair to state that the more an expense involves a moral and value based judgment on the part of the debtor, the more deference that will be accorded to the debtor's decision. Conversely, the more a decision is purely financial in character, the more scrutiny that will be accorded to that decision. For example, the decision to have a child, while undoubtedly having a financial component, is largely a moral decision, and thus it would be highly unusual for such a decision to have a negative impact on a debtor in a § 707(b)(3) analysis. In fact, deference to the debtor's decision to have a child may be constitutionally required. In re Edwards, 50 B.R. 933, 940 n.9 (Bankr. S.D.N.Y. 1985). On the other hand, a debtor's decision involving cable television, being largely a financial-based decision, would not be accorded much deference.

In this matter, the Court can only conclude that the Debtors' intention to retain their residence arises more from "want" as opposed to any "need." For example, no evidence was provided that the education or health of the Debtors' children would be impacted if they did not stay in their current residence. . . .

To be sure, the Debtors' have an emotional attachment to their home. However, while this is understandable, it does not justify overlooking the overall state of the Debtors' financial situation. In re DeRosear, 265 B.R. 196, 218 (Bankr. S.D. Iowa 2001). . . . Second, Mrs. Durczynski has not made a concerted effort to maximize her income, with the evidence showing that she has the ability to increase her income significantly, perhaps by 20% to 30%, if she were to work full-time. . . .

==

Do you agree that the mother of three children's decision to work part-time was not a moral or value-based judgment to which the judge should have accorded greater latitude under his own standard? If many would not agree, does that create some problems with this distinction? Despite the repeated rhetoric about "can-pay" debtors, is the means test really a normative identification of "should-pay" debtors? For example, look at § 707(b)(2)(D). Is that animated by a veteran's financial inability to pay?

Finally, if courts will be called upon regularly to scrutinize a debtor's budget with motions to dismiss under § 707(b)(3), how much has BAPCPA succeeded in streamlining scrutiny of abuse and getting judges out of the picture? Complexity and time consumption seem dubious triumphs.

2.   Discretionary Dismissal in Chapter 13: Good Faith

A longstanding requirement for chapter 13 confirmation is that a plan be "proposed in good faith and not by any means forbidden in law."

§ 1325(a)(3). Lest anyone have missed Congress's desire to imbue the chapter 13 system with this concept, BAPCPA added a second requirement requiring good faith in filing the petition (not just the plan). § 1325(a)(7). As innocuous as "good faith" may sound, it has defied consistent and simple application. The most straightforward invocation occurs when a debtor has engaged in shady behavior or been less than forthcoming in giving financial information; those cases are fun reading but largely raise issues of fact—either the debtor did or did not do the shady behavior.

The more contested use of the good faith requirement is to challenge a creative debtor's interpretation of the other statutory requirements for chapter 13 confirmation, and this process has become more complicated post-BAPCPA. Recall that Congress was trying to encourage the use of chapter 13, and so restrictions on chapter 13 filings present some tension with the ostensible purpose of the new regime. Recall too BAPCPA was designed to remove discretion, and so re-injecting that discretion through the good faith requirement raises the same concerns described above with § 707(b)(3). Unsurprisingly, there is some overlap between the § 707(b)(3)(B) "totality of the circumstances" standard and the chapter 13 "good faith" standard, as the next case shows. But like many other areas of the Code (and beyond), a charge of lack of good faith is often the last grasp of a disgruntled litigant, including trustees who dislike the attorney-friendliness of chapter 13.

In re CRAGER

691 F.3d 671 (5th Cir. 2012)

HIGGINBOTHAM, Circuit Judge.

The debtor, Patricia Ann Crager, is unemployed, and her main source of income is $1,060 per month in Social Security benefits plus $16 per month in food stamps. Her main asset is her primary residence, which is valued at $55,000 and encumbered by a $40,662 mortgage. Her mortgage payments are $327.10 per month. She also has $7,855.27 in credit card debt; her minimum monthly payments total $197. Prior to filing her Chapter 13 petition, Crager was current on all mortgage and credit card payments [suggesting reaffirming or riding through in chapter 7 would have been unproblematic—Eds.]. However, in early 2010, Crager learned that if she continued making the minimum payments on her credit cards, it would take her 17 to 20 years to pay off her balances. She contacted the loss mitigation departments of her credit card companies to seek an interest rate or monthly payment reduction but did not receive either.

Crager decided that her best course was to file for bankruptcy under Chapter 13 because it would have taken her over a year to save enough money to pay the up-front costs for a Chapter 7 bankruptcy and to do so she would have needed to stop making her minimum monthly credit card payments. She also was concerned that filing Chapter 7 would prevent her from declaring bankruptcy again for a longer period than would Chapter 13, and she believed that a Chapter 7 bankruptcy would stay on her credit report longer. Crager filed Chapter 13, with her attorney advancing the court costs of $274.

A few months after Crager filed her Chapter 13 petition and plan, the Trustee objected to confirmation of the plan. The objection asserted that Crager's petition and plan were not filed in good faith pursuant to 11 U.S.C. § 1325(a)(3) and (7) and that the amount of attorney's fees sought by Crager's attorney was unreasonable. After a contested hearing, the bankruptcy court overruled the Trustee's objection and approved Crager's Chapter 13 petition and plan and the requested legal fees and advanced legal costs.

The Trustee appealed, and the district court reversed the bankruptcy court's confirmation of Crager's Chapter 13 plan and entered an order requiring the bankruptcy court to find on remand that Crager's Chapter 13 plan was filed in bad faith. Crager appealed to this court.

. . .

In this circuit, courts apply a "totality of the circumstances" test to determine whether a Chapter 13 petition and plan are filed in good faith, and the bankruptcy court applied that standard when it approved Crager's plan. In approving the plan, the bankruptcy court focused on the rising cost of medical care and suggested that Crager had a legitimate fear that a future medical problem might leave her in a situation in which she had to take on more debt and might need to file another Chapter 13 petition. The court found that it would "border on malpractice" for Crager's attorney to advise her to file a Chapter 7.

The Trustee suggests that Crager's plan is against the spirit of Chapter 13, and indeed, one of the factors a court should consider in applying the totality of the circumstances test is "whether the plan shows an attempt to abuse the spirit of the bankruptcy code." But that is only one of at least seven factors. Moreover, the bankruptcy court had the opportunity to judge Crager's credibility as a witness and found credible her proffered reasons for filing a Chapter 13 petition. It was not clearly erroneous for the bankruptcy court to find that Crager's plan was not an attempt to abuse Chapter 13, but rather a responsible decision given her particular circumstances. There is no rule in this circuit that a Chapter 13 plan that results in the debtor's counsel receiving almost the entire amount paid to the Trustee, leaving other unsecured creditors unpaid, is a per se violation of the "good faith" requirement, and the district court erred when it reversed the bankruptcy court on that ground.

Alternatively, the Trustee argues that the bankruptcy court abused its discretion when it awarded $2,800 in attorney fees to Crager's counsel.

This issue turns on the relationship between the standard for awarding compensation to the debtor's attorney set forth in 11 U.S.C. § 330 and the "no-look" fee established by a Standing Order of the United States Bankruptcy Court for the Western District of Louisiana. [A "no-look" fee is an amount a court will generally approve as reasonable attorney charges without submission of a detailed fee application.—Eds.]

. . .

Under the Standing Order, a maximum no-look fee of $2,800 applies in a Chapter 13 case. The Standing Order allows the Trustee to file an objection to the presumptive fee and provides that, following notice to the debtor and a hearing, the bankruptcy court may adjust the fee. It notes that the no-look fee is not "an entitlement."

In this case, the Trustee objected to the bankruptcy court awarding the "no-look" fee on the basis that Crager's bankruptcy was "more simplistic and less complicated" than the average Chapter 13 case. Specifically: (1) the Trustee would make no disbursements to secured creditors; (2) there were only five unsecured creditors; (3) Crager's only sources of income were food stamps and Social Security benefits; (4) Crager had not filed an income tax return since 2004; and (5) Crager was judgment-proof and had no seizable assets. The bankruptcy court stated that it was the Trustee's burden not merely to raise a reasoned objection to the fee but to prove that the no-look fee should not apply, and it concluded that the no-look fee was reasonable.

The bankruptcy court was incorrect when it stated that it was the Trustee's burden to prove that the presumptive fee was unreasonable. As the Standing Order notes, the no-look fee is not an entitlement, and the Standing Order does not supplant the requirements of 11 U.S.C. § 330. Therefore, the bankruptcy court was obligated to consider the factors listed in the statute if the Trustee raised a reasoned objection.

However, we see no error in the bankruptcy court's finding that the no-look fee was reasonable under the circumstances. Most importantly, the Trustee's objection was based on the false premise that Crager's case was "more simplistic" than the average Chapter 13 bankruptcy. Indeed, the Trustee's own "bad faith" challenge to Crager's plan transformed the case from a routine Chapter 13 matter into a complicated proceeding. Given this added complexity, the reasoning of the Trustee's objection was not sound, and the bankruptcy court did not err in allowing the $2,800 no-look fee.

For the foregoing reasons, we REVERSE the ruling of the district court and AFFIRM the bankruptcy court's confirmation of Crager's Chapter 13 plan.

———————————

How far we've come from the means test! Recall that statutory brain-child was driven by a congressional desire to shunt debtors into chapter 13 by barring them from chapter 7. Here, we have a trustee complaining that the debtor was basically too poor for chapter 13 and was driven there by a rapacious attorney when she should have filed chapter 7. What would Congress have said? (We will look more at attorney incentives below.) While the debtor—and her attorney—were winners here, the court notes the costs and risks imposed by a multi-factored examination of whether bankruptcy relief is appropriate. The next case illustrates how good faith interacts with the means test's statutory expenses to create two bites at the apple for disgruntled creditors or tough trustees. Note the second bite mirroring the § 707(b)(3) cases above.

VEIGHLAN v. ESSEX (In re ESSEX)
452 B.R. 195 (W.D. Tex. 2011)

Rodriguez, District Judge.

On January 5, 2010, Appellees filed a petition for relief under Chapter 13 in the United States Bankruptcy Court for the Western District of Texas. Appellant filed an Objection to Confirmation of Appellees' Original

Chapter 13 Plan claiming in part that the Plan was not filed in good faith according to 11 U.S.C. § 1325(a)(3). Appellees then filed an Amended Chapter 13 Plan ("Plan") that included changes necessary for the Plan to meet feasibility requirements but did not address the good faith concerns that the Appellant raised.

The Plan "calls for payments of $3,717.00 for a period of sixty months and proposes to pay approximately a 1% dividend to non-priority unsecured creditors with the dollar amount to be paid to non-priority unsecured creditors a total of no less than $1,956.41." Appellant's Br. at 10. The basis of the good faith claim relates to the fact that in the Plan, "the debtors [Appellees] were proposing to retain a homestead with a mortgage of approximately $656,000.00 . . ." in which the Appellees have virtually no equity. *Id.* at 7, 24. To do so, Appellees would pay $6,770.00 towards the mortgage each month. *Id.* at 19. This amount constitutes 51% of Appellees' monthly income and represents a mortgage payment that "is over four times the amount of the IRS standard for housing *and* utilities for a family of five in San Antonio, Texas." *Id.* (emphasis included in original). In arguing that this proposal was not made in good faith, Appellant draws attention to the steep contrast between the high monthly mortgage payments and the low monthly dividend (1%) that Appellees propose to pay to unsecured creditors. Furthermore, it should be noted that before purchasing the home in 2006, Appellees had not paid income taxes for the years of 2003, 2004, or 2005 and continued this trend for 2006 as well. As a result of this failure to pay taxes, the Appellees owe the IRS $256,498.97, of which $136,681.46 is an unsecured claim. Based on the 1% dividend proposed in Appellees' Plan, the IRS will receive $1,366.82 of the unsecured debt.

Despite Appellant's objection, the Bankruptcy Court confirmed the Plan, citing the eligibility limits of 11 U.S.C. § 109(e) in conjunction with the Chapter 13 purpose of allowing debtors to retain their homes during bankruptcy. As the Court stated,

> We already know that we have a statute that's designed to help people keep their homes, and we already know that Congress also, de facto, put an upper limit on what kind of a home you can keep because they put an upper limit of how much secured debt you can take into Chapter 13. So, that's the de facto number. The de facto number for how much house can you have in Chapter 13 is set by the eligibility limits.

Ct. Tr. at 34-35. In response to the Court's Order confirming the Plan, Appellant filed an appeal and seeks reversal of the Order and denial of confirmation.

. . .

GOOD FAITH

Many courts disagree on what constitutes a violation of Section 1325(a)(3), particularly when the section is read in conjunction with Section 1325(b). While section 1325(a)(3) concerns whether ". . . the plan has been proposed in good faith and not by any means forbidden by law," Section

1325(b)(3) contemplates the determination of "[a]mounts reasonably necessary to be expended" by the debtor as it essentially factors into the overall "disposable income" calculation outlined in 1325(b)(2). 11 U.S.C. § 1325(a)(3), (b)(3). Section 1325(b)(3) provides that "amounts reasonably necessary to be expended" should be determined for debtors of certain income levels in accordance with 11 U.S.C. § 707(b)(2)(A)-(B) which outlines the "means test". . . . Section 707(b)(2)(A)(iii)(II) places no reasonableness requirement on the monthly payments necessary to "maintain possession of the debtor's primary residence." *Id.* Rather, any amount necessary to keep the residence is allowed by Section 707 and as a result, is considered an "amount[] reasonably necessary to be expended" under Section 1325(b)(3). *Id.*; 11 U.S.C. § 1325(b)(3).

As a result of this statutory language and the absence of a "reasonableness" component within Section 707(b)(2)(A)(iii)(II), courts have had difficulty determining whether a debtor's proposed monthly expenditures can be lawful under Section 1325(b)(3) yet constitute a violation of good faith under Section 1325(a)(3). During the confirmation hearing in this case, the Bankruptcy Court agreed that the proposed housing expenses in the Appellees' Plan comply with Section 1325(b)(3). Ct. Tr. 19. However, because the Court chose to overrule the good faith objection using Section 109(e), it did not reach the difficult question of whether the proposed plan nonetheless violated Section 1325(a)(3).

Appellant implores this Court to make that finding and to follow a line of cases from bankruptcy courts around the country holding that compliance with 1325(b)(3) is not determinative of compliance with 1325(a)(3). *See* In re Sandberg, 433 B.R. 837, 845-46 (Bankr. D. Kan. 2010) (" 'Notwithstanding the fact that the Debtors are entitled to account for the boat payments when calculating their disposable income under the means test, confirmation of a plan proposing to retain the boat is subject to the good faith test under 11 U.S.C. § 1325(a)(3). . . .' "); . . . In re McGillis, 370 B.R. 720, 750 (Bankr. W.D. Mich. 2007) ("Section 1325(b) is a hazard, not a harbor. Its avoidance does not mean clear sailing. Rather, all debtors still must establish that their plans exhibit the good faith demanded by Section 1325(a)(3).").

On the other hand, Appellees urge the Court to adopt the reasoning that expenditures in compliance with Section 1325(b)(3) automatically qualify as expenditures in compliance with Section 1325(a)(3) as long as no additional instances of bad faith are alleged. *See* In re Faison, 416 B.R. 227, 231-32 (Bankr. E.D. Va. 2008) ("The Court will not find that the Debtor acted not in good faith by doing what Congress has allowed in BAPCPA, even if the expenses taken result in a lower dividend to unsecured creditors than they would receive if the Debtor were forced to relinquish property that is worth far less than the debt securing it."); . . . In re Farrar-Johnson, 353 B.R. 224, 232 (Bankr. N.D. Ill. 2006) ("If the reasonable necessity of a debtor's expenses is no longer relevant, then plainly the debtor's 'good faith' in claiming them cannot be relevant. Disposable income is 'determined under section 1325(b) rather than as an element of good faith under section 1325(a)(3).' ").

In light of the Fifth Circuit precedent of applying the "totality of the circumstances" test to decide questions of good faith, overruling Appellant's

Section 1325(a)(3) objection solely on the basis of whether Appellees' proposed plan complies with Section 1325(b)(3) would be improper and would render Section 1325(b)(3) superfluous. However, to find that the Appellees proposed their plan in bad faith even though the housing expenses comply with Section 1325(b)(3) would also be inconsistent. In attempting to resolve this potential conflict within the statute, this Court finds the approach taken in In re Owsley to be persuasive. 384 B.R. 739 (Bankr. N.D. Tex. 2008). In that case, the Court concluded that "expenses deemed to be 'reasonably necessary' under subsection (b)(3) are presumed to be asserted in good faith under subsection (a)(3). The presumption of good faith can be negated by aggravating circumstances, an example of which might be a debtor's deduction of an ownership expense for a luxury vehicle purchased on the eve of bankruptcy." *Id.* at 750. Under this approach, the fact that Appellees' proposed monthly mortgage payments are lawful under Section 1325(b)(3) is important yet constitutes only one factor to be considered in addition to any "aggravating circumstances" that might arise within the overall "totality of the circumstances" test.

Appellant argues that there are aggravating circumstances in this case. Specifically, Appellant points to the fact that prior to purchasing their home, Appellees had not paid income taxes for three years. As Appellant states, ". . . the debtors clearly made the choice to live in a luxury home rather than pay their income taxes. . . . The trustee questions whether the debtors living in a $600,000.00 home while paying next to nothing on $136,681.46 of unsecured tax debt is the bargain that Congress intended between debtors and unsecured creditors." Appellant's Br. at 21. Furthermore, the Appellant points to recent cases in which bankruptcy courts have found Chapter 13 plans that allow debtors to keep highly valued homes in which they have very little equity while paying virtually nothing to unsecured creditors to be proposed in bad faith.

In the case of In re Namie, the debtor proposed to retain his $500,000 home even though his mortgage expenses amounted to five times more than the standard housing expenses in his community. 395 B.R. 594, 596-97 (Bankr. D.S.C. 2008). In fact, the debtor's mortgage expenses exceeded his personal net income. *Id.* The Court held that "debtor's retention of a home that consumes all of his net disposable income, to the detriment of his significant number of unsecured creditors, is not in good faith." *Id.* Although the case at issue is distinguishable from *Namie* in that Appellees' mortgage does not consume the entirety of their disposable income, Appellees' proposal to pay a 1% dividend to unsecured creditors is barely more substantial than the *Namie* debtor. . . .

Considering the "totality of the circumstances," this Court finds it necessary to reverse the order of the Bankruptcy Court to confirm Appellees' Chapter 13 Plan. Although Appellees' proposed housing expenses satisfy the standards outlined in Section 1325(b)(3) and thus are presumed to have been proposed in good faith, sufficiently aggravating circumstances serve to rebut that presumption. Appellees' proposal to retain a home valued at $600,000 while paying only 1% of the $136,681.46 unsecured debt owed to the IRS is a proposal in bad faith. Furthermore, in making this proposal, Appellees have not asserted a reason why it is necessary to retain a home for which the mortgage payments are over four times the amount of the IRS standard for their area despite the extremely low dividend they seek to pay to their unsecured creditors. . . . [T]hese Appellees seem "unwilling to engage in the kind of meaningful belt tightening" necessary for individuals in bankruptcy. As Appellant states, "debtors [Appellees] have not sought to change their spendthrift ways but rather seek to maintain their pre-petition lifestyle. . . . There is no reason why the debtors cannot find more affordable housing and pay their unsecured creditors a reasonable dividend while still living a comfortable lifestyle." Appellant's Br. at 19.

Although the Bankruptcy Court was correct to emphasize that a purpose of Chapter 13 bankruptcy proceedings is to allow debtors to keep their homes, it is doubtful that Congress intended to protect individuals, like the Appellees, who purchased the home during a time period when they evaded their income taxes. To allow the Appellees to retain their homestead while paying only 1% of the debt owed to unsecured creditors, including the IRS, would be to allow a bargain that too greatly favors the Appellees. In light of the totality of the circumstances, the Bankruptcy Court's Order confirming Appellees' Chapter 13 Plan is reversed.

The Essex family's low five-year payback suggests a net income that would pass the means test. If so, would there be any problem with them converting to chapter 7 (or filing a new chapter 7 case) given this dismissal from chapter 13? If they did, would they necessarily lose their home? Does the finding that there was a lack of good faith based on totality of the circumstances create law of the case requiring dismissal under § 707(b)(3), for bad faith, § 707(b)(3)(A), and/or a totality of the circumstances, § 707(b)(3)(B), or are there different considerations there?

3. Refiling Restrictions — *Made but necessary?*

Some debtors make multiple forays into bankruptcy. Some refile shortly after dismissal with the same attorney, while others wait out tough circumstances or shop for a new lawyer. While the repeat filer may not attract sympathy, the largest group of refilers, especially in chapter 13, actually appears to be people simply seeking a first discharge, not scoundrels coming back for a second bankruptcy discharge with newly acquired debt. This reality does not seem to echo in the halls of Congress, however, as BAPCPA tightened the rules to prohibit a discharge in chapter 13 for any debtor who has received a discharge in a chapter 7, 11, or 12 case in the preceding four years or for any debtor who received a discharge in a chapter 13 case in the preceding two years. § 1328(f). Congress also tightened the rules in chapter 7, extending the wait between chapter 7s to eight years, beyond the Biblical seven. § 727(a)(8). There are true "serial" filers out there, but they appear to be an exclusive clique. Jean Lown, New Study: Serial Bankruptcy Filers No Problem, ABI J. (June 2007) (finding 2.7% of chapter 13 debtors had filed four or more times). These restrictions on refiling are yet another factor to balance in chapter choice. Remember they drove Ms. Crager's lawyer's decision (at least if you take the explanation at face value) to have her file under chapter 13 rather than 7.

4.   *Scope of Discharge*

Chapter 13 has a somewhat more generous discharge provision than chapter 7. Compare § 1328 with § 727. But the differences are now so small only Old Timers still refer to chapter 13 as offering a "super discharge." These additional debts that can only be eliminated in chapter 13 are largely limited to various government fines and penalties, amounts from divorce or separation that are in the nature of property settlements (as opposed to support), and a few other oddities. Historically, the super discharge was designed to be a major carrot for filing chapter 13; the current screening test framework suggests sticks have now become *de rigueur* for incentives.

5.   *Coda: Chapter 11 for Individuals*

Having waded through the pros and cons of chapter 7 and chapter 13, you may be hoping for a magical third option to address one or more of the risks of chapter 7 or chapter 13. The good news is that individuals can file chapter 11. Sure, you may think about titans like General Motors and Delta Airlines, but individuals file chapter 11 too. Indeed, roughly one-third of all chapter 11 petitions in 2013 were filed by individuals. Richard Hynes, Anne Lawton & Margaret Howard, National Study of Individual Chapter 11 Bankruptcies, 25 Am. Bankr. Inst. L. Rev. 61, 71 (2017); see also id. n.48 (discussing findings of 2010 Harvard Bankruptcy Data Project).

Little is yet known about why individuals file chapter 11. Some of them flunk the means test or have debts that exceed the chapter 13 caps. They are essentially screened out by statute from both chapter 7 and chapter 13. Their choice is chapter 11 or nothing. Others choose chapter 11 voluntarily over chapter 7 or chapter 13 to deal with complicated financial issues beyond the scope of these materials; suffice it to say chapter 11 accords more flexibility and can deal with greater complexity. Precisely for these reasons, however, chapter 11 is slower and costlier.

And there is more bad news: Congress reduced incentives for individuals to use chapter 11 with BAPCPA by incorporating many aspects of the means test. Today, chapter 11 for individuals is now much closer to chapter 13—but that increased similarity by no means suggests identity. Chapter 11 is complex and involves special fiduciary obligations we will explore in the business assignments. Consumer practitioners used to mass-managing cases with legal software cannot just cross out "13" and write "11." Judge Jaroslovsky makes the point below.

Notice to Bar Regarding Individual Chapter 11 Cases

There has been a recent spate of individual Chapter 11 cases filed by attorneys who have neither the experience nor the education nor the competence to venture into Chapter 11. I believe that there are very few bankruptcy lawyers other than State Bar certified specialists who should be contemplating representation of Chapter 11 debtors in possession.

I see rampant errors being made in issues relating to cash collateral, conflicts of interest, and compensation. . . .

A Chapter 11 is not just a big Chapter 13. If you represent a Chapter 11 debtor in possession, your client is the *estate*, not the debtor personally. Failure to understand this results in serious liability exposure.

Forget about trying to fix your compensation. You will be paid what I allow, period. I suggest you not spend retainers until your fees are allowed to avoid having to return money you have already spent.

I see frequent malpractice in individual Chapter 11 cases and I am quick to note it on the record. Your employment will not be approved unless you have substantial current malpractice insurance. If you are going "bare," don't even think about taking a Chapter 11 case.

A complete understanding of the differences between chapter 11 and chapter 13 must await the detailed study of chapter 11 later in this book. To give you an idea of a few differences: (1) chapter 11 is much more expensive, both for the filing fee ($1,717 compared to $335 (chapter 7) or $310 (chapter 13)) and for attorneys' fees; (2) the retail valuation standard, § 506(a)(2), for property encumbered by a security interest does not apply; (3) creditors vote to confirm a plan in chapter 11 while confirmation in chapter 13 is determined solely by a judge; and (4) financial education is not a condition for discharge for chapter 11 debtors, as it is for chapter 7 and chapter 13 debtors. For further discussion, contending persuasively that individual chapter 11s are now so distinct they warrant a separate subchapter, see Bruce Markell, The Sub Rosa Subchapter: Individual Debtors in Chapter 11 After BAPCPA, 2007 U. Ill. L. Rev. 67.

Chapter 11 remains an odd fit for individuals. While individuals are a significant fraction of all chapter 11 cases, the converse is not true. Chapter 11 cases are a bare sliver of all bankruptcies filed by individuals each year. In 2013, 99.7% of cases filed by individuals were chapter 7 or chapter 13 cases, according to Hynes et al., supra. It makes little sense for the average family to use chapter 11 to propose a payment plan. We flag chapter 11 in this chapter choice discussion because post-BAPCPA more individuals may now be barred from both chapter 7 and chapter 13 and thus must turn to chapter 11 if they want any bankruptcy relief.

For space reasons, we omit any discussion of chapter 12, open only to family farmers or fishermen, a sort of chapter 11 and chapter 13 hybrid (as its number suggests) that may be more debtor-friendly. The filing numbers for this chapter are also very small. The empirical point is that the consumer system is largely dichotomous between chapter 7 and chapter 13.

B.   EXTRA-STATUTORY CONSIDERATIONS

Beyond the Code's provisions, various practice realities also influence chapter choice.

1. *Attorneys' Fees*

It has long been the practice of lawyers filing chapter 7 cases to demand their fees in cash from their bankrupt clients before filing. "Pay me next month? Well, er. . . ." Nonetheless, some lawyers did agree to be paid by the chapter 7 estate, at least until that practice was ended by the Supreme Court's decision in Lamie v. United States, 540 U.S. 526 (2004). *Lamie* did not apply to the reorganization chapters (11, 12, and 13), and it is routine in many districts in chapter 13 cases to include payment of the debtor's attorneys' fees as part of the monthly payments that go through the chapter 13 trustee, just like the filing fee and the trustee's fee. This difference in payment possibilities is another important distinction between the chapters.

The fee-only chapter 13 that survived challenge in *Crager* has actually fared even better in a post-BAPCPA world. The working theory seems to be that debtors who are paying even a pittance in chapter 13 are doing more to benefit creditors than if they just filed chapter 7 and so are "worthy." But as this excerpt from a First Circuit case shows, debtors who file fee-only cases do so under a watchful gaze.

===================== In re PUFFER =====================

674 F.3d 78 (1st Cir. 2012)

. . .

LIPEZ, Circuit Judge, concurring.

We have observed that the Bankruptcy Code's purposes are twofold: to give the deserving debtor a fresh start and to maximize the payment to creditors. A fee-only Chapter 13 plan may accomplish little toward the goal of satisfying creditors, but such a plan may nonetheless be essential to free "the honest but unfortunate debtor" from intolerable circumstances.

Bankruptcy judges evaluating a particular fee-only plan may properly take into account whether the plan "is consistent with the spirit and purpose of [Chapter 13]—rehabilitation through debt repayment,"—but I fear that circumscribing the totality of the circumstances assessment with the requirement of special circumstances [the majority opinion's proposed test to permit a fee-only plan—Eds.] will in practical effect impose on debtors the more daunting task of disproving bad faith rather than proving good faith. I am therefore reluctant to confine what should be, in the majority's apt words, a "holistic balancing of relevant factors."

. . . [A]s the majority observes, the fee-only structure may leave unknowledgeable debtors vulnerable to attorneys seeking to maximize their compensation. See Kerry Haydel Ducey, Note, Bankruptcy, Just for the Rich? An Analysis of Popular Fee Arrangements for Pre-Petition Legal Fees and a Call to Amend, 54 Vand. L. Rev. 1665, 1703 (2001) (hereinafter Just for the Rich?) (noting that, "[i]n some cases, self-interest . . . compels the attorney to advise debtors to file Chapter 13 or other high percentage payment plans when Chapter 7 would actually better serve the debtor" (footnote omitted)).

Nonetheless, we must keep in mind that a struggling debtor who lacks the resources to pay a Chapter 7 attorney's fee up front has limited options. Although he theoretically could proceed pro se, I doubt that bankrupt individuals will ordinarily be able to navigate the complexities of the bankruptcy process on their own. Indeed, an empirical study indicating that the percentage of pro se debtors has increased in the aftermath of BAPCPA shows that such cases are not succeeding. See Angela Littwin, The Affordability Paradox: How Consumer Bankruptcy's Greatest Weakness May Account for Its Surprising Success, 52 Wm. & Mary L. Rev. 1933, 1938 (2011) ("[T]he high pro se failure rate since 2005 suggests that it is reasonable to equate the inability to afford a lawyer with having less than full access to the bankruptcy system."); see also Just for the Rich?, 54 Vand. L. Rev. at 1667 ("Legal counsel is indispensable if a debtor is to effectively file for bankruptcy. The bankruptcy laws are complex, and legal counsel is often crucial in helping the debtor make an informed decision based on his unique circumstances and the available alternatives." (citing William C. Hillman, Personal Bankruptcy: What Every Debtor and Creditor Needs to Know 20 (1993) ("Many mistakes people make by trying to do it on their own often cannot be corrected later. Even the simplest choices involve uncertainties and risks if you are not thoroughly familiar with the law."))). Moreover, lawyers play an important role in the bankruptcy system beyond their direct assistance to clients.

A debtor could attempt to find cheaper, or free, legal services, but I have no reason to think that counsel fees vary widely or that competent bankruptcy legal advice is readily available for free. . . .

The fee-only cases underscore the difficult reality that modern chapter 7 practice requires up-front payment for cash-starved debtors. Many years of serious empirical work have failed to reveal whence stems the chapter 7 lawyer's fee. Some claim debtors are told to skip the next mortgage payment or two to fund the fee; others assert that the debtor is given to understand that it is time to get that one last loan from Mom or your bowling buddy. Another theory is that debtors time their filings to coincide with additional cash, usually a tax refund. Ronald J. Mann & Katherine Porter, Saving Up for Bankruptcy, 98 Geo. L.J. 289, 319-20 (2010). With the substantial increase of fees after BAPCPA, price constraints may shape chapter choice even more. In one countervailing maneuver, however, Congress added in BAPCPA the ability to file *in forma pauperis*. 28 U.S.C. § 1930(f). Such filings are now about 3% of all chapter 7 cases. Some have argued that anyone who needs a waiver of the filing fee should not be able to afford an attorney. Others have noted, consistent with the excerpt from *Puffer*, that *pro se* filings fare relatively poorly and that a debtor's attorney may be necessary for not just debtors but creditors. See, e.g., Angela K. Littwin, The Do-It Yourself Mirage, in *Broke*.

Another study observed a further serious issue with attorneys' fees — a huge regional disparity. Lois Lupica explains that the variations "go beyond: big city = expensive, small town = cheap." She explains the lawyers themselves may have input into setting attorneys' fees, even in chapter 13 where the Code seems to require court approval of any fees. Her study reproduces this attorney's description:

> [T]he judges get together with small filers, medium filers, and large filers and trustees and say, "Hey, what you guys need to do is let me know what you need to charge. Give me a figure, kind of roughly an average case. What we're going to do is put that as an average figure, which is $3,250. Now you can go with that if you want. And that's $3,250 at confirmation. Keep track of your time afterwards and do supplemental fees. Or you can just do it hourly, right from the start. We'll just pay you hourly, or you can do $4,500 for the life of the case."

Posting of Lois Lupica to Credit Slips, Mar. 29, 2011, www.creditslips.org.

For people in such serious financial trouble that bankruptcy looms, the cost of legal assistance is a serious burden. Based on cases filed in 2007 studied in the Consumer Bankruptcy Project the average chapter 7 attorney's fee was $1,284; the average chapter 13 attorney's fee was $2,883. Attorneys' fees implicate both access to justice concerns and the hard realities of chapter choice. Their post-2005 rise suggests that one of BAPCPA's most significant effects was that the law's complexity prices some debtors right out of representation. See, e.g., Lois R. Lupica, The Consumer Bankruptcy Fee Study: Final Report (American Bankruptcy Institute, 2012) 36-48, 51 (finding magnitude of cost increases varied considerably among judicial districts—with some districts even seeing fee decreases—but an overall clear upward trend). It is no wonder current scholarship describes the phenomenon of debtors essentially "too poor" to file bankruptcy. Angela Littwin, Low-income, low-asset debtors in the U.S. bankruptcy system, 29 Int. Insol. Rev. S116 (2020).

2. *Outcomes in Consumer Bankruptcy*

A good lawyer tells clients what to expect well beyond the immediate relief of an automatic stay. Likely outcomes are important to consider when planning the debtor's optimal debt relief strategy. Congress, too, hotly debates the respective outcomes of the different bankruptcy chapters, apparently holding firm to the belief that chapter 13 is just better for everyone. In this section, we offer a brief introduction to the wide literature on bankruptcy outcomes.

a. Chapter 7 Outcomes

A 2001 study of chapter 7 filers asked families one year after discharge: "Overall, since you filed for bankruptcy, has your financial situation improved, stayed about the same, or worsened?" The results were decidedly mixed. Although 64% reported improvement, more than one-third said their financial situation was the same or worse than when they sought bankruptcy relief. Katherine Porter & Deborah Thorne, The Failure of Bankruptcy's Fresh Start, 92 Cornell L. Rev. 67, 77 (2006). The authors conclude that for "many families, the fresh start either failed to materialize or dissipated within one year of the discharge of their debts in bankruptcy." Id. at 70.

The longer-term picture also showed enduring financial difficulties for debtors. Professors Jay Zagorsky and Lois Lupica compared bankruptcy filers with nonbankruptcy filers and found that even holding many differences between the groups constant, bankruptcy filers continue to work hard but struggle with income issues. Jay Zagorsky & Lois Lupica, A Study of Consumers' Post-Discharge Finances: Struggle, Stasis, or Fresh-Start?, 16 Am. Bankr. Inst. L. Rev. 283 (2007). The average filer earns $13,000 less in annual wages than the average non-filing peers; it is not until 13 years after bankruptcy discharge that bankruptcy filers catch up with their nonbankrupt peers. Id. at 310. The findings on wealth and savings show similar gaps. Of course, these data do not necessarily impugn the bankruptcy system; these people could be much worse off without the discharge. But the findings do give pause to the rosy assumption that the fresh start fixes all.

The slow recovery after bankruptcy could be a sign that bankrupt debtors are profligate and return to their old, bad habits after relief, miring themselves again in debt. While more research is needed, initial studies suggest that people are actually quite reluctant to borrow after bankruptcy—at least at the prices offered. Katherine Porter, Life After Debt: Understanding the Credit Restraint of Bankruptcy Debtors, 18 Am. Bankr. Inst. L. Rev. 1 (2010). These data are a reminder that the outcomes of bankruptcy may be more than a "radical adjustment to a debtor's balance sheet. Bankruptcy has behavioral effects that may be driven by psychological or social factors, not merely economic ones." Id. at 2. In the next assignment, we will consider the rehabilitative aims of consumer bankruptcy, along with competing goals.

b. Chapter 13 Outcomes

The conventional wisdom—borne out by multiple empirical studies, including groundbreaking work of the Consumer Bankruptcy Project back to 1981—is that only 33% of cases end in plan completion. Although as with all things chapter 13, there is wide variation from district to district, the hard fact remains that the majority of chapter 13 filers do not get to discharge unsecured debts because they do not complete their plans. Lack of discharge does not mean chapter 13 was useless; for example, the automatic stay may let the debtor find a new home by staving off a foreclosure and then the debtor can let her case voluntarily lapse. Still, the empirical evidence suggests that most incomplete plans reflect unhappy and difficult circumstances. Katherine Porter, The Pretend Solution: An Empirical Study of Bankruptcy Outcomes, 90 Tex. L. Rev. 103 (2011) (estimating that half of all filed chapter 13 cases are not successful when measured against debtors' self-reported goals of saving collateral or discharging unsecured debt).

The Code does permit a hardship discharge when the debtor has paid at least as much as creditors would have recovered in chapter 7, modification is not practicable, and the failure to complete the plan is outside the debtor's control. § 1328(b). This section is used with some regularity by savvy debtor's counsel, but note that it does not address secured debt problems, such as mortgage trouble, and has a different scope to the discharge.

Reconsidering our earlier discussion of good faith, § 1307(c) sets forth a non-exclusive list of "cause" that allows dismissal of a chapter 13 case. The same grounds apply to conversion of a petition from chapter 13 to chapter 7, but it is relatively uncommon, see Porter, *The Pretend Solution*, supra at 132 (finding that conversion accounts for fewer than 20% of non-completed cases). But again, it's not clear whether dismissal in chapter 13 reflects a bad outcome for the debtor. One key difference is between pre-confirmation and post-confirmation dismissal. The former usually occurs because the debtor never attempts confirmation, i.e., no plan is ever filed, or the debtor fails to complete a necessary step, such as pre-bankruptcy counseling or paying the filing fee. These cases likely reflect the limited options available to people at risk of losing their homes to foreclosure, cars to repossession, or other imminent collection activity. The upfront cost of chapter 7 deters them, so they file under chapter 13 for a temporary respite, perhaps to seek shelter while working on a nonbankruptcy solution, such as a loan modification, and then exit.

The post-confirmation dismissals reflect a different set of issues, with the cause for dismissal nearly always being the debtor's default on plan payments. Some debtors "intentionally" fail to pay the trustee, such as when a mortgage company has already lifted the stay and foreclosed for missed mortgage payments on a maintained-and-cured mortgage; with the home gone, many simply leave the bankruptcy system, unconcerned or unaware they have not discharged their unsecured debts. In the study reported in *The Pretend Solution*, supra, one debtor offered this advice to others considering bankruptcy.

> Be prepared for a rocky road. It's not an easy thing to go through. It's a longer process than what we thought it would be and there [are] unbelievable amounts of paperwork. We had creditors telling us that bankruptcy wouldn't solve our problems. We wanted to believe it would help us, but maybe they were telling us the truth.

Thus, while lawyers can truthfully tell their clients "only about a third of you will likely get to plan completion and discharge," that statement glosses over the factual nuance of each debtor's financial distress.

c.   Outcomes from the Creditor's Perspective

Creditors, of course, also care about bankruptcy outcomes, although their primary concern is getting paid as much as possible as fast as possible. It is difficult, however, to know how unsecureds really fare in chapter 13; the empirical evidence points in different directions. At an aggregate level, chapter 13 trustees distributed $1.58 billion to nonpriority unsecured creditors. U.S. Trustee Program, FY-2011 Chapter 13 Trustee

Audited Annual Report. That's a lot of dough. On the other hand, in the median case, the payment to unsecured creditors is zero. This was true in post-BAPCPA cases filed in 2007, based on Consumer Bankruptcy Project data, as well as cases filed in prior years, including 2001. Scott Norberg, The Chapter 13 Project: Little Paid to Unsecureds, 26 Am. Bankr. L.J. 1, 54-56 (2007). The actual median payout seems a wee bit higher because in many districts trustees capture new post-confirmation income, primarily tax refunds in subsequent years, in a confirmed plan with zero proposed payout.

The trend in congressional amendments to the Code has long been either to encourage chapter 13, or more stridently, to limit access to chapter 7, which makes a bizarre disconnect between the data and what people lobby for. Some have argued that the purpose of the BAPCPA reforms was not to promote chapter 13 but to discourage filings generally, in order to keep families longer in a "sweat box" of debt, where they continue to make payments under increasingly difficult circumstances. Ronald J. Mann, Consumer Bankruptcy and Credit in the Wake of the 2005 Act: Bankruptcy Reform and the "Sweat Box" of Credit Card Debt, 2007 U. Ill. L. Rev. 375. If so, then the poor outcomes in chapter 13 are of no concern to these creditors.

One thing creditors may care very much about with bankruptcy outcomes is the creation of future customers. Nobody wants to lend to someone about to go bankrupt; creditors use analytical products to try to identify those on the brink of bankruptcy. But what of the recently bankrupt? Some would argue that the clean balance sheets of these consumers should make them attractive borrowers, but others would argue their track records raise red flags. We let the market—at least as it was before 2008—speak. The *Washington Post* reported a 2005 story about Lenya Garcia, who filed for bankruptcy after being overwhelmed by $60,000 in credit card bills. She filed in July, got her discharge in January, and "less than a month later, a rash of new credit card offers began arriving in the mail." Caroline E. Mayer, Bankrupt and Swamped with Credit Offers; When Chapter 7 Filers Wipe Out Their Debts, Card Firms Jump, *Washington Post*, Apr. 15, 2005, at A1. Take, for example, this 2017 letter one of us received:

> Henna Chevrolet has the top finance department in Central Texas and can provide numerous options and lenders to assist your bankruptcy clients. We offer a unique approach with national lenders that will provide financing **DURING** and **AFTER** bankruptcy. Many people do not realize that even BEFORE the bankruptcy is discharged, they can obtain auto financing which can help begin rebuilding and re-establishing their credit to all 3 credit bureaus.

3. *The Lawyer's Role*

We end on a brief note underscoring the importance of lawyers in navigating this dizzying system. Counsel's "counseling" may range from offering full disclosure and free chapter choice on the one hand to an ultimatum that the attorney will only file the debtor under one chapter or the other. In this framework, deciding between chapter 7 and chapter 13 may be less about strategy and more about sorting or *steering* by counsel. Judges, trustees, the U.S. Trustee, and creditors also make decisions that affect chapter choice; the attorneys' fees discussion above is only one example. Attitudes and experiences about things like the importance of homeownership, the morality of repaying debts, and the efficacy of one chapter or the other all come into play.

Steering likely contains both conscious and subconscious components. As with many aspects of the legal system, the role of biases and preferences in the steering process implicate considerations of race, and bankruptcy is no exception. Indeed, recent research suggests that the race of the debtor is correlated with chapter choice, even after controlling for other likely explanations. For example, attorneys tend to steer African-Americans toward chapter 13 more often than white debtors in similar financial circumstances according to a study that presented attorneys with hypothetical debtors with identical financial characteristics but different race-cuing names. Jean Braucher, Dov Cohen & Robert M. Lawless, Race, Attorney Influence, and Bankruptcy Chapter Choice, 9 J. Empirical Legal Stud. 393 (2012). Indicia of subconscious influences are further supported by an eye-opening study of attorney beliefs that showed a marked disconnect between perception and practice. It found that the experts got the results exactly backward, believing that white debtors were more likely to file for chapter 13 than African-Americans. Dov Cohen, Robert M. Lawless & Faith Shin, Opposite of Correct: Inverted Insider, 91 Am. Bankr. L.J. 623 (2017). To be sure, prescient scholars have been flagging this issue for quite some time, see, e.g., A. Mechele Dickerson, Race Matters in Bankruptcy, 61 Wash. & Lee L. Rev. 1725 (2004). But a critical mass of attention is now being focused, and ongoing studies find that these important considerations of race and bankruptcy only multiply in complexity with further analysis. See, e.g., Robert M. Lawless & Angela Littwin, Local Legal Culture From R2D2 to Big Data, 96 Tex. L. Rev. 1353 (2018).

Collectively, the factors that shape chapter choice beyond a client's wishes (which may never be truly known in the presence of these other influences) are collectively called "local legal culture." See Jean Braucher, Lawyers and Consumer Bankruptcy: One Code, Many Cultures, 67 Am. Bankr. L.J. 501 (1993); Teresa Sullivan, Elizabeth Warren & Jay Westbrook, The Persistence of Local Legal Culture: Twenty Years of Evidence from the Federal Bankruptcy Courts, 17 Harv. J.L. & Pub. Pol'y 801 (1994). To give you just a taste of the disparities, the chapter 13 filing rate in some bankruptcy districts is 3% of consumer cases and more than 50% in others. Indeed, some judges or trustees let it be known they will grill debtors harder if they tried chapter 7 and were bounced into 13 than if they just filed for 13 from the outset. While there is debate about the benefits of diversity versus uniformity, we close by noting that much of local legal culture, and by extension the realities of consumer bankruptcy, reflect extra-legal considerations. So much for all that time spent studying the Code!

The map visually shows the striking variation in the use of chapter 13. For each judicial district, the probability of a debtor choosing a chapter 13 is shown as compared to the chapter 13 rate in the judicial district at the median (which happens to be 29.9% in the Middle District of Florida). The probabilities

Figure 1. Judicial District Fixed Effects from Regression, Probability of Filing Chapter 13 vs. Chapter 7 Relative to Median Judicial District.

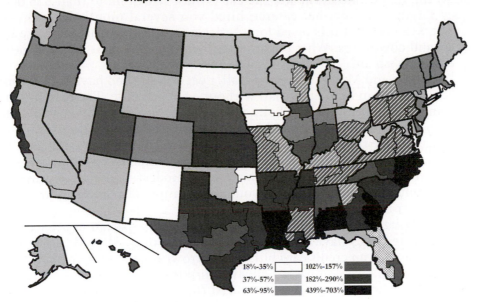

come from a statistical analysis of a database containing all bankruptcy filing from 2012-2016 and that controlled for many variables, such as income of the debtor and home ownership, that would affect the chapter 13 incidence within a district. Judicial districts with striped fill did not differ from the Middle District of Florida at a statistically significant level considering the number of judicial districts in the analysis (p < .0006, using a Bonferroni adjustment, for those who must know). See Robert M. Lawless & Angela Littwin, "Local Legal Culture from R2D2 to Big Data," 96 Tex. L. Rev. 1353, 1369 (2018).

Problem Set 13

13.1. A. You represent Angelica Ornelas, a realtor in Newport Beach, California. With bonuses and income from her share in a large real estate partnership, Angelica's total income is slightly over $200,000. She lives as if it were even higher. She has a million-dollar home almost completely encumbered by a mortgage, three credit cards on which she owes more than most people owe on their homes, and a bunch of home décor, such as a hot tub, subject to purchase money liens. In short, after she pays all these fixed obligations and expenses, plus a reasonable amount for food and clothing, the means test would leave her about $292 per month for her unsecured creditors in her chapter 13 plan. She owes these creditors almost $195,000. Her total five-year payout will be $12,000, about 6% of her unsecured debt. Because most of her assets are subject to heavy liens and her state has generous exemptions, the unsecured creditors would get nothing in chapter 7. What questions do you have to ask before advising Angelica about her choices under the Code? Can you get Angelica's plan confirmed? What are the weak spots? See § 1325.

B. In an alternative universe you represent two of Angelica's creditors. Perfection Motors, the Mercedes dealer who holds a $35,000 purchase money security interest on one of her cars, has called you for a consultation.

The lender is very concerned because the car market has slowed abruptly due to the real estate crash and the car is "not worth more than $25,000, tops." Divine Cuisine, her caterer, hired you several months ago to collect the $15,600 that it is owed for a series of receptions Angelica gave for bosses and coworkers. What position will you take on their behalf regarding Angelica's plan?

13.2. Mr. and Mrs. Poltz are a small, neat couple who have sat in front of your desk for an hour and a half without a single smile. They are hoping you can save their home. Mr. Poltz was an inventory control clerk for the Chicago school district, but was hurt about two years ago and has been "on disability" since that time. Because the school district has good disability benefits, he is receiving about $2,900 a month, which is far below the relevant state median income. They have only modest personal possessions worth about $4,000, all of which would be exempt. The small equity they have in their house would also be exempt.

Mrs. Poltz is not employed. After paying their spartan expenses and their mortgage, they have about $150 a month left over. After Mr. Poltz was injured, they ran up credit card bills and borrowed some money unsecured from a local finance company, "always thinking Mr. P. would be back to work in just a little time." They have $10,750.42 in unsecured debts. They missed three payments on the house when Mr. Poltz's disability checks were stopped because of a computer error. The bank filed a foreclosure suit and an answer is due tomorrow, but the bank officer called last week and said they would be willing to work things out. The Poltzes say they can pick up the current payments on the mortgage and pay the arrears within three months. They have heard about chapter 13 being used for saving a home, and they are willing to pay the full $150 a month to a plan "for as long as you say." You have no doubt you could get their chapter 13 plan confirmed. What is your advice?

13.3. Noah Zinner has labored tirelessly as a community organizer and social worker. To show for it, he has two advanced degrees, a slew of awards from foundations and government, and a lot of personal debt. Despite a very frugal lifestyle—he drives a beater, has used furniture, buys his clothes secondhand—he just can't seem to make ends meet on the $32,000 that he earns. He lives in Baltimore with his wife Emily, who stays at home with their four young kids. With the arrival of twins a couple of years ago, Noah started using credit cards for basic expenses, and paying just over the minimum each month. At this point, he owes $70,000 on his cards and his marriage is frayed from bickering over the bills. He wants to be an example to his community, many of whom struggle for years with low incomes and debts, and frankly is afraid of a tarnished reputation if he files bankruptcy. As a result, he adamantly insists on chapter 13 during your initial free consultation with him. What do you tell him? See §§ 1307, 1325(a), 1328, 1329.

13.4. Maggie Smith recently won a prestigious fellowship for young lawyers to develop innovative practices. She has purchased a "taco truck" and plans to drive the truck to streets near factories that employ large numbers of low-income workers. She and a paralegal will offer commonly needed legal services, including consumer bankruptcy, at a reduced cost based on a person's ability to pay (i.e., "low bono"). You were two years ahead of Maggie in law school and have escaped from the litigation division of your large firm into a niche practice in legal professional responsibility and malpractice. Maggie has asked you to donate time on a pro bono basis to help her draft the disclosures that she should give her bankruptcy clients. Besides a retainer agreement, what else will she need? What disclosures should she make and what language will you advise her to include? Are there additional disclosures that you would recommend based on norms of ethical practice? See §§ 526, 527, 528, 707(b)(4).

13.5. You are a member of a law reform commission that is tasked with reform of the consumer bankruptcy system. The Congressperson who funded the commission became interested in the issue after reading this passage in an article:

> I strongly believe that the current consumer bankruptcy system is unjust. I do not use that term lightly; the debate on whether and how much income contribution should be required in the context of debt relief is powerful evidence that "justice" in bankruptcy reflects very different normative beliefs. But the existing system of chapter 7 and chapter 13 is truly built on sand; its very foundation of informed consumer choice is not supported by any evidence. For thirty years, we have known that the sorting between chapter 7 and chapter 13 does not occur based on debtors having different financial circumstances or having different normative preferences. The research consistently shows that the selection of chapter—which itself determines the burdens of filing and the relief received—is determined by local legal culture, attorney steering, and often outright misinformation.

Assume that Congress is resolute that the two-chapter system must go. Your task is clear: recommend either solely a chapter 7 option or solely a chapter 13 option. Be prepared to vote on your position and offer reasons—based on law or policy—to support your position.

POLICY AND PRACTICE

The Bankruptcy Code is more than just a complex law; it is an expression of social policy. It reflects political compromise over conflicting theories of debt relief. While some view relief as morally compelled, others see it as a necessary evil, with a range of opinions in the middle on the risks and benefits of forgiving legal obligations. This assignment introduces theoretical frames for considering some of the contested and competing goals of the consumer bankruptcy system. It discusses the major justifications for the discharge, considering just why it is exactly that we allow families struggling with financial distress to shed their unsecured obligations. These theories are diverse, with economic, moral, and social considerations all in play. Although you had a brief introduction in the first assignment, we have saved this academic exploration until after you learned how the system works in practice. This way you can reflect back critically on what does, and does not, jibe with the theories you find most compelling.

After we present our categorization of the major theories of consumer discharge, we discuss prominent countervailing considerations—why we should *not* have a bankruptcy discharge (or, perhaps more accurately, why a discharge justified under any of the above theories should be narrowly constructed). Congress has gone back and forth over the years on whether we have too much or too little debt discharged in bankruptcy, and various amendments to the bankruptcy laws have reflected this struggle. We also offer a brief comparative look at what other systems do. As the United States wrestles with these issues, countries around the world are adopting consumer bankruptcy laws, sometimes for the first time in their nation's history, that are frequently based on the basic U.S. model of debt relief. All grapple with the tension captured in the quotation from the writer Simone Weil that begins this book: societies are torn between the economic necessity that most debts be paid and the equally compelling need to forgive debts.

Whatever the balance struck, a country needs a system to process debt relief. For better or worse, policymakers in our country have chosen a judicial model—one run by bankruptcy judges, trustees, and, of course, attorneys. We therefore close this reflective assignment with a hard look at the lawyer's role in consumer bankruptcy, with special emphasis on the ethical perils it brings.

Before we embark on this journey, however, we encourage you to think about the role of theory more generally in law. Theory is normative: what *should* the system be? When you switch to the descriptive (what *is* the system?), you will quickly note a normative gap. What we have today might seem like a bit of hodgepodge of various theories of discharge that lacks an overall coherence. But that should come as no surprise. No legal system is driven purely by theory. Congress is a political animal and succumbs to fads, lobbying, and fecklessness. Thus, in analyzing our bankruptcy laws, you must not only consider which theoretical justifications you find most compelling but also the reality of political process that generates those laws—laws that are fraught with both moral dimensions about the obligation to keep promises and the capitalist incentives of the high-profit consumer credit industry.

A. THE THEORIES SUPPORTING "FORGIVING OUR DEBTORS"

The heading of this section deliberately invokes the title of a book two of us (and our sociologist co-author) wrote trying to understand the characteristics of who goes bankrupt in the United States. Indeed, well after Biblical times, this country has embraced forgiveness of debts as an important policy. It has been woven into its social culture nearly from its inception. Our historical narrative is rife with the idea of a new beginning. Bruce H. Mann, Republic of Debtors (2002). Think of immigrants fleeing creditors to the new colonies in the United States, leaving behind the old classes, the old religion, the old ideas—and the old debts. The same pattern repeated itself with the Conestoga wagon setting off for Oregon, and the farmers fleeing the Dust Bowl. The year many historians identify as the close of the American frontier is 1898—the date of the first successful bankruptcy act in the United States.

With such a rich history of financial fresh starts, it is no accident that the United States was and remains perhaps the most debtor-friendly nation in the world.

Accordingly, it is no surprise one of the most oft-invoked quotes in judicial opinions discussing the consumer bankruptcy system is necessity of a bankruptcy law to facilitate a debtor's "fresh start." This concept is often traced to Local Loan Co. v. Hunt, 292 U.S. 234, 244 (1934), but therein the Court cited an earlier case in which it recited that a primary purpose of bankruptcy is to "relieve the honest debtor from the weight of oppressive indebtedness, and permit him to start afresh free from the obligations and responsibilities consequent upon business misfortunes." Williams v. U.S. Fidelity & Guaranty Co., 236 U.S. 549, 554-55 (1915). The idea is one of general forgiveness: honest but unfortunate debtors get a second chance and should not be consigned to a life of debt servitude. As we shall see below, however, many disagree as to whether the source of that forgiveness is economic incentivization, moral duty, or something else. As Professor Karen Gross laments, "Some scholars just reiterate the term *fresh start* in their justifications, saying, for example, that debtors should have an 'opportunity to begin anew' or a 'chance to start over'" without ever explaining their justification for what that fresh start is needed. Karen Gross, Failure and Forgiveness: Rebalancing the Bankruptcy Code 91 (1999). We will try to help you engage those justifications now, and so turn to the major theories of consumer bankruptcy relief and the concerns constraining that relief.

1. Forgiveness

Bankruptcy has always been laden with moral overtones:

> . . . [R]ehabilitation is a goal that says something about the moral instincts of American society. In part, society assists debtors on humanitarian grounds. Rehabilitating debtors is part of the responsibility to treat members of society humanely. It promotes values of human dignity and self-respect. It also enables people and business to be a part of the ongoing credit economy. As was stated in an 1822 letter to Congress on the desirability of a bankruptcy law, bankruptcy can be seen as an "essential attribute of active and humane society. . . . [It is necessary] in vindication of the national humanity." A *New York Times* editorial made a similar point, albeit in a different context, when it observed that a "community is only as strong as the care and respect it gives its weakest members." Debtors are among the weak members of a credit society. If our treatment of them were motivated by retaliation or retribution, we would not be showing care or respect.

Karen Gross, Failure and Forgiveness: Rebalancing the Bankruptcy System 102-03 (1997). Many share Professor Gross's view that the bankruptcy discharge is grounded in a moral obligation to the debtor—a deontic duty to treat that person with full dignity and respect. See Insolvency and Creditor/ Debtor Regimes Task Force, Report on the Treatment of the Insolvency of Natural Persons, World Bank 1, 43 (Dec. 14, 2012) (recommending adoption of insolvency regimes that incorporate human rights principles).

Others agree with the moral obligation to forgive debt, but come at it from a slightly different angle. Society benefits not just through vindication of the individual debtor's dignity, but also from the salutary effect on each person who forgives. As a matter of virtue ethics, forgiving debt can be seen as character-enhancing. Professor Heidi Hurd argues that releasing debtors from debts owed that the debtor cannot pay is an aretaic obligation—an act that cultivates a generous and forgiving character. She argues that "a desire to enforce obligations when doing so would impose upon debtors significant hardship and distress manifests attributes of character that are rightly condemned, rather than admired. Put inversely, the virtuous person does not press his rights against someone when doing so will inflict genuine suffering and psychological despair." Heidi Hurd, The Virtue of Consumer Bankruptcy, in A Debtor's World: Interdisciplinary Perspectives on Debt 221-22 (Ralph Brubaker, Robert Lawless & Charles Tabb eds., 2012).

Do you think Jamie Dimon feels virtuous when he approves writing off millions of dollars of consumer debt as uncollectible each quarter? Or do you think a profit-seeker simply recognizes that blood cannot be drawn from a stone? If the latter, then you are ready to consider our second cluster of considerations for the discharge.

2. *Rehabilitation*

Professor Gross mentioned rehabilitation and its role in human dignity. Other scholars identify rehabilitation as the animating concept of the fresh start, but look at it from a more utilitarian perspective. In this literature, the focus is on returning the debtor to "productive economic participation." Margaret Howard, A Theory of Discharge in Consumer Bankruptcy, 48 Ohio St. L.J. 1047, 1088 (1987). As one of us put it more colorfully, "[S]ociety as a whole also loses when moping bankrupt debtors are distracted from working at their highest and best use level of productivity because they are instead coping with financial ruin." John A.E. Pottow, Private Liability for Reckless Consumer Lending, 2007 U. Ill. L. Rev. 405, 412. This productivity notion of bankruptcy allows the individual debtor to keep future wages and sufficient property so as to stay off the public dole and to maximize society's labor resources.

This theory's deep utilitarianism is expressed by language praising the discharge's capacity to permit "the redeployment of the debtor's human capital." Ronald J. Mann, Making Sense of Nation-Level Bankruptcy Filing Rates, in Consumer Credit, Debt and Bankruptcy: Comparative and International Perspectives 225, 242 (Johanna Niemi, Iain Ramsay & William Whitford eds., 2009). For some, debt relief may be humane for the individual, but that help is given for the greater service of the collective, not out of a moral or social duty to relieve any one individual's suffering. Indeed, there is an almost amoral aspect to the theory. Advocates do not handwring about *why* the debtor went bankrupt. What they care about is that *given* the debtor cannot pay its debts, for whatever reason, what is the best thing for society to do about it today?

Rich sociological analysis has been devoted to the phenomenon of "overindebtedness." European countries—the United Kingdom in particular—are much further ahead on the research front, which considers overindebtedness as arising when existing and foreseeable resources are insufficient for a household to meet its financial commitments without lowering its living standards below what is regarded as a minimum acceptable threshold. Researchers are now trying to measure when the consequences of debt, both for an individual and society, impose unacceptable harms that warrant forgiveness as a policy prescription. See Study on Means to Protect Consumers in Financial Difficulty: Personal Bankruptcy, Datio in Solutum of Mortgages, and Restrictions on Debt Collection Abusive Practices, Fin. Servs. User Group (2012). This scholarly field is evolving, and shows that the division between a deontic and utilitarian explanation of a moral obligation to forgive debt may not be as crisp as one might at first think.

3. *Insurance*

There are clear economic undertones to a rehabilitation of human capital view of discharge. Those undertones become more explicit in a related idea that the bankruptcy discharge is really a form of (mandatory) financial disaster insurance. Sometimes honest but unfortunate debtors hit financial cataclysm, and bankruptcy's fresh start ensures they will not spend the rest of their lives suffering from this faultless economic shock. Barry Adler, Ben

Polak & Alan Schwartz, Regulating Consumer Bankruptcy: A Theoretical Inquiry, 29 J. Legal Stud. 585 (2000) (discussing social insurance theory). This is slightly different from the rehabilitation theory because it implicitly assumes that a substantial cause of bankruptcy is inevitable, i.e., just the nature of the beast when dealing with mass consumer credit (or living life in a financially risky world). Thus, this theory does "care" about the cause of the overindebtedness but from a somewhat actuarial perspective. If a meaningful portion of bankrupt debtors will find themselves in financial distress because of unforeseen or "exogenous" shocks, then protection in the form of public insurance may be efficient. Professor Feibelman summarizes this approach:

> Thus, at least in theory, bankruptcy should be thought of as a potential wage insurance, health insurance, disability insurance, workers' compensation, and divorce insurance program rolled into one. . . . Moving from the realm of theory to that of observation, it appears that bankruptcy does in fact serve the social insurance functions described above. . . . According to one prominent empirical study of consumer bankruptcy filings, nearly two-thirds of debtors cite job interruption or job loss, while 22% of individuals in bankruptcy cite family-related problems—including divorce—in the months leading up to their filing for bankruptcy. That same study found that nearly 20% percent of debtors cite medical problems, which in some cases were likely to be related to injury or disability. . . . It is important to note that some scholars are skeptical of these findings, however, and debate over the determinants of bankruptcy continues to be robust. Some writers have suggested that the causes of bankruptcy are likely to be more endogenous than recent empirical studies suggest. If so, recent studies may underestimate the extent to which over-consumption causes people to become insolvent.
>
> [E]ven the critics of recent empirical studies acknowledge that the causes of many bankruptcies are exogenous to some significant extent. In doing so, they acknowledge the underlying insight of the empirical data—that bankruptcy does function, at least in part, as a form of wage insurance, divorce insurance, disability insurance, and health insurance. To the extent it does so, it is important to bear in mind that bankruptcy serves the same social insurance functions as unemployment insurance, Medicare, disability insurance, workers' compensation, and spousal support laws.

Adam Feibelman, Defining the Social Insurance Function of Consumer Bankruptcy, 13 Am. Bankr. Inst. L. Rev. 129, 158-60 (2005).

A cognate of this insurance view of bankruptcy ties in research on entrepreneurship. Particularly in the United States, with its strong cultural norm of small business capitalism, restyling "consumer" bankruptcy as a necessary component of supporting self-employment and economic innovation is popular: discharge, thus conceived, provides a "cushion for the increased level of risk of financial failure associated with entrepreneurship." Rafael Efrat, The Rise & Fall of Entrepreneurs: An Empirical Study of Individual Bankruptcy Petitioners in Israel, 7 Stan. J.L. Bus. & Fin. 163, 167 (2002).

How realistic is the assumption that many debtors are at risk for financial dislocation? Research suggests that families today are saddled with more exogenous financial risks than in the 1950s or 1970s when filing rates were much lower. See Jacob Hacker, The Great Risk Shift (2006) (describing the higher likelihood of a significant income drop in recent decades); *Two-Income Trap* (explaining link of that financial risk to bankruptcy). Discharging or reorganizing debt can help families right themselves from the financial consequences of job loss, family break-up, or medical problems—factors commonly considered the "big three" of consumer collapse. See *Fragile Middle Class* (documenting the primary explanations that people give for their bankruptcy filings). Compounding the complexity of these empirical studies is uncertainty regarding causation: something may be both a cause and a consequence of financial distress. For example, does poor health cause unmanageable debt because of medical bills and lost wages, or do people in debt suffer poor health because of stress and forgone preventative care? See Melissa B. Jacoby, Does Indebtedness Influence Health? A Preliminary Inquiry, 30 J.L. Med. & Ethics 560 (2002). But it seems fair to conclude that the data suggest a considerable portion of debtors find themselves in bankruptcy not due to too many extravagant trips to the mall but to such less pleasant occurrences as divorce or lay-off.

One empirical point that seems inescapable is that consumer debt in itself seems to correlate with bankruptcy. For example, consumer bankruptcies rose sharply during the 1990s and early 2000s, then fell sharply in 2010, only to rise right back up again. Could those data simply reflect the effect of BAPCPA (effective 2005)? Not necessarily. These filing rates appear to reflect macro-economic trends, the most important of which was the growth in consumer debt. The graph below, courtesy of Professor Robert Lawless, shows the correlation between bankruptcy filings and household debt (data are population- and inflation-adjusted).

U.S. Bankruptcy Filings & Household Debt, 1946 - 2010

The solid line shows the annual number of U.S. bankruptcy filings per 1,000 population. The dashed line shows the amount of "household debt" (total consumer credit plus home mortgages) per capita and inflation-adjusted to 2010 dollars. All data are from U.S. government sources (Administrative Office of U.S. Courts, Census Bureau, Bureau of Economic Analysis, and the Federal Reserve).

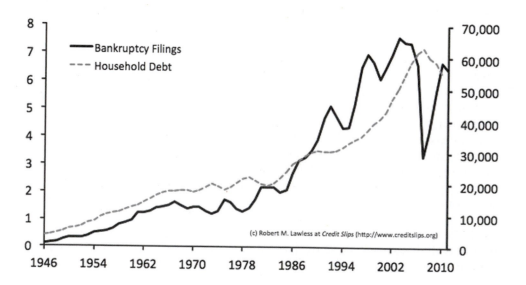

Thus, over a substantial period of time bankruptcy filings have increased hand-in-hand with the amount of debt that U.S. households carry. That trend of 65 years continues into data from 2017. See Robert Lawless, An Explanation for the Low Bankruptcy Rates: Debt, Credit Slips Blog (July 19, 2017, 7:05 AM), https://www.creditslips.org/creditslips/2017/07/an-explanation-for-the-low-bankruptcy-rates-debt.html.

These data suggesting a link between debt and bankruptcy may on the one hand seem obvious—more consumer debt leads to more bankruptcies. But they also support a characterization of the bankruptcy systems as serving an insurance function. Yet this raises even more questions, requiring analysis that depends upon how we conceive of the risk against which we insure. For example, if the insurance is "bad events" insurance, then it may be hard for the debtor to control such exogenous shocks. If the insurance is "debt" insurance, then it may be easier for the debtor to avoid the risks: don't take out debt. However, given that debt has a socially useful function (say, like driving), then the ideal prescription presumably isn't to ban the activity outright, but to minimize its accident costs when the related risks come to fruition. If the insurance covers an interaction between these two (i.e., the presence of debt makes it harder to absorb economic disruption when bad events happen), then the already complex considerations become even more complicated. Accordingly, at a broad level of abstraction, the idea that the bankruptcy discharge acts like a form of public, mandatory financial crisis insurance is surely coherent, but it raises many ancillary questions regarding the nature and scope of the risk insured against.

Moreover, even if we could agree on the nature and scope of risk we are insuring, we might have second-order disputes of how best to design "coverage." For example, adherents may be just as happy disposing with the bankruptcy discharge and implementing a "financial crisis" government assistance program, complete with a claims administration office. Note the comparison with unemployment insurance. Or those of a more mercantile bent note the Aflac duck is squawking away about such insurance being provided by the private market. And should such insurance be optional for the prudent, as is fire insurance, or mandatory for those who engage in inherently risky activity, as is automobile liability insurance? Those of a libertarian inclination chafe at mandatory insurance and they join those of a finger-wagging disposition to say that consumers should have the foresight to plan for their own distress (and their failure to do so should not be bailed out by those smart enough to do so), but others worry about the limited predictive capabilities of consumers and the social consequences of predictive errors.

One's inclination for policy intervention may depend upon whether one believes bankruptcy is a woe limited to the debtor and discharged creditors alone or whether others suffer as well. We know that creditors suffer, and those creditors vary substantially in their ability to spread risk (think of Big Bank vs. Widow Tort Victim). But as for others, "the case for negative bankruptcy externalities is more intuitive than empirical at this juncture." John A.E. Pottow, Private Liability for Reckless Consumer Lending, 2007 U. Ill. L. Rev. 405, 412. It is not even clear what we would try to measure as the "harm" of consumer debt problems. Katherine Porter, The Damage of Debt, 69 Wash. & Lee L. Rev. 979 (2012). Yet some "externalities" are well established. For example, foreclosures during the Great Recession tended to depress the neighboring property values, not just the home subject to the proceeding.

4. Creditor Conduct

The discharge is not just about debtors. Creditors' concerns also shape theories of bankruptcy. Professor Thomas Jackson is the major proponent of the collective action argument grounding the creditor-focused theory of bankruptcy we saw in Assignment 1 (namely, that bankruptcy helps corral hungry creditors into a value-maximizing group). But do those creditors need or want a system that discharges the debt? Jackson says yes, we need a discharge to police creditors from overleveraging debtors. If they go too far, the debtor will go bankrupt and the creditor will have the debt discharged. So the discharge threat "ex post" cabins creditors not to over-burden the debtor "ex ante."

> Discharge policy provides an alternative [to governmental oversight]: it leaves the determination of whether to extend credit to *creditors*, who presumably are better trained in credit policy than are legislators, and who are better able, by observing individual debtors or by employing specific contractual covenants, to monitor individuals' consumption of credit [and] . . . to oversee the individual's credit decisions even when the individual has not fully mortgaged his future. The availability of the right of discharge induces creditors to restrict the individual's credit intake and thus to ensure that he does not seriously underestimate his future needs.

Thomas H. Jackson, The Fresh Start Policy in Bankruptcy Law, 98 Harv. L. Rev. 1393, 1426 (1985). For a challenge to Professor Jackson's proposition that the market-based fear of charge-offs adequately polices lenders from lending to debtors who cannot repay, see, e.g., Pottow, Reckless Lending, supra (discussing literature on credit industry incentives). Professor Ronald Mann has shown that professional creditors like credit card issuers profit greatly from extending credit to financially weak debtors because the substantial fees and interest charges incurred by the debtor are sufficient to offset any losses from discharged principal caused by the unmanageable debt. See Ronald J. Mann, Bankruptcy Reform and the "Sweat Box" of Credit Card Debt, 2007 U. Ill. L. Rev. 375.

Another benefit of the bankruptcy discharge is aimed at creditors, one that they may find painful but that is important to regulators and the economy: it forces lenders to charge off losses from debtors who cannot or will not pay. "Value discovery" is how an economist might label this result. Bankruptcy's reckoning promotes proper account valuation. If this concept seems nebulous, consider how the bifurcation of secured debt in bankruptcy smokes out the value of the collateral.

5. Social Peace

The struggle between the necessity of payment and the necessity of non-payment appears throughout history. The reforms of Solon arose from a tumultuous time in the history of Athens when debtors revolted against their chains of debt, just as the reforms of the Bankruptcy Act arose from periodic financial panics in the United States. David A. Skeel, Debt's Dominion (2003). The social interest in debt rehabilitation is not just keeping people off the public dole, it's also keeping them off the parapets—and away from the polls. So perhaps the simplest "explanation" of the bankruptcy discharge's inclusion in a legal infrastructure largely designed by elites is that it placates the lower orders (or, in stylized economic parlance, reduces "pitchfork costs").

B.   COUNTERVAILING VALUES

All the preceding theories explained why a well-designed legal system might need a bankruptcy discharge. But you should not lose sight of the countervailing values that make the idea of discharging legal obligations unusual, even shocking. We began by considering Professor Gross's observation of the moral obligation to forgive debts, but others may quickly point out that there may be an equal and opposite moral obligation.

> [B]ankruptcy should not merely be a means of violating promises willy-nilly. A promise to repay money is an important legal and moral obligation, neither lightly to be undertaken nor lightly cast away. Filing bankruptcy represents a decision to repudiate promises made in exchange for goods, services, and other promises. Of such promises and reciprocity is the fabric of civil society woven.

Edith H. Jones & Todd J. Zywicki, It's Time for Means-Testing, 1999 BYU L. Rev. 177, 181.

It would be difficult to argue against the proposition that there is widespread support for a moral obligation to keep promises. The consequence of this, however, may be a form of moral stalemate, where each proponent is reduced to an axiomatic first principle. Consider, by way of thought experiment, how we would know whether our bankruptcy law's grounds for nondischargeable debt are immorally narrow—or immorally broad.

Nor are countervailing considerations constrained to the world of moral argument. Returning to the economically focused theory of the discharge premised on an insurance function, one versed in insurance theory may note the countervailing concerns with insurance coverage: fraud and moral hazard. As for fraud, you have seen by now the Code is rife with provisions designed to dismiss bankruptcy petitions of the unworthy.

Moral hazard raises more complex considerations. The concern of moral hazard is excessive activity distorted by the presence of insurance. (Have you driven more quickly over speed bumps in a rental car than your own?) Thus, even if one is all on board with the idea of the bankruptcy discharge providing much-needed insurance, one might also want to plan against moral hazard by preventing "over-use" of bankruptcy. Accordingly, the much-maligned means test might well be much-needed restraint to prevent over-use of the bankruptcy discharge, although it might be blatant overkill. Its proper categorization depends upon whether you believe we have the "correct" level of bankruptcy usage. Note that there are two ways we might worry that an inordinately generous discharge might tempt morally hazardous debtors into bankruptcy. First, we might worry that a debtor facing financial distress today, who must decide whether to belt-tighten or file bankruptcy, will just chose the easy out of bankruptcy if the outcome is too palatable. Second, we might worry about more "upstream" incentives, where debtors deciding whether to take out a big consumer credit loan—say, by buying a big home entertainment system on credit—or save for a rainy day might, again, go for broke (literally), secure in the comfort of bountiful "insurance coverage" by way of the discharge.

From what we know of consumers and their behavioral psychology, the prospect of them pricing in bankruptcy risk to upstream credit decisions is somewhere between unlikely and fanciful. (That is not to say researchers haven't tried—for example, with business-inclined entrepreneurs, see Wei Fan & Michelle J. White, Personal Bankruptcy and the Level of Entrepreneurial Activity, 46 J.L. & Econ. 543 (2003)—but it would be unwise to generalize.)

The current "downstream" incentives, however, may present a different story. Deciding whether to hunker down and struggle with bills or whether to seek refuge in bankruptcy may indeed be a context in which consumers respond to legal incentives. The Congress that enacted BAPCPA clearly thought consumers were so responsive and that there was "too much" bankruptcy. (To describe the debates leading up to BAPCPA's passage as "heated" is an understatement. Suffice it to say, it was a controversial law drafted by the credit industry that superseded the recommendations of the National Bankruptcy Review Commission.) And the number of bankruptcy filings did indeed decrease after that law's enactment, although a widely cited empirical study suggested that the reduction was regressively distributed. See John A.E. Pottow et al., Did Bankruptcy Reform Fail? An Empirical Study of Consumer Debtors, 82 Am. Bankr. L.J. 349 (2008).

Leaving aside whether Congress was correct that there was "too much" bankruptcy (and how we would even know how to assess that contention intelligently), note how the economic concerns of moral hazard intertwine with the moral concerns of declining commitment to promise-keeping discussed above (perhaps putting the "moral" in moral hazard). It could be that Congress thought we had too much bankruptcy because the discharge is too lenient and accessible, so the insurance "pricing" has not been accurately made. Or it could be that it thought we had too much bankruptcy because society was going to heck in a handbasket and losing its moral fiber, sliding down a slippery slope of immorality as slick debtors enjoy a rollicking lifestyle while racking up debts they have no intention of paying. Or it could have been both (or neither). What matters for present purposes is the overlap between the two sources of concern, which come to a head in considering the role social stigma plays in the consumer bankruptcy system. Bankruptcy stigma will both increase the "premium" of the bankruptcy discharge insurance cost and (rightfully, on one moral account) shame people into avoiding the easy way out of discharge vs. promise-keeping. This issue, once again, raises an empirical question: are consumers too willing or too reluctant to file bankruptcy?

The presence of stigma is probably easier to detect than its absence. That doesn't stop some from decrying the decline of stigma. Scant empirical support has been offered for this declining stigma hypothesis, however. See, e.g., F.H. Buckley & Margaret F. Brinig, The Bankruptcy Puzzle, 27 J. Legal Stud. 187 (1998) (using Roman Catholicism and divorce rates as proxies for social disinclination to file bankruptcy). And even those who allege stigma decline cannot agree on its cause. Some perceive it as a consequence of a general moral decline in our society, while others point to the laxity of the bankruptcy laws specifically as deserving the blame. Note that the 1978 Code intentionally sought to destigmatize bankruptcy, for example, by replacing the term "bankrupts" with "debtors."

Considerable empirical data suggest it is unlikely that stigma has declined or disappeared from the bankruptcy system. Most debtors try to hide, not trumpet as economically shrewd, their filings. E.g., Teresa A. Sullivan, Elizabeth Warren & Jay L. Westbrook, Less Stigma or More Financial Distress: An Empirical Analysis of the Extraordinary Increase in Bankruptcy Filings, 59 Stan. L. Rev. 213, 236-39 (2006); Nicola Howell & Rosalind F. Mason, Reinforcing Stigma or Delivering a Fresh Start: Bankruptcy and Future Engagement in the Workforce (2015) 38 U. New S. Wales L.J. 1529, 1530-31; Leon Anderson & Deborah J. Thorne, Managing the Stigma of Personal Bankruptcy, 39 Soc. Focus 77, 83 (2006). Recent research points to a highly complex cluster of consumer attitudes toward the bankruptcy discharge. See Sarah S. Greene, The Bootstrap Trap, 67 Duke L.J. 233, 272-86 (2017) (showing that consumers who embrace a self-sufficiency framework of debt management experience shame when accepting public assistance but end up worse off than those who seek out such assistance).

A related concern to moral hazard is cross-subsidy. Some suggest that allowing debtors to opt out of bankruptcy discharge will help lessen moral hazard. Barry Adler, Ben Polak & Alan Schwartz, supra (arguing that mandatory bankruptcy laws for consumers are inefficient and increase costs to all of us). The broader economic point is that tougher bankruptcy laws make moral hazard less likely and so lower the cost of credit. But also embedded in this reasoning is the idea that if I am smart and prudent, I should not have to shoulder the cost of a mandatory insurance program just because you are not. Although lenders try to credit score, it is tough to tell in advance who will go bankrupt, especially since many bankruptcies are driven by exogenous events unrelated to debtor conduct, such as a job loss at a closed factory. This means if the bankruptcy discharge imposes losses on the lender *ex post* (i.e., after the credit has been extended), those costs will be recouped *ex ante* (lenders do this by spreading costs to the next round of borrowers, pricing it into credit terms, or at the extreme, rationing credit), and those recoupments will be imposed on all borrowers, unfairly burdening the risk-tolerant ones.

Indeed, one claim that emerged during the BAPCPA legislative debates was that each debt-paying American incurs a $400 tax or subsidy in credit charges because of bankruptcy discharges, although no evidence supports the claim. On the other hand, if bankruptcy correctly addresses the moral hazard concern and identifies the honest but unfortunate debtor idealized in *Hunt*, then all is as it should be: losses are distributed among all who borrow, as a cross-subsidy from the nonbankrupt to the bankrupt. While some assert this is unfair to responsible promise-keeping debtors, most accept such loss-spreading as legitimate. As the World Bank Report explains:

> A society that has embraced the good of lending is in a similar position to one that has embraced the benefits of driving. Each carries inevitable risks and casualties, and some form of loss spreading is a healthy way of maximizing and smoothing the benefits for all. An insolvency regime thus represents the trade-off for deregulation of consumer lending.

World Bank, Report on the Treatment of the Insolvency of Natural Persons (2012).

In sum, there is an array of countervailing concerns that counsels caution in the implementation of a bankruptcy discharge. But, like many matters, these concerns often depend upon contestable propositions, some falsifiable with data and some not, but most at least resting on arguments that have a coherent foundation.

C.   COMPARATIVE LESSONS

One point of increasingly important reference is what other countries do, particularly as consumer credit grows rapidly around the world and United States law has had a growing influence. Few countries on the globe had personal debt relief laws of general application as recently in 1990. Most still do not. In 2012, the World Bank reported that two dozen nations have adopted full-fledged insolvency regimes for natural persons. World Bank Report, supra at 18. People in debt may face relentless collection pressures, or creditors may have no effective means for preserving or recovering from assets and income. Until 1984, when Denmark adopted a consumer law, even continental Europe with its highly developed economy had no equivalent to the longstanding chapter 7 and chapter 13 options for U.S. individuals. Comparatively, most bankruptcy systems are less friendly to debtors than the Code—even after BAPCPA imposed the means test. In the Scandinavian countries, for example, someone may only have one insolvency proceeding per lifetime. (That's one way to deal with refilings!) In other places, debtors must affirmatively prove their good faith in seeking relief, an aspect presumed with U.S. petitions unless and until raised by court or creditor objection. See Jason J. Kilborn, Comparative Consumer Bankruptcy (Michael L. Corrado ed., 2007) (surveying European approaches to consumer bankruptcy). On the other hand, the U.S. system may not be all that different from others in practice. Compare the treatment below with the approach taken in evaluating "abuse" under the Code.

Insolvency Applicants Who Can Get Bus Won't Be Allowed a Car

Tough lifestyle conditions to be imposed on people who attempt to write off mortgage debt under the [Irish] Government's new Insolvency regime include a warning that those living on public transport routes will not be allowed to include the running of a car as one of their expenses. The guidelines will also impose lifestyle conditions for families, who will be expected to eat healthily and cut back on leisure activities. Although those who avail of the service will be expected to drop pay-for-view television and private health care, they will be allowed enough money to at least purchase a newspaper and books. In spite of the banks' efforts to depress the level of personal expenditure allowed to those seeking an escape from mortgage arrears, the Insolvency Service has decided that while a "reasonable standard of living does not mean that a person should live at a luxury level neither does it mean that a person should only live at subsistence level." Instead, those attempting to write off mortgage debt "should be able to participate in the life of the community, as other citizens do." [John Drennan, Insolvency Applicants Who Can Get Bus Won't Be Allowed a Car, Independent.ie, Mar. 24, 2013, https://www.independent.ie/irish -news/insolvency-applicants-who-can-get-bus-wont-be-allowed-a-car -29150456.html.]

Some laws are confined to encouraging renegotiation of consumer debts, with little formal relief from the courts. Other nations permit courts to discharge unpaid debts, leaving creditors to accept whatever payment is approved by the court or mandated by statute. For an excellent and concise overview of European approaches, see Kilborn, *supra*.

Korea is an illustrative case study of the momentum toward more generous relief. After a consumer debt crisis that saw millions of South Koreans hopelessly indebted on credit cards and other consumer loans, Korea enacted a "rehabilitation" proceeding that provides for the debtor to keep paying the original debts without interest for eight years; at that point, the debtor receives a discharge. Before that regime, Korean consumer bankruptcy did not usually result in discharge but was a mechanism for enforcing and strengthening creditors' rights.

The U.S. Code's days as paragon may be waning. One particular trend of note is the development of special regimes for low-income, no-asset filings, such as the U.K.'s Debt Relief Order (https://www.gov.uk/options-for -paying-off-your-debts/debt-relief-orders). New Zealand and Canada have similar summary proceedings that avoid court and are purely administrative to save time and money for all. The World Bank's Working Group on the Treatment of the Insolvency of Natural Persons, however, was careful to avoid affirmative prescriptions, stating that its purpose was merely to offer "guidance" on the "opportunities and challenges encountered in the development of an effective regime." Id. at 3-4. You might reflect on the expedited processing these countries are using for "hopeless" cases and compare the fact that the 90+% full chapter 7 cases in the United States yield no unsecured creditor dividend.

D.   ETHICAL ISSUES IN CONSUMER PRACTICE

The theoretical complexity we have just explored means that any given judge may have a different idea of just what the bankruptcy system is trying to do, which makes representing debtors and creditors in the consumer system challenging (and fun). As if those challenges weren't enough, there are special ethical puzzles a lawyer must solve when working in this system that is built upon discharging debtors. While the general rules of professional responsibility apply in bankruptcy, there is an additional overlay of bankruptcy-specific rules and concerns, such as special rules for fee approval. Here, we see the consequences of those rules running up against a modern system dominated by high-volume practice.

In re SPICKELMIER
469 B.R. 903 (Bankr. D. Nev. 2012)

MARKELL, Bankruptcy Judge.

The hearing on this Rule 9011 Order to Show Cause did not start auspiciously. After reserving a half-day for the hearing, the court waited to call the matter to allow debtors' counsel, who was subject to the order and whose tardy arrival the court anticipated, extra time to arrive. After waiting almost ten minutes, the court took appearances, and only one lawyer—for a creditor—entered an appearance. One debtor was also present.

Without any appearance by the attorney or law firm named in the Order to Show Cause, the court indicated it would take the matter under submission and then prepared to adjourn. At this point, the debtor present asked to be heard, and the court allowed him to speak. As he was expressing his concerns about the poor quality of his counsel's representation, his attorney—Jeremy Mondejar of the law firm of Barry Levinson & Associates—finally arrived. He was approximately 15 minutes late. As he approached the lectern, he turned on his laptop computer, balanced it in one hand, and began scanning its screen apparently to determine what the hearing was about. He then made his appearance.

The lawyer's subsequent performance, as detailed below, shows that he was unaware of what had been filed in the case and ignorant of the contents of the Order to Show Cause at issue. He floundered, showing an almost complete lack of preparation. It was painful for all in the courtroom, from the client who saw his money being wasted, to the court staff who all too often had seen similar performances from the same attorney, to the court who had to endure silences—sometimes approaching 30 seconds—as Mr. Mondejar attempted to understand and answer the court's questions from information on his computer screen.

Were there ever a time to use "fail," as the contemporary vernacular permits, it is now, and in reference to this deplorable display of legal representation: it was an epic fail.

The Order to Show Cause

[The court] set an order to show cause given the circumstances under which Mr. Levinson's office submitted it. In particular, it required Mr. Levinson's office to appear and show cause why the filing of the OST [Order Shortening Time—Eds.] Motion did not violate Rule 9011. (*Id.* at 1). After the court informed counsel of its concerns, the order specifically advised counsel to be prepared to discuss the following at the hearing on the order to show cause:

(i) why he filed an OST Motion for the same motion, which was previously opposed and which this court denied on September 13, 2011,

(ii) why he has failed to disclose both the previous motion, and the order denying same, in his OST Motion; and

(iii) why he did not notify the party who opposed the previous motion in the attorney information sheet as required by Local Rule 9006(a) (and why the date of notification of the Office of the United States Trustee was in June, when the OST Motion is dated in September).

(*Id.* at 1-2). The court also warned counsel that he should be prepared to address "why the OST Motion, which does not contain any information that would help the court find a basis upon which to grant the relief requested, does not violate [Rule] 9011." (*Id.* at 2). In particular, the court requested that counsel be prepared to offer specific examples, supported by admissible evidence, of the prejudice referred to in the Levinson Affidavit. (*Id.*)

The Show Cause Hearing

The court scheduled the show cause hearing for October 12, 2011 at 9:30 A.M. (*Id.* at 1). It was the only matter on calendar, and the court had set aside a half day for it. The court, having anticipated that counsel would be late, waited to call the matter almost 10 minutes after its scheduled time. With only counsel for Bank of Nevada entering an appearance, the court took the matter under submission and prepared to adjourn. (*Id.* at 4). When one of the Debtors, Dr. James Spickelmier, asked to be heard, the court went back on the record. (*Id.*) Dr. Spickelmier expressed his dissatisfaction with the representation he had received from Mr. Levinson's office. (*Id.*) He stated that counsel had previously failed to appear in court, that counsel had twice assured him that he would appear at the show cause hearing, and that counsel had received payment of over $5,000 for services rendered in this case. (*Id.* at 4-5). At approximately 9:45 A.M., almost 15 minutes after the hearing's scheduled time, Mr. Mondejar, an attorney from Mr. Levinson's office, interrupted Dr. Spickelmier and entered an appearance as set forth in the introduction above. (*Id.* at 6).

When asked why he was 15 minutes late, Mr. Mondejar explained that he "just got caught up in traffic, and . . . was trying to look up some notes . . . online." (*Id.*) From that point, Mr. Mondejar continued to stare at his laptop computer as he struggled to respond to the simplest of queries by the court. As he read from his laptop, Mr. Mondejar successfully identified the matter before the court: "this is [the] order to show cause for the vacation of . . . the order to dismiss." (*Id.* at 7). But Mr. Mondejar only managed to tread water for so long; he painfully floundered through the remainder of the hearing.

When the court asked Mr. Mondejar for his response to the Order to Show Cause, eyes fixated on his computer screen, he replied:

> Okay. We were going to convert this. We're going to convert this to a Chapter 11, and he was over the debt limit for a 13. And we believe it's in the best interest, and it's just that we . . . didn't have the proper time to do all that stuff, and he's over the debt limit, so, I mean, we just need the time to do that stuff, your Honor.
> (*Id.* at 7-8).

In an attempt to shepherd Mr. Mondejar through the hearing, the court quoted portions from the Order to Show Cause. Specifically, the court directed Mr. Mondejar's attention to its request for admissible evidence demonstrating the existence of the prejudice referred to in the Levinson Affidavit, the prejudice which supposedly necessitated an order shortening time. (*Id.* at 8-9). The only evidence Mr. Mondejar was prepared to offer, after consulting with Dr. Spickelmier during the hearing, was that a notice of foreclosure had been placed on the Debtors' door two weeks before the hearing. This action, however, would have occurred *after* the filing of the OST Motion. (*Id.* at 11).

Similarly disappointing was Mr. Mondejar's explanation for why Mr. Levinson's office had filed a motion, to be heard on shortened time, that was identical to a previous motion, which the court had denied, and why the later filing contained no mention of the previous denial. (*Id.*) He had none. (*Id.*) All he had was what he could read from his computer screen. This was the lowest moment in attorney representation the court has ever witnessed.

II. ANALYSIS OF RULE 9011 VIOLATIONS

[The court examined the pleading and appearance under the standard for attorney conduct set forth in Fed. R. Bankr. P. 9011 and ruled that the firm had committed multiple violations.]

III. DISGORGEMENT OF FEES UNDER SECTION 329

Section 329(b) authorizes the court to "examine the reasonableness of a debtor's attorney fees and, if such compensation exceeds the reasonable value of any such services, the court may cancel any such agreement, or order the return of any such payment, to the extent excessive." Hale v. U.S. Trustee, 509 F.3d 1139, 1147 (9th Cir. 2007) (internal modifications and quotations omitted). The court's Order to Show Cause also put Mr. Levinson's office on notice of a potential disgorgement under this section. It stated that one of the sanctions the court could impose was an "order . . . to disgorge fees under the authority of 11 U.S.C. § 329." (Dkt. No. 71, p. 2).

The reasonable value of services rendered by a debtor's attorney "is a question of fact to be determined by the particular circumstances of each case. The requested compensation may be reduced if the court finds that the work done was excessive or of poor quality." 3 Collier on Bankruptcy ¶329.04[1] (Alan N. Resnick and Henry J. Sommer, eds., 16th ed. 2011) (citing *Hale*, 509 F.3d 1139). *See also* Hale v. U.S. Trustee (In re Basham), 208 B.R. 926, 933 (B.A.P. 9th Cir. 1997) (affirming bankruptcy court's order to disgorge fees that were unreasonable given the lack of contemporaneous time records and the failure to provide competent and complete representation).

The work counsel performed for the Debtors in this case reflects a lack of competence and diligence that does not deserve to be compensated. Initially, Mr. Levinson's office filed a case for Debtors for which they were not eligible. Their debts clearly exceeded the debt limit for Chapter 13; although the applicable debt limit at the time of filing permitted only $360,475 of unsecured debt, the Debtors' schedules, prepared by Mr. Levinson's office, listed a total of the non-contingent, liquidated unsecured debts of $583,888.13.

After filing for Debtors a petition for relief under a chapter for which they were not eligible, Mr. Levinson's office negotiated a stipulation for conversion or dismissal with the Chapter 13 Trustee, but failed to comply with it, resulting in the dismissal of the Debtors' case. Counsel then attempted to remedy this failing by moving for reconsideration, but he did not appear at the hearing on the motion. Thereafter, counsel moved for an order shortening time on a motion identical to the one the court previously heard and denied on regular time, without citing to any legal authority that supported the filing. Worse, when the court held the hearing on the Order to Show Cause issued with respect to these filings, counsel failed to provide any support for its actions, despite being warned to come to court prepared to provide such support. Given the poor quality of the services rendered by Mr. Levinson's office in this matter, the court finds that the reasonable value of those services is zero, that is, $0.00. Pursuant to Section 329, which provides the court a separate and independently sufficient basis upon which it can order the disgorgement of fees, the court hereby orders that Mr. Levinson's office disgorge all monies paid by the Debtors in this Chapter 13 case. [The court also imposed sanctions under Rule 9011, including referral to the State Bar of Nevada.]

———

While it is hard to make money at "zero, that is, $0.00" per case, the reality is that even the highest-quality bankruptcy attorneys are working with clients who are, to put it mildly, tight for cash. One solution to reduce attorneys' fees and increase access to representation is to automate much of the routine practice. Technology ranging from software to complete the bankruptcy forms to robo-dialers to remind debtors of appointments drives down the cost per case. But such capital investments only make sense if amortized over a high-volume practice. Yet certain "bankruptcy mills" draw scorn for behavior different only in degree, but not in kind, from that lambasted in *Spickelmier*, such as attorneys wandering around § 341 meetings politely asking people if they happen to be their client. One court faced with a "franchising" law firm that centrally processed cases but farmed out representation to local counsel was not impressed:

> Leaving it to a lay person to meet with the client, go over the petition and schedules, verify their accuracy, explain the ramifications, answer questions, and obtain the signature is beyond the pale in this Court. This is unacceptable practice. . . . Local attorneys joining multi-jurisdictional law firms as local or limited partners cannot be both tall and short. An attorney cannot claim to be a partner in the firm and file cases with the Court as lead counsel, but yet claim no responsibility for what happens in the main office on the files the attorney decides to take.

Robbins v. Delafield (In re Williams), 2018 Bankr. LEXIS 382, at *89–91 (Bankr. W.D. Va. Feb. 12, 2018).

On the other hand, presumably for fear of being overwhelmed, few legal services organizations help with bankruptcy cases, and *pro se* filers fare poorly, especially in chapter 13. Why should cost-saving technology be pooh-poohed in the consumer bankruptcy world when it is lauded as "efficient" and "competitive" in a high-end corporate legal practice? In *Spickelmier*, the debtor's counsel tried essentially the same argument. Neither sat well with the court, but the high-volume nature of the system is one of the very attributes that allows widespread representation in the first place. Is half a loaf better than none (assuming it is not filled with weevils)? On the third hand, we know personally a number of consumer debtor lawyers who would never wander into court unprepared and who appear to do a fine job for their clients, often under difficult circumstances, so perhaps these protestations, while grounded in reality, also have a touch of excusing-making.

Whatever may be the case, clearly consumer debtor representation is not for the faint of heart. The attorney has the usual duties of zealous representation but also faces additional obligations under the Code regarding the scope of representation that Congress has injected into the attorney-client relationship. §§ 524(c), 526. Add to this the scrutiny of their fees and practices that most other nonbankruptcy lawyers rarely have to endure, it's a wonder anyone is drawn to the field at all. (It must be the high esteem other members of the bar hold for these colleagues.) Attorneys are often one step away from landing in hot water. At the same time, it is not unusual to hear successful lawyers in this field describe their personal satisfaction with helping "real people" rather than giant corporations and making a quite decent living in the process.

Periodically over the last 50 years, there have been calls to eliminate or reduce the role of debtor's counsel. Some have proposed an administrative agency that would assist consumers and adjudge relief, thereby also eliminating courts and trustees. Others have called for greater simplicity in the bankruptcy system to make it more accessible for the *pro se* debtor.

> The new consumer bankruptcy system should be much simpler. It is not possible to solve every problem in a high-volume legal system. Undoubtedly, a simpler system would eliminate some of the "debtor friendly" tools of the

Bankruptcy Code. In its place would be a system of rough justice, but one in which the rough justice is nearly universally delivered. Policy makers need to move beyond the traditional model of sophisticated lawyers providing tailored legal advice and accept that cost concerns mean that consumers will have only very limited access to legal counsel. To make that counseling worthwhile, lawyers need to spend their time gathering factual information from clients. In the current system, counseling by a lawyer who is guided by conventional norms of professionalism likely entails mapping out the twists and turns of the Bankruptcy Code to help the client consider options.

See Katherine Porter, The Pretend Solution: An Empirical Study of Bankruptcy Outcomes, 90 Tex. L. Rev. 103 (2011). Other scholarship points to bankruptcy as unusually successful in aiding consumers in financial distress, comparing its procedures and results with public assistance systems such as disability and welfare. One big difference in bankruptcy is the presence of the debtors' lawyers, who enforce consumer protection statutes both inside and outside bankruptcy cases and lend professionalism and efficiency to the system. They even coalesce to lobby for pro-debtor legal reforms. See Angela Littwin, The Affordability Paradox: How Consumer Bankruptcy's Greatest Weakness May Account for Its Surprising Success, 52 Wm. & Mary L. Rev. 1933, 2009-20 (2011).

We revisit ethical issues in bankruptcy practice near the end of the book in the context of business reorganization. At that time, we will consider again whether the across-the-board nature of the rules of professional responsibility, including the bankruptcy-specific provisions related to fees and conflicts, work well in a system that covers everything from individual households to the largest corporations in the world. For now, we close by noting how the current consumer bankruptcy system, whether theoretically well-grounded or an unprincipled mess of legislative compromise, is a judicial one driven by lawyers.

Problem Set 14

14.1. Congresswoman Herring opposed BAPCPA, and her district has been pummeled hard in recent years by rising unemployment and plummeting home values. She wants your recommendation for one concrete consumer bankruptcy reform that she could introduce and push through. Longer term, there is a good think tank in her state that needs more government work, and she would like to include in her bill a requirement for a consumer bankruptcy study. For that purpose, she wants to know the most important factual question that could be answered by empirical research as well as some idea of what kind of data would be necessary to answer it. She's a practical woman, so suggest something that can actually be done.

14.2. You are thinking of doing an independent study with your bankruptcy professor, who said yes on the condition that you put together an outline of your proposed topic: identifying and documenting the harms of unmanageable debt. The professor suggested that you begin by identifying the possible effects of debt that might exist and that you include individual, economic, and social harms. To get you started, the professor pointed you to the discussion of debt's effects on health in the text. Make your list of areas for research.

14.3. Milton Hulme faced imminent home foreclosure. He had heard success stories from his neighbors about how bankruptcy helped them save their homes. Choosing not to base his decision whether to file bankruptcy solely on anecdotal evidence, he scheduled a free consultation with Chaz Chadbourne, a lawyer certified by the state bar in consumer bankruptcy. During the initial consultation, Milton was very clear about his motivation for considering bankruptcy: to save his home! Chaz explained how bankruptcy works generally and that chapter 7 is the type of bankruptcy with which he is most familiar given that "most people file under that chapter." Milton engaged Chaz to prepare and file his chapter 7 petition. When Milton's mortgage company moved for relief from the stay, Chaz filed an opposition and Chaz then requested an additional fee from Milton, explaining that it is his standard practice to charge an à la carte fee for contested matters and that $100 is the going rate. The initial retainer agreement expressly stated that "contested matters and adversary proceedings" were subject to additional fees. When Milton protested that he could not afford the $100, Chaz expressed his condolences, wished him luck, and withdrew for nonpayment. Nobody appeared at the hearing, and the bankruptcy court lifted the stay; Milton's home was sold.

Milton is devastated at the loss of his home and has called you, another board-certified local bankruptcy attorney asking if you'll file a malpractice action against Chaz. What is your analysis?

14.4. Rainbow and Blue Riley are married. They jointly filed two *pro se* bankruptcy petitions in the past 18 months. The court dismissed both petitions for failure to complete the required credit counseling. In the order dismissing the second case, the bankruptcy court warned that if the debtors filed another bankruptcy without first completing the required credit counseling, the couple would be barred under § 105 from ever filing for bankruptcy protection again. Preparing once again to file bankruptcy to prevent the imminent foreclosure of their home, the couple chose to retain a high-volume consumer bankruptcy firm, Silverman LLC, to get things right. They provided Silverman's staff with all of the information required to file the petition and schedules. After confirming that nothing further was needed on their part, the happy couple left the country on business. When Silverman reviewed the petition and schedules, he noticed the debtors had failed to complete the required credit counseling. Per the usual procedure, his staff had helped the Rileys create a log-in and work through the counseling at computer terminals in his office dedicated to this purpose. Using the Rileys' log-in, he signed into the counseling program, which showed that the Rileys had completed 95% of the course. To ensure the petition was filed in time to prevent the foreclosure, Silverman completed the last two screens on the computer test: inputting the Social Security numbers and confirming that all the information was correct. The program then generated a certificate of counseling, which was filed with the court. The § 341 meeting is in a week. What is Silverman's next step?

PART III

BUSINESS BANKRUPTCY: FOUNDATIONS

"It was 1961. Boom times, stability, easy credit . . . and of course none of the other entering classmen at law school thought of specializing in insolvency claims."

Section 1

Introduction

The upcoming assignments provide an overview of various responses to businesses that are not paying their debts or are facing other financial problems. We start, as we did in the consumer materials, by exploring a creditor's tools at state law. We then turn to the collective approach of liquidation bankruptcy, which is sometimes invoked involuntarily by creditors against the debtor. We close this introduction to business bankruptcy with an overview of chapter 11 reorganization, looking at the control of the "debtor in possession" as a crucial and distinguishing feature of the reorganization process. We spread these topics out over the next two assignments.

RECOVERING FROM BUSINESS DEBTORS

In this assignment, we first examine the legal tools under state and non-bankruptcy federal law that creditors and debtors have available in the event of financial default. We start with the most primal creatures, writs of execution used by unsecured creditors to levy on assets. We then move from one-off solitary collection techniques to collective ones at state law. We end the assignment by examining the ultimate collective collection technique: liquidation in bankruptcy, including the involuntary bankruptcy petitions that creditors can file. Knowledge of theoretical, empirical, and doctrinal concerns that arise in using chapter 7 for businesses is foundational to studying the reorganization bankruptcy most common with businesses.

A. BUSINESS COLLECTION TOOLS

At state collections law, the same rules apply to businesses when they do not pay their debts as to consumers, albeit with greater complexity. One important distinction is that many of the protective statutes regarding consumer debt collection have no application in the business context. It is fine to send a corporation a postcard to collect a debt or call them at all hours, and there is no minimum "wage" amount protected. Nor do corporations need exemptions for homesteads and heirlooms. On the one hand, this makes business debt collection simpler (and more ruthlessly fun). On the other hand, businesses are more likely to have multiple creditors with complicated loan provisions and overlapping claims to collateral (first, second, and third lien financing, with mezzanine debt, subordination agreements, cross-collateralization, and other financing exotica that might make English majors scramble to check the drop-add deadline for this course.)*

The writ remains the legal workhorse for collecting from a business, just as it is for consumers. While the writ of garnishment for employee-debtors

---

* Do not fear. Between us (including double and switched majors) we have: American Studies, Anthropology, Government, Philosophy, Psychology, Speech Therapy, and, of course, English. You'll be just fine.

studied in Assignment 2 is the most common, a veritable cornucopia of writs is available depending on the jurisdiction. Each has a specific purpose, often designed to collect a certain kind of property. In the business context, the variety of writs is important because of the diversity of businesses' assets. For example, specific property can be seized and held by a writ of *sequestration*, and a secured creditor seeking some judicial imprimatur of its repossession can go through the formal process of getting writ of *replevin*, just as a lienholder might file a writ *detinue*. Most of these have riveting statutory twists, so each state's laws must be consulted for the details of specific writs.

A creditor can keep coming back to these processes until the judgment is satisfied or can use different types of writs to try to collect as much as possible from as many assets as possible. If the creditor does not take any collection action, however, the judgment falls into *dormancy* and must be *revived* to permit new writs to be issued. If a judgment has been dormant for a long period, such as ten years in some jurisdictions, it expires under a limitation period, and a new judgment on the merits is needed to permit collection.

One area of fertile recovery from businesses for unsecured creditors is real estate. Recall that unsecured creditors fare poorly with real estate against consumers, whose real estate assets, if any, are often limited to mortgage-encumbered and/or exempt homesteads. But businesses often have multiple parcels of realty, some of which may be worth millions of dollars. To recover from a debtor's real property, the creditor *records* a judicial lien on a debtor's real property. This recordation often requires merely taking a copy of a judgment in the creditor's favor to the recorder's office in the county where the property is located. Recording a judgment against real property is often the fastest and cheapest post-judgment collection step a creditor can take. Recordation, like levy on personal property, ensures a creditor's place in the payment priority when the property is sold. For a nominal recording fee, the creditor effectively ties up the debtor's land, often preventing any resale because no purchaser will touch such title-clouded property. A few states, notably California, allow the recording of a judgment to create a lien on the debtor's personal property (such a recording is filed in the same office where security interests are perfected, not the county real estate offices). See Cal. Civ. Proc. Code § 697.510 (West 2010). When that personal property is a business's equipment, that recording can have some bite.

Writs and recording statutes supplement other tools. Many states allow "turnover" proceedings, in which a creditor can pursue a court order requiring the debtor to reveal assets and then turn over the assets to the creditor or the sheriff for sale. Disobedience is punishable by contempt. Another collection device is the statutory or common law lien. These liens give a creditor priority in certain debtor property by operation of law. The most common example is perhaps the artisan's lien, which is a possessory lien on personal property of the debtor. It entitles a garage mechanic (the artisan) to keep a car (the debtor's property) until the repair bill is paid or to sell the car if necessary to satisfy the charges (the lien). Another example, close to home for a law student, is the "charging lien," arising either by common law or by statute, given to an attorney with respect to the proceeds of a successful litigation. Mechanics' liens and construction liens can tie up real estate developments, too, so are frequently used in business disputes. Both state and federal law create certain statutory liens. The most significant for businesses are probably tax liens (although consumers get dinged with those too). The priorities accorded to statutory liens against competing consensual liens are specifically recognized in UCC § 9-333. Trust fund statutes also give certain creditors special priorities, notably in construction cases. These laws deem the debtor a "trustee" of certain property for the favored creditors, who, as "beneficiaries" of the statutory trust, effectively get a priority in that property. These arise frequently in tax and family law.

A final unique aspect of business collections is that larger businesses span multiple jurisdictions. For example, recording is usually by county, not by state, and any sizable business will own realty in multiple counties. For judgments, the common law method to collect in another state was to file a new lawsuit in the location of the asset, serving a summons, and so forth, resulting in a new local judgment in the enforcing state. Nearly all states have adopted the Uniform Enforcement of Foreign Judgments Act, which provides streamlined procedures. Moving farther afield, the Uniform Foreign Money-Judgments Recognition Act provides for enforcement in the United States of judgments from another country without a showing of reciprocity (a frequent requirement for cross-border judgment recognition). As for federalism, judgments obtained in a federal district court are enforceable in that court using procedures available in the state where the court sits, as well as any additional federal recovery tools. 28 U.S.C. § 1962; Fed. R. Civ. P. 64 and 69.

All these tools, of course, depend on the creditor's ability to find the debtor's assets. Law school hypotheticals about the collection process typically skip the hardest part: getting information about the existence, location, and ownership status of property subject to levy. Information is crucial not only to permit use of the execution process but also to avoid mistakes that might expose the judgment creditor to liability, such as damages for attaching a different debtor's property or seizing property in which a third party has a superior interest. Federal Rule of Civil Procedure 69 and most state rule analogues permit the judgment creditor to conduct discovery concerning the debtor's assets and affairs.

Sometimes businesses will even jump for pre-judgment remedies, fearful of rapidly dissipating assets. A writ of *attachment* helps here, but it is not as easy to get as a general writ of fi. fa. (short for *fieri facias*, which is the fancy-pants word for execution). Attachment usually requires a showing of facts to establish the likelihood of imminent concealment, harm, loss, or transfer of an asset. To guard against abuse of process, creditors are usually required to post a bond. The Constitution provides constraints, too. Indeed, while law developed in cases such as Mitchell v. W.T. Grant Co., 416 U.S. 600 (1974), and North Georgia Finishing, Inc. v. Di-Chem, Inc., 419 U.S. 601 (1975), were animated by consumer debtor plight and the risk of false deprivation prior to adjudication, businesses enjoy these sorts of protections as well. See, e.g., Grupo Mexicano de Desarrollo, S.A. v. Alliance Bond Fund, Inc., 527 U.S. 308 (1999) (rejecting the British-style "*Mareva* injunction" that freezes all a debtor's assets pending trial as beyond the equity jurisdiction of federal courts).

The final kicker is that even if a creditor can find assets, it still has to cajole the sheriff to levy on them. See Abercia v. Kingvision Pay-Per-View, Ltd., 217 S.W.3d 688 (Tex. Ct. App. 2007) (suing sheriff for declining to levy on bar in "rough part of town" after ten o'clock at night, even though cash receipts only arrived in the wee evening hours, and winning judgment *against the sheriff* for the underlying levy amount).

With all these legal tools, the business creditor can resort to numerous strategies to seek repayment when demand letters and leverage fail to do the job. But with the sophisticated businesses in the modern economy come complicated questions on what exactly is a collectible asset.

OFFICE DEPOT, INC. v. ZUCCARINI
621 F. Supp. 2d 773 (N.D. Cal. 2007)

ILLSTON, District Judge.

On December 14, 2000, the District Court for the Central District of California entered a judgment for Office Depot, against Zuccarini individually and d.b.a. "Country Walk," in the amount of $100,000 with an additional $5,600 due in attorney's fees. Office Depot subsequently assigned the right to receive all payments under the judgment, including interest, to DS Holdings. On December 19, 2006, this Court issued a Writ of Execution of Judgment, pursuant to California Code of Civil Procedure section 699.510, for the recovery of Zuccarini's outstanding debt. On February 20, 2007, this Court issued an order requiring the production and preservation of documents relating to Zuccarini's substantial domain name portfolio. . . . [O]n May 15, 2007, the Court denied DS Holdings' request for a turnover order from the Court requiring third-party domain name "registrars" to turn over internet domain names owned by Zuccarini. . . .

DISCUSSION

In opposition to DS Holdings' application . . . Zuccarini raises a more fundamental issue: whether the Northern District of California is the appropriate place to levy upon the domain names at issue. This is apparently an issue of first impression.

The California Code of Civil Procedure provides: "after entry of a money judgment, a writ of execution shall be issued by the clerk of the court upon application of the judgment creditor and shall be directed to the levying officer *in the county where the levy is to be made*. . . ." Cal. Code Civ. P. § 699.510(a) (emphasis added). . . . Under the California Code of Civil Procedure, levy is "made" in a variety of ways, depending on the type of property. See id. §§ 700.010-700.200. In all cases, however, the property exists in some form in the county. *See id.*

The first inquiry here, therefore, is whether domain names constitute "property" for purposes of the California Code of Civil Procedure. If they do, the second inquiry is where the property comprising or containing the domain names exists.

These inquiries first require a basic exploration of what a domain name is. Judge Whyte's decision in Coalition for ICANN Transparency, Inc. v. VeriSign, Inc., 464 F. Supp. 2d 948, 951-53 (N.D. Cal. 2006), provides a helpful explanation of domain names, registrars, and registries.

> The hierarchy of each domain name is divided by periods. Thus, reading a domain name from right to left, the portion of the domain name to the right of the first period is the top-level domain ("TLD"). TLDs include.com,.gov,. net., and .biz. Each TLD is divided into second-level domains identified by the designation to the left of the first period, such as "example" in "example. com" or "example.net." . . . Each domain name is unique and thus can only be registered to one entity. A domain name is created when it is registered with the appropriate registry operator. A registry operator maintains the definitive database, or registry, that associates the registered domain names with the proper IP numbers for the respective domain name servers. The domain name servers direct Internet queries to the related web resources. A registrant can register a domain name only through companies that serve as registrars for second level domain names. Registrars accept registrations for new or expiring domain names, connect to the appropriate registry operator's TLD servers to determine whether the name is available, and register available domain names on behalf of registrants. . . .

In this case, DS Holdings sought a writ of execution in this district because the .net and .com registry, VeriSign, is located here. The registrars of the domain names at issue, however, are not located in this district; they are located in Virginia, Germany, Washington, and Israel. One issue, therefore, is whether the domain names exist at the registry, or at the registrars. Before reaching this issue, however, the Court must address whether, even if they exist in this district, domain names are "property" subject to levy under the California Code of Civil Procedure.

In Kremen v. Cohen, 337 F.3d 1024, 1029 (9th Cir. 2003), the Ninth Circuit . . . answered in the affirmative, concluding that a registrant has "an intangible property right in his [or her] domain name. . . ." Id. at 1030.

As "intangible property," domain names appear to be covered by the California Code of Civil Procedure levy provisions. Section 695.010 thereof provides: "Except as otherwise provided by law, all property of the judgment debtor is subject to enforcement of a money judgment." Section 699.710 provides, in pertinent part, that "all property that is subject to enforcement of a money judgment . . . is subject to levy under a writ of execution to satisfy a money judgment." Accordingly, the Court concludes that domain names owned by Zuccarini and existing in California are subject to levy under a writ of execution.

As mentioned, the second issue is whether the domain names are located in this district. DS Holdings contends that because the.com and. net registry, VeriSign, is located in this district, the domain names at issue are also located here. DS Holdings' argument is strongly supported by the Anticybersquatting Consumer Protection Act of 1999 ("ACPA"), 15 U.S.C. § 1125(d). Under ACPA, Congress provided for in rem jurisdiction over domain names, in certain circumstances, "in the judicial district in which the domain name registrar, domain name registry, or other domain name authority that registered or assigned the domain name is located. . . .” 15 U.S.C. § 1125(d)(2)(A). ACPA also provides: “In an in rem action under this paragraph, a domain name shall be deemed to have its situs in the judicial district in which . . . the domain name registrar, registry, or other domain name authority that registered or assigned the domain name is located. . . .” Id. § 1125(d)(2)(C)-(C)(i). ACPA thus strongly suggests an intent on the part of the United States Congress to treat domain names as property existing in both the location of the registry, and the location of the registrar. See also Mattel v. Barbie-Club.com, 310 F.3d 293, 302 (2d Cir. 2002) (“it is the presence of the domain name itself—the ‘property that is the subject of the jurisdiction’—in the judicial district in which the registry or registrar is located that anchors the in rem action and satisfies due process and international comity.”).

While ACPA suggests this is the appropriate court to oversee levy of the domain names, Zuccarini argues that practical considerations suggest otherwise. The registrars handle the day to day management of domain names. The registry, in fact, apparently never interacts with domain name owners. Zuccarini argues, therefore, that anyone who wants to alter the ownership of a domain name, including a sheriff or marshal seeking to execute a judgment, must do so through the registrars. This practical consideration is highlighted by the fact that in this case DS Holdings has interacted solely with the registrars in its attempts to levy upon the domain names. To the Court's knowledge, DS Holdings has not interacted with the registry—VeriSign—and does not seek to do so.

As discussed above, writs of execution are directed to the county where levy is to be made. If these proceedings force the registrars to change the ownership of the domain names, then arguably levy will be made at the locations of the registrars, which in this case, all fall outside of the Northern District. See § 701.010 (“when levy is made . . . on a third person, the third person . . . shall deliver to the levying officer any of the property levied upon that is in the possession or under the control of the third person at the time of levy . . .”).

Despite the day to day control registrars exhibit over the ownership of domain names, however, the registry maintains the records that ultimately determine the existence and ownership of domain names. See Mattel, 310 F.3d at 296 n. 2 (“The domain name ‘registry’ . . . is the single official entity that maintains a list (‘a registry’) of all ‘top-level’ domain names and that maintains all official records regarding the registrations of such names.”) (citing David Bender, Computer Law § 3D.03[3] at 3D-56). In the internet hierarchy, registrars answer to the registries. Furthermore, under ACPA, at least one district court has forced a registry, rather than a registrar, to change the ownership of a domain name. See America Online, Inc. v. AOL .org, 259 F. Supp. 2d 449 (E.D. Va. 2003). Thus, if the location of a domain name is determined based on the location of the party with “control” over ownership of the domain name, then the location of the registry is as good as any.

In light of the foregoing, faced with the somewhat metaphysical question of where the intangible property comprising a domain name exists, this Court will follow Congress' suggestion in ACPA that a domain name exists in the location of both the registrar and the registry. As such, this is the appropriate Court to oversee levy upon domain names listed on the VeriSign registry.

======

Lest you forget, it may well be that some property is unseizable altogether, even if it is "property." For example, at common law only tangible property could be seized. This of course has been updated by statute, but even today, parties fight over what can be seized. See Itasca Bank & Trust Co. v. Thorleif Larsen & Son, Inc., 815 N.E.2d 1259 (Ill. App. Ct. 2004) (holding that although debtor enjoyed a "refund right" of $17,000 should he ever resign from a tony country club, there was no way to levy on that property; nor could the court order, as passionately requested by plaintiff, debtor to resign from the club, as gone was the reign of the "sequestrator," an officer who apparently could have done so in the good old days of the courts of equity).

B.   COMPETITION AMONG CREDITORS: PRIORITIES

In general, the rule in state collection law is the rule elsewhere in law: "First in time, first in right," or, in its earthier version, "The fastest dog gets fed first." The first creditor to levy on a particular piece of property will have the right to be paid in full from the sale proceeds of that property before any other creditor gets even a single dollar from the sale. But even these simple rules of thumb devolve into state-specific complexity.

BEEF & BISON BREEDERS, INC. v. CAPITOL REFRIGERATION CO., INC.
431 N.Y.S.2d 986 (N.Y. Sup. Ct. 1980)

CONWAY, Justice.

On February 8, 1980 petitioner [Beef & Bison Breeders, Inc.—there are two petitioners in this case—Eds.] entered into a security agreement with Kwik Serv whereby, as security for repayment of a certain promissory note of the same date, Kwik Serv granted petitioner a security interest in all of the personal property, furniture, fixtures, equipment and vehicles then owned or thereafter acquired by Kwik Serv. On February 20, 1980 petitioner filed the financing statement signed by Kwik Serv in [the wrong government office to create a properly perfected security interest]. The debtor, Kwik Serv, thereafter defaulted on the promissory note and petitioner commenced an action against said debtor.

On April 4, 1980 respondent Capitol Refrigeration entered a judgment in the Albany County Clerk's Office against Kwik Serv in the sum of $701.78. On April 16, 1980 a property execution was delivered to the Albany County Sheriff for service on the judgment debtor and on

August 15, 1980, the Albany County Sheriff levied upon the assets of the judgment debtor Kwik Serv at 700 New Loudon Road in Latham, New York and scheduled a sheriff's sale for August 25, 1980 which has been temporarily stayed.

Respondent Patrick Cornell is the owner of premises formerly occupied by Kwik Serv at 700 New Loudon Road. By virtue of the Sheriff's levy on behalf of Capitol Refrigeration as aforesaid, all the personal property, chattels and equipment owned by Kwik Serv remain on the premises owned by respondent Patrick Cornell who has advised petitioner and respondent Capitol Refrigeration that they would be charged $40 per day for storage of the property from July 28, 1980.

Petitioner Beef & Bison Breeders, Inc. (Beef & Bison) contends that it is the holder of a perfected security interest in the property sought to be levied on, and by virtue of UCC, Section 9-301 is entitled to priority over the lien creditors, respondents Capitol Refrigeration and Patrick Cornell.

This Court cannot agree with the contention of the petitioner. Petitioner does not have a duly perfected security interest in the subject property. . . . As petitioner has not properly perfected its security interest, respondent Capitol Refrigeration's levy continues and the execution sale of the Sheriff should be conducted immediately. . . .

The second motion is by Patrick Cornell for an order directing that petitioner (Cornell) have first priority to the proceeds of the levy made upon the bank accounts of the judgment debtor Kwik Serv, located in the Latham Branch of Key Bank, and that the Sheriff of Albany County apply the proceeds of the levy made upon said bank account to the satisfaction of the judgment of petitioner Patrick Cornell.

On June 30, 1980 a judgment was entered by petitioner Cornell in the Town of Colonie Justice Court against Kwik Serv in the sum of $4,469. A transcript of said judgment was filed with the Albany County Clerk on July 1, 1980 and on July 3, 1980 an execution was issued to the Albany County Sheriff.

On August 20, 1980 the petitioner's attorneys served an execution with notice to garnishee upon the Sheriff which specified the following property: "Kwik Serv Meats Key Bank checking account, balance $909.99; Kwik Serv Meats Key Bank checking account, balance $92.43." The Sheriff levied on said bank accounts on August 22, 1980.

On April 16, 1980 [as mentioned above—Eds.] respondent Capitol Refrigeration as judgment creditor in the amount of $701.80, filed a property execution with the Sheriff for service on the judgment debtor Kwik Serv. The proceeds of the bank accounts which have been turned over to the Sheriff under the levy of August 22, 1980 are sufficient to pay the aforesaid judgment of respondent Capitol Refrigeration.

The petitioner [Cornell] contends that while respondent Capitol Refrigeration admittedly has first priority to the proceeds of levies made on or before August 15, 1980, petitioner has first priority to the proceeds of the bank accounts which were levied upon on August 22, 1980 as the first priority was extinguished.

This Court cannot agree with the contention of the petitioner. CPLR Section 5234, subd. (b) provides that where two or more executions are issued against the same judgment debtor and delivered to the same enforcement officer, they shall be satisfied in the order in which they were delivered (6 Weinstein-Korn-Miller, N.Y. Civil Practice, Section 5234.05). It is not necessary for priority purposes that the sheriff or enforcement officer levy under the first execution before the delivery of or levy upon a second or subsequent execution. If the levy is made under a junior execution and the judgment debtor's property is sold, the judgment creditor who first delivered on execution does not lose his priority.

In view of the foregoing, the motion by petitioner Patrick Cornell is in all respects denied.

Delivery of the writ to the sheriff is all the creditor can do, and therefore in many states it is the delivery dates that determine priority, as in *Beef & Bison*. Some courts say that the filing creates an inchoate lien that becomes choate and relates back to the date of delivery upon actual levy that creates the lien, but others don't, saying that unless and until there's a levy, there's no lien. And sometimes there's even a fight about what even constitutes a "levy" by the sheriff. See Credit Bureau of Broken Bow, Inc. v. Moninger, 284 N.W.2d 855 (Neb. 1979) (determining whether the young deputy sheriff had to physically impound vehicle to effect levy or whether it sufficed when he "grabbed ahold the pickup and stated: 'I execute on the pickup for the County of Custer,'" rather like Columbus claiming the New World for Spain).

The timing of a creditor's levy is alas irrelevant if that property already has a consensual security interest on it granted in favor of another. Then, the secured creditor, so long as it properly perfected its interest, will win. By corollary, an unperfected secured creditor is in more trouble. Although it will still be able to repossess property pursuant to its lien if the debtor defaults, as in *Beef & Bison*, it will lose to a judgment creditor who properly levies on that property and becomes a *lien creditor* while the security interest remains unperfected. We touched on the importance of perfection of security interests back in Assignment 2, but we cannot spend the weeks that a good Article 9 course will devote to priority fights; these rules of thumb must suffice for now.

C.   COLLECTIVE REMEDIES

The fights between Capitol Refrigeration, Beef & Bison Breeders, Inc., and Patrick Cornell, all scrambling madly in the race for the assets of Kwik Serv, do not suggest efficiency. Is there a way to have an orderly resolution at state law of a debtor's multiple creditors without this mad dash? The short answer is "yes," but the longer answer is "not really." The traditional state-law remedy for an exhausted debtor or pokey creditor is an *assignment for the benefit of creditors* (or "ABC" in the trade). This is when the debtor assigns all its property to someone, usually a lawyer, and tells the creditors to go bug the lawyer. The lawyer then sells the assets and pays all the creditors pro rata. The problem is that ABCs do not discharge a debtor from the unpaid portion of the outstanding debts; that is the province of federal bankruptcy law.

A consensual discharge does not raise a federal-state supremacy problem, however, and there are a couple of state-law options, which are often used together. A *composition* is when the creditors agree to compromise their debts (take less than is owed). An *extension* is when creditors agree to let the debtor stretch out repayment. These tools help in limited circumstances because the creditors have to agree unanimously to their treatment. One or more creditors often holds out, a collective action problem that bankruptcy addresses.

A final collective procedure is a *receivership*, which creditors can impose against a debtor's will. Here the debtor's property becomes exempt from seizure as *custodia legis* (in the custody of the court) and then administered, with the hope of maximizing recovery from a collective process, to pay off creditors. Receiverships are especially prevalent for entities that cannot be put into bankruptcy by creditors (or file for bankruptcy). §§ 109(b), 303(a). When entities can do so, they may respond to a receivership by filing a bankruptcy petition, which invokes the automatic stay to prohibit the receiver from taking further action. Certain regulatory regimes require forms of receivership instead of a bankruptcy filing. The FDIC's role in insolvent banks is a common and important example.

Bankruptcy is often a better option for the debtor than these various state proceedings, but there are certain parts of the country and certain types of situations where there may be an advantage to the state system. For example, Professor Ronald Mann has found data showing that high-tech companies in Northern California are often liquidated under ABCs rather than put into bankruptcy, although similar high-tech companies in Texas almost always liquidate in bankruptcy. See Ronald Mann, An Empirical Investigation of Liquidation Choices of Failed High Tech Firms, 82 Wash. U. L. Rev. 1375 (2004).

We have not discussed one of the most powerful collection tools—a fraudulent conveyance action. Because the Bankruptcy Code has its own fraudulent conveyance section, we defer coverage, including of the state law Uniform Voidable Transactions Act ("UVTA"), to Assignments 20 and 21. The presence of the state laws on fraudulent conveyances means that an aggrieved creditor, even without bankruptcy law assistance, may be able to reverse a transaction that the debtor makes to "hinder, delay or defraud" other creditors, such as selling assets to an offshore affiliate with a secret repurchase right to try to claim that it's technically no longer the debtor's property.

We close our study of business collection law with a consideration of ethics. True, most of the consumer protections, such as the FDCPA, have no applicability to businesses, but that does not mean it is entirely a free-for-all. Attorneys are still governed by the codes of professional conduct, which temper the duty of zealous representation with a duty of civility. Consider the case of Qwest Business & Government Services v. Lawchek Ltd., 781 N.W.2d 101 (Iowa Ct. App. 2010) (unpublished table decision). Qwest had obtained a $3 million judgment against Lawchek, but when Lawchek said it was going to fight out an appeal, the parties entered into a settlement discussion (as they often do) over a reduced judgment. The stories diverge about what happened next, but things were looking good for settlement, with Lawchek ponying up $500,000 to its lawyers to hold onto "in anticipation of a settlement." After some languishing during back and forth on the settlement paperwork, however, Qwest apparently got fed up and swiftly exercised its collection rights as a judgment creditor owed $3 million—including a writ of garnishment on the $500,000 sitting in the Lawchek lawyers' account. Lawchek cried foul but lost in trial court when the parties took unsurprisingly contradictory positions on whether a settlement agreement had actually been reached. On appeal, the court split. The majority raised its eyebrows at what it thought was sharp conduct but eventually concluded that the debtor's property is the debtor's property, even if held by an attorney in an account:

> The $500,000 was, at all times material here, the unrestricted funds of Lawchek and, as such, subject to levy of execution. If a contrary result was reached in this or similar situations, it would create an unwarranted opportunity to place assets beyond the reach of creditors. This conclusion only applies to the $500,000 intended as settlement money [and not money, e.g., paid as a retainer for legal services—Eds.].

Id. at *5 (per DANLISON, J.).

The dissent, focusing on what it clearly thought was unprofessional conduct, noted that special purpose accounts are segregated and not free for creditor levy:

> SACKETT, C.J. (concurring in part and dissenting in part).
> I concur in part and dissent in part. I agree with the majority and the district court that what Qwest's attorney did here was distasteful. I also agree with the majority that what happened here does not follow the custom of the bar in this state of honoring oral agreements. That said, I cannot agree with the majority's decision that there was no error. The Lawchek money came into the attorney's trust account after an officer of Lawchek, who was an attorney, was of the opinion that he had reached a settlement with the attorney for Qwest that required Lawchek to pay $500,000. Qwest's attorney learned the deposit had been made in the attorney's trust account while discussing the documents necessary for the agreed settlement. Qwest's attorney knew that the money was deposited in the trust account for the specific purpose of paying an agreed settlement. Qwest's attorney levied while settlement papers were being prepared and without notifying Lawchek's attorney that the settlement was called off. Qwest's attorney never in clear written or spoken words indicated the terms of the settlement were denied, disputed, or unacceptable.
> Clearly the deposit in the attorney trust account was a special deposit for the purpose of settling the judgment. The attorney for Lawchek was restricted from releasing the money until the settlement was finalized. He could not have released it for any other purpose and the garnishment is subordinate to that purpose.

Id. at *6.

Even an appellate court could not agree whether this attorney deserved a medal for creative collection or bar disciplinary action for unethical conduct, and surely a different outcome could arise in a different state. Business collection often means pushing up to the line, and in a field lacking the pervasive regulation of consumer law, it is sometimes unclear where that line is.

D.   LIQUIDATING BUSINESSES IN CHAPTER 7 BANKRUPTCY

Given the limited usefulness of state collective remedies, bankruptcy is often a more attractive option to creditors. Some debtors may prefer it too when there is no hope of reorganization, because it is less of a headache with its painless euthanasia of a failed business. But few business leaders happily whistle their way into chapter 7 shutdown if there is even a glimmer of hope of reorganization (erstwhile Circuit City is the exception, not the rule). Most large businesses don't start, but end in chapter 7—after a failed reorganization attempt in chapter 11. Still, some do start there, but perhaps more by way of collapse at a finish line than a purposeful stride to the next mile marker for the business. Regardless of debtor preferences, many creditors definitely like chapter 7 because, to use an evocative metaphor, there is often more meat on the carcass for hungry creditors in a chapter 7 liquidation than there is in the drive-by meal that occurs with the race to levy at state law.

Before we begin discussing chapter 7, however, we want to add an introductory note on coverage. Our discussion of business liquidation is necessarily brief because you have already learned most key chapter 7 concepts in the consumer materials (automatic stay, appointment of trustee, priority of claims, etc.). But that does not mean chapter 7 issues are irrelevant for businesses. On the contrary, all businesses—even those who want to reorganize in chapter 11—need to know the chapter 7 liquidation rules. This is because all who give it a run in a chapter 11 reorganization do so with a keen eye to what will happen if things don't work out and they wind up in chapter 7. And they can get there multiple ways from chapter 11: the debtor usually has an absolute right to convert the case to chapter 7, § 1112(a); the creditors can do so on a proper showing, § 1112(b); and, most importantly, the debtor may be ordered there if the creditors do not approve a reorganization, § 1112(b)(4)(A). Thus, we say that chapter 11 negotiations occur "in the shadow" of chapter 7. Indeed, this chapter 7 "stress test" conducted by chapter 11 negotiators is so important that, as we will later learn, debtors must disclose to creditors who vote on a plan of reorganization what they would earn in a liquidation scenario under chapter 7. § 1129(a)(7)(A). Of course, sophisticated creditors already have their own assessments of what they will earn in such a hypothetical liquidation, declining to just take the debtor's word.

Even a nonbankruptcy workout occurs in the penumbra of the chapter 7 liquidation shadow. One can think of a negotiation with each side (debtor and creditor) threatening the other with bankruptcy—even though both really want to avoid it. Envision a conference room with the debtor standing in the window threatening to jump ("Stand back or I'll do it for sure!") while the creditors threaten to push ("We've had enough and we're coming over right now to end this mess!"). While the debtor may be planning to jump into chapter 11 and the creditor to push into chapter 7, vice versa is possible.

Thus, while our treatment of chapter 7 is brief, it should not be mistaken as trivial. It provides the basic rules of the game. Chapter 7 is the primal and ancient form of bankruptcy, developed against the state-law alternatives and assessed against the different opportunities that might be available in chapter 11 reorganization.

1. Voluntary Chapter 7: Why Do Failed Businesses Even Bother?

When a corporation enters liquidation, it is not loosed from its chains of debt by discharge and a fresh start. Instead, it quietly expires under state corporate law following its financial demise in bankruptcy. A corporate debtor almost never seeks liquidation given this lack of debt discharge except in final, exhausted resignation. When does this resignation kick in? Sometimes it is at the behest of creditors, and later in this assignment we will learn about the involuntary bankruptcy petitions that creditors can file against debtors, § 303, and the related incentive that gives corporations a reason to "quit before they are fired" by just filing bankruptcy themselves. Sometimes debtors themselves prefer it for finality and other reasons.

At this point, some of you may be wondering whether all creditors prefer bankruptcy to the collections race at state law, or only some. Obviously, if you're fast and furious, why not just whip the sheriff into action, get your own debt paid, and leave the other suckers behind? The reality, however, is that few know with absolute certainty in advance that they will be the fastest or best protected, and the race itself is highly costly and value-destructive when there are multiple competitors seeking repayment at the same time. Thus, many stakeholders in a business debtor's financial collapse often seek out bankruptcy. Their various goals include: (1) maximization of value; (2) fair, orderly, and predictable distributions; (3) final resolution of liability and title to property; and (4) discovery and remediation of fraud. In addition, bankruptcy has another potential: (5) vindication of various public interest concerns that transcend the immediate interests of the parties. The first two goals of bankruptcy are uncontroversial, the third and fourth minimally disputed, and the fifth a mix of the uncontroversial and the hotly contested.

The first three concepts turn on both the control of all of the debtor's assets and affairs and the imposition of bankruptcy-law results on all the claimants against the debtor. For a debtor that refuses to pay, those enforcement mechanisms may be the fastest and cheapest response. In case of an inability to pay any creditors, the collective creditor process in bankruptcy preserves value and assures an orderly procedure. A going-concern sale fetches higher dollar than the sale of individual factory equipment pieces. In addition, bankruptcy does not have the rigid timetables and procedures that are characteristic of state execution laws. The bankruptcy trustee can negotiate with buyers and, with court approval, pick the best method of disposition—discretion a sheriff often lacks. Value-maximizing sellers are sensitive to context. See generally Matt Campbell, Sex Toys to Be Auctioned to Pay Business's Delinquent Kansas Taxes, *Kansas City Star*, Sept. 24, 2014, 5:23 PM (noting that Kansas's conservative Republican governor authorized state seizure and sale of "Bang's" assets via [presumably anonymous] online auction), https://www.kansascity.com/news/politics -government/article2233475.html. It is common in larger cases to appoint professional liquidators who may have substantial experience in maximizing the payoffs from "going out of business" sales. The orderly assembly of the debtor's assets, flexible sale procedures, and set rules of distribution in bankruptcy are almost certain to yield higher returns for creditors and other claimants as a group than the mad scramble of executions and garnishments. Bankruptcy's results are also binding on everyone throughout the United States; the benefit of this approach is a clear, final, and universal resolution of ownership and liabilities. The Founders showed that they grasped this point when they allocated the power to make uniform bankruptcy law to the new national government. U.S. Const. art. I, § 8, cl. 4.

On the fourth goal, although, as we will see, fraud can be addressed and corrected at state law, great efficiencies are achieved by the appointment of an impartial trustee in bankruptcy who is owed a duty of cooperation by the debtor. § 521(a)(3). Trustees have experience, resources, and the incentive to discover fraud, recover property, and get damages for the benefit of creditors generally, which may be lacking in any one creditor's collection attorney.

As for the final, more contentious goal of bankruptcy proceedings, many believe there are public interest concerns that may arise when a business becomes financially troubled. For example, the priority system reflects normative preference for certain stakeholders in business failure, such as unpaid employees. Slow-moving tax and environmental authorities are given a better chance to collect in the collective system of bankruptcy when nobody's in a race. Hospitals and nursing homes often receive special treatment under specific rules in the Code that recognizes they are not just economic entities but care providers of vulnerable people. These are all examples of public concerns that bankruptcy law mediates—and in a transparent system that helps create and maintain public trust in the resolution of corporate financial distress. See Elizabeth Warren, Bankruptcy Policymaking in an Imperfect World, 92 Mich. L. Rev. 336 (1993).

What do we actually know about these chapter 7 cases filed by businesses? First, they make up 62.3% of the 22,231 cases that the Administrative Office of the U.S. courts denominated as business filings in calendar year 2018. Are these all corporate petitions? No. Not all business filings are by corporations. In fact, natural persons filed 69.3% of the chapter 7 cases that are designated business cases. Perhaps more surprisingly, individuals filed 13.0% of the chapter 11 cases that were designated as business cases. Integrated Database, Federal Judicial Center, https://www.fjc.gov/research/ idb (calculations made using 2018 data).

The overlap between business and consumer cases can also be studied from the other direction. The 2007 Consumer Bankruptcy Project data support estimates that between 14.0 to 20.2% of all the debtors listed as "consumers" on their bankruptcy petitions had recently operated small businesses. Striking Out on Their Own: The Self-Employed in Bankruptcy, in *Broke*. The distinction between consumer and business bankruptcy is fundamental but also blurs over a significant margin. From this point on, the discussion will assume that a business bankruptcy is a corporate bankruptcy unless specifically identified otherwise. One important reason for this assumption is that this rather technical material is easier to learn that way. It is also true that most of the largest and most interesting business bankruptcies are those in which the debtor is a corporation or, most often, a group of affiliated corporations.

A final dichotomy is important in business bankruptcies: the difference in the operation of the bankruptcy system depending on the size of the debtor's business. Assets, debts, or number of employees are commonly used measurements for size. A frequent distinction is between small and medium-sized companies on the one hand, and large companies on the other. See World Bank Group, Report by the Working Group on the Treatment of MSME Insolvency (2017) (discussing specific challenges of micro, small, and medium enterprises); see also Ronald B. Davis et al., The Modular Approach to Micro, Small, and Medium Enterprise Insolvency 6 (2016). But these broad categories are not commonly defined. Is a large business one with $1 million, $10 million, or $100 million in debt (or assets)? Smaller businesses not infrequently will start out in chapter 11 and then crash into chapter 7. By contrast, large corporations usually succeed in chapter 11, although "success" may well be asset sale of the whole business or of large pieces of it (and even big companies slide into liquidation too—Borders Books, to name one). Complicating further the picture is the fact that the study of large companies in the bankruptcy literature is limited almost entirely to large public companies (i.e., those with stock traded publicly on exchanges and regulated by the SEC). Very little research has been done into the bankruptcies of large privately held companies. So even what we think we know empirically must be tempered by cautious methodological caveats.

2.   *Involuntary Chapter 7: What Happens When Somebody Else Bothers?*

A business debtor seeking to start a chapter 7 has it easy: it files a petition, just as a consumer does. But because creditors may want to start a chapter 7 to capture its efficiency benefits as a collective proceeding, and probably are more motivated to do so than a dispirited manager of a failed business, the Code allows them to petition debtors into chapter 7 involuntarily. Knowing these involuntary rules is important, because sometimes debtors file the chapter 7 "quasi-voluntarily," meaning that they are volunteered by their creditors. Debtors have a strong incentive to resist filing bankruptcy, both because the natural optimism of a risk-taking entrepreneur who runs the business makes it likely that bankruptcy will be sought only as a last resort, but also because the manager fears the loss of control by the creation of an estate and concomitant vesting of power in a trustee that a filing will bring. There is a consensus that often companies do not file until it is too late to save them and much of their value has been dissipated.

Section 303 of the Code allows creditors to gang up on the debtor and initiate an *involuntary petition.* For example, creditors might be worried that a debtor in financial distress is wasting assets or paying certain favored creditors while ignoring the rest. Of course, when presented with the grim phone call that an involuntary petition is being circulated, debtors may take the plunge themselves (perhaps hiding in the comfort of chapter 11 rather than liquidating in chapter 7 as their more impatient creditors might prefer).

But the Code faces a problem with offering this power to creditors: creditors typically lack the necessary information to make a sound, efficient, and unbiased decision about the appropriateness of a bankruptcy remedy. If involuntary bankruptcy is too easy to commence, creditors have too much leverage. A single aggressive creditor could destroy a viable business. Yet if the law imposes stringent requirements as a precondition for an involuntary bankruptcy, creditors will find it difficult to initiate a case before debtors are completely financially moribund and the assets have all left the building. The difficulty in finding optimal balance is reflected in the variety of approaches used. In some countries, such as the United States, involuntary filings are rare; in other countries, such as England, they are commonplace. Some countries, such as those in Continental Europe, impose criminal fines on directors who do not comply with a *duty* to file upon insolvency (committing the wrong sometimes called "trading while insolvent"). See, e.g., Bruno M. Kübler & Karsten Otte, 2 Business Transactions in Germany § 17.04 (2014); Robert Weber, Can the Sauvegarde Reform Save French Bankruptcy Law?: A Comparative Look at Chapter 11 and French Bankruptcy Law from an Agency Cost Perspective, 27 Mich. J. Int'l L. 257, 285-86 (2005).

Section 303 reflects the decision in the United States to protect debtors by making involuntary bankruptcy relatively difficult and rare. In a study, Professor Susan Block-Lieb explained that the proportion of involuntary to voluntary petitions is low—and argued that it should continue to stay low. Why Creditors File So Few Involuntary Petitions and Why the Number Is Not Too Small, 57 Brook. L. Rev. 803 (1991). It may be that the primary use of the Code's involuntary filing provisions is as a credible threat during workout negotiations. Historically, an involuntary bankruptcy was always a chapter 7 case, but the Code permits a creditor to put a debtor into an involuntary chapter 11 as well. § 303(b).

The hesitancy in the United States about involuntary petitions recognizes that, even though they can serve salutary purposes, they can also be used to bully and threaten a debtor whose business may be destroyed by the mere filing of a petition. Recent innovations in financial markets have renewed concerns about creditors' motives in bringing a bankruptcy petition. Creditors can now buy financial products that pay them if a debtor defaults, and such creditors may have a powerful incentive to trigger payment by filing an involuntary petition against a debtor that might otherwise work its way out of a financial tailspin. These sorts of dangers explain the presence of § 303(b)(1), under which three creditors must join in most involuntary petitions. If that does not prevent abuse, § 303(i)(1) allows attorneys' fees and costs to be awarded against a petitioner who gets it wrong (i.e., when the petition is dismissed because the alleged debtor is not actually bankrupt), and § 303(i)(2) goes a step further and allows punitive damages against a petitioner who is not just wrong but in bad faith. This latter power was discovered the hard way by a colorful Michigander by the name of Mr. Adell whose strategy to gain a little leverage in a contract dispute by petitioning his adversary into bankruptcy blew up spectacularly.

In re JOHN RICHARDS HOMES BUILDING CO.
291 B.R. 727 (Bankr. E.D. Mich. 2003)

RHODES, Chief Bankruptcy Judge.

Following the dismissal of this involuntary petition, the Court conducted an evidentiary hearing on a request for compensatory and punitive damages by the alleged debtor, John Richards Homes Building Company, L.L.C. ("JRH"). . . .

JRH is in the business of constructing new homes priced at over $1 million. [Petitioning Creditor] Adell's claim against JRH arises from a contract for the sale of property and the construction of a new home. The parties signed this contract on December 28, 2001. Pursuant to the contract, JRH agreed to sell to Adell a 1.8 acre parcel of property in Bloomfield Hills, Michigan, and to construct a home for Adell on the property. Adell agreed to pay a total of $3,030,000. The contract required JRH to commence construction "within a reasonable time after this Agreement is signed and plans are completed and permit is issued."

The sale closed on February 28, 2002. The closing papers, signed by Adell, reflect that Adell agreed to allocate $1,750,000 for the purchase of the property and the balance to the building construction. The deed also reflects this purchase price. First Federal of Michigan financed the purchase for Adell.

In the next several months, two primary disputes developed. First, Adell asserted that the true value of the real property was $1 million rather than the $1.75 million stated in the closing papers and in the deed. Thus, he contended that the excess of $750,000 was actually an improper initial construction draw to which JRH was not entitled. Second, Adell asserted that the delays in commencing construction were unreasonable.

On June 6, 2002, Adell filed suit in the Oakland County Circuit Court against JRH, [JRH's principal] Shekerjian, First Federal and others, alleging fraud and misrepresentation, silent fraud, innocent fraud, breach of contract, Consumer Protection Act violations, unjust enrichment, accounting and constructive trust.

On June 18, 2002, JRH filed: (1) an answer denying the substance of Adell's claims; (2) affirmative defenses; and (3) a verified counter-complaint alleging breach of contract, business defamation, business libel, injurious falsehood, tortious interference with business relations and extortion. JRH also filed an emergency motion for a temporary restraining order and a preliminary injunction.

Six days later, on June 24, 2002, Adell filed this involuntary petition against JRH. This petition alleged that Adell's claim was $800,000 for fraud and breach of contract, and that he was eligible to file the petition under 11 U.S.C. § 303(b), i.e., that his claim was not subject to a bona fide dispute.

On July 1, 2002, JRH filed a motion to dismiss. JRH asserted that Adell's claim was the subject of a bona fide dispute, as it was still in the very early stages of contested litigation. JRH also asserted that the petition was filed in bad faith and that therefore, JRH was entitled to substantial compensatory and punitive damages. JRH also requested attorney fees and costs.

On July 15, 2002, after a hearing, the Court dismissed the petition, finding that Adell "knew or surely must have known that his claim was the subject of a bona fide dispute, and therefore that he was not qualified to be a petitioning creditor." The Court retained jurisdiction to resolve JRH's requests for compensatory and punitive damages and for attorney fees. . . .

After examining the totality of circumstances, the Court finds that JRH has established by a preponderance of the evidence that Adell filed the involuntary bankruptcy petition in bad faith. Indeed, the Court finds that the evidence overwhelmingly supports this conclusion:

1. As the Court found on July 15, 2002, when Adell filed this involuntary bankruptcy petition, he knew or should have known that his claims were the subject of a bona fide dispute. By then, JRH had responded to Adell's state court complaint by filing substantial defenses, affirmative defenses and counterclaims.

Adell testified that he was not aware of these responsive pleadings until after the involuntary bankruptcy petition was filed. There are [multiple] problems with this position:

First, his state court attorneys were aware of these pleadings before the petition was filed. His attorneys' failure to advise him of them in a timely way can be of no help to him.

Second, the nature of Adell's claims was such that he would certainly not require legal advice to understand that he and JRH would have real and substantial legal and factual disputes, and further that the litigation to resolve these disputes would be lengthy and costly. Even before JRH filed responsive pleadings, Adell could not have reasonably concluded that JRH would simply admit that it had committed the frauds and the other intentional wrongs that he had alleged.

Third, the evidence establishes that even if Adell was not aware of JRH's responsive pleadings, he already knew that his state court claims would be contested. At least twice before Adell filed the involuntary petition, JRH's attorneys specifically told Adell's attorneys that JRH would contest Adell's claims and that therefore an involuntary petition would be improper. First, after Adell threatened to file an involuntary bankruptcy petition during a meeting on June 3, 2002, attorney E. Michael Morris, representing JRH, sent a letter dated June 5, 2002, to attorney Dennis Dlugokinski, representing Adell. In that letter, Morris advised Dlugokinski that an involuntary petition would be improper and threatened "severe sanctions for damages in the event [Adell] files a frivolous petition for bankruptcy." . . .

2. Adell knew of the serious harm that JRH would suffer as a direct consequence of the involuntary filing. Indeed the evidence establishes that Adell intended to cause that harm. At a meeting on June 3, 2002, Adell specifically asked Shekerjian, "Can the company take the hit to its reputation if an involuntary bankruptcy was [sic] filed?" Adell denied this, but the Court finds that his denial lacks credibility.

Further evidence of Adell's intent to harm JRH is Adell's extraordinary effort and expense to hire a public relations firm, Marx Layne, to publicize the bankruptcy filing. For that purpose, Marx Layne contacted three newspapers, the Detroit News, the Detroit Free Press and Crain's Detroit Business. On June 25, 2002, the day after the involuntary petition was filed, a Marx Layne representative sent separate email messages to reporters for the Detroit News and the Detroit Free Press, apparently following up on conversations concerning the filing. . . .

Each message also attached a list of nine JRH customers whose contracts JRH had allegedly not fulfilled and outrageously stated that a state court hearing then scheduled for the following Wednesday "is sure to be worthy of coverage with plots and subplots and high-profile business people coming to the surface." In an attempt to maximize the probability of news coverage, each message falsely stated that the recipient was the only reporter in the area with this information. Finally, each message stated, "We would appreciate you keeping our name out of any conversations regarding this high-profile story." . . .

It is also noteworthy that at the hearing, two of JRH's customers on the list of nine customers stated to be dissatisfied with JRH, Jean McIntyre and Larry Gainer, testified that they were in fact satisfied with JRH's work.

3. On May, 31, 2002, attorney Dlugokinski, representing Adell, sent a letter to Shekerjian outrageously threatening *criminal prosecution.* . . .

5. Adell used improper threats and flaunted his wealth in an attempt to solicit creditors to join his petition. Two such creditors testified. Cynthia Weaver, credit manager of E.W. Kitchens, testified that Adell called her and stated that he was a very rich man, that he was angry and that he was trying to force JRH into bankruptcy. He then stated that he was looking for creditors to sign with him for the bankruptcy and that if she wanted to be paid, that would be the only way. . . .

Robert Clark of Motor City Stone, an excavating company testified that Adell called him twice to get him to sign on the bankruptcy petition. In the first call, Adell told him that only people who signed on would be paid. . . .

Adell told Shekerjian directly that he was worth $700 million and that he wanted his brother in law to finish the house. After their dispute surfaced, Adell also told Shekerjian that when the City of Franklin Hills had given him a hard time about certain permits required for a home that he wanted to build there, this made him mad, so he built "the ugliest home he could possibly think of just to piss them off." Shakerjian took this to mean that Adell was willing and able to spend significant money just to get back at someone who made him mad and he found it "scary."

6. Adell's testimony that he filed the petition in reliance on the advice of experienced bankruptcy attorneys and therefore in good faith must be rejected. The record certainly establishes that Adell's counsel did some substantial investigation before concluding that an involuntary petition would be proper [discussing explicitly the need for an undisputed debt amount over $12,000 under § 303(a) and saying there would be a "big problem" if there were not]. The difficulty here is that . . . Adell and his attorneys . . . withheld from [bankruptcy counsel] significant information that plainly would have, or should have, made a difference on the critical issue

of whether JRH either "admitted," or at least did not dispute, any portion of Adell's claim? . . . [M]ost inexplicably of all, Adell and his state court attorneys never gave Newman's firm a copy of JRH's answer to Adell's state court complaint or JRH's counterclaim.

It is fundamental that a client reasonably relies on an attorney's advice only when the client provides to the attorney all of the pertinent facts in the client's possession. *See* United States v. United Med. & Surgical Supply Corp., 989 F.2d 1390, 1404 (4th Cir. 1993) (One who willfully avoids the duty to disclose all material facts cannot rely in good faith on the advice of counsel.). . . . Here, Adell did not make a full disclosure, and apparently deliberately so. . . . Accordingly, Adell's defense of reliance on counsel must be rejected.

7. Adell falsely testified that in filing the involuntary petition, he was motivated by a concern for JRH's trade creditors. If he were indeed so charitably motivated, he would not have threatened at least two creditors that the only way they would be paid would be to join in the petition.

The totality of the circumstances compels the conclusion that Adell did not honestly believe that the involuntary bankruptcy petition would be appropriate. Adell did not file this petition in a sincere and honest belief that he was entitled to bankruptcy relief against JRH. Rather, he proceeded with the wrongful intent to intimidate Shekerjian into a settlement and, when that failed, to damage or destroy his business. This involuntary bankruptcy petition was not filed in good faith. . . .

Shekerjian credibly testified that the ability of JRH to compete in the market for high end homes is critically affected by its reputation. He further stated that in the five years preceding the filing his entities had built and sold 40 homes costing over $1 million each. However, since the involuntary was filed, JRH has not contracted with a single customer because of the damage to JRH's reputation that the filing caused. He also stated that two pending sales were lost as a result of the filing. . . .

Consequently, once the court has found bad faith, the court must decide whether punitive damages are appropriate and, if so, in what amount. . . . [T]he totality of the circumstances must be considered in fashioning an appropriate award under section 303(i)(2). . . .

It has already been determined that the evidence of Adell's bad faith is overwhelming. He was told and knew that JRH contested his claims. He withheld crucial information from his bankruptcy attorneys. He engaged in [a] campaign of publicity and disparagement with the specific intent to injure JRH. He threatened JRH with criminal prosecution. He flaunted his wealth. He cynically asserted a false concern for creditors. He presented no credible mitigating considerations. By any objective measure, this involuntary bankruptcy petition is an extreme case of abuse of the bankruptcy process. Adell's conduct was reprehensible and must be deterred and punished. . . .

The Court concludes that punitive damages of $2,000,000 are necessary and appropriate in this case. Such a punishment is approximately one-half of the compensatory damages of $4,100,000.

Mr. Adell responded to the adverse award by moving to Florida and buying a nice home—persuasively demonstrating his residence by procuring a fishing license—and shortly thereafter filing a voluntary petition for bankruptcy to stay enforcement, claiming his new homestead as exempt (all this was well before BAPCPA's restriction on homestead exemptions). His bankruptcy petition was eventually dismissed for bad faith. Emboldened, JRH asked the Florida bankruptcy court for sanctions, but was rebuffed, so it went back to the more sympathetic ear of Chief Judge Rhodes in Michigan. Adell's subsequent move back to Michigan in the interim, ostensibly prompted by the arrival of children who would miss grandparents, probably did not sit well with the Michigan bankruptcy court, which ordered further sanctions of a few more million dollars in punitive damages and cost reimbursements. This was partially reversed by the district court, which found punishment for the Florida proceedings beyond the Michigan court's equitable power (in contrast to the specific power to award punitive sanctions under § 303). In re John Richards Homes Bldg. Co., 475 B.R. 585 (E.D. Mich. 2012).

JRH raises the question whether a creditor whose debt was only in partial dispute counts as a petitioning creditor (because at least on the undisputed portion, it is clearly a creditor). BAPCPA made clear that a dispute about either the fact of liability *or* the amount owed is sufficient to classify the debt as "disputed," and so such a partially disputed creditor cannot count.

Once the sufficient number of petitioners qualifies under § 303(a), the court must proceed to decide if the debtor is "generally not paying" its debts under § 303(h). Of course, "generally not paying" could stem from a number of causes, including cash flow difficulties or sheer stubbornness. The "generally not paying" standard is more creditor-oriented than the traditional "inability to pay" test, since it encompasses the debtor who refuses to pay as well as the debtor who cannot pay. The standard resembles the one long applied to involuntary bankruptcy in European courts, where an analogous test is generally called "cessation of payments." Those courts enjoy varying levels of discretion in determining whether a "cessation" of payment by a particular debtor has actually taken place, in light of the debtor's general financial circumstances. See generally 1 J.H. Dalhuisen, Dalhuisen on International Insolvency and Bankruptcy, § 1.02[4] (1984).

Finally, consider that secured creditors in the United States rarely have to find two colleagues to join a petition to get the debtor to file. Most can force a "quasi-involuntary" bankruptcy filing by threatening repossession of key property. Without key collateral, the company will be kaput. Bankruptcy looks better by comparison to the debtor, often reducing the need for a true involuntary filing.

Problem Set 15

15.1. Rollins Home Appliances is in deep financial trouble. Three of its suppliers have sued and recovered judgments against Rollins, each in the amount of $100,000. Ace Machinery obtained its judgment on

November 1. You represent Blake Construction. You got a judgment for Blake on November 10 and delivered a writ of execution to the sheriff on November 15. Cratchett Parts got a judgment on November 20, delivered a writ to the sheriff on November 22, and on November 25 got a deputy to execute the writ by seizing all of the appliances at the Rollins store.

Your client estimates that the appliances will bring $150,000 at the sheriff's sale, which will be held next week. As things stand now, who will get the proceeds from the sale? Can you change that outcome?

15.2. Shoes Below Cost is a local shoe store that discovered too late that volume cannot offset losing money on each sale. Five creditors have obtained judgment against SBC, but only one has executed. Each judgment is for $50,000. You represent the executing creditor, Harry Kleson. On November 25, the sheriff went into the store and announced he was seizing all of the shoes pursuant to Kleson's *fi. fa.* However, SBC's lawyer arrived and explained that SBC had a plan for paying all of its creditors to be discussed at a meeting the next day. With your client's consent, you asked the sheriff to forbear actually seizing the shoes pending the results of the meeting.

At the meeting, SBC agreed to pay each creditor so much a month in exchange for each creditor's agreement to freeze its collection actions, leaving each creditor's execution efforts at the points described above. SBC agreed to a faster payment schedule for your client because he had gotten further along in collection. All the creditors went along with the plan.

Brisk Christmas sales completed the financial demise of SBC, which closed its doors on January 5. SBC just revealed that on December 1 that it granted a security interest in its entire inventory to the Solid State Bank to secure a loan of $200,000 additional operating capital. You have confirmed that the security interest was properly perfected on December 5. Your client estimates that the sale of the remaining shoes at the SBC store will produce $200,000. How will those proceeds be divided? How could you have better protected your client while going along with his decision to negotiate rather than shut the business down on November 25?

15.3. Gerald Barr is a personal injury lawyer who also invests in real estate. Over a period of years he acquired limited partnership interests in several profitable local real estate projects. Unfortunately, his most recent real estate investment has been less successful, and he was forced to drain his savings to meet repeated calls for additional cash by the developer, who eventually failed anyway and filed for bankruptcy. Gerald is behind on all his bills and maxed out on his credit. Recently, he wrote his creditors explaining his problem and assuring them that he would pay everyone in full, with interest, with contingent fees he expects to get in the next year, together with the sale, if necessary, of some of his successful real estate investments. Gerald furnished the creditors with a complete financial statement showing that his assets comfortably exceeded his liabilities and promised cooperation in verification.

All his creditors agreed to wait for payment, except the Solid State Bank, to which he owes $200,000 on a note that became due about two weeks ago. For some years he had a good relationship with SSB, but it became indirectly involved in a lawsuit Gerald brought last year, and the president felt Gerald acted in an unprofessional manner. Gerald has come to you because he fears that SSB may file an involuntary bankruptcy petition and that such a proceeding might destroy or severely harm his law practice even if it could be dismissed. Ask him key questions and give him your action plan. See § 303(h).

15.4. Ramsco is a mud supply company serving the United States and Canada. It supplies the compound that is injected under high pressure into oil and gas drilling lines for lubrication. Ramsco has been hard hit by a recent recession. Not only are orders off, but some customers who used Ramsco's mud are now as much as 20 months behind in payments.

As part of its attempt to collect more of the past-due debts, Ramsco consults your firm about one of its largest debtors, Greenhill, Inc. Greenhill is an independent drilling company in Louisiana that has used Ramsco's mud for three years now. It is currently $2.1 million in debt to Ramsco and has not made a payment in ten months. Informal collection efforts do not seem to have worked. Ramsco is concerned that Greenhill may not survive the recession, and that if it does not, the local creditors will get Greenhill's assets if Ramsco doesn't act soon. Ramsco is sure that it can get at least two other similarly unpaid creditors to join an involuntary petition.

Your firm has scheduled you to make a presentation at a planning session on whether to file for Greenhill's involuntary bankruptcy. You should develop several different theories of what constitutes "generally not paying" and which facts one might be able to uncover about a medium-sized firm in a high-risk industry that would support these theories. Be sure that you can tell your firm the strengths and weaknesses of each theory. See § 303(h). It might be a good idea to be prepared to identify the risks, if any, if your theories don't bear fruit. See § 303(i).

15.5. Harry Hopkins has come to see you about $50,000 he is owed by the Yearning for Mayor Campaign Committee. Hopkins is in the printing business and provided all the Yearning campaign material last spring. As it turned out, Fred Yearning was defeated in his mayoral bid. Even more distressing is the fact that Yearning, in defeat, turned to an "alternative lifestyle" and appears to have no interest in paying his campaign debts. The Yearning Committee had a treasurer and a secretary, as required by state law. The treasurer was George Simple, a small businessman (4'11" and 98 lbs.), and the secretary was Simple's own secretary. Hopkins doesn't know if the committee had any other members, although he is sure it was never incorporated. He believes that the committee still has considerable unspent funds, but fears that Simple may just contribute it to another candidate. Can bankruptcy help? See § 303(a).

15.6. Congresswoman Herring was intrigued by a law review article by Professor Lynn LoPucki, which was given to her by a staff member. Lynn LoPucki, A General Theory of the Dynamics of the State Remedies/Bankruptcy System, 1982 Wis. L. Rev. 311. In that article LoPucki discusses the implications of his empirical study of business bankruptcy in Kansas City. He found that often the owners of small businesses were so reluctant to relinquish their hopes for (and control over) their businesses that they tended to hang onto failing businesses far beyond the economically viable time, thus dissipating the assets that would have been available to creditors had they filed earlier. LoPucki argues that creditors should be encouraged to intervene earlier, through the filing of involuntary bankruptcy petitions.

While the "generally not paying" standard for filing petitions would remain in effect, under LoPucki's proposal petitioning creditors would be granted a priority repayment in bankruptcy to compensate them for the risks they must take in filing an involuntary petition. Explain to the congresswoman why you would or would not recommend an amendment to the Code along the lines suggested by Professor LoPucki.

REORGANIZING BUSINESSES

Business bankruptcy for most companies means use of chapter 11 to try to reorganize the business through recapitalizing its debts and changing its operations. Although the terms vary around the globe, from "administration" to "rescue" to "composition" (and even the noble-sounding French "*sauvegarde*"), all these proceedings aim to prevent liquidation by getting creditors to agree to a court-sanctioned workout plan. The newest version is American, the special, possibly radical version of chapter 11 that took effect in 2020 for small businesses, which we will discuss when we address the elements of a chapter 11 plan in subsequent assignments.

We discuss some of reorganization's variations and mechanics in the overview below. A key difference between liquidation and reorganization is that the latter normally involves continued operation of the company, and reworking its financing and operations, although it can also include a "going concern" sale of the company as a fully functioning unit. Liquidation is usually the piecemeal selling off of individual assets. Chapter 11's unique defining characteristic is leaving the existing management in control of the debtor company, a debtor in possession (or "DIP," in the trade), rather than giving control to a chapter 7 trustee. It's a tough job to stabilize a company in financial crisis and negotiate with creditors or buyers. We look at both what the DIP can do as controlling party of the bankruptcy and what happens when the DIP model of control breaks down.

A. OVERVIEW

1. What Is Reorganization?

Most students have seen the headline: "General Consolidated Corporation Files for Chapter 11," except the debtor was, say, American Airlines or Federal Mogul (the biggest company you never heard of). Chapter 11 is the reorganization form of bankruptcy designed for businesses. "Reorganization" in the business context is a somewhat vague and forbidding word to some students. Traditionally, it has described a process where the debtor "reorganizes" its debts by extending the time in which to pay them and reducing the total amount to be paid. In that way, it's similar to chapter 13 for individuals, but it has far more flexibility and fewer hard statutory constraints (e.g., no minimum repayment period of three to five years). Chapter 11, unlike chapter 13, is *an invitation to a negotiation.* Creditors get to participate in the court case and get a vote on the plan of reorganization. These topics are studied later; the key point for now is that chapter 11 permits creative lawyering and financial maneuvering.

To illustrate, a traditional chapter 11 "plan of reorganization" might provide that the debtor will pay only 75% of the amount of its bank loans and will have six years to do so rather than the two years according to the loans' terms. (In the jargon of the trade, the 25% forgiveness of the principal amount of the loans is called a "haircut," although the lender may feel the hair is being cut below the scalp.) Sometimes the debt itself may be converted into equity, so the bank loan may take a more dramatic haircut of 80% but also be issued a significant amount of stock in the reorganized company.

The statutory basis for reorganization was constructed in the Chandler Act amidst the Great Depression of the 1930s. Its origins lay in the railroad reorganizations in the 1800s, but those judge-made procedures broke down under the pressure of the near-collapse of the American economy in the Depression. In 1978, the Code reorganized reorganization, combining the specialized procedures created by the Chandler Act for public companies and private companies into one all-encompassing procedure, the chapter 11 we have today. It was the first successful reorganization procedure in the world and has been widely admired and copied around the globe.

Despite its longevity and influence, chapter 11 has also evolved over a quarter-century, producing species that are rather different from the parent genus. The very flexibility that makes reorganization a powerful mechanism for saving failing businesses also has permitted "reorganization" procedures that do not follow the traditional reorganization model or produce the same outcomes. For example, "prepacks" (short for "prepackaged") or "363 sales" (for the section in the Code that permits asset spin-off) are generally contrasted to a traditional chapter 11 when the business spends a while in chapter 11 and eventually emerges to operate with restructured debts. There is debate about the extent to which the traditional model is useful in today's economy and if so, for what types of businesses, which vary by size and industry. The Code follows the traditional model, and we think it remains viable. We start by learning the basic model before we advance to the innovative twists. Just remember that all these vehicles involve a petition under chapter 11 and are technically "reorganization" bankruptcies.

The debt of a business debtor is often much more complicated than that of a consumer. Debt structures may include public bondholders or noteholders, subordinated levels of debt, suppliers from around the country and the world, and institutional lenders such as banks, insurance companies, and pension funds. As mentioned earlier in Assignment 13, chapter 11 is available for individuals as well as corporations, but there we were thinking of consumer debtors who were forced into chapter 11 by ineligibility for chapter 7 or chapter 13. There are also many business debtors who are individuals, because sometimes enterprises are just sole proprietorships; by 2002, about 11% of chapter 11 business filers were natural persons. Elizabeth Warren & Jay Lawrence Westbrook, The Success of

Chapter 11: A Challenge to the Critics, 107 Mich. L. Rev. 603, 610 (2009). Although that is a fascinating and unexpected niche of debtors, worthy of further research, the typical chapter 11 debtor is corporate. Most individual debtors, even if saddled with business debts, are better off in chapter 13, which is less complex and less costly.

Nearly all of our ensuing discussion of chapter 11 will assume that the debtor is a corporation. Some reorganizations are purely financial. That is, the business operations remain the same, while the debts are written down, eliminated, and/or converted into equity. A business that has loaded up on debt may be operationally sound in the sense that revenues comfortably exceed marginal costs, but that business may have no hope of meeting its debt service. There is no reason in such a case to change the business operations. Instead, all that takes place is that the rights of various stakeholders must be readjusted. Old equity (i.e., the shareholders) may be wiped out, for example, while the unsecured creditors become the new owners of the stock. These reorganizations are sometimes called "balance sheet reorganizations" to reflect the fact that they take place on paper rather than by shifting operations.

Other reorganizations involve a wholesale reshuffling of the business operations. They can be called "business model reorganizations" because they result from a lack of sufficient earnings to support the enterprise. The debtor will use the breathing room provided by the automatic stay to close or substantially reduce money-losing divisions, restructure supply contracts, trim excess staff, refocus product lines, sell expendable assets, reduce the number of office parties, and so forth. In the retail industry, for example, which has been radically reshaped by online commerce, reorganization often involves closing the unprofitable stores while sprucing up the remainder. Steel companies have reorganized by dropping peripheral lines of business and closing their most out-of-date plants. Sometimes a merger is effected with a strategic competitor, which usually results in elimination of redundant or poorly performing aspects of the business.

A successful business-model reorganization in chapter 11 will usually produce a smaller, leaner company able to concentrate on the type of business that it does well. (Note that a key premise of a business model reorganization is that the new company can, in fact, be profitable. If it can't, say because there is insufficient demand for the product or unbearably high supply or labor costs, then many creditors will clamor for shutdown and liquidation, sometimes by converting the case to chapter 7.) Disagreements about a company's viability, and whether the focus should be on balance sheet or business model changes, can set up a hostile negotiating environment. An example was Borders Books, which eventually liquidated. A core function of bankruptcy law is to help structure the negotiations, keep them moving forward, and to offer tools to overcome recalcitrance or resistance, if necessary.

2. The Human Element

There is a human side to the chapter 11 process that is at least as important as legal doctrine and economic policy. The businesses that once were courted as the valued customers of banks and lending consortia see a different side of these lenders when the business begins to slip. For nearly every case and problem discussed in the following pages, there was once an amicable relationship that became frayed due to market changes, mismanagement, or both.

The collapse of the stock market bubble in 2000 and the Great Recession following the collapse of Lehman Brothers in 2008 evidenced widespread economic problems. Crippling unemployment and huge losses in retirement accounts once again made the general public aware of the personal trauma of financial failure. A vivid example was the sight of Enron employees in shock after learning that their life savings (pensions invested in the company stock) had been wiped out in a scandalous collapse. Outside of the national headlines, many other business bankruptcies also are stories of personal tragedy, ranging from shuttered car plants in the Midwest to vast half-finished housing developments in the desert.

Corporate cases revealing fraud represent a minority but an important one. Such situations raise interesting questions about the role of bankruptcy law, along with SEC investigations and criminal trials, in the policing of our financial markets and corporate boardrooms. A warehouse of books covers the subprime mortgage collapse and the rest of the 2008 financial debacle, one notable account being Michael Lewis's The Big Short (2010), which was made into an Oscar-winning movie of the same name. All these sources include a number of salutary lessons for lawyers and other professionals who advise public companies. Bethany McLean and Peter Elkind's treatment of Enron, The Smartest Guys in the Room (2003), and follow-up movie (with an appearance by bankruptcy law professor Nancy Rapoport) are also fascinating. We also recommend HBO's Too Big to Fail, which dramatizes the collapse of Lehman, and the PBS Frontline documentary The Untouchables (broadcast Jan. 22, 2013) for a hard look at the aftermath of the financial meltdown. Movie night, anyone?

Some of the most controversial chapter 11 cases do not involved fraud. For example, the government's role in supporting (some would say controlling) the bankruptcies of General Motors and Chrysler stirred much debate. See Steven Rattner, Overhaul: An Insider's Account of the Obama Administration's Emergency Rescue of the Auto Industry (2011); Bill Frezza, Obama to Secured Creditors: Drop Dead, Real Clear Markets, May 4, 2009, https://www.realclearmarkets.com/articles/2009/05/obama_to_secured _creditors_dro.html.

Business in the modern era has yet to find its Balzac or its Dickens, but Tom Wolfe has come closer than most in his novel A Man in Full. The following excerpt captures some of the human dynamics of the financial restructuring that often occurs in chapter 11, specifically that exquisite time before complete financial meltdown or bankruptcy when the relationship between debtor and creditor changes. Not all "workouts" are like this, but the debtor's fall from grace often yields similar emotions, on both sides of the table.

The protagonist of the novel is Charlie Croker, a larger-than-life Atlanta real estate developer who finds his empire in serious financial trouble. He is invited to a meeting with the bankers at his lead bank. (The developer, and the author's prose, are earthier and more vivid than this excerpt reveals. A full reading is highly recommended.)

Tom Wolfe, "The Saddlebags" from A Man in Full (1998)

Just then Croker's gaze wandered toward a far corner of the room and a doubtful, puzzled look came over his face.

Peepgass's colleague, Harry Zale, the workout artiste, leaned his huge head over and said out of the corner of his mouth:

"Hey, Ray, check out the big boffster. He just noticed the dead plant."

It was true. Croker's eyes had drifted over to the corner where, in a dismal gloaming, there stood a solitary tropical plant, a dracaena, in a clay pot, dying. Several long, skinny yellowish fronds drooped over like the tongues of the dead. The pot rested on an otherwise empty expanse of Streptolon carpet pocked with the mashed-in depressions of desk feet, chair casters, and office machines that had been moved somewhere else. The old man had to squint to make it out. He was puzzled. He could hardly see a thing. From where he was sitting, he should have been able to look out through the plate-glass wall and seen much of Midtown Atlanta . . . the IBM Tower, the GLG Grande, Promenade One, Promenade Two, the Campanile, the Southern Bell Center, Colony Square, and three of his own buildings, the Phoenix Center, the MossCo Tower, and the TransEx Palladium. But he couldn't. . . . It was the glare. He and his contingent had been seated so that they had to look straight into it.

Oh, everything about this room was cunningly seedy and unpleasant. The conference table itself was a vast thing, a regular aircraft carrier, but it was put together in modular sections that didn't quite jibe where they met, and its surface was not wood but some sort of veal-gray plastic laminate. On the table, in front of each of the two dozen people present, was a pathetic setting of paperware, a paper cup for the orange juice, a paper mug with foldout handles for the coffee, which gave off an odor of incinerated PVC cables, and a paper plate with a huge cold, sticky, cheesy, cowpie-like cinnamon-cheddar coffee bun that struck terror into the heart of every man in the room who had ever read an article about arterial plaque or free radicals. That, in its entirety, was the breakfast meeting's breakfast.

To top it off, on the walls a pair of NO SMOKING signs glowered down upon the Croker Global crew with the sort of this-means-you lettering you might expect to find in the cracking unit of an oil refinery, but not at a conference of twenty-four ladies and gentlemen of banking and commerce in the PlannersBanc Tower in Midtown Atlanta.

. . .

Harry began speaking in a softer, lower voice. "Listen, Mr. Croker, don't get me wrong. We're on your side here. We don't want this to turn into a free-for-all with nine lenders, either. And we wouldn't particularly look forward to the press coverage." He paused to let that terrorist threat, the press, stalk the room. "We're the agent bank in this setup, and that gives us the privilege of looking out for PlannersBanc first of all. But we gotta come up with something *concrete*." He extended his right fist up in the air as high as it would go and said, "Where's the money gonna come from? It ain't gonna come . . . *poof!*" — he sprung his fist open — "from outta the air! Mr. Stroock assures us you got a lot of sound assets. Okay . . . good. The time has come to make them liquid. The time has come to pay us back. The time has come to sell something. I'm with you — the tailgate has dropped."

At that point young Stroock jumped in, evidently to give his boss, Croker, time to get his breath back and his battered wits together. Just "selling something," said Stroock, was not such an easy proposition. Croker Global had considered this particular option. But in the first place there was a complex of interlocking ownerships. Certain corporate structures within Croker Global's real estate portfolio actually owned certain independently structured divisions of Croker Global Foods, each of which was a corporation in its own right, and—

"I'm aware of all that," said the Artiste. "I've got your organization chart. I'm entering it in the Org-off."

"The Org-off?" said Wismer Stroock.

"Yeah. That's a contest we have at PlannersBanc for the worst-looking organization chart. I thought nobody was gonna be able to beat Chai Long Shipping, out of Hong Kong. They got three hundred ships, and each ship is a separate corporation, and each corporation owns a fraction of at least five other ships, and each ship has a color code, and the chart is ten feet long. Looks like a Game Boy semiconductor panel, blown up. I thought Chai Long was a sure thing in the Org-off until I saw yours. Yours looks like a bowl of linguine primavera. You just gotta untangle it and sell something."

"Unh-huh. I see. Do you mind if I finish?"

"No, I don't mind, but why don't we entertain a few modest proposals first."

The Artiste turned to an assistant on his other side and said in a low voice, "Gimme the cars, Sheldon." The young man, Sheldon, snapped open a ring binder and handed Harry a sheet of paper.

The Artiste studied it for a moment, then looked up at Croker and said, "Now, in your last financial statement you list seven company automobiles, three BMW 750:L's valued at . . . what's it say here? . . . $93,000 each. . . . Two BMW 540:A's valued at $55,000 each, a Ferrari 355 valued at $129,000, and a customized Cadillac Seville STS valued at $75,000. By the way, how'd you get here this morning?"

Croker gave the Artiste a long death-ray stare, then said, "I drove."

"What'd you drive? A BMW? The Ferrari? The Customized Cadillac Seville STS? Which one?"

Croker eyed him balefully but said nothing. The steam was coming back into his system. His mighty chest rose and fell with a prodigious sigh. The dark stains were inching closer, from either side of his chest, toward the sternum.

Harry said, "Seven company cars. . . . Sell 'em."

"Those cars are in constant use," said Croker. "Besides, suppose we sold 'em—to the distinct disadvantage of our operations, by the way. What are we talking about here? A couple of hundred thousand dollars."

"Hey!" said the Artiste with a big smile. "I don't know about you, but I have great respect for a couple of hundred thousand dollars. Besides, your arithmetic's a little off. It's five hundred and ninety-three thousand. A thousand more insignificant items like that and we've got half a billion and plenty to spare. See how easy it is? Sell 'em."

He turned to his assistant again and said, "Gimme the airplanes." The ring binder snapped open, and the assistant, Sheldon, gave him several sheets of paper.

"Now Mr. Croker," said Harry, looking at the pages, "you also list four aircraft, two Beechjet 400A's, a Super King Air 350, and a Gulfstream Five." Then he looked up at Croker and, in a voice like W. C. Fields's, repeated: "a Gulfstream Five . . . a Gee-Five. . . . That's a $38 million aircraft, if I'm not mistaken, and I see here that yours has certain en*hance*ments. . . . A Satcom telephone system, $300,000 installed . . . a Satcom telephone enables you to telephone, while you're aloft from anywhere in the world, isn't that correct?"

"Yeah," said Croker.

"How many of Croker Global's operations are overseas, Mr. Croker?"

"As of now, none, but—"

"And I see you've also got a set of SkyWatch cabin radar display screens, worth $125,000 installed, and a cabin interior custom designed and furnished by a Mr. Ronald Vine for $2,845,000. And it says here there's a *painting* installed on that airplane worth $190,000." The Artiste raised his great chin and looked down his nose at Croker with a mixture of incredulity and disdain. "Are those figures correct? They come straight from your financial statement. You presented these items as collateral."

"That's right."

"That's $40 million tied up in that one aircraft." He turned to his assistant. "What's the total value of the other three planes, Sheldon?"

"Fifteen million, nine hundred thousand."

"Fifteen million, nine hundred thousand," said Harry. "So now we're talking about $58 million worth of airplanes. Where do you keep those airplanes, Mr. Croker?"

"Out at PDK," said Croker, referring to the airport for private aircraft in DeKalb County, just east of the city. PDK was short for Peachtree-DeKalb.

"You lease hangar space there?"

"Yeah."

"How many pilots do you employ?"

"Twelve."

"Twelve. . . ." The Artiste arched his eyebrows and whistled through his teeth in mock surprise. He smiled. "We're gonna save you a whole *lotta* money." He smiled again, as if this was all great fun. Then the smile vanished, and he said with a toneless finality, "Sell 'em."

"That we could always do," said Croker, "but it would be totally self-defeating. Those aircraft are not used in a frivolous manner. In Global Foods we got seventeen warehouses in fourteen states. We got—"

"Sell 'em."

"We got—"

"Sell 'em. From now on we're gonna be like the Vietcong. We're gonna travel on the ground and live off the land."

3. Mechanics of Chapter 11

After a business files a chapter 11 petition, an initial period of calm follows in which the automatic stay halts all creditor action. But that calm for the debtor lasts about two seconds, and so it is actually more accurate to say that the filing is often followed by an initial period of chaos when the debtor must juggle emergencies: stabilizing the failing business, finding new funds to finance the estate, and taking a swath of other critical actions to keep the company afloat (such as keeping key executives, getting out of burdensome contracts, and fighting secured creditors who plead a lack of adequate protection in their collateral). Once some stability has been achieved, the debtor then sets to negotiating a plan with its major creditors.

As the negotiations draw to a close, the debtor enters another whirlwind of activity as it attempts to have the plan confirmed by the bankruptcy court. Objectors may come out of the woodwork and urge the court to deny confirmation and convert the case to liquidation in chapter 7 or dismiss it entirely. Competing plans may sway some creditors, or the debtor may struggle to engage or pacify other constituencies including employees, tort victims, pension funds, or regulatory agencies. Corporate counsel for a major retailer that entered and successfully emerged from bankruptcy described the experience as similar to flying through a hurricane: initially chaotic and frightening, followed by a period of unreal calm, followed in turn by another period of chaos in which the survival of the enterprise was once again very much at stake.

The debtor's goal in chapter 11 is to confirm a plan of reorganization, in which it will promise to pay creditors a certain percentage of their claims over a stated period of time, with payment to be made in cash, in property, or in securities issued by the reorganized debtor. The proposed plan and an explanatory disclosure statement are distributed to all creditors who have filed, very much like a prospectus for a securities offering. A chapter 11 plan is put to a formal vote, with ballots and procedures for determining approval by the specified majorities of creditors in each class (creditors are divided into "classes" for voting purposes, which we will discuss later in Assignment 28). § 1126(c). If the creditors approve the plan, the court is likely to confirm it, provided that the plan also conforms to several other statutory requirements. § 1129. These include measures that will be familiar to those who mastered chapter 13, including a good faith requirement and satisfaction of a best interests of creditors test.

Upon confirmation of the plan in chapter 11, a corporate debtor is discharged from all its prepetition debts and released from all liens, except as provided in the plan. § 1141(c), (d). This chapter 11 discharge cannot be overstated in significance, because it means that with the requisite votes of creditors and confirmation by the court, a business debtor can be treated like an individual and get a "fresh start" as reorganized. This is a marked contrast to chapter 7, where businesses effectively die still smothered in debt. In fact, the chapter 11 discharge is even better than for some consumers. In chapter 11, the discharge kicks in upon the effective date of the plan (shortly after it is confirmed). § 1141(d)(1). By contrast, a chapter 13 debtor must complete all plan payments to receive a discharge.

All these myriad rules will be explained in the material that lies ahead. For now, we simply introduce you to some new terminology and crucial benchmarks in the chapter 11 process: filing a petition, the DIP, disclosure statement, the reorganization plan, and confirmation.

B. CONTROL: THE DEBTOR IN POSSESSION

Control of the debtor's assets and affairs lies at the heart of all bankruptcy law. Jay L. Westbrook, The Control of Wealth in Bankruptcy, 82 Tex. L. Rev. 795 (2004). In chapter 11, much of the control is given to the debtor in possession ("DIP"). The DIP is effectively deemed to be the trustee, with all the powers and most of the duties attendant to that role. § 1107(a). Thus, for example, the DIP has the power to sell assets, with court approval, and the duty to ensure that every claim made by creditors is valid ("allowable"). Above all, the DIP has the power to act for the estate in negotiating a plan of reorganization. The court has the ultimate control, but a good deal of power resides in the DIP, the debtor's corporate management.

The appeal of chapter 11 to a Charlie Croker is immediately apparent: in chapter 11, Charlie is back in control of his business, albeit known by the less glamorous moniker DIP. That single fact makes chapter 11 enormously attractive to management. Having said that, we noticed that PlannersBanc has security interests in many of the company's assets, so the Artiste will still have a lot to say about the fate of Croker Global. But Charlie, at least for now, keeps his reserved space in the company parking lot and the planes stay in the hangars. This is a marked contrast to many other legal systems, where the first thing an insolvency filing does is divest the management of any power over the corporate debtor. See, e.g., Jay Lawrence Westbrook, Christoph Paulus, Harry Rajak & Charles Booth, A Global View of Business Insolvency Systems (Martinus Nijhoff 2010).

The idea of DIP control came from the old Chapter XI, designed in the Depression for small proprietorships and closely-held companies where the management and owners were largely the same people. In passing the Code in 1978, Congress put a DIP in charge of every chapter 11 case as the legal stand-in for the trustee. The consequences in large public companies (in which management and ownership are routinely separated) are very different from the effects in the case of Porky's Tanning and Tax Service, where Ms. Porky is the DIP and resident expert on bronzing and Turbo Tax. In large companies, stockholders (who own the corporation) are not the people who manage it; managers of public corporations may own a small amount of stock to incentivize performance but they are nominally and functionally employees. This separation of ownership and control is the fundamental problem of governance in large companies. For the classic discussion, see A. Berle & G. Means, The Modern Corporation and Private Property (1932). The corporate structure means that technically when ABC, Inc. files chapter 11, ABC, Inc. is the DIP. But a corporation is a piece of paper that has to act through humans, and so ABC, Inc. acts through its shareholder-elected board of directors, which in turn delegates management to a CEO and other officers whose interests may at times diverge from those of the shareholders. This principal-agent tension can be especially pronounced in companies in financial trouble, when the interests of management and stockholders can diverge even more sharply. Recall for example that a bankruptcy trustee has a general duty to maximize recovery to unsecured creditors; a DIP inherits that same duty. By contrast, a board of directors elected by shareholders may not give two figs about creditors but only about maximizing their investments.

The DIP concept puts the existing pre-bankruptcy management in charge of the debtor and the chapter 11 process, but there is only skeletal guidance in the Code on management's role. As a result, chapter 11 gives management flexibility to exercise its control on behalf of several possible constituencies. It may act on behalf of stockholders, bondholders, trade creditors, bank lenders, or others, like employees and communities. Most likely, it will try to precariously balance the competing interests, subject to the power that each group has by virtue of bankruptcy law and negotiating leverage. Elizabeth Warren, Bankruptcy Policymaking in an Imperfect World, 92 Mich. L. Rev. 336 (1992). Finally, experience and economic theory combine to suggest that management will give considerable attention to protecting its own interests.

Some scholars have claimed that the DIP concept is antiquated formalism because today's large public-company chapter 11 cases are effectively controlled by lenders, a result that they applaud. See, e.g., David Skeel, Creditor's Ball: The "New" New Corporate Governance in Chapter 11, 152 U. Pa. L. Rev. 917 (2003); Douglas G. Baird & Robert K. Rasmussen, The End of Bankruptcy, 55 Stan. L. Rev. 751 (2002). These lenders possess important functional abilities to check the formal powers the DIP enjoys under chapter 11. Others have expressed concern about the increasing power of secured creditors when financing involves broad security interests and contractual provisions that limit management—even in bankruptcy—where there are more checks on such powers as discussed in Assignment 19. Elizabeth Warren & Jay L. Westbrook, Secured Parties in Possession, 22 Am. Bankr. Inst. L.J. 12 (2003); Westbrook, Control, supra.

Control of smaller businesses in chapter 11 is also not without controversy. Professor LoPucki has suggested that too often the owners of those businesses as DIPs use chapter 11 for their own purposes while abusing those powers vis-à-vis creditors. Lynn M. LoPucki, The Debtor in Full Control—Systems Failure Under Chapter II of the Bankruptcy Code? (pt 2), 57 Am. Bankr. L.J. 247 (1983). See also Douglas G. Baird & Edward R. Morrison, Serial Entrepreneurs and Small Business Bankruptcies, 105 Colum. L. Rev. 2310 (2005). Because a DIP is charged with steering the business out of troubled waters, its control is a key determinant of how the chapter 11 reorganization unfolds.

C. THE SCOPE OF THE DIP'S CONTROL

The drafters of chapter 11, and the judges and lawyers that apply it, have a strong practical streak. The Code and its application in thousands of cases to date recognize that it does no good to provide powerful legal tools for reorganization if the manager is too busy to use them because she has to run to court every time a business decision has to be made ("Your Honor, can the stores please have a sale on turkeys in early November?"). The Code acknowledges this reality by pragmatically authorizing the debtor to operate "in the ordinary course of business" without a hearing and permission from the court. § 363(c)(1). As with all things in human affairs, however, that phrase is subject to interpretation.

In re COOK AND SONS MINING, INC.
2005 WL 2386238 (E.D. Ky. 2005)

Caldwell, Judge.

Cook and Sons Mining, Inc. (the "Debtor") and South Carolina Public Service Authority ("Santee Cooper") appeal from a Memorandum Opinion and Order entered by the bankruptcy court on December 10, 2004 in which the bankruptcy court granted Santee Cooper an administrative expense claim in the amount of $5,150,284.62. With the December 10, 2004 Order, the bankruptcy court also ruled that the Debtor could not avoid its contract with Santee Cooper for the months of January 2004 to June 2004. . . .

DEBTOR'S CHAPTER 11 PETITION AND POST-PETITION CONTRACT WITH SANTEE COOPER

The Debtor filed its voluntary petition for relief under Chapter 11 of the Bankruptcy Code (the "Code") on August 26, 2003 (the "Petition Date"). The Debtor's business was the mining, cleaning and shipping of high quality coal to various end users which were mostly public or privately owned utilities via unit trains provided by CSX.

Santee Cooper is a South Carolina state agency operating as a public power and water utility. In November, 2003, Santee Cooper began taking bids for a six-month supply of up to 900,000 tons of coal or a one-year supply of up to 1,800,000 tons. On November 21, 2003, the Debtors submitted a proposal offering to deliver 60,000 tons of coal per month for a one-year period beginning January 1, 2004 at $35 per ton. Pat Runey of Santee Cooper sent an e-mail to the Debtor accepting the proposal and stating that he would send a purchase order after the holidays. . . .

The Debtor began shipping coal under the Contract in January 2004. In January, the Debtor shipped 21,233 tons of coal to Santee Cooper; in February, 50,811 tons; and in March, 11,047 tons. Thus, at no time during its months of performance did the Debtor ship 60,000 tons in one month as contracted. By April, 2004, the Debtor was running out of money and ultimately became administratively insolvent in April 2004. On April 26, 2004, Coal Extraction Company ("Coal X") took over all of the Debtor's operations.

SANTEE COOPER'S MOTION FOR ADMINISTRATIVE CLAIM AND DEBTOR'S MOTION TO AVOID SANTEE COOPER CONTRACT

On July 27, 2004, Santee Cooper filed a Motion for Allowance and Payment of Administrative Priority Claim in which Santee Cooper asked the bankruptcy court to enter an order allowing Santee Cooper an administrative priority claim in the amount of $10,815,484.62 pursuant to § 503(b)(1)(A) of the Code. Santee Cooper stated that this amount represented the damages it incurred as a result of the Debtor's breach of the post-petition contract. In response, the Debtor argued that Santee Cooper was not entitled to an administrative priority claim in any amount because the post-petition contract was not in the "ordinary course of business" pursuant to Code § 363(b) and was avoidable under Code § 549(a). The Debtor also filed a Motion to Avoid the contract on the same basis. . . .

In the Opinion and Order, the Bankruptcy Court ordered that, the Debtor could avoid the post-petition contract for the months of July 2004 to December 2004 but not for the months of January 2004 through June 2004. The Bankruptcy Court further granted Santee Cooper an administrative expense claim of $5,150,284.62 which represented its damages from the

Debtor's breach of the post-petition contract for the months of January to June, 2004. . . .

THE DEBTOR'S MOTION TO AVOID THE SANTEE COOPER CONTRACT

Pursuant to Code § 549, a debtor-in-possession[3] may avoid certain transfers of property that occur after the commencement of the case if the transfer was unauthorized. 11 U.S.C. § 549(a). Whether the post-petition contract with Santee Cooper was authorized is controlled by Code § 363(b)(1). Under that provision, a debtor-in-possession's transactions, other than those in the ordinary course of business, must be authorized by the court after notice and a hearing. In contrast, the debtor-in-possession may enter into transactions that *are* in the ordinary course of business. . . . Whether the contract was in the "ordinary course of business" is an issue of fact and will be reviewed under the clearly erroneous standard.

1) Horizontal and Vertical Dimension Tests

Neither the Code nor its legislative history provides a framework for analyzing whether particular transactions are or are not in the ordinary course of a debtor's business for the purpose of Code § 363. "Typically courts examine the 'horizontal' and 'vertical' dimensions of a debtor's business to address these policies reflected in the Code and to determine whether a transaction is outside the ordinary course of business." In re Crystal Apparel, Inc., 220 B.R. at 831.

The horizontal inquiry is an objective test asking whether, from an industry-wide perspective, the transaction is of the sort commonly undertaken by companies in that industry. For example, "raising a crop would not be in the ordinary course of business for a widget manufacturer." In re Waterfront Companies, Inc. v. Johnson, 56 B.R. 31, 35 (Bankr. D. Minn. 1985).

The vertical dimension examines "the reasonable expectations of interested parties as to this particular debtor-in-possession." In re Crystal Apparel, Inc., 220 B.R. at 831. . . . Creditors have a right to consider whether the proposed transaction "imposes a financial cost that exceeds the possible benefit of entering into the agreement and also exceeds the possible detriment that will occur if the debtor-in-possession does not enter into the agreement." *Id.* Thus, the issue is whether the transaction "is the type of transaction which creditors would expect to have advance notice of and have a chance to object to." In re Waterfront Co., Inc., 56 B.R. at 35. . . .

2) The Contract Was in the Ordinary Course of Business

Here, the parties have agreed that the contract meets the horizontal test for "ordinary." They have stipulated that "[c]ontracts of one year or

---

[3] Code § 549 specifically provides for the trustee's avoidance rights. Nevertheless, Code § 1107(a) grants a debtor-in-possession "all the rights" of a trustee with certain exceptions not applicable here.

more for the purchase of coal with fixed prices and/or escalating prices per ton are ordinary in the coal industry." There is no evidence to the contrary in the record. Accordingly, the court finds that the post-petition contract meets the horizontal test for "ordinary."

As to the vertical test, the Debtor's pre-petition business was mining and shipping coal to utilities. In the 12-month period prior to the Petition Date, the Debtor had contracts with 11 separate entities. Of those contracts, the highest monthly requirement was 60,000 tons to VEPCO over an 18-month period. Post-petition, the Debtor had contracts with at least four entities. Of these contracts, the highest monthly requirement was 60,000 tons over a 12-month period under the Santee Cooper contract. Thus, there is nothing in the record to indicate that the size of the Santee Cooper contract was inconsistent with the Debtor's pre-petition business. . . .

At the beginning of the case, the Debtor was able to produce as much as 170,000 tons of coal per month. Its post-petition contracts with Kentucky Utilities, Orlando and Santee Cooper required it to produce in aggregate 107,000 tons per month. . . . Accordingly, there is nothing in the record that indicates that, at the time the contract was formed, the Debtor was incapable of fulfilling its obligations under the Santee Cooper contract or that those obligations were extraordinary or unexpected.

Runey ("Runey") of Santee Cooper testified that in November 2003, when the parties entered into the post-petition contract, $35 per ton was a good price. . . . Accordingly, at the time the contract was formed, the purchase price was not extraordinary or unexpected.

Further, at the time the parties entered into the contract, there was no indication that the financial costs of the agreement would exceed the possible detriment if the Debtor did not enter into the contract. Again, it appeared at that time that the Debtor was capable of fulfilling its obligations under the contract. At the time that the Debtor entered into the contract, it was trying to and believed that it could continue operating and could reorganize. . . .

Creditors must have expected the Debtor to continue to enter into coal production contracts while reorganizing. There is nothing about the size or nature of the contract that renders it extraordinary or subjected the creditors to unexpected risks. Accordingly, the contract meets the vertical test for "ordinary course of business" and the Bankruptcy Court correctly concluded that, at the time the contract was formed, it was in the "ordinary course of business."

[The court disagreed with other rulings of the bankruptcy court concerning the Santee Cooper contract and ended by affirming in part and reversing in part—Eds.]

_____

Apparently, it is in the ordinary course for a coal company to sell coal. But not everything coal-related would cut it. For example, a "going out of business" sale would surely be extraordinary. And consider the case of that nefarious El Paso watering hole, The Three Legged Monkey. The neighbors hated it, begrudging the odd murder it hosted here and there, and repeatedly fought in the city council meetings to close it down, trying to convince oversight boards to pull its liquor license, etc. Eventually, the city leaned on the landlord to terminate the bar's lease. (The landlord was called a ground lease holder, meaning it didn't own the land outright on which it developed the strip mall. The underlying holder of the fee simple was the city's airport authority, making the bar technically a subtenant, so the city threatened to terminate the landlord's ground lease for the whole shopping mall if it didn't kick out the bar.) One problem: the landlord was already in chapter 11 itself, and when it ultimately terminated the lease at the city's behest, it did so without court approval. Fighting back—and jumping into its own chapter 11 to get an automatic stay for good measure—the bar argued that it was current on its lease and the landlord never had and never would terminate such a tenant's lease in the ordinary course of business. The court reluctantly agreed and voided the termination as an unauthorized act outside the ordinary course of business. In re Patriot Place, Ltd., 486 B.R. 773 (Bankr. W.D. Tex. 2013). (For Internet fun, explore the bar owner's influence on the subsequent mayoral campaign of the city representative who led the charge against the oddly limbed primate's bar.) No case could better illustrate the multi-constituency nature of a chapter 11 case.

Incidentally, when the DIP operates the business *in* the ordinary course under § 363(b), the outside world may see no day-to-day change. The DIP looks like the old debtor, but isn't the old debtor. Even though the envelopes bear the same corporate logo, the DIP controls a new legal entity—the estate—and has most of the legal rights and duties of the trustee. § 1107. So when most of the major airlines filed for chapter 11 in the early 2000s (some catching up a decade later), passengers continued cruising the skies, frequent flyer miles fully intact.

D.   LOSING CONTROL: WHEN THE DIP MODEL FAILS

If the DIP runs the show, you may ask whether the system relies on this fox alone to guard the henhouse. The answer is no. First, the U.S. Trustee is an important participant in chapter 11s, especially at the beginning of a case. The U.S. Trustee will weigh in on motions the debtor brings early in the proceedings, well before other stakeholders even know a case is up and running. Second, the Code provides for the appointment of an Official Committee of Unsecured Creditors, which has a right to scrutinize the debtor's activities (demanding financials, etc.) and negotiates with the debtor in securing a plan of reorganization. §§ 1102-1103. One reason a creditors' committee can play a central role is that its lawyers are ordinarily paid from the assets of the estate, just like the debtor's lawyers, so the committee has the funding to support an active role. § 330(a)(1). They also may have an enhanced entitlement to information from the debtor. Sometimes the committees or other stakeholders in the reorganization process will uncover debtor DIP misconduct.

Appointment of an unsecured creditors' committee is mandatory on the face of the statute, but often no creditor is willing to serve in smaller cases. Especially in larger cases, other stakeholders, notably equity shareholders, may seek "official" status. If they get it, their lawyers also get paid from the estate. For just that reason, however, the courts often hesitate to authorize such a committee unless it seems really necessary.

Despite the strong presumption that management will remain in control in chapter 11 as DIP, occasionally the courts will grant the motion of a U.S. Trustee or a creditor to appoint or displace the DIP and appoint an external trustee. Section 1104 authorizes appointment in situations of fraud or gross mismanagement or, more generally, when it is in the interests of all parties.

In re BIOLITEC, INC.

2013 WL 1352302 (Bankr. D.N.J. 2013) (not approved for publication)

STECKROTH, Bankruptcy Judge.

AngioDynamics, Inc. ("AngioDynamics") has moved for entry of an order directing the appointment of a chapter 11 trustee pursuant to 11 U.S.C. § 1104(a) ("Motion"). Opposition to the Motion was filed by Biolitec, Inc. ("Biolitec" or "Debtor"). . . .

AngioDynamics argues that "cause," as required by § 1104(a)(1), exists based upon: (i) the findings of the United States District Court for the District of Massachusetts; (ii) Biolitec's actions in the captioned bankruptcy case; and (iii) the inability of Biolitec's management to represent the best interests of Biolitec's creditors, and, alternatively, pursuant to § 1104(a)(2), arguing a trustee is in the best interests of the creditors.

Biolitec counters that AngioDynamics has not met its burden to establish clear and convincing evidence to overcome the strong presumption of leaving a debtor in possession of the estate. . . .

BACKGROUND AND FACTS

Biolitec is a member of a multi-national group of companies in the business of manufacturing and distributing fiber optic devices, medical lasers and fibers, photo-pharmaceuticals, and industrial fiber optics ("Biolitec Group"). The Biolitec Group serves global markets including Europe, Asia, the Middle East, and the United States. Biolitec is the United States affiliate of the Biolitec Group. Biolitec only engages in light manufacturing and acquires most of its products by purchasing them from the European Biolitec Group entities. [The debtor and "Related Entities" were all substantially controlled by Wolfgang Neuberger.] . . .

The New York Litigation

AngioDynamics and Biolitec were parties to a Supply and Distribution Agreement dated April 1, 2002. . . . In January of 2008, AngioDynamics brought suit against Biolitec for breach of the indemnification provisions of the Supply and Distribution Agreement. . . .

In November of 2012, the New York District Court awarded AngioDynamics just over $23 million. Biolitec perfected its appeal of the

New York Judgment in the United States Court of Appeals for the Second Circuit on January 18, 2013. The appeal is pending. [Biolitec filed its petition for Chapter 11 relief on January 22, 2013.]

The Massachusetts Litigation

In October of 2009, fearing that Biolitec was systematically funneling assets to certain of the Related Entities to make any potential judgment uncollectible, AngioDynamics brought suit in the United States District Court for the District of Massachusetts. The complaint alleges that Biolitec AG, BioMed, and Neuberger fraudulently removed assets amounting to $18 million from Biolitec to render the Debtor judgment proof. . . .

Judge Ponsor of the Massachusetts District Court first entered a temporary restraining order and then a preliminary injunction on September 13, 2012 ("Massachusetts Injunction"). The Massachusetts Injunction prevented Biolitec from transferring its assets and also prevented Biolitec AG from merging with its Austrian subsidiary, Biolitec AG Austria. No evidentiary hearing was held, but Judge Ponsor stated that the pleadings presented by AngioDynamics showed an

> extraordinarily dramatic diminution in [Biolitec's] assets and an increase in its debt just in the last three years. . . . All this points strongly to a deliberate course of conduct on the part of [Biolitec AG's] principals, including Mr. Neuberger . . . to move assets out of [Biolitec] in order to avoid having to pay the judgment that AngioDynamics has obtained in the Northern District of New York.

On December 14, 2012, the Massachusetts District Court denied a motion for reconsideration of the Massachusetts Injunction. In so ruling, Judge Ponsor found that there were "troubling questions about the Defendants' good faith" in light of the undisputed fact that, after the Massachusetts Injunction was entered, Biolitec AG and related entities had taken preliminary steps toward completing the merger between Biolitec AG and Biolitec AG Austria by securing a shareholder vote on the merger. The defendants filed an expedited appeal from the Massachusetts Injunction with the United States Court of Appeals for the First Circuit. That appeal was heard on April 1, 2013 and the First Circuit ruled the same day affirming the Massachusetts Injunction, finding the appeal to be without merit.

Subsequent to oral argument on the Motion in this Court, but prior to the decision of the First Circuit, counsel for Biolitec AG advised the Court that the downstream merger [to its Austrian subsidiary] had taken place. . . .

The New Jersey Litigation

In June of 2009, New Jersey Plaintiffs, Moran and Morello, former officers of Biolitec, filed an action in the Superior Court of New Jersey Chancery Division against Biolitec, Biolitec AG, Neuberger, and BioMed Technology Holdings, Ltd. The New Jersey Litigation was filed after Moran and Morello's termination in 2009. The complaint alleges, without verification, that the New Jersey Plaintiffs have been harmed by oppressive and illegal conduct of Biolitec's majority shareholders. Specifically, it alleges that Neuberger acted fraudulently, mismanaged the corporation for his personal benefit, abused his authority as an officer and director, and acted oppressively to the New Jersey Plaintiffs as minority shareholders. The New Jersey Plaintiffs contend that more than $15 million in cash and assets were fraudulently and illegally transferred from Biolitec.

. . .

DISCUSSION

AngioDynamics argues that the appointment of a trustee is required under 11 U.S.C. § 1104(a). Alternatively, AngioDynamics seeks the appointment of an examiner pursuant to § 1104(c)(2).

I. Whether a Trustee Shall Be Appointed . . .

Relying on In re Sharon Steel Corp., 871 F.2d 1217 (3d Cir. 1989), AngioDynamics argues that evidence of "systematic looting," as found by the Massachusetts District Court, together with common control, intercompany transfers, and intermingled business assets, creates a conflict among the Related Entities and the Debtor such that "cause" is established requiring the appointment of a trustee. Biolitec counters, arguing that the evidence relied on by AngioDynamics amounts to preliminary findings and mere allegations that do not support the appointment of a trustee and, therefore, consistent with the teachings of In re G-I Holdings, 385 F.3d 313 (3d Cir. 2004), AngioDynamics has not met its burden of showing clear and convincing evidence of "cause." . . .

While a bankruptcy court is required to appoint a trustee where it finds "cause," the determination of whether the moving party has satisfied its burden in showing "cause" is committed to the bankruptcy court's discretion. G-I Holdings, 385 F.3d at 318 (citing Sharon Steel, 871 F.2d at 1225-26). It is settled law in the Third Circuit that the appointment of a trustee is the exception, rather than the rule, and is relief granted only as a last resort. Sharon Steel, 871 F.2d at 1225. The movant must prove the need for a trustee by clear and convincing evidence. . . .

In Sharon Steel, a case with facts similar to those before the Court, the appointment of a trustee by the bankruptcy court was appealed by Posner as the Chairman, President and CEO of Sharon Steel, the debtor-in-possession, and DWG Corporation, an entity under common control with Sharon Steel. 871 F.2d at 1218. The Third Circuit reviewed the bankruptcy court's findings for an abuse of discretion. Those findings included numerous pre-petition transfers to insiders and secured creditors which "amounted at best to voidable preferences and at worst to fraudulent conveyances" and also that the debtor-in-possession had not sued on any of those transfers. Id. at 1220-21. Furthermore, "the bankruptcy court questioned the current management's ability to fulfill its fiduciary duty to pursue these claims since [the debtor] shares common management with the recipients of the transfers, who also owe conflicting fiduciary duties to recipients. . . .

Circumstances involving allegations of acrimony and conflicts of interest, like the case at bar, pose considerable challenges for bankruptcy courts. "A bankruptcy court cannot be expected to resolve all factual disputes that are the subject of various ongoing litigations in determining a motion for appointment of a trustee," even where, if proven, those factual disputes and challenged actions would mandate appointment of a trustee. . . .

The Court is not blind to the acrimony between AngioDynamics and Biolitec, two entities each with roles crucial to a successful reorganization of Biolitec. Even without considering whether the allegations and findings of the other litigations are true, there is no doubt that extreme acrimony exists between the parties. . . .

Most significant in the Court's judgment is that Biolitec, as debtor-in-possession, is intimately tied through common ownership and control with Neuberger and the Related Entities, the recipients of alleged fraudulent and preferential transfers. . . .

This Court is not faced with a scenario wherein the debtor-in-possession lacks experience in managing the debtor's business. To the contrary, and unlike the debtor-in-possession in *Marvel*, Biolitec management has been in place for years prior to the petition date running a multi-national manufacturer and distributor of high-tech medical and industrial devices. Current management has experience that may be critical to Biolitec as well as its creditors. It would be naive to think, however, that management can operate independent from the controlling ownership of Neuberger. Management's experience does not outweigh the challenges to reorganization and trust in the Debtor that flow from the commonality of control exercised by Neuberger and the Related Entities, particularly in light of their pre- and post-petition conduct. . . . It is clear a trustee is appropriate considering the relationship of the parties and their conduct before this and other courts.

Alternatively, AngioDynamics argues that appointment of a trustee is proper pursuant to 11 U.S.C. § 1104(a)(2). . . . [I]t being within the Court's discretion to appoint a trustee pursuant to § 1104(a)(2), sufficient evidence has been presented to determine that an appointment is in the best interests of creditors and the estate. Biolitec, while profitable under current management and control leading up to the current chapter 11 petition, fails to have sufficient independence from Neuberger and the Related Entities that engaged in conduct adverse to the interests of creditors. Considering the deep-seated conflicts between the parties and their inability to resolve them, the commonality among the Debtor, Neuberger, and Related Entities will likely be an obstacle to a successful reorganization and, therefore, appointment of a trustee is in the best interest of creditors and the estate. As such, the Motion is granted insofar as it seeks appointment of a trustee pursuant to § 1104(a)(2). . . .

———————————————

Enron (a case in which trustee appointment was defeated because new management took over the company and argued successfully they had cleaned house) and other scandal bankruptcies caused Congress in BAPCPA to insert new statutory language suggesting that the courts should be more aggressive in replacing DIPs with trustees where appropriate, but cases in which trustees are appointed remain relatively rare in the corporate setting. The *Sharon Steel* case relied on heavily by the court in *Biolitec* is one of the few prominent cases in which a trustee was appointed. The allegations against the DIP involved massive transfers of the debtor's assets to Victor Posner, the high-wheeling 1980s takeover specialist who took control of the company, and his related entities. A smattering of the problems:

> The bankruptcy court also faulted Sharon's day-to-day management of the estate. Sharon, which continued to rely on DWG [a Posner-controlled affiliate operating out of a Miami office building owned by Posner] for financial services, had not yet closed out its books for the period preceding reorganization. Thus, not only was the debtor continuing to hemorrhage money at an estimated $2 million per month at a time when steel prices were rising, but the debtor could not even measure the precise size of these losses since it had no postpetition profit and loss statements. . . .
>
> [T]he court also criticized Sharon's failure to renegotiate its $30 million working capital loan from the 28% to 30% interest rate originally agreed to a reasonable [then-market] 14% to 15%—an action that would save Sharon $4 million a year. It also impugned the wisdom (and the propriety) of Sharon's repayment . . . of $294 million in secured bank loans "in order to facilitate new loans from those banks to other Posner companies." Given Sharon's blast furnace crisis and the fact that the payments left Sharon so cash-poor that it was forced to enter into the $30 million high-interest working capital loan, it concluded that such actions amounted to gross mismanagement. . . .
>
> The bankruptcy court opinion conveys the image of a titanic industrial vessel foundering on the shoals of bankruptcy, steered there by at best careless management practices. These practices include payment of $294 million to secured creditors and $9.8 million and $970,000 without consideration to Victor and Stephen Posner respectively during a period when Sharon was so cash-poor that it could not afford to re-line the vital number 2 blast furnace. . . .
>
> Other questionable management actions . . . include transfer of Sharon's yacht and plane [to Posner entities]. [Again with the yachts? And the planes?—Eds.]

In re Sharon Steel Corp., 871 F.2d 1217, 1221, 1226 (3d Cir. 1989) (affirming bankruptcy court). While any or all of these likely justified the appointment of a trustee, rubbing salt in the wound was the use of estate funds to pay for counsel to fight the motion to appoint a trustee! Id. (Such practice may mortify in theory but seems to happen regularly.)

The court in *Biolitec* was notably candid in alluding to the risk of appointing a trustee for a debtor when management required specialized and technical knowledge, but opted for a trustee nonetheless. That difficult decision was no doubt aided by the fact that the movant held virtually all of the unsecured debt. If the trustee was incapable and the company cratered to the detriment of the creditors, AngioDynamics would have only itself to blame.

One reason for the rarity of a successful motion for appointment of a trustee may be the availability of an attractive alternative: an examiner appointed under § 1104(c). The case law has evolved to give the bankruptcy court broad discretion in deciding to appoint an examiner and in determining the scope of an examiner's work. Examiners' assignments range all the way from a sweeping investigation of the company's past and present to a narrowly focused inquiry about specific allegations of wrongdoing. But empirical data do not seem to confirm the appeal of an examiner alternative in practice. See Jonathan C. Lipson & Christopher Fiore Marotta, Examining Success, 90 Am. Bankr. L.J. 1 (2016). Their study finds that "[b]ankruptcy examination is a failure" because "[s]takeholders in chapter 11 cases rarely want examiners." This finding is odd given a further finding that examiners often improve outcomes. They hypothesize that control of cases by key insiders and lenders injects a distortion.

An examiner's report can produce a dramatic effect without ousting management, as demonstrated in the huge bankruptcy of the major gambling group of Caesar's Casinos. The examiner investigated a variety of prepetition transactions and reported as follows: "The principal question being investigated was whether in structuring and implementing these transactions assets were removed from [the subsidiary group] to the detriment of [the subsidiary] and its creditors. The simple answer to this question is 'yes.'" Final Report of Examiner, Richard J. Davis at 1, In re Caesars Entm't Operating Co., Inc., No. 15-01145 (ABG) (Bankr. N.D. Ill. Mar 15, 2016); In re Caesars, 2016 WL 7477566, at *1 (Bankr. N.D. Ill. Sept. 21, 2016) (1,787 pages). In response to this report, "Caesars and its backers agreed to contribute more than $5 billion to support the CEOC restructuring, up from a $1.5 billion pledge from Caesars. . . ." https://www.wsj.com/articles/caesars-unit-wins-court-approval-for-chapter-11-exit-plan-1484675918.

E. CONCLUSION

Most companies, like most people, are worth more alive than dead. More formally, operation or sale of a company as a going-concern business is likely to produce more for creditors than selling assets piecemeal. While those results are theoretically possible in a chapter 7 liquidation (certainly more so than at state law, which relegates creditors to an auction on the courthouse steps), the chapter 11 structure is more specifically designed to keep companies alive and running. In having extant management run the bankruptcy estate, Congress expressed its confidence that existing management would be far more expert in running the company than an outsider trustee. The obvious counterargument, one that perhaps carries the day in other nations' insolvency laws, is that management apparently was not so expert or it would not have needed bankruptcy. On the other hand, macroeconomic swells of recession swamp even the most expertly piloted corporate ships. Another factor in favor of DIP control is that management has little incentive to file chapter 7 if it means escorting each other out the exit door. The retention of existing management attracts earlier chapter 11 filings, when there is the best opportunity for a successful reorganization.

Through this DIP power, chapter 11 to some extent rebalances the debtor-creditor relationship when loan concessions are being sought. Outside bankruptcy, creditors enjoy tremendous power to call loans and seize assets; in bankruptcy, the automatic stay goes into effect while the debtor, as DIP, continues those negotiations. This facilitates a "workout" of the company's financial difficulties without extensive litigation disruptive to the business and often fatal to its value. (In and out of bankruptcy, such negotiations are often called "workouts," although many use this term only to refer to outside-bankruptcy talks.) As we will see later, in addition to the automatic stay, a crucial contribution that chapter 11 rules make is the ability to bind a minority of creditors who are "holdouts"; this is the key to chapter 11's reorganization power. In the process, chapter 11 produces significantly more transparency than a private workout. This exposure gives creditors (and shareholders, suppliers, and others) a higher degree of confidence in the negotiations and the results.

Let us not convey the impression that chapter 11 is without critics. Some decry its use as a union buster because the DIP is given power to abrogate collective bargaining agreements that would be forbidden outside chapter 11; others contend it provides cover for companies seeking to avoid environmental obligations because it permits the discharge of cleanup claims. Another branch of attack, also hotly contested, is that easy confirmation standards lead to soon-failed reorganizations, wasting assets and leaving the creditors worse off than if the company had liquidated sooner. Lynn M. LoPucki, Can the Market Evaluate Legal Regimes? A Response to Professors Rasmussen, Thomas, and Skeel, 54 Vand. L. Rev. 331 (2001). And we have already seen Professor LoPucki's charge (shared by others) that sometimes chapter 11 is used by management to shield themselves from the inevitable death of a business. And yet chapter 11 persists.

Problem Set 16

16.1. Porky Channing came to see you this morning about his company, Porky's Tanning and Tax Service, Inc. Porky and his two "tanistas" are the work force, and Porky owns all the stock. When the area's largest employer offered "wellness assessments" to its employees that offered reduced insurance premiums for those who abjured tanning, sales took a dive. A further blow was his wife Betty's recent illness. Although Porky draws no salary, he had to take almost $25,000 out of the corporate account to pay for Betty's treatment. She seems to be recovering, but Porky doubts the company can handle its accumulated debts without a substantial extension. The bank has said its regulators require full payment of the company's working capital loan and it can't justify a rollover given the current cash flow. The tanning equipment distributor is secured by the three machines and has gotten snarky after four missed payments. Just recently, business has picked up with the opening of a new junior college in town, and Porky is confident the company can make a go of it. Porky put his hand on yours and said, "I understand you are the best lawyer in town, so I'm hoping you can get me through this bad time." What's your advice?

16.2. Magellan Services is an Austin company that supplies diagnostic equipment to high-tech companies. Although it has been in business over 20 years, it faced declining revenues when other service companies got ahead of it in the latest technology. Its response was development of a new set of diagnostic machines that it thought would leap-frog its competitors' technology and put it out front for a good while. The development took longer than expected, however, and Magellan filed for chapter 11 nine months ago under creditor pressure. Shortly thereafter, it discovered that another local company, Dubinski Development, had perfected a device that solved a key remaining problem with the new Magellan system.

Magellan entered into a contract with Dubinski for supply of that key part for ten years at a fixed price and a fixed quantity of parts per quarter, the only deal Dubinski would accept. The contract was about the same size as the largest supply contract Magellan had granted to its other suppliers, but their terms permitted quantities and payments to fluctuate based on Magellan's sales. The minimum payments to Dubinski each quarter would amount to about 50% of Magellan's current revenues, but management expects sales to climb back to prior levels, which would make the payments comparable to the sales-based payments it makes to other licensors.

Since the contract was signed, Dubinski has done extremely well with its new device. It now can sell its products for far more than Magellan pays. Dubinski has come to you for advice about how to get out of the contract. What are your first questions? See §§ 102, 363, 1108.

16.3. You are counsel to the equity security holders of eBump, the dazzling new technology firm that dazzled its way right through $52 million of your clients' investment and right into chapter 11. The business filed owing another $20 million in debt and with hard assets valued at about $10 million. The reorganization has been pending for about eight months and talk of a plan is in the wind. The plan, as best you can figure it out from the negotiations, will give all the outstanding equity to the current creditors in return for forgiveness of their debts—wiping out your clients completely. Your clients think a better deal could be cut in which old equity invests a little more money and the current creditors take cash and some equity and forgive some debt, but your clients can't seem to get a seat at the negotiating table. Apparently, the current management team thinks that VentureLoan, the company that owns the biggest share of the outstanding debt, will be in the power position, and eBump's managers are doing everything they can to make VL happy. Your clients are also disgusted with executives' free-spending ways and have heard rumors about playhouses on Padre Island. They are also outraged because management's new-found loyalty may come from the fact that VL has announced that after the plan is confirmed, there will be a 5% stock distribution to "this fine management team."

Your client figures that for $52 million the investors are entitled to some upside if it comes along. You know the plan as described can be confirmed if the creditors vote for it, so you need to find another lever to push on behalf of your clients as leverage in these negotiations. What is your best idea? If you need to investigate for more information, what will you look for? See §§ 1102-1104.

Section 2

Operating in Chapter 11

Absent the sorts of circumstances that will justify the appointment of an external trustee, the debtor remains in control of the chapter 11 process and is allowed to run the business in the ordinary course. That control is important, critically so, but it would be a mistake to think that other stakeholders sit passively as the debtor continues to run things while negotiating a reorganization plan. Creditors, especially unsecured creditors, care deeply about how the business is being run pending the reorganization, because the amount they get paid depends in large part on the success of the business. Whether they admit it or not, debtors and creditors in almost all contexts are economic partners hoping for the success of the debtor's business both inside and out of bankruptcy, although a bankruptcy focuses everyone's attention on the fact that they are all sharing the same boat, watching the water start to rise.

Complicating matters, not all creditors share the debtor's goals, and bankruptcy can actually sharpen the differences. Consider a small wholesale food distributor whose hard assets consist of its refrigeration equipment, trucks, computers, and various office equipment, worth perhaps $5 million. Its real value is in its customer relationships, its supply lines, and its knowledge of the retail food industry. The bank that has a security interest in the hard assets looks at its outstanding debt of $4 million and sees an easy solution for this company: liquidate the business, sell off the hard assets, and pay the bank in full (with postpetition interest to boot); whatever is left over can go to the costs of administration and, if there is anything left after that, to pay something to the general unsecured creditors. The unsecured creditors, such as the suppliers who have sent vegetables and canned goods on credit, see this rather differently. They may recover something if the business is liquidated, but their returns may be much greater if the business succeeds. More importantly, they keep a customer, so future profits may offset current losses.

Moving beyond creditors to other stakeholders, the employees will have much the same interests and concerns as unsecured creditors. The investors in the debtor company are even further misaligned with the secured bank. They may have subordinated debt or only equity, which means that they will see no return on their investments unless the business succeeds. They are often enthusiastic about high-risk, high-reward options that may take them from no recovery to a large ownership stake in the business. Finally, the community where the business is located may have a strong interest in the continuation of the business. Not only are jobs at stake but also tax revenues. The community sometimes has leverage in the form of promised infrastructure for real estate, rezoning, and other benefits, but often it does not. While we learned in the previous assignment that the distinguishing feature of chapter 11 is that the debtor remains in control pending a reorganization, that control is exercised through an open judicial process where everyone gets to look over the debtor's shoulder and argue how things should be different.

In this assignment and the one that follows, we study the operation of a business in chapter 11. In the early stages of a traditional chapter 11, there is a chaos involved in just keeping the lights on and the employees at work before many debtors can even dream about proposing a recapitalized balance sheet to be voted on by creditors. The challenges come from two sources: first, some creditors may want to shut the debtor down right away, like the secured creditor in our wholesale food distributor example above, and so the debtor may be facing objections to every action it takes in bankruptcy court (e.g., arguments that something is not within the ordinary course of business); second, there is the actual business of running a business—the debtor has to convince suppliers to keep shipping critical supplies (a wholesaler's no good without product) and not just give up because they'd rather seek a nonbankrupt business customer. Especially critical is financing for the business's future months. To state the obvious, most companies that file bankruptcy are short of funds. Keeping the business running is the first and most important challenge in chapter 11.

First, we deal with how the DIP stabilizes the business so it can survive long enough to even propose a plan of reorganization. We call this "Getting Started" in Assignment 17, but the early-day focus continues in Assignment 18. We will look at orders that debtors seek on the very day of filing to permit smooth operation (and position things where they want them), such as authority to operate outside the ordinary course of business. We then proceed to the debtor's use of cash that is subject to a creditor's lien or right of setoff. We conclude with tools the debtor uses to ensure ongoing shipment of critical goods such as inventory and critical services such as plant maintenance from so-called trade creditors. In Assignment 19 we turn to the high-stakes and high-dollar task of getting financing to keep the cash-starved business afloat in chapter 11.

GETTING STARTED

Neither the maximization of values in an orderly liquidation nor any attempt at reorganization has any real hope of succeeding unless the court obtains immediate and complete control over the debtor and all of its assets. For that reason, the stay must be nationwide and must be strictly enforced. As we saw earlier in the consumer materials, unlike a regular injunction, the bankruptcy stay comes into effect automatically, instantly, and ex parte against a large number of people who had no prior notice or opportunity to contest it. We revisit the stay (and its protection of property of the estate) in these chapter 11 materials because it serves a different function. For consumers, the stay is chiefly a breathing spell that is only sometimes used to block secured creditor conduct (e.g., a home foreclosure sale). By contrast, the business stay is an important tool the debtor uses to protect against a creditor who can shut down the entire operations by levying or more likely repossessing critical property. The stay helps turn certain liquidation into possible reorganization.

Because of its importance to core purposes of bankruptcy, the automatic stay cannot be waived by contract before bankruptcy. See Farm Credit of Central Florida, ACA v. Polk, 160 B.R. 870 (M.D. Fla. 1993). Once in place, even actions taken in innocent violation of the stay, without notice of the bankruptcy filing, are void or voidable (usually void). E.g., In re Soares, 107 F.3d 969, 976 (1st Cir. 1997). We first saw the stay in Assignment 3, but in business cases, we encounter more complex legal entitlements that push the definition of just what estate "property" is protected.

A. SCOPE OF THE BANKRUPTCY ESTATE

An important type of dispute regarding "property of the estate" involves whether something is, in fact, property. Consider your driver's license. It represents a very valuable legal right to you. An economist would have fun calibrating at what strike price you would willingly forgo it. But the right exists at the pleasure of the state. You cannot sell it to that economist, regardless of your willingness to offer. Because it is a mere privilege, if the Secretary of State takes it away, say for failure to pay child support, you do not get just compensation (although you might be accorded due process, a question we leave for Con Law). If it is not property, it cannot go into the estate. Nevertheless, some types of licenses are considered estate property, so the question whether something is property of the estate cannot be answered just by use of labels like "license."

So how do we know whether a legal entitlement is property of the estate? You might think bankruptcy courts would look solely to state law to determine whether a legal right is "property." You would be wrong. State law is the starting, but not the ending, point. Because "property of the estate" is a concept of federal bankruptcy law, overriding federal bankruptcy policy can put a gloss on those state definitions. "Property interests are created and defined by state law. *Unless some federal interest requires a different result,* there is no reason why such interests should be analyzed differently simply because an interested party is involved in a bankruptcy proceeding." Butner v. United States, 440 U.S. 48, 55 (1979) (emphasis added). Many cite *Butner* for the proposition that bankruptcy follows state law but lazily (or intentionally) gloss over the important federal qualifier we emphasized.

Consider an economically valuable contract. A contract is not property in the ordinary sense. Absent a specific performance right on breach, we would generally not think of a contract holder as a property owner. But what is the bankruptcy consequence if a contract right is not property of the estate? If you prepaid for a car wash before filing bankruptcy, and the garage then insisted that a mere contractual right was not property that could enter your estate, the trustee would get the car, but not the right to have it cleaned—with the outcome being the garage gets a freebie release. Is that fair to the creditors hoping the trustee will have a chance to sell a clean car rather than a dirty one? (The policy concern is thus similar to that contained in § 541(c)(1).) Contract rights are bought and sold every day for millions, so the market surely sees them thus.

In the case that follows, notice how the court is clear about the definition of property and how it determines whether the legal prerogatives held by the debtor are properly defined as "property of the estate."

In re BURGESS

234 B.R. 793 (D. Nev. 1999)

REED, District Judge.

BACKGROUND

Since 1983, the debtor has operated a legal brothel (or "house of ill fame") in Storey County, Nevada. On July 30, 1997, the debtor filed a voluntary petition for bankruptcy under Chapter 11 of the Bankruptcy Code. On June 2, 1998, the Storey County Commission and the Sheriff of Storey County held a hearing to express their displeasure with the debtor's continuing association with the Hell's Angels motorcycle "club" (or, in the County's terminology, "outlaw motorcycle gang"). At the hearing, the Commissioners revoked the debtor's brothel license. . . .

[The bankruptcy court denied the debtor's request to undo the county's attempt to revoke his license, and the debtor appealed to the district court.

Under § 362 of the Code, which we consider in the next section, whether the debtor was entitled to a reversal of the revocation of his license and damages depended upon whether the license was property of the estate.—Eds.] In denying relief to the debtor, the bankruptcy court held that the brothel license was not "property," but rather a "personal privilege." . . .

DISCUSSION

When a bankruptcy petition is filed, an "estate" is created, consisting of all of the debtor's interests, both legal and equitable, in all property, both tangible and intangible. 11 U.S.C. § 541(a). Although "property" is not defined in the Code, it has been interpreted liberally in order to further the policies underlying the bankruptcy laws. See United States v. Whiting Pools, Inc., 462 U.S. 198, 202-04, 103 S. Ct. 2309, 76 L. Ed. 2d 515 (1983). "[T]he congressional goal of encouraging reorganizations . . . suggest[s] that Congress intended a broad range of property to be included in the estate." Id. at 204, 103 S. Ct. 2309. . . .

As noted above, the County did not provide any insight into the "property" issue. Likewise, we have not been overwhelmed with citations to cases involving the issue of whether a license to operate a legal brothel is "property" or not. The County cites to cases from the Nevada Supreme Court and this Court which indicate that Nevada law views prostitution as an activity that can be heavily regulated or forbidden altogether. From this, the bankruptcy court reasoned that the license was not property, but merely "a personal privilege granted to certain counties"—a "state matter . . . subject to discretionary control of the county."

Unfortunately, this analysis is incorrect. The fact that Nevada law may not consider brothel licenses to be property is not dispositive. The fact that the right/privilege to operate a brothel is defined by state law does not matter—most property rights are defined by state law. That does not mean that those rights receive no protection from federal law, bankruptcy and otherwise. In fact, state-created "rights" expressly denominated by the state as "privileges" have often been treated as "property" for purposes of the bankruptcy laws. While state law creates the right, federal law determines whether it is "property" for purposes of the federal bankruptcy laws, tax laws, etc. In re Nejberger, 934 F.2d at 1301-02 ("[W]hile state law creates legal interests and defines their incidents, the ultimate question whether an interest thus created and defined falls within a category stated by a Federal statute, requires an interpretation of that statute which is a Federal question." (internal quotations omitted)); In re Terwilliger's Catering, 911 F.2d at 1171-72 ("While the nature and extent of the debtor's interest are determined by state law 'once that determination is made, federal bankruptcy law dictates to what extent that interest is property of the estate.'" (quoting In re N. S. Garrott & Sons, 772 F.2d 462, 466 (8th Cir. 1985)).

While we have found no published bankruptcy decisions regarding brothel licenses, numerous cases have held that similar licenses issued by state agencies are property for bankruptcy purposes. Most of these cases involve liquor licenses, rather than brothel licenses, but the principle is the same. Most states or local governments require businesses that wish to sell alcoholic beverages to be licensed, and regardless of how the issuing state characterizes such licenses, most courts have held that they are property under the bankruptcy laws. Courts have also held that a license to operate a racetrack or a casino is property of the estate. In addition, many other cases have held similar licenses and certifications to be property. E.g., Ramsay v. Dowden (In re Central Arkansas Broadcasting Co.), 68 F.3d 213, 214-15 (8th Cir. 1995) (FCC license); Federal Aviation Admin. v. Gull Air, Inc. (In re Gull Air, Inc.), 890 F.2d 1255, 1260 (1st Cir. 1989) (airport landing slots); . . . Beker Indus. Corp. v. Florida Land & Water Adjudicatory Comm'n (In re Beker Indus. Corp.), 57 B.R. 611, 621-22 (Bankr. S.D.N.Y. 1986) (permission to truck phosphate ore). . . .

Of course, some courts have gone the other way. In In re Gammo, for instance, the court held that a state-issued license to sell lottery tickets was not property. In re Gammo, Inc., 180 B.R. 485, 487 (Bankr. E.D. Mich. 1995); see also Pension Benefit Guaranty Corp. v. Braniff Airways, Inc. (In re Braniff Airways, Inc.), 700 F.2d 935, 942 (5th Cir. 1983) (holding that airport landing slots are not property). . . . Clearly, though, the majority of cases examining the issue have held that liquor and similar licenses are property for bankruptcy purposes. The case that most concerns us, however, is Wade v. State Bar of Arizona (In re Wade), 115 B.R. 222 (9th Cir. BAP 1990), aff'd, 948 F.2d 1122 (9th Cir. 1991). In In re Wade, the Bankruptcy Appellate Panel of the Ninth Circuit held that an attorney's license to practice law was not property. In re Wade, 115 B.R. at 228. While the B.A.P.'s decision was affirmed by the Ninth Circuit, that court did not address the property question at all. The only question before the Circuit was whether the state bar was a government agency for purposes of the government exception. Thus the Ninth Circuit's decision is not particularly strong authority for the proposition that a license to practice law is not property. Nonetheless, we are convinced (although we suspect there may be some who would argue to the contrary) that a brothel license is more like a liquor license than a license to practice law.

Beyond the bankruptcy context, the Ninth Circuit has held that, for instance, a property right exists in license tags required for coin-operated "crane" games. Further, we note that the very license at issue here has recently been held by Judge Hagen, in the debtor's civil rights case, to constitute a property right for purposes of procedural due process analysis. Thus, we hold that the brothel license at issue here is "property." . . . The license has enormous value to the estate—in fact, without the license to operate as a brothel, there would essentially be no business left to reorganize. To hold that the license is not property would be to contravene the broad definition of property meant to further "the congressional goal of encouraging reorganizations." United States v. Whiting Pools, Inc., 462 U.S. 198, 204, 103 S. Ct. 2309, 76 L. Ed. 2d 515 (1983). . . .

[T]he order of the bankruptcy court . . . is reversed and remanded.

The study of bankruptcy property allows many new perspectives on the world, some more titillating than others. And what could be more salacious than a floating casino—involved in a corporate fight? The next case centers around "C" vs. "S" corporate tax status. In a C corporation, the corporate entity incurs and pays tax itself. In an S corporation, the shareholders elect to have the entity pay no tax and have the tax obligation flow through to the shareholders, payable on their own individual tax bills. Is the legal ability to allocate tax benefits and burdens property?

-------------------- In re THE MAJESTIC STAR --------------------
==================   CASINO, LLC   ==================
                        716 F.3d 736 (3d Cir. 2013)

JORDAN, Circuit Judge.

This case arises from a corporate reorganization under Chapter 11 of the Bankruptcy Code, 11 U.S.C. § 101 *et seq.* (the "Code"), and puts at issue whether a non-debtor company's decision to abandon its classification as an "S" corporation for federal tax purposes, thus forfeiting the pass-through tax benefits that it and its debtor subsidiary had enjoyed, is void as a postpetition transfer of "property of the bankruptcy estate." In November 2009, the Debtors, which had been controlled by Barden, filed petitions for relief under Chapter 11 of the Code. After the bankruptcy filing, Barden, as sole shareholder of BDI, successfully petitioned the IRS to revoke BDI's S-corp status. Under the Internal Revenue Code ("I.R.C."), that revocation also caused Majestic Star Casino II, Inc. ("MSC II"), an indirect and wholly-owned BDI subsidiary and one of the Debtors, to lose its status as a qualified subchapter S subsidiary (or "QSub"), which meant that it, like BDI, became subject to federal taxation.

The Debtors were by then effectively controlled by their creditors and, naturally, did not agree with shouldering a new tax burden. They filed an adversary complaint asserting that the revocation of BDI's S-corp status caused an unlawful postpetition transfer of property of the MSC II bankruptcy estate. The Bankruptcy Court agreed and ordered the Barden Appellants and the IRS to reinstate both BDI's status as an S-corp and MSC II's status as a QSub. The case was certified to us for direct appeal. . . .

At the Petition Date, both BDI and MSC II retained their status as, respectively, an S-corp and a QSub. Barden and BDI did not file bankruptcy petitions, nor did they participate as debtors in any of the petitions at issue in this case. In addition to certain events that automatically revoke an entity's election to be treated as an S-corp, that tax status may also be revoked if more than half of the corporation's shareholders consent to the revocation. I.R.C. § 1362(d)(1)(B). If S-corp status is revoked, the entity cannot elect such status again within five years of the revocation without the consent of the Secretary of the Treasury. *Id.* § 1362(g).

Sometime after the Petition Date, Barden, BDI's sole shareholder, caused and consented to the revocation of BDI's status as an S-corp, and BDI filed a notice with the IRS to that effect. The revocation was retroactively effective to January 1, 2010, the first day of BDI's taxable year. As a result, MSC II's QSub status was automatically terminated as of the end of the prior tax year (the "Revocation"), because it no longer met the requirement that it be wholly owned by an S-corp. Thus, both BDI and MSC II became C-corporations as of January 1, 2010. As a consequence of becoming a C-corporation, MSC II became responsible for filing its own tax returns and paying income taxes on its holdings and operations.

Neither BDI nor Barden sought or obtained authorization from the Debtors or from the Bankruptcy Court for the Revocation. . . . [As] of April 2011 (the first date federal taxes would have been due following the Revocation), the Debtors had paid no federal income taxes as a result of the Revocation.

. . .

1. QSub Status as "Property"

Section 541(a) of the Bankruptcy Code defines "property of the estate" as "all legal or equitable interests of the debtor in property as of the commencement of the case." 11 U.S.C. § 541(a)(1). "[W]e have emphasized that Section 541(a) was intended to sweep broadly to include all kinds of property, including tangible or intangible property, [and] causes of action[.]" In re Kane, 628 F.3d 631, 637 (3d Cir. 2010). "[T]he term 'property' has been construed most generously and an interest is not outside its reach because it is novel or contingent or because enjoyment must be postponed." In re Fruehauf Trailer Corp., 444 F.3d 203, 211 (3d Cir. 2006). "It is also well established that the mere opportunity to receive an economic benefit in the future is property with value under the Bankruptcy Code." *Id.* (internal quotation marks omitted).

However, "[f]iling for bankruptcy does not create new property rights or value where there previously were none." In re Messina, 687 F.3d 74, 82 (3d Cir. 2012); *cf.* Butner v. United States, 440 U.S. 48, 56, 99 S. Ct. 914, 59 L. Ed. 2d 136 (1979) (noting that the holder of a property interest "is afforded in federal bankruptcy court the same protection he would have had under state law if no bankruptcy had ensued"). Consequently, "[t]he estate is determined at the time of the initial filing of the bankruptcy petition. . . ." Kollar v. Miller, 176 F.3d 175, 178 (3d Cir. 1999).

This appears to be a matter of deliberate Congressional choice. Although the constitutional authority of Congress to establish "uniform Laws on the subject of Bankruptcies throughout the United States," U.S. Const., art. I, § 8, cl. 4, could, in theory, encompass a statutory framework defining property interests for purposes of bankruptcy, "Congress has generally left the determination of property rights in the assets of a bankrupt's estate to state law," *Butner*, 440 U.S. at 54, 99 S. Ct. 914. However, if "some federal interest requires a different result," *Butner*, 440 U.S. at 55, 99 S. Ct. 914, then property interests may be defined by federal law. *Cf.* McKenzie v. Irving Trust Co., 323 U.S. 365, 370, 65 S. Ct. 405, 89 L. Ed. 305 (1945) (noting that, "[i]n the absence of any controlling federal statute," a creditor may acquire rights to property transferred by a debtor "only by virtue of state law").

Given the importance of federal tax revenues, one might assume that the Internal Revenue Code determines whether tax status constitutes a property interest of the taxpayer, but it does not do so explicitly and the case law is not entirely clear. . . . [W]e conclude that the I.R.C., rather than state law, governs the characterization of entity tax status as a property interest for purposes of the Bankruptcy Code. . . .

i. S-Corp Status as "Property"

The Bankruptcy Court reasoned that QSub status is analogous to S-corp status and, based on a few cases holding that the latter is "property" for purposes of the Code, concluded that the former is "property" too. The principal case is In re Trans-Lines West, Inc., 203 B.R. 653 (Bankr. E.D. Tenn. 1996), which concerned whether a corporation's revocation of its S-corp status prior to filing for bankruptcy was a prepetition transfer of property avoidable by the trustee pursuant to Code § 548. . . . The court observed that "property refers . . . to the right and interest or domination rightfully obtained over [an] object, with the unrestricted right to its use, enjoyment, and disposition." *Id.* It then jumped to the conclusion that, once a corporation elects to be treated as an S corporation, I.R.C. § 1362(c) guarantees and protects the corporation's right to use and enjoy that status until it is terminated under I.R.C. § 1362(d). . . .

From that, the court concluded that "the Debtor possessed a property interest (i.e., a guaranteed right to use, enjoy and dispose of that interest) in its Subchapter S status. . . ." *Id.* at 662. Other courts that have considered the issue of S-corp status as a property right have all come to the same conclusion. *See* Halverson v. Funaro (In re Funaro), 263 B.R. 892, 898 (8th Cir. BAP 2001) ("[A] corporation's right to use, benefit from, or revoke its Subchapter S status falls within the broad definition of property [under the Code].").

. . .

A [conceptual] flaw in the S-corp-as-property cases is that they presume that "once a corporation elects to be treated as an S corporation, [the I.R.C.] guarantees and protects the corporation's right to use and enjoy that status . . . [and] guarantees and protects an S corporation's right to dispose of that status at will." *Trans-Lines West*, 203 B.R. at 662. That reflects an incomplete and inaccurate understanding of the law. The I.R.C. does not, and cannot, guarantee a corporation's right to S-corp status, because the corporation's shareholders may elect to revoke that status "at will." *See* I.R.C. § 1362(d)(1)(B) (providing for termination of S-corp status by revocation with the approval of shareholders holding more than one-half the corporation's shares). Even if the shareholders do not vote to revoke their corporation's S-corp status, any individual shareholder may at any time sell his interest—without hindrance by the Code or the I.R.C.—to another corporation, or to a nonresident alien, or to a number of new individuals sufficient to increase the total number of shareholders to more than 100. Any of those sales would trigger the automatic revocation of the company's S status because the corporation would no longer qualify as a "small business corporation." *See* I.R.C. § 1361(a)(1), (b)(1). . . .

Perhaps recognizing those flaws, some courts holding that S-corp status is "property" have defaulted to the argument that such status must be property because it has value to the estate. *See Prudential Lines*, 928 F.2d at 573

("[W]e must consider the purposes animating the Bankruptcy Code . . . [and] Congress' intention to bring anything of value that the debtors have into the estate." (internal quotation marks omitted)); *Bakersfield Westar*, 226 B.R. at 234 ("The ability to not pay taxes has a value to the debtor-corporation in this case."). Indeed, the Bankruptcy Court in this case essentially defined the Debtors' property interest as "the right to prevent a shifting of tax liability from the shareholders to the QSub through a revocation of the 'S' corporation's status." *Majestic Star Casino*, 466 B.R. at 678. But § 541 defines property only in terms of "legal or equitable interests of the debtor in property as of the commencement of the case." 11 U.S.C. § 541(a)(1). It goes without saying that the "right" of a debtor to place its tax liabilities on a non-debtor may turn out to have some value, but that does not mean that such a right, if it exists, is property. Capacious as the definition of "property" may be in the bankruptcy context, we are convinced that it does not extend so far as to override rights statutorily granted to shareholders to control the tax status of the entity they own. "[T]he Code's property definition is not without limitations. . . ." *Westmoreland*, 246 F.3d at 256. Even accepting that an interest that is "novel or contingent" may still represent property under the Code, *Segal*, 382 U.S. at 379, 86 S. Ct. 511, a tax classification over which the debtor has no control is not a "legal or equitable interest[] of the debtor in property" for purposes of § 541. [Reversed and remanded.]

As *Majestic* illustrates, a determination of property of the estate may be the first conceptual step in bankruptcy, but it is sometimes not an easy analysis. The exclusion of "non-property" is the first escape from bankruptcy control. The next creditor move is to argue a statutory exception to the stay, invoking § 362(b).

B.   EXCEPTIONS TO THE STAY

Notwithstanding the sweep of the Code language, the automatic stay provision is not absolute. A long list of exceptions to the stay is provided in § 362(b). We consider two, but in practice you are likely to encounter arguments over a number of the sections.

1.   *Exception for Police and Regulatory Power*

The Code has long contained a stay exception for government to act in its police and regulatory capacity. Murderers cannot hide from the District Attorney by filing a bankruptcy and invoking the stay. § 362(b)(1). The difficulty is in determining the boundaries of those powers when the government acts in a civil capacity. Section 362(b)(4)'s exception is not nearly so categorical as § (b)(1)'s.

=========================== In re FULTON ===========================
926 F.3d 916 (7th Cir. 2019)

FLAUM, Circuit Judge.

In this consolidated appeal of four Chapter 13 bankruptcies, we consider whether the City of Chicago may ignore the Bankruptcy Code's automatic stay and continue to hold a debtor's vehicle until the debtor pays her outstanding parking tickets. Prior to the debtors' filing for bankruptcy, the City impounded each of their vehicles for failure to pay multiple traffic fines. After the debtors filed their Chapter 13 petitions, the City refused to return their vehicles, claiming it [was excepted from the stay]. The courts [below] ordered the City to return debtors' vehicles and imposed sanctions on the City for violating the stay.

This is not our first time addressing this issue: in Thompson v. General Motors Acceptance Corp., 566 F.3d 699 (7th Cir. 2009), we held that a creditor must comply with the automatic stay and return a debtor's vehicle upon her filing of a bankruptcy petition. We decline the City's request to overrule Thompson. . . .

B. Exceptions to the Stay

The City next argues that even if the stay applies, it is excepted. . . . "We construe the Bankruptcy Code 'liberally in favor of the debtor and strictly against the creditor.'" Village of San Jose v. McWilliams, 284 F.3d 785, 790 (7th Cir. 2002) (quoting In re Brown, 108 F.3d 1290, 1292 (10th Cir. 1997)). The automatic stay is "one of the fundamental debtor protections provided by the bankruptcy laws." Midlantic Nat'l Bank v. N.J. Dep't of Envtl. Prot., 474 U.S. 494, 503, 106 S. Ct. 755, 88 L. Ed. 2d 859 (1986) (quoting S. Rep. No. 95-989, at 54 (1978), reprinted in 1978 U.S.C.C.A.N. 5787, 5840). We therefore narrowly construe exceptions "to give the automatic stay its intended broad application." In re Grede Foundries, Inc., 651 F.3d 786, 790 (7th Cir. 2011). . . .

2. Section 362(b)(4)

Alternatively, the City looks to § 362(b)(4) to except it from the stay. That section provides that a Chapter 13 bankruptcy petition does not operate as a § 362(a) automatic stay:

> of the commencement or continuation of an action or proceeding by a governmental unit . . . to enforce such governmental unit's or organization's police and regulatory power, including the enforcement of a judgment other than a money judgment, obtained in an action or proceeding by the governmental unit to enforce such governmental unit's . . . police or regulatory power.

11 U.S.C. § 362(b)(4). "This exception has been narrowly construed to apply to the enforcement of state laws affecting health, welfare, morals and safety, but not to 'regulatory laws that directly conflict with the control of the res

or property by the bankruptcy court.'" In re Cash Currency Exch., Inc., 762 F.2d 542, 555 (7th Cir. 1985) (quoting In re Missouri, 647 F.2d 768, 776 (8th Cir. 1981)). The City asserts its impoundment of vehicles is an exercise of its police power to enforce traffic regulations as a matter of public safety. The debtors respond that the impoundment of vehicles enhances the City's revenue collection rather than protects public safety, and it is therefore an enforcement of a money judgment which § 362(b)(4) does not permit.

Courts apply two tests to determine whether a state's actions fall within the scope of § 362(b)(4)—the pecuniary purpose test and the public policy test. Chao v. Hosp. Staffing Servs., Inc., 270 F.3d 374, 385-86 (6th Cir. 2001); In re First All. Mortg. Co., 263 B.R. 99, 107-08 (B.A.P. 9th Cir. 2001). Satisfying either test is sufficient for the exception to apply. See First All. Mortg., 263 B.R. at 108; see also 3 Collier on Bankruptcy ¶362.05.

The pecuniary purpose test requires the court to "look to what specific acts the government wishes to carry out and determine if such execution would result in an economic advantage over third parties in relation to the debtor's estate." Solis v. Caro, 2012 WL 1230824, at *5 (N.D. Ill. Apr. 12, 2012) (quoting In re Emerald Casino, Inc., 2003 WL 23147946, at *8 (N.D. Ill. Dec. 24, 2003)). "[I]f the focus of the police power is directed at the debtor's financial obligations rather than the [government's] health and safety concerns, the automatic stay is applicable." In re Ellis, 66 B.R. 821, 825 (N.D. Ill. 1986) (quoting In re Sampson, 17 B.R. 528, 530 (Bankr. D. Conn. 1982)). Though the City says its impoundment laws are "designed to further the safety and welfare of Chicago residents" with just an "ancillary pecuniary benefit," we disagree. In retaining possession of the vehicles until it is paid in full, the City is "attempting to satisfy a debt outside the bankruptcy process," which would give it an advantage over other parties interested in the debtors' estates. . . . The City's act is focused on the debtor's financial obligation, not its safety concerns, and thus fails the pecuniary purpose test.

Alternatively, the public policy test considers whether the state action is principally to effectuate public policy or to adjudicate private rights. Hosp. Staffing Servs., 270 F.3d at 385-86; Caro, 2012 WL 1230824, at *4. The public policy the City highlights is enforcing its traffic ordinances against repeat offenders "for the safety and convenience of the public." It explains the traffic ordinance system gradually escalates, beginning with the issuance of fines then intensifying to immobilization and impoundment only after an individual ignores repeat citations. Without impoundment as a general deterrence, the City argues, it cannot enforce its traffic regulations.

The debtors argue the balance between revenue collection and public safety weighs heavily toward the former. Additionally, prior to the 2016 Municipal Code amendment imposing a possessory lien on impounded vehicles, the City released impounded vehicles to Chapter 13 debtors. When the City recently amended the Code, it did not mention public safety concerns but rather stated the amendment was "in response to a growing practice of individuals attempting to escape financial liability for their immobilized or impounded vehicles." Chi., Ill., Ordinance, Amendment of M.C.C. § 9-100-120 (July 6, 2017).

We are persuaded that, on balance, this is an exercise of revenue collection more so than police power. As debtors observe, a not insignificant portion of the City's annual operating fund comes from its collection of parking and traffic tickets. See City of Chicago, 2019 Budget Overview 29, 192 (2018), https://chicago.legistar.com/View.ashx?M=F&ID=6683992&GUID=CAEFBC7F-7C1A-4B2E-9F8B-0CB931B3EE88 (fines, forfeitures, and penalties—primarily from parking tickets—constitute approximately nine percent of the 2019 fund). Moreover, the kind of violations the City enforces are not traditional police power regulations; these fines are for parking tickets, failure to display a City tax sticker, and minor moving violations. Even tickets for a suspended license, a seemingly more serious offense, are often the result of unpaid parking tickets and are thus not related to public safety. And the City impounds vehicles regardless of what violations the owner has accrued, without distinguishing between more serious violations that could affect public safety versus the mere failure to pay for parking. Most notably, the City imposes the monetary penalty on the owner of the vehicle, not the driver, which signals a seeming disconnect if the City actually has safety concerns about the offending driver. . . .

But even if we assume that the adjudication of these violations is the result of the City's exercise of police and regulatory power, the City cannot enforce these final determinations of liability if they are "money judgment[s]" as the term is used in § 362(b)(4). See S. Rep. No. 95-989, at 52 (1978), reprinted in 1978 U.S.C.C.A.N. 5787, 5838 ("Since the assets of the debtor are in the possession and control of the bankruptcy court, and . . . constitute a fund out of which all creditors are entitled to share, enforcement by a governmental unit of a money judgment would give it preferential treatment to the detriment of all other creditors."). A judgment is a "money judgment" that cannot be enforced without violating the automatic stay if it requires payment. 3 Collier on Bankruptcy ¶362.05 ("[T]he governmental unit still may commence or continue any police or regulatory action, including one seeking a money judgment, but *it may enforce only those judgments and orders that do not require payment.*" (emphasis added)); *First All. Mortg.*, 263 B.R. at 107 (same). . . .

I. Conclusion

For the foregoing reasons, we AFFIRM the judgments of the bankruptcy courts.

The Seventh Circuit's analysis seems straightforward enough, but recognize it may be reversed by the time you read this page. *Cert. granted*, City of Chicago v. Fulton, 140 S. Ct. 680 (2019).

→ SCOTUS overruled holding
Chicago did NOT violate
11 USC § 362(a)(3)

2. *Exception for Financial Contracts*

The Code contains several provisions that remove a class of financial contracts known as "derivatives" from all aspects of bankruptcy. That exemption starts with the automatic stay. § 362(b)(6), (7), (17). These texts are pretty technical to read but the trend in legislative intent is clear. Nearly every act that has amended the Bankruptcy Code has broadened these protections and the number and type of contracts to which they apply. For Wall Street wunderkinds, it may be enough to state that any repurchase agreement ("repo"), commodity contract, forward contract, swap agreement, or securities agreement (including master netting agreements) is excepted from the stay. The rest of the world might wonder exactly what those are but should not be put off by jargon.

Derivatives are contracts that "derive" their value from the outcome of specific events (such as the weather, the performance of a particular market, or even interest rates) or from the price of an underlying asset, such as stocks or bonds. In a "forward" contract, for example, a producer might contract to sell hogs in the future at a price locked in today. In a common type of interest rate swap, Vladimir agrees to pay a fixed rate of interest to Estragon, who agrees to pay a floating rate indexed to, say, the prime rate. The principal amount is typically not exchanged, just the difference in the rates. These contracts permit business actors to "hedge" for cost fluctuations (e.g., the hog buyer who wants to lock in a price now for the hogs because she's worried it might go up in the future). They also permit investors wholly unrelated to the hog industry to speculate (wager?) on hog prices. Since they are contracts, every derivative party needs a "counterparty" to be on the other side of the contract. Sometimes that's just a hog farmer, but sometimes that's a bank or insurance company that writes the contract and hence shoulders the offsetting risk. (Ask AIG and the taxpayers how that worked out.) One type of derivative that has contributed to many a bankruptcy is the credit default swap, which is in effect an insurance policy against default on a debt.

Derivatives are excepted from the stay, so when a debtor goes into bankruptcy, the counterparty can sue for collection immediately (i.e., if the debtor is on the losing end of the risk speculation and owes money to the counterparty) without worrying about the stay. This exemption often means that the counterparty can seize vital collateral from the estate without permission from the court. But how does the Code distinguish a derivative contract, which enjoys this special exception from the automatic stay, from a garden-variety contract (e.g., a secured car loan, the quintessential contract whose security enforcement is blocked by the stay)? Easily: a particular contract meets the criteria to be excepted from the stay if the financial industry says that it does. Sections 555 and 556, which are explicitly referenced in the automatic stay exceptions, define the "contractual rights" at issue to be those set forth in a rule or bylaw of a derivatives or multilateral clearing organization, a national securities exchange or association, a securities clearing agency, or a contract market, derivatives transaction execution facility, or board of trade registered under the Commodity Exchange Act. The effect is to create a form-over-substance type of approach. See Edward R. Morrison & Joerg Riegel, Financial Contracts and the New Bankruptcy Code: Insulating Markets from Bankrupt Debtors and Bankruptcy Judges, 13 Am. Bankr. Inst. L. Rev. 641, 657 (2005) ("Indeed, margin *loans*—loans secured by the debtor's securities portfolio—are now explicitly protected even though they are in form *and* in substance, simply loans.").

These financial contract provisions are collectively often called the "safe harbors," although they are actually sweeping exemptions from the bankruptcy laws ("shall not be stayed, avoided, or otherwise limited" by the Code). See, e.g., Mark J. Roe, The Derivatives Market's Payment Priorities as Financial Crisis Accelerator, 63 Stan. L. Rev. 539 (2011). Their effect is largely to shield an entire industry from the consequences of bankruptcy, including the stay, which would typically prohibit calling the contract or seizing collateral. Such contracts are "safe" from attack, not just from the stay, but also from litigation against fraudulent transfers and preferences (concepts studied in Assignments 21-24, respectively, that help the trustee or DIP augment the estate). Free to close out derivative contracts, the counterparty escapes from bankruptcy within minutes of learning of the filing with its cash or collateral in hand. Typical loan creditors and non-derivative contractual counterparties, by contrast, are bound by the stay and fight it tooth and nail.

The purported rationale for privileging derivative contracts is that a freeze on such contracts could create a market panic, leading to systemic failure (i.e., the entire Chicago Board of Trade could shut down), in large part because of the interconnectedness of the industry that writes them. There is debate about how real this risk is and whether it is outweighed by the other risk that allowing immediate collection by derivative counterparties can kill a fledgling chapter 11 reorganization. The safe harbor exceptions are controversial but remain a significant part of the Code.

C. LIFTING THE STAY

Most creditors readily acknowledge that the stay applies to them but ask the court to lift the stay under § 362(d). As you saw briefly in Assignment 10, § 362(d)'s tests are alternative; a secured party need only "win" one to get the stay lifted. And things happen fast; the court has to rule within 30 days. § 362(e).

1. Cause, Including Lack of Adequate Protection

The first alternative for stay relief is simply "cause." The statute provides one specific example of cause: "lack of adequate protection," by far the most common basis for a "lift stay" motion and a term that is itself defined (sort of) in § 361. Perhaps the most common counterargument offered to an adequate protection argument is the "equity cushion."

In re PANTHER MOUNTAIN LAND DEV., LLC
438 B.R. 169 (Bankr. E.D. Ark. 2010)

Evans, Bankruptcy Judge.
The Debtor, Panther Mountain Land Development, L.L.C. ("Debtor"), is an entity formed for the purpose of managing the development of two tracts of real estate. The business owners are Ms. Dana M. Kellerman [and family], with Ms. Kellerman being the primary business manager. . . .

The two properties owned and managed by the Debtor are located in Maumelle, Arkansas. Sunset Lake is an approximately 126-acre tract of land. This property is currently held in the form of vacant, undeveloped acreage and is zoned for both residential and commercial use. . . . The second property, Panther Mountain, is an approximately 79-acre tract of land. This property is held in the form of a developed subdivision, consisting of a total of 25 residential lots and an approximately 15-acre tract of undeveloped land. . . .

The Debtor had sold eight of the original 25 lots prior to filing this bankruptcy case. A total of 17 lots and the connected 15-acre undeveloped tract remain as property of the estate. The average lot size of the remaining 17 lots is slightly less than two acres per lot. No sales have taken place since the filing of the case.

National Bank is the holder of two claims against the Debtor's estate that arise out of two separate notes made payable to it by the Debtor. At the time of the filing of this bankruptcy case, the Debtor owed $1,206,736.65 on the loan secured by the Sunset Lake property and $689,442.11 on the loan secured by the Panther Mountain property. The last payment to National Bank was made on July 17, 2009, following the sale of Lot #14 of the Panther Mountain subdivision for $52,000.00.

. . .

II. RELIEF FROM STAY PURSUANT TO 11 U.S.C. § 362(d)(1)

. . .

B. Legal Standards

The Court can grant relief from the automatic stay "for cause." 11 U.S.C. § 362(d)(1). Section 362(d)(1) prescribes that cause exists where there is a lack of adequate protection. Id. Although there is not an exclusive list of circumstances under which cause exists, adequate protection is the argument most commonly employed to justify such requests. See United Sav. Ass'n v. Timbers of Inwood Forest Assocs., Ltd., 484 U.S. 365, 370-71.

The concept of adequate protection is derived from the property interest protections found in the Fifth Amendment. U.S. Const. Amend. V; In re Carson, 34 B.R. 502, 505 (D. Kan. 1983); In re Johnson, 90 B.R. 973, 979 (Bankr. D. Minn.1988). The purpose of adequate protection is to guard the secured creditor's interest from a decline in the value of the collateralized property. See 11 U.S.C. § 361; Timbers, 484 U.S. at 370. In exchange for providing protective assurances against a decline in property value, the debtor is allowed to retain the protections provided by the bankruptcy code. Timbers, 484 U.S. at 378 ("The debtor in process of reorganization . . . is given many temporary protections against the normal operation of the law.").

In order to establish a prima facie case of a lack of adequate protection, the moving party must provide evidence that the value of the collateralized property is declining, or at least threatened, as a result of the automatic stay. In re Elmira Litho, Inc., 174 B.R. at 902; In re Kowalsky, 235 B.R. 590, 595 (Bankr. E.D. Tex. 1999). The most direct and convincing proof that the value is "declining, or at least threatened" comes from a comparison of the property value at the time of the hearing to the property value on the date of filing. In re Elmira Litho, Inc., 174 B.R. at 903. Nonetheless, the prima facie case requirement is met if the creditor presents evidence, in any form, that effectively demonstrates that its position in the collateral is in jeopardy. In re Anthem, 267 B.R. at 874 ("Future interest accruals, property taxes and mechanic's liens are relevant to the extent that they demonstrate a post-petition erosion of the creditor's secured claim."); see also, e.g., In re Layne, 17 B.R. at 142 (Bankr. Ohio 1981) ("increasing tax debts, interest accruals, potential sudden loss, and 'sour' market conditions"); In re Kowalsky, 235 B.R. at 596 (vehicle driven by debtors' teenage son); In re Balco Equities Ltd., Inc., 312 B.R. 734 (Bankr. S.D.N.Y. 2004) ("wear and tear to the vessels").

Once the creditor evinces a decline in value, the debtor must either persuasively refute the evidence of the decline, or in the alternative, show that there are sufficient protections in place to guard against it. § 362(g). The methods of providing adequate protection fall broadly into one of the three following categories: cash payments, replacement liens, or any other form of protection that provides the creditor with the "indubitable equivalent" of its interest. See 11 U.S.C. § 361. The latter method opens the door to a boundless array of protective measures, the sufficiency of which must be determined on a case-by-case basis. In re Kowalsky, 235 B.R. at 595 ("The determination of whether a creditor's interest is adequately protected is not an exact science nor does it involve a precise arithmetic computation.").

A list of commonly influential factors is easily derived from prior court decisions on this topic. Of these factors, the most prevalent include the sufficiency of the equity cushion, periodic payments, additional liens, or a good prospect of a successful reorganization. By far the most determinative of these factors, however, is the existence of an equity cushion. In re Belton Inns, Inc., 71 B.R. 811, 816 (Bankr. S.D. Iowa 1987) ("[T]he classic protection for a secured debt . . . is the existence of an 'equity cushion,' . . ."). The "equity cushion" is a term of art defined as the amount by which the value of the collateral exceeds the liens—equity—which will operate as a shield to protect the creditor's interest—cushion—if the property value declines during the bankruptcy case. Whether the measure of the equity cushion is sufficient to provide adequate protection is ultimately decided on a case-by-case basis.

C. Analysis

National Bank urges that it is entitled to relief for cause pursuant to 11 U.S.C. § 362(d)(1). The only argument made by National Bank on this basis was lack of adequate protection. National Bank presented very little evidence in support of this argument, but the Court finds it sufficient to establish a prima facie case.

The Prima Facie Case

National Bank argues that it lacks adequate protection because there is an insufficient equity cushion to protect its claim. Specifically, National Bank asserts that any existing equity cushion will be depleted, over the next two years, as interest continues to accrue on the claim. Standing on its own, this argument fails. Even at a colossal interest rate, it is unlikely that the post-petition accrual of interest, on its own, could ever cause a lack of adequate protection.

Post-petition interest accruals are only allowed to the extent of the value of the collateral. 11 U.S.C. § 506(a). As such, post-petition interest accruals can have the effect of eroding the equity cushion, possibly even in its entirety, but can never actually impede the creditor's interest in the collateral. In re Chauncy St. Assoc. Ltd. P'ship, 107 B.R. 7, 8 (Bankr. D. Mass. 1989). Any argument to the contrary rebels against the fundamental and long-settled division of a creditor's secured and unsecured claims. See In re Lane, 108 B.R. at 8-9 ("If a creditor who is undersecured at the beginning of the case is nevertheless considered to have adequate protection, one who stands only to lose his equity cushion, largely through earning additional interest, hardly seems worse off.").

In order to supplement the deficiency in this argument, National Bank urges in its post-trial brief that there is a minimum equity cushion required in all adequate protection cases. In effect, National Bank's argument prescribes that the value of the collateral must exceed the liens by some minimum percentage before a claim of adequate protection can comfortably rest on the equity cushion. The Court declines to accept this broad suggestion. . . .

[I]t does not follow that even the most microscopic equity cushion would automatically fail to provide adequate protection if the chances of jeopardizing the creditor's interest were also de minimis. The sufficiency of the equity cushion must be evaluated on the facts of each individual case. [On the facts of this case,] National Bank's claim is sufficient to create a prima facie case for lack of adequate protection, and accordingly, the burden to prove the creditor is adequately protected shifts to the Debtor. . . .

The Equity Cushion and Other Factors of Adequate Protection

However, the calculations of equity provided by [the bank's] exhibits were based largely on the speculative outcome of yet undetermined events—the applicable rate of interest, the amounts taken out for real estate commissions, the amount taken out to fund the Debtor's plan, and the date on which the property sales will take place. Mr. Fisher admitted in his testimony that the figures he had used in the calculation were not certain to result, but only represented one possible scenario. This point is emphasized by a comparison to the similar, yet contradictory, calculations submitted by the Debtor. In stark contrast, the Debtor's exhibits reached the result that at the end of either of the one- or two-year periods, a sufficient equity cushion would remain to provide adequate protection. These contradictory conclusions are a byproduct of the parties' manipulation of several flexible variables, with each party trending the variable toward the maxim that most obtained its desired result. While the Court acknowledges that each party's calculation hypothesizes a plausible result, when viewed in contrast to one another it is clear that neither is largely determinative or persuasive of whether a sufficient equity cushion presently exists.

Nonetheless, the evidence provided by the Debtor on this matter was not limited to these exhibits. Through the testimony of its witnesses, the Debtor was able to provide persuasive support that there is an adequate equity cushion. Two different witnesses provided credible testimony on the value of the properties. In her testimony, Ms. Kellerman stated her valuation of the Panther Mountain lots to be, at a minimum, $50,000.00 per lot. With regard to the Sunset Lake acreage property, Ms. Kellerman testified that the value was around $15,000.00 per acre. The real estate agent for the property, Ms. Odom, made very similar valuations in her testimony. Ms. Odom stated that the Panther Mountain lots would likely sell in the range of $50,000.00 to $60,000.00, depending on the size variance of the lots, and that the Sunset Lake acreage property had a value of approximately $15,000.00 per acre. Further, circumstantial support can be drawn for each of these estimates from the fact that contract price on the Sunset Lake acreage property is $13,333.00 per acre, just below the value as assessed by the Debtor's witnesses, and from the fact that the average sales price of the previously sold Panther Mountain lots is in excess of $60,000.00.

Furthermore, the Debtor's witnesses provided persuasive testimony that the value of the property is likely to continue to increase. Both Ms. Kellerman and Ms. Odom are familiar with the subject properties and the real estate market in the Maumelle area. Each testified that Maumelle has experienced continuous growth despite a recent period of general economic downturn. . . . In rebuttal, National Bank pointed to the fact that none of the properties have sold in the last year despite the fact that the information on the new school and municipal facilities has been public during that time. While the Court agrees that this fact reduced the weight of the testimony provided by the Debtor on this issue, it notes that there is presently a contract to sell a large portion of the Sunset Lake property, which to some extent offsets this criticism. Additionally, the Debtor's witnesses both testified that the sale of this portion of the Sunset Lake property itself would likely inspire interest in the remaining acreage.

Finally, [beyond] the existence of an equity cushion, the Court finds that National Bank's interest is adequately protected. The Court is convinced that part of the reason the subject properties have not sold is owed to a reduction in Ms. Odom's ability to market the properties due to family members' health complications and that action has been taken to compensate for this reduced marketing opportunity. Ms. Odom testified that she has recently started an aggressive marketing campaign, consisting of printed materials, emails to registered builders in the area, and a mailing campaign. Ms. Odom stated that this campaign was producing interest in the properties and that she currently is talking with six different purchasers. . . . Additionally, . . . adequate measures are being taken to sell this property as quickly and efficiently as possible, which will provide protection to National Bank.

Therefore, the Court has determined that there is an equity cushion in the properties sufficient to provide adequate protection in this case. Although there is some possibility that the equity cushion will deteriorate over time due to the accrual of post-petition interest, this deterioration will only work to impugn the equity cushion and will not actually impair National Bank's claim. [T]he evidence was sufficient to persuade the Court that the increase in property value over time, the likelihood that the Debtor's plan of reorganization will be confirmed, and the Debtor's approach to marketing these properties in order to effect an expedient sale are sufficient to ensure that National Bank's interest will remain adequately protected. Accordingly, the Court finds that no cause exists sufficient to warrant that National Bank receive relief from the automatic stay.

The motion in *Panther* was the second one filed; there is no limit, other than the judge's patience, on how often a creditor can bring lift-stay motions as the case goes along. Also note how much effort was spent on both sides fighting about valuation, underscoring how critical a motion to lift the stay is. Lest you think these matters are decided fully accepting one side's numbers or the other's, we offer the Solomonic outcome of In re Rogers Development Corp., 2 B.R. 679 (Bankr. E.D. Va. 1980), in which debtor insisted the value of the property was $801,000 while the secured creditor insisted it was only $704,000. The court found as a matter of fact it was exactly $750,000.

A secured creditor's belief that it is not adequately protected does not require it to pursue the "capital punishment" remedy of lifting the stay. Instead, the secured creditor may simply ask for adequate protection payments to ensure it is covered against declining value while remaining subject to the stay. There, the litigation focuses on how much the debtor must pay to the creditor during the proceeding in order to provide adequate protection. In some districts, adequate protection payments are almost always agreed upon without a hearing as part of arranging financing during bankruptcy or settling a relief from stay motion outside of court.

2.   *No Equity and Not Necessary for Reorganization*

Section 362(d)(2) gives the secured creditor a second chance if it loses the adequate protection argument. The section's test has two prongs that both must be met, so a debtor can defeat a motion for stay relief under (d)(2) by showing *either* that equity exists *or* that the property is necessary. In the business context, the valuation issues are much more complex and so the existence of equity is more hotly contested. We explore valuation issues later in Assignment 30. The dispute often shifts to whether admittedly necessary property is needed for an "effective" reorganization; i.e., the judge takes an early look at a company's rehabilitation prospects. If the company looks fatally ill (despite the DIP's claim that the fever is just about to break), the judge can euthanize it quickly by lifting the stay.

Although the case below focuses on § 362(d)(2), note that the creditor—like all smart creditors—also pled under § 362(d)(1) that there was "cause" to lift the stay. Note also that the stay was opposed by certain other creditors as well.

CHRYSLER LLC v. PLASTECH ENGINEERED PRODS.

382 B.R. 90 (Bankr. E.D. Mich. 2008)

SHEFFERLY, Bankruptcy Judge.

This opinion addresses a motion to lift the automatic stay under § 362 of the Bankruptcy Code filed by Chrysler, LLC and related entities (collectively "Chrysler"). The motion was heard on February 14 and 15, 2008. The motion was opposed by the Debtor, many of its secured creditors and the Creditors' Committee ("Committee"). . . .

III. FACTS

Plastech Engineered Products, Inc. is a privately held entity engaged in business as a tier one automobile supplier and designer and maker of blow-molded and injected-molded plastic products primarily for use in the automotive industry. . . . (Plastech and its subsidiaries will be collectively referred to as the "Debtor.") The Debtor is the largest female-owned company in Michigan and it is certified as a minority business enterprise by the State of Michigan. The Debtor has been in business since 1988. . . . The Debtor's major customers are General Motors ("GM"), Ford Motor Company, Chrysler, and Johnson Controls, Inc. ("JCI") (collectively referred to as the "Major Customers").

In February 2007, . . . Chrysler [following other Major Customers] essentially gave $6,900,000 to the Debtor that Chrysler was not contractually obligated to give. [In exchange, Chrysler received not just a security interest in tooling equipment used to make Chrysler-bound goods, but the right to own this tooling equipment outright and to demand immediate possession thereof upon contract termination.] When the Debtor requested further financial accommodations from Chrysler in December 2007, "red flags" were going up at Chrysler. BBK [Chrysler's financial advisor hired to monitor the debtor] was advising Chrysler at that time that the Debtor's condition was deteriorating. By the middle of January, BBK was advising Chrysler that the Debtor was insolvent. Chrysler looked at the draft of the Third Accommodation Agreement and the Debtor's proposals and concluded that it would have to put in another $60,000,000 and perhaps up to $100,000,000 over the next four years. This was coming on the heels of a $1.6 billion loss in 2007 by Chrysler and Chrysler's decision was influenced greatly by the recent experience it had with [Collins & Akiman, another troubled bankrupt supplier Chrysler helped to the tune of $400 million]. In sum, Chrysler perceived the Debtor to be in a "meltdown" and determined that it would be less costly to Chrysler to implement its own plan "B" by moving its tooling from the Debtor to other suppliers to resource the parts previously made by the Debtor for Chrysler. [Accordingly, on Friday morning, February 1, 2008, Chrysler sent a letter terminating all contracts and demanding turnover of the tooling.]

Immediately after delivering the letter, Chrysler filed suit against the Debtor and obtained [an ex parte order of possession requiring delivering of the tooling used to produce Chrysler's parts]. . . . Later that same day, the Debtor filed this Chapter 11 case. On the next day, Saturday, February 2, 2008, Chrysler filed a motion for relief from the automatic stay so that it could be permitted to immediately enter onto the Debtor's premises and remove the tooling used by the Debtor in production of Chrysler's parts. . . .

B. Is There Cause to Lift the Stay Under § 362(d)(1)?

. . . The Bankruptcy Code does not define "cause" as used in § 362(d)(1). Therefore, under § 362(d)(1), "courts must determine whether discretionary relief is appropriate on a case by case basis." Laguna Associates L.P. v. Aetna Casualty & Surety Co. (In re Laguna Associates L.P.), 30 F.3d 734, 737 (6th Cir. 1994). "In determining whether cause exists, the bankruptcy court should base its decision on the hardships imposed on the parties with an eye towards the overall goals of the Bankruptcy Code."

. . .

The evidence [] shows that if Chrysler does not receive possession of its tooling, it will be forced to either continue to purchase parts from the Debtor on some basis that may require it to make additional accommodations going forward or, alternatively, close many of its plants and idle many of its employees while it begins the process of resourcing with new suppliers without being able to transfer possession of the tools used by the Debtor in making parts for Chrysler. Richard Schmidt, the senior manager of material supply operations at Chrysler, testified that if possession of the tools is not received at the end of the current interim agreement with the Debtor, it could be as little as five hours before Chrysler would see disruptions in its assembly lines, which would be followed by layoffs and, ultimately, substantial damages to Chrysler. . . .

On the other hand, if the stay is lifted and Chrysler is permitted to take possession of the tooling used to make parts for it, the evidence shows that many of the Debtor's plants will have to be immediately shut down. . . . If Chrysler is permitted to take immediate possession of all of its tooling at this time, [a witness] explained that 11 of the Debtor's plants would immediately turn to negative margin plants and 8 of them would immediately have to close. . . . The record demonstrates that Chrysler will suffer economic harm if the Court concludes there is not cause to lift the stay at this time. The record also demonstrates that the Debtor will suffer economic harm if the Court concludes that there is cause to lift the stay. But in the process of balancing the competing policies to determine whether sufficient cause has been shown, there are other facts in the record that are important to the Court. First, it is very early in this Chapter 11 case. The motion to lift stay was filed literally the day after the Debtor filed its Chapter 11 petition. This case is in its infancy. This is not a small case. It is a large case with 36 manufacturing facilities, 7,700 employees and many business entities who are suppliers to the Debtor and depend themselves upon the Debtor's business. The Debtor has approximately $500,000,000 of secured debt. It has projected annual sales of over $1 billion to its other Major Customers, without even considering the Chrysler sales volume. It is an important supplier to GM, Ford and JCI, that has been in business for over 20 years. There are other creditors in this case who claim an interest in the tooling Chrysler seeks to take. In short, there are many parties who have legitimate and substantial interests in this case that will be greatly affected if not destroyed by a lift of the automatic stay at this point in the case. Chrysler's rights and interests are valid and important, but so are those of the Debtor and the other constituents in this case. Determining cause is not a litmus test or a checklist of factors. It requires consideration of many factors and a balancing of competing interests. After carefully considering the evidence in this record, including the impact upon Chrysler, the Debtor, the Debtor's employees, other Major Customers, and secured and unsecured creditors, the Court concludes that Chrysler has not met its burden of proof to demonstrate "cause" to lift the automatic stay under § 362(d)(1).

. . .

C. Are There Grounds to Lift the Stay Under § 362(d)(2)?

In addition to requesting relief from the automatic stay based upon the "cause" standard under § 362(d)(1), Chrysler requests relief from the stay under § 362(d)(2). That section of the Bankruptcy Code provides that: "On request of a party in interest and after notice and a hearing, the court shall grant relief from the stay . . . such as by terminating, annulling, modifying, or conditioning [the] stay . . . with respect to a stay of an act against property . . ., if (A) the debtor does not have an equity in such property; and (B) such property is not necessary to an effective reorganization." Relief requires a showing of both elements. Chrysler has the burden of proof as to lack of equity. The Debtor has the burden of proof as to all other issues. See § 362(g).

"'Equity,' is the value, above all secured claims against the property, that can be realized from the sale of the property for the benefit of the unsecured creditors." Stephens Industries, Inc. v. McClung, 789 F.2d 386, 392 (6th Cir. 1986). . . . Establishing that property is "necessary to an effective reorganization" "requires [] not merely a showing that if there is conceivably to be an effective reorganization, this property will be needed for it[,] but that the property is essential for an effective reorganization *that is in prospect.* This means . . . that there must be a reasonable possibility of a successful reorganization within a reasonable time." United Savings Association of Texas v. Timbers of Inwood Forest Associates, Ltd., 484 U.S. 365, 375-76 (1988) (citations and internal quotation marks omitted).

The evidence in this case demonstrates that the Debtor does not have any equity in the tooling that Chrysler has paid for. . . . The tougher issue under § 362(d)(2) is whether the Debtor has met its burden of proof under § 362(g) to show that the tooling is necessary to an effective reorganization.

The record is clear that at the time that Chrysler sent its termination letter on February 1, 2008, there was no agreement between the Debtor and the Major Customers to provide any further financial accommodations. Further, the evidence shows that the Debtor was in breach of financial covenants with its secured lenders at that time and there was no agreement as of that date between the Debtor and its secured lenders for them to forbear from enforcing their rights and remedies against the Debtor. The evidence does not demonstrate that the Debtor had accomplished a restructuring on the date that it received the termination letter from Chrysler. However, the evidence does show that even though the Debtor had no firm agreement with the Major Customers and lenders, it was still engaged in good faith and intensive negotiations to try to reach an agreement for a restructuring plan.

Andrew Yearley, the managing director of Lazard Freres & Co. LLC ("Lazard") testified . . . that discussions had taken place between the Debtor and its customers, lenders and potential investors. Yearley could not say that a transaction had been agreed upon but he did testify to a high degree of confidence that a restructuring plan with the Debtor's customers, lenders and perhaps outside investors could have been accomplished over the next several days but for Chrysler's actions on February 1, 2008.

Donald MacKenzie, the Debtor's financial advisor . . . testified that at the time of the February 1, 2008 termination letter, the Debtor still had a "top line" of $1.2 billion or $1.3 billion and a proven capability to produce engineered component plastic injection molded and assembled parts with substantial customers, significant contracts, a strong work force and a supportive group of lenders. In MacKenzie's view, this Debtor "has a heart beat" and there are many ingredients present upon which a restructuring transaction could be built.

Permitting Chrysler to take possession of its tooling at this time will likely destroy the possibilities for an effective reorganization. [T]estimony established that an immediate turnover of possession of the tooling to Chrysler will result in 11 of the Debtor's plants becoming immediately negative margin contributors and will cause 8 plants to shut down and a substantial work force to be laid off. . . . [T]he Debtor will not be able to continue to provide parts uninterrupted to its other Major Customers and therefore any prospect of an effective reorganization will be lost. . . . [I]t is less than 3 weeks into this Chapter 11 case and the Debtor's efforts have largely been consumed with litigating with Chrysler. The Debtor does not have to demonstrate today that it has already accomplished a reorganization but only that it has a prospect for an effective reorganization and that the tools that Chrysler seeks to take at this time are necessary to an effective reorganization. It is possible that a reorganization may ultimately not involve the continued production of parts for Chrysler. But it is too early to say. At this stage, the Court is convinced that the Debtor has met its burden to show that the tooling is necessary to an effective reorganization. Without the tooling the Debtor will immediately close plants, interrupt the production of parts for its remaining customers and begin idling employees. With the tooling, while the Debtor cannot force Chrysler to do business with it if it is not contractually obligated, the Debtor has the prospect of an effective reorganization. That is all the law requires at this early stage in the case. After considering all of the evidence, the Court finds that, both the paid and unpaid tooling are necessary to an effective reorganization. That analysis may change in the future, but today the evidence establishes that they are necessary. Therefore, Chrysler is not entitled to relief under § 362(d)(2) of the Bankruptcy Code.

The protection from the automatic stay may help a debtor but doom a counterparty (the assertion animating the derivatives safe harbor). On April 30, 2009, Chrysler filed chapter 11. As for Plastech, just a few months after the above ruling, the debtor sold its business off in a couple of pieces with bankruptcy court approval. Some employees kept their jobs; many did not.

3. *Single Asset Real Estate Cases*

Not all debtors are created—or at least treated—as equals under the Bankruptcy Code. "Single asset real estate" ("SARE") debtors face additional challenges to remaining under the stay. §§ 101(51B), 362(d)(3). A special rule responds to complaints that real estate cases are often abusive, filed only to hide behind the stay while a local real estate market rebounds. The SARE rule forces the debtor in such cases either to propose a workable plan promptly or to start paying interest on the value of the collateral (regardless of whether the creditor is over- or undersecured). Failure results in the stay being lifted or modified.

In BAPCPA, Congress updated the rule, giving something to each side. SARE debtors get the right to use rents to make adequate protection payments, an area where case law had often gone against them, while mortgage lenders get the interest rate set at the pre-existing contract rate, which helps them in the typical falling markets when SARE strategic defaults are most likely.

Problem Set 17

17.1. Phoenix American Commercial Bank has a perfected security interest in all the equipment of Big City Bike Repair Shop, to secure a loan at prime plus 6% with a current balance of $180,000. Big City is currently in a chapter 11, and Phoenix Am wants your help.

The equipment consists mostly of specialized repair tools. The tools were purchased one year ago for $200,000 and have an expected life span of ten years, with no salvage value. Big City took a depreciation deduction on the tools of 20% for tax purposes last year. The wholesale value of similar new tools would be $140,000 and the retail value of such tools this year is $220,000. The owner of Big City thinks that she could sell the tool set to a bike repair shop just getting under way in another city for $160,000, but once this buyer has bought his tools, Big City's owner doesn't know anyone else who could use similar tools. What do you say? See §§ 361, 362.

17.2. Cameron Cohen is a major player in the high-stakes game of family entertainment. Cameron's World, Inc. ("CWI") now operates a number of theme parks in secondary markets. A series of nasty accidents on a rollercoaster in Tulsa, combined with a lengthy labor dispute, caused revenues to plummet, sending the company into chapter 11. Cameron is convinced he can turn things around, but cash is tight. He is furious when AtlantaFirst moves to lift the stay so that it can sell the corporate jet. At the time of the bankruptcy filing, AtlantaFirst was owed $8.8 million on a 12% note secured only by the jet. Cameron loves that jet, and he insists (his word) that you keep it for him. You had the jet appraised, and discover that it is worth about $8.1 million. According to the appraiser, a four-year-old jet has an expected lifespan of about 40 years, and if it is properly maintained that value isn't likely to change much for at least a couple of years. What will you argue at the hearing, and what will likely happen? See §§ 361, 362.

17.3. Although a liquor license is considered a license to print money in the state where Happy Harrison has his liquor store, Happy managed to run his store, Happy Hops, so badly that he was forced to file for bankruptcy. Liquor licenses are issued by the state to particular people, not to business entities such as Happy Hops, which is a sole proprietorship, so Harrison holds the license himself. Licenses are expressly nontransferable, although the State Alcohol Control Commission always has issued a new license to someone who buys a liquor store from a prior licensee unless the new owner is ineligible to hold one (e.g., as an ex-felon). Buying an old store is effectively the only way to get a new liquor license issued by the Commission, because the state does not wish to see any more liquor stores opened. Can Happy's trustee make any claim for the license? Why would she want the license? (Assume for this purpose that a "license" is not a contract; you will see why later.) See § 541.

17.4. DVD America is a DVD manufacturer. With the advent of streaming, DVDs are falling into almost total disuse, but owner Sharon Johnson-Cramer remains upbeat and has some great ideas for launching DVDA into the digital age. DVDA recently filed a chapter 11, and its creditor, Heathe Manufacturing, is trying to repossess the only remaining collateral of value: a $500,000 high-tech sound recording outfit. Heathe Manufacturing has a validly perfected PMSI in the equipment for $350,000, and Commerce Bank has a non-PMSI security interest in it for another $200,000. Can Heathe get the equipment? See § 362(d).

17.5. Billy D. Woodward is an experienced Denver commercial real estate developer. When the Denver real estate market crashed, Billy D. was badly over-committed and his fortune was wiped out. He now has $2.5 million in unsecured debt and deficiency judgments against him and $40 million in debt secured by his remaining assets.

Billy D.'s last remaining asset is a Denver office building. It cost $45 million to build three years ago, and occupancy was at 50% within the first year. But the economic crash forced many tenants out of business or to cheaper quarters, and occupancy fell back to 15% last year. Billy D. has scoured the town for tenants, getting the rate up to 30%. Rather than sell the building for $20 million earlier this year ("a giveaway price," said Billy D.), he filed chapter 11 a month ago.

Billy D. says that the building occupants now generate enough cash to pay the marginal cost of maintaining the building, but there is no extra income. As occupancy rises, deferred maintenance costs will consume the initial revenue, and marginal costs will increase somewhat. At a 65% occupancy rate, Billy D. estimates a sufficient profit to begin paying interest on the secured debt. At 80% there will be enough profit to begin paying the unsecured creditors.

You represent the FDIC, which has taken over the bank that made the loan to Billy D. If the Denver market rebounds, you will be paid in full. But you also recognize that if the market does not come back within a year, deferred maintenance will make the building less desirable and more expensive to repair. And the market could slip even further, so that in a year the FDIC might recover no more than $12.5 million.

Billy D. had his own bookkeeping "style." You are not sure that Billy D. is right about "breaking even" on a cash-flow basis, and you can't remember the last time Billy D. made eye contact with you. He shows no progress toward developing a plan of reorganization. Billy D. seems to want to stretch things out as long as possible, responding to your every call with a suggestion for a meeting in the next week or two. What strategy do you suggest for the FDIC? See §§ 361, 362.

RUNNING THE BUSINESS

Upon filing the petition, the debtor's managers may only get the time to breathe one sigh of relief before they must address a host of issues to get the case going. Chapter 11 is no place for the weary (as physically and emotionally drained as managers of floundering companies may be).

A.   FIRST DAY ORDERS

The debtor often has to ask for a judge's permission within hours, if not minutes, of filing on issues that imminently threaten to derail the business's operation. These requests are usually plopped onto the just-assigned judge's desk as "first day orders." (Some judges, bristling at this temerity, like to remind us that the pleadings are first day *motions* that request orders; note the terminology in the case below.) Common first day orders cover (1) additional injunctive relief, beyond the automatic stay; (2) the content of required operating reports; (3) authorization to buy or sell outside of the ordinary course; (4) authorization to pay employees wages; (5) use of cash collateral; and (6) approval of a postpetition financing arrangement (which we discuss in the next assignment). There may also be motions to employ other professionals, including investment bankers, valuation experts, or even a "turnaround manager" or "restructuring consultant" to run the company.

The first day orders are routinely entered with the slimmest of notice, without an opportunity to be heard for many of the stakeholders beyond the DIP. Most often they are presented to the court with a principal lender and perhaps a large creditor or crucial customer attending. In some cases, a creditors' committee has been formed in advance of filing and its counsel will attend as well; if not, the U.S. Trustee's office may appear. (In some megacases, the U.S. Trustee's office actually previews proposed first day motions for comments.) Not surprisingly, the debtor usually will have lined up the parties most likely to support the first day orders—that is, those who benefit from them or who are providing the financing and have already agreed that some of the money can be spent on the parties named. Judges try hard to police excesses right from the start, but when presented with two phone books' worth of motions claiming that a company will shut down if they are all not granted, this is a difficult task. To guard against a rush to judgment, most orders are now granted on an interim basis only, as a consequence of practices brought to light by the whistleblowing of cases like the following and protections incorporated into the Federal Rules of Bankruptcy Procedure.

In re COLAD GROUP, INC.
324 B.R. 208 (Bankr. W.D.N.Y. 2005)

BUCKI, Bankruptcy Judge.

This case provides an unusual opportunity to consider standards for the approval of first day motions in a case filed under chapter 11.

The Colad Group, Inc. ("Colad") is a specialty printer, whose primary business involves the production and sale of custom folders, binders and other stationery products. On the evening of Thursday, February 3, 2005, Colad electronically filed a petition for relief under chapter 11 of the Bankruptcy Code. The following day, debtor's counsel contacted the court to schedule an opportunity on an emergency basis to seek the court's approval of "first day orders." For this purpose, the court reserved time for both a conference and, if necessary, a hearing, on the afternoon of Tuesday, February 7. In attendance at those proceedings were counsel for the debtor; counsel from the Office of the United States Trustee; counsel for Continental Plants Group, LLC ("Continental"), the primary secured creditor in this case; and Daniel Williams, pro se.

Daniel Williams is the largest creditor in the chapter 7 bankruptcy case of William P. Brosnahan, Jr., an individual who at one time was affiliated with Colad. . . . The bankruptcy estate of Brosnahan [is Colad's] largest unsecured creditor. . . . For these reasons, this court directed that the Brosnahan trustee and its largest creditor receive notice of the conference and hearing relative to any first day motions in the Colad case. Mr. Williams participated in those proceedings, and his objections have served to focus the court's attention on a number of issues that have long had need for explication.

In bankruptcy practice, the phrase "first day motions" refers generally to any of a variety of requests made shortly after the filing of a chapter 11 petition, for prompt authorizations needed to facilitate the operation of the debtor's business. . . .

As of the present moment, this court has already rendered an oral decision with respect to all aspects of the above motions, with the exception of the application for final authority to obtain post-petition financing. Written orders have memorialized these oral decisions. With respect to post-petition financing, the debtor presently operates with benefit of an interim financing order. Primarily, the instant decision must address issues that relate to the terms of the final financing arrangement. However, to place the outstanding issues into context and to clarify the appropriate standard for first day orders, the court wishes to identify relevant principles and briefly recite the rationale for its ruling as to each of the motions.

. . .

First, the requested relief should be limited to that which is minimally necessary to maintain the existence of the debtor, until such time as the debtor can effect appropriate notice to creditors and parties in interest. In particular, a first day order should avoid substantive rulings that irrevocably determine the rights of parties.

Second, first day orders must maintain a level of clarity and simplicity sufficient to allow reasonable confidence that an order will effect no unanticipated or untoward consequences.

Third, first day orders are not a device to change the procedural and substantive rights that the Bankruptcy Code and Rules have established. In particular, first day orders should provide no substitute for the procedural and substantive protections of the plan confirmation process.

Fourth, no first day order should violate or disregard the substantive rights of parties, in ways not expressly authorized by the Bankruptcy Code.

Other principles may also apply with respect to certain first day motions, but the above list will help to explain the court's rulings with respect to the eight motions that the debtor presented in the instant case.

PAYMENTS TO EMPLOYEES AND TO TAXING AUTHORITIES

The debtor's first motion sought authority to pay pre-petition wages and benefits; its second motion sought to approve payment of pre-petition use and sales taxes. In papers filed with these motions, the debtor represented that nearly all of these wages, benefits and taxes would constitute priority claims; that the debtor had incurred these obligations in its ordinary course of operations; that the outstanding wages and benefits were pre-petition obligations that were not yet payable; that a disruption of wage and benefit payments could affect its ability to maintain its work force; and that the outstanding tax liabilities were ordinary obligations for use taxes and for sales taxes that the debtor had collected from its customers. In considering these two motions, the court was principally concerned for prejudice to the rights of other creditors. As against the interests of general unsecured creditors, the tax claims and nearly all of the employee claims held priority. No other priority claims appeared to be outstanding. Secured creditors might typically hold a superior interest in the cash that would be paid to the employees and taxing authorities [as a lien over cash—Eds.], but here, the secured creditor consented to the debtor's proposed distribution. Based upon that consent and upon the various representations made on behalf of the debtor, the court granted both motions in substantial part. With respect to employee wages and benefits, however, the distribution could not exceed the priority limits of 11 U.S.C. § 507(a)(3) and (4), except for an amount that the court deemed to be de minimis and with restrictions on payments to an insider.

POST-PETITION UTILITY SERVICES

[The court held the protections of § 366 of the Code to address whether continued utility services were adequate without more at that time, rejecting the debtor's request for further creditor assurances.—Eds.]

Key Employee Retention and Incentive Program

[The court approved special compensation for key employees, transactions that are outside the ordinary course of business, which have special rules under § 503(c).—Eds.]

Restructuring Consultant

Pursuant to 11 U.S.C. § 363(b), Colad asked the court to approve the continued employment of Getzler Henrich & Associates LLC ("Getzler Henrich") as a restructuring consultant. As part of this engagement, Getzler Henrich will also provide the services of a chief restructuring officer. In its moving papers, the debtor acknowledged that prior to the bankruptcy filing, its secured creditor had requested that Colad retain the services of a restructuring firm. Colad's president further represented that the debtor needed these consulting services "in order to maximize recovery for all parties in interest."

This court realizes that the designation of a particular restructuring manager may define the likely course of events in a bankruptcy proceeding. What inferences may be drawn from the fact that the debtor selected the proposed consultant upon the recommendation of the secured creditor? Do past practices reveal a history of recommendations which may have been made in good faith, but which nonetheless follow a pattern that Continental may now prefer? These questions suggest that even though the Debtor and Getzler Henrich signed a management agreement prior to the bankruptcy filing, the continued retention of the firm will involve the use of resources outside the ordinary course of the debtor's business. Accordingly, the debtor has properly moved for court approval of Getzler Henrich's appointment.

Section 363(b) provides that a debtor in possession "after notice and a hearing, may use, sell, or lease, other than in the ordinary course of business, property of the estate." By reason of the requirement for notice, this court denied the first day motion for final approval of the retention of Getzler Henrich. Instead, the court approved an interim retention, with direction for final hearing on notice to the twenty largest creditors and others who might request service. At that final hearing, debtor's counsel demonstrated the need for a consultant and that Colad had exercised sound discretion in its selection of Getzler Henrich. For these reasons, the court then gave its final approval to the retention proposal.

Retention of Counsel

In the absence of opposition from the office of the United States Trustee, this court will normally grant a first day motion for the appointment of counsel for the debtor in possession. . . .

CASH MANAGEMENT SYSTEM

Prior to its bankruptcy filing, Colad had established a cash management system, which required the deposit of receipts into a lockbox and the transfer of those funds to Continental, on account of its secured position. Essentially, this system facilitated the debtor's revolving credit agreement, under which Colad would direct all receipts toward payment on account of its secured obligations and Continental would continuously advance new funds into Colad's operating accounts. . . . In a separate first day motion, the debtor sought authority to maintain its cash management system. . . .

For reasons of convenience, I granted the debtor's request to maintain all of its existing accounts, but on condition that the debtor order new checks indicating Colad's status as a debtor in possession. Additionally, I allowed the processing of extant checks, in order to avoid disruption of relationships with employees who in any event would have claimed priority for the amount of their uncashed checks.

[Additional dispositions of first day motions are omitted, but some are discussed below.—Eds.]

As mentioned, the Federal Rules of Bankruptcy Procedure have since been revised to address some of these concerns. Rule 6003 prohibits a judge from, among other things, appointing counsel within 21 days of the commencement of the case, so what happened in *Colad* would no longer be allowed. Rule 4001 requires concise (five pages or less) motions or summaries and more extensive notice to interested parties. Rule 4001 also provides limits on what can be obtained under an interim order and restricts the use of cash collateral (the subject of the next section of this assignment) or DIP financing (the subject of the next assignment) to that required to "avoid immediate and irreparable harm to the estate. . . ." The U.S. Trustee has a new manual that includes provisions governing when it will object to certain first day motions, including specific guidance on payments to the so-called "critical vendors" you will see toward the end of this assignment. See United States Dep't of Justice, Trustee Program Policy and Practices Manual, Vol. 3 Ch. 3-2 § 8.6 (Feb. 2020). It seems like people were listening to Judge Bucki.

Incidentally, at first you might have thought that the power to conduct its business in the ordinary course surely meant Colad could pay its employees their back wages. But because these were wages owing for prepetition services, the debtor was asking permission for the estate (DIP) to pay not for services incurred in the ordinary course of its (the estate's) business, but for services incurred by the pre-estate debtor. These wages are unsecured claims *against* the estate, not postpetition expenses incurred *by* the estate. The debtor was quick to point out that those wages would almost all be priority claims, § 507(a)(3), and so would likely get 100% payment in a liquidation, even if unsecured. (If you wonder whether it would have been greedy for the debtor to request payment of unsecured nonpriority claims, keep reading this assignment.)

B.   CASH COLLATERAL

Cash is of course foremost on the DIP's mind at the initiation of a chapter 11 case (specifically, where did it all go and how can we get more?). Chapter 11 requires a balance between DIP control and the need of creditors to make sure the DIP doesn't do anything foolish with what remains of the company's assets. After all, many creditors will grumble that the debtor's management's skill and control are what drove the company into chapter 11.

The Code provides a couple of creditor backstops. First, as seen in the previous assignment, the DIP has to go to court for permission to engage in transactions outside the ordinary course of business. § 363(b). Second, the DIP has to go to court for permission to use "cash collateral." § 363(c)(2). This is the Code's term for money that is subject to a lien. You might wonder: if the bankruptcy estate is a fresh, new entity (a formalism demonstrated in *Colad*), how can that estate have any liens encumbering any of its property unless and until the DIP grants them? And you would be half right in your intuition. Section 552 provides that the debtor's previously granted liens that cover after-acquired property (e.g., "this loan is secured by all factory equipment of the debtor, now and hereafter acquired") encumber only the debtor, *not* the subsequent bankruptcy estate, making it one of the most-hated provisions of the Code by secured creditors. If the DIP buys a new machine for its factory, the secured creditor's after-acquired property clause, even if fully valid under Article 9, is nullified and will not attach to the estate's new machine. By contrast, a machine bought the year before the bankruptcy that has a duly perfected lien on it stays encumbered in bankruptcy. The estate can only acquire that property that the debtor has at filing—lien-encumbered warts and all. Debtors love § 552 just as much as secured creditors hate it because it frees up collateral that would otherwise be burdened by liens. As we will see in Assignment 19, free collateral can be critical to cash-starved debtors.

Before you get carried away thinking § 552 means every asset acquired after filing will be lien-free, remember that the Code does nothing to impair the tracing of proceeds. UCC § 9-315, Code § 541. If a lien-encumbered machine the debtor purchased a year before bankruptcy is sold in bankruptcy, Article 9 makes clear that the secured creditor's lien attaches to the proceeds, and nothing in the Code changes that result. True, the cash received upon the machine's sale is new debtor property acquired after bankruptcy (that cash was someone else's before filing), but that new property is the proceeds of old property that was subject to a security interest. Understand it as the transformation of a lien-encumbered machine into lien-encumbered cash, not the creation of a new lien on new property pursuant to a pre-bankruptcy pledge that would be blocked by § 552.

At the time of filing, the debtor frequently has cash in its estate that is encumbered by a lien, "cash collateral," § 363(a), which cannot be used without the court's permission. § 363(c)(2). The reason for this restriction is that while machines are easy to watch, working away in a factory while lawyers fight in court, cash is not. Indeed, one is hard-pressed to find an asset more liquid, and hence more "dissipatable," than cash: "cash flow" can flow right out of the debtor's accounts before a secured creditor even knows its collateral was sold. The classic example is a large retailer selling inventory where the security interest in inventory gets converted constantly into cash and credit card receivables. Telling a secured creditor not to worry because the lien will still be on the cash and other proceeds is cold comfort if the DIP spends all the cash. Recall that the DIP has lots of leeway given the ordinary course of business standard. On the other hand, to restrict use of that cash to the secured creditor's consent would likely doom a business's reorganization attempt before it even started. A chapter 11 filing is often precipitated not by some aggressive creditor lawsuit, but because the debtor simply runs out of cash to continue operations. The Code balances this tension by requiring court approval of the DIP's use of cash collateral. The DIP is free to use unencumbered cash, but cash that is subject to a secured creditor's lien requires a judge's OK before it gets spent. If a secured creditor can't agree to let the debtor use the cash collateral, then the fight has to go to court—with everything on the line for the debtor.

In re CARBONE COMPANIES, INC.
395 B.R. 631 (Bankr. N.D. Ohio 2008)

Baxter, Bankruptcy Judge.

Before the Court is the motion of Carbone Companies, Inc. . . . for authorization to use cash collateral pursuant to § 363(c)(2)(B) of the Bankruptcy Code. An objection to such relief was filed by the secured lender, Fifth Third Bank (the "Bank") on the basis that it is not adequately protected. The Official Committee of Unsecured Creditors (the "Committee") also filed an objection. . . .

Carbone Companies is in the construction business, with offices located in Cleveland, Ohio. Carbone Properties is a holding company and owns many other affiliated entities either directly or indirectly, including Carbone Properties of Audubon, LLC ("Carbone Audubon").

Presently, Carbone Companies has 13 ongoing projects and an additional six projects that are pending startup. Its main clients are the Ohio School Facilities Commission ("OSFC") and McTech Corporation ("McTech").

On August 1, 2004, R.P. Carbone obtained a loan from the Bank pursuant to a credit agreement (subsequently amended on May 3, 2006) in the principal amount of $15,000,000 ("Loan"). In return, the Bank received a security interest, pursuant to a security agreement dated August 1, 2004 (subsequently amended on May 3, 2006), in all accounts, inventory, equipment, general intangibles, investment property, negotiable instruments, personal property and other assets. . . .

According to the Bank, R.P. Carbone defaulted on the Loan on June 17, 2008. Debtors allege that after they defaulted on the Loan, the Bank agreed to a forbearance and proposed a budget for Debtors. When Debtors made several changes to the budget, the Bank ceased negotiations and swept Debtors' accounts. Debtors allege that after the Bank swept their accounts, Debtors were unable to pay their operating expenses, including payroll and taxes. On August 1, 2008, the Bank obtained a judgment in the Cuyahoga County Court of Common Pleas against Debtors and other related entities in the amount of $14,981,440, with default interest of $304,623.02, late charges of $749,072.03, and interest of $4,993.82 per day after July 31, 2008 ("Judgment"). Subsequently, on September 3, 2008, the Bank notified Carbone Companies in writing that it was executing its Judgment.

The next day, Debtors filed their respective Chapter 11 petitions and continued to operate their businesses as Debtors in Possession ("DIP"). . . .

The issue before this Court is whether the Debtors have satisfied the required elements for use of cash collateral under § 363(c)(2)(B) of the Bankruptcy Code. . . .

Debtors seek a final order authorizing their use of cash collateral in order to continue their business operations as DIPs. Following an earlier preliminary hearing, Debtors were granted limited use of cash collateral, while the Bank received replacement liens on the Debtors' postpetition assets. The present motion requests final court approval for continued use of cash collateral under § 363(c)(2)(B), since the Bank has refused consent to continued use of its cash collateral.

The Bank opposes the relief sought on the basis that it is not adequately protected. The Bank also alleged, in its objection to Debtors' limited use of cash collateral, that the Debtors were maintaining an inadequate cash management system, that Debtors' budgets were excessive, and that Debtors made improper transfers to insiders and affiliates. . . . As a remedy for the inadequate protection of its security interest, the Bank proposed liens on [possible lawsuits against the bank and others] that the Debtors may bring in their bankruptcy proceedings. . . .

A debtor requesting court approval to use cash collateral has the burden of proof as to the issue of "adequate protection." 11 U.S.C. § 363(p)(1). Although "adequate protection" is not defined in the Code, § 361 provides illustrative examples of adequate protection, specifically that the debtor may give cash, additional or replacement liens, or other relief that will result in the indubitable equivalent of the objecting party's interest in such property. 11 U.S.C. § 361. The test is whether the secured party's interest is protected from diminution or decrease as a result of the proposed use of cash collateral. In other words, if the debtor's proposed protections do not adequately preserve the creditor's interest in the cash collateral as it existed on the petition filing date, then the creditor is not adequately protected. Thusly, the Court may not authorize use of cash collateral without running afoul of the secured creditor's Fifth Amendment property right to a just compensation for a taking. See Wright v. Union Cent. Life Ins. Co., 311 U.S. 273, 61 S. Ct. 196, 85 L. Ed. 184 (1940).

. . .

Mr. Goddard, [an expert turnaround management specialist], testified that the net cash flow projections for the ensuing quarter, October to December 2008, reflect positive increases for Carbone Companies as opposed to negative cash flows. The net operating cash flow begins at $108,803 prepetition and increases to $196,630 by December 31, 2008. Likewise, the Debtors' accounts receivable will increase over the same period. The eligible accounts receivable begins at $453,432 prepetition and increases to $515,255 by December 31, 2008. In sum, the cash collateral (cash and accounts receivable) will increase during the next three months, from October to December 2008. Such an exhibition indicates adequate protection of the Bank's cash collateral. Further, Mr. Goddard opines that going forward, Debtors will be profitable. As such, the Bank is adequately protected because its cash collateral will not diminish during Debtors' proposed use; rather, it will increase because of Debtors' use. . . .

In support of the Debtors' positive cash flow projections, Debtors exhibited a report comparing its projected budget to its actual budget for the previous month, September 2008. . . . In sum, Debtors had more cash and accounts receivable and less expenses than projected for the month of September, meaning Debtors exceeded their projections. The Bank did not offer any persuasive evidence to refute the Debtors' budget for September.

As further adequate protection for the Bank's cash collateral, it is well understood that the Bank was entitled to postpetition replacement liens on its collateral, to the extent there was any diminution in its cash collateral. In support thereof, Mr. Scaparotti testified to the fact that the Debtors' main clients, OSFC and McTech, have indicated they would continue to do business with Debtors notwithstanding Debtors' pending bankruptcy proceedings. . . .

Although the objecting Bank's counsel argued strenuously that the Bank was not adequately protected, arguments of counsel are not to be construed as evidence. . . .

As partial support for its objection, the Bank alleged a diminution of Debtors' assets through a questionable transfer by McTech to an affiliate of the Debtor, Carbone Audubon, and another questionable transfer to a non-debtor third party, the law firm representing Carbone Audubon in its bankruptcy case in the Eastern District of Louisiana. Through testimony taken of McTech's chief financial officer ("CFO"), John George, it was not shown that the subject transfers by McTech involved any transfer of assets belonging to the Debtors. What was shown, and unrebutted by any evidence to the contrary, was McTech's transfer of certain of its own assets to third parties as an apparent favor to one Vincent Carbone, the former president of Carbone Companies. . . . In summary, no proof has been shown to demonstrate a decrease in Debtors' assets by virtue of the subject transfers acknowledged by McTech. . . .

Accordingly, the Debtors' motion for final authorization to use cash collateral is hereby granted. The objection of Fifth Third Bank is overruled, upon this Court's determination that the Bank's cash collateral is adequately protected. The objection of the Official Committee of Unsecured Creditors is also overruled. Each party is to bear its respective costs.

The evidence presented by the debtor of burgeoning cash flow was not offered merely to show that the company had a chance of success, although it surely had that effect. The true reason was to show the likelihood that the bank's collateral—cash—would be maintained at equal or greater amounts. Court permission to use cash collateral will be conditioned upon finding such adequate protection.

C.   SETOFF

Closely related to cash collateral is cash that is available for setoff. Setoff, for those of you dozing during Civ Pro, is when a party is both a creditor and debtor at the same time. For example, it arises when P sues D successfully for $\$X$, and before forlornly whipping out his checkbook, D realizes that P already owes him $\$Y$—$P$ is thus a creditor and a debtor of D. On these facts, D can "offset" $\$Y$ from the award and only pay P the net amount $\$(X - Y)$. By corollary, if P goes bankrupt and the bankruptcy trustee sues D to recover that $\$X$ for the estate, unhappy D will be stuck as a creditor and file an unsecured claim for $\$Y$ in P's case. Section 553 preserves the "right of setoff," which means that D can decline to pay the $\$X$ he owes P's bankruptcy estate and simply deduct that amount from his allowed claim of $\$Y$, netting his remaining claim to $\$(Y - X)$.

The right to set off is a very valuable one to unsecured creditors, since it enables them to obtain, in effect, full payment on their claims up to the amount of their debts to the debtor (i.e., $\$X$). For this reason, it is treated functionally the same as having a secured claim for that amount, where the "collateral" is the money in the creditor's pocket that it owes the debtor. Although the right to set off is not technically a security interest and is expressly excluded from the general rules of Article 9 of the UCC (except to the extent that the setoff rights of depositary institutions are specifically acknowledged, UCC §§ 9-109(d)(10), 9-340), a setoff is treated as security for the amount of the setoff right, § 506(a).

The most likely deployers of setoff are banks. Recall that a bank account is not actually a pile of dollar bills in a sack labeled "$$$." It is a promise (FDIC-insured) to pay the depositor upon demand the amount of money credited to the account (i.e., a debt from the bank to the depositor). When the setoff right arises from, for example, the cash in an operating account at a bank where the debtor does business and also owes money to the bank on a line of credit, that setoff "collateral" is of course cash collateral and governed by the already-discussed rules set forth in § 363(c). This is all good news for the unsecured bank, who gets to use its offsetting debt to the debtor effectively as security to provide for its recovery. That said, the creditor with a setoff right is also subject to the automatic stay, just like any other secured creditor, and may not exercise its right of setoff without the permission of the court. § 362(a)(7). Even these seemingly simple rules spark litigation.

In re OREXIGEN THERAPEUTICS, INC.
596 B.R. 9 (Bankr. D. Del. 2018)

GROSS, Bankruptcy Judge

The Court is ruling on McKesson Corporation's ("McKesson") and its wholly owned subsidiary McKesson Patient Relationship Solutions' ("MPRS") Motion for an Order Determining that McKesson Is Entitled to the Disputed Funds (the "Motion") (D.I. 654). McKesson seeks to affect a setoff under section 553 of the Bankruptcy Code. Specifically, McKesson asks to offset its $6,932,816.40 debt to the Debtor under the

Core Distribution Agreement ("Distribution Agreement") based on the Debtor's approximately $9,100,000 debt to MPRS under the Master Services Agreement ("Services Agreement"). For the reasons that follow, the Court finds that McKesson is seeking a triangular setoff which is prohibited in bankruptcy due to the lack of mutuality. An enforceable contractual right allowing a parent and its subsidiary corporation to affect a prepetition triangular setoff under state law does not supply the strict mutuality required in bankruptcy. The Court will therefore deny the Motion for the reasons that follow.

BACKGROUND

The material facts are relatively undisputed. The Debtor was a biopharmaceutical company that manufactured Contrave®, a drug that treats obesity. The United States Food and Drug Administration approved Contrave® in 2014. *Id.* ¶8. Prepetition, the Debtor entered into two agreements relevant here: one with McKesson, and one with MPRS. McKesson is the parent corporation and MPRS is its subsidiary corporation. It is undisputed that McKesson and MPRS are legally distinct entities.

On June 9, 2016, effective June 1, 2016, the Debtor entered into the Distribution Agreement with McKesson, which contemplated that McKesson would purchase and distribute Contrave® to various pharmacies in the United States. . . . More pertinently, the parties agreed that McKesson had certain rights, including a right to set off debts owed between the Debtor and its affiliates against debts owed between McKesson and its affiliates:

> . . .
> i. Notwithstanding anything to the contrary in this Agreement, each of McKesson Corporation and its affiliates is hereby authorized to *set-off*, recoup and apply any amounts owed by it to Manufacturer's [the Debtor's] affiliates against any all [*sic*] amounts owed by Manufacturer or its affiliates to any of McKesson Corporation or its affiliates, without prior written notice[.]

(emphasis added) (citation omitted). As of the petition date, McKesson owed the Debtor $6,932,816.40 under the Distribution Agreement.

On July 15, 2016, the Debtor entered into the Services Agreement with MPRS, which contemplated that MPRS would manage the Debtor's LoyaltyScript® program. The LoyaltyScript® program enabled patients to receive price discounts on Contrave® from retail pharmacies. MPRS would pay the retail pharmacies and patients for the Contrave® price discounts and other services under the LoyaltyScript® program. Consequently, the Debtor would reimburse MPRS. The Services Agreement does not incorporate or relate to the Distribution Agreement; they are wholly distinct. As of the petition date, the Debtor owed MPRS approximately $9,100,000.

On March 12, 2018, the Debtor voluntarily filed a petition for relief under Chapter 11. . . .

Setoff is a contractual or equitable right that "allows entities that owe each other money to apply their mutual debts against each other, thereby avoiding 'the absurdity of making A pay B when B owes A.'" Citizens Bank of Maryland v. Strumpf, 516 U.S. 16, 18 (1995). The Bankruptcy Code's Section 553(a) does not create a federal right of setoff but merely recognizes such party's right under state law. . . .

Whether a party has a setoff right under section 553 is a twofold inquiry. First, the party seeking setoff must acquire such right prepetition under applicable nonbankruptcy law. . . .

The parties do not dispute that McKesson had a prepetition setoff right pursuant to section VII.i. of the Distribution Agreement. . . .

Mutuality Under Section 553(a)

[Second, o]nce a party has a prepetition setoff right under applicable nonbankruptcy law, that party must then meet "[t]he additional restrictions imposed by section 553 [which are] well-settled." In re SemCrude, L.P., 399 B.R. 388, 396 (Bankr. D. Del. 2009). The plain language of Section 553(a) only allows a creditor to offset a "mutual debt." There is no statutory definition of "mutuality" or a "mutual debt" under the Bankruptcy Code. However, state and federal courts have found to a fare-thee-well that debts are "'mutual' only when 'they are due to and from the same persons in the same capacity.'"

Under section 553(a), "mutuality is strictly construed against the party seeking setoff." *Id.* at 396. . . .

McKesson does not have a mutual debt under section 553(a). As of the petition date, McKesson owed the Debtor $6,932,816.40 and the Debtor owed MPRS approximately $9,100,000. . . . A triangular setoff is a setoff between an affiliate of a contractual party and the counter-contractual party. McKesson's argument is that because the Debtor owes MPRS in excess of the amount of the Disputed Funds under the Services Agreement, section 553(a) enables McKesson to set off the MPRS claim against McKesson's payment under the Distribution Agreement. However, McKesson runs into fatal contrary bankruptcy precedent. A triangular setoff is impermissible under section 553(a) without mutuality. . . .

Furthermore, McKesson is the parent corporation and MPRS is its subsidiary corporation. They are legally distinct entities. Thus, their corporate structure poses another [not really—Eds.] issue preventing McKesson from affecting a triangular setoff. The Court wholly agrees with Judge Shannon's assessment on this point:

> Moreover, because each corporation is a separate entity from its sister corporations absent a piercing of the corporate veil, a "subsidiary's debt may not be set off against the credit of a parent or other subsidiary, or vice versa, because no mutuality exists under the circumstances." Sentinel Products Corp., 192 B.R. [41,] 46 [(N.D.N.Y. 1996)] (citing MNC Commercial Corp. v. Joseph T. Ryerson & Son, Inc., 882 F.2d 615, 618 n. 2 (2d Cir. 1989)). Allowing a creditor to offset a debt it owes to one corporation against funds owed to it by another corporation—*even a wholly-owned subsidiary*—would thus constitute an improper triangular setoff under the Code.

Id. at 393-94 (emphasis added). . . .

McKesson argues that when a creditor seeks to affect a setoff, the Bankruptcy Court's inquiry must begin and end with state law. That is, state law determines whether a creditor has a setoff right and also governs whether mutuality exists. Thus, McKesson's view that because California law governs the Distribution Agreement and California, according to McKesson, allows for an agreement between a parent and subsidiary to supply the requisite mutuality the latter needs to "be deemed a mutual debtor-creditor of the parent," Prudential Reinsurance Co. v. Superior Court, 842 P.2d 48, 60 (1992), a triangular setoff is permitted under section 553(a). For the following reasons, the Court rejects McKesson's argument as a matter of [federal] law and policy.

McKesson's point of departure is a precedential bankruptcy case, Butner v. United States, 440 U.S. 48, 55 (1979). *Butner* held that state law, not a federal law or a rule of equity, determined whether a security interest in property extends to rents and profits derived from the property [when the debtor is in bankruptcy]. *Butner* is eminent for its proposition that state law rights are respected in bankruptcy absent a contrary bankruptcy rule or policy. In its analysis, the Supreme Court explained with the oft-cited language:

> *Property interests are created and defined by state law. Unless some federal interest requires a different result, there is no reason why such interests should be analyzed differently simply because an interested party is involved in a bankruptcy proceeding.* Uniform treatment of property interests by both state and federal courts within a State serves to reduce uncertainty, to discourage forum shopping, and to prevent a party from receiving a "windfall merely by reason of the happenstance of bankruptcy."

Id. at 55 (emphasis added) (citation omitted).

. . .

McKesson also argues that *Butner*'s "federal interest" exception is inapplicable here. Specifically, McKesson "asserts that there is no federal interest that would impose a federal gloss on the application of state law to these [setoff] rights. . . . [T]he correct reading of section 553 is to conclude that the section does not create any federal right of setoff and it does not interfere with McKesson's rights under California law." The Court disagrees.

Congress in enacting section 553(a) recognized a federal interest. The statutory language is the point of departure for statutory interpretation. . . .

Here, section 553(a) is unambiguous in providing that a "mutual debt" must be "owing by such creditor to the debtor that arose before the commencement of the case under this title against a claim of such creditor against the debtor that arose before the commencement of the case" subject to certain exceptions. However, none of those exceptions state or imply a multi-party contractual exception exists to the mutuality requirement allowing a triangular setoff. *See* Section 553(a)(1)-(3) and (b). A contractual exception to mutuality would be incongruent with the express provision of section 553(a). McKesson is the *creditor* seeking to offset a debt of $6,932,816.40 it owes to the Debtor that arose prepetition under the Distribution Agreement against a $9,100,00 claim of MPRS against the debtor that arose prepetition. Statutorily speaking, that cannot happen.

Furthermore, section 553(a) aligns with the fundamental bankruptcy policy of ensuring similarly-situated creditors receive an equal distribution from the debtor's estate. If parties can contract around section 553(a)'s mutuality requirement, a creditor could receive a greater distribution than other equal-footed creditors and thus dilute the entire estate to the detriment of all creditors. Mutuality is the lynchpin of setoff under section 553(a). Thus, the cases the Court relies upon are not inconsistent with *Butner*. The Court refuses to read a contractual exception to strict mutuality allowing for triangular setoff in the face of contrary bankruptcy precedent and policy. . . .

———————————

One advantage to having decided the *Butner* caveat applies is avoiding the question whether setoff is best characterized as a substantive or procedural right. Some might find that debate *Erie*-ly familiar.

Once upon a time, there was a law professor named Richard Posner, who became a federal appellate judge. He liked to share his enthusiasm for the field of economics as broadly and in as many media as he could, most especially in cases that found their way to the U.S. Court of Appeals for the Seventh Circuit. He found few subjects that could not in his view benefit from this sharing of his thoughts, which were (and still are) often quite incisive, which is why he rightly became famous. Some might complain he occasionally blurred the line between the law reviews and the federal reporters, but many agree he offered cracking good reads. He once found himself puzzled by the bankruptcy protection of setoff and decided to share his intellectual musings with the world. See In re Elcona Homes Corp., 863 F.2d 483 (7th Cir. 1988) (remanding case for factual assessment whether setoff was mutual or triangular). His analysis of setoff and its conceptualization as a security interest is well worth reading in this abridged excerpt:

> The setoff provision in the Bankruptcy Code seems at first glance inconsistent with the usual result in bankruptcy, which is that all unsecured creditors are treated alike ("equity is equality"). . . .
>
> The principle is not absolute, as we have stressed, but its exceptions generally are intelligible; and we will be helped in determining the scope of the set-off exception—which on its face is arbitrary—if we can understand its rationale, too. Set offs outside of bankruptcy are in no wise anomalous or problematic; no third party's rights comparable to those of unsecured creditors in bankruptcy are affected, and circuitous proceedings are avoided. But in bankruptcy an unsecured creditor fortunate enough to owe his debtor as much as or more than the debtor owes him can, by setting off his debt against the debtor's, in effect receive 100 cents on the dollar, while the other unsecured creditors, who have nothing to set off against the debtor, might be lucky to collect 10 cents on the dollar. The difference in treatment seems based on a fortuitous difference among the unsecured creditors, and therefore arbitrary. Let us inquire further.
>
> Although the right of set off has been a part of Anglo-American bankruptcy law since 1705, see Act of 4 Anne, ch. 17, § 11, its rationale has never been made clear. . . . The only sense we can make of the rule is that it recognizes that the creditor who owes his debtor money is like a secured creditor; indeed, the mutual debts, to the extent equal, secure each party against the other's default. . . . The reasoning may seem circular, however, for it is only by virtue of the Bankruptcy Code's preserving the right of set off that the

creditor has, in the event of his debtor's bankruptcy, a form of security for the debt he is owed. (But of course not all defaulting debtors are bankrupt.) And one might suppose that if the theory of the set off is that it provides the creditor with security, the creditor would have to prove that the parties had intended a right of set off as a means of securing the creditor—that is, would have to prove that the creditor had been counting on the right in extending credit to the debtor on the terms he did. [We're not sure why this is so; security can arise involuntarily, such as through a statutory lien. Homer nodded?—Eds.] But such proof is not in fact required.

Banks argue that the right to set off deposits (a bank deposit is a debt of the bank to the depositor) against the depositor's debts to the bank facilitates the provision of bank credit and lowers the rate of interest, by giving the bank security in the event of the depositor's going broke. But the more secure the bank is, the less secure the depositor's other creditors will be, so they will charge higher interest rates. . . .

Yet if deposits are intended to secure the bank's loans, why not treat the bank [alone] as a secured creditor rather than creating a general right in all creditors to set off their debts against the bankrupt's debts to them? Maybe the answer is simply that set offs are just another form of secured financing that the Bankruptcy Code has decided to recognize, though under a different name and with different restrictions. But the underlying rights of creditors which are asserted in bankruptcy proceedings are the creation of state law, not of the Bankruptcy Code; for the general principle see Butner v. United States, 440 U.S. 48, 54-57 (1979). Maybe the right question to ask, therefore, is not why the Code allows set offs (for it also allows secured creditors to withdraw their collateral from the pool available to other creditors), but why it places restrictions on them.

Against this view of set offs as a species of secured financing, however, it can be argued that, apart perhaps from such special situations as that of banks dealing with their depositor-borrowers, set offs are recognized in state law for their procedural convenience—the consolidation of offsetting claims in the same suit—and that this convenience should receive little weight in bankruptcy. Professor Gilmore thought the express exemption of set offs from the filing requirements in Article 9 (secured financing) of the Uniform Commercial Code, see § 9-104(i), absurd: "Of course a right of setoff is not a security interest and has never been confused with one: the statute might as appropriately exclude fan dancing." 1 Gilmore, Security Interests in Personal Property § 10.7, at pp. 315-16 (1965). This view seems extreme and has been questioned, but certainly there is no evidence here that the existence of mutual debts (if that is what they were) between [the parties] reflected a desire by the parties to secure each other's obligations; it appears to have been an accident.

But we need not resolve these questions, or press our inquiry into the rationale for the Bankruptcy Code's treatment of set offs further, in order to decide this case [!!!!!—Eds.].

Id. at 484-86.

Judge Posner's apparent mystification by the "special treatment" of offsetting creditors is probably not shared by many non-lawyers (or even lawyers), who themselves might be mystified if told that when a debtor files for bankruptcy but a creditor happens to owe the debtor money as well, that creditor should cheerfully write a check for the full debt owed to the DIP and then file an unsecured claim for the amount it is owed back, hoping for the best: possession being nine-tenths of the law is surely a deep-seated conviction. (So too is mutuality of obligation. See Kingston v. Preston, 2 Doug. 689 (1773) [holding that parties' performances are presumptively construed as mutually dependent conditions such that one party's failure excuses the other from performance].) But on the other hand, he is surely correct that whatever its harmlessness as a procedural convenience outside bankruptcy, inside bankruptcy setoff has the substantive effect of conferring upon the offsetting creditor exclusive priority in the receivable owing to the estate—just as if it had a perfected security interest on that property. That's even more than an unsecured priority, *cf.* § 507, that's promotion to secured status—all on a theory that bears about as much sophistication as a middle-schooler yelling, "Dibs!"

As the *Elcona* court also notes, setoff is probably most relevant for banks. While the automatic stay requires the bank to get court permission before grabbing those debtor funds by setoff, it also says the debtor cannot use this cash collateral without court permission. With apparently no one able to use the money, the Supreme Court resolved the impasse by saying that the bank can "freeze" the account (but not take it) pending an application for setoff to the bankruptcy court. Citizens Bank of Maryland v. Strumpf, 516 U.S. 16 (1995). Returning to possession being nine-tenths of the law, we think this is a big win for banks. One area that the banks still cannot touch by common law, however, is special purpose accounts. Business debtors frequently have segregated accounts, such as accounts that hold the proceeds of cash withheld from employee paychecks. If the business gets into trouble, the bank cannot reach any such special account for a setoff. It is no surprise that substantial litigation persists over what constitutes a "special account."

D. TRADE SUPPLIERS AND VENDORS

The next thing on a debtor's mind for stabilizing the business in chapter 11 will be continuing shipments from its suppliers once it has permission to use cash collateral to pay them. Skeptical suppliers that are owed money on old invoices may be tempted to jump ship upon the debtor's filing, which can doom a reorganization before it even gets off the ground. Some may want to refuse to do further business with the debtor unless and until those old invoices are paid, but as we have seen, that violates the automatic stay. So they may try another weapon: their common law rights of *reclamation* to claw back recently shipped goods.

When sellers discover their buyers are insolvent, the common law treats it as a mistake and allows the sellers to rescind the contract and reclaim their goods within certain time periods, almost as if they have a pseudo-security interest in the goods. The UCC codifies this rule at UCC § 2-702. (Of course, this right is not an actual security interest, and so a properly perfected security interest in inventory would have superior rights to the reclaiming supplier's UCC rights.) This reorganization-imperiling right was one that the Code traditionally treated with hostility in chapter 11, but BAPCPA loosened the Code's restrictions on reclamation. Now, reclaiming sellers essentially get an opportunity to exercise such rights when a debtor enters chapter 11 within 45 days of shipment, § 546(c), even if state law provides for a shorter reclamation period. They also get a priority claim for invoices if the debtor files bankruptcy within 20 days of shipment, even if they cannot reclaim for some reason. § 503(b)(9).

The prospect of stripping the debtor's shelves of recently shipped goods under a reclamation order is powerful leverage for a mere "unsecured" supplier. And even those vendors who perform services, have shipped goods more than 45 days ago, or for other reasons cannot reclaim goods, still have a powerful tool: refusing to deal further with the debtor trying to stay on its feet in chapter 11. While the debtor can always promise to pay cash on demand going forward, that may not satisfy a supplier with a large unpaid prepetition invoice. Such a well-counseled trade creditor will be careful not to violate the stay, by having a conversation that goes something like this: "Of course I'd never *dream* of demanding payment of the old debt—respect the stay, man!—but this feeling is coming over me that I should discontinue our business relationship going forward. Sorry about your upcoming Memorial Day Sale." Surely that is an invitation for the debtor to come up with a "spontaneous" offer to repay the prepetition invoice, and under this scenario, the threatening creditor is not a stay-violator, just a tough cookie.

Can the debtor just fold and pay the vendor off? On the one hand, why not? It might want to do just that, especially if the vendor is critical to the business's survival in the exercise of sound business judgment. As a fiduciary to all the unsecured creditors, however, the DIP is not supposed to be in the favoritism business, giving one creditor 100% of prepetition debt when others go hungry. Courts are somewhat divided on this chapter 11 practice. "Many DIPs justify this creditor favoritism under a 'doctrine of necessity.' Based historically upon provisions of the Railway Labor Act, 45 U.S.C. § 151 et seq., the Doctrine of Necessity finds support from § 105(a) of the Bankruptcy Code, which authorizes the bankruptcy court to 'issue any order, process, or judgment that is necessary or appropriate to carry out the provisions of this title.'" In re Colad Group, Inc., 324 B.R. 208, 213 (Bankr. W.D.N.Y. 2005) (quoting Alan N. Resnick & Henry J. Sommer, Collier on Bankruptcy ¶105.04[5][a] (15 ed. rev. 2003)). Others are less convinced.

In re KMART CORP.

359 F.3d 866 (7th Cir. 2004)

EASTERBROOK, Circuit Judge.

On the first day of its bankruptcy, Kmart sought permission to pay immediately, and in full, the pre-petition claims of all "critical vendors." (Technically there are 38 debtors: Kmart Corporation plus 37 of its affiliates and subsidiaries. We call them all Kmart.) The theory behind the request is that some suppliers may be unwilling to do business with a customer that is behind in payment, and, if it cannot obtain the merchandise that its own customers have come to expect, a firm such as Kmart may be unable to carry on, injuring all of its creditors. Full payment to critical vendors thus could in principle make even the disfavored creditors better off: they may not be paid in full, but they will receive a greater portion of their claims than they would if the critical vendors cut off supplies and the business shut down. Putting the proposition in this way implies, however, that the debtor must prove, and not just allege, two things: that, but for immediate full payment, vendors would cease dealing; and that the business will gain enough from continued transactions with the favored vendors to provide some residual benefit to the remaining, disfavored creditors, or at least leave them no worse off.

Bankruptcy Judge Sonderby entered a critical-vendors order just as Kmart proposed it, without notifying any disfavored creditors, without receiving any pertinent evidence (the record contains only some sketchy representations by counsel plus unhelpful testimony by Kmart's CEO, who could not speak for the vendors), and without making any finding of fact that the disfavored creditors would gain or come out even. The bankruptcy court's order declared that the relief Kmart requested—open-ended permission to pay any [general unsecured] debt to any vendor it deemed "critical" in the exercise of unilateral discretion, provided that the vendor agreed to furnish goods on "customary trade terms" for the next two years—was "in the best interests of the Debtors, their estates and their creditors." The order did not explain why, nor did it contain any legal analysis, though it did cite 11 U.S.C. § 105(a). . . .

Kmart used its authority to pay in full the pre-petition debts to 2,330 suppliers, which collectively received about $300 million. This came from the $2 billion in new credit (debtor-in-possession or DIP financing) that the bankruptcy judge authorized, granting the lenders super-priority in post-petition assets and revenues. See In re Qualitech Steel Corp., 276 F.3d 245 (7th Cir. 2001). Another 2,000 or so vendors were not deemed "critical" and were not paid. They and 43,000 additional unsecured creditors eventually received about 10¢ on the dollar, mostly in stock of the reorganized Kmart. Capital Factors, Inc., appealed the critical-vendors order immediately after its entry on January 25, 2002. A little more than 14 months later, after all of the critical vendors had been paid and as Kmart's plan of reorganization was on the verge of approval, District Judge Grady reversed the order authorizing payment. 291 B.R. 818 (N.D. Ill. 2003). He concluded that neither § 105(a) nor a "doctrine of necessity" supports the orders. . . .

Appellants insist that, by the time Judge Grady acted, it was too late. Money had changed hands and, we are told, cannot be refunded. But why not? Reversing preferential transfers is an ordinary feature of bankruptcy practice, often continuing under a confirmed plan of reorganization. If the orders in question are invalid, then the critical vendors have received preferences that Kmart is entitled to recoup for the benefit of all creditors. Confirmation of a plan does not stop the administration of the estate, except to the extent that the plan itself so provides. Several provisions of the Code do forbid revision of transactions completed under judicial auspices. For example, the DIP financing order, issued contemporaneously with the critical-vendors order, is sheltered by 11 U.S.C. § 364(e): "The reversal or modification on appeal of an authorization under this section to obtain credit or incur debt, or of a grant under this section of a priority or a lien, does not affect the validity of any debt so incurred, or any priority or lien so granted, to an entity that extended such credit in good faith, whether or not such entity knew of the pendency of the appeal, unless such authorization and the incurring of such debt, or the granting of such priority or lien, were stayed pending appeal." Nothing comparable anywhere in the Code covers payments made to pre-existing, unsecured creditors, whether or not the debtor calls them "critical." Judges do not invent missing language.

Now it is true that we have recognized the existence of a longstanding doctrine . . . that detrimental reliance comparable to the extension of new credit against a promise of security, or the purchase of assets in a foreclosure sale, may make it appropriate for judges to exercise such equitable discretion as they possess in order to protect those reliance interests. Thus once action has been taken to distribute assets under a confirmed plan of reorganization, it would take some extraordinary event to turn back the clock. These appeals, however, do not question any distribution under Kmart's plan; to the contrary, the plan (which was confirmed after the district court's decision) provides that adversary proceedings will be filed to recover the preferences that the critical vendors have received. No one filed an appeal, which means that it is appellants in this court that now wage a collateral attack on the plan of reorganization.

Appellants say that we should recognize their reliance interests: after the order, they continued selling goods and services to Kmart (doing this was a condition of payment for pre-petition debts). Continued business relations may or may not be a form of reliance (that depends on whether the vendors otherwise would have stopped selling), but they are not detrimental reliance. The vendors have been paid in full for post-petition goods and services. If Kmart had become administratively insolvent, and unable to compensate the vendors for post-petition transactions, then it might make sense to permit vendors to retain payments under the critical-vendors order, at least to the extent of the post-petition deficiency. Because Kmart emerged as an operating business, however, no such question arises. The vendors have not established that any reliance interest—let alone any language in the Code—blocks future attempts to recover preferential transfers on account of pre-petition debts.

Section 105(a) allows a bankruptcy court to "issue any order, process, or judgment that is necessary or appropriate to carry out the provisions of" the Code. This does not create discretion to set aside the Code's rules about priority and distribution; the power conferred by § 105(a) is one to implement rather than override. Every circuit that has considered the question has held that this statute does not allow a bankruptcy judge to authorize full payment of any unsecured debt, unless all unsecured creditors in the class are paid in full. We agree with this view of § 105. "The fact that a [bankruptcy] proceeding is equitable does not give the judge a free-floating discretion to redistribute rights in accordance with his personal views of justice and fairness, however enlightened those views may be." In re Chicago, Milwaukee, St. Paul & Pacific R.R., 791 F.2d 524, 528 (7th Cir. 1986).

A "doctrine of necessity" is just a fancy name for a power to depart from the Code. Although courts in the days before bankruptcy law was codified wielded power to reorder priorities and pay particular creditors in the name of "necessity"—see Miltenberger v. Logansport Ry., 106 U.S. 286, 1 S. Ct. 140, 27 L. Ed. 117 (1882); Fosdick v. Schall, 99 U.S. 235, 25 L. Ed.

339 (1878)—today it is the Code rather than the norms of nineteenth century railroad reorganizations that must prevail. *Miltenberger* and *Fosdick* predate the first general effort at codification, the Bankruptcy Act of 1898. Today the Bankruptcy Code of 1978 supplies the rules. Congress did not in terms scuttle old common-law doctrines, because it did not need to; the Act curtailed, and then the Code replaced, the entire apparatus. Answers to contemporary issues must be found within the Code (or legislative halls). Older doctrines may survive as glosses on ambiguous language enacted in 1978 or later, but not as freestanding entitlements to trump the text.

. . .

That leaves § 363(b)(1): "The trustee [or debtor in possession], after notice and a hearing, may use, sell, or lease, other than in the ordinary course of business, property of the estate." This is more promising, for satisfaction of a pre-petition debt in order to keep "critical" supplies flowing is a use of property other than in the ordinary course of administering an estate in bankruptcy. . . . We need not decide whether § 363(b)(1) could support payment of some pre-petition debts, because this order was unsound no matter how one reads § 363(b)(1).

The foundation of a critical-vendors order is the belief that vendors not paid for prior deliveries will refuse to make new ones. Without merchandise to sell, a retailer such as Kmart will fold. If paying the critical vendors would enable a successful reorganization and make even the disfavored creditors better off, then all creditors favor payment whether or not they are designated as "critical." . . . For the premise to hold true, however, it is necessary to show not only that the disfavored creditors will be as well off with reorganization as with liquidation—a demonstration never attempted in this proceeding—but also that the supposedly critical vendors would have ceased deliveries if old debts were left unpaid while the litigation continued. If vendors will deliver against a promise of current payment, then a reorganization can be achieved, and all unsecured creditors will obtain its benefit, without preferring any of the unsecured creditors.

Some supposedly critical vendors will continue to do business with the debtor because they must. They may, for example, have long term contracts, and the automatic stay prevents these vendors from walking away as long as the debtor pays for new deliveries. See 11 U.S.C. § 362. Fleming Companies, which received the largest critical-vendors payment because it sold Kmart between $70 million and $100 million of groceries and related goods weekly, was one of these. No matter how much Fleming would have liked to dump Kmart, it had no right to do so. It was unnecessary to compensate Fleming for continuing to make deliveries that it was legally required to make. Nor was Fleming likely to walk away even if it had a legal right to do so. Each new delivery produced a profit; as long as Kmart continued to pay for new product, why would any vendor drop the account? That would be a self-inflicted wound. To abjure new profits because of old debts would be to commit the sunk-cost fallacy; well-managed businesses are unlikely to do this. Firms that disdain current profits because of old losses are unlikely to stay in business. They might as well burn money or drop it into the ocean. Again Fleming illustrates the point. When Kmart stopped buying its products after the contract expired, Fleming collapsed (Kmart had accounted for more than 50% of its business) and filed its own bankruptcy petition. Fleming was hardly likely to have quit selling of its own volition, only to expire the sooner.

Doubtless many suppliers fear the prospect of throwing good money after bad. It therefore may be vital to assure them that a debtor will pay for new deliveries on a current basis. Providing that assurance need not, however, entail payment for pre-petition transactions. Kmart could have paid cash or its equivalent. (Kmart's CEO told the bankruptcy judge that COD arrangements were not part of Kmart's business plan, as if a litigant's druthers could override the rights of third parties.) Cash on the barrelhead was not the most convenient way, however. Kmart secured a $2 billion line of credit when it entered bankruptcy. Some of that credit could have been used to assure vendors that payment would be forthcoming for all post-petition transactions. The easiest way to do that would have been to put some of the $2 billion behind a standby letter of credit on which the bankruptcy judge could authorize unpaid vendors to draw. That would not have changed the terms on which Kmart and any of its vendors did business; it just would have demonstrated the certainty of payment. If lenders are unwilling to issue such a letter of credit (or if they insist on a letter's short duration), that would be a compelling market signal that reorganization is a poor prospect and that the debtor should be liquidated post haste.

Yet the bankruptcy court did not explore the possibility of using a letter of credit to assure vendors of payment. The court did not find that any firm would have ceased doing business with Kmart if not paid for pre-petition deliveries, and the scant record would not have supported such a finding had one been made. The court did not find that discrimination among unsecured creditors was the only way to facilitate a reorganization. It did not find that the disfavored creditors were at least as well off as they would have been had the critical-vendors order not been entered. . . . Even if § 362(b)(1) allows critical-vendors orders in principle, preferential payments to a class of creditors are proper only if the record shows the prospect of benefit to the other creditors. This record does not, so the critical-vendors order cannot stand.

Affirmed.

═══════════
═══════════

Note on procedure that Judge Easterbrook made quick work of the suggestion that the settlement of the payments to the critical vendors would make it too hard to unscramble the eggs at this point. He is pushing back on a doctrine known as "equitable mootness," a doctrine under which prevailing parties argue for dismissal of bankruptcy confirmation appeals (at least ones that do not stay the effective date of the plan) by saying it's too late to so unscramble, especially in a complex chapter 11 with many moving parts and creditors. In re One2One Commc'ns, LLC, 805 F.3d 428, 432 (3d Cir. 2015) (upholding equitable mootness from constitutional attack but noting that it was bound by prior panel). Some appellate courts love this doctrine as a way to cleanse their dockets of what they consider boring bankruptcy appeals. Others worry that this is an abdication of appellate responsibility—one that bears, as we shall see in Assignment 37, constitutional dimensions. Matter of Sneed Shipbuilding, Inc., 916 F.3d 405,

409 (5th Cir. 2019) (internal citations omitted) ("We are more hesitant to invoke equitable mootness than many circuits, treating it as a scalpel rather than an axe.").

As for substance, many of the concerns raised by Judge Easterbrook are now addressed in the U.S. Trustee's Policy and Practices Manual cited earlier. As we will see later in Assignment 37, bankrupt companies with operations around the country can often choose where to file their chapter 11 petitions. Some question their enthusiasm for the Seventh Circuit.

Problem Set 18

18.1. Fredrick Fredrick is the president of Tiny Telephones, a retailer that is about to enter chapter 11. The Maine State Bank was the company's principal lender and has a security interest in its inventory. Fredrick wants to know if he can operate the business normally after filing without having to go to court. What do you tell him? See § 363, UCC § 9-315.

18.2. Gretchen Deaton is the owner of Funtime Vehicles, Ltd., a dealership for Winston motorbikes. Funtime is in severe financial difficulty and has sought your advice. You have recommended a chapter 11. On the day before the planned filing, Funtime has $61,000 in Citywide Bank, ready to meet its monthly payroll that is due four days later. As part of her explanation of Funtime's financial affairs, Gretchen tells you that she buys the motorbikes on unsecured credit from Winston, and that she owes them about $50,000. Gretchen said that last month she received a bill from Citywide Bank for the regular payment on the line of credit. She called the bank and learned that Winston had approached Citywide, saying it would continue to ship to Funtime on credit only if the bank agreed to "buy" Funtime's outstanding account payable to Winston for $40,000. The bank did so.

If a setoff right is cash collateral, how much, if any, right to a postpetition setoff does the bank have and why? How much of the cash in the checking account would Gretchen be able to use without getting court permission? What is your advice? See §§ 553(a)(2), 363(a).

18.3. The First National Bank has always been the principal bank of Teddy's Toasters, a local kitchen appliance dealer. Teddy's has always kept its checking accounts at the bank and has gotten its working capital and equipment loans there. As of June 1, Teddy's owed the bank about $450,000. The bank's loan is unsecured. By July 1, Teddy's was obviously in some financial trouble, and for the first time the bank demanded that Teddy's maintain a 10% "compensating balance," i.e., that it keep in its checking account at the bank (and never withdraw) an amount of money equal to at least 10% of its debt to the bank. From July 1 on, Teddy's complied by never letting its checking account balance fall below $45,000.

On September 5, Teddy's came to you for bankruptcy advice, and you filed a chapter 11 petition on September 10 on Teddy's behalf. On that date Teddy's had $100,000 in its checking account at the bank. The bank has brought a motion to set off the $100,000 and reduce its unsecured claim to $350,000. Will you object? On what grounds? See § 553(a)(3).

18.4. You filed a chapter 11 petition almost three weeks ago for Ben's Auto Parts. Ben Sauers had a solid auto parts business in a strip mall on the east side of town until the city started building a new overpass about three months before you filed. The city tore up the street and in the process tore up the businesses in the mall. Ben explained, "I'd hear that they were going to build the overpass, but they blocked access for months, and my business just collapsed. No one could get to me." This morning Ben's bookkeeper, Leo Bloom, brought you ten letters from suppliers of parts to Ben demanding return of their generators, spark plugs, wiper blades, etc., although with little documentation attached. He says he has gotten phone calls from five other suppliers with similar demands. Ben has more than 150 suppliers and expects more such letters every day, "even though I've never given any of those guys a lien or anything like that." On top of the letters, the biggest supplier, National Vehicle Wholesale Parts, arrived at the store with a letter demanding return of all "our parts" and a group of large men. They hauled off all of the National parts they could find. Ben protested but was ignored, and the police said it was up to the lawyers to sort it out. Leo wants to know what he should do about the letters, and Ben wants to know what you will do about National. See §§ 503(b), 546(c).

FINANCING THE REORGANIZATION

Even if the debtor were given unfettered access to the cash collateral and protection from setoff, many businesses seeking chapter 11 protection would still lack adequate resources to reorganize. For these businesses already suffocating from an inadequate cash flow, an increase in operating capital is essential for survival. Although the Code can do a great deal for debtors in trouble, it cannot magically produce cash, and so typically the debtor must find a lender who is willing to make new infusions in order for the business to survive. To facilitate this quest, the Code provides tools for the DIP to obtain postpetition financing. Indeed, along with the automatic stay, those financing tools are the principal reason that chapter 11 has been so successful and increasingly emulated around the world. This postpetition facility is called a DIP loan, or DIP financing, or, most confusing, sometimes just a DIP. (After the case, the DIP loan is retired and substituted with *exit financing*, the terms of which are often negotiated alongside the plan.)

While many if not most debtors need a cash injection, they do not all arrive at bankruptcy with similar encumbrances. Most business debtors have secured debt, but some have pledged only a portion of their assets (e.g., a floor-plan inventory loan alone) and so have other collateral ready to pledge. We could call these debtors traditionally secured. Others have granted blanket liens over all their assets to a dominant secured creditor. We like to think of this latter type as "hog-tied" debtors, whose secured creditors have so much control that they, not the debtor, effectively dictate the direction of the chapter 11 case. See Westbrook, *Control*.

A. SUPER-PRIORITY AND PRIMING LIENS

The first place a debtor goes knocking is its current lenders (Attention: Department of Sunk Costs), but some turn to creditors who specialize in high-risk business loans, such as those made to reorganizing companies. One such asset-based lender was CIT Group, which ironically went bankrupt in the Great Recession. When sufficient assurances can be offered, even very conservative institutions may be persuaded to lend. The likely success of any attempt to procure financing will, of course, depend on what inducements the debtor can offer, such as new security interests or priority repayments over other creditors should things go bad and the loan gets called. Deliberately rejecting the general norm of creditor equality, the Code offers special sweeteners to the creditors that are willing to provide postpetition financing, giving them the assurances they need to even think about lending to a bankrupt company.

Perhaps the most important protection a DIP can offer to a postpetition lender is a security interest in its property. As discussed previously, prepetition security interests with after-acquired property clauses cease to operate at the instant bankruptcy is filed. § 552. With the exception of any property locked up through tracing, the post-filing debtor will be able to offer as security for a postpetition loan both an interest in property that was not encumbered before bankruptcy plus, thanks to § 552, an interest in any new property it acquires after bankruptcy. Of course, the pre-bankruptcy lender will be loudly demanding adequate protection and that may get the lien imposed on the new property that way.

Sometimes, though, there are not enough assets to pledge to entice even the most risk-tolerant lender, and so the Code provides more tools for the debtor. The next case illustrates super-priority and priming liens. This case also shows that even in bankruptcy, when things are looking their darkest, you can always call Mom.

In re DEVLIN
185 B.R. 376 (Bankr. M.D. Fla. 1995)

FUNK, Bankruptcy Judge.

This Chapter 11 case came before the Court upon the debtor's motion for authority to incur secured debt with super priority status. Notice of the proposed financing was circulated to all creditors and parties in interest on May 13, 1995 and, pursuant to Local Rule 2.19A(a)(1) and (a)(3), creditors and parties in interest were given 15 days within which to serve objections. No written objections to Debtor's motion were received. The Court is also familiar with this case from the numerous prior hearings held and pleadings filed in this case. Based on the foregoing, and Debtor's proffered testimony, the Court finds as follows:

1. Debtor is the operator of a 220-room resort motel located at 900 North Atlantic Boulevard in Daytona Beach, Florida, which is commonly known as The Desert Inn Resort Motel (the "Resort").

2. The Resort utilizes a centralized air conditioning system to cool the interior of its buildings. The current air conditioning system was installed in 1967 and ceased to function in 1993. Debtor has since utilized on a temporary basis two 75 ton air conditioning units to cool the building. These units have proved to be inadequate and need immediate replacement. Similarly, the Resort's boiler and hot water heaters are antiquated and subject to frequent breakdown. The Debtor has requested authority to obtain financing to replace these items as well.

3. Debtor solicited bids for the replacement of the air conditioning system, boiler, and hot water heaters, and determined that the minimum cost of replacing these units is $123,920.

4. Debtor does not have the funds to pay for the replacement equipment and related work out of available cash flow and, accordingly, must obtain outside financing to replace these items. Irene L. Devlin, Debtor's mother, has agreed to provide such financing contingent on her receiving a first priority lien on the real property where the Resort is located.

5. Legal title to the property is currently vested in Nat Max & Associates, a Florida general partnership [which had contracted to sell the motel to the debtor]. Debtor's interests in the Resort are derived under a . . . purchase and sale contract which Debtor [in turn intends to sell] . . . to Deslin Hotels, Inc.

6. Nat Max & Associates has opposed assumption of the purchase and sale contract and the proposed plan of reorganization [on perhaps shaky standing grounds—Eds.]. If Nat Max & Associates' objections are sustained, there is a substantial risk that the Debtor's reorganization will fail and the case may convert to Chapter 7. In the event of a conversion, the prospects of a post-petition creditor being repaid in full are less than probable, even if such creditor were holding a Chapter 11 administrative expense claim superior to all others. There is also pending a foreclosure action by the Resolution Trust Corporation which stands to foreclose any subordinate interests in the Resort should the case convert to Chapter 7. Under these circumstances, therefore, the granting of a secured claim with super priority status is the only way the Debtor is likely to obtain financing to replace the air conditioning system, boiler and hot water heaters.

7. The Resort is currently encumbered by a first priority mortgage lien held by the Resolution Trust Corporation ("RTC") to secure a debt of approximately $2.3 million. The Court is unaware of any other liens against the Resort. The RTC's interests in the Resort will remain adequately protected if its mortgage lien is subordinated to a lien in favor of Irene Devlin for the cost of replacing the air conditioning system, boiler, and hot water heaters. The RTC did not oppose the Debtor's motion.

8. At the hearing on this motion, Nat Max & Associates orally objected to the motion for the first time contending that the Court has no authority to encumber property for which the Debtor does not hold legal title. With respect to this issue, the Court finds first that Nat Max & Associates' oral objection is untimely. Secondly, the bankruptcy estate is comprised of all property interests of the Debtor, both legal and equitable. 11 U.S.C. § 541. Under Florida law, the Debtor holds an equitable interest in the Resort [due to Nat Max's contractual obligation to sell the property to Debtor that could be enforced through specific performance—Eds.]. Section 364(d)(1) permits the Court to authorize financing secured by a senior lien on any property of the estate if the Debtor is unable to obtain such credit otherwise [which this debtor has shown he is unable to do]. . . .

10. Finally, the replacement of the air conditioning unit, the boiler, and the hot water heaters is necessary to preserve the value of the Resort and maintain ongoing operations. The replacement of these items will inure to the benefit of all persons claiming an interest in the Resort—including Nat Max & Associates—regardless of whether Debtor successfully reorganizes. The replacement of the air conditioning system, boiler,

and hot water heaters is in the best interest of the Debtor and its estate. It is therefore

ORDERED:

1. Debtor's motion for authority to incur secured debt with super priority status pursuant to 11 U.S.C. § 364(d)(1) is granted.

2. To secure the repayment of $123,920, Irene L. Devlin is hereby granted a first priority mortgage lien on the real property located at 900 N. Atlantic Boulevard, Daytona Beach, Florida . . . senior to all other secured indebtedness. . . .

———————————

Mom is no fool. She got not only a "priming" mortgage on the real estate but also a "super-priority" as to all other property under § 364(c)(1). The result was that Devlin the Younger could complete his contract with Nat Max and flip his interest in the hotel to Deslin Hotels for a price that reflected a working air-conditioning system. Priming RTC's mortgage means Mom recovered in full from the sale proceeds of the motel before RTC was paid. Presumably, RTC did not oppose because the cool air would greatly increase the value of its Florida motel collateral and that increased value would, as the court found, adequately protect its mortgage debt, even though Mom's loan would have priority when the property was sold. In other words, the increase in the value of the motel would be substantially greater than the cost of creating that value. Of course, ideally all investments should have positive net expected value, but § 364 actually requires the bankruptcy judge in a case like *Devlin* to enter a finding of fact to that effect. This determination of adequate protection as a precondition to approving a superseding lien protects the secured creditor who thinks it is the first mortgage holder but unexpectedly becomes the second after getting primed.

Not everyone's as easygoing as RTC, and so secured creditors object all the time to priming. For an example of such a less-enthusiastic lienholder getting primed, see the (overruled) objections in In re Hubbard Power & Light, Inc., 202 B.R. 680 (Bankr. E.D.N.Y. 1996). There, an electrical generating company on Long Island sought to get a DIP loan priming the following creditors, in ascending order, over its property: its landlord; the perfected secured bondholders who held a blanket first lien over all the debtor's property; the New York Department of Environmental Conservation (which held an injunction restraining the debtor from burning treated and painted wood chips in the generation of its power, a flagrantly illegal practice); and ultimately the County of Suffolk, which held a statutory lien trumping all others to secure the cleanup costs of a fire ($1,000,000 incurred by the City of Islip putting out a multi-day fire when the aforementioned wood chips burst into flames). Realizing they were so far out of the money, all the creditors gave up fighting except the County, which argued it had the top lien and thus sat to suffer most if primed by the DIP lender. The court explained that a shut-down power plant with a cleanup order hanging over its head was of no value to anyone, and so the risky DIP lender that was willing to extend $750,000 for cleanup costs and new working capital would necessarily be creating new value. Or, put another way, the County's lien requiring adequate protection was worth zero. It seems the County enjoyed the power under the local statute to jump ahead of first mortgages with a priming lien to recover certain fire extinguishment costs, an understandable public policy, but did not care for the prospect of being primed itself by the Bankruptcy Code's own policy of incentivizing DIP lenders. Irony can be pretty ironic. (Who, you might ask, was the crazy lender willing to take a gamble on such toxic property back in the late 1990s? A quiet postpetition financing entity named "Enron Capital & Trade Resources Corp.")

B. CROSS-COLLATERALIZATION AND ROLLUPS

Having looked at a relatively simple postpetition financing arrangement, we now return to Colad, the specialty printer in New York from Assignment 18. After the court had issued the other first day order about which we read earlier, it turned to the debtor's requests for emergency financing. Judge Bucki's opinion excerpted below divides into two parts: the first deals with the interim financing order, addressing what should and should not be done hurriedly, as an emergency, and under what procedures; the second part rules on the proposed final financing order, which the debtor asked for after notice had gone to all creditors and the court had considerably more information. The second part also confronts the sometimes controversial concept of "cross-collateralization" (and the related concept of "rollup"), which is when a postpetition lender gets a lien not just to secure its DIP loan but also its unsecured prepetition debt. Note how the undersecured lender uses the DIP loan to try to improve its position.

In re COLAD GROUP, INC.
324 B.R. 208 (Bankr. W.D.N.Y. 2005)

BUCKI, Bankruptcy Judge.

. . .

DEBTOR IN POSSESSION FINANCING AGREEMENT

The most important of the first day motions was the application for authority to obtain post-petition financing. Like most debtors in chapter 11, Colad had pledged nearly all of its assets as collateral to secure a pre-petition credit facility. Among these assets were Colad's inventory, receivables, and the proceeds of its inventory and receivables, all of which are deemed to constitute "cash collateral," as defined by section 363(a) of the Bankruptcy Code. . . .

Continental and Colad have proposed to link the post-petition financing facility to the debtor's pre-petition revolver loan. Under their agreement, proceeds of collateral would be applied first to the satisfaction of the balance due on the pre-petition loan. Meanwhile, Continental would fund the debtor's post-petition activities through new advances under the post-petition facility. Providing that post-petition advances would be secured by all assets of the debtor, the proposed facility would also create an obligation that would receive administrative and super priority status, as allowed under 11 U.S.C. § 364(c).

In a competitive and adversarial environment, one cannot fault a creditor for seeking an outcome that will maximize the return for itself. For this reason, this court has often approved the post-petition use of a revolving credit facility. From the lender's perspective, such an arrangement avoids the various legal problems of cross-collateralization. In a cross-collateralization arrangement, a lender advances new credit on condition that an enhanced set of collateral will secure both pre-petition and post-petition loans. Instead, the revolver arrangement permits a satisfaction of the pre-petition loan, so that an increasing percentage of the lender's total exposure will receive the security and benefits of the new post-petition credit facility. Although this court will approve a proper post-petition revolver facility, it will not allow a disregard of the procedural and substantive rights of other parties in interest.

Bankruptcy Rule 4001 imposes procedural rules for consideration of a motion for authority to obtain credit. Subdivision (c)(1) of this rule requires that the court treat such a motion as a contested matter under Rule 9014, and that notice of such a motion be served upon the members of the Official Committee of Unsecured Creditors, or if no committee has been appointed, then upon the twenty largest unsecured creditors. In a typical case, this requirement of notice presents practical challenges, in as much as most debtors have an immediate need for financing. For this reason, the following text of Bankruptcy Rule 4001(c)(2) attempts to find a balance that will accommodate both financial necessity and concerns for due process:

> The court may commence a final hearing on a motion for authority to obtain credit no earlier than 15 days after service of the motion. If the motion so requests, the court may conduct a hearing before such 15 day period expires, *but the court may authorize the obtaining of credit only to the extent necessary to avoid immediate and irreparable harm to the estate pending a final hearing.*

(emphasis added). Pursuant to this rule, therefore, the court may consider a first day motion to approve an emergency lending facility, but only if two conditions are satisfied. First, any emergency authorization must be limited only "to the extent necessary to avoid immediate and irreparable harm." Second, the authorization may be effective only until a final hearing on appropriate notice to creditors as required under Rule 4001(c)(1).

In support of its first day motion for authority to obtain post-petition financing, the debtor represented that it could not operate without a post-petition line of credit and that it had no ability to obtain such credit from any source other than Continental. Conceptually, this Court found that these representations were adequate to justify an appropriate form of emergency lending until the scheduled hearing for final approval. However, in the form that the debtor proposed, the emergency funding order was unacceptable for the following four reasons:

1. The order failed to reflect any effort to limit the conditions of credit only to those which would be absolutely necessary to avoid immediate and irreparable harm. See Bankruptcy Rule 4001(c)(2). Rather, the proposed

order would have approved an interim loan agreement with terms essentially identical to those contemplated for the final loan agreement. . . .

2. The interim order was inappropriately complex, and thereby denied to the court a sufficient basis of confidence in the reasonableness of its terms. On an emergency basis, the debtor wanted the court to sign a twenty-six page order, which incorporated the terms of a loan agreement that filled 93 pages of single space text, including exhibits. This court appreciates the dollar value of the proposed lending facility, and accepts the need for a comprehensive agreement. For this reason, as hereafter discussed, the court has carefully examined the terms of the final loan agreement. A first day order is inherently different, however. Without benefit of opportunities for comment from creditors on notice, the court must view with skepticism the exigent submission of any such complex instrument.

3. Based on its cursory review, the court discovered that the proposed order would change substantive and procedural rights, without allowing any reasonable opportunity for creditor objection. For example, the interim loan arrangement included a grant of relief from the automatic stay in the event of default, limitations on the debtor's right to propose a plan of reorganization, and a waiver of various claims that the debtor might assert against Continental. Particularly troublesome were the provisions of section 11.6 of the Loan Agreement, which purported to require, as a condition for interim funding, the disavowal and waiver of various "rights and remedies provided under the Bankruptcy Code, the Federal Rules of Civil Procedure, and the Bankruptcy Rules." Furthermore, paragraphs 2.1 and 11.1 of the Loan Agreement seemingly attempted to grant administrative priority to the pre-petition claims of Continental. Later in this opinion, the court will discuss whether certain of these terms are appropriately included into an order that authorizes lending on a final basis. As part of a first day order, where unsecured creditors have had no opportunity to object, such terms are unacceptable.

4. As originally submitted, the first day lending order proposed to authorize a potential violation of state law and to waive the substantive rights of other creditors without prior notice to them. By its terms, the proposed loan agreement contemplated a post-petition advance of $500,000, for a term of approximately 90 days. In addition to interest at the rate of 4.5 percent over prime, Colad was to pay loan fees totaling in excess of $135,000. Based upon these facts, the court questioned whether the cost of borrowing would exceed New York State's criminal usury rate of 25 percent. . . .

At the hearing to consider the debtor's first day motions, the respective attorneys for Colad and Continental responded to the above concerns, by asserting that the proposed lending arrangement represented the best and only terms available to the debtor. In my view, this position seemed disingenuous. Continental had recently acquired its secured position, with the stated desire to effect a purchase of assets as a going concern under section 363 of the Bankruptcy Code. With this objective, Continental would be obviously disinclined to compel a distressed liquidation of its position. As holder of a first lien in the debtor's inventory and receivables, Continental was positioned to dictate terms. Consequently, the proposed loan did not represent terms negotiated in any form of open market. Although the reality of circumstances might compel acceptance of these terms after a final hearing, this court was unwilling to disregard the above mentioned concerns until at least after the twenty largest unsecured creditors had opportunity to object.

The resolution of the motion for interim financing confirmed the court's perception of disingenuousness with regard to the assertion that the debtor could obtain no better terms of lending. After this court refused to approve an order in the form that the debtor had first presented, the parties negotiated an arrangement that the court could accept on an interim basis. Ultimately, I signed a simpler order authorizing the debtor to borrow funds needed to pay necessary expenditures. With respect to these advances, the lender received a super-priority administrative expense claim secured by a lien on all of the debtor's assets. . . .

Motion to Authorize a Final DIP Lending Facility

The debtor seeks authority to borrow funds under the terms of a final lending facility, whose present form incorporates changes designed to address some of the concerns that the court expressed to the parties at the hearing to approve interim lending. Appointed subsequent to the consideration of interim authorization, the Official Committee of Unsecured Creditors now supports the debtor's motion for final authority. However, [one objector] opposes the request. Primarily, he contends that the proposed facility entails excessive risk, particularly in light of the fact that the debtor's financial history indicates the improbability of a successful reorganization. The court might give greater consideration to this objection, if the debtor intended to reorganize as a going concern. In the present instance, however, the debtor has candidly indicated an intent to liquidate, most likely through a sale of assets under 11 U.S.C. § 363. Thus, the borrowing is designed only to maintain operations as a going concern for the short term, until a sale can be completed. Under these circumstances, the court is prepared to authorize borrowing under terms of an appropriate facility. However, the court cannot approve lending in the form that Colad and Continental have proposed.

In addition to his general opposition, [the objector] presented 27 objections to specific terms of the debtor's lending proposal. Except as stated herein, these objections are overruled. . . .

1. The Proposed Order Would Sanction Excessive and Usurious Interest

The debtor seeks to borrow a maximum of $494,000.00 for a term of less than ninety days. On this loan, the debtor would pay interest at an annual rate of four and one-half percent over "the Chase Bank Rate." In addition, however, the debtor would pay a non-refundable loan commitment fee of $50,000, a closing fee of $50,000, collateral management fees of $10,000 at closing and $1,500 per month thereafter, and an unused line fee based on a formula that would be calculated each month. All of these various fees would be deducted from the amount that the debtor proposes to borrow. Thus, the debtor would actually receive operating funds of less than $381,000 dollars. Because the term of the loan is less than ninety days, the fees alone would represent charges equivalent to an interest rate in excess of 100 percent per annum. . . .

2. The Debtor Proposes an Inappropriate Modification of Statutory Rights and Obligations in Bankruptcy

The debtor and its secured creditor do not constitute a legislature. Thus, they have no right to implement a private agreement that effectively changes the bankruptcy law with regard to the statutory rights of third parties. In three important respects, Colad and Continental have proposed terms that would impermissibly modify the laws and rules of bankruptcy.

First, the proposed order would prohibit any surcharge of collateral under section 506(c) of the Bankruptcy Code. This section provides that a trustee "may recover from property securing an allowed secured claim the reasonable, necessary costs and expenses of preserving, or disposing of, such property to the extent of any benefit to the holder of such claim." For example, if a sprinkler system extinguishes a fire that would otherwise have destroyed Continental's collateral, section 506(c) would allow the trustee to recover the resulting water bill. Instead, Colad and Continental would either deny the means to pay such charges, or would impose such costs on funds available for distribution to unsecured creditors. By its language, section 506(c) speaks only to the payment of reasonable and necessary costs. This court can discern no basis to allow a secured creditor to ignore its application.

Second, to the detriment of any future trustee, the proposed order would change the procedural requirements for stay relief. Section 362(d) of the Bankruptcy Code provides that the court may grant relief from the automatic stay "[o]n request of a party in interest and after notice and a hearing." Instead, the proposed order would create a default procedure, whereby the stay would automatically lift upon a failure by any interested party to demand a hearing within five business days following notice of an event of default. To the extent that the debtor and creditors' committee consent, this court would approve such a procedure for purposes of notice to the consenting parties. However, the court will not sanction a waiver of the controlling standard for a hearing on notice to any trustee that may hereafter be appointed. . . .

3. The Proposed Order Includes a Finding of Good Faith That the Parties Have Yet to Establish on the Record

Section 364(e) of the Bankruptcy Code provides generally that a reversal or modification on appeal of an order authorizing secured debt "does not affect the validity of any debt so incurred, or any priority or lien so granted, to an entity that extended such credit in good faith. . . ." For this obvious reason, the debtor has proposed an order which includes a finding that Continental is extending credit in good faith. At the hearing on this motion, the debtor offered only one witness and his statements about good faith were conclusory. Moreover, the order's other defects cause uncertainty about intent, particularly with respect to any attempt to discourage competitive bidding. Any finding of good faith is more appropriately made with the benefit of testimony and argument after a reversal or modification on appeal. This is not to say that the debtor would not be able to establish good faith at a future hearing. At this time, however, the court simply lacks an adequate basis to reach any conclusion about Continental's good faith.

Conclusion

For the reasons stated above, this court will not approve the form of the debtor's proposed order. Nonetheless, the court would sign an appropriate order authorizing a post-petition loan that avoids the various defects identified herein. With hope that the parties will negotiate the necessary changes, I will continue the interim financing authorization until further order of the court.

So ordered.

Although the creditor in *Colad* succeeded in getting a sort of "creeping cross-collateralization" through the revolving credit agreement (which many call "creeping rollup" of the unsecured prepetition debt into a secured postpetition DIP loan), Judge Bucki scrutinized the protections requested by the secured party closely, allowing only what he thought was absolutely necessary. His grumblings were shared by others, and Rule 4001 was amended in 2007 to require much more disclosure on financing motions. And local rules, such as the bankruptcy rules in the Southern District of New York, go even further, including specific provisions for rollups. S.D.N.Y. LBR 4001-2(a)(7) (requiring rollup provisions to be "prominently highlighted"), (e) (requiring notice to those "whose interests may be directly affected" by a rollup provision), (g)(5) (requiring language that allows the Court "to unwind" a rollup if it "unduly advantaged the lender"). All that said, the trend of secured lenders demanding—and getting—more and more shows no sign of abating.

In re MICHAEL DAY ENTERPRISES, INC.
2009 WL 7195491 (Bankr. N.D. Ohio Nov. 12, 2009)

Shea-Stonum, Bankruptcy Judge.
INTERIM ORDER FOR RELIEF [likely drafted by movant—Eds.]. This matter came before the Court for hearing on November 12, 2009 at 10:30 A.M. (the "Interim Hearing") on the Emergency Motion of the Debtors for Interim and Final Orders: . . .

(1) authorizing and approving, pursuant to section 364(c) and (d) of the Bankruptcy Code, the Debtors to obtain debtor-in-possession financing from the DIP Lender (as defined herein) pursuant to the terms and conditions of (a) this Interim Order and any Final Order (as defined herein), (b) the DIP Loan

Agreement (as defined herein) and all ancillary documents referred to in this Interim Order . . . (collectively, the "DIP Credit Facility");

(2) authorizing and approving, pursuant to section 363 of the Bankruptcy Code, the Debtors' use of Cash Collateral (as defined herein) of the Pre-Petition Lender or the Pre-Petition LC Issuer (as defined herein). . . .

The court hereby makes the following findings of fact and conclusions of law on an interim basis for purposes of entering this interim order:

. . .

C. Sufficient and adequate notice of the Motion has been provided under the urgent circumstances present and based upon the notice sent to the Interim Noticed Parties (defined below) . . .

D. KeyBank National Association [which was both the prepetition secured lender and the DIP lender] is willing to advance monies to the Debtors, and the Pre-Petition Lender [is] . . . willing to consent to the use of Cash Collateral, only upon the terms and conditions contained in this Interim Order.

E. The Debtors are unable to obtain sufficient levels of unsecured credit allowable as an administrative expense under section 503(b)(1) of the Bankruptcy Code to maintain and conduct their businesses.

F. The Debtors are unable to obtain the necessary financing as unsecured credit allowable under section 364(a), (b) or (c)(1) of the Bankruptcy Code or as secured credit pursuant only to section 364(c)(2) and (3). Additionally, the Debtors are unable to procure the necessary financing on more favorable terms than those offered by the DIP Lender or provided in this Interim Order.

G. The credit and financial accommodations to be extended under the DIP Credit Facility are being extended by the DIP Lender in good faith; the conditions required by the Pre-Petition Lender and the Pre-Petition LC Issuer in connection with the use of Cash Collateral are made in good faith; the Debtors, the DIP Lender, the Pre-Petition Lender and the Pre-Petition LC Issuer (collectively, the "Lenders") have negotiated the terms and conditions contained in this Interim Order in an arms' length, open and honest fashion; and the Lenders are entitled to the protection of section 364(e) of the Bankruptcy Code.

H. It is in the best interests of the Debtors' creditors and estates that they be allowed to finance their operations under the terms and conditions set forth herein. . . .

I. Notice of the relief sought by the Motion, and the Interim Hearing with respect thereto has been given to the following parties in interest: the United States Trustee; the DIP Lender, the Pre-Petition Lender, the Pre-Petition LC Issuer and Key Equipment Finance Inc. ("KEF") and their counsel, Squire, Sanders & Dempsey L.L.P.; the creditors holding the twenty (20) largest unsecured claims against the Debtors' estates on a consolidated basis; the Securities and Exchange Commission; the Internal Revenue Service; and all state and local taxing authorities concerning the Debtors (collectively, the "Interim Noticed Parties").

J. After consultation with their counsel and financial advisors, but without prejudice to the rights of parties in interest as set forth in paragraph 13 below, the Debtors admit, stipulate, acknowledge and agree that (collectively, paragraphs J(i) through J(v) hereof shall be referred to herein as the "Debtors' Stipulations"):

> (i) *Pre-Petition Obligations.*
> [Details omitted.]
> (v) *Cash Collateral.* All of the Debtors' cash, negotiable instruments, documents of title, securities, deposit accounts, or other cash equivalents, whether original collateral or proceeds, products, rents or profits of other Pre-Petition Collateral or the proceeds thereof (the "Cash Collateral"), constitute "cash collateral" as such term is defined in Bankruptcy Code section 363(a). . . .

K. The Debtors represent as follows:

> (i) that without the use of Cash Collateral and the financing proposed by the Motion, the Debtors will not have the funds necessary to pay post-petition payroll, payroll taxes, trade vendors, suppliers, overhead and other expenses necessary for the continued operation of the Debtors' business and the management and preservation of the Debtors' assets and properties. . . .

. . .

M. As of the date hereof, the Office of the United States Trustee has not appointed an official committee of unsecured creditors (a "Committee") under section 1102 of the Bankruptcy Code.

NOW, THEREFORE, IT IS HEREBY ORDERED:

. . .

4. *Payment of Pre-Petition Debt.* The Debtors are authorized to pay the [Pre-Petition Lenders] on account of the Pre-Petition Obligations in accordance with the DIP Financing Documents and the provisions of this paragraph [and] without further order of this Court, to pay or reimburse the Lenders for all present and future costs and expenses, including, without limitation, all reasonable professional fees and reasonable legal expenses, paid or incurred by the Lenders in connection with the financing transactions as provided in this Interim Order and the DIP Financing Documents, all of which shall be and are included as part of the principal amount of the Obligations, and shall be secured by the Collateral. . . .

8. *DIP Lender's Super Priority Claim.* . . . [S]ubject to the Carve-Out, the DIP Lender is hereby granted an allowed super priority administrative claim in accordance with section 364(c)(1) of the Bankruptcy Code, having a priority in right of payment . . . over any and all administrative expenses or priority claims of any kind . . . whether arising in the Cases or in any superseding chapter 7 cases concerning the Debtors ("Successor Cases").

9. *Post-Petition Lien.* Pursuant to Bankruptcy Code sections 362, 363(e) and 364(c) and (d), as security for the prompt payment and performance of any and all Obligations incurred by the Debtors to the Lenders, of whatever nature or description, the Debtors are hereby authorized to grant to the Lenders, and upon the entry of this Interim Order shall be deemed hereby

to have granted to the Lenders, effective as of the Petition Date, valid, binding, enforceable and perfected first priority liens, mortgages and security interests, superior to the liens, mortgages, security interests or other interests or rights of all other creditors of the Debtors' estates . . . including, but not limited to, on property owned or leased by the Debtors, in and upon all of the Pre-Petition Collateral and all of the Post-Petition Collateral. . . . It is understood that the Debtors may seek at the Final Hearing (as defined herein) to include as part of the Post-Petition Collateral, to secure the Post-Petition Obligations only, bankruptcy-related causes of action and recoveries thereunder, including, but not limited to [those based on the Code]. . . .

11. *Carve-Out.* Notwithstanding any contrary provision of this Interim Order, the liens, mortgages and security interests and super priority claims granted to the Lenders, and the Replacement Lien, shall be subject and subordinate to a carve-out consisting of: (a) up to $485,000 in the aggregate for the allowed fees and expenses, whether incurred before or after the occurrence of the Maturity Date or a Termination Event, of the following professionals of the Debtors . . . consisting of: (i) $350,000 to Brouse McDowell, proposed counsel to the Debtors . . . (c) up to $35,000 for the allowed fees and expenses of counsel and any other professionals of any Committee. . . . No portion of the Carve-Out may be used to litigate, object, contest or challenge in any manner or raise any defenses to the debt or collateral position of the Lenders. . . .

13. *Reservation of Certain Third Party Rights and Bar of Challenges and Claims.* [A Creditors' Committee, if one is formed, and perhaps other parties, are given 55 days to challenge the debtor's stipulations that all the lenders' security interests and other rights are invulnerable to legal attack of any kind.] . . .

17. *No Impairment by Plan.* The time of payment of any and all Post-Petition Obligations of the Debtors arising out of or incurred pursuant to the DIP Credit Facility shall not be altered, extended or impaired by any plan or plans of reorganization that may hereafter be accepted or confirmed or any further orders of the Court which may hereafter be entered. . . .

31. *Objection.* [The order became permanent unless an objection was filed within less than two weeks, even though no Creditors' Committee had yet been formed.]

Clause 4 was a doozy: the DIP lender got to have all its prepetition debt paid at 100 cents on the dollar before any other creditor was paid anything, even though that lender's debt was just a general, nonpriority claim if undersecured (a so-called rollup of the unsecured debt into the super-protected DIP loan). For good measure, Clause 9 "promoted" that prepetition claim from unsecured to secured by offering a lien on all the DIP's property as collateral ("cross-collateralizing" the unsecured debt with the collateral securing the secured DIP loan). And then for icing on the cake, the lender got a super-priority claim (like Mom's in *Devlin*) for any lingering undersecurity per Clause 8 (a sort of super-rollup).

C. THE SECURED PARTY IN POSSESSION

It could be that KeyBank had awesome negotiators, and/or Day was a shrinking violet. But more likely KeyBank had a dominant security interest over all the debtor's property. The dominant security interest means that Day had no unencumbered assets to offer as collateral because his estate was fully encumbered going into bankruptcy. Nor was there a clear value-creator, like an air-conditioning unit, to justify priming KeyBank. This means KeyBank was unlikely to be primed on its secured debt because it would be hard with these constraints for Day to show adequate protection. With an effective veto on any other DIP lender, KeyBank sat in the catbird's seat of either giving its own DIP loan to Day—on its terms—or watching Day get no financing and liquidate. This has led two of us to say that in situations with a hog-tied debtor, the Code's statutory conception of a DIP is often functionally replaced with a SPIP (secured party in possession). Elizabeth Warren & Jay Lawrence Westbrook, Secured Party in Possession, Am. Bankr. Inst. J., Sept. 2003, at 12. Although more empirical work needs to be done, we believe the SPIP is increasingly common, inverting the whole conception of reorganization that Congress enacted with the Code. See, e.g., David A. Skeel, Jr., Creditors' Ball: The "New" New Corporate Governance in Chapter 11, 152 U. Pa. L. Rev. 917, 919-20 (2003). Many scholars have begun to worry that dictating DIP financing orders is just the tip of the iceberg, and what we are really seeing is a quasi-privatization of chapter 11. See Melissa B. Jacoby, Corporate Bankruptcy Hybridity, 166 U. Pa. L. Rev. 1715 (2018); Jonathan C. Lipson, Controlling Creditor Control: Jevic and the End (?) of LifeCare, 27 Norton J. Bankr. L. & Prac. 563 (2018).

Lest you have any doubt that KeyBank was calling the shots as the holder of the DIP loan purse strings, consider that the loan's terms, approved by the court, required that "Revolving Credit Advances and Cash Collateral shall be used only to pay those expenditures identified in the Budget." This constraint was supplemented with many dictated grounds for default, such as a timeline of events ("milestones," in bankruptcy jargon), in addition to not meeting the budget. So much for the purportedly wide latitude accorded the DIP to run the business under § 363. ("I'm sorry, sir, but we have used up the transportation budget for this quarter under our DIP loan term sheet; I'm afraid you'll have to call the bank before you can call a cab.") Indeed, it seems that even the DIP's lawyers—priority creditors no less under § 507(a)(2)—only get paid at the beneficence of the secured DIP lenders. Being a priority unsecured creditor matters little if every asset is sucked up by the secured lender's lien. Because of that, the secured lender has to "carve out" some of its lien to allow any payment at all to unsecured creditors, even the debtor's lawyers. And the unsecured creditors' committee only got a carve-out of 10% of the amount for the DIP's lawyers. In a corporate chapter 11, $35,000 doesn't go far. Even at that, the unsecured creditors were ordered to not challenge any of the secured creditor's rights and defenses under restrictions that now probably run afoul local rules such as S.D.N.Y. LBR 4001-2(g)(4), (g)(11) (allowing ban on carve-out funds to challenge secured creditor liens, with disclosure, but effectively forbidding bans on other parties, such as creditors committee, to challenge the liens).

One famous case held that cross-collateralization is improper in chapter 11 and its logic would bar a rollup as well. Shapiro v. Saybrook Manufacturing Co., Inc., 963 F.2d 1490 (11th Cir. 1992). More recently, however, such extraordinary protections as rollups and milestones (far beyond § 364's quaint focus on priming liens) are becoming "routinely extraordinary," with judges put in a tough position as the debtors insist these concessions must be given or the lender will walk. See Frederick Tung, Financing Failure: Bankruptcy Lending, Credit Market Conditions, and the Financial Crisis, 37 Yale J. on Reg. (forthcoming 2020). Part of the reason is that an increasing number of cases are like *Day*, and unlike *Saybrook*, in that the lender already had a dominant security interest at the time of filing and was in complete control. The logic of approval of such financing orders is that there would be nothing for the unsecured creditors regardless and therefore no one is hurt by the financing order. On the contrary, keeping the debtor in business might maximize the value of its assets and benefit some other stakeholders (e.g., employees). Perhaps for those reasons, the SDNY Rules (as do the Federal Rules of Bankruptcy Procedure) expressly contemplate cross-collateralization, albeit with careful restrictions on its use. See S.D.N.Y. LBR 4001-2(a)(6), (g)(5); Fed. R. Bankr. P. 4001(c)(1)(B). (Perhaps these rules are invalid in the Eleventh Circuit?)

There has been little appellate scrutiny of these practices since *Saybrook*, because appellate review is nearly impossible: section 364(e) provides that a good-faith extension of DIP credit cannot be reversed on appeal, and the bankruptcy courts (excepting Judge Bucki in *Colad*) often include a finding of good faith when granting the orders. This appellate bar—or, good-faith safe harbor, depending on your perspective—is designed to ensure finality in time-sensitive bankruptcy cases. Absent a stay pending appeal, the order goes into effect and the good-faith lender can rely away. Section 363(m) provides the same protection to purchasers and lessees of estate property both within and without the ordinary course of business, and courts take its bar seriously. See, e.g., MOAC Mall Holdings LLC v. Transform Holdco LLC (In re Sears Holdings Corp.), 2020 U.S. Dist. LEXIS 82507, at *20 (S.D.N.Y. May 11, 2020) (decrying buyer's actions as "appall[ing]," but finding review barred by § 363(m)). Indeed, *Saybrook* itself had to finesse this on appellate review in a manner many condemned as disingenuous, proving even Congress has trouble stopping a motivated appellate court. Section 364(e)'s bar channels the cognate doctrine of equitable mootness, discussed in the prior assignment, which generally holds that appellate courts cannot review orders once parties have acted in reliance on them, unless the appealing party posts a bond to protect others against loss or otherwise secures a stay pending appeal. See, e.g., In re General Growth Properties, Inc., 423 B.R. 716 (S.D.N.Y. 2010). In a case of any size, such a bond is practically unobtainable, which means it's a stay or nothing. These bars explain the absence of appellate authority to guide cases like *Day*.

Chapter 11 practice now appears sharply divided between hog-tied and traditional debtors, creating two distinct types of proceedings with different implications in the markets and in the halls of public policy. The financing terms color many of the issues that arise later in the case. It is also bears mentioning that when the DIP gets steamrolled on loan terms, so too do the unsecured creditors to which the DIP is supposed to serve as a fiduciary. For that reason, the authors of Collier's tell us this:

> Although the debtor in possession may not have sufficient leverage to push back too hard, the bankruptcy court, in its role as final arbiter of whether the financing should be approved, often acts as the last and perhaps most effective negotiator against the secured lender. It is an awkward position for a judge who is supposed to resolve disputes and not become involved in the administration of the business of the estate, but it perhaps has become essential given the nature of the process.

Collier on Bankruptcy ¶364.04[2][d] (Alan N. Resnick & Henry J. Sommer eds., 16th ed. 2020).

Some courts do try to push back. For example, 9% in fees off the top that were unconditional, even in the absence of full approval of the loan, were deemed beyond the pale. See Jeff Montgomery, Addiction Center's 'Expensive' Ch. 11 Loan Gets A Trim, Law360 (June 23, 2020 5:59 PM), https://www.law360.com/delaware/articles/1285774/addiction-center-s -expensive-ch-11-loan-gets-a-trim. Indeed, for those drawn to drama, a bankruptcy judgeship may never look more attractive than at the make-or-break moment of financing review. Mindful of this difficulty, the ABI Business Bankruptcy Reform Commission proffered guidelines for DIP financing:

> A court should not approve any proposed postpetition financing under section 364 of the Bankruptcy Code that contains a provision to roll up prepetition debt into the postpetition facility or to pay down prepetition debt in part or in full with proceeds of the postpetition facility. This provision should not apply to postpetition financing, including a facility that refinances in part or in full prepetition debt, to the extent that—the postpetition facility (a) is provided by lenders who do not directly or indirectly through their affiliates hold prepetition debt affected by the facility or (b) repays the prepetition facility in cash, extends substantial new credit to the debtor, and provides more financing on better terms than alternative facilities offered to the debtor; and the court finds that the proposed postpetition financing is in the best interests of the estate.

Am. Bankr. Inst., American Bankruptcy Institute Commission to Study the Reform of Chapter 11: 2012-2014 Final Report and Recommendations 73 (2014). We note that Congress has yet to act on these suggestions.

Problem Set 19

19.1. You are the trustee for GoGo Properties, a real estate development firm that went, went. Despite its bad management and overleveraged debts, GoGo owns an excellent piece of suburban property. Although the "no growth" majority in the state legislature has adopted a statute that would make it impossible for a buyer to develop the property nearly as profitably, GoGo is the beneficiary of a grandfather clause that makes the restrictive statute inapplicable to existing owners and also makes it inapplicable to transferees if the property already has water and sewage service at the time of sale or transfer. GoGo's property does not have water and sewage service, and it will cost $100,000 to get them installed. The statute provides that "sale" is defined as the time the property is first advertised or the first negotiation is commenced concerning its possible transfer or sale. Thus, you cannot get a potential buyer to finance the work. How could you get someone to lend you the money to install the water and sewage service? See § 364.

19.2. Low Price, Inc. had a loan from the First State Bank for $5 million, fully secured by a lien on its inventory, when it entered chapter 11. Low Price's total unsecured debt was $2.5 million. Low Price got a postpetition loan from Hanratty Finance of $2.5 million secured by a lien on its equipment. FSB sought adequate protection by filing a stay-lifting complaint. The trustee offered an additional lien on Low Price's accounts receivable in order to provide adequate protection, and the court approved, refusing to lift the stay. FSB's fears were well founded: the inventory was depleted before FSB was successful in getting the case converted to chapter 7, and the accounts have proven to be almost impossible to collect because of customers' warranty claims.

FSB is still owed $2.5 million after sale of the inventory and collection of collectible accounts. Hanratty got only $1.5 million from the sale of the equipment. There is $3 million in other unencumbered assets. The only unpaid expense from the chapter 11 case is the $300,000 fee for the debtor's lawyer. The chapter 7 trustee and her lawyer are owed $110,000. How much will the trustee and her lawyer get? See § 726(b). How much will FSB, Hanratty, and the debtor's lawyer get? See §§ 364(c)(1), 507(b). (If you first consider the case as a chapter 11 and get those priorities worked out, and then consider what happens if it converts to chapter 7, the problem will be easier to work.)

19.3. Vehement Entertainment, Inc. (VEI) entered the "can't miss" business of interactive game manufacturing and distribution two years ago. It then entered chapter 11 last month. Your client, Murphy Investments, LP, holds the $6 million first mortgage on the company's principal manufacturing facility. At the time of the loan, the appraisal indicated that the facility was worth $4 million.

The company has $3 million in unencumbered assets. VEI has proposed to borrow $1.5 million in operating money from the Yankee State Bank, securing the loan with a lien on the unencumbered assets of the company. Murphy had refused any further financing prior to bankruptcy, and VEI entered bankruptcy because Yankee said it would facilitate its loan if it were a protected "DIP" loan approved by the court. Murphy complains that the interest rate Yankee proposes is "way too high" and is wondering if it should reconsider and offer to make the loan itself, at a lower rate, on the condition that all the money owed to it be secured by all of VEI's assets. What are the chances of getting court approval for Murphy's proposal if VEI's management agrees? What if Yankee takes another look at VEI's financials and decides to find some business somewhere else—will prospects improve? See § 364(c).

19.4. You had been mowing your yard late on Saturday afternoon, reviewing the events of your first week as a United States Bankruptcy Judge, when you received a call from counsel for Supertech Computers. Counsel asked for permission to come to your home to discuss a just-filed chapter 11 petition on an emergency basis. Counsel and several officers from the company arrived a few minutes ago. Aside from feeling a bit strange about your "X-Men" T-shirt amidst all the vests and ties, you are overwhelmed by the documents presented to you with the petition, which take up three full binders. Included are numerous requests for orders approving certain sales, leases, and the like, along with a request for approval of a Financing Order ("FO"). The FO would approve a loan to the company of $10 million by the Revere State Bank. Revere is interested in doing this because it has previously lent the company $20 million secured by substantially all of its assets. The new loan would be secured by the same collateral, with a priority over all prior liens, and would be given an administrative super-priority as well. The FO also contains a budget the debtor must follow strictly, including a carve-out for the fees of debtor's counsel up to $500,000. It even contains a stipulation that Revere's security interests are valid and may not be challenged. The FO will become final two weeks after notice of the order has been mailed to all creditors. No creditor's representative is present, although counsel represents that Revere has approved the transaction and form of order and has stated it will not make the $10 million loan except on the terms provided in the FO.

Debtor's counsel explains that the company has two pressing problems:

(1) a creditor has just obtained a judgment against it for $5 million and is threatening imminent enforcement, but the company cannot afford the bond required for the appeal; and

(2) the devices controlling toxic wastes from the plant have broken down, threatening a release of the wastes into the nearby river, but the company that supplies the devices refuses to install new ones unless paid in cash.

Each of these two threatened events may lead to the shutdown of the assembly line just five hours from now, although the two suppliers could act in time if guaranteed payment by Revere.

If the line shuts down, it will cost $3 million to restart it and Supertech will be forced to liquidate. Its 200 employees will lose their jobs and probably not be paid. On the other hand, shipping computers through next week will entitle Supertech to a $2.5 million payment of withheld customer funds and enable the company to survive. Supertech, you are told, now has 413 creditors (exclusive of Revere) owed a total of $24 million but has assets worth only $9 million. Finally, counsel says she called some of the major creditors at their offices this morning but couldn't reach anyone.

You ask Supertech's lawyer why she didn't call the major creditors sooner, but her answers are evasive and unsatisfactory. It seems to you that she really knew she was going to file the chapter 11 petition at least a couple of days ago. Next, you begin to pepper counsel with questions: What is the status of the Revere loan and is it validly and fully secured? What are the positions of other creditors to the extent they are known or reasonably predictable? Has the U.S. Trustee's office been consulted?

What other questions will you ask debtor's counsel before you rule? What would you need to hear before you would be willing to grant the debtor's motion? Are you wondering whether the fact that you are a new judge has anything to do with this emergency presentation?

19.5. In a section of the *Kmart* case not included in Assignment 18, Judge Easterbrook quickly rejected another statutory ground that the debtors and critical vendor argued justified the special treatment: the DIP financing provisions of § 364, on the theory that if Kmart was getting shipments on credit, that credit was a form of postpetition financing that could have the same sorts of protections rollups get. Rejecting this as a basis for unequal treatment, he wrote:

> Section 364(b) reads: "The court, after notice and a hearing, may authorize the trustee to obtain unsecured credit or to incur unsecured debt other than under subsection (a) of this section, allowable under section 503(b)(1) of this title as an administrative expense." This authorizes the debtor to obtain credit (as Kmart did) but has nothing to say about how the money will be disbursed or about priorities among creditors. To the extent that In re Payless Cashways, Inc., 268 B.R. 543 (Bankr. W.D. Mo. 2001), and similar decisions, hold otherwise, they are unpersuasive. Section 503, which deals with administrative expenses, likewise is irrelevant. Pre-filing debts are not administrative expenses; they are the antithesis of administrative expenses. Filing a petition for bankruptcy effectively creates two firms: the debts of the pre-filing entity may be written down so that the post-filing entity may reorganize and continue in business if it has a positive cash flow. *See* Boston & Maine Corp. v. Chicago Pacific Corp., 785 F.2d 562 (7th Cir. 1986). Treating pre-filing debts as "administrative" claims against the post-filing entity would impair the ability of bankruptcy law to prevent old debts from sinking a viable firm.

Do you agree with Judge Easterbrook? Does his logic equally apply to rollups and cross-collateralizations? What kinds of reforms or boundaries should be put on postpetition lending?

Section 3

Reshaping the Estate

A fair distribution of assets is a fundamental goal of bankruptcy. This is true for liquidation and reorganization. We have already studied how big of a slice of the asset pie is given to each creditor, which is determined by the calculation of claims and the priority statute. But the size of the asset pie is not permanently fixed at the moment of the bankruptcy filing. While bankruptcy law generally protects state law entitlements under contract or property, that's only half the story.

The Code gives the trustee/DIP important powers to augment and reshape that estate by allowing some pre-bankruptcy transactions entered into by the debtor to be reversed (the bankruptcy parlance is "avoid"). The consequence of these avoidances is to bring assets back into the estate to enhance its value. To be sure, the transferee of those assets will then have a claim against the estate for the avoided amount, but that claim will be general unsecured. In a world where the general unsecured get less than full payment, which is most of bankruptcy, the functional result is more money to share for all—and a sad transferee who has provided this augmentation of estate funds, involuntarily giving up full payment in exchange for a proportionate share of a bankruptcy estate.

Sometimes these powers come from the Code itself, other times from the Code's incorporation of state laws. We study these avoiding powers, along with a separate tool that can be used to save profitable contracts and evade burdensome ones, because they all have the same effect of "reshaping" the estate—for the better of all, on the back of one. While some fume over bankruptcy law's incursion into state-created property and contract rights by these avoiding powers, others see them as redistributive provisions essential to the vindication of various bankruptcy policies, the principal one being equal treatment of creditors.

Although these tools to reshape the estate are available in cases filed under all chapters of the Code, without regard to whether the debtor is a consumer or a business, we study them in our analysis of chapter 11 because they arguably hold greatest significance there. The power to claw back a transaction made with any given creditor gives the DIP strong leverage in negotiating a plan that requires creditor support. The power can also give leverage to savvy creditors. It only takes three to initiate an involuntary petition to get access to these Code-provided tools, and if the DIP is reluctant to avoid a transaction, the creditors can seek appointment of a trustee, who surely will (trustees get paid based on the recovery collected for the unsecureds).

Over the next batch of assignments exploring this reshaping of the estate, we address, in order: the power to invalidate problematic liens (Assignment 20), the power to reverse voidable preferences (Assignments 21-22), the power to set aside fraudulent conveyances (Assignments 23-24), and the power to assume or reject executory contracts (Assignments 25-26).

AVOIDING LIENS

In the study of the consumer materials, you learned the general rule that liens pass unaffected through bankruptcy. An individual might strip down the debt on the family's clunker to its value, but the title to the car remains encumbered with the lender's lien. Here we study some ways that bankruptcy allows the DIP to remove or limit liens, particularly in two situations. The first involves voluntary security interests. When the lender fails to comply with the requirements to perfect its lien, the DIP or trustee can avoid it in bankruptcy. The second scenario involves some statutory liens that arise under state law. There are three situations in which the Code simply tosses those liens aside as an exercise of Supremacy Clause might. This assignment looks at these powers. All these lien-limiting powers vindicate various policies, such as ensuring compliance with the notice filing system for liens designed in part to prevent secret liens and creditor confusion. The equally important policy in chapter 11 is to preserve the proceeds of the invalidated liens for the benefit of the estate, allowing the debtor to use such property to secure financing for the reorganization or increase payment to creditors.

A. THE STRONG ARM CLAUSE

As we saw back in the collection law materials, state law (both UCC Article 9 and real property law) controls priority fights when multiple creditors claim an interest in property of the debtor. One priority rule of thumb is that while a secured creditor who has perfected its lien is protected against a levying unsecured creditor who comes sniffing around for property, a secured creditor who has not yet perfected generally loses if the sheriff levies on the collateral for that unsecured creditor before perfection. (Recall that a levy perfects a lien, and that perfection is the specified legal act to give a lien its maximal priority.)

The Code confers upon the trustee the power of a hypothetical lien creditor who, as of the filing date of bankruptcy, makes an imaginary levy on every single piece of property the debtor has. Specifically, § 544(a) situates the trustee vis-à-vis all other creditors by treating it as a hypothetical judicial lien creditor, execution creditor, or, for real estate, a bona fide purchaser for value. This provision is known as the "strong arm clause," nicknamed to suggest its power to knock off unperfected liens. Using another evocative nickname, Professors White and Summers refer to the DIP or trustee as "the lien creditor from hell." James J. White & Robert S. Summers, Uniform Commercial Code, § 25-5, at 1297 (6th ed. 2010).

Once again the Code references state law, giving the trustee whatever priority rights a levying creditor would have against other creditors. Given the prevalence of Article 9, which is enacted in all 50 states, it is fair to generalize from the rule of thumb that a secured creditor (outside any grace period to perfect and enjoy retroactivity to a prior date) who has failed for some reason to perfect its security interest loses that lien—and a good deal of money—in bankruptcy. The strong arm thus illustrates the close interaction of state and federal law in bankruptcy. Article 9 establishes the rules for perfection, including the requirements of the official form, a financing statement, to be filed to perfect a security interest, but § 544(a) of the Code enforces it in bankruptcy. An Article 9 mistake is the nail in the coffin of a careless secured party; the strong arm clause is the hammer.

The following case introduces § 544(a) in its most familiar context, voiding an unperfected security interest in personal property. § 544(a)(1)-(2). It will be an introduction for those students who have not taken the UCC Article 9 course and a good review for those who have. (Note: The "Plan Agent" is the equivalent of the trustee in bankruptcy.)

In re DIABETES AMERICA, INC.
2012 WL 6694074 (Bankr. S.D. Tex. Dec. 21, 2012)

Isgur, Bankruptcy Judge.

The Plan Agent's Motion for Summary Judgment is granted. Basile's security interest is unperfected. The security interest is avoided. Basile's claim is unsecured. . . .

BACKGROUND

The parties do not dispute the relevant material facts. Diabetes America, Inc. (the Debtor) filed a chapter 11 bankruptcy petition on December 21, 2010.

On January 14, 2011, Frank Basile filed a fully secured proof of claim in the amount of $161,402.39. The claim relates to a promissory note and loan agreement entered into between Frank Basile and the Debtor. In exchange for lending $150,000.00 to the Debtor, Frank Basile received a security interest in essentially all of the Debtor's assets. Basile filed a UCC-1 financing statement only in Texas.

. . .

Law Governing Perfection

The Texas Business and Commerce Code states: "[e]xcept as otherwise provided in this section, while a debtor is located in a jurisdiction, the local law of that jurisdiction governs perfection, the effect of perfection or nonperfection, and the priority of a security interest in collateral." Tex. Bus. & Commerce Code § 9.301(1).

Under the Texas UCC, "[a] registered organization that is organized under the law of a state is located in that state." Tex. Bus. & Commerce Code § 9.307(e). The parties do not dispute that Diabetes America, Inc. is incorporated in Delaware (that is, organized under the laws of Delaware).

Basile argues that § 9.307(b)(3) governs the location of the Debtor. Section 9.307(b) explicitly states "except as otherwise provided in this section." Tex. Bus. & Commerce Code § 9.307(b). Section 9.307(e) explicitly provides otherwise. Diabetes America is located in Delaware.

Although Texas law governs the Loan Agreement, Texas law provides that Delaware law is the law governing perfection in this situation (absent an applicable exception).[4]

Perfection by Filing of a Financing Statement

The Delaware Uniform Commercial Codes requires that a filing statement be filed in the office of the Delaware Secretary of State in order for a security interest to be properly perfected. Del. Uniform Commercial Code § 9-501(A).

Basile does not dispute that he failed to file a financing statement in the Delaware Secretary of State's office. Basile instead argues that there is an applicable exception to this situation that makes the Texas Secretary of State's office the correct place to file the financing statement.

Basile points to Texas Business & Commerce Code § 9.301(3)(C), which provides exceptions to the general rule set forth in § 9.301(1). The general rule, as shown above, indicates that Delaware law governs perfection as Diabetes America (the debtor) is located in Delaware.

That section states, in pertinent part: "[W]hile tangible negotiable documents, goods, instruments, money, or tangible chattel paper is located in a jurisdiction, the local law of that jurisdiction governs . . . the effect of perfection or nonperfection and the priority of a nonpossessory security interest in the collateral." Tex. Bus. & Commerce Code § 9.301(3)(C).

Basile misreads the statute. Assuming § 9.301(3)(C) is applicable to any given item of collateral, Texas law would govern the *effect* of perfection or nonperfection and the priority of a nonpossessory security interest in the collateral. Texas law would not be the law governing perfection—that would remain Delaware law. In other words, if § 9.301(3)(C) were applicable, Delaware law would still be the law governing perfection (that is, determining what must be done in order to perfect a security interest in collateral) while Texas law would decide what the effect of perfection or nonperfection would be as well as certain questions of priority.

. . .

---

[4] The result would be the same if Delaware law governed the contract. Delaware Uniform Commercial Code § 9-301 is the same as § 9.301 of the Texas Business & Commerce Code, meaning that Delaware law also indicates that, to the extent Diabetes America is located in Delaware, Delaware law is the law governing perfection. . . .

As a result of Basile's failure to file a financing statement with the Delaware Secretary of State's office, Basile's security interest in the collateral was not properly perfected. Del. Uniform Commercial Code § 9-501(A).

Result of Nonperfection

Section 544 Strong-Arm Powers

. . .

In a chapter 11 case, the debtor in possession has these strong-arm powers instead of a trustee. 11 U.S.C. § 1107(a).

Section 544(a) (1) employs a legal fiction. As explained by the Second Circuit:

> The trustee hypothetically extends credit to the debtor at the time of the [bankruptcy] filing and, at that moment, obtains a judicial lien on all property in which the debtor has any interest that could be reached by a creditor. The advantage of this status derives not from the Bankruptcy Code, but from the relevant state law defining creditor rights.

Section 544(a)(1) gives the trustee (now the Plan Agent) the powers and rights of such a judgment lien creditor. It is the relevant state law that decides the advantages conferred upon the Plan Agent. Both Texas law and Delaware law give the Plan Agent priority over Basile's unperfected security interest in this situation. See Tex. Bus. & Commerce Code § 9.317(a)(2)(A); Del. Uniform Commercial Code § 9-317(A)(2)(A). As a result of this priority status, the Plan Agent may use § 544(a)(1) to avoid Basile's unperfected security interest. . . . Basile is a general unsecured creditor.

Basile's Equitable Arguments

. . . Basile argues that the Plan Agent (as the successor to the Debtor's rights and agreements) is estopped from denying the secured nature of Basile's claim. (ECF No. 11 at 6) ("The Debtor had actual knowledge of the Basile security grant and the filing in Texas. The Debtor intended the Basile claim to be secured by the designated collateral"). Section 544(a)(1) expressly forecloses these types of estoppel arguments. ("without regard to any knowledge of the trustee or of any creditor"). Furthermore, even if estoppel were applicable, this would not help Basile. The Loan Agreement cannot trump Texas law. . . .

═══════════

It is easy for a student to imagine that cases like the foregoing are rare and affect modest sums of money, given the care one assumes would be taken in large commercial matters. Not so. In some of the largest cases, lenders have been forced to settle for much-reduced recoveries because of improper UCC filings. The bankruptcy of one of the world's most massive and famous debtors, General Motors, presented the spectacle of a top-tier "Big Law" firm's filing of a UCC Termination Statement that mistakenly terminated (or at least purported to terminate) a security interest collateralizing a financing of $1.5 billion. This rendered the interest unperfected to the outside world checking the filings, who would have no way of knowing this was a mistake. (Think of the day someone walked into the responsible partner's office and said, "Uh, we may have a problem." If you are feeling something in the pit of your stomach, you are well on your way to becoming a lawyer.)

Although the bankruptcy court found a creative way to protect the lenders, the decision was controversial and certified for immediate appeal to the Second Circuit. In re Motors Liquidation Co., 486 B.R. 596, 646-48 (Bankr. S.D.N.Y. 2013). In turn, the Second Circuit did its own certification and asked the Delaware Supreme Court to advise whether Delaware law (the UCC) would permit the secured creditor to say, in effect, "Whoops! Just a little mistake; no intention to terminate by filing this notice of termination. Can we get a mulligan?" To the surprise of some, but not to others, the Delaware court answered that the official public filing was valid and binding regardless of subjective intent. The upshot was that JPMorgan Chase, the lead lender, and the members of its international lending group went from $1.5 billion secured to $1.5 billion unsecured—in a bankruptcy case. Official Comm. of Unsecured Creditors of Motors Liquidation Co. v. JPMorgan Chase Bank, N.A., 103 A.3d 1010 (Del. 2014). You can imagine the flurry of legal malpractice activity that followed. See Sally McDonald Henry, The $1.5 Billion General Motors Recalls at the Dangerous Intersection of Chapter 11, Article 9, and Tarp, 85 U. Cin. L. Rev. 131 (2017). A variety of interesting events followed, including a partial mitigation of the losses of the lending group by a neat legal maneuver involving characterizing some of the collateral as fixtures (which would not be covered by the termination statement). In re Motors Liquidation Co., 576 B.R. 325 (Bankr. S.D.N.Y. 2017). GM puts to rest any suggestion that the strong arm clause is a technical backwater of limited importance to unsophisticated rubes.

The Second Circuit's certification to Delaware underscores the interplay between state and federal law that is frequent under the Code but especially acute in the strong arm context. Sometimes there is not the luxury of certification. In *Diabetes America*, Judge Isgur had to look at Texas law to determine the validity of perfection (which in turn said look to Delaware law), but only because § 544(a) of the Code directed that. This interplay creates a political tension. Congress controls the Code, but state legislators control the content of state law. With personal property secured credit law, that authority is in large part outsourced to the drafters of Article 9 of the UCC. The Article 9 camp loathes the strong arm clause because it weakens the power of security interests. In their minds, Article 9 is premised on the virtues of facilitating secured lending. While the drafters of Article 9 have no jurisdiction to amend the federal Bankruptcy Code, they can and do amend Article 9 itself, usually to stymie the bankruptcy trustee by reducing the priority that lien creditors enjoy over unperfected security interests under Article 9. Whittling away at lien creditors' rights has the effect of making the bankruptcy trustee weaker in the arm. For example, Article 9 denies the lien creditor *qua* bankruptcy trustee the priority over unperfected interests enjoyed by, e.g., other secured creditors or buyers or fixture financers. See, e.g., UCC § 9-334. This dynamic and the Article 9 drafters' attempt to influence bankruptcy priorities is discussed in Ronald J. Mann, The Rise of State Bankruptcy-Directed Legislation, 25 Cardozo L. Rev. 1805, 1822-23 (2004).

Others, too, object to the strong arm clause, but on more theoretical grounds. Consider Professor White's insistence that it does nothing other than serve as a boondoggle to the obsessively technical and a windfall to the debtor. The federal bankruptcy laws, he suggests, should not be in the business of policing enforcement of state commercial law. See James J. White, Revising Article 9 to Reduce Wasteful Litigation, 26 Loy. L.A. L. Rev. 823 (1993).

The contentious debate about the scope of the bankruptcy trustee's power over Article 9 security interests should not distract from the other powers under § 544. The strong arm clause also has a provision applicable to real estate, § 544(a)(3), which gives the trustee even greater powers than against personal property interests. Against a holder of a real property interest, the trustee has the status of a "bona fide purchaser'" (BFP), whom we like to think of as a party with a white heart and an empty head—i.e., one in good faith and without relevant knowledge. Because a BFP generally has much greater rights under state law than a mere lien creditor, the avoiding power under the strong arm clause is also greater.

<hr/>

In re BOWLING
314 B.R. 127 (S.D. Ohio 2004)

AUG, JR., Bankruptcy Judge.

. . .

II. FACTS

Debtor Charles T. Bowling is the owner of the real estate located at 4340 West Street, Oxford, Ohio. The deed conveying the real estate to Mr. Bowling was recorded on September 26, 2000, and reflects that he was married at that time. The deed does not, however, include a spouse of Mr. Bowling as a grantee.

On July 12, 2001, Mr. Bowling executed a promissory note in favor of Alta Financial Corporation, predecessor to MERS [Mortgage Electronic Registration Systems, Inc., the company now holding the note—Eds.] in the amount of $116,073.00. On that same date, Mr. Bowling also executed a mortgage conveying the real estate as security for the promissory note. The mortgage was recorded on August 1, 2001, in the Butler County Recorder's Office. On its face, the mortgage reflects that Mr. Bowling's signature was notarized by Sharon R. Eisenhut. By her certificate, Ms. Eisenhut certifies that Mr. Bowling executed the mortgage in her presence. Debtor Cathy Bowling did not sign the promissory note or the mortgage.

The Debtors filed their chapter 7 petition on January 21, 2003. On July 30, 2003, the Trustee filed a complaint seeking to avoid MERS' mortgage on the basis that it was defectively executed under Ohio Revised Code § 5301.01 and thus avoidable pursuant to 11 U.S.C. §§ 544 and/or 547. In an affidavit attached to the Trustee's Cross Motion for Summary Judgment, Mr. Bowling states that

> The closing took place at my home, and the only parties present were my wife, Cathy J. Bowling and a gentleman named John. Sharon R. Eisenhut, the party signing the acknowledgement on the mortgage I executed at the time of closing was not present. I do not know Ms. Eisenhut, and certainly did not acknowledge the signing of that mortgage in her presence or to her at any time.

The Trustee also asserts that since Mrs. Bowling did not execute the mortgage, her dower interest in the real estate is property of the bankruptcy estate.

III. Discussion

This case involves a question of the validity of a mortgage concerning real property located in Ohio. Therefore, the law of Ohio governs the Court's decision on the following issues raised by the parties' summary judgment motions.

A. Is Mrs. Bowling's inchoate dower interest in the real estate property of the bankruptcy estate?

B. Do the amendments to Ohio Revised Code § 5301.01 eliminate the requirement that a notary must be present at the time the mortgage was signed?

C. If a notarized signature is required, is Mr. Bowling's testimony alone sufficient to establish that the notary was not present at the time the mortgage was executed? . . .

[The court works its way through Ohio law, determining that the mortgage was not executed according to Ohio law. — Eds.]

We now consider the Trustee's cross motion for summary judgment on the issue that the mortgage is defective because of the lack of presence of the notary at the time Mr. Bowling executed the mortgage; and, therefore, that the Trustee is entitled to avoid the mortgage pursuant to its strong-arm powers under § 544(a)(3).

The Trustee must show by clear and convincing evidence that the mortgage was not signed and notarized as purported. Ford v. Osborne, 45 Ohio St. 1, 12 N.E. 526, 527 (Ohio 1887); see also Weaver v. Crommes, 109 Ohio App. 470, 167 N.E.2d 661 (Ohio Ct. App. 1959) ("The presumption of validity . . . can be overcome only by clear and convincing proof; and he who challenges it must sustain the burden of such proof."). "Clear and convincing evidence may be defined as that measure or degree of proof which will produce in the mind of the trier of fact a firm belief or conviction as to the allegations sought to be established." Yoppolo v. Household Realty Corp. (In re Winland), 276 B.R. 773, 784 (Bankr. N.D. Ohio 2001) (citing Helbling v. Williams (In re Williams), 240 B.R. 884, 888 (Bankr. N.D. Ohio 1999) and Cross v. Ledford, 161 Ohio St. 469, 477, 120 N.E.2d 118 (1954)).

MERS contests Mr. Bowling's assertion that Ms. Eisenhut was not present when Mr. Bowling signed the mortgage. However, similar to the mortgagee in In re Collins, MERS has presented no evidence that Ms. Eisenhut was present. MERS has presented no evidence of the general business practices of MERS' predecessor. Mr. Bowling has testified by affidavit that the refinancing was done at his home and that there was only one other person besides Mr. and Mrs. Bowling present at the closing, that being a male by the name of "John." As the court in In re Zaptocky noted, a refinancing is an extraordinary event for a consumer. It would stick out in Mr. Bowling's mind. In particular, it seems that Mr. Bowling would remember whether the person coming to close the loan was male or female. See Simon v. Zaptocky (In re Zaptocky), 231 B.R. 260 at 264; see also In re Collins, 292 B.R. at 848.

MERS cannot rest on its pleadings alone, "but must identify specific facts supported by affidavits, or by depositions, answers to interrogatories, and admissions on file that show there is a genuine issue for trial." In re Gibson, 219 B.R. at 198. MERS' mere argument that the notary was present, is not sufficient. There is no per se rule in Ohio that Mr. Bowling's testimony alone is insufficient to overcome the notary's certification. We find that in the absence of MERS' presentation of any evidence to the contrary, that the Trustee has met his burden and presented clear and convincing evidence that a notary was not present at the time Mr. Bowling executed the mortgage. The Trustee's motion for summary judgment is GRANTED.

Finally, MERS has not addressed the Trustee's argument that contrary to assertions in MERS' answer, MERS is not entitled to a lien in the real estate pursuant to § 550. The Sixth Circuit has recently addressed this matter and determined that where the Trustee has avoided a mortgage pursuant to its strong-arm powers, the mortgagee's interest is preserved and becomes a part of the bankruptcy estate without the need for the trustee to resort to the recovery process pursuant to § 550(a). Therefore, the statutory provisions of § 550(e) providing for a replacement lien for the creditor are not triggered for the benefit of the mortgagee. Suhar v. Burns (In re Burns), 322 F.3d 421 (6th Cir. 2003). Based on this Sixth Circuit precedent and MERS' failure to address the issue in its pleadings, we further find that MERS is not entitled to a replacement lien pursuant to § 550.

======

The strong arm clause is effectively the acid test of the Bankruptcy Code for mortgagees — it tests the strength of the lock they have put on the property. If the mortgagee locked up the property so that it could prevail over a bona fide purchaser, then the lock will hold in bankruptcy. But if the property was unlocked at the time of bankruptcy, the creditor will find itself just one more floater in the general pool of unsecured creditors.

B.   FEDERAL TAX LIENS

Just as the strong arm clause establishes the trustee's place in the priority order, the clause also establishes the position regarding federal tax liens. The Code addresses repayment of taxes and discharge of tax debt in § 507 and § 523, respectively. These provisions apply to all state and federal taxes owed, whether the tax claim is secured or unsecured. Whether a tax is secured by a lien, however, and if so, its related priority to other creditors, turns on other federal law. 26 U.S.C. § 6323. Under this law, tax liens work somewhat differently from the Article 9 liens that are the primary subject of a secured credit course. A federal tax lien arises when an assessment is made; it springs to life automatically. At that point, and without any action by the IRS, it attaches to all the taxpayer's property and rights to property. Until the IRS files its lien (makes it "valid" in tax lien statute parlance), however, the lien is treated much like an unperfected security interest: good against the debtor, but not good against most other interested parties, including, for bankruptcy purposes, the trustee. Therefore, before the lien is filed, the strong arm provisions permit the trustee to exercise the rights of a judgment lien creditor or bona fide purchaser of real estate on the date of bankruptcy filing, giving it priority. After the tax lien is filed, however, the trustee (or DIP in a chapter 11 case) must recognize the lien in bankruptcy and treat the government as it does other perfected secured parties. The lien will get priority in that property. While tax liens do not have any different treatment under the Code, and indeed have to follow the automatic stay rules, they are so prevalent in the world (and in bankruptcy cases) that they merit special mention. Liens are a powerful tool that taxing authorities use, but they too must perfect them or else face the same bankruptcy grief as other tardy, sloppy, or laidback secured creditors: transformation from unperfected secured to outright unsecured.

C. STATUTORY LIENS

Section 545 operates somewhat like § 544, but is much narrower. Although the section is captioned "Statutory Liens," it does not have the blunderbuss reach of the strong arm clause to invalidate all liens created by statute. Instead, it targets three specific categories of state liens created by statute (other than Article 9). The first are landlords' liens, the second are what might be called "bankruptcy priority liens," and the last can be considered "unperfected liens."

Subsections 3 and 4 of § 545 permit the DIP to void state-law landlords' liens. Congress felt that these gave too much of the debtor's estate to landlords to the detriment of other creditors. If a landlord gets an automatic lien on all property of the debtor located on the premises for unpaid rent, it basically ties up all a debtor's assets the same way a hog-tied debtor is beholden to a dominant security interest (see Assignment 19). The congressional aversion to these liens is probably heightened in the consumer context, where residential tenants can be held hostage to a lien on their toothbrushes. Note that these are liens created by statute; a voluntary contractual lien (e.g., a security interest under Article 9) is not avoidable under § 545, even if it is given to a landlord. You may wonder: why is Congress cool with a dominant security interest but hostile to a dominant landlord lien for unpaid rent? The answer, at least in the business context, perhaps reflects concern over the automatic nature of these liens under some states' laws and the inefficiency of requiring unsecured creditors to investigate whether each business, often with opaque corporate names, owns or rents its business premises (as only in the latter case would a landlord's lien under state law apply). The invalidation of landlords' liens under § 545 is often complained about by commentators who say the job of bankruptcy law is to preserve state-law entitlements, and these powers expressly abrogate state-created rights by congressional authority under the Supremacy Clause. They serve as a reminder, however, that the Code vindicates federal policy that transcends state statutory leg-ups for favored creditors.

The second ground for voiding a statutory lien, under subsection 1 of § 545, is that the lien only applies in bankruptcy. Think of it this way: a statutory lien is an inherent jump up in priority and recovery for one type of creditor. As such, it must vindicate some sort of state policy (e.g., garage shops should get paid for the cars they work on and have a lock on the car until then). But when a state drafts a lien law that only applies sometimes, it illustrates, at best, a half-hearted policy commitment. Worse, when that "sometimes" is only when the debtor goes bankrupt, the state has basically gotten too big for its constitutional britches and decided it wants to control the bankruptcy priority scheme that Congress has constitutional trump power to author. The Code thus balks. We discussed a similar issue with regard to the bankruptcy-specific state exemption statutes back in Assignment 4.

Because the Code is clear about voiding statutory liens that are triggered on bankruptcy or near-bankruptcy conditions, one might expect no reasonable state would waste legislative ink creating them. But that assumption depends on rational state legislators and hence is flawed. For example, Arkansas, California, and North Carolina each have adopted laws to impose liens on continuing care health facilities (once known as nursing homes) only upon the bankruptcy, insolvency, or receivership of those businesses. Statutes such as these are readily avoided in bankruptcy.

Finally, subsection 2 of § 545 gives the trustee the same BFP status as under § 544(a)(3) against statutory liens that are not perfected at the time of bankruptcy. This basically confirms the trustee's hypothetical lien creditor power.

In re TWA INC. POST CONFIRMATION ESTATE
312 B.R. 759 (Bankr. D. Del. 2004)

WALSH, Bankruptcy Judge.

. . .

BACKGROUND

The USDA performed statutory inspections on aircraft owned by the Debtor, TWA Inc., during the period April 1, 2000 through January 9, 2001.

On January 10, 2001 the Debtor and twenty-six of its subsidiaries filed voluntary petitions for relief in this Court under chapter 11 of title 11 of the United States Code. The USDA filed a proof of claim for aircraft inspection services, reimbursable overtime inspections, and violations of animal welfare regulations. The USDA asserts that it has a claim for aircraft inspection services in the amount of $296,277.25 in principal and $9,047.66 in interest. The proof of claim asserts that it is secured by a statutory lien pursuant to 21 U.S.C. § 136a (1999 & Supp. 2004). . . .

The pivotal issue in this case is whether the USDA lien, effected pursuant to 21 U.S.C. § 136a, had to be recorded with the Federal Aviation Administration ("FAA") pursuant to Act §§ 44107, 44108 (1997). In relevant part, Act § 44107 provides:

> (a) Establishment of system.—The Administrator of the Federal Aviation Administration shall establish a system for recording—
> (1) conveyances that affect an interest in civil aircraft of the United States;
> (2) leases and instruments executed for security purposes, including conditional sales contracts, assignments. . . .

According to Act § 44108(a), the lien is given only limited effect until it is recorded:

> (a) Validity before filing.—Until a conveyance, lease, or instrument executed for security purposes that may be recorded under section 44107 (a) (1) or (2) of this title is filed for recording, the conveyance, lease, or instrument is valid only against—
> (1) the person making the conveyance, lease, or instrument;
> (2) that person's heirs and devisees; and
> (3) a person having actual notice of the conveyance, lease, or instrument.

The USDA argues that it did not have to record its lien with FAA because the lien was automatically imposed by 21 U.S.C. § 136a, which provides in relevant part:

> (a) Quarantine and inspection fees
> (1) Fees authorized
>
> The Secretary of Agriculture may prescribe and collect fees sufficient—
> (A) to cover the cost of providing agricultural quarantine and inspection services in connection with the arrival at a port in the customs territory of the United States. . . .
> (5) Leins [sic, in Code—Eds.]
> (A) In general
> The secretary shall have a lien against the [property] for which services have been provided under this section for the fees [etc.] assessed under this subsection.

According to the USDA, its "lien is set forth in the statute, and its plain words do not require USDA to take any additional steps to perfect its lien or enforce its rights." (Doc. #17 at 6.) I disagree.

As noted above, Code § 545(2) allows the trustee or debtor in possession to avoid statutory liens if the lien "is not perfected or enforceable at the time of the commencement of the case against a bona fide purchaser. . . ." 11 U.S.C. § 545(2). "Perfection is . . . generally designed to 'furnish [] public notice of the secured party's interest in the collateral, thereby protecting third persons against the secret or undisclosed lien.'" Clark v. Valley Fed. Sav. & Loan (In re Reliance Equities, Inc.), 966 F.2d 1338, 1341 (10th Cir. 1992) (citing Merrill Lynch v. Van Kylen (In re Van Kylen), 98 B.R. 455, 464 (Bankr. W.D. Wis. 1989)).

The concept of "public notice" is intertwined with Code § 545(2) because the avoidance right[s] given to the trustee or debtor in possession are those of a "bona fide purchaser." "Although the term 'bona fide purchaser' is not defined in the Bankruptcy Code, it is generally understood to mean 'one who has purchased property for value without notice of any defects in the title of the seller.'" United States v. Hunter (In re Walter), 45 F.3d 1023, 1030 (6th Cir. 1995) (citations omitted); Dietsch v. Long, 72 Ohio App. 349, 43 N.E.2d 906, 915 (Ohio Ct. App. 1942) ("The three essentials of a bona fide purchase being the absence of notice, a valuable consideration, and the presence of good faith."). These are the characteristics given to a bona fide purchaser by Code § 545(2), "whether or not such a purchaser exists." 11 U.S.C. § 545(2).

Since the USDA did not record its lien, there was no "public notice," and therefore the hypothetical bona fide purchaser of Code § 545(2) who purchased TWA's property at the time of commencement of TWA's bankruptcy case could not have had notice of the lien. . . .

The USDA argues that "neither the FAA Act nor the USDA statute requires that the USDA's statutory liens be recorded in the FAA registry system to render them unavoidable." I disagree. Nothing prevented USDA from recording its lien if it desired to make it good against purchasers without notice. Congress can be presumed to have been aware of the Bankruptcy Code and its predecessor at the time it enacted § 136a and since it did not provide a recording (i.e., perfection) requirement, it may be presumed that the lien was not meant to be enforceable against a purchaser without notice (unless USDA chose to make a public filing under the Act).

The USDA's position essentially ignores the Congressional intent in adoption of the Act. It was to create a "central clearing house for recordation of titles so that a person, wherever he may be, will know where he can find ready access to the claims against, or liens, or other legal interests in an aircraft." Philko Aviation, Inc. v. Shacket, 462 U.S. 406, 411, 76 L. Ed. 2d 678, 103 S. Ct. 2476 (1983); Southern Air Transport, Inc. v. Northwings Accessories (In re So. Air Transport, Inc.), 255 B.R. 715, 722 (Bankr. S.D. Ohio 2000) ("The Court concludes that FAA recording of all liens . . . is required for validity against third parties."); Crescent City Aviation, Inc. v. Beverly Bank, 139 Ind. App. 669, 219 N.E.2d 446, 448 (Ind. Ct. App. 1966) (Finding that any lien affecting aircraft will not be effective against property of third persons without knowledge unless and until lien is recorded with Administrator of the FAA).

Reading the Act along with its implementing regulations leaves no doubt that liens must be recorded to be valid against third parties. The Act establishes a system for recording, inter alia, "conveyances that affect an interest in civil aircraft of the United States." 49 U.S.C. § 44107(a). It is clear that "conveyances" include liens. . . .

According to Act § 44108, a conveyance that is not recorded with the FAA is only valid against (1) the person making the conveyance, (2) that person's heirs or (3) person[s] having notice. Here, the TWA estate does not fall within any of these exceptions and therefore the TWA estate is deemed a bona fide purchaser with authority under Code § 545(2) to avoid the lien.

The USDA claims that giving effect to the recordation requirement of Act will "repeal by implication the USDA's lien." The public notice requirement, however, does not nullify the statutory lien imposed by § 136a and its binding effect on the property owner and certain of its successors and parties with actual notice. The Act is not in direct conflict with § 136a, since § 136a does not address recordation or perfection; a § 136a statutory lien is still created, albeit with limited application, by the failure of a debtor to pay the inspection fees. Accepting the USDA position would have the effect of creating a specific exemption to the application of Code § 545(2) without any clear statutory or case law authority supporting such a result.

. . .

ORDER

For the reasons set forth in the Court's Memorandum Opinion of this date, the TWA Inc. Post Confirmation Estate's motion for summary judgment, is GRANTED. The USDA's claim is reclassified from secured to unsecured.

⸻

Once again we see a substantive law interplay, but this time between bankruptcy and nonbankruptcy federal law. Here, the USDA complained that it is supposed to get liens automatically and there is nothing in "its" law that requires perfection. But as the court observed, bankruptcy's strong arm law policy seems to require perfection, and there are lots of gaps and tensions in the U.S. Code between overlapping systems (e.g., food inspection and bankruptcy law). One tool to help confront such problems, used in *TWA*, is to engage in the necessary fiction that Congress knows all its laws.

Some courts show more sympathy for statutory lienholders. In Merchants Grain, Inc. v. Adkins, 184 B.R. 52 (S.D. Ind. 1995), the court confronted an Ohio statute that confers an automatic lien for grain suppliers who deposit their grain into storage facilities that "fail." The lien does not exist unless and until the failure but once it does, it is deemed to arise retroactively as of the delivery date of the grain to the elevator. Just as with the USDA lien in the preceding case, the statute is silent on perfection. When a bankruptcy trustee tried to set aside such an "unperfected" lien, the court adopted what some might call a creative solution. It held that the promulgation of the law by the Ohio legislature, warning all the world of such automatically enforceable liens, was all the notice that was required to forewarn (and defeat) subsequent purchasers under Ohio law and so satisfied the policy behind perfection. In other words, any lien under the statute was automatically perfected without need for further action.

So one court holds that an automatic lien is not enough to defeat the trustee if it's not perfected, even if there is no procedure in the relevant statute for perfection, while another holds that it is more than enough to defeat the bankruptcy trustee to have an automatic lien, because if the statute doesn't mention perfection the lien should just be deemed perfected automatically. We confess to having a hard time sorting that policy distinction other than noting that the first case involved the faceless USDA and the second a presumably sympathetic (and non-diversified) farmer whose grain was all in the elevator of a failed storage company. Surely the desire of local legislatures and courts to favor local farmers is intense. Feel free to take a crack at your own policy justification for the various twists and turns of the hundreds of statutory liens under various laws out there and let us know if you find a comprehensive or coherent theory.

Problem Set 20

20.1. Western Fliers runs a small charter airplane service. Eight months ago it bought a new ten-passenger Thunderbolt aircraft from Mitchell Aeronautics for $25 million. Western paid $2.5 million in cash and gave a promissory note for $22.5 million secured by the aircraft. When the deal was closed and Western had signed the security agreement and financing statement, MA's attorney gave the papers to her young assistant with the instructions "to file these right away." The assistant did so—in the filing cabinet drawer with the information on the Western sale.

Western Fliers has a major personal injury judgment against it, and it has just filed a chapter 11. When MA learned of the filing, it pulled out its files on Western and discovered the security agreement and financing statement. It called you immediately. What do you advise? See § 544(a), UCC § 9-317(a)(2).

20.2. Western Fliers, discussed in the previous problem, bought another plane a week before the filing. This plane was purchased from Aero for $1 million down and a promissory note for $16 million secured by the Aero Leader being purchased and "all Western Fliers' other planes, spare parts, and servicing equipment, including Western's ten-passenger Thunderbolt." When Aero learned of the chapter 11, it immediately filed copies of the financing statement in all the appropriate locations. What will Aero get in the chapter 11? See UCC § 9-317(e), §§ 362(b)(3), 544(a), 546(b).

20.3. Topson Air Conditioning sold Sally's Boutique a central air conditioning system for $12,200, taking a $3,000 down payment and a lien on the system for the balance. After Sally had paid about $500 more, Topson got a notice of the Boutique's chapter 7 bankruptcy. Topson's credit manager says a financing statement covering the lien was promptly filed in the Secretary of State's office immediately after sale of the AC unit. He wants to know if the company's lien will stand up in bankruptcy. What will you tell him? See § 544(a), UCC §§ 9-102(40), (41), 9-334, 9-501(a).

20.4. Chris Dombrowsky lent $300,000 to Pretty Printing, Inc., a start-up specialty printer run by his friend, Francine. He got a mortgage on a small building owned free and clear by PPI where the printing was done. He properly recorded the mortgage in the land records. A few months later, Francine hired Northern Interiors to do about $95,000 worth of work on the building. Despite the facelift to its building, Pretty Printer floundered because the economic downturn trumped preferences for fancy color font in its customers' minds. Chris knew there was trouble at PPI because Francine called four months ago to say that she hadn't been able to pay all she owed to Northern and it had threatened to file a mechanic's lien against the office building for $75,000. She thought at the time it would all work out, but now PPI has filed bankruptcy. Chris has come to see you about where he stands. You do a fair amount of real estate work and know that in your state a mechanic's lien trumps an ordinary mortgage and a bona fide purchaser, if it is properly recorded. Even if it is not recorded, it takes priority over a mortgage holder or purchaser who knew about the mechanic's lien. What's your analysis of Chris's legal situation? See §§ 544(a)(3), 545, 551.

20.5. A. You have filed a chapter 11 petition on behalf of Torrey's Day Spa, Inc. Although its principal owner, JJ Torrey, has been quite ill (his illness, indeed, was a major cause of the company's financial decline), he has come to consult with you about the company's bankruptcy.

The company's main shop is leased from Star Properties, Inc. The rent on the leased building was two months in arrears before bankruptcy. Not only does your state law give a landlord a lien for unpaid rent on all personal property within the leased premises, but the Torrey-Star lease has a similar provision as well. What can Star Properties claim? See §§ 545(3), 101(37), (51), (53).

B. Torrey's also owns a small two-room commercial unit from which it used to operate the spa in its very early days before it expanded. JJ still uses it as the spa's head office. Frank Gonzales, a former stockholder and employee of Torrey's, has obtained a $25,000 judgment against the company in a lawsuit over his disputed salary claim. The judgment was recorded almost six months ago in the county real estate offices, although Frank has not sought to enforce it pending settlement discussions with JJ. In addition, the company owes Clarence Plumbing about $13,500 for work done on the office after last winter's severe freeze. Clarence has demanded payment, but has not filed a notice of lien. Under your state law, an unfiled mechanic's lien for work done has priority over a judgment lien creditor, but it loses to a bona fide purchaser for value. How do these creditors stand? See § 545(2).

PREFERENCES I

A. GENERAL RULES

A commonly invoked power to reshape the estate is one that allows the trustee or DIP to "avoid a preference," by undoing certain transactions that took place shortly (generally 90 days) before the bankruptcy filing. Section 547(b) sets out the elements of a voidable preference.

This is the first of several two-part approaches to avoiding powers. As you'll discover, the second assignments in these paired sets tend to present issues that are more theoretical, appear in more complex financial situations, or are more hotly contested. In other words, they're harder. That said, you should find the job of learning these materials worth the candle (or, in today's world, worth your laptop's battery life).

By the way, do not be misled by the fact that this section uses consumer cases. Individual cases are more apt to lay out the fundamentals, while opinions in corporate cases often go straight to the most complex questions, so in this first section we use the cases that address the fundamentals. Exactly the same principles apply in a corporate chapter 11 and are more likely to be invoked.

In re PYSZ

2008 WL 2001753 (Bankr. D.N.H. May 7, 2008)

VAUGHN, Bankruptcy Judge.

. . .

The Defendant is the holder of a judicial lien in the amount of $43,723.14. This lien arose from a post-judgment attachment the Defendant obtained in the Sullivan County Superior Court. The Superior Court entered a judgment for unpaid professional services in favor of the Defendant against the Debtor and subsequently issued a writ of attachment on January 18, 2007. The attachment was on certain logging equipment and real property located at 415 E. Mountain Road in Newport (the "Newport Property") belonging to the Debtor. On January 19, 2007, the Defendant recorded the attachment in the Sullivan County Register of Deeds. The Debtor owns a fifty percent interest in the Newport Property, and his mother owns the other fifty percent interest.

On April 5, 2007, the Debtor filed for protection under Chapter 13 of the Bankruptcy Code. In his schedules, the Debtor lists the Newport

Property's fair market value as $300,000. The Defendant offered a separate appraisal report that values the Newport Property at $443,000 as of April 5, 2007.

DISCUSSION

The Plaintiffs move for summary judgment seeking to avoid the Defendant's judicial lien as a preference under 11 U.S.C. § 547(b). . . . [T]he trustee has the burden of proving the avoidability of a transfer under subsection (b) of this section[.] Id. § 547(g).

First, there is no issue that the obtainment of the attachment was a transfer of the Debtor's interest in property. Second, three of the five elements required to avoid a transfer under section 547(b) are unequivocally present here. It is undisputed that the subject lien was for the benefit of a creditor. (See Compl. ¶12; Answer.) It is also undisputed that the subject lien was for or on account of an antecedent debt. (See Compl. ¶13; Answer.) Finally, the attachment occurred during the ninety-day preference period. The Defendant obtained and recorded the writ of attachment on January 18th and 19th, respectively, in 2007, and the Debtor filed his voluntary petition on April 5, 2007. As such, the issues in this preference action are whether the Debtor was insolvent at the time of the attachment and whether the Defendant would receive more with the judicial lien than he would without the lien in a Chapter 7 case.

A. Insolvency Under Section 547(b)(3)

The term "insolvent" means "financial condition such that the sum of such entity's debts is greater than all of such entity's property, at a fair valuation[,]" excluding property that may be exempt under section 522. 11 U.S.C. § 101(32)(A). "For the purposes of this section, the debtor is presumed to have been insolvent on and during the 90 days immediately preceding the date of the filing of the petition." Id. § 547(f). The creditor bears the burden of overcoming this presumption. "A creditor may rebut the presumption by introducing some evidence that the debtor was not in fact insolvent at the time of the transfer." Roblin Indus., Inc. v. Ford Motor Co. (In re Roblin Indus., Inc.), 78 F.3d 30, 34 (2d Cir. 1996).

In reading the record most favorably to the Defendant, the Court finds that there is no genuine issue regarding the Debtor's insolvency during the preference period. A presumption of insolvency exists in the instant case pursuant to section 547(f). The Defendant attempts to rebut this presumption by (i) alleging that the fair market value of the Newport Property is $443,000 and (ii) identifying non-exempt assets that the Debtor failed to schedule, which are a 1999 Timberjack skidder, 1997 Timberjack skidder, and 1970 one-ton truck. First, the 1999 Timberjack skidder is a lease and not the Debtor's property. Thus, it is not part of the Court's insolvency calculation. Next, the following is a balance sheet of the Debtor's assets and liabilities, which incorporates the Defendant's fair market value for the Newport Property, the 1997 Timberjack skidder, and the 1970 one-ton truck:

ASSETS		LIABILITIES	
Newport Property	$ 443,000	Lake Sunapee Bank	$166,516
Cash	$ 500	Bank of NH 2002 Chevy 4x4	$ 14,000
Household Goods	$ 1,000	Capital One Auto Finance 2005 Chevy 4x4	$ 21,850
Wearing Apparel	$ 2,000	Capital One Auto Finance 2002 Escalade	$ 14,179
Fishing Equipment	$ 100	Internal Revenue Service	$ 11,253
2006 Federal Tax Refund	$ 4,172	Schedule F Debt	$126,044
2005 Chevy 4x4	$ 23,075	DSO	$ 3,175
2002 Chevy 4x4	$ 12,000	Town of Newport	$ 12,042
2002 Cadillac Escalade	$ 20,000	Creative Capital Arrearage	$ 12,555
1970 One-Ton Truck	$ 1,200		
Computer & Desk	$ 1,000	Total Liabilities	$381,614
10 Chainsaws and MISC Hand Tools	$ 6,000		
1997 Timberjack 240 Skidder	$ 3,500		
Dog	$ 100		
Subtotal	$ 517,647		
Less the Mother's 50% interest in the Newport Property:	$ 126,242		
[Less Homestead Exemption	$100,000]		
[Less Personal Property Exemptions	$ 20,000]		
[Total Assets	$271,405]		

As indicated above, the Debtor's total liabilities exceed his total assets. Thus, the Court finds that the Defendant fails to rebut the presumption, and the Debtor was insolvent during the ninety days preceding his bankruptcy in accordance with section 547(b)(3).

B. "Receive More" Analysis Under Section 547(b)(5)

The final element to avoid the Defendant's judicial lien as a preference under section 547(b) is a showing that the judicial lien "enables such creditor to receive more than such creditor would receive if—(A) the case were a case under chapter 7 of this title; (B) the transfer had not been made; and (C) such creditor received payment of such debt to the extent provided by the provisions of this title." 11 U.S.C. § 547(b)(5). Whether section 547(b)(5) "is met turns on the status of the creditor to whom the transfer was made." Boston Pub. Co., Inc. v. Chase (In re Boston Pub. Co., Inc.), 209 B.R. 157, 173 (Bankr. D. Mass. 1997). With respect to unsecured creditors, "'[a]s long as the distribution in bankruptcy is less than one-hundred percent, any payment "on account" to an unsecured creditor during the preference period will enable that creditor to receive more than he would have received in liquidation had the payment not been made.'" Id. "[A]s a matter of law, whenever a general unsecured creditor obtains, within the preference period, a judicial lien against a debtor who cannot fully repay his unsecured creditors, he has received a preference." Orth-O-Vision, Inc. v. Wometco Home Theatre, Inc. (In re Orth-O-Vision, Inc.), 49 B.R. 943, 945 (Bankr. E.D.N.Y. 1985).

In the instant case, the Debtor's liabilities exceed his assets. As such, under a hypothetical Chapter 7 liquidation analysis, the Debtor would be unable to repay his general unsecured creditors 100%.[3] The Defendant's judgment was for unpaid professional services, which, absent the attachment, is a general unsecured debt. By obtaining and recording the attachment, the Defendant converted an otherwise unsecured claim to a secured one. Thus, the lien enables the Defendant to receive more than he would without the lien in a Chapter 7 case. Therefore, the Court finds that section 547(b)(5) is satisfied.

CONCLUSION

For the reasons set out herein, the Court grants summary judgment in favor of the Plaintiffs.

Note that the remedy here, where no property physically changed hands, is to "void" or "avoid" the attachment lien and thus to render the defendant unsecured. This is one of the many dramatic powers accorded the debtor under § 547. Indeed, the voidable preference power is an important tool in reshaping the troubled business by permitting the debtor to avoid certain transfers and thus claw some property back into the estate to help facilitate reorganization. But its greatest importance may lie in its effect on pre-bankruptcy behavior because some debtors may be better able to resist demands from their creditors by pointing out that the transactions could be avoided in a subsequent chapter 11 filing. A creditor who has already received a transfer that will become a preference if the debtor files will be more inclined to come to the negotiating table for an informal workout. As one court summarized well, the preference power "is intended to discourage creditors from racing to dismember the debtor sliding into bankruptcy." Jones Truck Lines, Inc. v. Century State SE & SW Areas Pension Fund (In re Jones Truck Lines, Inc.), 130 F.3d 323, 326 (8th Cir. 1997). You

---

[3] Under a Chapter 7 liquidation analysis, general unsecured creditors stand to receive a 7.96% dividend. The Debtor's total liabilities less Schedule F debts is $255,570 ($381,614 – $126,044). The Debtor's assets total $271,405, leaving $15,835 ($271,405 – $255,570) or a 7.96% dividend ($126,044/$15,835) to pay general unsecured creditors.

should see its theoretical relationship to the automatic stay: don't rush the lifeboats (they'll swamp).

The second, perhaps more important policy behind the voidable preference power is vindicating bankruptcy law's equality norm. To the extent that Creditor *A* is worried that an insolvent debtor is giving favored payments (literally, "preferences," which is where the term comes from) to the debtor's good buddy, Creditor *B*, § 547 provides a safeguard. *A* can join Creditors *C* and *D*, file an involuntary petition, and force *B* to disgorge the voidable preference back to the newly created estate. (If the DIP refuses, *A* will have good grounds to request that the court appoint a trustee.) Voidable preference rules help police eve-of-bankruptcy circumvention of the bankruptcy equality principle. ("Get out, you coward! We're doing lifeboat seats by lot (with priority for women and children, *cf.* § 507), not by who gets there first.") These upstream effects of § 547 explain why, although it is one of the most important provisions of the Code, it produces few litigated cases.

While the policy behind the statute is easy to grasp, the mechanics of its application can be deceptively difficult. For example, while the 90-day rule may be clear enough as a matter of law, it can sometimes be difficult as a matter of fact to figure out when the relevant "transfer" took place.

CHASE MANHATTAN MORTGAGE CORP. v. SHAPIRO
530 F.3d 458 (6th Cir. 2008)

Cole, Circuit Judge.

Approximately six months before he filed a voluntary Chapter 7 bankruptcy petition, David Scott Lee ("Lee" or "Debtor") refinanced a residential mortgage loan with Chase Manhattan Mortgage Corporation ("Chase"), which was both the holder of the original mortgage and the refinanced mortgage. Seventy-seven days before Lee filed his bankruptcy case, and seventy-two days after Chase had distributed the funds that were used to discharge the original mortgage, a new mortgage on his residential real estate was recorded in favor of Chase to secure Lee's obligation to repay the new loan. At issue in this appeal is whether Chase's new mortgage lien may be avoided as a preferential transfer under 11 U.S.C. § 547 . . . .

. . .

[In determining when the transfer took place, we must first turn] briefly to § 547(b), specifically § 547(b)(2), under which a trustee must demonstrate that the transfer was made "for or on account of an antecedent debt owed by the debtor before such transfer was made." 11 U.S.C. § 547(b)(2). A debt is antecedent if it is incurred before the transfer in question. . . . Therefore, lenders who advance loan proceeds prior to the recording of the mortgage are undertaking "a transfer of an interest in the subject property for purposes of § 547." Superior Bank, FSB v. Boyd (In re Lewis), 398 F.3d 735, 746 (6th Cir. 2005). Such transfers are subject to preferential transfer liability.

Under this scenario, a borrower who later becomes a debtor incurs an antecedent [debt] and, at the time the mortgage is recorded, a transfer occurs for or on account of the debt that could be challenged as preferential by a trustee. Section 547(e) addresses this potential problem for lenders by providing a grace period for perfecting a security interest. As long as the mortgage is recorded within the [grace] period, the associated mortgage debt will not be deemed antecedent. On the other hand, if perfection occurs more than ten days after the transfer takes effect, the transfer occurs at the time of the perfection, and the debt thus will be an antecedent one.

. . .

Applying § 547(e) to the facts of this case, we first note that the Debtor incurred his obligation under the New Loan when Chase disbursed the loan proceeds on October 6, 2003. Next, we must determine when the New Mortgage was perfected and whether the perfection occurred within [the] grace period. Under § 547(e)(1)(A), the New Mortgage was perfected "when a bona fide purchaser of [the Property] from the debtor against whom applicable law permits such transfer to be perfected cannot acquire an interest that is superior to the interest of the transferee." Here, the "applicable law" referenced in § 547(e)(1)(A) is the law of Michigan. Under Michigan law, perfection occurs upon recording. See Mich. Comp. Laws Ann. § 565.29 (2007). Therefore, a bona fide purchaser of the Property from the Debtor could have acquired an interest superior to the interest of Chase up until the date that the New Mortgage was recorded. It is undisputed that the New Mortgage was recorded on December 17, 2003, which was 72 days after the loan proceeds were disbursed—well outside the . . . grace period. As a result, under § 547(e)(2)(B), a transfer of the Debtor's interest in the Property occurred "at the time such transfer [was] perfected," on December 17, 2003, and was accordingly made on account of an antecedent debt.

Arguing against this result, Chase relies on the undisputed fact that the [mortgage] Discharge was recorded after the New Mortgage was recorded. According to Chase, at all relevant times third parties were on notice of Chase's secured interest in the Property. But the fact that third parties may have been on notice of Chase's Original Mortgage is beside the point. A transfer of an interest in real estate is not necessarily perfected for purposes of § 547(e) when third parties have notice that there had been a mortgage on the property. Rather, a transfer of real property "is perfected when a bona fide purchaser of such property from the debtor against whom applicable law permits such transfer to be perfected cannot acquire an interest that is superior to the interest of the transferee." 11 U.S.C. § 547(e)(1)(A).

. . .

Under § 547(e)(2), if Chase had taken steps to ensure that the New Mortgage was perfected within [the grace period number of] days of the Debtor's granting it, the date on which the transfer would have been considered made would have been October 6, 2003—the date that the transfer "[took] effect between the transferor and the transferee." If Chase had done so, the New Mortgage would not have been for or on account of an antecedent debt. The New Mortgage, however, was recorded 72 days after the Debtor gave Chase the mortgage and thus constituted a transfer for or on account of an antecedent debt. Therefore the date the transfer was made is December 17, 2003.

We will come back to Chase and the extra-statutory arguments it tried in the next assignment, but for now note that the timing of the relevant transfer is critical: one day can be the difference between life and death.

B.   THE EXCEPTIONS

A literal application of § 547(b) could backfire and over-deter creditors in their dealings with businesses that may be at risk of bankruptcy. Without exceptions, even transactions that were beneficial to the ongoing business (and ultimately to all the other creditors) or transactions that by their nature were not attempts to prefer certain creditors in anticipation of demise would be avoided. To prevent this effect, the Code builds in nine exceptions. § 547(c). Each of the five most commonly used exceptions has its own moniker: (1) "contemporaneous exchange," (2) "ordinary course payments," (3) "purchase money," (4) "new value" rule, and (5) "floating lien."

1.   Contemporaneous Exchange

The idea behind the contemporaneous exchange exception is that a seller or lender should be able to deal with a buyer or borrower without worrying about whether the sequence in which the parties execute the transaction can inadvertently create a voidable preference. So, for example, even in a cash transaction, if the seller hands over the good first and the buyer hands over the cash second, in the intervening seconds between seller's and buyer's performance the seller is a general, unsecured creditor. The buyer's cash payment would be on account of an antecedent (from seconds ago) debt. The contemporaneous exchange exception tries to bless such transactions and protect them from avoidance. As the case below demonstrates, however, "near-cash" transactions (e.g., checks) cause some confusion.

═══════════ In re STEWART ═══════════

274 B.R. 503 (Bankr. W.D. Ark. 2002)

FUSSELL, Bankruptcy Judge.

. . .

STIPULATED FACTS

The parties filed the following stipulations of fact with the Court on December 7, 2001:

The Debtor, Gary Stewart, filed a chapter 13 bankruptcy case on April 11, 2000. . . . If the Debtor had filed a chapter 7 case without considering the preference action, the case would be considered a no asset case and no distribution would be anticipated for unsecured creditors. . . .

On January 29, 2000, the Debtor purchased cattle from [Barry County Livestock Auction, Inc. ("Barry County"), a livestock auction facility] by personal check number 4029 from the Bank of Pea Ridge, Arkansas, in the amount of $17,580.70. Check No. 4029 was issued to pay Barry County Invoice Nos. 15, 16 and 17, also dated January 29, 2000. When Check No. 4029 was returned to Barry County for insufficient funds on February 12,

2000, the Debtor tendered a cashier's check numbered 83582 drawn on the Bank of Pea Ridge in the amount of $17,580.70 on February 12, 2000, to satisfy the obligation owing from the insufficient Check No. 4029. [Same story with a second check.]

Cashier's Check Nos. 83582 and 83692 were purchased with monies belonging to the Debtor and constituted property of the Debtor.

The payments made with Cashier's Check Nos. 83582 and 83692 were made while the Debtor was presumed insolvent and was insolvent.

The payments made with Cashier's Check Nos. 83582 and 83692 were made within 90 days immediately preceding the Debtor's bankruptcy filing.

The payments made with Cashier's Check Nos. 83582 and 83692 enabled Barry County to receive more than it would have received if this case had been a chapter 7 case; if the payments had not been made; and if Barry County had received payment of its debt as allowed under the Bankruptcy Code.

Barry County and Bill Younger [owner of Barry County Livestock Auction] received notice of the Debtor's bankruptcy filing as a result of the Notice of Commencement of Case sent on April 14, 2000. The first meeting of creditors for the Debtor's case was conducted and concluded on June 6, 2000. Bill Younger, Dayne Galyen and Dayne Galyen, Jr., all representatives and officers of Barry County, attended and participated in the first meeting of creditors.

On or about the evening of June 6 or 7, 2000, Bill Younger, Dayne Galyen and Dayne Galyen, Jr., acting individually and on behalf of Barry County, went to the Debtor's residence. The parties' recollection of the events differ; however, a disagreement occurred and the Benton County Sheriff's Department was contacted and subsequently appeared on the scene. A few days later, Debtor's mother, Janet Scott, paid $15,000 to Barry County toward the Debtor's debt owing Barry County. Bill Younger then returned an insufficient check that had been received from the Debtor prior to the bankruptcy filing to the Debtor's mother.

. . .

A debt is antecedent if the debt was incurred prior to the allegedly preferential transfer. Jones Truck Lines, Inc. v. Central States, Southeast and Southwest Areas Pension Fund (In re Jones Truck Lines, Inc.), 130 F.3d 323, 329 (8th Cir. 1997). A debt is incurred " 'on the date upon which the debtor first becomes legally bound to pay.' " Id. (quoting In re Iowa Premium Serv. Co., 695 F.2d 1109, 1111 (8th Cir. 1982)). In this case, Dayne Galyen Jr. testified, and the Court credits his testimony, that all buyers at the auction barn were required to pay for their purchases on the date of the sale. Therefore, the debts were incurred two weeks before the delivery of the cashier's checks and were antecedent debts.

The Court finds that Barry County Livestock Auction is a creditor for purposes of 11 U.S.C. § 547(b)(1), and that cashier's checks number 83582 and 83692 were given by the debtor to Barry County Livestock Auction for antecedent debts. Because the parties have stipulated to the other elements of a preferential transfer, the Court finds that the trustee has met her burden of proof as to the preferential transfer of the two cashier's checks. The creditor may avoid preference liability if it can prove that it falls within one of the exceptions set forth in § 547(c). . . .

CONTEMPORANEOUS EXCHANGE FOR NEW VALUE EXCEPTION

To qualify for the contemporaneous exchange for new value exception under § 547(c)(1), a creditor must prove that an otherwise preferential transfer was "(A) intended by the debtor and the creditor . . . to be a contemporaneous exchange for new value given to the debtor; and (B) in fact a substantially contemporaneous exchange." 11 U.S.C. § 547(c)(1). "New value" is defined as "money or money's worth in goods, services, or new credit, or release by a transferee of property previously transferred to such transferee in a transaction that is neither void nor voidable by the debtor or the trustee under any applicable law, including proceeds of such property, but does not include an obligation substituted for an existing obligation." 11 U.S.C. § 547(a)(2).

Before the Court can determine whether the payments made by the debtor with cashier's checks payable to Barry County Livestock Auction were contemporaneous exchanges for new value under the bankruptcy code, the Court must determine as a matter of law when the transfer of cattle occurred. If the transfer of the cattle did not occur until the cashier's checks were presented to Barry County Livestock Auction, the transactions may have been contemporaneous exchanges for new value. If, on the other hand, the transfer of the cattle occurred on the day of the sale, two weeks before the debtor presented the cashier's checks to Barry County Livestock Auction, the Court must determine whether the subsequent delivery of the cashier's checks to replace the insufficient funds checks constituted contemporaneous exchanges for new value.

. . . The Court finds that under the UCC, title to the cattle passed upon delivery of the cattle on the day of the respective sales. At best, Barry County Livestock Auction retained only a security interest in the cattle.

Having found that the transfer of cattle occurred on the date of the sale, the Court must now determine whether the delivery of the cashier's checks two weeks after the transfer of the cattle is a contemporaneous exchange for purposes of § 547(c)(1). The legislative history of § 547(c)(1) specifically references transactions in which checks are involved:

> Normally, a check is a credit transaction. However, for the purposes of this paragraph, a transfer involving a check is considered to be "intended to be contemporaneous," and if the check is presented for payment in the normal course of affairs, which the Uniform Commercial Code specifies as 30 days, U.S.C. § 3-503(2)(a), that will amount to a transfer that is "in fact substantially contemporaneous." . . .

Goger v. Cudahy Foods Co. (In re Standard Food Serv., Inc.), 723 F.2d 820, 821 (11th Cir. 1984) (quoting S. Rep. No. 989, 95th Cong., 2d Sess. 88). The debtor's payment by personal check constituted a contemporaneous transfer only if the check was presented and paid within a reasonable time. Hall-Mark Electronics Corp. v. Sims (In re Lee), 179 B.R. 149, 163 (9th Cir. B.A.P. 1995). Had the debtor's personal checks cleared, Barry County Livestock Auction's argument that a contemporaneous exchange for value occurred would prevail.

However, other portions of the legislative history indicate that the bank's dishonor of the personal checks changed the nature of the transaction:

> Contrary to language contained in the House report, payment of a debt by means of a check is equivalent to a cash payment unless the check is dishonored. Payment is considered to be made when the check is delivered for purposes of sections 547(c)(1) and (2).

Standard Food Serv., Inc., 723 F.2d at 821 (quoting 124 Cong. Rec. H11,097 (daily ed. Sept. 28, 1978); 124 Cong. Rec. S17,414 (daily ed. Oct. 6, 1978)). A contemporaneous exchange defense cannot involve a dishonored check. *Lee*, 179 B.R. at 163. When the checks were dishonored by the bank, the transactions became credit transactions and created an antecedent debt. Id.; *Standard Food Serv., Inc.*, 723 F.2d at 821. Any subsequent payment, no matter how quickly made, would satisfy that antecedent debt. *Lee*, 179 B.R. at 163 (quoting In re Barefoot, 952 F.2d 795, 800 (4th Cir. 1991)). When the debtor delivered the cashier's checks to Barry County Livestock Auction, the cashier's checks satisfied the antecedent debt, and were not contemporaneous exchanges for new value. Hence, Barry County Livestock Auction's contemporaneous exchange for new value exception fails.

COUNT 2 — VIOLATION OF AUTOMATIC STAY

. . . By separate order, the Court has set a hearing on Count 2 of the plaintiffs' complaint on March 1, 2002, at 9:00 A.M. in the United States Bankruptcy Court, Fayetteville, Arkansas.

We would like to get a look at the Barry County Livestock Auction management team. They seem to have found some very persuasive ways to encourage both the debtor and the debtor's mother to come up with quick cash, although they may be returning it soon under a contempt award for violating the stay.

Cases like *Stewart* are a reminder that the intent of the parties to be contemporaneous is insufficient; the transaction must in fact be contemporaneous as well. If wishes were horses, beggars would ride.

2.   *Ordinary Course of Business*

Subsection 547(c)(2) balances two competing concerns: the need to discourage preferences in favor of certain creditors pre-bankruptcy and the need to encourage pre-bankruptcy transactions that are essential to keep the business alive. The Code therefore provides a voidable preference exception to permit some ordinary course transactions to stand, notwithstanding the fact that they permitted some unsecured creditors to be paid in full. This exception has gone through several iterations. Initially, the Code set a bright-line rule: within 45 days was ordinary course; later was not.

Like all bright-line rules, it had the problem of being both over- and under-inclusive. Congress then redrafted it in 1984, to make it more of a standard.

More pedagogical help arrives from our friends at Barry County Livestock Auction:

====================== In re STEWART (cont'd) ======================

ORDINARY COURSE OF BUSINESS EXCEPTION

Barry County Livestock Auction also raised the ordinary course of business exception pursuant to § 547(c)(2). To qualify for the ordinary course of business exception, a creditor must prove that the transfer was "(A) in payment of a debt incurred by the debtor in the ordinary course of business or financial affairs of the debtor and the transferee; (B) made in the ordinary course of business or financial affairs of the debtor and the transferee; and (C) made according to ordinary business terms." 11 U.S.C. § 547(c)(2).

The parties did not specifically stipulate that the transfers were in payment of a debt incurred by the debtor in the ordinary course of business between the debtor and Barry County Livestock Auction. However, the parties did stipulate that the debtor engaged in a business relationship with Barry County Livestock Auction in July 1997 that continued until the debtor filed his chapter 7 bankruptcy petition on April 11, 2000. They also stipulated that in the course of their business relationship, the debtor purchased cattle from Barry County Livestock Auction and was required to pay for the cattle purchased the same day of the purchases. Because the payments were made to satisfy debts that the debtor incurred in the ordinary course of his business dealings with Barry County Livestock Auction, the Court finds that Barry County Livestock Auction meets the [first] elements of subsection (c)(2).

[The second element] deals with the way the parties actually conducted their business dealings. According to the Eighth Circuit Court of Appeals, a court must engage in a "peculiarly factual analysis" to determine whether payments made by the debtor during the 90 day preference period were made in the ordinary course of business. Lovett v. St. Johnsbury Trucking, 931 F.2d 494, 497 (8th Cir. 1991). Specifically, the court must look at the "consistency of the transaction in question as compared to other, prior transactions between the parties." Concast Canada, Inc. v. Laclede Steel Co. (In re Laclede Steel Co.), 271 B.R. 127, 131 (8th Cir. B.A.P. 2002). Sufficient alteration of any one of four factors may be sufficient for a court to conclude that a payment was made outside the ordinary course of business. 271 B.R. at 132. The factors are:

(1) the length of time the parties were engaged in the transactions at issue;
(2) whether the amount or form of tender differed from past practices;
(3) whether the debtor or the creditor engaged in any unusual collection or payment activity; and (4) whether the creditor took advantage of the debtor's deteriorating financial condition.

Id. n.3. The Eighth Circuit has found that the timing of the payments to the creditor to be of overriding importance, and stated that review of the

12 months preceding the 90-day preference period and the 90-day period itself was an appropriate standard for determining the ordinary course of business. *Lovett*, 931 F.2d at 498.

The Court will first look at all of the dealings the debtor had with Barry County Livestock Auction. . . . The debtor only presented one check during the 12-month period preceding the 90-day preference period that was dishonored by the bank when presented for payment. In fact, that was the only check that was not honored when presented to the bank during the entire 42 months the debtor had been purchasing cattle from Barry County Livestock Auction prior to the preference period. That one check was written within three weeks of the preference period, and the debt was paid three days before the preference period. On the other hand, the debtor presented four checks during the preference period that were dishonored by the bank when presented for payment, two of which were later paid by cashier's checks. Despite the one dishonored check right before the preference period, the Court finds that the ordinary course of business between the debtor and Barry County Livestock Auction was that the debtor paid for his purchases with a personal check on the date of sale that was honored when presented for payment. The payments by personal checks made during the preference period that were dishonored by the bank when presented for payment, but later paid with cashier's checks, were not sufficiently consistent with the payments made during the prior 12 months. Because of this, the Court finds that Barry County Livestock Auction has failed to meet the [second] element of subsection (c)(2).

Subsection (c)(2)(C) requires that the transfers be made according to ordinary business terms; in other words, "whether the transaction was ordinary pursuant to terms in the industry." *Laclede Steel Co.*, 271 B.R. at 133. To make this determination, the Court must compare the payment record of the debtor with the general practice in the industry regarding time of payment. *Lovett*, 931 F.2d at 499. The only testimony presented regarding the general practice in the industry was from Dayne Galyen Jr. He testified that cattle purchases were always paid on the day of purchase and that this practice was typical in the industry. Upon cross examination, he again stated that "by law," a buyer is required to pay on the day of the sale. Based on Mr. Galyen's testimony, which the Court credits, and in the absence of any contrary evidence, it is clear that payment by cashier's check two weeks after the date of sale is not typical in the industry. Because of this, the Court finds that Barry County Livestock Auction has failed to meet the elements of [the third] subsection (c)(2).

Based on the above findings of facts and conclusions of law, the Court finds that the payments made by the debtor to Barry County Livestock Auction with cashier's check number 83582 and cashier's check number 83692, in the total amount of $46,749.55, were preferential transfers in favor of Barry County Livestock Auction.

After *In re Stewart* was decided, Congress tweaked the 547(c)(2) exception in 2005. The first element, that the debt be incurred in the debtor's ordinary course of business, remained the same, but now the creditor need only prove *either* the second element (that the transfer was in the ordinary course of the debtor's business) *or* the third element (that the transfer was made according to ordinary business terms), not both. Other than seeming generally pro-creditor, it is not clear why this change was made and who was lobbying for it—maybe banks that know nothing about their clients' businesses? We think that most trade creditors, just like the Barry County Livestock Auction folks, either pass or flunk both, so we doubt much has changed.

3.   The Purchase Money Exception

For those conversant with Article 9 of the UCC, the easiest voidable preference exception to understand is § 547(c)(3), which provides that purchase money creditors will receive special protection in bankruptcy, just as they do under the UCC. The policy reasons are similar: transactions that give the debtor additional property are regarded as the most beneficial and therefore deserve the greatest protection.

Perhaps Congress thought it was being helpful to these creditors by expanding the perfection grace period from 20 days under state law to 30 days under bankruptcy law, but the problem is that this is now longer than the UCC's § 9-317(e) PMSI grace period of 20 days. A PMSI lender that perfects on Day 25 might lose to a lien creditor outside bankruptcy under UCC § 9-317(e) but nevertheless be protected against preference attack in bankruptcy under § 547(c)(3). But wait a minute, doesn't the strong arm clause allow the trustee/DIP to step into the shoes of a hypothetical lien creditor at state law, in which case it beats the PMSI lender? Hmm. . . .

4.   The New Value Exception

Subsection 547(c)(4), the "new value" preference exception, shelters preference payments that come *before* a particular extension of new value, analyzed on a payment-by-payment basis. Here are the steps:

1. Identify a payment (or other transfer) that is preferential under subsection 547(b). (This is the first step because otherwise there is no reason to look to the exceptions.)
2. See if the avoidable amount of the preference can be reduced by the amount of ("to the extent that") later-advanced new value that qualifies under subsection (c)(4). For example, if a creditor received a $100,000 preferential payment, then made a $70,000 delivery of new supplies on credit, when the debtor filed bankruptcy a preference of $100,000 would presumptively exist, but this preference is reduced to $30,000 under subsection (c)(4).
3. Check for the caveats of Parts (A) and (B). For example, a creditor that received a $100,000 preference and then delivered $70,000 of new supplies, paid in cash on delivery, could not use the new value exception because of the caveat of Part (B): it was accompanied by a $70,000 cash payment that is not otherwise an avoidable transfer (because it is a contemporaneous exchange payment for the new supplies).

The new value exception implements the policy that helpful creditors who, after the preferential payment, extended new, unsecured credit to the debtor and who will thus already suffer in bankruptcy as an unsecured creditor to the extent of that new credit should not face an additional whammy of having to return the payments. The notion is at least arguably consistent with the idea that preference policy is designed to encourage creditors to work with a financially troubled debtor. On the other hand, if the creditor insists that the debtor grant a security interest or pay in cash for the new goods, then the creditor warrants no such solicitude.

5.   The "Floating Lien"

The final major category of voidable preference is perhaps the most daunting: the protection of floating liens. To understand the provision, it is helpful to know the historical "problem" of floating liens, the case law's fix of that problem, and the Code's fix of that fix.

First, the problem: floating liens are liens that attach to a seething mass of property, like inventory in a retail store. Unlike a lien on one piece of fixed property, such as manufacturing equipment, a lien on inventory is in a constant state of flux because the old inventory goes out the front door and new inventory comes in the back. These changes in the collateral create a conceptual difficulty.

An example sets up the issue. If a lender takes a lien on the toothpaste inventory of a drugstore, as soon as any given tube is sold, consider what happens. The customer pays in cash or by credit card, and under the UCC: (1) the customer will take free of the lien, as buyer in the ordinary course, and (2) the lien carries over to the proceeds of the sale (cash or credit card receivable). UCC §§ 9-320(a), 9-315. But then when the proceeds get commingled, such as cash that the store deposits into a general operating account, the lender generally loses its lien altogether. A prudent lender has to get another security interest in the new toothpaste tube that the store orders, which it does perhaps by having an after-acquired property clause in its security agreement, securing "toothpaste, now and hereafter acquired" (or more likely a blanket lien on inventory).

Now run that transaction through what you know of preference law. To secure the outstanding loan, the debtor has granted a lien on the newly acquired tube of toothpaste, albeit pursuant to a security agreement executed years ago. That new lien on freshly acquired toothpaste is a transfer of an interest in property of the debtor, as explained in the *Shapiro* case, and clearly on account of antecedent debt. This in turn means that the toothpaste arriving within 90 days before bankruptcy of an insolvent debtor gives rise to a preferential transfer to the inventory lender. But from the inventory lender's perspective that is absurd: the lender just wants a lien on the store's inventory so if the store defaults it can repossess the toothpaste. The lien is not intentionally preferential; it simply attaches to all toothpaste and "floats" up and down on the dentifricial tide as the inventory shifts: a fat lien when toothpaste is selling slow and crowding the shelves, but a lean lien when there's been a clearance sale and the shelves are near bare.

Absurd or not, the lender was subject to preference recovery. While some courts tried to futz with ordinary course of business, the landmark fix stemmed from seminal cases, such as *Grain Merchants v. Union Bank and Savings Co.*, 408 F.2d 209 (7th Cir. 1969), and its more aggressive cousin, *DuBay v. Williams*, 417 F.2d 1277 (9th Cir. 1969). The fix was essentially to say that the relevant "transfer" actually occurred at the initial execution of the security agreement—way back, well before the 90-day period—and not when the new tube of toothpaste was acquired, thus saving from preference attack all the recently acquired pre-bankruptcy toothpaste. (The logic relied on "relation back" doctrines.) While this fix was hailed by many as an innovation that ratified modern lending practices, a sizeable number of commentators argued that *Grain Merchants* and *DuBay* eliminated the application of preference law to all after-acquired property as a per se rule, creating the potential for abuse. A powerful creditor—as the inventory and receivables creditors often are—could "encourage" the debtor to pour assets into the acquisition of inventory or the development of accounts at the expense of using those assets to pay other creditors. ("The business is facing tough times and losing money fast? Why not order ten times your normal toothpaste needs on unsecured credit? No, really, *order ten times your normal toothpaste.* 'Feed' our undersecured lien with more collateral. If we get hungry, we get cranky and exercise our remedies.") This nefarious and very real scenario is exactly what preference law is supposed to combat.

Subsections 547(e)(3) and 547(c)(5) of the Code are the fix to the fix. The language of § 547(e)(3) represents a firm rejection of the relation back approach by flatly forbidding for preference purposes any dating of a security interest in a piece of property prior to the debtor's acquisition of an interest in that property. Under this rule, the time of the "transfer" of a security interest in after-acquired property is the date the debtor acquires the property, regardless of an earlier perfected security agreement, i.e., when the new toothpaste arrives. That sounds like a step backward, which is why Congress also added § 547(c)(5), which grants an exception for transfers resulting from the attachment of liens on inventory and receivables. Security interests in inventory and accounts—but not in any other type of after-acquired property—are saved by § 547(c)(5) (but not categorically, as under *Grain Merchants*).

The Code protects the lien on recently acquired inventory, but only partially—not to the extent the lender improves its position during the 90-day lookback period. The formal text speaks of "reduction" of the "amount by which the debt secured . . . exceeded the value" of the collateral, § 547(c)(5), which we find painful and so prefer to think of in our heads as "reducing the degree to which they are underwater." If the floating lien coverage stays flat or goes down, it's fine. If it goes up, it's disallowed to the extent of improvement. Some (mathletes) may find it helpful to express it as a formula:

> Let I = the insufficiency of collateral coverage (i.e., balance of loan *minus* value of collateral),
> let BD = the date the bankruptcy petition is filed ("Bankruptcy Day"),
> let LBD = the date computed under § 547(c)(5)
> ("Look-Back Day," generally 90 days prior), and
> let VP = the amount of preference avoidable.

The § 547(c)(5) Rule:

If $I_{LBD} > 0$ and $I_{LBD} > I_{BD}$, then $VP = I_{LBD} - I_{BD}$. Else, $VP = 0$.

For the rest of us, we simply say that a lienholder on inventory or accounts receives a voidable preference to the extent it has reduced its underwateredness over the 90 days.

In the next case, the creditor with an interest in accounts receivable admits that the value of the accounts increased during the 90 days before bankruptcy but argues that the debt increased as well, leading to no improvement—and in fact a worsening—of its position.

In re QMECT, INC.
373 B.R. 100 (Bankr. N.D. Cal. 2007)

TCHAIKOVSKY, Bankruptcy Judge.

. . .

SUMMARY OF UNDISPUTED FACTS

The Debtor filed a chapter 11 bankruptcy petition on February 27, 2004. Prior to the filing and during the chapter 11 phase of the case, before the case was converted to chapter 7, the Debtor operated an electroplating business. Customers of the Debtor would supply objects to the Debtor which the Debtor, using chemicals, would electroplate and return to their owners. These operations generated accounts receivable. Although not held for sale, the chemicals qualified as the Debtor's inventory. See Cal. Comm. Code § 9102(48)(D) ("materials used or consumed in a business").

At the beginning of the preference period—on December 27, 2003—the Debtor had two secured creditors. The senior secured creditor was Comerica Bank ("Comerica"). The junior secured creditor was Burlingame. Both Comerica and Burlingame had security interests in virtually all of the Debtor's assets, which included accounts receivable and inventory.

At all times during the preference period, Burlingame was undersecured: i.e., the value of its collateral, taking into account the amount of the senior secured debt, was less than the amount of Burlingame's debt. During the preference period, some, if not all, of the accounts receivable in which Burlingame held a security interest at the beginning of the preference period generated cash proceeds. These proceeds were then spent in the continued operation of the business, and new accounts receivable were generated.

Pursuant to the after-acquired property clause in Burlingame's security agreement, Burlingame automatically acquired liens in the new accounts receivable generated during the preference period. On the petition date, the value of Burlingame's security interest in the Debtor's accounts receivable and inventory then in existence was greater than the value of its security interest in the accounts receivable and inventory in existence at the beginning of the preference period.

. . .

B. "Improvement in Position" Defense

Burlingame's [] ground for its motion for summary judgment was that, even if the transfers did constitute preferences, it is entitled to a complete defense to their avoidance under 11 U.S.C. § 547(c)(5). . . . This defense is generally referred to as the "improvement in position" defense. Thus, the value of an undersecured creditor's collateral in relationship to its debt on the petition date is compared with the value of its collateral in relationship to its debt at the beginning of the preference period. The transfers during the preference period are only avoidable to the extent that its undersecured position on the earlier date is greater than its undersecured position on the later date.

The Trustee presented evidence that the value of the Debtor's accounts receivable and inventory increased by $156,939 during the preference period. Burlingame presented no evidence to the contrary. Nevertheless, Burlingame contended that it was entitled to a complete defense because the Trustee would be unable to prove that the preferential transfers prejudiced unsecured creditors. . . .

Burlingame argued that its "position" had not "improved" because its debt had increased during the preference period, due to the accrual of interest and late fees, even more than the value of its collateral had increased.

In his post-hearing brief, the Trustee asserted that, for purposes of determining a secured creditor's "improvement in position" pursuant to 11 U.S.C. § 547(c)(5), the only changes in the "debt" during the preference that should be considered were increases due to additional "advances" or decreases pursuant to additional "payments." Increases in the debt other than additional advances should not be considered. The Trustee conceded that he had found no express support for this proposition in legal treatises or case law. He based his assertion primarily on policy grounds.

The Trustee noted that, if the transfers attacked as preferences had been payments rather than transfers of security interests and Burlingame were asserting a "new value" defense pursuant to 11 U.S.C. § 547(c)(3), increases due to interest, late charges, and attorneys' fees would not qualify as "new value." See 11 U.S.C. § 547(a)(2) (defining "new value" as "money or money's worth in goods, services, or new credit"). He also observed that 11 U.S.C. § 506(b) excludes post-petition interest and attorneys' fees from an undersecured creditor's secured claim. . . .

Burlingame responded to each of these arguments. First, it noted that statutory construction must begin with the language of the statute, not with policy. When the language of the statute is clear, policy need not and should not be consulted. Burlingame correctly noted that 11 U.S.C. § 547(c)(5) refers only to "debt," not to "advances" or "new value." Second, unless otherwise indicated, the definition of terms used in the Bankruptcy Code are governed by state law. Under state law, the additional interest, late fees, and attorneys' fees incurred during the preference period would clearly be considered part of the "debt." Moreover, 11 U.S.C. § 506(b) excludes only "post-petition" interest and attorneys' fees from an undersecured creditor's secured debt.

. . .

The Court finds the arguments made and authority cited by Burlingame more persuasive than those advanced by the Trustee. Section 547(c)(5) refers to "debt." "Debt" is defined as "liability on a claim." See 11 U.S.C. § 101(12). "Claim" is defined extremely broadly and would certainly include pre-petition interest, late fees, and attorneys' fees. See 11 U.S.C. § 101(5).

Section 506(b), which excludes post-petition interest and attorneys' fees from an undersecured creditor's secured claim, has no bearing on the amount of the secured creditor's debt, either as of the petition date or 90 days before that date. Finally, the determination of Burlingame's debt was actually litigated. Because the Court found that the form of Burlingame's proof of claim was inadequate to shift the burden of production to the Debtor and at the insistence of the Debtor, Burlingame was required to prove each element of its claim in excruciating detail.

CONCLUSION

For the reasons stated above, Burlingame's motion for reconsideration will be granted . . . . [T]he Trustee does not contend that value of Burlingame's collateral increased during the preference period by more [than] $157,000. The Court has already determined the amount of Burlingame's debt increased during the same period by at least $165,184. Therefore, the Court finds that Burlingame is entitled to a complete defense under 11 U.S.C. § 547(c)(5). Thus, the Court will grant summary judgment in favor of Burlingame.

===

You might think that any inventory lender who is fully secured on Day T-90 can never receive a voidable preference under the improvement in position test. You would be mostly right. But consider In re Qualia Clinical Servs., Inc., 652 F.3d 933 (8th Cir. 2011), in which the receivables lender argued just that—and that its failure to perfect its security interest for months until it did so during the preference period created no vulnerability because it was fully secured at T-90 days. The court made quick work of that argument: "A creditor who . . . enters the test period unperfected is properly deemed, for purposes of section 547(c)(5), to have an interest of zero." Id. at 939. It's hard to argue you have not improved from zero.

When improvement does occur, however, it still may not be a voidable preference. In re Nivens, 22 B.R. 287 (Bankr. N.D. Tex. 1982), addresses the eternal question: does the sun shine for the benefit of the unsecured or the secured? In *Nivens*, the trustee battled creditors with perfected security interests in the cotton crop (more precisely, over "low yield" and "disaster" payments paid to the debtor-farmer just before bankruptcy under government support programs). The court distinguished crops from toothpaste:

[I]f there is only an increase in *value* of the inventory due to market fluctuations, without an accompanying increase in volume of inventory, there is no avoidable preference. A crop as "inventory" is different from the grocery store inventory example. A crop is continuously undergoing change. Its existence commences as soon as the seed is planted and starts to germinate. It undergoes daily change until it finally matures and is ready for harvest. The lien which was initially fixed against the crops in its embryonic stages continues against the crop in all stages of development. It is the same lien and the same crop. Although the crop is increasing in value the crop was in existence at all relevant times. While there might be an increase in the value of the crop between the different stages of its development, the "inventory" itself is not increased. There is nothing added within the prohibited period which would mandate avoidance of lien against increase.

Id. at 293-94.

The court in *Nivens* seems clearly correct in ruling that a mere increase in value of collateral does not generate an improvement in position under § 547(c)(5). More precisely, an increase in value, whether from a rising market or a good rainfall, does not involve a *transfer* and therefore cannot constitute a preference under § 547. On the other hand, the crop did not increase in value merely by the bounty of nature; there was value added to it by the labor of the farmers and the application of fertilizers. That additional value raises some subtle and interesting issues. For example, as discussed in Assignment 3, if the farmers worked during a pending chapter 7, they should have been compensated by the trustee. But we have plowed that field already.

6.   *And the Rest**

Four other exceptions to the voidable preference rules are in § 547(c). Statutory liens that violate the voidable preference provisions can survive if they are otherwise unavoidable. § 547(c)(6). In effect, this provision means that statutory liens will be dealt with in § 545, notwithstanding that they technically meet the preference criteria. Subsection 547(c)(7) clarifies that alimony and support payments, although made to an unsecured creditor, will not be recoverable as voidable preferences, further implementing the Code's policy of protecting family law creditors.

Subsections 547(c)(8) and (c)(9), sometimes called the "small potatoes" exceptions, were added at the insistence of creditors who did not want to have to fight voidable preference actions for modest amounts of money. In effect, the provisions permit creditors to keep preferential transfers if the amount in question is less than $600 in consumer cases and less than $6,825 in business cases (subject to inflation adjustment). The justification is not principled so much as pragmatic: the creditors whine that they can't afford to litigate. Some have argued, however, that these exceptions were added to make it harder for the trustee to get money at the start of a case. Because trustees get paid a portion of the amounts distributed to unsecured creditors, an easy-win, low-dollar preference helps "seed" the trustee's budget to do a more thorough investigation of the debtor's estate, especially in a possible low-asset case. Whatever the reason for the change, it proves that

* http://ebb.org/bkuhn/blog/2011/06/28/gilligans-island.html.

even creditors are just human with behavioral foibles: creditors lobbied for these preference protections, evidently motivated by vivid memories of the few times they had to give up money as a voidable preference rather than the marginally larger distribution in the many cases in which other fellow creditors got tagged.

Problem Set 21

21.1. **A.** Underdown is a wildcat driller. His last three holes have been dry, and he fears he is insolvent. On June 1, one of his principal suppliers that ships on unsecured credit, OKC Supply, calls on him to discuss payment on an outstanding $140,000 invoice. He immediately sends them $14,000. On August 15, Underdown files for chapter 11 but on December 15 the case is converted to a chapter 7. The trustee ends up paying unsecured creditors a 10% dividend. Is the OKC payment a voidable preference? See § 547(b).

B. What if, instead of the payment, Underdown had just let OKC take some of the loose equipment worth around the same amount that was left at the warehouse and drilling sites, knowing OKC could spruce it up and resell it? See § 547(b).

C. Another creditor of Underdown's, Iverson Bank of Commerce, saw the writing on the wall. Although it had an unsecured term loan of $600,000 outstanding for over a year, it asked Underdown to pledge one of his unencumbered drillers as security on May 20, which he does by signing the security agreement Iverson sends over, and it perfects later that afternoon. Is there a voidable preference? See § 547(b).

21.2. North Woods, Inc. is an insolvent logging concern but believes that a current upturn in the construction industry will allow the company to become profitable again. It persuades VenCap, a venture capital company, to lend it an emergency $500,000 to survive the next few months. On June 1, VenCap makes the loan and takes a security interest in North Woods's unencumbered equipment, which it perfects on July 6. On September 15, North Woods cannot meet its payroll and it declares chapter 11. Voidable preference? See § 547(b), (e).

21.3. On February 1, Hartford Baking, Inc. has two secured creditors. One, Magic Chef Co., sold Hartford four $100,000 specialized ovens one year earlier and perfected its security interest before delivery. On February 1, the loan balance was $350,000 and the value of the ovens was $300,000. The other creditor, Commercial Bank, made a loan to Hartford six months earlier. Commercial took a security interest in Hartford's other baking equipment and perfected at the time of the loan. On February 1, Commercial's loan had a balance of $400,000 and Commercial's collateral was worth $500,000. On February 2, Hartford paid each creditor $50,000. On April 2, Hartford filed for bankruptcy. Hartford was insolvent throughout, and the value of the collateral was stable. Would either creditor face a voidable preference action? See § 547(b).

21.4. Virginian Air Conditioning Service owes $250,000 to First Richmond Bank. The loan is secured by a perfected security interest in "all Virginian's current and after-acquired equipment," which on March 1 is worth about $150,000. On April 15, Virginian acquires another $200,000 in equipment from a supplier who sells on credit but who declines to take a security interest in these goods (relying on its reclamation rights). On May 25, after having been insolvent for six months, Virginian files for bankruptcy. Has there been a voidable preference? See § 547(b), (e)(3).

21.5. A. The principal asset of Clear Springs Bottling Company was a two-ton bottle-capping machine. As of June 1 last year, Clear Springs owed $2.8 million to Hillside Bank. Under an agreement with an after-acquired property clause, the loan was secured by a perfected security interest in the bottle-capping machine, which was then valued at $3 million. On July 1, Clear Springs made a $200,000 payment to Hillside. On July 15, a fire swept through the plant and the bottle-capping machine was completely destroyed. Contrary to the requirements of the security agreement, Clear Springs had tried to save cash by permitting the insurance on the machine to lapse. Clear Springs was already in serious financial trouble, and the fire finished it. It declared bankruptcy on August 1. Has there been a voidable preference? See § 547(b).

B. If Clear Springs had purchased another used bottle-capping machine after the fire using unsecured credit from the seller, and the new machine was worth $3 million, would there have been a voidable preference? See § 547(b).

21.6. Fun City Go-Karts was in failing financial condition and legally insolvent. Its chief supplier, Exaco, knew of the difficulties and told Fun City it would only make gasoline deliveries for cash payments. Fun City and Exaco completed about two deliveries per week for about $3,400 each during the 90 days preceding bankruptcy. Three times during that period, however, the delivery truck arrived and Fun City did not have cash available. Rather than take Fun City's check, the Exaco driver agreed simply to collect payment on his next run, which was accomplished each time. When Fun City files for bankruptcy within 90 days of these transactions, can the trustee recover any of these payments? See § 547(b), (c)(1), (c)(8)-(9).

21.7. GoldenView Nursing Home filed for bankruptcy in September. The trustee later reviewed the books and found among the entries evidence of the following transactions:

1. $34,200 in utility bills were paid four weeks before filing. It seems that GoldenView had been more than three months behind in its utility payments, and when the power company threatened to shut them off, GoldenView took a large portion of the August receipts and paid them off in full.
2. The June, July, and August mortgage payments were due on the first, but made between the twentieth and twenty-fifth of each month and each included a $50 late penalty charge. The mortgage is undersecured.
3. Solid State Bank received a payment in full of a $500,000 unsecured, six-month loan. The payment was made on July 15, the date it was due.

Which of these payments can the trustee recover? See § 547(b), (c)(2).

21.8. Odd Notions is a button manufacturer that specializes in fine bone and shell buttons. It has been insolvent since January 1, but it has continued to operate based on an emergency line of unsecured credit from the Des Moines People's Bank. (The bank does not usually make such loans, but one of the bank's vice-presidents, Chris Weil, is a neighbor of Notions' CFO, Chris Wawro, and pulled a few strings.) The arrangement has been that whenever Notions needs money to make its payroll or pay bills, it will call on its line of credit and whenever Notions receives payments from its buyers, it deposits them directly to pay down the balance.

The current year's accounts between Notions and DMPB can be summarized as follows:

Date	Transaction	Amount	Balance owed to DMPB
1/1	beginning balance		$80,000
1/3	payment from Notions	$5,000	$75,000
1/15	new credit from DMPB	$4,000	$79,000
2/10	payment from Notions	$2,000	$77,000
2/28	new credit from DMPB	$8,000	$85,000
3/4	new credit from DMPB	$9,000	$94,000
3/10	payment from Notions	$1,000	$93,000
3/17	new credit from DMPB	$6,000	$99,000
3/20	payment from Notions	$10,000	$89,000
4/1	payment from Notions	$9,000	$80,000
4/10	Notions files bankruptcy		

How much of the payments from Notions can DMPB keep? See § 547(b), (c)(4).

21.9. Metal Traders, Inc. is a buyer and seller of gold and silver. It currently owes $10 million to SpecVest, a capital investment company specializing in speculative industries. SpecVest has a perfected security interest in Metal Traders's inventory, which was worth $8 million on April 1. A federal investigation into allegations that Metal Traders was involved in an investment scam put a freeze on all of Metal Traders's operations so that no gold or silver was bought or sold. The good news is that the freeze resulted in a bonanza to Metal Traders: the price of gold jumped 42% in the interim. The bad news is that the Feds figured out the scam. The business filed for bankruptcy on June 30. Assuming it was insolvent throughout, can the trustee sue SpecVest for a preference? See § 547(b), (c)(5).

21.10. On September 10, Klocinski's Restaurant Supply has an inventory valued at $950,000 and a loan of $930,000 from Nowlin Investors secured by that inventory. Active sales during September deplete the inventory to $800,000, but subsequent threats from other creditors cause all the cash raised to go elsewhere and no payments are made to Nowlin. Following threats from Nowlin, Klocinski's replenishes its stock despite its insolvency, so that on December 10 the inventory is valued at $1 million, with the loan still $930,000. If Klocinski's files bankruptcy on December 10, does Nowlin face a voidable preference problem? See § 547(b), (c)(5).

PREFERENCES II

Beyond the basics, preference law presents a number of more complicated and interesting issues. This assignment explores four of the most important ones, along with another advanced doctrine, "equitable subordination," for setting aside special advantages enjoyed by certain favored creditors.

A.   STATE LAW

The Uniform Voidable Transactions Act ("UVTA") is mostly devoted to fraudulent transfers, and those exciting transactions are the subject of the next assignment. But the concepts of preferences and fraudulent transfers arise from common historical roots, and the UVTA has a special preference provision as well. (We cover it here rather than with the UVTA discussion in the next assignment because it really is a preference rule, not a fraudulent conveyance rule.) The trustee or DIP, for reasons we will also see in the fraudulent conveyance materials (*spoiler!* § 544(b)!), gets to use the UVTA state-law powers in bankruptcy, including this voidable preference provision.

Specifically, the UVTA provides that a transfer is avoidable whenever it is made (1) in payment of an antecedent debt (2) by an insolvent debtor (3) to an insider (4) who had reasonable cause to know of the insolvency. UVTA § 5(b). (We often call these "fraudulent conveyances" or "fraudulent transfers," but they aren't really fraudulent at all—they sound at worst negligent—but that's what they were called for centuries and we have some linguistic path-dependence. Perhaps to solve this, the former Uniform Fraudulent Transfer Act was renamed as the UVTA—but only in 2014.) Section 5(b) means that an insolvent debtor's repayment of debt to an insider can be set aside by other creditors at state law, just as it can by the trustee or DIP in bankruptcy, too, § 544(b).

The UVTA's approach is noteworthy in two respects. First, it treats insiders with much greater suspicion than arm's-length creditors. The Code does this too, by extending the lookback period for voidable preferences from 90 days to one year for transfers to insiders. § 547(b)(4)(B). The second, and more striking, innovation is to inject culpability into the insider-repayment rule. Generally, the drafters of § 547 were indifferent about culpability. Voidable preference recipients have no mens rea defenses. Under the UVTA preference rule, by contrast, insider repayment is only attackable if the insider *knew or had reason to know* of the insolvency (a provision that incidentally used to be in the preferences rules of the Code too but was taken out).

By making a preference provision available at state law, the UVTA undercuts some of the need to push a debtor into an involuntary bankruptcy to claw back assets that some creditors feel were distributed inequitably. The provision also extends the restrictions on insider payments to entities that are not subject to involuntary bankruptcy filings, such as charitable organizations. And perhaps most importantly for a business debtor, the UVTA requires no coordination among three creditors, which is required to initiate a bankruptcy petition; the rights are enforceable by anyone who was a creditor of the debtor at the time of the transfer.

B. INDIRECT PREFERENCES

Moving on to the higher levels of federal preference law, we come to "indirect" preferences. Suppose there are two secured lenders secured by the same piece of collateral. The senior lender, *A*, is oversecured. The junior lender, *B*, is undersecured, with only 50% of its loan covered. We know that any payments to *B* during the lookback period while the debtor is insolvent are presumptively voidable preferences. But what about payments to *A*? Since *A* is oversecured, any payments to it will not improve its position — so no preference, right? Reconsider those payments from *B*'s perspective. If *A* is paid a big chunk of money to whittle down its loan balance, then it has a concomitant lesser claim on the collateral, which improves *B*'s coverage (say, to 75% coverage of its undersecured loan). While of course *B* would prefer the debtor use that money to pay down *B*'s loan directly instead of *A*'s, it's better than a slap in the face with a wet haddock. Payments to *A* are called an indirect preference to undersecured *B*.

The concept of the indirect preference was a major focus of controversy for a number of years because of a case called Levit v. Ingersoll Rand Financial Corp. (In re V.N. Deprizio Constr. Corp.), 874 F.2d 1186 (7th Cir. 1989). This was an ordinary dry and technical bankruptcy case, with Mr. Deprizio, the debtor's president, assassinated in a parking lot and that sort of thing. The real source of the case's notoriety is that it held that a payment made more than 90 days, but less than one year, before bankruptcy to an arm's-length bank was a preference, even though not made to an insider. How? The transfer occurred within the longer one-year preference period applicable to insiders, § 547(b)(4)(B), and it was deemed to be an indirect transfer to an insider. In the case, the benefit to the insider was even more tangential than the "promotion" of a junior secured lender's position when a senior secured is paid. The insider was merely an officer of the debtor corporation who had guaranteed the corporate debt to the bank (a commonplace term of small business financing).

The *Deprizio* case, as it is popularly known, is based on the theory that payment to the bank of the guaranteed debt reduced the exposure of the insider guarantor, thus "benefiting" the insider, even though the transfer was not "to" him. (Textualists among you will revel at the relevance of the statute's clarity in catching payments disjunctively "to or for the benefit of a creditor," § 547(b)(1).) Since the insider was a creditor, on account of his contingent right to reimbursement by the corporation if required to perform under the guaranty, the transfer *to* the bank was *for the benefit* of the insider creditor and thus fell under the preference statute. The final kicker in such situations is that the trustee doesn't even have to sue the insider creditor if the deeper pockets of the transferee seem more attractive. Look carefully at the language of § 550(a)(1): recovery is available from *either* the transferee *or* the creditor who benefits indirectly. Any surprise the trustee preferred an arm's-length bank to the individual guarantor?

Congress tried to address these indirect preference situations by amendments to the Code in 1994 and in 2005. Sections 547(i) and 550(c) insulate the non-insider creditor from the effects of an insider benefit for transfers made more than 90 days before bankruptcy. It didn't quite protect everyone, however.

In re DENOCHICK

287 B.R. 632 (W.D. Pa. 2003)

CINDRICH, District Judge.

This bankruptcy appeal fulfills the old adage, "No good deed goes unpunished." It also illustrates the wisdom of Proverbs 22:26: "Be not one of those who give pledges, who become surety for debts." Revised Standard Version.

In this case, appellants [Sandra Krasinksi et al.] agreed to guarantee a debt consolidation loan from NBOC to Sandra Krasinski's sister, Susan Lee Denochick (the debtor). The debtor made $1,713.35 in loan payments to NBOC in the year prior to filing bankruptcy. Appellants received none of this money, but the payments had the indirect effect of reducing their exposure on the guarantee they gave to NBOC. The trustee commenced an adversary action to avoid as a preference and recover from appellants the money Denochick paid to NBOC. After a trial, at which appellants did not testify, the bankruptcy court concluded by a memorandum order dated September 10, 2001 that appellants fell within the definition of "creditors" and that they had failed to establish the applicability of the "ordinary course of business" exception. Thus, the court concluded that the trustee could avoid the $1,713.35 and recover that amount from appellants.

We affirm. As the bankruptcy court thoroughly explained, the definition of a "creditor" under the bankruptcy code and Pennsylvania law is very broad and encompasses a guarantor of a debt. Appellants were "creditors," even though their claim was derivative of NBOC's and was contingent upon the debtor's default. Ms. Denochick's payments to NBOC conferred a benefit upon appellants, to the detriment of her other creditors. . . .

Nothing in the BAPCPA amendments seems to help sister Denochick, who remains an insider of her sister, which sounds vaguely sinister or even lewd, but is the language of the Code.

C.   EXTRA-STATUTORY DEFENSES TO PREFERENCES

As we have seen repeatedly, a host of equitable and other common law doctrines exist alongside the statutory regime of the Code. These non-Code laws can provide defenses to a voidable preference attack. The most significant extra-statutory defense is the "earmarking" doctrine. In its simplest application, it applies when there is a substitution of one creditor for another. For example, assume the debtor wants to refinance its loan from Siskel Bank to a more attractive one offered by Ebert Savings & Loan. Mechanically, Ebert may wire funds to Siskel directly to retire the old loan and become the debtor's new lender. Or it may even wire the money to the debtor directly and have the debtor in turn retire the Siskel loan. The point is, for the trustee to attack Siskel for receiving a preference by this loan repayment seems odd, because Ebert jumped in as a new creditor for the same amount. Some courts have said this isn't really a transfer of the debtor's property at all, it's a transfer of Ebert's property to Siskel, "earmarked" directly for Siskel's use even if it happens to pass through the debtor's accounts en route. You might think of the doctrine as related (albeit as a third cousin) to a constructive trust, with the debtor briefly holding "Ebert's" money in constructive trust for Siskel.

In the previous assignment, Chase Manhattan ran headlong into a preference problem with its belated perfection of a mortgage refinancing. But their well-compensated lawyers tried another tack.

CHASE MANHATTAN MORTGAGE CORP. v. SHAPIRO (cont'd)

B. The Earmarking Doctrine — Transfer of an "Interest of the Debtor in Property"

Development and Elements of the Earmarking Defense

When the other elements of a preferential transfer are established, § 547(b)'s prefatory language sweeps into the bankruptcy estate any transfer "of an interest of the debtor in property." Although this provision has a potentially expansive reach, it is not without limits. In addition to the exceptions to preference liability set forth in § 547(c) — none of which are at issue here — this Court adopted another limitation on § 547(b), the judicially-crafted "earmarking doctrine":

[T]here is an important exception to the general rule that the use of borrowed funds to discharge the debt constitutes a transfer of property of the debtor: where the borrowed funds have been specifically earmarked by the lender for payment to a designated creditor, there is held to be no transfer of property of the debtor even if the funds pass through the debtor's hands in getting to the selected creditor. See In re Hartley, 825 F.2d at 1070; In re Smith, 966 F.2d [1527, 1533 (7th Cir. 1992)]; In re Bohlen Enters., Ltd., 859 F.2d 561, 564-66 (8th Cir. 1988). "The courts have said that even when the lender's new earmarked funds are placed in the debtor's possession before payment to the old creditor, they are not within the debtor's 'control.'" *Bohlen*, 859 F.2d at 565 (citing cases).

McLemore v. Third Nat'l Bank in Nashville (In re Montgomery), 983 F.2d 1389, 1395 (6th Cir. 2005).

The earmarking doctrine applies whenever a third party transfers property to a designated creditor of the debtor for the agreed-upon purpose of paying that creditor. Under such circumstances, the property is said to be "earmarked" for the designated creditor. As a result, there is deemed to have been no transfer of an interest of the debtor in property, even if the property passes through the hands of the debtor on its way to the creditor. The earmarking doctrine, then, is a judicially-created defense that may be invoked by a defendant to a preference action in an attempt to negate § 547(b)'s threshold requirement—a transfer of an interest of the debtor in property. In order for the doctrine to apply, however, it must be that: (a) the agreement is between a new creditor and the debtor for the payment of a specific antecedent debt; (b) the agreement is performed according to its terms; and (c) the transaction according to the agreement does not result in a diminution of the debtor's estate.

The Earmarking Defense Applied to Refinancing Transactions

When applying the earmarking doctrine in the context of a refinancing transaction, courts have split over whether to characterize the refinancing as a single unitary transaction or as a number of parts. . . .

As an initial matter, we note that Chase is not a "new creditor," and that this alone precludes it from successfully invoking the earmarking doctrine. Because Chase refinanced its own loan with the Debtor, it cannot establish this preliminary element of the earmarking defense. See, e.g., In re Lazarus, 334 B.R. 542, 549 (Bankr. D. Mass. 2005) ("The earmarking doctrine requires three specific parties: the 'debtor,' an 'old creditor,' and a 'new creditor' who pays the debtor's obligation to the old creditor.").

Yet even if we were to deem Chase to be a new creditor, the earmarking doctrine would not shield it from preference liability under the circumstances of this case. As did the First Circuit in In re Lazarus [478 F.3d 12 (1st Cir. 2008)] and the clear majority of courts that have decided the issue, we conclude that the earmarking doctrine does not protect the late-perfecting refinancer from preference exposure. We reach this conclusion because we find the analysis in In re Lazarus persuasive, and because we find [Kaler v. First Community Nat'l Bank (In re Heitkamp), 137 F.3d 1087

(8th Cir. 1998)]'s unitary-transaction approach to be fundamentally flawed in several respects.

First, In re Heitkamp's unitary-transaction theory ignores the plain meaning of the Bankruptcy Code. The common theme in the Supreme Court's bankruptcy jurisprudence over the past two decades is that courts must apply the plain meaning of the Code unless its literal application would produce a result demonstrably at odds with the intent of Congress. . . . In re Heitkamp's extension of the earmarking defense to a debtor's transfer of a lien interest has been rightly criticized as a violation of this cardinal principle. . . . Specifically, In re Heitkamp's unitary-transaction approach ignores the definition of "transfer" set forth in § 101(54), as supplemented by § 547(e). Application of this definition to Lee's refinancing transaction with Chase leads to the inescapable conclusion that it was comprised of two transfers by the Debtor — a transfer of the proceeds of the New Loan to Chase to pay off the Original Loan and the grant of the New Mortgage to Chase to secure his obligation to repay the New Loan.

> . . .

Chase urges us to follow In re Heitkamp and turn a blind eye to the plain meaning of the term "transfer" contained in §§ 101(54) and 547(e). We decline Chase's invitation to conflate the two transfers made by Lee in the refinancing transaction and treat them as one for purposes of applying the earmarking defense. To do so would ignore what actually occurred in the transaction and disregard the Bankruptcy Code's plain meaning.

Second, applying earmarking to the transfer of a lien interest — as opposed to a transfer of funds — extends the doctrine beyond its logical limits. A debtor's grant of a mortgage lien in a refinancing transaction does not involve a transfer of "earmarked" property. Here, Lee did not serve as a conduit for the transfer of property from a third party to Chase. Rather, the transfer challenged by the Trustee — Lee's grant of a mortgage to Chase — was most assuredly that of a property interest owned and controlled by the Debtor.

Third, to successfully invoke the earmarking defense, a preference defendant must demonstrate that the transfer in question did not result in a diminution of the debtor's bankruptcy estate. Although Chase claims no diminution, it arrives at this conclusion by pointing to its status at the inception of the refinancing transaction, a time when it indisputably had a perfected mortgage on the Property, and its status at the conclusion of the transaction — when it again had a perfected mortgage — and ignoring everything that happened in between. But focusing on the actual transfer at issue, Chase's perfection of the New Mortgage, clearly reveals that Lee's bankruptcy estate was in fact diminished. From the point that the New Loan was made and the Original Mortgage discharged up until such time as the New Mortgage was recorded, Chase did not hold a perfected lien interest. Thus, Chase's subsequent perfection of the New Mortgage diminished Lee's estate because the non-exempt equity in the Property that otherwise would have been available for distribution to Lee's unsecured creditors became encumbered, and unavailable to unsecured creditors, by the New Mortgage that Chase received.

Finally, applying the earmarking doctrine to insulate Chase from preference liability would essentially write § 547(e) out of the Bankruptcy

Code and, in the process, defeat the sound policy the statute was intended to promote—the discouragement of secret liens. By enacting § 547(e) and establishing a definite and firm 10-day time period for lien perfection (now expanded to 30 days by BAPCPA), Congress sought to promote the Bankruptcy Code's policy of discouraging secret liens on property of the estate.

For all these reasons, we conclude that the earmarking doctrine does not protect Chase from preference liability.

. . .

Chase argues that imposing preference liability on it would be unfair and against public policy because the refinancing transaction involved a mere substitution of its New Mortgage for the Original Mortgage and ultimately benefitted the Debtor's other creditors, not Chase. According to Chase, the refinancing reduced the amount of the Debtor's monthly mortgage payments, causing more funds to be available for other creditors. Moreover, Chase argues, it derived no benefit from the refinancing transaction and should not be penalized for assisting the Debtor in his attempt to avoid bankruptcy. However, "whatever equitable powers remain in the bankruptcy courts must and can only be exercised within the confines of the Bankruptcy Code." Norwest Bank Worthington v. Ahlers, 485 U.S. 197, 206, 108 S. Ct. 963, 99 L. Ed. 2d 169 (1988).

The problems that arise when courts effectively rewrite bankruptcy statutes in order to reach a result deemed "equitable" are illustrated by the bankruptcy court's decision that was reversed by In re Lazarus. Apparently recognizing the potentially open-ended effect of its ruling, the bankruptcy court there stated that it was not holding "that the earmarking doctrine necessarily applies to a refinancing transaction where the length of time between the transfer of value to the old creditor and the perfection of the new security interest is so extensive that a material issue of fact has arisen relative to the parties' intention." In re Lazarus, 334 B.R. at 553. But that begs the question: What length of time period would be too extensive—six months, one year, longer? The approach taken by that court, overturned by the First Circuit in In re Lazarus, and the approach advocated by Chase here substitutes the judgment of the courts for that of Congress. Congress, by enacting § 547(e)(2), has determined the appropriate length of time between a creditor's transfer of value and perfection: originally 10 days, now expanded to 30 days by BAPCPA. By hewing to the plain meaning of the Code and respecting Congress's judgment in enacting § 547(e)(2), our holding today fosters predictability in the law of preferences.

Moreover, the result in this case, although arguably harsh, could have readily been prevented by Chase. On this point, our prior decision in In re Lewis is instructive. There, a late-perfecting mortgagee argued that we should apply the doctrine of equitable subrogation to insulate it from preference liability. In re Lewis, 398 F.3d at 746-47. In declining to apply the equitable subrogation doctrine to shield the late-perfecting mortgagee from preference liability, we noted that the mortgagee was a sophisticated creditor facing a problem of its own making:

[The late-perfecting mortgagee] is a sophisticated creditor who had complete control over the recording of the signed mortgage. It offers no explanation for the more than seven-month delay between the signing and recording of the mortgage. Its own negligence led to the dilemma created by the debtor's filing for bankruptcy.

Id. at 747. See also In re Lazarus, 478 F.3d at 16 ("[T]he penalty [of lien avoidance] is not without a general benefit—*pour encourager les autres*—and is easily avoided by recording within 10 days as the statute directed.").

Chase is a sophisticated lender well aware of the consequences of failing to perfect its security interest within the grace period afforded by § 547(e)(2)—a deadline in effect since the enactment of the Bankruptcy Code more than a quarter century ago. We simply are not at liberty to rewrite the Code's preference provision under the rubric of doing equity to protect late-perfecting secured creditors.

III. Conclusion

For the foregoing reasons, we hold that the recording of the New Mortgage is a preferential transfer under § 547(b). Accordingly, we REVERSE the decision of the district court and AFFIRM the opinion of the Bankruptcy Court.

Merritt, Circuit Judge, dissenting.

Our court's opinion in this case, in my judgment, is wrong and further establishes a split in the circuits on the preference issue in mortgage refinancing transactions. I agree with the District Court and the Eighth Circuit in Kaler v. Community First Nat'l Bank (In re Heitkamp), 137 F.3d 1087 (8th Cir. 1998), that we should look to the purpose, consequences, details, and common sense of the complete financing transaction at issue here and not just one little part of the transaction, i.e., the recording of the second mortgage more than 10 days after the execution of the second note and mortgage. We should look to see whether anyone was misled or whether the bankruptcy estate was diminished for reasons prohibited by Congress. . . .

Earmarking defenses have gained in popularity, based on the creditor's appeal to "the equities of the case." But as the Sixth Circuit noted, equity may be in the eye of the beholder, so that substitution of one obligation for another may nonetheless trigger a voidable preference action if the debtor ends up in bankruptcy. The earmarking doctrine does have an intuitive appeal resting on a "no harm—no foul" intuition that the replacement of Siskel with Ebert is a matter of irrelevance to all the other creditors and so does not engage the policies animating the voidable preference rules. But some question whether this analysis is too quick. If Ebert is willing to offer unsecured credit to the debtor—even on the condition that the debtor retire other debt—why is it fair for a third creditor of the debtor (Shalit?) not to be taken out the same way Siskel was? Presumably because the debtor (or maybe Ebert) favors Siskel, but that sort of favoritism is precisely what the voidable preference rules seek to police. As a result, the equitable doctrine of earmarking is far from uniformly embraced, let alone applied.

D.   SETOFF PREFERENCES

For some setoff holders, the amount subject to setoff may fluctuate over time, such as when the setoff right attaches to funds in a debtor's bank account. Just like a floating lien on inventory, the setoff lender may have an incentive for the debtor to "feed" its bank account in the worrisome days before a bankruptcy filing. The drafters of the Code try to police such improvements in position as they do with inventory and receivables lenders. Their tool to do so is § 553(b). This constraint empowers the trustee to recover from an offsetting creditor the amount by which the creditor's setoff position improved during the 90 days before bankruptcy.

While the formula in § 553(b) is similar in concept to that in § 547(c)(5), the application is somewhat different. The most important difference is that the avoidance power applies only if the creditor *actually* offsets before bankruptcy. The patient creditor who holds back from dismembering the debtor in the lookback period and waits until bankruptcy to ask the judge to lift the stay to allow setoff is rewarded. Such a creditor is not required to surrender any improvement in setoff position obtained during the 90-day period, even though the first day order depleting the account by setoff may have the exact same effect. Other than generally promoting patience, the policy at work here remains, shall we say, opaque. Nonetheless, banks that use setoffs seem determined to hang onto this favorable provision. Also worthy of brief note is the long line of exclusions from the operation of § 553. All of the referenced sections deal with financial contracts whose traders have persuaded Congress that they must be excluded from almost all bankruptcy provisions lest the markets crash and the sky fall. See Assignment 17, where we saw their exclusion from the automatic stay.

═══════════════ In re HURT ═══════════════

579 B.R. 765 (Bankr. W.D. Va. 2017)

BLACK, Bankruptcy Judge.
This matter comes before the Court on cross-motions for summary judgment filed by the Debtors, Adam and Jessica Hurt ("Debtors"), and the United States Department of Housing and Urban Development ("HUD"). The Debtors filed an adversary proceeding pursuant to 11 U.S.C. §§ 542(a) and 547(b) seeking to recover a federal tax refund the United States Department of the Treasury ("Treasury") setoff prepetition within ninety (90) days of their petition date in partial satisfaction of a foreclosure deficiency that the Debtors owed to HUD. HUD contends that the setoff is not recoverable under either section, nor is it recoverable under 11 U.S.C. § 553, the provision of the Bankruptcy Code governing setoffs.

On or about March 1, 2011 the male debtor, Adam Andrew Hurt, obtained a Title I loan ("the Loan") from HUD, an agency of the United States, to purchase a manufactured home. . . . The Loan fell into arrears as a result of the Debtors' failure to make payments. As of July 20, 2016, the outstanding balance due on the Loan was $18,301.93. *Id.* at ¶3. On or about August 22, 2016, HUD sent a "Notice of Intent to Collect by Treasury Offset" to the male debtor. No response or objection to the Notice was received by HUD or Treasury in response to the Notice, and HUD referred the matter to the Treasury, an agency of the United States, in October 2016.

Prior to February 23, 2017, the Debtors filed their 2016 income tax return with the Internal Revenue Service, a component agency of the Treasury Department. Because the Debtors had overpaid taxes due to the United States, it was determined that Treasury owed a debt, namely, a tax refund to the Debtors in the amount of $5,267.00. On February 23, 2017, Treasury processed the request from HUD and offset the tax refund amount due to the Debtors and, instead, paid it to HUD to satisfy a portion of the indebtedness due on the Loan. The Debtors filed a Chapter 7 bankruptcy petition on March 3, 2017, listing the tax refund as exempt under Schedule C. . . .

II. *Analysis*

The Debtors ask the Court to enter summary judgment in their favor, contending that they are eligible to recover their 2016 federal income tax refund pursuant to 11 U.S.C. §§ 522 and 542. [The court noted that individual debtors, not the trustee, get to recover voidable preferences or setoffs when the property recovered is exempt, § 522(h), in the exercise of the trustee's turnover power under § 542.—Eds.]

A. 11 U.S.C. § 547 [Is] Not Applicable

The Debtors assert that under § 547 of the Bankruptcy Code, the intercepted funds constitute a preference. . . . [Following many other cases and Supreme Court dictum, the court held that the setoff does not involve a transfer of the debtors' property, the second element in § 547(b), only a refusal of the offsetting party to pay a mutual obligation.—Eds.]

B. The Treasury Did Not Improve Its Position Within the Scope of Section 553(b)

Section 553 of the Bankruptcy Code does not create a right of setoff. Rather, it recognizes a right of setoff established by non-bankruptcy law and establishes limits on the exercise of that right before bankruptcy or during bankruptcy. The Supreme Court in Citizens Bank of Maryland v. Strumpf, 516 U.S. 16 (1995), described the right of setoff as follows: "The right of setoff (also called 'offset') allows entities that owe each other money to apply their mutual debts against each other, thereby avoiding the 'absurdity of making A pay B when B owes A.'" 11 U.S.C. § 506(a) places setoff rights on similar footing to that of a lien holder in terms of secured status. Section 553(b) of the Bankruptcy Code provides a basis for recovering a pre-bankruptcy setoff in which the creditor improved its position within 90 days of bankruptcy. . . .

HUD argues that section 553(b) simply limits a creditor's right of setoff and establishes an "improvement in position" test designed to ensure that a creditor will not improve its position during the 90-day period before bankruptcy and then protect its position by completing a setoff prior to a debtor filing for bankruptcy. *See* 4 *Collier on Bankruptcy* ¶553.09[2] (Alan N. Resnick & Henry J. Sommer eds., 16th ed.). HUD points to the district court's opinion in In re Lopes, [211 B.R. 443, 444 (D.R.I. 1997),] the facts of which are substantially similar to the case at bar. . . .

The Debtors argue that because the setoff occurred within the 90 days of the filing of the petition, Section 553(b) compels the government to turn over the tax refund. They argue that the deficiency amount on the date of the offset was $14,386.38, and the deficiency amount 90 days before the filing of the petition was zero. The Debtors state that the deficiency became $19,653.38 during the 90-day period and the difference between the two amounts, $5,267.00, is the recoverable amount. . . .

Following the analysis in *In re Lopes*, on the first day of the 90-day pre-petition period, which is December 3, 2016, the government did not owe the Debtors any money for their overpayment of taxes in the 2016 tax year. At this point in time, the Debtors owed HUD, an agency of the federal government, $19,653.38 by virtue of their obligations under the loan. There were no mutual debts, therefore no insufficiency arose. The Debtors' refund was only an expectancy. The right to the refund arose at the end of the taxable year to which it relates, in this case, December 31, 2016.

On December 31, 2016, during the 90-day pre-petition period, a mutual debt arose because of overpayment of taxes by the Debtors to the United States. The "insufficiency" established at that time was $14,386.38, the difference between $19,653.38 and the refund due of $5,267.00. "[S]ection 553(b) requires a comparison between the creditor's setoff position at the initial reference point . . . and the day on which any setoff was actually taken." Section 553(b) permits the trustee to recover any improvement in the creditor's position measured by any decrease in the creditor's insufficiency on the date of setoff." On February 23, 2017, when the Treasury processed the request from HUD and offset the tax refund amount due to the Debtors an insufficiency of at least $14,386.38 remained. There was no change favorable to the creditor. If anything, the insufficiency increased with the accrual of interest. HUD did not improve its position over that amount. . . .

Both the Hurts and HUD seemed to agree that while the Hurts owed the government almost $20,000 90 days before bankruptcy, the government at that point had no countervailing obligation to offset. The Hurts concluded that exposure meant the insufficiency was therefore almost 20 "large ones" on that date. The government took the dramatically opposite view that the insufficiency was zero (or perhaps "not applicable"), because there was no "mutual debt" to trigger the term "insufficiency" in the statute as a matter of law. Take a look at § 553(b)(2) and see if you agree. Now pretend the government had just been the traditional setoff party, a bank, and the debtor had no money in its account 90 days before bankruptcy. A big deposit of $20,000 arrives the day before setoff. Would you allow that to be offset, or would you say the bank improved its position under § 553(b)? If you would, would your answer change if the debtor had a penny in the account on the Day T-90? If so, you may have to ask yourself why Congress would intend a different result with the penny. To be sure, the court had to take account of the statutory definition of "insufficiency," § 553(b)(2), which requires a "mutual" debt at the beginning of the calculation, but the text must not be applied absurdly. Could this finally be that special juncture where the court is allowed to consider the purpose of the statute and what makes sense? Regardless of your answer to this contested question, note what may be the more important setoff issue: HUD and IRS may sound like different initials of different creditors, but they are only one creditor with initials often chanted at the Olympic Games.

E. EQUITABLE SUBORDINATION (AND ITS KIN)

The final topic involving preferential treatment of creditors is another equitable doctrine: subordination. A creditor that finds its claim "equitably subordinated" goes to the back of the line and has to wait until everyone else is paid in full before receiving anything (which is the functional equivalent of death): in other words, it's a judicially created "negative" priority, and it offers the DIP another powerful tool in policing creditor conduct. A voidable preference recipient has to spit out the eve-of-bankruptcy payment but still gets to partake in the unsecured creditor's pot (now enhanced by the preference recovery). An equitably subordinated creditor, by contrast, has to give the payment back *and* wait to get paid anything at all — a wait that usually lasts forever.

"Equitable" subordination was developed by bankruptcy courts over the years using their general equitable powers. While some commentators debate whether and to what extent bankruptcy courts possess general equitable authority, the broad statutory grant of power under § 105(a) of the Code now makes this a debate of diminished relevance. Suffice it to say, the term "equity" and its cognates (e.g., equitable) appear no less than 19 times in the Bankruptcy Code. In fact, so accepted is this doctrine that it is explicitly mentioned in § 510(c), although it is a stretch to call this terse reference a "codification" of the doctrine. It remains subject to various judicially crafted tests, jurisdiction by jurisdiction.

Generalizing from the cases, equitable subordination has been applied in some recurrent fact patterns: (1) an insider extracts favorable treatment from the debtor; (2) a seeming outsider acts like an insider (e.g., a bank sending in a "workout officer" to start calling the shots as the debtor runs into trouble) and extracts favorable treatment from the debtor; (3) a creditor does something just too icky for comfort. This last category is important because a recent trend has been for courts to put the "equitable" back into equitable subordination. Although "equitable" probably is meant to refer to the use of the court's equitable power to quash the creditor's claim against the bankruptcy estate, this new trend is to require wrongfulness—inequity—as a trigger.

A doctrine related to equitable subordination (and sometimes subsumed within it) is the power of (equitable) *recharacterization*. This is the traditional substance-over-form power that courts have to enter an order calling something that quacks a duck rather than whatever fowl the parties have named it. See, e.g., In re Vanguard Airlines, Inc., 298 B.R. 626, 636-37 (Bankr. W.D. Mo. 2003) ("Pursuant to the express wording of the statute, the prohibition on the Court's power is limited to actions by the secured party, lessor or conditional vendor. . . . There is no prohibition in the statute preventing the court from exercising its equitable power to recharacterize a creditor's interest as something *other than* a secured party, lessor, or conditional vendor.") (emphasis added). This longstanding equitable power has been codified in familiar statutory contexts, too, such as the classic example of the power to recharacterize a purported lease as a security interest. UCC § 1-203. Recharacterization might lead to subordination of a creditor's claim if, for example, a business insider tries to mask what is clearly an equity investment into a company as a "loan" in the hopes of getting paid back with the creditors pro rata in bankruptcy. See In re Carolee's Combine, 3 B.R. 324 (Bankr. N.D. Ga. 1980) (calling such a scheme "inventive" in invoking equitable subordination of the investor's claims).

Equitable subordination should not be confused with commonplace *contractual subordination*, which arises when lenders by contract agree to subordinate a higher priority loan to a lower one. For example, a secured lender may want a struggling debtor to survive but not enough to pour more money into the company. All states' laws (and Article 9) allow the prior lender to subordinate its lien voluntarily to a new lender that might be willing to throw the debtor a bone. The subordinated creditor pledges not to take any distribution from the debtor until the other creditor has been paid in full (and to hand over any payments received from the debtor for whatever reason). The Code blesses these arrangements. § 510(a). But equitable subordination remains a murkier and more controversial doctrine on which courts sometimes diverge in their applications.

In re SI RESTRUCTURING, INC.

532 F.3d 355 (5th Cir. 2008)

DAVIS, Circuit Judge.

. . .

This dispute arises from the loans made by John and Jeffrey Wooley ("the Wooleys") to Schlotzsky's, Inc. ("Schlotzsky's"). At the time of the events giving rise to this appeal, the Wooleys were officers and directors and the largest shareholders of Schlotzsky's. In order to relieve a critical cash crunch faced by Schlotzsky's, the Wooleys made two loans to the corporation: one in April 2003 for $1 million and another in November 2003 for $2.5 million.

The Wooleys made the April loan after other financing options fell through. This loan was secured with the company's royalty streams from franchisees, the company's intellectual property rights, and other intangible property. Schlotzsky's and the Wooleys were represented by separate legal counsel for the April loan negotiations. The loan terms were approved by the audit committee and Schlotzsky's board of directors as a related-party transaction, and the transaction was disclosed in the company's filings with the SEC.

Throughout 2003, the company continued to experience severe cash flow problems, and the Wooleys continued their efforts to obtain financing. The board of directors was keenly aware of these efforts. In the fall of 2003, Schlotzsky's general counsel approached the International Bank of Commerce ("IBC") about a loan to the company. IBC declined to make the loan to the company but agreed to allow the Wooleys to borrow the funds directly from the bank so that the Wooleys could, in turn, lend the proceeds to Schlotzsky's. The need for this additional financing and the possibility of this loan by the Wooleys was discussed at an October 31, 2003 board meeting. The loan to the company was approved by the board and made on November 13, 2003.

In finding the Wooleys' conduct to be inequitable, the bankruptcy court focused on this second loan ("the November loan") and attached significance to the short notice given to the board for approval. IBC formally approved the loan to the Wooleys on November 10, 2003. The following day, the board was provided notice of a special meeting scheduled for November 13, 2003 to approve the Wooleys' loan to the company. Before the special meeting, the board members were provided with copies of the proposed promissory note and the security agreement along with e-mails from the company's assistant general counsel. As with the April loan, the November loan was secured with the company's rights to the royalty streams from franchisees, intellectual property rights, and, and general intangibles.

When the loan was made, the Wooleys had in place personal guarantees which guaranteed pre-existing Schlotzsky's debt in the amount of $4.3 million. As part of the November loan package, the Wooleys also secured this potential liability under the guarantees with the same collateral that secured the April and November loans.

At the November 13, 2003 board meeting, conducted via telephone conference call, the board was told that without the infusion of additional funds, payroll could not be met and that the company would default on a payment to a secured creditor. All of the non-interested directors in attendance approved the loan without objection. An independent audit committee also approved the loan, and the transaction was publicly disclosed in SEC filings.

In mid-2004, the Wooleys were removed as officers of the corporation and resigned their positions as directors. The financial condition of the company deteriorated further, and a Chapter 11 Bankruptcy proceeding was filed in August 2004. The Wooleys filed secured claims relating to the April and November loans. The committee of unsecured creditors brought an adversary proceeding against the Wooleys, challenging their right to be treated as secured creditors with respect to these claims.

The bankruptcy court found that John and Jeffrey Wooley, as fiduciaries, engaged in inequitable conduct in relation to the November transaction and that their conduct conferred an unfair advantage upon them. This inequitable conduct stemmed from a breach of fiduciary duties that the Wooleys owed to Schlotzsky's as officers and directors. According to the bankruptcy court, the Wooleys breached their fiduciary duties in part by the manner in which they presented the November loan transaction to the board. The court found that the transaction was presented as the only option available, at the eleventh hour, as a *fait accompli*. In other words, the board was given the option, "approve the loan or the company collapses tomorrow." Additionally, the judge questioned why the Wooleys required that the loan be secured if it was truly meant to be a temporary loan to secure permanent financing. By securing the loan with the income stream of the franchise company, the crown jewel of the Schlotzsky's complex, the bankruptcy court concluded that the Wooleys "grabbed for as much as they could get[,] and they got it all." The final straw to the bankruptcy court was the Wooleys' insistence on securing their pre-existing contingent liability on their personal guarantees with the revenue stream of the franchise company. The bankruptcy court found that securing the Wooleys' contingent liability effectively released them as guarantors on the debt at the expense of the corporation and its unsecured creditors. In the words of the bankruptcy court: "[t]hat's unfair advantage." The bankruptcy court, however, made no specific findings that the Wooleys' actions in securing either of the 2003 loans or their pre-existing contingent liability on the guarantees resulted in harm to the corporation or to the unsecured creditors.

The bankruptcy court ordered that the Wooleys' claims based on both the April and November loans be equitably subordinated and thus converted from secured to unsecured status. The district court agreed with the bankruptcy court and affirmed. The Wooleys then lodged this appeal.

. . .

Appellants argue that the bankruptcy court's application of the "extraordinary remedy" of equitable subordination is not warranted in this case. The Wooleys assert that none of the bankruptcy court's findings of inequitable conduct relate to the April transaction and that the court's findings do not support subordination of their claim based on this loan. They also argue that they did not act inequitably in structuring the loan to the corporation as they did and that the record does not support the finding that they breached their fiduciary obligations. They contend that their November loan to Schlotzsky's was an arms-length transaction with approval of the board, including disinterested directors and independent audit committee members. They point out that the company had its own in-house counsel and outside securities counsel who reviewed the transaction. The Wooleys assert that all members of the board of directors and audit committee knew of the precarious financial condition of the company, that they were not surprised about the urgent need for the loan, and that the bankruptcy court improperly faulted them for obtaining the board's quick approval of the transaction. They argue that the bankruptcy court improperly found that the transaction occurred at the "eleventh hour" or that the timing of the loan justified equitable subordination of the Wooleys' claims.

The Wooleys also assert that they did nothing improper in negotiating an agreement with the company to obtain security as a condition of making the loan. The Wooleys contend that no evidence was presented that the November transaction resulted in an unfair advantage to them. They contend that the bankruptcy court's conclusion amounts to a *per se* rule that an insider creditor cannot obtain security for a loan or for preexisting contingent liability from a solvent company. The Wooleys emphasize that the bankruptcy court found that the November loan was real money that was used by the company to pay off its debts, and it, therefore, benefitted the company's creditors. We now turn to a consideration of the law that applies to the issues these arguments raise. . . .

The Bankruptcy Code does not otherwise set forth the circumstances under which equitable subordination is appropriate; however, the case law has formulated a number of requirements to guide courts in their application of this remedy. This Court in [Benjamin v. Diamond (In re Mobile Steel Corp.), 536 F.2d 692, 700 (5th Cir. 1977)], articulated the widely quoted three-prong test for equitable subordination: (1) the claimant must have engaged in inequitable conduct; (2) the misconduct must have resulted in injury to the creditors of the bankrupt or conferred an unfair advantage on the claimant; and (3) equitable subordination of the claim must not be inconsistent with the provisions of the Bankruptcy Code. In re Mobile Steel Corp. adds an additional requirement, critical to the decision in this case: a claim should be subordinated only to the extent necessary to offset the harm which the debtor or its creditors have suffered as a result of the inequitable conduct. . . .

The bankruptcy court made no findings of inequitable conduct by the Wooleys with respect to the April loan. As to the November transactions, we assume, without deciding, that the record supports the finding of inequitable conduct and unfair advantage. However, the bankruptcy court made no finding of harm, and the record does not support a finding that either the debtor or the unsecured creditors were harmed by the November transaction.

Appellee argues that when the company secured the Wooleys' loan with the assets of Schlotzsky's Franchisor, L.L.C., this reduced the assets available to the unsecured creditors and injured them. This argument fails because neither the record nor the bankruptcy court's findings support a view that general unsecured creditors as a class were harmed. Indeed, the bankruptcy court found that the proceeds of the loan were used to pay the unsecured creditors and keep the company in operation. . . .

Because the loan proceeds were used to pay current unsecured creditors, unsecured creditors, as a class, were not harmed when the Wooleys obtained security for the November loan. The general unsecured creditors who were paid from the proceeds of the November loan may have benefitted to the detriment of another group of unsecured creditors, but this does not mean that unsecured creditors were harmed when the Wooleys obtained security for their loan. Further, the unsecured creditors who remain unpaid have advanced no theory supporting a view that they were entitled to payment over the creditors who were paid from the proceeds of the April and November loans. . . .

Appellee further argues that by [securing] their existing personal guarantees, the Wooleys were effectively released from liability for the guarantees, thus securing an unfair advantage. This argument could have merit if the company had defaulted on the underlying debt and the Wooleys' potential liability under the guarantees had been triggered. The record reveals, however, that the Wooleys' potential obligation on the guaranty agreements was never triggered because the company never defaulted on its principal obligation covered by the guarantees. Because no claim ever arose on these guarantees, no harm resulted.

Appellee also asserts that the unsecured creditors were harmed because the value of the company deteriorated as a result of the November loan transaction, thus decreasing the amount of funds available for the creditors. Although Appellee denies seeking damages under a "deepening insolvency theory," the expert on which appellee relies to quantify the harm acknowledged that his calculation was based on this theory. Deepening insolvency has been defined as prolonging an insolvent corporation's life through bad debt, causing the dissipation of corporate assets.

Appellee's expert estimated the value of the company at the time of the November 2003 loan and conducted a later evaluation in August of 2004, at the time the bankruptcy petition was filed. He testified that because the Wooleys made the November loan to the company, the company lost value and unsecured creditors were damaged as a result. He suggests that the Wooleys lent $2.5 million to the company in the face of obvious evidence that the financial condition of the company was deteriorating and they had no reason to believe that the loan would allow the company to survive. He assessed the lost value at $3.5 million.

The bankruptcy court did not accept this testimony. The court recognized that the Wooleys were "highly committed" to keeping the company going, and in its oral reasons the bankruptcy court stated: "Did they try to continue to make the company work? Yes, of course, they did. I have no question about that. Did they try to put this company back together? Yes, of course, they did."

A deepening insolvency theory of damages has been criticized and rejected by many courts. We agree with the Third Circuit Court of Appeals, which recently concluded that deepening insolvency is not a valid theory of damages. [See In re CitX Corp., 448 F.3d 672, 678 (3d Cir. 2006).] The court recognized that deepening insolvency as a measure of harm depends on how the company uses the proceeds of the loan in question and "looks at the issue through hindsight bias." [Id.; see also High McDonald et al., Lafferty's Orphan: The Abandonment of Deepening Insolvency, Am. Bankr. Inst. J., Dec. 2007/Jan. 2008, at 59.]

In the Delaware Court of Chancery, the doctrine of deepening insolvency as an independent cause of action or as a theory of damages was also considered and rejected:

> Even when a firm is insolvent, its directors may, in the appropriate exercise of their business judgment, take action that might, if it does not pan out, result in the firm being painted in a deeper hue of red. The fact that the residual claimants of the firm at that time are creditors does not mean that the directors cannot choose to continue the firm's operations in the hope that they can expand the inadequate pie such that the firm's creditors get a greater recovery. By doing so, the directors do not become a guarantor of success. . . .

[The court is quoting Trenwick America Litigation Trust v. Ernst & Young, LLP, 906 A.2d 168 (Del. Ch. 2006), which the Delaware Supreme Court affirmed in an order adopting Vice-Chancellor's Strine's opinion.—Eds.]

The bankruptcy court made no finding that the company was under-capitalized or insolvent. The bankruptcy court's findings on this point, which are fully supported by the record, undermine the expert's conclusion that the loans caused deepening insolvency. In sum, the Trustee's deepening insolvency theory—in addition to having little legal support—is not supported by the record or the bankruptcy court's findings.

CONCLUSION

The bankruptcy court made no finding that the Wooleys breached any obligations to the company or its creditors or that they engaged in inequitable conduct of any kind in connection with the April loan. With respect to the November loan, the bankruptcy court made no finding that Appellants' transactions with the debtor caused harm to either the debtor or the unsecured creditors. We have carefully considered the Trustee's damage theories and conclude that none are legally cognizable or supported by the record. Thus, neither claim should have been subordinated.

═══════════
═══════════

The Wooleys got caught right in the middle of the tension that runs through bankruptcy: what benefits one creditor (getting paid now) may hurt others (those who are owed payments when the business later collapses). The bankruptcy judge saw harm to current creditors, while the Fifth Circuit saw the benefit of another chance for the business to survive—and plenty of benefit to the creditors who were paid off.

The opinion also discusses the tort of deepening insolvency, popular in some foreign jurisdictions but not in Delaware. Trenwick America Litigation Trust v. Ernst & Young, LLP, 906 A.2d 168, 205 (Del. Ch. 2006) ("[T]he fact of insolvency does not render the concept of 'deepening insolvency' a more logical one than the concept of 'shallowing profitability.'"); but cf. Official Committee of Unsecured Creditors v. Baldwin (In re Lemington Home for the Aged), 659 F.3d 282 (3d Cir. 2011) (reaffirming existence of cause of action for deepening insolvency under Pennsylvania law). The premise of the tort is that by artificially prolonging the life of a debtor beyond its natural death, the principals harm the corporation (and, indirectly, its stakeholders). Creditors, for example, might have incurred smaller losses if the company had been shut down or sold while it still had some unencumbered assets or potential as an ongoing business. Hostility toward the tort stems from concerns about hindsight bias, so some jurisdictions permit it only in situations of intentional misconduct (but we question whether this simply collapses it into fraud or breach of fiduciary duty). The United Kingdom and a number of Commonwealth countries have a doctrine of "wrongful trading" (or "fraudulent trading"). Roughly, this doctrine makes directors liable if a company continues in business after the directors should have known it was insolvent and unlikely to survive. Germany and other civil law countries have analogous rules.

In the United States, deepening insolvency is a kindred spirit to another state law tort: lender liability, under which a lender can get tagged for wrongfully killing a debtor's business (e.g., by calling a loan in bad faith that results in the debtor's business going bust). See, e.g., K.M.C. Co. v. Irving Trust Co., 757 F.2d 752, 766 (6th Cir. 1985) (affirming $7.5 million verdict). Such an action—more often threatened than invoked—freaks the heck out of banks because unlike a voidable preference or even an equitably subordinated claim, when the maximum downside is zero recovery, a tort judgment of liability for unjust destruction of a business is unrelated to the cost of the loan; it's the going-concern cost of the business, which could be orders of magnitude more than the loan. State torts, like deepening insolvency and lender liability, creep into the DIP's arsenal by way of § 544(b), which gives it the state-law rights of a creditor.

Considering all these actions together, one might think of a continuum of bad news to a creditor: lien avoidance (lose priority treatment), voidable preference (disgorge money received), equitable subordination (get paid last), and finally tort liability (pay money to the debtor who originally borrowed money). The facts will sometimes support more than one option. Sometimes more extreme ones are alleged than best fit the facts—even when a knock-down argument exists for a lesser one—simply to spook creditors and increase debtor leverage in negotiations.

Problem Set 22

22.1. David Sheinfeld is president and owner of 50% of the stock of Sheinfeld's Model Trains Inc. A large highway has virtually cut off access to the model train store. The business has rocked around for several months, making some late payments, having some of the inventory repossessed, and so forth. On April 20, Sheinfeld, as president, repaid himself for an unsecured loan of $22,000 that he had made to the company. This transaction completely wiped out the last of the liquid assets in the business. In the ten weeks since that time, Sheinfeld has simply quit paying the store's bills.

A group of the train store's creditors visit you on July 15 for advice. One found out about the large payment to Sheinfeld, and they are ready to act. What do you advise? Does it matter whether they file an involuntary petition now or later? See § 547(b), (f), UVTA § 5(b).

22.2. Wendorf's Hardware was a small, family-owned hardware store. Two new, large home centers moved into the same locality, and Wendorf's was insolvent for several months before filing for chapter 7. Eric Wendorf, the owner and president, was especially upset about the injury to some of his creditors, including Granny Wendorf, who made a $200,000 unsecured loan to the business, and First Oregon City Bank, which extended $300,000 in unsecured credit and whose president is a golfing buddy of Eric's. Eric doesn't feel at all bad, however, about some of his other creditors, including Minnesota Manufacturing, a materials supplier and unsecured creditor for $450,000, and Rebecca Marston, a local painter who did extensive remodeling for Wendorf's and who is still owed $50,000, but who got into an argument with Eric over paint splatters on the store's inventory.

Eric Wendorf recently obtained a $500,000 loan from New York Bank to consolidate some of the store's debt, giving the bank a lien on the company's forklifts, display cases, and other equipment, worth about $600,000. The bank recorded its security interest and wired checks directly to Granny Wendorf and First Oregon repaying their loans in full. Two months later Wendorf's Hardware filed for bankruptcy. Can the trustee recover the payments to Granny and First Oregon? If so, would the result be different if New York Bank had not taken the security interest on the debt? See §§ 541(a), 547(b), (i), UVTA § 5(b).

22.3. Your firm represents Consolidated Bank. Angelika Glogowski is the bank's loan officer for Matthew Thornburg's Major Mobile, Inc., a local mobile-home dealer that is in financial trouble. Angelika calls the partner you work for, explaining that she is about to set off against the company's account with Consolidated in order to stem its likely loan losses, but thought she should check with the firm first. The partner has transferred the call to you. What questions should you ask Angelika? Be ready to advise her when she answers them.

22.4. You represent Liberty Bank, working chiefly with its commercial accounts. Liberty consults you about an open line of credit it has maintained with Tulsa Pool Supplies and Service. The current balance on the loan is $900,000 and Tulsa Pool is four months behind on its payments. The loan is secured by Tulsa Pool's inventory of pool chemicals and supplies.

The bank officials monitoring the loan have tried to pressure Tulsa Pool into paying on the loan by threatening to call the loan. Tulsa Pool points out that it is now barely the "pool season" (it is May), but that they have geared up for an active summer. In late April they were able to make an extremely favorable purchase of pool chemicals on unsecured credit (which the bank officials feel sure has not been paid). The purchase boosted the value of the inventory on hand from $300,000 to $1 million, most of which still remains in the store.

The bank thinks that the business has been insolvent for quite some time and that it is not going to survive. They see that the business's checking account is overdrawn and that two paychecks have just been dishonored. Because the loan payments are late, the analysts have recommended that the bank call the loan and repossess the collateral. What do you advise?

22.5. A. Big Rig Equipment is an Oklahoma rental company that has been insolvent for several months. It decided to take a final gamble and order ten new pieces of heavy equipment, begin an aggressive advertising campaign, trim its office staff, etc. A John Deere dealership was willing to finance the sale of ten new pieces of industrial and farming equipment to the business, taking a purchase money security interest in the new equipment. The deal worked as follows:

On July 1 Big Rig placed the order for the equipment (specifications in the contract) and agreed to pay $2 million, giving John Deere a security interest in the new equipment.

On July 12 the equipment was identified to the Big Rig contract at the JD factory.

On July 20 custom work was completed.

On July 24 the equipment was delivered to the local dealer.

On July 28 the dealer delivered the equipment to Big Rig.

On August 21 the JD dealership filed a financing statement in the Office of the Secretary of State as required under Oklahoma law to perfect properly.

Sadly, Big Rig's new plans never got off the ground, and on September 30 it filed for chapter 11. The only valuable asset in the estate is the new equipment. Oklahoma has adopted the standard version of Article 9. Does JD get the equipment? See § 547(b), (c)(3), (e)(2).

B. Liberty National Bank has an outstanding, perfected security interest in all of Big Rig's equipment, current and after-acquired, under a financing agreement that was duly perfected more than a year ago. When the Big Rig case is converted to a chapter 7, the bank files a motion to lift the stay so it can sell the equipment, citing its superior lien. Does it win? See § 551, UCC § 9-317(e).

22.6. Audrey Roberts runs "Audrey's," a hair salon, and has a $50,000 term loan from Norris Cole & Associates, a local factoring agent specializing in small business loans. Norris's loan is secured by a duly perfected lien on Audrey's salon equipment, such as specialty hairdryers, and has an after-acquired property clause. Sadly, David Platt, Audrey's grandson who works with Audrey and to whom she is slowly turning over the reins, has made some highly questionable decisions. The salon has now filed for chapter 11, after having been insolvent for four months.

In the 90 days before the filing: (1) Norris received an extraordinary payment of $10,000 on its loan, reducing the balance to $40,000, and (2) an unusual new hairdryer worth $10,000 was purchased on unsecured credit, increasing the total equipment value to $50,000. Ken Barlow is another creditor of the salon. He has come to you to see if you can get any of these transfers to Norris undone. Can you? See § 547(b).

FRAUDULENT CONVEYANCES I

Fraudulent conveyances may seem to have an evocatively self-explanatory moniker—asset transfers tinged with fraud—and there certainly is no shortage of sketchy asset-hiding. But the doctrine also has a broader reach than you might think. We'll start at the beginning, because shifty debtors are as old as time—or at least as old as recorded common law.

A. HISTORY OF FRAUDULENT CONVEYANCE LAW

TWYNE'S CASE

3 Coke 806, 76 Eng. Rep. 809 (Star Chamber, 1601)

In an information by Coke, the Queen's Attorney General, against Twyne of Hampshire, in the Star-Chamber, for making and publishing of a fraudulent gift of goods: the case on the stat. of 13 Eliz. cap. 5. was such; Pierce was indebted to Twyne in four hundred pounds, and was indebted also to C. in two hundred pounds. C. brought an action of debt against Pierce, and pending the writ, Pierce being possessed of goods and chattels of the value of three hundred pounds, in secret made a general deed of gift of all his goods and chattels real and personal whatsoever to Twyne, in satisfaction of his debt; notwithstanding that Pierce continued in possession of the said goods, and some of them he sold; and he shore the sheep, and marked them with his own mark: and afterwards C. had judgment against Pierce, and had a *fieri facias* directed to the Sheriff of Southampton, who by force of the said writ came to make execution of the said goods; but divers persons, by the command of the said Twyne, did with force resist the said sheriff, claiming them to be the goods of the said Twyne by force of the said gift; and openly declared by the commandment of Twyne, that it was a good gift, and made on a good and lawful consideration. And whether this gift on the whole matter, was fraudulent and of no effect by the said Act of 13 Eliz. or not, was the question. And it was resolved by Sir Thomas Egerton, Lord Keeper of the Great Seal, and by the Chief Justice Popham and Anderson, and the whole Court of Star Chamber, that this gift was fraudulent, within the statute of 13 Eliz. And in this case divers points were resolved:

1st. That this gift had the signs and marks of fraud, because the gift is general, without exception of his apparel, or any thing of necessity; for it is commonly said, *quod dolus versatur in generalibus.*

2nd. The donor continued in possession, and used them as his own; and by reason thereof he traded and trafficked with others, and defrauded and deceived them.

3rd. It was made in secret, *et dona clandestina sunt semper suspiciosa.*

4th. It was made pending the writ.

5th. Here was a trust between the parties, for the donor possessed all, and used them as his proper goods, and fraud is always apparelled and clad with a trust, and a trust is the cover of fraud.

6th. The deed contains, that the gift was made honestly, truly, and *bona fide; et clausulae inconsuet semper inducunt suspicionem.*

Secondly, it was resolved, that notwithstanding here was a true debt due to Twyne, and a good consideration of the gift, yet it was not within the proviso of the said Act of 13 Eliz. by which it is provided, that the said Act shall not extend to any estate or interest in lands, &c. goods or chattels made on a good consideration and *bona fide;* for although it is on a true and good consideration, yet it is not *bona fide,* for no gift shall be deemed to be *bona fide* within the said proviso which is accompanied with any trust; as if a man be indebted to five several persons, in the several sums of twenty pounds, and hath goods of the value of twenty pounds, and makes a gift of all his goods to one of them in satisfaction of his debt, but there is a trust between them, that the donee shall deal favorably with him in regard of his poor estate, either to permit the donor, or some other for him, or for his benefit, to use or have possession of them, and is contented that he shall pay him his debt when he is able; this shall not be called *bona fide* within the said proviso; for the proviso saith on a good consideration, and *bona fide;* so a good consideration doth not suffice, if it be not also *bona fide:* and therefore, reader, when any gift shall be to you in satisfaction of a debt, by one who is indebted to others also; 1st, Let it be made in a public manner, and before the neighbors, and not in private, for secrecy is a mark of fraud. 2nd, Let the goods and chattels be appraised by good people to the very value, and take a gift in particular in satisfaction of your debt. 3rd, Immediately after the gift, take the possession of them; for continuance of the possession in the donor, is a sign of trust. . . .

The Statute of Fraudulent Conveyances, 13 Eliz. c.5, 1571, was passed to protect creditors against debtors who would obstruct collection efforts by conveying away all their property, usually with an intent to have it reconveyed back to them at a future date. The statute was supplemented by a second act against fraudulent conveyances, designed to protect purchasers, in 27 Eliz. c.4, 1584-1585. Both statutes imposed fines for fraudulent conveyances and permitted the court to set such transfers aside.

Much of the subsequent case law turned on whether there had been sufficient proof of the debtor's "intent to delay, hinder or defraud" creditors or purchasers. Courts dealt with the difficult problems of proof by developing the "badges of fraud" that raise a presumption (rebuttable or otherwise) that the transaction was fraudulent. One obvious factual setting that raises the presumption of fraud is a sale or gift without transfer of possession. Recall that blackguard Pierce, notwithstanding his purported gift to Twyne, had shorn the sheep and marked them as if they were his own. This presumption has had an enormous impact on the development of non-possessory security interests, inspiring a judicial hostility to such interests that persisted well into the twentieth century. The problem can be seen by imagining a replay of *Twyne's Case*, but with Pierce saying he had granted a lien on all his sheep to Twyne, and so although it looked to C. like Pierce had all sorts of property, he was actually leveraged up to the chops in mut-tonly security interests. This problem of creditors' potential deception by "secret liens" was solved with public filing requirements, and as discussed before in Assignment 20, the strong arm clause is thought by many to be the key to ensuring compliance with that public filing requirement.

American jurisdictions adopted the Statute of Elizabeth either by enacting statutes based on it or through the common law. In the 1910s, the National Conference of Commissioners on Uniform Laws drafted a uni-form act to clarify the substantive issues and streamline the procedures: the Uniform Fraudulent Conveyance Act (UFCA). In 1984, a new statute was promulgated to replace the UFCA, the Uniform Fraudulent Transfer Act (UFTA), which in 2014 changed its name to the less-pejorative Uniform Voidable Transactions Act. The UVTA has been adopted in 22 states, but some have not gotten around to it yet. And some, such as Maryland, have resisted and clung to the UFCA. (New York just caved as of 2020 and dumped the UFCA for the UVTA.) While the core principles are similar between UFCA and UVTA, with many of the changes being in the nature of technical and procedural clarifications, the differences can sometimes be outcome dispositive. See In re Panepinto, 487 B.R. 370 (Bankr. W.D.N.Y. 2013) (holding that transfer of exemptible homestead could be attacked under New York's UFCA statute, despite widespread authority that a trans-fer of exemptible property cannot be fraudulent under then-UFTA).

B.   ACTUAL INTENT FRAUD

The UVTA is mercifully short compared to the Code. It can be deceptively complex to apply, however, and sometimes one has the additional diffi-culty of a factually dense transaction. Structurally, there are several liabil-ity sections. We begin with one of the biggies—liability for actual fraud, proven by intent under § 4(a), often with help of the tools in § 4(b) that codify (after 300 years) a modern version of the old badges of fraud begun in *Twyne's Case*.

ACLI GOVERNMENT SECURITIES, INC. v. RHOADES
653 F. Supp. 1388 (S.D.N.Y. 1987)

LASKER, District Judge.

This case concerns the validity of a conveyance of property from defendant Daniel Rhoades to his sister defendant Norma Rhoades, which occurred the day before a judgment of over $1,500,000 was entered against Daniel Rhoades in favor of plaintiff ACLI Government Securities, Inc. ("AGS") in ACLI Government Securities, Inc. v. Rhoades, 81 Civ. 2555 (MEL) ("the AGS securities action"). After hearing the testimony of six witnesses and examining a number of documents presented at a three-day non-jury trial, I conclude that the conveyance was fraudulent and that AGS is entitled to judgment accordingly.

The significant facts are not in dispute. AGS is a government securities trader. Daniel and Norma Rhoades, both New York State residents and attorneys licensed to practice in New York, are brother and sister who are also partners in the law firm of Rhoades & Rhoades. After a lengthy jury trial, on May 10, 1983 the jury in the AGS securities action returned a verdict in favor of AGS and against Mr. Rhoades in the amount of $1,285,598.28. On May 20, 1983, a judgment on the verdict against Mr. Rhoades was signed and it was filed three days later. After a technical amendment, the total judgment was for $1,519,898.59, of which $1,385,401.06 plus post-judgment interest remains outstanding and unpaid.

On June 30, 1959, Daniel and Norma Rhoades became the owners of the property which is the subject of this suit, consisting of 68 acres of land located at Route 124 and Turk Hill Road in Brewster, Putnam County, New York ("the Putnam County Property"), as "tenants-in-common, Daniel Rhoades having an undivided three-fifths . . . thereof . . . and Norma Rhoades having an undivided two-fifths . . . thereof." In 1981-1982 a house was constructed on the property, and as of May, 1983, the property was appraised to have a value of $325,000. On May 19, 1983, the day before the judgment against Daniel Rhoades referred to above was signed, defendants executed a deed in which Daniel and Norma Rhoades conveyed the Putnam County property to Norma Rhoades, for $1.00 and unspecified "other good consideration." . . .

Defendants contend that the May 1983 conveyance was based on fair consideration because it was in satisfaction of an antecedent debt owed by Daniel Rhoades to Norma Rhoades. Ms. Rhoades testified at trial that she had entrusted her brother with half a million dollars in treasury bonds so that he could convert them from 4.25 percent to 9 percent treasury bonds via his AGS account, and that the bonds were never returned to her. The only proof offered of this transaction was evidence that Norma Rhoades owned $40,000 of over $350,000 in treasury bonds that Daniel Rhoades had forwarded to his AGS account in August-September 1980. . . .

The evidence here was not sufficient to establish the existence of *any* antecedent debt, let alone a debt proportionate to Mr. Rhoades' interest in the Putnam County property. First, while on deposition Ms. Rhoades stated that she "loaned" bonds to her brother, at trial she testified that she "entrusted them" to her brother "[t]o return to [her] 9 percent Treasury Bonds or an equivalent amount." Ms. Rhoades' trial testimony, then, suggests the conclusion that the transaction between her and her brother, if any, was a bailment rather than a loan. Furthermore, even if Norma Rhoades did make bonds available to her brother, this would not necessarily have created a creditor-debtor relationship between them. . . . Finally, Daniel Rhoades' own statements and those of his counsel further support the conclusion that he was not in debt to his sister at the time of the conveyance. In December 1982, Mr. Rhoades' then-attorney represented that he was unaware of any significant liabilities faced by Mr. Rhoades, and Mr. Rhoades himself swore out an affidavit on the issue of his financial condition which failed to mention any debt owed to Norma Rhoades.

In sum, the evidence presented on the transfer of bonds from Norma to Daniel Rhoades established at most a bailment of indeterminate size, and I conclude that there was no antecedent debt owed by Daniel Rhoades to Norma Rhoades which could have served as fair consideration for the conveyance of property in question. . . .

> Every conveyance made . . . with actual intent . . . to hinder, delay, or defraud either present or future creditors, is fraudulent. . . .

N.Y. Debt. & Cred. Law § 276 (McKinney 1945) [see UVTA § 4(a)(1)—Eds.]. The burden of proof to establish "actual intent" is on the creditor who seeks to set aside the conveyance, and he must do so by clear and convincing evidence. Actual fraudulent intent, by its very nature, is rarely susceptible to direct proof, and normally is established by inference from the circumstances surrounding the allegedly fraudulent act. Factors from which fraudulent intent can be inferred include (1) a close relationship among the parties to the transaction; (2) secrecy and haste of the sale; (3) inadequacy of consideration; and (4) the transferor's knowledge of the creditor's claim and his own inability to pay it [see UVTA § 4(b)—Eds.]. In this case, I find and conclude that the conveyance of the Putnam County property was made by Daniel Rhoades with actual intent to defraud AGS, and that Norma Rhoades knew of his intent.

This case has all of the classic indicia of fraudulent intent. Intrafamily transfers are scrutinized carefully, and Daniel and Norma Rhoades are not only brother and sister but have been law partners together for almost forty years. Both defendants knew of the jury verdict against Daniel Rhoades at the time of the conveyance. Indeed, Norma Rhoades testified on deposition that she demanded that her brother turn over his interest in the property to her precisely because she was angry "that a verdict had been rendered in this matter, an unconscionable verdict, which was full of error," and she was concerned that "a sheriff should not come up and try to sell this interest improperly." Second, the conveyance was made in secret, and was contrary to the court order of December 15, 1982, which required Daniel Rhoades to notify counsel and the court before transferring any assets. Moreover, the timing of the transaction, which occurred nine days after the jury verdict against Mr. Rhoades was announced and one day before judgment was signed against him, could not more strongly support the finding of fraudulent intent. Finally to be noted are the inadequacy of consideration involved and Daniel Rhoades' knowledge of his inability to pay the judgment. . . .

In sum, I conclude that AGS has established by clear and convincing evidence that the defendants' joint intent in conveying Daniel Rhoades' interest in the Putnam County property to Norma Rhoades was to defraud AGS, and that the conveyance was fraudulent under N.Y. Debt. & Cred. Law § 276 [see UVTA § 4(a)(1)—Eds.].

Norma Rhoades claims that if the conveyance is declared fraudulent she is nevertheless entitled to an equitable lien on the property in the amount of the property taxes, maintenance and utility bills she has paid since the conveyance took place. . . . Even if Ms. Rhoades were entitled, despite her participation in the fraud, to an equitable lien on the property, a conclusion which is far from obvious, she would be entitled only to reimbursement for expenses essential to the preservation of the property and for tax payments beyond the reasonable value of her use and occupation of the land. Here, there is no evidence that the $50,000 paid by Norma Rhoades in taxes for the Putnam County property for the years 1983 through 1987 exceeds the fair rental value of the estate for four years, nor that payment of the other bills was essential for the preservation of the property. . . .

The cheerful-sounding "badges of fraud" are not the sort earned by Cub Scouts. Rather, they serve as recognition, true since Elizabethan times, that few inclined to fraud will memorialize their intent with direct evidence. In fact, "actual intent" fraud is so hotly contested that defendants sometimes insist on their jury trial rights. (One wonders whether Daniel and Norma Rhoades still view juries with such favor, given their alleged capacity to generate unconscionable verdicts riddled with error.) Here's one loveless court that found actual intent fraud more recently. In Citizen State Bank Norwood Young America v. Brown, 829 N.W.2d 634 (Minn. Ct. App. 2013), *aff'd in part, rev'd in part on other grounds*, 849 N.W.2d 55 (Minn. 2014), a 94-year old man divorced his 55-year old wife, transferring $2 million in assets to her and leaving himself with a negative $8.5 million net worth. Because a court had entered a judgment approving the terms of their marital dissolution, Mr. Brown argued that a fraudulent conveyance action on the $2 million transfer would be an "impermissible collateral attack" on the divorce. Id. at 641. The court upheld liability for a fraudulent transfer. The major persuasive fact to the court in concluding that Mr. Brown had an actual intent to hinder, delay, or defraud his creditors was that the legally divorced "Browns continue to live together in their marital home," id. at 636. The Browns apparently chose love over money, an expensive decision. In many situations, particularly in larger companies with less colorful management, actual intent is hard to prove. The UVTA's second big ground for undoing transfers gets around the problem of showing actual intent.

C.   CONSTRUCTIVE FRAUD

Section 5(a) codifies a concept called "constructive fraud" or "presumptive fraud," which are horrible names because they cover transactions that are not remotely fraudulent at all, which probably explains why they changed the name of the statute. They do, however, cover transactions, like voidable preferences, that benefit some creditors at the expense of others. Specifically, § 5(a) permits a creditor to avoid any transfer made (1) in exchange for an unfairly low consideration, (2) at a time when the debtor was insolvent. Notice the absence of any requirement of intent, fraudulent or otherwise. Adding the term "fraud" to these situations may actually exacerbate litigation (wouldn't you rather be sued for an innocuous-sounding "preference" than finger-wagging "fraud"?), especially since the recipients have done absolutely nothing wrong. The following New York case is under the UFCA, but it makes no difference; the UVTA analysis would be identical.

FED. NAT'L MORTGAGE ASS'N v. OLYMPIA MORTGAGE CORP.

792 F. Supp. 2d 645 (E.D.N.Y. 2011)

GERSHON, District Judge.

Federal National Mortgage Association ("Fannie Mae") initiated this action on November 16, 2004. On October 18, 2005, Olympia Mortgage Corporation ("Olympia") filed an Amended Answer and Crossclaims asserting four crossclaims against [several individuals], ("the Donner Relatives") for: . . . violation of New York Debtor and Creditor Law ("N.Y. Debt. & Cred. Law") § 276 [and] violation of N.Y. Debt. & Cred. Law § 273. . . . [The Donner Relatives are the wife, sons, daughters, and daughters-in-law of Abe Donner, the former president and 32% shareholder of Olympia.]

Olympia has been put into receivership by this court and has entered into a consent judgment with Fannie Mae concerning its breach of contract claims. On May 11, 2011, by Stipulation and Order, the remaining six claims against Olympia were dismissed without prejudice.

BACKGROUND AND FACTS

The following facts are undisputed unless otherwise noted.

Olympia was insolvent at least from December 31, 1997, and possibly for its entire existence. Karen Kincaid Balmer Decl. Ex. 40, May 23, 2008.

Abe Donner was the President of [Olympia.] The Donner Relatives consist of Toby Donner, Abe Donner's wife; Naftali and Chaim Donner, Abe Donner's sons; Perry Lerner and Yocheved and Sarah Donner, Abe Donner's daughters; and Nachema Donner, Abe Donner's daughter-in-law and Chaim Donner's wife. Olympia transferred sums of money to and on behalf of the Donner Relatives from 1998 through 2004. These transfers from Olympia took the form of payments evidenced by W-2 Wage and Tax Statement forms, as well as payments for healthcare insurance and mortgage payments made on their behalf. . . .

[The court lists several Donner Relatives and the amounts of the transfers. We preserve the most intriguing one below.—Eds.] . . . (5) There is a disagreement among the parties as to the amount of money that should be attributed to Yocheved. Yocheved calculates the amount she received to include only the money she directly received from Olympia.

Olympia, however, correctly includes mortgage payments it made on Yocheved's behalf in the transfers it seeks to recover. In support of its position, Olympia has submitted an undisputed ledger showing that it made mortgage payments on Yocheved's behalf. Therefore, the undisputed facts establish that Yocheved directly received or benefitted from a total of $136,155.41. . . .

Despite the existence of W-2s for some of the Donner Relatives, they do not claim to have provided any services to Olympia in exchange for the monies or benefits they have received. Rather, they claim that all of the transfers were part of Abe Donner's compensation for the services that *he* provided as President of Olympia.

Between 1998 and 2003, Abe Donner himself received between $99,814.55 and $143,261.12 in compensation each year. The sole evidentiary support for the Donner Relatives' claim that Abe Donner's salary nonetheless included the money transferred to the Donner Relatives, is his affidavit. He states:

> "[A]ny transfers [the Donner Relatives] may have received from Olympia [are] part of the compensation I received as President of Olympia. . . . [T]he amount of compensation I received from Olympia, as president, was well under the average of what the President of a company such as Olympia would receive. This is because the benefits my family [the Donner Relatives] received from Olympia were part and parcel of my compensation as President of Olympia. . . . Thus, it is evident that the transfers that Olympia alleges went to me alone cannot constitute my total salary. Indeed, this is borne out by the amount of the alleged transfers solely to myself, which range from as low as $99,814.55 in 2001, to a maximum of only $143,261.12 in 1998. These salaries are significantly below the salary that a President of a company such as Olympia normally makes. Thus, as illustrated, the transfers to my family were part and parcel of my compensation as President of Olympia."

Abe Donner Aff. ¶¶1-11. During his deposition, citing the Fifth Amendment, Abe Donner refused to answer any questions relating to his role or responsibilities at Olympia.

Undisputed evidence establishes that, although he had the title "President," Abe Donner did not have a large role, or spend much time working, at Olympia. Patricia Trinidad, an Olympia employee who most recently held the title of Director of Operations, explained that Abe Donner did not have an office at Olympia and was not involved in day-to-day operations at Olympia. Both Marcus Pinter, Olympia's accountant, and Alan Braun, Olympia's auditor, confirmed that Abe Donner had a very limited role at Olympia and was not involved in the company's daily operations. Marcus Pinter Dep. Barry Goldstein, Olympia's Managing Director and a part-owner, stated that Abe Donner had "in essence no responsibilities for [Olympia]." The Donner Relatives do not contest that Abe Donner's role and responsibilities at Olympia were limited. In their reply papers, the Donner Relatives add an argument that, in addition to Abe Donner's salary, the transfers in question also included shareholder profits disbursed to Abe Donner. They offer no evidence in support of this position.

. . .

New York Debtor and Creditor Law § 273 ("§ 273") states: "Every conveyance made and every obligation incurred by a person who is or will be thereby insolvent is fraudulent as to creditors without regard to his actual intent if the conveyance is made or the obligation is incurred without a fair consideration." [The UVTA would say "reasonably equivalent value."—Eds.]

Under § 273, "if a conveyance is made without fair consideration and the transferor is a debtor who is insolvent or will be rendered insolvent by the transfer, the conveyance is deemed constructively fraudulent." Capital Distrib. Servs., Ltd. v. Ducor Express Airlines, Inc., 440 F. Supp. 2d 195, 203 (E.D.N.Y. 2006); Zanani v. Meisels, 78 A.D.3d 823, 910 N.Y.S.2d 533 (2d Dep't 2010). Therefore, in order to succeed under this Section, Olympia must show (1) that it transferred money; (2) that the money was transferred while Olympia was insolvent or that the transfers rendered Olympia insolvent; and (3) that the transfers were not made in exchange for fair consideration. See In re Sharp Inter. Corp., 403 F.3d 43, 53 (2d Cir. 2005).

As explained above, there is some uncertainty as to the appropriate standard of proof required to prove constructive fraud pursuant to § 273. The court need not decide which standard is correct because Olympia would prevail under either standard. [The UVTA now clarifies that the standard of proof required to establish a voidable transfer is preponderance of the evidence. UVTA § 8(h).—Eds.]

Money Transfers

The record establishes, without dispute, that the Donner Relatives received the transfers from Olympia or benefitted from transfers Olympia made on their behalf. So, the first element is satisfied.

Olympia's Insolvency

Olympia was insolvent at least from December 31, 1997, which is prior to any of the transfers at issue, and possibly for its entire existence. The Donner Relatives make the bald assertion that the transfers to them, and the transfers from which they benefitted, did not occur while Olympia was insolvent and did not contribute to Olympia's insolvency, but offer no evidence in support of their position. . . .

Fair Consideration

"Under section 273 of the Debtor and Creditor Law, any transfer made by an insolvent debtor for less than 'fair consideration' is fraud as against his creditors without regard to the actual intent of the transferee." Schmitt v. Morgan, 98 A.D.2d 934, 471 N.Y.S.2d 365 (3d Dep't 1983). In order to satisfy the statutory requirement for "fair consideration" under § 273, a conveyance must satisfy an antecedent debt or constitute a present exchange. HBE Leasing Corp. v. Frank, 61 F.3d 1054, 1061 (2d Cir. 1995). The value of the consideration may not be disproportionately small when compared with the value of the conveyance. Lippe v. Bairnco Corp., 249 F. Supp. 2d 357, 377 (S.D.N.Y. 2003).

It is undisputed that the Donner Relatives themselves gave no consideration for the transfers to them or benefits they received from transfers made on their behalf. The Donner Relatives argue that the transfers to them and benefits they received from transfers made on their behalf were for fair consideration because the transfers were part of Abe Donner's compensation as President of Olympia. The only affidavit provided was that of Abe Donner in which he states in a most conclusory fashion that the payments the Donner Relatives received were part of his salary. Olympia, however, has submitted copies of Abe Donner's W-2s from 1998 through 2003. The money transferred to the Donner Relatives was not included in Abe Donner's W-2 forms. These W-2s contradict Abe Donner's conclusory affidavit that the transfers were part of his salary; any money that Olympia paid Abe Donner as salary should have been on Abe Donner's own W-2s. Olympia also submitted various Donner Relatives' W-2 forms from 1998 through 2003, showing that Olympia declared the transfers as some of the Donner Relatives' own salary; while these W-2s were improperly issued, as the Donner Relatives acknowledge they never worked for Olympia, they do serve to further contradict Abe Donner's statement that the transferred money was part of *his* salary.

The Donner Relatives do not contest that Abe Donner spent little time at Olympia or that he had very few responsibilities at Olympia. Rather, they argue that his compensation should not be a function of his role or responsibilities but a function of his unidentified contributions to Olympia. In the absence of any but the most conclusory evidence—an affidavit from someone who refused to testify on the subject at his deposition but pled the Fifth Amendment—and in the presence of undisputed contrary evidence in the form of Abe Donner's own W-2s, no reasonable jury could conclude that the transfers to the Donner Relatives constituted salary payments to Abe Donner.

In their reply papers, the Donner Relatives make a new argument, that the money transferred to them, and transfers from which they benefitted, included Abe Donner's profits for being a 32% shareholder of Olympia. None of the Donner Relatives has provided any affidavit or documentary evidence supporting the argument that the transfers to them were in fact a return on profits owed to Abe Donner. In any event, as a matter of law, they could not be entitled to transfers or benefits from transfers made on their behalf under this theory. Under New York Business Corporations Law, "[a] corporation may declare and pay dividends . . . except when [] the corporation is insolvent or would thereby be made insolvent. . . ." N.Y. Bus. Corp. Law § 510(a). "A corporation holds its assets in trust for the benefit of the corporation's creditors, and cannot lawfully distribute its assets to shareholders to the prejudice of those creditors." In re Trace Intern. Holdings, Inc., 289 B.R. 548, 560 (Bankr. S.D.N.Y. 2003). An insolvent corporation cannot make distributions to shareholders, and such distributions are "classic fraudulent conveyances [] prohibited by law." In re Adelphia Communications Corp., 323 B.R. 345, 377 fn. 104 (Bkrtcy. S.D.N.Y. 2005) *citing* In re Trace Intern. Holdings, Inc., 289 B.R. at 561. Given

Olympia's poor financial condition, any transfers to, or on behalf of, a corporation's shareholders would have been illegal and therefore recoverable.

For the above reasons, the Donner Relatives' motion for summary judgment is denied. Applying either standard of proof, clear and convincing evidence or the preponderance of the evidence, Olympia has established by undisputed evidence that the transfers were made by Olympia to the Donner Relatives, or on their behalf, while Olympia was insolvent and without fair consideration. Because there remain no issues of fact, Olympia's application for summary judgment on its § 273 claims is granted. . . .

Recovery of Damages

The Donner Relatives argue that, even if Olympia prevails on its claims, it cannot recover money damages from the Donner Relatives because none of them participated in the fraud. . . . Courts . . . have repeatedly noted that one need *only* be a transferee or beneficiary to be a participant in a fraudulent transfer; not either a transferee or beneficiary of a fraudulent conveyance *and* a participant in the underlying fraud. See, e.g., Chemtex, LLC v. St. Anthony Enterprises, Inc., 490 F. Supp. 2d 536, 548 (S.D.N.Y. 2007). [The court also suggested they did participate in the fraud.—Eds.]

Finally, the New York Uniform Fraudulent Conveyance Act, which is set forth in N.Y. Debt. & Cred. Law §§ 270-281, protects the rights of certain transferees who paid "fair consideration" for assets without "knowledge of the fraud at the time of the purchase." N.Y. Debt. & Cred. Law § 278(1); HBE Leasing v. Frank, 48 F.3d 623, 636 (2d Cir. 1995) (noting the statute's "policy of protecting innocent creditors or purchasers for value who have received the debtor's property without awareness of any fraudulent scheme"). This is not one of those instances, as the Donner Relatives did not offer any fair consideration in exchange for the money transfers. Thus, money damages for the entire amount of the fraudulent transfers are recoverable against the Donner Relatives.

. . .

CONCLUSION

For the reasons set forth above, the Donner Relatives' motion for summary judgment is denied. Summary judgment is granted to Olympia on its crossclaims against the Donner Relatives on constructive and actual fraud pursuant to New York Debtor and Creditor Law §§ 273 and 276.

This Donner Family's plight hardly attracts sympathy. We wonder whether Honest Abe offered to produce his gift tax returns to show that the money was really a big gift of his salary to the kids. Regardless, you should note how insolvency is a requirement for constructive fraud. Giving away property without fair consideration (or, as UVTA §§ 4(a)(2) & 5 state, a "lack of reasonably equivalent value" (REV)) is either foolish or generous, or even possible tax evasion, but it is not avoidable in most instances. Only if you do so when insolvent do you trigger the UVTA. Indeed, even the legal wonder twins of Rhoades & Rhoades knew the significance of solvency as a defense to constructive fraudulent conveyance. They fought tooth and nail on the issue, arguing that Daniel Rhoades's ownership of a parcel of real estate left him solvent by hundreds of thousands of dollars and so incapable of constructive fraud. The argument did not fare well:

> Karl Kenyon, a South Carolina lawyer who also invests in real estate in Anderson County, testified for Mr. Rhoades that in his opinion the property, which consisted of about 425 acres of undeveloped land, could have been sold as "ranchette" sites for a net of approximately $700,000. However, Kenyon's opinion was undercut in several ways. First, the South Carolina property was actually sold in 1984 or 1985 at auction for only about $200,000, and the actual price which the property brought on the open market is far better evidence of its value than Kenyon's speculation as to what price the land might have brought had it been marketed in a particular way. Second, the only appraisal of the property which was put into evidence was an estimate made in 1983 by a South Carolina real estate broker that the property was worth approximately $475–500 per acre, or about $212,500 in all. Finally, Kenyon's limited experience in the real estate field—which is not his profession—and his business relationship and friendship with Daniel Rhoades, weaken the value of his opinion. I find that the South Carolina property had a value of approximately $212,500 in 1983.

ACLI Gov't Sec. v. Rhoades, supra, at 1393 (finding constructive fraud in addition to actual intent fraud).

As for what constitutes "reasonably equivalent value," you can probably guess that that fact-dependent question is litigated 'til the cows come home. In one seminal case, Durrett v. Washington National Insurance Co., 621 F.2d 201 (5th Cir. 1980), the court held that a legally conducted, non-judicial foreclosure sale that had brought a low price could be a "transfer" for "less than reasonably equivalent value" to the bona fide purchaser and hence set aside in bankruptcy. This created the anomaly that a debtor who had lost a piece of property in a state foreclosure proceeding could file bankruptcy and suddenly become, much like Superman emerging from the telephone booth, a debtor in possession who could reclaim the property from the buyer. Now acting on behalf of all the creditors, the DIP could pay off the small price paid by the buyer and reclaim the property for the estate.

To understate things, *Durrett* was controversial. The argument became unavailable under the then-UFTA when the 1984 revision added § 3(b) to foreclose the outcome in *Durrett*. Congress in turn then amended § 548, the Bankruptcy Code fraudulent conveyance provision, but failed to resolve the issue. The Supreme Court then decided BFP v. Resolution Trust Corporation, 511 U.S. 531 (1994), under § 548. The Justices ruled 5-4 (each side insisting, without apparent irony, that it was adhering to the Code's plain meaning) that "reasonably equivalent value" exists per se when offered as the purchase price at a properly conducted, noncollusive judicial foreclosure sale. True market value, said Justice Scalia, "has no applicability in the forced sale context; indeed, it is the very *antithesis* of forced-sale value." Id. at 537.

We confess to having been critical of *Durrett* when it was decided with its seeming overreach of federal law, but Justice Souter offered a compelling dissent in *BFP* (yes, the best case name of all time for a dispute involving the rights of a bona fide purchaser) that has made some of us rethink: while certainty is important in state-law foreclosure proceedings, federal policies that arise in bankruptcy are also important, and they may require some yielding of state law. Sometimes, thoughtful analysis beats contested "plain" meaning.

Finally, before leaving the UVTA, note that two other provisions of the UVTA trigger liability in situations other than the actual-intent situation. Sections 4(a)(2)(i) and (ii) rely on something that might be thought of as a "negligently fraudulent transfer" or "quasi-constructive fraud." These provisions seem to capture an interim level of mens rea and culpability and are explored in analyzing leveraged buyouts in the next assignment.

D. FRAUDULENT CONVEYANCE LAW IN BANKRUPTCY

As we have seen, the UVTA or similar state laws allow a creditor to attack a transfer of assets under certain conditions. Section 544(b) of the Code preserves those state-law rights, but gives them to the trustee (or DIP acting as a trustee in chapter 11). This makes state fraudulent conveyance law an important tool for the trustee for reshaping the estate. Under § 544, the trustee's rights are derivative; there must be an actual unsecured creditor (creditor with an unsecured claim under § 502) eligible to bring the avoidance action under state fraudulent conveyance law into whose shoes the trustee can step.

In addition to embracing state avoidance laws through § 544(b), the Code provides its own fraudulent conveyance provisions in § 548, addressed by the Supreme Court in *BFP*. While state laws tend to be very similar, § 548 creates a federal fraudulent conveyance law to ensure baseline protection in bankruptcy for all creditors, regardless of variations in state law.

One key difference between the state fraudulent conveyance law (§ 544) and federal bankruptcy law (§ 548) is the statute of limitations. State law, while not entirely uniform, is typically more favorable to creditors. The UVTA allows four years to bring an action, § 9, while the Code has a two-year limitation. § 548(a)(2).

E. REMEDIES FOR FRAUDULENT CONVEYANCES

Sections 7 and 8 of the UVTA essentially allow two types of remedies: a property-recovery action against the asset *in rem* and a monetary claim against a transferee *in personam*. The Code takes the same approach in § 550, which is the general remedy clause for avoiding powers, applying to preferences, fraudulent conveyances, lien invalidations, and the like. Both the UVTA and the Code offer certain transferees safe harbors, setoffs, and other protections, adopting similar but not identical approaches. For example, § 548(c) gives an innocent transferee a setoff for value to the extent given in exchange for the fraudulent transfer. If an insolvent debtor sells a $1,000 piano to you for $10 and the trustee unwinds the transfer, you get your $10 back (assuming no cahoots). Creditors considering avoidance of a fraudulent conveyance will want to carefully study the remedial options, as well as consider the statute of limitations and liability provisions, in gauging the likelihood of recovering a transferred asset. But the real meat of the Code's remedial revisions depends upon the identification of who is the initial transferee of that property that the trustee wants back. § 550(a), (b).

In re VIDEO DEPOT, LTD.
127 F.3d 1195 (9th Cir. 1997)

NELSON, Circuit Judge.

Kenneth Schafer, the trustee of Video Depot, Ltd., brings this fraudulent conveyance action to recover the proceeds of a cashier's check purchased by Video Depot and paid to the Las Vegas Hilton in partial satisfaction of gambling debts incurred by Jeffrey Arlynn, Video Depot's principal. Hilton appeals the district court's decision affirming the bankruptcy court's judgment in favor of the trustee. We have jurisdiction pursuant to 28 U.S.C. § 1291, and we affirm.

FACTUAL AND PROCEDURAL BACKGROUND

Most of the relevant facts are not in dispute. Jeffrey Arlynn was the president of Video Depot, a consumer electronics company. Arlynn controlled virtually all of Video Depot's operations.

Arlynn was also an active gambler. Between 1985 and 1990, he made approximately 60 trips to the Las Vegas Hilton. Initially, Arlynn gambled on funds he brought with him, or against credit that Hilton extended to him for the duration of each individual trip. In 1987, however, Arlynn obtained a permanent line of credit with Hilton in the amount of $50,000, which was increased to $75,000 in 1990.

Prior to 1990, Arlynn regularly repaid his losses in full either at the end of each stay or at the beginning of the next trip. While he occasionally retained a balance, the balance was always substantially less than his credit limit. In addition, Arlynn carefully controlled the size of his accumulated credit losses. Until 1990, Arlynn's balance only twice exceeded $100,000 and never exceeded $125,000.

In early May of 1990, however, Arlynn incurred a debt of $225,000, and he did not make a payment towards this debt before he left Las Vegas. On June 15, Video Depot purchased a cashier's check payable to Hilton in the amount of $65,000. The check clearly indicated that Video Depot was the purchaser. When Arlynn returned to Las Vegas on June 16, he gave two checks to Hilton: the $65,000 cashier's check from Video Depot, and a personal cashier's check in the amount of $10,000. Arlynn had never before presented either a cashier's check or a check purchased by Video Depot to cover his gambling losses.

Video Depot commenced bankruptcy proceedings on September 14, 1990, and the trustee was appointed shortly thereafter. The trustee then filed suit against Hilton to recover the proceeds of the $65,000 cashier's check. After an initial round of litigation, both parties stipulated that the check was a fraudulent transfer within the meaning of 11 U.S.C. § 548, and the bankruptcy court proceeded to determine whether Hilton was an initial transferee under 11 U.S.C. § 550(a) or a subsequent transferee lacking good faith knowledge of the voidability of the transfer within the meaning of 11 U.S.C. § 550(b). . . .

The central issue before us is whether Hilton was the initial transferee of the $65,000 cashier's check purchased by Video Depot.

The Statutory Scheme

The parties have stipulated that the $65,000 payment to Hilton was a fraudulent transfer within the meaning of 11 U.S.C. § 548. Once a transfer has been determined to be voidable as a fraudulent conveyance under section 548, the trustee of the debtor may recover it from either

1.   the initial transferee of such transfer or the entity for whose benefit such transfer was made; or
2.   any immediate or mediate transferee of such initial transferee.

11 U.S.C. § 550(a). The distinction between the two, however, is a critical one. The trustee's right to recover from an initial transferee is absolute. On the other hand, the trustee may not recover from a subsequent transferee if the subsequent transferee accepted the transfer for value, in good faith, and without knowledge of the transfer's voidability. 11 U.S.C. § 550(b). Subsequent transferees therefore have a defense unavailable to initial transferees.

The purpose of this scheme is to protect creditors "from last-minute diminutions of the pool of assets in which they have interests," while at the same time to guard against "the waste that would be created if people either had to inquire how their transferors obtained their property or to accept a risk that a commercial deal would be reversed for no reason they could perceive at the time." Bonded Fin. Servs., Inc. v. European American Bank, 838 F.2d 890, 892 (7th Cir. 1988). Section 550 balances these two goals by imposing on the initial transferee the "burden of inquiry and the risk if the conveyance is fraudulent." Id. While the initial transferee is in the best position to monitor the transaction, "subsequent transferees usually do not know where the assets came from and would be ineffectual monitors if they did." Id. at 892-93.

In this case, the bankruptcy court determined, and the district court agreed, that Hilton was the initial transferee. On appeal, Hilton makes two arguments to the contrary. First, Hilton contends that Arlynn, not Hilton, was the initial transferee because Arlynn controlled Video Depot and directed that the funds be transferred to Hilton. Alternatively, Hilton argues that Arlynn was the initial transferee because Video Depot's ledger appears to indicate that the cashier's check was a "loan" to Arlynn. We address each of these arguments in turn.

I. Arlynn's Control over Video Depot

While the Bankruptcy Code does not define "transferee," it is widely accepted that a transferee is one who, at a minimum, has "'dominion over the money or other asset, the right to put the money to one's own purposes.'" In re Bullion, 922 F.2d at 548 (quoting *Bonded Fin. Servs.*, 838 F.2d at 893). The bankruptcy court determined that Arlynn did not have dominion over the $65,000. The court reasoned that although Arlynn controlled Video Depot's operations and arranged for the check to be issued, the check was a direct transfer from Video Depot to Hilton. Once the check was issued, Arlynn no longer had legal control over the funds, even if he retained physical control over them. Arlynn therefore did not have the right to use the money for any other purpose than to give it to Hilton. Hilton maintains that Arlynn had dominion over the $65,000 because he was Video Depot's principal and, in that capacity, directed Video Depot to purchase the cashier's check.

The bankruptcy courts are split on the question of whether the principal of a debtor corporation necessarily is the initial transferee of corporate funds used to satisfy a personal obligation. . . . In Nordberg v. Arab Banking Corp. (In re Chase &. Sanborn Corp.), 904 F.2d 588 (11th Cir. 1990), on which the bankruptcy court in the present case relied, the Eleventh Circuit held that a bank was the initial transferee of loan payments made by a corporation even though the corporation's principal directed the transfer and the loan was the principal's private debt. Id. at 599-600. The court determined that "the extent of [the principal's] control over [the corporation] generally, and over [the corporation's] actions in transferring the disputed funds to [the bank] in particular, is entirely irrelevant to the 'initial transferee' issue." Id. at 598.

Since the bankruptcy court's decision, two other circuits, citing *Lucas Dallas* and the district court's opinion in this case, also have concluded that a principal who directs a debtor corporation to issue a certified check to pay for a personal debt is not an initial transferee. See Bowers v. Atlanta Motor Speedway, Inc. (In re Southeast Hotel Properties Limited Partnership), 99 F.3d 151 (4th Cir. 1996); Rupp v. Markgraf, 95 F.3d 936 (10th Cir. 1996). These courts have held that a principal or agent does not have "dominion and control" over funds unless he or she has *legal* dominion and control," in other words, the "right to put those funds to one's own purpose." *Bowers*, 99 F.3d at 155 (emphasis in original); see also *Rupp*, 95 F.3d at 941. The mere power of a principal to direct the allocation of corporate resources does not amount to legal dominion and control. . . .

In the present case, however, Video Depot purchased a cashier's check payable to Hilton, with Video Depot listed as the purchaser. Legal control over the funds consequently passed directly from Video Depot to Hilton.

Hilton contends that this view elevates form over substance. Whether Video Depot, at Arlynn's direction, purchased a cashier's check payable directly to Hilton or, instead, issued the funds to Arlynn, enabling him then to write a personal check for the sum, there is, so the argument goes, the same result—that Arlynn used corporate funds to satisfy a personal debt. What Hilton's argument fails to acknowledge, however, is the basic rationale for distinguishing in section 550 between initial and subsequent transferees. An initial transferee is exposed to stricter liability than a subsequent transferee because an initial transferee is in the best position to evaluate whether the conveyance is fraudulent. Where, as here, a transferee receives funds directly from a debtor, the transferee's capacity to monitor—and, accordingly, its burden to monitor—is at its greatest. Thus, Hilton's receipt of a cashier's check clearly purchased by Video Depot subjects it to a burden of inquiry that it may not have had upon receipt of a check from Jeffrey Arlynn's personal account.

Moreover, the rule advocated by Hilton would have the anomalous result that every agent or principal of a corporation would be deemed the initial transferee when he or she effected a transfer of property in his or her representative capacity. See *Bowers*, 99 F.3d at 156. Such a rule "gives too much power to an unscrupulous insider to effect a fraudulent transfer . . . without allowing a trustee to have the means for avoiding the transfer for the benefit of the debtor's creditors." In re Mitchell, 164 B.R. at 128. . . . Thus, we conclude that Arlynn's control over the business operations of Video Depot does not, in itself, compel a finding that Arlynn had dominion and control over the funds transferred from Video Depot to Hilton.

II. Video Depot's "Loan" to Arlynn

Hilton next contends that the transfer of funds from Video Depot constituted a loan to Arlynn, giving Arlynn control over how the funds were spent and making him, not Hilton, the initial transferee. The bankruptcy court rejected this argument, citing insufficient evidence. Because we find nothing in the record to support a finding that Arylnn had dominion over the funds after they were disbursed by Video Depot, we agree with the bankruptcy court.

Hilton's argument rests on two documents that it submitted in support of its motion for summary judgment: excerpts from a ledger that appear to track payments by Video Depot on Arlynn's behalf and an affidavit from Arlynn. In the affidavit, Arlynn maintains:

> On or about June 15, 1990, I borrowed the sum of $65,000.00 from Video Depot and caused this loan transaction to be recorded in the records of the corporation. The $65,000.00 in corporate funds was used to purchase a cashier's check in the amount of $65,000 made payable to the Las Vegas Hilton in partial satisfaction of a debt I owed. . . . Prior to the commencement of involuntary bankruptcy proceedings against Video Depot, I repaid this specific loan to the corporation.

The ledger lists payments to Jeffrey Arlynn in the amount of $10,000 and $65,000 on June 15. On the credit side of the ledger, a $75,000 payment from Arlynn is shown.

Simply referring to the transfer as a "loan" in the company ledger does not suffice, however, to demonstrate that at any point in time Arlynn exercised independent control over the funds. So long as the money remained in Video Depot's account, Arlynn's legal right to it was circumscribed by his duties to the corporation and its creditors. Once the funds were disbursed, Arlynn could use them only to pay Hilton. Regardless of how Hilton chooses to characterize the transfer, Hilton has failed to explain how Video Depot's issuance of a check earmarked expressly for the purchase of a cashier's check to the Las Vegas Hilton gave Arlynn dominion over the funds.

Arlynn was a courier, not a transferee. Particularly in view of the fact that Arlynn, as principal of Video Depot, could direct that the transfer be called anything he pleased in the company ledger, we require more substantial evidence that he exercised independent control over the funds after they left Video Depot's account. The bankruptcy court gave Hilton ample opportunity to present such evidence, and Hilton failed to do so.

<h2 style="text-align:center">CONCLUSION</h2>

The bankruptcy court had adequate grounds for determining that Hilton was an initial transferee under section 550(a). Accordingly, we affirm the district court's decision affirming the bankruptcy court. Since we find Hilton to have been an initial transferee, we do not reach Hilton's section 550(b) argument.

Affirmed.

———————————

The analysis of just who is characterized as the initial transferee is obviously important to the differing defenses available, and the Ninth Circuit's analysis took great care to resolve that important question. Less care was taken by their superiors in an important case upending the scope of the derivatives safe harbors of § 546(e), Merit Mgmt. Group, LLC v. FTI Consulting, Inc., 138 S. Ct. 883 (2018). In that case, the debtor made transfers to Merit through financial intermediaries, namely by executing a transfer to one bank, then another, then ultimately to Merit. The safe harbors, discussed first in Assignment 17 in relation to exceptions from the automatic stay, protect transfers "to or for the benefit" of certain financial intermediaries as an attempt to exclude these entities (and their transactions) from the bankruptcy system. Clearly the transfers were not for the benefit of the banks, but were they to the banks? In other words, just like *Video Depot*, was a fact-dependent analysis of dominion and control required? Apparently not, as the Court created a new category of "ultimate" transfer, which here was from the debtor to Merit ("through" the banks, a preposition the Code declines to use). It appears the Supreme Court's view is that identifying which of a train of transfers is the one that matters is something you just have to know when you see it, an approach that has a storied pedigree. See Jacobellis v. Ohio, 378 U.S. 184, 197 (1964) (Stewart, J., concurring).

The comparative equities of equal innocents (unknowing transferees vs. hapless creditors) requires exquisite policy balancing. *Video Depot* articulates the policy justification for the less favorable treatment of initial transferees: they have a better monitoring capacity than subsequent transferees. Apparently, a casino should know better when it gets a corporate cashier's check. How often do corporations gamble? (OK, how often do they gamble in Las Vegas casinos?) Consider in a similar case the fraudulent conveyance loss of a clothing retailer that shipped for full retail value some swanky designer outfits to a corporate customer. The court held that selling designer clothes is all well and good in the stream of commerce—but not to *a marine engine business*. The REV is not the value of the transferred property in the abstract (here, the clothes were sold and paid for at their full and fair price), but the value of the transfer to the debtor (and a marine engine business derives zero value from fancy clothes, lovely as they might be). In re Keith Eichert Power Products LLC, 344 B.R. 685 (Bankr. M.D. Fla. 2006). These aspects of "benefit" and "value" become fine pinheads upon which to dance. In Janvey v. The Golf Channel, 487 S.W.3d 560 (Tex. 2016), the Fifth Circuit decided no REV, then reversed itself, then certified to the Texas Supreme Court whether a Ponzi scheme's purchasing of Golf Channel sponsorship conferred value upon the debtor when, by definition of a Ponzi scheme, the debtor was not interested in acquiring any value, only diverting any and all cash through fraud. The Lone Star court held that "the reasonably equivalent value requirement in [the equivalent of § 8(a) UVTA] is satisfied when the transferee fully performed in an arm's-length transaction in the ordinary course of its business at market rates." That standard applies "without regard to the subjective needs or perspectives of the debtor or transferee and without the wisdom hindsight often brings." Id. at 582.

Problem Set 23

23.1. Adrienne Leiske is insolvent. She owes $50,000 to Family Finance. In order to raise money so she can make her rent payments and eat, she sells her grand piano. Although the piano is valued at $40,000, she lists it on popular sales website Franz's List for $20,000. When offered $15,000, Adrienne accepts. Does Family Finance have a viable cause of action for a fraudulent conveyance? UVTA §§ 4, 5.

23.2. Bonney O'Hare is insolvent and she feels the tightening web of creditors. She decides to sell her coin collection to her friend, Susan Mallory. Although the collection would bring $75,000 if she sold it to a dealer, Bonney sells it to Susan for $5,000 so that "it will stay in the family." Bonney also knows that Susan has no real interest in the collection and will undoubtedly be willing to sell it back when Bonney's financial troubles are over. The day after her conveyance to Susan, Bonney uses her American Express card to purchase $25,000 in new furnishings. Can American Express successfully assert that a fraudulent conveyance occurred? UVTA §§ 4, 5.

23.3. Jeremiah Stoke owns a homestead in Suffragette City free and clear worth $200,000. His other assets total $55,000; his debts, all unsecured, total $75,000. Under state exemption law his homestead is safe from his creditors. He has made a mess of his own affairs, but his favorite son, Quentin, has just married, and Jeremiah would like to do just one thing right. So he conveys the homestead to Quentin as a gift and settles down to await the battles with his creditors over his debts. Can Jeremiah's current creditors reach the conveyed homestead? See UVTA §§ 1, 2, 5.

23.4. Yesterday Diana Saliceti Moran, one of the partners of Commercial Investors, called you to ask about an investment that has clearly gone sour. It appears that Barry Held, the president of Held Real Estate, has gone completely round the bend. Barry has had a severe alcohol abuse problem, and he let the company fall to pieces. Although Held's second-in-command, a frightened young bookkeeper, managed to keep paying the company's creditors, including your client, during most of the decline, the business has fallen apart. Brokers have left, income is off sharply, and the business is essentially over. CI's collateral, accounts receivable, is virtually worthless.

The only substantial, unencumbered asset was the office building where the business operated. Moran says the building is worth about $8.5 million and was outraged to find that it was sold last Tuesday at a sheriff's auction. It seems that the business had failed to pay a plumber's bill of $1,600. The plumber got a judgment, and the property was auctioned off last Tuesday. The only bidder was the plumber who had brought the action, and he bid in the unpaid bill of $1,600. The bookkeeper remembers getting some kind of notice for the sale, which he gave to Held, but Held didn't even show up for the sale.

Moran says that CI will gladly pay the plumber the $1,600 plus expenses and share the value obtained from the business with the other unsecured creditors. Without that building, CI is staring at a $1.2 million loss on its loan. What advice do you give her?

23.5. Almost Homes, Inc., a mobile home dealer, is insolvent. Its chief creditor is Vampire Squid Bank. S.R. Wilson, the business's president and owner, sold one unit, valued at approximately $160,000, to his neighbor Sam for $90,000 cash. Sam moved into the home, cleaned it up, spent $10,000 for repairs, thereby enhancing the value by 20%, so it's now worth around $192,000. Vampire Squid successfully claims that the conveyance was fraudulent. What can the bank get its tentacles on? UVTA § 8.

23.6. For 26 years, Burt DiAngelo has owned and operated Be Well, Inc., a health products manufacturing concern. Burt now employs 106 people ("all like family"), but Burt is the business. He makes all the decisions, keeps the books, runs the show. After years of successful operation, last year was a disaster. Bad press over rodent droppings seemed to be the principal problem, and Burt has taken the company into chapter 11.

As you and Burt are plotting strategies, Burt mentions ruefully that only six months ago today he spent nearly $40,000 cash from the business to take his extended family on a cruise to celebrate his parents' fiftieth wedding anniversary. He knew that the business was faltering, but he thought it would recover. He can't believe that a few bad news stories have brought him so low so fast.

You are getting a tingling feeling in the back of your neck. What's wrong? See §§ 548(a)(1), (2), 550.

23.7. You are counsel to the trustee for Advant Advertising, Inc., which has filed a chapter 7 petition. Advant had grown rapidly under the leadership of its dynamic chief executive, Cheri Schneider, who made money by a combination of clever ad copy and wheeling and dealing with her clients.

Unfortunately, Cheri's "golden touch" eventually turned to lead, and the company was forced to file for bankruptcy.

Jefferson and Jefferson, a CPA firm that the court has appointed to investigate the chaotic records of the company, has sent you a file on one of Cheri's deals. In this transaction, Cheri swapped a small office building that the company owned for stock in Sure Fire Investments, a local development company for which Advant did the advertising. What Cheri did not know was that Sure Fire was in financial trouble when the trade was made and the stock that Advant got was worth only $90,000. In all fairness, however, it must be said that the management of Sure Fire was also unaware of its financial problems. The Sure Fire management thought it was giving stock actually worth $900,000, which was the appraised value of the building at the time of the building-for-stock swap.

Sure Fire got the building about six months before Advant filed its chapter 7. Sure Fire wanted the building in order to renovate and sell it, which it did, spending about $300,000 on refurbishments. Unfortunately, the real estate market turned down and it was only able to get $1 million for the building. The buyer of the building was S. Eric Wang, a real estate genius who made his first million playing professional hockey in Detroit.

Against whom will you take action and what relief will you ask for? See §§ 548(a), (c), 550.

FRAUDULENT CONVEYANCES II

Still more fraudulent conveyances, but more sophisticated issues. Both statutes—the UVTA, via § 544, and its federal equivalent, § 548—target similar conduct that has been going on for centuries. We now examine the evolution of fraudulent conveyance law to cover more modern commercial developments, such as corporate transfers, leveraged buyouts, and even settlement payments. While we've come a long way from Pierce's sheep, the principles are still the same. We start with application of fraudulent conveyance law to the corporate form and restrictions on the trustee's power in that context.

A. CORPORATE TRANSFERS

Fraudulent conveyance law has important application both to transfers from corporations and transfers between corporations. We look at both.

1. Single Corporate Transfers

Corporations can only act through humans, as Jeffrey Arlynn reminded us when Video Depot, Inc. "decided" to pay for some casino romps. This creates some difficulty when individuals act to make corporations do bad things. Are they acting as rogue agents, or are they acting in a way that somehow inures to the benefit of the corporation sufficiently to justify tagging the corporation with liability, too? Equitable doctrines, such as *in pari delicto*, sometimes impute bad acts of one legal person (a principal) over to another (a corporation). But what should happen in bankruptcy? If we impute bad acts from one to another, but the other's assets are now in an estate being administered for the benefit of innocent third parties, is it less equitable to exercise this equitable power? Consider this question of innocence as you read the next case, which presents the by-now familiar constructive fraudulent conveyance posture: a bankruptcy trustee for innocent creditors suing an innocent transferee.

In re THE PERSONAL AND BUSINESS INSURANCE AGENCY
334 F.3d 239 (3d Cir. 2003)

BECKER, Circuit Judge.

. . .

The Debtor, PBI, was an insurance brokerage firm in the business of obtaining coverage for trucking companies and their cargo by placing such coverage with various insurers. Between March 1997 and November 1998, [Emil] Kesselring, the sole owner and chief executive officer of PBI, took advantage of PBI's operating procedures to use the company in an illegal money-making scheme . . . .

Beginning in March 1997, Kesselring began to take advantage of this established procedure as a way to illegally obtain funds for himself. He prepared false applications for finance company loans in the name of actual PBI clients or fictitious entities, either forging the borrower's signature or signing as the borrower's agent/broker. He then submitted the applications to [Premium Finance Services ("PFS")] and obtained the loan proceeds. Rather than paying for insurance coverage with these funds, however, Kesselring pocketed the money. To avoid detection, Kesselring caused PBI to make payments on the fraudulent loans using PBI funds. Kesselring made a total of $580,000 in such payments to PFS.

Kesselring's malfeasance was nonetheless uncovered and he was indicted by a grand jury for mail and wire fraud. In August 1999, PBI's Chapter 7 bankruptcy trustee, James McNamara, filed a complaint against PFS, seeking to recover the funds Kesselring had transferred to PFS pursuant to his illegal scheme. The Trustee then filed an amended complaint, alleging a claim for fraudulent conveyance under 11 U.S.C. § 548 and the Pennsylvania Uniform Fraudulent Conveyance Act, 12 Pa. C.S.A. § 5104 *et seq.* . . .

. . .

The Bankruptcy Court determined that the transfers in question in this case were neither actually nor constructively fraudulent because they were made in repayment of a debt owed to PFS [by PBI, even though PBI had gotten no benefit whatsoever from the loan PFS gave "it" — Eds.]. The District Court agreed and rejected the Trustee's argument. In rejecting this argument, the District Court was guided by the analysis laid out in Waslow v. Grant Thornton L.L.P. (In re Jack Greenberg, Inc.), in which the Court held that:

> the fraud of an officer of a corporation is imputed to the corporation when the officer's fraudulent conduct was (1) in the course of his employment, and (2) for the benefit of the corporation. This is true even if the officer's conduct was unauthorized, effected for his own benefit but clothed with apparent authority of the corporation, or contrary to instructions. The underlying reason is that a corporation can speak and act only through its agents and so must be accountable for any acts committed by one of its agents within his actual or apparent scope of authority and while transacting corporate business.

212 B.R. 76, 83 (Bankr. E.D. Pa. 1997).

The District Court correctly found that the first prong of this test was satisfied because Kesselring committed the fraud in the course of his employment; applying for loans from PFS was part of Kesselring's standard work at PBI. The second prong proved more difficult, however. Under what is known as the "adverse interest [corollary]," "fraudulent conduct will not be imputed if the officer's interests were adverse to the corporation and 'not for the benefit of the corporation.'" *Lafferty*, 267 F.3d 340, 359 (3d Cir. 2001) (citations omitted). This [corollary] applied to the situation at hand, as Kesselring's illegal actions redounded only to his own benefit, not to the corporation's. There is however, an exception to this [corollary], which states that:

> [I]f an agent is the sole representative of a principal, then that agent's fraudulent conduct is imputable to the principal regardless of whether the agent's conduct was adverse to the principal's interests. The rationale for this rule is that the sole agent has no one to whom he can impart his knowledge, or from whom he can conceal it, and that the corporation must bear the responsibility for allowing an agent to act without accountability.

Id.

The District Court determined that this "sole actor" exception applied because Kesselring was the sole representative of PBI in the alleged fraudulent scheme. On the basis of this determination, the Court concluded that the transfers of money from PBI to PFS were not constructively fraudulent because the corporation, through Kesselring's imputed conduct, received a reasonably equivalent value for them (the loan proceeds disbursed by PFS to PBI and appropriated by Kesselring), and therefore the transfers were made in payment of an antecedent debt. The Court further held that there was no actual fraud here as the "'badges of fraud,' the most significant of which include the adequacy of the consideration," were not present. Specifically, the Court explained that "after having determined that Kesselring's alleged fraud is imputable to the Debtor corporation, we have little difficulty concluding that the transfers made in repayment of this debt were given for adequate consideration."

III.

A.

As it did before the District Court, PFS argues that the Trustee's fraudulent conveyance claim was properly dismissed because PBI transferred the $580,000 in question in payment of an antecedent debt owed to PFS. PFS advances two theories for how this debt was created. First, it argues that PFS transferred the loan monies directly to PBI's general checking account, not to Kesselring, and therefore PBI was responsible for using the funds appropriately and for making repayment to PFS. We cannot agree. To the extent that PBI held the loan monies, it did so only as a conduit; Kesselring appropriated the monies for his own uses and PBI exercised no control over them. Therefore, PBI's transitory possession of the loan funds did not create a debt owed to PFS.

PFS next asserts that even if the transfer of funds to the PBI account did not create a debt, the District Court was correct in holding that, on the basis of the "sole actor" exception, Kesselring's fraud, and therefore his debt, must be imputed to PBI, thereby creating a debt owed to PFS. The Trustee responds that even if Kesselring's fraud may be imputable to PBI, it is not imputable to the Trustee, who is now bringing this claim. . . .

[T]he Trustee submits that we must consider his claim in light of a post-petition event, namely his appointment as Trustee in place of the "bad actor" Kesselring, in determining whether the transfers were fraudulent under § 548. This Court's ability to take the Trustee's appointment into account is the pivotal issue in this case because the Trustee comes to us with clean hands, whereas prepetition, PBI bore the taint of Kesselring's fraud. . . .

As the Trustee points out, there are strong equitable arguments that favor courts' consideration of post-petition events. A number of courts have applied these arguments in concluding that the defense of *in pari delicto* should not be applied when a bad actor has been removed and the defense is serving only to bar the claims of an innocent successor.

[I]n Scholes v. Lehmann, 56 F.3d 750, 754 (7th Cir. 1995), the Court noted that "the defense of *in pari delicto* loses its sting when the person who is *in pari delicto* is eliminated." Similar equitable considerations apply here as the bad actor, Kesselring, has been eliminated and the Trustee comes to us with clean hands, representing the interests of innocent creditors. If the doctrine of imputation were applied to bar PBI's recovery, that application would lead to an inequitable result (loss to innocent creditors).

We agree that "under Pennsylvania law equitable defenses such as the doctrine of imputation that may be sustainable against the corporation may fail to act as a total bar to recovery when the beneficiaries of the action are the corporation's innocent creditors," and find that the same logic applies to suits brought under § 548 of the Code, and we therefore conclude that we may take the appointment of the Trustee into account when evaluating his fraudulent conveyance claim. In re Jack Greenberg, 240 B.R. at 506. There is no limiting language in § 548 similar to that in § 541, and without that language there is no reason not to follow the better rule, under which Kesselring's conduct would not be imputed to the Trustee because it would lead to an inequitable result in this case.

D.

In sum, nothing in the language of § 548 precludes us from considering the replacement of Kesselring by the Trustee and the concomitant removal of the taint of Kesselring's fraud from PBI, and we hold that Kesselring's conduct will not be imputed to the Trustee. In that event, the Trustee had no "antecedent debt," and consequently no value was received for the payments made by PBI to PFS. The District Court's order granting the motion to dismiss will therefore be vacated and the matter remanded to the District Court, which we assume will remand the matter to the Bankruptcy Court for further proceedings consistent with this opinion.

PBI shows the difficulty in applying fraudulent transfer law to corporations, who can only act through human beings. Just as the trustee can avoid a lien that the debtor would be bound by under the strong arm clause, *PBI* holds that a trustee may not even be bound by knowledge that would be equitably charged to a DIP under common law doctrines, such as *in pari delicto*. Some courts have gone the other way, with regard to fraudulent transfers in other contexts, and have tagged bankruptcy trustees on the basis of *in pari delicto*. For a collection of such cases, see William McGrane, The Erroneous Application of the Defense of In Pari Delicto to Bankruptcy Trustees, 29 Cal. Bankr. J. 275 (2007). Historically, a transferor was barred from attacking its own fraudulent transfer by the doctrine of unclean hands, but the trustee acting for creditors was immune from that. Official Comm. of Unsecured Creditors of PSA, Inc. v. Edwards, 437 F.3d 1145, 1151-52 (11th Cir. 2006) (fraudulent conveyances are an "exception to the general rule that the trustee takes the debtor estate as it is at the commencement of the bankruptcy").

The impropriety of imputing prior debtor conduct to the trustee is highlighted by the language in § 544(b), which sounds in subrogation. The famous statement is that "[t]he trustee stands in the shoes of the [debtor]," but in "the overshoes of the creditors." Schneider v. O'Neal, 243 F.2d 914, 918 (8th Cir. 1957). For that reason, it could be assumed that the trustee can only avoid a transfer or obligation to the extent of that actual "subrogor" creditor's claim. The Supreme Court in Moore v. Bay, 284 U.S. 4 (1931), held to the contrary: the trustee could avoid the transaction completely, even if the actual creditor in whose stead the trustee sued was owed much less than the transaction amount. Furthermore, the transaction is avoided for the benefit of all unsecured creditors, § 550, not just the subset of creditors who could have brought the avoidance action under state law. This result of according the trustee extraordinary power that nobody has under state law—pursuant to a Code provision (§ 544(b)) purportedly based on state law—was thought extreme by many scholars in the bankruptcy field (and federalism buffs), but the debate quieted with a growing disuse of § 544(b). Then again, it may be coming back. Giuliano v. Schnable (In re DSI Renal Holdings, LLC), 2020 WL 550987, at *4 (Bankr. D. Del. Feb. 4, 2020) (restricting avoidance recovery to amount of creditors' hypothetical state-law claims); see also Douglas J. Whaley, The Dangerous Doctrine of *Moore v. Bay*, 82 Tex. L. Rev. 73 (2003) (predicting, accurately, that the issue would take on increased vitality as the number of state and federal laws that permit avoidance of transactions under § 544(b) was increasing).

2. *Intercorporate Transfers*

You now know that if you sell your car to your roommate for $1 when insolvent, that's constructive fraud; $1 is not REV (yes, even for your car). If you do so in a rush when you hear the sheriff's on her way to levy, that's probably actual fraud to boot. UVTA §§ 4, 5; § 548(a)(1). As the following case shows, a transfer may fail the test of REV because even though plenty of value is given, it is given to the wrong party.

In re IMAGE WORLDWIDE, LTD.

139 F.3d 574 (7th Cir. 1998)

ESCHBACH, Circuit Judge.

Image Worldwide, Ltd. guaranteed loans paid to an affiliate corporation, Image Marketing, Ltd. Both corporations were owned by the same person, but only Image Marketing received funds from the loan. The Image Worldwide's bankruptcy trustee filed suit to avoid the guarantees as a fraudulent transfer, alleging that the guarantees made Image Worldwide insolvent, and that Image Worldwide did not receive reasonably equivalent value in exchange for its guarantees. . . .

Richard Steinberg was the sole shareholder, sole officer, and sole director of Image Marketing, Ltd. (IM), an Illinois corporation incorporated in June 1991. IM was in the commercial printing business, primarily dealing in wholesale sales of music and sports merchandise. IM leased space from FCL Graphics, a printing company that did all of the printing for IM.

In 1992, IM obtained a line of credit from Parkway Bank secured by a first lien against substantially all of IM's assets (IM loan). The line of credit allowed IM to borrow against up to 70% of its eligible accounts receivable, and required IM to reduce its indebtedness to 70% of its accounts receivable in the event that its eligible accounts receivable declined. By June 1993, IM had borrowed $300,000 on its line of credit.

At the end of 1993, IM was several hundred thousand dollars in debt to trade creditors. So in December 1993, Steinberg incorporated a new Illinois corporation, Image Worldwide, Ltd. (IW). Steinberg was the sole shareholder, officer, and director of IW as well. IW leased the same space from FCL as IM, used the same suppliers, and had many of the same customers. In early 1994, Steinberg liquidated IM. Parkway knew of and cooperated in the liquidation of IM. Instead of demanding that IM pay off its loan under the terms of the agreement, however, Parkway allowed Steinberg to use the money obtained from the liquidation of IM to pay down IM's trade debts. Parkway never required IM to pay off its loan, even when its accounts receivable declined to zero in 1994.

Instead, Parkway demanded that IW guarantee IM's $300,000 debt. IW executed the guarantee on May 27, 1994. The guarantee was secured by a first lien on substantially all of IW's assets. IW never borrowed any money from Parkway on its own. Parkway's consideration for the guarantee was its allowing IW to stay in business. Between May 27, 1994 and when IW was forced into bankruptcy, IW paid principal and interest on the loan as it became due.

Even after IM was wound down, IM still owed $200,000 to FCL Graphics. Parkway lent $200,000 to Steinberg to pay this debt (Steinberg loan). The bank paid the proceeds from this loan directly to FCL.[1] The loan was secured by all of IW's accounts receivable. As of the date of its bankruptcy, IW had paid down $72,076.49 in principal and $26,863.45 in interest on the loan.

---

[1] The Bankruptcy Court found that "FCL Graphics was an important customer of Parkway Bank and its sole shareholder, Frank Calabrese, was also a shareholder of Parkway Bank."

IW was no more successful than IM. At trial, Parkway stipulated that the guarantees made IW insolvent. In August 1995, FCL stopped doing work for IW, and filed an involuntary Chapter 7 petition for bankruptcy against IW. David Leibowitz was appointed as the trustee of IW's bankruptcy estate. Over the trustee's objection, Parkway obtained relief from the automatic stay, and collected IW's accounts receivable to pay down the debts guaranteed by IW. All told, Parkway collected $444,507.55 from IW, including the amounts paid prior to the bankruptcy.

The trustee instituted this adversarial proceeding in July 1996 to recover the amounts transferred to Parkway. Pursuant to 11 U.S.C. § 544(b), the trustee charged that the transfers to Parkway were fraudulent transfers in violation of the Uniform Fraudulent Transfer Act (UFTA), 740 ILCS 160/5, because IW never received reasonably equivalent value for its guarantees to Parkway. . . .

The federal fraudulent transfer statute, 11 U.S.C. § 548, contains a one year [now two years—Eds.] statute of limitations that barred the trustee from using that section to avoid the transfer. However, under the strong-arm provision of the Bankruptcy Code, 11 U.S.C. § 544(b), the trustee can avoid any transaction of the debtor that would be voidable by any actual unsecured creditor under state law. The trustee need not identify the creditor, so long as the unsecured creditor exists. Thus, the trustee proceeded against Parkway under the constructive fraud provision of the UFTA [§ 5(a)]. Because Parkway has stipulated that the transaction rendered IW insolvent, the key issue in this case is whether IW, as guarantor, received reasonably equivalent value for its guarantee when the direct benefits of the transaction were received by a third party, IM. Parkway argues that its allowing IW to stay in business constituted reasonably equivalent value for IW's guarantee of IM's debt. Parkway also attempts to argue that IM and IW were the same entity.

A

Because the UFTA is a state law, we must predict how the Illinois courts would handle Parkway's claims. The Illinois courts have not yet elaborated on what "reasonably equivalent value" is for purposes of § 160/5. . . . Thus, we can look to interpretations of "reasonably equivalent value" from § 548 cases, as well as cases from courts interpreting other states' versions of the UFTA for assistance in predicting what an Illinois court would do.

B

The bankruptcy court determined as a matter of law that "a conveyance by a corporation for the benefit of an affiliate is not regarded as given [sic] fair consideration to the creditors of the conveying corporations," citing Rubin v. Manufacturers Hanover Trust Co., 661 F.2d 979 (2d Cir. 1981). This determination is an overly narrow statement of law, and misreads the holding of *Rubin*. Nevertheless, under the appropriate law, the bankruptcy court did not clearly err in ruling that the guarantees were fraudulent transfers.

The transactions in question are known in corporate law lingo as an "intercorporate guarantee." These fall into three types: "upstream," "downstream," and "cross-stream." An upstream guarantee is when a subsidiary guarantees the debt of its parent; a downstream guarantee is when a parent corporation guarantees a debt of its subsidiary; a cross-stream guarantee is when a corporation guarantees the debt of an affiliate. See Jack F. Williams, The Fallacies of Contemporary Fraudulent Transfer Models as Applied to Intercorporate Guaranties: Fraudulent Transfer Law as a Fuzzy System, 15 Cardozo L. Rev. 1403, 1419-20 (1994) [hereinafter Williams, Fallacies]. IW's guarantees in this case were cross-stream guarantees.

Intercorporate guarantees are a routine business practice, and their potential voidability creates a risk for unwary lenders. See generally Blumberg, Intragroup Guarantees; Williams, Fallacies, 15 Cardozo L. Rev. at 1418-20; Barry L. Zaretsky, Fraudulent Transfer Law as the Arbiter of Unreasonable Risk, 46 S.C. L. Rev. 1165 (1995); Scott F. Norberg, Comment, Avoidability of Intercorporate Guarantees Under Sections 548(b) and 544(b) of the Bankruptcy Code, 64 N.C. L. Rev. 1099 (1986). Intercorporate guarantees are common because they benefit both the creditor and debtor in a loan transaction. Within a corporate group, some units will often have better credit ratings than others. The units which are perceived as credit risks by lenders will be either unable to obtain loans, or able to obtain a loan only at a higher interest rate. However, when the corporate group exploits the units with good credit ratings by having them guarantee the debt of the weaker unit, the weaker unit will benefit from either obtaining the loan, or getting the loan at a better rate. The creditor benefits from greater security in repayment. So between creditor and debtor, the guarantee is a win-win situation.

However, the creditors of the guarantor making a cross-stream guarantee can sometimes lose out in the transaction, because the guaranteeing corporation may not receive a direct economic benefit from the guarantee. See *Rubin*, 661 F.2d at 991. Should the guarantee push the guarantor into insolvency, these transactions will be scrutinized under a fraudulent transfer analysis. Fraudulent transfer law seeks to preserve assets of the estate for creditors. Some courts applying traditional fraudulent transfer rules to intercorporate guarantees therefore found that the guarantor had not received reasonably equivalent value for the guarantee, because from the standpoint of the unsecured creditor, the guarantor had received no consideration for the guarantee.

However, requiring a direct flow of capital to a cross-guarantor to avoid a finding of a fraudulent transfer "is inhibitory of contemporary financing practices, which recognize that cross-guarantees are often needed because of the unequal abilities of interrelated corporate entities to collateralize loans." TeleFest, Inc. v. Vu-TV Inc., 591 F. Supp. 1368, 1379 (D.N.J. 1984). Often, these guarantees are legitimate business transactions, and not made to frustrate creditors. In recognition of this economic reality, courts have loosened the old rule that transfers primarily for the benefit of a third party invariably give no consideration to the transferor. Thus, even when there has been no direct economic benefit to a guarantor, courts performing a fraudulent transfer analysis have been increasingly willing to look at whether a guarantor received indirect benefits from the guarantee if there has been an indirect benefit. See, e.g., *Xonics*, 841 F.2d at 201; *Rubin*, 661 F.2d at 991-92; *TeleFest*, 591 F. Supp. at 1377-81. "One theme permeates the authorities upholding guaranty obligations: that the guaranty at issue was the result of arm's length negotiations at a time when the common enterprise was commercially viable." Williams, Fallacies, 15 Cardozo L. Rev. at 1438.

Generally, a court will not recognize an indirect benefit unless it is "fairly concrete." See Heritage Bank Tinley Park v. Steinberg (In re Grabill Corp.), 121 B.R. 983, 995 (N.D. Ill. 1990). The most straightforward indirect benefit is when the guarantor receives from the debtor some of the consideration paid to it. See *Rubin*, 661 F.2d at 991; *Grabill*, 121 B.R. at 995-96. But courts have found other economic benefits to qualify as indirect benefits. For example, in Mellon Bank, N.A. v. Metro Communications, Inc., 945 F.2d 635, 646-48 (3d Cir. 1991), the court found reasonably equivalent value for a debtor corporation's guarantee of an affiliate's debt when the loan strengthened the corporate group as a whole, so that the guarantor corporation would benefit from "synergy" within the corporate group. The *Mellon* court stated that indirect benefits included intangibles such as goodwill, id. at 647, and an increased ability to borrow working capital. Id. at 648. *TeleFest* indicated that indirect benefits to a guarantor exist when "the transaction of which the guaranty is a part may safeguard an important source of supply, or an important customer for the guarantor. Or substantial indirect benefits may result from the general relationship" between affiliates. 591 F. Supp. at 1380-81 (quoting Normandin, "Intercorporate Guarantees and Fraudulent Conveyances," in Personal Property Security Interests Under the Revised UCC 361, 370-71 (1977)). In *Xonics*, we recognized the ability of a smaller company to use the distribution system of a larger affiliate as an indirect benefit as well. See *Xonics*, 841 F.2d at 202. . . .

The Steinberg loan presents a [close] case, because IW may have received an indirect benefit from this guarantee. FCL Graphics was IW's printer, and thus its most important supplier. FCL also allowed IM and FW to operate their business on FCL's premises. At trial, Steinberg testified as follows about the benefits to IW from the Steinberg loan:

Q: What, if any, benefit was there to Image Worldwide for you to pay FCL
     Graphics $200,000? . . .
A: It was allowed to continue doing business remaining on FCL's premises
     and having FCL as a supplier.
Q: Is it your testimony that if you hadn't paid FCL the $200,000, it would
     have put Image Worldwide out of business?
A: Yes.
Q: It would have moved Image Worldwide off the premises?
A: Yes.
Q: It would not have supplied product to Image Worldwide?
A: Yes.

Transcript at 44-45, Leibowitz v. Parkway Bank & Trust Co., 210 B.R. 298 (Bankr. N.D. Ill. 1997) (No. 97 C 923). If the Steinberg loan had not been made to pay off IM's debt to FCL, FCL Graphics clearly posed a substantial threat to IW because of its ability to evict IW and discontinue providing services to IW. *TeleFest* states that:

> [Some courts have] rationalized upholding various transfers against fraudulent conveyance challenges by finding that sufficient consideration passed to the transferor because an opportunity had been given to it to avoid bankruptcy through the strengthening of an affiliated corporation that received the benefit of the transfer. Such an approach seems indisputably proper when a weak but still solvent entity is rendered insolvent only because of the inclusion of the guaranty on the liability side of the balance sheet. This permits the analysis to focus upon economic reality in the appropriate factual context without rewarding legal laxity or inflexibly ignoring real benefits merely because they have no place on the company's balance sheet.

TeleFest, 591 F. Supp. at 1379 (quoting Rosenberg, Intercorporate Guarantees and the Law of Fraudulent Conveyances: Lender Beware, 125 U. Pa. L. Rev. 235, 245-46). Under the broad reading of the indirect benefit doctrine laid down in cases like *TeleFest*, IW received an indirect benefit from the payment of the Steinberg loan because the loan kept FCL Graphics from kicking Steinberg and his companies off of FCL's property, and from refusing to do business with Steinberg. True, the balance sheet showed that IW was insolvent after taking on the IM loan and the Steinberg loan, but IW was not finished as a going concern, as IW was able to remain in business for 17 months after guaranteeing the Steinberg loan.

On the other hand, the circumstances of this case do not fit the circumstances when indirect benefits from a guarantee are found to constitute reasonably equivalent value. As indicated above, courts that uphold cross-stream guarantees generally do so when the transaction strengthens the viability of the corporate group. In this case, though, there were not two functioning corporations that benefitted mutually from the loan. By the time IW guaranteed the Steinberg loan, IM had been wound down. Even though it was not officially dissolved, the company had been liquidated and was inactive. IW became insolvent to pay an inactive affiliate's debts. Indeed, while IW was able to timely pay the bank pursuant to the loans for a time after guaranteeing the loans, IW eventually fell behind in payments to trade creditors just like IM had. In effect, by paying off IM's debts, IW kept IM out of bankruptcy by bankrupting itself. This shift of risk from the creditors of the debtor to the creditors of the guarantor is exactly the situation that fraudulent transfer law seeks to avoid when applied to guarantees. See *Rubin*, 661 F.2d at 991. Thus, while IW received an indirect benefit from the transaction, it did not receive reasonably equivalent value.

We therefore hold that indirect benefits to a guarantor may be considered when determining whether a corporation receives reasonably equivalent value for a guarantee. However, we do not believe that the bankruptcy court clearly erred when it found that IW did not receive reasonably equivalent value for its guarantees. Thus, the judgment of the district court is affirmed.

―――――――――――――――

While Steinberg and Parkway Bank's lawyers may have pitched the benefits of incorporation, such as insulation from liability so long as the corporate form is respected, they may not have realized the fraudulent conveyance law flip side: each entity is its own debtor, requiring its own transfers to be for REV when insolvent.

A fraudulent transfer issue similar to intercorporate guarantees is a change of tax status for corporations vis-à-vis their shareholders. Recall *Majestic Star Casino* from Assignment 17 and its discussion of the difference between C corporations and S corporations. In a case that came to a contrary result, In re Bakersfield Westar, Inc., 226 B.R. 227 (B.A.P. 9th Cir. 1998), the focus was on fraudulent conveyance law. The debtor's principals made an "irrevocable" IRS election to convert an S corp. into a C corp., largely to have the soon-to-be-bankrupt corporation shoulder the tax burden versus the pass-through shareholders. The corporation's chapter 7 trustee said the debtor got nothing out of this election—and in fact incurred a substantial tax to pay. Agreeing that "tax status" was property subject to fraudulent transfer, the court set aside the election as a constructive fraud as the company was insolvent. The IRS jumped in as strange bedfellow to the debtor and said the election couldn't be undone thus because the IRS is very clear that the only way to revoke tax status election is through IRS procedures, not use of the federal bankruptcy laws, and there was no ground to revoke the election under IRS regulations. The court told the astonished IRS that even it yields to the Code.

A final wrinkle with intercorporate transfers and fraudulent conveyance law raises the reverse problem of *Image Worldwide*. Whereas in *Image Worldwide*, the issue was whether the wrong entity received the REV exchanged for another entity's transfer, in other cases the question is whether the seemingly distinct entities are actually so indistinct that they must be treated as one. This concept should be familiar for those who have studied veil-piercing doctrines of corporate law. It reaches special poignancy for financial whizzes seeking to set up so-called "bankruptcy-remote vehicles," which is just a doublespeak way of saying separate entities. Why do they try to do so? Because if a lender wants to take a security interest in accounts receivable, and the debtor goes into bankruptcy, the lender has to deal with that pesky automatic stay and, perhaps worse, a bankruptcy judge with decision-making authority. But if the lender instead gets the debtor to sell the same receivables to a separate entity, and that entity borrows money from the bank (secured by its newly acquired receivables), then if the original debtor goes bankrupt, but the affiliated special entity does not, there is no automatic stay or anything to deal with if a default entitles the lender to collect on the receivables collateral.

PALOIAN v. LASALLE BANK
619 F.3d 688 (7th Cir. 2010)

EASTERBROOK, Chief Judge.

Doctors Hospital of Hyde Park was founded (as "Illinois Central Hospital") to provide medical care as a fringe benefit for workers of the Illinois Central Railroad. Construction began in 1914; the architects were Schmidt, Garden & Martin. The building is on several lists of memorable designs. But the Illinois Central, like other railroads, eventually decided that it did not have a comparative advantage in providing medical care and sold the business.

Between 1992 and 2000 the Hospital was a Subchapter S corporation controlled by James Desnick, an ophthalmologist with a checkered past. Desnick once operated a chain of eye-care clinics, whose business practices garnered adverse publicity. See Desnick v. American Broadcasting Cos., 233 F.3d 514 (7th Cir. 2000). Following charges of misconduct during the 1980s, Desnick gave up his medical practice in 1991 and bought the Hospital the next year. In 1999 and 2000 Desnick paid civil penalties of some $18.5 million to the Medicare and Medicaid programs on account of the Hospital's excessive bills—not only "upcoding" to put services in categories that led to greater reimbursement, but also claims for medically unnecessary procedures or work never done at all. The Hospital also was inefficient. . . .

Like other medical providers, the Hospital furnished services well before it received payment from patients or their insurers. This created a cash-flow problem, which the Hospital addressed by borrowing money. The current dispute arises from two of these loans. The Hospital's trustee in bankruptcy proposes to recover, as fraudulent conveyances, some of the payments made during the last years before the Hospital entered bankruptcy.

In March 1997 Daiwa Healthco extended a revolving $25 million line of credit to MMA Funding, L.L.C., which made the money available to the Hospital for operating expenses. (Desnick owned 99% or more of MMA Funding and all other Hospital-related entities mentioned in this opinion. . . .) The Hospital transferred all of its current and future accounts receivable to MMA Funding, which gave Daiwa a security interest in them. The plan of this transaction was to use MMA Funding as a "bankruptcy-remote vehicle" so that Daiwa could be assured of repayment even if the Hospital entered bankruptcy. . . .

[O]ne issue that is sure to recur [on remand] is whether Daiwa and Desnick succeeded in making MMA Funding a bankruptcy-remote vehicle. For, if they did not, and the Hospital went insolvent before April 2000, then payments routed through or for the account of MMA Funding potentially could be recaptured for the benefit of creditors in general (if § 550(b) does not foreclose relief).

The idea behind the bankruptcy remote vehicle is that, if a debtor sells particular assets to a separate corporation, the lender can rely on those assets without the complications (such as preference-recovery actions) that attend bankruptcy. See, e.g., Kenneth N. Klee & Brendt C. Butler, Asset-Backed Securitization, Special Purpose Vehicles and Other Securitization Issues, ALI-ABA Course of Study Materials SJ082 (June 2004). Bankruptcy remote entities are among several devices that borrowers and lenders have adopted to make corporate reorganization more a matter of contract and less a matter of judicial discretion. See Alan Schwartz, A Contract Theory Approach to Business Bankruptcy, 107 Yale L.J. 1807 (1998); Robert K. Rasmussen, Debtor's Choice: Menu Approach to Corporate Bankruptcy, 71 Tex. L. Rev. 51 (1992). See also Douglas G. Baird & Robert K. Rasmussen, The End of Bankruptcy, 55 Stan. L. Rev. 751 (2002).

To make the idea work, the separate entity must be, well, separate. It must buy assets (here, accounts receivable). It must manage these assets in its own interest rather than the debtor's. It must observe corporate formalities, to prevent the court from rolling it back into the debtor under the approach of a decision such as United Airlines v. HSBC Bank USA, N.A., 416 F.3d 609 (7th Cir. 2005), which holds that debtors and creditors can't evade bankruptcy law through clever choice of words, but must structure their transactions so that their economic substance lies outside particular sections of the Bankruptcy Code.

If Daiwa had loaned $25 million to Vehicle, a corporation independent of Desnick, which then purchased the Hospital's accounts receivable for $22 million (using the proceeds of the loan) and stood to make a profit, or suffer a loss, depending on how much eventually came in, there would be little ground to treat Vehicle's payments on the loan as preferential transfers by the Hospital. The transfer by the Hospital would have occurred with the initial sale of the receivables, and, if that sale predated the Hospital's insolvency (or the bankruptcy filing) by enough time, it would be outside the bankruptcy trustee's avoiding powers, even though particular payments occurred within the look-back periods (90 days or one year under 11 U.S.C. § 547(b), two years under § 548(a)). And the parties agree that, if MMA Funding became a legitimate bankruptcy-remote vehicle as part of the Daiwa loan, this prevents recovery of payments made on the Nomura loan from July 1998 forward.

As far as we can tell from this record, however, MMA Funding lacked the usual attributes of a bankruptcy-remote vehicle. It was not independent of Desnick or the Hospital; Desnick owned MMA Funding (99% of which was owned by the Hospital, and 1% of which was owned by a firm that Desnick owned directly or through some trusts), and MMA Funding operated as if it were a department of the Hospital. It did not have an office, a phone number, a checking account, or stationery; all of its letters were written on the Hospital's stationery. It did not prepare financial statements or file tax returns. It did not purchase the receivables for any price (at least, if it did, the record does not show what that price was). Instead of buying the receivables at the outset, MMA Funding took a small cut of the proceeds every month to cover its (tiny) costs of operation. The Hospital continued to carry the accounts receivable on its own books, as a corporate asset; it told other creditors that Daiwa had a security interest in the receivables, which is of course the sort of structure that makes the payments amenable to an [avoidance] action whether or not the receivables are remitted to a lockbox at a bank.

There is scarcely any evidence in this record that MMA Funding even *existed*, except as a name that Daiwa's and Desnick's lawyers put in some documents. Daiwa can't complain; it knew that MMA Funding was a shell or could have found out easily enough. See Fusion Capital Fund II, LLC v. Ham, 614 F.3d 698 (7th Cir. Aug. 2, 2010). But a trustee in bankruptcy can step into the shoes of any hypothetical lien creditor, see 11 U.S.C. § 544—which for current purposes may mean a creditor ignorant of the contracts signed by the Hospital, Daiwa, Nomura, LaSalle Bank, and MMA Funding. If a hypothetical creditor could have obtained an interest in assets that the Hospital's books declared belonged to it, then a bankruptcy trustee can maintain an avoidance action. And the interests of these outside creditors can't be ignored. The bankruptcy and district judges observed that treating MMA Funding as a bankruptcy-remote vehicle allowed Daiwa and Nomura to charge lower rates of interest—which is true enough but overlooks the fact that, if some creditors are protected from [avoidance] actions and thus can charge lower interest, other creditors bear higher risk and must charge higher interest. The net effect for operating firms is unclear. See Barry E. Adler, A Re-Examination of Near-Bankruptcy Investment Incentives, 62 U. Chi. L. Rev. 575 (1995). The Code allows the trustee to look out for the interests of these other creditors, who may not appreciate that they should have charged extra to offset the effects of a bankruptcy-remote vehicle that was hidden in the weeds.

Perhaps LaSalle Bank can offer on remand evidence to show that there was a bona fide sale of accounts receivable from the Hospital to MMA Funding in March 2007, and that MMA Funding was more than a name without a business entity to go with it. Or perhaps the Bank could contend that the hypothetical lien creditor must be charged with knowledge of those aspects of the earlier transactions that were matters of public record. See In re Professional Investment Properties, 955 F.2d 623, 627-28 (9th Cir. 1992); Collier on Bankruptcy ¶544.02[2]. . . .

The judgment of the district court is vacated, and the case is remanded. . . .

_____

The substance-over-form analysis of *Paloian* segues us nicely to our next topic.

B.   LEVERAGED BUYOUTS

The problem of matching up the entity that gave value with the entity that received value is at the heart of corporate fraudulent conveyance law. The apotheosis of this difficulty lies in the application of fraudulent conveyance law to leveraged buyouts ("LBOs"). Without LBOs, many marginal corporate takeovers could not be financed. As the economy cycles, LBOs go in and out of fashion, but even in the moments of the loosest credit, there is usually someone attracted to the device.

The essence of the LBO financing device is fairly simple. If you buy something for cash, you have to have the cash to do it; if you buy something for a down payment plus debt, you "leverage" your equity investment to allow you to build up a portfolio of assets that exceeds your available cash. Now assume you go to a bank to borrow money to buy a business. Just as banks demand mortgages for homeowners who buy on debt, so too do they demand collateral from business purchasers.

What assets might investors pledge? You might think their own, but that would be naïve. Here's a stylized example that captures the essence.

Old Shares wants to sell her company, Lunch, Inc., that she built up over the years to Hedgie Fund. They decide $100 million is a fair price for the company that has great goodwill, lots of hard assets, and very little debt—mostly unsecured trade. Hedgie and Old Shares agree that Hedgie will buy Old Share's stock in Lunch for $100 million. But because Hedgie wants neither to pay cash nor to pledge its own assets to secure a loan for $100 million, it comes up with a clever two-step. It buys the company for $100 million by signing a (short-lived) I.O.U. to Old Shares and then does its dance. Step One: Lunch borrows $100 million from lender and pledges all its assets to secure the loan. Lunch now has a ton of debt, no free collateral, but also $100 million in cash. (When outside investors rather than a bank provide the financing for an LBO, it is often through the issuance of aptly named "junk bonds.") Step Two: Hedgie declares a $100 million dividend—to itself as 100% shareholder—and pays that money to retire the I.O.U. to Old Shares. Result: Old Shares has $100 million and Hedgie owns Lunch, just as the two had planned. But Lunch now has $100 million of secured debt and nothing to show for it. If Lunch flourishes, Hedgie makes a killing for no money down. If Lunch tanks, Hedgie's lost nothing, the lender comes and gets repaid by liquidating all the assets, but there's nothing left over for the unsecured trade debt. They complain that if we cut through all the malarkey, what *really* happened, in substance, was that Lunch, Inc. took on a huge debt and got nothing in return. Sound familiar?

In the next case, the planners tried to be even sneakier. Instead of Hedgie buying Old Share's stock of Lunch, Hedgie bought all the *assets* of Lunch, including the intellectual property right to use the name "Lunch." Hedgie formally left it up to (Old) Lunch to decide whether it would pay a dividend to Old Shares. (*Spoiler*: it did.) Hedgie financed the deal for only $500, a $3 million bank loan—promptly secured by all the assets it bought from Lunch, and an I.O.U. of dubious worth. A distracted court or busy judge might have let it slip by, but look who's back.

BOYER v. CROWN STOCK DISTRIBUTION, INC.
587 F.3d 787 (7th Cir. 2009)

POSNER, Circuit Judge.

These appeals arise from the Chapter 7 bankruptcy of Crown Unlimited Machine, Inc. The trustee in bankruptcy filed an adversary action charging the defendants—a defunct corporation and its shareholders, members of a family named Stroup—with having made a fraudulent conveyance in violation of Ind. Code § 32-18-2-14(2) (section 4(a)(2) of the Uniform Fraudulent Transfer Act), a statute enforceable in a bankruptcy proceeding. See 11 U.S.C. § 544(b). After an evidentiary hearing, the bankruptcy judge awarded the trustee $3,295,000 plus prejudgment interest. The district judge affirmed and the defendants have appealed. The trustee has cross-appealed, seeking an additional $590,328.

Crown was a designer and manufacturer of machinery for cutting and bending tubes. Most of the machinery it made was custom-designed to the buyer's specifications, and only two other companies manufactured custom-designed machinery of that type. In January 1999 the defendants agreed to sell all of Crown's assets to Kevin E. Smith, the president of a company in a similar line of business. The price was $6 million. Crown agreed to employ Smith until the closing, so that he could assure himself of the value of the business before committing to buying it.

He decided to go through with the deal. At the closing, on January 5, 2000, Crown received from a new corporation, formed by Smith, $3.1 million in cash and a $2.9 million promissory note. The new corporation (also named Crown Unlimited Machine, Inc., the name being among the assets sold to the new Crown) had borrowed the $3.1 million from a bank. Although the loan was secured by all of Crown's assets, the annual interest rate (a floating rate) initially exceeded 9 percent. The rate suggests—since inflation expectations were low at the time—that the bank considered the risk of default nontrivial.

The promissory note was payable [to old Crown] on April 1, 2006, with interest at an annual rate of 8 percent. Although that translates into an interest expense of $232,000 a year, the agreement of sale specified that the new corporation would be required to pay only $100,000 a year on the note, with the first payment due in April 2001, unless new Crown's sales exceeded a specified high threshold. The note, like the bank loan, was secured by all of Crown's assets, but the promise's (old Crown's) security interest was subordinated to the bank's. Although the interest rate on the note was lower than the interest rate on the bank loan, even though the note was not as well secured, there was, as we'll see, little chance that the note would ever be paid; and after the first two $100,000 interest payments, it wasn't.

Smith's personal assets were meager. He contributed only $500 of his own money toward the purchase.

Just prior to the closing, old Crown transferred $590,328 from its corporate bank account to a separate bank account so that it could be distributed to Crown's shareholders as a dividend. This was done pursuant to an understanding of the parties that, depending on the company's performance between the initial agreement and the closing, the Stroups would be permitted to keep some of Crown's cash that would otherwise have been transferred to the new corporation as part of the sale; the sale, since it was of all of Crown's assets, included whatever money was in the corporation's bank account.

After the closing, old Crown (renamed [evocatively—Eds.] Crown Stock Distribution, Inc.) distributed the entire $3.1 million in cash that it had received to its shareholders, and ceased to be an operating company.

New Crown was a flop. It declared bankruptcy in July 2003, and its assets were sold pursuant to 11 U.S.C. § 363 (which authorizes a sale, if approved by the bankruptcy judge, of assets of the debtor) for $3.7 million. The buyer was a new company of which Smith is now the president. Most of the money realized in the sale was required for paying off the bank; very little was left over to pay the claims of new Crown's unsecured creditors, who were owed some $1.6 or $1.7 million and on whose behalf the trustee in bankruptcy brought the adversary action. The action was timely, despite the length of time since the alleged fraudulent conveyance, because the bankruptcy petition was filed within the four-year "look back" period of the Uniform Fraudulent Transfer Act, Ind. Code § 32-18-2-19(2), and the trustee initiated this suit within the period specified in 11 U.S.C. § 546 for bringing a section 544 avoidance action and the one-year deadline for bringing a section 550 action to recover improperly transferred funds, a deadline that runs from the date on which the transfer was set aside. 11 U.S.C. § 550(f)(1).

The bankruptcy judge ruled that the $6 million that new Crown had paid (the $3.1 million in cash), or obligated itself to pay (the $2.9 million promissory note), for old Crown's assets had been paid "without [new Crown's] receiving a reasonably equivalent value in exchange." As a result, New Crown had embarked upon "a business . . . for which [its] remaining assets . . . were 'unreasonably small in relation to the business,'" in the language of the Uniform Fraudulent Transfer Act. The judge did not think the assets, including intangible assets such as goodwill that made old Crown a going concern and not just a pile of machinery, had been worth more than $4 million tops on the date of the closing. And he thought that new Crown had been so depleted by the debt it had taken on that it had been, in his words, on "life support" from the get-go. So old Crown and its shareholders could neither enforce the promissory note nor keep either the $3.1 million in cash received at the closing or the two $100,000 interest payments made on the note.

But the $590,328 dividend, the judge ruled, was legitimate, because it had been paid out of cash that belonged to old Crown rather than to the debtor (new Crown). In so ruling he rejected the trustee's argument that the purchase of old Crown's assets had been an LBO (a leveraged buyout), that it should be "collapsed" and the sale thus recharacterized as a sale by the shareholders of old Crown, and that once it was collapsed in this fashion the $590,328 "dividend" would be seen as an asset of the debtor's estate and thus would be available to help satisfy the claims of the unsecured creditors. If the transaction was not collapsed—and the bankruptcy judge thought it should not be because he refused to recharacterize the sale of assets as an LBO—the debtor was not entitled to the return of the dividend because, when it was paid, the money out of which it was paid belonged to old Crown.

We begin our analysis with the trustee's argument for recharacterizing the transaction. In a conventional LBO, an investor buys the stock of a corporation from the stockholders with the proceeds of a loan secured by the corporation's own assets. In re Image Worldwide, Ltd., 139 F.3d 574, 580 (7th Cir. 1998); In re EDC, Inc., 930 F.2d 1275, 1278 (7th Cir. 1991); Mellon Bank, N.A. v. Metro Communications, Inc., 945 F.2d 635, 645-46 (3d Cir. 1991). It follows that if all the assets are still fully secured when the corporation declares bankruptcy, the unsecured creditors cannot satisfy any part of their claims from a sale of the assets. If the trustee loses this suit, the unsecured creditors will have recovered only $150,000—less than 10 cents on the dollar.

Should the acquired company be doomed to go broke after and because of the LBO—if the burden of debt created by the transaction was so heavy that the corporation had no reasonable prospect of surviving—the payment to the shareholders by the buyer of the corporation is deemed a fraudulent conveyance because in exchange for the money the shareholders received they provided no value to the corporation but merely increased its debt and by doing so pushed it over the brink. HBE Leasing Corp. v. Frank, 48 F.3d 623, 635-37 (2d Cir. 1995). . . .

Some courts have been reluctant to apply the Act as written to leveraged buyouts. See Kupetz v. Wolf, 845 F.2d 842, 847-50 (9th Cir. 1988); United States v. Tabor Court Realty Corp., supra, 803 F.2d at 1297; Wieboldt Stores, Inc. v. Schottenstein, 94 B.R. 488, 503 (N.D. Ill. 1988). They sympathize with minority shareholders who have no power to prevent such a deal. They may also agree with the scholars who have argued that many LBOs are welfare-enhancing transactions because by making the managers owners (managers are often the buyers in an LBO [often called MBOs—Eds.]) and thus fusing ownership with control, an LBO increases the managers' incentive to operate the corporation with a view to maximizing its value rather than their salaries and perks. . . .

The reluctance of the courts in the decisions we cited is not easy to square with the language of the Uniform Fraudulent Transfer Act. And anyway the "equities" as we shall see, do not favor lenient treatment in this case. Moreover, although before the LBO Smith was briefly a member of Crown's management, the LBO did not close a gap between managers and shareholders. . . . [Discussion omitted exploring the possible virtues of LBOs to fuse manager-owner alignment of incentives.—Eds.]. [B]oth old and new Crown were closely held corporations. And while the economic literature also argues that the increased risk of bankruptcy that an LBO creates concentrates the minds of the managers (just as, according to Samuel Johnson, the prospect of being hanged concentrates the mind of the condemned person), this is hard to take seriously in the present case; for the owner-manager had only a $500 stake in the company.

But the critical difference between the LBO in this case and a bona fide LBO is that this LBO was highly likely to plunge the company into bankruptcy. There was scant probability that the transaction would increase the firm's value; on the contrary, it left the firm with so few assets that it would have had to be extremely lucky to survive.

The transaction differed, however, in two formal respects from a conventional overleveraged LBO: the buyer bought the assets of the corporation, rather than stock in the corporation; and despite a load of debt and a dearth of cash, the corporation limped along for three-and-a-half years before collapsing into the arms of the bankruptcy court. The defendants urge these as grounds for not reclassifying the asset purchase as an LBO.

Now whether one calls it an LBO or not is not critical, although both the bankruptcy court and the defendants have called it that. Some LBOs are legitimate; others are fraudulent conveyances . . . . If the dividend was part and parcel of the transaction that fatally depleted new Crown's assets, it was part and parcel of a fraudulent conveyance. But if one has to call the overall transaction something, the something is an LBO.

. . .

New Crown thus had made payments and incurred obligations without receiving "reasonably equivalent value" in return. Even if it was not actually insolvent ab initio, as a result of the lack of equivalence it began life with "unreasonably small" assets given the nature of its business. That was what the bankruptcy judge meant when he said that new Crown survived as long as it did only on "life support." That was a finding of fact to which we defer.

The difference between insolvency and "unreasonably small" assets in the LBO context is the difference between being bankrupt on the day the LBO is consummated and having at that moment such meager assets that bankruptcy is a consequence both likely and foreseeable. Focusing on the second question avoids haggling over whether at the moment of the transfer the corporation became "technically" insolvent, a question that only accountants could relish having to answer. Moody v. Security Pacific Business Credit, supra, 971 F.2d at 1070 n. 22; Bruce A. Markell, "Toward True and Plain Dealing: A Theory of Fraudulent Transfers Involving Unreasonably Small Capital," 21 Ind. L. Rev. 469, 498 (1988).

But one has to be careful with a term like "unreasonably small." It is fuzzy, and in danger of being interpreted under the influence of hindsight bias. One is tempted to suppose that because a firm failed it must have been inadequately capitalized. The temptation must be resisted. . . . As we said in a related context in Baldi v. Samuel Son & Co., 548 F.3d 579, 582 (7th Cir. 2008), "of course many start-ups fail, but if a significant probability of failure sufficed to pronounce a start-up insolvent, how would any start-up finance its operations?" But new Crown started life almost with no assets at all, for all its physical assets were encumbered twice over, and the dividend plus new Crown's interest obligations drained the company of virtually all its cash. It was naked to any financial storms that might assail it. So the statutory condition for a fraudulent conveyance was satisfied—or so at least the bankruptcy judge could and did find without committing a clear error.

The fact that mistakes by the buyer hastened the company's demise is not a defense. Whether a transfer was fraudulent when made depends on conditions that existed when it was made, not on what happened later to affect the timing of the company's collapse. Not that the length of the interval between the LBO and the collapse is irrelevant to determining the effect of the transfer. It is pertinent evidence. The longer the interval, the less likely that the collapse was fated at the formation of the new company, although we are skeptical of cases that can be read to suggest that ten or twelve months is a long enough interval to create a presumption that the terms of the LBO were not responsible for the company's failure. An inadequately capitalized company may be able to stagger along for quite some time, concealing its parlous state or persuading creditors to avoid forcing it into a bankruptcy proceeding in which perhaps only the lawyers will do well. . . .

[T]he defendants are unable to sketch a plausible narrative in which new Crown could have survived indefinitely despite being cash starved as a result of the terms of the LBO that brought it into being. The fact that Smith made mistakes in running the company does not weigh as strongly as the defendants think. Everyone makes mistakes. That's one reason why businesses need adequate capital to have a good chance of surviving in the Darwinian jungle that we call the market.

As for the "dividend," it was an integral part of the LBO, although the trustee stumbled by failing to present evidence concerning old Crown's dividend policy. . . . [T]he dividend represented 50 percent of Crown's 1999 profits, which was unreasonably high given the cash needs of the business. Crown's [former] owners drained it of cash—all unbeknownst to the corporation's present and future unsecured creditors. These indications that the dividend was part of the fraudulent transfer rather than a normal distribution of previously earned profits—that it wasn't an ordinary dividend but rather the withdrawal of an asset vital to the acquiring firm—were sufficient to place a burden on the defendants of producing evidence that it was a bona fide dividend, a burden they failed to carry . . . .

Determining that the transfer of assets to new Crown was fraudulent was only the first stage of the adversary action. The second stage was to restore to new Crown (which is to say the trustee) the money that new Crown had paid for the Crown assets. The bankruptcy judge based the award of that money to the trustee on section 550 of the Bankruptcy Code, which defines the right of the trustee in bankruptcy to recover money transferred in a transaction that he is authorized by section 544 to nullify, as the trustee in this case was Section 550(b)(2) denies recovery of property that was transferred to "any immediate or mediate good faith transferee" of the initial transferee of a fraudulent transfer if the subsequent transferee took for value and "in good faith and without knowledge of the voidability of the transfer avoided." § 550(a)(2). If the asset sale is recharacterized as a sale of old Crown by its shareholders, as is implicit in our characterization of the sale as an LBO (remember that a conventional LBO is a stock acquisition), the shareholders lose the protection of section 550(b) because they then are initial rather than subsequent transferees and the "dividend"—the retention of cash by old Crown—becomes an adjustment in the purchase price. But we are now considering the bankruptcy judge's theory.

If the transaction is not collapsed, the initial transferee of the $3.3 million was old Crown and the second-stage transferees were the shareholders. But they gave no "value" in the transfer and so are not protected by section 550(b). As the bankruptcy judge put it, "the individual defendants gave nothing in exchange for their distributions from Crown Stock. Those distributions were made, not in return for some exchange of property or services, or the payment of an antecedent debt, but solely on account of their status as shareholders of the company."

. . .

The trustee is entitled to the judgment awarded by the bankruptcy judge, plus the $590,328 dividend. After the claims of all creditors have been satisfied and the costs of administering the bankruptcy paid, any money remaining in the hands of the trustee must be returned to the defendants. The judgment of the district court is therefore affirmed in part and reversed in part (the part relating to the dividend), and the case remanded for further proceedings consistent with this opinion.

Note that if the transaction is "collapsed," then there was either an insolvent corporation paying a shareholder dividend, a no-no under corporate law (e.g., New York's, as we saw in the *Olympia* case in Assignment 23), or a corporation (New Crown) undertaking debt not for its own benefit but for the benefit of another party (the Stroups), which is a no-no under fraudulent transfer law. But as Judge Posner explained in this treatise, the use of fraudulent conveyance statutes to attack LBOs is not without critics. They have asserted that some transactions are benign (or even beneficial) in their effects on a debtor and its creditors, and it is relatively easy for a creditor to contract against the risk of a harmful fraudulent conveyance, but difficult for a debtor and its creditors to contract out of fraudulent conveyance law to protect a beneficial transaction. See, e.g., Douglas G. Baird, Fraudulent Conveyances, Agency Costs, and Leveraged Buyouts, 20 J. Legal Stud. 1 (1991). Perhaps a less theoretical concern, which gives even those who support application of the doctrine pause, is the potential of strict liability against innocent, unknowing transferees. The Stroups were all in on the scam, but think of public shareholders who get bought out in a tender offer and have no idea about the financing. Indeed, the UVTA's quasi-constructive fraud provisions address just that. Thus, while Judge Posner frets somewhat over the potential fuzziness of "unreasonably small capital," he misses the good work that such fuzziness performs: a culpability escape for those parties who are acting "reasonably" in predicting capital needs.

LBOs go to the max in In re OODC, LLC, 321 B.R. 128 (Bankr. D. Del. 2005), at least according to the trustee. The company bought up smaller businesses, then sold them using LBOs to strip asset value and leave the resulting companies with unreasonably small capital to pay the debtor's existing and maturing debts. The court said it would be possible to view the LBO as one integrated transaction—the business of LBO'ing. We note that the Great Recession started shortly afterward.

C. SAFE HARBORS FOR SETTLEMENT PAYMENTS

The UVTA and Bankruptcy Code both provide safe harbors for certain transactions. Section 546(e), adopted in 1982 but steadily expanded since that time, limits the ability of a trustee to avoid many transactions that reshape the estate:

> Notwithstanding sections 544, 545, 547, 548(a)(1)(B), and 548(b) of this title, the trustee may not avoid a transfer that is a margin payment, . . . or settlement payment, . . . or that is a *transfer made by or to (or for the benefit of)* a commodity broker, forward contract merchant, stockbroker, *financial institution*, financial participant or securities clearing agency, in connection with a securities contract . . . that is made before the commencement of the case, except under section 548(a)(1)(A) of this title.

§ 546(e) (emphasis added). Moreover, the definitions of "securities contract" and "settlement payment" are remarkably wide. § 741(7), (8). Because of its presumptive focus, the section is sometimes called the "stockbroker's defense." Most courts adhered to its text.

> The Frosts contend on appeal, and the bankruptcy and district courts held, that the payments they received in exchange for their privately-held Contemporary Industries stock are exempt from avoidance within the plain meaning of the

[safe harbors]. CIC contends, however, that the payments are not settlement payments within the meaning of § 546(e), because that section was enacted to protect the stability of the financial markets and only protects payments made to settle public securities transactions. CIC also contends the payments were not "made by or to a . . . financial institution" within the meaning of § 546(e), because First National never obtained a beneficial interest in the funds.

CIC . . . points out that several courts have concluded the statutory definition of settlement payment does not encompass payments for [as here] privately held securities. The general rationale behind those holdings, which rely in part on legislative history, is that § 546(e) was enacted to protect the nation's financial markets against instability caused by the reversal of settled securities transactions, that undoing private transactions does not implicate those concerns, and therefore, that Congress did not intend for payments like the ones at issue to fall within the purview of the exemption. CIC suggests we should also review legislative history to determine whether these payments qualify as settlement payments, either because § 741(8)'s definition of that term is ambiguous or because extending § 546(e)'s protection to these payments would lead to an absurd result.

CIC . . . contends it is unreasonable to construe § 546(e) as exempting these payments, the reversal of which would in no way impact the stability of the financial markets, solely because the parties utilized a financial institution as an escrow agent to complete the transaction. . . .

Contemporary Indus. Corp. v. Frost, 564 F.3d 981, 984-87 (8th Cir. 2009).

One sentence suffices to show the case's result: "As noted above, however, our analysis begins—and where the language is plain, usually ends—with the statutory text. . . ." Id. at 986.

When the Supreme Court got its hands on the issue, it surprised everyone by rejecting this dominant approach. But its analysis had little to do with the policy concerns cogently articulated in the passage above:

FTI maintains that the only relevant transfer for purposes of the § 546(e) safe-harbor inquiry is the overarching transfer between Valley View [buyer] and Merit [seller] of $16.5 million for purchase of the stock, which is the transfer that the trustee seeks to avoid under § 548(a)(1)(B). Because that transfer was not made by, to, or for the benefit of a financial institution [such as the one that Valley View transferred its payments to as escrow agent], FTI contends that the safe harbor has no application.

The Court agrees with FTI. The language of § 546(e), the specific context in which that language is used, and the broader statutory structure all support the conclusion that the relevant transfer for purposes of the § 546(e) safe-harbor inquiry is the overarching transfer that the trustee seeks to avoid under one of the substantive avoidance provisions.

Merit Management Group v. FTI Consulting, 138 S. Ct. 883, 892-93 (2018).

We're still waiting to see how the securities industry will respond.

Problem Set 24

24.1. Kim Winick called you this morning about a broken friendship. It was just one year ago that Kim lent $500,000—the money she had inherited from her mother—to help her friend, Pat Rafferty, start a small dry cleaning business: Magic Clean, Inc. Kim lent the money to the company at a good interest rate, with only the interest payable for six years. At the end of six years, which was Pat's estimate of the time needed for the business to become established and profitable, the company would repay Kim in full. Two weeks ago Kim got a letter from Pat saying that he had sold all the stock of the company to Rick Lance, a recently retired navy man. Kim knows Lance and says he has no business experience. As Kim put it, "Cash flow is not one of the flows he knows about." Lance paid $100,000 for the equity, a price that seems more than adequate for a business that has not yet turned a profit. The stock sale was entirely on credit, with the company guaranteeing Lance's payments to Pat and all of the company's assets securing the guarantee. Pat included a balance sheet showing the value of the company's assets exceeding its liabilities, even if the guarantee to Pat is included as a liability.

Pat's letter explains that the business is struggling and its bills from suppliers are piling up. It concludes, "I have been without a salary for a whole year, Kim, and I just can't go on like this. But I'm proud of the fact that I'm up to date on your interest and I'm sure everything will be fine with Lance running the shop." Kim does not feel at all fine and wants to know what she can do "to cancel my ticket on the *Titanic*." What's your advice? See UVTA §§ 2, 4, 5.

24.2. Illinois Vacuum is an old client of yours, a long-time manufacturer of high-quality cleaning equipment. The Credit Director, Shirley Lo, has come to you this afternoon because of a serious credit problem with Springfield Appliances and Aluminum Siding, a major customer of IV. IV has sold vacuum cleaners to Springfield for a long time on open account. Springfield has been suffering from competition in two new malls and has been in increasing financial difficulty. It is now 90 days behind in its payments to IV, with a total owed of about $90,000.

Lo claims the troubles at Springfield really go back to the retirement of Sam Kirwin, the principal owner of the business, and the takeover of operations by his son, Scott. Lo recently talked with Sam at his new Florida retirement home, but Sam refuses to believe that the business is in trouble, citing the very substantial dividend he had just received as the owner of 75% of the common shares. The news of this dividend hit Lo really hard, prompting her to seek your advice. Aside from the numerous other questions you would have, advise Lo about the possible remedies available to IV with regard to the dividend. Would your analysis be any different if the dividend were a regular preferred stock dividend in the amount provided for by the terms of the preferred stock (e.g., $100 per share each year, cumulatively)?

24.3. Mr. and Mrs. Young are members of the Crystal Evangelical Free Church. They are active in the church, attending services weekly with their children, serving as officers, and contributing their time. They tithe regularly, following the Biblical injunction to contribute 10% of their income to the church. Last year, their church contributions totaled $13,450, all made while the Youngs were legally insolvent. They are eligible for and have filed a chapter 7 petition, and their trustee has asked the church to return the contributions. You represent the church; what do you advise? (We don't make this stuff up. To see a more complete discussion of the case, brought by a trustee named Christians, where the court relied on a case styled In re Moses, see Christians v. Crystal Evangelical Free Church (In re Young), 148 B.R. 886 (Bankr. D. Minn. 1992), *aff'd*, 152 B.R. 939 (D. Minn.), *rev'd*, 82 F.3d 1407 (8th Cir. 1996), *vacated*, 521 U.S. 1114 (1997), *on remand, sub nom.* In re Young, 141 F.2d 854 (8th Cir.), *cert. denied*, 525 U.S. 811 (1998).)

24.4. Marcel Du Champs fraudulently conveyed his beloved prize racehorse Jonquil to his friend, Travis Winchel, for $100 to keep it safe from creditor attachment. The two had a signed understanding that when Marcel's business difficulties were over, Travis would reconvey the horse, which is worth about $900,000. Ultimately, Marcel was able to revive his business, become solvent, and pay all his creditors in full. He offers $100 to Travis, plus a generous bonus to cover the horse's stable fees, but Travis refuses to reconvey. He has grown fond of the horse and of life in the fast lane, and no longer wishes to sell. Does Marcel have any legal recourse?

EXECUTORY CONTRACTS I

A. THE ECONOMIC DECISION

To an ever-increasing extent, the wealth of our society is in contracts, and valuable contracts are found in every aspect of economic life. Any business is likely to have a number of agreements that were negotiated long before bankruptcy, with performance continuing or due after the filing. As the DIP decides what direction the ongoing business should take, a review of the pending contracts becomes essential. Some of the debtor's pre-bankruptcy contracts may have turned out to be good bargains, while others may have turned out to be losers. Even among the good bargains, some may be worth more to someone else than they are to the debtor and so might be sold (assigned) for needed cash. Escaping burdensome contracts can be thought of as another way of "reshaping" the bankruptcy estate by the DIP, and protecting beneficial contracts is another way to help the debtor stabilize operations and resuscitate the business.

A prepetition contract may be *assumed* under the Code, § 365(a); that is, the DIP may agree to perform the contract, which of course forces the other party to honor the contract as well, even if it were secretly hoping that the debtor's bankruptcy would be the end of a soured contractual relationship. This assumption power helps a business continue its operations during and after filing, but the assumption also transforms the contract into an obligation of the estate, and so any subsequent breach by the debtor would become a breach by the estate and hence a priority administrative expense under §§ 503(b) and 507(a)(2). This means that a DIP will not assume lightly; it will want to scrutinize all the company's contracts to understand how they fit into the business's future and assess the current state of the market for the goods or services that are the subject of the contractual arrangement.

If the DIP decides a contract is a loser, the Code provides an out. It permits the estate to *reject* the contract, § 365(a), which means to breach it. That breach gives rise to a claim for damages by the debtor's counterparty under nonbankruptcy law, of course, but those damages are just another general unsecured claim, § 365(g), payable in tiny bankruptcy dollars. The justification for payment in tiny bankruptcy dollars is that the rejection is deemed to have occurred at the moment of filing and thus is accorded the same treatment as all other aggrieved creditors. Cherry-picking winning and losing contracts is a major tool for reshaping the estate.

While it is simple enough to understand that the estate will assume good bargains and reject (breach) bad ones, it is considerably more complicated to translate the basic economic idea into the Code. As a preliminary matter, note that assumption or rejection requires the approval of the court. § 365(a).

B.   THE STATUTE

Section 365 is one of the longest and most detailed provisions of the Code. So many specifics have been added that the section is tough to parse. And the real kicker is that it applies only to "executory" contracts, a term defined nowhere in the Code but which we will explore in the next assignment. (It also applies to unexpired leases, the real property analogue.) The analysis should begin, however, in the more fundamental § 541(a), which brings all property of the debtor, of whatever kind, into the estate. As we have seen, even such ethereal intangibles as "tax status" can be property of the estate, so despite what you may have learned in the first-year curriculum, contracts can indeed be property—at least in bankruptcy. Preempting an argument that an anti-assignment clause might render an assignment from the debtor into the estate impermissible, § 541(c)(1) invalidates anti-assignment clauses' efforts to keep matters out of the estate. Once the contract is property of the estate, § 365 becomes applicable to provide the rules of rejection and assumption.

The statute gives the chapter 11 debtor (and thus its body of creditors) great advantages in both assumption and rejection, especially as to timing, over the contractual counterparty. The debtor may take its time all the way up to confirmation to decide whether to assume or reject, while the counterparty stews or even has to continue performing its own contractual obligations in the interim. § 365(d)(2). This "free option" is underscored by §§ 365(g) and 502(g), which set any damage claim at the filing date, regardless of how long the debtor takes to decide what to do.

If the contract is a winner, the debtor will want to assume it. But that does not mean the debtor itself will perform. It might be that the debtor simply wants to capture the economic benefit of the winning contract but "outsource" performance to someone else. Consider a painter who has a contract to paint a garage for $500, and the going rate is $300. That contract is a winner and should be assumed pronto. But if the debtor has gotten stuck in another job that's taking longer than expected and won't have time to perform this lucrative contract when it comes time, she may want to sell the contract to a fellow painter for, say, $100. By *assuming* and then *assigning* the contract, the painter turned what was going to be a lawsuit for breach against her into a quick $100 for the estate. The fellow painter is happy, too, picking up for $100 the right to a $500 paint job that usually only earns $300—the same as if he had negotiated to be paid $400 for that job. And the counterparty is revenue-neutral to this transaction. Everyone wins, or at least nobody loses. (Were the painter hired for a portrait, we might have a different analysis, but we will get to that later.) Thus, debtors may exercise their assumption power under the Code even if they have no intention of performing the contracts themselves. "Winning" contracts have value.

The parties might have thought in advance about assignment and written their contract in many possible ways. For example, they might have prohibited assignments, just as they might have allowed them freely. They might have conditioned assignments upon approval of the counterparty, "that approval not to be unreasonably withheld" to quote a boilerplate contractual clause. Or they have gotten creative and decided in advance how to allocate any assignment surplus (e.g., "this contract may be assigned by painter *provided* that any profit upon such assignment be divided 50/50 between painter and garage owner"). The Code, however, has something to say about such terms.

═══════════════ In re JAMESWAY CORP. ═══════════════

201 B.R. 73 (Bankr. S.D.N.Y. 1996)

GARRITY, JR., Bankruptcy Judge.

FACTS

The facts are not disputed. On October 18, 1995 ("petition date"), Jamesway and its affiliates (collectively, the "debtors") filed separate petitions for relief under chapter 11 of the Bankruptcy Code in this district. At that time, debtors operated discount department stores under the "Jamesway" name. Debtors are in possession of their businesses and properties as debtors-in-possession pursuant to §§ 1107 and 1108 of the Bankruptcy Code.

As of the petition date, Jamesway and Mass Mutual, as successor-in-interest to Valley Green Mall Co., were parties to an agreement dated July 16, 1986, as amended (the "Newberry Lease"), whereby Jamesway, as tenant, leased certain retail space located in the Newberry Commons shopping center in Etters, Pennsylvania. Paragraph 17 of that lease states in relevant part that:

> [i]f Tenant assigns this Lease . . . then during the first twenty (20) years . . . Tenant shall pay Landlord 50% of the "profits" received by Tenant from the assignee or sublessee. Thereafter, Tenant shall pay Landlord 60% of such profits. . . .

Newberry Lease ¶ 17. On or about February 9, 1996, Jamesway moved under § 365 of the Bankruptcy Code to assume and assign the Newberry Lease to Rite Aid of Pennsylvania, Inc. ("Rite Aid") for $100,000 (the "Rite Aid Motion"). Over Mass Mutual's objection, we granted the motion. . . . [Two other leases had similar provisions, and the court had permitted their assignments as well. — Eds.]

DISCUSSION . . .

Section 365(a) of the Bankruptcy Code authorizes a debtor-in-possession to assume or reject, subject to the court's approval, any executory contract or unexpired lease of the debtor. 11 U.S.C. § 365(a). A debtor-in-possession may assign an unexpired lease of the debtor only if it assumes the lease in accordance with § 365(a), and provides adequate assurance of future performance by the assignee, whether or not there has been a default under the lease. See 11 U.S.C. § 365(f)(2).

Except as otherwise provided in the Bankruptcy Code, an executory contract or unexpired lease is assumed cum onere. . . . Jamesway contends that the subject lease provisions are void and unenforceable under § 365(f)(1) because they limit its ability to realize the full economic value of the Leases for the benefit of all unsecured creditors. . . . Mass Mutual argues that § 365(f)(1) does not empower us to nullify the profit sharing provisions in the lease, but merely permits us to authorize the assignment over its objection. It argues that our power to invalidate lease provisions is limited by § 365(f)(3) to "ipso facto" or forfeiture provisions and that to hold otherwise will read § 365(f)(3) out of the statute. Courts do not have carte blanche to rewrite leases under §§ 365(f)(1) and (f)(3) or any provision of the statute. Simpson, Leases and the Bankruptcy Code: Tempering the Rigors of Strict Performance, 38 Bus. Law. 60, 75.

However, § 365 reflects the clear Congressional policy of assisting the debtor to realize the equity in all of its assets. Toward that end, § 365(f)(1) permits assignment of an unexpired lease despite a clause in the lease prohibiting, conditioning or restricting the assignment. Subsection (f)(3) goes beyond the scope of subsection (f)(1) by prohibiting enforcement of any clause creating a right to modify or terminate the contract because it is being assumed or assigned, "thereby indirectly barring an assignment by the debtor." In re Howe, 78 B.R. at 226 (citing In re J.F. Hink & Son, 815 F.2d at 1317-18; In re Sapolin Paints, Inc., 20 B.R. 497, 509 (Bankr. E.D.N.Y. 1982)). "The essence of Subsections (1) and (3) is that all contractual provisions, not merely those entitled 'anti-assignment clauses' are subject to the court's scrutiny regarding their anti-assignment effect." Id. at 229-30 (citing Matter of U.L. Radio Corp., 19 B.R. 537, 543 (Bankr. S.D.N.Y. 1982)). While they operate in tandem to promote the Congressional policy favoring a debtor's ability to maximize the value of its leasehold assets, subsections (f)(1) and (f)(3) deal with different problems; (f)(1) with provisions that prohibit, restrict or condition assignment, and (f)(3) with provisions that terminate or modify the terms of a lease because it has been assumed or assigned.

For this reason, construing the former to invalidate provisions that directly or indirectly restrict the debtor's ability to assign the subject lease does not render § 365(f)(3) superfluous.

Moreover, Mass Mutual's literal construction of § 365(f)(1) makes nonsense of the statute while undermining its purpose. For Mass Mutual, even if assignment of an assumed lease were expressly conditioned upon the payment of a portion of the proceeds realized upon assignment to the lessor, § 365(f)(1) would permit assignment but would not affect any lease term associated with the condition. As applied herein, it would mean that

Jamesway could assign the Leases provided it paid the Landlords the relevant percentages of the profits realized through the assignments. In other words, Jamesway would be complying with the very condition that subsection (f)(1) was designed to invalidate. This is not the correct reading of the statute.

In furtherance of Congressional policy favoring the assumption and assignment of unexpired leases as a means of assisting the debtor in its reorganization or liquidation efforts, we interpret § 365(f)(1) to invalidate provisions restricting, conditioning or prohibiting debtor's right to assign the subject lease. No court has read the statute as narrowly as Mass Mutual. Rather, lease provisions conditioning a debtor-in-possession's right to assignment upon the payment of some portion of the "profit" realized upon such assignment are routinely invalidated under § 365(f)(1).

Mass Mutual distinguishes those cases arguing that ¶17 is enforceable under § 365(f)(1) because it does not prevent Jamesway from assigning the Newberry Lease to Rite Aid, does not alter any term in the lease based upon the assignment and is not triggered by the filing of Jamesway's chapter 11 case. It urges that the only effect of ¶17 is to allocate funds between Jamesway and the landlord upon assignment of the lease and that it is relevant only as it may impact on Jamesway's business judgment in electing to assume or reject the leases. The practical effect of the profit sharing clause in the Newberry Lease is the same as those at issue in the cited cases: it limits Jamesway's ability to realize the intrinsic value of the lease. . . .

Finally, the Tri-State and Monticello landlords contend that § 365(f)(1) bars enforcement of profit sharing provisions that are so burdensome as to constitute penalties. They urge that we should conduct a balancing test and enforce the provisions at issue here as reasonable fees payable upon assignment.

Some cases contain language leaving open the possibility that the courts might have ruled differently had the amounts payable by the debtor upon assignment been less. None of these courts ruled that the contract provisions in question would be enforced if the debtors had to pay a "reasonable" percentage of the assignment proceeds. Nothing in § 365(f)(1) supports the Landlord's position.

CONCLUSION

We grant debtor's request for an order declaring that the profit-sharing provisions of the Leases are unenforceable and direct that the $50,000 currently held in escrow from the assignment proceeds of the Newberry Lease be released to debtor.

———————

Lessors suffer further grief because § 502(b)(6) caps landlords' damage claims following rejection, while at the same time providing the landlord no relief from the duty under state law to mitigate damages (i.e., re-letting the premises as soon as possible). The cap and mitigation obligations apply to the allowed amount of the claim, which then, to add insult to injury, is of course paid in tiny bankruptcy dollars. Depending on state law and the economic circumstances of a particular case, the opportunity to reject leases and limit damages in this way may be a major advantage of a chapter 11 filing to a debtor with many retail locations that are losing money, although BAPCPA's imposition of a new time limitation has somewhat reduced the options available to the debtor in a chapter 11. § 365(d)(4).

C. CONSEQUENCES OF ASSUMPTION AND REJECTION

Whenever the debtor does decide to reject (or when the contract is deemed rejected in chapter 7 under § 365(d)(1)), a recurrent question is how much the DIP owes to the counterparty who provided goods, services, or the use of real property to the DIP during the decision period. One starting point might be to pay the contract rate—after all, that's what they agreed. But if the contract is one that is unwanted by the estate, it makes no sense to saddle the estate and its creditors with a burdensome contract rate for the estate's usage when the estate never entered into that contract and doesn't want it. All that is required is to prevent unjust enrichment by the DIP while it made its decision to reject, which leads most courts to adopt a "restitutionary" measure in *quantum meruit*. While the case below deals with a specific compromise in the Code to this problem for nonresidential landlords (yet another addition grafted onto § 365), it explores the general *quantum meruit* measure that many courts use.

=============== In re TSB, INC. ===============

302 B.R. 84 (Bankr. D. Idaho 2003)

MYERS, Bankruptcy Judge.

BACKGROUND AND FACTS

TSB, Inc. ("Debtor") was a chapter 11 debtor in possession in a case filed on April 9, 2003. Debtor ran a tavern ("The Interlude") on 8th Street in Boise, Idaho. On June 2, 2003, the Court converted the case to a chapter 7 liquidation. Richard Crawforth ("Trustee") was appointed the chapter 7 Trustee and immediately took possession of the business.

Debtor's tavern was operated on premises leased from Knapp-Block 44, LLC ("Lessor"). The Lessor has filed an application for allowance of administrative expenses for rent it alleged accrued both in the chapter 11 and chapter 7 periods. . . .

The Lessor's claims are, initially, based on a written lease agreement dated February 27, 2002. The lease was on a month-to-month basis and indicates that, "in the event Tenant fails to pay rent on time, the New Lease shall terminate and Tenant shall vacate the premises." It provides for a lease rate of $20.00 per square foot, applicable to 2287 square feet of space, for a total of $3,811.67.

Upon the June 2 conversion to chapter 7, the Trustee immediately re-keyed the locks and took possession of the premises. On June 4, the Trustee met with the Lessor, and with parties who were prospective purchasers of estate assets as well as prospective new tenants of the space. Somewhere between June 5 and June 10, the Lessor advised the Trustee that it had decided to lease the property to one of these parties ("City Grill").

The Trustee removed some of the personal property of the estate located on the premises. He left the tables, chairs, and bar equipment on site. It was understood by the Trustee and the Lessor that City Grill would seek to purchase that property from the estate, and would enter into a lease with the Lessor. On June 16, the Trustee surrendered to the Lessor all keys to the premises, and City Grill soon commenced remodeling the property.

The Trustee concedes that personal property of the estate was stored on the premises until September 19. He indicates that this was with the tacit, if not express, consent of the Lessor, since all parties understood that City Grill would acquire the personal property in connection with the new lease of the premises that it was actively remodeling. The Trustee and Debtor both indicate that no more than 10% of the premises was required to store such property.

Discussion and Disposition

. . .

The Chapter 11 Administrative Expense

Debtor was obligated to timely perform under the terms of its lease with the Lessor during the first 60 days of the chapter 11 case. See § 365(d)(3). The Lessor is entitled to an administrative expense claim for the full amount of the rent called for in that period. Towers v. Chickering & Gregory (In re Pacific-Atlantic Trading Co.), 27 F.3d 401, 403-05 (9th Cir. 1994) (determining that a post-petition, pre-rejection claim be valued and asserted according to contract terms, not according to reasonable value or benefit bestowed).

The lease reflects a basic monthly rent obligation of $3,430.50. This establishes not just a starting point for the § 365(d)(3) rent claim; given the lack of requirement in the lease that Debtor pay any other amounts, it caps the expense as well.

Debtor's chapter 11 case lasted from April 9, 2003 through June 2, 2003, a period of 54 days. At best, two month's worth of lease charges could have accrued. This amounts to $6,861.00. Debtor paid the Lessor $6,100.00 during the chapter 11. *See* Ex. 1. Thus, the unpaid chapter 11 administrative expense is $761.00.

1. Pre-Rejection Rent Claim

Under § 365(d)(4), a lease of nonresidential real property must be assumed within 60 days of the date of the order for relief or it will be deemed rejected. When Debtor's case was converted to chapter 7, only some 7 days of this period remained. [The 60th day from the April 9 filing was Sunday, June 8. See Fed. R. Bankr. P. 9006(a).—Eds.] The conversion of the case did not start the clock anew. Section 348(a) provides that conversion of a case does not change the date of the order for relief except as provided in subsections (b) or (c). Section 348(b)'s exceptions do not make the conversion date the date of the order for relief when dealing with § 365.

The Trustee did not assume the lease, nor did he seek to extend the time for assumption or rejection. Therefore, on June 9, the lease was deemed rejected by operation of law. See § 365(d)(4)[.] As noted above, the obligation arising in a pre-rejection period is established by § 365(d)(3) and the terms of the lease itself. Here, the lease required rent of $3,430.50 per month. The Trustee held the premises under the unrejected lease for one week. The Court thus concludes that the post-conversion, pre-rejection administrative claim is $857.63 ($3,430.50 ÷ 4 = $857.63).

2. Post-Rejection Use Claim

The Trustee did not "immediately surrender" the premises upon rejection as § 365(d)(4) requires. He instead (a) effectively surrendered control and use of the premises on June 16, some 7 days after rejection, and (b) retained some use of a portion of the premises after rejection for the purpose of storage of estate personal property pending its sale.

The Lessor did not demand compliance with the surrender requirement. Instead, it allowed the personal property to remain on site, knowing that City Grill, the prospective new tenant, wished to buy those chattels from the bankruptcy estate. The Lessor also entered into a new lease agreement with City Grill on June 25, and it allowed City Grill access to the premises to start remodeling. The Trustee in no way (other than leaving the furniture and equipment on site) interfered with the Lessor's total control over the premises.

An additional chapter 7 administrative expense accrued during this post-rejection period, however it arises under § 503(b)(1)(A) and not under § 365(d)(3). Instead of being calculated per the lease terms (as is the case for postpetition, pre-rejection rent under § 365(d)(3) and *Pacific-Atlantic*), the benefit conferred on the estate from the continued possession and use of the real property after lease rejection must be determined on competent proof, consistent with the several limitations articulated in Custom Spray Technologies, 00.3 I.B.C.R. at 160.

In In re PYXSYS Corp., 288 B.R. 309 (Bankr. D. Mass. 2003), a nonresidential real property lessor made a claim under § 365(d)(3) for the 60-day period from filing the petition through automatic rejection, and also a claim for use and occupancy through the date the debtor vacated the premises. 288 B.R. at 310-11. The latter claim (which the court characterized as a "use claim") was allowed against the estate under § 503(b)(1)(A) because the use provided an objective benefit to the estate. 288 B.R. at 316-18. Insofar as the amount of such claim was concerned, the court concluded that "the terms of the lease should be used to value the benefit conferred by the use of the premises in the absence of evidence that said terms were unreasonable." Id. at 318 (citing In re Rare Coin Galleries of Am., 72 B.R. 415, 417 (D. Mass. 1987)); accord In re Trak Auto Corp., 277 B.R. 655, 666-67 (Bankr. E.D. Va. 2002) (noting that the post-rejection presumption in favor of the rental contract rate can be rebutted by showing the reasonable worth of the premises).

Here, using the monthly base rent amount under the lease of $3,430.50 provides an excessive and unreasonable measure of the benefit conferred for the limited use of a portion of the premises for storage. The Lessor had virtually unfettered control of the premises from and after June 16; in fact, it allowed its prospective new tenant access for remodeling, and entered into a lease with that tenant on June 25. The Trustee's use of the premises for storage was not shown to be disruptive to the plans and efforts of either the Lessor or City Grill. The Lessor made no demand on the Trustee for rent or storage charges, or for removal of the personal property. Treating the situation as a "continued lease" of the entire premises at the prebankruptcy commercial rate is not warranted. Doing so would lead to an unjustified windfall to the Lessor and an unreasonable detriment to the estate.

PYXSYS' "benefit conferred [on the estate] by the use of the premises" or Trak Auto's "reasonable worth of the premises" standards apply to the period from June 9 through September 19 (the date the personal property was sold to City Grill, and the Trustee no longer incurred any storage costs). These standards can be calculated in one of two ways under the evidence. On the one hand, the Trustee competently testified that off-site storage for the amount of personal property here at issue could have been obtained for $75.00 per month. On the other hand, an argument could be advanced that storage costs should be calculated on the presumptive value of the commercial premises under the lease, but only for the portion of the premises reasonably utilized for the estate's benefit. Here, that amounts to 10% (given the testimony of the Trustee and Debtor's principal) of the monthly rent, or $343.05 per month.

Since the Trustee did not opt to move the personal property off the premises into less expensive, noncommercial storage, the Court deems it appropriate to use the second methodology. The period of use ran from June 9 through September 19, or about 3 1/3 months. The use claim is therefore determined to be $1,145.00.

When this chapter 7 "use claim" of $1,145.00 is added to the post-conversion, pre-rejection expense under § 365(d)(3) of $857.63, the Lessor's total chapter 7 administrative expense claim is $2,002.63.

CONCLUSION

Upon the foregoing, the Lessor will be allowed a chapter 11 administrative expense of $761.00, and a chapter 7 administrative expense of $2,002.63.[10] The Lessor's Application will be granted to that extent, but

---

[10] Segregating the claims between the chapter 11 and chapter 7 time frames is important in converted chapter 11 cases because §726(b) gives higher priority in distribution to the chapter 7 administrative expenses than to similar expenses incurred in the superseded chapter 11 case.

otherwise denied. Counsel for the Trustee may submit an order in accord herewith.

═══════════════

The court's care in parsing the different types of claims in the case came not just from the conversion but also from the fact that in real life, people do not always act on the exact day prescribed by the Code. The result is some sausage-making to come up with the appropriate amount of claims.

D.   RESTRICTIONS ON ASSUMPTION AND REJECTION

Section 365 also imposes certain constraints on the debtor's right to assume or reject (perform or breach) a pre-bankruptcy contract or to assign it to a third party under § 365(f). Three of the most important constraints on assumption (and assignment) are:

1.   The trustee must cure or arrange to cure most defaults as a condition of assumption. § 365(b)(1)(A). The trustee or its assignee also may be required to provide "adequate assurance of future performance." § 365(b)(1)(C), (f)(2)(B). This requirement should not be overread, however, because while on the one hand it means the trustee cannot assume until a default is cured, on the other hand, it means, quite significantly, that the trustee *can* assume so long as it cures any default. This ability to cure contractual defaults is one of the most important powers conferred upon debtors in bankruptcy. We already saw it back in Assignment 9 with the consumer debtor's power to cure a mortgage default and de-accelerate its loan in chapter 13.

2.   The trustee may not assume a contract for a loan or "financial accommodations." § 365(c)(2).

3.   Section 365(c)(1) forbids assignment of a contract that could not have been assigned by the debtor under applicable non-bankruptcy law. The classic example is the personal services contract—remember our portrait painter? NHL defenseman Jack Johnson had a $30 million five-year contract to play for the L.A. Kings when he went bankrupt. In re Johnson, 2016 WL 8853601 (Bankr. S.D. Ohio Nov. 10, 2016). Every state's common law of contract would not allow Johnson to sell that deal to a hockey enthusiast—even a rich hockey enthusiast willing to pay $29 million for it. Performance by Johnson is "personal" to the regal counterparty, and the law protects it from assignment, even if the terms of their contract are silent on the matter. Section 365(c)(1) implements this protection, too, but in language that has hung some courts up and led to bizarre results.

_In re_ TAYLOR INVESTMENT
PARTNERS II, LLC

533 B.R. 837 (Bankr. N.D. Ga. 2015)

MURPHY, Bankruptcy Judge

This case is before the Court on Movant's Motion for Relief from Stay. Movant asserts Debtors are legally barred from assuming their franchise agreements with Movant without Movant's consent, and Movant withholds such consent; therefore, Movant seeks relief from the automatic stay of 11 U.S.C. § 362 to terminate the franchise agreements. . . . For the reasons set forth below, the Motion is granted.

A. BACKGROUND

TIP II–Ansley, LLC and TIP II–Suburban, LLC operate Moe's Southwestern Grill franchises in Atlanta, Georgia and Decatur, Georgia, respectively. Taylor Investment Partners II is an affiliated entity through which the other two entities pay various common expenses, and also appears to be the franchisee of record with respect to both locations.

Pursuant to the franchise agreements, Movant is entitled to terminate the franchise agreements if certain defaults occur, including if Debtors repeatedly fail to meet certain franchise standards. To that end, Movant performs unannounced Restaurant Operation and Standards Evaluations ("ROSE"). Failing two consecutive ROSE inspections places Debtors in default with a 30-day opportunity to cure. If Debtors fail three ROSE inspections in a 12-month period, Movant may terminate the franchise agreement without a cure period.

Movant alleges Debtors failed consecutive ROSE inspections in June and December of 2012. As a result, Movant placed Debtors in default and conducted follow-up inspections in February of 2013, which, according to Movant, Debtors again failed. Debtors disputed the results of the ROSE inspections. After several termination deferrals, Debtors and Movant arbitrated their dispute. The arbitrator recommended an additional inspection. Movant asserts Debtors' Decatur location failed the final inspection; accordingly, Movant sent a termination notice regarding the Decatur franchise agreement, giving Debtors six months to sell or vacate. Debtors filed their Chapter 11 petitions January 22, 2015, shortly before the termination deadline.

B. DISCUSSION

1. Debtors May Not Assume the Franchise Agreement Without Movant's Consent

Movant now argues, pursuant to 11 U.S.C. § 365(c), Debtors may not assume the franchise agreements without Movant's consent, which it withholds. . . .

Section 365(c) restricts a trustee's power to assume an executory contract if, under applicable law, the other party to the contract would be excused from rendering performance to an entity other than the debtor. Movant argues that because applicable trademark law would prevent Debtors from assigning the franchise agreement without Movant's consent, a trustee could not assume the franchise agreement. And because Debtors, as debtors in possession, exercise the powers of a trustee subject to the same limitations as a trustee, Movant argues that Debtors are similarly restricted from assuming the franchise agreement. Debtors apparently do not contest that the franchise agreements are executory contracts or that applicable trademark law would bar Debtors from transferring the agreements without Movant's consent; instead, the sole issue before the court is whether the restriction of § 365(c) applies to debtors in possession. A circuit split exists as to that issue, and the parties disagree as to whether this Circuit has precedential authority on the topic.

Movant's interpretation of the interaction of § 365(c) and § 1107 is supported by decisions of the 3d Circuit, Matter of West Electronics, Inc., 852 F.2d 79 (3d Cir. 1988), the 4th Circuit, In re Sunterra Corp., 361 F.3d 257 (4th Cir. 2004), and the 9th Circuit, In re Catapult Entertainment, Inc., 165 F.3d 747 (9th Cir. 1999).

Of the appellate courts to have faced the issue, Debtors point only to the 1st Circuit as adopting a test contrary to Movant's interpretation. In Summit Inv. & Development Corp. v. Leroux, 69 F.3d 608 (1st Cir. 1995), . . . [f]inding more than one plausible interpretation of the statutes, the *Leroux* court looked to the legislative history of § 365(c), and determined that § 365(c), and by analogy § 365(e)(2), was not meant to apply unless the executory contract would *actually* be assumed or assigned by a non-debtor party, as opposed to whether a *hypothetical* assignment would be barred by applicable law. . . .

A third approach comes to the same result as the 1st Circuit's "actual" test, but under different reasoning. In In re Footstar, 323 B.R. 566 (Bankr. S.D.N.Y. 2005), the court distilled the circuit split down to whether the word "or" in the statutory language "assume or assign" should be read literally in the disjunctive, as in the 3d Circuit's "hypothetical" test, or construed as the functional equivalent of "and," as in the 1st Circuit's "actual" test. . . . [T]he *Footstar* court reasons that the restriction of § 365(c), as applied to a debtor in possession pursuant to § 1107, does not logically restrict a debtor in possession from assuming the executory contract in question. The statute "is quite logical and sensible as written" when applied to trustees, because it "is vindication of the right under applicable law of the contract counterparty to refuse to accept performance from or render performance to an entity 'other than the debtor or the debtor in possession.'" Id. at 573. However, reading the statute to restrict a debtor in possession from assuming such a contract simply "makes no sense." Id.

The pragmatic approach of *Footstar* certainly has appeal, but Movant argues that we are bound to the "hypothetical" test by the 11th Circuit's decision in In re James Cable Partners, L.P., 27 F.3d 534 (11th Cir. 1994). . . .

James Cable unequivocally holds that a plain reading of the statute burdens a debtor in possession with the restriction of § 365(c). . . . Debtors may not assume the franchise agreement if (1) applicable law would excuse Movant from accepting performance from a party other than Debtors, and (2) Movant does not consent to Debtors' assumption of the executory contract. The Lanham Act excuses Movant from accepting performance from a party other than Debtors, and Movant does not consent to Debtors' assumption of the executory contract. Accordingly, Debtors are barred from assuming the franchise agreement.

Courts taking this side of the split like to pat themselves on the back for following the clear text of the statute that says "the trustee may not assume *or* assign" in holding that the trustee may not assume such contracts, but they do not, at least on our analysis, adequately address the compelling argument that the result is absurd—which even the staunchest textualist concedes is an outcome to be avoided. It makes perfect sense to say if the applicable law prohibits assignment, the bankruptcy power to assume and assign executory contracts cannot trump those prohibitions and allow assignment over counterparty objection. It makes no sense to say that a contract or law that prohibits assignment also forbids a debtor to continue performing under the contract—by operation of the Bankruptcy Code no less. If anything, this result offends bankruptcy policy. Contractual provisions that trigger default automatically upon filing for bankruptcy are invalid for the powerful reason that bankruptcy rehabilitation would be impossible were such penalties enforced. § 365(e)(1)(A). Courts using the "hypothetical test" read the bar on § 365(c) to mean that the debtor forfeits its contractual rights—rights that it wishes to continue exercising by prompt assumption—solely due to its filing for relief under the Code, flatly contradicting the command of § 365(e)(1)(A). The circuit split may send the issue to the Supreme Court. At least some who matter think it should be there. Statement of Kennedy, J., N.C.P. Mktg. Group, Inc. v. BG Star Prods., Inc., 556 U.S. 1145 (2009) (joined by Breyer, J.).

Problem Set 25

25.1. PetroCo, Inc. is an independent oil refinery. Bad market predictions and excessive overhead have caused the company to lose money for several consecutive quarters. Finally, it has filed a chapter 11. Indicative of its difficulties in the highly volatile market for fuel oil is its contract with ConEd. This contract provides that PetroCo will furnish 100,000 barrels of oil, nearly six months' output from the small refinery, for $30 a barrel, a price that looked lucrative when it was proposed 11 months ago. Now, two weeks from delivery, the contract appears to be a disaster. The resolution of a price war between OPEC and Russia and an increase in global demand following the end of a pandemic have caused the price of oil to surge, so that if PetroCo could sell that six-month supply of oil on the current market, it would be able to get $50 per barrel. What should PetroCo do? See § 365(a). Assuming PetroCo will ultimately pay its unsecured creditors 30 cents on the dollar, what will ConEd get if PetroCo rejects? See § 502(g). What will PetroCo get from rejection? In a chapter 7 liquidation of PetroCo, who functionally benefits? In PetroCo's chapter 11, who benefits?

25.2. Duke & Duke Distributors has long specialized in supplying citrus fruits from Florida throughout the country. High interest rates and bad market predictions have put D&D in a tenuous financial position, and its co-founders, Mortimer and Randolph Duke, recently made the difficult decision to put the company into chapter 11. At the time of filing, D&D has one large contract outstanding: it has agreed to buy 750,000 bushels of oranges for $37.52 per bushel from Valentine Growers, a Tallahassee co-op.

Speculation on the futures market for oranges is dynamic right now. No one is sure how big this year's crop will be, but the citrus count (a federal census of the oranges currently on the trees) will be announced next Monday. Mortimer asks you, as bankruptcy counsel to the company, what will happen when the census is revealed. A high orange count will result in orange prices below the $37.52 in his contract, whereas a low count will result in a price well above $37.52. What are D&D's options? Valentine is also concerned about the effect of the orange count. It has asked another attorney what will happen if the count is high and D&D does not want the fruit. If that lawyer is even half as good as you are, what will she have explained to Valentine about its economic position? See § 365(a) and (d)(2). (Ignore §§ 555-556, which have to do with certain financial and commodity contracts, including the securities safe harbors (such as futures contracts, which these plausibly are)—they are beyond the scope of the basic course.) How, if at all, does § 365(d) add to the DIP's options? See generally, if inclined, 7 U.S.C. § 6(c)(a) (implementing so-called "Eddie Murphy Rule" against using confidential information in commodities trading).

25.3. Jacky Pell has a small electronics repair shop in town. His shop is in rented space in a small office building. He has come to you because he has just received notice of cancellation of the lease from his landlord. Although the notice says "vacate immediately," you have read the lease and it provides for a five-day "notice and cure" period prior to final cancellation. He explains that he has fallen two months behind on the rent (a total of $4,200) because of a fire that damaged the repair room and destroyed some of his equipment. He had to use the rent money to fix the room and replace the tools. He has offered to catch up on the rent over the next three months, but the landlord told him, "I don't trust you anymore, now that I know you didn't keep insurance like the lease says you're supposed to."

Jacky admits he had slipped up and forgotten the insurance, but says he has already reinstated the policy by making the past due premium payments. Although Jacky, in his words, is otherwise "all right" financially, he says that eviction would destroy his business and "I'd probably never be able to build it back in another location." What good would bankruptcy do Jacky? What would you try to do in bankruptcy to save the lease? What arguments would the landlord's attorney make against you, and how could you reply? See § 365(b)(1), (3), and (c)(3). An hour after he left your office, you are going through the documents he gave you when you find he is also leasing a diagnostic machine for locating defects in appliances. You can see that the lapse of the insurance breached that lease as well. Does that present a different problem for Jacky in a bankruptcy? See § 365(b)(1)-(2).

25.4. Novelty Industries leased a manufacturing facility from Alfred Bucks for a 20-year term at $2 million per year. Novelty's president tells you that the lease provides that

1. it terminates automatically upon Novelty's making an assignment for benefit of creditors or entering receivership or bankruptcy;
2. it can be assigned only with the written approval of Bucks; and
3. it can be terminated if Novelty's outstanding debts ever exceed twice its equity investment, upon ten days' written notice of termination from Bucks.

Shortly after Novelty sent Bucks its most recent financial statement as required by the lease, Bucks sent a notice of termination based on the statement's revelation that Novelty's debts exceed twice its equity. Novelty has come to seek your advice since the ten days provided in the notice expire today. Just before coming to your office, Novelty's president talked to Bucks about an assignment of the lease to Monster Toys, who would be willing to pay $3 million per year for the space. Bucks said he would agree to the assignment if he got an extra million each year, i.e., all of the increase. Novelty has decided to get out of the toy business and will not have a further need for the facility. What can you advise Novelty? See § 365(b), (e), (f).

25.5. A. When you had a chance to read the Novelty lease yourself, you discover that provision 2 above actually permits free assignability but does require that Bucks get one-half of any increase in rent. Does your analysis change?

B. You then discover what may be a "poison pill" in the lease, although in the form of a benefit to Novelty: the lease grants Novelty a license to use Bucks's patented Auto Fork Lift machine, which automates much of the inventory movement and greatly increases the value of the lease. Can Novelty assume the license? If so, can it assign it? If the answer to either question is negative, does its presence make the whole lease unassumable and unassignable?

25.6. Last year's hottest new fast-food franchise was Don's Duck Enchiladas. It became the darling of Wall Street because it had an upscale market and could expand quickly by offering franchisees very generous terms: "All they supply is the hard work." Jane Stover got the coveted franchise for Newport, Rhode Island. Her franchise contract provides for:

(a) her purchase of food and other supplies from Don's on easy credit terms for the first two years (no payment for 90 days and a low interest rate);
(b) a one-year lease for the store;
(c) at the end of the first year, her purchase of the store and the land it sits on from Don's, Inc., the franchisor, for 5% down and the rest of the purchase price on a 20-year mortgage; and
(d) her option after the first year to borrow up to $100,000 from Don's at a low interest rate, repayable in easy installments.

Unfortunately, only six months after she signed the contract and opened for business, a Nor'easter damaged her store and closed it for several weeks. Now she has reopened, but her insurance was inadequate and she is almost out of working capital. She is current on her high franchise fees to Don's, but her bank is pressing her and she is afraid Don's is itching for an excuse to terminate. Can she keep the franchise contract in chapter 11? See § 365(a), (c).

EXECUTORY CONTRACTS II

Despite its painful length, § 365 omits certain key rules. For example, a contract may only be assumed if it is "executory," but nowhere does the Code tell us what that means. This assignment plunges into the world of "executoriness," one of the most theoretically complex topics of bankruptcy law. Courts have struggled mightily with this concept, and at high stakes, since only executory contracts are subject to the debtor's powerful toolkit in § 365. Because executoriness is not defined by the Code, it functions as an "extra-statutory" constraint on the trustee's power to assume or reject contracts for the estate. This assignment explores executoriness, and two other equally complex extra-statutory doctrines: the limitation of state-law remedies against the bankruptcy estate and the protection of pre-bankruptcy property rights (legal and equitable) held by the counterparty.

A.   EXECUTORINESS

Section 365 only allows the debtor to assume or reject an "executory" contract or "unexpired" lease. This presumably means that if a lease is not unexpired ("expired," as normal people would say), there's nothing a debtor can do under § 365. The same general idea underlies the word "executory," which finds its linguistic roots as a contrast to a fully "executed" contract. So at the big picture level, the executoriness doctrine means nothing more than that if a contract is fully performed or terminated before bankruptcy, the trustee gets no special powers under § 365. The statute provides for this explicitly in § 365(c)(3) for commercial leases, a codification that most think is redundant given that a contract or lease that is already "dead" cannot be executory. Commercial landlords perhaps wanted this belt-and-suspenders protection to curb judges from using equitable powers to revive concluded leases to a debtor's benefit.

   The requirement of executoriness is of considerable importance to the counterparty to the debtor's contract. If the counterparty hates doing business with the debtor and wants out of a bad deal, it may try to argue that the debtor cannot assume the contract in bankruptcy because it is not executory. To do so, it will try to come up with reasons why the contract already came to an end well before the debtor's bankruptcy started. So, too, will counterparties who love a contract with the debtor similarly insist in entirely different cases—apparently without irony—that those arrangements are not executory and hence cannot be rejected. Executoriness thus serves as a much-litigated constraint on the DIP's power in bankruptcy.

The combination of its economic importance with its doctrinal confusion means there is a great deal of case law wrestling with the concept, yet all that spilled ink has not left behind a coherent approach. Serious difficulties exist in the cases as courts struggle to explain clearly the elements that make up the quality of executoriness that a contract supposedly must have before it is eligible for assumption or rejection under § 365. Some contracts are simple: if you hire a painter to paint your garage door for $300 next month, all would agree that that contract is executory. Now what if next month the painter fully performs but you have yet to pay the $300—and then bankruptcy occurs? Executory? Half-executory? Or what if the painter offered you a three-year warranty and finished the job two years ago and you haven't talked to each other since? Executory? One-third executory? Contingently executory depending on whether she's a good painter? It is tempting to equate "executory" with "incomplete," but that just begs a host of complicated further questions.

The lack of an intelligible definition of executoriness was the status quo for years until Professor Vern Countryman published his seminal articles on executory contracts in the mid-1970s. Vern Countryman, Executory Contracts in Bankruptcy: Part I, 57 Minn. L. Rev. 439 (1973); Part II, 58 Minn. L. Rev. 479 (1974). In the face of this intellectual morass, Professor Countryman's articles distilled the case law and provided the first persuasive test of executoriness. His test: a contract is executory if it is "a contract under which the obligation of both the bankrupt and the counterparty to the contract are so far unperformed that the failure of either to complete performance would constitute a material breach excusing the performance of the other." Countryman, Part I, at 460. The "material breach" test became one of the most widely adopted scholarly contributions to bankruptcy law in its history. Most circuit courts have explicitly adopted it, and it was cited favorably in the legislative history to the Code, even though it was not actually codified in the statute. H.R. Rep. No. 595, 95th Cong., 1st Sess. 347 (1977). It seems clear that the Countryman test dramatically improved the courts' analyses of these problems.

The material breach analysis, however, fails to resolve many contemporary bankruptcy contract problems. The case that follows is one such example (and also provides a nice review of the fact that the court has the ultimate power to review the debtor's business decision to assume or reject under § 365(a)).

In re RIODIZIO, INC.
204 B.R. 417 (Bankr. S.D.N.Y. 1997)

BERNSTEIN, Bankruptcy Judge

Riodizio, Inc. (the "debtor") seeks, inter alia, to reject a stock option agreement and a shareholders agreement, both entered into in June, 1995. Riodizio Company, LLC ("LLC"), the optionee as well as a party to the shareholders agreement, opposes the motion. The motion thrusts us into the "psychedelic" world of executory contracts, Jay Lawrence Westbrook,

A Functional Analysis of Executory Contracts, 74 Minn. L. Rev. 227, 228 (1989) ("Westbrook"), and reinforces the prophecy that the time that litigants and the courts spend searching for "executoriness" can be put to better use analyzing the benefits and burdens of the contract itself. . . .

FACTS

The debtor commenced this chapter 11 case on August 19, 1996. It owns and operates a Brazilian grill restaurant (called a "Riodizio" in Brazil) at 417 Lafayette Street in New York, New York. Prior to commencing business, the debtor and its two shareholders, Alan Berfas and Frank Ferraro, entered into numerous agreements with LLC to secure financing and equipment for the restaurant. These included a Loan and Lease Agreement, dated June 1, 1995 (the "Loan and Lease"), a Shareholders Agreement, dated June 23, 1995 (the "Shareholders Agreement"), and an undated stock option (the "Warrant") that the debtor granted to the LLC.

1. The Loan and Lease

Under the Loan and Lease, LLC advanced $200,000.00 to the debtor to operate the business. The terms of the loan, as evidenced by a promissory note, called for 15% interest, with principal and interest payable in 42 monthly installments. As security for the advances, the debtor gave LLC a priority security interest in all office equipment including, without limitation, computer equipment, kitchen equipment, fixtures, mailing lists, bank accounts, Transmedia agreements and proceeds, and accounts receivable. Berfas and Ferraro also provided a limited guaranty by depositing into escrow, in favor of LLC, their respective shares in the debtor, general stock powers, and their resignations as officers, directors and employees. . . .

2. The Warrant and Shareholders Agreement

As part of the underlying transaction, the debtor also executed the Warrant. It states, in its entirety, as follows:

> Riodizio, Inc. (the "Corporation") hereby grants to the holder of this warrant the right to purchase all or part of an aggregate of 93 common shares of the Corporation for the consideration of one dollar ($1.00) per share.
> This warrant may be exercised for a period of twenty-five years.

The Warrant was signed on behalf of the debtor by Berfas and Ferraro, each of whom own 33 shares of the debtor's common stock. If LLC exercises its warrant (and the debtor delivers the shares), LLC will own approximately 60% of the debtor's outstanding shares based upon an additional investment of only $93.00.

Finally, the debtor, Berfas, Ferraro and LLC entered into the Shareholders Agreement. According to the introductory "WHEREAS" clauses, they did so at LLC's request "as an additional safeguard to its collateral." Further, LLC is made a party "solely for the purpose of granting the Company the legal and equitable right to sue for the enforcement of the agreement and/or seek damages for the breach of this Agreement; and to protect the value of the warrants." The Shareholders Agreement protects LLC's financial stake in the debtor, or otherwise benefits it, in several ways. First, it requires Berfas and Ferraro to establish a four person board of directors which will include two LLC nominees in addition to themselves. Second, it requires a two-thirds shareholders vote to take certain "extraordinary" actions. If LLC exercises its warrants and controls nearly 60% of the outstanding stock, it will be able to veto these "extraordinary" actions. Third, if the shareholders open a different type of restaurant, they must first offer LLC the right to participate in the venture.

The balance of the Shareholders Agreement concerns rights and obligations running between the debtor and the shareholders. For example, Berfas and Ferraro cannot open a similarly-styled restaurant within ten miles of any restaurant operated by the debtor unless the debtor gives its written consent. Under those circumstances where they can operate a similarly styled restaurant, they must first offer the debtor the right to participate in the venture. The debtor must purchase Key Man Life Insurance on the lives of the individual shareholders. Finally, the Shareholders Agreement contains a series of provisions relating to the sale or transfer of the shares, giving the non-selling shareholder and/or the debtor a right of first refusal.

DISCUSSION

1. Introduction

Section 365(a) states that "the trustee, subject to the court's approval, may assume or reject any executory contract or unexpired lease of the debtor." 11 U.S.C. § 365(a). The Bankruptcy Code does not define the term "executory contract." The legislative history regarding this section states that "[t]hough there is no precise definition of what contracts are executory, it generally includes contracts on which performance remains due to some extent on both sides." H.R. Rep. No. 95-595, at 347 (1977); S. Rep. No. 95-989, at 58 (1978), U.S. Code Cong. & Admin. News 1978, pp. 5787, 5844, 6303. . . . Finding this definition too broad and sweeping, . . . most courts have adopted Professor Countryman's definition of an executory contract as "a contract under which the obligation of both the bankrupt and the counterparty to the contract are so far unperformed that the failure of either to complete performance would constitute a material breach excusing performance of the other." Vern Countryman, Executory Contracts in Bankruptcy: Part 1, 57 Minn. L. Rev. 439, 460 (1973).

Under Countryman's "material breach" test, a prepetition contract is executory when both sides are still obligated to render substantial performance. Where such performance remains due on only one side, the contract is non-executory, and hence, neither assumable nor rejectable. The materiality of the breach is a question of state law. Thus, if applicable non-bankruptcy law permits either party to sue for breach because of the counterparty's failure to perform, the contract is executory. . . .

Some have found the Countryman "material breach" test too constraining and static. . . . In this same vein, some advocate a functional analysis which eliminates the requirement of executoriness. See Westbrook, supra, 74 Minn. L. Rev. 227; see also Michael T. Andrew, Executory Contracts in Bankruptcy: Understanding Rejection, 59 U. Colo. L. Rev. 845 (1988) ("Andrew I"); Michael T. Andrew, Executory Contracts Revisited: A Reply to Professor Westbrook, 62 U. Colo. L. Rev. 1 (1991) ("Andrew II"). Under the functional approach, "the question of whether a contract is executory is determined by the benefits that assumption or rejection would produce for the estate." Sipes v. Atlantic Gulf Communities Corp. (In re General Dev. Corp.), 84 F.3d 1364, 1375 (11th Cir. 1996) (affirming on the basis of the district court's opinion, 177 B.R. 1000 (S.D. Fla. 1995)).

The functional approach does not repudiate the Countryman rule; it merely recognizes its limitations. It also conserves the time and effort that the parties and the court otherwise spend resolving the question of executoriness. But it has its critics. To be subject to assumption or rejection, the statute, 11 U.S.C. § 365, expressly requires that the contract be executory. Ignoring executoriness rewrites the statute in a fundamental way. See In re Child World, Inc. 147 B.R. at 851 ("manifestly, th[e functional] approach ignores the statutory requirement that the contract to be assumed or rejected must be 'executory.'").

2. The Warrant

Options agreements, such as the Warrant, demonstrate the shortcomings of the Countryman definition. "[A]n option contract is essentially an enforceable promise not to revoke an offer." In re III Enterprises, Inc. V, 163 B.R. 453, 460-61 (Bankr. E.D. Pa.), aff'd, 169 B.R. 551 (E.D. Pa. 1994). It is a unilateral contract until exercised; upon exercise, it becomes a bilateral contract. An option contemplates performance by both parties but requires it from only one. The optionor must keep the offer open. The optionee may but need not exercise the option; if he does, each party must perform its obligations under the resulting bilateral contract. The optionee's failure to exercise the option constitutes a failure of condition rather than a breach of duty. The failure to perform a condition which is not also a legal duty cannot give rise to a material breach, and hence, an option contract is not executory under the Countryman definition.

Most courts, however, consider an option contract to be executory although they reach their conclusions through different routes. In In re Waldron, 36 B.R. 633 (Bankr. S.D. Fla. 1984), aff'd without op., (S.D. Fla.), rev'd on other grounds, 785 F.2d 936 (11th Cir.), cert, dismissed, 478 U.S. 1028 (1986), the debtors granted a real estate option to the Shell Oil Company. The debtors subsequently filed a joint chapter 13 petition in order to reject the contract since the value of the property exceeded the option price.

The *Waldron* court held that the option was executory, but relied on the "some performance due" standard cited in the legislative history rather than the more rigorous Countryman test. . . . The option cases that came after *Waldron*, but adopted the Countryman definition, faced a dilemma. The optionor's obligation—to keep the option open—was substantial, but the optionee did not owe any substantial obligation that could result in a material breach. Andrew II, supra, 62 U. Colo. L. Rev. at 32. To fit the option contract within the "material breach" test, they conflated the option contract with the contingent bilateral contract, finding the optionee's duty of substantial performance in the contingent obligation to perform under the bilateral contract created by the exercise of the option.

The case law confirms that executoriness lies in the eyes of the beholder. Despite the contrary case law discussed above, the Warrant, an option contract, is not an executory contract under Countryman's "material breach" test. The debtor granted the option to LLC as additional consideration for the loan. LLC fully performed any legal obligation in connection with the Warrant when it funded the loan. While the exercise of the Warrant is a condition to the debtor's obligation to deliver the shares to LLC, LLC is not legally obligated to exercise the Warrant or do anything (or refrain from doing anything).

If the "some performance due" test in the legislative history is overly inclusive, the Countryman test excludes too much. It imposes a "material breach" requirement, raising the threshold of executoriness above what Congress seemed to intend. In the case of options, it excludes contracts under which the debtor has benefits and burdens, each party must still perform as a condition to the counterparty's performance, and assumption or rejection may confer a net benefit on the estate. Under the circumstances, we should question the test rather than condemn the contract to a "legal limbo" in which it can be neither assumed nor rejected. See Westbrook, supra, 74 Minn. L. Rev. at 239.

A test less exclusive than Countryman's that takes into account the mutual performance requirement embodied in the legislative history should be substituted. Under this test, a contract is executory if each side must render performance, on account of an existing legal duty or to fulfill a condition, to obtain the benefit of the counterparty's performance. Weighing the relative benefits and burdens to the debtor is the essence of the decision to assume or reject; if each party must still give something to get something, the contract is executory, and the debtor must demonstrate whether assumption or rejection confers a net benefit on the estate. If the debtor has done everything it needs to do to obtain the benefit of its bargain, assumption serves no purpose, and the debtor may simply sue to enforce its rights. Similarly, if the counterparty has done everything necessary to require the debtor to perform, the debtor's performance adds nothing to the estate, the debtor will not assume the contract, and the counterparty can file a prepetition claim. Here, the Warrant is executory; each party must perform under the Warrant in order to obtain the benefits under the contingent bilateral contract of sale. To sell the shares and receive payment, the debtor must keep the offer open. To make payment and acquire the shares, LLC must first exercise the option granted under the Warrant.

Having concluded that the Warrant is executory, the Court must determine whether its rejection will benefit the estate. While a court will ordinarily defer to the business judgment of the debtor's management, Berfas and Ferraro have an interest in preventing LLC from exercising the option and diluting their personal stakes in and control over the debtor.

Consequently, the debtor cannot rely on the presumptions of [the] business judgment rule to support its decision.

The Court's independent review nevertheless confirms that rejection benefits the estate without any significant downside. Proper business reasons for rejecting a contract include the following: (1) the contract is uneconomical to complete according to its terms; (2) the contract is financially burdensome to the estate . . . and (5) in the case of a stock option contract, the debtor can market the shares and receive a higher or better price than the option offers.[9]

The Warrant provides a de minimis benefit to the debtor, granting it the right to receive $93.00 if LLC exercises its option. On the other hand, it deprives the debtor of the possibility that it can sell the same shares for more money to another investor during the next twenty-three years of its remaining life. It does not matter whether this hypothetical investor exists; a $93.00 payment is so de minimis that the mere possibility outweighs any benefit in performing the Warrant.

Breaching the Warrant through rejection produces a minimal, adverse effect on the estate. Rejection constitutes a breach of contract immediately prior to the petition date. 11 U.S.C. § 365(g)(1). At the outset, the Warrant does not create any property interest in LLC's favor that would survive rejection. A breach leaves LLC with a claim for damages equal to the difference between the option price and the market value of the shares at the time of the breach. If LLC suffered any damage, this goes far to proving the wisdom of rejection; the debtor can sell the shares (to LLC or a third party) for more than the per share price of $1.00, and pay LLC's claim in tiny bankruptcy dollars. Further, LLC's claim is arguably subordinated under 11 U.S.C. § 510(b) to the payment of its other unsecured creditors.

3. The Shareholders Agreement

Consideration of the Shareholders Agreement is far more straightforward. Manifestly, it is executory. . . . The record is insufficient, however, to determine whether the debtor should be permitted to reject this contract. Having outlined only some of the relevant benefits and burdens of the Shareholders Agreement, the Court must leave it to the parties to quantify these rights and obligations, and provide an evidentiary basis to support the decision to reject. For instance, the parties have not revealed the cost of the insurance. It may represent a burdensome administrative expense. On the other hand, the existence of the restrictions on competition and the rights of first refusal may enhance the value of the debtor to a potential investor. . . .

---

[9] Some courts refer to a balancing of equities, suggesting that rejection should be refused if it will cause disproportionate harm to the non-debtor party. The right to assume or reject an executory contract is designed to permit the debtor to shed its obligations under burdensome and uneconomical contracts. Section 365 does not require any balancing of the equities.

The Court grants the debtor's motion to reject the Warrant, and directs the parties to contact chambers to schedule an evidentiary hearing. . . .

===

As the *Riodizio* court notes, any contract that has any consequence for the bankruptcy case will have something about it that is unperformed, especially if one is willing to count obligations *not* to do something. This suggests infinite flexibility in the executoriness requirement, which undermines its capacity for analytical utility. The court settles on a test that might be described as "Countryman Lite." But perhaps even that is progress?

As the court also demonstrates, the material breach test leaves enormous problems for seemingly "one-way" contracts like options. They may have huge value for the debtor, but apparently do not require any more performance by the debtor as option holder, who *may* exercise the option, but also may just let an option quietly expire and do nothing. So too with the common right of first refusal to buy out co-member interests held by members of an LLC. That right may be worth millions, but where is the material obligation to perform? See Jay Lawrence Westbrook & Kelsey Stayart, The Demystification of Contracts in Bankruptcy, 91 Am. Bankr. L.J. 481 (2017), which analyzes a wide sample of cases in addressing the theoretical problems.

Despite the general acknowledgment of these shortcomings and other difficulties, executoriness continues to confuse the cases. The ABI Commission recommended continuing the status quo by following the material-breach test and actually proposed that it be codified for the first time, ignoring the views of its own advisory committee and virtually every academic commentator and major professional association. It further recommended a discretionary element be added into the definition, perhaps conceding both the inadequacy of that definition and a desire to bring in through the back door an ability to adjust for felt equities not found in the statute.

B.   THE ROLE OF STATE CONTRACT
AND PROPERTY LAW

Assuming the debtor rejects a contract, the Code deems that a breach. § 365(g). The remedies for contract breach are generally governed by state law, and so pursuant to the *Butner* principle, federal bankruptcy courts should look to state law to determine the proper remedy, unless some federal bankruptcy policy trumps. For example, consider a debtor that would like to reject a contract, but state law would grant specific performance to the counterparty as a remedy for that breach. If the bankruptcy court applies state remedies law to the breach-by-rejection, the counterparty would effectively be able "to reject the rejection" as the debtor would have to perform. Some courts have applied the safety valve of *Butner* and ruled that there is a countervailing federal bankruptcy policy, namely, equality of creditors, so that specific performance should be barred as a remedy. Perhaps for this reason, historically bankruptcy trustees were not subject to orders of specific performance. See, e.g., Leasing Serv. Corp. v. First Tenn. Bank Nat'l Ass'n, 826 F.2d 434, 436 (6th Cir. 1987) (specific performance cannot be ordered against trustee as remedy for rejection). Specific performance is the financial equivalent of 100% payment (full performance), which seems unfair to the other creditors crying over their pro rata payment in tiny bankruptcy dollars.

Consider this illustrative colloquy:

DIP: I'm going to reject your executory contract under § 365(a).
Counterparty: Curses! OK, I guess I'm just a poor victim of breach and have to ask the court for my breach remedies under § 365(g).
DIP: I agree. By the way, what are your state-law remedies for breach of this contract?
Counterparty: Specific performance.
DIP: Wait, you mean I have the power under bankruptcy law to reject your contract, but you have the remedial power to force me to perform anyway?
Counterparty: Hey, I'm just a states' rights guy in a federalist system.
DIP: Then my rights under § 365 would be meaningless!
Counterparty: Boo-hoo for you, poor debtor that is trying to duck my contract.
DIP: So you expect to get full performance while the other unsecured creditors get 10 cents on the dollar?

While the debtor's last rejoinder—why should one contract party get full performance—is a powerful federal policy, the counterparty sometimes can invoke an even more powerful response: state-law property rights, albeit created by contract. Specific performance is often a remedy when property rights are at issue. Consider a contract to sell Blackacre. After the sale but before closing, the law in many states would say that the purchaser of land in a given set of circumstances (e.g., having already taken possession of the land) has a right to specific performance by way of conveyance of the land. Not only does that state-law right look, smell, and taste like a property right in the land, it is often called "vendee's title," a recognition that it is a form of property. Bankruptcy blows away contract rights cheerfully, but if the buyer's right is a vested *property* right, then bankruptcy's cavalier attitude toward state law becomes more problematic: abrogating a property right may run into difficult questions about unconstitutional takings and the interaction between the Takings Clause and the Bankruptcy Clause. (Many would say that the same principle undergirds the right of the secured party to its security interest in bankruptcy.) So two principles come crashing into conflict: equality of creditors under federal bankruptcy law and vindication of property rights under state remedies law.

You may wonder what all this has to do with executoriness. The answer is that many courts, goaded by self-interested parties, avoid confronting these difficult policy questions by hiding behind the executoriness doctrine. For example, if they do not want to order specific performance in a case (say, because of binding circuit precedent barring specific performance against the bankruptcy estate) but nevertheless want the debtor to perform, they simply say the contract is non-executory and hence cannot be rejected, period. But this distortion has led to madness, as other courts will hold that a given contract is not executory and therefore cannot be assumed by the debtor. Leaving aside the doctrinal incoherence, both of the arguments are troubling because the seeming consequence of inability to assume is a forced termination, and the consequence of inability to reject is forced performance. Such compulsions seem nowhere directed by the Code, which on the contrary confers upon the trustee the discretion to decide what is in the best interests of the estate.

But worse, these arguments prove too much. When viewed together, they suggest non-executory contracts can *neither* be assumed (performed) *nor* rejected (breached) by the estate. Exactly what option remains for such purgatory-consigned "zombie" contracts? One of us has taken up the challenge and proposed that even when the parties playing games convince courts that some contracts are "non-executory" and cannot be assumed or rejected (depending on what the party is trying to achieve), the proper outcome is to use other provisions of the Code beyond § 365 to impose the same results as assumption or rejection would achieve. As such, if the outcome is the same, the parties will give up on the game. See John A.E. Pottow, A New Approach to Executory Contracts, 96 Tex. L. Rev. 1437 (2018) (presented at Festschrift celebrating one of the other authors who is old enough to have a Festschrift).

1.   *Vested Rights in Property Law*

There is hope. Increasingly, courts are turning away from executoriness as a *deus ex machina* for the problem of conflicting state and federal rights. Here is one court that tries to set the record straight regarding intellectual property rights vested in a trademark licensee that came into question when its licensor went bankrupt and rejected the licensing contract. Rather than argue the license was not executory and hence could not be rejected, the licensee tried another approach: it agreed the license was executory but argued it would be unfair to reject the trademark agreement because the licensee had invested capital in reliance on its ability to use the mark. The bankruptcy court agreed and ordered the debtor to allow the licensee to keep using the mark, notwithstanding rejection (de facto rendering it unrejectable). The Seventh Circuit analyzed the question from scratch with welcome analytic clarity that needed none of the foregoing complications.

SUNBEAM PRODUCTS, INC. v. CHICAGO AMERICAN MFG., LLC
686 F.3d 372 (7th Cir. 2012)

EASTERBROOK, Circuit Judge
Lakewood Engineering & Manufacturing Co. made and sold a variety of consumer products, which were covered by its patents and trademarks.

In 2008, losing money on every box fan, Lakewood contracted their manufacture to Chicago American Manufacturing (CAM). The contract authorized CAM to practice Lakewood's patents and put its trademarks on the completed fans. Lakewood was to take orders from retailers such as Sears, Walmart, and Ace Hardware; CAM would ship directly to these customers on Lakewood's instructions. Because Lakewood was in financial distress, CAM was reluctant to invest the money necessary to gear up for production—and to make about 1.2 million fans that Lakewood estimated it would require during the 2009 cooling season—without assured payment. Lakewood provided that assurance by authorizing CAM to sell the 2009 run of box fans for its own account if Lakewood did not purchase them.

In February 2009, three months into the contract, several of Lakewood's creditors filed an involuntary bankruptcy petition against it. The court appointed a trustee, who decided to sell Lakewood's business. Sunbeam Products, doing business as Jarden Consumer Solutions, bought the assets, including Lakewood's patents and trademarks. Jarden did not want the Lakewood-branded fans CAM had in inventory, nor did it want CAM to sell those fans in competition with Jarden's products. Lakewood's trustee rejected the executory portion of the CAM contract under 11 U.S.C. § 365(a). When CAM continued to make and sell Lakewood-branded fans, Jarden filed this adversary action. It will receive 75% of any recovery and the trustee the other 25% for the benefit of Lakewood's creditors.

The bankruptcy judge held a trial. After determining that the Lakewood-CAM contract is ambiguous, the judge relied on extrinsic evidence to conclude that CAM was entitled to make as many fans as Lakewood estimated it would need for the entire 2009 selling season and sell them bearing Lakewood's marks. In re Lakewood Engineering & Manufacturing Co., 459 B.R. 306, 333-38 (Bankr. N.D. Ill. 2011). Jarden contends in this court—following certification by the district court of a direct appeal under 28 U.S.C. § 158(d)(2)(A)—that CAM had to stop making and selling fans once Lakewood stopped having requirements for them. The bankruptcy court did not err in reading the contract as it did, but the effect of the trustee's rejection remains to be determined.

Lubrizol Enterprises, Inc. v. Richmond Metal Finishers, Inc., 756 F.2d 1043 (4th Cir. 1985), holds that, when an intellectual-property license is rejected in bankruptcy, the licensee loses the ability to use any licensed copyrights, trademarks, and patents. Three years after *Lubrizol*, Congress added § 365(n) to the Bankruptcy Code. It allows licensees to continue using the intellectual property after rejection, provided they meet certain conditions. The bankruptcy judge held that § 365(n) allowed CAM to practice Lakewood's patents when making box fans for the 2009 season. That ruling is no longer contested. But "intellectual property" is a defined term in the Bankruptcy Code: 11 U.S.C. § 101(35A) provides that "intellectual property" includes patents, copyrights, and trade secrets. It does not mention trademarks Some bankruptcy judges have inferred from the omission that Congress codified *Lubrizol* with respect to trademarks, but an omission is just an omission. . . . See also In re Exide Technologies, 607 F.3d 957, 966-67 (3d Cir. 2010) (Ambro, J., concurring) (concluding that § 365(n) neither codifies nor disapproves *Lubrizol* as applied to trademarks). . . .

The bankruptcy judge in this case agreed with Judge Ambro that § 365(n) and § 101(35A) leave open the question whether rejection of an intellectual-property license ends the licensee's right to use trademarks. Without deciding whether a contract's rejection under § 365(a) ends the licensee's right to use the trademarks, the judge stated that she would allow CAM, which invested substantial resources in making Lakewood-branded box fans, to continue using the Lakewood marks "on equitable grounds." 459 B.R. at 345; see also id. at 343-46. This led to the entry of judgment in CAM's favor, and Jarden has appealed.

What the Bankruptcy Code provides, a judge cannot override by declaring that enforcement would be "inequitable." "The Bankruptcy Code standardizes an expansive (and sometimes unruly) area of law, and it is our obligation to interpret the Code clearly and predictably using well established principles of statutory construction." RadLAX Gateway Hotel, LLC v. Amalgamated Bank, 566 U.S. 639, 132 S. Ct. 2065, 2073, 182 L. Ed. 2d 967 (2012).

Although the bankruptcy judge's ground of decision is untenable, that does not necessarily require reversal. We need to determine whether *Lubrizol* correctly understood § 365(g), which specifies the consequences of a rejection under § 365(a). . . . [A]ll that matters [for the purposes of this case] is the opening proposition [in § 365(g)]: that rejection "constitutes a breach of such contract." Outside of bankruptcy, a licensor's breach does not terminate a licensee's right to use intellectual property. . . . CAM had bargained for the security of being able to sell Lakewood-branded fans for its own account if Lakewood defaulted; outside of bankruptcy, Lakewood could not have ended CAM's right to sell the box fans by failing to perform its own duties, any more than a borrower could end the lender's right to collect just by declaring that the debt will not be paid.

What § 365(g) does by classifying rejection as breach is establish that in bankruptcy, as outside of it, the other party's rights remain in place. After rejecting a contract, a debtor is not subject to an order of specific performance. See NLRB v. Bildisco & Bildisco, 465 U.S. 513, 531, 104 S. Ct. 1188, 79 L. Ed. 2d 482 (1984); Midway Motor Lodge of Elk Grove v. Innkeepers' Telemanagement & Equipment Corp., 54 F.3d 406, 407 (7th Cir. 1995). The debtor's unfulfilled obligations are converted to damages; when a debtor does not assume the contract before rejecting it, these damages are treated as a pre-petition obligation, which may be written down in common with other debts of the same class. But nothing about this process implies that any rights of the other contracting party have been vaporized. . . .

Bankruptcy law does provide means for eliminating rights under some contracts. For example, contracts that entitle creditors to preferential transfers (that is, to payments exceeding the value of goods and services provided to the debtor) can be avoided under 11 U.S.C. § 547, and recent payments can be recouped. A trustee has several avoiding powers. See 11 U.S.C. §§ 544-51. But Lakewood's trustee has never contended that Lakewood's contract with CAM is subject to rescission. The trustee used § 365(a) rather than any of the avoiding powers—and rejection is not "the functional equivalent of a rescission, rendering void the contract and requiring that the parties be put back in the positions they occupied before the contract was formed." Thompkins v. Lil' Joe Records, Inc., 476 F.3d 1294, 1306

(11th Cir. 2007). It "merely frees the estate from the obligation to perform" and "has absolutely no effect upon the contract's continued existence." Ibid. (internal citations omitted).

Scholars uniformly criticize *Lubrizol*, concluding that it confuses rejection with the use of an avoiding power. See, e.g., Douglas G. Baird, Elements of Bankruptcy 130-40 & n.10 (4th ed. 2006); Michael T. Andrew, Executory Contracts in Bankruptcy: Understanding "Rejection," 59 U. Colo. L. Rev. 845, 916-19 (1988); Jay Lawrence Westbrook, The Commission's Recommendations Concerning the Treatment of Bankruptcy Contracts, 5 Am. Bankr. Inst. L. Rev. 463, 470-72 (1997). *Lubrizol* itself devoted scant attention to the question whether rejection cancels a contract, worrying instead about the right way to identify executory contracts to which the rejection power applies. . . .

AFFIRMED.

════════════════

As Judge Easterbrook explained, Congress roundly repudiated the holding in *Lubrizol* by enacting § 365(n), which confirms that the property rights that exist in intellectual property, such as patents, do not "vaporize" upon a licensor's breach of the IP license by way of rejection. Some clung to belief that the Code's definition of "intellectual property" to exclude trademarks meant that Congress indirectly upheld *Lubrizol* for that specific type of IP, an argument Judge Easterbrook emphatically rejected in insisting on the application of the baseline rules of § 365(g) ("An omission is just an omission.").

When the First Circuit disagreed and decided to follow *Lubrizol* in holding that the trademark holder's rejection of the trademark license in its bankruptcy stripped the licensee of its vested rights to use the mark, the Supreme Court took the case. Adopting Judge Easterbrook's conclusion that nothing gets "vaporized" by § 365, it applied the same reasoning to hold that trademark licenses do not get magically rescinded but continue to exist post-rejection. Mission Product Holdings, Inc. v. Tempnology, LLC, 139 S. Ct. 1652, 1662-63 (2019). Justice Kagan specifically noted that "Congress's repudiation of *Lubrizol* for patent contracts does not show any intent to *ratify* that decision's approach for almost all others." Id. at 1665. This should hearten those of you who purchased laptop computers to know that if your vendor, whom you haven't had contact with for years, files for bankruptcy tomorrow and decides to reject the remaining term of your executory three-warranty contract, the consequence is that you have a breach of contract claim against that vendor's estate, not that the contract is vaporized and you have to return the computer to revert to the pre-contractual status quo.

What *Sunbeam* and many of the land-sale cases have in common is the conclusion that § 365(a) cannot be used to extinguish a property right held by the counterparty (be they simple land rights in Blackacre or complex IP rights in a patent), even though the right was created by contract. The Supreme Court specifically noted that abrogation of property rights can only be properly found in the avoiding powers. Id. at 1663. In other words, if the trustee wants to take back your computer, she would have to show it was a voidable preference or some other ground allowing for avoidance of a transfer of an interest in *property*.

2. Remedial Rights in Contract Law

In addition to real property and IP cases, there is a third category that creates a special level of tension between state remedies law and the rejection power: those involving contracts not to compete. Here, however, there is not a specific property right held by the counterparty, but there may be an equitable right to injunctive relief that has the same economic effect of compelling performance. Again, while some courts wade into executoriness to try to get to what they think is the "right" result, the proper analysis, as the following case demonstrates, starts with what state law provides about remedies that may have to be balanced against countervailing considerations about the federal bankruptcy policy of discharge.

======= In re ORTIZ =======

400 B.R. 755 (C.D. Cal. 2009)

MORROW, District Judge.

. . .

I. FACTUAL AND PROCEDURAL BACKGROUND

Ortiz is a professional boxer; Top Rank is a boxing promoter. In 2005, Ortiz and Top Rank entered into a five-year promotional agreement, pursuant to which Ortiz agreed to fight annually in a minimum number of bouts promoted by Top Rank and Top Rank agreed to pay Ortiz a guaranteed minimum purse per bout. The agreement contained an exclusivity provision, requiring that Ortiz fight only in televised bouts promoted by Top Rank. The contract prohibited Ortiz from fighting in bouts for another promoter for ninety days before or after a televised appearance promoted by Top Rank.

On January 2, 2008, Ortiz filed a voluntary Chapter 7 bankruptcy petition. On April 21, 2008, he filed an adversary action against Top Rank, seeking declaratory relief, a permanent injunction, and attorneys' fees and costs. Ortiz argued that the promotional agreement was rejected by operation of law on March 3, 2008, because the bankruptcy trustee did not assume his obligations under the contract within sixty days after the bankruptcy action was filed, and Top Rank took no action to prevent its rejection within that period.

Ortiz asserted that Top Rank had interfered with his efforts to enter an agreement with Golden Boy Productions, another boxing promoter, by advising Golden Boy that the promotional agreement was still valid. Ortiz sought a declaration that he was no longer required to perform his obligations under the promotional agreement and an injunction prohibiting Top Rank from interfering with future negotiations between Ortiz and third parties. On August 18, 2008, the bankruptcy court entered judgment in Ortiz's favor on the declaratory and injunctive relief claims. It concluded that the trustee's rejection of the promotional agreement terminated all of Ortiz's obligations under the agreement; and that Top Rank's rights under the agreement were limited to seeking monetary damages against the bankruptcy estate. The court also found that even if the trustee's rejection of the contract did not terminate Ortiz's obligations, the exclusivity provision was unenforceable under Nevada law as an unreasonable non-competition agreement.

1. Standards Governing Rejection of Executory Contracts in Bankruptcy

The parties agree that the promotional agreement was an "executory contract" as that term is defined in bankruptcy law, and do not dispute that it was "deemed rejected" by the trustee's failure to assume it.

Top Rank argues that rejection merely constitutes a pre-petition breach of the contract, which does not [a]ffect the substantive rights and obligations of the parties. Thus, it asserts that in addition to filing a claim against the estate, it may also seek injunctive relief enforcing the agreement's exclusivity provision. . . .

Although rejection also serves to relieve a debtor from certain financial obligations, the breach created by rejection under the Bankruptcy Code does not terminate rights and obligations under the contract. Rather, the debtor is relieved because monetary claims for breach are treated as claims against the estate rather than the debtor. . . . While courts have explained the rule as providing protection for the debtor, therefore, it is clear that rejection in itself does not eliminate the non-debtor's rights under the contract.

2. Whether Rights to Equitable Relief Survive Rejection

To determine whether a claim for non-monetary relief under an executory contract can be asserted post-bankruptcy against the debtor, a court must look elsewhere than section 365. The "breach" created by rejection is deemed to have occurred immediately prior to the filing of the bankruptcy petition. For this reason, to the extent that breach of an executory contract gives rise to a claim for money damages, that claim can be asserted only against the bankruptcy estate, not against the debtor. Whether the non-debtor party has a right to an equitable remedy that survives bankruptcy turns on whether such right constitutes a "claim" that is dischargeable in bankruptcy. . . .

Bankruptcy law provides for the discharge of a bankrupt's "debts," defined as "liabilit[ies] on [] claim[s]." 11 U.S.C. § 101(12). The Bankruptcy Act defines a "claim" in relevant part as a "right to an equitable remedy for breach of performance if such breach gives rise to a right to payment, whether or not such right to an equitable remedy is reduced to judgment, fixed, contingent, matured, unmatured, disputed, undisputed, secured, or unsecured." 11 U.S.C. § 101(5)(B). Thus, "[a]n equitable remedy, such as an injunction, will 'give rise to a right to payment,' and therefore be discharged, if payment of a monetary remedy is an alternative to the equitable remedy." [In re Mitchell, 249 B.R. 55, 59 (Bankr. S.D.N.Y. 2000) (citing In re Ben Franklin Hotel Assocs., 186 F.3d 301, 305 (3d Cir. 1999)]. . . .

3. *The Bankruptcy Court's Decision Regarding the Effect of Rejection . . .*

In sum, the court concludes that the bankruptcy court's decision that rejection of the promotional agreement, by itself, "terminated" the contract and extinguished Top Rank's ability to seek equitable relief for breach of contract was error. . . . To determine whether any provisions of the contract remain enforceable against the debtor, rather than as claims against the estate, courts must assess whether the right to an equitable remedy is a "claim" dischargeable in bankruptcy. This in turn requires an inquiry as to whether an equitable remedy is available under state law. Section 365 simply does not speak to which obligations may and may not be enforced post-bankruptcy against the debtor. Consequently, the bankruptcy court's conclusion that the trustee's rejection of the contract between Ortiz and Top Rank terminated the contract and extinguished any claim for breach that Top Rank may have was erroneous. . . .

[The court remanded to the bankruptcy court the question of the enforceability of the covenant not to compete under Nevada law. If the covenant was not enforceable under state law, presumably it would not be necessary to determine if state law permitted damages as an alternative to injunctive relief. If the covenant was enforceable under state law, the bankruptcy court would next decide if damages were available as an alternative to an injunction, in which case Top Rank's contract right would be a "claim" and therefore dischargeable, as the court had discussed earlier in the opinion.—Eds.]

━━━━━━━━━

Not only did the court in *Ortiz* agree with Judge Easterbrook that rejection is not vaporization, the court also eschewed executoriness as a pseudo-solution—although that may be because it didn't have a choice as the parties agreed the contract was executory. The *Ortiz* court identified a key distinction in understanding the state-federal conflict in remedies: the difference between relief against the estate, where specific performance will frequently be denied because of the creditor inequality issue discussed earlier, and relief against the debtor, where the key question becomes one of discharge. Note, however, that even the question of discharge, on its face a classic bankruptcy issue, rests in large part on the state law about the availability of equitable relief or of damages as an alternative to equitable relief in the definition of "claim" and "debt" within the interplay among §§ 101(5), (12), 524(a), and 727(a). Thus, the wide power conferred on debtors by § 365 is ultimately cabined extra-statutorily by state laws pertaining to remedies under their law of contract and vested rights under their law of property.

Problem Set 26

26.1. Rancho Industries was in the business of raising horses and other livestock on its 10,000-acre ranch. About a year ago, it leased 1,000 acres for a five-year term to your client, Fledgling Breeders, Inc., for similar purposes. The agreed rent was $100,000 per year. Rancho promised in the lease to ensure a steady supply of water from its wells through the existing irrigation system to FB land. Rancho has recently filed a chapter 7 petition. There is no water on the land FB leases and it would cost $120,000 per year to bring the necessary water by truck. Can Rancho reject the lease? If so, what remedies will FB have? See § 365(h).

26.2. A. Your client is Roxanna Gonzales, the trustee who was appointed in the PetroCo case (Problem 25.1) after it failed and was converted to a chapter 7, despite the cash infusion resulting from rejection of the ConEd contract and resale of the oil at the market price. While going through the PetroCo records, she has found a contract whereby PetroCo agreed to sell its Queens office building to J-Mart, a large local retailer. The sale price was $17.5 million, but Gonzales thinks the building would bring at least $25 million in the overheated market that has resulted from the construction of new luxury apartments in the area. Under the contract, the closing was to take place on June 5, but the chapter 11 was filed on June 1, and nothing has been done since. The chapter 7 conversion took place 55 days ago. Can she still reject the contract? Can she resell the building? What arguments will J-Mart likely make? What do you need to learn about state law to resolve this issue? What other economic facts might be important? To prepare for your meeting with Gonzales, come up with a list of issues, questions to be resolved, and possible outcomes. See § 365(a), (i), (j).

B. When Roxanna came to see you, she brought a second problem/opportunity as well. PetroCo has a pre-bankruptcy option contract to buy gravel from Jones Materials, Inc., for $40 a ton up to 10,000 tons. On June 30, the State will announce an award of a major highway contract. Roxanne, who has spent her life in the construction business, is confident she can sell the gravel to Romano Construction for $80 a ton if Romano gets the big contract. She explained to you that "the option is perfect, because I have no use for the gravel as we liquidate, but if I could sell the gravel for a net of $40 a ton we could pay a substantial dividend to the unsecured creditors." The problem is that Jones knows about the Romano opportunity as well, and the sales manager told her to forget the contract: "Like it says in the contract, I don't have to deal with no bankrupt bums." Is he right?

26.3. CL, Inc., patented a new bug extermination chemical, "Death Spray," which combines high toxicity to insects with safety to humans to an unparalleled degree. Its CEO, Calvin Looper, came to you 18 months ago to represent CLI in licensing negotiations with FuturVista Technologies, a growing mini-conglomerate. In the negotiations, FuturVista agreed to pay CLI a small initial fee, plus a royalty based on net profits of its exterminator division, in exchange for a 20-year license that would be exclusive for the first year. In the license contract CLI agreed it could not assign its patent or the FuturVista contract to any other entity, directly or through merger or acquisition, for the life of the contract.

Calvin was very tough in the negotiations. FuturVista wanted CLI to agree to defend any suits attacking its patent or at least to cooperate in their defense. Although you told him that such agreements by inventors were standard, he refused to permit CLI to incur that or any other obligation. CLI also refused to agree to license future improvements. The contract thus provided "Licensor shall have no other or further obligation whatsoever and no defect in its patent shall be any defense to its rights under this contract."

Calvin came to see you this morning about a new deal. Gigantic Oil has acquired a pest-extermination service and has heard about Death Spray. It has offered CLI a very large royalty fee for a license for both patent and trademark, but is only interested in an exclusive license. "If CLI can just junk those jerks at FuturVista, our stock will skyrocket," Calvin explained in asking you how CLI can get the deal with Gigantic. He also explained that FuturVista has yet to turn a profit on Death Spray, although he thinks they will do so in the next year or two. You have done some research in your state's contract law since Calvin left your office and found that it is very hard to prove and recover future profits ("too speculative," the cases say), although in licensing cases specific performance or other equitable relief is often granted. What advice should you give Calvin and why? Would Calvin be better or worse off if he had been less tough in the negotiations with FuturVista? Should you recommend further negotiations with FuturVista at this time? See § 365(n).

26.4. Sweet Sarah Kaminsky is one terrific cook. She ran her restaurant, Sweet Sarah's, for many years, making it the center of neighborhood dining in the Clarksville area of Austin. Three years ago Sarah sold out to Harold Bonker, who bought the restaurant for $4 million. The contract of sale included a covenant that Sarah would not compete in the restaurant business in Austin or its suburbs for five years. Sadly, within six months both Sarah and Hank, her husband, were struck by cancer. After two years of massive drug interventions and radiation treatments, she made it but he didn't. The medical bills beyond the insurance coverage were enormous. Sarah now finds herself broke and seeking a job doing the only thing she knows how to do, cooking. She's been offered a high-paying job as head chef at an upscale restaurant in the western Austin suburb of Bee Cave. Harold heard about the offer and came to you, saying, "My business is doomed if Sarah accepts the position as a chef because all of her old friends and customers will want to help her out by going over there." You did some research and determined the covenant would likely be considered reasonable and enforceable under state-law precedents. At Harold's request, you sent a letter warning Sarah not to violate her covenant. This morning you got a notice of her chapter 11 bankruptcy filing. What can you tell Harold about his chances of preventing Sarah from taking the job? See §§ 365(a), 1141(d)(1)-(2), (5). (Assume for now that Sarah as an employee does not meet the definition of "small business debtor.")

PART IV

BUSINESS BANKRUPTCY: PLANS AND BEYOND

"Ladies and gentlemen, is there a bankruptcy attorney on board?"

Section 1

Traditional Chapter 11

After assessing the debtor's financial condition, stabilizing operations, shoring up liquidity, and reviewing the legal tools available to reshape the estate, the debtor's counsel should have a solid picture of the prospects for reorganizing the business. A "traditional" chapter 11 involves negotiating and confirming a plan of reorganization to keep the company operating. (In Section 2, we consider "modern" chapter 11 strategies, often involving a sale of the business.) Although a number of reorganization structures and tools may be used, the essence of a traditional chapter 11 is reorganizing the debtor into a profitable business going forward that can pay its plan obligations to creditors from future revenues.

In 2019, Congress enacted the Small Business Reorganization Act (SBRA), subchapter V of chapter 11. The effective date was in early 2020, just about the same time the COVID-19 pandemic began sweeping across the globe. (It has already been amended, in response to the economic crisis, in laws that nominally will sunset.) The SBRA, as its name implies, applies only to small business debtors. Unpublished data from the Business Bankruptcy Project show, however, that even in the megacorporation stronghold of the Southern District of New York, those businesses that would be eligible for the SBRA constitute more than 40% of the chapter 11 filers and over half the cases when the temporary legislation is applied. Thus, the SBRA should not be viewed as the quaint backwater its name may lull you into believing: its regime may well be selected by the vast majority of chapter 11 users. Despite this special and broad-reaching subchapter within chapter 11, it is crucial to recognize that its core is premised upon developing a plan of reorganization, the bailiwick of traditional chapter 11. Accordingly, the traditional rules for classification, voting, best interests, and the like that you will learn in these next few assignments regarding chapter 11 apply in the SBRA. That said, the point of the SBRA is to develop special rules for small business cases, so there will be important exceptions to these traditional rules that we will point out along the way.

Regardless the size of the business, a debtor's use of chapter 11 is a means to an end. In other words, chapter 11 reorganization is best seen as a *process*, despite its culminating moment in a litigation event—*confirmation*. Negotiation exists at every step, from designing a plan to classifying voting groups to determining sufficient disclosures to getting requisite support to pass the plan. Moreover, this process is often iterative; debtor companies sometimes have to go back to the drawing board if creditors exercise leverage or the court throws down a legal gauntlet to derail a reorganization effort. Because this bankruptcy course cannot take years (as some chapter 11 cases do), we present the chapter 11 stages sequentially, with greater linearity than real life.

NEGOTIATING THE PLAN

Chapter 11 is sometimes described as *an invitation to a negotiation.* Both operational matters (whether to close the West Coast office) and financing matters (whether to give unsecured creditors warrants for 80% of the company's equity) are up for grabs, and so those negotiations are far-reaching. The key requirement for confirmation—and certainly the one that drives most negotiations—is that a statutory majority of each class of creditors must vote in favor of the plan for the plan to be confirmed. §§ 1126, 1129(a)(8). Thus, before presenting a plan, a debtor must negotiate to arrive at a plan that is acceptable to most creditors. The negotiations may be formal, with the creditors' committee (if there is one) and other stakeholders, such as the secured lenders, exchanging correspondence or sitting around a table, but plenty of emails, texts, and phone calls—of varying emotions—abound. All this negotiation, however, takes place with the players knowing the ground rules of what they can insist upon under the Code, which negotiations jocks call their "bargaining endowments." These entitlements are generally spelled out in §§ 1122 and 1129.

Before we turn to those rules, however, it is important to understand that the negotiation covers much more than just how much of a haircut a creditor will take. As mentioned, operational control of the debtor will be open for consideration. The very composition of a debtor can change. Sometimes a debtor emerges with just a restructured balance sheet, other times with new ownership altogether. Additionally, "extra-bankruptcy" considerations arise for some debtors, such as regulatory compliance with government entities ranging from utility boards to the Federal Aviation Administration.

Often the most important extra-bankruptcy consideration is the Internal Revenue Code. In a complex chapter 11, legions of tax advisers will pore over the plan and often have final say in its content. There are two basic tax rules important to reorganizations. First, "Cancellation of Indebtedness" income is taxable income that is triggered when your creditor says you don't have to pay. The idea may seem silly: I'm broke and the IRS says I had a big income? The reason is that the IRS considers you richer by the amount of the forgiven debt and taxes you accordingly. Cancellation of debt is income because it increases the debtor's wealth as surely as if the debtor had won the lottery. We all understand that if Jane wins $10,000 in the Massachusetts lottery, she must pay income tax on the winnings. The win increased her net wealth by $10,000 and that is taxable income. On the other hand, if Jane borrows $10,000, the loan does not constitute income because it has to be paid back. The debt she owes balances out the cash she receives, so there is no net increase in Jane's wealth. But suppose Jane's creditor calls her and says, for whatever reason, "Jane, forget about paying me back." At that moment, Jane has $10,000 in the bank with no offsetting obligation to pay it back. The disappearance of the debt has increased her net wealth by $10,000. The cancellation of the debt is income and is taxable as such.

Because liquidity-starved bankrupt debtors would have difficulty paying such a tax bill, the Tax Code forgives it. IRC § 108. Second, ensuring no free lunch, the IRS makes you reduce any pre-existing tax benefits in exchange. For example, Net Operating Losses ("NOLs"), which debtors naturally tend to have, get sopped up, just as the tax basis for the company's assets must be reduced. IRC § 1017. These tax benefits ("attributes" in tax-talk) are big deals. Writing down basis means both a reduced depreciation expense deduction on tax returns and a higher capital gain tax if the asset is ever sold. Because NOLs can be applied to reduce future income, there used to be a brisk business in bankrupt companies—buy it, merge into it, and protect the profit from your real business. NOLs are now much harder to transfer. This may be sound tax policy, but it pits that policy against bankruptcy policy favoring reorganization. IRC § 382.

When these negotiations are all done, the plan will be put to a vote. Section 1129(a)(8) sets out the voting thresholds that must be reached for confirmation. Creditors vote by "class" in chapter 11, and the debtor gets to construct the classes, subject to court approval. § 1122. However, the Code requires that the debtor must provide detailed disclosure of its plans for the reorganized company, which hopefully ensures an informed electorate. § 1125.

A.   CAMPAIGNING FOR THE VOTE: DISCLOSURE AND SOLICITATION

Information is often a crucial advantage in a negotiation. If one party has more information than another, it will be in a stronger position to negotiate a favorable outcome. Chapter 11 is concerned about such a dynamic for several reasons. First, information asymmetries will undermine the principle of equality as equity. Certain creditors, although of the same status (for example, trade creditors) could vote differently simply because they have different information about the company's management, financials, and strategy. Second, bankruptcy is a public process, overseen by a court. Confidence in the fairness of the judicial process would be undermined if side deals dominated. This concern is even more acute when the debtor is a publicly traded company, subject to securities regulation (just ask the SEC if it thinks disclosure is important). Third, information sharing makes negotiation more efficient. Parties often drag out deal making if they do not have the necessary information. A shared set of information speeds things along. Finally, forced *ex ante* disclosure minimizes disharmony with the deal that could arise after confirmation if relevant information were not revealed until then. For all these reasons, voting in chapter 11 is intended to be well informed under the Code.

1.   *Disclosure*

The Code requires disclosure at several points prior to the reorganization plan. The petition and accompanying schedules, the § 341 meeting of creditors, quarterly reports during the chapter 11, and proofs of claim are all disclosures. The creditors' committee has the right to access the debtor's otherwise proprietary financial records. §§ 1102, 704. But the apotheosis of this is the disclosure statement. The Code takes disclosure so seriously that the statement must be approved by the bankruptcy court before any solicitation of votes can even begin. § 1125. This inclines lawyers to be garrulous; disclosures are a fruitful source for young associate billing.

Do not think disclosure is all boilerplate. The disclosure requirement can produce heated litigation and go through numerous amendments. Most often, an objecting creditor claims the debtor failed to disclose important financial and business information that is necessary for an informed vote on the plan. Behind this argument—or in the following case, front and center—is the fact that a creditor wants to defeat a plan. Disclosure can provide a preview of confirmation issues. From an unhappy creditor's point of view, the sooner the parties are sent back to the negotiating table, the better.

==================== In re PUFF ====================

2011 WL 2604759 (Bankr. N.D. Iowa June 30, 2011)

COLLINS, Bankruptcy Judge.

. . .

Wells Fargo Financial Leasing (WFFL) and Farmers Savings Bank (FSB) objected to Debtor's Third Amended Disclosure Statement. WFFL made two separate arguments regarding the sufficiency and adequacy of the Third Amended Disclosure Statement. FSB raised similar objections and added arguments about the information in the Disclosure Statement being insufficient to determine feasibility [a requirement of confirmation—Eds.] . . .

PROCEDURAL BACKGROUND AND FACTUAL RECORD FROM DISCLOSURE STATEMENT HEARING AND AUTOMATIC STAY HEARING

Debtor filed a Third Amended Disclosure Statement in this Chapter 11 case on March 18, 2011. WFFL and FSB raised the objections stated above. Both creditors filed objections on their own behalf, not on behalf of unsecured creditors or equity holders.

At the request of the parties, the Court held an evidentiary hearing to address the objections. The focus of the hearing was the valuation of the numerous parcels of property involved in Debtor's Chapter 11 reorganization. Debtor has both residential and commercial property in the rural area surrounding Hazleton, Iowa.

The Court received testimony from Debtor, Debtor's expert witnesses on valuation, an officer of FSB, and expert witnesses on valuation from both WFFL and FSB. The evidence disclosed a sharp and significant difference in the valuation between Debtor and her secured creditors on the secured property in her reorganization. The disagreement is meaningful because it affects the treatment and ultimate payment to both WFFL and FSB under the Plan. Secured claims are largely to be paid in full. Unsecured claims will receive approximately one cent on the dollar. The valuation of the property determines the amount of security available upon which the security interests of WFFL and FSB could attach. Under Debtor's valuation, the secured claims of both WFFL and FSB are reduced significantly from what each of them claim, resulting in a larger unsecured claim for each. Under the valuations offered by WFFL and FSB, their secured claims would be greater because of the higher valuations. This would result in smaller unsecured claims paid at the nominal rate.

Both WFFL and FSB (by virtue of their joinder of WFFL's arguments) also argue that Debtor erroneously treats some of WFFL's claims as security agreements instead of "true leases." WFFL and FSB argue that some or all of WFFL's claims are in fact true leases and not secured claims. This is significant because "true leases" would require either substantially greater payments than those offered on the secured portions of WFFL's claims, or repossession by WFFL of property critical to the reorganization if those leases were ultimately rejected. In sum, if WFFL's obligations are true leases and not secured claims, the Plan proposed by Debtor may not be feasible.

. . .

Conclusions of Law

The requirements for and adequacy of disclosure statements are governed by § 1125(b) of the Bankruptcy Code.

"Adequate information" is defined to mean:

information of a kind, and in sufficient detail, as far as is reasonably practicable in light of the nature and history of the debtor and the condition of the debtor's books and records . . . *that would enable a hypothetical reasonable investor typical of holders of claims* or interests of the relevant class to *make an informed judgment about the plan.*

11 U.S.C. § 1125(a)(1) (emphasis added). The hypothetical reasonable investor is also defined:

"investor typical of holders of claims or interests of the relevant class" means investor having—

(A) a claim or interest of the relevant class;

(B) such a relationship with the debtor as the holders of other claims or interests of such class generally have; and

(C) such ability to obtain such information from sources other than the disclosure required by this section as holders of claims or interests in such class generally have.

11 U.S.C. § 1125(a)(2). It is thus specifically presumed that such an investor will have the "ability to obtain such information from sources other than the disclosure required by this section as holders of claims or interests in such class generally have." In re The New Power Company, 438 F.3d 1113, 1118 (11th Cir. 2006) (quoting 11 U.S.C. § 1125(a)(2)(C)).

"Numerous courts have prescribed a list of disclosures which typically should be included in a disclosure statement." In re Cardinal Congregate I, 121 B.R.760, 765 (Bankr. S.D. Ohio 1990). These cases and others have developed a list of factors which may be necessary to meet the statutory requirement of adequate information. These factors are:

(1) the events which led to the filing of a bankruptcy petition;
(2) a description of the available assets and their value;
(3) the anticipated future of the company;
(4) the source of information stated in the disclosure statement;
(5) a disclaimer;
(6) the present condition of the debtor while in Chapter 11;
(7) the scheduled claims;
(8) the estimated return to creditors under a Chapter 7 liquidation;
(9) the accounting method utilized to produce financial information and the name of the accountants responsible for such information;
(10) the future management of the debtor;
(11) the Chapter 11 plan or a summary thereof;
(12) the estimated administrative expenses, including attorneys' and accountants' fees;
(13) the collectability of accounts receivable;
(14) financial information, data, valuations or projections relevant to the creditors' decision to accept or reject the Chapter 11 plan;
(15) information relevant to the risks posed to creditors under the plan;
(16) the actual or projected realizable value from recovery of preferential or otherwise voidable transfers;
(17) litigation likely to arise in a nonbankruptcy context;
(18) tax attributes of the debtor; and
(19) the relationship of the debtor with the affiliates.

Cardinal Congregate I, 121 B.R. at 265-66. Disclosure of all factors, however, is not necessary in every case. *Id.* Cases have specified that these factors are only a general "yardstick" and need to be modified as the circumstances and size of each case warrant.

. . .

"Courts generally have agreed that it may, on occasion, be appropriate to consider issues at the disclosure hearing stage which could otherwise be raised at confirmation, if the described plan is fatally flawed so that confirmation would not be possible." *Phoenix Petroleum Co.*, 278 B.R. at 394. . . . However, "[s]uch action is discretionary and must be used carefully so as not to convert the disclosure statement hearing into a confirmation hearing, and to insure that due process concerns are protected." *Cardinal Congregate I*, 121 B.R. at 762.

ANALYSIS

WFFL and FSB raised essentially identical arguments regarding the sufficiency of information provided in the Disclosure Statement. They both argued about Debtor's valuation of the parcels of property and the failure to disclose the possible issue arising from Debtor's proposed treatment of WFFL's claim as a security interest instead of a true lease. . . . They are both creditors that have "had access to adequate information regarding the treatment of [their] claims and interests" sufficient to satisfy disclosure requirements. *New Power Co.*, 483 F.3d at 1120-21. The Court finds that the "additional information" that they seek will not help either of them to form an opinion on how to vote on the Plan. It is clear from the record that both of them simply disagree with their treatment in the Plan and intend to vote no even if all the information they seek from Debtor in the Disclosure Statement is ultimately provided.

Their arguments that the additional information they seek disclosure of is critical to determine Plan feasibility suffers from the same and an additional flaw. Feasibility of the Plan is specifically an issue for the confirmation stage. See 11 U.S.C. § 1129. In fact, underlying much of the argument and presentation of evidence at this stage is simply a preview of confirmation arguments on feasibility. The Court will decide those issues there, not here.

In post-hearing briefing, WFFL and FSB changed their approach slightly and argued that the additional information they sought disclosure of was for other unsecured creditors. While the Court believes there is some legal infirmity in attempting to rely on arguments that the other interested parties have not made, the Court sets those concerns aside for the purpose of this opinion. The Court agrees with both WFFL and FSB that general unsecured creditors—specifically treated as a separate class under the proposed Plan—may not be aware of the valuation issues and/or the true lease/security agreement issues that have been raised and argued. It is conceivable that unsecured creditors would find the disclosure of these facts useful in making their decision on how to vote on the Plan.

While the Court concludes that additional information on the disputed valuation is appropriate, the Court does make any final decision on valuation on any of the assets. Instead, the Court adopts and incorporates the alternative suggestions of WFFL and FSB. Debtor should be required to disclose that there are serious valuation disputes, that conflicting testimony and evidence has been offered, and that there are competing appraisals and valuations for both sides. The Court believes that it is appropriate for Debtor to disclose the specific values offered by each side on each parcel of property. The Court believes such disclosure will provide sufficient information for all parties to determine how they will vote on the plan.

The Court reaches a similar conclusion on the "true lease" versus "security agreement" issue . . . . It is a complicated issue. In re Warne, 2011 WL 1303425 at *2 (Bankr. D. Kan.) ("Much ink has been spilt over the intriguing question of what is a true lease."). . . . The Disclosure Statement should also state that if the Court ultimately determines that the claims of WFFL are in whole or in part based on "true leases," this could change both the analysis of feasibility and the ultimate payout available to unsecured creditors.

Based on the above analysis, the Court concludes that the Disclosure Statement is approved in all regards except for those specifically noted above. Debtor has ten (10) days to amend her Disclosure Statement on those specific issues. When those amendments are made, Debtor can move into the process of solicitation for confirmation as provided under the Bankruptcy Code. Under the authority provided in § 105(d)(2)(B)(vi), the Court will hear any further objections on the amended disclosure statement limited to those specific areas discussed above—and no others—at the hearing on confirmation.

The creditors in this case "won" on the disclosure issue, forcing an amendment, but they did not get the summary judgment they wanted. They may try again at confirmation to block the plan. In this way, a disclosure fight, by those who can finance counsel, may just be posturing. Many creditors, however, such as those being told they will receive a whopping penny for a dollar of debt, will not actively participate in a bankruptcy case, with the result that chapter 11 disclosures can find themselves lining a recycling bin along with office supply catalogs. In other instances, creditor victory at disclosure will prompt a debtor to sweeten the reorganization plan to discourage further disclosure objections and hopefully ensure a positive vote on the plan.

Because it is the basis on which the creditors vote, the disclosure statement should be comprehensive, taking into account the facts of the case. For large, publicly traded companies, disclosure statements may run thousands of pages. For a small business, disclosure may be accomplished in less than a dozen pages. Length does not ensure nor even necessarily correlate with accuracy. In a study of 201 large firms that completed chapter 11 reorganizations between 1982 and 1993, Professors Betker, Ferris, and Lawless concluded that there was a "significant optimistic bias in the earnings projections" of the disclosure statements:

> The annual pretax and post-tax incomes of reorganized firms are systematically overestimated for each of the four years following plan confirmation. . . . By the fourth year following plan confirmation, the cumulative forecast error for pretax income (e.g., EBIT) is 170% of the average annual projected income examined in the study.

Brian Betker, Stephen Ferris & Robert Lawless, Warm with Sunny Skies: Disclosure Statement Forecasts, 73 Am. Bankr. L.J. 809, 834 (1999).

The title of their article says it all. The authors recommend that those who rely on disclosure statements "should discount the projected income figures prior to a determination of the plan's ultimate feasibility." Of course, as one side increases the discount factor, the other may just ratchet up the gloriousness of the projections.

The problem with inaccurate disclosure is not limited to overstated value. Management may sometimes understate the value of the debtor company in order to persuade creditors to accept payouts that are lower than those they would be entitled to if the firm were correctly valued. If the firm is undervalued, of course, the effective distribution to the equity owners of the emerging business will have been far in excess of their legal entitlement. In the chapter 11 case of National Gypsum Corporation, for example, a short time after the chapter 11 plan was confirmed, a group of creditors sued management and equity. The creditors alleged that the business was grossly (and fraudulently) undervalued in the chapter 11 documents, causing the creditors to settle for too little money. The problem of management *under*valuation was documented in Stuart Gilson, Edith Hotchkiss & Richard Ruback, Valuation of Bankrupt Firms, 13 Rev. Fin. Stud. 43 (2000), and continues to provoke research today. See, e.g., Jared Ellias, Regulating Bankruptcy Bonuses, 92 S. Cal. L. Rev. 653 (2019).

Disclosure is where we see the first innovation of the SBRA. Building upon the premise that the capital structure and business plans of a small business cannot be excessively complicated, Congress dispatches the requirement of a disclosure statement as a separate litigation moment (and expense). The SBRA instead requires only that a list of critical information be disclosed within the plan itself, not as a separate document. § 1181(b).

2.   *Solicitation and the "Safe Harbor"*

When a business attempts to reorganize in chapter 11, it makes statements about the operations of the company, projections, and proposed distributions of stock for money or for forgiveness of debt. Depending on whether the business is large enough or in certain lines of work, those statements and distributions could be subject to the state and federal laws regulating the sale of securities. Bankruptcy laws displace the regulations governing disclosure as part of the vote solicitation for a chapter 11 plan. This exemption is referred to as a "safe harbor," because companies can make disclosure and solicit votes exempt from securities regulations. "No person connected with the solicitation of plan acceptances and rejections is liable for a violation of the securities laws, so long as that person acts in good faith and in compliance with the Code." § 1125(e). The general purpose is to avoid the impact of the strict and time-consuming disclosure requirements of the securities laws. The exemption from SEC and state registration requirements in § 1125(d) is similar to exemptions provided in other specialized fields. The exemption from fraud liability given by § 1125(e), however, is more unusual.

It is worth noting that because the Supreme Court has already interpreted Rule 10b-5 and § 10(b) of the Securities and Exchange Act of 1934 to shield good faith actors from private causes of action, the principal effect of the § 1125(e) exemption is to block SEC injunctive actions, in which the SEC seeks to enjoin a defendant "from further violations of the securities laws." This is no technical sidebar. The legislative history is unusually candid in stating that its authors feared not merely the adverse effects of such an injunctive action, but also the "leverage" that the SEC had derived from threatening such actions prior to the enactment of the 1978 Code.

B.   ELIGIBILTY TO VOTE: IMPAIRMENT

The first rule about voting is that some creditors are barred from the polls. The Code deems *unimpaired* classes to have accepted the plan. § 1126(f). For *impaired* classes, acceptance of the plan is required. § 1129(a)(8). (Additionally, the Code requires for confirmation the acceptance by *at least one impaired class*, § 1129(a)(10), which may seem silly and gratuitous to § 1129(a)(8), which requires acceptance by *all* impaired classes. The "at least one impaired class" rule will have its relevance described when we turn to non-consensual plan confirmation—so-called cramdown—in Assignments 29 and 30.)

The logic behind eliminating the vote for unimpaired classes of creditors is fairly obvious. If creditors in a class are not being deprived of their nonbankruptcy rights by the plan, why should their approval of the plan be required? But it is still possible for an angry creditor to derail a reorganization that would benefit the collective whole. Thus, creditors fighting confirmation (either because they prefer liquidation or simply to gain leverage for a greater payout) will resist their classification as unimpaired. In the following case, the creditors held a contractual right to penalty interest at a default rate and other payments that were likely unmatured interest in a contract otherwise enforceable under state law but arguably unclaimable under (pre-emptive) § 502(b)(2).

In re ULTRA PETROLEUM CORPORATION
943 F.3d 758 (5th Cir. 2019)

On Petition for Rehearing
OLDHAM, Circuit Judge.

These bankruptcy proceedings arise from exceedingly anomalous facts. The debtors entered bankruptcy insolvent and now are solvent. That alone makes them rare. But second, the debtors accomplished their unlikely feat by virtue of a lottery-like rise in commodity prices. The combination of these anomalies makes these debtors as rare as the proverbial rich man who manages to enter the Kingdom of Heaven.

The key legal question before us is whether the rich man's creditors are "impaired" by a plan that paid them everything allowed by the Bankruptcy Code. The bankruptcy court said yes. In that court's view, a plan impairs a creditor if it refuses to pay an amount the Bankruptcy Code independently disallows. . . . We reverse and follow the monolithic mountain of authority holding the Code—not the reorganization plan—defines and limits the claim in these circumstances.

. . .

I.

Ultra Petroleum Corporation ("Petroleum") is an oil and gas exploration and production company. To be more precise, it's a holding company.

Petroleum's subsidiaries—UP Energy Corporation ("Energy") and Ultra Resources, Inc. ("Resources")—do the exploring and producing. [T]o finance its operations, [b]etween 2008 and 2010 Resources issued unsecured notes worth $1.46 billion to various noteholders. And in 2011, it borrowed another $999 million under a Revolving Credit Facility. Petroleum and Energy guaranteed both debt obligations.

In 2014, crude oil cost well over $100 per barrel. But then Petroleum's fate took a sharp turn for the worse. Only a year and a half later, a barrel cost less than $30. The world was flooded with oil; Petroleum and its subsidiaries were flooded with debt. On April 29, 2016, the companies voluntarily petitioned for reorganization under Chapter 11. . . .

During bankruptcy proceedings, however, oil prices rose. Crude oil approached $80 per barrel, and the Petroleum companies became solvent again. So, the debtors proposed a rare creature in bankruptcy—a reorganization plan that (they said) would compensate the creditors in full. As to creditors with claims under the Note Agreement and Revolving Credit Facility (together, the "Class 4 Creditors"), the debtors would pay three sums: the outstanding principal on those obligations, pre-petition interest at a rate of 0.1%, and post-petition interest at the federal judgment rate. Accordingly, the debtors elected to treat the Class 4 Creditors as "unimpaired." Therefore, they could not object to the plan. 11 U.S.C. § 1126(f).

The Class 4 Creditors objected just the same. They insisted their claims *were* impaired because the plan did not require the debtors to pay . . . additional post-petition interest at contractual default rates [and thus] an additional . . . $186 million in post-petition interest. Both sides chose to kick the can down the road. Rather than force resolution of the impairment issue at the plan-confirmation stage, the parties stipulated the bankruptcy court could resolve the dispute by deeming the creditors unimpaired and confirming the proposed plan. Meanwhile, the debtors would set aside $400 million to compensate the Class 4 Creditors if necessary "to render [the creditors] Unimpaired." The bankruptcy court agreed and confirmed the plan.

The Bankruptcy Code provides that a class of claims is not impaired if "the [reorganization] plan . . . leaves unaltered the legal, equitable, and contractual rights to which such claim . . . entitles the holder." 11 U.S.C. § 1124(1). Elsewhere the Code states that a court should disallow a claim "to the extent that [it seeks] unmatured interest." *Id.* § 502(b)(2). The debtors argued . . . [t]he Bankruptcy Code entitles creditors, at most, to post-petition interest at the "legal rate," not the rates set by contract. 11 U.S.C. § 726(a)(5). And the legal rate, they said, is the federal judgment rate under 28 U.S.C. § 1961.

The bankruptcy court rejected the premise that it must bake in the Code's [limits on postpetition and unmatured interest] before asking whether a claim is impaired. Instead it concluded unimpairment "requires that [creditors] receive all that they are entitled to under state law." In other words, if a plan does not provide a creditor with all it would receive under state law, the creditor is impaired even if the Code disallows something state law would otherwise provide outside of bankruptcy. . . .

II.

We consider first whether a creditor is "impaired" by a reorganization plan simply because it incorporates the Code's disallowance provisions. We think not.

A.

Chapter 11 lays out a framework for proposing and confirming a reorganization plan. Confirmation of the plan "discharges the debtor from any debt that arose before the date of such confirmation." 11 U.S.C. § 1141(d)(1). Because discharge affects a creditor's rights, the Code generally requires a debtor to vie for the creditor's vote first. *Id.* § 1129(a)(8). And when it does, the creditor may vote to accept or reject the plan. *Id.* § 1126(a). But the creditor's right to vote disappears when the plan doesn't actually affect his rights. If the creditor is "not impaired under [the] plan," he is "conclusively presumed to have accepted" it. *Id.* § 1126(f). The question, then, is whether the Class 4 Creditors were "impaired" by the plan.

Let's start with the statutory text. Section 1124(1) says "a class of claims or interests" is not impaired if "the plan . . . leaves unaltered the [claimant's] legal, equitable, and contractual rights." The Class 4 Creditors spill ample ink arguing their rights have been altered. But that's both undisputed and insufficient. The plain text of § 1124(1) requires that "the plan" do the altering. We therefore hold a creditor is impaired under § 1124(1) only if "*the plan*" itself alters a claimant's "legal, equitable, [or] contractual rights."

The only court of appeals to address the question took the same approach. In *In re PPI Enterprises (U.S.), Inc.*, a landlord (creditor) argued the reorganization plan of his former tenant (debtor) impaired his claim because it did not pay him the full $4.7 million of rent he was owed over the life of the lease. 324 F.3d 197, 201-02 (3d Cir. 2003). The Third Circuit disagreed. Because the Bankruptcy Code caps lease-termination damages under § 502(b)(6), the plan merely reflected the *Code's* disallowance. *Id.* at 204. At the end of the day, "a creditor's claim outside of bankruptcy is not the relevant barometer for impairment; we must examine whether the plan itself is a source of limitation on a creditor's legal, equitable, or contractual rights." . . .

B.

The Class 4 Creditors' counterarguments do not move the needle. First, they focus on § 1124(1)'s use of the word "claim." They note the Code elsewhere speaks of "*allowed* claims." *See, e.g.,* 11 U.S.C. §§ 506(a)(1), 506(a)(2), 510(c)(1), 1126(c). Then they suggest the absence of "allowed" in § 1124(1) means "claim" there refers to the claim *before* the Code's disallowance provisions come in and trim its edges. But the broader statutory context cuts the other way. Section 1124 is not just (or even primarily) about the allowance of claims. It is about rights—the "legal, equitable, and contractual rights to which [the] claim . . . entitles the holder." *Id.* § 1124(1). That means we judge impairment after considering everything that defines the scope of the right or entitlement—such as a contract's language or state law [and also the Code]. . . . "The Bankruptcy Code itself is a statute which, like other statutes, helps to define the legal rights of persons." *Solar King,* 90 B.R. at 819-20. . . .

★ ★ ★

[W]e REVERSE in part, VACATE in part, and REMAND for further proceedings consistent with this opinion.

———————————

The broad language of § 1124 suggests that any legal impairment would count, irrespective of economic effect. For example, a creditor might be given additional security for its debt, which leaves it far more confident of payment. At the same time, the creditor might be subjected to a "cure" period before it can foreclose, whereas before it could have foreclosed immediately. An economist might say that the creditor's economic condition has stayed the same or even improved, but § 1124 would probably count this as impaired (although note some wiggle room for fixing defaults in § 1124(2), which is necessary for any reorganization to get off the ground). The drafters of the Code wanted very much to avoid valuations whenever possible. The desire to avoid valuation favors focusing solely on legal impairment, rather than economic effect, because measurement of economic impairment will often require valuation. On the other hand, to ignore economic impairment risks elevating form over substance. But that is the balance Congress chose.

Sometimes, however, courts are worried about impairment "the other way." That is, if read literally to mean that *any* impairment, no matter how small, crosses the line under § 1124, then a debtor could impose a 0.0000000000000001% haircut on a friendly creditor, classify it as impaired, and get it to join the electorate—perhaps as the swing vote to carry confirmation over the finish line. To jump the gun a bit on a future assignment, this risk is especially acute with aforementioned § 1129(a)(10), which requires at least one impaired class accept the plan as a precondition to cramdown. Thus, to use our democracy analogy, we see litigation over disenfranchisement (being wrongfully called unimpaired) and padding the voter rolls (being wrongly called impaired). Notice the tightrope on the latter: the padding must be generous enough to retain the creditor's favorable vote on the plan but stingy enough to leave the class "substantively" unimpaired. Below is an example of walking this thin, nigh invisible, line of class impairment, with the interesting wrinkle that the line-walking was done by a non-debtor's proposed plan (after the debtor's exclusive period to propose and solicit votes on the plan expires, § 1121(c), anyone can jump into the fray and propose a plan and canvass the electorate).

In re MANGIA PIZZA INVESTMENTS
480 B.R. 669 (Bankr. W.D. Tex. 2012)

GARGOTTA, Bankruptcy Judge.

BACKGROUND

Mangia Pizza is a locally owned pizza restaurant. Prior to filing bankruptcy, it had several locations in Austin; but as the economy worsened, Mangia scaled back its operations to one location in Austin, Texas, and licensed its name to operations at Austin-Bergstrom International Airport and Georgetown, Texas.

Mangia Pizza filed Chapter 11 bankruptcy on November 10, 2010. The Chapter 11 case continued with little dispute until the disclosure statement hearing in July 2011. At the Debtor's disclosure statement hearing, the Court learned that Cloud Cap had purchased the claim of Knife Sharpest for $244.66 and, because exclusivity had terminated, filed a competing disclosure statement. Cloud Cap's disclosure statement adopted much of the information contained in the Debtor's disclosure statement; but Cloud Cap provided more disclosure regarding the pizza industry nationally and locally. Further, Cloud Cap articulated its business plan for the Debtor, which included a revised menu, improved décor for the restaurant, and a proposed expansion of the restaurant. Cloud Cap also objected to the Debtor's lack of disclosure, focusing on feasibility and an apparent inability to confirm a plan.

The Court reset consideration of approving both disclosure statements to allow the parties to come to an agreement regarding the adequacy of disclosure under 11 U.S.C. § 1125. The parties did agree on a form of disclosure statement for both sides. The Court approved the amended disclosure statement for both Cloud Cap and the Debtor. The parties further agreed that one plan packet would be sent to all creditors that included copies of both amended disclosure statements and plans. Creditors were given the option of voting for either plan, voting for both plans, or rejecting both plans. If claimants voted to accept both plans, they were to indicate which plan they preferred. The parties further agreed that the Court would consider confirmation of both plans, allowing the Debtor to present its plan first and Cloud Cap second.

. . .

The Cloud Cap Plan tracks the Debtor's Plan but for a few notable differences. [T]he Cloud Cap Plan created an additional class of claims for HEB in ¶4.4, Class 2(a) as follows:

Class 2(a): Allowed HEB Secured Claim. This Class shall consist of Allowed Secured Claim of HEB Grocery Company secured by a security deposit related to the rejected lease between HEB and the Debtor. Pursuant to 11 U.S.C. § 506(a), HEB's claim is a secured claim for which separate classification is required. The Allowed HEB Secured Claim shall be paid in full on or before 30 days after the Effective Date. Pending payment of

HEB's Secured Claim, HEB shall retain its liens on any Collateral Securing its Claim. The Reorganized Debtor shall pay the Allowed Class 2(a) Claim with Cash from funds available from the Membership Purchase Agreement and operations of the Reorganized Debtor.

Prior to confirmation, Cloud Cap reached an agreement with HEB regarding the treatment of HEB's secured claim. The proposed treatment allows HEB to set off its security deposit against its pre-petition rent claim. . . .

[T]he Debtor had a legitimate concern about the Plan's modification for voting purposes. Cloud Cap asserted that the HEB secured claim was impaired. The Debtor argued that Class 2(a) is Cloud Cap's attempt at manufacturing an impaired accepting class where one simply does not exist. The Debtor argued that HEB's secured claim is not impaired. HEB holds in its account cash in the amount of $9,497.33 plus any accrued interest since its possession of the deposit, which will offset its claim against the Debtor on the Effective Date. HEB has held these funds since the inception of the lease, and its rights at this time, and under the Cloud Cap Plan, are no different than on the Petition Date.

Cloud Cap states that HEB's secured claim will be paid in full within 30 days with cash from funds available from the Membership Purchase Agreement and operations of the Reorganized Debtor. Cloud Cap does not state that HEB will release and/or offset the security deposit it holds as collateral. By a plain reading of Cloud Cap's Plan, HEB will retain the $9,497.33 cash security deposit and will be paid in full from funds of the Debtor. Arguably, rather than recognize the setoff, Cloud Cap has tried to create an impairment by delaying payment to HEB for 30 days. However, with HEB continuing to retain the cash collateral, HEB retains full rights to the collateral, including any accrual of interest.

The Court agrees with the Debtor that HEB's secured claim is not impaired, and, therefore, Class 2(a) is not an eligible voting class under § 1129(a)(10). Under both plans, HEB will be paid the full amount of its secured claim. In fact, HEB already has the funds, so there is no risk that it will not get paid nor is there any impairment of HEB's rights under the Cloud Cap Plan. Because the Debtor was in default of the HEB lease prior to the bankruptcy filing, HEB's rights to the deposit, pursuant to paragraph 3(b) of the HEB lease, vested prior to the bankruptcy. Only the bankruptcy automatic stay posed a statutory restriction on HEB's ability to offset the deposit. The Court finds that Cloud Cap cannot create an impairment by simply stating that HEB will be paid within 30 days when it will actually be paid on the Effective Date.

A class of claims is deemed unimpaired if the plan leaves unaltered the legal, equitable, and contractual rights to which such claim or interest entitles the holder of such claim or interest. 11 U.S.C. § 1124(1). HEB's legal right to the security deposit will be the same on the Effective Date as it was upon the Debtor's default. Any impairment to the funds thus far has been the result of the automatic stay provisions of the Bankruptcy Code, not because of the treatment under the Plan. Therefore, HEB's rights remain unaltered. Although Cloud Cap labeled HEB's secured claim "impaired" and solicited HEB's vote, the Class 2(a) class is unimpaired, and therefore, not a voting class.

We wonder whether HEB's counsel shared the view of the court that it was just as protected legally as it was before bankruptcy. But presumably HEB's decision makers who call the shots were down with it, because they got on board the Cloud Cap plan. Other courts have proposed bright-line rules for ferreting out such "artificial impairment."

> [Allowing artificial impairment] would directly undermine one of the primary functions of bankruptcy law: to discourage "side dealing" between the shareholders of a corporation and some creditors to the detriment of other creditors. See Posner, Economic Analysis of Law 375. A similarly situated debtor, with the knowledge that impairment under section 1129(a)(10) might be manufactured, would be encouraged to make arrangements with small, unsecured creditors, and to seek their approval when a plan is filed that leaves their interests only marginally affected. It is exactly such "side dealing" that prompted the adoption of a bankruptcy code, and to allow it would defeat "'the purposes Congress sought to serve.'" *Norfolk Redevelopment*, 464 U.S. at 36, quoting *Chapman*, 441 U.S. at 608. Accordingly, we hold that, for purposes of 11 U.S.C. § 1129(a)(10), a claim is not impaired if the alteration of rights in question arises solely from the debtor's exercise of discretion.

In re Windsor on the River Associates, Ltd., 7 F.3d 127, 132 (8th Cir. 1993). This may be sound policy, but many courts have disagreed. See, e.g., In re Village at Camp Bowie, L.P., 710 F.3d 239, 245 (5th Cir. 2013) (stating that *Windsor* "warps" the text of the Code); In re L & J Anaheim Assocs., 995 F.2d 940 (9th Cir. 1993). See also ABI Commission to Study the Reform of Chapter 11, 23 Am. Bankr. Inst. L. Rev. 1, 225 (2015) (arguing that "the potential delay, cost, gamesmanship and value destruction attendant to section 1129(a)(10)" weigh in favor of eliminating the section from the Code).

Here we see our next innovation of the SBRA. Cloud Cap proposed a rival plan, which means the debtor's exclusivity period expired. § 1121(c). The SBRA cuts a different balance. On the one hand, exclusivity never expires (the SBRA debtor gets "exclusive exclusivity"). § 1189. On the other hand, the reason for that is the debtor has to get hustling. The plan—albeit exclusively negotiated without fear of rivals—must be proposed within 90 days. § 1189(d). We guess that means that simplicity is a two-way street: no need for lengthy disclosure statements, but also no need to puzzle for months over how to restructure the debts while creditors wait without interest payments.

C.   GERRYMANDERING THE VOTE: CLASSIFICATION

Voting is done by class in reorganization. A class votes in favor of a plan only when a two-part majority is achieved: a simple majority by number of creditors and a two-thirds majority by amount of debt. § 1126(c). Both thresholds must be met. This voting system is critical to chapter 11: the super-majority is allowed to bind the dissenting minority, which eliminates the value-destructive incentive to hold out. In a workout there will be a great temptation to be the last one to agree and then hold out for better treatment than everyone else. Such incentives can make agreement impossible to reach, leaving aside the risk of pure cussedness on the part of one creditor or a small group. Every bankruptcy system around the world that contemplates court-approved workouts provides for some form of majority rule. It is the lack of such a rule that often defeats attempts at out-of-court workouts. Thus, a majoritarian vote rule is not surprising. What may be surprising is that the Code allows the debtor to design the classes that vote.

As in congressional redistricting, the debtor wants to ensure "safe" votes by putting dissenting creditors into classes where they can be outvoted (or sometimes making sure that one separate impaired class can be hived off from other creditors and vote yes to permit cramdown). The Code has remarkably little guidance on how the debtor can populate the classes that vote on the plan. On one side, the Code is clear. Section 1122, by its express language, prohibits dissimilar claims from being put into the same class. The opposite problem has proven more difficult: the circumstances under which claims that are at least arguably similar in some dimensions can be classified separately for presumably strategic purposes. The Code offers no clue on when—or if—legally similar creditors might be allocated to separate classes, with the unremarkable exception of explicitly sanctioning putting small creditors into a separate class for convenience. § 1122(a), (b). But not all is nefarious.

In re BERNHARD STEINER PIANOS USA, INC.
292 B.R. 109 (Bankr. N.D. Tex. 2002)

HALE, Bankruptcy Judge.

I. EVENTS LEADING UP TO THE PLAN

Bernhard Steiner Pianos was established in Europe in 1886. In 1903, the company moved operations to South Africa. Bernhard Steiner Pianos was a part of the Kahn Pianos Group, a family business owned by the Kahn family. The Kahn family enjoys an international reputation in the piano industry, with Ivan Kahn being the fourth generation of piano makers in the family.

In 1976, Ivan Kahn and members of his family relocated to the United States and established Bernhard Steiner Pianos USA, Inc. ("Debtor") in North Dallas. The company deals in the sale and service of new and used pianos of all descriptions. The company sells new pianos, consigns used pianos, and repairs and refurbishes pianos. By 2001, annual sales had reached over $3.3 million.

Unfortunately, the Kahn family also entered into other areas of commerce in Africa. Ivan Kahn's father and mother contracted with the Nigerian government relating to certain construction. The Kahn family was to provide services and the Nigerian government would then submit payment for those services. Apparently, after some political upheaval in Nigeria, the new government refused to pay the debts of the old government. Much time, energy, and money has been spent by the Kahn family to remedy that situation.

. . .

In a self-described "misguided" attempt to aid his family, Kahn began borrowing funds from the Debtor without repaying on a timely basis, if at all. To further compound the situation, the events of September 11, 2001 were far-reaching and even impacted negatively a piano store in Dallas, Texas. After the terrorist attacks, piano sales fell dramatically for Mr. Kahn. In late 2001 and early 2002, sales were also dismal. Due to the Debtor's cash crunch, funds were not turned over to the lenders providing the floor plan financing. The collateral for the floor plan lenders was exceeded by the debt owed to those entities. Debtor, and Kahn, found themselves out of trust with the floor plan lenders.[2]

Debtor filed this bankruptcy proceeding on March 14, 2002. Debtor remained open for business during the pendency of this bankruptcy. Early in the case, the Objecting Creditors obtained relief from the automatic stay, and repossessed their remaining collateral.

During this bankruptcy case, Debtor entered into a Court-approved agreement with a third party whereby the third party would provide pianos to Debtor and would also pay for the cost of operations for a 90-day period. In return, Debtor and the third party split the profits from the sale. During this 90-day period, Debtor sold $1 million worth of pianos and netted $45,000. Thereafter, Debtor entered into another Court-approved agreement with another third party who presently provides pianos to Debtor for sale.

Debtor filed its Debtor's Plan of Reorganization dated September 13, 2002 (the "Plan"). The Plan contemplates repayment of Debtor's creditors on a 100% basis. Kahn testified that in order for Debtor to repay its creditors, Debtor must maintain a successful operation. Kahn further testified that Debtor's ability to continue successfully in business will require that the Debtor attract good consignment pianos; the sale of new pianos alone will not suffice.

Typically, consignment pianos come from individual owners. Most of the consignment business is by word of mouth. In the piano industry, if a consignee gets the reputation that it is unwilling or unable to pay consignors, the consignee won't be able to attract good consignment pianos. Kahn testified that it would be very difficult to supplement any lost consignment income through other operations. Kahn testified that the quicker the Debtor repays the consignment class, the quicker they will get new consignment pianos.

Kahn testified that he will remain the president of the company after confirmation. Largely speaking, Mr. Kahn is all that is left of the Debtor. The company's only tangible assets are some desks and some old wood. At the confirmation hearing, the parties were complimentary of Mr. Kahn's heroic efforts at keeping the Debtor in operation. Through his management during the pendency of the bankruptcy, Kahn singlehandedly managed to

---

[2] Although the Court has approved the Plan, such approval does not extend to the unauthorized use of cash collateral of the Objecting Creditors.

keep the Debtor's doors open. The Bernhard Steiner Pianos name is closely associated with Kahn and the Kahn family in the minds of the piano-buying public. The public identifies the Debtor and Mr. Kahn as one and the same.

The Plan was ultimately approved by all the impaired classes except for Class 6, of which the Objecting Creditors, the floor plan lenders, are members.

II. Analysis

A. Separate Classification of Certain Unsecured Creditors

The Plan separately classifies creditors whose claims arose from consigned goods and general unsecured claims, including the claims of the floor plan lenders. The floor plan lenders object to this separate classification. Both classes are unsecured creditors.

The consignment creditors, Class 4, will be repaid over a term of 10 months beginning on the effective date of the plan. The floor plan lenders are part of the allowed general unsecured class, Class 6. Under the Plan, as originally drafted, their scheduled payments begin after full payment to Class 4 (and the convenience class, Class 5), approximately one year after the effective date. Under an agreed modification made in Court after the effective date, the Class 6 creditors will also begin to receive a portion of excess cash flow. Based on the record, the excess cash flow payments should begin before the Class 4 consignment claims are paid in full. Despite the favorable change in the payment schedule, the Objecting Creditors still object and argue that both Class 4 and Class 6 should be placed in the same class.

All unsecured claims outstanding as of the commencement of the case, and claims arising from the rejection of executory contracts or unexpired leases, may be classified together as general unsecured claims. 7 Collier on Bankruptcy ¶1122.03[4][a] (15th ed. rev. 2000). However, the Code does not require that all such claims be placed within a single class. . . .

The Fifth Circuit has taught that, as a general premise, substantially similar claims, or those which share common priority and rights against the debtor's estate, should be placed in the same class. Small unsecured claims may be classified separately from their larger counterparts if the court so approves for administrative convenience. Id. Substantially similar claims are not permitted to be separately classified "in order to gerrymander an affirmative vote on a reorganization plan." Id.

Nevertheless, in this Circuit, separate classification is permitted for "good business reasons." Heartland Fed. Sav. & Loan Ass'n v. Briscoe Enterprises, Ltd., II (In re Briscoe Enterprises, Ltd., II), 994 F.2d 1160, 1167 (5th Cir.1993) (citing Matter of Greystone, 995 F.2d 1274 (5th Cir. 1991), cert. denied, 506 U.S. 821, 113 S. Ct. 72, 121 L. Ed. 2d 37 (1992)). In *Briscoe*, the Court found that where a continuing relationship with an unsecured creditor who had a distinct interest in the debtor's business was essential to the continued operations of the debtor, separate classification of that creditor was for a good business reason.

In the present case, the Debtor has met the good business reason test. Selling consigned pianos has historically been an important part of the

Debtor's business and is contemplated to be an integral part of the Debtor's future. Debtor presented evidence, which was not rebutted, that its consignment business had suffered significantly since word had leaked out that Debtor did not remit the proceeds from the sale of consigned pianos. Kahn testified that the consignment market is local and small, and adverse local community opinion affected whether pianos would be consigned to the Debtor or to its competitors. Kahn also testified that competitors were informing potential consignors that Debtor had failed to remit the sale proceeds to its past consignors. The undisputed testimony is that the Class 4 consignment creditors were separately classified so as to accelerate repayment to them so Debtor could begin expeditiously to repair its tarnished consignment name in a small market. Improving the consignment public's perception of this Debtor and restoring trust in the Debtor among potential consignors as soon as possible is important to the success of the reorganization overall.

No evidence of gerrymandering was offered at the confirmation hearing. Debtor's principal, Mr. Kahn, testified that the development of future consignment business was necessary to its successful reorganization and accordingly, for the repayment of its creditors. Further, the Plan, on its face, treats the consignment class and the general unsecured class differently. The Debtor has presented a good business reason for the separate classification and treatment of consignment creditors in Class 4 from the claims of the general unsecured creditors; therefore, the Court overrules the classification objection. . . .

—————————————

A small sampling of cases, presented in the dreaded string cite, is actually useful here for seeing the kinds of differences that might spawn separate classification. See, e.g., Steelcase Inc. v. Johnston (In re Johnston), 21 F.3d 323, 327-28 (9th Cir. 1994) (proper to classify separately an unsecured claim subject to hotly disputed litigation); Frito-Lay, Inc. v. LTV Steel Co. (In re Chateaugay Corp.), 10 F.3d 944, 956-57 (2d Cir. 1993) (finding permissible the separate classification of tax lessors (a status resulting from a special type of tax transactions popular in the early 1980s) based upon whether they independently provided DIP financing); In re Jersey City Medical Ctr., 817 F.2d 1055, 1061 (3d Cir. 1987) (permitting separate classification of medical malpractice tort claims, non-priority pension claims, and trade creditors); Teamsters Nat'l Freight Indus. Negotiating Comm. v. United States Truck Co. (In re United States Truck Co.), 800 F.2d 581, 587 (6th Cir. 1986) (upholding separate classification of labor union based on such entity's "non-creditor" interests in reorganization—namely, threatening to vote no as leverage in collective bargaining).

Academics have generally been less bothered by such manipulations than courts have. See Bruce A. Markell, Clueless on Classification: Toward Removing Artificial Limits on Claim Classification, 11 Bankr. Dev. J. 1 (1995) (arguing that a court should permit any classification that does not combine claims with different nonbankruptcy priorities, such as intermingling secured and unsecured claims in a class). The National Bankruptcy Review Commission wrestled with this question and concluded that

"Section 1122 should be amended to provide that a plan proponent may classify legally similar claims separately if, upon objection, the proponent can demonstrate that the classification is supported by a 'rational business justification.'" NBRC Recommendation 2.4.16 (1997). While "rational business justification" does not provide an obvious checklist for parties and courts to use, such an amendment would make it clear that separate classification of legally similar claims is permissible, and it would provide a direction for the courts to look in as they evaluate different classification schemes. While this may vindicate Mr. Kahn, we note the recommendation has not yet become part of the statute.

Problem Set 27

27.1. Country Smokes, Inc., is a manufacturer of corn cob pipes for the souvenir trade. Although it has been in business for over 50 years, it has been badly wounded by a recent hike in the price of gasoline. Decreased vacation driving has seriously depressed souvenir sales. It filed its chapter 11 petition on June 1 of this year.

Your client is Pany Chemicals, which supplies the various chemicals needed in the production of Country's pipes. It is owed $1,000,000 on an unsecured basis. Your negotiations with the debtor went quite well, due to the power of your legal arguments blended with your winning smile, and a plan of reorganization for Country Smokes paying 70% to the unsecured creditors has been proposed. The rumor is that the necessary majorities of creditors have voted for the plan.

You were therefore startled when Talbert Pany, the president of Pany Chemicals, burst into your office yesterday, the veins on his neck like tree trunks. He is upset because he was just contacted by Brian Nelson, Country Smoke's "preference counsel." Nelson had explained to Pany that he was "reaching out to discuss an opportunity" for Pany to settle with Country Smokes. When Pany explained that he was only interested in getting his money back as set forth in the plan, Nelson clarified the purpose of his call. Pany Chemicals is about to be sued to recover $250,000 that Country paid to Pany on March 15 of this year.

"They are stiffing me for 30% of what they owe me and now they say I am a *preferred* creditor," as Talbert put it. He could not believe that Country could get him to vote for the plan without saying a word about recovering any preferences and then "sandbag me."

You explained that the plan didn't release Pany. He demands to know why you didn't flag that for him. You note, gently, that you didn't know about the payment. "You didn't ask," Talbert replied. There followed a long and painful silence.

You and Talbert agreed that you would try to think of a way to defend the preference action and call him back today. Talbert told you as he left that he was particularly upset about the whole situation because he has learned that Country's backlog of orders was actually considerably less than had been claimed in the solicitation materials. He said he isn't sure if Country's president, Sam Pickens, is "a liar or a dummy," but either way the prospects for Pany aren't good, even if the plan is confirmed. What should you do? See §§ 1123, 1125.

27.2. Talbert Pany, the company's president, is back in your office, madder than ever. After much back and forth, including Brian Nelson's conclusion that most of the "preferences" would not be recoverable, the debtor has proposed an amended plan that offers exactly 60 cents on the dollar to the unsecureds (down from the 70 cents in the first plan). It is re-balloting the creditors, and Talbert has poured over the disclosure statement this time. He took note that the amended plan offers the possibility of full payment if certain profit levels are reached in future years, but he says the profit levels required for any additional payments are utterly ridiculous ("Couldn't make that if they put a pipe in every mouth in America"), so effectively the plan only offers 60% plus interest. He trumpets, "If those deadbeats are going to give me the same amount as if they closed down, then let's close 'em down and let 'em look for honest work."

Talbert has been out "working the electorate" to defeat the amended plan. He tells you that he has found one other unsecured creditor who agrees with him and is now willing to vote against the amended plan. This other creditor is owed $600,000. Talbert also says that the holder of the mortgage on Country's real estate might be talked into voting against the plan, but that holder has been classified separately under the plan as unimpaired because the plan will cure the default within 30 days of plan confirmation, de-accelerate the debt, and pay it according to its original terms.

Talbert has been further upset by "Country's latest maneuver." Of the total unsecured debt of $5,000,000 (of which Pany Chemicals is owed $1,000,000 and the other dissenting creditor $600,000), some $300,000 consists of a number of small claims of less than $10,000 each. Talbert has talked to some of these small creditors and reports that Sam Pickens, the president of Country, has personally guaranteed these debts in order to convince these small creditors to vote for the plan. Talbert says, "This is just the sort of cheap trick a snake like Pickens would pull."

Talbert wants to know if he can "stop this steamroller." What is your strategy and on what theories does it rest? (Ignore any question of "cramdown" under § 1129(b) for now.) See §§ 1122, 1129.

27.3. You don your robe and take the bench for the chapter 11 confirmation hearing in the consolidated cases of debtors John Paul Smith, and his wholly-owned companies Gurganus Milling (grain storage), JPS Holdings (real estate), and JPS Farms (seed store). You already denied confirmation once, because in between balloting and confirmation, the debtor proposed changing the distribution to a class of farmers, from full payment on favorable terms down to 50% payment. Upon re-balloting, the farmers are apparently on board with this reduced treatment, but the bank is not happy. Below is what you heard from Mr. Oliver, counsel for the debtors, and Mr. Pryor, counsel for the undersecured bank, BB&T. How would you rule? Be prepared to rule from the bench (in class) and give a few sentences, including some authority, to justify your ruling.

Mr. Oliver: We have come before you several times with confirmation and this ought to be the last, telling Mr. Pryor, just before we came up, to wait to continue it, but I think that's alright. Last time what we did, we amended the plan in each of these four cases; we propose to pay farmer class differently from the general unsecured creditor class and at the prior confirmation hearing, we proposed to pay the unsecured class in full which is different from how they'd been proposed.

Judge: As I recall, what you had agreed to do was to pay the unsecured class in full, and then you created the farmer class, but you are only going to pay them half, and that's where I said: "You can't do that, you can't send somebody a ballot saying we are going to pay you in full, vote, and then come to the confirmation hearing and say oh, by the way we are only going to pay you half." So I made you re-ballot and that's where we are.

Mr. Oliver: That's right. And we have proposed modified treatments for the farmer classes and got the ballots on those creditors and have those here today. We have acceptances from all creditors in all four cases with the exception of Mid State Mills in the Gurganus Mills case, your honor. But everybody else in all the other cases all say yes, the ones that have voted are all saying yes, and so if I could just again for recap purposes tell you what the differences are in the farmer classes versus the general unsecured classes.

General unsecured classes were proposed to be paid in full, with 4% interest, and those we paid from the cash flow of various debtors and we included a kind of chart in the amended treatments in the unsecured class that says which debtors are responsible for each of the unsecured creditors.

We are going to pay in semi-annual installments over a period of 25 years at 4% interest, and just continue to give you an idea these payments would be. The payments for JPS Farms, which is the grain elevator debtor, would be $46,743 every six months, starting the year after the effective date. The payments for general unsecured creditors of JPS Holdings will be much smaller, $207.30 every six months. Gurganus Milling payments will be $59,470 every six months. Now let me describe to you what the farmers class would get.

We do propose to pay half of [the farmer class] claims without interest, over a 10-year period in semi-annual payments, every six months. And listed in the amended treatment for these farmers' plans for each of the four debtors we list the similar chart which says which debtors are responsible for these debts. Because some of them had claims only against one debtor, sometimes had claims against all four debtors, so it is a similar payment structure. JPS Farms will make payments every six months to this class of $10,148 dollars. JPS Holdings will make payments every six months of $937.50, Gurganus Mills will make payments every six months of $15,211 and John Paul Smith will make payments every six months of about $6,800. That will pay 50% of the total of farmer claims in these classes and all of the farmers who voted for the payments had they have been treated in the unsecured class they would have been paid 100% with interest over a longer period of time. Mr. Smith will give testimony about the reason for having the separate class; it is because the farmers recognize the benefit for operations to stay in business. These farmers are owed money because they sold grain to Mr. Smith and his entities and were not paid. Arguably they each have a dischargeability action and have not brought them. They want him to stay in business, they want to be paid half of their money, but they also want to continue to sell grain through his operation.

Judge: Mr. Pryor, I would be glad if you make an opening statement; it does seem to have devolved into a dispute between BB&T and the debtors.

Mr. Pryor: It has, and I think the initial thing that probably we'll address is whether there is an accepting class, Your Honor, because of the gerrymandering issue. The treatment of the farmer claims in the prior plan and the treatment of the farmer claims as amended here are identical.

Mr. Oliver: No, no, no. Now we're paying them it over a shorter period of time. Before, I think it was 15 maybe 20 years, now it's 10.

Mr. Pryor: Where we got to when we were here before is that Mr. Oliver said BB&T was supposed to be getting nothing on the unsecured claim. And Mr. Oliver came in and orally modified the plan so that BB&T would be paid in full over 25 years deferring out a year at 4% interest.

Judge: Right.

Mr. Pryor: They re-balloted everybody and the question was whether there should be separate classifications for farmer claims which are just unsecured creditors versus other unsecured creditors.

Mr. Pryor: Their [original] justification at that point for having a separate classification for the farmer claims [that treated them more favorably under the first ballot was] we've got to treat them better than the other unsecured creditors because we've got to continue to do business with them. Now I did the math in the response [to the reduced treatment]. For example, if you take a fictitious farmer with a $100,000 claim, he would get 20 semi-annual installments of $2,500 each. Whereas if that farmer was treated with all the other unsecured creditors similarly situated, they would get 50 semi-annual payments in excess of $3,200 each; so not only are the farmers getting many fewer payments, they are also getting lower amounts of these payments. So the justification for having a separate class simply falls back on, we wanted to find some friendly folks who would vote in favor of our plan.

Judge: Well, which is precisely why I required to be re-balloted since it was unfavorable, I thought. I understand your point, Mr. Pryor, but I do think this is not an easy issue. I do think it is factually intensive and I hear your argument, but I want to hear the evidence before we get to the legal argument. Let's go ahead, Mr. Oliver.

Mr. Oliver: Thank you, your Honor. I call Mr. John Paul Smith to the stand.

Court clerk: Mr. Smith, please come forward. Place your left hand on the Bible, raise your right. Do you solemnly swear that the testimony which you are about to offer will be the truth, the whole truth and nothing but the truth, so help you God?

Mr. Smith: Yes, Ma'am.

Mr. Oliver: Good morning, Mr. Smith, how are you, Sir?

Mr. Smith: Good morning. Chair don't move back, do it?

Mr. Oliver: I'm afraid not. Mr. Smith, I think you were last in that chair when we had the first hearing in this case back in July of last year. Is that right?

Mr. Oliver: I talked about how these farmers were owed money prior to filing and I said they might be subject to dischargeability actions. Do you know what I mean by that?

Mr. Smith: Not really.

Mr. Oliver: You remember you had a 2004 exam with Mr. Bingham when you came to my office and were asked a bunch of questions?

Mr. Smith: Yeah.

Mr. Oliver: And he was inferring that maybe you did something wrong by not paying the debts back as opposed to just not paying the debts. Remember that?

Mr. Smith: Yeah, I sure do.

Mr. Oliver: Do you know whether, those farmers, have any of them have pursued that and tried to say that you can't discharge their debts?

Mr. Smith: No.

Mr. Oliver: Are they all pretty satisfied about what you are doing here to pay them back?

Mr. Smith: Yeah, they want me to stay in business and keep on buying grains so we to try to get as much as we can with the market. The market is up $0.50 one day and down another day $0.40, it's hard to predict the market and we do something different than our competitors and if a farmer is gonna need more $4 grains, then we will put in for another $4 truck.

Mr. Oliver: How important is it to your business that these farmers do business with you?

Mr. Smith: It's very important to keep the farmers, the farmers is the backbone, they bring the grains, that's where the money's coming in.

Mr. Oliver: If these farmers, that you owed money to, they did not do businesses with JPS Farmers going forward, are there enough other farmers out there to even make your minimum that you owe the grain dealer?

Mr. Smith: Yeah, oh yeah.

Mr. Oliver: If you didn't have the farmers that you owed money to, would you be able to make the financial predictions that you made in the plan.

Mr. Smith: Yes.

CONFIRMING THE PLAN

In general, acceptance of the plan by most creditors is the heart of the chapter 11 process. Section 1129(a) has several other requirements, however, that apply regardless of whether the creditor consents required by paragraphs (8) and (10) are achieved. Some of these promote generalized policy, such as system integrity, and others implement specific bankruptcy goals, such as the priority repayment hierarchy. The most important non-voting requirements for confirmation derive from pre-Code bankruptcy cases and include those found in § 1129(a)(7) and (11). Called by the non-Code names of the "best interests" and "feasibility" requirements, respectively, these rules have similar purpose to the identically named requirements in chapter 13 (see Assignment 11). This assignment focuses on these additional confirmation requirements and briefly discusses their special application to small businesses.

A. BEST INTERESTS

The best interests test can be raised by any single creditor. This individual protection, as opposed to a right of a "class," is important because § 1129(a)(7) is one of the few protections for the minority that is otherwise bound by the majority's vote. If chapter 11 is likened to a democratic voting process, the best interests test can be thought of as a constitutional protection that safeguards against the tyranny of the majority. The best interests test requires a finding that the objecting creditor will receive at least as much under the plan as that creditor would have received in a liquidation under chapter 7. The consequence is that the court (and debtor in its disclosure statement) must do a hypothetical liquidation analysis, estimating the amount that could be obtained by selling each asset of the estate and then calculating the resulting dividend that would be paid to the nonaccepting creditor. This absolute entitlement gives creditors that are outvoted in their class a minimum dividend, albeit with the corollary that if the plan is at least as good as liquidation in terms of recovery, the objecting creditors should shut their yaps.

Best interests, like so many issues in bankruptcy, thus turns on valuation. But it also turns on speculations as to what would happen in chapter 7. The following case shows a dizzying (but not uncommon) array of intercorporate dealings that resulted not just in substantive consolidation but

also, in light of the generation of inter-affiliate debts made when some affiliates were known to be insolvent, in claim subordination (contractual—
and likely equitable, too). In chapter 11, the debtors saw the writing on
the wall and proposed simply subordinating these sketchy claims to "real"
trade creditors. When one of those affiliates ended up in its own proceeding subject to the control of a frisky receiver, the receiver argued it had a
perfectly good claim on behalf of the affiliate that it would prosecute and
surely would have honored in chapter 7. The chapter 11 plan to fold and
give up on this claim therefore violated its best interest rights, or at least
so it argued.

In re ABENGOA BIOENERGY BIOMASS OF KANSAS, LLC
2018 WL 812941 (Bankr. D. Kan. Feb. 8, 2018)

Nugent, Bankruptcy Judge.

Debtor['s] plan separately classifies the claims of its affiliates, classifying them below non-affiliate general unsecured creditors and denying them
payment. The holder of four such claims . . . contends that the separate
classification was done to gerrymander the unsecured creditors' class and
is improper. It also objects that its four claims on behalf of related companies that did business with this debtor would be paid pro rata in a chapter 7
case and that they will receive less under the debtor's plan. . . .

ABBK is one of over 700 affiliates and subsidiaries in a global concern, Abengoa, S.A., a Spanish corporation organized in 1941 and located in
Seville, Spain ("Abengoa"). In late 2015, Abengoa and several of its Spanish
subsidiaries and affiliates filed a proceeding under Article 5bis of the Spanish
Insolvency Act. This is a pre-insolvency proceeding to allow companies
to negotiate with creditors for restructuring their financial affairs without
filing for insolvency; it culminated in a Master Restructuring Agreement
("MRA"). This foreign proceeding was recognized in the United States in a
chapter 15 filing in Delaware.

ABBK is part of Abengoa's United States bioenergy group. ABBK is
wholly owned by Abengoa Bioenergy Hybrid of Kansas (ABHK), a Kansas
limited liability company. ABBK's upstream corporate parent is Abengoa
Bioenergy US Holding, LLC (ABUSH). Its sibling affiliates include ABC
(Abengoa Bioenergy Company, LLC), ABEC (Abengoa Bioenergy Engineering
& Construction, LLC), ABT (Abengoa Bioenergy Trading, LLC), and ABO
(Abengoa Bioenergy Outsourcing, LLC), all of whom are part of the bioen-
ergy group and chapter 11 debtors in Missouri (collectively the "Missouri
Debtors."). The Missouri cases began as voluntary petitions filed in the
Eastern District of Missouri (including ABUSH, ABBK's upstream parent)
in late February, and were jointly administered. When their combined plan
was confirmed, these debtors' estates were substantively consolidated.
Abeinsa Holding Inc. and other related subsidiaries and affiliates (including
ABHK, ABBK's direct corporate parent) filed voluntary chapter 11 cases in
the District of Delaware in late March and early April of 2016.

This case began when several mechanic's lien creditors filed an involuntary chapter 7 petition against ABBK on March 23, 2016. ABBK converted

the case to chapter 11 and sought a transfer of its venue to the District of Delaware with the other Delaware cases. After the Court denied the transfer motion and the venue order became final, ABBK prepared to sell its principal asset, a 25 million gallon capacity, second-generation cellulosic ethanol and cogeneration plant that it had built at Hugoton, Kansas. ABBK built this plant as a demonstration project to be used by its upstream corporate parents to demonstrate their design-build capabilities and new technology developed in the alternative fuels and power cogeneration fields. The initial construction was funded in part by a $95 million grant and a $45,000,000 loan guaranty by the United States Department of Energy (DOE). ABBK substantially completed the plant in late 2014, but only after extensive cost overruns. At start up, ABBK experienced operational and equipment problems. The Hugoton plant produced 75,000 gallons of ethanol in 2015, but never approached commercial viability.

By 2015 all of the DOE funds had been expended and ABBK was wholly reliant on its affiliates and Abengoa S.A. for funding its operations. . . . In November of 2016, ABBK sold its Hugoton plant at auction for $48.5 million. . . .

ABBK filed its . . . plan and disclosure statement on April 14, 2017. The plan provides for the classification of unsecured third party trade creditors in Class 2, paying them pro rata, but relegates all unsecured intercompany claims by other Abengoa entities [such as Objectors] to Class 3 and pays them nothing. Class 4 consists of the equity interests in ABBK, including the DOE's interest under its grant to ABBK, but the equity interests are canceled and will receive no distribution. Classes 2, 3, and 4 are impaired. Class 1 consisting of secured claims is unimpaired. Only Class 2 claims were entitled to vote on ABBK's plan [as Classes 3 and 4 were deemed to vote no on account of their zero dividend]. . . . After ABBK's Amended Disclosure Statement was approved, the debtor solicited acceptances of its plan in late May, 2017. Balloting of the ABBK plan was completed on July 7, 2017 and the unsecured creditors accepted it by a wide margin. . . .

How the Intercompany Claims Are Different

The evidence shows that many of the U.S. Abengoa bioenergy affiliates did business with one another. While [Objectors] focused on the Missouri Debtors' claims it holds, ABBK recognized and scheduled other intercompany transactions and claims. Because it was not intended to be a revenue producer, ABBK relied on financing through ABC [another affiliate] which operated as a cash manager for the domestic bioenergy affiliates. That reliance increased when ABBK ran out of DOE funds at the end of 2014. ABC accessed credit and funding mechanisms from Abengoa's "central treasury" in Spain and provided those funds to ABBK (and other affiliates) when funds were available. ABO provided shared services for the bioenergy group (management, legal, administrative, accounting, IT, etc.), including ABBK. ABEC supplied engineering and construction management services. ABT procured and supplied ABBK with biomass for the plant, mostly corn stalks.

. . .

Mr. Santos served as Executive Vice President of the debtor since 2008. He also served in that role for Abengoa Bioenergy New Technology (ABNT), meanwhile serving on the Board of Directors for ABUSH. In his testimony about the treatment of the affiliate claims, he noted that ABBK and the other bioenergy affiliates operated in an integrated manner, sharing the same management and services. Their financials were ultimately consolidated as were budgets and cash management functions. He described the flow of funds as follows: ABBK would ask ABO for money for some purpose. If ABO could not source that money domestically, it would request a draw from Central Treasury in Seville, Spain. If that was approved, the funds would disburse to ABC who would then disburse to ABBK. These transfers would be booked as short-term loans. He described the debtor as being "totally one hundred percent dependent on . . . the affiliates and the corporate entity." . . .

Santos also stated that while it might be possible to analyze each companies' respective obligations to and entitlements from one another, that binary analysis might disregard the larger picture. Given that money and property flowed among both U.S. and Spanish entities with impunity, untangling that web might prove more difficult than its cost would merit. Moreover, by the time the ABBK plan was drafted in April of 2017, the Delaware case was complete and those debtors' claims against ABBK had been released. He stated that, early on, the debtors considered subordinating one another to be the most efficient way to treat the intercompany claims. Those claims were different and deserved to be treated differently from those of third-party creditors who had none of the inside knowledge that the affiliates shared. As for providing for each affiliate to claim against the others, Santos stated that they were "better off not going there." Santos also said that none of these affiliates ever expected to be paid, particularly after the beginning of 2015 when the Hugoton project became plagued with problems and "everybody" knew it would not be profitable. . . .

Even though the claims may have had contractual foundation, and even though the debtor did not oppose their being allowed, the affiliates knew of ABBK's condition when the debts were incurred, they understood ABBK's dependence upon them, and they understood that ABBK was a demonstration project, not a revenue-producing entity like the other bioenergy affiliates that operated first generation plants. This understanding was facilitated by the board meetings among the shared leadership of the entities at which its condition was regularly discussed. This demonstrates that these managers had access to financial and other information about ABBK that no non-affiliate could hope to attain.

. . .

[In all the related bankruptcy proceedings] at least among the debtors, there was an understanding that each other's debts would be released and not paid (except where specified). Mr. Santos testified that the exchange of these releases for the subordination of intercompany claims was "part of the strategy from the beginning . . . that the [shared bioenergy] management team had from the time that these cases were filed, probably from the beginning of 2016." . . .

. . .

ABBK's Plan Satisfies the Best Interests of Creditors Test, § 1129(a)(7)

Section 1129(a)(7)(A)(ii), commonly referred to as the "best interests of creditors" requirement, provides with respect to each non-accepting impaired class of claims that: (A) each holder of a claim . . . of such class—. . . (ii) will receive or retain under the plan on account of such claim . . . property of a value, as of the effect date of the plan, that is not less than the amount that such holder would so receive or retain if the debtor were liquidated under chapter 7 of this title on such date. [Objectors] assert[ ] that the liquidation analysis submitted with the ABBK's disclosure statement, along with the subsequently produced footnotes to the analysis, unequivocally demonstrates that the affiliated intercompany claims would receive substantially more in a chapter 7 liquidation than under ABBK's plan. I disagree.

Applying the best interests test requires that "the court must take into consideration the applicable rules of distribution of the estate under chapter 7." I must also "engage in rational speculation" of what may occur in a chapter 7 liquidation, including whether certain claims may evoke an objection by the chapter 7 trustee[ ]. To do that, a court must take into account potential claims against insiders, subordinations, and disallowed claims under § 502(d). Even without considering whether the Delaware, Missouri, and Kansas debtors agreed that intercompany debt would be subordinated, my "rational speculation" must certainly include the likelihood that a chapter 7 trustee would question paying the claims of four affiliated companies who shared information, management, and objectives at par with unaffiliated and less informed third-party creditors. Having found as a fact that there was a shared intention among ABBK, the Delaware debtors, and the Missouri Debtors to subordinate these claims, I conclude that the Code honors that agreement under § 510(a). As Santos stated, the affiliate intercompany creditors understood when they extended credit or made advances to ABBK that trade creditors would be paid first. Indeed, the evidence suggests that there was no corporate expectation of any payment unless and until the Hugoton plant achieved commercially profitable production. . . . [N]ot a single member of Abengoa's bioenergy group's shared management refuted Mr. Santos' testimony regarding the agreed upon treatment of intercompany claims.

The debtor's liquidation analysis supports this conclusion. In preparing that analysis, debtors should consider subordination agreements or any other events (such as claims objections) that may occur in a chapter 7 liquidation and how they may affect distributions, just as a chapter 7 trustee would [consider], in determining the hypothetical distribution in a chapter 7 liquidation to the affiliate intercompany claimants. ABBK's plan satisfies the best interests of creditors test. . . . [The] objection to confirmation is overruled and ABBK's plan is CONFIRMED.

═══════════════

The conglomerate appears to have weathered the storm and still survives today. See http://www.abengoa.com/web/en/index3.html.

B.   FEASIBILITY

One generalization about the "feasibility" test of § 1129(a)(11) is that no general statements can be made about it. Feasibility goes to the likelihood that the plan will succeed and that the business will survive and prosper—at least long enough to make the scheduled payments. The test is applied on a case-by-case basis and reflects the best business judgment of the bankruptcy judge based on the testimony (often including expert testimony) of witnesses.

In one sense, the feasibility requirement is wildly paternalistic: if most creditors believe that the business can succeed, they—with skin in the game—should be permitted to go forward under the plan. On the other hand, a dissenting creditor will regard feasibility as the ultimate protection against the hopeless naïveté of its deluded peers. And as with the best interests requirement, feasibility can be raised by a single creditor, even when it has been outvoted in its class. Indeed, technically the bankruptcy judge must ensure that all requirements of § 1129 have been met regardless of what the parties raise, but as a practical matter, if no one challenges a plan's feasibility, the court's limited time and resources will tend to constrain judicial inquiry. Finally, in such an amorphous area, courts want to give debtors every benefit of the doubt. A difficult balance must be found distinguishing good ol' American optimism from terminal euphoria. In this next case, the gas station entrepreneur had high hopes—high apple pie, in the sky hopes—but the creditors were not singing his song.

═══════ In re CHEERVIEW ENTERPRISES, INC. ═══════
586 B.R. 881 (Bankr. E.D. Mich. 2018)

SHEFFERLY, Bankruptcy Judge.

INTRODUCTION

The debtor in this Chapter 11 case owns a gas station and convenience store. The debtor seeks final approval of its disclosure statement and confirmation of its plan of reorganization. Two objections were filed: one by the debtor's largest secured creditor, and another by a large unsecured creditor. The secured creditor also filed a motion for relief from the automatic stay.

. . .

On April 20, 2018, the Court held a hearing on Cheerview's request for final approval of the first amended disclosure statement and confirmation of the first amended plan. At the same time, the Court also held a hearing on the Motion for Stay Relief. Just prior to the hearing, Cheerview filed a second amended combined disclosure statement and plan of reorganization. After listening to arguments by lawyers for Cheerview, Stockbridge [secured creditor] and U.S. Oil [unsecured creditor], the Court found that there are disputed issues of material fact that require the Court to hold an evidentiary hearing. Cheerview also informed the Court that it intended to file a third amended combined disclosure statement and plan of reorganization. The Court adjourned the hearings and set some deadlines. . . .

On May 1, 2018, Cheerview filed a third amended combined disclosure statement and plan of reorganization. Stockbridge and U.S. Oil filed supplements to their objections.

FACTS

Cheerview is a Michigan corporation that owns a gas station and convenience store located at 700 South Waverly, at the corner of St. Joseph, in a busy traffic area in Lansing, Michigan ("Property"). In early 2015, Mohamad Berro ("Berro"), then a 26-year old individual who owned an oil change business, learned that the stock in Cheerview was for sale. Ali Damsaz ("Damsaz"), a shareholder in Cheerview, told Berro this was a good location and that Berro could basically run the business from his home if he kept the same employees. Berro purchased the stock sometime in 2015 and became the sole owner of Cheerview. . . . Berro formed a new corporation known as Mikey's Fuel Mart, Inc. ("Mikey's") to operate the gas station and convenience store.

Berro was an absentee owner. After acquiring Cheerview, he continued to work full time in his oil change business and only went out to the Property about once a month. He also took Damsaz's advice and kept the existing Cheerview employees to run the business. That turned out to be a big mistake. At least one of those employees, and maybe more, were stealing from the business. It took awhile for Berro to discover the theft. Once he did, he fired the employees and filed a police report.

Sometime in 2016, Mikey's hired Hassan Ouza ("Ouza"), a long time personal friend of Berro, to help him deal with Cheerview's problems. Although only in his early 30's, Ouza had managed and otherwise worked in gas stations for over 15 years. However, Berro and Ouza were unable to turn Cheerview's business around. U.S. Oil's records (exhibit 14) show that the gas station at the Property sold approximately 35,000 gallons of gas per month during 2016. The largest sales month was March, 2016, with 51,392 gallons sold. The 2016 federal income tax return for Mikey's (exhibit 11) shows that Mikey's lost $75,428.00 on gross receipts of $1,056,341.00 in 2016. Losing money and unable to make its payments to . . . U.S. Oil and its other creditors, Mikey's shut down the operation of both the gas station and the convenience store in August, 2017. The Property has been shuttered since that date.

Although the precise date is not clear from the record, [secured creditors] began foreclosure proceedings on their respective mortgages in mid-2017. . . . Despite the failure of the business, and even though the value of the Property is far less than the mortgages on it, the Property is still considered by others in the gas station industry to be a good location for a gas station and convenience store. . . . As the foreclosure proceedings brought by Stockbridge and U.S. Oil came to a head, Cheerview filed its Chapter 11 petition. . . .

Since the filing of this Chapter 11 case, Cheerview has not transacted any business. But the Third Amended Disclosure Statement and Plan states that Cheerview intends to now reopen the gas station and convenience store. Toward that end, Cheerview has entered [a] specific transaction[], subject to Court approval, that Cheerview believes will enable it to reopen the business and become profitable going forward. . . . [O]n April 13, 2018, Cheerview entered into a series of agreements ("RPF Agreements") (exhibit 18) with RPF Oil Company ("RPF"), a gas supplier for approximately 85 gas stations, that primarily sells BP products. Under Cheerview's prior agreement with U.S. Oil, Cheerview purchased gas from U.S. Oil and then Cheerview set its own price to sell the gas at the Property. In contrast, under the RPF Agreements, Cheerview will not purchase any gas, but instead RPF will provide gas to Cheerview and then pay Cheerview a 4% commission on any gas that Cheerview sells. Under this arrangement, RPF will determine the price at which Cheerview sells the gas and RPF will also maintain the pumps and control all aspects of the sale of gas by Cheerview. The RPF Agreements require Cheerview to sell a minimum of 70,000 gallons per month, because that is what BP requires, and give RPF the right to terminate the RPF Agreements if the minimum sales are not met. . . .

The Third Amended Disclosure Statement and Plan is accompanied by projections. . . . Except for the 4% commission to be received from RPF for the gas sold by Cheerview, the other line items on the Projections for income and expenses are largely taken from the historical experience of Mikey's, as shown on its financial statement for 2016 (exhibit 11). . . . The Projections assume that Ouza and Berro will both work full time at the gas station and convenience store and that they will have one part-time employee as well. The Projections assume net revenue more than double the net revenue of Mikey's, and show how that net revenue will be used to pay Cheerview's creditors. . . .

The Plan

. . .

Section 1129(a)(11)

Stockbridge and U.S. Oil next argue that the Plan does not meet the requirement of § 1129(a)(11) that "[c]onfirmation of the plan is not likely to be followed by the liquidation, or the need for further financial reorganization, of the debtor or any successor to the debtor under the plan[.]" Section 1129(a)(11) embodies what is commonly understood and referred to as feasibility. The purpose of the feasibility requirement is to protect creditors against unrealistic plans that have little or no chance of success. The debtor has the burden to prove by a preponderance of the evidence that the plan is not likely to fail in order to meet the feasibility test. In re Griswold Building, LLC, 420 B.R. at 697. Feasibility is fundamentally a factual question that depends on the determination of the reasonable probability of payment. A feasibility determination "must be firmly rooted in predictions based on objective fact," showing that "the plan offers a reasonable assurance of success." Id. (citations omitted). "Reasonable assurance of success" requires that the "plan must provide a realistic and workable framework for reorganization," rather than "'visionary promises.'" Id. (quoting In re Made in Detroit, Inc., 299 B.R. 170, 176 (Bankr. E.D. Mich. 2003)). Stockbridge and U.S. Oil argue that the evidence at trial does not show that the Plan is feasible.

The Plan proposes payments to Class 1 of $533.87 per month; Class 2 of $1,679.17 per month; Class 3 of $139.33 per month; and Class 4 of $472.50 per month. The total monthly Plan payments are $2,804.87. The Plan proposes 60 monthly payments to Classes 1, 3, and 4, and 240 monthly payments on the Stockbridge mortgage that makes up Class 2. The evidence establishes that the Plan depends entirely on the RPF Agreements. . . .

The RPF Agreements require that Cheerview sell a minimum of 70,000 gallons of gas per month, and a total of 8,400,000 gallons of gas over the ten year span of the RPF Agreements. Berro and Ouza testified that 70,000 gallons of gas per month is realistic. Their testimony is corroborated by the testimony of Zerka, the Branded Sales Manager for RPF, who is confident that the Property is a very good location for a gas station and, if the gas is priced right, a gas station at the Property can be a "gold mine." The Projections show that there is sufficient money available each month to make all of the Plan payments based on the RPF Agreements. . . .

Stockbridge and U.S. Oil argue that the Projections are not realistic. The Court agrees. There is no evidence in the record that the gas station at the Property has ever come anywhere close to 70,000 gallons of gas for even one month, let alone every month. As noted earlier, during the time that Mikey's operated the business, it sold an average of approximately 35,000 gallons of gas per month, with the largest month, March, 2016, producing sales of 51,392 gallons of gas.

Berro and Ouza brush aside the historical sales volume by Mikey's and say that once reorganized, Cheerview will be able to hit the 70,000 gallons of gas per month marker every month because RPF will be able to set the price for the gas to be sold at the Property and can undercut Speedway, its main competition in the Lansing area. That testimony is persuasively controverted by [creditor witness] Beydoun's testimony. Beydoun testified—and even Zerka agreed—that Speedway is the predominant gas station in the Lansing area and that it historically sets the lowest price. The notion that Cheerview will be able to double its historical sales volume immediately following confirmation based on RPF undercutting Speedway's price is not supported by objective fact, but instead appears to be the product of wishful thinking. Even Cheerview's own Projections do not project that it will sell 70,000 gallons of gas on a monthly basis, but instead project that it will sell only 54,000 gallons of gas on a monthly basis for the entire duration of the Plan. If the Projections are accurate, that means that when the Plan is confirmed, Cheerview will immediately be in default under the RPF Agreements beginning with the very first month after confirmation and will go into default each and every month for the entire length of the Plan.

One of the RPF Agreements, the "Complete Contract of Sale (Branded)," specifies in paragraph 25(b)(xi), that RPF can terminate the RPF Agreements if Cheerview fails to purchase the minimum 70,000 gallons of gas in any month during the life of the RPF Agreements. At the trial, Berro and Ouza seemed only vaguely familiar with this contractual provision, but dismissed it in any event because of their belief that if Cheerview does not hit the 70,000 gallons of gas per month, RPF would simply forego its contractual remedies and agree to extend the life of the RPF Agreements to let Cheerview make up the lost sales. There is nothing in the RPF Agreements that gives Cheerview the option to make up insufficient sales by extending the contract, despite Berro's and Ouza's firm belief to the contrary. The RPF Agreements are clear in stating that RPF can terminate the RPF Agreements if Cheerview misses even one month of 70,000 gallons of gas sold.

The Projections are unrealistic in other respects, too. Berro and Ouza explained that for the line items of income and expenses other than the commission to be paid by RPF, they simply took the historical information from Mikey's and assumed that the line items containing that information will remain constant for the life of the Plan. As a result, there are no changes in any of the other line items on the Projections during the life of the Plan, not on the income side, not on the expense side and not even a cost of living increase. Most surprising is that the entire monthly payroll projected for Cheerview is $3,800.00 per month and remains $3,800.00 per month for the entire 60 month length of the Projections. Berro and Ouza testified that they each intend to work full time at Cheerview and that their compensation is included in that payroll. Further, they testified that they intend to hire one more employee. Paragraph 17 of the Complete Contract of Sale (Branded) requires that the gas station be open 24/7 throughout the year except for three holidays. That means that three employees will work for $3,800.00 every month, covering three shifts per day, for at least the next 60 months, and perhaps many more since the Plan proposes to make monthly payments on Stockbridge's Class 2 claim for 240 months—in other words, 20 years. That is not a realistic projection of payroll to run Cheerview's business post-confirmation.

When asked about the inconsistencies both internally in the Projections and when compared to the terms of the RPF Agreements, Berro and Ouza displayed a surprising lack of familiarity. Sometimes they could not answer the questions and explain the inconsistencies, and other times they indicated they needed to talk to their accountant or lawyer. Their lack of familiarity with the information contained in the Projections, and the assumptions made in those Projections, does not instill much confidence that the Projections are attainable.

To the extent that Berro and Ouza have a track record, it is not a good one. Berro readily admits that his absentee ownership contributed to Cheerview's failure that led to the bankruptcy filing. And Ouza was brought on by Berro at Mikey's during 2016, yet he too had no success in turning around the business. Berro and Ouza seem well intentioned and enthusiastic, but their management track record at the Property is poor, particularly when considered in light of the Projections which do not seem to the Court to be attainable even with experienced and capable management.

. . .

Feasibility does not demand that a debtor guarantee that every payment under a plan of reorganization will be made in the future. But there must be some evidence of objective facts to show that all plan payments are likely to be made. . . . After considering all of the evidence, the Court finds that Cheerview did not meet its burden to prove that the Plan is feasible. The plan does not meet the requirement of § 1129(a)(11).

CONCLUSION

The Disclosure Statement contains adequate information under § 1125(a)(1). However, the Plan cannot be confirmed because it does not meet the requirements of § 1129(a)(8) and (11) and because it violates the absolute priority rule of § 1129(b)(2)(B). There are grounds to grant the Motion for Stay Relief under both § 362(d)(1) and (2). The Court will enter a separate order consistent with this opinion.

It's never good when a court talks about "visionary schemes" at a confirmation hearing. Sometimes those schemes are so fanciful the creditors will not even wait until the confirmation hearing.

In re AURORA MEMORY CARE, LLC

589 B.R. 631 (Bankr. N.D. Ill. 2018)

GOLDGAR, Bankruptcy Judge.

AMC operates a health care facility in Aurora, Illinois. The 100% owner of [the various corporate affiliates is] Taher Kameli, a Chicago immigration lawyer. . . . AMC is one of several health care facilities in Illinois and Florida with which Kameli is involved. These facilities, or more specifically the investment funds Kameli established in connection with them, have served as investment vehicles for foreign nationals interested in gaining U.S. citizenship though the U.S. Citizenship and Immigration Service's EB-5 Program. Created under the Immigration Act of 1990, the EB-5 Program extends citizenship to immigrants who invest in designated U.S. businesses that create a certain number of jobs.

Kameli's investment scheme has not sat well with the federal government. In April 2017, the SEC brought a civil enforcement action (the "SEC action") against Kameli and others alleging that the handling of the investment funds violated the Securities Act of 1933 and the Securities Exchange Act of 1934. AMC was named in the action as a "relief defendant[]". . . .

Foreign investment was not the only one source of AMC's funding. In 2015, the Bank loaned AMC $6.5 million. The loan was secured by a mortgage on AMC's property as well as pledges of [] Kameli's ownership interest[s]. Kameli also personally guaranteed the loan. The loan matured on December 1, 2016. When AMC failed to repay it on the maturity date, the Bank filed an action in Illinois state court to foreclose on the mortgage and recover on the note [upon which chapter 11 ultimately followed]. . . .

To date, AMC has filed no monthly operating reports in the case, as sections 1106(a)(1) and 704(a)(8) require. 11 U.S.C. §§ 1106(a)(1), 704(a)(8). AMC also has yet to propose a plan. . . .

2. DISCUSSION

. . .

[T]he Bank has shown that AMC has no reasonable likelihood of successfully confirming a plan of reorganization [and therefore the case should be converted to chapter 7 or dismissed]. The reorganization AMC proposes—indeed, the only one it has ever mentioned—entails refinancing its $8.4 million debt to the Bank. But AMC has no financing currently available and has shown no prospect of obtaining any. AMC claims in its response to the Bank's motion that it has "secured financing through T2 Investments." (Resp. at 2). As evidence, AMC attaches T2's March 28 letter of intent. The letter, though, declared that it was "presented for discussion purposes only and does not constitute an offer, agreement, or commitment to lend." At most, then, T2 expressed an interest in discussing a loan. T2 made no financing commitment. AMC has produced no financing commitment from T2 or anyone else. . . .

Confirmation cannot be based on "speculation" or "visionary projections" of a plan's success. *Repurchase Corp.*, 332 B.R. at 343. When a plan depends on post-petition financing, as AMC's does, it is not possible to satisfy the feasibility requirement in section 1129 without "evidence of a firm commitment of financing." In re Ralph C. Tyler, P.E., P.S., Inc., 156 B.R. 995, 997 (Bankr. N.D. Ohio 1993); see also In re Save Our Springs (S.O.S.) Alliance, Inc., 632 F.3d 168, 173 n.8 (5th Cir. 2011). "Optimistic but hollow declarations from [a debtor's principal] about hopes for funding" do not do the job. *Repurchase Corp.*, 332 B.R. at 343. A plan will not be confirmed based on a debtor's "hope against hope" that financing will materialize. Id. (internal quotation omitted). Hope is all AMC has and all it has ever had.

Although the prospects for confirming a plan are not evaluated as stringently early in a case as they are later on, a debtor facing a motion under § 1112(b) must still show that a reorganization is plausible and not "a mere financial pipe dream." *Ramreddy*, 440 B.R. at 115 (internal quotation omitted). With no financing available, and with no other means of reorganizing suggested, AMC has not made that showing. . . .

═══════════════

Note the difference between a letter of intent and an actual commitment of postpetition financing. Many entrepreneurs seem to have trouble distinguishing the two. That said, these cases should not create the impression that feasibility objections routinely derail plans. Far from it, feasibility challenges are often thrown in as kitchen-sink objections, or perhaps brought up in menacing tones during plan proposals in just another attempt to exert leverage in negotiations; any motion can be withdrawn—for a price.

Feasibility determinations are not perfect. All too often companies emerge from chapter 11 only to fail again. In the jargon of the trade, these repeaters are in "chapter 22." Data show that about one in four of the publicly traded companies that confirmed a chapter 11 plan ended up back in bankruptcy. See UCLA School of Law, UCLA-LoPucki Bankruptcy Research Database, *available at* http://lopucki.law.ucla.edu. These repeated failures lead to concern that the courts are finding feasibility where it does not exist. See Stuart Gilson, Transaction Costs and Capital Structure Choice: Evidence from Financially Distressed Firms, 52 J. Fin. 161 (1997). A very interesting article (later book) reported that Delaware and the Southern District of New York, which attract a disproportionate number of the largest public company chapter 11 cases, have substantially higher rates of chapter 22s than courts elsewhere. Lynn M. LoPucki & Sarah D. Kalin, The Failure of Public Company Bankruptcies in Delaware and New York: Empirical Evidence of a "Race to the Bottom," 54 Vand. L. Rev. 231 (2001). The authors speculate that these two jurisdictions approve riskier plans and thus attract filings by debtors who seek approval of plans they know are marginal. It seems at least equally plausible that the debtors are pressured to file in such a jurisdiction by creditors unwilling to accept a sufficient "haircut" to permit the business to survive. A spate of scholarship has disputed the so-called "Delaware" effect on refiling, and it indeed appears that the problem may have abated in recent years—or at least is now spread more evenly across courts. The chapter 22s are a reminder that feasibility needs to have real bite if debtors are to survive after confirmation. Creditors and courts need to push reality in the face of debtor optimism.

C. SPECIAL RULES FOR SMALL BUSINESSES

Confirming chapter 11 plans under the SBRA is much different—and by design, easier—than it is with regular chapter 11 plans. The SBRA is Congress's latest move in its recurrent but confused insistence that small business should be treated differently in bankruptcy. Back in the Great Depression, Congress first developed special rules for small businesses under the former Bankruptcy Act by having enacting a special Chapter XI, which allowed reorganization without the mandatory involvement of the SEC that it still required for large corporations under Chapter X. This proved so popular (and the SEC so unpopular) that everyone tried to squeeze into Chapter XI, and so in its comprehensive reform in 1978, chapter 11 under the Code became available for all, regardless of size. Under the modern Code, most business bankruptcy procedures apply to all debtors, from Tina's Tax Preparation & Tanning Salon, a Tupperware party planner, and a lawn service guy who has lost his mower (all companies from the Business Bankruptcy Project sample), right up to such better-known entrants as Sears, General Motors, and nearly every major airline in the country.

In 2005's BAPCPA, however, Congress decided it was time to clamp down on small business debtors and added a slew of stricter rules that applied only to small businesses, apparently animated by a concern they were just dilly-dallying in chapter 11 to the waste of everyone's time. As with chapter 13, "eligibility" was defined by a cap on debt (around $2 million, but always adjusting due to indexing). Compare § 1182 with § 109(e). We use quotes around "eligibility" deliberately, however, because unlike chapter 13, debtors did not clamor for admittance but were often anxious to escape the scarlet "SB" of Small Business's definitional reach. E.g., In re Roots Rents, Inc., 420 B.R. 28 (Bankr. D. Idaho 2009) (debtor failed in its attempt to prove it owed more money than it had initially claimed and therefore exceeded the statutory maximum to be designated a "small business").

In 2019, however, Congress changed its collective, bipartisan mind and adopted new provisions permitting small businesses to bypass almost all of the onerous BAPCPA rules by opting into the new subchapter V of chapter 11, created by the SBRA. Now that you have learned most of the general voting rules designing, canvassing support for, and confirming a chapter 11 plan, you can appreciate the different SBRA rules. (Not yet all, though, because the SBRA's most significant innovation is its upending of the cramdown rules you will learn over the next two assignments.) Starting with what has not changed, nobody gets out of the "constitutional protections" for voting creditors of best interests and feasibility. Every debtor, big or small, has to pass that. But there are lots of other rules that help small business debtors. You have already seen, for example, in the previous assignment that the SBRA excuses disclosure statements. § 1181. It also abolishes the need for a creditors' committee (unless a court "for cause" orders otherwise), id., and gives the debtor more exclusivity to design the plan (albeit on a shorter timeline). The debtor can also pay off counsel over the terms of the plan; it need not do so right on the effective date of the plan. Compare § 1191(e) (SBRA) with § 1129(a)(9) (traditional).

Perhaps most significantly, however, both to help the debtor and police the proceeding, the statute establishes a trustee to be appointed in each case rather like those in chapters 12 and 13 — a sort of "trustee lite." § 1183. The estate vests in the DIP, as with a regular chapter 11, but a trustee is also involved. This trustee has important but limited duties of inspection, advice to the court, and the like. This strikes a balance between giving creditors confidence that in lower-stakes cases where they may not be able to monitor cost-effectively someone will be watching over the debtor's shoulders, while at the same time assuring the debtor that this officer will stay out of the debtor's hair and leave the entrepreneur free to make the business decisions of how to run the company. The SBRA trustee will opine on the debtor's plan, either supporting or objecting to it, and if the debtor must move to cramdown, serve as the conduit of payments to creditors. §§ 1183, 1194. (We will discuss these and other cramdown-specific SBRA rules in the next assignments.)

As mentioned in the previous assignment, the SBRA will have a large reach. Small businesses in their millions constitute the great majority of enterprises in the United States. These businesses are the median and modal debtors in chapter 11, even if they are not the exemplars of chapter 11 on the pages of the *Wall Street Journal*. Data from the 2002 Business Bankruptcy Project (BBP), reported in Elizabeth Warren & Jay Westbrook, The Success of Chapter 11, 107 Mich. L. Rev. 603 (2009), showed the median debt for chapter 11 was about $1.8 million, not tiny, but of pretty modest size in the business world. Unreported figures from the 2014 and 2018 databases of the BBP show that even in the Southern District of New York (mostly Manhattan), 40% of the chapter 11 businesses that filed had debt below the statutory small business cap in the Bankruptcy Code, $2.725 million.

For the foreseeable future, that proportion of eligible debtors will be much, much higher, because the CARES Act bumps that debt limit up to $7.5 million. The CARES amendments to the Code will sunset on March 27, 2021 — perhaps much the same way Congress "temporarily" raised estate tax limits that were to sunset after a decade. (Wouldn't you know it, a Congress that came along later decided to make those heightened limits that everyone grew accustomed to permanent.)

The specifics of the debt cap are different from the chapter 13 eligibility rules, which differentiate secured and unsecured debt. Under § 1182(1)(A), all debt must be included, although there is still the exclusion of the contingent and unliquidated. Moreover, if the debtor is an individual, at least half the total debts must arise from "commercial or business activities," a new and undefined term under the Code. Id. This cap includes the aggregate debt of "affiliates," who also file, but affiliates whose debt exceeds the cap may not file and thus are not included in the cap. Id. Real estate businesses are eligible, but not single asset ones. Id. Needless to say, public companies are also excluded even if small. Id. As such, we think contrary to the *Roots* case cited above, where debtors shunned the small business designation under BAPCPA, debtors will now flock to the SBRA, especially when they consider the relaxation of the cramdown requirements we will address in the next assignments.

Problem Set 28

28.1. Talbert Pany, the president of Pany, came storming back into your office this morning. (You are beginning to consider locking your office door, or at least acquiring a burly receptionist.) He was waving a copy of Country Smoke's Third Amended Plan of Reorganization, furious because Country now proposes to pay only 50 cents on the dollar to the unsecured creditors, including on Pany's $1,000,000 claim. When he shouts that he "thought the whole point of negotiation was to get more money," you kind of see his point about how this case is going. But your job is to know the law, not puzzle over the mysteries of the universe. So you remind Talbert that he could vote against the plan.

He is sure the other unsecured creditors will support the plan. He thinks that they are afraid of losing Country as a customer if it liquidates. Since the other unsecureds are owed a total of $4,000,000, Pany will be outvoted in its class. Talbert remains annoyed at various things he has learned from reviewing the multiple disclosure statements in this case. Particularly, it stuck in his craw that Country never told Pany Chemicals during their prepetition dealings that it had a $10,000,000 working capital loan from the First State Bank or that the loan was secured by a lien on all of Country's equipment. The equipment, which is worth about $2,500,000, is Country's only important asset, other than some real estate that is encumbered for its full value. The plan provides that First State will keep its lien on the equipment and the remaining balance of its loan will be paid in full.

Talbert says that the bank is still calling the shots in the chapter 11 because of its secured position. He feels that Country would never have been forced into chapter 11 in the first place until First State insisted on payment of $7,500,000 of the $10,000,000 loan in April, just when Country needed cash to start acquiring inventory. (That is why the bank is now only owed $2,500,000.) He cannot understand "how a bank can force a company into bankruptcy and then get paid in full while the rest of us get only 50%."

Talbert asked you to call the bank's lawyer and "insist" (his word) on a better deal for the unsecureds. You know the bank's lawyer will tell you to get lost unless you have some potent legal ammunition. What have you got to say? See § 1129(a).

28.2. BB&T is back hurling more stones at John Paul Smith in his battle for confirmation. Will you rule in the bank's favor and deny confirmation based on the transcript below? Again, be prepared to rule from the bench, citing evidence and law. See § 1129.

[Direct by] Mr. Oliver: We are going to talk today about what's happened since then, and we're going to talk about what's going to happen going forward. But before we do, I know there's some things that you'd like to tell the Judge about what happened before you filed for bankruptcy, is that right?

Mr. Smith: Yeah.

Mr. Oliver: Mr. Smith, you owed BB&T a lot of money, you and your entities, is that right?

Mr. Smith: Yes.

Mr. Oliver: What did you do before bankruptcy to try and pay down the BB&T debt?

Mr. Smith: We met Mr. Tucker and Edmund Gore and they had an associate they wanted us to hire to sell assets, and we started doing that to restructure the business.

Mr. Oliver: Did you hire the consultant that they wanted you to hire?

Mr. Smith: Yeah.

Mr. Oliver: And who was that?

Mr. Smith: John Toller was the one that worked with us.

Mr. Oliver: How much did you pay Mr. Toller?

Mr. Smith: I paid him about $32,000. He charged $60,000 for his whole fee to do what he needed to do to help restructure our business.

Mr. Oliver: And did you start selling assets of these different businesses?

Mr. Smith: Yes, John Toller, you know, he got prices for the different land, the warehouse, the trucks, and the trailers, and he distributed and then we'd sell them.

Mr. Oliver: Why did you think you were going to sell these assets?

Mr. Smith: Well, we was trying to do everything we can to restructure the business, get it back on its feet, so we started down south, selling every asset that weren't making money whatever we needed to sell to get the money back to BB&T.

[Cross by] Mr. Pryor: In each of these exhibits you have what you call a profit and loss statement, and you also have an ending balance in the operating account?

Mr. Smith: Hmhm.

Mr. Pryor: Mr. Smith, I want to show you what I have marked BB&T exhibit 9, and you ignore the first page the top of proof of claim but there are three promissory notes attached to that. If you would look at those and see if those are the copies of BB&T notes that you signed.

Mr. Smith: Yeah, these are the ones I signed, and dated in person.

Mr. Pryor: Okay, and they were all matured, I believe, in May 15, 2007.

Mr. Smith: Yes, yes.

Mr. Pryor: And you had trouble giving the bank accurate financial reporting at that point, hadn't you?

Mr. Smith: That's what that says.

Mr. Pryor: As matter of fact you gave them a financial statement showing you had made substantial money over a period of time and then it would come back revised to show that you had lost substantial money over the same period of time.

Mr. Smith: That's right.

Mr. Pryor: You were having great difficulty figuring out whether you were making or losing money?

Mr. Smith: Well, you might buy $200,000 worth of grain this month; you might sell $200,000 that month. It would be hard for it to be an even number, I mean, showing a profit.

Mr. Pryor: But you were having trouble figuring out whether you were losing or making money, right?

Mr. Smith: No, I wouldn't say that.

Mr. Pryor: Ok, well you were having trouble writing BB&T checks that didn't have the funds to be covered.

Mr. Smith: We had a few instances where he had . . ., we had one case there in [inaudible] that a check was supposed to have been deposited in our account, but it didn't and they had a problem on it. Several others had the same thing. It showed it where it was positive, so I did have an issue in that area.

Mr. Pryor: So you were keeping account of what your check book showed versus what money you had in the account to be able to write checks on?

Mr. Smith: Well, we worked to a certain extent: we got ACH on automatic direct deposit. So it was some cases where it was supposed to be deposited in the account, we got a fax that it was supposed to be, and it didn't happened till the next day so we did have some bad checks in that situation.

Mr. Pryor: The bigger issue here, is the feasibility issue for us, Your Honor, especially with the one year we are not going to get paid anything, on our secured claim for one year.

Judge: They are paying your secured claim now, right?

Mr. Pryor: They are paying the secured claim now; they have finally paid the secured claim every month since the court order.

Judge: Right.

Mr. Pryor: Adequate protection payments. And, not to belabor the point, but I think that the Court will look at the monthly operating account balance summaries and the monthly P&L summaries, and look at how these companies have struggled to even make that payment and where they have run negative balances, where they have run negative P&L and just sort of look at how, how low the numbers are. I understand the debtor has high hopes that this will turn around and work greatly, but the truth of the matter is history is a pretty good indication of what we're looking at in the future and from BB&T's perspective, for us is that there is a grain bin here that has some value, we believe that it has more value now with respect with what is going on out in the market that than it is going to have a year from now, if we have to sit here for a year and not receive, and I do not think they can make the secured payments, they have made so far, I don't know.

Judge: Right.

Mr. Pryor: The problem is, there are huge amount of payments they have to make beginning at the end of that one year that history has shown there is absolutely no ability to do it. And the reason I went back and went through their monthly projections for August is that, if you look, and I did the math, if you look at the difference between what they said they were going to have and what they actually had, and what they said they were actually going to pay as far as they were going to start paying claims, there is a, I did the math here, hold on a second, I wrote it down somewhere here, $120,731 is the difference between what they said August was going to look like and what August looked like.

Judge: But they also bought $100,000 more inventory in August, than they said they were going to buy?

Mr. Pryor: But August looks remarkably similar to the last fourteen months, that's the point, is that if you look at the history of what is gone on and, just, from our standpoint is for negative amortization they can't be shifting the burden on BB&T and according to the case law that's really where it is. They are going to make us sit here for a year for . . .

Judge: All right.

Mr. Pryor: There were a series of loans over years that led up to this one that got in trouble, and the debtor was having trouble figuring out where he was financially. There is no better way to say it: they couldn't figure out whether they had a problem loan. The bank would get statements with a profit one month, and the next month something would arrive and it would show a loss. In December of '06, I believe it was, whatever period of '06 when these loans were made, the bank consolidated the loans to give this debtor an opportunity to try to get his financial house in order. The debtor attempted but never got there, and a decision was made at that point that there is really no restructuring that was possible; they could never get the books and records, and the debtors still don't have anybody helping them with their books and records.

28.3. An old law school friend, José Garcia, has come to see you this morning about one of his business clients, Slick and Shiny, a Capital area cleaning service. Because of difficulties in the local economy of late, revenues have dropped by 25% and Melissa Jacoby, the owner, is having trouble finding the money to pay the monthly minimums she promises to her workers and still keep current on her commercial debts. "Melissa is a very hard worker and her people are loyal, so she will get through this if we can buy her some time." José knows you have a business bankruptcy practice and have been successful reorganizing small businesses in chapter 11.

Before he tries to negotiate a workout with the creditors, he wants to know his options. Can the four corporations that make up S&S (separate branches in Fairfax, Silver Spring, D.C., and Greenbelt) use the new procedures? The business has a total of $2.7 million in commercial loans and trade credit, all of it cross-guaranteed, not counting the $200,000 Melissa recently loaned to the Fairfax branch from her personal funds. Melissa owns 100% of all these entities. If José tells you Melissa is sure she can get most, but not all, creditors on board, will Melissa's business get any special benefits from the SBRA? See §§ 101(51D), 1121(e). (Ignore the temporary changes to the caps enacted in 2020.)

CRAMMING DOWN UNSECURED CREDITORS

In this assignment we turn to the rights of unsecured creditors against cramdown in chapter 11. Cramdown is a dramatic power wielded by debtors and so the creditors' protections are similarly strong. Secured and unsecured creditors are protected by different standards. We discuss cramdown against unsecured creditors in this assignment and cramdown against secured creditors in the next one. The rights are powerful in regular cases and even more so under the new SBRA.

A. THE CONCEPT OF CRAMDOWN: CONFIRMATION WITHOUT CONSENT

Even if a plan satisfies the best interests test of § 1129(a)(7) as to every non-accepting creditor and meets the test of feasibility, § 1129(a)(11), the plan nonetheless must be accepted by the statutory majority of creditors in each impaired *class* under § 1129(a)(8). If any class rejects the plan, then the plan cannot be confirmed as a consensual plan under § 1129(a). The remaining shot at confirmation is "cramdown" under § 1129(b). Once again, the word "cramdown" is jargon that everyone uses but is found nowhere in the statute.

Cramdown is the available strategy to reorganize when despite the debtor's best efforts at gerrymandering-cum-classification, the debtor faces a recalcitrant class that insists on voting no. Cramdown gives the debtor a second chance at reorganization by overriding that otherwise confirmation-precluding vote. § 1129(b) (providing an exception only to § 1129(a)(8) (all impaired classes approve the plan)). Cramdown, as the name suggests, is high energy and involves stuffing a plan down unhappy throats.

Don't get too excited about cramdown, though; most plans are consensual. See Arturo Bris, Ivo Welch & Ning Zhu, The Costs of Bankruptcy: Chapter 7 Liquidation versus Chapter 11 Reorganization, 61 J. Fin. 1253, 1274 (2006) (finding no cramdown plans in a sample of corporate bankruptcies filed in Arizona and Southern District of New York between 1995 and 2001). On the other hand, here as elsewhere, the hard legal alternative of cramdown shapes the negotiation for all the parties.

As we saw in Assignment 26, to qualify for a cramdown the plan must attract at least one consenting class of impaired creditors. Without the consent of at least one class with skin in the game (impairment), a plan cannot be confirmed, even by cramdown. § 1129(a)(10). But with an impaired class's affirmative vote, the debtor may confirm a plan even over the vigorous objections of another class (or classes). Against an unsecured creditor class, cramdown of the rejecting class can be approved only if the plan does "not discriminate unfairly" between classes *and* is "fair and equitable." § 1129(b)(1).

B. THE "UNFAIR DISCRIMINATION" BAR

The statutory proscription against unfair discrimination admits of tolerance of fair discrimination, once again being tested in advance in the disclosure statement.

In re DEMING HOSPITALITY, LLC
2013 WL 1397458 (Bankr. D.N.M. Apr. 5, 2013)

THUMA, Bankruptcy Judge.

This opinion addresses the argument of . . . the United States Small Business Administration ("SBA") that the debtor's Amended Disclosure Statement, filed March 1, 2013, doc. 95 (the "Disclosure Statement") should not be approved because the Debtor's reorganization plan (the "Plan") is facially unconfirmable. The alleged defects in the plan [include:] The disparate treatment of SBA's deficiency claim violates § 1129(b)(1)'s prohibition against unfair discrimination. . . . At a hearing held February 20, 2013, the Court set a briefing schedule on the Plan's alleged facial unconfirmability. . . . SBA filed briefs, Debtor responded, and a hearing was held March 11, 2013.

I. THE PLAN

Debtor's Plan, filed January 7, 2013, provides for eight classes of claims: Four classes of secured claims (SBT, SBA, TRD, and Luna County); a class for Choice Hotels; a class for non-priority unsecured claims other than the SBA's deficiency claim; a class for SBA's deficiency claim; and an equity class. The Plan provides, in pertinent part:

. . .

3. Class 5 (Choice Hotels): Choice Hotels is the franchisor under a certain Licensing Agreement, an executory contract with a $67,000 pre-petition arrearage. Debtor proposes to assume the contract and pay Choice Hotels $50,000 in full satisfaction of the arrearage;

> 4. Class 6 (General Unsecured Claims): General unsecured claims are to be paid 75% of their claim amounts within 30 days of the effective date;
>
> 5. Class 7 (SBA Deficiency Claim): SBA is to be paid $25,000 on its $1,500,000 deficiency claim, within 30 days of the effective date. . . .

SBA [has] stated in [its] brief[] and in open court that [it] would vote to reject, and would object to, the Plan. . . .

. . .

IV.   DISPARATE TREATMENT OF SBA's DEFICIENCY CLAIM

Under the Plan, general unsecured creditors would be paid 75% of their claims within 30 days of the Plan's effective date. In contrast, by the same deadline SBA would receive a lump sum payment of $25,000 on its approximate $1,500,000 claim, or about 1.67%. SBT and SBA argue that this disparate treatment violates 11 U.S.C. § 1129(b)(1)'s prohibition against "unfair discrimination."[3]

There is no controlling Tenth Circuit authority on what "discriminate unfairly" means. Other courts have developed a variety of tests to distinguish between "fair" and "unfair" discrimination. Some have followed In re Aztec Co., 107 B.R. 585, 590 (Bankr. M.D. Tenn. 1989), and considered (1) whether the discrimination is supported by a reasonable basis; (2) whether the debtor can confirm and consummate a plan without the discrimination; (3) whether the discrimination is proposed in good faith; and (4) the treatment of the classes discriminated against. *See, e.g.,* In re Riviera Drilling & Exploration Co., 2012 Bankr. LEXIS 5991, 2012 WL 6719591 (Bankr. D. Colo. 2012). . . .

A refinement of the test changes the fourth factor to "the degree of the discrimination is directly related to the basis or rationale for the discrimination." In re Ambanc La Mesa L.P., 115 F.3d 650, 656 (9th Cir. 1997), cert. denied, 522 U.S. 1110, 118 S. Ct. 1039, 140 L. Ed. 2d 105 (1998). . . .

A condensed version of this test is whether there is a reasonable basis for the discrimination and whether the debtor can confirm a plan without it. See In re Lernout & Hauspie Speech Products, N.V., 301 B.R. 651, 660 (Bankr. D. Del. 2003), aff'd, 308 B.R. 672 (D. Del. 2004), citing In re Ambanc La Mesa; In re Crosscreek Apartments, Ltd., 213 B.R. 521, 537 (Bankr. E.D. Tenn. 1997) ("at a minimum there must be a rational or legitimate basis for the discrimination and the discrimination must be necessary for the reorganization").

---

[3] Section 1129(b)(1) provides that "Notwithstanding section 510(a) of this title, if all of the applicable requirements of subsection (a) of this section other than paragraph (8) are met with respect to a plan, the court, on request of the proponent of the plan, shall confirm the plan notwithstanding the requirements of such paragraph if the plan does not discriminate unfairly, and is fair and equitable, with respect to each class of claims or interests that is impaired under, and has not accepted, the plan."

Other courts have adopted a "rebuttable presumption test" proposed by Professor Bruce Markell.[4] See In re Tribune Co., 472 B.R. 223, 241 (Bankr. D. Del. 2012) [Yes, that *Tribune*, as in *The Chicago*.—Eds.]. . . . For the plan proponent to rebut the presumption, it must show that outside of bankruptcy, the dissenting class would receive less than the class receiving greater recovery, or that the alleged preferred class had infused new value which offset its gain.

Regardless of the standard used to determine unfair discrimination, courts agree that if the treatment of substantially similar claims is "grossly disparate," it is very difficult for the plan proponent to show "fair" discrimination. See *Tribune*, 472 B.R. at 243 (defining grossly disparate as a difference of 50% or more in the recovery (e.g. 10% versus 60% recovery), and saying that courts have "roundly rejected plans" proposing such treatment). . . .

In In re Crawford, 324 F.3d 539, 542 (7th Cir. 2003), Judge Posner, reviewing whether a Chapter 13 plan discriminated unfairly, reviewed tests developed in Chapter 13 practice, including one very similar to the Aztec/Ambanc La Mesa test. He was critical of the test,[6] and stated:

> We haven't been able to think of a good test ourselves. We conclude, at least provisionally, that this is one of those areas of the law in which it is not possible to do better than to instruct the first-line decision maker, the bankruptcy judge, to seek a result that is reasonable in light of the purposes of the relevant law, which in this case is Chapter 13 of the Bankruptcy Code; and to uphold his determination unless it is unreasonable (an abuse of discretion).

324 F.3d at 542. See also In re Pracht, 464 B.R. 486, 491 (Bankr. M.D. Ga. 2012) (citing *Crawford* and reviewing the attempts courts have made to formulate tests for "unfair" discrimination); In re Orawsky, 387 B.R. 128, 141 (Bankr. E.D. Pa. 2008) (reviewing the various tests used in Chapter 13).

The Court agrees with *Crawford* that none of the tests (in this case for Chapter 11) is helpful or tailored enough to be adopted. The Aztec/Ambanc La Mesa test, for example, while somewhat helpful, is general and vague (e.g. using "reasonable basis" and "good faith"), and therefore gives insufficient guidance. Judge Markell's "rebuttable presumption" test, on the other hand, seems restrictive, and could exclude treatment that is fair.

---

[4] I propose that a court should not confirm a nonconsensual plan, even if it provides fair and equitable treatment for all classes, when there is: (1) a dissenting class; (2) another class of the same priority; and (3) a difference in the plan's treatment of the two classes that results in either (a) a materially lower percentage recovery for the dissenting class (measured in terms of the net present value of all payments), or (b) regardless of percentage recovery, an allocation under the plan of materially greater risk to the dissenting class in connection with its proposed distribution. . . . In either case—disparity of recovery or disparity of risk—the plan proponent can rebut the presumption of unfairness by proving that the difference in treatment is attributable to differences in the prepetition status of the creditors. In the case of a difference in the present value of the recovery, the presumption may also be overcome by a demonstration that contributions will be made by the assenting classes to the reorganization, and that these contributions are commensurate with the different treatment. In such cases, while discrimination exists, it is not unfair.

Bruce A. Markell, A New Perspective on Unfair Discrimination in Chapter 11, 72 Am. Bankr. L.J. 227, 249-50 (1998).

[6] Judge Posner stated: "With respect, this test is empty except for point 2, which does identify an important factor bearing on the reasonableness of a classification. . . ." 324 F.3d at 542.

In the Court's opinion the only helpful general rules are (1) if the disparate treatment is "grossly disproportionate" the plan proponent will have a heavy burden to justify the treatment, and (2) if a plan is feasible and could be confirmed without materially disparate treatment, then the burden on the plan proponent to justify disparate treatment will be particularly heavy. Apart from these rules, the determination whether any discriminatory treatment is "unfair" will be left to the sound discretion of the Court.

Here, there is a gross disparity between the proposed dividend to non-priority unsecured creditors (75%) and the proposed dividend to SBA (1.67%).[7] In addition, it appears it may be possible to draft a plan that would not discriminate against the SBA (e.g. a plan that treats all unsecured claims the same, which SBA would agree to vote for). Thus, while the current Plan is not unconfirmable on its face, the Debtor will carry a heavy burden to justify SBA's disparate treatment. . . .

An appropriate order will be entered.

"Unfair discrimination" surely makes the short list for most discretion-conferring provisions of the Code. While it seems unlikely Deming's plan is going to work, "The Trib" case, cited in the opinion, was a case of dizzying complexity. The plan proposed lumping one group of unsecured creditors, who were entitled to an extra distribution under a subordination agreement, in the same class as another group of unsecureds who were not. The objectors argued the dilution of their extra dividend (by having it shared by the whole class) was unfair discrimination. Noting that they only fell from an estimated 35.9% to 33.6%, the court swiftly dispatched the objection and was affirmed. In re Tribune Co., 472 B.R. 223, 243 (Bankr. D. Del. 2012). Even more dramatic differentials are frequently upheld when there are "stronger" reasons beyond complexity. For example, in one recent case, the court allowed paying unsecured bondholders 4-6% while paying trade creditors 100% for the simple reason that the debtor needed an ongoing relation with those trade creditors to keep its business alive. Hargreaves v. Nuverra Envtl. Sols., Inc. (In re Nuverra Envtl. Sols., Inc.), 590 B.R. 75, 98-99 (D. Del. 2018). In sum, two parts bankruptcy court flexibility plus one part business judgment rule make a potent cocktail. Unlike with civil rights, in bankruptcy it appears discrimination is often fair; cases like *Deming*, with its brazen differential headed for likely unconfirmability, are rare.

C. THE "FAIR AND EQUITABLE" REQUIREMENT

The "fair and equitable" constraint does more work, although not for the reason you might think. Despite its loosey-goosey language, the "fair and equitable test" mostly follows a line of case law under the old Chapter X that has been semi-codified in § 1129(b)(2). Northern Pacific R. Co. v. Boyd,

---

[7] In other words, other non-priority unsecured creditors are preferred over the SBA at a rate of almost 45 to 1.

228 U.S. 482, 508 (1913). Under § 1129(b)(2)(B), unsecured creditors must either get paid in full (rare), § 1129(b)(2)(B)(i), or be protected by the "absolute priority rule." Again, that term is not found in the Code, but is a central idea of chapter 11.

1.   *The Absolute Priority Rule*

The Code says that no parties "junior" to the objecting class can get a distribution under the plan. § 1129(b)(2)(B)(ii). Thus, if the plan proposes to pay a dividend to the equity holders of the company, the plan cannot be crammed down over the objection of the unsecured creditor class. Because equity is "junior" to unsecured creditors (stockholders only get paid after the creditors), a plan already sufficiently repugnant to the unsecured creditors to trigger a negative vote cannot be confirmed through the vote-overriding bypass of cramdown. The unsecured creditors can insist on ensuring their "absolute priority" over equity.

At first glance, you may think the absolute priority rule does nothing more than vindicate petty schadenfreude of the objecting class (*If we're not happy, no one beneath us can be happy!*). But the rule has greater elegance. An example is a plan proposed by managers who own significant equity stakes in the debtor as stockholders. The plan's proponents will evince a strong temptation to treat equity more generously than unsecured creditors. This is magnified by the DIP's exclusive right to design the reorganization proposal for the first four months. § 1121(b). Absolute priority helps the unsecureds fight back, adding a layer of protection that applies in cramdown.

Consider a stock-holding CEO who proposes, "How about you general unsecureds take a 70% haircut, and we stockholders will generously let you have 10% of the shares of 'our' company as a sweetener?" (The CEO reveals no irony in suggesting the stockholders still own the insolvent company as "theirs.") This proposal would allow the stockholders to keep their shares of the company post-bankruptcy, albeit with a 10% dilution. The creditors might well reply, "No, we'd prefer to take only a 10% haircut, thanks. If you really want us to take a 70% haircut on our debt, we want half of the shares of the company in exchange." The negotiations can go back and forth, and the unsecured creditors' leverage is threatening to vote as a class against the plan. If that happens, the CEO cannot use cramdown to override the vote *and* keep equity owning stock (which the CEO desperately wants).

The absolute priority rule guarantees dissenting creditors that if confirmation of the plan will be crammed down over their objection, all the stockholders, including that CEO, will have their shares cancelled—they get nothing. The rule is that stark. Yet it makes sense in a world where equity isn't allowed to get paid until creditors have been paid in full. You might wonder: who owns the company if all the stock is wiped out? Under a sort of conservation of financial mass, it doesn't just disappear, unless the debtor liquidates. The answer is the next most junior class—in this example, the unsecureds—must receive the new equity for a reorganization plan to be confirmed.

These cramdown cases pitting the unsecured creditors against equity should not be overread. While the absolute priority rule seems to give creditors an unconditional option to squeeze equity out, not so many unsecured creditors are actually willing to do so if it means a dispirited owner-manager just walks away rather than continuing to pour talent and work into the company. While some creditors, such as the oversecured, are sanguine about and perhaps even impatient for liquidation, others see reorganization as the best chance for building value and getting paid. For them, threats to vote no may be mere bluster. Especially with small businesses, because the owner and manager are the same, these creditors often know that unless the manager stays on, the business is worthless. Antoinette's Tonight, Home of Antoinette LaPierre's Genuine Authentic Handpacked Blackened Redfish (a real business from one of our empirical studies), may be worth very little if Antoinette is out and Sam Bump is in. In other cases, the equity owner is critical because the owner's business connections are what make the business go. Holstrom's Athletic Supply Equipment depends on having Red Holstrom, a retired coach of a four-time state champion football team, around to make calls on the high school coaches. Chapter 11, as we have said before, is just an invitation to a complex negotiation in which both sides will play chicken.

Absolute priority thus ensures that the equity owners get the unsecured creditors to support the plan (or else they lose everything in cramdown). While a CEO may be upset about losing stock options but still has a nice investment portfolio to fall back on, a small business owner whose entire life is the company is unlikely to respond well to a scenario of losing all the equity. (The new SBRA, discussed below, may upend that power dynamic.) This is just one reason why consensual plans are more common than cramdowns: equity works hard to get to yes. But cramdowns do happen, even with small businesses, *and* the equity players sometimes manage to stay alive in the post-reorganization debtor. How? Good question!

2.   Equity's Reprieve: The New Value "Corollary"

The Code says that equity may not "receive or retain" anything under the reorganization plan "on account of" their junior interests in the event of a cramdown. § 1129(b)(2)(B)(ii). But analogous to causation arguments in tort law, that doesn't speak to whether equity can retain ownership on account of something else. Recall that the debtor has several postpetition financing options. In addition to seeking DIP loans in return for security interests or the like, the debtor may look for a new investor to put money into the business and become the new equity owner. And, not surprisingly, that new equity owner who will provide the cash to resuscitate the failing business through reorganization is often the old equity owner, still running the show. (Old equity has inside information—cheaper information costs, in the words of economists—that will both make them more excited about bidding on the company and scare others off from doing so for the same reason.) For an appropriate infusion of badly needed cash, old equity can become post-bankruptcy new equity, even in a cramdown. The theory is that they get ownership "on account of" this injection of new value.

Supporters call this a corollary to the absolute priority rule: while you can't get anything under the plan *on account of being a stockholder*, you can *on account of being a new investor* (whether you were an old stockholder or not).

This issue divided courts—hotly—with some seeing it as an end run around the absolute priority rule driven by nothing more than legal mumbo-jumbo, but others seeing it as a simple question of causation. The issue finally worked its way to the Supreme Court, which offered a sort of glancing blow. The somewhat cryptic opinion is one of the most important bankruptcy cases decided by the Court. Note that in this case the dissenting unsecured class consisted of the deficiency claim of an undersecured creditor.

BANK OF AMERICA NAT'L TRUST & SAV. ASS'N v. 203 NORTH LASALLE STREET PARTNERSHIP

526 U.S. 434 (1999)

Justice SOUTER delivered the opinion of the Court.

The issue in this Chapter 11 reorganization case is whether a debtor's prebankruptcy equity holders may, over the objection of a senior class of impaired creditors, contribute new capital and receive ownership interests in the reorganized entity, when that opportunity is given exclusively to the old equity holders under a plan adopted without consideration of alternatives. We hold that old equity holders are disqualified from participating in such a "new value" transaction by the terms of 11 U.S.C. § 1129(b)(2)(B)(ii), which in such circumstances bars a junior interest holder's receipt of any property on account of his prior interest.

I.

Petitioner, Bank of America National Trust and Savings Association (Bank), is the major creditor of respondent, 203 North LaSalle Street Partnership (Debtor or Partnership), an Illinois real estate limited partnership. The Bank lent the Debtor some $93 million, secured by a . . . first mortgage on the Debtor's principal asset, 15 floors of an office building in downtown Chicago. In January 1995, the Debtor defaulted, and the Bank began foreclosure in a state court.

In March, the Debtor responded with a voluntary petition for relief under Chapter 11 of the Bankruptcy Code, which automatically stayed the foreclosure proceedings, see § 362(a). The Debtor's principal objective was to ensure that its partners retained title to the property so as to avoid roughly $20 million in personal tax liabilities, which would fall due if the Bank foreclosed. The Debtor proceeded to propose a reorganization plan . . . .

The value of the mortgaged property was less than the balance due the Bank. . . . Under the plan, the Debtor separately classified the Bank's secured claim, its unsecured deficiency claim, and unsecured trade debt owed to other creditors. See § 1122(a). The Bankruptcy Court found that the Debtor's available assets were prepetition rents in a cash account of $3.1 million and the 15 floors of rental property worth $54.5 million. The secured claim was valued at the latter figure, leaving the Bank with an unsecured deficiency of $38.5 million.

So far as we need be concerned here, the Debtor's plan had these further features:

1. The Bank's $54.5 million secured claim would be paid in full between 7 and 10 years after the original 1995 repayment date.
2. The Bank's $38.5 million unsecured deficiency claim would be discharged for an estimated 16% of its present value.
3. The remaining unsecured claims of $90,000, held by the outside trade creditors, would be paid in full, without interest, on the effective date of the plan.
4. Certain former partners of the Debtor would contribute $6.125 million in new capital over the course of five years (the contribution being worth some $4.1 million in present value), in exchange for the Partnership's entire ownership of the reorganized debtor.

The last condition was an exclusive eligibility provision: the old equity holders were the only ones who could contribute new capital.[11]

The Bank objected and, being the sole member of an impaired class of creditors, thereby blocked confirmation of the plan on a consensual basis. See § 1129(a)(8). The Debtor, however, took the alternate route to confirmation of a reorganization plan, forthrightly known as the judicial "cramdown" process for imposing a plan on a dissenting class. § 1129(b).

There are two conditions for a cramdown. First, all requirements of § 1129(a) must be met (save for the plan's acceptance by each impaired class of claims or interests, see § 1129(a)(8)). Critical among them are the conditions that the plan be accepted by at least one class of impaired creditors, see § 1129(a)(10), and satisfy the "best-interest-of-creditors" test, see § 1129(a)(7). Here, the class of trade creditors with impaired unsecured claims voted for the plan, and there was no issue of best interest. Second, the objection of an impaired creditor class may be overridden only if "the plan does not discriminate unfairly, and is fair and equitable, with respect to each class of claims or interests that is impaired under, and has not accepted, the plan." § 1129(b)(1). As to a dissenting class of impaired unsecured creditors, such a plan may be found to be "fair and equitable" only if the allowed value of the claim is to be paid in full, § 1129(b)(2)(B)(i), or, in the alternative, if "the holder of any claim or interest that is junior to the claims of such [impaired unsecured] class will not receive or retain under the plan on account of such

---

[11] The plan eliminated the interests of noncontributing partners. More than 60% of the Partnership interests would change hands on confirmation of the plan. See Brief for Respondent 4, n.7. The new Partnership, however, would consist solely of former partners, a feature critical to the preservation of the Partnership's tax shelter. Tr. of Oral Arg. 32.

junior claim or interest any property," § 1129(b)(2)(B)(ii). That latter condition is the core of what is known as the "absolute priority rule." . . .

We granted certiorari to resolve a Circuit split on the issue. The Seventh Circuit in this case joined the Ninth in relying on a new value corollary to the absolute priority rule to support confirmation of such plans. See In re Bonner Mall Partnership, 2 F.3d 899, 910-916 (C.A. 9 1993). The Second and Fourth Circuits, by contrast, without explicitly rejecting the corollary, have disapproved plans similar to this one.[15] We do not decide whether the statute includes a new value corollary or exception, but hold that on any reading respondent's proposed plan fails to satisfy the statute, and accordingly reverse.

II.

The terms "absolute priority rule" and "new value corollary" (or "exception") are creatures of law antedating the current Bankruptcy Code, and to understand both those terms and the related but inexact language of the Code some history is helpful. The Bankruptcy Act preceding the Code contained no such provision as subsection (b)(2)(B)(ii), its subject having been addressed by two interpretive rules. The first was a specific gloss on the requirement . . . that any reorganization plan be "fair and equitable." The reason for such a limitation was the danger inherent in any reorganization plan proposed by a debtor, then and now, that the plan will simply turn out to be too good a deal for the debtor's owners. See H.R. Doc. No. 93-137, pt. I, p.255 (1973) (discussing concern with "the ability of a few insiders, whether representatives of management or major creditors, to use the reorganization process to gain an unfair advantage"); ibid. ("It was believed that creditors, because of management's position of dominance, were not able to bargain effectively without a clear standard of fairness and judicial control"); Ayer, Rethinking Absolute Priority After *Ahlers*, 87 Mich. L. Rev. 963, 969-973 (1989). Hence the pre-Code judicial response known as the absolute priority rule, that fairness and equity required that "the creditors . . . be paid before the stockholders could retain [equity interests] for any purpose whatever." Northern Pacific R. Co. v. Boyd, 228 U.S. 482, 508 (1913).

The second interpretive rule addressed the first. Its classic formulation occurred in Case v. Los Angeles Lumber Products Co., in which the Court spoke through Justice Douglas in this dictum:

> It is, of course, clear that there are circumstances under which stockholders may participate in a plan of reorganization of an insolvent debtor. . . . Where the necessity [for new capital] exists and the old stockholders make a fresh contribution and receive in return a participation reasonably equivalent to their contribution, no objection can be made. . . .
> We believe that to accord "the creditor his full right of priority against the corporate assets" where the debtor is insolvent, the stockholder's

---

[15] All four of these cases arose in the single-asset real estate context, the typical one in which new value plans are proposed.

participation must be based on a contribution in money or in money's worth, reasonably equivalent in view of all the circumstances to the participation of the stockholder. 308 U.S. at 121-122.

Although counsel for one of the parties here has described the *Case* observation as "'black-letter' principle," Brief for Respondent 38, it never rose above the technical level of dictum in any opinion of this Court, which last addressed it in Norwest Bank Worthington v. Ahlers, 485 U.S. 197 (1988), holding that a contribution of "'labor, experience, and expertise'" by a junior interest holder was not in the "'money's worth'" that the *Case* observation required. 485 U.S. at 203-205. . . . Hence the controversy over how weighty the *Case* dictum had become, as reflected in the alternative labels for the new value notion: some writers and courts . . . have spoken of it as an exception to the absolute priority rule, while others have characterized it as a simple corollary to the rule. . . .

III.

Three basic interpretations have been suggested for the "on account of" modifier. The first reading is proposed by the Partnership, that "on account of" harks back to accounting practice and means something like "in exchange for," or "in satisfaction of,". On this view, a plan would not violate the absolute priority rule unless the old equity holders received or retained property in exchange for the prior interest, without any significant new contribution; if substantial money passed from them as part of the deal, the prohibition of subsection (b)(2)(B)(ii) would not stand in the way, and whatever issues of fairness and equity there might otherwise be would not implicate the "on account of" modifier.

This position is beset with troubles, the first one being textual. Subsection (b)(2)(B)(ii) forbids not only receipt of property on account of the prior interest but its retention as well. . . .

The second difficulty is practical: the unlikelihood that Congress meant to impose a condition as manipulable as subsection (b)(2)(B)(ii) would be if "on account of" meant to prohibit merely an exchange unaccompanied by a substantial infusion of new funds but permit one whenever substantial funds changed hands. "Substantial" or "significant" or "considerable" or like characterizations of a monetary contribution would measure it by the Lord Chancellor's foot, and an absolute priority rule so variable would not be much of an absolute.

Since the "in exchange for" reading merits rejection, the way is open to recognize the more common understanding of "on account of" to mean "because of." This is certainly the usage meant for the phrase at other places in the statute, see [e.g., — Eds.] . . . § 547(c)(4)(B) (barring trustee from avoiding a transfer when a creditor gives new value to the debtor "on account of which new value the debtor did not make an otherwise unavoidable transfer to . . . such creditor"). So, under the commonsense rule that a given phrase is meant to carry a given concept in a single statute, the better reading of subsection (b)(2)(B)(ii) recognizes that a causal relationship between holding the prior claim or interest and receiving or retaining property is what activates the absolute priority rule.

The degree of causation is the final bone of contention. We understand the Government, as amicus curiae, to take the starchy position not only that any degree of causation between earlier interests and retained property will activate the bar to a plan providing for later property, but also that whenever the holders of equity in the Debtor end up with some property there will be some causation; when old equity, and not someone on the street, gets property the reason is res ipsa loquitur. An old equity holder simply cannot take property under a plan if creditors are not paid in full.

There are, however, reasons counting against such a reading. If, as is likely, the drafters were treating junior claimants or interest holders as a class at this point, then the simple way to have prohibited the old interest holders from receiving anything over objection would have been to omit the "on account of" phrase entirely from subsection (b)(2)(B)(ii). . . .

A less absolute statutory prohibition would follow from reading the "on account of" language as intended to reconcile the two recognized policies underlying Chapter 11, of preserving going concerns and maximizing property available to satisfy creditors. Causation between the old equity's holdings and subsequent property substantial enough to disqualify a plan would presumably occur on this view of things whenever old equity's later property would come at a price that failed to provide the greatest possible addition to the bankruptcy estate, and it would always come at a price too low when the equity holders obtained or preserved an ownership interest for less than someone else would have paid. A truly full value transaction, on the other hand, would pose no threat to the bankruptcy estate not posed by any reorganization, provided of course that the contribution be in cash or be realizable money's worth, just as *Ahlers* required for application of *Case*'s new value rule.

IV.

Which of these positions is ultimately entitled to prevail is not to be decided here, however, for even on the latter view the Bank's objection would require rejection of the plan at issue in this case. It is doomed, we can say without necessarily exhausting its flaws, by its provision for vesting equity in the reorganized business in the Debtor's partners without extending an opportunity to anyone else either to compete for that equity or to propose a competing reorganization plan. Although the Debtor's exclusive opportunity to propose a plan under § 1121(b) is not itself "property" within the meaning of subsection (b)(2)(B)(ii), the respondent partnership in this case has taken advantage of this opportunity by proposing a plan under which the benefit of equity ownership may be obtained by no one but old equity partners. At the moment of the plan's approval the Debtor's partners necessarily enjoyed an exclusive opportunity that was in no economic sense distinguishable from the advantage of the exclusively entitled [offeree] or option holder. This opportunity should, first of all, be treated as an item of property in its own right. While it may be argued that the opportunity has no market value, being significant only to old equity holders owing to their potential tax liability, such an argument avails the Debtor nothing, for several reasons. It is to avoid just such arguments that the law is settled that any otherwise cognizable property interest must be treated as sufficiently valuable to be recognized under the Bankruptcy Code. Even aside from that rule, the assumption that no one but the Debtor's partners might pay for such an opportunity would obviously support no inference that it is valueless, let alone that it should not be treated as property. And, finally, the source in the tax law of the opportunity's value to the partners implies in no way that it lacks value to others. It might, indeed, be valuable to another precisely as a way to keep the Debtor from implementing a plan that would avoid a Chapter 7 liquidation.

Given that the opportunity is property of some value, the question arises why old equity alone should obtain it, not to mention at no cost whatever. . . .

[E]ven if we assume that old equity's plan would not be confirmed without satisfying the judge that the purchase price was top dollar, there is a further reason here not to treat property consisting of an exclusive opportunity as subsumed within the total transaction proposed. On the interpretation assumed here, it would, of course, be a fatal flaw if old equity acquired or retained the property interest without paying full value. It would thus be necessary for old equity to demonstrate its payment of top dollar, but this it could not satisfactorily do when it would receive or retain its property under a plan giving it exclusive rights and in the absence of a competing plan of any sort.[27] Under a plan granting an exclusive right, making no provision for competing bids or competing plans, any determination that the price was top dollar would necessarily be made by a judge in bankruptcy court, whereas the best way to determine value is exposure to a market. See Markell, 44 Stan. L. Rev., at 73 ("Reorganization practice illustrates that the presence of competing bidders for a debtor, whether they are owners or not, tends to increase creditor dividends."). . . .

Whether a market test would require an opportunity to offer competing plans or would be satisfied by a right to bid for the same interest sought by old equity, is a question we do not decide here. It is enough to say, assuming a new value corollary, that plans providing junior interest holders with exclusive opportunities free from competition and without benefit of market valuation fall within the prohibition of § 1129(b)(2)(B)(ii).

The judgment of the Court of Appeals is accordingly reversed, and the case is remanded for further proceedings consistent with this opinion.

It is so ordered.

Justice THOMAS, with whom Justice SCALIA joins, concurring in the judgment.

---

[27] The dissent emphasizes the care taken by the Bankruptcy Judge in examining the valuation evidence here, in arguing that there is no occasion for us to consider the relationship between valuation process and top-dollar requirement. While we agree with the dissent as to the judge's conscientious handling of the matter, the ensuing text of this opinion sets out our reasons for thinking the Act calls for testing valuation by a required process that was not followed here.

I agree with the majority's conclusion that the reorganization plan in this case could not be confirmed. However, I do not see the need for its unnecessary speculations on certain issues and do not share its approach to interpretation of the Bankruptcy Code. I therefore concur only in the judgment. . . .

Our precedents make clear that an analysis of any statute, including the Bankruptcy Code, must not begin with external sources, but with the text itself. The relevant Code provision in this case, 11 U.S.C. § 1129(b), does not expressly authorize prepetition equity holders to receive or retain property in a reorganized entity in exchange for an infusion of new capital. . . .

Unfortunately, the approach taken today only thickens the fog.

Justice STEVENS, dissenting.

Prior to the enactment of the Bankruptcy Reform Act of 1978, this Court unequivocally stated that there are circumstances under which stockholders may participate in a plan of reorganization of an insolvent debtor if their participation is based on a contribution in money, or in money's worth, reasonably equivalent in view of all the circumstances to their participation.[1]

As we have on two prior occasions, we granted certiorari in this case to decide whether § 1129(b)(2)(B)(ii) of the 1978 Act preserved or repealed this "new value" component of the absolute priority rule. I believe the Court should now definitively resolve the question and state that a holder of a junior claim or interest does not receive property "on account of" such a claim when its participation in the plan is based on adequate new value. . . .

I.

Section 1129 of Chapter 11 sets forth in detail the substantive requirements that a reorganization plan must satisfy in order to qualify for confirmation. In the case of dissenting creditor classes, a plan must conform

---

[1] As Justice Douglas explained in Case v. Los Angeles Lumber Products Co., 308 U.S. 106 (1939):

> It is, of course, clear that there are circumstances under which stockholders may participate in a plan of reorganization of an insolvent debtor. This Court, as we have seen, indicated as much in Northern Pacific Ry. Co. v. Boyd[, 228 U.S. 482 (1913),] and Kansas City Terminal Ry. Co. v. Central Union Trust Co.[, 271 U.S. 445 (1926)]. Especially in the latter case did this Court stress the necessity, at times, of seeking new money "essential to the success of the undertaking" from the old stockholders. Where that necessity exists and the old stockholders make a fresh contribution and receive in return a participation reasonably equivalent to their contribution, no objection can be made. . . .
>
> In view of these considerations we believe that to accord "the creditor his full right of priority against the corporate assets" where the debtor is insolvent, the stockholder's participation must be based on a contribution in money or in money's worth, reasonably equivalent in view of all the circumstances to the participation of the stockholder.

308 U.S. at 121-122 (footnote omitted).

to the dictates of § 1129(b). With only one exception, the requirements of §§ 1129(a) and 1129(b) are identical for plans submitted by stockholders or junior creditors and plans submitted by other parties. That exception is the requirement in § 1129(b)(2)(B)(ii) that no holder of a junior claim or interest may receive or retain any property "on account of such junior claim or interest."

When read in the light of Justice Douglas' opinion in Case v. Los Angeles Lumber Products Co., 308 U.S. 106 (1939), the meaning of this provision is perfectly clear. Whenever a junior claimant receives or retains an interest for a bargain price, it does so "on account of" its prior claim. On the other hand, if the new capital that it invests has an equivalent or greater value than its interest in the reorganized venture, it should be equally clear that its participation is based on the fair price being paid and that it is not "on account of" its old claim or equity. . . . In every reorganization case, serious questions concerning the value of the debtor's assets must be resolved. . . . I believe that we should assume that all valuation questions have been correctly answered. . . .

II.

As I understand the Court's opinion, it relies on two reasons for refusing to approve the plan at this stage of the proceedings: one based on the plan itself and the other on the confirmation procedures followed before the plan was adopted. In the Court's view, the fatal flaw in the plan proposed by respondent was that it vested complete ownership in the former partners immediately upon confirmation, and the defect in the process was that no other party had an opportunity to propose a competing plan.

These requirements are neither explicitly nor implicitly dictated by the text of the statute. As for the first objection, if we assume that the partners paid a fair price for what the Court characterizes as their "exclusive opportunity," I do not understand why the retention of a 100% interest in assets is any more "on account of" their prior position than retaining a lesser percentage might have been. Surely there is no legal significance to the fact that immediately after the confirmation of the plan "the partners were in the same position that they would have enjoyed had they exercised an exclusive option under the plan to buy the equity in the reorganized entity, or contracted to purchase it from a seller who had first agreed to deal with no one else." Ante, at 19.

As to the second objection, petitioner does not challenge the Bankruptcy Judge's valuation of the property or any of his other findings under § 1129 (other than the plan's compliance with § 1129(b)(2)(B)(ii)). Since there is no remaining question as to value, both the former partners (and the creditors, for that matter) are in the same position that they would have enjoyed if the Bankruptcy Court had held an auction in which this plan had been determined to be the best available. . . .

Accordingly, I respectfully dissent.

Justices Thomas and Scalia seem to want a simple textual solution and they note that nowhere does the Code expressly authorize the new value corollary—but that just leaves them subject to the retort that nowhere does the Code expressly prohibit the new value corollary, so we're back to the problem of what "on account of" means. Problems-to-solve 1, Textualism 0. The real problem, as the majority alludes, is one of valuation—and how valuation indirectly speaks to causation. If new value can break the causation chain and eliminate the affront to absolute priority, how much new value suffices—and how do we find out? For example, if old equity proposed contributing one shiny penny and keeping in exchange 100% ownership of the company under a cramdown plan, nobody would fall for the penny as "purchasing" the post-bankruptcy equity. We'd call it a sham or a peppercorn and say that on account of this insufficient value, old equity isn't purchasing the company—it's keeping its ownership intact through the structure of a sham purchase in flagrant violation of the absolute priority rule.

Because nobody's going to be that flagrant, the real question is whether the same scheme works when the contribution is $1 million. The causation question is inextricably intertwined with the valuation one. Thus, a nominal causation question is really a valuation one. If it's the right value, there's no problem with old equity buying (unless you are as "starchy" as the Solicitor General); if it's under-valued, the creditors are being denied their cramdown protection of absolute priority. To solve this concern of valuation, in an ideal world we'd have a well-attended auction, teeming with fully informed bidders because the best place to test value is in the marketplace. Reality rarely matches such idealism, however, and so often the old equity holders actually are best positioned to gauge the enterprise value of the company. The question is: do we trust them? This seems to be the concern that the Court is trying to police with its non-exclusivity auction requirement. But while this may be sensible as a solution, surely Justice Stevens has a point (which doubtless Justices Thomas and Scalia would support) that such an auction requirement is nowhere in the Code and such clever innovations should be forwarded to Congress. And as Justice Stevens goes on to say, if our concern is about ascertaining the true value of the company, isn't that the sort of factual issue that we leave for the bankruptcy judge in our legal system?

The National Bankruptcy Review Commission proposed to resolve the debate over equity participation in the post-reorganization business with two amendments. The first was to amend § 1129(b)(2)(B)(ii) to make it clear that a junior class could purchase a new interest in the reorganized debtor. The second was to amend § 1121 to provide that if the debtor moved to cram down a plan that provided for the sale of an interest in the business to old equity then exclusivity should be terminated so that any party in interest could propose a competing plan. NBRC Recommendation 2.4.15. The proposal addressed much the same concern expressed in *203 North LaSalle*, but the remedy was fashioned in a different way. The ABI, by contrast, just suggested amending the statute to clarify new value purchases were allowed by old equity provided they are "reasonably proportionate" exchanges as determined by being subjected to a "reasonable market test." Am. Bankr. Inst., American Bankruptcy Institute Commission to Study the

Reform of Chapter 11: 2012-2014 Final Report and Recommendations 224-26 (2014). The statute, however, remains unaltered.

3. *"Valuing" the New Value*

After *203 North LaSalle*, skirmishes continue, as the next case will show. One thing that is off the table, however, is so-called "sweat equity." In In re Ahlers, 485 U.S. 197 (1988), discussed in *203 North LaSalle*, the Court rejected the plea of farmer-debtors trying to save their family farming operation that they would buy the old equity for no money up-front but for their ongoing efforts as labor. Calling the debtor's proposed contribution "intangible, inalienable, and in all likelihood unenforceable," the Court found that "a promise of future services cannot be exchanged in any market for something of value to the creditors today." 485 U.S. at 204. Compare In re Chrysler LLC, 405 B.R. 84, 92 (Bankr. S.D.N.Y. 2009) ("[To acquire its equity stake in New Chrysler,] Fiat will contribute to New Chrysler access to competitive fuel-efficient vehicle platforms, certain technology, distribution capabilities in key growth markets and substantial cost saving opportunities [but not one red cent in cash—Eds.].").

Another parade on which the Court rained was the farmers' argument that because the fair value of the farm was zero due to its hopeless insolvency, they only had to come up with zero in cash to buy that equity for its fair value. The Court noted that there is always some value in the control of an enterprise; more importantly, the possibility that the property will rebound, even in an insolvent enterprise, means that the debtor who keeps it without paying at least something for this upside violates the absolute priority rule. 485 U.S. at 207-08. As the next case reveals, however, this issue is still up for grabs post–*203 North LaSalle*.

========= In re RED MOUNTAIN MACHINERY CO. =========
448 B.R. 1 (Bankr. D. Ariz. 2011)

HAINES, Bankruptcy Judge.
Pending before the Court is confirmation of the Debtor's First Amended Plan of Reorganization. The only objections to confirmation are those filed by the secured creditor Comerica Bank. Comerica objects . . . that the plan does not satisfy the new value corollary to the absolute priority rule with respect to Comerica's deficiency claim.

BACKGROUND FACTS

The Debtor is an Arizona corporation formed in 1986 by Owen and Linda Cowing, who are the Debtor's only shareholders. Although they are no longer married, the Cowings jointly manage the Debtor's business operation in their respective capacities as president and secretary.

The Debtor's business consists of the rental of large earth moving equipment, primarily Caterpillars often referred to as "yellow iron," almost exclusively to licensed contractors. Its equipment is used primarily in four business sectors: commercial building, road building, other infrastructure construction, and residential building. During the height of the housing boom perhaps as much as 30% of Debtor's business was in residential construction, but today it is only about 1%.

The Debtor's business model is to purchase and rent out older, used equipment but to maintain it extremely well according to regular maintenance schedules. In addition, the Debtor has maintenance staff that can respond quickly if a machine breaks down on the job, either to repair it or to substitute replacement equipment. Over the past quarter century the Debtor has built a reputation for reliability and minimal downtime, and because it does not buy or use new equipment it can charge lower rental rates than its principal competitor.

By 2001, the Debtor had expanded its operations both into southern California and southern Nevada, owned more than 300 machines, employed more than 140 people, and produced annual gross revenues in excess of $43 million. As a result of the economic downturn beginning in 2007, however, its annual revenues declined to $10 million for 2008.

Since 2003, the Debtor has been financed by a revolving line of credit with Comerica Bank. By the time the Chapter 11 was filed in August, 2009, the Comerica debt was approximately $33 million. The debt is guaranteed by Owen and Linda Cowing.

In the spring of 2008, the decline in revenues caused non-monetary defaults in the Comerica debt, which led to a series of forbearance agreements and workout negotiations. At about that same time Owen Cowing was diagnosed with leukemia, and therefore turned over primary responsibility for the workout negotiations to the Debtor's then-Chief Financial Officer Darren Dierich. Dierich continually advised that no workout solution could be negotiated with Comerica, and that Comerica insisted that the Debtor wind down its business operations, substantially reduce the amount of equipment it owned, and that it prepare for liquidation.

Although not directly at issue at this confirmation hearing, the Debtor contends that in June, 2009, Owen Cowing discovered that Comerica had published a notice of the UCC sale of the Debtor's business. Subsequently, he discovered secret e-mails between Comerica and his CFO Dierich that revealed a plan for Comerica to sell the Debtor's assets to an entity owned and controlled by Dierich, with the purchase to be financed by Comerica, so that Dierich could take over the Debtor's business for his own benefit. Comerica and Dierich had agreed to keep their plan secret from the Cowings, according to the Debtor.

In June, 2009, the Debtor advised Comerica of its discovery of the secret sale plan and that it might have claims against Comerica as a result. In August, 2009, Comerica advised that it would not approve payment of any weekly expenses, including payroll, that had routinely been paid out of Comerica's revolving line. Because it could not fund payroll or pay trade vendors, the Debtor filed this Chapter 11 petition on August 11, 2009.

The Debtor has filed an adversary proceeding asserting claims against Comerica arising from the secret sale scheme, including equitable subordination and damages for aiding and abetting breaches of fiduciary duty. That adversary proceeding is currently pending before Bankruptcy Judge Case and is not scheduled for trial until 2012. Comerica's primary defense is not to deny the facts as alleged by the Debtor, but to argue that there was no damage to the Debtor because the scheme was discovered before the sale could be concluded. . . .

THE PLAN . . .

Class 10 consists of the equity ownership of Owen and Linda Cowing. The plan provides that their equity ownership shall be extinguished and that on the effective date the Cowings shall contribute the $480,000 cash payable on their administrative claim in exchange for 100% of the equity of the reorganized debtor. A modification filed shortly before the confirmation hearing clarified that this is to be a cash contribution. In addition, there is an exit loan facility in the amount of $1.25 million to be funded by the Cowings. Together with cash on hand, this will be much more than sufficient to pay all administrative claims, including the Cowings', which will enable them to make their cash contribution to the Debtor, and also to fund a capital reserve.

The only rejections of the plan were cast by Comerica, both in Class 2 and Class 7. . . .

NEW VALUE COROLLARY

Finally, Comerica objects that the plan violates the absolute priority rule and its new value corollary that both the Supreme Court and the Ninth Circuit have recognized and defined. . . .

The issue here, therefore, is whether the equity interests that the Cowings will obtain under this plan are "on account of" their former equity ownership, or instead are "on account of" their new value contribution of $480,000. And it is important to recognize that under controlling Ninth Circuit law, this is a purely factual determination, not a legal question. . . .

In *Bonner Mall*, the Ninth Circuit held that "if a proposed plan satisfies all of these [five] requirements, i.e., the new value exception, it will not violate section 1129(b)(2)(B)(ii) of the Code and the absolute priority rule. Such a plan, [we agree], will *not* give old equity property '*on account of*' prior interests, but instead will allow the former owners to participate in the reorganized debtor *on account of* a substantial, necessary, and fair new value contribution." The five requirements are that the new value be "1) new, 2) substantial, 3) money or money's worth, 4) necessary for a successful reorganization and 5) reasonably equivalent to the value or interest received.". . .

Comerica presented no evidence that the contributions required of the old equity holders were either not new or not money or money's worth. At closing argument, Comerica's counsel conceded that the contribution was both new and money or money's worth. . . .

The Disclosure Statement estimates that administrative claims will be approximately $880,00 (inclusive of the Cowings' $480,000 administrative claim). Mr. Gonzales' Declaration, which is in evidence, establishes that the Debtor's cash position as of March 22, 2011 was $522,000. The Code unequivocally requires that administrative expenses be paid in full, in cash, on the effective date of the plan. Because the evidence is undisputed that the Debtor does not otherwise have access to cash to pay the administrative claims in the approximate amount of $880,000, the Court finds that the new value contributions are necessary to the reorganization of the Debtor. Without them, the reorganization could not occur.

Comerica argues in a heading, but provided no evidence in support, that the new value contribution of either $480,000 or $1.2 million is not "sufficient." It . . . is merely described as being too "meager" without any attempt to compare it to the value of the equity interest the Cowings will receive under the plan.

Particularly in the absence of any evidence to the contrary, the Court finds, as a fact, that $480,000 is "substantial." To paraphrase Senator Everett Dirksen, a half million here and there pretty soon adds up to real money. I can take judicial notice that it is more than three times the annual gross salary of a U.S. Bankruptcy Judge. . . . It is more than four times the contribution the Seventh Circuit found insufficient in *Woodbrook,* and almost 22 times larger than the contribution found insufficient in *Snyder.* Second, although the Ninth Circuit expressly declined to hold that the comparison is appropriate, it is approximately 3% of the unsecured debt being discharged, more than six times the percentage that was found insufficient in *Ambanc.*

Finally, the Court finds, as a fact, that the $480,000 effective date cash contribution is more than reasonably equivalent to the value of the equity interests received by the Cowings and, in light of the expiration of exclusivity, satisfies the "top dollar" requirement of *203 North LaSalle.*

[T]he Ninth Circuit noted that the fifth new value requirement— equivalence to the value of the interest received—is the "most conceptually difficult prong of the new value corollary." The conceptual difficulty exists because, from the inception of the absolute priority rule, the Supreme Court has indicated that there may be value being retained by equity interests due to retention of control of an insolvent enterprise, but has never indicated how the amount of that value is to be determined. On a balance sheet analysis, there is no value to the equity interest in a corporation when its debts exceed its assets. Yet in *Boyd,* and reiterated in both *Case* and *Ahlers,* the Supreme Court held the absolute priority rule to be violated if old equity retained its interests "only for purposes of control," even if no dividends were in prospect. So we know there is value to such retained equity interests, and we are required to determine whether that value exceeds the amount of the new value contributions, but the Court has never suggested any legal, accounting or economic analysis or methodology by which that determination could be made.

The answer to this conceptual difficulty may be found in *203 North LaSalle.* . . . Like *Boyd, Case* and *Ahlers, 203 North LaSalle* also focused on the value of control of the debtor and its assets. But unlike those precedents, *203 North LaSalle* for the first time pinpointed exactly where that value is found, and why it is not found in a balance sheet. While declining to define it as constituting "property," the Court found the problematic value to subsist in the plan's "provision for vesting equity in the reorganized business in the Debtor's partners without extending an opportunity to anyone else either to compete for that equity or to propose a competing reorganization plan." The Court made clear that it was the retention in the equity holders of the "exclusive opportunity to propose a plan" that caused a violation of the absolute priority rule. While declining to find it to be a "formal" "express option" right, the Court held that because "no one else could propose an alternative" plan, "the Debtor's partners necessarily enjoyed an exclusive opportunity that was in no economic sense distinguishable from the advantage of the exclusively entitled offeror or option holder."

Thus Justice Souter's analysis in *203 North LaSalle* explains why the Court has always found (in *Boyd*, *Case* and *Ahlers*) a retention of value that violates the absolute priority rule even when that value does not appear on a GAAP-prepared balance sheet—it exists in the option value of the exclusive right to propose a new value plan. It is not surprising that it has taken over a hundred years for the Court to start to identify the basis of that value. Economic analysis of option value is a relatively recent development, both in academia and in the markets, that was certainly not understood when the absolute priority rule was originally adopted or when it was partially codified.

But if the option value of the exclusive right to propose a plan is why the Court has always rejected the "no value" argument in the context of a new value plan, then it also means there is no reason to reject the "no value" analysis when exclusivity has expired and there is no option value to the right to propose a plan. In other words, once exclusivity has expired, the value of the interest being retained should be determined based on either a pro forma balance sheet of the reorganized debtor or a capitalization of the reorganized debtor's projected income.

Neither expert who testified at confirmation attempted to determine an enterprise value of the reorganized debtor based on a present value of its projected income stream. Nor has either expert opined as to an enterprise value based on a multiple of the projected EBITDA, another common method of valuing an operating business based on its projected earnings. Either of those methods is probably sounder than determining value of the new equity interests simply based on a reorganized balance sheet. [Both these methods are discussed in Assignment 30.—Eds.]

[W]hen expert opinion evidence of a discounted cash flow valuation is not available, the balance sheet approach supplies sufficient evidence to satisfy the preponderance of evidence standard applicable to confirmation of a plan, at least when there is no evidence to the contrary.

It is stipulated that Comerica's claim that must be paid under the plan is in excess of $15 million, and that the value of the Debtor's assets is $10 million. Consequently upon the effective date of the plan the reorganized debtor will be insolvent on a balance sheet basis, even considering the new value contribution, whether it be regarded as having a balance sheet value of $480,000 or $1.2 million. Because the reorganized debtor will be balance sheet insolvent, there will be no value to its equity interests. Compared to this zero value for the equity in the reorganized Debtor, the new value contributions substantially exceed that value, whether they be regarded as having a value of either $480,000 or $1.2 million. . . . Therefore the Court finds as a fact that the value of the new value contributions substantially exceeds the value of the equity interests that the Cowings will receive under the plan.

Conclusion

For these reasons, the Court finds and concludes that the First Amended Plan satisfies all of the requirements of § 1129(a) and (b), that the objections of Comerica must be denied, and that the plan must be confirmed. . . .

As Judge Haines's opinion reveals, courts that do allow new value plans are still faced with the difficulty of how to assess that new value when there is no auction. Recall that the Supreme Court did not require an auction in *North LaSalle*; it only held that when there is no auction during the plan's exclusivity period, a plan allowing only old equity to bid on buying the new equity violates the absolute priority rule. The court in *Red Mountain* decided an auction was neither necessary nor warranted. In the absence of valuation evidence on discounted cash flow and EBITDA (terms we will explore in the next assignment), it went with the balance sheet valuation to decide whether the injection of $480,000 was real or a sham. Unsurprisingly for an insolvent corporation, that balance sheet value was zero, which means that the Cowings' purchase price of $480,000 (or $1.2 million) was more than real—it exceeded the equity value by a factor of infinity. Perhaps Judge Haines found corroboration in Comerica's (or anyone's) demurral to bid on the company when anybody could have proposed a rival plan after the exclusivity period lapsed.

Other courts have taken a simpler approach to the valuation question post–*203 North LaSalle*, believing that precedent now compels an auction, period.

> [T]he rationale of *203 North LaSalle* [does not] depend on who proposes the plan [or whether the proposal occurs during exclusivity]. Competition helps prevent the funneling of value from lenders to insiders, no matter who proposes the plan or when. An impaired lender who objects to any plan that leaves insiders holding equity is entitled to the benefit of competition. If, as [the debtors and insiders] insist, their plan offers creditors the best deal, then they will prevail in the auction. But if, as [the lender] believes, the bankruptcy judge has underestimated the value of [debtor's] real estate, wiped out too much of the secured claim, and set the remaining loan's terms at below-market rates, then someone will pay more than $375,000 (perhaps a lot more) for the equity in the reorganized firm.

In re Castleton Plaza, LP, 707 F.3d 821, 824 (7th Cir. 2013) (Easterbrook, C.J.) (remanding case with instructions to "order competitive bidding"), *cert. denied*, 2013 WL 2458345 (U.S. Oct. 7, 2013).

Justice Thomas's predicted fog appears to have thickened some more.

4.   *Coda: Single Asset Real Estate Cases and Cramdown Jurisprudence*

203 North LaSalle was a single asset real estate case ("SARE") bankruptcy, and indeed the Supreme Court noted that all four of the circuit court opinions creating the conflict were also SAREs. This is not surprising. Unlike most reorganizations, SAREs can end up in protracted litigation. To see why, consider that they are dominated by a mortgage lender with a deficiency claim so vast it dominates the other unsecured trade creditors (e.g., the landscaping service for the building). This means the mortgage lender can force a no vote on its deficiency claim, either as a dominant unsecured vote in a general class of unsecured creditors or in its own class. Either way, the debtor ends up in the cramdown world. Consensual plans are less frequent in this context because the dominant lender just wants to get paid and has no interest in an ongoing relationship with the debtor, the way a supplier might want to keep an operating business alive (think of John Paul Smith and his farmers). Consequently, SAREs skew cramdown jurisprudence—and indeed all bankruptcy jurisprudence—by settling less frequently through consensus. According to the data collected for the Business Bankruptcy Project, in the mid-1990s, SARE cases comprised about 7% of all business bankruptcies. Calculated from Financial Characteristics at 521, table 1; 543, table 10.

Because of this pattern, appellate courts view bankruptcy as a domain in which auctions can be run as efficiently as in the real estate context and where equity should be viewed suspiciously as trying to extract value. On the other hand, SAREs involve what are functionally two-party disputes, in which case the need for an automatic stay to resolve collective action creditor problems seems attenuated and delaying a lender from its right to foreclose at state law upon default is questionable as a policy matter. (For all these reasons, real estate cases used to have their own chapter, Chapter XII of the 1898 Bankruptcy Act.) In BAPCPA, Congress tried to address some of these concerns by speeding up SAREs—plans must be filed in 30 days, mortgagees can more easily lift the stay, and lenders can get their contract interest rate while waiting. § 362(d)(3). Sections 101(51B) and 362(d)(3) effectively mean that only SARE cases with substantial cash flow can survive in bankruptcy for more than a short time. Somewhat paradoxically, however, the case law built upon SARE considerations, like *203 North LaSalle*, remains good and governing law even in non-SARE cases.

D.   CRAMDOWN UNDER THE SBRA

We have called cramdown "confirmation without consent," but that is both overstatement and understatement. It is overstatement because at least one impaired class must consent as a prerequisite to cramdown, § 1129(a)(10), but it is understatement because lack of consent abounds already—many creditors may dissent but get outvoted within their respective class, §§ 1126(c), 1129(a)(8). The SBRA dispenses with the one-impaired-class rule, § 1191(b), and thus may literally permit cramdown where no single creditor consents. Furthermore, unlike the absolute priority rule, which wipes out the business owner's equity if a consensual plan cannot be reached, the SBRA abolishes the previously sacred absolute priority rule and allows the equity owners to hold on to ownership of the business in cramdown in exchange for committing to contribute projected disposable income (of the business or of the individual, depending on the enterprise organization) over the duration of the plan. §§ 1181(a), 1191(c). In the case of a corporate debtor, that means its profits; for an individual debtor, it means net income after "reasonable and necessary" expenses.

If that sounds familiar, it should, because it is what is required under most chapter 13 plans to cram down over unsecured creditor objection. But note the differences here. First, it does not matter whether the business owner's income is below, above, or exactly on the median income. There is no means test statutory budget, just the old-fashioned "weak" test (§ 1325(b)(2) of reasonable and necessary (read: "what works for the judge")). Second, the plan length can be up to five years (§ 1192(c)(2)), but can also be shorter; there is no minimum five-year "applicable commitment period" forced upon some filers as there is in chapter 13. Third, the debtor can be a corporation, an entity that would be allowed nowhere near chapter 13. Congress is really trying hard to allow smaller business debtors to hold onto their life's work, even if creditors object.

It is difficult to overstate how dramatic we think this change is to chapter 11 (and perhaps to chapter 13 as well). All the handwringing of *203 North LaSalle* has been swept by the wayside as equity holds on, over creditor protest, with no new contribution of money or money's worth. Perhaps the best way to think about it is that the SBRA overrules *Ahlers* for many businesses and says that even if an impaired class objects, the debtor *can* buy the equity of the business through "sweat" alone and no cash—and that sweat will be measured by projected disposable income over a three-to-five-year period under the plan. To combat against overuse of cramdown, Congress adds some carrots for debtors who can get the creditor classes to accept a consensual plan: discharge comes upon plan confirmation (not completion), § 1181(c), and the debtor (not the trustee) oversees creditor disbursements, §§ 1183(c), 1194(b). The "trustee lite" will also help "facilitate" a consensual plan. § 1183(b)(7). It remains anyone's guess how these will play out in the years to come.

Problem Set 29

29.1. You are still counsel to Pany Chemicals in the Chapter 11 proceeding of Country Smokes, Inc. (see Problem Sets 27-28). Somewhat ironically, in under two weeks after your motion to reject the disclosure statement was granted on account of the overstatement of the backlogs, Country just got a big contract with a corporation that owns a number of theme parks around the country, improving Country's prospects dramatically. As a result, Country has amended its disclosure document, which now looks even better because of the big contract. It is proposing the same plan as before, the bank to be paid in full, with interest, and the unsecureds to get 70 cents on the dollar.

Talbert remains furious with Country and with Sam Pickens, its president, and is determined to defeat the plan. Although Talbert's objection to the plan — that Country can now afford to pay more than 70% on unsecured claims — is a plausible one, his reaction is also emotional, because of the "sandbagging" preference action. Talbert believes that enough other unsecured creditors now agree with him that the plan can be defeated.

He wants to know if the plan could be confirmed even over the protest of a majority of the unsecureds. Although you continue to urge Talbert to let you use his electoral leverage to negotiate a better deal, he insists on knowing if "this cramdown stuff" will work against him here. What is the answer, as things stand now? If the bank agreed to less than full payment, might the analysis change? What position might Country take with the unsecureds who are threatening to vote against the plan? What leverage does Pany have? What deal might you propose to the bank and Country on behalf of Pany based on that leverage?

29.2. Angie Littwin has built Basset Babies, Inc. (BB), an online retailer specializing in basset hound–themed clothing, toys, and knickknacks, into a thriving business with $4 million annual revenues (and $500,000 in annual profit after expenses). But when a scandal erupted over Linus, her prize-winning hound and the model for the signature trademark on all her merchandise, business took a nosedive. A losing competitor in the Westminster finals sued Linus's legal owner, Basset Babies, Inc., alleging that Linus had had cosmetic surgery in violation of Westminster rules and that his lineage papers were forged. Angie absolutely did not fiddle with Linus's beautiful snout, nor are his papers phony, but the wealthy woman who is suing is suffering from bruised pride and is unwilling to let go of the litigation. As the lawsuit has dragged on, Angie has fallen behind on all BB payments. When Angie comes to see you, BB has about $2.7 million in commercial debts. Angie is fairly certain BB can win the pending suit eventually, but legal fees are mounting, and she really needs to launch a public relations blitz to win back clients right away. DogStar, Inc., the PR firm BB uses, will bill BB after the PR campaign is complete, so BB's current financial situation is not necessarily hopeless. What can she do in chapter 11, both with and without her tort suitor's support?

CRAMMING DOWN SECURED CREDITORS

If a secured creditor refuses to consent to the plan, the debtor can turn to § 1129(b)(2)(A) to confirm the plan. The cramdown rule for a secured party seems simple. It is the same standard as in chapter 13: the secured creditor must receive the amount of its allowed secured claim (namely, the amount of the debt or the value of its collateral, whichever is less) at its present value (i.e., with interest). Yet in reality the two variables—value and interest rate—may be as immeasurable as beauty and truth. Trials feature battles of experts along each axis. Big money is at stake, and big theory, so buckle up not just to learn the Code but for a crash introduction to corporate and real estate finance.

A. VALUATION OF CLAIMS AND COMPANIES

As one of us has written:

> In practice, no problem in bankruptcy is more vexing than the problem of valuation. Volumes have been written on it, literally thousands of cases each year involve disputes about it, and virtually every aspect of the bankruptcy system turns on it. Nonetheless, there is little conceptual guidance for valuing most assets, beyond some general sense of liquidation values and going-concern values. Both parties and courts try to scrape together a coherent picture of the business with a variety of numbers and an overriding sense of skepticism about the accuracy of any valuation estimates.

Elizabeth Warren, A Theory of Absolute Priority, 1991 Ann. Survey Am. L. 9, 13.

The central problem with valuing the secured creditor's collateral in cramdown is that there is no sale to test value on the open market. The Supreme Court held in Associates Commercial Corp. v. Rash, 520 U.S. 953 (1997) (see Assignment 10) that in a reorganization, where the debtor keeps the property over creditor protest, the proper valuation standard is *replacement* value, not *liquidation* value, a rule that Congress tried to codify for consumer cases in § 506(a)(2). Putting policy to one side, that simple instruction may work great for an old truck (the collateral in *Rash*), but less well for a hotel. (How much did your last hotel cost you to replace when you lost it?) But bankruptcy judges face these issues every day. They do their best, borrowing methodologies from the world of corporate finance and dissecting the expert valuation opinions with which they are bombarded.

<hr>

In re BUENA VISTA OCEANSIDE, LLC
479 B.R. 342 (Bankr. W.D. Pa. 2012)

FITZGERALD, Bankruptcy Judge.

INTRODUCTION

The matter before this court is a Motion for Valuation of Secured Claim and Avoidance of Lien filed by Buena Vista Oceanside, LLC (hereafter "Debtor"). On April 9th and 10th of 2012, a trial was held to hear evidence regarding the value of the Buena Vista Hotel and the Courtyard Villa Hotel (hereafter "Properties"). The Properties are owned by the Debtor and are operated as two small hotels located in Lauderdale-By-The-Sea, on El Mar Drive, Fort Lauderdale, Florida. Optimum Bank, the creditor in this matter, (hereafter "Optimum") has a first priority mortgage lien on the Properties.

FACTS

Debtor is a limited liability company that owns and operates the Properties. The first of the two Properties, the Buena Vista, consists of fourteen units and is located across the street from the beach. The second, the Courtyard Villa, consists of eight units and is situated on the beach front.

On or about November 30, 2005, Optimum made a loan to the Debtor in the amount of $4,368,000 evidenced by a Promissory Note executed by Debtor in favor of Optimum.

. . .

On September 1, 2011, Optimum filed a Proof of Claim in the amount of $4,977,984.70, which was docketed as Proof of Claim #1. On October 5, 2011, the Debtor filed a Motion for Valuation of Secured Claim and Avoidance of Lien.

. . .

To prepare for the April 2012 Valuation Hearing, the parties hired professional appraisers. Debtor retained Jesse Vance (hereafter "Vance") who rendered an opinion on the market value of the Buena Vista as $770,000. Debtor also used the opinion of Ronald Ames (hereafter "Ames") who rendered separate opinions on the market value of the Buena Vista as $750,000 and the Courtyard Villa as $805,000. Optimum retained Lawrence Pendleton (hereafter "Pendleton") who rendered an opinion on the value of the Buena Vista as $1,950,000 and the Courtyard Villa as $1,425,000. Based on these appraisals, the Debtor asserts that the collective value of the Properties is $1,690,000, and Optimum asserts that the value is $3,375,000.

The experts submitted their reports prior to the trial and all three experts testified at trial regarding their opinions. The three experts are all MAI-certified appraisers. . . .

All three appraisers utilized two methods to value the properties: the Sales Comparison Approach and the Income Capitalization Approach. They agreed that the Cost Approach was not appropriate for this case. This court concludes that the most reliable method for this particular property is the Income Capitalization Approach and will rely on that method in determining the value of the properties.

WEIGHT OF THE TESTIMONY

"[A] bankruptcy court is not bound by valuation opinions or reports submitted by appraisers, and may form its own opinion as to the value of property in bankruptcy proceedings." In re 210 Ludlow Street Corp., 455 B.R. 443, 447 (Bankr. W.D. Pa. 2011). . . .

While the court sees minor flaws impacting the reliability of each appraiser's opinion, none is so severe that we find it necessary to reject any of the three opinions in toto. We have considered all of the evidence, evaluated each appraiser's numbers and examined each appraiser's rationale, including responses to questions posed by the parties regarding validity. Although we do not rely on any one appraiser exclusively, we find that certain aspects of the appraisers' opinions are more reliable than others. Thus, the court will utilize the Income Capitalization Approach as discussed by the experts and select the numbers and rates which best estimate fair market value in a "piecemeal" manner. . . .

DEFERRED MAINTENANCE

Before coming to a conclusion on the value of the Properties we will discuss the role of deferred maintenance in the valuation process. Deferred maintenance has been described by the witnesses as work that should have been completed on particular property, but was not, and must be completed in order to get that property back into good condition. The costs of such maintenance should be deducted from the value of the property to which it applies. . . .

INCOME CAPITALIZATION APPROACH

As mentioned above, the court will rely on the Income Capitalization Approach in determining the value of the properties. Generally, with this approach "an investor looks at a proposed one-year income and applies a capitalization rate to it." Trial Tr., 178:24-179:2, (Apr. 9, 2012), ECF No. 233.

The first step of this method is to project the Potential Gross Income (hereafter "PGI") to determine what the total potential income for each property would be at full occupancy. This number is determined by selecting an Average Daily Rate (hereafter "ADR") attainable by the hotel. The process involves analyzing the rental rates of the property concerned, as well as the rates of the most similar properties available in the subject market.

Once the PGI at 100% occupancy is determined a realistic occupancy rate must be selected. This rate is derived by reviewing the rates in the market and the subject's actual vacancies.

After the selected occupancy rate is applied to the PGI, the Net Operating Income (hereafter "NOI") is established by deducting operating expenses.

. . .

[As the experts surely explained, one way to value the equity ownership of a cash-producing asset like a hotel—especially if there is no simple Zillow on hotels to consult—starts by conceiving the asset as something that spit out money every year. A *capitalization rate* can then be calculated by dividing that annual cash generation—Net Operating Income—by the asset's value, which is expressed as a percentage and functions analogously to a return on investment rate. By corollary, when you don't know the value of the income-generating asset, you can take its NOI and divide it by the cap rate. How do you find its cap rate? Look at similar-return assets (e.g., comparable hotels of comparable riskiness) and borrow their rate of return, which is why you need to hire expert witnesses.—Eds.]

The NOI is then divided by the selected Capitalization Rate. This is the "process of converting income into value." Ames Appraisal 2011, Ex. 16, at 68. . . . "The higher the risk the higher the rate you would use." Trial Tr., 37:20-21, (Apr. 10, 2012), ECF No. 235. Capitalization Rate data can be derived from national survey data and from local sales data, when available.

. . .

This basic formula was applied by each of the appraisers, with slight variations, addressed below. We have utilized this formula in determining the final value of the Properties.

Buena Vista Hotel

The court finds that the most difficult part of the valuation process (and the biggest discrepancy between the parties) is the determination of the ADR. However, based upon the evidence, the court finds that a fair and accurate PGI can be established by utilizing the ADR chosen by Optimum Bank's appraiser, Pendleton, and making a slight adjustment. Pendleton's ADR is based on average room rate data gathered by researching competitive lodging facilities in the market area. He discovered that the Buena Vista's rates were generally higher than the lowest rates offered at comparable lodging facilities and selected a more reasonable figure. He utilized a different rate for in season and off season rentals and determined that in season the ADR should be $179 and off season it should be $99. Although Pendleton's analysis is rational, the rates he selected are "rack rates." Ames' report, which we credit on this point, explained that in order to determine the ADR of a comparable property based on the comparable's "rack rates" the rate should be reduced by 10% to 20%, as that reflects the actual rents received. We will therefore deduct 15% from the rates selected by Pendleton in order to more accurately project the rates achievable by the Buena Vista. After deducting 15% from the ADR, at 100% occupancy, the PGI for the Buena Vista is $568,046.50.

We must next determine the appropriate occupancy rate for the Buena Vista. Pendleton's research showed that in 2010 the average occupancy in the Broward County Lodging Segment, where the Properties are located, grew to 70.9% from 62.9% the year before. Based on these numbers, he chose to use a 65% occupancy rate. Ames also looked to Broward County for a determination of the occupancy rate. According to Ames' research, from October 2008 through March 2011 the occupancy rates in Broward County were roughly between 63% and 68% as annual averages. Ames selected a rate below the averages his own research disclosed and chose to use a 60% occupancy rate.

Unlike the approach used by Pendleton and Ames, Vance utilized the actual occupancy at the Buena Vista, 30.84%, as well as the actual ADR. However, over the past few years it has been difficult to reasonably calculate the occupancy at the Buena Vista because it has been closed for several months during the off-season. We therefore accept the approach used by Ames and Pendleton which is based on market data. We accept the occupancy rate of 65% as chosen by Pendleton to be most credible and reasonable as it falls in the range of occupancy rates determined by both Pendleton's and Ames' research. Using our selected ADR and 65% occupancy rate, the projected room revenue is $369,230.23.

Pendleton increased the projected revenue by adding a category of "Other Revenues," which he describes as "a small amount of telephone revenue and other miscellaneous revenues." Pendleton Appraisal 2011, Ex. 19, at 45. However, the testimony does not support income from these items. Such revenues are too speculative and inconsistent to be added to the projected income at the Buena Vista. Thus, only room revenues will be included as income in our valuation.

The next step in the process is to determine the amount of operating expenses which must be deducted from projected revenue.

. . .

In determining the operating expenses, we have considered market data and reviewed the expense to income ratio for comparable properties as explained by the appraisers. However, we also considered the fact that the Buena Vista has unutilized space which results in a higher expense to room revenue ratio. Thus, the court determines that 60% of the gross income should be deducted as operating expenses. The 60% we have chosen is close to the high end of Pendleton's research (58%) and matches the most similar of Vance's comparables. This is a deduction of $221,538.14 and establishes the NOI at $147,692.09.

Finally, we address capitalization. The estimated NOI is capitalized by dividing it by an appropriate Capitalization Rate. According to Ames, who considered national and market trends, a Capitalization Rate between 10% and 12% is an optimistic, but not unrealistic, expectation. Ames chose to be highly optimistic using 10%. Pendleton also contends that most Capitalization Rates in the South Florida Hospitality market range from

10% to 12% and he selected a rate of 11%, which this court adopts. We find that a 10% rate is too optimistic for this property, recognizing that the property has excess space, is not beach front and does not have a swimming pool. Vance selected a 6% Capitalization Rate, which differs greatly from those selected by Ames and Pendleton. His rate is based on five comparable sales, not national and local market trends. We believe that a rate of 6% for this property is too low and, if applied to the numbers selected by this court, the value of the Buena Vista would be unrealistic.

Applying the 11% Capitalization Rate, the estimated subject value is $1,342,655.36 [$147,692.09/0.11—Eds.] and, as explained above, we will deduct $125,000 from the value for deferred maintenance. The final value of the Buena Vista is $1,217,655.36.

. . .

[The Court went through the same sort of analysis for the second property, Courtyard Villa.—Eds.]

Conclusion

Debtor asserts that the value of the Properties is $1,690,000 and Optimum asserts that the value is $3,375,000. This court finds that the value of the Properties lies somewhere between these two numbers. After reviewing the appraisal reports submitted by the experts, the testimony of the witnesses at trial and the deposition testimony of Zimmer we determine that the combined value of the Properties is $2,238,182.63. Thus, Optimum Bank has a secured claim in the amount of $2,238,182.63 and an unsecured claim in the amount of $2,739,802.07.

———

While the court looks to the future in *Buena Vista*, other courts have made clear that at least formally valuation is about the present. In re Heritage Highgate, Inc., 679 F.3d 132 (3d Cir. 2012), holds that a budget in a plan is "simply a set of projections" to demonstrate feasibility, not a substitute for a rigorous fair market valuation. It rejected a "wait and see what the future holds" approach in favor of replacement value of the cost the debtor would incur to obtain similar assets. *Heritage Highgate* also emphasizes the burden of proof matters in valuation, and that it rests on the party challenging valuation.

Maybe our favorite real estate valuation case is In re Mirada Del Lago, LLC, 2013 WL 2318411 (Bankr. D.N.M. May 28, 2013), where the value of real estate in the thinly populated county had dropped 70% in the Great Recession. The battling appraisers made wildly different estimates of the half-completed development subject to the secured creditor's mortgage, but the big difference between them was their "estimates" of the number of jobs that would be brought to the county by several "potential" startups, including "Spaceport America." The court then weighted the two appraisals, counting one-third for the optimistic one and two-thirds for the pessimistic one, and cited Denmark's Nobel Prize–winning quantum physicist Neils Bohr: "Prediction is very difficult, especially concerning the future." (And we thought that was Yogi Berra.)

Every expert agrees that the best approaches for real estate cases differ from the best ones to use for other sorts of companies. So what is the best appraisal practice for a huge, multinational industrial company whose batteries are running low? The next case shows us. It is deeply technical, so we try to pave the way with an extra dose of intra-case commentary.

In re EXIDE TECHNOLOGIES

303 B.R. 48 (Bankr. D. Del. 2003)

CAREY, Bankruptcy Judge.

The Debtor asks that this Court confirm its Fourth Amended Joint Plan of Reorganization Under Chapter 11 of the Bankruptcy Code (the "Plan"). Objections to the Plan have been filed by various parties, including, the Official Committee of Unsecured Creditors. . . .

BACKGROUND

. . .

2. Summary of the Debtor's Business

The Debtor manufactures and supplies lead acid batteries for transportation and industrial applications worldwide, with operations in Europe, North America and Asia. The Debtor's operations outside the United States are not included in the chapter 11 proceedings. The Debtor's transportation segment represented approximately 63% of its business in fiscal year 2003. Transportation batteries include starting, lighting and ignition batteries for cars, trucks, off-road vehicles, agricultural and construction vehicles, motorcycles, recreational vehicles, boats, and other applications. In North America, Exide is the second largest manufacturer of transportation batteries. . . .

On September 29, 2000, the Debtor acquired GNB Technologies, Inc. ("GNB"), a U.S. and Pacific Rim manufacturer of both industrial and transportation batteries, from Pacific Dunlop Limited.

4. The Creditors Committee's Adversary Proceeding

. . . After conducting its own investigation and analysis, the Creditors Committee took the position that the estate had significant causes of action against the Prepetition Lenders and, on January 16, 2003, the Creditors Committee commenced a suit against the Prepetition Lenders. . . . The Adversary Proceeding alleges that, in financing the Debtor's purchase of GNB in 2000, the Prepetition Lenders were able to obtain significant control over the Debtor, enabling the Prepetition Lenders to force the Debtor to provide them with additional collateral ["feeding their lien"—Eds.] and to control the Debtor's bankruptcy filing. [Additionally, the Creditors Committee alleged that the Debtor was in cahoots with, or at least beholden to, the Prepetition Lenders on account of this power dynamic and thus proposed a plan that gave everything to the Prepetition Lenders and peanuts to the general unsecured creditors, on the assertion that the company just wasn't worth that much so there was not a lot left over for the lower orders. — Eds.]

. . .

The Voting Report clearly shows that Class P3 (Prepetition Credit Facility Claims) voted overwhelmingly in favor of the Plan, while Class P4 (General Unsecured Claims) voted overwhelmingly against the Plan (regardless of how General Unsecured Claims are grouped).

DISCUSSION

. . .

Because the parties' competing views of Exide's enterprise value permeate all of these issues, I first consider valuation.

2. The Debtor's Enterprise Valuation

The Debtor and the Creditors Committee each offered their own expert to testify about the Debtor's enterprise value. The Debtor presented the expert testimony and valuation analysis of Arthur B. Newman ("Newman"), a senior managing director and founding partner of the Restructuring and Reorganization Group of The Blackstone Group, L.P. ("Blackstone"), who has over 38 years of experience in the merger and acquisitions market for restructuring companies. The Creditors Committee presented the expert testimony and analysis of William Q. Derrough ("Derrough"), a managing director and co-head of the Recapitalization and Restructuring Group of Jefferies & Company, Inc. ("Jefferies"), who also was qualified as an expert based upon his experience in numerous restructuring, financings, and merger and acquisition transactions.

Both experts used the same three methods to determine the Debtor's value: (i) comparable company analysis; (ii) comparable transaction analysis; and (iii) discounted cash flow. However, the end results of their valuations were far from similar. Newman, the Debtor's expert, set the Debtor's value in a range between $950 million and $1.050 billion, while Derrough, the Creditors Committee's expert, set the value in a range between $1.478 billion and $1.711 billion. [Surprise, surprise. — Eds.][23] It becomes necessary, therefore, to delve deeper in the parties' respective approaches to valuation, so that the court may make its own determination.

The Debtor argues that its expert used a "market-based approach" to valuation that determines value on a going concern basis by analyzing the

---

[23] The parties also disagree about the "hurdle" amount, i.e., the amount that the Debtor must be worth to enable it to pay all secured, administrative and priority claims and have some value left to distribute to the unsecured creditors. The Creditors Committee used a hurdle amount of $1.190 billion based upon Exhibit C to the Debtor's Disclosure Statement See Ex. C-152, Expert Valuation Report by Jefferies & Company, Inc. (the "Derrough Report"), p. 13. At the confirmation hearing, the Debtor argued that its expert had "updated" the hurdle amount and set it at $1.285 billion.

price that could be realized for a debtor's assets in a realistic framework, assuming a willing seller and a willing buyer. The Debtor claims that Newman's application of the valuation methods in this case "reflects the manner in which he believes real world purchasers will view the Company." The Debtor also argues that Newman's value is confirmed by the "private equity process" conducted by the Debtor during the chapter 11 case, during which offers were solicited from potential purchasers, including private equity firms and one strategic buyer. The Debtor claims that the process fixed the total enterprise value of the Debtor in a range of $782 million and $950 million. *See* The Newman Report, pp. 6, 17-18.[24]

The Creditors Committee, on the other hand, argues that the most accurate way to determine the enterprise value of a debtor corporation is by the straightforward application of the three standard valuation methodologies. To support its position, the Creditors Committee presented expert testimony of Professor Edith Hotchkiss ("Hotchkiss"), a professor of finance at Boston College who, in addition to teaching the topic of how to value companies, has performed research and written articles specifically related to valuation of companies in bankruptcy. Hotchkiss agreed with the Creditors Committee's argument in favor of objective application of the valuation methods. . . . Hotchkiss noted that, in this case, the input information chosen by the experts was not significantly different; what caused the variance was that Newman made a subjective determination to reduce further the multiples determined from the input information prior to applying the valuation formula.

The Creditors Committee argues, too, that Hotchkiss' research also supports its argument that the Debtor has undervalued the company. In her research, Hotchkiss compared the value of chapter 11 debtor companies prior to confirmation, which she determined by applying the valuation methods to the cash flows in the Debtor's disclosure statements, to the market price of the debtor companies after exiting chapter 11. Her research showed that, in some cases, the debtors' disclosure statement cash flows were significantly overvaluing or undervaluing the debtors and, from those findings, she extrapolated certain factors that tended to predict when debtors were being overvalued or undervalued. She noted that plans providing management and/or senior creditors with the majority of stock or options in the reorganized company (as in the Debtor's Plan) is a strong indicator that the company is being undervalued, resulting in a windfall for management and the senior creditors.

. . . The Creditors Committee argues that the Debtor's expert has undervalued the company. . . . The Debtor, on the other hand, argues that the Creditors Committee's expert has overvalued the company. . . . The

---

[24] The "private equity process" was conducted by Newman's employer, Blackstone, for the purpose of raising $2 to $3 million in cash in exchange for some percentage investment in the reorganized Exide. (Tr. 10/22/03, p. 212). Blackstone approached approximately 75 equity firms. . . . Blackstone informed the participating parties the Debtor was unlikely to consider seriously offers in which the enterprise value of the Debtor was considered to be under $900 million. However, the enterprise value was set by the highest second round bid at approximately $950 million. . . . A subsequent round of telephone calls to the lower bidders did not generate any interest in continuing the process to attempt to increase the bids. . . .

following is a detailed review of the competing experts' valuation reports, keeping in mind each side's incentive to either overvalue or undervalue the Debtor.

A. Comparable Company Analysis

The key components of a comparable company analysis are the Debtor's EBITDA (i.e., earnings before interest, taxes, depreciation and amortization) and the selection of an appropriate multiple to apply to the EBITDA to arrive at enterprise value. ["Multiple" is what the market thinks companies are worth as a function of their EBITDA. Just as hotels can be valued as a function of the income they generate annually, so too can battery companies. The private equity whizzes prefer to multiply by a positive number than divide by a percentage (as one does with cap rate), but the premise is the same. The "market" for a publicly traded stock is, unsurprisingly, the stock market. "It" values the equity ownership of a company, by definition, as the price investors are currently willing to pay for shares of that ownership. Thus, the market capitalization ("market cap") of a public company is the price per share multiplied by the number of shares outstanding. If ABC Corp. has a million shares outstanding trading at $10 per share, the market thinks that company is worth $10 million. That may be crude, but it's a great quick-and-dirty, and refinements like "enterprise value" can be used to back out cash and debt, but we will leave that for the Corporate Finance course. Accordingly, analysts can look at how the market values a company in relation to its EBITDA, i.e., does its market cap trade at 5 *times* its EBITDA (a respectable multiple) or is the market frothy so the analysts capitalize the company at 12 *times* its EBITDA (the hottest new tech stock)? If one has a moribund company, like de-listed Exide, one can reverse-engineer a multiple by looking at the multiple of comparable peers.—Eds.] The appropriate multiple is determined by comparing the enterprise value of comparable publicly traded companies to their trailing twelve months EBITDA.[27] A subjective assessment is required to select the comparable companies and, here, the parties argue about which comparable companies are more appropriate to use.

However, as pointed out by the Creditors Committee, regardless of the comparables used, both experts arrived at similar EBITDA multiples, with Newman at 7.2x and Derrough at 7.7x. However, Newman then reduced his multiple to a range between 5.0x and 6.0x, because he determined that his comparable for the Debtor's industrial division (C & D Technologies) should be given less weight. The Debtor also argues that Newman's reduced multiple is more in line with the implied EBITDA multiples that can be derived from the Debtor's private equity process.

. . .

The experts significantly differed on their choice of the data to use for the Debtor's EBITDAR.[28]

. . .

---

[27] Exide is held publicly, but was delisted by the New York Stock Exchange sometime around February 2002.

[28] For the Debtor, EBITDAR is used to add "restructuring charges" to the metric.

In determining the Debtor's value for purposes of deciding whether the Debtor's Plan is fair and equitable, it is appropriate to include the benefit of the Debtor's restructuring. Part of the purpose of this exercise is to determine whether the Debtor's intent to give common stock to the Prepetition Lenders results in paying the Prepetition Lender more than 100% of the value of their claims [which would violate, inter alia, the best interests test—Eds.]. This requires a forwardlooking valuation and I conclude that it is appropriate to use projected, rather than historic, EBITDAR. Because the Debtor has revised its projections, the most appropriate EBITDAR to use would be for the trailing twelve months ending December 31, 2003 as set forth in the October 2003 business plan ($188.2 million). [Note this opinion's publication date of October 2003, which means these are projections of future earnings.—Eds.]

Based on the foregoing comparable company analyses, Newman determined that the Debtor's enterprise value was a range between $897 million to $1.076 billion, while Derrough determined that the Debtor's enterprise value was $1.515 billion. However, because I find that it is appropriate to calculate value based upon the EBITDAR for the trailing twelve months ending December 31, 2003 ($188.2 million), and the appropriate multiple is between 7.2x (the multiple calculated by Newman before subjectively reducing it) and 7.7x (Derrough's multiple), the comparable company value should be in the range between $1.355 billion (using 7.2x) [well over Newman] and $1.449 billion (using 7.7x) [below, but near, Derrough].

B. Comparable Transaction Analysis

The comparable transaction analysis is similar to the comparable company analysis in that an EBITDA multiple is determined from recent merger and acquisition transactions in the automotive and industrial battery industries and that multiple is then applied to the appropriate trailing twelve months of the Debtor. . . .

C. Discounted Cash Flow ["DCF"]

The experts' valuations based on a discounted cash flow analysis differed greatly, with Newman calculating value in a range between $1.023 and $1.254 billion and Derrough calculating value in a range between $1.583 and 1.837 billion. Derrough applied the discounted cash flow analysis in a straightforward manner (see Tr. 10/25/03, pp. 135-36 (Hotchkiss)), while Newman adjusted his formula based upon his "market-based approach" to valuation to account for the manner in which he believed prospective purchasers would view the Debtor.

. . . DCF is calculated by adding together (i) the present value of the company's projected distributable cash flows (i.e., cash flows available to all investors) during the forecast period, and (ii) the present value of the company's terminal value (i.e., value of the firm at the end of the forecast period). In this case, the experts relied on the Debtor's projected cash flows for the fiscal years ending March 31, 2004 through March 31, 2008, as set forth in the Debtor's five-year business plans. The DCF factors which the parties dispute are (1) the discount rate; and (2) the multiple used to calculate terminal value. [The discount rate thus serves the same function as the cap rate in the income capitalization valuation from *Buena Vista Oceanside.*—Eds.]

Newman used a discount rate in the range of 15% to 17%, while Derrough used a discount rate in the range of 10.5% and 11.5%. Both experts relied on a weighted average cost of capital (the "WACC") to determine the discount rate, which is based upon a combined rate of the cost of debt capital and the cost of equity capital [i.e., the (prorated) combined cost of debt, which can be found from the company's loan documents and bond indentures, and its "cost" of equity—the price it must pay to bribe its stockholders not to sell off their shares—which is much harder to estimate and so requires even more assumptions and calculations. Read on!—Eds.]. In determining the cost of equity, Derrough used the generally accepted method known as the capital asset pricing model or "CAPM." [This widely accepted model determines the expected return of a stock, i.e., what the shareholders expect to earn for their shares through dividends or appreciation to prevent them from dumping the investment. It estimates that expected return by starting with the risk-free rate of return (such as U.S. treasury notes, say 2%) and adding to it the risk-adjusted return for the particular stock, which itself is calculated in reference to a risk measure called the stock's *beta.* The higher the *beta* (which measures volatility and covariance with the general stock market's variance), the greater the risk that requires an upward adjustment to determine how much more than average the company will have to pay to raise capital as calculated by CAPM. A company that generates annual free cash flow at a lower cost of capital is valued higher than a company with higher capital costs that generates that same cash flow.—Eds.]*

Newman, however, chose not to use CAPM [to calculate WACC] because he noted that CAPM can be inaccurate when applied to company that is not publicly traded. [Although] in such cases, comparable companies are used to determine the "beta" for a CAPM valuation, . . . Newman felt that comparable companies are inappropriate in this instance because the Debtor is emerging from chapter 11 and will face substantial risk in executing its five-year projected business plan.

Therefore, Newman determined cost of equity based upon information showing the rate of return on equity that a prospective purchaser would demand. Based upon the private equity process . . . Newman used a cost of equity between 20% and 30%; while the standard CAPM method employed by Derrough resulted in a cost of equity between 13.6% and 14.6%.

---

*This is beyond the scope of this course, but for those interested in corporate finance, *beta* is a co-efficient, either below 1.0 if the stock varies less than the stock market average, or greater than 1.0 if it varies more than the market. The stock market, *en masse*, has a *beta* of exactly 1.0 (by definition). *Beta* can also be negative if the stock moves contra-cyclically in inverse relation to the market. It is calculated as a ratio of comparative variance: the *individual stock's* rate of return less the risk-free rate of return divided by the *overall stock market's rate of return* less the risk-free rate of return. *Beta* is used in the CAPM as follows: a company's cost of equity is found by (1) calculating the difference between the overall stock market's rate of return and the risk-free rate of return, (2) multiplying that difference by the company's *beta*, and then (3) adding that "risk premium" to the risk-free rate of return.

Furthermore, in calculating WACC, Newman determined the cost of debt at 7.5%, while Derrough's calculation resulted in a cost of debt at 5.9%. The Debtor's own five-year plan assumes a cost of debt at 6.2%.

Discounted cash flow analysis has been used to determine valuation in many chapter 11 cases. Newman's numerous subjective adjustments to the analysis stray too far from the generally accepted method of determining the discount rate. Therefore, I will rely on Derrough's more straightforward determination of the discount rate.

Newman determined the terminal value in his discounted cash flow analysis by using the same adjusted EBITDA multiple as used in his comparable company analysis (i.e., 5.0x to 6.0x). Derrough, however, used the actual multiple which he derived from his comparable company analysis. Again, Newman's terminal value multiple was adjusted, causing his calculation to depart from the standard discounted cash flow methodology.

The Debtor argues that in the final determination of enterprise value, Derrough accorded too much weight to his DCF analysis. Derrough elected to attribute 60% of his total valuation to his DCF analysis. The Debtor argues that a DCF analysis is dependent on a company's ability to meet long-range projections, in this case the Debtor's FY 2008 projections. Because the long-range projections are the most speculative and uncertain, and because testimony of the Debtor's officers showed that the Debtor's past and current performance has not met the projections in its business plans, the Debtor argues that Derrough's strong reliance on his DCF is misplaced.

Courts often rely upon DCF analyses in valuing reorganizing debtors. I conclude that it is appropriate to consider DCF when determining such value and no less weight should be accorded to DCF because it relies upon projections. When other helpful valuation analyses are available, as in this case, each method should be weighed and then all methods should be considered together.

D. Valuation Summary

. . .

The Third Circuit Court of Appeals [has written]:

> That argument [that market value should not be used] has considerable force when the securities in issue represent equity in, or long term interest bearing obligations of, a reorganized debtor. In such cases, the market value of the security will depend upon the investing public's perception of the future prospects of the enterprise. That perception may well be unduly distorted by the recently concluded reorganization and the prospect of lean years for the enterprise in the immediate future. Use of a substitute "reorganization value" may under the circumstances be the only fair means of determining the value of the securities distributed.

Matter of Penn Central Transportation Co., 596 F.2d 1102, 1115-16 (3d Cir. 1979).

The stated purpose for Newman's numerous adjustments to the valuation methodologies were to bring value calculations in line with current market value. This is not appropriate when seeking to value securities of a reorganized debtor since the "taint" of bankruptcy will cause the market to undervalue the securities and future earning capacity of the Debtor. The more appropriate method, in this instance, is a straightforward application of the valuation methodologies to arrive at a better understanding of whether the Debtor's Plan treats creditors fairly and equitably.

E. Valuation Conclusion

The Debtor advocates an enterprise value in the range of $950 million to $1.050 billion; the Creditors Committee advocates a range of $1.5 billion to $1.7 billion. After considering the various methods employed by the experts and their resultant valuations, the competing incentives of the parties to either overvalue or undervalue the company, and the extensive, divergent evidence offered in support of valuation, and consistent with the above analysis of all of these, I determine the Debtor's enterprise value to be in the range of $1.4 billion to $1.6 billion. . . .

[In addition to agreeing with the Committee's objection to valuation, thus finding increased value for the unsecureds, the court upheld other objections to the plan as well.—Eds.]

For all of the reasons set forth above, I conclude that the Debtor's Plan cannot be confirmed.

B. INTEREST RATE

The interest rate required on a loan makes an enormous difference as to the number of dollars that must be repaid, a much greater difference than most people realize when they make a purchase on credit. It is not surprising that chapter 11 debtors and secured parties tussle mightily over the right interest rate required to "discount" the payment owed to the secured party to its present value.

The Supreme Court addressed how to calculate the interest rate payable on allowed secured claims in chapter 13 cases in Till v. SCS Credit Corp., 541 U.S. 465 (2004), although without a solid majority for one formula. In dicta, the plurality suggested the formula might also apply in chapter 11 cases. Deep in the heart of Texas, there seems to be some skepticism about *Till*, yet it still rules the range with various twists.

In the Matter of TEXAS GRAND PRAIRIE HOTEL REALTY, L.L.C.
710 F.3d 324 (5th Cir. 2013)

HIGGINBOTHAM, Circuit Judge.

Wells Fargo Bank National Association ("Wells Fargo") appeals from a district court decision affirming confirmation of a Chapter 11 cramdown plan. Finding no error in the bankruptcy court's judgment, we affirm.

I.

In 2007, Texas Grand Prairie Hotel Realty, LLC . . . obtained a $49,000,000 loan from Morgan Stanley Mortgage Capital, Inc., applying the proceeds to acquire and renovate four hotel properties in Texas. Morgan Stanley—not a party to this case—took a security interest in the hotel properties and in substantially all of the Debtors' other assets. Wells Fargo eventually acquired the loan from Morgan Stanley.

In 2009, the Debtors' hotel business soured. Unable to pay Wells Fargo's loan as payment came due, the Debtors filed for Chapter 11 protection and proposed a plan of reorganization. When Wells Fargo rejected the proposed reorganization, the Debtors sought to cram down their plan under 11 U.S.C. § 1129(b). The plan valued Wells Fargo's secured claim at roughly $39,080,000, in accordance with Wells Fargo's own appraisal. Under the plan, the Debtors proposed to pay off Wells Fargo's secured claim over a term of ten years, with interest accruing at 5%—1.75% above the prime rate on the date of the confirmation hearing.

The bankruptcy court held a two-day evidentiary hearing to assess whether it could confirm the Debtors' plan under § 1129(b) over Wells Fargo's objection. Among other things, Wells Fargo challenged the Debtors' proposed 5% interest rate on its secured claim. Both parties stipulated that the applicable rate should be determined by applying the "prime-plus" formula endorsed by a plurality of the Supreme Court in *Till v. SCS Credit Corp.* However, the parties' experts disagreed on the application of that formula: whereas the Debtors' expert—Mr. Louis Robichaux—testified that it supported a 5% rate, Wells Fargo's expert insisted that it mandated a rate of at least 8.8%. [Again, surprise, surprise.—Eds.]

. . .

IV.

Wells Fargo claims that the bankruptcy court erred in setting a 5% cramdown rate. We turn first to the standard under which this Court reviews a Chapter 11 cramdown rate determination, then to its application.

A.

Under 11 U.S.C. § 1129(b), a debtor can "cram down" a reorganization plan over the dissent of a secured creditor only if the plan provides the creditor—in this case Wells Fargo—with deferred payments of a "value" at least equal to the "allowed amount" of the secured claim as of the effective date of the plan. In other words, the deferred payments, discounted to present value by applying an appropriate interest rate (the "cramdown rate"), must equal the allowed amount of the secured creditor's claim.

. . .

In *Till*, a plurality of the Supreme Court ruled that bankruptcy courts must calculate the Chapter 13 cramdown rate by applying the prime-plus formula. . . . *Till* was a splintered decision whose precedential value is limited even in the Chapter 13 context. While many courts have chosen to apply the *Till* plurality's formula method under Chapter 11, they have done so because they were *persuaded* by the plurality's reasoning, not because they considered *Till* binding. Ultimately, the plurality's suggestion that its analysis also governs in the Chapter 11 context—which would be dictum even in a majority opinion—is not "controlling . . . precedent."

. . . We will not tie bankruptcy courts to a specific methodology as they assess the appropriate Chapter 11 cramdown rate of interest; rather, we continue to review a bankruptcy court's entire cramdown-rate analysis only for clear error.

B.

At length, we turn to address whether the bankruptcy court clearly erred in assessing a 5% cramdown rate under § 1129(b). While both parties stipulate that the *Till* plurality's formula approach governs the applicable cramdown rate, they disagree on what that approach requires.

Under the *Till* plurality's formula method, a bankruptcy court should begin its cramdown rate analysis with the national prime rate—the rate charged by banks to creditworthy commercial borrowers—and then add a supplemental "risk adjustment" to account for "such factors as the circumstances of the estate, the nature of the security, and the duration and feasibility of the reorganization plan." Though the plurality "d[id] not decide the proper scale for the risk adjustment," it observed that "other courts have generally approved adjustments of 1% to 3%."

In ruling that the formula method governs under Chapter 13, the *Till* plurality was motivated primarily by what it viewed as the method's simplicity and objectivity. First, the plurality reasoned, the method minimizes the need for costly evidentiary hearings, as the prime rate is reported daily, and as "many of the factors relevant to the [risk] adjustment fall squarely within the bankruptcy court's area of expertise." Second, the plurality observed, the approach varies only in "the state of financial markets, the circumstances of the bankruptcy estate, and the characteristics of the loan" instead of inquiring into a particular creditor's cost of funds or prior contractual relations with the debtor.

For these same reasons, the plurality "reject[ed] the coerced loan, presumptive contract rate, and cost of funds approaches," as "[e]ach of these approaches is complicated, imposes significant evidentiary costs, and aims to make each individual creditor whole rather than to ensure the debtor's payments have the required present value." . . .

Having explained its prime-plus formula, the plurality applied it to the case before the Court, in which the secured creditor—an auto-financing company—objected to the bankruptcy court's assessment of a cramdown rate at 1.5% over prime. The creditor claimed that this cramdown rate was woefully inadequate to compensate it for the risk that the debtor would default on its restructured obligations, presenting evidence that the subprime financing market would demand a rate of at least prime plus 13% for a comparable loan. The plurality rejected the creditor's arguments and affirmed the bankruptcy court's 1.5% risk adjustment, observing that the debtor's expert had testified that the rate was "very reasonable given that Chapter 13 plans are supposed to be feasible."

In a spirited dissent, Justice Scalia warned that the plurality's approach would "systematically undercompensate" creditors. Justice Scalia observed that "based on even a rudimentary financial analysis of the facts of this case, the 1.5% [risk adjustment assessed by the plurality] is obviously wrong—not just off by a couple percent, but probably by roughly an order of magnitude." As for the plurality's reference to the testimony of the debtors' economics expert, Justice Scalia noted that "[n]othing in the record shows how [the expert's] platitudes were somehow manipulated to arrive at a figure of 1.5 percent." Justice Scalia concluded that it was "impossible to view the 1.5% figure as anything other than a smallish number picked out of a hat."

While *Till* was an appeal from a Chapter 13 proceeding, the plurality observed that "Congress [likely] intended bankruptcy judges and trustees to follow essentially the same [formula] approach when choosing an appropriate interest rate under [Chapter 11]," reasoning that the applicable statutory language was functionally identical in both contexts. However, in Footnote 14, the plurality appeared to qualify its extension of the prime-plus formula to Chapter 11, observing that as "efficient markets" for exit financing often exist in business bankruptcies, a "market rate" approach might be more suitable for making the cramdown rate determination under § 1129(b).

In spite of Justice Scalia's warning, the vast majority of bankruptcy courts have taken the *Till* plurality's invitation to apply the prime-plus formula under Chapter 11. While courts often acknowledge that *Till*'s Footnote 14 appears to endorse a "market rate" approach under Chapter 11 *if* an "efficient market" for a loan substantially identical to the cramdown loan exists, courts almost invariably conclude that such markets are absent. Among the courts that follow *Till*'s formula method in the Chapter 11 context, "risk adjustment" calculations have generally hewed to the plurality's suggested range of 1% to 3%. Within that range, courts typically select a rate on the basis of a holistic assessment of the risk of the debtor's default on its restructured obligations, evaluating factors including the quality of the debtor's management, the commitment of the debtor's owners, the health and future prospects of the debtor's business, the quality of the lender's collateral, and the feasibility and duration of the plan.

Returning to the proceedings in this case, both Wells Fargo and the Debtors presented the bankruptcy court with expert testimony on the appropriate prime-plus cramdown rate. Mr. Louis Robichaux, the Debtors' expert, began his analysis by quoting the prime rate at 3.25%. He then proceeded to assess a risk adjustment by evaluating the factors enumerated by the *Till* plurality, looking to "the circumstances of the [D]ebtors' estate, the nature of the security, and the duration and feasibility of the plan." Robichaux concluded that the Debtors' hotel properties were well maintained and excellently managed, that the Debtors' owners were committed to the business, that the Debtors' revenues exceeded their projections in the months prior to the hearing, that Wells Fargo's collateral was stable or appreciating, and that the Debtors' proposed cramdown plan would be tight but feasible. On the basis of these findings, Robichaux assessed the risk of default "just to the left of the middle of the risk scale." As *Till* had suggested that risk adjustments generally fall between 1% and 3%, Robichaux reasoned that a 1.75% risk adjustment would be appropriate.

Wells Fargo's expert, Mr. Richard Ferrell, corroborated virtually all of Robichaux's findings with respect to Debtors' properties, management, ownership, and projected earnings. Ferrell also agreed that the applicable prime rate was 3.25%. However, Ferrell devoted the vast majority of his cramdown rate analysis to determining the rate of interest that the market would charge to finance an amount of principal equal to the cramdown loan. Because Ferrell concluded that there was no market for single, secured loans comparable to the forced loan contemplated under the cramdown plan, he calculated the market rate by taking the weighted average of the interest rates the market would charge for a multi-tiered exit financing package comprised of senior debt, mezzanine debt [as its name implies, mid-level debt subordinated to senior debt—Eds.], and equity. Ferrell's calculations yielded a "blended" market rate of 9.3%.[56]

To bring his "market influenced" analysis within the form of *Till*'s prime-plus method, Ferrell purported to "utilize the [3.25%] Prime Rate as the Base Rate," making an upward "adjustment" of 6.05% to account for "the nature of the security interest." This calculation yielded Ferrell's 9.3% blended market rate.[57] Mr. Ferrell then adjusted the blended rate in accordance with the remaining *Till* factors, making a downward adjustment of 1.5% to account for the sterling "circumstances of the bankruptcy estate" and an upward adjustment of 1% to account for the plan's tight feasibility. Ultimately, Mr. Ferrell concluded that Wells Fargo was entitled to a cramdown rate of 8.8%.

. . .

We agree with the bankruptcy court that Robichaux's § 1129(b) cramdown rate determination rests on an uncontroversial application of the *Till* plurality's formula method. As the plurality instructed, Robichaux engaged in a holistic evaluation of the Debtors, concluding that the quality of the bankruptcy estate was sterling, that the Debtors' revenues were exceeding projections, that Wells Fargo's collateral—primarily real estate—was liquid and stable or appreciating in value, and that the reorganization plan would be tight but feasible. On the basis of these findings—which were all independently verified by Ferrell—Robichaux assessed a risk adjustment of 1.75% over prime. This risk adjustment falls squarely within the

---

[56] More precisely, Mr. Ferrell determined that the market could finance the first $23,448,000 of the cramdown loan at a rate of 6.25%, in exchange for a first mortgage on the Debtors' hotel properties. He then determined that the balance of the cramdown loan could be financed through a combination of mezzanine debt, at a rate of 11%, and equity, at a constructive rate of 22%. The weighted average of the interest rates on these three financing tranches was 9.3%.

[57] As Wells Fargo's briefs on appeal implicitly concede, Mr. Ferrell thus effectively chose the *market* rate, and not the prime rate, as the starting point of his cramdown rate analysis. *Cf.* C.B. Reehl & Stephen P. Milner, *Chapter 11 Real Estate Cram-Down Plans: The Legacy of Till*, 30 Cal. Bankr. J. 405, 410 ("[I]f the risk adjustment could take on any value, *Till* would have no relevance since cram-down interest rates could be determined reverse engineered through application of other methodologies. . . . In other words, the same market factors used to develop cram-down interest rates before *Till*, could now be used to determine the value of the risk adjustment.").

range of adjustments other bankruptcy courts have assessed in similar circumstances.

We also agree that Ferrell predicated his 8.8% cramdown rate on the sort of comparable loans analysis rejected by the *Till* plurality. . . .

Wells Fargo complains that Robichaux's analysis produces "absurd results," pointing to the undisputed fact that on the date of plan confirmation, the market was charging rates in excess of 5% on smaller, over-collateralized loans to comparable hotel owners. While Wells Fargo is undoubtedly correct that no willing lender would have extended credit on the terms it was forced to accept under the § 1129(b) cramdown plan, this "absurd result" is the natural consequence of the prime-plus method, which sacrifices market realities in favor of simple and feasible bankruptcy reorganizations. . . .

Notably, Wells Fargo makes no attempt to predicate Ferrell's "market-influenced" blended rate calculation on the *Till* plurality's Footnote 14, which suggests that a "market rate" approach should apply in Chapter 11 cases where "efficient markets" for exit financing exist. Footnote 14 has been criticized by commentators, who observe that it rests on the untenable assumption that the voluntary market for forced cramdown loans is somehow less illusory in the Chapter 11 context than it is in the Chapter 13 context. Nevertheless, many courts—including the Sixth Circuit—have found Footnote 14 persuasive, concluding that a "market rate" approach should be used to calculate the Chapter 11 cramdown rate in circumstances where "efficient markets" for exit financing exist.

Even assuming, however, that Footnote 14 has some persuasive value, it does not suggest that the bankruptcy court here committed any error. Among the courts that adhere to Footnote 14, most have held that markets for exit financing are "efficient" only if they offer a loan with a term, size, and collateral comparable to the forced loan contemplated under the cramdown plan. In the present case, Ferrell himself acknowledged that "there's no one in this market today that would loan this loan to the debtors—one to one loan-to-value ratio, 39 million dollars, secured by these properties." While Ferrell concluded that exit financing could be cobbled together through a combination of senior debt, mezzanine debt, and equity financing, courts including the Sixth Circuit have rejected the argument that the existence of such tiered financing establishes "efficient markets," observing that it bears no resemblance to the single, secured loan contemplated under a cramdown plan. . . . On this record, we cannot conclude that the bankruptcy court's cramdown rate calculation is clearly erroneous. However, we do not suggest that the prime-plus formula is the only—or even the optimal—method for calculating the Chapter 11 cramdown rate.

─────────────

Till clearly leaves lots of disagreement on interest rate. As Justice Scalia noted in his dissent: "Eight Justices are in agreement that the rate of interest set forth in the debtor's approved plan must include a premium for risk. Of those eight, four are of the view that beginning with the contract rate would most accurately reflect the actual risk, and four are of the view that beginning with the prime lending rate would do so.

The ninth Justice takes no position on the latter point, since he disagrees with the eight on the former point; he would reverse because the rate proposed here, being above the risk-free rate, gave respondent no cause for complaint." Till v. SCS Credit Corp., 541 U.S. 465, 508 (2004). "Today's judgment is unlikely to burnish the Court's reputation for reasoned decisionmaking." Id.

C.   INDUBITABLE EQUIVALENCE

Section 1129(b)(2)(A)(iii) provides a plan proponent with a wildcard to satisfy cramdown of a secured creditor in the form of an exchange that offers the "indubitable equivalent" of the collateral. The most common use of this workaround is "dirt for debt," in which the debtor gives a piece of property to the secured creditor as payment for all or part of its debt, whether the creditor wants to be a real estate investor or not. See, e.g., Sandy Ridge Dev. Corp. v. La. Nat'l Bank (In re Sandy Ridge Dev. Corp.), 881 F.2d 1346 (5th Cir. 1989). Often the creditor claims the property is not worth what the debtor claims as payment and off we go to another valuation hearing. It is even more complex when the debtor offers the property in partial payment, plus some cash. See, e.g., Bate Land Company LP, Creditor v. Bate Land & Timber LLC, 877 F.3d 188 (4th Cir. 2017).

D.   THE § 1111(b) ELECTION

Congress gave a special cramdown protection to undersecured creditors: the "§ 1111(b) election." It is designed to keep the debtor from lien-stripping the secured party's interest at a low point in the market, with the debtor hoping to reap all of the benefit of a near-term price rise as the market recovers.

For the usual undersecured creditor with its combined secured-unsecured bifurcated claim under § 506(a), § 1111(b) gives the creditor the option of *waiving* any unsecured deficiency claim that exists by virtue of the creditor's collateral being worth less than the debt. This waiver prohibits the creditor from participating in the plan—voting—as an unsecured creditor. That sounds like a terrible "protection," but in exchange for this waiver, the debtor must pay the secured creditor the *full nominal dollar amount of its entire (unbifurcated) claim*. The debtor is not required to pay the present *value* of the entire claim, just its nominal amount in total dollars. Present value is required only for the allowed secured claim, which, by definition, is lesser than the total allowed claim for an undersecured creditor whose collateral is underwater. (You can refresh on "present value" by looking back at Assignment 10.) Note that the election is in § 1111(b)(1)(B), but the two-part payment test is stated in the last two sentences of § 1129(b)(2)(A)(i)(II), which we edit to make the two component parts clear:

> (II) that each holder of a claim of such class receive on account of such claim deferred cash payments totaling at least the allowed amount of such claim, [and whose present value must be] a value, as of the effective date of the plan, of at least the value of such holder's interest in the estate's interest in [the securing collateral].

The effect of a § 1111(b) election can be illustrated as follows. A creditor is owed $1,000,000 secured by a building worth $400,000. In the normal course under § 506, the creditor has a secured claim for $400,000, which is the allowed secured claim, and an unsecured deficiency claim for the remaining $600,000. If the plan calls for all payments to be made at the end of one year and the applicable rate of interest at the time is 10%, then the creditor must be paid $400,000 plus 10% interest (total $440,000) at the end of the year. If unsecured creditors are receiving a 40% payout also at the end of one year, the creditor will get an additional $240,000 from its deficiency claim, for a total of $680,000 paid in the bankruptcy.

If the secured creditor instead makes a § 1111(b) election, it waives its unsecured claim, but it gets a secured claim for $1,000,000. As to that claim, it must be paid $1,000,000 by the end of the plan—in our example, one year. As to the $400,000 value of its collateral, it is guaranteed not less than $40,000 interest (the present value applicable rate) for the one-year period under the plan, for a total of $440,000. Thus, if it gets $1,000,000 by the end of the year, both tests will have been fulfilled: the number of dollars it received was equal to the full number of dollars in its claim ($1,000,000) and was at least as great as the value of collateral plus interest for the period ($440,000). It will be much better off by taking the election, $1,000,000, versus $680,000 without the election.

Note that the debtor can stretch out an electing creditor's payments over a long period and thus pay that creditor much less on a present value basis than the full claim. Suppose the debtor agrees to pay our exemplary creditor $1,000,000 over ten years and pay unsecured creditors 40% of their claims at the end of one year. The payment of $1,000,000 in nominal dollars satisfies the first test—payment of the face value of the note. Because $1,000,000 is greater than $400,000 plus 10% interest for ten years, which is $800,000 (ignoring the declining balance, it is $400,000 in principal plus $40,000 interest per year for ten years), the second test is also satisfied: the $1,000,000 payment over ten years is not less than $800,000, which is the present value of an allowed secured claim of $400,000 stretched out over ten years. Because the unsecured claim is waived in a § 1111(b) election, the creditor in our ten-year example is actually worse off financially with the election because it missed the 40% payment on the unsecured claim that it would have had at the end of the first year ($240,000). That unsecured dividend would have made its total payout $1,040,000—greater than the $1,000,000 payment that would pass the § 1111(b) test(s). (The loss is even greater in reality, because of the loss of interest that could have been earned on the $240,000 payment over ten years, another $240,000 even without compounding.) In addition, the creditor that made the § 1111(b) election forfeited its ability to vote as an unsecured creditor and perhaps to force a liquidation of the business and the resulting seizure of its collateral.

On the other hand, the undersecured creditor that waives its deficiency under § 1111(b) gains an advantage against a debtor that confirms a plan and must pay off the loan in a short time frame. If some economic circumstance forces the debtor to repay the loan in a year or two (can't stretch over ten years), then the requirement that it pay the full nominal amount of the claim has real bite. As in our previous example, a debtor that pays over just one year must pay at least $1,000,000 to pass the first test, which is way more than the $400,040 present value of the $400,000 collateral one year out. This prevents a debtor from "cashing out" the creditor on the quick when the collateral's value has temporarily collapsed (think real estate slump).

A second type of undersecured creditor that may benefit from § 1111(b) is the nonrecourse creditor. Recall that a loan is nonrecourse if the original security agreement provided that the creditor cannot pursue a deficiency judgment against the debtor (the phrase often used is "the debtor has no personal liability") and can only recover by selling the collateral. To protect such a creditor's § 1111(b) rights, the Code deems the creditor to have full recourse like any other secured creditor. § 1111(b)(1)(A). No election is needed; it happens automatically.

E. HOME MORTGAGE CRAMDOWN REDUX: SPECIAL RULES FOR SMALL BUSINESS OWNERS

As noted earlier, individual debtors are statutorily barred from cramming down their home mortgages to the current value of the allowed secured claim in chapter 13. § 1322(b)(2). So too in chapter 11. § 1129(b)(2). This process is called "lienstripping." (In chapter 7, there is no cramdown; the equivalent for cashing out at market value would be redemption, which is not allowed for real property, § 722.) A potentially critical provision in the SBRA lifts this bar and permits lienstripping for a small business debtor under particular circumstances, namely, the classic small business transaction where the lender demands a mortgage (often a second mortgage) on the borrower's home to secure the homeowner's personal liability on the business loan, either directly or by guarantee of a loan to the corporate business. In the latter scenario, the individual debtor will have to be the next docket entry in bankruptcy court after the corporation to take advantage of the lienstripping opportunity, but a personal filing will often be a practical necessity anyway. The key joint requirements are that the debt be "(A) not used primarily to acquire the real property; and (B) used primarily in connection with the small business of the debtor." § 1190(3). We think these two requirements may collapse into one because most business borrowers do not use their business loans as a PMSI on the family home. And "primarily"? Sounds like time for litigation. And let the games begin! See In re Ventura, 2020 WL 1867898 (Bankr. E.D.N.Y.

Apr. 10, 2020) (fact question whether small business debtor's PMSI on historic home used as B&B qualifies for a SBRA exception to anti-cramdown rules on home mortgages).

<h2 style="text-align:center">Problem Set 30</h2>

30.1. As you continued to interview Angie Littwin (Problem 29.2), she admitted that she was lying awake nights thinking about her business "and, let's face it, the fact that I guaranteed $500,000 of the debt personally." Worse still, her guarantee is secured by a second mortgage she granted on her home. (Her home is worth $1 million, and the first mortgage is for $700,000.) Now that you know that, what else should she consider doing?

30.2. Feasibility and classification were initial arrows that BB&T Bank shot at John Paul Smith and his assorted companies' bankruptcies to derail confirmation. (See Problem Sets 27-28.) Its nuclear bomb, however, was the cramdown objection. Below is the hearing transcript of the parties' legal arguments on that issue.

You must now make a ruling, and as is always your practice when possible, you are going to give an oral ruling before the parties tomorrow morning. Begin your ruling by summarizing the plan's proposed treatment of the unsecured BB&T class and BB&T's assertion of what it should be paid. How far apart are they? How will you rule? What legal or factual issues shape your ruling? (Ignore the CARES Act temporary amendments to the SBRA.)

Mr. Oliver: Your Honor, we move for confirmation. The evidence with the court is that based on the changes made to these companies and where they have been able to operate, and the projections going forward, they should be able to cash flow the proposed plans.

Judge: Okay, all right, tell me exactly, we didn't go through like we normally do because we have done it before, so I don't have it right at my fingertips. Go through, since the objecting class here is BB&T, go through exactly how you are proposing to treat BB&T in the plan that you have proffered today.

Mr. Oliver: It's about $2.4 million in total secured claims of BB&T across the 4 debtors. That is broken out in these disclosure statements to how much the assets are for that particular debtor . . . and we have used these numbers to figure out the amortizing payments listed on the objections. In addition, we would propose an 8-year balloon to BB&T.

Judge: . . . Amortized over what? At what rate?

Mr. Oliver: We said 6% per year with a 30-year amortization and I, we were, I don't want to say being generous, but the contract rate is prime plus 1, which is right now would work out to 4.25%. And so in order to achieve a fixed rate, we thought we were being realistic by saying 6%. To be higher than prime plus 1, now four and a quarter. So that's where that came from, 6%, and it's in line with what we have seen in other cases and what's been proven these are not debtors that can afford to bring in experts, we haven't done that, we are just relying on what the court has done in recent past, 6%.

With respect to BB&T's unsecured claim, it would be in the unsecured class, paid out over a 25-year period, every 6 months there would be a payment, 4% for interest, of interest per annum, and that 4% just came up from a plan that we had confirmed in September of last year if you remember the Franklins. There was 4% interest paid, I believe on those claims and those actually were where there was sufficient equity in the case that they were going to be paid in full. So we did 4% there, not based on expert testimony just based on what we have seen the court do in the past year. BB&T will be paid those payments from cash flow from Farms & Gurganus.

Judge: What if, for instance, it was prime plus 1 over 20 years, what would that do to the payments in this case?

Mr. Oliver: Your Honor I don't, I could figure out what it would be in the cash flow, but it's hard, it's always changing. But it obviously would be a higher payment. I would say, looking at the cash flow of Gurganus it doesn't appear that it would be a problem because, particularly with the storage of the grain that they have been able to do, they have such a large cash flow at the end; Farms would be more problematic, showing a positive of $166 at the end of the period. I guess, (indecipherable), if that's the interest rate that Your Honor thinks it's appropriate then we would agree to it, and then if it gets out of control. . . .

Judge: Well my experience it's been in this and some other cases, it is that frankly no one knows what this market is going to do, and banks have very severe inflationary concerns that to get a fixed rate right now it's not down at prime and prime plus 1, but it's upwards of where it was a year ago.

Mr. Oliver: I can tell you the debtor would agree to that, what interest rate you think is fair and if they get to a point where they can't do it, they will have to refinance those debts.

Judge: I understand, all right. Mr. Pryor, several issues here, I know.

Mr. Pryor: We got a lot of issues, I will try to be brief, you've heard them before. In summary BB&T has joint and several liability claims against all four debtors in the amount of approximately $5.2 million. The treatment under the plan breaks the secured claim down into little over $2.4 million over a 30-year period at interest rate, the plan says is approximately 6%. It's divided the way they want to between the four debtors. On the unsecured portion of it, we need to recall the debtor changed the treatment, the absolute priority rule issues. And under 1129 they have to pay that full claim at a market rate interest over some period of time the court finds reasonable. Those installments are deferred per year so we got a negative amortization issue, and we cited the law on that issue.

Judge: Right.

Mr. Pryor: In the unsecured claim part of it is divided out between two, the primary debtors and the other debtors, although Mr. Oliver says they remain joint[ly] and severally liable, that provision is not in the plan. Mr. Oliver says there are default provisions in the plan, but there are no default provisions in the plan, Your Honor, there are no provisions in the plan for the retention of BB&T liens, it's just not in there.

Judge: Okay.

Mr. Pryor: And I think the law is very clear that you apply, and they're trying to get by the absolute priority rule. . . . They are paying you in full, but it also says, and the statute says, they have to pay it with interest at the market rate. And that issue I think has been litigated and seems, pretty definitive about it. That the language tracks exactly the language which is for the secured portion on cram down. In most of the case law will be applicable to similar issues to ensure that the interest rate provided in the plan was below the market rate of interest a stream of critical payments equal to the allowed amount of the unsecured claim will not be fair and equitable.

Judge: All right.

Mr. Pryor: So again, let's let me just before Mr. Oliver jumps up, we also have the market rate of interest. I think the only evidence is, if it's going to be a fixed rate, which you don't offer when it goes out this far, but the closest we got to it is a 8.5% interest rate and if it was stretched out that amount of time it would go up and that was an interest rate that we would offer to a good customer. The interest rate with respect to the unsecured claim would even be, I mean, it is common sense that unsecured loan interest rates are a lot higher than secured ones.

Mr. Oliver: Excuse me, Your Honor, if I may. Just briefly on this negative amortization issue. I have a case decided that might fit in footnote 59. It does say here that this form of cram down will often be used for solvent or near-solvent debtors attempting to realign their capital structure in need of better terms not to accomplish this task something we have here. Obviously, that's the case like when you have enough equity and property where you have to pay it all in full. This is one where if it were to liquidate today, there's zero.

Judge: Right.

Mr. Oliver: So if you look at fair and equitable you have to look at the whole picture and you have to say what is fair and equitable to this debtor?

Judge: Yeah, but fair and equitable includes as a minimum, this provision. You can't override this provision by fair and equitable, you can add to it. Fair and equitable that means you got to do this. What you have chosen to do here is to try to confirm this plan by paying BB&T in full.

Mr. Oliver: Yes.

Judge: . . . so you can get around their rejecting unsecured class, which means that Mr. Smith can't keep any interest in his property. And when you do that, you got to do what the Code says, you got to pay 'em a fair rate in order to go forward.

Mr. Oliver: Right, but again it's a fair rate in the light of everything and if this were liquidated today this unsecured claim is worth nothing. Worth absolutely nothing because BB&T has it all and question whether we even bring what the values are for the postpetition secured claims and again it says, total, the totality of circumstances what is fair and equitable, and what is in the best interest of creditors.

30.3. Bilene Hinajosa is one exciting lady. Among other things, she has become a well-known race car driver and the first woman to win or place in a number of the top NASCAR races. Like some NFL players, she incorporated herself as Bilene, Inc. ("BI") which owns her winnings and endorsement income. She sold shares to about 100 fans and used the money to build the *Flaming Arrow*, her race car, also owned by BI. After winning a major race, the value of her car shot up to over $1 million and much of her endorsement income comes from videos of her and the car doing various things (e.g., tooling up to the take-out window of a famous burger joint while multitudes ooo and ahhh). To expand her brand, BI borrowed $800,000 from the Los Angeles Celebrity Finance Company ("LAC"), secured by the car. The interest rate was a floating rate, prime plus 8%, "admittedly high but the collateral is somewhat unusual," according to the LAC loan officer. Among other things, the car is uninsurable as a practical matter, given its primary use and Bilene's reputation for utter fearlessness.

Bilene suffered a major injury last year and is just now back to racing in a restored *Flaming Arrow*. Her visibility and income fell off in tandem. BI has missed three payments on the car and is not current on its trade debt to suppliers either, but Bilene's back on the track and ready to roll. BI has filed chapter 11 and proposes a plan that would pay its secured debt to LAC at an interest rate of 2% above prime over five years based on an appraised value of $500,000 for the car. BI still owes $600,000 on the LAC loan and has missed three monthly payments totaling $54,000. The proposed payment schedule would require monthly payments of about $10,900 a month.

LAC uses your firm for its bankruptcy work. It doesn't like anything about this plan and wants to know what arguments it can make against it.

30.4. A chapter 11 case was filed by Fong Properties #21 ("FP#21"), one of many LLCs established by Jamey Fong, a remarkably successful local real estate investor. FP#21 owns land near the proposed (but very controversial) new arm of the Central Artery in Boston. He plans to develop it with a mix of apartments and retail stores and has about 80 investors who have contributed the funds to buy the land and provide the equity underlying the $120 million secured construction loan from your client, the Boston Bean Bank ("BBB"). However, the delay in approvals for the new highway alarmed the BBB and caused FP#21 to file chapter 11 to buy time.

Yesterday at lunch with another client, Kevin Snorguson ("Everybody calls me Snorgy!"), you learned that Snorgy had been offered a chance to buy into the FP#21 as soon as a plan was confirmed. The value of the building, he was told, would be $200 million in a year, when it was rented out. Snorgy is considering the investment and told you to tell no one about the conversation.

When you got back to the office, you got a call from Hank Ferrell, the lawyer for FP#21, who explained that they would be filing a plan in the near future valuing the building at $80 million on the basis of two appraisals from top MAI appraisers, so BBB's loan would be deeply underwater. The value would be as of the effective date of the plan, at which time the approval process would still be uncompleted and uncertain. The plan would promise to pay the unsecured creditors, including BBB's $40 million unsecured claim, about 50%, while a small additional class of unsecured construction contractors will be paid 90% of their claims (and, unstated, get lots of future business from Fong). But Hank assured you that the secured claim would be paid in full over ten years at the going rate for local real estate loans on safe projects.

Ten minutes later, Mary Nguyen, the Loan Officer from BBB, called you to say that a friend of hers had just told her that many of the unsecured creditors in the case were mad about getting only 50% and thus the vote of the unsecured class would be close.

What do you tell Mary and what advice do you give her? See § 1111(b). (Assume that §§ 101(51B) and 362(d)(3) do not apply here.)

Section 2

New Chapter 11

Now that you have learned all about the negotiation, voting, and confirming of chapter 11 plans, it is time to unlearn all that a bit. The reality is that in the "new" world of chapter 11, many companies reorganize their balance sheets, change ownership structures, and even adapt new operational models without the fanfare of a full election cycle. Some have gone so far as to say this trend is the "death" of chapter 11. Douglas G. Baird & Robert K. Rasmussen, The End of Bankruptcy, 55 Stan. L. Rev. 751 (2002). Others have retorted that the trends are sector- and company-specific and far from universal. Lynn M. LoPucki, The Nature of the Bankrupt Firm: A Response to Baird and Rasmussen's The End of Bankruptcy, 56 Stan. L. Rev. 645 (2003); A. Mechele Dickerson, The Many Faces of Chapter 11: A Reply to Professor Baird, 12 Am. Bankr. Inst. L. Rev. 109 (2004); see also Jay L. Westbrook, Secured Creditor Control and Bankruptcy Sales: An Empirical View, 2015 Ill. L. Rev. 831 (finding secured creditor control—an assumed predicate to bankruptcy sales—not as pervasive as commonly believed).

Deferring this academic debate for now, the point for the bankruptcy student is that chapter 11 practice is sufficiently flexible to permit a variety of less than full-blown reorganization models. These uses of chapter 11 cases raise some eyebrows but are now commonplace in the real world. Sometimes this flexibility may allow the private parties to construct their own ad hoc distributions, untethered from the priority hierarchy of the Code. And increasingly—some would say nearly always—these new cases amount to the sale of a business rather than a traditional reorganization. In this next section we look at these newer, light-form chapter 11s, focusing on bankruptcy sales and other innovations. In the first assignment, we start with a discussion of "prepackaged" reorganizations before focusing on § 363 of the Code—the sales provision—and the judicial and statutory constraints on its use and on cognate attempts to use the Code "flexibly" in the "new chapter 11." In the second assignment, we look at more advanced issues, such as the proper design of auction sales procedure and the market for distressed debt claims. (You might think of the discussion as taking the seller's perspective in the first assignment and then switching to the buyer's in the second.)

SALES AND BEYOND I

This assignment is about selling off a business by using chapter 11 and other "reorganizations" that do not track the traditional negotiating and voting model you learned in the previous assignments. This might cause you to wonder at the outset, "Why would companies use the 'reorganization' chapter for sales, especially sales of virtually all the businesses' assets?" A good question. Although the Code explicitly permits liquidation of companies in chapter 11, § 1125(a)(5)(D), chapter 7 is generally considered the liquidation chapter. Indeed, some of the main justifications for chapter 11 turn on saving the old business, retaining jobs, and so on, not putting it on the auction block. In the United Kingdom, for example, reorganizations are called "rescues," and the great enthusiasm in other countries that are adopting versions of chapter 11 rests on the traditional justifications of entity-preservation. Yet here in the United States, the birthplace of chapter 11, we increasingly use it for liquidation.

The increased use of chapter 11 to sell businesses rests on several arguments. Some are normative, which we will discuss in Assignment 39, when we explore theoretical considerations of reorganization and whether sales are the long-overdue apotheosis of efficiency. For now, we focus on the practical. Chapter 7 is not necessarily the best way to sell a complex business as a going concern. A newly appointed chapter 7 trustee chosen from a panel of lawyers may not have the same skills to organize the sale of a whole business as the prior managers or a turnaround specialist appointed for the purpose. Those managers may also prefer to control who purchases the business and thus push the court for that approach.

In this assignment, we work through the governing law of this "new chapter 11," which has both "internal" statutory constraints and "external" judicially created ones on its use for selling the business. Before we do that, however, we examine *prepackaged* bankruptcies, which share with bankruptcy sales a common desire to bypass the full apparatus of a chapter 11 disclosure and voting procedure.

A. PREPACKAGED REORGANIZATIONS

Many negotiating parties, knowing what awaits them in a traditional chapter 11, manage to come to a deal before a bankruptcy petition is even filed. In such cases, the debtors arrive in bankruptcy with their plans already drafted, filing their disclosure statements the same day as their petitions, nonchalantly mentioning that the creditors already support the plan. These "prepacks" often sail quickly through the bankruptcy process. Sometimes, if the deal is so obviously acceptable—say, for example, the holder of a huge claim representing 95% of the outstanding unsecured debt thinks the workout proposal is great—then the confirmation of the plan is foreordained. The role of bankruptcy at that point is primarily to bind any minority of dissenting creditors to the confirmed plan and, if necessary, use the stay to hold off such creditors while the negotiations are wrapped up. For some prepacks, the Code even excepts some of the extensive financial disclosures generally required in chapter 11. § 1125(b).

Generalization of prepacks is difficult. Like many other innovations, prepacks tend to trend up and down. In 2012, 14 publicly traded companies filed a prepackaged chapter 11 case. While that is double from 2011, it is still a relatively small number in absolute terms. On the other hand, some of these were quite large, including the $15.6 billion filing of Residential Capital, LLC. In a 2018 sample drawn from unreported data of the Business Bankruptcy Project involving cases in the Southern District of New York and District of Delaware, only 11 of 87 were prepacks. It also appears that prepacks tend to be more common in some sectors than others (and for companies of a certain size).

Aside from these descriptions, there are three main attributes about prepacks that are fair to observe. First, prepacks likely correlate with "hog-tied" debtors whose debt is all wrapped up with a dominant lender. Because a dominant lender is a dominant voter for chapter 11 purposes under § 1129, the writing's on the wall once the lender reveals its vote, and so a protracted negotiation and vote-lobbying process becomes unnecessary.

Second, prepacks occupy one end of a range of pre-filing preparation. Many debtors are engaged in frantic negotiations with lenders as they approach default. Whether they can reach a full out-of-court "workout" agreement that obviates bankruptcy, whether they have a partially or fully "prepackaged" plan ready for the judicial confirmation when they file, or whether they have "prenegotiated" the plan with certain major creditors—even though they haven't had time to solicit the votes officially before filing—are really points along a continuum rather than a dichotomy of prepack-versus-traditional. Indeed, companies regularly try to line up their ducks before the bankruptcy press announcement. So often is this true that cases where there are no preliminary agreements with key creditors are now commonly known as "freefalls." The hope is to reduce the inevitable drop in share value as much as possible when filing news hits the wire. For example, many DIP loans are already arranged and ready for approval (even if only on an interim basis) in time for the first day orders.

That said, not everyone who wants a prepack gets one. Sometimes negotiations are ongoing but a default is triggered and "the baby comes early," as Jim White says. See James J. White, Death and Resurrection of Secured Credit, 12 Am. Bankr. Ins. L. Rev. 139, 177 n.154 (2004). This causes the company to file a freefall petition, scurrying to seek protection behind the automatic stay, which underscores the fact that pre-filing preparation ranges along a continuum. The press releases issued upon filing are pretty revealing of the degree of prepackedness (yes, we made that word up). If a prepack is lined up, they trumpet that fact proudly, often announcing a ready financing line and how many creditors support the plan, spinning confirmation as a fait accompli. If not, we enter the world of tap-dancing and spin, and the press releases talk about the filing for chapter 11 as a "base for exploring new capital structures in the current economic climate to maximize stakeholder value."

Finally, prepacks are related to the type of plan. A plan to liquidate the debtor or sell its assets as a going concern lends itself to up-front agreement amenable to prepackaging: the "plan" of reorganization might be little else than, "We're going to run a sale, get the most money we can, and divide up the proceeds by priority." By contrast, when parties are negotiating over what stake of a new company they will get in exchange for debt write-down, the process can become more drawn out and hamstring any effort to prepack the bankruptcy. To be sure, these are generalizations; the empirical data are developing on how these bankruptcies work. See Stephen J. Lubben, What We "Know" About Chapter 11 Cost Is Wrong, 17 Fordham J. Corp. & Fin. L. 141 (2012) (finding that prepacks are not, as concluded by first-wave studies in the 1990s, cheaper than regular chapter 11s and that case complexity is a primary determinant of case costs).

Not everyone loves prepacks. For a skeptical (debate-inciting) account of their utility, see Lynn M. LoPucki & Joseph W. Doherty, Why Are Delaware and New York Bankruptcy Reorganizations Failing?, 55 Vand. L. Rev. 1933, 1973 (2002) (finding prepacks significantly more likely to fail and prepack debtors more likely to refile for bankruptcy); see also Foteini Teloni, Chapter 11 Duration, Preplanned Cases, and Refiling Rates: An Empirical Analysis in the Post-BAPCPA Era, 23 Am. Bankr. Inst. L. Rev. 571 (2015) (finding BAPCPA associated with both increased use of prepacks and increased refiling rates). Others object that the debtor is trying to pull a fast one by rushing through a plan, and some just complain out of sheer frustration that a blindsided creditor not in the inner circle simply has insufficient time to process the proposed prepackaged plan. Sometimes the speed is amazing.

FullBeauty Files, Exits Bankruptcy in 24 Hours

FullBeauty announced in early January that it expected to obtain support from debt and equity holders to file Chapter 11. What was not anticipated was the company's plan to exit bankruptcy in under 24 hours. The proposal depends on the bankruptcy court's approval, which was not obtained as of press time.

Restructuring is expected to slash the company's debt by nearly $900 million, based on earlier information provided by FullBeauty, allowing it to continue operations as it turns around the business.

While the company conducts all its business online versus relying on physical locations, FullBeauty has experienced increased competition as more apparel companies move to inclusive sizing. In the past year, Universal Standard expanded its size range from 00 to 40, Old Navy added extended sizes to stores and Target introduced a wider size range to two of its private label apparel lines, among others.

According to court documents, the company's largest unsecured creditor is Hong Kong-based KGS Sourcing Ltd, which is owed $38.9 million, followed by FedEx, to which it owes $6.7 million.

FullBeauty is owned by Apax Partners and Charlesbank Capital Partners, and has a number of brands under its umbrella including Woman Within, Roaman's, Jessica London, Swimsuits for All, Ellos, KingSize, BrylaneHome and fullbeauty.com.

UPDATE: February 5, 2019: FullBeauty Brands won approval of its prepackaged bankruptcy in 24 hours. The restructuring plan hands over the company's ownership to a group of lenders and slashes $900 million in debt. [Kaarin Vembar, https://www.retaildive.com/news/fullbeauty-files -chapter-11-aims-to-exit-in-24-hours/547639/ (Feb. 5, 2019).]

FedEx was probably estopped to begrudge the speed of these proceedings.

B. GOING-CONCERN SALES

Recall from our study of DIP powers that § 363(c) allows the sale of property in the ordinary course of business without court approval and that § 363(b) allows a sale of property even outside the ordinary course, after the bankruptcy court approves the sale. Clever lawyers realized that with no textual constraint on what an "extraordinary" sale of estate property is under § 363(b), there was nothing that explicitly prohibited them from selling the *entire debtor* though § 363 (or, more accurately, selling every single asset of the debtor). If that happens, the debtor, Widget Co, transforms from being a company owning widget makers, inventory, and valuable customer lists into a company that holds a big pile of post-sale cash, notes, or maybe even stock as proceeds for its erstwhile assets that have all been sold. Recall that *Crown* back in Assignment 24 even sold its name as part of its (ill-fated) going-concern sale. As such, the "reorganization plan" of Widget Co after such a sale becomes nothing more than a discussion of how to distribute the pile of cash and other proceeds.

The real appeal may be that selling all or nearly all assets under § 363 does not require a creditor vote, just a motion by the debtor and approval by the court. § 363(b). A creditor who does not want the debtor to sell all of its assets can't lobby an electorate to vote down the plan; it must file an objection at the § 363 motion hearing and argue to the judge. Section 363 thus grants great control to the DIP. It also provides the potential for a very speedy process. A motion and sale can be done in a couple of weeks or months. In fact, § 363 can be used additively with a prepack: a debtor might file a prepack plan saying everyone agrees on a § 363 sale of all the assets, which we plan to do (and here's the motion attached, which includes proposed auction procedures), and here's our plan for how the proceeds should be distributed (and here's the proposed disclosure statement attached).

There are two general constraints on the use of this § 363 power. First, some case law has developed on when a judge should withhold approval of the § 363 "reorganization" as improper. Second, § 363 itself has internal constraints on when its powers can be deployed, assuming the judicial tests for the section's use have been passed.

1. *Judicial Constraints*

Some judges feel that to liquidate outright or sell substantially all of a company through § 363 is an end run around the voting rules of chapter 11. Even allowing for a healthy judicial ego, they are concerned that a judge's approval is no substitute for the elaborate statutory procedures of voting and confirmation. If the debtor wants a liquidating plan, which the Code allows, § 1123(b)(4), it should put that proposal to a vote to see if it carries the creditor poll, not try to sneak through the same result using a § 363 motion. The classic case requiring a justification to sell an entire company through a § 363 sale was In re Lionel Corp., 722 F.2d 1063 (2d Cir. 1983), with its now widely referenced "*Lionel* test" that is discussed in the upcoming *Chrysler* case.

Over the years, various refinements of the *Lionel* test have been added and tweaked, and a cognate doctrine developed pertaining to the *proceeds* of the § 363 sale. Unsatisfied with merely having power to sell the entire company, some power brokers wanted to go a step further and dictate the distribution of the proceeds of a § 363 sale. They would ask the court for permission to authorize the sale and casually throw in that the proceeds of the sale would be distributed, say, to favored creditors A and C, but leave B out in the cold. The Second Circuit blinked when a proposed settlement of a litigation included a term of the deal that paid the proceeds only to some creditors in violation of the Bankruptcy Code's distribution rules, vacating the settlement and remanding for an explanation of what the extraordinary circumstances were that would justify departing from the Code (although not closing the door with a categorical bar as had other circuits). In re Iridium Operating LLC, 478 F.3d 452 (2d Cir. 2007). *Iridium* also addressed the related doctrine that prohibits "*sub rosa*" plans of reorganization, under which privatizing the chapter 11 process was only allowed to go so far.

To help keep these doctrines distinct, it might help to think about it this way: *Lionel* says you have to have a good business reason to sell the chapter 11 assets quickly through § 363 rather than wait and make the sale a term of your chapter 11 plan that gets subjected to vote. The *sub rosa* doctrine says if you do sell those assets, you cannot circumvent the chapter 11 process by pre-dictating who gets paid what from the sale's proceeds. Working backward, then, a party with a *sub rosa* objection would naturally raise it at the § 363 hearing and fold it into an argument that the impermissible *sub rosa* incentive is not a sufficient justification to sell the assets in the first place and hence flunks the *Lionel* test. The next case invokes both judicial creations of the *Lionel* test and the *sub rosa* plan doctrine, candidly conceding that their conceptual overlap is significant.

In re CHRYSLER LLC
576 F.3d 108 (2d Cir. 2009)

JACOBS, Chief Judge.

The Indiana State Police Pension Trust, the Indiana State Teachers Retirement Fund, and the Indiana Major Moves Construction Fund (collectively, the "Indiana Pensioners" or "Pensioners"), along with various tort claimants and others, appeal from an order entered in the United States Bankruptcy Court for the Southern District of New York, Arthur J. Gonzalez, *Bankruptcy Judge,* dated June 1, 2009 (the "Sale Order"), authorizing the sale of substantially all of the debtor's assets to New CarCo Acquisition LLC ("New Chrysler"). On June 2, 2009 we granted the Indiana Pensioners' motion for a stay and for expedited appeal directly to this Court, pursuant to 28 U.S.C. § 158(d)(2). On June 5, 2009 we heard oral argument, and ruled from the bench and by written order, affirming the Sale Order "for the reasons stated in the opinions of Bankruptcy Judge Gonzalez," stating that an opinion or opinions would follow. This is the opinion.

In a nutshell, Chrysler LLC and its related companies (hereinafter "Chrysler" or "debtor" or "Old Chrysler") filed a pre-packaged bankruptcy petition under Chapter 11 on April 30, 2009. The filing followed months in which Chrysler experienced deepening losses, received billions in bailout funds from the Federal Government, searched for a merger partner, unsuccessfully sought additional government bailout funds for a stand-alone restructuring, and ultimately settled on an asset-sale transaction pursuant to 11 U.S.C. § 363 (the "Sale"), which was approved by the Sale Order. The key elements of the Sale were set forth in a Master Transaction Agreement dated as of April 30, 2009: substantially all of Chrysler's operating assets (including manufacturing plants, brand names, certain dealer and supplier relationships, and much else) would be transferred to New Chrysler in exchange for New Chrysler's assumption of certain liabilities and $2 billion in cash. Fiat S.p.A agreed to provide New Chrysler with certain fuel-efficient vehicle platforms, access to its worldwide distribution system, and new management that is experienced in turning around a failing auto company [but no actual cash of its own, the ultimate LBO! What sort of patsy bank would finance such a brazen deal with no money down?—Eds.]. Financing for the sale transaction—$6 billion in senior secured financing, and debtor-in-possession financing for 60 days in the amount of $4.96 billion—would come from the United States Treasury and from Export Development Canada. The agreement describing the United States Treasury's commitment does not specify the source of the funds, but it is undisputed that prior funding came from the Troubled Asset Relief Program ("TARP"), 12 U.S.C. § 5211(a)(1), and that the parties expected the Sale to be financed through the use of TARP funds. Ownership of New Chrysler was to be distributed . . . [such that] 55% [would] go to an employee benefit entity created by the United Auto Workers union, 8% to the United States Treasury and 2% to Export Development Canada. Fiat, for its contributions, would immediately own 20% of the equity with rights to acquire more (up to 51%), contingent on payment in full of the debts owed to the United States Treasury and Export Development Canada.

At a hearing on May 5, 2009, the bankruptcy court approved the debtor's proposed bidding procedures. No other bids were forthcoming. From May 27 to May 29, the bankruptcy court held hearings on whether to approve the Sale. Upon extensive findings of fact and conclusions of law, the bankruptcy court approved the Sale by order dated June 1, 2009.

After briefing and oral argument, we affirmed the bankruptcy court's order on June 5, but we entered a short stay pending Supreme Court review. The Supreme Court, after an extension of the stay, declined a further extension. The Sale closed on June 10, 2009. . . .

The Sale Order is challenged essentially on four grounds. First, it is contended that the sale of Chrysler's auto-manufacturing assets, considered together with the associated intellectual property and (selected) dealership contractual rights, so closely approximates a final plan of reorganization that it constitutes an impermissible *"sub rosa* plan," and therefore cannot be accomplished under § 363(b).

We consider this question first, because a determination adverse to Chrysler would have required reversal. . . .

Discussion . . .

I

The Indiana Pensioners characterize the Sale as an impermissible, *sub rosa* plan of reorganization. *See* Pension Benefit Guar. Corp. v. Braniff Airways, Inc. (In re Braniff Airways, Inc.), 700 F.2d 935, 940 (5th Cir. 1983) (denying approval of an asset sale because the debtor "should not be able to short circuit the requirements of Chapter 11 for confirmation of a reorganization plan by establishing the terms of the plan *sub rosa* in connection with a sale of assets"). As the Indiana Pensioners characterize it, the Sale transaction "is a 'Sale' in name only; upon consummation, new Chrysler will be old Chrysler in essentially every respect. It will be called 'Chrysler.' . . . Its employees, including most management, will be retained. . . . It will manufacture and sell Chrysler and Dodge cars and minivans, Jeeps and Dodge Trucks. The real substance of the transaction is the underlying reorganization it implements." Indiana Pensioners' Br. at 46 (citation omitted).

Section 363(b) of the Bankruptcy Code authorizes a Chapter 11 debtor-in-possession to use, sell, or lease estate property outside the ordinary course of business, requiring in most circumstances only that a movant provide notice and a hearing. 11 U.S.C. § 363(b). We have identified an "apparent conflict" between the expedient of a § 363(b) sale and the otherwise applicable features and safeguards of Chapter 11. Comm. of Equity Sec. Holders v. Lionel Corp. (In re Lionel Corp.), 722 F.2d 1063, 1071 (2d Cir. 1983); *cf. Braniff*, 700 F.2d at 940.

In *Lionel*, we consulted the history and purpose of § 363(b) to situate § 363(b) transactions within the overall structure of Chapter 11. The origin of § 363(b) is the Bankruptcy Act of 1867, which permitted a sale of a debtor's assets when the estate or any part thereof was "of a perishable nature or liable to deteriorate in value." *Lionel*, 722 F.2d at 1066 (citing Section 25 of the Bankruptcy Act of 1867, Act of March 2, 1867, 14 Stat. 517) (emphasis omitted). Typically, courts have approved § 363(b) sales to preserve " 'wasting asset[s].' " *Id.* at 1068 (quoting Mintzer v. Joseph (In re Sire Plan, Inc.), 332 F.2d 497, 499 (2d Cir. 1964)). Most early transactions concerned perishable commodities; but the same practical necessity has been recognized in contexts other than fruits and vegetables. "[T]here are times when it is more advantageous for the debtor to begin to sell as many assets as quickly as possible in order to insure that the assets do not lose value." Fla. Dep't of Revenue v. Piccadilly Cafeterias, Inc., ___ U.S. ___, 128 S. Ct. 2326, 2342, 171 L. Ed. 2d 203 (2008) (Breyer, J., dissenting) (internal quotation marks omitted); *see also* In re Pedlow, 209 F. 841, 842 (2d Cir. 1913) (upholding sale of a bankrupt's stock of handkerchiefs because the sale price was above the appraised value and "Christmas sales had commenced and . . . the sale of handkerchiefs depreciates greatly after the holidays"). Thus, an automobile manufacturing business can be within the ambit of the "melting ice cube" theory of § 363(b). As *Lionel* recognized, the text of § 363(b) requires no "emergency" to justify approval. *Lionel*, 722 F.2d at 1069. For example, if "a good business opportunity [is] presently available," *id.*, which might soon disappear, quick action may be justified in order to increase (or maintain) the value of an asset to the estate, by means of a lease or sale of the assets. Accordingly, *Lionel* "reject[ed] the requirement that only an emergency permits the use of § 363(b)." *Id.* "[I]f a bankruptcy judge is to administer a business reorganization successfully under the Code, then . . . some play for the operation of both § 363(b) and Chapter 11 must be allowed for." *Id.* at 1071.

At the same time, *Lionel* "reject[ed] the view that § 363(b) grants the bankruptcy judge *carte blanche*." *Id.* at 1069. The concern was that a quick, plenary sale of assets outside the ordinary course of business risked circumventing key features of the Chapter 11 process, which afford debt and equity holders the opportunity to vote on a proposed plan of reorganization after receiving meaningful information. *See id.* at 1069-70. Pushed by a bullying creditor, a § 363(b) sale might evade such requirements as disclosure, solicitation, acceptance, and confirmation of a plan. *See* 11 U.S.C. §§ 1122-29. "[T]he natural tendency of a debtor in distress," as a Senate Judiciary Committee Report observed, is "to pacify large creditors with whom the debtor would expect to do business, at the expense of small and scattered public investors." *Lionel*, 722 F.2d at 1070 (quoting S. Rep. No. 95-989, 2d Sess., at 10 (1978), *as reprinted in* 1978 U.S.C.C.A.N. 5787, 5796 (internal quotation marks omitted)).

To balance the competing concerns of efficiency against the safeguards of the Chapter 11 process, *Lionel* required a "good business reason" for a § 363(b) transaction. [The court offered a long list of factors "not intended to be exclusive, but merely to provide guidance."—Eds.]

After weighing these considerations, the Court in *Lionel* reversed a bankruptcy court's approval of the sale of Lionel Corporation's equity stake in another corporation, Dale Electronics, Inc. ("Dale"). The Court relied heavily on testimony from Lionel's Chief Executive Officer, who conceded that it was "only at the insistence of the Creditors' Committee that Dale stock was being sold and that Lionel 'would very much like to retain its interest in Dale,'" *id.* at 1072, as well as on a financial expert's acknowledgment that the value of the Dale stock was not decreasing, *see id.* at 1071-72. Since the Dale stock was not a wasting asset, and the proffered justification for selling the stock was the desire of creditors, no sufficient business reasons existed for approving the sale.

In the twenty-five years since *Lionel*, § 363(b) asset sales have become common practice in large-scale corporate bankruptcies. *See, e.g.,* Robert

E. Steinberg, *The Seven Deadly Sins in § 363 Sales*, Am. Bankr. Inst. J., June 2005, at 22, 22 ("Asset sales under § 363 of the Bankruptcy Code have become the preferred method of monetizing the assets of a debtor company."); Harvey R. Miller & Shai Y. Waisman, *Does Chapter 11 Reorganization Remain A Viable Option for Distressed Businesses for the Twenty-First Century?*, 78 Am. Bankr. L.J. 153, 194-96 (2004). A law review article recounts the phenomenon:

> Corporate reorganizations have all but disappeared. . . . TWA filed only to consummate the sale of its planes and landing gates to American Airlines. Enron's principal assets, including its trading operation and its most valuable pipelines, were sold within a few months of its bankruptcy petition. Within weeks of filing for Chapter 11, Budget sold most of its assets to the parent company of Avis. Similarly, Polaroid entered Chapter 11 and sold most of its assets to the private equity group at BankOne. Even when a large firm uses Chapter 11 as something other than a convenient auction block, its principal lenders are usually already in control and Chapter 11 merely puts in place a preexisting deal.

Douglas G. Baird & Robert K. Rasmussen, *The End of Bankruptcy*, 55 Stan. L. Rev. 751, 751-52 (2002) (internal footnotes omitted). In the current economic crisis of 2008-09, § 363(b) sales have become even more useful and customary. The "side door" of § 363(b) may well "replace the main route of Chapter 11 reorganization plans." Jason Brege, Note, *An Efficiency Model of Section 363(b) Sales*, 92 Va. L. Rev. 1639, 1640 (2006).

Resort to § 363(b) has been driven by efficiency, from the perspectives of sellers and buyers alike. The speed of the process can maximize asset value by sale of the debtor's business as a going concern. Moreover, the assets are typically burnished (or "cleansed") because (with certain limited exceptions) they are sold free and clear of liens, claims and liabilities. *See infra* (discussing § 363(f) and tort issues). A § 363 sale can often yield the highest price for the assets because the buyer can select the liabilities it will assume and purchase a business with cash flow (or the near prospect of it). Often, a secured creditor can "credit bid," or take an ownership interest in the company by bidding a reduction in the debt the company owes. *See* 11 U.S.C. § 363(k) (allowing a secured creditor to credit bid at a § 363(b) sale).

This tendency has its critics. *See, e.g.*, James H.M. Sprayregen et al., *Chapter 11: Not Perfect, but Better than the Alternative*, Am. Bankr. Inst. J., Oct. 2005, at 1, 60 (referencing those who "decr[y] the increasing frequency and rise in importance of § 363 sales"). The objections are not to the quantity or percentage of assets being sold: it has long been understood (by the drafters of the Code, and the Supreme Court[8]) that § 363(b) sales may encompass all or substantially all of a debtor's assets. Rather,

---

[8] The transaction at hand is as good an illustration as any. "Old Chrysler" will simply transfer the $2 billion in proceeds to the first lien lenders, and then liquidate. The first lien lenders themselves will suffer a deficiency of some $4.9 billion, and everyone else will likely receive nothing from the liquidation. Thus the Sale has inevitable and enormous influence on any eventual plan of reorganization or liquidation. But it is not a *"sub rosa* plan" in the *Braniff* sense because it does not specifically "dictate," or "arrange" *ex ante*, by contract, the terms of any subsequent plan. *Id.*

the thrust of criticism remains what it was in *Lionel*: fear that one class of creditors may strong-arm the debtor-in-possession, and bypass the requirements of Chapter 11 to cash out quickly at the expense of other stakeholders, in a proceeding that amounts to a reorganization in all but name, achieved by stealth and momentum. *See, e.g.,* Motorola, Inc. v. Official Comm. of Unsecured Creditors and JPMorgan Chase Bank, N.A. (In re Iridium Operating LLC), 478 F.3d 452, 466 (2d Cir. 2007) ("The reason *sub rosa* plans are prohibited is based on a fear that a debtor-in-possession will enter into transactions that will, in effect, short circuit the requirements of Chapter 11 for confirmation of a reorganization plan." (internal quotation marks and alteration omitted)); Brege, *An Efficiency Model of Section 363(b) Sales,* 92 Va. L. Rev. at 1643 ("The cynical perspective is that [§ 363(b)] serves as a loophole to the otherwise tightly arranged and efficient Chapter 11, through which agents of the debtor-in-possession can shirk responsibility and improperly dispose of assets."); *see also* Steinberg, *The Seven Deadly Sins in § 363 Sales,* Am. Bankr. Inst. J., at 22 ("Frequently, . . . the § 363 sale process fails to maximize value.").

As § 363(b) sales proliferate, the competing concerns identified in *Lionel* have become harder to manage. Debtors need flexibility and speed to preserve going concern value; yet one or more classes of creditors should not be able to nullify Chapter 11's requirements. A balance is not easy to achieve, and is not aided by rigid rules and prescriptions. *Lionel*'s multifactor analysis remains the proper, most comprehensive framework for judging the validity of § 363(b) transactions.

Adopting the Fifth Circuit's wording in *Braniff,* 700 F.2d at 940, commentators and courts—including ours—have sometimes referred to improper § 363(b) transactions as "*sub rosa* plans of reorganization." *See, e.g.,* In re Iridium, 478 F.3d at 466 ("The trustee is prohibited from such use, sale or lease if it would amount to a *sub rosa* plan of reorganization."). *Braniff* rejected a proposed transfer agreement in large part because the terms of the agreement specifically attempted to "dictat[e] some of the terms of any future reorganization plan. The [subsequent] reorganization plan would have to allocate the [proceeds of the sale] according to the terms of the [transfer] agreement or forfeit a valuable asset." 700 F.2d at 940. As the Fifth Circuit concluded, "[t]he debtor and the Bankruptcy Court should not be able to short circuit the requirements of Chapter 11 for confirmation of a reorganization plan by establishing the terms of the plan *sub rosa* in connection with a sale of assets." *Id.*

The term "*sub rosa*" is something of a misnomer. It bespeaks a covert or secret activity, whereas secrecy has nothing to do with a § 363 transaction. Transactions blessed by the bankruptcy courts are openly presented, considered, approved, and implemented. *Braniff* seems to have used "*sub rosa*" to describe transactions that treat the requirements of the Bankruptcy Code as something to be evaded or subverted. But even in that sense, the term is unhelpful. The sale of assets is permissible under § 363(b); and it is elementary that the more assets sold that way, the less will be left for a plan of reorganization, or for liquidation. But the size of the transaction, and the residuum of corporate assets, is, under our precedent, just one consideration for the exercise of discretion by the bankruptcy judge(s), along with an open-ended list of other salient factors. *See Lionel,* 722 F.2d at 1071 (a bankruptcy judge should consider "such relevant factors as the proportionate value of the asset to the estate as a whole"). . . .

The Indiana Pensioners argue that the Sale is a *sub rosa* plan chiefly because it gives value to unsecured creditors (*i.e.*, in the form of the ownership interest in New Chrysler provided to the union benefit funds) without paying off secured debt in full, and without complying with the procedural requirements of Chapter 11. However, Bankruptcy Judge Gonzalez demonstrated proper solicitude for the priority between creditors and deemed it essential that the Sale in no way upset that priority. The lien holders' security interests would attach to all proceeds of the Sale: "Not one penny of value of the Debtors' assets is going to anyone other than the First-Lien Lenders." Opinion Granting Debtor's Motion Seeking Authority to Sell, May 31, 2009 ("Sale Opinion") at 18. As Bankruptcy Judge Gonzalez found, all the equity stakes in New Chrysler were entirely attributable to *new* value—including governmental loans, new technology, and new management—which were not assets of the debtor's estate. *See, e.g., id.* at 22-23.

The Indiana Pensioners' arguments boil down to the complaint that the Sale does not pass the discretionary, multifarious *Lionel* test. The bankruptcy court's findings constitute an adequate rebuttal. Applying the *Lionel* factors, Bankruptcy Judge Gonzalez found good business reasons for the Sale. The linchpin of his analysis was that the only possible alternative to the Sale was an immediate liquidation that would yield far less for the estate—and for the objectors. The court found that, notwithstanding Chrysler's prolonged and well-publicized efforts to find a strategic partner or buyer, no other proposals were forthcoming. In the months leading up to Chrysler's bankruptcy filing, and during the bankruptcy process itself, Chrysler executives circled the globe in search of a deal. But the Fiat transaction was the *only* offer available. Sale Opinion at 6; *see id.* at 16-17 ("Notwithstanding the highly publicized and extensive efforts that have been expended in the last two years to seek various alliances for Chrysler, the Fiat Transaction is the only option that is currently viable. The only other alternative is the immediate liquidation of the company.").

The Sale would yield $2 billion. According to expert testimony—not refuted by the objectors—an immediate liquidation of Chrysler as of May 20, 2009 would yield in the range of nothing to $800 million. *Id.* at 19. Crucially, Fiat had conditioned its commitment on the Sale being completed by June 15, 2009. While this deadline was tight and seemingly arbitrary, there was little leverage to force an extension. To preserve resources, Chrysler factories had been shuttered, and the business was hemorrhaging cash. According to the bankruptcy court, Chrysler was losing going concern value of nearly $100 million each day. Sale Order at 7.

On this record, and in light of the arguments made by the parties, the bankruptcy court's approval of the Sale was no abuse of discretion. With its revenues sinking, its factories dark, and its massive debts growing, Chrysler fit the paradigm of the melting ice cube. Going concern value was being reduced each passing day that it produced no cars, yet was obliged to pay rents, overhead, and salaries. Consistent with an underlying purpose of the Bankruptcy Code—maximizing the value of the bankrupt estate—it was no abuse of discretion to determine that the Sale prevented further, unnecessary losses. . . .

[Moreover, the] Indiana Pensioners exaggerate the extent to which New Chrysler will emerge from the Sale as the twin of Old Chrysler. New Chrysler may manufacture the same lines of cars but it will also make newer, smaller vehicles using Fiat technology that will become available as a result of the Sale—moreover, at the time of the proceedings, Old Chrysler was manufacturing no cars at all. New Chrysler will be run by a new Chief Executive Officer, who has experience in turning around failing auto companies. It may retain many of the same employees, but they will be working under new union contracts that contain a six-year no-strike provision. New Chrysler will still sell cars in some of its old dealerships in the United States, but it will also have new access to Fiat dealerships in the European market. Such transformative use of old and new assets is precisely what one would expect from the § 363(b) sale of a going concern.

CONCLUSION

. . . We have considered all of the objectors-appellants' contentions on these appeals and have found them to be without merit. For the foregoing reasons, we affirm the June 1, 2009 order of the bankruptcy court authorizing the Sale.

The unhappy Indiana pension fund appealed its case to the Supreme Court, which did not just loftily deny certiorari but took the noteworthy step of a *Munsingwear* order (named after the famous underwear company). Indiana State Police Pension Trust v. Chrysler LLC, 558 U.S. 1087 (2009). That is when subsequent developments—here, Chrysler's confirmation of its plan—moot out a petition, but the Supreme Court does not want the lower court opinion to stand as precedent. It grants certiorari, vacates the lower court opinion without comment, and remands for instructions to dismiss as moot. Many see this as a signal that the Court saw an important issue it did not want to let a lower court get first dibs on with a binding precedent. General Motors' similarly momentous § 363 sale also survived various attacks before it too was rendered moot. See, e.g., In re Motors Liquidation Corp., 829 F.3d 139 (2d Cir. 2016) (discussing case history and noting *Chrysler* was *Munsingwear*ed, so did not bind *GM* case as precedent).

The bankruptcy court allowing *GM*'s sale tried to flesh out *Lionel* with a bit more guidance:

As the *Lionel* court expressly stated that the list of salient factors was not exclusive, this Court might suggest a few more factors that might be considered, along with the preceding factors, in appropriate cases: Does the estate have the liquidity to survive until confirmation of a plan? Will the sale opportunity still exist as of the time of plan confirmation? If not, how likely is it that there will be a satisfactory alternative sale opportunity, or a stand-alone plan alternative that is equally desirable (or better) for creditors? And is there a material risk that by deferring the sale, the patient will die on the operating table? Each of these factors goes to the ultimate questions that the *Lionel* court identified: Is there an "articulated business justification" and a "good business reason" for proceeding with the sale without awaiting the final confirmation of a plan[?]

In re Gen. Motors Corp., 407 B.R. 463, 490 (Bankr. S.D.N.Y. 2009).

Other courts express concern with perceived rushing too fast. "I do not think the scheduled three-day trial on these motions is adequate to protect the creditors and the other interests involved. Rather, the transactions proposed in those motions should properly be examined in the disclosure statement and confirmation processes. This is how Congress intended to deal with bankruptcy entities proposing major restructuring, and I must respect that decision." In re New Hampshire Elec. Coop., Inc., 131 B.R. 249, 252 (Bankr. D.N.H. 1991). Some academics agree, noting that urgency is easily fabricated and can sometimes be a cover for rushing through a sale of a company where focused scrutiny might be embarrassing. And even genuine urgency can be used to hurry through a sale that might end up unfairly transferring value from creditors to insiders (incumbent managers, purchasers, and/or the senior secured lenders). See Melissa B. Jacoby & Edward J. Janger, Ice Cube Bonds: Allocating the Price of Process in Chapter 11 Bankruptcy, 123 Yale L.J. 862 (2014) (proposing to diminish this "melting ice cube" leverage to rush through sales outside voted plans of reorganization by setting aside a disputed claims reserve). Empirical work also now questions the premise for hurrying, noting that sales cases may not actually proceed any faster than traditional ones. Lynn M. LoPucki, Chapter 11: Changes in Chapter 11 Success Levels Since 1980, 87 Temp. L. Rev. 989, 997 (2015) (confirmed by unreported data from Business Bankruptcy Project's 2018 sample of chapter 11 cases from Southern District of New York and District of Delaware). Suffice it to say, sales add drama to an already fast-paced arena. For a gripping overall account of the auto bailouts via bankruptcy by the head of the head of the task force, see Steven Rattner, Overhaul: An Insider's Account of the Obama Administration's Emergency Rescue of the Auto Industry (2010).

While some courts and commentators resist what they see as excessive party control over the new chapter 11, the parties themselves push back. They say that so long as *A* has the right to all the proceeds (say, it has a dominant first security interest), what business is it of *B*'s if *A* decides to share some of its bounty with *C* as a gift—"gifting," for those who can countenance use of that word as a verb—even though *B* is next in the priority chain? Even tougher: can the Purchaser, *P*, as a conditional offer say, "I'll buy those assets from the bankruptcy estate for a handsome sum—but only if the proceeds go to *A* and *C*, but not horrible *B*, whom I detest!"? (Assume, e.g., that *B* is the IRS.) If *P* has a lot of money, and there are a lot of unsecured creditors in Class *C* who will get nothing in a piecemeal liquidation, then the judge decides Rock v. Hard Place.

===== **CZYZEWSKI v. JEVIC HOLDING CORP.** =====

137 S. Ct. 973 (2017)

Justice BREYER delivered the opinion of the Court.

Bankruptcy Code Chapter 11 allows debtors and their creditors to negotiate a plan for dividing an estate's value. See 11 U.S.C. §§ 1123, 1129, 1141.

But sometimes the parties cannot agree on a plan. If so, the bankruptcy court may decide to dismiss the case. § 1112(b). The Code then ordinarily provides for what is, in effect, a restoration of the prepetition financial status quo. § 349(b).

In the case before us, a Bankruptcy Court dismissed a Chapter 11 bankruptcy. But the court did not simply restore the prepetition status quo. Instead, the court ordered a distribution of estate assets that gave money to high-priority secured creditors and to low-priority general unsecured creditors but which skipped certain dissenting mid-priority creditors. The skipped creditors would have been entitled to payment ahead of the general unsecured creditors in a Chapter 11 *plan* (or in a Chapter 7 liquidation). See §§ 507, 725, 726, 1129. The question before us is whether a bankruptcy court has the legal power to order this priority-skipping kind of distribution scheme in connection with a Chapter 11 *dismissal*.

I

. . . It is important to keep in mind that Chapter 11 foresees three possible outcomes [confirmation; failure and conversion to chapter 7; or (voluntary or involuntary) dismissal]. A dismissal typically "revests the property of the estate in the entity in which such property was vested immediately before the commencement of the case"—in other words, it aims to return to the prepetition financial status quo. § 349(b)(3).

Nonetheless, recognizing that conditions may have changed in ways that make a perfect restoration of the status quo difficult or impossible, the Code permits the bankruptcy court, "for cause," to alter a Chapter 11 dismissal's ordinary restorative consequences. § 349(b). A dismissal that does so (or which has other special conditions attached) is often referred to as a "structured dismissal," defined by the American Bankruptcy Institute as a "hybrid dismissal and confirmation order . . . that . . . typically dismisses the case while, among other things, approving certain distributions to creditors, granting certain third-party releases, enjoining certain conduct by creditors, and not necessarily vacating orders or unwinding transactions undertaken during the case." American Bankruptcy Institute Commission To Study the Reform of Chapter 11, 2012-2014 Final Report and Recommendations 270 (2014). Although the Code does not expressly mention structured dismissals, they "appear to be increasingly common." *Ibid.*, n. 973. . . .

2

The Code also sets forth a basic system of priority, which ordinarily determines the order in which the bankruptcy court will distribute assets of the estate. Secured creditors are highest on the priority list, for they must receive the proceeds of the collateral that secures their debts. 11 U.S.C. § 725. Special classes of creditors, such as those who hold certain claims for taxes or wages, come next in a listed order. §§ 507, 726(a)(1). Then come low-priority creditors, including general unsecured creditors. § 726(a)(2). The Code places equity holders at the bottom of the priority list. They receive nothing until all previously listed creditors have been paid in full. § 726(a)(6).

The Code makes clear that distributions of assets in a Chapter 7 liquidation must follow this prescribed order. §§ 725, 726. It provides somewhat more flexibility for distributions pursuant to Chapter 11 plans, which may impose a different ordering with the consent of the affected parties. But a bankruptcy court cannot confirm a plan that contains priority-violating distributions over the objection of an impaired creditor class. §§ 1129(a)(7), 1129(b)(2).

The question here concerns the interplay between the Code's priority rules and a Chapter 11 dismissal. Here, the Bankruptcy Court neither liquidated the debtor under Chapter 7 nor confirmed a Chapter 11 plan. But the court, instead of reverting to the prebankruptcy status quo, ordered a distribution of the estate assets to creditors by attaching conditions to the dismissal (*i.e.*, it ordered a structured dismissal). The Code does not explicitly state what priority rules—if any—apply to a distribution in these circumstances. May a court consequently provide for distributions that deviate from the ordinary priority rules that would apply to a Chapter 7 liquidation or a Chapter 11 plan? . . .

B

In 2006, Sun Capital Partners, a private equity firm, acquired Jevic Transportation Corporation with money borrowed from CIT Group in a "leveraged buyout." . . . Just two years after Sun's buyout, Jevic . . . filed for Chapter 11 bankruptcy. At the time of filing, it owed $53 million to senior secured creditors Sun and CIT . . ., and over $20 million to tax and general unsecured creditors.

The circumstances surrounding Jevic's bankruptcy led to two lawsuits. First, petitioners, a group of former Jevic truckdrivers, filed suit in bankruptcy court against Jevic and Sun. Petitioners pointed out that, just before entering bankruptcy, Jevic had halted almost all its operations and had told petitioners that they would be fired. Petitioners claimed that Jevic and Sun had thereby violated state and federal Worker Adjustment and Retraining Notification (WARN) Acts—laws that require a company to give workers at least 60 days' notice before their termination. See 29 U.S.C. § 2102; N.J. Stat. Ann. § 34:21-2 (West 2011). The Bankruptcy Court granted summary judgment for petitioners against Jevic, leaving them (and *this* is the point to remember) with a judgment that petitioners say is worth $12.4 million. See In re Jevic Holding Corp., 496 B.R. 151 (Bkrtcy. Ct. D. Del. 2013). Some $8.3 million of that judgment counts as a priority wage claim under 11 U.S.C. § 507(a)(4), and is therefore entitled to payment ahead of general unsecured claims against the Jevic estate.

Petitioners' WARN suit against Sun continued throughout most of the litigation now before us. But eventually Sun prevailed on the ground that Sun was not the workers' employer at the relevant times. See In re Jevic Holding Corp., 656 Fed. Appx. 617 (C.A.3 2016).

Second, the Bankruptcy Court authorized a committee representing Jevic's unsecured creditors to sue Sun and CIT. The Bankruptcy Court and the parties were aware that any proceeds from such a suit would belong not to the unsecured creditors, but to the bankruptcy estate. See §§ 541(a)(1), (6); Official Comm. of Unsecured Creditors of Cybergenics Corp. v. Chinery, 330 F.3d 548, 552-553 (C.A.3 2003) (en banc) (holding that a creditor's committee can bring a derivative action on behalf of the estate). The committee alleged that Sun and CIT, in the course of their leveraged buyout, had "hastened Jevic's bankruptcy by saddling it with debts that it couldn't service." In re Jevic Holding Corp., 787 F.3d 173, 176 (C.A.3 2015). In 2011, the Bankruptcy Court held that the committee had adequately pleaded claims of preferential transfer under § 547 and of fraudulent transfer under § 548. In re Jevic Holding Corp., 2011 WL 4345204 (Bkrtcy. Ct. D. Del., Sept. 15, 2011).

Sun, CIT, Jevic, and the committee then tried to negotiate a settlement of this "fraudulent-conveyance" lawsuit. By that point, the depleted Jevic estate's only remaining assets were the fraudulent-conveyance claim itself and $1.7 million in cash, which was subject to a lien held by Sun.

The parties reached a settlement agreement. It provided (1) that the Bankruptcy Court would dismiss the fraudulent-conveyance action with prejudice; (2) that CIT would deposit $2 million into an account earmarked to pay the committee's legal fees and administrative expenses; (3) that Sun would assign its lien on Jevic's remaining $1.7 million to a trust, which would pay taxes and administrative expenses and distribute the remainder on a pro rata basis to the low-priority general unsecured creditors, *but which would not distribute anything to petitioners* (who, by virtue of their WARN judgment, held an $8.3 million mid-level-priority wage claim against the estate); and (4) that Jevic's Chapter 11 bankruptcy would be dismissed.

Apparently Sun insisted on a distribution that would skip petitioners because petitioners' WARN suit against Sun was still pending and Sun did not want to help finance that litigation. See 787 F.3d, at 177-178, n. 4 (Sun's counsel acknowledging before the Bankruptcy Court that " 'Sun probably does care where the money goes because you can take judicial notice that there's a pending WARN action against Sun by the WARN plaintiffs. And if the money goes to the WARN plaintiffs, then you're funding someone who is suing you who otherwise doesn't have funds and is doing it on a contingent fee basis' "). The essential point is that, regardless of the reason, the proposed settlement called for a structured dismissal that provided for distributions that did not follow ordinary priority rules.

Sun, CIT, Jevic, and the committee asked the Bankruptcy Court to approve the settlement and dismiss the case. Petitioners and the U.S. Trustee objected, arguing that the settlement's distribution plan violated the Code's priority scheme because it skipped petitioners—who, by virtue of their WARN judgment, had mid-level priority claims against estate assets—and distributed estate money to low-priority general unsecured creditors.

The Bankruptcy Court agreed with petitioners that the settlement's distribution scheme failed to follow ordinary priority rules. App. to Pet. for Cert. 58a. But it held that this did not bar approval. *Ibid*. That, in the Bankruptcy Court's view, was because the proposed payouts would occur pursuant to a structured dismissal of a Chapter 11 petition rather than an approval of a Chapter 11 plan. *Ibid*. The court accordingly decided to grant the motion in light of the "dire circumstances" facing the estate and its creditors. *Id.*, at 57a. Specifically, the court predicted that without the settlement and dismissal, there was "no realistic prospect" of a meaningful distribution for anyone other than the secured creditors. *Id.*, at 58a. A confirmable Chapter 11 plan was unattainable. And there would be no funds to operate, investigate, or litigate were the case converted to a proceeding in Chapter 7. *Ibid.* . . . The Third Circuit affirmed the District Court by a vote of 2 to 1. 787 F.3d, at 175; *id.*, at 186 (Scirica, J., concurring in part and dissenting in part). The majority held that structured dismissals need not always respect priority. Congress, the court explained, had only "codified the absolute priority rule . . . in the specific context of plan confirmation." *Id.*, at 183. As a result, courts could, "in rare instances like this one, approve structured dismissals that do not strictly adhere to the Bankruptcy Code's priority scheme." *Id.*, at 180.

Petitioners (the workers with the WARN judgment) sought certiorari. We granted their petition. . . .

III

We turn to the basic question presented: Can a bankruptcy court approve a structured dismissal that provides for distributions that do not follow ordinary priority rules without the affected creditors' consent? Our simple answer to this complicated question is "no."

The Code's priority system constitutes a basic underpinning of business bankruptcy law. Distributions of estate assets at the termination of a business bankruptcy normally take place through a Chapter 7 liquidation or a Chapter 11 plan, and both are governed by priority. In Chapter 7 liquidations, priority is an absolute command—lower priority creditors cannot receive anything until higher priority creditors have been paid in full. See 11 U.S.C. §§ 725, 726. Chapter 11 plans provide somewhat more flexibility, but a priority-violating plan still cannot be confirmed over the objection of an impaired class of creditors. See § 1129(b).

The priority system applicable to those distributions has long been considered fundamental to the Bankruptcy Code's operation. See H.R. Rep. No. 103-835, p. 33 (1994) (explaining that the Code is "designed to enforce a distribution of the debtor's assets in an orderly manner . . . in accordance with established principles rather than on the basis of the inside influence or economic leverage of a particular creditor"); Roe & Tung, Breaking Bankruptcy Priority: How Rent-Seeking Upends The Creditors' Bargain, 99 Va. L. Rev. 1235, 1243, 1236 (2013) (arguing that the first principle of bankruptcy is that "distribution conforms to predetermined statutory and contractual priorities," and that priority is, "quite appropriately, bankruptcy's most important and famous rule"); Markell, Owners, Auctions, and Absolute Priority in Bankruptcy Reorganizations, 44 Stan. L. Rev. 69, 123 (1991) (stating that a fixed priority scheme is recognized as "the cornerstone of reorganization practice and theory"). . . .

[W]e would expect to see some affirmative indication of intent if Congress actually meant to make structured dismissals a backdoor means to achieve the exact kind of nonconsensual priority-violating final distributions that the Code prohibits in Chapter 7 liquidations and Chapter 11 plans. We can find nothing in the statute that evinces this intent. The Code gives a bankruptcy court the power to "dismiss" a Chapter 11 case. § 1112(b). But the word "dismiss" itself says nothing about the power to make nonconsensual priority-violating distributions of estate value. Neither the word "structured," nor the word "conditions," nor anything else about distributing estate value to creditors pursuant to a dismissal appears in any relevant part of the Code. . . .

Section 349(b), we concede, also says that a bankruptcy judge may, "for cause, orde[r] otherwise." But, read in context, this provision appears designed to give courts the flexibility to "make the appropriate orders to protect rights acquired in reliance on the bankruptcy case." H.R. Rep. No. 95-595, at 338; cf., *e.g.*, Wiese v. Community Bank of Central Wis., 552 F.3d 584, 590 (C.A.7 2009) (upholding, under § 349(b), a Bankruptcy Court's decision not to reinstate a debtor's claim against a bank that gave up a lien in reliance on the claim being released in the debtor's reorganization plan). Nothing else in the Code authorizes a court ordering a dismissal to make general end-of-case distributions of estate assets to creditors of the kind that normally take place in a Chapter 7 liquidation or Chapter 11 plan—let alone final distributions that do not help to restore the *status quo ante* or protect reliance interests acquired in the bankruptcy, and that would be flatly impermissible in a Chapter 7 liquidation or a Chapter 11 plan because they violate priority without the impaired creditors' consent. . . .

The Third Circuit also relied upon In re Iridium Operating LLC, 478 F.3d 452 (C.A.2 2007). But *Iridium* did not involve a structured dismissal. It addressed an *interim* distribution of settlement proceeds to fund a litigation trust that would press claims on the estate's behalf. See *id.*, at 459-460. The *Iridium* court observed that, when evaluating this type of preplan settlement, "[i]t is difficult to employ the rule of priorities" because "the nature and extent of the Estate and the claims against it are *not yet fully resolved.*" *Id.*, at 464 (emphasis added). The decision does not state or suggest that the Code authorizes nonconsensual departures from ordinary priority rules in the context of a dismissal—which is a *final* distribution of estate value—and in the absence of any further unresolved bankruptcy issues. . . .

We recognize that *Iridium* is not the only case in which a court has approved interim distributions that violate ordinary priority rules. But in such instances one can generally find significant Code-related objectives that the priority-violating distributions serve. Courts, for example, have approved "first-day" wage orders that allow payment of employees' prepetition wages, "critical vendor" orders that allow payment of essential suppliers' prepetition invoices, and "roll-ups" that allow lenders who continue financing the debtor to be paid first on their prepetition claims. See *Cybergenics*, 330 F.3d, at 574, n. 8. . . . In doing so, these courts have usually found that the distributions at issue would "enable a successful reorganization and make even the disfavored creditors better off." In re Kmart Corp., 359 F.3d 866, 872 (C.A.7 2004) (discussing the justifications for critical-vendor orders). . . . By way of contrast, in a structured dismissal like the one ordered below, the priority-violating distribution is attached to a final disposition; it does not preserve the debtor as a going concern;

it does not make the disfavored creditors better off; it does not promote the possibility of a confirmable plan; it does not help to restore the *status quo ante*; and it does not protect reliance interests. In short, we cannot find in the violation of ordinary priority rules that occurred here any significant offsetting bankruptcy-related justification.

Rather, the distributions at issue here more closely resemble proposed transactions that lower courts have refused to allow on the ground that they circumvent the Code's procedural safeguards. See, *e.g.,* In re Braniff Airways, Inc., 700 F.2d 935, 940 (C.A.5 1983) (prohibiting an attempt to "short circuit the requirements of Chapter 11 for confirmation of a reorganization plan by establishing the terms of the plan *sub rosa* in connection with a sale of assets"); In re Lionel Corp., 722 F.2d 1063, 1069 (C.A.2 1983) (reversing a Bankruptcy Court's approval of an asset sale after holding that § 363 does not "gran[t] the bankruptcy judge *carte blanche*" or "swallo[w] up Chapter 11's safeguards"); In re Biolitec, Inc., 528 B.R. 261, 269 (Bkrtcy. Ct. N.J. 2014) (rejecting a structured dismissal because it "seeks to alter parties' rights without their consent and lacks many of the Code's most important safeguards"); cf. In re Chrysler LLC, 576 F.3d 108, 118 (C.A.2 2009) (approving a § 363 asset sale because the bankruptcy court demonstrated "proper solicitude for the priority between creditors and deemed it essential that the [s]ale in no way upset that priority"), vacated as moot, 592 F.3d 370 (C.A.2 2010) (*per curiam*).

IV

We recognize that the Third Circuit did not approve nonconsensual priority-violating structured dismissals in general. To the contrary, the court held that they were permissible only in those "rare case[s]" in which courts could find "sufficient reasons" to disregard priority. 787 F.3d, at 175, 186. Despite the "rare case" limitation, we still cannot agree.

For one thing, it is difficult to give precise content to the concept "sufficient reasons." That fact threatens to turn a "rare case" exception into a more general rule. Consider the present case. The Bankruptcy Court feared that (1) without the worker-skipping distribution, there would be no settlement, (2) without a settlement, all the unsecured creditors would receive nothing, and consequently (3) its distributions would make some creditors (high- and low-priority creditors) better off without making other (mid-priority) creditors worse off (for they would receive nothing regardless). . . . [O]ne can readily imagine other cases that turn on comparably dubious predictions. The result is uncertainty. And uncertainty will lead to similar claims being made in many, not just a few, cases. See Rudzik, A Priority Is a Priority Is a Priority—Except When It Isn't, 34 Am. Bankr. Inst. J. 16, 79 (2015) ("[O]nce the floodgates are opened, debtors and favored creditors can be expected to make every case that 'rare case.'").

The consequences are potentially serious. They include departure from the protections Congress granted particular classes of creditors. See, *e.g.,* United States v. Embassy Restaurant, Inc., 359 U.S. 29, 32, 79 S. Ct. 554, 3 L. Ed. 2d 601 (1959) (Congress established employee wage priority "to alleviate in some degree the hardship that unemployment usually brings to workers and their families" when an employer files for bankruptcy); H.R. Rep. No. 95-595, at 187 (explaining the importance of ensuring that employees do not "abandon a failing business for fear of not being paid"). They include changes in the bargaining power of different classes of creditors even in bankruptcies that do not end in structured dismissals. See Warren, A Theory of Absolute Priority, 1991 Ann. Survey Am. L. 9, 30. They include risks of collusion, *i.e.*, senior secured creditors and general unsecured creditors teaming up to squeeze out priority unsecured creditors. . . .

We cannot "alter the balance struck by the statute," Law v. Siegel, 571 U.S. ___, ___, 134 S. Ct. 1188, 1198, 188 L. Ed. 2d 146 (2014), not even in "rare cases." Cf. Norwest Bank Worthington v. Ahlers, 485 U.S. 197, 207, 108 S. Ct. 963, 99 L. Ed. 2d 169 (1988) (explaining that courts cannot deviate from the procedures "specified by the Code," even when they sincerely "believ[e] that . . . creditors would be better off"). The judgment of the Court of Appeals is reversed, and the case is remanded for further proceedings consistent with this opinion.

The jury is still out on what *Jevic* means for chapter 11 cases, as the Court's reference to allowed departures for the betterment of all suggests the sheltering of the critical vendors doctrine that so irked the Seventh Circuit in *Kmart*. But *Jevic*'s tone sends a shot across the bow of crafty practitioners, who will continue to try to get around priority rules they dislike. For example, some lawyers use "gift" as a verb and contend there is a "gifting" exception to the absolute priority rules that allows senior creditors to donate some of their recovery to lower-tiered creditors.

2.   *Statutory Constraints*

Earlier in the consumer materials, you learned how liens on collateral generally survive bankruptcy, and how those liens cloud title to and lower the valuation of the lien-encumbered property by prospective purchasers. In a chapter 11 plan, the lienholder can consent in a plan of reorganization to relinquishing a lien in exchange for a payout or stake in the reorganized company, and the judge's entry of confirmation thus cleans the title. But what if the property is sold through a § 363 sale? While of course the creditor would like its lien to continue, as it would under state law, UCC § 9-315(a)(1), the inability to convey lien-free title to purchasers lowers value. Bankruptcy law seeks to maximize value.

Consequently, § 363(f) expressly allows the trustee to sell or lease estate property "free and clear" of liens. The liens don't just disappear, of course—that would violate the Law of Conservation of Liens—it just means, as under state law, that the liens carry over to the proceeds of the sale. The ability to convey clean property free from liens is great news for purchasers and for the estate trying to maximize value: collateral can be sold for its true worth, undiscounted by the probability a lingering lien on it will be realized and foreclosed upon. Great news for the debtor and the purchaser, however, can be bad news for the secured creditor, who may want to hold onto the collateral, either smelling appreciation or enjoying the leverage that a lien on key collateral accords. To protect the secured creditor, § 363(f) has restrictions that must be satisfied before the power to remove liens is exercised. These restrictions protect not just secured creditors, but anyone else who has a legally cognizable interest encumbering the property to be sold, such as a leasehold. You should look at the five situations in which it allows sales free and clear and then see how the court in the following case had to engage several of them.

In re BRIDGE ASSOCIATES OF SOHO, INC.
589 B.R. 512 (Bankr. E.D.N.Y. 2018)

GROSSMAN, J.

Before the Court is the Debtor's motion to sell an occupied residential loft building located in the SOHO district of New York City free and clear of liens claims and encumbrances including any rights of existing occupants pursuant to 11 U.S.C. § 363(b) and (f). . . .

The Debtor is the owner of real property located at 99 Vandam Street a/ka 533 Greenwich Street, New York (the "Building" or the "Property") which has been designated an "interim multiple dwelling" or "IMD" under Article 7-C of the New York Multiple Dwelling Law (the "Loft Law"). The Debtor seeks to sell the Property free and clear of any liens, claims and encumbrances, including any possessory rights that may be held by the current occupants of the Building. The Building's occupants ("Statutory Tenants") object. The Statutory Tenants argue that they have possessory rights under the Loft Law which cannot be altered by a § 363 sale. The New York City Loft Board also objects to the sale arguing that the Debtor should not be permitted to use the Bankruptcy Code to strip the Property of otherwise valid and controlling statutory regulations. Finally, the Debtor's senior secured creditors, tax lien holders, object to the sale and seek relief from stay in order to complete a foreclosure sale of the Property which was stayed by the Debtor's bankruptcy filing on the eve of foreclosure.

The Debtor proposes to conduct an auction sale of the Property with a reserve price of $12.5 million which, according to the Debtor, will be sufficient to ensure payment of secured claims thus satisfying § 363(f)(3) as to the secured creditors. As for the Statutory Tenants, according to the Debtor applicable nonbankruptcy law permits the sale of the Property free of their interests, and/or such a sale is permissible because the Statutory Tenants' interests are subject to bona fide dispute. See § 363(f)(1) and (4). The Debtor argues that the Statutory Tenants have no possessory interest in the Property, and are merely holdover tenants who have not paid rent in decades and are subject to eviction under state law.

The Loft Law was enacted in 1982 to address illegal conversions of a large number of buildings within New York City that wanted to transition from commercial to residential use. The Laws were enacted order to bring these buildings into conformity with governing statutory, regulatory and/or code requirements for residential occupancy, protect tenants in those buildings and protect public health, safety and general welfare. . . .

The Debtor's Property has been subject to coverage under the Loft Law since approximately 1991 when prior owners of the Building conceded coverage as an "interim multiple dwelling" or "IMD" and formally registered the Building with the "Loft Board" in 1993. The Debtor acquired the Property in 2002, subject to the rules and regulations of the Loft Law.

All parties agree that the Building does not have, and never has had, a certificate of occupancy for residential use, nor is the Debtor currently in compliance with the process to bring the Building into compliance. Pursuant to §§ 301 and 302 of the Multiple Dwelling Law, if a building is occupied without a certificate of occupancy, no rent may be collected. In recognition of the process needed to convert IMD's to legal multiple dwellings, the Loft Law allows an owner to collect rent even if there is no certificate of occupancy, **as long as** it is in compliance with the rules and regulations of the Loft Law necessary to move the Building towards legalization. N.Y. Mult. Dwell. Law § 285. If the owner is not in compliance then it may not collect rent. . . .

The Debtor argues that absent the payment of rent, the Statutory Tenants have no possessory rights to occupy the premises. In response, the Statutory Tenants cite to § 286 of the Multiple Dwelling Law which provides that:

> Prior to compliance with safety and fire protection standards of article seven-B of this chapter, residential occupants qualified for protection pursuant to this article shall be entitled to **continued occupancy provided that the unit is their primary residence, and shall pay the same rent**, including escalations. . . .

N.Y. Mult. Dwell. Law § 286(2)(i) (emphasis added).

The Debtor and the Statutory Tenants disagree on the construction of this statute. The Statutory Tenants argue that their continued occupancy rights are conditioned only upon the requirement that the unit they occupy be their primary residence. The Debtor argues that any occupancy rights conferred by this statute are conditioned upon both the primary residence requirement **and** upon the payment of rent. The Court agrees with the Statutory Tenants. The comma inserted before the phrase "and shall pay the same rent," in this Court's view, distinguishes the reference to rent from the residency requirement. The discussion of rent in § 286 addresses what rents an owner may collect assuming the owner is permitted to collect rent. This conclusion is supported by the decision of the New York Court of Appeals in Chazon LLC v. Maugenest, 19 N.Y.3d 410, 948 N.Y.S.2d 571, 971 N.E.2d 852 (2012). In that decision, the Court found that statutory tenants under the Loft Law could not be evicted based on non-payment of rent where the owner was not in compliance with the Loft Laws.

The Debtor further argues that notwithstanding the Loft Law and caselaw which prevent an out-of-compliance owner from collecting rent, or evicting based on nonpayment of rent, or evicting based on holdover status, a § 363(f) "free and clear" sale can be used to cut off the Statutory Tenants rights of possession because they have no "substantive right" to remain at the Property. The Court disagrees and finds that the rights of possession conferred by § 286 of the Multiple Dwelling Law are rights that cannot be stripped without satisfaction of the requirements of § 363(f)(1) or (4). The Debtor has failed to show the Court that applicable nonbankruptcy law would allow the sale of the Property free and clear of the Statutory Tenants' interests, and has failed to present arguments here which would rise to the level of a "bona fide" dispute as to the Statutory Tenants' rights under the Loft Law. Finally, in its most recent submission to the Court, the Debtor argues that the Statutory Tenants could be compelled, in a legal or equitable proceeding, to accept a money satisfaction of their interests and as such a sale free and clear of their tenancies is permitted. § 363(f)(5). This last minute argument is premised on § 286(12) of the Multiple Dwelling Law which allows "an owner and a residential occupant [to] agree to the purchase by the owner of such person's rights in a unit." N.Y. Mult. Dwell. Law § 286(12). This section was cited by the Loft Board in support of its position that the Statutory Tenants have protected property interests in their respective units. However, § 286(12) does not state that the Statutory Tenants can be *compelled* to accept a monetary settlement of their interests, nor does the Debtor cite any case interpreting § 286(12) as requiring the Statutory Tenants to accept a money satisfaction of their interests. . . .

Based on the foregoing, the Court finds that the Statutory Tenants have possessory rights granted to them under the Loft Law which the Debtor cannot disturb under § 363 of the Bankruptcy Code. The Debtor's motion is therefore denied.

So ordered.

Bridge Associates went 0 for 3 under the possibilities of § 363(f). Lest you believe the other two channels to a sale are any easier under the statute, think again.

In re CHRYSLER (cont'd)

II

The Indiana Pensioners next challenge the Sale Order's release of all liens on Chrysler's assets. In general, under § 363(f), assets sold pursuant to § 363(b) may be sold "free and clear of any interest" in the assets when, *inter alia*, the entity holding the interest consents to the sale. 11 U.S.C. § 363(f)(2). The bankruptcy court ruled that, although the Indiana Pensioners did not themselves consent to the release, consent was validly provided by the collateral trustee, who had authority to act on behalf of all first-lien credit holders.

When Chrysler went into bankruptcy, the trustee had power to take any action necessary to realize upon the collateral—including giving consent to the sale of the collateral free and clear of all interests under §§ 363. . . . The Indiana Pensioners argue that, by virtue of a subclause in one of the loan agreements, Chrysler required the Pensioners' written consent before selling the collateral assets. The clause in question provides that the loan documents themselves could not be amended without the written consent of *all* lenders if the amendment would result in the release of all, or substantially all, of the collateral property. This clause is no help to the Indiana Pensioners. The §§ 363(b) Sale did not entail amendment of any loan document. To the contrary, the §§ 363(b) sale was effected by implementing the clear [consent] terms of the loan agreements. . . .

[T]he Indiana Pensioners argue as a last resort that the majority lenders were intimidated or bullied into approving the Sale in order to preserve or enhance relations with the government, or other players in the transaction. Absent this bullying, the Pensioners suggest, the majority lenders would not have requested the agent to direct the sale of the collateral, and the Sale would not have gone through. The Pensioners argue that this renders the lenders' consent ineffective or infirm.

The record before the bankruptcy court, and the record before this Court, does not support a finding that the majority lenders were coerced into agreeing to the Sale. On the whole, the record (and findings) support the view that they acted prudently to preserve substantial value rather than risk a liquidation that might have yielded nothing at all. . . .

With so much at stake, it is no wonder § 363(f) is heavily litigated. Indeed, recall from Assignment 16 our friends at the Three-Legged Monkey, who rebuffed a lease termination by demonstrating it was outside the ordinary course of business of their bankrupt landlord under § 363(b). The landlord's Plan B was to sell the property "free and clear" of the leasehold under § 363(f) over 3LM's objection. The court demurred, frowning upon the argument that generalized acrimony was a "bona fide dispute" over the legality of the leasehold under § 363(f)(4). (By the way, the 3LM saga, as perhaps was inevitable, had a sad ending. http://kisselpaso.com/death-of-a-monkey-the-3-legged-monkey-is-gone-forever.)

Problem Set 31

31.1. When Adam Levitin's baby daughter was ill, Adam set aside everything to be with his family. After several frightening months, the child recovered, but Adam's dental practice, Happy Smiles, Inc., did not. Adam tried to resuscitate the business through chapter 11, but all the assets are tied up with security interests in favor of his current lender, EnBanc, and he is concerned that his creditors may be difficult to deal with, particularly the rival dentist, Orin Bar-Scrivello, who sold Adam six X-ray machines on unsecured credit and who has since made it clear he would like to put Adam out of business. Adam says he has nothing to offer but his hands— everything else has already gone into the business. Adam is sure he can start again, but he needs the lease on the dental offices, the customer list, the trade name, and the equipment including the X-ray machines. Adam has a new bank, First Wave, which is willing to lend Adam about $3,500,000, if it can have a first lien against all the assets. Three and a half million dollars is a fair liquidation price for these assets. He owes EnBanc about $3,000,000 and his unsecured creditors another $1,000,000. What do you advise? See §§ 363(f), 1129(b). (Ignore the CARES Act temporary modifications to the SBRA.)

31.2. Your client, Finger Lakes Capital, holds a $40 million first mortgage on the Oneida Resort Hotel in upstate New York. The most recent appraisal a couple years ago showed the property as only worth $37 million and that was before the COVID-19 pandemic decimated tourist travel. It came as no surprise when the debtor's counsel, Conor MacNamara, called you to discuss a prepackaged 11. The debtor wants to sell the resort to Chelberg Properties for $26 million free and clear of your lien and wants your assent. Chelberg is a rival hotel operator and insists (as reported by Conor) that the offer will only be good for two weeks with no extensions, so he needs your answer by Monday morning. You were blindsided when Conor also dropped the following: "We also have to discuss those rumors out there someone at Finger Lakes bribed the registrar of deeds to backdate its mortgage recordation." How should you respond? See § 363(f)(3), (4).

SALES AND BEYOND II

In this assignment we continue to look at the sale of a distressed business, focusing on the procedures used to auction companies in bankruptcy. We also look at how a prospective buyer might trade in the burgeoning market of distressed debt as a strategic lever in approaching, or even instigating, those auctions. In fact, so thick is the market for claims in bankrupt companies that chapter 11 has now become an important part of merger and acquisition practice. (Also, this assignment gives you the chance to learn how to use chapter 11 to get to the World Series.)

A. AUCTIONS

Assuming the debtor can jump through § 363's hoops and related case law, it still must come up with a sale procedure that the court is willing to approve. The easiest sale procedure is an auction. Even before the decision in *203 North LaSalle*, auctions were frequently used for § 363 sales. Among other things, auctions provide the court and the parties with some comfort that insiders have not rigged the game.

Most debtors envisioning an auction-type sale will bring a motion to approve a proposed sale procedure, just to make sure the judge is on board with how the DIP's planning to run the bids—and to foreclose Monday-morning objections. Sometimes, the sale is what you would think of as a real auction, with a pool of bidders all showing up to make offers. But buying a large, public company is different from picking up a car at a sheriff's auction. Extensive due diligence is required; bidders don't just show up with a checkbook. Moreover, often a debtor will be approached by a strategic competitor in the same business who wants to get the debtor's assets and is willing to pay good money for them. A debtor may well want to take that bird in the hand rather than run a full auction. But for the reasons we saw in *203 North LaSalle*, bankruptcy judges like to see thick exposure to the market before signing off on a sale, in which case the first-moving bidder, such as the strategic competitor, may not want to undertake all the due diligence costs and come up with a price only to let other bidders freeload off its work by bidding one dollar more. *Cf. The Price Is Right*. The solution is to ordain the first bidder—often hand-picked by the debtor or controlling secured creditor—as the "stalking horse," who gets to set the pace of the auction and establish the presumptive purchase price. Others might then be given a time period to match or exceed that price. What's in it for the stalking horses to perform this public service? Generally, they insist on putting in the sale procedures order an authorization to be paid "breakup fees" if they end up being jilted—getting their lawyers, investment bankers, and other advisors paid for ("buzzards," in the eyes of some, Chris Cumming, Consultants Emerge as Big Beneficiaries of Bankruptcy Sales, American Banker (July 8, 2014)), plus maybe a little something extra for the effort themselves ("hyenas," id.). They might also try to tilt the playing field just a bit. It has been noted that the Chrysler auction order permitted only "qualified bidders" to bid, and one qualification was a willingness to accept the union contracts with the UAW, which some decried as a pro-labor thumb put on the scale by the Obama administration (as DIP lender whispering in the debtor's ear).

Let's look at an auction in practice, with a case that puts the business page right next to the sports page, just like *The New York Times.* This case features the Texas Rangers baseball club, formerly headed by a businessman named George W. Bush. Baseball is a complicated game (try explaining it to a foreign visitor), but the business of baseball is more complex still.

The human protagonists themselves have star power. Thomas Hicks is a famous Texas businessman of the "I take large steps" variety. He was struggling with his leveraged buyout of Liverpool F.C., a highly ranked club in the English Premier Football [soccer] League. At the same time, his Texas Rangers baseball club had consumed $100 million from him and his investors and still needed more. The partnership that owned the club ("Equity Owners"), represented later by a turn-around specialist named William Snyder ("Snyder"), entered into a classic workout agreement—the Asset Purchase Agreement ("APA")—to sell the Rangers to an entity called "Express," whose central figure was the legendary fastball pitcher Nolan Ryan. The Express sale (pun likely intended) under the APA was blessed by the Commissioner of Baseball ("BOC"), whose blessing was necessary because for oligopolistic reasons related to Major League Baseball, 75% of the baseball club owners must approve the sale of any team. The Hicks empire, however, was heavily in debt to the "Lenders," a group that included heavyweights of the finance world like JPMorgan Chase, who were equally insistent that their financing agreement gave them the right to veto any proposed sale of their collateral, regardless of what the Commissioner had to say. Although the Rangers club had guaranteed only $75 million of the Hicks group debt, any additional value from the sale would, according to the court, flow through to the Lenders. Thus, the potentially undersecured Lenders were anxious to maximize the price obtained for the team, and they thought the price in the APA was way too low, so they balked (sorry). When they announced their refusal to approve the sale to Ryan et al. envisioned by a prepack, the club did the only natural thing: file chapter 11 anyway, with the plan of a quick sale to cram down a liquidation plan on the Lenders, where the purchaser under § 363 would be unfettered by any bank veto over sales—vindicating the paranoia of everyone who worries § 363 sales are a way to run roughshod over secured creditors' contractual rights.

In an earlier decision well worth reading, In re Texas Rangers Baseball Partners, 434 B.R. 393 (Bankr. N.D. Tex. 2010), Judge Lynn made several crucial holdings, including that the sell-to-Express-and-liquidate plan was modified enough from the initial APA that the equity owners would have to re-approve it. After Mr. Snyder was hired as chief restructuring officer and sniffed around a bit for other offers, it became less clear what equity would want or even whether it would continue its support of the Express sale—and it was as clear as a Texas night that the Lenders would certainly not. The opinion that follows offers as a bonus a sense of the rapid, dynamic nature of the sales process as the "operation upon a living patient" (or maybe here, a "pitcher's duel"?).

In re TEXAS RANGERS BASEBALL PARTNERS

431 B.R. 706 (Bankr. N.D. Tex. 2010)

LYNN, Bankruptcy Judge.

Before the court is the *Emergency Joint Motion of Lender Parties for Reconsideration of Court's Order Adopting Bidding Procedures* (the "Motion") . . . by which the Lenders ask that the court reconsider its *Order Adopting Bidding Procedures* (the "Procedures Order"). . . .

I. BACKGROUND

. . .

Prior to commencement of this case, Debtor and Express entered into an asset purchase agreement (the "APA") by which Express would purchase the assets of Debtor including the Rangers. Upon filing its chapter 11[] petition[,] Debtor also filed a plan of reorganization (the "Plan") by which it proposed to implement the APA. In the Prior Opinion the court made clear that, in order to confirm the Plan, either the Rangers Equity Owners (*i.e.*, Snyder) would have to accept the Plan or it would have to be proven at the confirmation hearing that the Rangers Equity Owners would receive in a chapter 7 case no more from a sale of the Rangers than the price provided in the APA. *See* Code § 1129(a)(7).

Following his appointment, Snyder learned of and made contact with several potential bidders interested in acquiring the Rangers. Having concluded that the best proof of the adequacy of the price to be paid by Express pursuant to the APA would be an auction of the team, in which other bidders might participate, Snyder negotiated with Express, Debtor and other parties, seeking to agree on bidding procedures to market-test the APA. . . .

[T]he court held a hearing on July 13, 2010. At that time, the court presented to the parties a draft of proposed bidding procedures, based on the form used by Express and Debtor and modified by the court. Following argument by the parties, the court announced that it would adopt its procedures with certain further modifications. It directed the Rangers Equity Owners to make modifications to the existing draft and invited parties to comment by the afternoon of July 14 on the result. Following receipt of the revised draft and review of comments received, the court completed its formulation of procedures, in the form of the Approved Procedures, which it then implemented by the Procedures Order.

Noting that the court adopted the Approved Procedures without the benefit of an evidentiary record, the Lenders then filed the Motion. Though the court, for reasons given below, believed it necessary to enter the Procedures Order as soon as possible, and though the court believed it had sufficient basis for doing so, it promptly set the Motion and allowed the parties to address the fairness of the Approved Procedures at the Hearing.

II. The Court's Exercise of Authority

[The court explained its authority under §§ 363(b)(1) and 105 for the bidding procedures it had imposed and set an auction date of August 4. — Eds.] As to why it would exercise that authority as it did, the court believed (and now finds) that the APA is subject to severe time constraints. Specifically, if Express does not close under the APA by August 12, 2010, its ability to finance the transactions contemplated by the APA will end. While it may well be that, as the Lenders maintain, a better offer than that represented by the APA will materialize, the court does not at this writing have sufficient evidence before it to so conclude.

Thus, while the Lenders are content to let the Plan proceed to a confirmation hearing on the assumption that the Plan cannot be confirmed absent a test of the APA in the market, and so would accept the loss of the APA and Express as a potential purchaser of the Rangers, the court is not so inclined. Rather, the court concluded that it was necessary to have in place bidding procedures that would provide a reasonable opportunity for the APA to be tested against the market. If, as the court anticipates, the Approved Procedures prove a sufficient test of Express's purchase price, then this case may be concluded without the necessary loss of the APA.

. . . [The court] saw no other way to establish procedures in the time available than through its imposition of them. After taking account of arguments made at the July 13 hearing and the comments submitted on July 14, the court concluded that entry of the Procedures Order was appropriate — and, given the time constraints, necessary to be done without delay. . . .

III. Issues

The Lenders and Snyder raise two issues with the Approved Procedures. First, they argue that the time allowed other bidders under the Approved Procedures is inadequate for completion of due diligence and for competing bidders to obtain financing. Second, they contend that the stalking horse protections afforded Express are unnecessary and overly generous.

IV. Discussion

A. Timing

. . .

Prospective bidders have been on notice since immediately following commencement of Debtor's chapter 11 case (by May 26, 2010) that other bids than that of Express for purchase of the Rangers would be entertained. Indeed, other potential bidders have been in contact with Debtor and Snyder, and at least two of them participated in a mediation session among the parties on July 6. The court concludes that the small universe of potential bidders and the common knowledge that the Rangers are for sale offsets in large part the shortness of time between the adoption of the Approved Procedures and the August 4 auction.

1. Due Diligence

The court does, however, appreciate the concern of Snyder and the Lenders respecting due diligence. From adoption of the Approved Procedures to the date of auction is less than a three-week period. Further, before a bidder may commence due diligence it must be qualified by the BOC.

On the other hand, two or more potential bidders have been qualified, the BOC has promised to act promptly (and has done so) as to other potential bidders, and the court will promptly, on motion, review a refusal by the BOC to grant clearance. Moreover, those two qualified potential bidders as well as others had access to Debtor's data room during the prepetition auction that resulted in selection of Express as purchaser of the Rangers and ultimately Debtor's execution of the APA. Finally, Cofsky [from Perella Weinberg, debtor's investment bankers] testified that none of the potential bidders with which he has communicated have expressed that they would be unable to make a bid by August 4. He also testified that one potential bidder affirmatively told him that it would have sufficient time to submit a bid if it chose to do so. . . .

Given that the Rangers are constantly in public view and that their principal obligations—players' contracts—are the subject of endless news stories, the court believes due diligence by bidders is not the sort of inquiry that would, by reason of mystery surrounding Debtor's assets and liabilities, daunt a serious prospective purchaser.

For the foregoing reasons, the court concludes that, notwithstanding difficulties prospective bidders may encounter in completing due diligence, the time period leading up to the August 4 auction is sufficient and a necessary limitation in the Approved Procedures.

2. Financing

The court is less concerned about prospective bidders finding financing. The necessary wealth of potential purchasers is only part of the reason for this. . . .

B. The Breakup Fee

The Approved Procedures establish Express and the APA as a stalking horse bid. The court also established protections, including, as an alternative to proving rejection damages should the APA not be consummated, an all-inclusive breakup fee of the greater of $10,000,000 [or] 12.5% of Express's actual costs and damages. The Lenders contend that the breakup fee is unnecessary, is too much and will chill bidding by allowing Express a type of credit bid. . . .

[T]he breakup fee is provided as an alternative to litigation.[27] Avoidance of litigation and the inherent benefits of having a stalking horse justify a breakup fee in this case. . . . [T]he magnitude of the breakup fee is not excessive. Cofsky testified that the amount of the fee, at approximately 2% of the purchase price, is in line with similar, non-bankruptcy transactions. The court has found other bankruptcy cases in which breakup fees of as much as 4% have been approved. Furthermore, it is not uncommon for an agreement to provide for payment of the stalking horse's expenses in addition to a breakup fee. The breakup fee provided for in the Approved Procedures is inclusive of all claims Express might make.

However, the court erred in establishing the 125% alternative to the $10,000,000 breakup fee. By providing that Express would be entitled to the *greater of* $10,000,000 [or] 125% of its allowable costs and expenses, the court guaranteed that Express could seek to enhance its recovery by proving up excessive costs. Nor did the court intend that the breakup fee might approach, let alone exceed, the $15,000,000 initial overbid provided for in the Approved Procedures. Thus those procedures must be modified such that (1) Express must elect whether to rely on the 125% calculation or accept the $10,000,000 *before* the court determines which of its costs and expenses are allowable; and (2) in no event may the 125% calculation exceed $13,000,000. . . .

The court is acutely aware that Debtor is under the indirect control of Thomas O. Hicks ("Hicks"), for whose benefit it is alleged that the pre-filing transactions were undertaken. Further, Debtor's president—Ryan—is a principal of Express. The Approved Procedures leave much control of disposition of the Rangers under Debtor's control. The court assumes Debtor will act in good faith, on the advice of Perella, its financial advisor, in evaluating bids under the Approved Procedures; Hicks's legitimate interest in Debtor's chapter 11 case is limited to ensuring that claims and rights he may have that are ultimately sustained by the court are protected: *i.e.*, that he will receive any moneys he is eventually found to be entitled to. Should Debtor, contrary to the court's expectations, prove overly attentive to Hicks's interests and opinions in administering the Approved Procedures, the court will act to expand Snyder's authority or otherwise protect the interests of the Lenders and Debtor's other creditors.

V. Conclusion

The court recognizes the Approved Procedures are not necessarily the optimal way to resolve this chapter 11 case. It is possible, as the Lenders and the Ranger Equity Owners argue, that no bidder will come forward to

---

[27] Because the APA was entered into prepetition, if it is not performed by Debtor—*i.e.*, if it is rejected—Express may assert an unsecured claim against Debtor. Code §§ 365(g)(1) and 502(g)(1). The Lenders argue that such a claim is limited to a $1,500,000 breakup fee provided to Express by the APA (Express contends its breakup fee under the APA is $10,000,000). Express, on the other hand, argues that its rejection claim would be for the difference between its bid under the APA and the Successful Bidder's bid. The court reaches no conclusion here as to which, if either, interpretation of Express's potential unsecured claim is correct.

compete with Express at the auction. Should that be the case, Debtor and Express will have the burden of showing that the Approved Procedures indeed provided an effective market test of the APA.

While such a showing may not be a low bar, it is by no means impossible to make. First, the evidence elicited at the Hearing provides substantial support for the conclusion that the Approved Procedures will satisfactorily market-test the APA. Second, it might be shown (though, of course, the court at this time makes no such finding) that prosecution of the Motion may have chilled bidding under the Approved Procedures in two ways, thus explaining the potential absence of competing bidders. In the first place, rather than working toward a sale of the Rangers, the parties spent the first week after entry of the Procedures Order distracted by the Motion and the Hearing. In the second place, by highlighting the Lenders' opposition to and the deficiencies in the Proposed Procedures, the Motion and the Hearing may have dissuaded bidders from participating in the process. Not only were potential bidders' attention called to weaknesses in the Approved Procedures, but they may well also have been left with the impression that the Approved Procedures will lead not to a sale of the Rangers but rather to yet another round of negotiation and bidding leading to an auction sometime in the distant future.

No bidder should so assume. Indeed, if even one bidder appears to compete with Express, the court will most likely conclude the market-test of the APA was fair. Certainly if there is a second bidder, any party contending the Approved Procedures were nevertheless inadequate will bear a heavy burden. It is thus in every party's interest to make a success of the Approved Procedures. . . .

The court seems to be saying that if the auction fails, it will not be because the procedures it designed were too restrictive, but because the objectors *complained* that the procedures it designed were too restrictive. The court's blamelessness thus appears unfalsifiable. As for the need for speed in prepacks and § 363 sales, consider this excerpt from footnote 12 of the court's opinion, authored by, one presumes, a Rangers fan: "The court is also concerned that a hiatus between now and September 30, during which disposition of the Rangers is so uncertain, would have an adverse effect on the team's performance, on-field and otherwise. *See, e.g.*, Ryan, 7/21, 12:21-13:18; Washington, 7/22, 10:2-19. The Rangers, at this writing, are in first place in their division. If they continue to win, they are likely to be serious contenders in post-season play." Lest there be an allegation the court was considering extraneous factors in rendering its decision, the judge was also quick to tie matters back to bankruptcy by his conclusion on this effect of a World Series run: "This will substantially enhance the team's value."

How did it turn out? They made it to the Series but lost to the Giants. The auction's outcome was more propitious:

Following the commencement of Debtor's bankruptcy case on May 24, 2010, and until July 15, 2010, Perella [the debtor's financial advisor] did not actively seek to market the Rangers. However, once the court entered its order adopting bidding procedures, Perella, using both its own resources and lists of potential bidders provided by Raine and Merrill [other investment bankers], undertook to find persons interested in bidding on the Rangers. Once potential bidders had been located, Perella assisted them in going through the necessary steps to qualify to participate in the auction of the Rangers set by the court for August 4, 2010 (the "Auction").

Two bidders appeared at and participated in the Auction: Express and Radical Pitch LLC ("Pitch"). [The principal of Pitch was Mark Cuban, billionaire owner of the Dallas Mavericks—Eds.] Prior to actual commencement of the Auction, Pitch had to qualify its bid [with the other owners]—a process in which Perella, through Cofsky, played an important part. Cofsky also was active in determining the discount to be applied to Pitch's bid—a function the Objectors contend was less than beneficial.

Express proved to be the winning bidder. The price resulting from the Auction was over $90,000,000 more than Express's opening, stalking-horse bid, and the direct and indirect return to creditors (through equity) improved by approximately $120,000,000. . . .

In re Texas Rangers Baseball Partners, 2011 WL 1323777 (Bankr. N.D. Tex. Apr. 6, 2011).

With prepacks and sales, considerable control of the government-conferred discharge in bankruptcy is doled out to the debtor and its controlling stakeholders, including lenders. In the Rangers case, these principals had a sale all sewn up to Express and ready to go. But the guiding hand of the bankruptcy court had the result of upping the return from the sale by a cool $90 million and the ultimate payoff for creditors increased about $120 million. Perhaps the presence of a public watchdog can indeed make a difference. Still, there is an ongoing tension between the virtues of stalking horses in stirring up auctions interest and the concern that they don't just line their pockets with exorbitant breakup fees compensated by the bankruptcy estate. See In re Energy Future Holdings Corp., 904 F.3d 298 (3d Cir. 2018) (affirming sua sponte reconsideration and denial of $275 million breakup fee).

B.   CLAIMS TRADING

We have seen that one result of a chapter 11 filing by an insolvent business may be that the shareholders are "out of the money" and disappear, while the ownership of the company moves up to the next priority level, the unsecured creditors. If unsecured creditors are likely to inherit the ownership of the company, it's not much of a leap to see that buying unsecured claims may be a method of buying the business and, bankruptcy being bankruptcy, buying it at a steep discount. Of course, buying a secured claim may be an even surer way to getting control of a debtor's assets, especially when that secured claim hog-ties all of them. It is thus not surprising that buying claims has become a significant approach to buying companies or their assets in bankruptcy.

The development of large and liquid markets for distressed debt has provided another important avenue for avoiding the elaborate procedures of chapter 11. See Michelle M. Harner, Trends in Distressed Debt Investing: An Empirical Study of Investors' Objectives, 16 Am. Bankr. Inst. L. Rev. 69 (2008) (finding funds specializing in distressed debt investing are actually both concentrated and successful in influencing the outcome of chapter 11 cases). For an updated discussion, see the American Bankruptcy Institute Law Review Volume 22 (Winter 2014) symposium featuring eight papers discussing hedge funds in bankruptcy. E.g., Keith Sharfman & G. Ray Warner, Hedge Funds in Bankruptcy, 22 Am. Bankr. Inst. L. Rev. 61 (2014); see also Edward I. Altman, The Role of Distressed Debt Markets, Hedge Funds, and Recent Trends in Bankruptcy on the Outcomes of Chapter 11, 22 Am. Bankr. Inst. L. Rev. 75 (2014) (estimating as of time of writing more than 200 financial institutions collectively investing between $400-450 billion in the U.S. distressed debt market since late 1980s).

In a world of all-encompassing security interests, a putative acquirer through the distressed-debt trading route would be well placed to start with buying up secured debt. Secured creditors have an entitlement to credit bid at a § 363 sale, which means, just as outside bankruptcy, they can bid more than the true value of the collateral—all the way up to the face amount of the secured debt that is owed. This power means a credit-bidding undersecured creditor can easily win any foreclosure auction. The ability to credit bid thus in many cases can be a functional right to buy the debtor. This functional control can even lead to a shadow auction (all private and unregulated by the bankruptcy court) where suitors bid for the secured debt of the debtor's pre-existing lender with an eye to using that acquired secured debt in a subsequent credit bid for the debtor's assets at a § 363 sale.

A market for trading in claims against the debtor has thus developed, and not just for secured debt. Buying up unsecured debt allows a purchaser to control any chapter 11 voting that might unfold—including proposing a plan, rival to the DIP plan if necessary, to sell control of the company. This growth of claims trading has unsurprisingly transformed the negotiations in chapter 11 in many cases. Traditional lenders are increasingly anxious to sell their loans early in the game, take their losses, and move on. (The only thing bankers hate more than losing money is protracted uncertainty about how much money they will lose.) Some buyers are merely looking for relatively short-term returns and have little interest in the long-term potential of the debtor company as a customer or as an investment. The buyers are often called "vulture investors," but like their avian namesakes they play an important part in the ecology of the financial world. See Paul M. Goldschmid, More Phoenix than Vulture: The Case for Distressed Investor Presence in the Bankruptcy Reorganization Process, 2005 Colum. Bus. L. Rev. 191. (See, we cite student notes, too!) While sometimes vulture funds will buy a position in the debtor because they think the distressed debt is trading at a bargain and hope to make a quick profit, other times they do more: sometimes the strategy is to buy the debt to control the outcome of the bankruptcy and force a sale, and sometimes it is to buy the debt and hold onto the company, spruce it up, and sell it a higher exit multiple in a few years. Much of the posture of the vulture fund will depend on whether the DIP is planning to sell the company. When the DIP is on board with a sale, the claims acquirers are perhaps trying to buy stakes to ground a credit bid or otherwise help them win the auction. When the DIP is fighting a sale—trying in the traditional sense to reorganize the company and keep it going with current management—the vultures are buying up debt to vote against the DIP's rescue plan and counter-propose a sale. These latter cases tend to be more fractious.

1.   *Buying Claims to Buy Companies*

The first case below looks at a claims trading investor that bought debt to get a leg up in a management-supported sale. It found, however, that the "right" to credit bid in a § 363 sale may not be as inviolable as it sounds.

In re FISKER AUTOMOTIVE HOLDINGS, INC.
510 B.R. 55 (Bankr. D. Del. 2014)

GROSS, Bankruptcy Judge.

. . .

The Debtors were founded in 2007 with the goal of designing, assembling, and manufacturing premium plug-in hybrid electric vehicles in the United States. Debtors faced many difficulties that prevented the Debtors from operating as planned. The challenges included safety recalls related to battery packs supplied by a third party vendor, the loss of a material portion of their existing unsold vehicle inventory in the United States during Hurricane Sandy in 2012, and the loss of their lending facility provided through the United States Department of Energy ("DOE").

UNCONTESTED FACTS

The following facts are uncontested and will describe the origination and essence of the conflict at hand.

1. The Debtors expressly filed these cases to accomplish the sale of substantially all their assets to Hybrid Tech Holdings, LLC ("Hybrid") and then to administer these chapter 11 estates through the Debtors' proposed chapter 11 plan of liquidation.

2. As of the Petition Date, November 22, 2013, the Debtors had approximately $203.2 million in indebtedness and related obligations outstanding. [$168.5 million of senior debt to DOE and $34.7 million to various other creditors.—Eds.]

3. Debtors and the United States of America, through DOE, are parties to that certain Loan Arrangement and Reimbursement Agreement, dated as of April 22, 2010 (as amended, supplemented or otherwise modified, "Senior Loan Agreement"). Pursuant to the Senior Loan Agreement, DOE agreed to, among other things: (a) arrange for the Federal Financing Bank ("FFB") to purchase notes from Fisker Automotive in an amount not to exceed $169.3 million to fund the development, commercial production,

sale and marketing, and all related engineering integration of the Debtors' "Karma" model automobile, the Debtors' premium-priced [plug-in hybrid electric vehicle] (the "Karma Lending Facility"); and (b) arrange for FFB to purchase notes from Fisker Automotive in an amount not to exceed $359.4 million to fund the development, commercial production, sale and marketing of the Debtors' "Nina" model automobile, a moderately priced version of the Karma, including the establishment and construction of an assembly and production site in the United States (the "Nina Lending Facility," and together with the Karma Lending Facility, the "Senior Loan Facility").

4. On October 11, 2013, Hybrid purchased DOE's position of outstanding principal of $168.5 million ($.15/$1.00) under the Senior Loan Facility for $25 million and, for all practicable purposes, succeeded to DOE's position as the Debtors' senior secured lender.

5. With the Senior Loan sale by DOE to Hybrid, the Debtors entered into discussions with Hybrid regarding Hybrid's potential acquisition of the Debtors' assets through a credit bid of all or part of the Senior Loan. These discussions led to the Asset Purchase Agreement, pursuant to which Hybrid proposes to acquire substantially all of the assets of Debtors for consideration which includes $75 million in the form of a credit bid. The Debtors determined that a sale to a third party other than Hybrid was not reasonably likely to generate greater value than the Debtors' proposed sale transaction or advisable under the facts and circumstances of these chapter 11 cases. The DOE Loan purchase made Hybrid the Debtors' senior secured lender holding approximately $168.5 million in claims. What collateral is thereby secured remains at issue [and hence the precise amount of the "credit" to bid—Eds.].

6. The Debtors decided that the cost and delay arising from a competitive auction process or pursuing a potential transaction with an entity other than Hybrid would be reasonably unlikely to increase value for the estates. The Sale Motion therefore reflects Debtors' decision to sell its assets to Hybrid through a private sale.

7. The Official Committee of Unsecured Creditors (the "Committee") opposes the Sale Motion and is seeking an auction along the lines contained in the Bidding Procedures Motion. In particular, the Committee opposes Hybrid's right to credit bid. The Committee has proposed an alternative to the Hybrid private sale: an auction with Wanxiang America Corporation ("Wanxiang").

8. While the offers are evolving and improving, the Wanxiang proposal at the time the Sale Motion was pending was extremely attractive both economically and in its significant non-economic terms. The Committee strongly endorsed Wanxiang's participation in an auction.

9. At the hearing on January 10, 2014, at which the Court was to consider the Sale Motion and the Bidding Procedures Motion, the Debtors and the Committee announced on the record an agreement to limit the areas of dispute. The Debtors and the Committee agreed that (emphasis supplied):

Stipulated Agreements

. . . [I]f at any auction Hybrid either would have no right to credit bid or its credit bidding were capped at $25 million, there is a strong likelihood that there would be an auction that has a material chance of creating material value for the estate over and above the present Hybrid bid. . . . [I]f Hybrid's ability to credit bid is not capped; it appears to both the Debtors and the Committee that there is no realistic possibility of an auction. . . . [W]e agree that limiting of Hybrid's ability to credit bid, for these reasons alone, would likely foster and facilitate a competitive bidding environment. . . .

[A]ll of the work here has shown to both the Debtors and the Committee that the highest and best value for the estate is achieved only in the sale of all of the Fisker assets as an entirety. . . .

[W]ithin that entirety of the assets offered for sale are (i) material assets that we believe consist of properly perfected Hybrid collateral, (ii) material assets that are not subject to properly perfected liens in favor of Hybrid and (iii) material assets where there is a dispute as to whether Hybrid has a properly perfected lien. . . .

[If] the Court rules that there is no basis to limit Hybrid's ability to credit bid as proposed, the Committee will withdraw all of its oppositions to the Debtors' present sale. . . .

10. The Stipulated Agreements are highly significant to the credit bidding issue. If Hybrid is entitled to credit bid more than $25 million at an auction, Wanxiang will not participate—and there will be no auction.

11. Wanxiang has made it clear it is prepared to increase its bid if there is an auction.

DISCUSSION

The Sale Motion and the Bidding Procedures Motion require the Court to determine whether Hybrid is entitled to credit bid its claim and, if so, whether the Court may properly limit, or cap, the amount that Hybrid may credit bid. If the answer to the second question, the capping of the credit bid, is "no," it is clear there will be no auction. The Committee will withdraw its objection to the Sale Motion and Hybrid will have a clear path to purchase the Debtors' assets in a private sale, subject to the Court's approval.

It is beyond peradventure that a secured creditor is entitled to credit bid its allowed claim. . . .

Hybrid paid $25 million for its claim. It will be entitled to credit bid. The only question is: in what amount.[2]

The law is equally clear, as § 363(k) provides, that the Court may "for cause order[] otherwise." In [In re Philadelphia Newspapers, LLC, 599 F.3d 298 (3d Cir. 2010)], the Third Circuit Court of Appeals captured the law as follows:

As an initial matter, the Code plainly contemplates situations in which assets encumbered by liens are sold without affording secured lenders the right to credit bid. The most obvious example arises in the text of § 363(k),

---

[2] The Committee argues Hybrid should not be permitted to credit bid at all, or in any event no more than the $25 million it paid for the $168.5 million claim Hybrid purchased from DOE. Hybrid insists on credit bidding $75 million.

under which the right to credit bid is not absolute. A secured lender has the right to credit bid "unless the court for cause orders otherwise." 11 U.S.C. § 363(k). In a variety of cases where a debtor seeks to sell assets pursuant to § 363(b), courts have denied secured lenders the right to bid their credit. . . .[14]

The evidence in this case is express and unrebutted that there will be *no* bidding—not just the chilling of bidding—if the Court does not limit the credit bid. The Committee, which strongly opposes any credit bidding by Hybrid, will abandon its opposition to the Sale Motion if there is no auction—and there will be no auction if the credit bid is not capped. It is through the Committee's efforts that Wanxiang is now prepared to bid. Wanxiang is also prepared to increase its offer in an auction.

Wanxiang is a highly attractive and capable participant. Wanxiang recently purchased in bankruptcy, through an auction, certain assets of A123 Systems for almost $300 million, most importantly, the primary component of the Fisker electric cars, which is the lithium ion battery. This means that Wanxiang has a vested interest in purchasing Fisker.

Thus, the "for cause" basis upon which the Court is limiting Hybrid's credit bid is that bidding will not only be chilled without the cap; bidding will be frozen.

Hybrid if unchecked of its purchase, might well have frozen out other suitors for Fisker's assets. Debtors filed these cases on Friday, November 22, 2013, a mere three business days before the Thanksgiving holiday, and insisted that the Sale Motion and confirmation hearings occur not later than January 3, 2014, i.e., immediately after the New Year holiday.[4] The schedule therefore allowed only 24 business days for parties to challenge the Sale Motion and even less time for the Committee, which was not appointed until December 5, 2013, to represent the interests of unsecured creditors. Neither Debtors nor Hybrid, when the Court asked, ever provided the Court with a satisfactory reason why the sale of the non-operating Debtors required such speed. Nor did Debtors or Hybrid respond to the Court's repeated admonition that the timing of the Sale Motion was troublesome. It is the Court's view that Hybrid's rush to purchase and to persist in such effort is inconsistent with the notions of fairness in the bankruptcy process. The Fisker failure has damaged too many people, companies and taxpayers to permit Hybrid to short-circuit the bankruptcy process.

Finally, the Committee has raised concerns that the amount of Hybrid's secured claim is uncertain. In their Stipulated Agreements, the Debtors and the Committee agree that Hybrid's claim is partially secured,

---

[14] The Lenders argue that the "for cause" exemption under § 363(k) is limited to situations in which a secured creditor has engaged in inequitable conduct. That argument has no basis in the statute. A court may deny a lender the right to credit bid in the interest of any policy advanced by the Code, such as to ensure the success of the reorganization or to foster a competitive bidding environment. *See, e.g.,* 3 Collier on Bankruptcy 363.09[1] ("the Court might [deny credit bidding] if permitting the lienholder to bid would chill the bidding process.").

[4] It is now clear that Hybrid's "drop dead" date of January 3, 2014, was pure fabrication, designed to place maximum pressure on creditors and the Court. Today is January 17, 2014. Hybrid is still working to acquire Debtors' assets.

partially unsecured and of uncertain status for the remainder [a hybrid claim.—Eds.]. Hybrid argues that under case law in this Circuit, Hybrid is yet entitled to credit bid its entire claim. Hybrid cites In re Submicron Systems Corp., 432 F.3d 448 (3d Cir. 2006). . . . In *Submicron* the classification of the claim to be credit bid was clear. The claim was secured, albeit the secured collateral was deficient as to the entirety of the claim. But here we do not yet know how much of Hybrid's claim is secured. The law leaves no doubt that the holder of a lien the validity of which has not been determined, as here, may not bid its lien. *Submicron* addresses an allowed claim. No one knows how much of the claim Hybrid purchased from DOE will be *allowed* as a secured claim.

CONCLUSION

As discussed, the Court will limit, for cause, Hybrid's credit bid to $25 million. To do otherwise would freeze bidding. Hybrid as the proposed sale purchaser insisted on an unfair process, i.e., a hurried process, and the validity of its secured status has not been determined. In reaching its decision, the Court has followed precedent. A decision to authorize an uncapped credit bid under the facts of this case would be unprecedented and unacceptable.

Hybrid appealed the order, but the district court affirmed, with this caustic footnote:

> At the outset, the court notes that Hybrid filed four emergency motions in the space of three days. This barrage of "emergency" motions of dubious merit and even more doubtful urgency has served only to unnecessarily burden the court and impede resolution of Hybrid's contentions regarding the Bankruptcy Court's credit bid order. It appears that Hybrid's persistent haste is not entirely out of character and may be part of the "rush to purchase" and attempt to "short-circuit the bankruptcy process" for which the Bankruptcy Court chastised Hybrid in its January 17th order. *Hybrid is hereby precluded from filing additional motions regarding the credit bid order.*

In re Fisker Auto. Holdings, Inc., 2014 WL 576370, at *1 n.1 (D. Del. Feb. 12, 2014) (emphasis added).

Fisker highlights a serious policy concern about the power of credit bidding that is heightened in a world of claims trading. When a debtor runs a § 363 sale, the secured creditor's right to credit bid gives it extra leverage in winning the auction. But that only seems fair: it lent that full amount to the debtor and never got it back; it risked that much, so why shouldn't it get to bid that as "banked credit" in trying to get the debtor's assets? If, by contrast, a risk-averse secured creditor sells its note for 40 cents on the dollar to a vulture fund, then the secured creditor eats a loss right away while the vulture (unless the court orders otherwise) gets the power to credit bid the full face amount of the note, enjoying 60 cents of "free" leverage, with only 40 ever put at risk. Functional control of an auction, all pursuant to a sale perhaps never seen by the bankruptcy court, may be what irks some judges, even without facts as stark as *Fisker*'s.

Some downplay *Fisker* and make the contrary argument: that it chills the market for secured debt to the collective economic loss of all. See, e.g., In re Aéropostale, Inc., 555 B.R. 369 (Bankr. S.D.N.Y. 2016). The ABI suggested constraining *Fisker* by recommending the court address any chilling concerns through approving well-designed auction and sale procedures rather than tinkering with the secured creditor's bidding rights under § 363(k)'s "for cause" language. ABI Commission to Study the Reform of Chapter 11, 2012-2014 Final Report and Recommendations 147 (2014). So maybe the *Fisker* courts have it all wrong. Was Judge Gross making much ado about nothing? He forbade a credit bid for $75 million because he wanted to have a real auction, albeit one that would start at $25 million. But could an auction that only had two interested suitors really treble the price paid for the debtor?

> China's Wanxiang Group won an auction for Fisker Automotive Holdings Inc., the maker of luxury plug-in hybrid cars, with a $149.2 million bid, almost six times what Fisker was seeking when it filed for bankruptcy. Wanxiang topped Hybrid Tech Holdings LLC during the auction, which began three days ago and went through 19 rounds of bidding, with an offer that includes $126.2 million in cash and $8 million in assumed liabilities, Fisker said yesterday in a statement.

http://www.bloomberg.com/news/2014-02-14/wanxiang-s-149-million-fisker-bid-tops-hybrid-tech-in-auction.html. A similar fate befell another American company, Bumble Bee Foods, which was sold to Fong Chun Formosa (FCF) Fishery Company, making Bumble Bee perhaps the "Fisker of the Sea." For some reason, though, this case did not raise the same level of national defense concerns, which surprises at least one of us.

2. Buying Claims to Sell (or Shut Down) Companies

Say what you want about Hybrid, but at least it believed in the debtor and wanted to buy it, albeit on the cheap. The next case looks at another claims-trading investor who scooped up the debt with a much different agenda in mind.

=========== In re DBSD NORTH AMERICA, INC. ===========

634 F.3d 79 (2d Cir. 2011)

LYNCH, Circuit Judge.

These consolidated appeals arise out of the bankruptcy of DBSD North America, Incorporated and its various subsidiaries (together, "DBSD"). The bankruptcy court confirmed a plan of reorganization for DBSD. . . .

DISH [Dish Network Corporation—Eds.] . . . argues that the bankruptcy court erred when it found DISH did not vote "in good faith" under 11 U.S.C. § 1126(e) and when, because of the § 1126(e) ruling, it disregarded

DISH's class for the purposes of counting votes under 11 U.S.C. § 1129(a)(8). DISH also argues that the bankruptcy court should not have confirmed the plan because the plan was not feasible. On DISH's appeal we find no error, and conclude (1) that the bankruptcy court did not err in designating DISH's vote, (2) that, after designating DISH's vote, the bankruptcy court properly disregarded DISH's class for voting purposes, and (3) that the bankruptcy court did not err in finding the reorganization feasible. . . .

BACKGROUND

. . .

ICO Global Communications founded DBSD in 2004 to develop a mobile communications network that would use both satellites and land-based transmission towers. In its first five years, DBSD made progress toward this goal, successfully launching a satellite and obtaining certain spectrum licenses from the FCC, but it also accumulated a large amount of debt. Because its network remained in the developmental stage and had not become operational, DBSD had little if any revenue to offset its mounting obligations.

On May 15, 2009, DBSD (but not its parent ICO Global), filed a voluntary petition in the United States Bankruptcy Court for the Southern District of New York, listing liabilities of $813 million against assets with a book value of $627 million. Of the various claims against DBSD, three have particular relevance here:

1. The First Lien Debt: a $40 million revolving credit facility that DBSD obtained in early 2008 to support its operations, with a first-priority security interest in substantially all of DBSD's assets. It bore an initial interest rate of 12.5%.
2. The Second Lien Debt: $650 million in 7.5% convertible senior secured notes that [DBSD] issued in August 2005, due August 2009. These notes hold a second-priority security interest in substantially all of DBSD's assets. At the time of filing, the Second Lien Debt had grown to approximately $740 million. It constitutes the bulk of DBSD's indebtedness.
3. [Omitted]

After negotiations with various parties, DBSD proposed a plan of reorganization which, as amended, provided for "substantial de-leveraging," a renewed focus on "core operations," and a "continued path as a development-stage enterprise."

[The court described the plan and objections made by parties other than DISH.—Eds.] Meanwhile, DISH, although not a creditor of DBSD before its filing, had purchased the claims of various creditors with an eye toward DBSD's spectrum rights. As a provider of satellite television, DISH has launched a number of its own satellites, and it also has a significant investment in TerreStar Corporation, a direct competitor of DBSD's in the developing field of hybrid satellite/terrestrial mobile communications. DISH desired to "reach some sort of transaction with [DBSD] in the future if [DBSD's] spectrum could be useful in our business."

Shortly after DBSD filed its plan disclosure, DISH purchased all of the First Lien Debt at its full face value of $40 million, with an agreement that the sellers would make objections to the plan that DISH could adopt after the sale. As DISH admitted, it bought the First Lien Debt not just to acquire a "market piece of paper" but also to "be in a position to take advantage of [its claim] if things didn't go well in a restructuring." Internal DISH communications also promoted an "opportunity to obtain a blocking position in the [Second Lien Debt] and control the bankruptcy process for this potentially strategic asset." In the end, DISH (through a subsidiary) purchased only $111 million of the Second Lien Debt—not nearly enough to control that class—with the small size of its stake due in part to DISH's unwillingness to buy any claims whose prior owners had already entered into an agreement to support the plan.

In addition to voting its claims against confirmation, DISH reasserted the objections that the sellers of those claims had made pursuant to the transfer agreement, arguing, among other things, that the plan was not feasible under 11 U.S.C. § 1129(a)(11) and that the plan did not give DISH the "indubitable equivalent" of its First Lien Debt as required to cram down a dissenting class of secured creditors under 11 U.S.C. § 1129(b)(2)(A). Separately, DISH proposed to enter into a strategic transaction with DBSD, and requested permission to propose its own competing plan (a request it later withdrew).

DBSD responded by moving for the court to designate that DISH's "rejection of [the] plan was not in good faith." The bankruptcy court agreed, finding that DISH, a competitor to DBSD, was voting against the plan "not as a traditional creditor seeking to maximize its return on the debt it holds, but . . . 'to establish control over this strategic asset.'" *DBSD II*, 421 B.R. at 137 (quoting DISH's own internal presentation slides). The bankruptcy court therefore designated DISH's vote and disregarded DISH's wholly-owned class of First Lien Debt for the purposes of determining plan acceptance under 11 U.S.C. § 1129(a)(8). The court also rejected DISH's objections to the plan, finding that the plan was feasible and that, even assuming that DISH's vote counted, the plan gave DISH the "indubitable equivalent" of its First Lien Debt claim and could thus be crammed down over DISH's dissent.

After designating DISH's vote and rejecting all objections, the bankruptcy court confirmed the plan. The district court affirmed. . . .

DISCUSSION

. . .

A. The Treatment of DISH's Vote

1. Designating DISH's Vote as "Not in Good Faith"

To confirm a plan of reorganization, Chapter 11 generally requires a vote of all holders of claims or interests impaired by that plan. See 11 U.S.C. §§ 1126, 1129(a)(8). This voting requirement has exceptions, however, including one that allows a bankruptcy court to designate (in effect, to disregard) the votes of "any entity whose acceptance or rejection of such plan was not in good faith." Id. § 1126(e).

The Code provides no guidance about what constitutes a bad faith vote to accept or reject a plan. Rather, § 1126(e)'s "good faith" test effectively delegates to the courts the task of deciding when a party steps over the boundary. Case by case, courts have taken up this responsibility. No circuit court has ever dealt with a case like this one, however, and neither we nor the Supreme Court have many precedents on the "good faith" voting requirement in any context; the most recent cases from both courts are now more than 65 years old and address § 1126(e)'s predecessor, § 203 of the Bankruptcy Act. Nevertheless, these cases, cases from other jurisdictions, legislative history, and the purposes of the good-faith requirement give us confidence in affirming the bankruptcy court's decision to designate DISH's vote in this case.

We start with general principles that neither side disputes. Bankruptcy courts should employ § 1126(e) designation sparingly, as "the exception, not the rule." In re Adelphia Commc'ns Corp., 359 B.R. 54, 61 (Bankr. S.D.N.Y. 2006). For this reason, a party seeking to designate another's vote bears the burden of proving that it was not cast in good faith. Merely purchasing claims in bankruptcy "for the purpose of securing the approval or rejection of a plan does not of itself amount to 'bad faith.'" In re P-R Holding, 147 F.2d at 897. Nor will selfishness alone defeat a creditor's good faith; the Code assumes that parties will act in their own self interest and allows them to do so. Section 1126(e) comes into play when voters venture beyond mere self-interested promotion of their claims. . . .

Here, the debate centers on what sort of "ulterior motives" may trigger designation under § 1126(e), and whether DISH voted with such an impermissible motive. The first question is a question of law that we review de novo, and the second a question of fact. . . .

Clearly, not just any ulterior motive constitutes the sort of improper motive that will support a finding of bad faith. After all, most creditors have interests beyond their claim against a particular debtor, and those other interests will inevitably affect how they vote the claim. For instance, trade creditors who do regular business with a debtor may vote in the way most likely to allow them to continue to do business with the debtor after reorganization. And, as interest rates change, a fully secured creditor may seek liquidation to allow money once invested at unfavorable rates to be invested more favorably elsewhere. We do not purport to decide here the propriety of either of these motives, but they at least demonstrate that allowing the disqualification of votes on account of any ulterior motive could have far-reaching consequences and might leave few votes upheld.

The sort of ulterior motive that § 1126(e) targets is illustrated by the case that motivated the creation of the "good faith" rule in the first place, Texas Hotel Securities Corp. v. Waco Development Co., 87 F.2d 395 (5th Cir. 1936). In that case, Conrad Hilton purchased claims of a debtor to block a plan of reorganization that would have given a lease on the debtor's property — once held by Hilton's company, later cancelled — to a third party. Hilton and his partners sought, by buying and voting the claims, to "force [a plan] that would give them again the operation of the hotel or otherwise reestablish an interest that they felt they justly had in the property." The district court refused to count Hilton's vote, but the court of appeals reversed, seeing no authority in the Bankruptcy Act for looking into the motives of creditors voting against a plan.

That case spurred Congress to require good faith in voting claims. As the Supreme Court has noted, the legislative history of the predecessor to § 1126(e) "make[s] clear the purpose of the [House] Committee [on the Judiciary] to pass legislation which would bar creditors from a vote who were prompted by such a purpose" as Hilton's. . . . Modern cases have found "ulterior motives" in a variety of situations. In perhaps the most famous case, and one on which the bankruptcy court in our case relied heavily, a court found bad faith because a party bought a blocking position in several classes after the debtor proposed a plan of reorganization, and then sought to defeat that plan and to promote its own plan that would have given it control over the debtor. See In re Allegheny Int'l, Inc., 118 B.R. 282, 289-90 (Bankr. W.D. Pa. 1990). . . .

Although we express no view on the correctness of the specific findings of bad faith of the parties in those specific cases, we think that this case fits in the general constellation they form. As the bankruptcy court found, DISH, as an indirect competitor of DBSD and part-owner of a direct competitor, bought a blocking position in (and in fact the entirety of) a class of claims, after a plan had been proposed, with the intention not to maximize its return on the debt but to enter a strategic transaction with DBSD and "to use status as a creditor to provide advantages over proposing a plan as an outsider, or making a traditional bid for the company or its assets." DBSD II, 421 B.R. at 139-40. In effect, DISH purchased the claims as votes it could use as levers to bend the bankruptcy process toward its own strategic objective of acquiring DBSD's spectrum rights, not toward protecting its claim.

We conclude that the bankruptcy court permissibly designated DISH's vote based on the facts above. This case echoes the *Waco* case that motivated Congress to impose the good faith requirement in the first place. In that case, a competitor bought claims with the intent of voting against any plan that did not give it a lease in or management of the debtor's property. In this case, a competitor bought claims with the intent of voting against any plan that did not give it a strategic interest in the reorganized company. The purchasing party in both cases was less interested in maximizing the return on its claim than in diverting the progress of the proceedings to achieve an outside benefit. In 1936, no authority allowed disregarding votes in such a situation, but Congress created that authority two years later with cases like *Waco* in mind. We therefore hold that a court may designate a creditor's vote in these circumstances.

We also find that, just as the law supports the bankruptcy court's legal conclusion, so the evidence supports its relevant factual findings. DISH's motive—the most controversial finding—is evinced by DISH's own admissions in court, by its position as a competitor to DBSD, by its willingness to overpay for the claims it bought, by its attempt to propose its own plan, and especially by its internal communications, which, although addressing the Second Lien Debt rather than the First Lien Debt at issue here, nevertheless showed a desire to "to obtain a blocking position" and "control the bankruptcy process for this potentially strategic asset."

The Loan Syndications and Trading Association (LSTA), as amicus curiae, argues that courts should encourage acquisitions and other strategic transactions because such transactions can benefit all parties in bankruptcy. We agree. But our holding does not "shut[] the door to strategic transactions," as the LSTA suggests. Rather, it simply limits the methods by which parties may pursue them. DISH had every right to propose for consideration whatever strategic transaction it wanted—a right it took advantage of here—and DISH still retained this right even after it purchased its claims. All that the bankruptcy court stopped DISH from doing here was using the votes it had bought to secure an advantage in pursuing that strategic transaction.

DISH argues that, if we uphold the decision below, "future creditors looking for potential strategic transactions with chapter 11 debtors will be deterred from exploring such deals for fear of forfeiting their rights as creditors." But our ruling today should deter only attempts to "obtain a blocking position" and thereby "control the bankruptcy process for [a] potentially strategic asset" (as DISH's own internal documents stated). We leave for another day the situation in which a preexisting creditor votes with strategic intentions. We emphasize, moreover, that our opinion imposes no categorical prohibition on purchasing claims with acquisitive or other strategic intentions. On other facts, such purchases may be appropriate. Whether a vote has been properly designated is a fact-intensive question that must be based on the totality of the circumstances, according considerable deference to the expertise of bankruptcy judges. Having reviewed the careful and fact-specific decision of the bankruptcy court here, we find no error in its decision to designate DISH's vote as not having been cast in good faith.

2. Disregarding DISH's Class for Voting Purposes

DISH next argues that the bankruptcy court erred when, after designating DISH's vote, it disregarded the entire class of the First Lien Debt for the purpose of determining plan acceptance under 11 U.S.C. § 1129(a)(8). Section 1129(a)(8) provides that each impaired class must vote in favor of a plan for the bankruptcy court to confirm it without resorting to the (more arduous) cram-down standards of § 1129(b). Faced with a class that effectively contained zero claims—because DISH's claim had been designated— the bankruptcy court concluded that "[t]he most appropriate way to deal with that [situation] is by disregarding [DISH's class] for the purposes of section 1129(a)(8)." *DBSD I*, 419 B.R. at 206. We agree with the bankruptcy court. Common sense demands this result, which is consistent with (if not explicitly demanded by) the text of the Bankruptcy Code. . . .

B. The Feasibility of the Plan

[The court found the plan feasible. Judge Pooler approved of the portion of the opinion reproduced here, but dissented on other grounds.—Eds.]

Is the standard for knowing when votes are not cast in good faith similar to the Supreme Court's obscenity jurisprudence—judges just know it when they see it? In one Ninth Circuit case, the court held that the secured creditor of a condo-apartment complex, Teachers Insurance and Annuity Association of America, had acted in good faith when it purchased 21 of the 34 claims in an unsecured class in order to block the debtor's plan of reorganization (enough claims to vote no and kill a consensual plan). In re Figter Ltd., 118 F.3d 635 (9th Cir. 1997). Rubbing salt in the wound, Teachers counter-proposed a liquidating plan where it would credit bid its secured claim at a foreclosure sale. The debtor cried foul that Teachers was buying up claims from creditors for the sole purpose of torpedoing the reorganization and facilitating its own business-destroying plan, contrary to the purposes of the Code.

The court was unmoved, proclaiming that "we do not condemn mere enlightened self-interest, even if it appears selfish to those who do not benefit from it." There was no bad faith problem because Teachers was acting to "preserve what [it] reasonably perceive[d] as [its] fair share of the debtor's estate." Id. at 639. Indeed, Teachers pointed out that the debtor's plan—to convert the rental units to condos—might leave it with a hybrid building of half-condos, lowering the value of its real estate collateral. "[P]ure malice, 'strikes' and blackmail, and the purpose to destroy an enterprise in order to advance the interest of a competing business" would all be examples. Id. at 639-40. Does this provide any more or less guidance than the Second Circuit's attempt? If so, can you tell whether it is a more stringent or lenient standard?

Struggling to put structure into something as equitable as good faith may be bootless. The ABI Commission's recommendation did not specify the boundaries of good faith, but recommended amending § 1126(e) to permit courts to consider both whether the creditor's vote was "manifestly adverse" to the interests of the other creditors within the class or was otherwise cast in bad faith. ABI Commission to Study the Reform of Chapter 11, 2012-2014 Final Report and Recommendations 264 (2014). One area where good faith has arisen, and been upheld, is with Restructuring Support Agreements (RSAs), whereby parties in a workout discussion privately contract with each other to take concerted action (e.g., agree to payment X, and agree to vote in support of a chapter 11 plan implementing X). Does this pre-commitment suggest a prejudice incompatible to voting in good faith? Courts facing disputes have looked at a host of factors, including the sophistication of the parties, but generally blessed RSAs. See, e.g., In re Indianapolis Downs, LLC, 486 B.R. 286 (2013). Academics are more skeptical. See Edward J. Janger & Adam J. Levitin, Badges of Opportunism: Principles for Policing Restructuring Support Agreements, 13 Brook. J. Corp. Fin. & Com. L. 169 (2020). To continue our political voting analogy, we guess voting absentee ballot in advance before the final debate is not bad faith.

Lest you be concerned that good faith scrutiny is only directed toward creditors, rest assured chapter 11 debtors, just like their chapter 13 peers, must also propose and confirm their plans in good faith. § 1129(a)(3). For example, what if you have enough money to pay all your creditors, but want to file bankruptcy anyway to take advantage of a bankruptcy-only power? Recall from Assignment 31 the landlord trying to sell its property under § 363 "free and clear" of the Three-Legged Monkey lease as a way to try to boot the tenant. Might that be "bad faith"? One (in)famous case involving a bad faith challenge to a solvent debtor's filing involved the cap on landlord-creditor's damages under § 502(b)(6) (a section you should take three seconds now to look at and appreciate its animating policy in a world of 99-year leases). The Third Circuit, in an oft-cited opinion, held that while in some circumstances it might be impermissible, it was not per se bad faith to file a plan primarily to take advantage of that rent cap. In re PPI Enterprises (U.S.), Inc., 324 F.3d 197, 211-12 (3d Cir. 2003) (noting division of business assets was ancillary reason for debtor's filing and noting bankruptcy court's four-day evidentiary hearing probing good faith). The landlord, you might expect, had a different view. An arguably closer case was In re AAGS Holdings, LLC, 608 B.R. 373 (Bankr. S.D.N.Y. 2019) (filing purchaser's chapter 11 morning of real estate closing to trigger § 108(b)(2)'s 60-day extension period not bad faith on totality of circumstances).

3.   *Regulating Claims Trading*

Good faith is just one way that courts fight back against perceived improprieties with the bankruptcy sales process. The *Lionel/sub rosa* plan doctrine(s) are animated by similar concerns. What is especially difficult, as Judge Lynch reminds, is that judges have been left to go at it alone in balancing the policy concerns in this area, unaided by Congress. One of the biggest issues that lurks with claims trading is whether there should be any regulation of the sale of claims. For example, when parties buy and sell publicly traded stock, they do so subject to the rules of stock exchanges, federal and state securities laws, and the oversight of the SEC and other agencies. *But cf.* § 1125(e) (preempting securities laws).

When parties buy and sell claims against companies in bankruptcies, they may be trading in what can be effectively the residual ownership—the equity—of the business. Many of the same market problems that prompt regulation of stock markets also exist when the subject of the sale is a bankruptcy claim. What should be the regulations governing secret purchases, failure to buy all the shares in a class, strategic purchases at different prices, disclosure, blocking positions, and control stakes? All the concerns that arise in the sales of securities can arise in the sale of claims. The difference is that in chapter 11 there is no equivalent to the SEC and the securities laws to protect traders in these markets. Instead, the courts are left to fashion a common law of regulation around the Code.

Disclosure seems to be the *de rigueur* solution for securities market regulation. The need for its role in bankruptcy law has become more pressing because of the growth of credit derivatives and other financial contracts that permit a creditor to remain the legal owner of a claim while transferring the risk to a counterparty. The creditor pays a fee for what amounts to insurance, while the counterparty generally acquires the right to control the voting of that claim in a chapter 11. The fact that the other parties to a chapter 11 negotiation do not know the identity or interests of the real owner of the claim makes the negotiations far more difficult. Another possibility is that the voting rights of a claim may be sold to someone who has no economic interest in the company or who has some other motive for wanting to influence its future, or perhaps even an economic interest in the failure of the company. Consider that a credit default swap is like fire insurance against economic failure. The buyer of that insurance might want to burn the place down and file a claim. See Henry T.C. Hu & Bernard Black, Equity and Debt Decoupling and Empty Voting II: Importance and Extensions, 156 U. Pa. L. Rev. 625, 728-35 (2008). The bankruptcy system's somewhat tepid approach involves the rules. Rule 2019 requires disclosure of identity of committees of bankruptcy stakeholders who start to act in potentially bankruptcy-market-moving manners. Its expansion in 2009 now requires:

> (a) Definitions. In this rule the following terms have the meanings indicated:
>
>> (1) "Disclosable economic interest" means any claim, interest, pledge, lien, option, participation, derivative instrument, or any other right or derivative right granting the holder an economic interest that is affected by the value, acquisition, or disposition of a claim or interest.
>> (2) "Represent" or "represents" means to take a position before the court or to solicit votes regarding the confirmation of a plan on behalf of another.
>
> (b) Disclosure by groups, committees and entities.
>> (1) In a chapter 9 or 11 case, a verified statement setting forth the information specified in subdivision (c) of this rule shall be filed by every group or committee that consists of or represents, and every entity that represents, multiple creditors or equity security holders that are (A) acting in concert to advance their common interests. . . .
>
> (c) Information required. The verified statement shall include:
>> . . . with respect to an entity, and with respect to each member of a group or committee: (A) name and address; (B) the nature and amount of each disclosable economic interest held in relation to the debtor as of the date the entity was employed or the group or committee was formed; and (C) with respect to each member of a group or committee that claims to represent any entity in addition to the members of the group or committee, other than a committee appointed under § 1102 or § 1114 of the Code, the date of acquisition by quarter and year of each disclosable economic interest, unless acquired more than one year before the petition was filed. . . .

Fed. R. Bankr. P. 2019.

Some disagreement exists over the scope of this Rule. Whatever its scope, the Rule probably requires the disclosure of a derivative position like the example given above where the party may be a creditor but has a strong economic interest in the company's failure. The Rule is a compromise that does not go far enough in the view of some, however, because it no longer requires disclosure of the price paid for the economic interest being revealed or the date of acquisition (except for those few actors who fall under the reach of (c)(2)(C)). On the other hand, some actors, especially vulture funds themselves, complain that disclosure of these sorts of prices will destroy proprietary trade secrets and run some of them out of business. The first group probably does not see that as a problematic outcome.

Problem Set 32

32.1. Your client, Heartland Haul Holdings (HHH), and its subsidiaries filed for chapter 11 several months ago. The companies provide logistics, distribution and transportation services in the Midwest. The reorganization headed quickly for an asset sale, which attracted two bidders: Flying F Inc., an expanding competitor of the debtor, and Hedge Co, current lender to HHH. At a duly scheduled Friday afternoon auction, Hedge Co made an opening cash bid of $100 million and Flying F bid $200 million in cash. Repairing to their respective conference rooms at your law firm, the bidders reassessed their positions. Flying F held fast at $200 million but Hedge Co came back with a "restructured" bid at $220 million, but with $120 million of that amount a credit bid—a right it contended it had under a contested interpretation of HHH's first-lien credit agreement.

Flying F went ballistic and filed an emergency objection, threatening debtor's counsel with personal liability if they did not cancel the auction immediately for alleged violations of the sales procedure order, or in the alterative, declare Flying F the victor. The court calendared the motion for first thing Monday morning. After two days of intense negotiations, the debtor allowed Flying F to submit a "belated" bid and the emergency motion was withdrawn. Flying F went up to $210 million but preserved its rights to object to the sale. That afternoon, HHH instructed you to declare Hedge Co's bid to be superior and to calendar a sales confirmation hearing despite objections from several other parties-in-interest, including the Creditors Committee, the U.S. Trustee, and of course Flying F. Flying F beat HHH to the punch by filing a Motion Objecting to Sale and Request to Reopen Bidding.

The hearing is set for three days from now. After a heart-to-heart (or wallet-to-wallet) with Flying F yesterday, HHH's management has assurances from Flying F that it will not destroy HHH and truly wants a strategic partnership. They now regret their support for Hedge Co and want to support Flying F's objection to their own sale. Is this pure folly? What arguments will dominate the hearing? If HHH has received a letter from the DOJ Antitrust Division regarding its possible upcoming sale, will that affect matters?

32.2. After months of building a case at the antitrust division of the DOJ, you finally filed a civil action against SLUG Carbon, a manufacturer of graphite electrodes used in steel production. The complaint alleges that SLUG has been engaged in price-fixing and seeks to reimburse actual pecuniary loss. Your supervisor, Stewart Malcolm, wants you to make an example of this corporate defendant in line with the Attorney General's goal of demonstrating a "tough on corporate wrongdoing" stance. "I want to give the AG a victory by the end of the year!"

You have dutifully taken an aggressive litigation strategy, rebuffing the settlement offer of Douglas Drallward-Heimeir, SLUG's general counsel, that would have resulted in a sizable payment but no admission of wrongdoing. Stewart is known in government circles for his fiery disposition and once told you regarding SLUG's CEO, Curtisa Gannon, "I want you to drive her and SLUG into the ground." Later, in a cooler mood, he clarified, "I'm not asking you to do anything you think is wrong, but go after her as hard as the law allows. She deserves it."

Gannon has just finished her third deposition session, and you are going to court to complain about gaps in her answers for the third time. You expect to bring her back for more. You have filed three motions for partial summary judgment on various aspects of the case and otherwise kept E. George Brunstain, the lead partner from the outside firm retained by SLUG to defend the suit, in court every week. You've just given notice of three experts you've hired for testimony at the trial, including a famous antitrust professor, Herb Hovercraft. Yet another settlement Drallward-Heimeir forwarded you and Stewart was rejected last week; Stewart snorted to you, "How about Gannon sells all SLUG's inventory and equipment and has just enough to pay DOJ and her lawyers in full? Then we'd be paid, she'd be out of business, and that would be that."

This morning you got a notice that SLUG has filed a chapter 11, retaining top-shoe firm Weil, Kirkland & Arps as bankruptcy counsel. The petition lists just two debts, about $1 million owed to lawyers and the disputed debt claim to DOJ. You call Drallward-Heimeir, who explains that SLUG had to file because the legal expenses were getting out of hand and Gannon couldn't run her business while spending so much time in court and in deposition. Plus he claims the stress and anxiety made it impossible for Gannon to generate new business and that business was falling off as other customers heard about the case. "We might still be able to make this go away," offers Drallward-Heimeir, "but now I'd have to involve the bankruptcy guys. They say they're in for the long haul."

What should you tell the furious Stewart about the effect of the SLUG filing? What steps can you tell him DOJ can take to get the litigation back on track? See §§ 362, 363(f), 1112(b)(1), 1129(a)(3).

Section 3

Governance and Practice in Chapter 11

As we have seen, flexibility is central to chapter 11 in theory and practice, but that characteristic also creates the danger of abuse by insiders, traders, and yes, even lawyers. This final section of the chapter 11 story focuses on the legal constraints and guidelines imposed on officers, directors, buyers/sellers, and lawyers. Its two chapters introduce the practical and theoretical challenges in understanding the nature and role of that remarkable legal concept, the debtor-in-possession—and all its management and legal attendants with their inevitable conflicts of interest. We have already discussed the DIP in Assignment 16 when looking at how chapter 11 operates, but it is time for a deeper look at some of the governance and ethics challenges. We must focus on the interaction between corporate law (often from management-friendly Delaware) and bankruptcy law, where there are numerous stakeholders, but creditors have pride of place. We then shift to the women and men who represent these actors in court and out, conflicts of interest and all, who try to race through an ethical environment that sometimes resembles the nerve-wracking progress of Indiana Jones through a new temple-cave. And very often the journey is in real time.

GOVERNANCE IN CHAPTER 11

This assignment examines the governance of companies in chapter 11, which requires reconsideration of the nature and role of the debtor-in-possession. The control of the debtor and its assets has been a central focus all along, but here we are less concerned with the fact of control and more with the legal obligations of those who exercise that control, although concededly the two questions cannot be cleanly separated. At issue are the legal responsibilities and liabilities of a host of corporate actors and advisors, including counsel to the chapter 11 debtor, as well as the prospects for an efficient and socially useful reorganization system. It is closely related to a central bankruptcy issue to which we often have returned: who is in control?

A. GOVERNANCE RULES: FIDUCIARY DUTIES IN CHAPTER 11

The detor-in-possession (DIP) in a modern bankruptcy system was invented almost entirely in the United States. Even though reorganization à la chapter 11 has had enormous influence on bankruptcy reform all over the world, until very recently few countries have been willing to give control of a reorganization to a DIP rather than a trustee in bankruptcy or "administrator."

The DIP concept began during the Depression with the notion of a "mom-and-pop" business that could not support an expensive trustee, so Chapter XI permitted these proprietors to run their own companies during reorganization. As time went on, Congress became dissatisfied with Chapter X, in which a trustee was appointed to preside over a public company, in part because the SEC kept insisting on special treatment for public bondholders and shareholders. Fewer companies were filing Chapter X, while many large ones struggled to qualify under Chapter XI to evade the trustee requirement. The 1978 Code extended the DIP idea to all companies under the consolidated reorganization process, chapter 11. It was thought that management would be more likely to file in time to save the company if management could keep the key to the executive washroom. Further, persuasive arguments were offered that pre-bankruptcy management would be more competent at running the business than some lawyer or other outsider who knew nothing about it. The change largely sidelined the SEC as an actor in cases involving publicly owned companies.

This all sounded great on paper. But nobody really worked through how this concept would work overlaid upon an already developed system of corporate governance under state law. For example, bright-eyed MBAs are indoctrinated into the norm that their raison d'être is representing the best interests of shareholders once they become CEOs. But economists will tell us that the "residual owners" of an insolvent firm—the ones whose money is at stake—are the impaired class of creditors. Does that mean that upon filing bankruptcy managers must shift governance gears and report to new constituents? And if they fail, who gets to replace them? The shareholders? The creditors? The bankruptcy judge as advised by the U.S. Trustee?

Just as the bankruptcy law concept of "property of the estate" starts with analysis of legal rights under state law, so, too, do bankruptcy governance obligations begin with state law.

1.   *Corporate Law Fiduciary Duties*

Chapter 11 governance implicates the most fundamental corporate law issue, often called the "agency problem"—that is, the difficulty of aligning the interests of management (the agents of the company) with the interests of the owners of the company. The agency problem is manifest both in closely-held companies, where the management-owners may ignore the interests of minority owners, and in large companies, where management may not own any significant portion of the company's shares and thus may diverge in its interests from shareholders. The problem was most famously articulated around 90 years ago in the midst of the Great Depression. Adolph A. Berle, Jr. & Gardiner C. Means, The Modern Corporation and Private Property (1932). The question, near insoluble, has consumed a vast amount of scholarship and public debate ever since, with mixed results at best.

One approach to the agency problem is the statutory and common law imposition of fiduciary duties. It is well-settled corporate law that management (directors and officers) owes fiduciary duties of care and loyalty to shareholders. Of course, comportment with these duties is generally policed by a tolerant *business judgment rule*, which is "a presumption that in making a business decision the directors of a corporation acted on an informed basis, in good faith and in the honest belief that the action taken was in the best interests of the company." Aronson v. Lewis, 473 A.2d 805, 812 (Del. 1984); see also Robert W. Hamilton, Jonathan R. Macey & Douglas K. Moll, The Law of Business Organizations 425-44 (13th ed. 2017) (discussing rule). Critics argue that nowadays management is mostly immune from liability for all but the most egregious misconduct. Defenders say that incentive alignment arises through tools other than legal duties, such as compensation tied to performance.

Whatever the outcome of that corporate law debate in the ordinary course for a solvent corporation, the problem becomes far more complicated when a company is in financial distress. The courts in Delaware (the jurisdiction of greatest significance to corporate law) wrestled mightily with whether the fiduciary duties typically reserved for shareholders should extend to creditors when the company becomes insolvent, or is in the "zone of insolvency." After some confusion, the Delaware Supreme Court wrapped this riddle in a mystery by saying that the fiduciary obligation upon insolvency is to the "corporation," dodging the fact that the various stakeholders in the corporation may have quite different interests. North Am. Catholic Educ. Programming Found. v. Gheewalla, 930 A.2d 92 (Del. 2007). But which is it: does the duty that the officers and directors owe to creditors replace the duty to shareholders or just add more beneficiaries? See, e.g., Henry Hu & Jay L. Westbrook, Abolition of the Corporate Duty to Creditors, 107 Colum. L. Rev. 1321 (2007). The *Gheewalla* case's position is that creditors can only sue on behalf of an insolvent corporation for breach of fiduciary duties to the corporation; officers and directors do not owe any duty to creditors distinct from their obligations to the corporate entity itself. As the Delaware Chancery Court has held:

> When directors of an insolvent corporation make decisions that increase or decrease the value of the firm as a whole and affect providers of capital differently only due to their relative priority in the capital stack, directors do not face a conflict of interest simply because they own common stock or owe duties to large common stockholders. Just as in a solvent corporation, common stock ownership standing alone does not give rise to a conflict of interest. The business judgment rule protects decisions that affect participants in the capital structure in accordance with the priority of their claims.

Quadrant Structured Prods. Co. v. Vertin, 115 A.3d 535, 547-48 (Del. Ch. 2015).

One argument for switching management's allegiance from shareholders to creditors (rather than just adding creditors as another, conflicting constituency) rests on the idea that shareholders are out of the money; because the corporation is insolvent, shareholders have no further interest in its future. But likening bankruptcy shareholders to the dead voters popular in some Chicago elections is too quick a comparison; it ignores the instability and ambiguity of insolvency. A corporation can be solvent today, insolvent tomorrow, and solvent again next Monday. If the concept of "no shareholder interest" is based on a prediction that the corporation will never be solvent again, it is subject to all the uncertainties attendant upon prediction. (Hat tip, Niels Bohr.) At any given moment, a finding of insolvency depends on a valuation of the company's assets as against its liabilities (we've seen how simple that is) or its capacity to pay its bills currently, both metrics full of unknowns and difficult predictions. During the Great Recession in 2008, banks would not lend to other banks because the solvency of the borrowers was simply unknowable, even though many banks were public companies, and continue to thrive today.

Nowadays, there may be a greater percentage of companies that wait to file for chapter 11 until they are greatly distressed, meaning that by the time they do file, they are clearly insolvent and highly likely to remain that way without a debt haircut. But there are still plenty of filings in which insolvency is far from clear even at the moment of bankruptcy. Fluctuating solvency is beautifully illustrated by *Quadrant*, where the court held that insolvency at the date the lawsuit was filed was the crucial fact necessary for a creditor derivative suit, despite the assertion by the defendants that they could show it had since regained solvency.

2.   *Bankruptcy Law Fiduciary Duties*

Bankruptcy law offers disappointingly little additional guidance. The DIP's fiduciary duties in chapter 11 start with chapter 7, because formally the DIP is vested with most of the powers and obligations of a trustee. 11 U.S.C. § 1107. The Code, in turn, charges the trustee with a list of duties, but nowhere discusses fiduciary obligations or governance norms. 11 U.S.C. § 704. These duties thrust the trustee into a role that is sometimes supportive of creditors but sometimes antithetical to them. Creditors that emerge in bankruptcy are often heterogenous in nature, and the denial of one claim increases the pool of money for the other creditors. The trustee thus often finds herself opposed to certain creditors, demonstrating the inherently conflicting nature of the multiparty bankruptcy system. John A.E. Pottow, Fiduciary Duties in Bankruptcy and Insolvency, in The Oxford Handbook of Fiduciary Law (Evan J. Criddle, Paul B. Miller & Robert H. Sitkoff, 1st ed. 2019). Yet courts cheerfully pronounce that the trustee bears a fiduciary obligation to the estate, whose constituents' interests may diverge markedly. Consider: what would "the estate" want regarding avoiding one creditor's security interest for the benefit of other (unsecured) creditors? The secured creditor will surely give you a different answer from an unsecured creditor. (Perhaps tying your compensation to a percentage of the liens you avoid may incline you toward avoidance. See 11 U.S.C. § 326(a).) Thus, an agency problem of a different order arises regarding governance.

General corporate law does not help much. The primary concern of Berle & Means was upon misdirection of resources: the management/trustee lining their pockets at the expense of the shareholders. That may explain the corporate law focus on harm to the corporation as a whole and thus avoidance of the question *qui bono*? Bankruptcy, to be sure, also has its maximization-of-value goal (the resources question) and over the centuries has had its share of frauds and defalcators, but the agency problem also involves making decisions that inevitably benefit some stakeholders more than others. That is bankruptcy's "internal" agency problem: a well-intentioned chapter 7 trustee has no guidance as to which conflicting constituency's interests to maximize *within* the estate. A duty to multiple constituencies within the estate may be the equivalent of no enforceable duty at all. Hu & Westbrook, supra at 1349-54. Giving a fiduciary a mandate to serve multiple parties with divergent interests, such as telling corporate managers to serve creditors instead of, or in addition to, shareholders, may make it impossible to measure their loyalty and care to either constituency, so that they may become legally irresponsible even as we hope they are ethically responsible. A trustee as fiduciary has little assistance from the Code, and the bankruptcy system's response has largely been to immunize trustees from suit. See Barton v. Barbour, 104 U.S. 126, 128 (1881) (promulgating the "*Barton* doctrine," which requires that "before suit is brought against a receiver leave of the court by which he was appointed must be obtained").

Indeed, moving from a chapter 7 trustee to a chapter 11 corporate DIP only magnifies the problems, because now there are both internal and external agency conflicts. Internally, the tensions of multiple taskmasters are just as bad as with the poor chapter 7 trustee. Externally, on the resource side, the real women and men who manage corporations may be tempted to avoid chapter 11 altogether, even if it's best for the company to maximize its value. Among other things, they may be deterred by the prospect of losing their jobs once the company enters chapter 11. That fear is hardly irrational according to data reported by empirical studies, including widely cited work done by Stuart Gilson at the Harvard Business School. See Stuart C. Gilson, Management Turnover and Financial Distress, 25 J. Fin. Econ. 241 (1989). It may be for this reason that the chapter 11 DIP rule no longer seems to produce the early-stage-of-distress filings envisioned by its advocates when the Code was written. Another empirical study suggests that managers of a distressed company are probably going to lose their jobs in or out of bankruptcy. Ethan S. Bernstein, All's Fair in Love, War and Bankruptcy? Corporate Governance Implications of CEO Turnover in Financial Distress, 11 Stan. J.L. Bus. & Fin. 298 (2006). Management, therefore, may see a bankruptcy filing as the definitive path to the unemployment office, while struggling with the creditors outside bankruptcy may offer some hope or at least buy a little time. Throughout, the agency problem makes protection of either shareholders or creditors (much less other stakeholders) more difficult.

In the next case, note the traditional corporate law governance rule that the shareholders get to vote for the board of directors, the humans who implement the fiduciary duties of the DIP in chapter 11. But then notice that a separate, bankruptcy law argument is being made that the shareholders' votes to replace those fiduciaries should be enjoined because they are doing so just to gain advantage in the chapter 11 negotiations (presumably dissatisfied with the way the incumbent DIP directors are exercising their fiduciary duties by not giving these stakeholders as much as they would like under the unfolding plan).

In re MARVEL ENTERTAINMENT GROUP, INC.
209 B.R. 832 (D. Del. 1997)

McKelvie, District Judge.

I. Factual and Procedural Background

The following facts are drawn from the parties' briefs and the record of proceedings below. Approximately 80% of [Debtor] Marvel's common stock is owned or controlled by three holding companies: Marvel Holdings, Inc. ("Marvel Holdings"), Marvel (Parent) Holdings, Inc. ("Marvel (Parent)"), and Marvel III Holdings, Inc. All three holding companies (collectively referred to herein as "the Marvel Holding Companies") are owned by Mr. Ronald O. Perelman. The balance of Marvel's common stock is held by public stock-holders (18.84%) and entities owned or controlled by Mr. Perelman (2.35%).

In 1993 and 1994, the Marvel Holding Companies raised $894 million through the issuance of bonds. The bonds were issued pursuant to three separate indentures and were secured by a pledge of approximately 80% of Marvel's stock and by 100% of the stock of Marvel (Parent) and Marvel Holdings. An indenture trustee was appointed to act for the bondholders under the indentures. LaSalle is the current indenture trustee.

On December 27, 1996, [Marvel Entertainment] and certain of its sub-sidiaries (collectively referred to herein as "the Debtors") filed separate petitions for relief under Chapter 11 of the United States Bankruptcy Code in the United States Bankruptcy Court for the District of Delaware. The Debtors' cases have been procedurally consolidated and are being jointly administered. On the same day, the Marvel Holding Companies also filed petitions for relief under Chapter 11 in the bankruptcy court. . . . LaSalle (hereinafter referred to as "the Indenture Trustee") filed several proofs of claims against Marvel on behalf of the bondholders so that they may recover against Marvel in the event Marvel is liable for any wrongdoing with respect to the amounts owed by the Marvel Holding Companies under the indentures.

. . .

On February 26, 1997, after two days of evidentiary hearings, the bankruptcy court entered an order lifting the stay in the Marvel Holding Companies' cases to permit the bondholders and the Indenture Trustee to foreclose on and vote the pledged shares. In lifting the stay, however, the bankruptcy court noted that the issue of whether the automatic stay imposed in the Debtors' cases would be implicated by any subsequent action taken by the bondholders and the Indenture Trustee with respect to the pledged shares was not yet before the court.

On March 19, 1997, the Bondholders Committee and the Indenture Trustee notified the Debtors of the intent of the bondholders and the Indenture Trustee to vote the pledged shares to replace Marvel's board of directors. Subsequently, on March 24, 1997, the Debtors instituted an adversary proceeding in the Debtors' cases by filing a complaint for declar-atory and injunctive relief and a motion for a temporary restraining order ("TRO") and a preliminary injunction enjoining the bondholders and the Indenture Trustee from voting the pledged shares to replace Marvel's board of directors. Also on that day, Chase Manhattan Bank, as agent for the senior secured lenders in the Debtors' cases, commenced a similar adver-sary proceeding in the Debtors cases wherein it sought substantially the same relief.

. . .

At the conclusion of the hearing, the court held that § 362(a)(3) pre-vented the bondholders and the Indenture Trustee from voting the pledged shares to replace Marvel's board of directors until they first sought and obtained relief from the automatic stay pursuant to § 362(d) of the Bankruptcy Code. The court denied the Debtors' and Chases' motions for a

TRO pursuant to § 105(a) because neither the Debtors nor Chase made any showing of irreparable harm.

Shortly after the bankruptcy court issued its March 24, 1997 order, appellants filed a motion to lift the stay pursuant to § 362(d). A hearing on that motion is currently scheduled in bankruptcy court for June 6, 1997. In addition, a hearing with respect to the relief sought by appellees in the adversary proceedings is currently scheduled for June 16, 1997. . . .

B. The Bankruptcy Court's Decision

. . .

It is well settled that the right of shareholders to compel a shareholders' meeting for the purpose of electing a new board of directors subsists during reorganization proceedings. The right of shareholders "to be represented by directors of their choice and thus to control corporate policy is paramount." In re Potter Instrument Co., Inc., 593 F.2d 470, 475 (2d Cir. 1979) (quoting In re J.P. Linahan, Inc., 111 F.2d 590, 592 (2d Cir. 1940)). . . . As a result, the election of a new board of directors may be enjoined only under circumstances demonstrating "clear abuse" [citing *Manville*]. . . . The fact that the shareholders' action may be motivated by a desire to arrogate more bargaining power in the negotiation of a reorganization plan, without more, does not constitute clear abuse.

It follows from these principles that the automatic stay provisions of the Bankruptcy Code are not implicated by the exercise of shareholders' corporate governance rights.

. . .

The Debtors rely heavily on two cases in support of the automatic stay. . . . The courts in [In re Fairmont Communications Corp., No. 92-B-44861 (Bankr. S.D.N.Y. Mar. 3, 1993)] and [In re Bicoastal Corp., 1989 Bankr. LEXIS 2046 (Bankr. M.D. Fla. Nov. 21, 1989)] thus applied the automatic stay provisions of § 362(a)(3) in order to prevent creditors of debtors from gaining control of the debtors' estates through the exercise of corporate governance rights. The Debtors argue that here, too, the bondholders are seeking to exercise rights accruing to them as creditors rather than traditional shareholder rights because the shares were pledged as security for the payment of the bonds issued by the Marvel Holding Companies. Appellants, however, did not acquire shareholder rights in Marvel as creditors of Marvel, but rather as creditors of the Marvel Holding Companies. Because the pledged shares were property of the Marvel Holding Companies' estates, appellants were required to seek and, indeed, obtained relief from the automatic stay in the Marvel Holding Companies case that prevented them from exercising control over those shares. The fact that they acquired shareholder rights in Marvel by exercising creditor remedies in the Marvel Holding Companies case is of no moment. . . . Should a new board elected by the bondholders attempt to take any action that would run afoul of § 362(a), they can be enjoined from doing so.

Finally, Chase suggests that Marvel is insolvent and that as a result the automatic stay applies. Chase cites dicta in *Johns-Manville* [In re

Johns-Manville Corp., 801 F.2d 60 (2d Cir. 1986)] to the effect that, if a debtor is insolvent, it would probably be inappropriate to permit shareholders to call a meeting because they would no longer have equity in the debtor and thus [not] be real parties-in-interest. Even if that proposition were correct, however, the bankruptcy court has never found that Marvel is insolvent. Accordingly, that issue is not a proper subject of this appeal.

. . .

[The court vacated the injunction against the pledged shares being voted.—Eds.]

The court seems to say that shareholders have a right to control the DIP unless their rights come from being creditors—which stands on its head the canon of bankruptcy law that the interests of creditors should dominate. In addition, *Marvel* implies that the DIP is indeed the prepetition debtor corporation, which manages the estate through its agents, the managers of the corporation. Management's duties to creditors are thus indirect, "through" the corporation. Yet management still presumably has duties owed directly to the shareholders, who haven't gone anywhere. What should they do if the creditors think the best reorganization plan is an orderly sale of all assets and the shareholders think the best answer is put all the chips on red, what have we got to lose?

It is clear that while bankruptcy law addresses many of the same governance concerns as corporate law, it does so pursuant to its own substantive source of law. That law does not track Delaware (or any state's) law perfectly. Consider just one issue: should fiduciary duties extend to non-management parties, such as entities in actual control of the debtor, as sometimes happens under corporate law but has generally not happened under the Bankruptcy Code? A. Mechele Dickerson, Privatizing Ethics in Corporate Reorganizations, 93 Minn. L. Rev. 875 (2009).

Moreover, bankruptcy law may impose its own policies that restrict ordinary state governance law, building upon the theme in *Marvel* that sometimes federal bankruptcy policies must reign supreme (*cf.* the *Butner* principle, where property rights are presumptively determined by state law unless some federal bankruptcy policy commands otherwise). This clash occurs dramatically in the "golden share" cases, so named because many states' corporate laws allow special voting privileges to be enshrined in the corporate charter, such as requiring all shareholders, or a special class of them, to consent to major transactions of the corporation. Thus, even one "golden" shareholder in such cases can veto a bankruptcy filing otherwise approved by the board. When that party is also a creditor, bankruptcy courts worry consent to file might be withheld to garner repayment advantage, contravening an arguable federal right to file bankruptcy. If such a debtor files over golden shareholder objection, the weight of authority appears to be that bankruptcy policy voids such governance rights and permits the filing to be effective despite the corporate charter violation, but an important Fifth Circuit case ruled the other way and granted a dismissal motion by a golden shareholder who did not consent to a chapter 11 filing. In re Franchise Services of

North America, Inc., 891 F.3d 198 (5th Cir. 2018). A 2020 Bankruptcy Court opinion in Delaware disagrees. The debate rages on.

3.   *Public Oversight of Fiduciary Duties*

Increasing attention has been devoted to the obligations of "private trustees"—that is, persons appointed to manage chapter 11 cases by nomination of the existing management or control persons. See, e.g., Dickerson, supra. They can be called private trustees because they were not part of prior management and their expertise lies in managing insolvencies rather than the substantive business of the corporate debtor. Often the person is appointed as a "Chief Restructuring Officer," or CRO. The appointment of private trustees has become common in recent years, despite the statutory scheme that places the selection of trustees in the United States Trustee Program. (The statute contemplates the UST appointment of a trustee only if creditors do not elect one, but that electoral power has been largely unexercised. §§ 702, 1104(b)(1).) That scheme was meant to eliminate the "bankruptcy ring" scandals of the past, by separating the bankruptcy judge's judicial role from administrative (or patronage) duties, such as appointment of lawyers to prestigious and lucrative trusteeships, as they previously did. H. Rep. No. 95-595, at 6011 (Sept. 8, 1977). But it appears that courts readily accept private trustees in a great many cases. The idea of the private trustee as the DIP circumvents the statutory procedure and gives both control persons (e.g., large shareholders or secured creditors) and the judge a role in trustee selection that the Code drafters ostensibly sought to avoid.

In re BLUE STONE REAL ESTATE, CONSTR. & DEV. CORP.
392 B.R. 897 (Bankr. M.D. Fla. 2008)

McEwen, Bankruptcy Judge.

. . .
[T]he Debtors request an expedited hearing for the Court to consider the entry of an order approving their retention of Steven S. Oscher, C.P.A., and Oscher Consulting, P.A. ("the firm") as their Chief Restructuring Officer ("CRO") to, inter alia, (i) review the Debtors' books and records and conduct the necessary investigation to ensure that the schedules and statements of financial affairs are accurately prepared and, if not, prepare and file corrected ones, (ii) conduct a thorough inventory of the assets, (iii) negotiate with and verify the financial viability of all potential purchasers of any of the Debtors' assets, and (iv) oversee and monitor the liquidation of the Debtors' assets.

BACKDROP—THE TRUSTEE MOTION

At the time of the Hearing, then pending for trial on August 15, 2008, was the United States Trustee's Emergency Motion to Appoint a

Chapter 11 Trustee Pursuant to 11 U.S.C. Section 1104(a)(1) or (2), or in the Alternative to Appoint an Examiner, pursuant to U.S.C. Section 1104(c)(1) or (2) (Docket No. 51) ("Trustee Motion"). The Trustee Motion seeks relief only in the lead consolidated case, the case filed by Blue Stone Real Estate, Construction & Development Corp. ("Blue Stone"). Some background about the Trustee Motion is necessary to gain an understanding of the record before the Court at the time of the Hearing.

The bases of the Trustee Motion largely relate to alleged acts or omissions of James W. DeMaria, the Debtors' principal, as well as document deficiencies that have plagued the lead case since its inception. The allegations of the Trustee Motion can be summarized as follows: (i) Blue Stone's schedules and statement of financial affairs are incomplete and have been constantly evolving through several amendments (almost like a work in progress), with some amendments having been made only after testimony of Mr. DeMaria at meetings of creditors had been shown to be inaccurate or incomplete; (ii) Mr. DeMaria has not fully accounted for prepetition use of Blue Stone credit cards and for prepetition distributions made by Blue Stone to Mr. DeMaria or for his benefit; (iii) a $100,000 deposit that should have been received by Blue Stone for a sale of a gas station has not been fully accounted for; (iv) after several opportunities for compliance, Mr. DeMaria has not provided all documents requested by the United States trustee; and (v) due to the document deficiencies and lack of cooperation, the meeting of creditors has been continued many times and remains pending.

At the preliminary hearing on the Trustee Motion, an additional basis for the Trustee Motion was proffered by the United States trustee: Within two years of the filing of the Blue Stone bankruptcy petition, Blue Stone transferred or attempted to transfer four parcels of property located in Arkansas and one parcel of property located in Missouri. None of these alleged transfers was disclosed in Blue Stone's schedules and statement of financial affairs. Additionally, none of the property, to the extent Blue Stone has an interest in such property, is disclosed in Blue Stone's schedules and statement of financial affairs. An issue of fact exists as to whether the ultimate transferees of the Arkansas and Missouri properties are affiliates of or controlled by, either directly or indirectly, Mr. DeMaria.

Mr. DeMaria's contention is that all of the transfers were made in the ordinary course of business and, thus, did not require disclosure in the statement of financial affairs. Notwithstanding this assertion, however, at the meetings of creditors, Mr. DeMaria failed to disclose the transfers in response to direct questioning about all transfers of property from Blue Stone (i.e., regardless of their possible characterization as ordinary course transactions). At the time of the Hearing on the CRO Motion, Mr. DeMaria had not had the opportunity to rebut the allegations in the Trustee Motion, explain his conduct, or comment on his responses at the meetings of creditors.

Based on the allegations summarized by the Court above, the Trustee Motion argues that Mr. DeMaria, as "current management" of Blue Stone, "engaged in fraud, dishonesty, gross mismanagement, or is incompetent with regard to managing the affairs of [Blue Stone] both before and after the filing." If true, these allegations would require appointment of a Chapter 11 trustee under section 1104(a)(1). The Trustee Motion also claims that

Mr. DeMaria's alleged lack of cooperation and his alleged dissipation of assets "have clearly not been in the interest of the creditors of [Blue Stone]." If true, these allegations would require appointment of a Chapter 11 trustee under section 1104(a)(2). The Trustee Motion also seeks appointment of an examiner pursuant to section 1104(c) if a Chapter 11 trustee is not warranted.

Opposition to the CRO Motion

A. Objecting Parties Argue That the Proposed CRO Is Not Independent or Disinterested and Cannot Perform as Effectively as a Chapter 11 Trustee

During the Hearing on the CRO Motion, the United States trustee and two secured creditors opposed the relief requested by the Debtors. All three parties argued that Mr. Oscher would be controlled or directed by Mr. DeMaria and that Mr. DeMaria would be able to hide assets or documents from Mr. Oscher. However, in open court, Mr. DeMaria agreed to act only as directed by Mr. Oscher and agreed to withdraw from all management functions. Notwithstanding those concessions, the opposing parties insisted that an "independent" and "disinterested" Chapter 11 trustee would be better able to perform the functions that Mr. Oscher would perform as a CRO, including the charge to discover any assets or transfers that remain hidden.

The record made during the Hearing clearly demonstrates that Mr. Oscher and the firm are disinterested, do not hold an interest adverse to the Debtors, and do not represent an interest adverse to the Debtors. Mr. Oscher's engagement was proposed by counsel to the Debtors in the exercise of their fiduciary duty to the Debtors' estates and creditors. Mr. Oscher did not even meet Mr. DeMaria until after the engagement was proposed.

Mr. Oscher's substantial experience with the bankruptcy process, both as a trustee and an authorized professional with various functions or expertise would be extremely beneficial to these Debtors, especially if the allegations of the Trustee Motion are true. Mr. Oscher is a respected and "well known quantity" to the Court, the United States trustee, and all of the parties in interest represented at the Hearing except for one party represented by out-of-town counsel.[5]

No party in interest was able to articulate any credible difference between the skill set of a Chapter 11 trustee and the skill set that Mr. Oscher would bring to the table as a CRO. No party in interest was able to identify any power possessed by a Chapter 11 trustee that would not be available or could not be made available under section 1107(a)—concerning the rights, powers, and duties of a debtor in possession—to a CRO whose

---

[5] . . . Even the United States trustee's counsel conceded, at the Hearing, "Mr. Oscher's high standing in the community and the high regard in which he is held" and indicated that "a person of Mr. Oscher's expertise would clearly be the type of person we would appoint [as a Chapter 11 trustee]."

engagement was authorized by an order of this Court to act on behalf of a debtor in possession.

The United States trustee argued that a fundamental difference between a Chapter 11 trustee and a CRO is that by its terms, section 1107(a) limits the ability of a CRO to perform the functions of a Chapter 11 trustee under section 1106(a)(2), (3), and (4). This is a misreading of the statute. The statute states in pertinent part: "Subject . . . to such limitations or conditions as the court prescribes, a debtor in possession . . . shall perform all the functions and duties [of a Chapter 11 trustee], except the duties described in sections 1106(a)(2), (3), and (4). . . ." 11 U.S.C. § 1107(a). A proper reading of this statute is that a debtor in possession is not mandated to undertake certain investigative and reporting duties, but the bankruptcy court in its discretion can nonetheless prescribe such action—as well as other actions not encompassed within section 1106. See In re Adelphia Communications Corp., 336 B.R. 610, 665 (Bankr. S.D.N.Y. 2006) (lengthy discussion of how courts should construe the nature of the limitations and conditions they are permitted to impose pursuant to section 1107(a)). In these cases, the Court is inclined to require Mr. Oscher to undertake the duties specified in sections 1106(a)(2) and (3). He may, but need not absent further order of the Court, undertake the duties specified in section 1106(a)(4).

On whole, the contentions that Mr. Oscher is not or cannot be independent, is not disinterested, and cannot perform as effectively as a Chapter 11 trustee are not credible and border on being frivolous. These arguments are without any basis in fact or law and are rejected by the Court.

B. United States Trustee Argues That a Corporate Debtor in Possession Can Act Only Through a Board of Directors

Perhaps in part to persuade the Court that Mr. Oscher is compelled to serve at the direction of Mr. DeMaria and, therefore, cannot be free of Mr. DeMaria's control, the United States trustee also disputed the Court's ability to enter an order imposing conditions or limitations under section 1107(a) that would, in effect, leave the Debtors that are corporations without boards of directors.

A debtor in possession operating in Chapter 11 is not conducting "business as usual" during the time between the commencement of the case and its emergence from bankruptcy as a reorganized debtor (assuming the debtor reorganizes and is not liquidated). The Bankruptcy Code is laden with express requirements of and limitations on business operations of a debtor in possession, not to mention discretionary requirements and limitations that may be imposed by the bankruptcy court where permitted. As touched on above, section 1107(a) specifically contemplates the use of the court's discretion in the context of what a debtor in possession must do or cannot do because it states that "[s]ubject . . . to the limitations or conditions as the court prescribes, a debtor in possession shall have all the rights . . . and powers . . . of a trustee serving in a case under this chapter." 11 U.S.C. § 1107(a) (emphasis added). Accordingly, the Bankruptcy Code contemplates that the state law powers of a corporation's board of directors can be altered while the corporation is a debtor in bankruptcy.

This Court concludes that the plain meaning of section 1107(a) permits the Court to alter the powers of the Debtors' boards of directors (and managers, in the cases of the Debtors that are limited liability companies) and impose requirements that will alleviate any concern, however unfounded, of a party in interest that Mr. Oscher as CRO will be some toady or crony of Mr. DeMaria instead of an independent professional with absolute control over the Debtors.

C. United States Trustee Argues That the Proposal to Engage a CRO Is a Disguised Selection of a Chapter 11 Trustee by the Debtors, Invading the Province of the United States Trustee

It quickly became apparent to all at the Hearing that the real concern of the United States trustee is its own organizational interest in maintaining control when it seeks the appointment of a Chapter 11 trustee, never mind that the Debtors' retention of this particular CRO in these particular cases just might be (and the Court determines it is, clearly) in the best interest of the Debtors. The United States trustee argued that the CRO Motion is effectively an "end run" on section 1104's mandate that only the United States trustee is empowered to select a Chapter 11 trustee. Therefore, the United States trustee submits, the Court has no power to authorize the engagement of a CRO that would be the functional equivalent of a Chapter 11 trustee. The United States trustee urges the Court to, instead of granting the CRO Motion, wait for a determination on the Trustee Motion some weeks hence before authorizing a change in management.

In essence, the United States trustee argues that once its office has filed a motion to appoint a Chapter 11 trustee, there are no facts or circumstances that would allow a debtor in possession to change management, even if a change in management would obviate the perceived need for a Chapter 11 trustee. Stated alternatively, if a debtor in possession is guided by management that can be proved to be incompetent, or to have engaged in fraud or dishonesty or to have grossly mismanaged the debtor, then the appointment of a Chapter 11 trustee is fait accompli and no salutary action can be taken by the debtor to cure that problem.

. . .

In these administratively consolidated cases, the protection afforded by a Chapter 11 trustee in containing or overcoming Mr. DeMaria's alleged conduct would not be needed if a CRO with Mr. Oscher's particular talents is authorized to have sole control over the management of the Debtors without interference by Mr. DeMaria. Moreover, case law supports the view that the appointment of a Chapter 11 trustee is an "extraordinary remedy." . . .

Furthermore, there is little question that equity holders of a corporate debtor-in-possession may change the debtor's management; there is nothing in the Bankruptcy Code prohibiting equity from doing so. In re The 1031 Tax Group, 374 B.R. 78, 89 n.11 (Bankr. S.D.N.Y. 2007). However, if a motion to appoint a trustee has been made, as in these cases, then section 1104(a)(1) does compel the Court to "examine the integrity of the new management." Id. And this Court has done precisely that.

For these reasons, the Court rejects the United States trustee's position that a proposed change of management following the filing of a still pending motion to appoint a Chapter 11 trustee is proscribed by section 1104(a).[7] See also In the Matter of Gaslight Club, Inc., 782 F.2d 767 (7th Cir. 1986) (approving replacement of debtor's president and majority shareholder with individual exercising debtor in possession powers, without appointing trustee, but where the individual who had been replaced consented).

A troubling aspect of the United States trustee's argument that authorization of a CRO treads on its domain is that it elevates a parochial policy concern over the potential harm that could come to these Debtors' estates and creditors if the status quo continued pending the trial on the Trustee Motion. If the alarming allegations in the Trustee Motion and the United States trustee's supplemental proffer on the record are true (and the Court must assume the United States trustee believes them to be so), then it is disappointing that the United States trustee has shown more regard for its "turf"—its territorial or organizational interests—than the larger interests of the bankruptcy system it is designed to serve. In other words, the United States trustee has sought to advance its own view of its role in preserving the integrity of the system ahead of the apparently critical need of the Debtors to change management immediately.

As applied to these cases, the United States trustee's view of the facts and the law is shortsighted. It ignores the reality of what the United States trustee accomplished by the very filing of the Trustee Motion—the triggering of a voluntary response that will undoubtedly cure the problems noted in that motion. This reality demonstrates that the United States trustee has effectively functioned to preserve the integrity of the system in these cases, just as it has done in other cases before this Court, time and time again. The United States trustee's view also ignores the reality of what the Debtors require if the Trustee Motion is accurate—an immediate change in management. Yet the Court is prevented from taking immediate action on the Trustee Motion because the contested matter arising from that motion involves disputes of fact that require the parties be given the usual elements of due process, such as discovery and a trial. The CRO Motion presents the perfect opportunity to address the Debtors' problems, as identified by the United States trustee, immediately.

. . .

Authority Under Which the CRO in These Cases Should Be Engaged

Mr. Oscher is clearly a "professional" within the meaning of section 327(a) for purposes of these cases. As a professional, Mr. Oscher's retention or engagement (however it is characterized) should be

---

[7] This conclusion is buttressed by section 1105, coupled with section 105(a), which would permit the Court, on its own motion, to terminate a Chapter 11 trustee and "restore the debtor to possession and management of the property of the estate and operation of the debtor's business." If the Court can revoke the appointment of a Chapter 11 trustee, then certainly the Court can consider a motion that would eliminate the need for one in the first place.

subject to approval by the Court pursuant to section 327(a).[8] Likewise, his compensation should be subject to review and authorization by the Court.[9]

ORDERED that:

1. The CRO Motion is granted, effective at 5:15 P.M. EDT on July 24, 2008.
2. The Debtors are authorized to retain Steven S. Oscher, C.P.A., as Chief Restructuring Officer of the Debtors pursuant to section 327(a) coupled with section 105(a), and not pursuant to section 363 as requested by the Debtors.

Blue Stone is one of the few reported opinions addressing the private trustee issues. Note the court does not discuss whether Mr. Oschler has the same fiduciary duties that it attributes to the DIP, although perhaps that is implied by its cite to Wolf v. Weinstein, 372 U.S. 633, 649-50 (1963) ("[I]t is clear that the [debtor in possession] bears essentially the same fiduciary obligation[s] to the creditors as does the trustee for a debtor out of possession."). On the other hand, the original justification for putting the DIP in charge of chapter 11 cases under the Code was that the existing managers would do a better job of actually operating the company. That justification having been mooted (if not turned on its head) in a case like *Blue Stone*, why is the choice of current management—or shareholders or a secured party, for that matter—entitled to as much weight as the statutory power given to the UST? In fact, why is it entitled to any weight? Perhaps the appointment power "trickling down" to the existing management is a half-vindication of the idea of private party control over its governance in chapter 11, or perhaps it is an unprincipled abdication. A creditor has a right to object to an appointment, but *Blue Stone* shows that even the UST may have an uphill battle resisting appointment of a private trustee because of the presumption in favor of a DIP. The power to control successor management seems often to be the last element that maintains the

---

[8] The two main purposes of section 327 are to permit the Court to control administrative expenses in the form of professionals' compensation and ensure that the professional is conflict free and impartial. Absent such judicial oversight and the opportunity for continuing party-in-interest scrutiny of both a professional's retention and compensation, these important goals of the Bankruptcy Code cannot be met. The so-called "Jay Alix" protocol that depends upon section 363 for retention of an executive officer does not provide the Court the same ability to meet the twin goals of section 327 when the candidate for employment is also a professional. Indeed, one part of the protocol abdicates to a board of directors the decision to employ executive officers who may be professionals, as Mr. Oscher would be in these cases, as well as the decision to remove professionals. Somewhat surprisingly, this protocol is apparently embraced by the United States trustee's office even in a case where an executive officer would be deemed to be a professional subject to section 327(a) under the *First Merchants* and *Bartley Lindsay* analyses. This is a failing of the protocol in such cases. See https://www.justice.gov/ust-regions-r02/region-2-chapter-11-3.

[9] The CRO Motion does not seek authorization for Mr. Oscher's engagement pursuant to section 327, but rather section 363. The Court employs its power under section 105(a) to grant the CRO Motion pursuant to section 327(a).

power of a control person in chapter 11. That control begins with choice of the management that is empowered as the DIP, continues with the business judgment rule insulating management's actions, and may finally protect against the appointment of a trustee selected by the United States Trustee even when private control has gone badly wrong.

Most often the persons appointed as private trustees are "turnaround specialists," although in many cases they are appointed in cases where the debtor is going to be liquidated through bankruptcy sales and are therefore liquidators (turning the debtor right around to the auction house). Their turnaround firms are also appointed as part of the DIP team in an advisory role rather than as private trustees replacing or supervising management. It is a thriving business. See e.g., the Turnaround Management Association, https://turnaround.org. As one testified, his "title as 'chief transformation officer' was not magical and could have easily been 'chief transformation person' or 'head minion.'" In re McDermott Int'l, Inc., 2020 Bankr. LEXIS 1323, at *3 (Bankr. S.D. Tex. 2020). The Jay Alix firm, mentioned in *Blue Stone*, is a well-known example. Although in *Blue Stone* Mr. Oschler was clearly intended to be appointed as the contracted manager of the company in chapter 11, the court insisted he be appointed as an advisory "professional" under § 327 of the Code (like a lawyer or accountant). This allows more oversight, both of conflicts, § 327, and compensation, § 328.

In many other cases, however, turnaround specialist appointments are made under § 363 (probably outside the ordinary course), without the pesky requirements of disinterestedness or compensation authorization. In those cases, the Jay Alix protocol, blessed by the U.S. Trustee's office, is often used. But as seen in footnote 8 of *Blue Stone*, some courts have suspicion regarding its use, especially when it anticipates appointment not just of a corporate officer but of a restructuring advisor who really bears all the hallmarks of a professional for whom the protections of §§ 327-328 seem designed. "The two primary goals of § 327(a) are to ensure the impartiality of the professional and to provide court oversight in the determination of the reasonableness of the professional's compensation. These goals are best achieved through the transparent process of § 327(a) that governs the employment of all professional persons employed by a debtor." *McDermott*, at *11. But the genesis of the protocol was not as some sneaky way to skirt § 327 and its rules for employed professionals. Rather, it arose out of concern that restructuring advisors helping a debtor pre-bankruptcy might be statutorily disqualified from serving the debtor in bankruptcy under § 327(a)'s requirement of disinterestedness (although there is some wiggle room depending on how one reads § 1107(b)). The protocol thus synthetically recreates many—but, importantly, not all—of the §§ 327-328 protections for agents employed under ho-hum § 363 as a way to fill the policy gap. According to Bankruptcy Judge David Jones, however, the question is what it has transformed to become: "While innovative at its inception, the Alix Protocol has become a tool to avoid transparency and create inequity." Id. at *8.

The most searching examination of the private trustee system and CRO retention has arisen in a series of lawsuits brought by Jay Alix, founder of the eponymous consulting company that often serves as a private trustee. The charges were levied against a formidable competitor,

McKinsey & Co., a famous management consulting company that has gone into the "restructuring consultancy" business in a big way. Alix contends that McKinsey has repeatedly failed to disclose conflicting interests, often those relating to a private hedge fund it controls, and some even involving the representation (as business consultants) of parties who were major creditors in the chapter 11 cases where they were representing the debtor. On the one hand, McKinsey has been successful in procedurally rebuffing several of these challenges; on the other, Alix has been joined by the U.S. Trustee's office, and McKinsey has settled some allegations with a $15 million payment. See As McKinsey Sells Advice, Its Hedge Fund May Have a Stake in the Outcome, N.Y. Times (Feb. 19, 2020). Matters have come to a head in a trial conducted in the winter of 2020 in Houston, by the same judge who heard *McDermott*.

Somewhat sadly, we must end this section floating on a sea of doubt and inconsistency. Cosmopolitans that we are, we look at other countries for ideas. In Canada, for example, the CCAA (Companies' Creditors Arrangement Act) has such broad provisions that it is often called "Chapter 11 without rules," which suggests even less corporate governance oversight. Our Canadian friends, however, have a key institutional player who is absent in chapter 11: the *monitor*. A monitor is appointed to oversee management's stewardship and reports to the court on a regular basis. Thus, we see something like a DIP plus a quasi-trustee, perhaps something akin to the SBRA trustee, with the debtor having control, but the monitor having the ear of the court from the powerful posture of a disinterested expert. The monitor system has been subject to criticism, including additional expense, but may offer useful food for thought. To the south, the Mexican system has an official called a *conciliador*, who serves similar functions but with more explicit power to affect the proceeding. Keep in mind, too, that each country's bankruptcy rules overlie general corporate law rules. (Indeed, in many countries corporate bankruptcy is part of corporation law, not a separate insolvency law.) Foreign laws are generally far less favorable to pre-bankruptcy owners or managers. For example, few U.S. executives would envy their peers in countries where director misconduct—or even failure to file bankruptcy by a given time after the company becomes insolvent—can result in jail.

B.   GOVERANCE INCENTIVES: COMPENSATION IN CHAPTER 11

We turn in this section from general governance concerns to a very specific, salient one: guidelines for compensation of corporate management in chapter 11 cases. Too low, and the managers will either refuse to file for chapter 11 or flee to other employment when the storm clouds gather. Too high, and the creditors, employees, and others will cry that the shepherds are making off with all the wool.

In a system that gives so much power to corporate management, it is not surprising that there are concerns about management compensation and incentives. This concern exists outside bankruptcy and is reflected in state corporate law. In bankruptcy, the concern is enhanced by the fact that workers often lose jobs or are asked to accept major financial sacrifices. The law may not want to accord the management the self-policing compensation latitude enjoyed in the ordinary state of affairs. When the big corporate scandals of the early twenty-first century hit, such as Enron and Worldcom, observers began to question the compensation that managers were awarding themselves, especially fraudulent managers, and that criticism persists today. BAPCPA via § 503(c) imposed stringent (some would say insurmountable) restrictions on executive retention plans (a bonus scheme designed to keep "key employees" from deserting the ship in chapter 11), while plans designed to retain non-executive personnel are functionally permissible given the statute's focus on median compensation of corporate employees. 11 U.S.C. § 503(c). Chapter 11 lawyers hamstrung in preserving Key Employee Retention Plans (KERPs), like all good lawyers do, came up with a workaround: style the package a Key Employee *Incentive* Plan. Let's see how they fared in the next case.

<hr>

In re HAWKER BEECHCRAFT, INC.
479 B.R. 308 (Bankr. S.D.N.Y. 2012)

BERNSTEIN, Bankruptcy Judge.

The Debtors filed a motion seeking approval of their proposed key employee incentive plan (the "KEIP") and their non-insider key employee retention plan (the "KERP"). Following an evidentiary hearing, the Court approved the KERP from the bench, and reserved decision on the KEIP. Although the KEIP includes elements of incentive compensation, when viewed as a whole, it sets the minimum bonus bar too low to qualify as anything other than a retention program for insiders. Accordingly, the Court concludes that the Debtors have failed to sustain their burden of proof and denies the KEIP part of the Motion without prejudice.

BACKGROUND

A. Introduction

At all relevant times, the Debtors have been engaged in the business of manufacturing and servicing business jets, trainer/attack aircraft and propeller and piston aircraft under the Hawker and Beechcraft brands. Burdened with excessive secured and unsecured debt, they filed chapter 11 petitions in this Court on May 3, 2012 (the "Petition Date").

Prior to the Petition Date, the Debtors had entered into a Restructuring Support Agreement (the "RSA") with the majority of their creditors (the "Consenting Creditors") which, in substance, would convert 100% of their prepetition debt into equity (the "Standalone Transaction"). The Debtors also agreed prior to the Petition Date but in contemplation of bankruptcy to (a) file a plan of reorganization and disclosure statement by June 30, 2012, (b) obtain an order approving the disclosure statement by August 31,

2012, (c) confirm the plan by November 15, 2012 and (d) consummate the plan by December 15, 2012.

The RSA did not preclude the Debtors and their advisors from engaging in a marketing process to pursue a sale or other strategic transaction with a third party ("Third-Party Transaction"). The Debtors proceeded on a dual track pursuing the plan contemplated by the Standalone Transaction (the "Standalone Plan") while contemporaneously seeking a Third-Party Transaction that would provide greater value to the estates. On or about July 2, 2012, the Debtors received a Second Revised Proposal from Superior Aviation Beijing, Co., Ltd. ("Superior") to purchase substantially all of the Debtors' assets (excluding its defense business) on a cash free, debt-free basis for $1.79 billion in cash (the "Superior Proposal"). The Superior Proposal was subject to several conditions including a 45 day exclusive access period during which the Debtors would cease soliciting or negotiating with other third parties, the parties would execute a definitive agreement; the Debtors would hold a bankruptcy auction and the parties would obtain the necessary regulatory approvals.

On July 10, 2012, the Debtors filed the Superior Exclusivity Motion which sought Court authorization to grant the 45 day exclusivity sought by Superior. Following an evidentiary hearing, the Court granted the Superior Exclusivity Motion over the objection of the International Associations of Machinists and Aerospace Workers, AFL-CIO ("IAM"), the union that represented 45% of the Debtors' workforce as of the Petition Date.

B. The Motion

The Debtors historically maintained incentive plans that paid certain key employees additional compensation through an annual cash incentive program based on certain cash and percentage profit targets and through equity-based awards. . . .

As they contemplated bankruptcy, the Debtors opted to develop a senior management incentive program, and retained Towers Watson, executive compensation experts, to assist in its development. According to the testimony of Nick Bubnovich, a former director of Towers Watson who testified as an expert, the Debtors' senior management's base salary stood at 58% below the market median, substantially below market. Working in conjunction with the Official Committee of Unsecured Creditors (the "Committee") and the Consenting Creditors, the Debtors' developed the KEIP and filed the Motion seeking its approval.

The KEIP applies to eight "insiders" within the meaning of 11 U.S.C. § 101(31), denominated as the senior leadership team, or SLT. They include the Debtors' Chairman, the Executive Vice President of Operations, the Vice President of Human Resources, the Vice President of Engineering, the Executive Vice President and General Counsel, the Senior Vice President of Global Customer Support, the Chief Financial Officer and the Executive Vice President of Customers. The KEIP offers two mutually exclusive paths for awarding bonuses to the SLT depending on whether the Debtors consummate the Standalone Plan or a Third-Party Transaction. To be eligible to receive payment of any award, the SLT member must be employed on the effective date of the plan unless the SLT member has been terminated without cause or resigned for good reason prior to the date that payment is due.

1. The Standalone Plan

Each member of the SLT can earn up to 200% of his annual base salary, or the aggregate amount of $5,328,000, in the event the Debtors' consummate the Standalone Plan (the "Standalone Transaction Award"). The award is comprised of two independent components with 50% based on the timing of the consummation (the "Consummation Award") and 50% based on the achievement of financial targets (the "Financial Performance Award"). The Consummation Award provides for a sliding scale of recovery under which the SLT members can earn a bonus if the Debtors consummate the Standalone Plan on or before December 15, 2012. The earlier the consummation, the greater the award. [Omitted is a table with dates for determining bonus amounts due.—Eds.]

These dates can be extended without notice or Court approval at the discretion of the Debtors and with the agreement of the Consenting Creditors and the Committee. In addition, the target consummation dates will automatically be extended by the number of days (but not to exceed 30 days) beyond August 31, 2012, in which the Debtors have not resolved the treatment of their three defined benefit pension plans.

The second component of the Standalone Transaction Award is the Financial Performance Award. The computation of this award is set out in a complicated chart at paragraph 23 of the Motion; it is based on a sliding scale of targets relating to the Debtors' cumulative net cash flow starting on July 9, 2012, and ending as of the end of the week in which the plan is consummated. The lowest target level, which pays 50% of the base salary to each member of the SLT, corresponds to the projections under the Debtors' business plan.

2. Third-Party Transaction

The KEIP includes a separate set of incentives if the Debtors consummate a plan based on a Third-Party Transaction. Each member of the SLT would receive a sale bonus of 200% of his base salary upon Court approval of a Third-Party Transaction prior to December 15, 2012 that (a) results in a purchase price of at least $1.79 billion and (b) closes no later than January 15, 2013 (the "Third-Party Transaction Award"). As with the Consummation Award, these dates can be extended with the consent of the Committee and the Consenting Creditors. If the Court-approved Third-Party Transaction results in a purchase price of less than $1.79 billion, the Third-Party Transaction Award would decrease by 25% of each SLT member's base salary for each $100 million in purchase price below $1.79 billion. However, there would not be any downward adjustment if (a) the decrease in purchase price is the result of a purchase price adjustment triggered by the assumption of certain liabilities (which is not currently contemplated) and (b) the assumption of such liabilities is supported by the Committee. In the event the Debtors determine to pursue the Third-Party Transaction, but through no fault of management, the Third-Party Transaction does not close, the Debtors will award the Standalone Transaction Awards, but the level of cumulative net cash flow that needs to be reached for 50% of the bonus will be adjusted to reflect the costs expected to be incurred while the Debtors pursue the Third-Party Transaction.

Discussion

The Debtors concede that the members of the SLT are "insiders," and accordingly, the threshold question raised by the objections to the Motion is whether the KEIP is a true incentive plan, or instead, a disguised retention plan. Section 503(c)(1) of the Bankruptcy Code governs retention plans applicable to insiders. Congress enacted § 503(c) as part of the 2005 BAPCPA amendments to the Bankruptcy Code to "eradicate the notion that executives were entitled to bonuses simply for staying with the Company through the bankruptcy process," In re Global Home Prods., LLC, 369 B.R. 778, 784 (Bankr. D. Del. 2007) (internal quotation marks omitted) and to "limit the scope of 'key employee retention plans' and other programs providing incentives to management of the debtor as a means of inducing management to remain employed by the debtor." 4 Alan N. Resnick & Henry J. Sommer, Collier On Bankruptcy ¶ 503.17, at 503-105 (16th ed. 2012).

A debtor is, of course, free to propose a KERP for the benefit of insiders that satisfies the rigorous criteria in § 503(c)(1). Furthermore, § 503(c)(1) does not prevent a debtor from adopting a plan that rewards insiders for achieving financial or other targets, rather than for simply remaining in the employment of the debtor, even though the incentive plan has a retentive effect. See In re Dana Corp., 351 B.R. 96, 102 (Bankr. S.D.N.Y. 2006) ("*Dana I*"). The concern in the type of motion presented in this case is that the debtor has dressed up a KERP to look like a KEIP in the hope that it will pass muster under the less demanding "facts and circumstances" standard in 11 U.S.C. § 503(c)(3). [S]ee *Dana I*, 351 B.R. at 102 n.3 ("If [a bonus proposal] walks like a duck (KERP), and quacks like a duck (KERP), it's a duck (KERP)."). The Court must examine a proposed KEIP mindful of the practice that Congress sought to eradicate and, at the risk of oversimplification, determine whether the proposed targets are designed to motivate insiders to rise to a challenge or merely report to work. The proponent of the KEIP bears the burden of proving that the plan is not a retention plan governed by § 503(c)(1).

Here, the Debtors have failed to sustain their burden of proof. At the outset, they did not identify the roles of each member of the SLT or why, individually or as part of a team, they will contribute services that are necessary to achieve the targets. Beyond that, although the KEIP includes incentivizing targets, the lowest levels are well within reach. The SLT will earn a bonus under either of two transactions, one of which is bound to occur. The Debtors are on target to meet the confirmation and consummation deadlines under the RSA and KEIP pertaining to the Standalone Transaction, but in any event, the deadlines under each alternative can be extended with the consent of the parties.

Each alternative includes a financial target (cumulative net cash flow or sale price), but the Debtors do not have to hit any financial target to pay a bonus under the Standalone Transaction, and the sale price target does not seem to be much of a challenge in light of the Superior Proposal and the fact that the Debtors must still pay a bonus even if a Third-Party Transaction is consummated at a substantially reduced price. In essence, the KEIP pays a bonus for consummating a plan that is likely to occur. . . .

Furthermore, the SLT member does not earn a bonus if the member quits prior to consummation of the transaction (the effective date of a plan). Thus, if the SLT member does everything required of him and more, but the effective date is delayed because of an appeal, and the SLT member takes another job in the interim, he sacrifices his bonus. In other words, he has to stay for his pay.

Finally, the Debtors' Chief Executive Officer Robert S. Miller confirmed the retentive purpose of the Third-Party Transaction Award. He opined that in its absence, "the SLT could seek alternative employment opportunities and, as a result, immediately undermine the Debtors' restructuring efforts at a critical juncture of the Debtors' chapter 11 cases and in the Debtors' business cycle."

The Debtors' authorities do not support a contrary conclusion. In In re Borders Group, 453 B.R. 459 (Bankr. S.D.N.Y. 2011), the debtors proposed a KEIP for the benefit of insiders that required them to confirm an ongoing (non-liquidating) business plan or consummate a sale of the business as a going concern under 11 U.S.C. § 363 and meet specific financial targets relating to annual rent reductions or other cost reductions as well as distributions to unsecured creditors.

. . .

In In re Dana Corp., 358 B.R. 567 (Bankr. S.D.N.Y. 2006) ("*Dana II*"), the Court approved a long term incentive plan that awarded bonuses if the company reached a specific EBITDAR, and the bonuses increased as EBITDAR increased. The plan represented substantial reductions from the long-term incentive plans that were available pre-petition. The Court approved the incentive plan based upon evidence showing that the debtors' pro forma EBITDAR was $210 million, and achieving the financial target of $250 million was difficult and not a "lay-up." Here, the minimum target level matches the business plan projections, the Debtors' Chief Executive Officer testified that they should hit at least the minimum target if they don't encounter any "whoopsies," and the Debtors failed to compare their pre-petition plans to the KEIP.

. . .

[T]he proposed KEIP in this case keys the minimum 50% Financial Performance Award under the Standalone Plan to the business projections. In addition, the Debtors offered general testimony that the SLT members will be required to provide the services necessary to move down dual plan paths. . . . However, the SLT members can earn a 50% Consummation Award through the Standalone Plan under an indefinite deadline without meeting any financial targets. In addition, they can earn a 200% bonus under the Third-Party Transaction by consummating the transaction under a flexible deadline at a price that Superior has already offered, or a lesser bonus at a substantially lower price.

Nothing in this opinion is meant to denigrate the efforts of the SLT or minimize their contributions to the success of the case. Nevertheless, the BAPCPA changes impose a high standard that requires challenging goals that insiders must meet in order to earn a bonus under an incentive plan that is not subject to § 503(c)(1). The targets at the higher end of the KEIP meet this requirement but the goals at the lower end do not.

======

Near the end of American Airlines' flight through chapter 11, it sought approval of its merger with US Airways. Once it had that approval, it would seek confirmation of its plan of reorganization based on the merger. In the merger agreement was a provision for a $20 million exit package for the outgoing CEO of American parent company AMR Corp. (Whatever happened to a gold watch and a hearty handshake?) The debtor conceded that § 503(c) would preclude approval of the exit package if it were paid by the debtor, but said that the section would not apply to this payment because it would be paid by the merged, post-bankruptcy airline after the merger and plan approval. In effect, the court said, "Fine. Award it after the merger and exit from bankruptcy." But unstated was the important fact that without a binding agreement as part of the merger, the former president would be old news at the new company, no longer in control of the merger process and without a contract for his bonus enforceable against the emerged company.

There is virtually unanimous agreement that the provisions of § 503(c)(1) are between very difficult and impossible to satisfy, so the primary hope for management bonuses is to craft a bonus to which it does not apply. It makes a lawyer feel good to be needed.

Problem Set 33

33.1. Rafael Guitar often jokes that "With my name, I was going to play the piano?" Instead, he has become a very successful flamenco guitarist based in Greenwich Village. He has a line of guitars sold by his company, Guitar's Guitars, Inc. (GGI) that he has promoted with tours and PBS appearances. The recession, however, caught GGI in the midst of a major expansion just as demand for its products plummeted. It has now filed chapter 11 with over $15 million in debt. Rafael is the president and the company's shareholders are various members of his extended family and close friends. All very much want for GGI to survive. Because the company has hired Manuel Hinajosa, an MBA with a good track record, to run the business side, Rafael thinks there is every chance for a recovery as the economy picks up. However, "I also have to look out for my family," which includes child support times seven children.

A much larger company based in Boston has offered to hire him to become the lead promoter of their guitars at his prior salary with a $400,000 signing bonus. (He has taken no salary from GGI during the last six months because of its difficulties.) He wants a new contract with GGI that would grant him the same bonus. He thinks the board, which is made up of leading music industry figures (but only one member of his family other than himself), would be glad to approve such a contract. He is sure the creditors' committee will concur. "They know that it is my name and promotion that will produce the sales." What is your advice? See §§ 101(31)(B), 503(c).

33.2. Now a thought experiment. Imagine yourself the lawyer from the U.S. Trustee's office on your feet before Judge McEwen in Tampa at the hearing involving *Blue Stone Development*. It is increasingly apparent that the judge is frustrated and a bit disgusted with your position, as her opinion suggests, and you feel there is no hope for your argument as stated so far. You ask for and get a recess to think about what to do and to confer with your boss back at the UST's office. What are your possible courses of action? See § 1104(a), (d), (e), Fed. R. Bankr. P. 8002. What are the key issues at stake here and how can they best be addressed?

33.3. Reggie McFlintock is deeply divided about what to do. A year ago he was a fast-rising star in the electronics industry when he was offered the job of CEO of XKX Corp. XKX is a large publicly owned consumer electronics company that survived a brutal industry shakeout, but only by a hair. He knew there was a serious risk that XKX was beyond saving, so he asked for a $3 million signing bonus and a $800,000 salary with big performance incentives added. The XKX board was deeply divided by his demand. Bill Finley, a nonmanagement board member, said, "Given a little time to get our new products to market, this company will be worth easily $250 million, but Reggie is the only guy who can do it." However, Ethel Cinchley, another independent director, thought such compensation for a CEO of a deeply troubled company made no sense and that the company should accept a recent offer from Maximum Cap, Inc. of $100 million for all its assets, "which would pay all our debts and leave something for the shareholders." Bill carried the day, and Reggie got the job. Ethel and her supporters resigned. Now, a year later, they both appear to have been right. The first of the new products has gone to market and is doing very, very well. On the other hand, overall revenue is down and losses are mounting. It is not clear if the company is solvent on a balance sheet basis, although it is paying its bills.

Recently, Maximum has made a new offer of $40 million for all the XKX assets, tying the lower price to the continued decline in XKX's financials. The $40 million would pay all creditors in full but the shareholders would get nothing. Maximum also promised to take over Reggie's contract and make him the head of its new XKX division, although Reggie notes that Maximum executives don't seem to have much job security. Bill Finley is firmly opposed to the offer, telling Reggie that a turnaround is just ahead, "although we on the board will support whatever decision you finally make, even though it will be a terrible disappointment to the shareholders if you sell, plus you will be giving up a lot personally under your contract incentives." Reggie agrees there is a good chance of recovery, but XKX's bank lenders are pressing him hard to accept the deal so they will be paid off. Because of revenue problems, XKX might miss a payment and face default anytime in the next six months, likely forcing the company to go into chapter 11 to hold off the banks and other creditors.

Reggie got a call this morning from the lawyer for the bank lenders emphasizing his fiduciary duty to creditors and urging him "not to take any stupid risks when you've got $40 million on the table in front of you." Now Reggie has called you, as the company's outside counsel. He wants to know what legal considerations should affect his decision. Especially, he wants you to explain to him whose interests he is supposed to put first. See §§ 503(c), 548(a)(1), 1121(d)(2).

PRACTICING IN CHAPTER 11

Bankruptcy is a messy place to apply the standard rules of professional responsibility on conflicts, compensation, privilege, and the like. Part of the difficulty is the context of reorganization itself, with parties coming and going and their negotiating positions changing so quickly that it is often hard to keep track. "Bankruptcy courts often need to act quickly, and should be able to assume that counsel are truthful." In re Hoover, 827 F.3d 191 (1st Cir. 2016) (upholding substantial sanctions under Fed. R. Bankr. P. 9011, bankruptcy's analogue of Fed. R. Civ. P. 11, for bankruptcy lawyer's misleading citations and arguments in a lift-stay motion). Another aspect of the difficulty is that the Code and Bankruptcy Rules add another layer of ethical requirements beyond all the good stuff you will learn for the MPRE. The cardinal rule in bankruptcy is disclose, disclose, disclose. Omissions are always interpreted adversely in the ethics context. And rest assured there will be plenty of opportunities to bring matters to the court's attention: the court must approve all professional fees before the estate may pay them. § 330.

A. CONFLICTS

1. Duties of DIP Counsel

One of the first differences an attorney representing a debtor in bankruptcy notices is that the court has a much more active role in supervising the attorney-client relationship than it does in ordinary litigation. As discussed in the previous assignment, the attorney represents a new legal entity, the DIP, and court supervision of the attorney is conceptually akin to supervision of attorneys of decedents' estates and of minors. The attorney for the DIP represents the bankruptcy estate, not the debtor, and so fiduciary duties are imposed to police the attorney from freely doing the bidding of the debtor's managers or owners (the only human beings through whom the inanimate estate gets to talk to its lawyer). The difficulty for the DIP attorney is hewing to the estate's best interests while fielding directives from the debtor's managers and at the same time facing off against the unsecured creditors, who are often the true residual owners of the estate. These issues are sufficiently thorny that the American

Bankruptcy Institute convened an ethics task force. The first part of its report parses the issues and comes up with best practices. The simplest, but most important advice might be the first recommendation: "An attorney for a debtor-in-possession must be proactive in counseling her client with respect to its compliance with its fiduciary duties to the bankruptcy estate." Final Report of the ABI National Ethics Task Force 25 (2013). Easier said than done, however, because while the potential conflicts between a corporation and its owner or manager may be fundamental and pervasive (as corporate law scholarship reminds us repeatedly), they are not always easy to see in practice, especially in a smaller, private corporation where proxy fights and contested board elections simply don't exist. Consider the following excerpt from a game invented by Professor Lynn LoPucki.

The Debtor's Lawyer as Trojan Horse
(Player's Manual for Debtor-Creditor Game (West 1984))

Shares is the sole shareholder of Corps, a corporation which is now in financial difficulty. He comes to Lawyer for advice. Shares describes the problems of the business, and after some discussion they conclude that the corporation should file for reorganization under chapter 11 of the Bankruptcy Code. Among the papers which Lawyer prepares for that filing is the standard "Application of Debtor-in-Possession to Employ Attorney." The "Debtor-in-Possession" referred to is, of course, the corporation; the attorney to be employed is Lawyer. Included in the application is the usual recitation that Lawyer "represents no interest adverse to the estate." See Bankruptcy Code § 327(a).

Shortly after the proceeding is filed, Lawyer comes to three very disturbing realizations. First, the heart of Corps' problem may be that Shares is a poor manager. Second, it is in the corporation's best interests to have the Court seriously consider replacing Shares as manager. Third, Shares would be a fool to voluntarily step down, since if he does creditors will seize control of the proceedings and oust him from his ownership position. He will lose everything. What should Lawyer do?

Since Lawyer, in this example, led Shares to believe that he would represent Shares' interests as well as those of the corporation, and those interests are now in direct conflict, Lawyer probably is bound to withdraw from both representations. He has lost his clients and the fees he might have earned during the remainder of the proceedings. If Lawyer had been conscious of the likelihood of such a conflict from the beginning could he have reached a better result? Let's give Lawyer another try.

Shares comes to Lawyer for advice about the Corps' financial difficulties. Lawyer carefully explains that here is a potential conflict of interest between Shares and Corps, and that he should not represent both. Since it is Corps that needs to file the chapter 11 proceeding, he suggests that he should represent Corps before filing as "debtor" and after filing as "debtor-in-possession." Lawyer advises Shares that, should an actual conflict of interest arise, he will notify Shares and Shares can then obtain separate counsel. He also cautions Shares that while Shares' communications to him will be protected by the attorney-client privilege, the privilege will be owned by the corporation, not by Shares. A trustee appointed at some later time could compel Lawyer to disclose Shares' communications to Lawyer, over the objection of both Lawyer and Shares.

Shares is absolutely astounded. "I brought my legal problem to you and asked for help. You seem to be telling me not only that you cannot help me, but that you may be 'ethically' bound to work against my interests. And you expect to be paid out of the corporation that I own 100 percent of! If that is correct, wouldn't I (or any other owner of a closely held corporation in financial difficulty) be a fool to authorize the hiring of an attorney for the corporation?"

"That's certainly a problem," says Lawyer, "but a corporation is a person, a separate legal entity, and needs to have the undivided loyalty of its attorney, just as you would want to have the undivided loyalty of your attorney." (If Lawyer is conscious of any irony, his face does not betray it.)

"You may *say* that a corporation is a 'person,' but that doesn't make it so," Shares responds. "I started the business, I supplied the capital, I hired the people who did the work. There is no one in the business but a bunch of short-term employees and me. There is no other person who might be injured by your loyalty to me."

"What about the creditors?" Lawyer replies.

"Are you supposed to represent them?" Shares asks. "Most of them already have their own attorneys and wouldn't be interested. The law purports to be worried about the interests of the corporation, but a corporation is nothing but a legal fiction. There's nobody in this corporation except me." Shares pauses, grins, then adds, "And you, of course, if I were dumb enough to let you in."

Lawyer is obviously offended. "I don't make the rules," he says. "But as an attorney I have ethical obligations to the Court as well as to the client." The sound of these familiar words enables Lawyer to regain his composure. He continues, "If you don't want me in your corporation, possibly working against you, you'll just end up with somebody else doing the same thing. Worse yet," Lawyer chuckles, "you might get some lawyer who's not as ethical as I am!"

Shares ignores Lawyer's attempt at humor. "Since I'm ultimately going to be paying your fees anyway, couldn't I just hire you as my attorney—and let the corporation be the one without counsel?"

Lawyer thought about that for a few minutes. "I don't think that will work unless the corporation is also represented. Who would sign the pleadings? Who would make the arguments in court? Oh, I suppose it could be done, but it would be very clumsy. I've never heard of anyone else doing it. It would be very unusual for a corporate debtor in a chapter 11 proceeding to have no attorney. The creditors and the Bankruptcy Judge wouldn't like it. They would think we were up to something, and in a way, they would be right. You'd run a very high risk that a trustee would be appointed. If that happened, you'd probably lose your ownership interest in the business."

There is a long silence before Shares speaks. "So then the real problem isn't that the corporation needs an attorney. It's that the creditors and the Judge want it to have one. Then aren't you telling me that the lawyer for a debtor-in-possession is really a sort of Trojan horse—brought in by a shareholder like myself for the ostensible purpose of representing my interests—but whose real function is to spy on me for the creditors and the court?"

"That's not really a fair description," Lawyer protests. "We also do a lot of other things. . . ."

Shares interrupts. "This is ridiculous," he fumes. "I read in a newspaper article that about 90 percent of all corporations that file under chapter 11 are owned and managed by a single owner or a family, and that in about 90 percent of the cases the cause of the debtor's problems is that the businesses have bad managers. What you are telling me is that your Code of Professional Responsibility requires that their lawyers work in the interests of the corporations even if it means working against the men or women who hired them. Why that means that in at least 81 percent of all chapter 11 proceedings in this country the attorney for the debtor-in-possession has an 'ethical' duty to work to oust his own client from control!"

"Almost correct," says Lawyer, "but that guy he's ousting *isn't* his client."

Some lawyers would try to avoid the hard issues in this dialogue by saying that management competence is not a legal issue. Aside from the fact that such "business" issues are often intertwined with legal issues, unavoidable conflicts of a purely legal sort are commonplace with closely-held companies in financial distress. Insider preference and fraudulent conveyance issues are obvious examples, and they routinely arise despite the lack of any evil motive or sense of wrongdoing on the part of the owner-officer of the business. Paying suppliers to keep the business afloat or asking dad to lend money very short term to the business in order to make payroll are business decisions with powerful legal implications if the company heads into bankruptcy. In larger corporations, management compensation and shareholder lawsuits can similarly create tension between the concerns of management and the best interests of the estate. Perhaps the most important lesson to be drawn from Professor LoPucki's story is that it is the lawyer—not the client—who is responsible for dealing with these conflicts.

Lawyers can also find themselves ensnared in another ethical issue when they represented the debtor company prepetition and now serve as DIP counsel: who can exercise or waive the attorney-client privilege? In bankruptcy, the issue can arise in several situations because of the shifting dynamics of control and the sharp division between prepetition and postpetition duties. Perhaps the thorniest privilege problem comes from trying to determine whether a particular attorney-client conversation was between counsel and the client-DIP, or between counsel and the non-client management/owners. The attorney in both conversations is looking into the same beady eyes of the feckless or stressed (or both) corporate manager.

The Supreme Court weighed in on "ownership" of the privilege in the context of a corporate chapter 7 bankruptcy. *Commodity Futures Trading Comm'n v. Weintraub*, 471 U.S. 343 (1985). At a deposition, the company's former counsel asserted attorney-client privilege on behalf of the debtor corporation. The investigating agency briskly secured a waiver of privilege from the trustee. The Court ruled that the power to exercise the privilege with respect to pre-bankruptcy communications passes to a chapter 7 bankruptcy trustee, comparing the trustee to "successor management" in a corporate takeover. But a chapter 7 trustee arguably only inherits the right to control the property of the corporation (the estate), not the right to control its governance or any rights that it has in bankruptcy independent of its property. The difference with a chapter 11 DIP may limit *Weintraub*'s applicability. As a practice note, we caution that receiving the protection of privilege requires more than merely invoking the word. Many an attorney is tripped up by an inquiring court that requests a thorough privilege log or by an inadvertent waiver of privilege.

2. *Employment*

The Code requires that counsel can serve only with court approval, § 327(a), that counsel's fees must be approved by the court, §§ 328(a), 329(b), 330(a), that only "disinterested persons" may serve as counsel, § 327(a), and that the representation and fee arrangements must be disclosed to the court and creditors, § 329(a). To ensure the court's role in supervising this absence of conflicts, Rule 2014(a) requires professionals to disclose "all connections" with the debtor.

In re LEE

94 B.R. 172 (Bankr. C.D. Cal. 1989)

BUFFORD, Bankruptcy Judge.

I. FACTS

Debtors Chile B. Lee and Hae Sook Lee filed this voluntary Chapter 11 bankruptcy case on August 23, 1988. They are apparently the sole shareholders of Seoul Corporation, whose Chapter 11 bankruptcy case was filed in this Court on August 16, 1988. Seoul Corporation is engaged in the sale of general merchandise and costume jewelry at wholesale. Chile Lee is the president and Hae Sook Lee is the secretary of Seoul Corporation. Presumably the debtors are also the only directors of Seoul Corporation, although this is not disclosed in the papers filed with the Court. Both of the petitions were signed by Jang W. Lee [no apparent relationship to the debtors—Eds.], as counsel for debtors.

A brief review of the schedules filed by the Lees and Seoul Corporation discloses that there is a substantial overlap of creditors for the individuals and for the corporation. However, it appears that a number of creditors are not shared.

The debtors in each case have filed an application for the appointment of the law firm Lee, Scott & Young ("LSY"), in which Jang W. Lee is a partner, as general counsel for the debtors, pursuant to Bankruptcy Code § 327. . . .

The employment applications also make no disclosure whatever of the relationship between these two cases, or that LSY is seeking employment in both of them, notwithstanding the conflicts that such employment could raise. The declaration of Jang W. Lee in the employment application in each case states:

1. To the best of my knowledge, I am not connected with the debtors, their creditors, or any other party in interest except I am the attorney for the debtors in this Chapter 11 case. . . .
2. No member or associate of this law firm represents any interest in this estate, adverse or otherwise, except the interest of the applicants.

The parallel applications for appointment as legal counsel came to the Court's attention because they arrived in chambers and were reviewed on the same day. If this had not occurred, the problem would likely not have come to the Court's attention.

After noting the similar employment applications in the two cases, the Court obtained and reviewed the respective bankruptcy case files and thus learned of the conflicting interests that LSY seeks to represent. The Court then issued an order to show cause why LSY should not be disqualified in both cases because of its failure to disclose the parallel employment applications. In response to the order to show cause, LSY disclosed for the first time its retainer in this case.

II. ANALYSIS

This is not an isolated instance of a potential conflict in interest by prospective counsel for related debtors. This Court has received similar applications for appointment as counsel for related debtors from many law firms in Los Angeles that represent bankruptcy debtors.

The failure to disclose the potential conflict is also not an isolated instance. In this Court's experience, prospective counsel infrequently discloses that appointment is sought in a related case.

. . .

LSY's parallel employment applications in this case and in the *Seoul Corporation* case raise two problems. First, the failure to disclose the parallel applications is a violation of Rule 2014(a). Second, appointment of LSY in both cases would result in its representation of conflicting interests, which is prohibited.

1. Non-Disclosure

LSY's failure to disclose its application to represent Seoul Corporation is also a violation of Rule 2014(a). Rule 2014(a) requires the disclosure in an application for employment of "all the [applicant's] connections with . . . any other party in interest. . . ." . . . The failure to disclose the employment application in a related case is alone a sufficient basis for disqualifying counsel in both cases. While the Court does not impose total disqualification in this case, it will not hesitate to disqualify counsel in the future in all related cases, or to impose other appropriate sanctions, for similar nondisclosure.

2. LSY's Adverse Interests

LSY does not meet the requirements of Bankruptcy Code § 327(a), for the appointment of attorneys in both of these cases. Section 327(a) authorizes a trustee to employ "one or more attorneys . . . that do not hold or represent an interest adverse to the estate, and that are disinterested persons. . . ." Section 1107(a) gives a debtor in possession the rights and powers of a trustee (with certain exceptions not material here), including the power to employ attorneys.

Section 327 requires the application of a two-pronged test for the employment of professional persons. A debtor in possession or trustee may employ attorneys with court approval only if (1) they do not hold or represent an interest adverse to the estate, and (2) they are disinterested persons. Both prongs of this test must be met. LSY fails to meet the first of these requirements.

The term "adverse interest" is not specifically defined in the Bankruptcy Code. The reported cases have defined what it means to hold an adverse interest as follows:

(1)   to possess or assert any economic interest that would tend to lessen the value of the bankrupt estate or that would create either an actual or potential dispute in which the estate is a rival claimant; or

(2)   to possess a predisposition under circumstances that render such a bias against the estate.

To "represent an adverse interest" means to serve as agent or attorney for entities holding such adverse interests. . . .

Seoul Corporation has an interest adverse to the estate of the debtors in this case because, according to the schedules filed in the respective cases, there is joint liability on many of the debts owing by the respective estates. Thus it is in the interest of Seoul Corporation, as debtor in possession, to have these debts paid by the estate of the Lees. In contrast, it is in the interest of the debtors in this case to have Seoul Corporation's estate pay these debts. If LSY is appointed to represent the debtors in both cases, it will be representing these conflicting interests. . . .

3. Counsel's Response

Jang W. Lee contends that the representation of the debtors in the two cases does not involve the representation of conflicting interests, because Seoul Corporation is not a creditor of Chile B. Lee, and Lee is willing to waive any claims he has against the corporation.

First, Chile B. Lee does not have the power unilaterally to waive a claim of his estate against the corporation. The filing of a bankruptcy case creates an estate, which includes all legal and equitable interests of the debtor in property as of the commencement of the case. § 541. This property includes all causes of action that belong to the debtor on the date of filing. Thus any claim available to Chile B. Lee against the Seoul Corporation belongs to his estate, and presumptively to his creditors. As a debtor in possession he has a fiduciary duty to assert any such claim on their behalf. The filing of the bankruptcy case terminated his power unilaterally to waive claims, including any claims that he may have against Seoul Corporation.

Second, it is too early to determine whether Seoul Corporation has any claim against Chile B. Lee, its shareholder and president (and presumably also a director). Careful scrutiny of Chile B. Lee's actions as a shareholder, director and officer is necessary before such a determination can be made. The financial status of the corporation makes it quite likely that such a claim may be available to the corporation.

. . .

[M]ost important . . . in this case LSY has been dishonest and has hidden the conflict from the Court. This fact alone justifies the disqualification of LSY as counsel in both cases. . . .

LSY also pleads that the debtors in these two cases cannot afford separate counsel. This rationale has often been used in the past to justify the appointment of counsel to represent related debtors. However, lack of financial resources is no justification for representing conflicting interests.

Lack of financial resources is often a reason for waiving a conflict of interest. Rule 5-102 permits an attorney to represent conflicting interests upon the written consent of all parties concerned. An attorney who desires to represent a debtor in possession and a conflicting interest must obtain a written waiver from the debtor, all creditors and the United States trustee. No such waiver has been offered in this case. . . .

Judge Bufford made clear that bankruptcy is not a game of catch-me-if-you-can. Disclosure is required in the employment application, both initially and on a going-forward basis as the representation unfolds. Note too that the easy-multiple choice answer of the MPRE—written waiver of a conflict—hits bumps in the real world of bankruptcy, where such waiver must be executed by *all* creditors. But some cases disagree. See, e.g., In re Professional Dev. Corp., 140 B.R. 467 (W.D. Tenn. 1992) (approving dual representation of sole shareholder and corporate debtor due to lack of actual conflicts).

The next case is a liquidating chapter 11 in which divvying up the assets is the only remaining task. When a creditor unearths a jaw-dropping conflict between the debtor and the debtor's counsel, does the counsel's attempt to address the conflict make matters better or worse?

In re SONICBLUE INC.

2007 WL 926871 (Bankr. N.D. Cal. Mar. 26, 2007)

MORGAN, Bankruptcy Judge.

SONICblue . . . designed and marketed consumer electronic products. Pillsbury Winthrop Shaw Pittman LLP ("PWSP") served as SONICblue's longtime general corporate and litigation counsel. On January 3, 2001, SONICblue formed S3 Graphics Co., Ltd., a joint venture with VIA Technologies, Inc., to operate SONICblue's graphics chip business. Among the assets that SONICblue contributed to the joint venture was its graphics intellectual property, specifically including rights under a 1998 patent cross-license with Intel Corporation. The rights to use Intel's graphics patents were so important that the joint venture agreement included a liquidated damages clause at article 5.6 entitling the joint venture and VIA each to damages of up to $70 million if the joint venture were ever enjoined from using the Intel cross-license. From the inception of the joint venture, there were serious disputes, including the threat of litigation, between SONICblue and VIA. . . .

Issuance of Senior Debentures and Related Opinion Letter by PWSP

In April 2002, SONICblue raised financing in a private placement issuance of $75 million in 73/4 % senior secured subordinated convertible debentures [bonds—Eds.]. Three institutional bondholders, Portside Growth & Opportunity Fund Ltd., Smithfield Fiduciary LLC, and Citadel Equity Fund Ltd., acquired the senior debentures at a discount for $62.5 million. . . . Importantly, the indenture provided for the subordination of the senior debentures to [certain obligations to VIA, principally the Intel cross-license "guarantee" to VIA and S3 Graphics—Eds.]. . . .

In its capacity as counsel to SONICblue, on April 22, 2002, PWSP issued to the senior bondholders a written opinion as to the enforceability of the debentures. This opinion letter reads in pertinent part:

> 2. . . . Each of . . . the Purchase Agreement, the Registration Rights Agreement, the Indenture, the Pledge and Security Agreement and the Option Agreement, when duly executed and delivered by the Buyers, will each constitute a valid and binding agreement of the Company, enforceable against the Company in accordance with its terms.
>
> . . .
>
> 3. The issuance and sale of the Debentures have been duly authorized. Upon issuance and delivery against payment therefor in accordance with the terms of the Indenture and the Purchase Agreement, the Debentures will constitute valid and binding obligations of the Company, enforceable against the Company in accordance with their terms.
>
> . . .
>
> 9. . . . (b) Our opinion in paragraph 2 above is subject to and limited by (i) the effect of applicable bankruptcy, insolvency, reorganization, fraudulent conveyance, receivership, conservatorship, arrangement, moratorium or other laws affecting or relating to the rights of creditors generally. . . .

In what may have been a scrivener's error, the bankruptcy limitation in paragraph 9 referenced only paragraph 2 and not paragraph 3 of the opinion letter.

Chapter 11 Filing and PWSP's Bankruptcy Rule 2014 Disclosures

Just six months after the issuance of the senior debentures, SONICblue was unable to meet its maturing financial obligations and entered into a retainer agreement for PWSP to "represent it in its effort to restructure its obligations to certain of its existing [debt]. . . . The Firm's engagement will also include representation of SONICblue in . . . any case prosecuted under Title 11 of the United States Code." . . .

On April 11, 2003, PWSP filed an employment application accompanied by a verified statement pursuant to Bankruptcy Rule 2014, which disclosed:

> 3. The Firm has been engaged as the Debtors' corporate and litigation counsel since approximately 1989. During that time, the Firm has provided legal representation to the Debtors in a variety of areas, including corporate and securities matters, mergers and acquisitions, litigation, and intellectual property matters. The Firm has been working with the Debtors in connection with

their restructuring since approximately October 25, 2002 when the Firm was retained to provide advice concerning the restructuring of the Debtor's liabilities and business operations. . . .

However, PWSP failed to disclose its connection resulting from the issuance of the opinion letter to the senior bondholders one year earlier. It added, "The Firm will continue to monitor its relationship with the creditors and other parties in interest in these cases and, as it discovers additional information requiring disclosure, will promptly supplement this application with any appropriate disclosures." The court appointed PWSP as counsel for the debtors. Marcus Smith, the Chief Financial Officer of SONICblue, was designated its responsible individual. PWSP diligently filed supplemental disclosures on May 30, 2003, January 23, 2004, October 27, 2004, July 13, 2005, July 27, 2005, November 4, 2005, and June 5, 2006, none of which mentioned the opinion letter.

The Office of the United States Trustee appointed an Official Committee of Unsecured Creditors on March 21, 2003. . . . Including the anticipated distribution collectable from the junior bondholders, the senior bondholders effectively control approximately two-thirds of the claims in these cases. . . .

Objection to Claim of Senior Bondholders

Since substantially all assets have been liquidated, PWSP has been prosecuting avoidance actions and objections to claims. It has divided and shared the work with LNBRB [Counsel for the Unsecured Creditors' Committee]. However, PWSP retained the more complex litigation or litigation requiring some knowledge of the background of the debtor's operations. PWSP initially examined the claims of the senior bondholders and the junior bondholders. It expended 49.50 hours, incurring $23,237.50 in legal fees, to complete its analysis of the senior bondholders' claims, including research on the applicability of fraudulent transfer law and usury law to the transaction. Based on its analysis, it identified a significant problem with the original issue discount granted the bondholders. . . . [The problem was that the bondholders might arguably be getting postpetition interest on their unsecured claim, contravening the prohibition in § 502(b)(2).—Eds.] . . .

Bennett [counsel for the bondholders] contacted PWSP partner Craig Barbarosh on August 24, 2006 to discuss SONICblue's challenge to the bondholders' claim. He also brought to Barbarosh's attention that PWSP had issued the opinion letter to the bondholders in connection with the issuance of the debentures. Bennett asserted that the bondholders had relied on the opinion letter, which they interpreted as assuring that their claims were allowable in a subsequent bankruptcy case. He further indicated that the bondholders would demand that PWSP defend and indemnify them for any losses resulting from SONICblue's challenge to their claim. Bennett's partner followed up on September 5, 2006 with a letter to the managing partner of PWSP demanding indemnification from PWSP for any shortfall to which the senior bondholders may be subjected as a result of SONICblue's objection to their claim. In the letter, he indicated that to the extent the bondholders are unable to recover in the bankruptcy case the full principal amount of the debentures, they intended to pursue PWSP for negligent misrepresentation and negligence, among other claims. . . .

PWSP immediately contacted [LNBRB] and turned over to the committee the task of prosecution of the objection to the claims of the senior bondholders [and presumably began work on its own cross-claim indemnification defense—Eds.]. On September 6, 2006, it forwarded its work file containing its analysis to LNBRB. PWSP did not, however, file a supplemental Bankruptcy Rule 2014 disclosure to address the claim of the senior bondholders. . . .

The Best Interests of Creditors Mandate the Disqualification of PWSP from Its Representation in the Case and the Appointment of a Chapter 11 Trustee

Under § 327(a) of the Bankruptcy Code, a debtor in possession may employ attorneys that do not hold an interest adverse to the estate and that are disinterested persons. Thus, to serve as debtor's counsel, counsel must be free of all conflicting interests that might impair the impartiality and neutral judgment that they are expected to exercise. In re Bellevue Place Associates, 171 B.R. 615, 626 (N.D. Ill. 1994). "Conflicting loyalties produce inadequate representation, which threatens the interests of the debtor, the trustee and the creditors, and compromises the ability of courts to mete out justice." . . .

[I]t is clear that PWSP knew it had a continuing duty to update its Rule 2014 disclosures upon learning of any undisclosed connections or conflicts. It is also apparent that as of late August 2006, PWSP knew it had a disabling conflict of interest because it immediately sought the aid of LNBRB in an attempt to resolve the conflict. Yet, PWSP failed to apprise the court of these facts. PWSP's attempt to characterize its failure as inadvertent oversight rings hollow in the face of its previous history of supplemental disclosures. PWSP argued in court that the partner in charge "assumed" a supplemental disclosure had been made, but the firm has not offered any evidentiary foundation for that assumption. . . .

The entirety of the undisputed facts also provides clear and convincing evidence that the appointment of a chapter 11 trustee is necessary to restore creditor confidence in the bankruptcy system and to assure that there is no lingering taint from PWSP's representation of the debtor. Neither the court nor the creditors may ever learn why PWSP or Smith, as debtor's responsible individual, failed to bring PWSP's conflict to the court's attention. But, that unanswered question is less important with the appointment of a strong, neutral trustee, who has no connections to any interested party.

[A creditor] also expresses concern that LNBRB may have failed to fulfill its role as a watchdog on behalf of the unsecured creditors. First, it appears that LNBRB failed to independently review the settlement agreement. . . . Second, when the actual conflict arose between PWSP and the senior bondholders, . . . LNBRB accepted responsibility for prosecuting the objections to the bondholders' claims without considering its own connections to the bondholders and the fact, or at least appearance, that it might also be conflicted. Professionals retained by an official committee of unsecured creditors owe fiduciary duties to the committee and its constituency. . . . It is not clear at this juncture whether LNBRB's handling of the objections of the bondholders was an actual conflict of interest. . . . If not an actual conflict, these facts certainly raise questions regarding LNBRB's suitability to vigorously pursue the claims objections on behalf of the estate. . . .

There have been serious allegations that the case is being run by and for the benefit of counsel. As a result, an active trustee who will formulate an independent strategy and direct its own counsel is critical. . . .,

CONCLUSION

The issue of disgorgement of fees is reserved for a later hearing after review by the appointed trustee. . . .

As the case shows, the conflicts nightmare is not limited to small and obscure law firms. The largest, most prestigious firms in the country face the same risks. The difficulty for debtor's counsel in the case began with a single misstated reference in an opinion letter of the sort firms issue regularly. (It was the sort of tiny, yet potentially catastrophic, mistake that gives lawyers cold sweats.) Notice how conspicuous the court felt the one decision not to disclose a "slight wrinkle" in the representation of the debtor was in the context of voluminous disclosure reports filed to date. Yet it is not always dramatic events that lead to conflicts issues. If the lawyer has sat on the company's board of directors and suits might be filed against the directors, or if the firm is owed large amounts of money for fees at the time of bankruptcy, the courts may well find the firm disqualified as bankruptcy counsel. In that case, the company may be forced to educate new counsel in complex operations and pending lawsuits just at the moment of extreme financial emergency. Balancing competing policy interests in this context is excruciating.

3.   *Conflicts Counsel*

Lawyers have designed a different solution to the conflicts problem: ask the court to approve the appointment of "conflicts counsel." The general idea is to allow one firm to do the bulk of the work and refer any issues that present conflicts of interest to separate, independent counsel. As LNBRB learned the hard way in *SONICblue*, however, "separate, independent counsel" for the DIP suing one specific creditor does not include counsel for the committee that represents all creditors—both the defending creditor *and* all others who gain if the defending creditor loses. While debtors' lawyers who want to continue with their former client frequently use conflicts counsel in large cases, the same procedure may be proposed by firms vying to be selected as counsel to a creditors committee. The prize for the runner-up in the so-called beauty contest for main committee counsel is that the runner-up may often be appointed as conflicts counsel. The runner-up gets a slice of the professional fee pie, and the winner eats the remainder.

Section 327(e) of the Code explicitly authorizes conflicts counsel, but the legislative history suggests that its scope was anticipated to be narrow. "[It] will most likely be used when the Debtor is involved in complex litigation, and changing attorneys in the middle of the case after the bankruptcy case has commenced would be detrimental to the progress of that other litigation." H.R. Rep. No. 595, 95th Cong. 1st Sess. 328 (1977). Modern practice has left such quaint predictions behind. Had PSWP disclosed the conflict and turned the prosecution of the objection to the bondholders' claim to a truly neutral third-party law firm, they might—*might*—have been allowed to stay on as counsel, perhaps depending on the dollar amount and complexity of the indemnification demand.

B.   COMPENSATION

Getting paid in chapter 11 is far from a sure bet. The problem is not only that the estate may run out of funds—that is just the obvious concern. Court approval of employment and compensation creates an additional barrier to payment, even from a willing and able client.

1.   Permissible Structures

For a client on the brink of bankruptcy, the bill to the law firm trying to negotiate a debt workout or do its general corporate, employment, securities, etc. work is likely to be unpaid. The firm is a creditor at the moment of bankruptcy, seemingly flunking the disinterestedness requirement right out of the gate. This payment "conflict" can be addressed in several ways. The easiest—from an ethical perspective, although it is surely painful—is for the firm to waive all prepetition fees. (Be forewarned: the junior associate who suggests this course at the firm's retreat is likely to be met with cold stares.) The work, the fees, and the waiver must all still be disclosed. § 329(a). If so, this is widely held to be sufficient to allow pre-existing counsel to be appointed as DIP counsel. In such situations, the firm is making a business decision that it will ultimately net higher profits with the time-intensive bankruptcy work than by sitting on the sidelines and filing a proof of claim in the case handled by a competitor firm. Of course, other, canny firms may be especially diligent in making sure that their monthly invoices are paid on time in the ordinary course of business to prevent precisely this sort of predicament. (The SBRA contains a limited exception to this rule in small business cases. § 1195.)

That's past payments, but what about future ones—from a financially distressed client no less? Can the attorney deal with the problem of adequate assurance of future payment by doing what many other businesses do at the inception of a business relationship: take a security interest to ensure timely payment? That may be fine for a bank or a supplier, but it injects a possibly tense dynamic between the client and its legal champion. Not surprisingly, at minimum, such interests must be disclosed. The leading case declined to rule that security interests are *per se* impermissible, In re Martin, 817 F.2d 175 (1st Cir. 1987). After dismissing the argument that a failure to appeal an engagement order barred challenging a security interest as "jejune," the *Martin* court held that there is a fine balance. On the one hand, lawyers' judgments may be shaded by their own economic welfare; counsel may cherry-pick the best estate assets as collateral before filing the case. On the other hand, the debtor may not get a competent lawyer without being able to provide some financial assurance of payment. It held that a security interest for fees was not per se unreasonable but should be scrutinized and policed by the bankruptcy court (and remanded to the bankruptcy court to figure out that balance). Perhaps due to the uncertainty of this balancing test, security interests of real or personal property are relatively rare ways to be paid, especially in larger cases where scrutiny is likely to be high—and more practically, a secured creditor likely already has a lien on everything of value.

Generally, attorneys in all areas of practice rely frequently on taking a retainer and billing the client against the retainer for future services. When the retainer is exhausted, the attorney may ask for another one before work continues, or the attorney may decide to bill the client as services are performed, expecting payment after the fact. Bankruptcy courts routinely recognize the validity of retainer agreements, although courts require that the agreement be disclosed as part of the general requirements for disclosure of fee arrangements. § 329(a); Bankruptcy Rule 2014(a). Most courts also make it clear that if the attorneys want to draw against the retainer, they must still seek court approval before taking as fees the money in the retainer account. There are a host of different approaches to fee protection by debtors and creditors' committees. See, e.g., In re Pan American Hosp. Corp., 312 B.R. 706 (Bankr. S.D. Fla. 2004) (outlining different retainer types).

In re HUNGRY HORSE

574 B.R. 740 (Bankr. D.N.M. 2017)

THUMA, Bankruptcy Judge.

. . .

I. FACTS

Debtor is a limited liability company engaged in oilfield services in southeastern New Mexico. Debtor filed this chapter 11 case on May 17, 2016[.] . . .

[After a substitution of counsel] the Debtor seeks approval, pursuant to § 328(a), of the engagement agreement between it and the Gorman firm, and of the following paragraph in particular:

> The Client agrees to pay all reasonable legal fees incurred in obtaining Court approval of all employment and fee applications including dealing with any

objections to any of the applications is [sic] also compensable to [the Gorman firm]. The Client agrees to pay all reasonable legal fees including dealing with any objections to court approval. . . . The Client agrees that all reasonable fees and expenses incurred by [the Gorman firm] in collecting and/or obtaining approval of its fees and costs by bankruptcy or any other court shall be added to the total fees and costs due from the Client. All such fees and costs if disputed shall be resolved by the Court.

[Discussion of hourly rates omitted. —Eds.]

1. Baker Botts v. ASARCO. The [Unsecured Creditors' Committee] argues that the proposed fee defense provision is barred by the Supreme Court's decision in Baker Botts LLP v. ASARCO LLC, 135 S. Ct. 2158 (2015). In *ASARCO*, the reorganized debtor objected to the final fee application of its bankruptcy counsel. After a six-day trial on the fee application and objection, the bankruptcy court for the Southern District of Texas awarded counsel $120 million in fees, plus an additional $5.2 million in fees incurred defending the fee application. The reorganized debtor appealed. The district court affirmed the $5.2 million fee award, but the Fifth Circuit Court of Appeals reversed. On further appeal, the Supreme Court affirmed the Fifth Circuit. The Supreme Court stated:

> Our basic point of reference when considering the award of attorney's fees is the bedrock principle known as the American Rule: Each litigant pays his own attorney's fees, win or lose, unless a statute or contract provides otherwise.

135 S. Ct. at 2164. The dispute in *ASARCO* was whether § 330 could be read as a "statutory exception" to the American Rule. No party argued the "contract exception" to the American Rule.

ASARCO's bankruptcy counsel filed fee applications under "§ 330(a)(1), which provides that a bankruptcy court 'may award . . . reasonable compensation for actual, necessary services rendered by' professionals hired under § 327(a)." 135 S. Ct. at 2163. The counsel argued that its fee defense fees were compensable under § 330(a)(1) as "reasonable compensation." The Supreme Court disagreed. . . .

The Supreme Court was not focused on whether the fee charged was "reasonable," but instead on whether it was for "services" rendered to the estate:

> § 330(a)(1) provides compensation for all § 327(a) professionals—whether accountant, attorney, or auctioneer—for all manner of work done *in service of* the estate administrator. More specifically, § 330(a)(1) allows "reasonable compensation" only for "*actual, necessary services rendered.*" (Emphasis added.) That qualification is significant. The word "services" ordinarily refers to "labor performed for another." . . . Thus, in a case addressing § 330(a)'s predecessor, this Court concluded that the phrase " 'reasonable compensation for services rendered' necessarily implies loyal and disinterested service in the interest of" a client. Time spent litigating a fee application against the administrator of a bankruptcy estate cannot be fairly described as "labor performed for"—let alone "disinterested service to"—that administrator.

135 S. Ct. at 2165.

2. In re Boomerang Tube, Inc. After *ASARCO*, bankruptcy professionals began including fee defense provisions in their retention agreements. Such provisions, it was hoped, would come within the contract exception to the American Rule, since ASARCO had foreclosed the statutory exception. The leading post-*ASARCO* case to address this attempt is In re Boomerang Tube, Inc., 548 B.R. 69 (Bankr. D. Del. 2016). . . .

After analyzing *ASARCO*, other case law, and §§ 327-330, the Delaware bankruptcy court sustained the U.S. Trustee's objection to the fee defense provision. First, the court held that § 328 is not a statutory exception to the American Rule. . . .

Next, the court held that the retention agreement could not come within the contract exception to the American Rule:

> [T]he retention agreements in this case are not contractual exceptions to the American Rule. Here, there is not a contract between two parties providing that each will be responsible for the other's legal fees if it loses a dispute between them. Rather, here there is a contract between two parties (the Committee and Committee Counsel) that in the event Committee Counsel win a challenge to their fees, a third party (the estate) will pay their defense costs even if the estate is not the party who objected. As the UST notes, this is not the typical contract modifying the American Rule. . . .

4. The Interplay of §§ 328 and 330. The Debtor asks that the fee defense provision be approved under § 328(a), which provides:

> The trustee, or a committee appointed under section 1102 of this title, with the court's approval, may employ or authorize the employment of a professional person under section 327 or 1103 of this title, as the case may be, on any reasonable terms and conditions of employment, including on a retainer, on an hourly basis, on a fixed or percentage fee basis, or on a contingent fee basis. Notwithstanding such terms and conditions, the court may allow compensation different from the compensation provided under such terms and conditions after the conclusion of such employment, if such terms and conditions prove to have been improvident in light of developments not capable of being anticipated at the time of the fixing of such terms and conditions.

If employment terms and conditions are approved by a bankruptcy court under § 328(a), then the professional's compensation is governed by those terms and conditions, rather than the general "reasonable compensation for services rendered" language of § 330(a)(1)(A). See § 330(a)(1) ("After notice to the parties in interest and the United States Trustee and a hearing, *and subject to* section 326, *328*, and *329*, the court may award. . . .") (emphasis added). Case law makes clear that the "subject to" qualification in § 330(a)(1) means that the previously approved § 328(a) terms and conditions control the professional's compensation. . . .

Does *ASARCO* Foreclose Approval of a Fee Defense Provision under § 328(a)? The question here is whether *ASARCO* prevents the Court from approving a fee defense provision in a retention agreement as a "reasonable term and condition" under § 328(a)? . . .

ASARCO does not hold that a fee defense provision can never be a "reasonable term" under § 328(a). Nothing in the Code says that an employment term must benefit the estate to be reasonable. A typical employment agreement between a lawyer and client has many terms; some benefit the client, while others benefit the lawyer. Considered together, they may be reasonable. For example, the following are included in the engagement agreements submitted by attorneys and other professionals in this case:

- The client agrees to pay New Mexico gross receipts tax, even though it is a tax on the lawyer, not the client;
- Retainer requirements, including initial retainers and replenishing retainers;
- Allowing the lawyer to withdraw if the retainer is not replenished;
- Prompt payment of monthly bills;
- Returned check fees;
- Interest on any advanced costs not reimbursed within 30 days;
- Guarantees of payment;
- Granting or acknowledging a lien on any recovery; and
- Granting a power of attorney to endorse settlement checks.

Do these terms benefit the client? Not directly. The direct beneficiary is the lawyer. The client benefits indirectly, however. By agreeing to the terms, the client obtains the services of needed, able professionals. For that reason, many of these terms could be reasonable under § 328(a).

In jurisdictions such as New Mexico, which typically have smaller bankruptcy cases with smaller fees, fee defense can be a sizeable percentage of the total fees billed. If estate counsel were forced to successfully defend its fees "on its own dime," the net compensation in a bankruptcy case could be substantially reduced.

. . .

6. The Proposed Fee Defense Provision in this Case. The Court concludes that the contract exception to the American Rule remains viable in bankruptcy cases. In the Court's view, a properly drafted fee defense provision could be a "reasonable term" under § 328(a), violating neither the letter nor spirit of *ASARCO*. Such a provision should:

- Be agreed to by the bankruptcy estate (thus avoiding the problem addressed in *Boomerang Tube*);
- Allow the bankruptcy court to review and approve the reasonableness of any fee defense fees sought;
- Provide that the estate will also agree to a similar provision for committee counsel; and
- Provide that no fees will be allowed for unsuccessful fee defense work. . . .

———————————————

As a practical matter, a threat by a major adversary to oppose the fee application of the debtor's lawyers can be a potent weapon in negotiation, especially if the other party is seeking to avoid or settle an avoidance lawsuit or other claim by the debtor on behalf of the estate. Of course, the threat will usually be subtle and hard to prove.

Another restriction in bankruptcy is on fee-sharing arrangements. § 504(a) (prohibiting most). Judge Chapman spent more than 100 pages examining the interplay of § 504 and Fed. R. Bankr. P. 2016(a) in assessing the conduct of a financial advisor in a large chapter 11. It did not go well:

> As reflected in its multiple pleadings, arguments, and testimony, Capstone's attitude toward its duty of disclosure falls somewhere on the continuum between lackadaisical and arrogant, and its conduct violating the fundamental teaching . . . that it is up to the court, and not the professionals, to decide such disclosure issues."

In re GSC Group, Inc., 502 B.R. 673, 737-38 (Bankr. S.D.N.Y. Dec. 12, 2013). The court held that although the advisor's relationship with the firm was sufficiently close to allow fee-sharing under § 504(b), there should have been disclosure of the contract and fee-sharing in the employment application. The sanction: forgoing pending fees of $367,000 and disgorging $600,000 already paid fees. That's a lost million, although the firm still kept $4.4 million for its work on the case. Unless the firm had unusually cushy margins in its fees, a loss of 19% of the total is pretty painful.

2. Judicial Oversight

As the above cases emphasize, the court scrutinizes fees at multiple stages in the proceedings. The initial employment application is only the first hurdle. Then there is getting paid, hopefully on an interim basis, as a draw against the final fee review, which comes at the very end of the case. There is a labyrinth of law as well as the Code provisions. The cases have already highlighted the importance of the Rules, particularly 2014 and 2016. Local orders are also important in this realm because judges take different approaches to reviewing fees. The UST office also takes an active role in fee hearings, citing its role as a watchdog of the system. Indeed, the UST issued detailed guidelines for chapter 11 cases with $50 million or more in assets and $50 million or more in liabilities. While not binding on courts, a failure to follow the guidelines—or at least negotiate the blessing of the UST to deviate from them—will normally guarantee an objection from the UST at one or more points in the employment process. One particular practice that raises the UST's ire is "lumping," which is billing entries that contain several work entries but only a single time entry. The objection comes back to the need for the court to find the fees reasonable. Without knowing how much time was spent on each separate task, perhaps some tasks were overbilled. While lumping may make for short and sweet bills to clients, it often will not pass muster in bankruptcy court.

The focus of the fee guidelines is disclosure (tiring of this theme, yet?). But here the disclosure is framed around the market for professional fees. Among other things, the firm is to create a budget and staffing plan, use rates that are based on the attorney's home office location (not where the case is filed), and justify any rate increases that occur during the case. A controversial guideline is that the firm is to make a showing that the rates charged reflect market rates outside bankruptcy. For attorneys, this requires a disclosure of an average or "blended" hourly rate charged by other attorneys in their firm, who will regard it as proprietary information. But some practice areas, and some attorneys, charge a premium, and the market outside bankruptcy is evidence of this. Is bankruptcy sufficiently complex, risky, and specialized that a higher fee may be justified compared to other practice areas? Surely an economist would tell us that the risk of nonpayment— a theme in the ethics of compensation cases—requires a premium on that basis alone. The guidelines are, of course, just that—guidelines. Fee practices continue to evolve, so there is likely to be flexibility as the guidelines deploy.

Below, however, is one judge's perception of practice "evolving" in the wrong direction. Apparently everything is not always bigger in Texas.

In re ENERGY PARTNERS, LTD.
409 B.R. 211 (Bankr. S.D. Tex. 2009)

Воhm, Bankruptcy Judge.

Oblivious to recent congressional and public criticism over executives of publicly-held corporations who are paid monumental salaries and bonuses despite running their companies into the ground, two investment banking firms now come into this Court requesting that they be employed under similarly outrageous terms. They do so because two committees in this Chapter 11 case have filed applications to employ these investment banking firms to perform valuation services even though two other independent firms have already performed similar valuations. These investment bankers, who wish to have their fees and expenses paid out of the debtor's estate, have sworn under oath that they will render services only if they immediately receive a nonrefundable fee aggregating $1.0 million. This Court declines the opportunity to endorse such arrogance. The purse is too perverse. . . .

On May 1, 2009, Energy Partners, Ltd. (the Debtor), a publicly-held entity in the oil and gas industry, filed a voluntary Chapter 11 petition on behalf of itself and its affiliated entities. Eleven days thereafter, the Debtor filed an Expedited Application for Order Pursuant to 11 U.S.C. §§ 327(a) and 328(a) Authorizing Employment and Retention of Parkman Whaling LLC as Financial Advisors for the Debtors, *Nunc Pro Tunc* to the Petition Date. In its Order granting the Application to Employ Parkman Whaling, the Court expressly approved the terms of the engagement letter between the Debtor and Parkman Whaling. The amount of monthly compensation that this Court approved is $75,000.00, plus expenses. The professional services that Parkman Whaling LLC has provided include, among other things, developing an enterprise valuation of the Debtor.

On May 27, 2009, the Court issued an Order Granting Motion to Establish Procedure for Monthly and Interim Compensation and Reimbursement of Expenses for Case Professionals (the Procedure for Professionals Order). Pursuant to the Procedure for Professionals Order, all professionals retained by the estate in these jointly administered cases may seek interim compensation on a monthly basis, subject to (a) a 20%

holdback of monthly fees incurred, (b) any party-in-interest's right to object to the compensation sought, and (c) the obligation to file quarterly fee applications. The Procedures for Professionals Order operates in conjunction with the Agreed Final Order (I) Authorizing the Debtors' Use of Cash Collateral. . . .

On May 15, 2009, the Debtor filed its initial Disclosure Statement. Birch Run Capital, LLC (Birch Run) thereafter filed its Objection to this Disclosure Statement. Birch Run owns stock in the Debtor and is a party-in-interest, which will apparently participate in the plan confirmation process. Among other things, Birch Run objects to Parkman Whaling's valuation of the Debtor and has argued that since Parkman Whaling's March 31, 2009 valuation, the spot price of oil has increased and forward price curves for both oil and natural gas have increased significantly; therefore, according to Birch Run, Parkman Whaling's valuation is too low and outdated.

On June 11, 2009, the Debtor filed its Second Amended Joint Plan of Reorganization and its Second Amended Disclosure Statement. Under the Second Amended Plan, Class 9-EPL Other Equity Interests will be "cancelled" and equity holders with interests in that class will "not receive or retain any property or interest in property on account of their EPL Other Equity Interests."

This Court has approved the Second Amended Disclosure Statement and has set the confirmation hearing for July 29, 2009. The Second Amended Disclosure Statement references two valuation reports for the Debtor's assets: (1) the Parkman Whaling report; and (2) the Birch Run report. . . . According to Birch Run's valuation report, "the current EPL Common Shares are estimated to be worth in excess of $212 million" whereas "Parkman Whaling estimates the current value of these interests at zero ($0)." . . . [T]hese two reports reflect a clear and distinct disagreement over the value of the Debtor's common stock.

On July 13, 2009, the Equity Holders' Committee filed the Tudor Pickering Application. The proposed fee terms in the Tudor Pickering Application are as follows: (a) a nonrefundable advisory fee of $500,000.00 payable pursuant to the Court's Procedure for Professionals Order; (b) a nonrefundable expert witness fee of $25,000.00 per day, payable each day that a Tudor Pickering Holt & Co. Securities, Inc. (Tudor Pickering) employee is requested, and made available, for the purpose of deposition or testimony; (c) a nonrefundable extended assignment fee of $100,000.00 per month, payable beginning September 1, 2009, and each month thereafter; and (d) any out-of-pocket expenses.[7] According to the Tudor Pickering Application, the services Tudor Pickering will render to the Equity Holders' Committee include, but are not limited to, the following: (a) analyzing the Debtor's assets and liabilities, the valuation of the Debtor's businesses and objecting to the plan of reorganization; (b) attending meetings and negotiating with representatives of the Debtor and creditors; (c) assisting in the review, analysis, and negotiation of the plan of reorganization; (d) appearing before this

---

[7][The court observed that Tudor Pickering expected to be paid without further court oversight—unlike the other professionals under the court's pre-existing procedures order—such that its fees would effectively be absolute and "nondisgorgable."—Eds.]

Court and other courts and protecting the Equity Holders' Committee's interests; and (e) performing all other necessary valuation services in this case. . . .

[The court describes the application of the Unsecured Noteholders' Committee to retain Houlihan Lokey, on financial terms and for services to be performed very similar to those described above with respect to Tudor Pickering.—Eds.]

On July 14, 2009, Bank of America, N.A., as agent for itself and on behalf of the Prepetition Secured Lenders, (the Agent) filed its objections to the Applications. The Agent's objections are four-fold: (1) the proposed fees are too high; (2) the proposed fees are nonrefundable; (3) the proposed fees are to be paid from the Debtor's cash collateral on which the Agent has a lien; and (4) the amount of cash collateral that would have to be used to pay the fees would violate the limitations set forth in the Budget for paying consultants.

On July 15, 2009, the Official Committee of Unsecured Creditors also filed objections to the Applications. The Unsecured Creditors' Committee essentially objects that the proposed fees are too high and nonrefundable.

On July 15, 2009, this Court held a hearing on, among other things, the Applications. . . . In support of the Tudor Pickering Application, the Court heard testimony from two witnesses: (1) Donald Randolph Waesche, a shareholder of the Debtor and chairman of the Equity Holders' Committee; and (2) Lance Gilliland, an investment banker and partner at Tudor Pickering.

Tom A. Howley, counsel for the Unsecured Noteholders' Committee, proffered the testimony of Dunayer in support of the Houlihan Lokey Application. Dunayer gave no testimony regarding Houlihan Lokey's hourly rates and made no comparison of fees Houlihan Lokey charges for similar projects within similar time frames. Dunayer merely listed other matters where Houlihan Lokey has been retained. The proffered testimony indicated that the engagement letter "was the culmination of robust negotiations between the Unsecured Noteholders' Committee and Houlihan Lokey" and that the proposed fees were "vigorously negotiated." . . .

The Equity Holders' Committee chose Tudor Pickering because of that firm's "attractive fee level" and its "concentration in oil and gas." When the Debtor's counsel asked Waesche why the Equity Holders' Committee is not satisfied to use the higher valuation from Birch Run in the plan confirmation process, Waesche testified that Birch Run was not an oil and gas "expert" or "in the business of valuation." Waesche testified that the Equity Holders' Committee wants a "reputable valuation" of the Debtor.

Gilliland testified that Tudor Pickering has been in existence for approximately six years and has operated as an investment banking firm with a focus on the energy industry for approximately two and a half years. [Tape recording of July 15, 2009 hearing at 12:03 p.m.] He stated unequivocally that the terms in the engagement letter are typical in the industry and the proposed fees are even lower than some of the other fee arrangements that Tudor Pickering has negotiated in similar situations. . . .

Two valuation reports concerning the Debtor already exist: (1) the Parkman Whaling report; and (2) the Birch Run report. It is not uncommon to have competing valuations of the Debtor in Chapter 11 cases. Birch Run disagrees with Parkman Whaling's valuation of the Debtor's assets. Birch Run argues that the Parkman Whaling valuation, which was prepared on March 31, 2009, is outdated and too low given that the spot price of oil has increased and the forward price curves for both oil and natural gas have increased significantly. Birch Run's report indicates that the Debtor's equity value is approximately $212 million whereas Parkman Whaling's report values the equity at zero. The Debtor strongly disagrees with the Birch Run valuation and, as of July 15, 2009, believes that there is no equity value. The Birch Run report, if accurate, would allow the Class 9-EPL Other Equity Interests to be paid rather than be "cancelled" and "not receive or retain any property or interest in property on account of their EPL Other Equity Interests."

The Equity Holders' Committee, believing that there is equity in the Debtor but dissatisfied with the credentials of those who prepared the Birch Run valuation, filed the Tudor Pickering Application requesting permission to employ Tudor Pickering to conduct an independent valuation. Meanwhile, counsel for the Unsecured Noteholders' Committee, Howley, represented to this Court that the Unsecured Noteholders' Committee, which believes there is no equity, is convinced it must retain Houlihan Lokey in order to obtain an appraisal that will rebut the anticipated valuation that Tudor Pickering will produce.

. . .

WHETHER HOULIHAN LOKEY AND TUDOR PICKERING SHOULD BE EMPLOYED PURSUANT TO 11 U.S.C. § 328

The parties who file the applications to employ . . . have the burden to prove that the investment bankers should be retained. See In re Interwest Bus. Equip., Inc., 23 F.3d 311, 318 (10th Cir. 1994). . . . This Court does not take § 328(a) applications lightly because "[o]nce the bankruptcy court has approved a rate or means of payment, such as a contingent fee, the court cannot on the submission of the final fee application instead approve a 'reasonable' fee under § 330(a), unless the bankruptcy court finds that the original arrangement was improvident due to unanticipated circumstances as required by § 328(a)." In re Tex. Sec., Inc., 218 F.3d 443, 445-46 (5th Cir. 2000). . . .

Therefore, this Court, in its duties as a gatekeeper, must have a sufficiently strong record when deciding whether to approve a professional under § 328(a). See In re High Voltage Eng'g Corp., 311 B.R. at 333 (holding that a committee seeking to retain the professional must present evidence not conclusory statements). Unfortunately for the two investment banking firms now seeking employment in this case, the Court has a woefully insufficient record. . . .

[In In re High Voltage Eng'g Corp., 311 B.R. 320, 333 (Bankr. D. Mass. 2004)], the court . . . set forth a non-exclusive list of factors . . . which should be considered when determining whether to approve employment subject to § 328(a):

> (1) whether terms of an engagement agreement reflect normal business terms in the marketplace; (2) the relationship between the Debtor and the professionals, i.e., whether the parties involved are sophisticated business entities with equal bargaining power who engaged in an arms-length negotiation; (3) whether the retention, as proposed, is in the best interests of the estate; (4) whether there is creditor opposition to the retention and retainer provisions; and (5) whether, given the size, circumstances and posture of the case, the amount of the retainer is itself reasonable, including whether the retainer provides the appropriate level of "risk minimization," especially in light of the existence of any other "risk-minimizing" devices, such as an administrative order and/or a carve-out. . . .

First, this Court has virtually no evidence that the committees in the case at bar could not have obtained comparable services without paying the excessive fees demanded by Houlihan Lokey and Tudor Pickering. . . .

[T]he amount of compensation that Houlihan Lokey and Tudor Pickering believe to be standard in the industry does not, in and of itself, render the compensation reasonable under § 328. Rather, the Court needs specific evidence in the record to determine whether the proposed compensation is reasonable under § 328. For example, the committees' respective counsel needed to adduce testimony about the specific compensation earned by investment bankers other than Tudor Pickering in engagements similar in size and circumstance to the engagement proposed in this case. Yet, the Court heard no such testimony on this point. Indeed, the only information in the record on this point is that a competitor of Houlihan Lokey and Tudor Pickering—i.e. Parkman Whaling—has been willing to render services for $75,000.00 per month, which is a figure substantially lower than the six-figure fees requested by Houlihan Lokey and Tudor Pickering. Given the wholly insufficient record in this case on such points, the Court concludes that this factor weighs against approval of the Applications.

Second, proof that arms-length negotiations took place between the committees and the investment bankers is another factor that should be considered when determining whether to approve the employment of a professional pursuant to § 328(a). . . . With respect to the negotiations between the Unsecured Noteholders' Committee and Houlihan Lokey, Dunayer's proffered testimony indicated that "robust negotiations" took place and that the proposed fees were "vigorously negotiated." Such testimony is extremely generalized and too conclusory. . . .

Third, the proposed retention of Houlihan Lokey and Tudor Pickering is not in the best interest of the estate. . . . These professionals may not just simply appear at the hearing, give conclusory testimony, and then expect to walk out of the courtroom with nonrefundable checks aggregating $1.0 million. . . .

Fifth, aside from the unreasonableness of expecting to be paid an up-front, nonrefundable $500,000.00 fee, the Court is also extremely discouraged that Tudor Pickering has also requested a $25,000.00 per day witness fee. It is noteworthy that this fee is to be paid regardless of whether the witness testifies for one hour or eight hours, or somewhere in between. In these dire financial times, a request to be paid a $25,000.00 per day witness fee out of the coffers of a publicly traded company in bankruptcy is not only excessive, but unconscionable—particularly when the amount of this *daily* fee is compared to the *annual* compensation earned by certain Americans who provide arguably more essential services to society.[16] . . . [T]he Court concludes that the $25,000.00 per day witness fee that Tudor Pickering has requested is *per se* unreasonable. No witness is worth such an absurd amount regardless of the dollars at stake in the case. . . .

At some point, this Court must draw the line between what is reasonable and what is not. To quote the Fifth Circuit: "'[W]hen a pig becomes a hog it is slaughtered.'" In re Swift, 3 F.3d 929, 930 (5th Cir. 1993) (quoting In re Zouhar, 10 B.R. 154, 157 (Bankr. D.N.M. 1981)). "As the finder of fact, the bankruptcy court has the primary duty to distinguish hogs from pigs." Id. . . . These two investment banking firms have become hogs. . . .

The exorbitant fees requested by Houlihan Lokey and Tudor Pickering are similar to the "appearance fees" which certain of the world's top athletes—for example, Tiger Woods—are able to command. However, unlike Tiger Woods, whose presence does guarantee a financial benefit at any event where he appears, neither of these two investment banking firms introduced any testimony or exhibits guaranteeing some benefit to the estate in this case. . . .

For all of the reasons set forth herein, the Houlihan Lokey Application and the Tudor Pickering Application should both be denied. An order consistent with this Opinion will be entered on the docket simultaneously with the entry on the docket of this Opinion.

Neither are lawyers immune from withering scrutiny, particularly when asking for reimbursement for a $378 Jimmy John's lunch and $22,748 "telephone" charge (emphasis in original), among other items. Coal Bankruptcy Judge Asks Company to Explain Attorney Costs, Associated Press (Dec. 4, 2019), https://apnews.com/49a97beb48d8ecb1bf53b4c500e20eb7.

Problem Set 34

34.1. Jesse's Jet Clean, a multi-state chain of car washes, has been a client of the firm since the first location opened 22 years ago. You have been in charge of Jesse's account for about a year. Recently, you've been consulting with Jesse over a possible chapter 11 filing. You have been a little slow in billing the company since you took over, so it owes about $800,000 to the firm for work over the last six months. You've gotten to know Jesse

---

[16] For example, the men and women of our nation's armed forces, who risk their lives to preserve and protect the abundant freedoms of this country, earn an annual salary that barely exceeds Tudor Pickering's proposed $25,000.00-per-day appearance fee. *See* United States Army Public Website, Benefits—Total Compensation, http://www.goarmy.com/benefits/total_compensation.jsp (listing the average annual salary for a military police sergeant as $26,967.00). . . .

pretty well working on his retirement plan and real estate investments, as well as the company's problems, and you know he would faint at the thought of getting a new lawyer at this point. Is there a problem with filing chapter 11 for Jesse? If so, how best to solve it? See §§ 327, 329.

34.2. You are part of one of the most successful bankruptcy boutiques in Minneapolis. Your firm has a thriving debtor practice, but the firm is barely able to break even. A review of your books shows the reason: more than 30% of the hours and expenses the firm bills in bankruptcies are never paid. This compares unfavorably with a bad debt rate of less than 5% on estate work completed and less than 10% on general corporate work undertaken by comparable area firms. A major partners' meeting is called for next week. What do you recommend? See §§ 328, 330, 331.

34.3. Tiring of law practice after only a few years, you joined a communications strategy firm. You just took an intake call from the nation's preeminent restructuring lawyer, Mr. Solomon. He's hopping mad about a recent interview he did with a major paper. The topic was supposed to be "Mr. Solomon's work in the first few months of the Big Co. ongoing bankruptcy" but when he tried to talk to the reporter about the legal issues, the reporter seemed only interested in the interim fee application for $363 million. You ask Mr. Solomon if he can recall any specific questions. "Well," he says, "I definitely remember him mentioning the $2,100 for September's late-night rides home after work. And there was something about $263,000 in copy charges."

He wants you to call the reporter to try to "spin" the story. "I was accused of greed," he seethes. "It is not my fault that saving companies from failure takes time and costs money." Drawing on your lawyerly smarts and savvy analytical thinking, what information, arguments, analogies, etc. do you use to try to soften the reporter's approach to the story? Be prepared to have a dialogue with the reporter and anticipate likely questions.

34.4. Your firm has represented Summer Enterprises for over a decade. Summer is a large conglomerate (sales exceeding $5.3 billion last year) that generates millions of dollars in yearly revenue for the firm. Your experience with struggling firms and workouts has brought you to the attention of Ella Roland, the senior partner managing the Summer account. Roland calls you in to ask you to take on a very important assignment: go over the Summer books, interview the employees, and try to determine if some nefarious activity is afoot that is causing Summer's devastating quarterly losses despite record sales. The chairman of the board of Summer says that you are to be given carte blanche by the company, bringing in your own accounting team and any other assistance you need. No one else is to know of your task, except that you are working under the chairman's authority.

You make a preliminary review of the records and you see that Summer may have a high-placed embezzler. You also have heard rumors about irregularities in Summer's government contracts (kickbacks, competitive contract manipulation, etc.). You have identified a large group of employees to interview. What will you say to the employees as you begin your interviews? Does it matter whether Summer seems to be on sound financial footing despite the problems under investigation?

Section 4

The Finality of Chapter 11

This final section, just one assignment, considers the power of chapter 11 as a tool to resolve financial distress once and for all. Specifically, it examines what claims can be conclusively and comprehensively addressed in the name of reorganization, and what claims run into concerns of fairness and constitutional protections when the debtor tries to discharge what might be called "future claims" against the debtor. It also turns 90 degrees to study which claims against third parties not in bankruptcy can be addressed in the name of finality and the need to provide meaningful financial resolution.

THE DISCHARGE OF FUTURE CLAIMS

Some creditors are simple. A banker with a debtor in chapter 11 has a stiff drink, books the loss on the loan's write-down, and moves on. But the invitation to a chapter 11 negotiation goes to *all* creditors, and some have complicated legal relationships with the debtor. Think of the potential mass tort claimants whose injuries have not manifested by the time a bankruptcy might be filed, yet some organized approach to compensation needs to be addressed before the tortfeasor goes broke. Similarly, think of the appliance that proves dangerous only years later when a part proves defective: what do owners of that appliance (or car) do when their manufacturer goes bankrupt? What is the government's role in enforcing environmental cleanup costs for contamination that may have been done by a company that was bankrupt decades ago? This assignment addresses bankruptcy law's struggle with these "future" claims.

A. THE EFFECT OF DISCHARGE ON FUTURE CLAIMS BY CREDITORS

As previously emphasized, the definition of "claim" is capacious, encompassing not only all current obligations, but any "right to payment, whether or not such right is reduced to judgment, liquidated, unliquidated, fixed, contingent, matured, unmatured, disputed, undisputed, legal, equitable, secured, or unsecured." § 101(5)(A). The approach lets bankruptcy accelerate debts and deal with the total possible liability, rather than just the payments currently due.

This broad sweep is necessary to achieve the goal of clearing the debtor's financial decks, but it also means that bankruptcy has to confront obligations that may not come to fruition until years hence—if ever. The Code allows judges to estimate claims to address these elusive and uncertain liabilities. § 502(c). Nonetheless, a great intellectual and practical burden arises in exercising this task. The theoretical difficulty partly stems from the fact that state law is the source of claims, but that law rarely permits those liabilities to be litigated before a cause of action accrues, which means there is little legal guidance on how to estimate them. Complicating matters, many of these exotic creditors are "game changers," such as the massive tort that can shut a debtor down with claims overwhelming in quantity and complexity, many involving unknown parties. Closely related is the problem of contribution from third parties not in bankruptcy (e.g., insurers), who want releases against the world, including future claimants.

1.   The Problem of the Future Claim

The adoption of the 1978 Code shepherded in the arrival of the mass tort case, and asbestos, the Dalkon Shield, Bhopal, Fen-Phen, Vioxx, and breast implants are all members of the mass injury hall of fame, forcing many of their makers to seek refuge in bankruptcy. The next generation includes the talc supplier for Johnson & Johnson baby powder, likely followed by the opioid manufacturers, wildfire defendants, and maybe COVID-19 claims, among others. The reason is that the Code's definition of claim is not merely broad, but eliminated the ancient concept of "provability," which had previously excluded certain claims from being cognizable under a ripeness concept. The classic unprovable claim was an unlitigated tort. The bad news for a tort victim was that no claim meant no distribution could be had in the bankruptcy case, but the good news was that the victim's cause of action also was not discharged (no claim). In a liquidation, that news was all bad. If it was a personal bankruptcy or corporate reorganization, however, the silver lining was that the victim could sue the post-discharge debtor and collect in full postpetition dollars when the claim ripened into litigability. Congress's expansion of the definition of claim was a conscious decision to abolish this concept, deciding everything ("contingent, unmatured") was a claim and so torts would be resolved with all the other claims on the debtor.

The bankruptcy assistance to companies with mass-tort problems may have moved beyond payment relief to a mass joinder device. See Alexandra D. Lahav, The Continuum of Aggregation, 53 Ga. L. Rev. 1393 (2019), building upon Troy A. McKenzie, Toward a Bankruptcy Model for Nonclass Aggregate Litigation, 87 N.Y.U. L. Rev. 960 (2012). Some companies are not in immediate financial trouble but file because the class-action system makes it very difficult for a defendant to resolve all claims in one lawsuit. See, e.g., In Amchem Products v. Windsor, 521 U.S. 591 (1997) (voiding famous *Georgine* asbestos settlement under Fed. R. Civ. P. 23 for insufficient commonality of class given the disparate tort laws of the hundreds of thousands of members across 50 states). Bankruptcy presents an attractive alternative for repose.

Consider the asbestosis crisis. Johns-Manville had produced and distributed asbestos for ages. Who had been exposed and what would be the consequences of that exposure was unknown. Outside bankruptcy, each plaintiff could line up and sue when his or her cause of action ripened under state tort law. The first claimants to discover their problems would be paid in full, but at some point the business would run out of money. Even though the company engaged in the same wrongful behavior that injured each potential victim, some victims would be made whole while others would receive squat. When all claimants are collected together, however, the distribution is smoothed. Payment is likely to be smaller to the present claimants than under first-come, first-served state law rules but larger for those claimants who would have been left at the end of the line with nothing (a point you will see animating the plaintiff in the next case). Chapter 11 reorganization can bind everyone with a "claim": those already with judgments against the company, those with pending claims, those who had been exposed but were not yet sick, and even those who did not yet know of their exposure. The *Johns-Manville* bankruptcy became one of the most publicized cases filed in the wake of the Code. The company managed to confirm a plan of reorganization to deal with all the claimants at once—both those currently known and those who would become known in the future—all thanks to handy little § 105.

KANE v. JOHNS-MANVILLE CORP.
843 F.2d 636 (2d Cir. 1988)

NEWMAN, Circuit Judge.

This appeal challenges the lawfulness of the reorganization plan of the Johns-Manville Corporation ("Manville"), a debtor in one of the nation's most significant Chapter 11 bankruptcy proceedings. Lawrence Kane, on behalf of himself and a group of other personal injury claimants, appeals from an order . . . that confirmed a Second Amended Plan of Reorganization (the "Plan"). Kane and the group of 765 individuals he represents (collectively "Kane") are persons with asbestos-related disease who had filed personal injury suits against Manville prior to Manville's Chapter 11 petition. The suits were stayed, and Kane and other claimants presently afflicted with asbestos-related disease were designated as Class-4 creditors in the reorganization proceedings. Kane now objects to confirmation of the reorganization Plan on several grounds: it discharges the rights of future asbestos victims who do not have "claims" within the meaning of 11 U.S.C. § 101(4) (1982), it was adopted without constitutionally adequate notice to various interested parties, the voting procedures used in approving the Plan violated the Bankruptcy Code and due process requirements, and the Plan fails to conform with the requirements of 11 U.S.C. § 1129(a) and (b) (1982 & Supp. IV 1986). We determine that Kane lacks standing to challenge the Plan on the grounds that it violates the rights of future claimants and other third parties, and we reject on the merits his remaining claims that the Plan violates his rights regarding voting and fails to meet the requirements of section 1129(a) and (b). The order of the District Court affirming the Bankruptcy Court's confirmation of the Plan is affirmed. . . .

[The eventual plan of reorganization included a trust to compensate victims, funded by more than half of the Manville stock. In negotiations, the future claimants—that is, those who would learn about their asbestos-related illnesses in the future—were represented by a court-appointed Legal Representative.—Eds.]

Manville was directed to undertake a comprehensive multimedia notice campaign to inform persons with present health claims of the pendency of the reorganization and their opportunity to participate. Potential health claimants who responded to the campaign were given a combined proof-of-claim-and-voting form in which each could present a medical

diagnosis of his asbestos-related disease and vote to accept or reject the
Plan. For voting purposes only, each claim was valued in the amount of
one dollar. Claimants were informed that the proof-of-claim-and-voting
form would be used only for voting and that to collect from the Trust, they
would have to execute an additional proof of claim establishing the actual
value of their damages.

The notice campaign produced a large number of present asbestos
claimants. In all, 52,400 such claimants submitted proof-of-claim-and-
voting forms. Of these, 50,275 or 95.8% approved the Plan, while 2,165 or
4.2% opposed it. In addition to these Class-4 claimants, all other classes
of creditors also approved the Plan. Class 8, the common stockholders,
opposed the Plan. . . . On December 18, 1986, the Bankruptcy Court issued
a Determination of Confirmation Issues in which it rejected all objections
to confirmation. . . .

Discussion

A. Standing

The Legal Representative of the future claimants challenges Kane's
standing to bring this appeal. The Legal Representative contends that Kane
is not directly and adversely affected by the confirmation order and that
his appeal improperly asserts the rights of third parties, namely the future
claimants. We conclude that Kane is sufficiently harmed by confirmation
of the Plan to challenge it on appeal but that his appeal must be limited
to those contentions that assert a deprivation of his own rights. . . . The
question we must consider is whether on this appeal of the confirmation
order, Kane may assert claims of these third parties. We conclude that he
may not. . . . Prudential concerns weigh heavily against permitting Kane
to assert the rights of the future claimants in attacking the Plan. First,
Kane's interest in these proceedings is potentially opposed to that of the
future claimants; both Kane and the future claimants wish to recover from
the debtor for personal injuries. To the extent that Kane is successful in
obtaining more of the debtor's assets to satisfy his own claims, less will
be available for other parties, with the distinct risk that the future claimants will suffer. Thus, we cannot depend on Kane sincerely to advance the
interests of the future claimants. Second, the third parties whose rights
Kane seeks to assert are already represented in the proceedings. Though
it is true, as Kane points out, that the future claimants themselves are
not before the Court, they are ably represented by the appointed Legal
Representative. Therefore, it is not necessary to allow Kane to raise the
future claimants' rights on the theory that these rights will be otherwise
ignored. The Bankruptcy Court appointed the Legal Representative specifically for the purpose of ensuring that the rights of the future claimants would be asserted where necessary. Certainly as between Kane
and the Legal Representative, there is no question that the latter is the
more reliable advocate of the future claimants' rights, and we may confi-
dently leave that task entirely to him. Finally, and significantly, the Legal
Representative has expressly stated in this appeal that he does not want

Kane to assert the future claimants' rights. This is precisely the situation where the third-party standing limitation should apply. . . .

Kane argues that he ought to be permitted at least to challenge the Injunction because his claim is "inextricably bound up with" the rights of the future claimants. Kane reasons that his own recovery from the Trust depends upon Manville's financial stability, which in turn could be jeopardized by a future claimant's successful challenge to the Injunction. If future claimants are not bound by the Injunction, then, Kane predicts, they will sue Manville's operating entities directly, Manville will be unable to meet its funding commitments to the Trust, and Kane will lose his rights to compensation under the Plan. Kane therefore contends that he should be able to test the validity of the Injunction as to the future claimants now so as to avoid a successful challenge detrimental to him in the future. . . . The flaw in Kane's analysis is that it assumes that an onslaught of future victims' suits could impair the Trust before Kane is paid. Such is not the case. Kane and the other present claimants are, by definition, currently afflicted with asbestos disease. They may all initiate claims against the Trust immediately after confirmation. Resolution and payment of these claims is expected to take approximately ten years. The bulk of the future victims, in contrast, are not presently afflicted with disease. Many of them will not become ill until well into the 1990's or later. While some of the last of the present claimants may overlap with the first of the future claimants in presenting their damage claims, the claims of these groups will be presented essentially consecutively. By the time enough future claimants develop asbestos-related disease, challenge the Injunction, and, if successful, collect damages directly from Manville to an extent sufficient to impair the long-term funding of the Trust, Kane will have had years to enforce his own claims. Kane's concern that he will be precluded from collecting from the Trust because of future claimants' suits against Manville is therefore too speculative a basis on which to grant third-party standing. . . .

Like so many other bankruptcy cases, *Manville* has its own M. Night Shyamalan twist. Less than two years after the plan was confirmed, serious difficulties arose in the operation of the Manville trust, the most important being that the trust was running out of cash as settlements were achieved (earning Kane the I-Told-You-So Award). The Manville settlement had to be coordinated with the massive remaining litigation against other asbestosis defendants. Very few people had been careful to breathe only Manville's asbestos, and other manufacturers wanted contribution from Manville. Manville's lawyers continued to worry about whether the bankruptcy court had adequate jurisdictional reach to solve its problems, particularly regarding the injunctions issued as part of its plan that forced victims to deal with the trust and prevented them from suing Manville's insurers and co-defendants directly. These injunctions were crucial to the whole scheme and the cornerstones of the insurance companies' and co-defendants' contributions to the Manville trust.

Uncertain that the injunctions would hold up, Manville's lawyers lobbied for special legislation to sanction its "bankruptcy class action" treatment of its victims. The effort was rewarded in a 1994 amendment that added to the Code a special section for those claiming "personal injury, wrongful death, or property-damage actions seeking recovery for damages allegedly caused by the presence of, or exposure to, asbestos or asbestos-containing products." § 524(g). The statute by its own terms is limited to asbestos cases only, so other suitors have to follow the judicial path blazed in *Manville*. Companies in other industries have indeed successfully used bankruptcy trusts to pay those injured by their products, which has helped support a developing specialty among the practicing bar. A.G. Robins filed bankruptcy to address liability, including punitive damages, related to its intrauterine contraceptive device, the Dalkon Shield. National Gypsum, another manufacturer of products that contained asbestos, settled claims estimated at between $270 million to $3.7 billion by its insurers funding a trust to pay $1 billion over several years. The trust was administered by the Center for Claims Resolution, a company established in Princeton, New Jersey, to handle this type of dispute. Another new industry is born. But note the house of cards: Manville's injunctions were upheld only by gadfly Kane's lack of standing, and then Congress stepped in to moot it all. What of these other industries?

2. *The Solution of Limiting Claims*

Some debtors have obvious and long-standing environmental issues, such as strip miners and chemical manufacturers. Others may operate businesses for decades before they discover that their trash or their energy source contains substances that subject them to environmental regulations. Still others may inherit environmental obligations when they buy already-polluted land. All of these may be unripe torts, or unripe bases for statutory liability. Thus, they may be "claims," as unmatured obligations. But what if the parties entitled to compensation do not yet know of their legal rights (likely for the very reason that those rights are so unripe)? To address this conundrum, some courts try to graft a knowledge or notice element into the Code's definition of "claim."

===== SIGNATURE COMBS, INC. v. UNITED STATES =====
253 F. Supp. 2d 1028 (W.D. Tenn. 2003)

DONALD, District Judge.
This matter is before the Court on Defendant Mason and Dixon Lines, Inc. ("MDL")'s motion for judgment on the pleadings. . . . MDL contends that Plaintiffs' claims against it were discharged pursuant to MDL's Chapter 11 bankruptcy reorganization. . . . For the following reasons, this Court denies MDL's motion. . . .
Pursuant to the Comprehensive Environmental Response, Compensation and Liability Act ("CERCLA"), 42 U.S.C. § 9601 et seq., Plaintiffs seek to recover response costs allegedly incurred by Plaintiffs at the South 8th Street Landfill Superfund Site and the Gurley Pit Superfund Sites

(collectively, the "Gurley Sites"). These response costs stem from remedial measures taken to alleviate hazardous waste dumped at the Gurley Sites in the 1950s-1970s. . . .

[The EPA and the Arkansas environmental agency cleaned up the Gurley Pit sites and forced the Plaintiffs to reimburse them for their costs in doing so. Plaintiffs now sue MDL for contribution to those costs.—Eds.]

This question of when a party's contingent CERCLA liability may be discharged through bankruptcy constitutes an issue of first impression within this Circuit. Courts in other Circuits have split on this issue, adopting different standards for determining when contingent CERCLA claims "arise" for the purpose of bankruptcy discharge. Before adopting an approach, the Court will briefly outline the varying approaches other courts have taken.

A. Right to Payment Approach

At one end of the jurisprudential spectrum, some courts have held that a claim does not arise until all four CERCLA elements exist.[3] Under this approach, known as the "right to payment" approach, a debtor's CERCLA liability will be discharged only if all four CERCLA elements exist prior to bankruptcy. This approach therefore focuses on substantive, non-bankruptcy law to determine when a claim arises.

The right to payment approach has been criticized for failing to address bankruptcy law and policy. . . . Requiring courts to determine when a bankruptcy claim arises based on whether all four CERCLA elements have been satisfied in effect reinserts a "provability" requirement which was expressly repealed under the 1978 Bankruptcy Code.

B. Underlying Act Approach

At the other end of the spectrum, some courts have maintained that a pre-bankruptcy "claim" subject to the Code's discharge provisions exists so long as the underlying polluting act occurred prior to the debtor's bankruptcy. Thus, under this "underlying act" or "debtor's conduct" approach, even if the EPA does not yet know of a potential CERCLA claim against the debtor, the debtor's liability is discharged so long as the debtor's conduct relating to the contamination concluded prior to its bankruptcy petition. Rather than looking to substantive nonbankruptcy law to determine when a CERCLA claim arises, these courts emphasize substantive bankruptcy law and policy.

This underlying act standard has been criticized as patently unfair to creditors because it would allow a polluting party to undergo bankruptcy

---

[3] These four elements are: 1) the defendant falls within one of the four categories of responsible parties; 2) hazardous substances are disposed at a facility; 3) there is a release or threatened release of hazardous substances from the facility into the environment; and 4) the release causes the incurrence of response costs including removal activities and enforcement activities related thereto. See In re Reading Co., 115 F.3d at 1118, 1125.

proceedings and receive a discharge from any liabilities before the EPA—or any other credit[or]—ever has a reason to know about the debtor's involvement in the release or threatened release of hazardous waste. . . .

. . .

C. DEBTOR-CREDITOR RELATIONSHIP APPROACH

A few courts have adopted a third approach, known as the "debtor-creditor relationship" standard, for determining when a CERCLA claim arises. This standard posits that any CERCLA liability is discharged if the creditor and debtor began a relationship before the debtor filed for bankruptcy, so long as the underlying act occurred before the bankruptcy petition was filed. . . . The Second Circuit, in In re Chateaugay Corp., found that discharge of CERCLA liability was appropriate despite the EPA's lack of knowledge of the full extent of the hazardous waste dumped by or removal costs attributable to the debtor because of the relationship between the EPA and LTV, the debtor. . . . [T]he regulatory relationship between the EPA and those subject to regulation in and of itself is sufficient "to bring most ultimately maturing payment obligations based on pre-petition conduct within the definition of 'claims.'" Id.

The primary criticism of this approach is that courts using the relationship test, such as In Re Chateaugay Corp., have defined "relationship" so broadly that they have made it the equivalent of the underlying acts approach. . . .

D. FAIR CONTEMPLATION APPROACH

Reflecting on the shortcomings of the first three approaches, subsequent courts and commentators have developed an alternative standard seeking to accommodate the policy aims of both bankruptcy law and CERCLA. This "fair contemplation" or "foreseeability" standard posits that a contingent CERCLA claim arises pre-petition only if it is "based upon pre-petition conduct that can fairly be contemplated by the parties at the time of the debtors' bankruptcy." Jensen, 995 F.2d at 930 (quoting In re Nat'l Gypsum Co., 139 B.R. 397, 404 (N.D. Tex. 1992)). Thus, a claim accrues when the potential CERCLA claimant, at the time of bankruptcy, "could have ascertained through the exercise of reasonable diligence that it had a claim" against the debtor for a hazardous release.

This standard allows a claim to accrue earlier than the right to payment standard because the potential claimant need not incur response costs (the fourth CERCLA element) for a contingent claim to arise under this standard. At the same time, the standard requires more awareness of a potential CERCLA claim by a potential creditor than do the underlying act or debtor-creditor relationship standards, both of which allow claims to accrue even if the potential creditor had no idea that it might have a CERCLA claim against the debtor. In so doing, this standard attempts to reconcile the goals of both the bankruptcy courts and CERCLA. . . .

E. Adopting a Standard

After reviewing the above theories, the Court finds the fair contemplation standard to be the appropriate standard to apply in the case at bar. It is the only test which tries to accommodate both the fresh start goal of bankruptcy and the speedy cleanup and polluter accountability CERCLA goals. Moreover, unlike other standards, the fair contemplation approach does not violate Fifth Amendment and Bankruptcy Code notice requirements because creditors must be aware of potential claims against debtors before such claims can be discharged. Finally, while this standard slightly prioritizes CERCLA's goals over the fresh start bankruptcy goal, the Court finds this prioritization to be justifiable. . . .

MDL's bankruptcy reorganization plan was finalized in 1986. Nothing in the Complaint or in MDL's bankruptcy reorganization order suggests that, as of that time, the EPA fairly contemplated or had reason to foresee MDL's potential liability to the EPA for the Gurley Sites. Without additional facts, the Court cannot conclude that the EPA had a contingent claim against MDL at the time MDL discharged its "claims" in its bankruptcy reorganization. Thus, MDL, as the moving party, has failed to meet its burden of proof. . . .

As if the foregoing analysis were not complicated enough, there are greater problems with environmental claims than simply finding their starting points. For example, pollution may occur at Time 1, but remediation may occur at Time 2—and the pollution may be ongoing or wholly ceased in the interim. If the business is struggling to confirm a chapter 11 plan, the difference is great between dealing with a multimillion dollar cleanup claim as an administrative expense priority (which must be paid in full at confirmation under § 1129(a)(9)) or as a general prepetition debt (which receives only pro rata treatment with other unsecured creditors under § 1129(a)(7)). The proper categorization of various permutations of prepetition and postpetition actions and remediations is still debated, but the majority of circuit courts have, at least on certain facts, allowed cleanup costs as administrative priority expenses. The likelihood of that approach is particularly strong when the remediation costs are first incurred postpetition and relate to the reorganization. See, e.g., In re Virginia Builders, Inc., 153 B.R. 729 (Bankr. E.D. Va. 1993) (allowing administrative claim for cleanup when contamination—oil leaching out of tanks and contaminating ground—continued prepetition and postpetition, with conditions becoming "deplorable" by time of reorganization).

3. The Solution of Ensuring Due Process

The previous section involved restricting the definition of "claim" to ensure fairness to unknowing creditors in discharging future claims. Another approach to future claims is to acknowledge that these parties may well hold claims at the time of bankruptcy, but that the process by which they are discharged must comport with the Constitution, which can serve as its own check on potential unfairness. This is equally true for a traditionally reorganizing debtor and a § 363-sale purchaser who want to scrub off those claims. Recall Judge Newman's lofty unconcern for such future intrigues: let's worry about that in the future. Well, sometimes the future comes.

In re MOTORS LIQUIDATION CO.
829 F.3d 135 (2d Cir. 2016)

CHIN, J.

BACKGROUND

I. Bailout

In the final two quarters of 2007, as the American economy suffered a significant downturn, [the debtor,] Old GM posted net losses of approximately $39 billion and $722 million. In 2008, it posted quarterly net losses of approximately $3.3 billion, $15.5 billion, $2.5 billion, and $9.6 billion. Id. In a year and a half, Old GM had managed to hemorrhage over $70 billion. The possibility of Old GM's collapse alarmed many. Old GM employed roughly 240,000 workers and provided pensions to another 500,000 retirees. The company also purchased parts from over eleven thousand suppliers and marketed through roughly six thousand dealerships. A disorderly collapse of Old GM would have far-reaching consequences.

After Congress declined to bail out Old GM, President George W. Bush announced on December 19, 2008 that the executive branch would provide emergency loans to help automakers "stave off bankruptcy while they develop plans for viability." In Old GM's case, TARP loaned $13.4 billion on the condition that Old GM both submit a business plan for long-term viability to the President no later than February 17, 2009 and undergo any necessary revisions no later than March 31, 2009. If the President found the business plan unsatisfactory, the TARP funds would become due and payable in thirty days, rendering Old GM insolvent and effectively forcing it into bankruptcy.

On March 30, 2009, President Obama told the nation that Old GM's business plan was not viable. At the same time, the President provided Old GM with another $6 billion loan and sixty more days to revise its plan along certain parameters. . . .

II. Bankruptcy

The federal aid did not succeed in averting bankruptcy. But entering bankruptcy posed a unique set of problems: Old GM sought to restructure and become profitable again, not to shut down; yet if Old GM lingered in bankruptcy too long, operating expenses would accumulate and consumer confidence in the GM brand could deteriorate, leaving Old GM no alternative but to liquidate and close once and for all. On June 1, 2009, with these risks in mind, Old GM petitioned for Chapter 11 bankruptcy protection in the United States Bankruptcy Court for the Southern District of New York.

A. Mechanics of the § 363 Sale

The same day, Old GM filed a motion to sell itself to New GM (also dubbed "Vehicle Acquisition Holdings LLC" or "NGMCO, Inc."), complete with a 103-page draft sale agreement and 30-page proposed sale order. Through this proposed sale, Old GM was attempting not a traditional Chapter 11 reorganization, but a transaction pursuant to 11 U.S.C. § 363—a less common way of effecting a bankruptcy. . . . In contrast in a § 363 sale of substantially all assets, the debtor does not truly "reorganize." Instead, it sells its primary assets to a successor corporation, which immediately takes over the business. As evidenced by the GM bankruptcy, a § 363 sale can close in a matter of weeks.

The proposed sale was, in effect, a complex transaction made possible by bankruptcy law. GM's sale would proceed in several parts. First, Old GM would become a "debtor-in-possession" under the Code. See 11 U.S.C. § 1101. . . . Second, there would be New GM, a company owned predominantly by Treasury (over sixty percent). As proposed, New GM would acquire from Old GM substantially all of its business—what one might commonly think of as the automaker "GM." But New GM would not take on all of Old GM's liabilities. . . . Other than a few liabilities that New GM would assume as its own, this "free and clear" provision would act as a liability shield to prevent individuals with claims against Old GM from suing New GM. Once the sale closed, the "bankruptcy" would be done: New GM could immediately begin operating the GM business, free of Old GM's debts.

Third, Old GM would remain. The proposed sale would leave Old GM with some assets, including $1.175 billion in cash, interests in the Saturn brand, and certain real and personal property. Old GM would also receive consideration from New GM, including a promise to repay Treasury and Canadian government loans used to finance the business through bankruptcy and a ten-percent equity stake in New GM. Old GM would retain, however, the bulk of its old liabilities. Fourth, Old GM would liquidate. Though liquidation is not formally part of a § 363 sale, the sale would result in two GM companies. Old GM would disband: it would rename itself "Motors Liquidation Company" and arrange a plan for liquidation that addressed how its remaining liabilities would be paid. See 11 U.S.C. § 1129(a)(11). Thus, while New GM would quickly emerge from bankruptcy to operate the GM business, Old GM would remain in bankruptcy and undergo a traditional, lengthy liquidation process.

B. Sale Order

One day after Old GM filed its motion, on June 2, 2009, the bankruptcy court ordered Old GM to provide notice of the proposed sale order. Old GM was required to send direct mail notice of its proposed sale order to numerous interested parties, including "all parties who are known to have asserted any lien, claim, encumbrance, or interest in or on [the to-be-sold assets]," and to post publication notice of the same in major publications, including the Wall Street Journal and New York Times The sale notice specified that interested parties would have until June 19, 2009 to submit to the bankruptcy court responses and objections to the proposed sale order.

The bankruptcy court proceeded to hear over 850 objections to the proposed sale order over the course of three days, between June 30 and July 2, 2009. On July 5, 2009, after addressing and dismissing the objections, the bankruptcy court approved the § 363 sale. Among those objections were arguments against the imposition of a "free and clear" provision to bar claims against New GM as the successor to Old GM made by consumer organizations, state attorneys general, and accident victims.

Next, the bankruptcy court issued the Sale Order, which entered into effect the final sale agreement between Old GM and New GM (the "Sale Agreement"). In the Sale Agreement, New GM assumed fifteen categories of liabilities. As relevant here, New GM agreed to assume liability for accidents *after* the closing date for the § 363 sale and to make repairs pursuant to express warranties issued in connection with the sale of GM cars—two liability provisions present in the initial draft sale agreement. The Sale Agreement also provided a new provision—resulting from negotiations among state attorneys general, the GM parties, and Treasury during the course of the sale hearing—that New GM would assume liability for any Lemon Law claims. With these exceptions, New GM would be "free and clear" of any and all liabilities of Old GM.

On July 10, 2009, the § 363 sale officially closed, and New GM began operating the automaker business. As a matter of public perception, the GM bankruptcy was over— the company had exited bankruptcy in forty days.

C. Liquidation of Old GM

. . .

The bankruptcy court set November 30, 2009 as the "bar date" for any individual or entity to file a proof of claim—that is, to assert a claim as to Old GM's remaining assets. Old GM filed its liquidation plan [and amended] on March 29, 2011. . . . [U]nder the plan, Old GM would establish GUC Trust, which would be administered by the Wilmington Trust Company. Once GUC Trust (and other like trusts) was established, Old GM would dissolve.

GUC Trust would hold certain Old GM assets—including New GM stock and stock warrants that could be used to purchase shares at fixed prices, along with other financial instruments. Creditors with unsecured claims against Old GM would receive these New GM securities and "units" of GUC Trust (the value of which would be pegged to the residual value of GUC Trust) on a pro rata basis in satisfaction of their claims. The Sale Agreement also imposed an "accordion feature" to ensure that GUC Trust would remain adequately funded in the event that the amount of unsecured claims grew too large. The accordion feature provided that if "the Bankruptcy Court makes a finding that the estimated aggregate allowed general unsecured claims against [Old GM's] estates exceed $35 [billion], then [New GM] will . . . issue 10,000,000 additional shares of Common Stock . . . to [Old GM]." . . .

As of March 31, 2014, GUC Trust had distributed roughly ninety percent of its New GM securities and nearly 32 million units of GUC Trust. . . . The GM bankruptcy that began five years earlier appeared to be approaching its end.

III. Ignition Switch Defect

On February 7, 2014, New GM first informed the National Highway Traffic Safety Administration ("NHTSA") that it would be recalling, among other vehicles, the 2005 Chevrolet Cobalt. A defect in the ignition switch could prevent airbags from deploying [the first of ultimately 25 million recalls]. New GM hired attorney Anton Valukas of the law firm Jenner & Block to investigate; he did so and prepared an extensive report (the "Valukas Report"). [The court summarized the damning report, which suggested knowledge of the defects was widespread but GM downplayed or hid their significance, including testing of "the switch from hell" going back to the 1990s, in part due to a dysfunctional corporate culture of "the 'GM salute,' [where] employees would attend action meetings and literally cross their arms and point fingers at others to shirk responsibility." As the court summarized, "Old GM personnel considered the problem to be a matter of customer satisfaction, not safety. These personnel apparently also did not then fully realize that when a car shuts off, so do its airbags. But as early as August 2001, at least some Old GM engineers understood that turning off the ignition switch could prevent airbags from deploying."—Eds.]

Then came reports of fatalities. In late 2005 through 2006, news of deaths from airbag non-deployments in crashes where airbags should have deployed reached the desks of Old GM's legal team. Around April 2006, Old GM engineers decided on a design change of the ignition switch to increase the torque. Old GM engineers did so quietly, without changing the ignition switch's part number, a change that would have signaled that improvements or adjustments had been made.

IV. Proceedings Below

On April 21, 2014, Steven Groman and others (the "Groman Plaintiffs") initiated an adversary proceeding against New GM in the bankruptcy court below, asserting economic losses arising from the ignition switch defect. The same day, New GM moved to enforce the Sale Order to enjoin those claims, as well as claims in other ignition switch actions then being pursued against New GM. [A]fter receiving further briefing and hearing oral argument on the motion to enforce, on April 15, 2015 the bankruptcy court decided to enforce the Sale Order in part. . . . In other words, the bankruptcy court held that New GM could not be sued—in bankruptcy court or elsewhere—for ignition switch claims that otherwise could have been brought against Old GM, unless those claims arose from New GM's own wrongful conduct. . . . [T]he bankruptcy court certified its decision for appeal to this Court pursuant to 28 U.S.C. § 158.

. . . Here, no party seeks to undo the sale of Old GM's assets to New GM, as executed through the Sale Order. Instead, plaintiffs challenge the extent to which the bankruptcy court may absolve New GM, as a successor corporation, of Old GM's liabilities . . . In particular, they dispute whether New GM may use the Sale Order's "free and clear" provision to shield itself from claims primarily arising out of the ignition switch defect and other defects.

[Appellants contest] the scope of the power to sell assets "free and clear" of all interests [and] the procedural due process requirements with respect to notice of such a sale. . . .

II. Scope of "Free and Clear" Provision

We turn to the scope of the Sale Order. The Sale Order transferred assets from Old GM to New GM "free and clear of liens, claims, encumbrances, and other interests . . ., including rights or claims . . . based on any successor or transferee liability." [Successor liability doctrine imposes liability for torts, employment obligations, and the like upon purchasers who acquire a critical mass of a corporation's assets and continue operations.—Eds.]

A. Applicable Law

The Code allows the trustee or debtor-in-possession to "use, sell, or lease, other than in the ordinary course of business, property of the estate." 11 U.S.C. § 363(b)(1). A sale pursuant to § 363(b) may be made "free and clear of any interest in such property" if any condition on a list of conditions is met. Id. § 363(f). "Yet the Code does not define the concept of 'interest,' of which the property may be sold free and clear," 3 Collier on Bankruptcy ¶ 363.06[1], nor does it express the extent to which "claims" fall within the ambit of "interests."

Rather than formulating a single precise definition for "any interest in such property," courts have continued to address the phrase "on a case-by-case basis." In re PBBPC, Inc., 484 B.R. 860, 867 (B.A.P. 1st Cir. 2013). At minimum, the language in § 363(f) permits the sale of property free and clear of *in rem* interests in the property, such as liens that attach to the property. But courts have permitted a "broader definition that encompasses other obligations that may flow from ownership of the property." 3 Collier on Bankruptcy ¶ 363.06[1]. Sister courts have held that § 363(f) may be used to bar a variety of successor liability claims that relate to ownership of property: an "interest" might encompass Coal Act obligations otherwise placed upon a successor purchasing coal assets, In re Leckie Smokeless Coal Co., 99 F.3d 573, 581-82 (4th Cir. 1996), travel vouchers issued to settle an airline's discrimination claims in a sale of airline assets, Trans World Airlines, 322 F.3d at 288-90, or a license for future use of intellectual property when that property is sold, FutureSource LLC v. Reuters Ltd., 312 F.3d 281, 285 (7th Cir. 2002). See generally Precision Indus., Inc. v. Qualitech Steel SBQ, LLC, 327 F.3d 537, 545 (7th Cir. 2003) ("[T]he term 'interest' is a broad term no doubt selected by Congress to avoid 'rigid and technical definitions drawn from other areas of the law.' "). In these instances, courts require "a relationship between the[] right to demand . . . payments from the debtors and the use to which the debtors had put their assets." *Trans World Airlines*, 322 F.3d at 289.

We agree that successor liability claims can be "interests" when they flow from a debtor's ownership of transferred assets. See 3 Collier in Bankruptcy ¶¶ 363.06[1], [7]; *Trans World Airlines*, 322 F.3d at 289. But successor liability claims must also still qualify as "claims" under Chapter 11. Though § 363(f) does not expressly invoke the Chapter 11 definition of "claims," see 11 U.S.C. § 101(5), it makes sense to "harmonize" Chapter 11 reorganizations and § 363 sales "to the extent permitted by the statutory language." *Chrysler*, 576 F.3d at 125; see *Lionel*, 722 F.2d at 1071 ("[S]ome play for the operation of both § 363(b) and Chapter 11 must be allowed for."). Here, the bankruptcy court's power to bar "claims" in a quick § 363 sale is plainly no broader than its power in a traditional Chapter 11 reorganization. Compare 11 U.S.C. § 363(f) ("free and clear of any interest in such property"), with § 1141(c) ("free and clear of all claims and interests"). We thus consider what claims may be barred under Chapter 11 generally.

Section 101(5) defines "claim" as any "right to payment, whether or not such right is reduced to judgment, liquidated, unliquidated, fixed, contingent, matured, unmatured, disputed, undisputed, legal, equitable, secured, or unsecured." 11 U.S.C. § 101(5). A claim is (1) a right to payment (2) that arose before the filing of the petition. If the right to payment is contingent on future events, the claim must instead "result from pre-petition conduct fairly giving rise to that contingent claim." In re Chateaugay Corp. ("*Chateaugay I*"), 944 F.2d 997, 1005 (2d Cir. 1991).

This Court has not decided, however, "the difficult case of pre-petition conduct that has not yet resulted in detectable injury, much less the extreme case of pre-petition conduct that has not yet resulted in any tortious consequence to a victim." Id. at 1004. *Chateaugay I* considered a hypothetical bankrupt bridge building company, which could predict that out of the 10,000 bridges it built, one would one day fail, causing deaths and other injuries. Id. at 1003. If that bridge did fail, the individuals might have tort claims resulting from pre-petition conduct, namely the building of the bridge.

Recognizing these claims would engender "enormous practical and perhaps constitutional problems." Id. Thus, " 'claim' cannot be extended to include . . . claimants whom the record indicates were completely unknown and unidentified at the time [the debtor] filed its petition and whose rights depended entirely on the fortuity of future occurrences." Lemelle v. Universal Mfg. Corp., 18 F.3d 1268, 1277 (5th Cir. 1994); see In re Chateaugay Corp. ("*Chateaugay IV*"), 53 F.3d 478, 497 (2d Cir. 1995) (stating that, in "common sense," "claim" is "not infinite"). To avoid any practical and constitutional problems, courts require some minimum "contact," *Chateaugay I*, 944 F.2d at 1003-04, or "relationship," *Chateaugay IV*, 53 F.3d at 497, that makes identifiable the individual with whom the claim does or would rest.

To summarize, a bankruptcy court may approve a § 363 sale "free and clear" of successor liability claims if those claims flow from the debtor's ownership of the sold assets. Such a claim must arise from a (1) right to payment (2) that arose before the filing of the petition or resulted from pre-petition conduct fairly giving rise to the claim. Further, there must be some contact or relationship between the debtor and the claimant such that the claimant is identifiable.

B. Application

[T]he pre-closing accident claims clearly fall within the scope of the Sale Order. Those claims directly relate to the ownership of the GM automaker's business—Old GM built cars with ignition switch defects. And those plaintiffs' claims are properly thought of as tort claims that arose before the filing of the petition; indeed, the claims arise from accidents that occurred pre-closing involving Old GM cars.

Second, the economic loss claims arising from the ignition switch defect or other defects present a closer call. Like the claims of Pre-Closing Accident Plaintiffs, these claims flow from the operation of Old GM's automaker business. These individuals also, by virtue of owning Old GM cars, had come into contact with the debtor prior to the bankruptcy petition.

Yet the ignition switch defect (and other defects) were only revealed some five years later. GUC Trust thus asserts that there was no right to payment prior to the petition. We disagree. The economic losses claimed by these individuals were "contingent" claims. 11 U.S.C. § 101(5). That is, the ignition switch defect was there, but was not yet so patent that an individual could, as a practical matter, bring a case in court. The contingency standing in the way was Old GM telling plaintiffs that the ignition switch defect existed. In other words, Old GM's creation of the ignition switch defect fairly gave rise to these claims, even if the claimants did not yet know. See *Chateaugay I*, 944 F.2d at 1005.

III. *Procedural Due Process*

The Sale Order covers the pre-closing accident claims and economic loss claims based on the ignition switch and other defects. The Sale Order, if enforced, would thus bar those claims. Plaintiffs contend on appeal that enforcing the Sale Order would violate procedural due process. We address two issues: (1) what notice plaintiffs were entitled to as a matter of procedural due process, and (2) if they were provided inadequate notice, whether the bankruptcy court erred in denying relief on the basis that most plaintiffs were not "prejudiced." . . .

A. Notice

The bankruptcy court first concluded that plaintiffs were not provided notice as required by procedural due process. The bankruptcy court held that because Old GM knew or with reasonable diligence should have known of the ignition switch claims, plaintiffs were entitled to actual or direct mail notice, but received only publication notice. The parties dispute the extent of Old GM's knowledge of the ignition switch problem.

1. APPLICABLE LAW

The Due Process Clause provides, "No person shall . . . be deprived of life, liberty, or property, without due process of law." U.S. Const. amend. V. Certain procedural protections attach when "deprivations trigger due process." Connecticut v. Doehr, 501 U.S. 1, 12, 111 S. Ct. 2105, 115 L. Ed. 2d 1 (1991). Generally, legal claims are sufficient to constitute property such that a deprivation would trigger due process scrutiny. Indeed, a fundamental purpose of bankruptcy is to discharge, restructure, or impair claims against the debtor in an orderly fashion. See Lines v. Frederick, 400 U.S. 18, 19, 91 S. Ct. 113, 27 L. Ed. 2d 124 (1970). "The general rule that emerges . . . is that notice by publication is not enough with respect to a person whose name and address are known or very easily ascertainable and whose legally protected interests are directly affected by the proceedings in question." Schroeder v. City of New York, 371 U.S. 208, 212-13. In other words, adequacy of notice "turns on what the debtor . . . knew about the claim or, with reasonable diligence, should have known." DPWN Holdings (USA), Inc. v. United Air Lines, Inc., 747 F.3d 145, 150 (2d Cir. 2014).

> "An elementary and fundamental requirement of due process in any proceeding which is to be accorded finality is notice reasonably calculated, under all the circumstances, to apprise interested parties of the pendency of the action and afford them an opportunity to present their objections."

Mullane v. Cent. Hanover Bank & Tr. Co., 339 U.S. 306, 314 (1950).

If a debtor reveals in bankruptcy the claims against it and provides potential claimants notice consistent with due process of law, then the Code affords vast protections. Both § 1141(c) and § 363(f) permit "free and clear" provisions that act as liability shield. These provisions provide enormous incentives for a struggling company to be forthright. But if a debtor does not reveal claims that it is aware of, then bankruptcy law cannot protect it. . . .

2. APPLICATION

The bankruptcy court found that because Old GM knew or reasonably should have known about the ignition switch defect prior to bankruptcy, it should have provided direct mail notice to vehicle owners. We find no clear error in this factual finding.

As background, federal law requires that automakers keep records of the first owners of their vehicles. 49 U.S.C. § 30117(b)(1) ("A manufacturer of a motor vehicle . . . shall cause to be maintained a record of the name and address of the first purchaser of each vehicle"). This provision facilitates recalls and other consequences of the consumer-automaker relationship. . . . The facts paint a picture that Old GM did nothing, even as it knew that the ignition switch defect impacted consumers. From its development in 1997, the ignition switch never passed Old GM's own technical specifications. Old GM knew that the switch was defective, but it approved the switch for millions of cars anyway. . . . At minimum, Old GM knew about moving stalls and airbag non-deployments in certain models, and should have revealed those facts in bankruptcy. Those defects would still be the basis of "claims," even if the root cause (the ignition switch) was not clear.

New GM argues in response that because plaintiffs' claims were "contingent," those individuals were "unknown" creditors as a matter of law. But contingent claims are still claims, 11 U.S.C. § 101(5), and claimants are entitled to adequate notice if the debtor knows of the claims. Moreover, as discussed above, the only contingency was Old GM telling owners about the ignition switch defect—a contingency wholly in Old GM's control and without bearing as to *Old GM's* own knowledge. New GM essentially asks that we reward debtors who conceal claims against potential creditors. We decline to do so. . . .

While the desire to move through bankruptcy as expeditiously as possible was laudable, Old GM's precarious situation and the need for speed did not obviate basic constitutional principles. Due process applies even in a company's moment of crisis.

[The bankruptcy court nonetheless ruled against the plaintiffs because it held that the unconstitutional lack of notice did not create prejudice as it would have affirmed the sales order anyway; this court reversed holding (alternatively) *either* prejudice is not required when constitutional due process is violated *or* the plaintiffs were prejudiced because it was not clear the outcome would have been the same had the plaintiffs been given proper notice, and the burden of proof to show an absence of prejudice would be on due-process deprivers.—Eds.]

To conclude, we reverse the bankruptcy court's decision insofar as it enforced the Sale Order to enjoin claims relating to the ignition switch defect. Because enforcing the Sale Order would violate procedural due process in these circumstances, the bankruptcy court erred in granting New GM's motion to enforce. . . .

Note the distinction between known and unknown. Because GM knew the car purchasers due to recordkeeping requirements, direct notice through mail was required by the Constitution's Due Process Clause. The publication notice of a newspaper cattle call suffices only for "known unknowns," where the debtor knows it has a class of claimants out there, it just doesn't know who they individually are. But this raises the specter of unknown unknowns, as one former Secretary of Defense used to remind us. What about people who bought cars after confirmation, perhaps used? The court said this:

> [T]he Sale Order likewise does not cover the Used Car Purchasers' claims. The Used Car Purchasers were individuals who purchased Old GM cars *after* the closing, without knowledge of the defect or possible claim against New GM. They had no relation with Old GM prior to bankruptcy. Indeed, as of the bankruptcy petition there were an unknown number of unknown individuals who would one day purchase Old GM vehicles secondhand. There could have been no contact or relationship—actual or presumed—between Old GM and these specific plaintiffs, who otherwise had no awareness of the ignition switch defect or putative claims against New GM. We cannot, consistent with bankruptcy law, read the Sale Order to cover their claims.

In re Motors Liquidation Co., 829 F.3d at 157.

Other courts have agreed. In dealing with a similar Sales Order purporting to inoculate a purchaser prospectively from liability for debtor's aircraft made before confirmation, the court noted that future claimants (sadly, the estates of passengers on flights that had not yet crashed) could not be expected to have their claims extinguished by a prior bankruptcy without due process, and whether that process was sufficient can only be litigated by those litigants when they get around to suit.

> Regretfully, the successor in this case cannot enjoy the fruits of our analysis. That is really no one's fault. How, after all, could any of the litigants in this case know how these issues would shake out back in 1990, before the Fifth Circuit had ever spoken on the issue. Yet it is the nature of the beast that, in all likelihood, it will never be possible for a debtor emerging from bankruptcy (or any successor entity), to know of a certainty that the provisions of a given plan will effectively cut off claimants such as these unless and until a challenge is mounted. In no other way can the due process rights of such claimants be fully vindicated.

Fairchild Aircraft Corp. v. Fairchild Aircraft Inc. (In re Fairchild Aircraft), 184 B.R. 910, 934 (Bankr. W.D. Tex. 1995), *vacated upon party consent*, 220 B.R. 909 (Bankr. W.D. Tex. 1998).

Yet note that in *Fairchild*, unlike *GM*, there was no evidence that the old debtor knew of the defects leading to the crash, so post-sale liability was a definite step further along the road. The necessary result of these cases allowing future liability to remain undischarged is that the purchasers of assets (and those who finance those purchases) must lower the price paid to adjust for these contingencies. The cost might be calculated in terms of the premiums on the insurance against old claims they would be wise to buy—if such a coverage market exists.

B.   THE EFFECT OF DISCHARGE ON FUTURE CLAIMS OF NON-CREDITORS

The future claims puzzles also bedevil claims by the debtor and against third parties.

1.   The Effect of Discharge on Future Claims by the Debtor

Debtors who contemplate bringing lawsuits after bankruptcy have to consider the other side of confirmation-and-discharge: defendants may raise its shield. While claims by the debtor are not discharged under § 1141, plenty of other legal doctrines may step in. In particular, the confirmed plan of reorganization looks like a general settlement of claims, while the order of confirmation itself may give rise to an assertion of res judicata as to claims (or compulsory counterclaims) that were or should have been raised in the chapter 11 proceeding. For example, an early case under the Code involved a confirmed chapter 11 plan that settled both the lender's claims for payment and the debtors' counterclaims seeking on various prepetition grounds to void the lender's mortgage and block its right to collect. In re Howe, 913 F.2d 1138 (5th Cir. 1990). Five years later, the debtors brought a lender liability suit arising out of the same facts. The court dismissed the case, although lender liability was neither raised nor addressed in the bankruptcy.

Note that Old GM gave the creditors shares in a litigation trust. This trust could then assert all the causes of action held by the estate (e.g., voidable preferences) and prosecute them at its leisure without worrying about delaying the new life of GM. The trust may even raise money to finance litigation by selling shares in the trust to third parties or to some subset of creditors. Any recovery is distributed to the trust unitholders. Champerty, you say? Cash, respond bankruptcy creditors.

The "disembodied" litigation from trusts is becoming ever more structurally complex, and perhaps problematic. One reason is that Wall Street's endless creativity has spawned the possibility of public offerings of securities that are essentially contingent interests in bankruptcy litigation trusts. At some point, questions about champerty in jurisdictions that still recognize it do need to be taken seriously. Another reason is that increasingly trustees and debtors are assigning lawsuits that are unique to bankruptcy, like the power to recover a preference. Although the motive is the same as in the sale of a prepetition cause of action arising under non-bankruptcy law—to generate recoveries for creditors—the separation of bankruptcy actions from the special context in which they arise may lead to serious problems of legal concept and public perception. For example, a citizen might see the fairness of a trust recovering a preferential payment to even up the pain from a recent bankruptcy by spreading the recovery among all the creditors. That same citizen may react differently to a news story explaining how an innocent party had to pony up a lot of money for the benefit of Vulture, Inc., because of some legal tool available in a distant bankruptcy. Despite all the reasonable arguments that can be made about the useful role of investors in permitting the widows and orphans to bail out with early payment, context may matter to fairness perceptions about the outcomes from such litigation.

2. *The Effects of Discharge on Future Claims Against Non-Debtors: "Third-Party Releases"*

Third-party releases rose to prominence in the asbestos cases, where insurance companies agreed to settle with the insureds and their claimants by contributing large amounts to the trusts that were formed, but only if they were shielded from any additional liability. See, e.g., Johns-Manville Corp. v. Chubb Indem. Ins. Co. (In re Johns-Manville Corp.), 517 F.3d 52, 57 (2d Cir. 2008). Similar settlements releasing contributing third parties were approved in Canada in connection with the collapse of commercial paper markets, and those settlements were enforced in the United States despite objections about third-party releases. In re Metcalfe & Mansfield Alt. Invs., 421 B.R. 685 (Bankr. S.D.N.Y. 2010).

But third-party releases also arise with entities affiliated with the debtor. Because modern legal systems permit the creation of new corporate entities freely and cheaply, a considerable range of choice often exists as to which affiliates in a group go into bankruptcy. In an interrelated group, however, persons and entities other than the debtor may contribute money or talent that is essential to a reorganization—including directors and officers. Often, they will want to be released from future liability in return for their contributions.

Generally, consensual releases of third parties in a reorganization plan will be enforced. § 1141. An unwelcome release where a creditor objects, however, is quite a different matter. Those non-debtor releases rest on shakier legal grounds. Section 524(e) is a stumbling block that some believe forecloses non-debtor releases. Indeed, the Tenth Circuit has flatly refused to approve them outside the asbestos context. Other circuits have scrutinized them carefully. In re Metromedia Fiber Network, Inc., 416 F.3d 136 (2d Cir. 2005), explains the courts' concerns:

> At least two considerations justify the reluctance to approve nondebtor releases. First, the only explicit authorization in the Code for nondebtor releases is 11 U.S.C. § 524(g), which authorizes releases in asbestos cases when specified conditions are satisfied, including the creation of a trust to satisfy future claims. . . .
>
> Second, a nondebtor release is a device that lends itself to abuse. By it, a nondebtor can shield itself from liability to third parties. In form, it is a release; in effect, it may operate as a bankruptcy discharge arranged without a filing and without the safeguards of the Code. The potential for abuse is heightened when releases afford blanket immunity. Here, the releases protect against any claims relating to the debtor, "whether for tort, fraud, contract, violations of federal or state securities laws, or otherwise, whether known or unknown, foreseen or unforeseen, liquidated or unliquidated, fixed or contingent, matured or unmatured."
>
> Courts have approved nondebtor releases when: the estate received substantial consideration; the enjoined claims were "channeled" to a settlement fund rather than extinguished; the enjoined claims would indirectly impact the debtor's reorganization by way of indemnity or contribution, and the plan otherwise provided for the full payment of the enjoined claims, id. Nondebtor releases may also be tolerated if the affected creditors consent.

Id. at 142.

The court in *Metromedia* notes that the injunction there was not like the "channeling" injunction approved in *Manville*, which did not prevent suit against the insurance companies for asbestos claims but channeled them first to the overall settlement fund to which those companies had contributed.

Despite the lack of a statutory foundation in most instances, nondebtor releases occur fairly frequently. We met Ivan Kahn earlier as he successfully overcame an objection to the classification of creditors in the reorganization plan of his family's century-old piano business in Dallas back in Assignment 27. A later portion of the opinion addresses his personal future as the company struggles to survive.

══════ In re BERNHARD STEINER PIANOS USA, INC. ══════
292 B.R. 109 (Bankr. N.D. Tex. 2002)

HALE, Bankruptcy Judge.

. . .

THE EFFECT OF CONFIRMATION UPON CLAIMS AGAINST THIRD PARTIES: THE REACH OF 11 U.S.C. § 524(e)

Textron and Transamerica objected to Plan ¶¶ 10.03, 10.04 and 12.04. . . . Debtor subsequently modified the Plan in open court on November 20, 2002, by omitting paragraph 10.04 and replacing 10.03 with the following language:

> 10.03 Notwithstanding anything contained herein to the contrary, neither debtor, reorganized debtor, the officers, guarantors, and directors of the debtors nor the shareholders shall be discharged and released from any liability for claims and debts under this plan, however, absent further court order upon notice and hearing, the exclusive remedy for payment of any claim or debt so long as the plan is not in default shall be the plan. To the extent necessary, any applicable statute of limitations against collection from any third party is specifically tolled from the period of time from the bankruptcy petition date until the date upon which debtor fails to cure any written notice of default as set forth in the plan.

(Debtor's Plan of Reorganization Dated Sept. 13, 2002 and attached to Order Confirming Debtor's Plan of Reorganization, as Modified at 8-9.) The Confirmation Order provides for a ten-day cure period and relief from modified ¶ 10.3 upon "changed circumstances."

Textron and Transamerica are not satisfied with the modification and continue to argue that modified ¶ 10.3 of the Plan (hereinafter "¶ 10.3") violates § 524(e) to the extent it acts as a release of their claims against Debtor's principal, Kahn. . . .

1. Availability of the Relief Requested

Generally, a plan of reorganization cannot be confirmed if the Plan purports to release guarantors of the debtor's debts and a creditor objects to the release. Paragraph 10.3 specifically states that guarantors are not discharged or released from any liability under the plan. Therefore, on its face, the Plan does not purport to grant a release for third parties, such as Mr. Kahn. Further, nothing in ¶ 10.3 affects Kahn's ultimate liability under any guaranty agreement. Instead, ¶ 10.3 merely controls the timing of when a claim, if any, against Kahn, can be brought. And, under the Plan, as modified, the temporary stay could lift upon uncured default under the plan, or upon a change in circumstances for Mr. Kahn, i.e. recovery of the Nigerian Funds. If the Objecting Creditors are not paid under the Plan, they may pursue their guarantor, Mr. Kahn. If his circumstances improve, or if the situation warrants, the Objecting Creditors can seek relief from the stay imposed by the Plan.

On the issue of the effect of confirmation on the claims against third parties, this Court does not write on a clean slate. The Fifth Circuit has held that post-confirmation *permanent injunctions* that effectively release a non-debtor from liability are prohibited. Feld v. Zale Corp. (In re Zale Corp.), 62 F.3d 746, 761 (5th Cir. 1995). However, temporary injunctions may be proper under unusual circumstances. These circumstances include (1) when the non-debtor and debtor enjoy such an identity of interest that the suit against the non-debtor is essentially a suit against the debtor, and (2) when the third-party action will have an adverse impact on the debtor's ability to accomplish reorganization. *Id.* . . .

The *Zale* unusual circumstances test has been met in this case. The success or failure of the Debtor lies mainly, if not exclusively, with the efforts, reputation, and dedication of Mr. Kahn. For all practical purposes, at this time, he is the Debtor. This Debtor will survive and creditors will be paid under the plan only if Mr. Kahn is allowed to conduct the business of the Debtor without distraction. Debtor and Kahn enjoy such an identity of interest that the prosecution of the claims, or attempted collection of any judgments against Kahn would be tantamount to prosecuting and/or seeking collection from the Debtor. Further, Textron and Transamerica's pursuit of judgment or recovery against Kahn individually would have an adverse impact on the successful reorganization of the Debtor. . . .

The harm to Transamerica and Textron, on the other hand, is simply that they are not being repaid as quickly as they would like. They are free to pursue Kahn on his guaranties in the event Debtor defaults on its Plan payments and the default is not cured within 10 days. At that time, they need only to obtain an order from this Court lifting the "stay" and allowing them to proceed against Kahn directly. The harm to Debtor far outweighs the harm to Transamerica and Textron.

Anyone who reviews the contents of their email spam folder may be concerned that part of Kahn's plan involved the recovery of apparently bountiful funds from Nigeria.

Problem Set 35

35.1. Strosnider Sunrise Farm, Inc., has been in Kim Strosnider's family for three generations, growing into a 1,600-acre fruit and vegetable operation. Kim works hard and the business is profitable, but Kim is worried. The state EPA has found contamination in the soil and water on her property. Kim explains that she can't even begin to list the pesticides and chemical fertilizers they have used on the crops over the past 60 years. The EPA has told her to clean it up and explained that if she doesn't, they will clean it up and send her a bill for about $10.1 million. Kim says that the business can't pay that kind of money. "It might as well be $10.1 trillion—we can't even make interest payments on ten million dollars. The land and the equipment are already over-mortgaged. We make a profit some years, but only because I work 18 hours a day." She asks for your help. What do you tell her? (Kim would not qualify for chapter 12 or the SBRA.)

35.2. You have been Chris Rosekrans's chief legal advisor as he has taken on one business challenge after another. He's put together a group of investors to buy Kewanee Boiler, a 70-year-old company that specialized until recently in heavy industrial boilers. The plant is shuttered and in chapter 11. Current management has abandoned the business, and the liquidating trustee had recommended a piecemeal sale. Rosekrans is willing to invest $40 million to revitalize the factory and shift its output to a more varied industrial supply line. The 550 workers who would be recalled are delighted to see high-skill, high-wage jobs return, creditors see the promised 50% repayment as an unexpected windfall, and the mayor sees this as a chance to turn around a decaying part of the city. The only hitch is that Rosekrans has read the *GM* case. He knows about the old problems with the Kewanee boilers produced back in the 1970s. Forty-six of the 10,000 sold that were manufactured from 1971 to 1975 have simply blown up, averaging about two a year once the boilers reach ten years old. Rosekrans says his investors are willing to take full responsibility for every product they produce, but not for the products manufactured long before they took over. He says that unless you can guarantee that if an old boiler blows up and someone gets hurt, he won't face a judge who later decides that Kewanee is liable, then he won't invest. Everyone—investors, creditors, employees, the mayor—awaits your answer.

35.3. Universal Chips is a major supplier of standard microchip circuits for thermostat control units in home heating and cooling systems. After years of rapid growth, however, UC is now in financial trouble. Its difficulties arise from its sluggish adoption of technical advances (a mistake its R&D department is rapidly correcting) but also from a failure of quality control during a two-year period of over-rapid expansion. During that period, UC produced a number of defective chips for the thermostat market. The company's engineers estimate that about 30% of the chips produced during that period are subject to sudden, unpredictable failure, with varying consequences ranging from a simple need for replacement to serious damage to an entire home heating system. Because the central microchip is a unit with an expected lifespan far greater than the system as a whole, it is installed in a way that makes it difficult and expensive to remove.

UC recently filed chapter 11. In general, its prospects for reorganization look good, except that its principal lenders and the public debt markets are very concerned about its potential long-term liabilities arising from the thermostat chip problem. You have been retained by the Heating Repair Association (HRA) as bankruptcy counsel. HRA members have installed hundreds of thousands of the thermostats with suspect chips. To replace them all would cost at least $500 million, and much of that cost would be wasted, at least in the sense that many of the chips would last the normal 20 years with no problem. On the other hand, HRA sees the likelihood of expensive replacement costs and warranty claims from members' homeowner-customers for years in the future. Unfortunately, it is very hard to predict what those costs will be or when they will be incurred. (For example, the experts are bitterly divided over the likely "peak" failure year; some say year five after installation, while others think it will be year nine.)

What claim will you file on behalf of HRA members? How might the court rule on the claim? How might your members be treated in a plan of reorganization? Do homeowners have a claim? If some lawyer representing a small group of potentially affected homeowners should file a purported "class" claim, how should you react on behalf of HRA members? Should you support or oppose? If you or the company opposes the class claim, what arguments can be made against it, and how will counsel for the class respond?

35.4. Suppose in Problem 35.3 neither consumers nor the contractors' association (HRA) knew of the problem with the home thermostats at the time of UC's chapter 11 filing. The debtor published a notice of the bankruptcy and the bar date for filing claims in all major newspapers around the country and there were many news stories about the filing as well. A year after confirmation, the HRA discovered the problem with the thermostats. They come to you as counsel to the association asking (a) Can their members sue UC for their damages for replacement of the chips in response to the demands of their customers, the homeowners? and (b) Can the homeowners sue the contractors, even if the contractors cannot sue UC for indemnity? Does either question turn on whether UC knew about the problem? Would it matter if there were some low-key news stories about a possible problem with the thermostats? See §§ 1141, 523(a)(3), 524.

35.5. Do you have any new thoughts on the saga of the DOJ and SLUG Carbon from Problem 32.2?

35.6. Evelyn Brewer of the Missing Children Foundation called you this morning in shock. The foundation has been sued by Morris Mangle, the former president of Associated Fundraisers (AF), for return of money the foundation received from AF. Until it filed chapter 11 last year, AF's business was raising money for charities by telephone solicitations. The reorganization failed and converted into a chapter 7. Evelyn explains that the foundation was paid $35,000 by AF about a month before AF's chapter 11 filing. The money had been owed for nine months after completion of a successful money-raising campaign by AF for the foundation. "I only got it by threatening to go to the newspapers and I was so relieved after the bankruptcy that we were out of it and didn't have to make a claim," Evelyn told you. A phone call to one of the lawyers involved in the case has gotten you the explanation for the lawsuit: Mangle made a deal with the chapter 7 trustee that he would pay the trustee $10,000 in return for an assignment of all the preference and fraudulent conveyance actions the estate might have. The trustee distributed the money, net of her fee, to the creditors who had filed claims and closed the case. As a result of the deal, Mangle not only keeps whatever he can get, but now doesn't have to worry about being sued for the real estate he transferred from AF to his daughter Susan six months before the bankruptcy. What can you do for the foundation?

FUNCTIONS AND BOUNDARIES

It is said that the world is in a state of bankruptcy,
that the world owes the world more than the world can pay . . .

       —Ralph Waldo Emerson, "Gifts," in Essays: Second Series *(1844).*

This final part of the book plays on the title of Thomas Jackson's seminal book, The Logic and Limits of Bankruptcy Law (1986). Although we disagree with his analysis in important ways, his book is a landmark in modern theorizing because it attempts to define the proper scope of bankruptcy by examining its functions. Part V is an introductory exploration of these issues. In a fact- and statute-intensive area such as bankruptcy, the big picture can sometimes be elusive, so we end with these materials now that the nitty-gritty has been digested. Here, we step back a bit and think about broader, system-wide aspects of the business reorganization system, focusing on scope: the scope of chapter 11, the scope of the bankruptcy court system, the scope of the U.S. regime in an increasingly internationalized world, and finally the very theory behind the function of bankruptcy law.

It's a big place to close a big book, but you have come a long way and eaten many vegetables. Enjoy the dessert.

BEYOND CHAPTER 11

Certain important types of financial distress are resolved in distinctly different ways under the Code or are excluded from the Code entirely. The underlying policy is that some institutions and systems are sufficiently unique to require their own reorganization (or liquidation) systems outside the tools of chapter 11. This assignment explores these debtors that are "beyond chapter 11." It then turns the telescope around and, using labor law as a case study, examines a federal regulatory system that might certainly justify similarly exceptional treatment but is nevertheless resolved "within chapter 11." (Recall the policy debates that we encountered in the resolution of mass tort and environmental claims in the previous assignment.) Together, these enable us to reconsider some of the issues that we have addressed in the chapter 11 materials but that are, or perhaps should be, excluded from chapter 11 — issues that sometimes rest just outside the walls.

A. REORGANIZING PRIVATE DEBT OUTSIDE CHAPTER 11

Several entities that hold private debt are either excepted from eligibility to file for bankruptcy — shunted to their own regulatory regimes — or governed by special rules within the Code. An important example of an entity whose financial distress resolution occurs outside bankruptcy altogether is a bank. (Bankers love euphemisms, so we call a process that deals with the financial distress of a bank a "resolution," not a "bankruptcy.") Another is an insurance company. Insurance companies and banks go broke, but not bankrupt, § 109(b)(1)-(2), because they have their own specialized insolvency systems. Although these systems resemble bankruptcy law in many ways, the key difference is that they include government guarantees or complete distributional priority to one preferred class of creditors — policyholders and depositors, respectively. The other stakeholders, such as ordinary creditors and shareholders, may lose all they had risked when one of these entities fails because the focus is on paying the preferred classes. One explanation for this treatment is an apparent assumption that depositors and policyholders are risk-averse and poor risk-spreaders, so that full repayment for them is central to the smooth working of the financial system. In the case of banks, the protection is nearly ironclad (at least up to a certain amount) because of the deposit insurance provided by the federal government through the FDIC. Similarly, state laws often provide for compulsory compensation funds to cover policyholder losses in insurance insolvencies.

The most important example of companies who are able to file for bankruptcy but are governed by special Code rules is the securities industry. The Securities Investor Protection Act of 1970, 84 Stat. 1636, 15 U.S.C. § 78aaa et seq., gives coverage to brokerage customers who deposit their stocks and bonds with the broker through the Securities Investor Protection Corporation ("SIPC") system. See, e.g., Securities Investor Protection Corp. v. Barbour, 421 U.S. 412, 421 (1975). SIPC offers something like the protection that the FDIC offers to bank depositors, although its coverage is not as complete. Securities investors who deposit money into brokerage accounts are presumably thought willing to take the risk of the markets but not the risk of the financial mismanagement or venality of the brokers themselves. When a brokerage fails, it resides in sort of an insolvency ghetto in the Code. It is not permitted to file for chapter 11 at all, and special rules apply to a stockbroker (or commodity broker) that files chapter 7. §§ 741-766. In particular, the customers who leave stock deposited with a stockbroker in chapter 7 represent a preferred class of creditors to the extent of the value of that property. § 752. SIPC is the key party in stockbroker cases, and the rules are sufficiently different from ordinary bankruptcy that such cases tend to attract specialty lawyers.

Securities firms and banks share two characteristics that explain their exceptional treatment: they hold large amounts of value deposited—as opposed to invested—by the public, and they are heavily regulated at all times, not just when in financial distress. Thus, a common thread for chapter 11 exclusions seems to be "highly regulated financial institutions that take deposits of money or valuables from the public." While we take a brief look at the resolution of banks in default, stockbrokerages are so specialized and insurance companies so regulated state-by-state that we leave their treatment to financial regulation texts.

Finally, some private debtors get exceptional treatment for solely historical reasons perhaps difficult to justify by modern policy. Railroads, for example, are forbidden from filing in chapter 7, § 109(b)(1), and are governed by a separate subchapter in chapter 11, §§ 1161-1174, even though more modern common carriers—like airlines—have flown through chapter 11.

1. Traditional Banks

The United States has a large number of banks, although nowadays just a few dominate the national market. One reason for the plethora of banks is that bank charters are granted at both the state and federal levels. Although these banks are heavily regulated by states and by the federal government, including the Federal Reserve, the central agency in the resolution of a distressed bank is the FDIC, which stands behind the sign on the front door of nearly every bank: "Deposits Insured by the FDIC." In exchange for that insurance, which is necessary as a practical matter if a bank wants to attract depositors, the bank is subject to summary procedures in case of financial difficulty. Typically, once the FDIC and the other regulators agree there is a serious problem, the FDIC enters the bank on a Friday afternoon after closing (a bit like Butch Cassidy and the Sundance Kid), takes over the bank as the "receiver," and reopens it on Monday morning, at which point everyone's payments and deposits go through just fine, thank you, and the bank does business apparently just as before. The receiver normally does a quick sale of the "good" loans and other assets to another bank and then does a drawn-out "workout" of the bad ones. As noted, the bank does not have the option of filing chapter 11. § 109(b)(2), (d). Remember, this is a last resort: the FDIC tries to stop all this from happening by regular inspections, making banks keep certain minimum capital reserves, and so on.

Any bank resolution process has to operate at top speed to restore the confidence when a bank fails, both to prevent a run on the individual bank and a "contagion" panic at other banks. For this reason, the FDIC is given extraordinary summary powers to act (and actually arrives at the bank in unmarked, nondescript cars). For an excellent description of the functioning of this system in response to the Great Recession, see Sheila Bair, Bull by the Horns: Fighting to Save Main Street from Wall Street and Wall Street from Itself 186 (2012). FDIC insurance is funded like most insurance— through premiums paid by the insured: banks. In good times, the fund is ample. In bad times, ironically when the insurance is needed most, the fund may get overwhelmed. When that happens, the U.S. government stands behind the fund with its general taxation power to shore up the balance. If that government backing should ever cease to assuage market panic, we will have much more pressing problems than our bank deposits.

The following case gives an example of the granularity of the statutes governing the bank resolution regime (and protections accorded the FDIC).

C&C INVESTMENT PROPERTIES, L.L.C. v. TRUSTMARK NATIONAL BANK
838 F.3d 655 (5th Cir. 2016)

Costa, Circuit Judge.

At the height of the savings & loan crisis, we considered a number of cases involving the *D'Oench, Duhme* doctrine. That doctrine, which originated in the federal common law and is now codified at 12 U.S.C. Section 1823(e), prevents borrowers from relying on oral agreements they allegedly had with a failed bank to defend against collection efforts of a federal receiver like the Federal Deposit Insurance Corporation (FDIC). D'Oench, Duhme & Co. v. FDIC, 315 U.S. 447, 459-60, 62 S. Ct. 676, 86 L. Ed. 956 (1942). The failure of a Mississippi bank in the aftermath of the 2008 financial crisis requires us to again consider the doctrine.

In 2004, Glen and Charlotte Collins formed C&C Investment Properties, LLC to buy, rent, and flip real estate. Between 2006 and 2009, C&C bought several foreclosed properties from Heritage Banking Group. C&C financed these purchases through promissory notes payable to Heritage, which were secured by deeds of trust encumbering the properties and guaranteed personally by the Collinses. According to the Collinses, the purchases were subject to the following side agreement: C&C would pay Heritage amounts equal to what Heritage paid for the properties at foreclosure and Heritage would later refinance the properties to account for their renovation value.

C&C stopped making payments on the loans because Heritage purportedly did not live up to the side agreement. As a result, it defaulted on the notes and guaranties. In response, Heritage foreclosed on the properties. Aggrieved, Glen Collins and C&C sued Heritage for breach of contract and fraudulent inducement.

While the suit was pending, Heritage was declared insolvent and the FDIC was appointed as receiver. That same day, the FDIC entered into a Purchase and Assumption Agreement with Trustmark National Bank, under which it transferred to Trustmark various Heritage assets and liabilities, including the C&C notes and guaranties.

Upon being substituted for Heritage as a defendant, the FDIC moved to dismiss the case. Before the court could rule on the motion, however, Mr. Collins and C&C sought and obtained leave to amend, adding Trustmark as a defendant. The FDIC thereafter renewed its motion, which was granted.

Once added as a party, Trustmark pleaded section 1823(e) as a defense and filed counterclaims against C&C and the Collinses (hereafter referred to jointly as the "borrowers") for the amount still owing on the notes. Trustmark also sought reimbursement for its costs and expenses related to collection and enforcement of the loans.

Trustmark filed a motion for summary judgment, arguing that because the claims against it and the defenses to its counterclaims are based on an unwritten side agreement between C&C and Heritage, section 1823(e) bars them. The borrowers objected, asserting that Trustmark either affirmatively or by being dilatory waived this defense. They further argued that, even if there was no waiver, there is a material fact dispute about whether the side agreement exists in a written form sufficient to overcome section 1823(e). The district court granted Trustmark's motion.

I.

. . .

Enacted in 1950, not long after the Supreme Court decided *D'Oench, Duhme*, section 1823(e) codifies that common law ruling. The statute provides that any "agreement which tends to diminish or defeat the interest of the [FDIC] in any asset acquired by it under this section" shall not "be valid against the [FDIC] unless such agreement" is: (1) in writing; (2) contemporaneously executed by the depository institution and the person claiming an adverse interest; (3) approved by the board of directors of the depository institution and reflected in the minutes of the board; and (4) continuously, from the time of its execution, an official record of the depository institution. We have extended these protections to private parties, like Trustmark, that purchase the assets of insolvent banks from the FDIC.

There are two reasons for the *D'Oench, Duhme* rule. First, it "allow[s] federal and state bank examiners to rely on a bank's records in evaluating the worth of the bank's assets." Langley v. FDIC, 484 U.S. 86, 91, 108 S. Ct. 396, 98 L. Ed. 2d 340 (1987). Second, it "ensure[s] mature consideration of unusual loan transactions by senior bank officials, and prevent[s] fraudulent insertion of new terms, with the collusion of bank employees, when a bank appears headed for failure." *Id.* at 92, 108 S. Ct. 396.

The borrowers do not dispute these general principles of section 1823(e) or their applicability to this case. Instead, they attempt to avoid the defense in three ways. The first two involve waiver, as the borrowers contend that Trustmark substantively waived the defense in its agreement for the purchase of the Heritage assets and also procedurally waived the defense by asserting it too late in this lawsuit.

. . .

Apart from their unsuccessful waiver arguments, the borrowers argue that a material fact dispute exists that should have precluded summary judgment: whether the side agreement is in a written form sufficient to overcome section 1823(e). They point to the testimony of a Heritage division president who, when asked whether something in writing described the arrangement between C&C and Heritage, replied, "there may have been—well, I would have . . . gotten—and I can't remember whether it was an e-mail or something from Tim Leitaker saying it was okay for me to do that." The executive was then asked whether there was something in writing other than the email, to which he replied, "I don't remember the exact communication, but, yeah . . . I guess I'm positive that it was communicated in writing. If not, it still had to be signed off on every time I turned a loan in for it."

Even viewing the executive's testimony about the purported side agreement in favor of the borrowers, there is no evidence from which a jury might conclude that all of the conditions necessary to overcome section 1823(e) are present. At most, the statements are evidence of communications describing the purported side agreement. We have doubts whether such writings would meet even the first requirement: that the "agreement" itself be in writing—not other communications referring to it. That the agreement be in writing, however, is only one requirement of section 1823(e). The written agreement must also meet the three other non-secrecy requirements. The bank executive does not state that the communication was signed by Heritage and the borrowers, approved by Heritage's Board of Directors, or continuously kept as an official Heritage record. Nor do the borrowers point to any other evidence supporting these additional statutory requirements. See Resolution Trust Corp. v. McCrory, 951 F.2d 68, 72 (5th Cir. 1992) (holding that a copy of an agreement executed by an insolvent bank found in the draft documents of the bank's attorney did not satisfy section 1823(e)'s requirements because it was not an official record of the failed bank); Twin Constr., Inc. v. Boca Raton, Inc., 925 F.2d 378, 383-84 (11th Cir. 1991) (holding that a written form, despite outlining the obligations of both parties and existing in the insolvent bank's records, did not meet section 1823(e)'s requirements because it had not been executed by the failed bank); FDIC v. Gardner, 606 F. Supp. 1484, 1488 (S.D. Miss. 1985) (finding that a written agreement executed by a failed bank president could not be enforced against the FDIC because it was not specifically approved by the board).

To complete the picture, we note that the United States has a quite different system of bank ownership from most countries. A U.S. bank is generally owned by a "bank holding company" ("BHC"). There are several reasons for that. One important one is that the structure permits the BHC to engage in nonbanking businesses that a bank is forbidden by regulation to enter. The feds have struggled for many years to be sure that the BHC is a good parent, responsible for its bank subsidiary, while the BHCs have striven to stay a step away. One consequence is that the FDIC may be doing an assumption and sale, as in *C&C*, while another federal regulator is suing the BHC trying to hold it responsible for the bank's liabilities. Section 365(o) applies to such guarantees to make them survive bankruptcy (deemed assumption), which indirectly demonstrates another point: a BHC may file under chapter 11. It can do this because, obviously, it is not a bank. And so begins *The Dance of the Regulatory Flight*: Congress excludes banks from the Code, sending them off to the FDIC; the banks respond by having BHCs, which can file for bankruptcy. Then Congress counters by enacting § 365(o). And so on. The degree to which a BHC can succeed in distancing itself from its bank can leave bank regulators frustrated. Nonetheless, the FDIC resolution system worked for most failed banks throughout the Great Recession, the crisis of 2008-2010. Yet the crisis also revealed some serious gaps in the resolution regime. We discuss below two of the most significant problems: "nonbank" banks and the so-called "SIFIs."

2. *Nonbanks*

This awkward term is used to describe financial institutions that perform many of the functions of banks but are importantly different. They are not "banks" primarily because they do not take insured deposits. They are like banks because they present many of the same risks to the financial system that arise from their failure, yet they are much more lightly regulated. If they fail, their place in the financial system can cause losses throughout the banking system. Because they are similar to banks, the Code is not well devised to deal with their financial distress, even though they are technically eligible to file chapter 11. Among other things, both BHCs and nonbanks are often parties to derivative contracts (discussed in Assignment 17). Those contracts are exempt from the Code, which means often the most important bankruptcy tools, like the automatic stay, are unavailable to a BHC in bankruptcy, which reduces the Code's attraction.

Light regulation tends to attract capital to nonbanks due to greater flexibility and lower costs. Yet the very risks that justify imposing regulations on banks make it dangerous to leave nonbanks too unregulated. In effect, the benefits of limited regulation, which often enable nonbanks to pay higher interest rates to customers, arise from the externalities they impose on the financial system when they fail, up to and including the possibility of government bailouts.

The common and simplest example of a nonbank is a money-market fund. Its customers (sometimes mutual fund or other brokerage customers looking to park cash in a high-yielding account) "invest" their money in the fund and are promised their money whenever they want it, plus a good rate of interest in the meantime. Thus, they look much like a bank and the financial chaos that might result from their failure is much the same as well. During the Great Recession, customers were reminded that these bank-like accounts are not, in fact, bank accounts with FDIC insurance. There was one very serious run on such a fund. More were probably prevented by the emergency decree of a government guarantee for customers, much like the FDIC guarantee, which some might say is the worst of both worlds: moral hazard without prudential regulation.

3. Systematically Important Financial Institutions (SIFIs)

SIFIs used to be called "Too Big to Fail." (You should see the eponymous HBO movie *Too Big to Fail* (HBO Studios 2011).) These banks (and some nonbanks) that present widespread risk are now termed "SIFIs," Systemically Important Financial Institutions. The Dodd-Frank Wall Street Reform and Consumer Protection Act, Pub. L. No. 111-103, 124 Stat. 1376 (2010) ("Dodd-Frank"), a huge piece of legislation enacted in response to the financial disasters of 2007-2009, imposes the new moniker and special rules that cover these banks and nonbanks alike.

SIFIs of both varieties present special problems for at least two reasons. First, they're huge. In case of financial distress, finding another bank to buy one of them (and assume its obligations) would be difficult. Plus, such a sale would make highly concentrated markets even more highly concentrated. Thus, the standard FDIC strategy—take over a bank, strip the bad loans, and quickly sell it to another bank—is probably not workable for SIFIs. The second and equally serious problem is that these banks are international, so extraordinary cooperation would be required among sovereign governments to assure a soft landing after default. The term "SIFI" highlights the degree to which the affairs of a bank are intertwined with those of other institutions and the financial system in general, so that failure of even one SIFI to meet its obligations might threaten a wholesale crippling of that system. Of course, the bank's size affects the likelihood of such systematic importance. In fact, many if not most U.S. SIFIs are G-SIFIs, where the "G" stands for global and rhymes with "T": a G-SIFI's failure is real Trouble, because its failure threatens the world economy. United States institutions that were included in the first official list of 29 G-SIFIs were Bank of America, Bank of New York Mellon, Citigroup, Goldman Sachs, JPMorgan Chase, Morgan Stanley, State Street, and Wells Fargo. A generation ago there were no banks in the United States of this size.

Dodd-Frank strives to prevent a recurrence of 2008, when multiple Too Big to Fail financial institutions actually failed, a "black swan" occurrence of such rarity it sent the markets into panic for fear that the interrelationship of the financial sector would cause other SIFIs to fail, too. This put pressure on the government to bail these organizations out with financial assistance. It did so, but that in turn raised concerns of moral hazard—that these institutions had become too inter-related and risktaking, knowing that the government would always stand behind them should things go bad. For a discussion about SIFIs, public debt, and the interaction between them, see Symposium, The Nation State and Its Banks: Sovereign Debt and International Regulation, 49 Tex. Int'l L.J. 145 (2014). Dodd-Frank attempts to put the costs of financial failure on bank creditors, including bondholders and other financial institutions owed money by a bank at the time of its failure, underscoring the contagion risk. See Thomas H. Jackson & David A. Skeel, Jr., Dynamic Resolution of Large Financial Institutions, 2 Harv. Bus. L. Rev. 435 (2012). The hope is to reduce the fears of depositors and the losses to taxpayers. The SIFIs have filed the "living wills" required by Dodd-Frank. These documents are supposed to show how the SIFI could be resolved under various circumstances of financial crisis and are conceived as blueprints for the reorganization or sale of the SIFI should it become distressed. The fact that major institutions, such as MetLife, litigate voraciously against their designation as SIFIs suggests that the regulation has some real bite.

B. REORGANIZING PUBLIC DEBT OUTSIDE CHAPTER 11

Debts owed by governments or quasi-governmental agencies are fundamentally different from private sector debts in a host of ways. Among other things, they are often difficult or impossible to collect by traditional legal tools because public entities—from cities to countries—often enjoy sovereign immunity. Thus, a sovereign frequently may not be sued, much less suffer seizure of property, unless it consents.

One policy behind these traditional rules is that the entities involved in most cases perform vital public services and their assets are ultimately owned by the people. The implications of permitting ordinary collection devices are problematic. ("Sorry, Colonel, I'm here to repo that missile defense system.") The source of repayment of public debt in many instances is a levying of taxes, or the diversion of revenue from schools, roads, pensioners, or other public purposes, and promises; allowing private creditors power to force these public decisions raises difficult questions. Then again, many public entities issue bonds on the public markets and, to entice investors, waive sovereign immunity or even pledge tax increases to secure their obligations.

1. Public Debt Within the United States: Chapter 9

The federal government always has the power not to default on its debt by printing money; not so for states. State government default is rare (but not unprecedented); only one American state has defaulted since the Civil War era. See David A. Skeel, Jr., States of Bankruptcy, 79 U. Chi. L. Rev. 677, 678 (2012). Indeed, 49 of 50 states have constitutional or statutory provisions that require a balanced budget each year. Nat'l Conference of State Legislatures, NCSL Fiscal Brief: State Balanced Budget Provisions (2010). Even if that were not the case, "state bankruptcy" would be an unlikely addition to the Code. There has been a complete lack of political interest in a federal bailout of a state, despite the great difficulties in California and other states during the Great Recession, although the COVID-19 pandemic is triggering some rumblings. More importantly, the Tenth and Eleventh Amendments make any legal control of state finance awkward at best.

Local government entities within a state, however, can and do go broke all the time. Decades ago during the Great Depression, when many municipalities defaulted on their bonds and other debt, Congress enacted a special provision for such public debtors in what has developed into chapter 9. Only a few pages long, chapter 9 is a modified chapter 11 for local entities that cannot pay their debts. (Chapter 7 provides no help, because cities generally cannot be liquidated, which is also why there are no involuntary petitions.)

Discussion of chapter 9 must start with the fact that every city, water district, and other local entity is a creature of the state where it is located. (For ease, we'll call them "cities.") Chapter 9 recognizes a state's sovereignty over the internal affairs of its own political entities by setting certain eligibility criteria for a city even to file a petition, the most important of which is that the relevant state must consent to a city's use of chapter 9. § 109(c)(2). Some states deny their cities access to chapter 9, while some other states' statutes are vague. See, e.g., Ga. Code § 36-80-5 (explicitly denying access to chapter 9); Cal. Gov't Code § 53760 (authorizing access to chapter 9 if one of two conditions exists). A state's reason for not allowing free access to chapter 9 might be to ensure that a federal bankruptcy court proceeding is truly a "last resort" when creditor negotiations stall and state-initiated actions fail. *Cf.* § 109(c)(5).

If a city is eligible to file, chapter 9 provides many, but not all, of the tools available in chapter 11. You should look at § 901 to see which provisions are imported. For example, the city can bring its creditors to the table by imposition of the automatic stay. § 901(a) (applying § 362 to chapter 9). The most important tool chapter 9 offers is to allow a vote on a plan of adjustment, which if approved by the court can be binding on all parties, just like a chapter 11 plan. § 944. That said, the court's power is limited:

> The bankruptcy court in a Chapter 9 case does not have as much power to influence a debtor's conduct as it has in a Chapter 11 case. Moreover, the bankruptcy court is not permitted to "interfere with . . . any of the political . . . powers of the debtor; . . . any of the property or revenues of the debtor; or . . . the debtor's use or enjoyment of any income-producing property." 11 U.S.C. § 904(1)-(3). These provisions recognize the separation of powers in the United States' federal system and express deference to the political power of a state as delegated to its municipalities, including a city's judgment about what is a fair plan of debt adjustment.

Zack A. Clement & R. Andrew Black, How City Finances Can Be Restructured: Bankruptcy Debt Discharge and Contract Impairment Cases Follow a Similar Approach, 88 Am. Bankr. L.J. 41, 47 (2014).

Possibly the biggest difference between chapters 9 and 11 is that there is no liquidation alternative to failure to confirm a plan in chapter 9. If the creditors cannot agree, then the case ends and they go back to the asset race at state law. Thus, chapter 9 is essentially a court-supervised negotiation process for an "unliquidatable" debtor, with few rules or even precedents spelled out. For this reason, as an opening salvo, many creditors who would prefer to grab assets, fight a city's petition on the grounds that it is ineligible to access chapter 9 under the five components of § 109(c), and the court must rule on this threshold matter before the case can even get off the ground.

> The eligibility test for chapter 9 has five components. First, the chapter 9 debtor must actually be a municipality. Second, applicable state law must authorize the municipality to file for chapter 9 bankruptcy. Third, the municipality must be insolvent. The fourth and rather subjective requirement is that the municipality "desires to affect a plan to adjust such debts"; no specific metric measures this prong's satisfaction. Fifth, the municipality must meet one of four alternative tests relating to good faith pre-filing negotiations.

Melissa B. Jacoby, The Detroit Bankruptcy, Pre-Eligibility, 41 Fordham Urb. L.J. 849, 852 (2014).

In the next case, the objectors threw in an additional eligibility challenge: that the debtor was barred by the state constitution (via its application in chapter 9 through the Tenth Amendment). That law provided: "The accrued financial benefits of each pension plan and retirement system of the state and its political subdivisions shall be a contractual obligation thereof which shall not be diminished or impaired thereby." Mich. Const. art. IX, § 24. A chapter 9 plan that might seek to reduce those benefits and impose those reductions on out-voted pensioners was argued to be illegal, especially in a special chapter of the Code that's supposed to be sensitive to state sovereignty.

In re CITY OF DETROIT, MICHIGAN
504 B.R. 97 (Bankr. E.D. Mich. 2013)

RHODES, Bankruptcy Judge.

. . . The City of Detroit was once a hardworking, diverse, vital city, the home of the automobile industry, proud of its nickname—the "Motor City." It was rightfully known as the birthplace of the American automobile industry. In 1952, at the height of its prosperity and prestige, it had a population of approximately 1,850,000 residents. In 1950, Detroit was building half of the world's cars. The evidence before the Court establishes that for decades, however, the City of Detroit has experienced dwindling population, employment, and revenues. This has led to decaying infrastructure, excessive borrowing, mounting crime rates, spreading blight, and a deteriorating quality of life. The City no longer has the resources to provide its residents with the basic police, fire and emergency medical services that its residents need for their basic health and safety. Moreover, the City's governmental operations are wasteful and inefficient. Its equipment, especially its streetlights and its technology, and much of its fire and police equipment, is obsolete. To reverse this decline in basic services, to attract new residents and businesses, and to revitalize and reinvigorate itself, the City needs help. . . .

Although variously cast, the primary thrust of these [constitutional] arguments is that if chapter 9 permits the State of Michigan to authorize a city to file a petition for chapter 9 relief without explicitly providing for the protection of accrued pension benefits, the Tenth Amendment is violated. The Court concludes that these arguments must be rejected. . . . The basis for this result begins with the recognition that the State of Michigan cannot legally provide for the adjustment of the pension debts of the City of Detroit. This is a direct result of the prohibition against the State of Michigan impairing contracts in both the United States Constitution and Michigan Constitution, as well as the prohibition against impairing the contractual obligations relating to accrued pension benefits in the Michigan Constitution. The federal bankruptcy court, however, is not so constrained. . . .

"The Bankruptcy Clause necessarily authorizes Congress to make laws that would impair contracts. It long has been understood that bankruptcy law entails impairment of contracts." [In re City of Stockton, 478 B.R. 8, 15 (Bankr. E.D. Cal. 2012)] (citing Sturges v. Crowninshield, 17 U.S. 122, 191, 4 Wheat. 122, 4 L. Ed. 529 (1819)). The state constitutional provisions prohibiting the impairment of contracts and pensions impose no constraint on the bankruptcy process. The Bankruptcy Clause of the United States Constitution, and the bankruptcy code enacted pursuant thereto, explicitly empower the bankruptcy court to impair contracts and to impair contractual rights relating to accrued vested pension benefits. Impairing contracts is what the bankruptcy process does. . . . For Tenth Amendment and state sovereignty purposes, nothing distinguishes pension debt in a municipal bankruptcy case from any other debt. If the Tenth Amendment prohibits the impairment of pension benefits in this case, then it would also prohibit the adjustment of any other debt in this case. . . .

The [objecting Pension] Plans seek escape from this result by asserting that under the Michigan Constitution, pension debt has greater protection than ordinary contract debt. The argument is premised on the slim reed that in the Michigan Constitution, pension rights may not be "impaired or diminished," whereas only laws "impairing" contract rights are prohibited [under the Contracts Clause]. There are several reasons why the slight difference between the language that protects contracts (no "impairment") and the language that protects pensions (no "impairment" or "diminishment") does not demonstrate that pensions were given any extraordinary protection. . . .

It was within [the pre-existing] framework of rights, expectations, scenarios and possibilities that the newly negotiated, proposed and ratified Michigan Constitution of 1963 explicitly gave accrued pension benefits the status of contractual obligations. That new constitution could have given pensions protection from impairment in bankruptcy in several ways. It could have simply prohibited Michigan municipalities from filing bankruptcy. It could have somehow created a property interest that bankruptcy would be required to respect under Butner v. United States, 440 U.S. 48 (1979) (holding that property issues in bankruptcy are determined according to state law). Or, it could have established some sort of a secured interest in the municipality's property. It could even have explicitly required the State to guaranty pension benefits. But it did none of those.

Nevertheless, the Court is compelled to comment. No one should interpret this holding that pension rights are subject to impairment in this bankruptcy case to mean that the Court will necessarily confirm any plan of adjustment that impairs pensions. The Court emphasizes that it will not lightly or casually exercise the power under federal bankruptcy law to impair pensions. Before the Court confirms any plan that the City submits, the Court must find that the plan fully meets the requirements of 11 U.S.C. § 943(b) and the other applicable provisions of the bankruptcy code. . . .

[The court then worked through the § 109(c) eligibility requirements and found each to be present. For example, regarding the insolvency prong of § 101(32)(C), the court found that after "deferring" tens of millions of required payments and borrowing even more money to try to fund essential services, Detroit was broke. In fact, "[a]s of May 2013, the City stopped paying its trade creditors to avoid running out of cash. But for these and other deferments, the City would have completely run out of cash by the end of 2013." But it went on to find insolvency under an alternative, broader test, pursuant to the next paragraph.—Eds.]

Most powerfully, however, the testimony of Chief Craig established that the City was in a state of "service delivery insolvency" as of July 18, 2013, and will continue to be for the foreseeable future. He testified that the conditions in the local precincts were "deplorable." "If I just might summarize it in a very short way, that everything is broken, deplorable conditions, crime is extremely high, morale is low, the absence of leadership." He described the City as "extremely violent," based on the high rate of violent crime and the low rate of "clearance" of violent crimes. He stated that the officers' low morale is due, at least in part, to "the fact that they had lost ten percent pay; that they were forced into a 12-hour work schedule," and because there was an inadequate number of patrolling officers, and their facilities, equipment and vehicles were in various states of disrepair and obsolescence. In *Stockton*, the Court observed: "While cash insolvency . . . is the controlling chapter 9 criterion under § 101(32)(C), longer-term budget imbalances [budget insolvency] and the degree of inability to fund essential government services [service delivery insolvency] also inform the trier of fact's assessment of the relative degree and likely duration of cash insolvency." [493] B.R. at 789. Service delivery insolvency "focuses on the municipality's ability to pay for all costs of providing services at the level and quality that are required for the health, safety, and welfare of the community." Id. at 789. Indeed, while [other financial factors] might more neatly establish the City's "insolvency" under 11 U.S.C. § 101(32)(C), it is the City's service delivery insolvency that the Court finds most strikingly disturbing in this case. . . .

After this decision, the real negotiations began, a combination of the legal and the political unique to chapter 9. Given the state of the finances of a number of American cities, chapter 9 may be an increasingly important area of practice in the future.

2. *Public Debt Beyond the United States: The Debt of Nations*

Because there is no bankruptcy system that covers the public debts owed by nations (although some have been proposed), a sovereign default is generally followed by a complex series of high-level negotiations involving the country in question, the IMF (the ultimate banker), and various groups of creditors. (The most exclusive creditor group is the "Paris Club," which consists of the other countries to which the defaulting sovereign owes money.) Frequently, the IMF imposes certain conditions, for example, to raise taxes or lower expenditures, to access funds. These negotiations are often effective because of the sovereign immunity impediments to the traditional levying process discussed above.

Sovereign immunity is not absolute. The U.S. government has consented to be sued in various ways and it has limited the sovereign immunity accorded foreign sovereigns in U.S. courts by adoption of the Foreign Sovereign Immunities Act (FSIA), 28 U.S.C. § 1602 et seq. FSIA starts with a presumption of immunity and then provides exceptions for certain kinds of suits. For business purposes, the most important instance in which suit is permitted is for debts arising from the commercial activities in the United States or having a "direct effect" in the United States. The Supreme Court has interpreted that exception fairly broadly in commercial cases, although rather more narrowly in tort cases. In Republic of Argentina v. Weltover, Inc., 504 U.S. 607 (1992), the Court held that bonds issued by Argentina in New York and payable there had a direct effect in the United States and thus Argentina could be sued in U.S. courts for collection of those bonds. Liability, however, is only half the battle. Sovereign immunity has been left more in place when it comes to collections. The other country's military is generally off limits, as are its embassies and similar governmental units. But some property can be seized. In Republic of Austria v. Altmann, 541 U.S. 677 (2004), the Court held that works of art on exhibit in the United States but belonging to the Austrian government could be seized and returned to the families from whom they were stolen by the Nazis.

The problem is, stray works of art aside, foreign governments tend to have most of their assets at home, and so a judgment would have to be recognized by the defaulting sovereign's courts to provide the basis of any meaningful recovery. That is sometimes, shall we say, "challenging." So lawyers keep trying to use their creativity.

NML CAPITAL, LTD. v. REPUBLIC OF ARGENTINA

699 F.3d 246 (2d Cir. 2012)

PARKER, Circuit Judge.

The Republic of Argentina appeals from permanent injunctions entered by the United States District Court for the Southern District of New York (Griesa, J.) designed to remedy Argentina's failure to pay bondholders after a default in 2001 on its sovereign debt. The district court granted plaintiffs summary judgment and enjoined Argentina from making payments on debt issued pursuant to its 2005 and 2010 restructurings without making comparable payments on the defaulted debt. We hold that an equal treatment provision in the bonds bars Argentina from discriminating against plaintiffs' bonds in favor of bonds issued in connection with the restructurings and that Argentina violated that provision by ranking its payment obligations on the defaulted debt below its obligations to the holders of its restructured debt. Accordingly, we affirm the judgment of the district court; we find no abuse of discretion in the injunctive relief fashioned by the district court, and we conclude that the injunctions do not violate the Foreign Sovereign Immunities Act ("FSIA"). . . .

BACKGROUND

In 1994, Argentina began issuing debt securities pursuant to a Fiscal Agency Agreement ("FAA Bonds"). A number of individual plaintiffs-appellees bought FAA Bonds starting around December 1998. The remaining plaintiffs-appellees, hedge funds and other distressed asset investors, purchased FAA Bonds on the secondary market at various times and as recently as June 2010. The coupon rates on the FAA Bonds ranged from 9.75% to 15.5%, and the dates of maturity ranged from April 2005 to September 2031.

The FAA contains provisions purporting to protect purchasers of the FAA Bonds from subordination. The key provision, Paragraph 1(c) of the FAA, which we refer to as the "*Pari Passu* Clause," provides that:

> [t]he Securities will constitute . . . direct, unconditional, unsecured and unsubordinated obligations of the Republic and shall at all times rank *pari passu* without any preference among themselves. *The payment obligations of the Republic under the Securities shall at all times rank at least equally with all its other present and future unsecured and unsubordinated External Indebtedness.* . . .

"External Indebtedness" is limited to obligations payable in non-Argentine currency.[2] We refer to the second sentence of the *Pari Passu* Clause as the "Equal Treatment Provision." Following the 2001 default on the FAA Bonds, Argentina offered holders of the FAA Bonds new exchange

---

[2] The practical significance of an equal ranking obligation is readily apparent in the event of the bankruptcy or insolvency of a corporate debtor. Lee C. Buchheit & Jeremiah S. Pam, The Pari Passu Clause in Sovereign Debt Instruments, 53 Emory L.J. 869, 873 (2004). In a corporate bankruptcy, holders of senior obligations have a priority claim over the debtor's assets. Id. In the case of sovereign borrowers, however, the impact of the clause is less clear because creditors cannot force them into bankruptcy-like proceedings, and no comparable asset distribution plan applies. Thus, in the event of a debt crisis, sovereigns wishing to honor some portion of their defaulted debt must negotiate with individual creditors or groups of creditors to effectuate restructurings. Typically, these proceedings leave in their wake so-called "holdout" creditors who refuse to restructure, opting instead to seek judgments against the sovereign. See generally William W. Bratton, Pari Passu and a Distressed Sovereign's Rational Choices, 53 Emory L.J. 823, 828-33 (2004).

bonds in 2005 and 2010 (the "Exchange Bonds"). Argentina continued to make payments to holders of those Exchange Bonds while failing to make any payments to persons who still held the defaulted FAA Bonds.

After Argentina defaulted, its President in December 2001 declared a "temporary moratorium" on principal and interest payments on more than $80 billion of its public external debt including the FAA Bonds. Each year since then, Argentina has passed legislation renewing the moratorium and has made no principal or interest payments on the defaulted debt. Plaintiffs estimate that, collectively, their unpaid principal and prejudgment interest amounts to approximately $1.33 billion. . . .

In 2005, Argentina initiated an exchange offer in which it allowed FAA bondholders to exchange their defaulted bonds for new unsecured and unsubordinated external debt at a rate of 25 to 29 cents on the dollar. In exchange for the new debt, participants agreed to forgo various rights and remedies previously available under the FAA. To induce creditors to accept the exchange offer, Argentina stated in the prospectus under "Risks of Not Participating in [the] Exchange Offer" the following:

> *Existing defaulted bonds eligible for exchange that are not tendered may remain in default indefinitely.* As of June 30, 2004, Argentina was in default on approximately U.S. $102.6 billion of its public indebtedness. . . . *The Government has announced that it has no intention of resuming payment on any bonds eligible to participate in [the] exchange offer . . . that are not tendered or otherwise restructured as part of such transaction.* Consequently, if you elect not to tender your bonds in an exchange offer there can be no assurance that you will receive any future payments in respect of your bonds.

2005 Prospectus, J.A. at 465 (second emphasis added). . . .

The 2005 exchange offer closed in June 2005 with a 76% participation rate, representing a par value of $62.3 billion. Plaintiffs did not participate. [A subsequent offering got the acceptance rate to 91%.—Eds.]

An important new feature of the Exchange Bonds was that they included "collective action" clauses. These clauses permit Argentina to amend the terms of the bonds and to bind dissenting bondholders if a sufficient number of bondholders (66 2/3% to 75% of the aggregate principal amount of a given series) agree. With the inclusion of collective action clauses, the type of "holdout" litigation at issue here is not likely to reoccur.

Argentina has made all payments due on the debt it restructured in 2005 and 2010 [and none of the unexchanged FAA debt]. . . . Plaintiffs sued Argentina on the defaulted FAA Bonds at various points from 2009 to 2011, alleging breach of contract and seeking injunctive relief, including specific performance of the Equal Treatment Provision. The FAA is governed by New York law and further provides for jurisdiction in "any state or federal court in The City of New York." . . . In February 2012, the district court granted injunctive relief, ordering Argentina to specifically perform its obligations under the Equal Treatment Provision (the "Injunctions"). The Injunctions provide that "whenever the Republic pays any amount due under the terms of the [exchange] bonds," it must "concurrently or in advance" pay plaintiffs the same fraction of the amount due to them (the "Ratable Payment").

I.

We first address Argentina's argument that the district court erred in its interpretation of the Equal Treatment Provision. . . . Argentina argues that the *Pari Passu* Clause is a boilerplate provision that, in the sovereign context, "has been universally understood for over 50 years . . . to provide protection from *legal subordination* or other discriminatory *legal ranking* by preventing the creation of *legal priorities* by the sovereign in favor of creditors holding particular classes of debt."

We are unpersuaded that the clause has this well settled meaning. Argentina's selective recitation of context-specific quotations from arguably biased commentators and institutions notwithstanding, the preferred construction of *pari passu* clauses in the sovereign debt context is far from "general, uniform and unvarying," Law Debenture Trust Co. of N.Y. v. Maverick Tube Corp., 595 F.3d 458, 466 (2d Cir. 2010). Argentina's primary authorities and Argentina itself appear to concede as much. See Appellant's Reply Br. 21 n.9 ("*[N]o one knows* what the clause really means" (emphasis in Appellant's Reply Br.)); . . . Philip R. Wood, *Project Finance, Subordinated Debt and State Loans* 165 (1995) ("In the state context, the meaning of the clause is uncertain because there is no hierarchy of payments which is legally enforced under a bankruptcy regime."). In short, the record reveals that Argentina's interpretation of the *Pari Passu* Clause is neither well settled nor uniformly acted upon.

Once we dispense with Argentina's customary usage argument, it becomes clear that the real dispute is over what constitutes subordination under the *Pari Passu* Clause. Argentina contends the clause refers only to legal subordination and that none occurred here because "any claims that may arise from the Republic's restructured debt have no priority in any court of law over claims arising out of the Republic's unrestructured debt." Plaintiffs, on the other hand, argue that there was "de facto" subordination because Argentina reduced the rank of plaintiffs' bonds to a permanent non-performing status by passing legislation barring payments on them while continuing to pay on the restructured debt and by repeatedly asserting that it has no intention of making payments on plaintiffs' bonds.

We disagree with Argentina because its interpretation fails to give effect to the differences between the two sentences of the *Pari Passu* Clause. . . . Instead, we conclude that in pairing the two sentences of its *Pari Passu* Clause, the FAA manifested an intention to protect bondholders from more than just formal subordination. See Riverside S. Planning Corp. v. CRP/Extell Riverside, L.P., 13 N.Y.3d 398, 404, 892 N.Y.S.2d 303, 920 N.E.2d 359 (2009). The first sentence ("[t]he Securities will constitute . . . direct, unconditional, unsecured, and unsubordinated obligations. . . .") prohibits Argentina, as bond *issuer*, from formally subordinating the bonds by issuing superior debt. The second sentence ("[t]he payment obligations . . . shall at all times rank at least equally with all its other present and future unsecured and unsubordinated External Indebtedness.") prohibits Argentina, as bond *payor*, from paying on other bonds without paying on the FAA Bonds. Thus, the two sentences of the *Pari Passu*

Clause protect against different forms of discrimination: the issuance of other superior debt (first sentence) and the giving of priority to other payment obligations (second sentence). . . .

. . . [I]t is clear to us that monetary damages are an ineffective remedy for the harm plaintiffs have suffered as a result of Argentina's breach. Argentina will simply refuse to pay any judgments. It has done so in this case by, in effect, closing the doors of its courts to judgment creditors. In light of Argentina's continual disregard for the rights of its FAA creditors and the judgments of our courts to whose jurisdiction it has submitted, its contention that bondholders are limited to acceleration is unpersuasive. . . .

Next, we conclude that because compliance with the Injunctions would not deprive Argentina of control over any of its property, they do not operate as attachments of foreign property prohibited by the FSIA. Section 1609 of the FSIA establishes that "the property in the United States of a foreign state shall be immune from attachment arrest and execution." 28 U.S.C. § 1609. . . . The Injunctions at issue here are not barred by § 1609. They do not attach, arrest, or execute upon any property. They direct Argentina to comply with its contractual obligations not to alter the rank of its payment obligations. They affect Argentina's property only incidentally to the extent that the order prohibits Argentina from transferring money to some bondholders and not others. . . .

Nor will the district[] court's judgment have the practical effect of enabling "a single creditor to thwart the implementation of an internationally supported restructuring plan," as the United States contends. It is up to the sovereign—not any "single creditor"—whether it will repudiate that creditor's debt in a manner that violates a *pari passu* clause. . . . In any event, it is highly unlikely that in the future sovereigns will find themselves in Argentina's predicament. Collective action clauses—which effectively eliminate the possibility of "holdout" litigation—have been included in 99% of the aggregate value of New York-law bonds issued since January 2005, including Argentina's 2005 and 2010 Exchange Bonds. Only 5 of 211 issuances under New York law during that period did not include collective action clauses, and all of those issuances came from a single nation, Jamaica. Moreover, none of the bonds issued by Greece, Portugal, or Spain— nations identified by Argentina as the next in line for restructuring— are governed by New York law.

The court in *NML* conceded that the plaintiffs were holdouts in a restructuring that attracted the approval of 91% of the creditors (although of course some of those may have simply been resigned), but then decided that it was not the conduct of the holdouts that was blocking the workout, but the conduct of the *debtor*—in not succumbing to the holdout's demands—that was the problem. Isn't that blaming the victim? Bondholders and others will surely be emboldened after this decision to stand their ground and hold out rather than settle with sovereign debtors by accepting a haircut once they hear about this case. Yet the court doubts this worry, suggesting sovereign debt holdout has been cured by collective action clauses, which contractually create a majoritarian-vote rule similar to chapter 11. Do they solve the problem? Among other problems, collective action clauses may only apply to the bonds within a specific issuance. Sovereigns (like most corporations) regularly sell a number of different issues of bonds, so that majority acceptance by one set of bondholders may not bind another. And with maturity terms spanning decades there are still plenty of non-CAC sovereign bonds out there. Some argue that we really need a collective proceeding—not just a clause—to bind creditors legally and therefore solve the holdout problem in sovereign defaults. International Monetary Fund, Proposed Features of a Sovereign Debt Restructuring Mechanism, SM/03/67 (Feb. 13, 2003). Those proposals have been too politically sensitive to take root, but in Europe, where Greece's default sent ripples around the continent, sentiment may be changing. See Christoph G. Paulus, Should Politics Be Replaced by a Legal Proceeding?, in A Debt Restructuring Mechanism for Sovereigns (Christoph G. Paulus ed., Hart Publ'n, 2014).

C.   RECONCILING OTHER FEDERAL REGIMES WITHIN CHAPTER 11

Just as the Code is blocked from providing relief for certain types of debtors, so too do other fields of federal law have to yield to chapter 11 and its policies. We saw this a bit with "special claimants" holding tort and environmental claims against the debtor in the previous assignment. But those are infrequent cases. Other cases in chapter 11 raise more recurrent issues that affect other federal regulatory regimes. For example, you have seen how the IRS has to take the priority offered it under § 507 and forgo its standard collection tools. Securities regulation raises overlap problems too, when the SEC wants to prioritize reimbursement for defrauded investors, but the Code favors creditors over equity. See Official Comm. of Unsecured Creditors of WorldCom, Inc. v. S.E.C., 467 F.3d 73, 85 (2d Cir. 2006) (Sotomayor, J.) (holding SEC did not need to follow bankruptcy priority rules when distributing recovered funds from bankrupt debtor with defrauded equity holders). The same issues arise with energy regulation, where federal regulators' approval power may take a back seat to the bankruptcy court's authority to allow rejection of pre-bankruptcy contracts. In re FirstEnergy Sols. Corp., 945 F.3d 431 (6th Cir. 2019).

For this discussion we examine labor law's encounter with chapter 11 as a specific case study. Labor negotiations are highly regulated under federal law. National Labor Relations Act of 1935, 49 Stat. 449, 29 U.S.C. § 151 et seq. Summarizing crudely in a way that would horrify our labor law colleagues, one rule of thumb is that collective bargaining agreements (CBAs) are ironclad ways to buy the peace: for the duration of a CBA's term, the workers agree not to strike and the management agrees not to impose changes in employment terms. But CBAs are, at root, just contracts. What happens when a debtor goes into bankruptcy? Can they be rejected if burdensome (as surely many bankrupt debtors will argue)? Recognizing the sensitive policy issues at play, the Code tries to cut a delicate balance by making labor law yield to chapter 11, but with "extra protections" for CBAs.

The Code does this through § 1113. Section 1113 governs the process of rejecting or modifying collective bargaining agreements in chapter 11. Congress enacted § 1113 in response to the Supreme Court's decision in NLRB v. Bildisco & Bildisco, 465 U.S. 513 (1986), in which the Court held that a debtor could unilaterally reject a CBA under § 365 without violating § 8(a) and § 8(d) of the National Labor Relations Act. Under pressure from labor unions to overturn *Bildisco*, Congress passed § 1113, which provides that "[n]o provision of this title shall be construed to permit a trustee to unilaterally terminate or alter any provisions of a collective bargaining agreement prior to compliance with the provisions of this section." § 1113(f). Subsections 1113(b) and 1113(c) contain procedural and substantive requirements that must be satisfied prior to rejection of a CBA, as a form of "labor law lite."

In re ALPHA NATURAL RESOURCES, INC.
552 B.R. 314 (Bankr. E.D. Va. 2016)

HUENNEKENS, Bankruptcy Judge.

. . .

This matter comes before the Court on the motion (the "Rejection Motion") of the Debtors for entry of an order authorizing the Debtors to i) reject certain collective bargaining agreements with the United Mine Workers of America (the "UMWA" or "Union") under § 1113 of the Bankruptcy Code and ii) modify certain retiree benefits under § 1114 including the elimination of the Debtors' liabilities under the Coal Industry Retiree Health Benefit Act of 1992 (the "Coal Act"). . . .

FACTUAL BACKGROUND

The Debtors, headquartered in Bristol, Virginia, are the largest domestic producers of coal by volume in the United States. The Debtors sell both metallurgic coal and steam coal to international and domestic consumers. At their height, the Debtors operated 145 mines and employed 14,500 individuals, generating $7 billion in revenue annually.

Beginning in 2010, the coal industry began to experience serious market challenges that ultimately affected every major operator in the coal industry. Both the price of and the demand for coal began to fall. That trend has continued to this day. Between 2011 and 2015, the price of metallurgic coal fell 72%. During the same period, the price of steam coal fell 44%. Factors leading to the decline of coal prices are lengthy. The genesis of the problem is simple: too much supply and too little demand.

. . .

Following the Petition Date, the price of coal continued to fall. . . . During the first two months of 2016, the Debtors incurred a net book loss of $126 million. The Debtors' present cash burn amounts to $10 million each week. The Debtors have sustained over $300 million in losses since the Petition Date. While many of the Debtors' non-union employees have suffered through these difficult times, the Debtors' union-ized workers have largely avoided this fate due to their collective bargain-ing agreements. . . .

The Debtors' Labor and Retiree Obligations

The collective bargaining agreements generally provide certain protec-tions and benefits in favor of the collective body of workers covered there-under. The terms and conditions of each collective bargaining agreement vary, but in many instances, the collective bargaining agreements result in higher labor costs for the Debtors compared to non-union workers. For example, the collective bargaining agreements restrict the Debtors' abil-ity to utilize subcontractors and to modify work schedules. The Debtors' average labor cost for an Active Union Employee is $92,442 as compared to $69,068 for a non-union employee.

The collective bargaining agreements require the Debtors to make payments to the four different UMWA Funds for the benefit of the Retired Union Employees. . . .

The Chapter 11 Case

. . .

The direction of the case switched course on February 8, 2016, when the Debtors filed a motion with the Court seeking authorization for a going-concern sale of substantially all of the Debtors' core, revenue gen-erating assets (the "Core Assets") under § 363 of the Bankruptcy Code. Included among the Core Assets were substantially all of the Debtors' coal mining related complexes throughout the United States. The Debtors' pre-petition lenders agreed to serve as a stalking horse for the sale of the Debtors' Core Assets (the "Stalking Horse Bidder"). The pre-petition lend-ers initially agreed to credit bid $500 million for the Debtors' Core Assets (the "Stalking Horse Bid"). The Debtors proposed to sell their Core Assets as a going concern, free and clear of liens, claims, and encumbrances as detailed in the asset purchase agreement executed by the Debtors and the Stalking Horse Bidder (the "APA"). [The prepetition lenders, as is common, became the DIP lenders. — Eds.]

The Stalking Horse Bidder has refused to assume any of the Debtors' liabilities and obligations under the Coal Act or to the UMWA Funds. The Stalking Horse Bidder will not close the sale unless it can receive the Core Assets free and clear of the Debtors' obligations under their collective bargaining agreements. The collective bargaining agreements that are subject to the Rejection Motion each contain a successorship clause that would bind a subsequent purchaser of the Debtors' business operations. The successorship provisions need to be either waived by the UMWA or rejected by the Debtors in order to consummate a sale to the Stalking Horse Bidder.

UMWA Negotiations

Leading up to and following the filing of the Rejection Motion, the Debtors and the UMWA attempted to negotiate modifications to the collective bargaining agreements that would prevent an outright rejection of the agreements by the Debtors. The Debtors and the UMWA met in person and over the telephone on a number of occasions from December 2015 through March 2016. Both sides exchanged proposals and information. As the Hearing Date approached, the UMWA initiated negotiations directly with the Stalking Horse Bidder. These discussions proved to be encouraging. . . .

§§ 1113 and 1114 Apply to the Debtors

Both Objectors argue that this Court cannot grant relief to the Debtors under §§ 1113 and 1114 of the Bankruptcy Code because the Debtors are liquidating and §§ 1113 and 1114 are only available to a debtor that is involved in a "reorganization."

Courts unanimously hold that relief under § 1113 is available to liquidating debtors in Chapter 11.

The Debtors Have Met the Substantive Requirements of §§ 1113 and 1114

While the Objectors' primary focus is that it is not "necessary" that the Debtors obtain the requested relief, see § 1113(b)(1)(A) (requiring that the debtors proposal be "necessary to permit the reorganization of the debtor); § 1114(g)(3) (conditioning any relief unless the court finds that the modification "is necessary to permit the reorganization of the debtor"). . . . [The court went through each of the other requirements of the two sections. — Eds.]

. . .

The Relief Is Necessary to Permit a Reorganization

. . .

The Court of Appeals of the Fourth Circuit has not adopted a definition for "necessary." The Court of Appeals for the Third Circuit, relying in large measure upon the legislative history behind § 1113, construed the term to mean modifications necessary to prevent the debtor's liquidation. The Court of Appeals for the Second Circuit found the Third Circuit's interpretation "troubling" and went on to "conclude that the necessity requirement places on the debtor the burden of proving that its proposal is made in good faith, and that it contains necessary, but not absolutely minimal, changes that will enable the debtor to complete the reorganization process successfully." Courts have found that the "necessary" standard has been satisfied when a debtor has proven that modification or rejection is necessary to achieve a sale under § 363 of the Bankruptcy Code. . . . [The court found that no going-concern sale was possible without elimination of the CBA. — Eds.]

Finally, the UMWA argues that it is unnecessary to eliminate the UMWA collective bargaining agreements because the UMWA operated mine complexes are cash flow positive. The Court is not persuaded. The Debtors business does not operate as a confederation of individual mines—the Debtors operate as a single, fully integrated enterprise. No such mine-by-mine analysis is appropriate.

. . .

The Court finds that the Debtors have met their burden to prove that the rejection of the collective bargaining agreements and the modification of their retiree benefits are necessary under both the Second Circuit and the Third Circuit tests. The Court finds that the relief requested in the Rejection Motion is necessary for the Debtors to have any hope for effectuating a reorganization in this case.

. . .

The threat of liquidation and loss of every union and non-union job permeates the Court's concern in this case, and overrides the other equitable considerations. Without a rejection of the collective bargaining agreements, the sale to the Stalking Horse Bidder will not close. There has been no indication that any other party is willing to step forward and assume the collective bargaining agreements. The Debtors desperately need to bring their cash bleed under control if they have any hope of avoiding liquidation. No party has suggested how the Debtors might replace the $60 million in expected savings from the Rejection Motion with savings from some other source. The Court finds that the balance of equities weighs in favor of the Debtors.

———————————

Just as § 1113 sets hurdles a company must clear before rejecting a CBA, § 1114 sets up similar (but not identical) hurdles before a company can modify retiree benefits. In another part of the opinion, the court in *Alpha Resources* confirmed that § 1114 can encompass retiree benefits created by statute even if that statute bars modification of the benefits arising under it. Of course, neither of these provisions can give employees rights they don't have. For example, if the CBA has expired on its own terms, §§ 1113-1114 do not confer additional rights that debtors must overcome through procedural and substantive requirements. That said, the debtor-employer should be careful what it wishes for. One consequence of a CBA being rejected in chapter 11 before it would have run its natural course is that the workers are freed from their obligation not to strike. On the other hand, if the court in that case is right that everyone's job would be lost absent rejection of the CBA, why is the union fighting to maintain it?

If the debtor succeeds in rejecting the CBA, then what? Following § 1113's adoption, courts have been divided over whether a claim for damages is even permitted after successfully rejecting a CBA. Compare In re Moline Corp., 144 Bankr. 75 (Bankr. N.D. Ill. 1992) (reasoning § 1113's silence on consequence of assumption or rejection of CBA means "§ 365 must apply to fill in the gap"), with In re Blue Diamond Coal Co., 147 B.R. 720 (Bankr. E.D. Tenn. 1992) (dismissing claim for damages upon successful termination of CBA under § 1113 because statute places CBAs in entirely different framework without apparent redress for rejection). And yet other courts have nailed debtors for abrogating a CBA without court authority under § 1113, saying not only is there a damages claim, but it has administrative priority. In re Unimet Corp., 842 F.2d 879 (6th Cir. 1989).

Sections 1113 and 1114 have been at the forefront of debates over the role of unions in today's workplaces, especially financially struggling businesses. When Hostess Brands, beloved maker of the "food" called Twinkies and Wonder Bread, went bankrupt (again), management made it clear it was due to a standoff with its bakers' union. While the largest union, the Teamsters, agreed to concessions, the bakers held out. Management said that after having already tried reorganization once, if it could not come to a consensual labor agreement, it would not bother anymore and file bankruptcy to close down the company. Both sides dug in and the company shut its doors. Some decried the bankruptcy as the product of intransigent unions, who would rather see an 82-year-old company liquidate than make long-overdue concessions, but others saw it as the product of financial mismanagement and excessive executive compensation. An example of the former category of commentators was Fox Business News, who pointed to ossified, downright "ugly" union work rules as a source of the downfall and noted that management had the unenviable task of negotiating with 372 different collective bargaining units, 40 pension plans, and 80 health and benefits plans. See Elizabeth MacDonald, Wal-Mart and Hostess: Two Union Stories, FOXBusiness (Nov. 23, 2012), https://www.foxbusiness.com/features/wal-mart-and-hostess-two-union-stories (noting that "[u]nion rules said no Hostess delivery trucks could have both bread and snacks on board, despite the fact the goods were going to the same stores" and that "[d]rivers were not allowed to load the snacks onto their trucks," and "certain workers could only load snacks not bread, and vice versa").

Others were less willing to place all the blame for the company's downfall on the unions. The company had already experienced a 20% drop in sales. Given that, the bakers were not being irrational (just demoralized) as low-paying jobs were under pressure to go lower. Moreover, these concessions were being sought, in the views of critics, by at best tone-deaf or at worst cynical executives who were just trying to squeeze the last company dollars out for themselves. Indeed, before the company filed for bankruptcy, it tripled its CEO's pay and increased other executives' compensation by as much as 80%. When the closing was announced, the bakers' union was unapologetic:

> BCTGM members are well aware that as the company was preparing to file for bankruptcy earlier this year, the then CEO of Hostess was awarded a 300 percent raise (from approximately $750,000 to $2,550,000) and at least nine other top executives of the company received massive pay raises. One such executive received a pay increase from $500,000 to $900,000 and another received one taking his salary from $375,000 to $656,256.
>
> Certainly, the company agreed to an out-sized pension debt, but the decision to pay executives more while scorning employee contracts during a bankruptcy reflects a lack of good managerial judgment.

Annie-Rose Strasser, Hostess Blames Union for Bankruptcy After Tripling CEO's Pay, ThinkProgress (Nov. 16, 2012), https://archive .thinkprogress.org/hostess-blames-union-for-bankruptcy-after-tripling -ceos-pay-9d92a07738d/.

Although §§ 1113 and 1114 would have possibly allowed termination of the CBAs, the Hostess Brands management had had enough and didn't even want to try, preferring to sell the assets off to buyers (which it did—to buyers who declined to assume the union contracts). To describe §§ 1113 and 1114 as sensitive policy compromises is understatement.

A much more sweeping solution is to recognize that "you cannot effectively fix a non-bankruptcy problem with a bankruptcy-specific solution." Daniel Keating, Ten Lessons for Congress to Ponder About the Labor/ Bankruptcy Intersection, 22 ABI L. Rev. 35, 38 (2014). But defining what is a "bankruptcy problem" and a "nonbankruptcy problem" may beg the question on these difficult issues at the boundary of chapter 11. As you think about them more in digesting these materials, also park them in the back of your head for when you get to Assignment 39.

Problem Set 36

36.1. You have a substantial practice representing SME (small and medium-sized enterprises) in chapter 11 cases, most often as debtor's counsel. Yesterday, Jim Norris walked into your office with a problem quite different from your usual case. He is head of the Ector County Water District. The county is rural but lies next to your rapidly growing city and is beginning to feel the effects of growth. Several years ago it signed a contract with a local aquaculture operation to provide water for its fish farming. Back then, the farm provided a healthy percentage of the jobs in the county (albeit low-paying) and the District was happy to oblige. The contract gave the farm first claim on the county's aquifer wells over all other users. It has another 20 years to run before it expires by its terms.

A huge new suburb is growing on the edge of the county, including a number of new homes and various businesses and light industries. Everyone is excited by this growth but worried about the availability of enough water to sustain it. The problem is worse because the farm is expanding rapidly, too, and demanding more and more water. "The major developers will not invest," Jim told you, "unless we can promise them access to the District's water." The farm's management hasn't so far been much interested in negotiating.

For the last three years the District has been buying water from neighboring districts and city utilities to serve both its old and new customers, but it loses money on each purchase and is running out of cash. The water pressure is falling in parts of the county and long-time customers are starting to complain. Is there a possible solution for the District under the Code? What is the first thing you must learn to answer that question? Assuming a favorable answer, what is the key set of gateway issues for the District and how would you argue for your desired resolution? See §§ 101(40), 365(a), 901.

36.2. Sandra Yao is general counsel to your client, San Diego A/C Suppliers. SD has supplied Renaud with special fittings required for air conditioners, sold in several sub-Saharan African countries. A dispute arose about the specifications required for recent shipments and the companies are at loggerheads. "They won't pay us and told us to just try to sue them," according to Sandra. Renaud is supposed to wire payments to the Third Bank of San Diego within forty days of each shipment, but now has skipped three payments because of the dispute.

Sandra has confirmed that the Ruritanian government is the largest single shareholder of Renaud and therefore the company might be able to claim sovereign immunity from suit as an "instrumentality" of the Ruritanian state. Sandra has also called around to friends and found that several other companies in California who are owed money by Renaud are being paid through prompt wires from Third; most of them also owe money to Renaud for various products they buy from Renaud. Assuming Renaud does enough business in California to be subject to personal jurisdiction under the usual rules, can you find a way to sue locally for the unpaid bills?

36.3. Wachovia Regional Airline filed chapter 11 in May of this year. This month it sought to reject its collective bargaining agreements with each of its employee unions, including the machinists, flight attendants, and pilots. It sent a proposal to each providing for a 30% reduction in pay and an end to the "working-conditions" seniority systems for each. (For example, the flight attendants' working-conditions seniority system permits a flight attendant to claim priority for more desirable flights or flight schedules based on seniority.) After negotiations, all the unions accepted the proposals except for the pay reduction and the termination of the seniority systems. At yesterday's hearing before the court, the debtor presented evidence that showed that the proposed changes would eliminate its losses and increase its profits going forward to $20,000,000 per year.

You represent the flight attendants union. Its President, Thor Quick, has told you that he can show that the pay reductions and the ending of seniority systems are unnecessary, because the other proposals for changes in the CBA are sufficient to yield a pretty sure profit of $10,000,000 per year based on historical performance. Thor told you that at the meeting the company's labor-relations guy, Norris LaGuardia, rejected the proposal, saying, "That is too little profit for our investors and we would have trouble raising capital for expansion." Thor says the real problem "is paying those fancy salaries for the directors and officers." What are your strongest arguments at today's continuation of the hearing and how do you anticipate debtor's counsel will respond? Thor is anxious to know the union's likelihood of success, so break it down for him. See § 1113(b)(1), (e).

DOMESTIC JURISDICTION

The byzantine jurisdictional rules of the bankruptcy court system are enough to make grown lawyers cry. The most important point to remember in learning them is that the term "jurisdiction" is used by many—such as the Supreme Court, and even us sometimes, to be honest—inaccurately to refer to two distinct doctrines: (1) real jurisdiction, i.e., the *subject matter jurisdiction* of the federal courts sitting in bankruptcy, and (2) what we will call for lack of a better name "allocation," i.e., the *allocation of judicial business* properly within the subject matter jurisdiction of the federal courts between federal district judges and federal bankruptcy judges. Many refer to the second topic as a question of jurisdiction, but you should resist this sloppiness. (Try correcting senior partners when they do this as you start in practice; they will love this and you will surely become popular in the office.) Real jurisdiction in bankruptcy is covered by 28 U.S.C. § 1334 (not the Code). Allocation is covered by § 157 of the same title, which bears the Delphic description "Procedures." This assignment will cover both subjects, as well as touching upon venue and alternative dispute resolution within bankruptcy.

A. BANKRUPTCY JURISDICTION OF THE FEDERAL COURTS

Before the Code, jurisdictional matters were chiefly governed by the 1898 Act. Its jurisdictional scheme harkened back to Georgian England, dividing bankruptcy matters into "summary" and "plenary" proceedings. To oversimplify, summary matters involved administering the bankruptcy estate itself and bringing actions against property in the debtor's actual or constructive possession. Summary matters were tried before inferior judicial officers in the federal courts, who over history have been called commissioners, registers, referees, and, eventually, bankruptcy judges. Plenary matters were everything else and were tried before regular state judges, or, if there was an independent jurisdictional basis (e.g., diversity of citizenship), federal district judges.

The summary-plenary division was complex and confusing, and the Act was maddeningly terse on the subject. For instance, a fraudulent conveyance action, if filed against a party who was a creditor in the bankruptcy, was designated summary and tried by a federal bankruptcy judge, but if filed against a third-party non-creditor was plenary and litigated in state court. (The theory was that by filing a claim, the creditor had consented to the bankruptcy judge's adjudication.)

When enacting the Code, Congress responded to complaints about this antiquated system by abolishing the summary-plenary distinction. Exercising its power to regulate bankruptcy, Congress conferred on the federal courts expansive federal question jurisdiction over all bankruptcy cases (exclusive jurisdiction) and all proceedings "arising under . . . or arising in or related to" a bankruptcy case (nominally concurrent jurisdiction but the overwhelming majority proceed in federal court). § 1334(b). No more running to state court! In addition to some federalism buffs, general commercial litigators did not like this dramatic extension of federal court jurisdiction, chiefly because they found themselves suddenly litigating in a fantastical "bankruptcy court," where rumors of debtor solicitude abounded. But the real grumblers were the tort bar, who really, *really* liked state court jury awards. Congress, in the name of federalism (never politics), thus amended the Code to claw back federal bankruptcy jurisdiction a bit. It added *mandatory abstention* of federal court jurisdiction over certain types of state law actions, § 1334(c)(2), and allowed *permissive abstention* in others, § 1334(c)(1).

The federalism buffs seethe at the broad grant of jurisdiction that remains. They have a point, because there is a constitutional dimension to the jurisdictional grant. It's one thing for Congress to have a bankruptcy power, but you can't put lipstick on a pig and call it "bankruptcy." If Congress had passed the jurisdictional statute conferring federal bankruptcy jurisdiction on "all cases in bankruptcy and any other commercial disputes in which a plaintiff's name begins with the letter 'B,'" states would rightly take affront to this over-stepping of Congress's enumerated powers. Observe the next case's struggle with the statutory and constitutional components of the term "related to." (Note: the statute discussed in the opinion refers to "core proceedings." We explore these in glorious detail below; for now, think of them as the equivalent to modern-day "summary" proceedings.)

In reading this first case, you might also consider the following as a general legal framework for assessing bankruptcy jurisdiction questions:

(1) Is the matter sufficiently "related to" bankruptcy to exercise federal jurisdiction?

(2) If so, is the federal court nevertheless (i) required or (ii) permitted to abstain from exercising that jurisdiction in deference to a state court with concurrent jurisdiction?

=== In re DOW CORNING CORP. ===

86 F.3d 482 (6th Cir. 1996)

MARTIN, JR., Circuit Judge.

This is an appeal to determine the subject matter jurisdiction of federal . . . courts, over proceedings "related to" a case filed under Chapter 11 of the Bankruptcy Code. . . . The principal issue presented is whether the district court erred, as a matter of law, in its determination that claims for compensatory and punitive damages asserted in tens of thousands of actions against numerous nondebtor manufacturers and suppliers of silicone gel breast implants could have no conceivable effect upon, and therefore were not related to, the bankruptcy estate of The Dow Corning Corporation. The district court held that it did not have "related to" jurisdiction over those claims pursuant to 28 U.S.C. § 1334(b) and [therefore] concluded that they could not be transferred to it pursuant to 28 U.S.C. § 157(b)(5). For the following reasons, we reverse and remand for further proceedings consistent with this opinion.

I.

Until it ceased their manufacture in 1992, Dow Corning was the predominant producer of silicone gel breast implants, accounting for nearly 50% of the entire market. In addition, Dow Corning supplied silicone raw materials to other manufacturers of silicone gel breast implants. In recent years, tens of thousands of implant recipients have sued Dow Corning, claiming to have been injured by autoimmune reactions to the silicone in their implants. Dow Chemical Company, Corning Incorporated, Minnesota Mining and Manufacturing Company, Baxter Healthcare Corporation and Baxter International Incorporated, and Bristol-Myers Squibb Company and Medical Engineering Corporation are other manufacturers and suppliers of silicone gel-filled implants, and are codefendants with Dow Corning in a large number of personal injury actions.

On June 25, 1992, prior to Dow Corning's filing of its Chapter 11 petition, the Federal Judicial Panel on Multidistrict Litigation ordered the consolidation of all breast implant actions pending in federal courts for coordinated pretrial proceedings, and transferred those actions to Chief Judge Pointer of the Northern District of Alabama. On September 1, 1994, Chief Judge Pointer certified a class for settlement purposes only, and approved a complex agreement between members of the class and certain defendants that contemplated the creation of a $4.25 billion fund to cover, among other things, the costs of treatment and other expenses incurred by breast implant recipients. Each class member was given the opportunity to opt out of the class and to pursue her individual claims separately. Several thousand plaintiffs opted out of the settlement class, while approximately 440,000 elected to register for inclusion in the Global Settlement.

Due to the litigation burden imposed by what is one of the world's largest mass tort litigations, and the threatened consequences of the thousands of product liability claims arising from its manufacture and sale of silicone breast implants and silicone gel, Dow Corning filed a petition for reorganization under Chapter 11 of the Bankruptcy Code on May 15, 1995, in the [bankruptcy court of the] United States District Court for the Eastern District of Michigan. The court had jurisdiction over that proceeding pursuant to 28 U.S.C. § 1334(a). As a result of Dow Corning's Chapter 11 filing, all breast implant claims against it were automatically stayed pursuant to 11 U.S.C. § 362(a). Claims against Dow Corning's two shareholders, Dow Chemical and Corning Incorporated, and the other nondebtor defendants were not stayed. Dow Chemical, Corning Incorporated, Minnesota Mining,

Baxter and Bristol-Myers Squibb subsequently removed many [pending] opt-out claims in which those companies were named defendants with Dow Corning from state to [the local] federal court pursuant to 28 U.S.C. § 1452(a).

On June 12, 1995, Dow Corning filed a motion pursuant to 28 U.S.C. § 157(b)(5) to transfer to the Eastern District of Michigan opt-out breast implant claims pending against it and its shareholders, Dow Chemical and Corning Incorporated. Dow Corning's motion covered claims that had been removed to federal court and were pending in the multidistrict forum, as well as claims pending in state courts which were in the process of being removed to federal courts pursuant to 28 U.S.C. § 1452(a). Dow Corning envisioned its transfer motion as the first step in ensuring a feasible plan of reorganization, and indicated that it would seek to have the transferred actions consolidated for a threshold jury trial on the issue of whether silicone gel breast implants cause the diseases claimed. . . .

On September 12, 1995, the district court issued two opinions and companion orders regarding the . . . transfer motions. With respect to opt-out breast implant cases pending against Dow Corning, the district court asserted jurisdiction under Section 1334(b) and permitted transfer pursuant to Section 157(b)(5). The district court, however, denied the remainder of the transfer motions [i.e., those against Dow's parent companies and other non-affiliated co-defendants—Eds.] on the ground that, as a matter of law, it lacked subject matter jurisdiction over the claims sought to be transferred because they were not "related to" Dow Corning's bankruptcy proceeding pursuant to 28 U.S.C. § 1334(b). . . .

III.

The first issue to be resolved is whether the district court has subject matter jurisdiction over breast implant claims pending not only against the debtor, Dow Corning, but also over certain claims pending against the nondebtor defendants. . . .

In addressing the extent of a district court's bankruptcy jurisdiction under Section 1334(b) over civil proceedings "related to" cases under title 11, we start with the premise that the "emphatic terms in which the jurisdictional grant is described in the legislative history, and the extraordinarily broad wording of the grant itself, leave us with no doubt that Congress intended to grant to the district courts broad jurisdiction in bankruptcy cases." [In re Salem Mortgage Co., 783 F.2d 626, 634 (6th Cir. 1986).] . . . "[S]ituations may arise where an extremely tenuous connection to the estate would not satisfy the jurisdictional requirement" of Section 1334(b). . . .

The definition of a "related" proceeding under Section 1334(b) was first articulated by the Third Circuit in *Pacor*[, Inc. v. Higgins, 742 F.2d 984 (3d Cir. 1984)]. As stated in that case, the "usual articulation of the test for determining whether a civil proceeding is related to bankruptcy is whether the outcome of that proceeding could conceivably have any effect on the estate being administered in bankruptcy." Id. at 994. An action is "related to bankruptcy if the outcome could alter the debtor's rights, liabilities, options, or freedom of action (either positively or negatively) and which in any way impacts upon the handling and administration of the bankrupt estate." Id. A proceeding "need not necessarily be against the debtor or against the debtor's property" to satisfy the requirements for "related to" jurisdiction. Id. However, "the mere fact that there may be common issues of fact between a civil proceeding and a controversy involving the bankruptcy estate does not bring the matter within the scope of section [1334(b)]." Id. (also stating that "[j]udicial economy itself does not justify federal jurisdiction"). . . . The majority of our sister circuits have[, like us,] adopted the *Pacor* test for "related to" jurisdiction. . . .

In addition, the Supreme Court recently cited *Pacor* with approval in addressing the broad scope of the jurisdictional grant in Section 1334(b). The Court stated:

> Congress did not delineate the scope of "related to" jurisdiction, but its choice of words suggests a grant of some breadth. The jurisdictional grant in [Section] 1334(b) was a distinct departure from the jurisdiction conferred under previous acts, which had been limited to either possession of property by the debtor or consent as a basis for jurisdiction. We agree with the views expressed by the Court of Appeals for the Third Circuit in *Pacor* that "Congress intended to grant comprehensive jurisdiction to the bankruptcy courts so that they might deal efficiently and expeditiously with all matters connected with the bankruptcy estate," . . .

Celotex, 514 U.S. at [307-08]. . . .

1. Claims for Contribution and Indemnification

Dow Corning, Dow Chemical and Corning Incorporated argue that the district court erred in its determination that "related to" jurisdiction does not exist over certain breast implant claims asserted against Dow Chemical and Corning Incorporated because, in addition to the claims asserted by the personal injury claimants, Dow Chemical and Corning Incorporated have asserted cross-claims against each other and Dow Corning in the underlying litigation, which will have an effect on the bankruptcy estate. Minnesota Mining, Baxter, and Bristol-Myers Squibb argue that, despite the fact that they have not yet filed contribution and indemnification claims or proofs of claim relating to implant litigation in Dow Corning's bankruptcy case, they have contingent claims for contribution and indemnification [against the debtor] that will have a conceivable effect on the bankruptcy proceedings. . . . The companies argue that these claims need to be resolved as part of Dow Corning's bankruptcy proceedings and reorganization plan, and certainly will affect the debtor's rights, liabilities, options, and freedom of action in the administration of its estate.

Pacor involved John and Louise Higgins' claim against the Philadelphia Asbestos Co. (Pacor) in state court seeking damages allegedly caused by Mr. Higgins' work-related exposure to asbestos supplied by the company. In response, Pacor filed a third-party complaint impleading the Johns-Manville Corporation, which Pacor claimed was the original manufacturer of the asbestos. After Johns-Manville filed for Chapter 11, a dispute ensued as to whether the Higgins-Pacor action was "related to" the Manville bankruptcy so that the entire controversy could be removed to bankruptcy court. The Third Circuit held that the primary Higgins-Pacor action would not affect the Manville bankruptcy estate, and therefore was not "related to" the bankruptcy proceedings. The court stated that the Higgins-Pacor action was, "[a]t best, a mere precursor to the potential third party claim for indemnification by Pacor against Manville," and held that, because all issues with regard to Manville's possible liability would be resolved in a subsequent third party impleader action, "there would be no automatic creation of liability against Manville on account of a judgment against Pacor." *Pacor*, 743 F.2d at 995 (stating also that "[t]here would therefore be no effect on administration of the estate, until such time as Pacor may choose to pursue its third party claim"). Thus, the court in *Pacor* viewed the absence of "automatic" liability on the part of the debtor as dispositive in determining that Section 1334(b) "related to" jurisdiction did not exist.

It has become clear following *Pacor* that "automatic" liability is not necessarily a prerequisite for a finding of "related to" jurisdiction. The Third Circuit itself has emphasized that:

> A key word in [the] test is "conceivable." Certainty, or even likelihood, is not a requirement. Bankruptcy jurisdiction will exist so long as it is possible that a proceeding may impact on "the debtor's rights, liabilities, options, or freedom of action" or the "handling and administration of the bankrupt estate."

In re Marcus Hook Dev. Park Inc., 943 F.2d 261, 264 (3d Cir. 1991) (citation omitted). . . . [W]e believe the district court has "related to" subject matter jurisdiction over the breast implant claims pending against the nondebtor defendants in this case. Thousands of suits asserted against Dow Corning include claims against the nondebtors, and the nature of the claims asserted establishes that Dow Corning and the various nondebtor defendants are closely related with regard to the pending breast implant litigation. . . .

Claims for indemnification and contribution, whether asserted against or by Dow Corning, obviously would affect the size of the estate and the length of time the bankruptcy proceedings will be pending, as well as Dow Corning's ability to resolve its liabilities and proceed with reorganization. . . . [The court also found "related to" jurisdiction based on a $1 billion joint insurance policy that the parents might deplete and leave nothing left for Dow Corning if they made the first claims.—Eds.]

IV.

[Having federal jurisdiction, 28 U.S.C. § 157(b)(5) authorized a transfer of the tort cases to the district where the bankruptcy was pending in Michigan.—Eds.]

V.

Finally, a Section 157(b)(5) motion "requires an abstention analysis." The abstention provisions of 28 U.S.C. § 1334(c) qualify Section 1334(b)'s broad grant of jurisdiction. In re Salem, 783 F.2d at 635. It is for the district court to "determine in each individual case whether hearing it would promote or impair efficient and fair adjudication of bankruptcy cases." Id.

Section 1334 provides for two types of abstention: discretionary abstention under 28 U.S.C. § 1334(c)(1) and mandatory abstention under 28 U.S.C. § 1334(c)(2). . . .

For mandatory abstention to apply, a proceeding must: (1) be based on a state law claim or cause of action; (2) lack a federal jurisdictional basis absent the bankruptcy; (3) be commenced in a state forum of appropriate jurisdiction; (4) be capable of timely adjudication; and (5) be a non-core proceeding. Non-core proceedings under Section 157(b)(2)(B) (i.e. liquidation of personal injury tort or wrongful death case) are not subject to Section 1334(c)(2)'s mandatory abstention provisions pursuant to 28 U.S.C. § 157(b)(4).

The district court in this case determined that Section 157(b)(4) rendered exempt from the mandatory abstention requirement all personal injury tort claims pending solely against Dow Corning, and decided not to abstain discretionarily with regard to those claims at this time. . . . Because we believe the district court is in a better position to make the necessary abstention determinations, as to both mandatory and discretionary abstention, we remand the case to the district court for further proceedings on this issue. . . .

———————————

On remand, the district court remained reluctant to take on the massive and complex package of litigation, exercising both mandatory and discretionary abstention in an omnibus three-page analysis. The circuit court was not amused by what it saw as shirking a tough case, granting a writ of mandamus requiring an abstention ruling upon each claim individually. In re Dow Corning Corp., 113 F.3d 565, 568, 570, 571 (6th Cir. 1997) ("It is undisputed that some of the cases do not meet the requirements of mandatory abstention. Indeed, in many of the cases, there does not even appear to have been a motion for abstention filed by the plaintiff in the proceeding.").

B. ALLOCATION OF BANKRUPTCY PROCEEDINGS AMONG FEDERAL JUDGES

1. Constitutional Considerations

a. The 1978 Code

Once federal jurisdiction attaches, the next question is who gets to decide the case: a bankruptcy judge or a district judge? And if the answer is a bankruptcy judge, the follow-up question is whether that judge can enter final judgment on the matter or only enter a recommendation of the proposed disposition to the district judge.

Under the old Act, bankruptcy judges were clearly subservient to district judges, hearing bankruptcy cases only when district court judges wanted them to; they were even appointed by district judges for fixed terms as inferior judicial officers of the federal judiciary. When Congress adopted the Code in 1978, it not only expanded the reach of federal courts in bankruptcy to "related to" matters but upped the stature of the bankruptcy judges, deeming them "adjuncts" to the district courts with full powers to enter judgments as if a district court, subject only to appeal to the circuit courts. Striking a compromise between the House, which wanted full Article III status for these judges, and the Senate, which reflected the views of many district judges who saw this as a dilution of their prestige, the Code had bankruptcy judges appointed by the President, not the district judges, but only for a term of years. For an excellent historical account of these negotiations and the involved pettiness, see Geraldine Mund, Appointed or Anointed: Judges, Congress, and the Passage of the Bankruptcy Act of 1978 Part Two: The Third Branch Reacts, 81 Am. Bankr. L.J. 165 (2007) (recounting how some courts reprogrammed judges' elevators not to stop at the magistrate/bankruptcy floors, changed access to the judges' lunchroom, and how even Chief Justice Burger forbade addressing letters to bankruptcy courts with "Judge" but only "Mr.," "Mrs.," or "Sir").

Problem solved! Well, there was one, slight problem with this compromise. It was unconstitutional. No sooner than the ink dried on the Code, a breach-of-contract defendant who did not file a claim as creditor (and therefore could not have been dragged into bankruptcy court with a summary proceeding under the old Act) objected to being forced to defend itself before a bankruptcy court when it wanted nothing to do with the debtor's bankruptcy. It claimed it had a constitutional right under Article III to have its legal defense heard in federal court by a full-fledged district judge, appointed by the Senate, confirmed by the President, and life-tenured. The Supreme Court agreed, but splintered badly. Northern Pipeline Construction Co. v. Marathon Pipe Line Co., 458 U.S. 50 (1982). Justice Brennan, writing for a four-member plurality, had a hard time explaining just what the problem was. It's easy to say bankruptcy judges were not Article III judges, but neither were myriad other "non-Article III" jurists populating the federal government, from military courts-martial to the NLRB's administrative law judges. Gamely, Justice Brennan propounded a taxonomy of categorical "exceptions" to the seemingly absolute text of Article III: courts of the territories and the District of Columbia, courts-marital, and legislative courts and administrative agencies "created by Congress to adjudicate cases involving 'public rights.'" Id. at 63-67. The first two categories are straightforward and indeed conform with tradition. The final category is a bit amorphous, but the idea is that if Congress creates a system of radio licenses, it can also create an adjudicative network to administer disputes over them. And even common law actions, if against the United States, can be consigned to non-Article III courts, on the theory that the greater power of sovereign immunity includes the lesser power of creating a judicial dispute mechanism when the Sovereign deigns to be sued (hence, non-Article III tax courts). He then considered whether the appeal fell under the "public rights" branch and found it came up short.

Appellants argue that a discharge in bankruptcy is indeed a "public right," similar to such congressionally created benefits as "radio station licenses, pilot licenses, and certificates for common carriers" granted by administrative agencies. But the restructuring of debtor-creditor relations, which is at the core of the federal bankruptcy power, must be distinguished from the adjudication of state-created private rights, such as the right to recover contract damages that is at issue in this case. The former may well be a "public right," but the latter obviously is not. Appellant Northern's right to recover contract damages to augment its estate is "one of private right, that is, of the liability of one individual to another under the law as defined." [Crowell v. Benson,] 285 U.S. [22, 51 (1932)].

Id. at 71-72 (plurality opinion).

The plurality also rejected the idea that bankruptcy judges were "adjuncts," assisting Article III judges, because unlike the deputy commissioners in *Crowell v. Benson* (cited in the excerpt above and seen by many as the constitutional foundation of the modern administrative state), bankruptcy judges could preside over the full case and enter judgment, thus exercising "the 'essential attributes' of the judicial power of the United States. . . ." Id. at 84-85.

Precluding a majority, Justices Rehnquist and O'Connor concurred only in the result, avoiding the larger constitutional question (hinting at their skepticism that the watertight compartments proposed by Justice Brennan would work for an evolving federal judiciary). They simply said that this particular exercise of jurisdiction was beyond the scope of the bankruptcy judge. The dissenters thought there was adequate authority for the adjudication of the claim by a bankruptcy judge, with Justice White arguing that bankruptcy courts derived authority as adjuncts of the district courts. Chief Justice Burger also in dissent lamented that the delicate compromise by Congress on the proper power and scope of the newly designed bankruptcy courts was being junked by the Court. Supreme Court 1, Congress 0.

The opinion has been read and re-read by generations, but remains, charitably, "opaque." Consider that Justice Brennan talks of the "core" of the bankruptcy power and says that it might well be a "public right," suggesting that *some* bankruptcy judge power might be okay, at least if at the "core" of bankruptcy. How's that for helpful dictum?

b.   The 1984 Amendments

Congress was unable to act promptly (despite two Supreme Court stays) and *Marathon* went into effect on Christmas Eve 1982, invalidating the bankruptcy courts. The Judicial Conference acted through the Administrative Office of the U.S. Courts to issue an "Emergency Rule," which each district court was urged to adopt (and did), effectively permitting bankruptcy judges to serve as district court assistants. Congress then copied this as the basis for the 1984 Amendments Act, with no real guidance—let alone a clear opinion of the Court—on just precisely what was unconstitutional. Little helpful legislative history exists on the 1984 Amendments, and the final statutory language is, at best, unartful. The gist is that Congress, grasping at language from the Supreme Court's tea leaves, divided the bankruptcy universe into "core" and "non-core" proceedings (although the latter term does not appear in 28 U.S.C. § 157).

Core proceedings preserve for bankruptcy judges the power to hear and decide matters like district judges. § 157(b)(1). Appeals, however, go to district court judges, § 158(a), adding a level of federal appellate review (although a majority of circuits have designated bankruptcy appellate panels ("BAPs") that substitute for district courts on appeal, § 158(b)); further appeals go to the circuit court and then through the certiorari process.

In "non-core" proceedings, bankruptcy judges can only offer recommendations for district judges, who maintain responsibility for entering final judgments upon de novo review of the recommendations. § 157(c)(1). The parties can always consent, however, to bankruptcy court adjudication of a non-core case if they want to skip the recommendation stage. § 157(c)(2). If this is starting to sound a bit familiar, you are not alone. Some have argued this is basically a return to the summary-plenary divide of the old Act. Ralph Brubaker, A "Summary" Statutory and Constitutional Theory of Bankruptcy Judges' Core Jurisdiction After *Stern v. Marshall*, 86 Am. Bankr. L.J. 121 (2012). Because Congress chose not to define core proceedings, however, and instead offered only a non-exhaustive illustrative list, § 157(b)(2), the parties may have to ask the judge whether any given proceeding is core, a determination contemplated by § 157(b)(3). Some of the "core" proceedings sound pretty all-encompassing to us, § 157(b)(2)(O), leaving some to opine that non-core is merely a residual of whatever the bankruptcy judge does not want to hear (or, we suppose, that the district judge wants to hear).

The 1984 Amendments also returned power to the Article III judiciary to control bankruptcy judges as true assistants, removing the President from the picture. Circuit court judges now appoint bankruptcy judges for 14-year terms. § 152. District court judges decide whether to "refer" cases to bankruptcy judges in their district as a standing order, § 157 (every district so refers), and whether, in any given case referred to bankruptcy court, the district court wants to "withdraw" that case's reference and hear the case itself. § 157(d). Congress also provided that district courts *must* withdraw the reference in any matter involving federal statutes "regulating organizations or activities affecting interstate commerce." § 157(d). While that seems to us to describe a big chunk of the U.S. Code, mandatory withdrawal of the reference is not routine.

Problem solved (again)! So many thought, especially as the Court seemed in some subsequent nonbankruptcy cases to give more room to the public rights exception. But then the Court decided Granfinanciera, S.A. v. Nordberg, 492 U.S. 33 (1989), a dispute about the Seventh Amendment right to jury trial for a fraudulent conveyance action brought in bankruptcy court. In a passage of dictum, the Court seemed to suggest that any matter that carried a jury trial right, like a fraudulent conveyance, also carried an Article III right and hence couldn't be decided by a bankruptcy judge over party objection. Supreme Court 2, Congress 0. But rather than doom the bankruptcy jurisdiction scheme, the Court maneuvered. It purported to limit the holding of *Granfinanciera* to the Seventh Amendment. Congress responded by adding a jury trial right for private-rights matters in bankruptcy. § 157(e). Problem solved (again)! While *Granfinanciera*'s dictum sword remained hanging over the bankruptcy courts' constitutionality, as the years accumulated to decades, calm descended and the bankruptcy courts hummed along adjudicating their million-odd bankruptcy petitions per year. Then another ho-hum bankruptcy jurisdiction case came along—you know the type: beautiful but somewhat zany Playmate of the Year marries "the richest man in Texas." An epic, multi-year and multi-court struggle with his family over his estate ensues. (The plot pretty much writes itself.)

══════ STERN v. MARSHALL ══════
564 U.S. 462 (2011)

Chief Justice ROBERTS delivered the opinion of the Court.

This "suit has, in course of time, become so complicated, that . . . no two . . . lawyers can talk about it for five minutes, without coming to a total disagreement as to all the premises. Innumerable children have been born into the cause: innumerable young people have married into it"; and, sadly, the original parties "have died out of it." A "long procession of [judges] has come in and gone out" during that time, and still the suit "drags its weary length before the Court." Those words were not written about this case, see C. Dickens, Bleak House, in 1 Works of Charles Dickens 4-5 (1891), but they could have been. This is the second time we have had occasion to weigh in on this long-running dispute between Vickie Lynn Marshall and E. Pierce Marshall over the fortune of J. Howard Marshall II, a man believed to have been one of the richest people in Texas. . . .[1] Although the history of this litigation is complicated, its resolution ultimately turns on very basic principles. Article III, § 1, of the Constitution commands that "[t]he judicial Power of the United States, shall be vested in one supreme Court, and in such inferior Courts as the Congress may from time to time ordain and establish." That Article further provides that the judges of those courts shall hold their offices during good behavior, without diminution of salary. Ibid. Those requirements of Article III were not honored here. . . .

I

Known to the public as Anna Nicole Smith, Vickie was J. Howard's third wife and married him about a year before his death. Although J. Howard bestowed on Vickie many monetary and other gifts during their courtship and marriage, he did not include her in his will. Before J. Howard passed away, Vickie filed suit in Texas state probate court, asserting that Pierce—J. Howard's younger son—fraudulently induced J. Howard to sign a living trust that did not include her, even though J. Howard meant to give her half his property. Pierce denied any fraudulent activity and defended the validity of J. Howard's trust and, eventually, his will. After J. Howard's death, Vickie filed a petition for bankruptcy in the Central District of California. Pierce filed a complaint in that bankruptcy proceeding, contending that Vickie had defamed him

---

[1] Because both Vickie and Pierce passed away during this litigation, the parties in this case are Vickie's estate [Howard K. Stern, Executor] and Pierce's estate [Elaine T. Marshall, Executrix]. We continue to refer to them as "Vickie" and "Pierce."

by inducing her lawyers to tell members of the press that he had engaged in fraud to gain control of his father's assets. The complaint sought a declaration that Pierce's defamation claim was not dischargeable in the bankruptcy proceedings. Pierce subsequently filed a proof of claim for the defamation action, meaning that he sought to recover damages for it from Vickie's bankruptcy estate. Vickie responded to Pierce's initial complaint by asserting truth as a defense to the alleged defamation and by filing a counterclaim for tortious interference with the gift she expected from J. Howard.

On November 5, 1999, the Bankruptcy Court issued an order granting Vickie summary judgment on Pierce's claim for defamation. On September 27, 2000, after a bench trial, the Bankruptcy Court issued a judgment on Vickie's counterclaim in her favor. The court later awarded Vickie over $400 million in compensatory damages and $25 million in punitive damages. In post-trial proceedings, Pierce argued that the Bankruptcy Court lacked jurisdiction over Vickie's counterclaim. In particular, Pierce renewed a claim he had made earlier in the litigation, asserting that the Bankruptcy Court's authority over the counterclaim was limited because Vickie's counterclaim was not a "core proceeding." . . . The Bankruptcy Court in this case concluded that Vickie's counterclaim was "a core proceeding" under § 157(b)(2)(C), and the court therefore had the "power to enter judgment" on the counterclaim under § 157(b)(1). Id., at 40. The District Court disagreed. It recognized that "Vickie's counterclaim for tortious interference falls within the literal language" of the statute designating certain proceedings as "core," see § 157(b)(2)(C), but understood this Court's precedent to "suggest[] that it would be unconstitutional to hold that any and all counterclaims are core." The District Court accordingly concluded that a "counterclaim should not be characterized as core" when it "is only somewhat related to the claim against which it is asserted, and when the unique characteristics and context of the counterclaim place it outside of the normal type of set-off or other counterclaims that customarily arise."

Because the District Court concluded that Vickie's counterclaim was not core, the court determined that it was required to treat the Bankruptcy Court's judgment as "proposed[,] rather than final," and engage in an "independent review" of the record. 28 U.S.C. § 157(c)(1). Although the Texas state court had by that time conducted a jury trial on the merits of the parties' dispute and entered a judgment in Pierce's favor, the District Court declined to give that judgment preclusive effect and went on to decide the matter itself. Like the Bankruptcy Court, the District Court found that Pierce had tortiously interfered with Vickie's expectancy of a gift from J. Howard. The District Court awarded Vickie compensatory and punitive damages, each in the amount of $44,292,767.33.

[On the case's remand from the first Supreme Court visit], the Court of Appeals reasoned that allowing a bankruptcy judge to enter final judgments on all counterclaims raised in bankruptcy proceedings "would certainly run afoul" of this Court's decision in *Northern Pipeline*. With those concerns in mind, the court concluded that "a counterclaim under § 157(b)(2)(C) is properly a 'core' proceeding . . . only if the counterclaim is so closely related to [a creditor's] proof of claim that the resolution of the counterclaim is necessary to resolve the allowance or disallowance of the claim itself." The court ruled that Vickie's counterclaim did not meet that test. That holding made "the Texas probate court's judgment . . . the earliest final judgment entered on matters relevant to this proceeding," and therefore the Court of Appeals concluded that the District Court should have "afford[ed] preclusive effect" to the Texas "court's determination of relevant legal and factual issues." . . .

II

A . . .

The manner in which a bankruptcy judge may act on a referred matter depends on the type of proceeding involved. Bankruptcy judges may hear and enter final judgments in "all core proceedings. . . ." "Core proceedings include, but are not limited to" 16 different types of matters, including "counterclaims by [a debtor's] estate against persons filing claims against the estate." § 157(b)(2)(C). Parties may appeal final judgments of a bankruptcy court in core proceedings to the district court, which reviews them under traditional appellate standards. When a bankruptcy judge determines that a referred "proceeding . . . is not a core proceeding" the judge may only "submit proposed findings of fact and conclusions of law to the district court." § 157(c)(1). It is the district court that enters final judgment in such cases after reviewing de novo any matter to which a party objects. Ibid.

B . . .

Vickie's counterclaim against Pierce for tortious interference is a "core proceeding" under the plain text of § 157(b)(2)(C). That provision specifies that core proceedings include "counterclaims by the estate against persons filing claims against the estate." . . . [Yet] we agree with Pierce that designating all counterclaims as "core" proceedings raises serious constitutional concerns. Pierce is also correct that we will, where possible, construe federal statutes so as "to avoid serious doubt of their constitutionality." Commodity Futures Trading Comm'n v. Schor, 478 U.S. 833, 841 (1986). But that "canon of construction does not give [us] the prerogative to ignore the legislative will in order to avoid constitutional adjudication." Ibid. In this case, we do not think the plain text of § 157(b)(2)(C) leaves any room for the canon of avoidance. We would have to "rewrit[e]" the statute, not interpret it, to bypass the constitutional issue § 157(b)(2)(C) presents. Id., at 841. That we may not do. . . .

III

Although we conclude that § 157(b)(2)(C) permits the Bankruptcy Court to enter final judgment on Vickie's counterclaim, Article III of the Constitution does not.

A

Article III, § 1, of the Constitution mandates that "[t]he judicial Power of the United States, shall be vested in one supreme Court, and in such inferior Courts as the Congress may from time to time ordain and establish." The same section provides that the judges of those constitutional courts "shall hold their Offices during good Behaviour" and "receive for their Services[] a Compensation[] [that] shall not be diminished" during their tenure.

As its text and our precedent confirm, Article III is "an inseparable element of the constitutional system of checks and balances" that "both defines the power and protects the independence of the Judicial Branch." *Northern Pipeline*, 458 U.S., at 58 (plurality opinion). . . . In establishing the system of divided power in the Constitution, the Framers considered it essential that "the judiciary remain[] truly distinct from both the legislature and the executive." The Federalist No. 78, p. 466 (C. Rossiter ed. 1961) (A. Hamilton). . . . Those limitations serve two related purposes. "Separation-of-powers principles are intended, in part, to protect each branch of government from incursion by the others. . . . [Additionally, these] structural principles secured by the separation of powers protect the individual as well. By appointing judges to serve without term limits, and restricting the ability of the other branches to remove judges or diminish their salaries, the Framers sought to ensure that each judicial decision would be rendered, not with an eye toward currying favor with Congress or the Executive, but rather with the "[c]lear heads . . . and honest hearts" deemed "essential to good judges." 1 Works of James Wilson 363 (J. Andrews ed. 1896). Article III could neither serve its purpose in the system of checks and balances nor preserve the integrity of judicial decisionmaking if the other branches of the Federal Government could confer the Government's "judicial Power" on entities outside Article III. . . .

C

Vickie and the dissent argue that the Bankruptcy Court's entry of final judgment on her state common law counterclaim was constitutional, despite the similarities between the bankruptcy courts under the 1978 Act and those exercising core jurisdiction under the 1984 Act. We disagree. . . . Here Vickie's claim is a state law action independent of the federal bankruptcy law and not necessarily resolvable by a ruling on the creditor's proof of claim in bankruptcy. *Northern Pipeline* and our subsequent decision in *Granfinanciera* rejected the application of the "public rights" exception in such cases. . . .

Vickie's counterclaim cannot be deemed a matter of "public right" that can be decided outside the Judicial Branch. As explained above, in *Northern Pipeline* we rejected the argument that the public rights doctrine permitted a bankruptcy court to adjudicate a state law suit brought by a debtor against a company that had not filed a claim against the estate. Although our discussion of the public rights exception since that time has not been entirely consistent, and the exception has been the subject of some debate, this case does not fall within any of the various formulations of the concept that appear in this Court's opinions. . . .

[T]his Court [has] contrasted cases within the reach of the public rights exception—those arising "between the Government and persons subject to its authority in connection with the performance of the constitutional functions of the executive or legislative departments"—and those that were instead matters "of private right, that is, of the liability of one individual to another under the law as defined." Crowell v. Benson, 285 U.S. 22, 50, 51 (1932). . . . Shortly after *Northern Pipeline*, the Court rejected the limitation of the public rights exception to actions involving the Government as a party. The Court has continued, however, to limit the exception to cases in which the claim at issue derives from a federal regulatory scheme, or in which resolution of the claim by an expert government agency is deemed essential to a limited regulatory objective within the agency's authority. In other words, it is still the case that what makes a right "public" rather than private is that the right is integrally related to particular federal government action. . . .

The most recent case in which we considered application of the public rights exception—and the only case in which we have considered that doctrine in the bankruptcy context since *Northern Pipeline*—is Granfinanciera, S.A. v. Nordberg (1989). In *Granfinanciera* we rejected a bankruptcy trustee's argument that a fraudulent conveyance action filed on behalf of a bankruptcy estate against a noncreditor in a bankruptcy proceeding fell within the "public rights" exception. . . . We explained that, "[i]f a statutory right is not closely intertwined with a federal regulatory program Congress has power to enact, and if that right neither belongs to nor exists against the Federal Government, then it must be adjudicated by an Article III court." Id., at 54-55. We reasoned that fraudulent conveyance suits were "quintessentially suits at common law that more nearly resemble state law contract claims brought by a bankrupt corporation to augment the bankruptcy estate than they do creditors' hierarchically ordered claims to a pro rata share of the bankruptcy res." Id., at 56. . . .[7]

Vickie's counterclaim—like the fraudulent conveyance claim at issue in *Granfinanciera*—does not fall within any of the varied formulations of the public rights exception in this Court's cases. . . . What is plain here is that this case involves the most prototypical exercise of judicial power: the entry of a final, binding judgment by a court with broad substantive jurisdiction, on a common law cause of action, when the action neither derives from nor depends upon any agency regulatory regime. If such an exercise of judicial power may nonetheless be taken from the Article III Judiciary simply by deeming it part of some amorphous "public right," then Article III would be transformed from the guardian of individual liberty and separation of powers we have long recognized into mere wishful thinking.

---

[7] We noted that we did not mean to "suggest that the restructuring of debtor-creditor relations is in fact a public right." 492 U.S., at 56, n.11. Our conclusion was that, "even if one accepts this thesis," Congress could not constitutionally assign resolution of the fraudulent conveyance action to a non-Article III court. Ibid. Because neither party asks us to reconsider the public rights framework for bankruptcy, we follow the same approach here.

Vickie and the dissent next attempt to distinguish *Northern Pipeline* and *Granfinanciera* on the ground that Pierce, unlike the defendants in those cases, had filed a proof of claim in the bankruptcy proceedings. Given Pierce's participation in those proceedings, Vickie argues, the Bankruptcy Court had the authority to adjudicate her counterclaim under our decisions [such as] Langenkamp v. Culp, 498 U.S. 42 (1990) (per curiam) [holding *Granfinanciera* jury trial right does not apply to fraudulent conveyance defendant who *does* file a claim in the bankruptcy case—Eds.]. We do not agree. As an initial matter, it is hard to see why Pierce's decision to file a claim should make any difference with respect to the characterization of Vickie's counterclaim. Pierce's claim for defamation in no way affects the nature of Vickie's counterclaim for tortious interference as one at common law that simply attempts to augment the bankruptcy estate—the very type of claim that we held in *Northern Pipeline* and *Granfinanciera* must be decided by an Article III court. . . . Our per curiam opinion in *Langenkamp* . . . explained . . . that a preferential transfer claim can be heard in bankruptcy when the allegedly favored creditor has filed a claim, because then "the ensuing preference action by the trustee become[s] integral to the restructuring of the debtor-creditor relationship." 498 U.S., at 44. If, in contrast, the creditor has not filed a proof of claim, the trustee's preference action does not "become[] part of the claims-allowance process" subject to resolution by the bankruptcy court. Ibid. . . .

[To be sure, t]here was some overlap between Vickie's counterclaim and Pierce's defamation claim that led the courts below to conclude that the counterclaim was compulsory, or at least in an "attenuated" sense related to Pierce's claim. But there was never any reason to believe that the process of adjudicating Pierce's proof of claim would necessarily resolve Vickie's counterclaim. . . . The only overlap between the two claims in this case was the question whether Pierce had in fact tortiously taken control of his father's estate in the manner alleged by Vickie in her counterclaim and described in the allegedly defamatory statements. From the outset, it was clear that, even assuming the Bankruptcy Court would (as it did) rule in Vickie's favor on that question, the court could not enter judgment for Vickie unless the court additionally ruled on the questions whether Texas recognized tortious interference with an expected gift as a valid cause of action, what the elements of that action were, and whether those elements were met. . . .

Vickie additionally argues that the Bankruptcy Court's final judgment was constitutional because bankruptcy courts under the 1984 Act are properly deemed "adjuncts" of the district courts. We rejected a similar argument in *Northern Pipeline*, and our reasoning there holds true today. To begin, as explained above, it is still the bankruptcy court itself that exercises the essential attributes of judicial power over a matter such as Vickie's counterclaim. . . . It is thus no less the case here than it was in *Northern Pipeline* that "[t]he authority—and the responsibility—to make an informed, final determination . . . remains with" the bankruptcy judge, not the district court. 458 U.S., at 81 (plurality opinion). Given that authority, a bankruptcy court can no more be deemed a mere "adjunct" of the district court than a district court can be deemed such an "adjunct" of the court of appeals. . . . It does not affect our analysis that, as Vickie notes, bankruptcy judges under the current Act are appointed by the Article III courts, rather than the President. . . . The constitutional bar remains. . . .

D . . .

[W]e are not convinced that the practical consequences of such limitations on the authority of bankruptcy courts to enter final judgments are as significant as Vickie and the dissent suggest. . . . If our decision today does not change all that much, then why the fuss? Is there really a threat to the separation of powers where Congress has conferred the judicial power outside Article III only over certain counterclaims in bankruptcy? The short but emphatic answer is yes. A statute may no more lawfully chip away at the authority of the Judicial Branch than it may eliminate it entirely. "Slight encroachments create new boundaries from which legions of power can seek new territory to capture." Reid v. Covert, 354 U.S. 1 (1957) (plurality opinion). . . . We cannot compromise the integrity of the system of separated powers and the role of the Judiciary in that system, even with respect to challenges that may seem innocuous at first blush. . . . We conclude today that Congress, in one isolated respect, exceeded that limitation in the Bankruptcy Act of 1984. . . .

Justice SCALIA, concurring.

I agree with the Court's interpretation of our Article III precedents, and I accordingly join its opinion. I adhere to my view, however, that—our contrary precedents notwithstanding—"a matter of public rights . . . must at a minimum arise between the government and others," Granfinanciera, 492 U.S. at 65 (1989) (Scalia, J., concurring in part and concurring in judgment). The sheer surfeit of factors that the Court was required to consider in this case should arouse the suspicion that something is seriously amiss with our jurisprudence in this area. I count at least seven different reasons given in the Court's opinion for concluding that an Article III judge was required to adjudicate this lawsuit. . . . I agree that Article III judges are not required in the context of territorial courts, courts-martial, or true "public rights" cases. See Northern Pipeline, 458 U.S. at 71 (1982) (plurality opinion). Perhaps historical practice permits non-Article III judges to process claims against the bankruptcy estate, see, e.g., Plank, Why Bankruptcy Judges Need Not and Should Not Be Article III Judges, 72 Am. Bankr. L.J. 567, 607-609 (1998); the subject has not been briefed, and so I state no position on the matter. But Vickie points to no historical practice that authorizes a non-Article III judge to adjudicate a counterclaim of the sort at issue here.

Justice BREYER, with whom Justice GINSBURG, Justice SOTOMAYOR, and Justice KAGAN, join dissenting. . . .

In my view, the majority overstates . . . the importance of an analysis that did not command a Court majority in Northern Pipeline, and that was subsequently disavowed. . . . Rather than leaning so heavily on the approach taken by the plurality in *Northern Pipeline*, I would look to this Court's more recent Article III cases, [in which the] Court took a more pragmatic approach to the constitutional question. [Those cases instruct us] to determine whether, in the particular instance, the challenged delegation of adjudicatory authority posed a genuine and serious threat that one branch of Government sought to aggrandize its own constitutionally delegated authority by encroaching upon a field of authority that the Constitution assigns exclusively to another branch. . . . [I]n [Commodity Futures Trading Commission v.] Schor, the Court described in greater detail how this Court should analyze this kind of Article III question. . . . In doing so, the Court expressly "declined to adopt formalistic and unbending rules." *Schor*, 478 U.S. [833, 851 (1986)]. Rather, it "weighed a number of factors, none of which has been deemed determinative, with an eye to the practical effect that the congressional action will have on the constitutionally assigned role of the federal judiciary." Ibid. Those relevant factors include (1) "the origins and importance of the right to be adjudicated"; (2) "the extent to which the non-Article III forum exercises the range of jurisdiction and powers normally vested only in Article III courts"; (3) the extent to which the delegation nonetheless reserves judicial power for exercise by Article III courts; (4) the presence or "absence of consent to an initial adjudication before a non-Article III tribunal"; and (5) "the concerns that drove Congress to depart from" adjudication in an Article III court. Id., at 849, 851. The Court added that where "private rights," rather than "public rights" are involved, the "danger of encroaching on the judicial powers" is greater. Id., at 853-854. Thus, while non-Article III adjudication of "private rights" is not necessarily unconstitutional, the Court's constitutional "examination" of such a scheme must be more "searching." Ibid. . . .

II . . .

Applying *Schor*'s approach here, I conclude that the delegation of adjudicatory authority before us is constitutional. A grant of authority to a bankruptcy court to adjudicate compulsory counterclaims does not violate any constitutional separation-of-powers principle related to Article III. . . . Moreover, in one important respect Article III judges maintain greater control over the bankruptcy court proceedings at issue here than they did over the relevant proceedings in any of the previous cases in which this Court has upheld a delegation of adjudicatory power. The District Court here may "withdraw, in whole or in part, any case or proceeding referred [to the Bankruptcy Court] . . . on its own motion or on timely motion of any party, for cause shown." 28 U.S.C. § 157(d). . . .

[Pierce's voluntary filing of a claim in Vickie's estate is fatal.] Compare *Granfinanciera*, supra, at 58-59 ("Because petitioners . . . have not filed claims against the estate" they retain "their Seventh Amendment right to a trial by jury"), with *Langenkamp*, supra, at 45 ("Respondents filed claims against the bankruptcy estate" and "[c]onsequently, they were not entitled to a jury trial"). . . .

III

The majority predicts that as a "practical matter" today's decision "does not change all that much." But I doubt that is so. Consider a typical case: A tenant files for bankruptcy. The landlord files a claim for unpaid rent. The tenant asserts a counterclaim for damages suffered by the landlord's (1) failing to fulfill his obligations as lessor, and (2) improperly recovering possession of the premises by misrepresenting the facts in housing court. . . . [U]nder the majority's holding, the federal district judge, not the bankruptcy judge, would have to hear and resolve the counterclaim. Why is that a problem? Because these types of disputes arise in bankruptcy court with some frequency. . . . Because under these circumstances, a constitutionally required game of jurisdictional ping-pong between courts would lead to inefficiency, increased cost, delay, and needless additional suffering among those faced with bankruptcy. For these reasons, with respect, I dissent.

Supreme Court 3, Congress 0. (Law Students, –10.) *Stern* has titillating facts, to be sure, but is so confusing that even the Supreme Court disagreed on its scope. In Executive Benefits Insurance Agency v. Arkison, 573 U.S. 25 (2014), the Court recognized that in addition to core and non-core, it had created a third category of "*Stern* claims" — statutorily core but unconstitutional to treat as core — and held they should be treated as if non-core claims (i.e., subject to proposed findings of fact and recommended conclusions of law under § 157(c)(1)). And in Wellness International Network, Ltd. v. Sharif, 575 U.S. 665 (2015), the Court decided that the consensual adjudication of non-core claims under § 157(c)(2) by bankruptcy judges, which mirrors the system of consensual adjudication by magistrate judges, is constitutional, although this time with a 6-3 split. Chief Justice Roberts, in dissent, grumbled that *Stern* was being ignored, Justice Sotomayor for the Court made great use of *Stern*'s insistence that it did not change all that much, and Justice Breyer presumably smiled quietly to himself that the majority anchored its analysis on the *Schor* test he found missing from *Stern*. While some drama has thus abated, the problem of identifying a *Stern* claim remains, perhaps with Justice Scalia chuckling from afar over the suspicious "surfeit of factors" required for that task. In *Wellness*, the dissent suggested the test for a *Stern* claim—a question the majority avoided by holding party consent solves any *Stern* problem—should likely mirror the historical test for summary vs. plenary jurisdiction. Historians 1, Bankruptcy Administration Simplicity 0. (Textbook Authors, Scratch.)

2.   *Statutory Considerations*

Leaving aside its constitutionality, § 157 is a challenge to decipher. For example, personal injury and wrongful death claims *against* the estate receive special treatment. On the one hand, they are not core proceedings before a bankruptcy judge, § 157(b)(2)(B), but on the other hand, they are not subject to mandatory abstention under § 1334(c)(2), § 157(b)(4). As a result, such non-core cases will be tried by the district judge, unless the parties consent to bankruptcy jurisdiction, § 157(c)(2), or the district court abstains on a discretionary basis and permits a state court to try the case, § 1334(c)(1). The next case takes a crack at deciding just what is a "core proceeding." Although it is a mass-tort chapter 11, the issue presented is a contract question involving interpretation of policies of insurance. In 1993, in an opinion referred to in the following case, the Second Circuit was seen as greatly narrowing the "core" jurisdiction of the bankruptcy courts in contract matters. Orion Pictures Corp. v. Showtime Networks, Inc. (In re Orion Pictures Corp.), 4 F.3d 1095 (2d Cir. 1993). In the case that follows, six years after *Orion*, the judges of that circuit court disagree considerably about the proper articulation of the applicable rule, although they all agree on the result in the case presented, which proves this is hard for everyone.

In re UNITED STATES LINES, INC.
197 F.3d 631 (2d Cir. 1999)

WALKER, Circuit Judge.

The United States Lines, Inc. and United States Lines (S.A.) Inc. Reorganization Trust (the "Trust") sued in the Bankruptcy Court for the Southern District of New York (Francis G. Conrad, Bankruptcy Judge) seeking a declaratory judgment to establish the Trust's rights under various insurance contracts. The bankruptcy court held that the action was within its core jurisdiction and denied the defendants' motion to compel arbitration of the proceedings. The District Court for the Southern District of New York (Sidney H. Stein, District Judge), reversed and held that the insurance contract disputes were not core proceedings. . . . We now reverse and remand.

BACKGROUND . . .

On November 24, 1986, United States Lines, Inc. and United States Lines (S.A.) Inc., as debtors, filed a voluntary petition for bankruptcy relief under Chapter 11 of the Bankruptcy Code, 11 U.S.C. §§ 101 et seq. The Trust is their successor-in-interest pursuant to a plan of reorganization that was confirmed by the bankruptcy court on May 16, 1989.

Among the creditors are some 12,000 employees who have filed more than 18,000 claims, most of which are for asbestos-related injuries sustained while sailing on different ships in debtors' fleet over four decades. Many additional claims are expected to mature in the future. The Trust asserts that these claims are covered by several Protection & Indemnity insurance policies (the "P & I policies") issued by four domestic and four foreign mutual insurance clubs ("the Clubs"). . . . All of the P & I policies were issued before the debtors petitioned for bankruptcy relief.

The proceeds of the P & I policies are the only funds potentially available to cover the above employees' personal injury claims. At the heart of each of the P & I policies is a pay-first provision by which the insurers' liability is not triggered until the insured pays the claim of the personal injury victim. The deductibles for each accident or occurrence vary among the different policies, ranging from $250 to $100,000.

On December 8, 1992, the Bankruptcy Court entered a stipulation of conditional settlement between the Trust and an initial group of 106 claimants, and on January 5, 1993, the Trust began this action as an adversarial proceeding in bankruptcy, pursuant to 28 U.S.C. § 2201, seeking a declaratory judgment of the parties' respective rights under the various P & I policies. Nine of the ten counts in the complaint seek a declaration from the court of the Clubs' contractual obligations under the P & I policies in light of the stipulation of conditional settlement. The tenth claim seeks punitive damages for creating an "insurance maze."

1. Whether the Declaratory Judgment Action Is "Core"

The Bankruptcy Code divides claims in bankruptcy proceedings into two principal categories: "core" and "non-core." . . . Proceedings can be core by virtue of their nature if either (1) the type of proceeding is unique to or uniquely affected by the bankruptcy proceedings, or (2) the proceedings directly affect a core bankruptcy function. . . .

[T]he question [is] whether the underlying insurance contract claims are core. Some arguments for deeming the contract claims core are unavailing. While "[t]he debtors' rights under its insurance policies are property of a debtor's estate," St. Clare's Hosp. & Health Ctr. v. Insurance Co. of N. Am. (In re St. Clare's Hosp. & Health Ctr.), 934 F.2d 15, 18 (2d Cir. 1991), the contract claims are not rendered core simply because they involve property of the estate. "The issue [in the contract claims] is the scope of the insurance policies, an issue of contractual interpretation, not their ownership." In re United States Brass Corp., 110 F.3d 1261, 1268 (7th Cir. 1997). A general rule that such proceedings are core because they involve property of the estate would "create[] an exception to Marathon that would swallow the rule." Orion Pictures Corp. v. Showtime Networks, Inc. (In re Orion Pictures Corp.), 4 F.3d 1095, 1102 (2d Cir. 1993).

The Trust argues that the proceedings are core because not all of the insurance claims have been fully developed pre-petition. However, the critical question in determining whether a contractual dispute is core by virtue of timing is not whether the cause of action accrued post-petition, but whether the contract was formed post-petition. The bankruptcy court has core jurisdiction over claims arising from a contract formed post-petition under § 157(b)(2)(A). But a dispute arising from a pre-petition contract will usually not be rendered core simply because the cause of action could only arise post-petition. In Orion, for example, we held to be non-core Orion's cause of action for anticipatory breach of a pre-petition contract that sought declaratory and other relief from Showtime even though the event that triggered Orion's claim occurred post-petition. See In re Orion Pictures Corp., 4 F.3d at 1097, 1102.[1]

---

[1] This paragraph expresses the views of the author. Each of the other members of the panel has filed a concurring opinion setting forth his separate views.

Notwithstanding that the Trust's claims are upon pre-petition contracts, we conclude that the impact these contracts have on other core bankruptcy functions nevertheless render the proceedings core. . . . [R]esolving disputes relating to major insurance contracts are bound to have a significant impact on the administration of the estate. In *Orion*, we concluded that where the insurance proceeds would only augment the assets of the estate for general distribution, the effect on the administration of the estate was insufficient to render the proceedings core. See *Orion*, 4 F.3d at 1102 ($77 million potential debt which admittedly would ease administration and liquidation of the estate still encompassed by *Marathon* prohibition). Resolving the disputes over the P & I policies here has a much more direct impact on the core administrative functions of the bankruptcy court.

The insurance proceeds are almost entirely earmarked for paying the personal injury claimants and represent the only potential source of cash available to that group of creditors. However, under the pay-first provisions of the P & I policies, those proceeds will not be made available until the Trust has paid the claims. . . . The insolvent insured is therefore often forced to satisfy the pay-first requirement by means of complex, creative payment schemes. In addition to the difficulties involved in paying the claims, the Trust faces a significant risk that the payment scheme ultimately employed will be deemed not to satisfy the pay-first requirement. . . .

NEWMAN, Circuit Judge, concurring:

I concur in the result and in all aspects of Judge Walker's opinion except his individual statement of the view that whether a lawsuit alleging a post-petition breach of a pre-petition contract is a core proceeding depends on the impact the contract has on core bankruptcy functions. In my view, the efficient functioning of the bankruptcy system will be better served by a bright-line rule that treats as core proceedings all suits alleging post-petition breaches of pre-petition contracts.

This Circuit's approach to the issue of whether post-petition breaches of pre-petition contracts are core has not been consistent. . . . On this inconclusive state of the law in the Second Circuit, I believe the issue of whether a suit for a post-petition breach of a pre-petition contract is core remains open. . . . I agree, as Judge Walker's opinion demonstrates, that this suit affects core functions and, for that reason, can be considered core, but I would deem it core simply because it involves a post-petition breach. . . . There can be nothing unconstitutional in permitting a non-Article III bankruptcy court to adjudicate a cause of action for a post-petition breach of a pre-petition contract, a cause of action that did not exist until the jurisdiction of the bankruptcy court attached. . . .

Since a cause of action for a post-petition breach can constitutionally be considered core, it always should be in order to promote the efficient functioning of the bankruptcy system. That efficiency will be substantially impeded by injecting into numerous bankruptcy proceedings the fact-specific and somewhat nebulous issue of whether a particular post-petition breach of a pre-petition contract has a sufficient impact on core functions to render the cause of action core. . . .

CALABRESI, Circuit Judge, concurring:

I too "concur in the result and in all aspects of Judge Walker's opinion except the portion indicating that whether a lawsuit alleging a post-petition breach of a pre-petition contract is a core proceeding depends on the impact the contract has on core bankruptcy functions." But my reasons for not joining fully in that part of Judge Walker's opinion are different from Judge Newman's. . . .

Were I to reach the question, I would be inclined to favor a case-by-case approach. But since we do not need to resolve the issue to decide the case before us, I would defer the matter to another day and to a case that raises the question squarely. Like Judges Walker and Newman, I have no doubt that this particular post-petition breach of a pre-petition contract is core. That is all I need to decide the instant case. . . .

Slicing the bologna even thinner, a subsequent case in the Second Circuit distinguished *U.S. Lines* based on the type of insurance contract, holding that a non-pay-first policy's breach fight could be a non-core proceeding. In re Residential Capital, LLC, 563 B.R. 756 (Bankr. S.D.N.Y. 2016). But why so much bother over locating the insurance-contract dispute within the core jurisdiction of the bankruptcy judge when the Article III district judge could just take over the dispute by withdrawing the reference and resolving it on its own? Is it worthwhile to note that withdrawal is rare, which means under the equitable mootness doctrine discussed earlier in Assignment 18, many cases involving huge companies, massive intellectual property, and large amounts of money never see the light of Article III day?

C.   VENUE

Venue rules provide for debtors to file where they live or where they have their assets. 28 U.S.C. § 1408(1). Big businesses may be interested in "shopping" for venues that they find congenial. (Small debtors might, too, but they usually can't afford to move just to court-shop.) Id. § 1409(b) (requiring bankruptcy actions under $25,000 to be brought in venue of defendant's residence). Sometimes venues are desirable due to precedent: Second Circuit case law that makes rejecting a CBA easier under its multi-factored test than the Third Circuit's makes New York more attractive than Delaware for an airline seeking to avoid its union obligations. Sometimes the forum appeals due to its procedures (recall the local rules discussed in Assignment 19) or even for the reputation and experience of its judges. Those of a cynical bent might speculate that courts with "flexibility" in approving counsel's fee applications are especially sought after for their "predictability and good sense."

Fortunately for these large debtors, Congress has made shopping for a favorable forum both expeditious and expedient. A debtor may file in its "domicile, residence, or principal place of business [or] principal assets." Id.

§ 1408(1). But the real sleeper is § 1408(2), which allows filing wherever an affiliate, general partner, or partnership has already filed. Thus, a large corporate debtor with 50 affiliates incorporated in 50 states can pick whichever state it prefers, file the appropriate affiliate first, and then piggyback all the other parts of the enterprise in that venue under § 1408(2); there is no requirement the holding company or "main" corporate entity must be the first to file.

Even if a filing is properly located in one jurisdiction, the court may transfer a case to another district "in the interest of justice or for the convenience of the parties." Id. § 1412. The standards are highly flexible. "In considering the convenience of the parties, the Court weighs a number of factors: 1. The proximity of creditors of every kind to the Court; 2. The proximity of the debtor to the Court; 3. The proximity of the witnesses necessary to the administration of the estate; 4. The location of the assets; 5. The economic administration of the estate; and 6. The necessity for ancillary administration if liquidation should result." In re Enron Corp., 274 B.R. 327, 343 (Bankr. S.D.N.Y. 2002) (citation omitted). With so many choices, it would be reasonable to assume that there are many hard-fought lawsuits over venue. Reasonable, but wrong. If a party protests venue, courts are unlikely to transfer the case elsewhere. Consider the *Enron* case just cited, from the dot-com collapse early this millennium. Enron was a company born, bred, and managed in Texas, albeit with operations all over the world. But Enron chose a New York filing, despite the vigorous protests of, among others, Enron's employees, many Texas-based creditors, tax authorities, and the Texas state attorney general. A comprehensive opinion authored by a well-respected bankruptcy judge explained that despite the Texas connection, many creditors and decision makers lived in New York and so some parties were going to have to travel in any case. Id. at 345-47 (noting specifically that New York has three airports). That said, there is some venue pushback. See, e.g., In re Patriot Coal Corp., 482 B.R. 718 (Bankr. S.D.N.Y. 2012) (venue transfer granted from New York to location of parent corporation's headquarters when New York affiliates were incorporated on eve of their filing bankruptcy).

The big winners of the flexibility of bankruptcy venue have evolved over time. By the mid-1990s, Delaware had an 87% market share of big chapter 11 cases. By the mid-2000s, New York and Delaware together took about half of all the public company cases that were shopped out of other locations around the country. Bankruptcy Research Database at http://lopucki.law.ucla.edu (database of large public companies). These data are in flux. Although New York and Delaware continue to have many large cases filed in their venues, by 2018 New York appeared out of the game, having only three cases filed by "travelers"—companies whose headquarters were located elsewhere. Business Bankruptcy Project (unpublished data). Delaware, by contrast, remained steadfast, without a single filing involving a company with Delaware headquarters. Id. Why would the people who decide where to file a bankruptcy choose Delaware over the local jurisdiction? Some debtors may want to escape unhappy employees who can march in front of the courthouse or the scrutiny of the local press. Others may be looking for judges who are sympathetic to debtors on first day orders or who will readily extend debtor exclusivity. Perhaps it is the expertise and efficiency of the Delaware courts that attracts big cases. See, e.g., Kenneth Ayotte & David Skeel, An Efficiency-Based Explanation for Current Corporate Reorganization Practice, 73 U. Chi. L. Rev. 425 (2006). Or maybe the big case lawyers who are disproportionately located in New York and Delaware are calling the shots. Or perhaps, as one Delaware supporter claimed in hearings before the National Bankruptcy Review Commission, it is the proximity to the Philadelphia airport. Perhaps.

It is not just "demand," but also "supply" that may affect forum shopping. A big bankruptcy case generates lawyers' and professionals' fees, along with hotels, meals, messenger services, stenography, and enough other services that chapter 11 is now estimated to be a $2-to-4-billion-a year industry. See, e.g., In re Nortel Networks Inc, 532 B.R. 494, 531 (Bankr. D. Del. 2015) (fees and expenses in excess of $1.3 billion). Moreover, a big case can secure a national reputation for a bankruptcy judge. Professor LoPucki concludes that pressures on judges to make decisions that favor the people who decide where the cases will be placed forces courts into a destructive competition. His book, Courting Failure: How Competition for Big Cases Is Corrupting the Bankruptcy Courts (2005), makes for lively reading, although many were dismayed by the provocative label of "corruption." He relies on an empirical analysis of cases filed in the 1990s to show that holding other factors constant in regression models, companies filing in Delaware or New York are much more likely to refile chapter 11. A subsequent study looking at later cases concludes that the refiling rate is converging among jurisdictions. Ruth Sara Lee, Delaware's Relevance in Chapter 22: Who Is "Courting Failure" Now?, 31 Rev. Banking & Fin. L. 443 (2011). The controversy stirred up by LoPucki, and the resulting firestorm of defense, may itself have shaped judicial behavior. While the controversy about *Courting Failure* has abated a bit, we still recommend not mentioning the book in job interviews at New York or Delaware law firms.

Venue reform remains a political hot potato. In 2019, a bipartisan bill was proposed restricting corporate affiliate venue to a proceeding afoot only if that debtor is parent or owner of more than 50% of the would-be piggyback debtor that files first. See Bankruptcy Venue Reform Act of 2019, 116 H.R. 4421. It was filed by a most unlikely pair, Senators Cornyn and Warren, and has been supported by 42 states so far (conspicuously not among them are New York or Delaware). It is difficult to tell whether the political winds will blow toward corporate bankruptcy venue reform. Congress may have bigger fish to fry.

D.   ALTERNATIVE DISPUTE RESOLUTION

Perhaps the only topic to rival the political volatility of venue reform is the use of arbitration, where the Supreme Court and state lawmakers have been engaged in an ongoing war on the scope of regulation of boilerplate arbitration clauses in contracts under the development of a sort of "federal common law of arbitration"—nominally interpreting the cryptically terse Federal Arbitration Act. See, e.g., Epic Sys. Corp. v. Lewis, 138 S. Ct. 1612 (2018). The use of arbitration in bankruptcy is especially complicated, because on the one hand, arbitration's speed commends it to a field where time is of the essence, but on the other hand, arbitration is at root a creature of contract (party consent, whether one doubts the robustness of that consent in consumer contracts or not), and it is difficult to conceive the debtor's pre-consenting on behalf of various stakeholders for which it may become a fiduciary as a DIP. Furthermore, bankruptcy courts are well versed in quick resolution, making arbitration perhaps less necessary than elsewhere. But most important is the in rem nature of bankruptcy, where the Code's structure anticipates a comprehensive, centralized dispute resolution that arbitration may, or may not, impede. As the Second Circuit put it, "Disputes that involve both the Bankruptcy Code and the Arbitration Act often present conflicts of 'near polar extremes: bankruptcy policy exerts an inexorable pull towards centralization while arbitration policy advocates a decentralized approach toward dispute resolution.'" MBNA America Bank, N.A. v. Hill, 436 F.3d 104 (2d Cir. 2006) (quoting *U.S. Lines*).

The dominant approach in the lower courts considers whether the Bankruptcy Code "repeals" parts of the FAA. It generally allows arbitration agreements in bankruptcy when the matter is non-core, but allows bankruptcy courts to stay arbitration on some, but not necessarily all, core matters: those "matters central to the purposes and policies of the Bankruptcy Code." Id. at 110. Courts have wide latitude to disagree under this test, which means it is an invitation to litigation. Compare In re Anderson, 884 F.3d 382 (2d Cir. 2018), *cert. denied sub nom.* Credit One Bank, N.A. v. Anderson, 139 S. Ct. 144 (2018) (affirming bankruptcy court's discretion to deny motion to compel arbitration of discharge injunction complaint) with In re Trevino, 599 B.R. 526 (Bankr. S.D. Tex. 2019) (holding that compelling arbitration of a core bankruptcy matter was appropriate under *Epic*, as the debtors failed to "carry their heavy burden of showing a clear and manifest expression of congressional intention" for the Bankruptcy Code to displace the Arbitration Act). This standard of "central to the purposes and policies of the Bankruptcy Code" presumably envisions "super-core" bankruptcy proceedings, as if the jurisdictional scheme weren't complicated enough. The Supreme Court's general enthusiasm to cart cases off to arbitration, when applied by the lower courts in bankruptcy cases, seems somewhat in tension with the jealous guarding of the Article III judicial function expressed in *Stern*. Did the late Mrs. Marshall get the last laugh?

Problem Set 37

37.1. As counsel for the trustee in a chapter 7 liquidation bankruptcy of the Mullen Company, you have been reviewing the claims filed by creditors. One is a claim by Atlantic Supply for goods it sold under contract to Mullen. On examining the Mullen files, you have concluded that the goods were defective and that substantial damages may be due Mullen from Atlantic. What action may you take, in what court, and before what judge? If you also find a basis for an antitrust action against Atlantic in connection with these transactions, how would that affect the answers to the foregoing questions? What if Atlantic had not filed a claim in the bankruptcy case? See 28 U.S.C. §§ 157(b)(2)(C), 1334(a), (c)(2).

If Mullen had filed a chapter 11 reorganization, reconsider your position. As attorney for the DIP, you recognize that no plan can be confirmed until these disputes with Atlantic are resolved. It would take six months to get to trial in bankruptcy court, eighteen months in state court, and thirty months in federal district court. How would these facts affect your litigation decisions? 28 U.S.C. See §§ 157(b), 1334(c)(2).

37.2. You represent the trustee in the chapter 7 bankruptcy case filed by Ingrid Schupbach. She appears to have valid prepetition claims against her former employer, who fired her after she asserted that he had sexually harassed her. In addition to a Title VII civil rights claim, she probably had an action for breach of her employment contract. She also has a Truth in Lending Act claim against her bank, and an assault suit against her former husband. Can the trustee's claims be brought in federal court and, if so, before which judge? Would it matter if the defendants also wanted to be in federal court and before the same judge you want? 28 U.S.C. See §§ 157, 1334(c)(2).

37.3. Stan Johnson had enough financial trouble even before he was sued in state court by Ethel Cannon. Ethel had blocked Stan's car in a mall parking lot. He got mad and deliberately backed into her car, breaking several of her favorite bones. Feeling the pressure mounting, he bought a book called "Doing Your Own Bankruptcy and Auto Body Repairs" and filed for chapter 7. He has now received a notice of trial from Ethel's state court case against him and has decided to ask a lawyer where he stands. When he asks you, what do you tell him? 11 U.S.C. See § 523(a)(6), 28 U.S.C. §§ 157(b)(2)(B), 1334(c)(2), 1452.

37.4. No one is quite sure how to describe what Alden Industries does anymore. The old chemical company and its two dozen subsidiaries have morphed into consumer electronics, cattle feed, and industrial fasteners businesses (just to name a few). In fact, maybe that's why the billion-dollar company is in enough trouble to be thinking about a chapter 11 filing. You have just made partner at your firm and have been asked to put together a strategy meeting, beginning with where to file. As you put together your notes for the agenda, what is on your list?

TRANSNATIONAL BANKRUPTCIES

As companies become more multinational in their capital structures and operations, the insolvency system needs to be increasingly multinational in its scope to work. Traditionally, bankruptcy has been one of the most parochial and nationalistic areas of the law because it was often seen as a last chance to reap value from a soon-to-be-liquidated business. Each nation followed a "grab rule" approach: seizing local assets and distributing them to the claimants in a local proceeding, with little concern for the overall result for the company or for claimholders outside the domestic jurisdiction. The trend now, however, is firmly in the direction of a collective and cooperative approach to addressing financial distress in global businesses.

Traditionally, two opposite theories anchored an intellectual debate on international bankruptcy: territorialism and universalism. Territorialism justifies the "grab rule" on the grounds that local creditors have legitimate expectations that any financial crisis should be resolved by applying local policies and preferences. Its proponents argue that those expectations give rise to vested local rights that should be respected. Universalism rests on the position that bankruptcy resolution must be symmetric to a debtor's market; it should be a collective proceeding that extends to all of a debtor's assets and all the stakeholders, regardless of location. In liquidation, this is the only approach that will maximize the collection of assets and permit a coherent and just distribution of those assets. Reorganization ups the ante; it is nearly impossible without one central, supervising court. Just as a national market (such as the United States) requires a national bankruptcy regime, a globalizing world requires a globalizing bankruptcy regime.

Territorialism has a long pedigree. For example, the seminal *Gibbs* case holds that British debt contracts may only be compromised by British insolvency proceedings, which functionally precludes cooperation with foreign insolvency proceedings. Antony Gibbs & Sons v. La Societe Industrielle et Commerciale des Métaux [1890] QB 399 (affirmed as still good law in Bakhshiyeva v. Sberbank of Russia [2018] EWCA Civ 2802, although with a hint it should be overruled); see also Re Pacific Andes Resources Dev. Ltd. [2016] SGHC 210 (rejecting *Gibbs* as antiquated). The great majority of scholars agree, however, that universalism is the right long-term goal. In the interim, the approach that is generally accepted in an increasing number of courts is "modified universalism," which takes universalism's worldwide perspective as a start and then asks what concessions are required by local laws and creditors to "modify" that perspective to assuage nations sensitive about their sovereignty. The American Law Institute endorses modified universalism as "universalism tempered by a sense of what is

869

practical at the current stage of international legal development." Am. L. Inst., Transnational Insolvency Project, Principles of Cooperation in Transnational Bankruptcy Cases Among Members of the North American Free Trade Agreement 11-12 (2000). The United States is a poster child for modified universalism. It engaged in it ad hoc under former § 304 of the Code by applying principles of comity before the landmark UNCITRAL Model Law on Cross-Border Insolvency was adopted as chapter 15.

The management of the general default of a multinational company (called a "bankruptcy proceeding" in the United States and an "insolvency proceeding" in the rest of the English-speaking world, where "bankruptcy" is usually reserved for liquidation of individuals) engages two central questions: choice of forum and choice of law. The two are often confused in the literature and in the cases. We divide the assignment along just those lines: choice of forum and choice of law.

A.   THE CHALLENGES OF COOPERATION IN CROSS-BORDER INSOLVENCY

Universalism (and modified universalism) requires a choice of forum to be the primary one to run the show. In a territorial system, the question is moot, because every court administers the assets it controls. Choice of forum in a universalist system, however, does not mean that only one court is involved in the case; effective liquidation or reorganization requires assistance from every ancillary jurisdiction court that has control over important segments of the company's assets. Choice of forum really means choice of a lead court.

Universalism's assumption of a main forum anticipates centralized control. United States bankruptcy law embraces that assumption through its application of a stay covering a debtor's worldwide assets. §§ 362; 541(a)(1). The legislative history to that subsection's predecessor in the old Act makes it clear that the Code asserts jurisdiction over the assets of the bankrupt "wherever located" in the world. A number of other countries employ the same rule. See, e.g., Insolvency Act 1986, c. 45, § 436 (United Kingdom); Trib. Comm. Seine 2 Fev. 1882 (France); R.S.C., 1985, c. B-3, s. 67 (Canada).

The following case provides the standard citation both for the long reach of U.S. jurisdictional claims with respect to the debtor's property abroad and for the serious practical difficulties of cross-border enforcement. Although the style of the case is "In re McLean Industries, Inc.," the principal operating company was United States Lines (yes, from Assignment 37), then one of the largest shipping companies in the world.

In re McLEAN INDUSTRIES, INC.
68 B.R. 690 (Bankr. S.D.N.Y. 1986)

BUSCHMAN, Bankruptcy Judge.

United States Lines, Inc., a debtor herein (the "debtor") seeks from this Court a preliminary injunction restraining defendant GAC Marine Fuels

Ltd. ("GAC Marine") from taking any action to arrest or interfere with vessels and other property of this estate. It further seeks an order holding GAC Marine in civil contempt for violating both the automatic stay applicable to this proceeding by the filing of the petition, 11 U.S.C. § 362, and the restraining order issued by this Court. GAC Marine, although essentially admitting the underlying facts, opposes these motions, declaring that it, as a non-domiciliary corporation organized under the laws of the United Kingdom and with a principal place of business in London, is not subject to the in personam jurisdiction of this Court. . . .

The debtor filed a voluntary petition for relief under Chapter 11 of the Bankruptcy Code, 11 U.S.C. §§ 101 et seq. (1984) (the "Code") on November 24, 1986. On that date, this Court issued an order, which restated the automatic stay provided by § 362(a) of the Code and not excepted by § 362(b) of the Code. The Debtor has remained in possession and continues to operate its trans-Pacific and western hemisphere cargo shipping services. It is in the process of terminating its around the world and North Atlantic services.

The facts are not in dispute. On December 4, 1986, ten days after the petition was filed, GAC Marine commenced an in rem admiralty action in the Supreme Court of Hong Kong against the debtor, pursuant to a Writ of Summons, for the payment of $173,750 allegedly owed it for fuel oil delivered on board the *American Utah*, a vessel owned by the debtor, in October 1986 in Khorfakkan Port, United Arab Emirates. On December 9, 1986, upon application of GAC Marine, the Hong Kong court issued a warrant of arrest against the *American California*, also owned by the debtor. As a result, this vessel has since been restrained from leaving Hong Kong harbor. [A similar seizure of another debtor ship happened a few days later in Singapore. — Eds.]

. . .

GAC Marine took these actions with knowledge of the debtor's filing of its reorganization petition and the resultant automatic stay provided by § 362 of the Code, and after being informed by the debtor that such actions would be improper, carried out a threat contained in a telex from GAC Marine to the debtor dated November 28, 1986. That telex stated:

> . . . On request by agents for payment of these invoices, we have been informed of your refusal to settle all outstandings as your company has filed for bankruptcy under Chapter 11 of the U.S. Law. . . . Chapter 11 procedure in the USA is not enforceable in foreign jurisdictions. Therefore we are entitled to arrest any U.S. Lines ship abroad and unless prompt settlement is made to us, we will have no recourse other than to take such action as is deemed necessary by our lawyers for the protection of our interests. We will therefore arrest your ships one-by-one unless settlement is made immediately. . . .

GAC Marine is, we are told by its counsel, a subsidiary of a Liechtenstein corporation, apparently known as Gulf Agency Company ("GAC"), which has its central office in Athens, Greece. GAC Marine's principal offices are located in London, England but its invoices state that it also has offices in Hong Kong, Norway, United Arab Emirates and Basking Ridge, New Jersey. The New Jersey office is apparently located in the same office as that of G.A.C. Shipping (North America) Ltd. ("GAC Shipping"), another GAC subsidiary. That office is staffed by one Norman Schmidt, Georgianne Temple and Marilyn Taylor, who are paid by GAC Shipping with funds supplied by GAC. But Schmidt styles himself as manager of GAC's U.S. office and his business card is under the name of the defendant GAC Marine. GAC and GAC Marine, according to Schmidt, "apparently are run by the same people." Schmidt describes his duties for GAC Marine as "sales and contact and follow through." . . .

. . .

The limits of . . . in personam jurisdiction are apparently conceded by both sides to be tested by due process. This is not a case in diversity where state law concepts govern the extent of personal jurisdiction. Rather, this is a case involving the violation of a federal statute and related court order.

Two grounds for the exercise of such jurisdiction consistent with due process are asserted here: (i) transactional jurisdiction as set forth in 1 Restatement (Second) of Conflicts of Laws § 47(1)(1971)(the "Restatement") ["specific jurisdiction" in U.S. parlance—Eds.] and (ii) general "doing business" jurisdiction as set forth in § 47(2) of the Restatement ["general jurisdiction"—Eds.].[4]

Here it is clear that the defendant transacts business in the United States. It regularly affords, in the United States, quoted prices and terms for delivery of bunkers abroad. Agreements for the same are reached in the United States upon the acceptance of the quoted prices and terms. Its representative in the United States is apparently empowered to sign letters and to deliver documents on its behalf with respect to U.S. customers. It repeatedly holds itself out to the world as having an office in the United States.

It is also clear that the second half of the [transactional] test, i.e., that the cause of action asserted arose from business done here, has also been satisfied. . . . [The court alternatively found jurisdiction under the "doing business" test of § 47(2), but on an analysis of general jurisdiction that would likely not survive. See Daimler AG v. Bauman, 571 U.S. 117 (2014).—Eds.]

We thus find that, with the debtor's success on the merits being virtually conceded on this motion and with its injury being, and deemed to be, irreparable, a preliminary injunction should issue since in personam jurisdiction is established. We further find that a contempt citation should issue since all that need be shown is a knowing violation of the automatic stay. Although willfulness is not required in view of the remedial nature of the remedy, the brazenness of GAC Marine's conduct makes that remedy particularly appropriate.

---

[4]No claim is made on this motion that in personam jurisdiction may be posited on the notion that the interest of the United States in administering bankruptcy proceedings of domestic corporations is so strong as to justify the right of its courts, in the exercise of exclusive jurisdiction over the property of the estate afforded by 28 U.S.C. § 1334(d), to enjoin attempts to divest them of that jurisdiction and to determine the rights of all creditors wherever they may be. Nor is any claim made on this motion that jurisdiction may be found on the basis that the warrant and arrest of the two vessels had a substantial, direct and foreseeable effect on the administration of this estate of exactly the type that 11 U.S.C. § 362(a) was designed to prevent. Those highly interesting issues are left to another day.

An injunction and finding of contempt notwithstanding, the fish continued to wiggle on the hook. GAC Marine subsequently objected that it could not comply with the court's order because it assigned its prepetition claims to another entity, so it no longer had standing to desist the foreign attachments. The court was not amused, outlining some questionable timing of the alleged transfers and noting that GAC Marine never mentioned in the initial proceeding that it had apparently divested itself of all claims. In re McLean Industries, 76 B.R. 291, 295-97 (Bankr. S.D.N.Y. 1987) (ordering contempt sanctions for stay violation to be paid to the debtor).

In *McLean*, the recalcitrant creditor had enough contacts with the United States to permit the court to enforce its worldwide stay — "an indirect global stay." Jay Lawrence Westbrook, Global Insolvency Proceedings for a Global Market: The Universalist System and the Choice of a Central Court, 96 Tex. L. Rev. 1473 (2018). When that is not true, restraint of creditors will depend on the cooperation of foreign courts. If that cooperation is not forthcoming, then an orderly reorganization or a value-maximizing liquidation may be impossible. Note the tension at work. The global aspirations of the primary court's jurisdiction corrals control into one forum but also creates a serious risk of conflict, and even resentment, with other countries.

You may have noticed an even bigger problem. If U.S. law enables universalism by extending its reach to worldwide assets, but U.K. law does the same, then how can both be the "primary" forum? Jurisdictions responded to this by allowing "ancillary" proceedings, such as former § 304 — bankruptcy cases of limited scope, to assist a foreign proceeding. The ancillary case then offers its assistance to the foreign primary court under principles of comity. See, e.g., Roberts v. Picture Butte Municipal Hospital, [1999] 4 W.W.R. 443 (Alberta Q.B.) (directing Canadian tort claimants to file their claims in U.S. main reorganization proceedings). But nothing forces a debtor to file an ancillary case. If global conglomerate Maxwell Communications files for administration in England, nothing stops it from also filing in the United States under chapter 11. This gives rise to "parallel proceedings," with co-primary courts, each of which might bask in its own sovereignty. At that point, there is no primary court to seek assistance from an ancillary court. Rather, there are two primary courts who must cooperate with each other without logical hierarchy and the potential for chaos.

Sometimes this goes badly. Compare Perpetual Trustee Co Ltd v. BNY Corporate Trustee Services Ltd, [2009] EWCA Civ 1160, with In re Lehman Brothers Holdings Inc., 422 B.R. 407 (Bankr. S.D.N.Y. 2010): the courts rendered flatly conflicting decisions concerning the effect of contract clauses that reverse priorities in event of bankruptcy. (The case fortunately settled before the gunboats met mid-Atlantic.) Other times courts muddle through. See generally ALI Principles, Procedural Principle 4: Stay Upon Recognition, at 56 (suggesting rules for resolving conflicts of overlapping stays).

In sum, a transnational debtor often has many choices of where and how (i.e., through which proceedings) to file bankruptcy. Recall that a chapter 11 petition can be opened by a foreign debtor if it has "a place of business or property" in the United States. § 109(a). This may encourage international "forum shopping," although sometimes courts rebuff truly brazen stretches. See, e.g., In re Yukos Oil Co., 321 B.R. 396, 410-11 (Bankr. S.D. Tex. 2005) (dismissing U.S. chapter 11 of Russian oil company with negligible U.S. assets, notwithstanding defected corporate officer's residence in Houston, in favor of Russian proceedings). But "forum shopping" is a more complex phenomenon in transnational insolvency than a pejorative label suggests, because jurisdictions vary in their legal infrastructures' capacities to process sprawling reorganizations. In the *China Fishery* case, a holding company was incorporated in the Cayman Islands, but the primary asset was a billion-plus dollar fishing license for anchovies in Peru, a venue whose legal ability to manage a complex cross-border insolvency was questionable. All this was resolved in a bankruptcy case in Battery Park on the shores of New York Harbor. In re China Fishery Grp. Ltd. (Cayman), 2016 WL 6875903, at *20 (Bankr. S.D.N.Y. Oct. 28, 2016) (appointing a chapter 11 trustee to sell Peruvian assets). You may take note that the United States, United Kingdom, and, increasingly, Singapore capture the lion's share of cross-border bankruptcy cases—and compete for them vigorously.

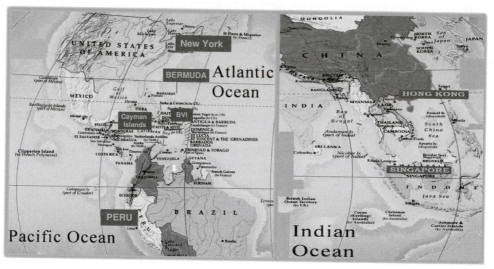

China Fishery Group filing locations

B.   THE UNCITRAL MODEL LAW ON CROSS-BORDER INSOLVENCY

The messiness of overlapping claims to jurisdiction, which peaks with parallel proceedings, was likely a driving force behind international bankruptcy reform at the United Nations. Converging beliefs led to promulgation by the United Nations Commission on International Trade Law (UNCITRAL) in 1997 of a Model Law on Cross-Border Insolvency for international cooperation in bankruptcy matters (based on a parallel-developed EU Insolvency Treaty that was enacted as an EU Regulation, Council Regulation 1346/2000 European Union Regulation on Insolvency

Proceedings, 2000 O.J. (L 160), at http://eur-lex.europa.eu/LexUriServ/
LexUriServ.do?uri=CELEX:32000 R1346:en:HTML). The United States
was an active participant in the development of the Model Law, which
was enacted in 2005 as chapter 15 of the Code. The key innovation of this
Model Law, increasingly adopted around the globe, is to develop a hierarchy of jurisdictions by coming up with rules to designate one insolvency
forum as the primary and encouraging others to assist it.

1. Designating a Primary Forum: COMI and Recognition of a Foreign Main Proceeding

Chapter 15 contemplates a limited U.S. bankruptcy case ancillary to a "foreign main proceeding," which is a proceeding in the center of main interests ("COMI") of the debtor. Absent evidence to the contrary, the debtor's
registered office ("place of incorporation" in U.S. parlance) is presumed to
be its COMI. § 1516(c). A "foreign representative," § 101(24), may file for
recognition of a foreign proceeding in the United States under § 1515, and
recognition will be granted quickly in most cases, pursuant to various presumptions. §§ 1515-1517. Upon recognition, an automatic stay goes into
effect with similar force and limitations to that under § 362. § 1520(a)(1).
In addition to these automatic consequences, the recognizing court in a
chapter 15 case is given broad powers to grant further "relief" (which we
explore below), including the grant of additional injunctive remedies, the
use of U.S. discovery tools, and the turnover of assets within its control to
the foreign representative. §§ 1520(a)(1), 1521(a)-(b). Recognition of a foreign main proceeding triggers automatic relief, such as a local stay of proceedings in the recognizing jurisdiction. § 1520(a)(1).

"Foreign non-main proceedings," pending in non-home countries
where the debtor nonetheless has an "establishment," are also recognized
but granted more limited, discretionary relief, § 1521(c), implementing
chapter 15's goal of corralling maximal authority to the primary jurisdiction. Thus, chapter 15 cuts a middle ground of sorts between universalism
and territorialism, although with a thumb firmly on the universalist side
of the scale. It generally defers to the COMI court for dominant control on
the universalist side, but on the territorialist side conditions relief upon
the "protection" of creditor interests, § 1522 (a concept left deliberately
vague), and permits the opening of local proceedings under local law in
parallel to a foreign main proceeding, § 1529. John A.E. Pottow, Procedural
Incrementalism: A Model for International Bankruptcy, 45 Va. J. Int'l
L. 935, 935-1015 (2005).

Recognition under chapter 15 has been granted to the great majority
of foreign representatives so requesting, although that does not stop litigation, especially when COMI moves or connections seem wispy. In reading the next case, it will help to think of the Cayman Islands debtor as a
"grandchild" investment fund, whose principal assets were investments
in a "parent" Delaware investment fund, whose own assets were in turn
invested in the "grandparent," Bernie Madoff's $64 billion international
Ponzi scheme fund. The grandchild debtor (along with its parent) was sued
by the trustee for the Madoff fund to claw back massive distributions made

by the Madoff fund to the parent and onto the grandchild-debtor before the fraud was revealed. (The theory for the clawbacks was that they were fraudulent transfers because there was no reasonably equivalent value for fake investment returns.) But the grandchild-debtor was also entitled to a share of the parent's estate—which was also, of course, bankrupt—and so there was inter-bankruptcy litigation over the dividend due from the parent to the grandchild and the amount of any setoff for clawbacks. As part of a settlement of all that, it was determined the grandchild-debtor was entitled to a net recovery. The question in the case was whether a New York bankruptcy court or the Cayman insolvency court would get to control the determination of the formula for allocating the distribution of that net recovery—millions of dollars—among the shareholders of the grandchild fund ("great-grandchildren," under our taxonomy). One such shareholder objected to the Cayman court's control.

In re ASCOT FUND LTD.
603 B.R. 271 (Bankr. S.D.N.Y. 2019)

Bernstein, Bankruptcy Judge.

The debtor, Ascot Fund Ltd. ("Ascot Fund"), an investment fund organized under Cayman Islands law, invested all or substantially all of its assets in Ascot Partners L.P. ("Ascot Partners"), a Delaware limited partnership. Ascot Partners, in turn, invested all or substantially all of its assets with Bernard L. Madoff Investment Securities, LLC ("BLMIS"), the vehicle through which Bernard Madoff ran his notorious Ponzi scheme. When Madoff's fraud was revealed in December 2008 and the scheme collapsed, the BLMIS investors, direct (e.g., Ascot Partners) and indirect (e.g., Ascot Fund), lost their investments.

As a result of certain settlements described below [with, inter alia, BLMIS], Ascot Partners now holds substantial assets available for distribution and some of that money will be down streamed to Ascot Fund, and ultimately, Ascot Fund's shareholders. Ascot Fund is currently in liquidation in the Cayman Islands ("Cayman Proceeding") and one of its Joint Official Liquidators ("JOLs"), Mr. Michael Penner ("Petitioner"), has filed a petition under chapter 15 of the United States Bankruptcy Code ("Petition") seeking recognition of the Cayman Proceeding as a foreign main proceeding. HFC Limited ("Objector"), an Ascot Fund investor, opposes the Petition. It contends that Ascot Fund's center of main interests, or COMI, is not in the Cayman Islands and the Cayman Proceeding cannot, therefore, be recognized as a foreign main proceeding. The Court conducted a one-day trial, overrules the objection and grants the Petition.

BACKGROUND . . .

The Picard Litigation

Also in 2009, Irving H. Picard, as trustee ("Trustee") for the liquidation of BLMIS under the Securities Investor Protection Act ("SIPA"), commenced an adversary proceeding against inter alia . . . Ascot Partners and Ascot Fund. [Picard sued to recover various distributions to the two funds by the Madoff fund, alleging they were fraudulent conveyances as part of the Ponzi scheme.]

On July 3, 2018, this Court approved a settlement ("Picard Settlement") in the Picard Litigation. Pursuant to the Picard Settlement, Ascot Partners received an allowed customer claim in the sum of $501,734,338.00. From its catch-up distribution of $320,628,311.35, it paid the Trustee $280 million, leaving a balance of $40,628,311.35. In addition, Ascot Partners will be entitled to receive additional distributions on a pari passu basis with other customers holding allowed customer claims. Don Seymour, a director of Ascot Fund, signed the Picard Settlement on Ascot Fund's behalf. Based on its receipt of the settlement proceeds and possible future distributions, Ascot Partners has a substantial amount of money to distribute to its investors.

The Distribution Dispute

Although the JOLs have not adopted and the Cayman Court has not approved a distribution methodology, the Objector, a shareholder of the Ascot Fund, is concerned that a distribution methodology adopted by the Ascot Fund Board will be less favorable to it than any distribution methodology a New York court might adopt governing distributions from Ascot Partners to Ascot Fund or directly to Ascot Fund's shareholders [and hence prefers a U.S chapter 11 to govern the debtor's insolvency under U.S. rules rather than a U.S. chapter 15 that recognizes and assists a Cayman proceeding under Cayman rules—Eds.]. . . .

The Liquidation Proceeding

[T]he sole voting shareholder, DMS Bank & Trust Ltd. ("DMS Bank"), appointed the Petitioner and Timothy Derksen as Ascot Fund's Joint Voluntary Liquidators ("JVLs"). The appointment of the JVLs commenced Ascot Fund's liquidation and provided the JVLs with authority . . . to manage Ascot Fund in the course of its liquidation. . . .

Immediately upon assuming their duties, the JVLs wrote to the Ascot Fund shareholders. Their letter advised the shareholders of the dispute relating to the distribution methodology and explained that the dispute prompted the filing of the voluntary liquidation. The letter also stated that the dispute may require the JVLs to bring the liquidation proceeding under the supervision of the Grand Court of the Cayman Islands ("Cayman Court") and seek recognition under chapter 15 of the Bankruptcy Code.

. . .

On January 16, 2019, the Petitioner and Derksen [commenced] the Cayman Proceeding. . . . At the February 14, 2019 hearing, which . . . the Objector attended . . . the Cayman Court entered an order (the "Appointment Order") pursuant to section 131(b) of the Companies Law, bringing Ascot Fund's liquidation under court supervision and appointing the Petitioner and Derksen to act as JOLs with authority to act jointly and severally. Among other things, the Appointment Order granted the JOLs the power to file a chapter 15 case. . . .

DISCUSSION

. . .

Standards Governing Recognition

Section 1517(a) of the Bankruptcy Code establishes the statutory requirements for recognition. Subject to a narrow public policy exception, see 11 U.S.C. § 1506, which the Objector does not contend applies, the Court must grant recognition, if it finds that:

(1)   such foreign proceeding for which recognition is sought is a foreign main proceeding or foreign nonmain proceeding within the meaning of section 1502;

(2)   the foreign representative applying for recognition is a person or body; and

(3)   the petition meets the requirements of section 1515.

The Objector has not challenged the Petitioner's satisfaction of the second or third factors (arguing the Court need not reach them), and the Petitioner has plainly met them. Bankruptcy Code § 101(23) defines a "foreign proceeding" as "a collective judicial or administrative proceeding in a foreign country, including an interim proceeding, under a law relating to insolvency or adjustment of debt in which proceeding the assets and affairs of the debtor are subject to control or supervision by a foreign court, for the purpose of reorganization or liquidation." The Cayman Proceeding is a collective proceeding governed by the Companies Law through which Ascot Fund's financial affairs will be wound up and its assets distributed to creditors, here the shareholders. In addition, the Cayman Proceeding is overseen by the Cayman Court. Moreover, courts in this district have consistently recognized Cayman Islands liquidation proceedings as "foreign proceedings" for purposes of chapter 15 of the Bankruptcy Code.

Next, the Petitioner is a "foreign representative." Bankruptcy Code § 101(24) defines "foreign representative" as "a person or body, including a person or body appointed on an interim basis, authorized in a foreign proceeding to administer the reorganization or the liquidation of the debtor's assets or affairs or to act as a representative of such foreign proceeding." . . .

COMI

The sole question disputed and litigated by the parties is whether the Cayman Proceeding can be recognized as a "foreign main proceeding." . . . "The relevant principle . . . is that the COMI lies where the debtor conducts its regular business, so that the place is ascertainable by third parties." Morning Mist Holdings Ltd. v. Krys (In re Fairfield Sentry Ltd.), 714 F.3d 127, 130 (2d Cir. 2013) ("Fairfield Sentry"). "In the absence of evidence to the contrary, the debtor's registered office . . . is presumed to be the center of the debtor's main interests." 11 U.S.C. § 1516(c). The following non-exclusive group of factors guides the analysis, "but consideration of these specific factors is neither required nor dispositive": the location of the debtor's headquarters; the location of those who actually manage the debtor (which, conceivably could be the headquarters of a holding company); the location of the debtor's primary assets; the location of the majority of the debtor's creditors or of a majority of the creditors who would be affected by the case; and/or the jurisdiction whose law would apply to most disputes.

The Location of Ascot Fund's Headquarters and Management

Ascot Fund's registered address has been located in the Cayman Islands since its formation in 1992, and hence, the Cayman Islands is presumed to be its COMI. As further proof of its pre-liquidation Cayman Islands COMI, the Board directed Ascot Fund's affairs, and the Board members resided or were based in the Cayman Islands. . . . Additionally, Ascot Fund's sole voting shareholder, DMS Bank, is a Cayman Islands entity, as is Sackville Bank, the Enforcer under the STAR Trust arrangement governing Ascot Fund.

The Board conferred regularly in the Cayman Islands to conduct Ascot Fund's business. . . . Both before and after the liquidation, Ascot Fund has employed Estera Fund Services ("Estera") to provide administrative services. Estera has offices throughout the world, including the Cayman Islands, but the principal Estera employee responsible for Ascot Fund is located in the Isle of Man where it maintains Ascot Fund's register of shareholders. The Objector places great significance on the fact that Estera works out of the Isle of Man, but does not contend that Estera played any role with respect to the activities that the Objector relies on to argue that Ascot Fund's pre and post-liquidation activities have been centered in New York or that the Isle of Man is its COMI.

. . . Immediately upon the commencement of the voluntary liquidation, a representative of Deloitte reached out to Ascot Fund's New York lawyers to advise them that the JVLs had assumed control of Ascot Fund. . . .

The Objector's central argument in opposition is that Ascot Fund has been engaged in a "soft wind-down" since December 2008 and its only activities have occurred in New York where it has "piggybacked" on the . . . liquidation activities in New York. . . . ¶ 41 ("The question before the Court now is whether the minor, ministerial actions that the Cayman Liquidators have conducted since their appointment—such as providing investors with banal updates and producing a statutorily-required report, in addition to initiating the Cayman Island Proceeding and participating in the chapter 15 process to seek recognition . . . —are sufficient to shift Ascot Fund's COMI to the Cayman Islands.") . . .

It is certainly true that Ascot Fund has not been engaged in the investment business since the BLMIS Ponzi scheme came to light. The same may be said of the other offshore funds and fund-of-funds, including Fairfield, Kingate, Harley, etc., that invested all of their money with BLMIS and are now in liquidation in their home countries. Since then, Ascot Fund's only significant activity has been its participation in New York litigation. Not coincidentally, New York was where BLMIS operated and where the SEC, the Securities Investor Protection Corporation, the United States Attorney and Mr. Picard have commenced their various proceedings relating to Madoff and BLMIS. As a result of its direct relationship to Ascot Partners and its indirect relationship to BLMIS, Ascot Fund was dragged into [litigation] as a relief defendant and . . . as an initial and subsequent [fraudulent conveyance] transferee of BLMIS [as well as, on the other hand, an ultimate beneficiary of some recovered funds]. . . .

This does not mean that the New York litigations define Ascot Fund's COMI or, as the Objector implies, Ascot Fund [is a] silent partner in the [litigations] or the resulting settlements. In [one] Litigation, the New York Attorney General did not seek any relief against the Ascot Fund, but instead, sought and obtained relief on behalf of the Ascot Fund shareholders as well as other indirect investors in BLMIS. As noted, Ascot Fund, not the Receiver, approved the . . . Settlement and granted the releases on behalf of Ascot Fund.

Nor did Ascot Fund "piggyback" on the Receiver's defense of the Picard Litigation. While both were represented by the same counsel, they had different rights and faced different potential liabilities. Ascot Fund (but not Ascot Partners) stipulated with Picard to dismiss the initial fraudulent transfer claims but remained a defendant on the subsequent transfer claims. In a subsequent motion for summary judgment made by the defendants, the Court dismissed the subsequent transfer claims brought against Ascot Partners but denied the same motion by Ascot Fund. . . .

The Objector's principal authorities, *SPhinX, Ltd.*, 351 B.R. 103 and In re Bear Stearns High-Grade Structured Credit Strategies Master Fund, Ltd., 374 B.R. 122 (Bankr. S.D.N.Y. 2007), aff'd, 389 B.R. 325 (S.D.N.Y. 2008), are distinguishable. In *SPhinX*, the JOLs sought recognition of a Cayman proceeding, inter alia, as a foreign main proceeding. The Court noted that the debtors' business had been managed outside the Cayman Islands and the business transacted in the Cayman Islands was primarily ministerial, the debtor had no employees, managers, or offices in the Cayman Islands, the debtors' board did not include any Cayman Islands residents and never met in the Cayman Islands, most of its assets were in the United States and most of the investors and creditors were located outside of the Cayman Islands.

Despite these facts, the Court nonetheless stated that it would still normally recognize the Cayman Islands proceeding as a foreign main proceeding [but for the fact that] the chapter 15 petition had been filed as a litigation tactic. . . .

Initially, the Sphinx Court focused on the debtor's business activities before the petition date, but since Fairfield Sentry, courts are required to assess COMI on the date the chapter 15 petition is filed with a lookback period to the date of the commencement of the foreign proceeding to decide whether COMI has been manipulated. By the time the JOLs filed Ascot Fund's chapter 15 case, Ascot Fund had not carried on any investment activity in New York or anywhere else for over ten years. Further, unlike the non-resident directors in that case, Ascot Fund has always had directors that reside or were based in the Cayman Islands.

. . . COMI has not been manipulated as Ascot Fund's principal place of business has always been in the Cayman Islands and the documents and agreements discussed immediately below provided that the liquidation of Ascot Fund would occur in the Cayman Islands under Cayman law.

Accordingly, the location of the Ascot Fund's headquarters and management weigh in favor of recognition.

The Governing Law, Appropriate Forum and the Creditors' Expectations

From the Ascot Fund investors' point of view, and as a matter of fact and law, they invested in a Cayman fund and their rights were to be determined under Cayman law. . . .

The Objector seems to imply that New York law will determine any dispute between the Ascot Fund and its shareholders because Ascot Fund's principal asset is its limited partner interest in Ascot Partners. This assertion conflates two distinct distributions. The first, from Ascot Partners to Ascot Fund, will be determined presumably under either Delaware or New York law and in accordance with the relevant Ascot Partners documents and will be subject to the approval of the New York court. The second, from Ascot Fund to its shareholders should be determined under Cayman law in accordance with the Ascot Fund documents and will be subject to the approval of the Cayman Court. . . .

The Location of the Creditors

Ascot Fund's sixty-six creditors (i.e., its shareholders) are scattered throughout the world. This is not surprising given the nature of Ascot Fund's business as an offshore investment fund designed to attract non-U.S. Persons. The largest group, numbering fourteen, have registered addresses in Switzerland. Only nine shareholders are registered in New York. Five shareholders are registered in the Cayman Islands. They include the Objector. This factor is neutral.

The Location of Assets

As noted, Ascot Fund's only significant asset is its limited partner interest in Ascot Partners. The value of this asset ultimately depends on the value of Ascot Partners' customer claim in the BLMIS liquidation and the distribution that the Receiver makes to Ascot Fund as a limited partner of Ascot Partners. Thus, Ascot Fund's principal asset is located either in Delaware where Ascot Partners was formed or in New York, where its Receiver operates, but not in the Cayman Islands. This factor weighs against recognition.

Nevertheless, it does not follow, as the Objector argues, that the location of this asset is "the key piece of evidence 'ascertainable by third parties.'" While the Objector bought shares in Ascot Fund in 2017, those who invested pursuant to the 2006 Confidential Offering Memorandum had no idea that they would become embroiled in New York litigations involving a Ponzi scheme or depend on the SIPA liquidation of BLMIS with whom they never dealt. Rather, the only situs ascertainable as Ascot Fund's COMI, based on the fund documents described above, was the Cayman Islands. . . . [T]he Cayman Proceeding is recognized as a foreign main proceeding. . . .

An empirical study has shown that the goal of routine recognition of a foreign main proceeding has been largely achieved in the United States under chapter 15. Jay L. Westbrook, An Empirical Study of the Implementation in the United States of the Model Law on Cross-Border Insolvency, 87 Am. Bankr. L.J. 247 (2013). Only in true letterbox corporation cases like *SPhinX* and *Bear Stearns*, cited in *Ascot*, is recognition usually denied. *Bear Stearns* also holds, importantly, that the presumption of registered office being the debtor's COMI can be rebutted by the court on its own, even if no party objects, when the record shows the COMI location is clearly elsewhere. See In re Bear Stearns High-Grade Structured Credit Strategies Master Fund, Ltd., 374 B.R. 122, 129 (Bankr. S.D.N.Y. 2007), *aff'd*, 389 B.R. 325 (S.D.N.Y. 2008).

There is an important caveat to the Model Law's jurisdictional hierarchy favoring the debtor's COMI with the designation of being the main proceeding: nothing stops a debtor from opening a full-blown plenary insolvency proceeding in any place where jurisdiction properly lies. Thus, parallel proceedings persist and are acknowledged by chapter 15. But the statute adds a twist: where the debtor's COMI is elsewhere, such a U.S. plenary proceeding will not have worldwide effect; its stay must be limited to assets situated within the territorial jurisdiction of the United States. Furthermore, nothing stops a domestic judge from dismissing the local case in the interests of all creditors. § 1507(b). And any parallel proceeding imposes an obligation to cooperate with the other court(s). §§ 1525-1526.

The idea of an obligation to cooperate and to encourage direct communication between courts was a radical one when included in the ALI Statement of Principles, but was enacted in chapter 15, and is now frequent. Certain leading courts have formed the Judicial Insolvency Network ("JIN") and adopted "Guidelines for Communication and Cooperation between Courts in Cross-Border Insolvency Matters." See, e.g., Bankr. D. Del. R. 9029-2 (effective Feb. 1, 2017).

An example of successful parallel proceedings in which the courts communicated well is the *Nortel* case. Although there were three loci of control (Canada, United States, Europe and beyond), the parties—with the encouragement of the courts—were able to coordinate their parallel proceedings and orchestrate a worldwide sale of $7 billion in intellectual property assets, realizing far more than could have been achieved in separate sales controlled by each jurisdiction. (Such agreements in international insolvency cases that hammer out coordination procedures are often called "protocols.") Of course, the parties then squabbled over the proceeds and burned through $1 billion in expenses, but the preservation of the intellectual property value was a testament to how much cross-border insolvency had evolved. The ultimate dispute resolution was itself an international milestone, with the first joint trial before a U.S. and Canadian court televised live in courtrooms in Toronto and Wilmington, including evidence presented and witnesses cross-examined simultaneously. The single decision about worldwide distribution was set forth in two separate opinions from the two courts. In re Nortel Networks, Inc., 532 B.R. 494, 502 (Bankr. D. Del. 2015); Nortel Networks Corp. (Re), 2015 ONSC 2987, 2015 CanLII 2987, ¶ 40 (Can. Ont. Super. Ct. J.). It is heralded as landmark. John A.E. Pottow, Two Cheers for Universalism: Nortel's Nifty Novelty, in Annual Review of Insolvency Law, 333-68 (J.P. Sarra & B. Romaine eds. 2015).

2. *Guiding the Ancillary Jurisdiction: Obligation and Discretion to Order Relief*

Deciding to recognize a foreign proceeding is just the first step in chapter 15. The next question, and the tougher one, is determining the relief to be granted. As mentioned, some relief, like the implementation of a domestic stay, is automatic. In re Hanjin Shipping Co., Ltd., 2016 WL 6679487, 2016 A.M.C. 2126 (Bankr. D.N.J. Sept. 20, 2016) (triggering U.S. stay upon recognition of foreign main proceeding of Korean shipping company to protect assets from seizure—involving ships literally cruising outside U.S. harbors for fear of admiralty arrests upon docking until relief could be assured).

Other relief is discretionary, such as enforcement of a foreign reorganization plan. § 1521(a). Plan enforcement requires granting a discharge of the original debts and ordering substitution of the new debts set forth in the plan. That means for a foreign reorganization to be effective in the United States, a U.S. court must enter an order enforcing the foreign discharge against assets and creditors located domestically. Under chapter 15, a foreign representative, once recognized, might ask for such an injunction as "relief." (There may be a time lag between recognition and relief requests—not all foreign reorganizations are prepacks.) Or the representative may ask, as in the insurance liquidation case coming later in this assignment, for local assets to be turned over for distribution in the foreign proceeding. Even before chapter 15, U.S. courts had a good track record of providing relief for foreign reorganizations. See, e.g., In re Board of Directors of Telecom Argentina, S.A., 528 F.3d 162 (2d Cir. 2008) (finding foreign plan had been adopted with adequate due process for creditors and could be given the same effect against U.S. bondholders as if it had resulted from a domestic proceeding) (per Sotomayor, J.). But relief is not a rubber stamp. The Fifth Circuit drew the line when it felt the foreign main proceeding was not giving the creditors a fair shake.

=========================== In re VITRO S.A.B. DE C.V. ===========================
701 F.3d 1031 (5th Cir. 2012)

KING, Circuit Judge.
Consolidated before us are three cases relating to the Mexican reorganization proceeding of Vitro S.A.B. de C.V., a corporation organized under the laws of Mexico. . . . Vitro and one of its largest third-party creditors, Fintech Investments, Ltd., each appeals directly to this court the bankruptcy court's decision denying enforcement of the Mexican reorganization plan because the plan would extinguish the obligations of non-debtor guarantors. We . . . affirm the bankruptcy court's order denying enforcement of the Mexican reorganization plan.

I. Factual and Procedural Background

A. *Vitro S.A.B. de C.V. and the 2008 Financial Crisis*

Vitro S.A.B. de C.V. ("Vitro") is a holding company that, together with its subsidiaries, constitutes the largest glass manufacturer in Mexico. Originally incorporated in 1909, Vitro operates manufacturing facilities in seven countries, as well as distribution centers throughout the Americas and Europe, and exports its products to more than 50 countries worldwide. Vitro employs approximately 17,000 workers, the majority of whom work in Mexico. Between February 2003 and February 2007, Vitro borrowed a total of approximately $1.216 billion, predominately from United States investors. Vitro's indebtedness is evidenced by three series of unsecured notes . . . (collectively the "Old Notes").

Payment in full of the Old Notes was guaranteed by substantially all of Vitro's subsidiaries (the "Guarantors"). . . .

B. *Vitro Restructures Its Obligations*

After Vitro stopped making payments on the Old Notes, it entered into a series of transactions restructuring its debt obligations. . . .

Partly as a result of these transactions, Vitro generated a large quantity of intercompany debt. Previously, certain of Vitro's operating subsidiaries directly and indirectly owed Vitro an aggregate of approximately $1.2 billion in intercompany debt. As a result of a series of [allegedly manufactured—Eds.] financial transactions in December of 2009, that debt was wiped out and, in a reversal of roles, Vitro's subsidiaries became creditors to which Vitro owed an aggregate of approximately $1.5 billion in intercompany debt. Despite requests by holders of Old Notes, Vitro did not disclose these transactions. . . .

Only in October of 2010, approximately 300 days after completing the transactions with its subsidiaries, did Vitro disclose the existence of the subsidiary creditors. This took the transactions outside Mexico's 270-day "suspicion period," during which such transactions would be subject to additional scrutiny [as fraudulent conveyances—Eds.] before a business enters bankruptcy.

C. *Vitro Commences a* Concurso *Proceeding in Mexican Court . . .*

1. Terms of the *Concurso* Plan

On December 5, 2011 the *conciliador* [a court-appointed expert—Eds.] submitted to the Mexican court a proposed restructuring plan (the "*Concurso* plan" or "Plan") substantially identical to the one Vitro had originally proposed. Under the terms of the Plan, the Old Notes would be extinguished and the obligations owed by the [non-debtor] Guarantors would be discharged. Specifically, the Plan provides that:

> [O]nce this Agreement is approved by the Court . . . this Agreement . . . will substitute, pay, replace and terminate the above obligations, instruments, securities, agreements and warranties in which were agreed upon Approved

Credits and, therefore . . . will terminate personal guarantees granted a third and/or direct and indirect subsidiaries [sic] of Vitro with regards to the obligations, instruments, securities and agreements that gave rise to the Approved Credits.

The Plan further provides that Vitro would issue new notes payable in 2019 (the "New 2019 Notes"), with a total principal amount of $814,650,000. . . .

2. The *Concurso* Plan Is Approved

Under Mexican law, approval of a reorganization plan requires votes by creditors holding at least 50% in aggregate principal amount of unsecured debt. As distinguished from United States law, Mexico does not divide unsecured creditors into interest-aligned classes, but instead counts the votes of all unsecured creditors, including insiders, as a single class. As a result, although creditors holding 74.67% in aggregate principal amount of recognized claims voted in favor of the plan, over 50% of all voting claims were held by Vitro's subsidiaries in the form of [allegedly manufactured] intercompany debt. The 50% approval threshold could not have been met without the subsidiaries' votes. . . .

The bankruptcy court denied relief under 11 U.S.C. §§ 1507, 1521, and 1506 because approval of the Plan would extinguish claims held by the Objecting Creditors against the [solvent, guarantor] subsidiaries. Vitro and Fintech appeal this decision solely on the issue of whether the bankruptcy court erred as a matter of law in refusing to enforce the *Concurso* plan because the Plan novated guaranty obligations of non-debtor parties. While the relief available under Chapter 15 may, in exceptional circumstances, include enforcing a foreign court's order extinguishing the obligations of non-debtor guarantors, Vitro has failed to demonstrate that comparable circumstances were present here. Because Vitro has not done so, we affirm the bankruptcy court's decision denying the Enforcement Motion. . . .

Central to Chapter 15 is comity. Comity is the "recognition which one nation allows within its territory to the legislative, executive or judicial acts of another nation, having due regard both to international duty and convenience, and to the rights of its own citizens, or of other persons who are under the protections of its laws." Hilton v. Guyot, 159 U.S. 113, 164, 16 S. Ct. 139, 40 L. Ed. 95 (1895). . . . Comity considerations are explicitly included in the introduction to § 1507, and § 1509(b)(3) further provides that our courts "shall grant comity or cooperation to the foreign representative" of a foreign proceeding. . . .

[W]hether any relief under Chapter 15 will be granted is a separate question from whether a foreign proceeding will be recognized by a United States bankruptcy court. . . .

In the Enforcement Motion, Vitro sought broad relief pursuant to 11 U.S.C. §§ 105(a), 1507, and 1521. Specifically, Vitro sought an order giving full force and effect in the United States to the Mexican court's order approving the *Concurso* plan. . . . Given Chapter 15's heavy emphasis on comity, it is not necessary, nor to be expected, that the relief requested by a foreign representative be identical to, or available under, United States law.

We have previously cautioned that the mere fact that a foreign representative requests relief that would be available under the law of the foreign proceeding, but not in the United States, is not grounds for denying comity. Nevertheless, Chapter 15 does impose certain requirements and considerations that act as a brake or limitation on comity, and preclude granting the relief requested by a foreign representative. . . .

We conclude that a court confronted by this situation should first consider the specific relief enumerated under § 1521(a) and (b). If the relief is not explicitly provided for there, a court should then consider whether the requested relief falls more generally under § 1521's grant of any appropriate relief. We understand "appropriate relief" to be relief previously available under Chapter 15's predecessor, § 304 [which had its own case law on the permissibility of cooperation—Eds.]. Only if a court determines that the requested relief was not formerly available under § 304 should a court consider whether relief would be appropriate as "additional assistance" under § 1507.

We start by acknowledging that "[t]he relationship between § 1507 and § 1521 is not entirely clear." In re Toft, 453 B.R. at 190. . . . § 1521(a) empowers a court to "grant any appropriate relief" at the request of the foreign representative when necessary to "effectuate the purpose of [Chapter 15] and to protect the assets of the debtor or the interests of the creditors." 11 U.S.C. § 1521(a). In addition, § 1521 lists a series of non-exclusive forms of relief. . . . Section 1522 provides an important limiting factor: relief under § 1521 may be granted "only if the interests of the creditors and other interested entities, including the debtor, are sufficiently protected," and a court may impose appropriate conditions on relief. 11 U.S.C. § 1522(a)-(b).

Unlike § 1521's "any appropriate relief" language, § 1507 gives courts the authority to provide "additional assistance." . . . We are thus faced with two statutory provisions that each provide expansive relief, but under different standards. To clarify our resolution of requests for relief under Chapter 15 we adopt the following framework for analyzing such requests.

First, because § 1521 lists specific forms of relief, a court should initially consider whether the relief requested falls under one of these explicit provisions. . . .

Second, if § 1521(a)(1)-(7) and (b) does not list the requested relief, a court should decide whether it can be considered "appropriate relief" under § 1521(a). This, in turn, requires consideration of whether such relief has previously been provided under § 304. . . .

Third, only if the requested relief appears to go beyond the relief previously available under § 304 or currently provided for under United States law should a court consider § 1507. . . .

3. Availability of Relief Under § 1521 and § 1507

Applying our analytic framework to Vitro's request for relief, the bankruptcy court did not err in denying relief. Sections 1521(a)(1)-(7) and (b) do not provide for discharging obligations held by non-debtor guarantors. Section 1521(a)'s general grant of "any appropriate relief" also does not provide the necessary relief because our precedent has interpreted the Bankruptcy Code to foreclose such a release, and because when such relief has been granted, it has been granted under § 1507, not § 1521. Even if the relief sought were theoretically available under § 1521, the facts of this case run afoul of the limitations in § 1522. Finally, although we believe the relief requested may theoretically be available under § 1507 generally, Vitro has not demonstrated circumstances comparable to those that would make possible such a release in the United States, as contemplated by § 1507(b)(4). . . .

We conclude that § 1507 theoretically provides for the relief Vitro seeks because it was intended to provide relief not otherwise available under United States law. But the devil is in the details, and in this case, the bankruptcy court correctly determined that relief was precluded by § 1507(b)(4). Under that provision, the bankruptcy court had to consider whether the relief requested was comparable to that available under the Bankruptcy Code. We conclude below that, although a non-consensual, non-debtor discharge would not be available in this circuit, it could be available in other circuits. We also hold that because Vitro has failed to show the presence of the kind of comparable extraordinary circumstances that would make enforcement of such a plan possible in the United States, the bankruptcy court did not abuse its discretion in denying relief. . . .

Vitro cannot rely on the fact that a substantial majority of unsecured creditors voted in favor of the Plan. Vitro's majority depends on votes by insiders. To allow it to use this as a ground to support enforcement would amount to letting one discrepancy between our law and that of Mexico (approval of a reorganization plan by insider votes over the objections of creditors) make up for another (the discharge of non-debtor guarantors).[42] . . .

On the basis of the foregoing analysis, we hold that Vitro has not met its burden of showing that the relief requested under the Plan—a non-consensual discharge of non-debtor guarantors—is substantially in accordance with the circumstances that would warrant such relief in the United States. In so holding, we stress the deferential standard under which we review the bankruptcy court's determination. It is not our role to determine whether the above-summarized evidence would lead us to the same conclusion. Our only task is to determine whether the bankruptcy court's decision was reasonable.

This downer case for the cooperation champions among you should not suggest that U.S. courts regularly deny recognition and relief. The United States offers relief regularly, even in circumstances where its own domestic law might not. In re Metcalfe & Mansfield Alt. Invs., 421 B.R. 685, 696 (Bankr. S.D.N.Y. 2010). "The issue in chapter 15 cases then is whether to recognize and enforce the foreign court order based on comity." In re Avanti Communications Group PLC, 582 B.R. 603 (Bankr. S.D.N.Y. 2018) (approving release of insider guarantees but without objection).

---

[42] For the same reasons we conclude that, even if § 1521 did provide the broad relief Vitro seeks, enforcement of this Plan would be precluded under § 1522 for failing to provide an adequate "balance between relief that may be granted to the foreign representative and the interests of the persons that may be affected by such relief." In re Int'l Banking Corp. B.S.C., 439 B.R. at 626 [citation omitted—Eds.].

A final safety valve on assistance is § 1506, which permits withholding assistance when to do so would be "manifestly contrary" to "the public policy of the United States." Almost all chapter 15 cases in the United States have either declined to find a § 1506 public policy violation when asked, or, as in *Vitro*, denied recognition on other grounds to avoid the issue. The decisions, following UNCITRAL's Guide to Enactment, speak of the high bar of "manifestly" transgressing a "fundamental" policy of the assisting jurisdiction to withhold recognition, which explains the scarcity of this exception's use and increasing prevalence of cooperation.

3.   *Universalism's Challenge: Accepting Outcome Differences for Local Creditors*

Some relief is easier to grant than others. Enforcing a foreign plan approved by huge majorities of creditors over the objections of a few whiners is not tough. But the Model Law has several open-ended safeguards that come into play for trickier circumstances. Consider a foreign creditor who asks the U.S. court to authorize a U.S. bank to wire over funds in a U.S. account to be distributed in the foreign proceeding. The account has a valid lien on it by a U.S. secured creditor that would not be recognized in the foreign proceeding. That creditor, understandably, objects, complaining it would not be fair to have all that money it would have first dibs on with the lien evaporate to the benefit of a foreign pool (itself included, albeit greatly diluted). §§ 1522(a) (allowing relief "only if the interests of the creditors and other interested entities . . . are sufficiently protected"); 1507(a) (". . . the court, if recognition is granted, may provide additional assistance," (b)(4) (including, specifically, as one factor whether distribution would be substantially in accordance of the provisions of this title). But that is just one factor, and substantial does not mean identical. Yet it underscores perhaps the thorniest hurdle to international cooperation: local court acceptance of different priority rules that will sometimes disadvantage local creditors. Intrinsic in this concern is a choice of law issue assumption: that local courts apply local insolvency law, which is often true but not inevitably so. Given the wide latitude in the ancillary court's discretion to cooperate, whether to accept such outcome difference really boils down to how committed to the cause of universalism the jurisdiction is.

In the next case, the House of Lords confronts just such a test case: an Australian insurance liquidator asking for remission of U.K. funds—to the horror of U.K. creditors who realized Australia did not match their priority under U.K. insolvency law.

=========== McGRATH v. RIDDELL ===========

[2008] UKHL 21 (House of Lords)

LORD HOFFMANN [with whom LORD WALKER OF GESTINGTHORPE agrees]. My Lords,

1. This appeal arises out of the insolvent liquidation of the HIH group of Australian insurance companies. On 15 March 2001 four of them presented winding up petitions to the Supreme Court of New South Wales.

Some of their assets—mostly reinsurance claims on policies taken out in London—were situated in England. To realize and protect these assets, provisional liquidators were appointed in England. In Australia, the court has made winding up orders and appointed liquidators. The Australian judge has sent a letter of request to the High Court in London, asking that the provisional liquidators be directed, after payment of their expenses, to remit the assets to the Australian liquidators for distribution. The question in this appeal is whether the English court can and should accede to that request. The alternative is a separate liquidation and distribution of the English assets in accordance with the Insolvency Act 1986.

2. The English and Australian laws of corporate insolvency have a common origin and their basic principles are much the same. . . . But Australia has a different regime for insurance companies. I need not trouble your Lordships with the details. . . . It is agreed that if the English assets are sent to Australia, the outcome for creditors will be different from what it would have been if they had been distributed under the 1986 Act. Some creditors will do better and others worse. Approximate figures are given in para 17 of the judgment of the Chancellor in the Court of Appeal. Generally speaking, [policy holders] will be winners and other creditors will be losers.

3. The Australian court made its request pursuant to section 426(4) of the Insolvency Act 1986:

> "The courts having jurisdiction in relation to insolvency law in any part of the United Kingdom shall assist the courts having the corresponding jurisdiction in . . . any relevant country . . .".

4. The Secretary of State has power under subsection (11) to designate a country as "relevant" and has so designated Australia. Subsection (5) describes the assistance which a UK court may give. A request from the court of a relevant country is—

> "authority for the court to which the request is made to apply, in relation to any matters specified in the request, the insolvency law which is applicable by either court in relation to comparable matters falling within its jurisdiction." . . .

. . .

6. [Prior to the adoption of section 426], some degree of international co-operation in corporate insolvency had been achieved by judicial practice. This was based upon what English judges have for many years regarded as a general principle of private international law, namely that bankruptcy (whether personal or corporate) should be unitary and universal. There should be a unitary bankruptcy proceeding in the court of the bankrupt's domicile which receives world-wide recognition and it should apply universally to all the bankrupt's assets.

7. This was very much a principle rather than a rule. It is heavily qualified by exceptions on pragmatic grounds; . . . Professor Jay Westbrook, a distinguished American writer on international insolvency has called it a principle of "modified universalism": see also Professor Ian Fletcher, Insolvency in Private International Law (2nd ed 2005) at pp. 15-17. Full

universalism can be attained only by international treaty. Nevertheless, even in its modified and pragmatic form, the principle is a potent one. . . .

9. [T]he judicial practice which developed in [ancillary cases] was to limit the powers and duties of the liquidator to collecting the English assets and settling a list of the creditors who sent in proofs. The court, so to speak, "disapplied" the statutory trusts and duties in relation to the foreign assets of foreign companies. . . .

10. . . . Sir Richard Scott V-C held in Re Bank of Credit and Commerce International SA (No 10) [1997] Ch 213, 247 that an English court had power in an ancillary liquidation (provisional or final) to authorize the English liquidators to transmit the English assets to the principal liquidators. The basis for the practice could only be . . . principles of international comity, the desirability of a single bankruptcy administration which dealt with all the company's assets. . . .

21. It would in my opinion make no sense to confine the power to direct remittal to cases in which the foreign law of distribution coincided with English law. In such cases remittal would serve no purpose, except some occasional administrative convenience. And in practice such a condition would never be satisfied. Almost all countries have their own lists of preferential creditors. . . .

24. It follows that in my opinion the court had jurisdiction at common law [wholly apart from section 426], under its established practice of giving directions to ancillary liquidators, to direct remittal of the English assets, notwithstanding any differences between the English and foreign systems of distribution. These differences are relevant only to discretion. . . .

28. The power to remit assets to the principal liquidation is [not necessarily] a decision on the choice of the law to be applied to those questions. . . .

30. . . . The primary rule of private international law which seems to me applicable to this case is the principle of (modified) universalism, which has been the golden thread running through English cross-border insolvency law since the eighteenth century. That principle requires that English courts should, so far as is consistent with justice and UK public policy, co-operate with the courts in the country of the principal liquidation to ensure that all the company's assets are distributed to its creditors under a single system of distribution. That is the purpose of the power to direct remittal. . . .

36. In my opinion, therefore, this is a case in which it is appropriate to give the principle of universalism full rein. There are no grounds of justice or policy which require this country to insist upon distributing an Australian company's assets according to its own system of priorities only because they happen to have been situated in this country at the time of the appointment of the provisional liquidators. I would therefore allow the appeal and make the order requested by the Australian court.

Lofty language indeed, but Lord Hoffmann and Lord Walker did not garner a majority in their view of the common law power to cooperate in the name of universalism. Two others felt that there was no common law power to "disapply," in their words, U.K. insolvency law in favor of Australian law when U.K. creditors objected; however, given the express statutory provision, § 426, that allowed for explicit cooperation to scheduled common law countries (Australia among them), they concurred in the result. The fifth Law Lord ducked the question by noting since everyone agreed § 426 supplied the authority to remit the funds, determining the existence and extent of the common law power could be left to another day.

The skeptics got the last laugh in another opinion after Lord Hoffmann retired and the House of Lords was reconstituted as the U.K. Supreme Court. In Rubin v. Eurofinance S.A., [2012] UKSC 46, a U.S. bankruptcy court had entered a default judgment for fraudulent conveyances against non-U.S. defendants who were sponsors of a company in a chapter 11 proceeding that was alleged to have defrauded American consumers. The judgement was for transfers paid to the defendants by the chapter 11 debtor. When the U.S. insolvency representative requested assistance under the Model Law in England by way of recognizing the judgment, the British Court refused on the ground that the U.S. proceeding did not follow U.K. (highly restrictive) rules on personal jurisdiction. In other words, recognizing a bankruptcy court judgment was not "relief" available under the Model Law in the U.K. Supreme Court's interpretation. As for an earlier Lord Hoffmann opinion saying the flexible nature of bankruptcy requires relaxation of in personam jurisdictional rules when the debtor is located abroad, Cambridge Gas Transportation Corp. v. Official Committee of Unsecured Creditors of Navigator Holdings plc [2006] UKPC 26, the *Rubin* Court suggested the precedent was wrongly decided, an opinion it re-affirmed in Singularis Holdings Ltd. v. PricewaterhouseCoopers [2014] UKPC 36 (Privy Council). So much for universalism's "golden thread."

But maybe the last laugh has not yet been had. UNCITRAL in 2018 promulgated a Model Law on Recognition and Enforcement of Insolvency-Related Judgements. It noted in its Guide to Enactment:

> The work on this topic had its origin, in part, in certain judicial decisions [Rubin] that led to uncertainty concerning the ability of some courts, in the context of recognition proceedings under MLCBI, to recognize and enforce judgments given in the course of foreign insolvency proceedings, such as judgments issued in avoidance proceedings, on the basis that neither article 7 nor 21 of MLCBI explicitly provided the necessary authority. Moreover, there was a concern that decisions by foreign courts determining the lack of such explicit authority in MLCBI for recognition and enforcement of insolvency-related judgments might have been regarded as persuasive authority in those States with legislation based upon article 8 of MLCBI, which relates to international effect.

UNCITRAL Model Law on Recognition and Enforcement of Insolvency-Related Judgements, Guide to Enactment, ¶ 2, U.N. Doc. E.19.V.8 (2018). The U.K. delegation at UNCITRAL fully supported the adoption of this new model law. John A.E. Pottow, The Dialogic Aspect of Soft Law in International Insolvency: Discord, Digression, and Development, 40 Mich. J. Int'l L. 479 (2019).

C.   CHOICE OF LAW IN CROSS-BORDER INSOLVENCY

As Lord Hoffmann pointed out, remitting the reinsurance proceeds to the Australian main proceedings did not necessarily mean they would be distributed under Australian bankruptcy rules (although it was surely likely). Thus, technically a second, explicit analysis would have to be done in Australia regarding which bankruptcy priority rules should govern—a "private international law" question in much of the world, or a "choice of law" or "conflicts" question in the United States. For example, suppose the insurance proceeds were covered by a special contract with a choice of law clause. In that case, the Australian court might choose to distribute the proceeds in accordance with the contractually selected bankruptcy law, not Australian law. The worst-case scenario is when there is a conflict in conflicts. Thus, had Australia not been a § 426 country, the House of Lords may have decided that the English reinsurance proceeds would have to be distributed under English bankruptcy law priority rules (no authority to cooperate), while an Australian court of a more universalist bent might order the proceeds to be distributed under Australian priority rules (as COMI), creating a nightmare for the debtor.

Just as difficult as priority conflicts are questions of avoidance law, where there is usually a specific transaction that the debtor or trustee wishes to avoid and a creditor wishes to uphold. Specific transactions give rise to the traditional "contacts-based" analysis of many private international law regimes, e.g., Restatement (Second) of Conflict of Laws §§ 6, 47, 188 (1971), but some have argued that bankruptcy raises different policy concerns.

Note that we are discussing choice of which *bankruptcy* law to apply. In any cross-border bankruptcy case the court will also be required to choose which *nonbankruptcy* law to apply to a particular dispute. Thus, for example, if a trustee in such a case attacks the enforceability of a security interest, the court must ascertain first which jurisdiction's secured-credit law applies to determine the validity of the security interest (e.g., in the United States, whether the creditor has met the obligations imposed by Article 9 of the UCC), and second, which nation's bankruptcy avoidance provisions apply (e.g., in the United States, when would §§ 544 or 547 of the Code void an otherwise enforceable security interest?). Similar permutations multiply in contract law, if, for example, Canadian nonbankruptcy law applies to determine the underlying substantive right (e.g., validity of a contract), but German insolvency law determines the effect of the right once the debtor has filed for bankruptcy (e.g., treatment of executory contracts). Chapter 15—probably as a necessity to garner international consensus in passing the Model Law—is mostly silent on the subject.

A seminal case on this issue is In re Maxwell Commc'n Corp., 93 F.3d 1036 (2d Cir. 1996)—another routine insolvency case, with the English press baron falling from his yacht in Spanish waters under questionable circumstances. His death and the collapse of his global empire in scandal led to parallel bankruptcy proceedings in the United States and United Kingdom and to extraordinary cooperation between the courts in the two countries, a triumph of comity. Transfers of large pre-bankruptcy payments from U.S. subsidiaries to the principal bank lenders raised questions of voidable preference, however, and litigation commenced in both countries to set them aside. But a choice of law analysis was required: under U.S. law, the payments were probably avoidable, whereas they were unlikely to be avoidable under the narrower British statutes, where debtor intent to prefer is required for liability. The British Court (Mr Justice Hoffmann, as he then was) declined to issue an anti-suit injunction requested by the British banks who were afraid U.S. law might require them to cough up their payments. Instead, he said it was up to the U.S. court to decide as a choice of law matter which preference law to apply. There, the Second Circuit affirmed that British law should control, largely on grounds of cooperation and comity rather than a true choice of law analysis, based on the essential "Englishness" of the dispute, and dismissed the action on a sort of forum non conveniens ground.

A much more recent authority is In re Picard, 917 F.3d 85 (2d Cir. 2019), *cert. denied sub nom.* HSBC Holdings v. Picard, 2020 WL 2814770 (U.S. June 1, 2020). We met Trustee Picard in *Ascot*, above, but in this case there was no settlement. Trustee Picard sued where no trustee had gone before: he sued direct transferees of the fraudulent transfers, like Ascot Partners, and then subsequent transferees, like Ascot Fund. Far enough down the chain, this meant he was suing foreign transferees for distributions under 11 U.S.C. § 548. The lower courts dismissed the suits, holding such remote application of the Code was an impermissible exercise of U.S. law, unable to overcome the presumption against "exterritoriality." Morrison v. Nat'l Austl. Bank Ltd., 561 U.S. 247, 266-67 (2010). Although the lower court thought the relevant transfer was from foreign fund to foreign investor, and thus extraterritorial, the Second Circuit thought the relevant transfer was the initial one: from debtor to first transferee, which was in its view a domestic transfer with no extraterritoriality problem at all. *Cf. Merit Management* (Assignment 23)! This seems like the right outcome (assuming no misled foreign parties relying on local law), but highly formalistic. If a U.S. debtor carries a briefcase of cash to Mexico and uses it to repay a Mexican creditor, is that a foreign transfer, but if the same transaction is done by bank wire initiated from a U.S. bank, is that a domestic transfer? How can choice of law turn on that?

Just to end on a note showing how truly complicated choice of law can be in this area, consider that applicable bankruptcy law may itself depend on the type of proceeding in which it is to be deployed. In one case, the Fifth Circuit held that §§ 1521(a)(7) and 1523(a) block use of U.S. avoiding powers in chapter 15; a full-fledged chapter 7 or chapter 11 must be opened to access those provisions. By corollary, a foreign representative in chapter 15 might well be able to bring an avoidance action in U.S. court applying the foreign main proceeding's avoidance law. In re Condor Insurance Ltd., 601 F.3d 319 (5th Cir. 2010). Only now are international bankruptcy reform efforts turning to choice of law issues. They are so desperate in these uncharted waters, they are even looking for the help of academics. John A.E. Pottow, Beyond Carve-Outs and Toward Reliance: A Normative Framework for Cross-Border Insolvency Choice of Law, 9 Brook. J. Corp. Fin. & Com. L. 197 (2014).

The framers of the U.S. Constitution recognized that a new national market required that the national legislature be empowered "to Establish . . . uniform Laws on the subject of Bankruptcies throughout the United States." U.S. Const., Art. I, § 8, cl. 4. Just as surely, the growth of international trade and transnational enterprise requires the achievement of international agreement on the rules of cross-border insolvency. If the U.S. precedent illustrates the need, it also illustrates the difficulty; it took 100 years to fulfill the constitutional command, failing to enact a permanent bankruptcy law until 1898. We must hope that the international community will not be so long delayed.

Problem Set 38

38.1. Maple Leaf Components, Inc., a consumer electronics company based in Calgary, Alberta, has a plant there and another in York, Ontario, along with warehouses in several other Canadian cities and four U.S. locations. Maple Leaf filed liquidation bankruptcy in Calgary yesterday under the Bankruptcy and Insolvency Act. Your client, CompuTech, Inc., based in Detroit, wants to obtain pre-judgment attachments against each of the U.S. warehouses to secure payment of the $775,000 Maple Leaf owes to it. Nadan ("Dan") Nadal, the CompuTech general counsel, has lots of questions. Does the Canadian stay affect the client's right to seize the inventory? What is the likely next step by the Canadian bankruptcy trustee, Bev McLachlin, for Maple Leaf? What effect will it have on the client? Overall, Dan wants to know your take on their likelihood of success in grabbing the inventory. See § 1501 et seq.

BUSINESS BANKRUPTCY THEORY

Although we introduced some general ideas in the introduction to business bankruptcy assignment, we now can look at the more advanced conversation threads, armed with an understanding of what the tools and strategies within the system actually are. A preliminary note of caution, however, is in order before you start taking notes: bankruptcy theory is intrinsically interesting, like the life cycle of the honeybee or the moons of Jupiter, but it also serves a legislative policy function. If we understand the purpose and function of bankruptcy law, we might better evaluate proposals for its reform. Yet the over-arching "purpose" of business bankruptcy law (if any) is contestable and controversial. Even methodology is in dispute. For some scholars, bankruptcy theories present highly abstract issues best understood through models, while others want those models to be grounded in empirical reality, and still others believe in social interest exploration ill-suited for modeling. Each approach builds upon its own premises, nearly all of which are disputed. Thus, there is a rich and robust debate in progress about these questions. We offer an introduction to that debate, by necessity having to ignore a number of excellent contributions and many interesting riffs on the central arguments. Our hope is that an overview of the debates will seduce the student into exploring them further. Consider whether the following use of corporate reorganization law is to be lauded or derided.

From a private newsletter, June 22, 2000:

> Cheval Golf & Country Club in Tampa filed chapter 11 last week. The club says it has no financial difficulty but is using bankruptcy to change its governing bylaws which specify that any changes must be approved unanimously by the membership. The club blames its problems on a former lawyer who drafted the original documents.

A. SYSTEMIC THEORIES

We might break theoretical bankruptcy scholarship into three waves for simplicity. In the first wave, commentators engaged in lofty debate on the very purpose of bankruptcy law itself. As discussed already, a prominent theory of business reorganization is that it serves to solve the collective action problem of general default by corralling atomistic creditors into a state-controlled renegotiation process. See Thomas Jackson, The Logic and

Limits of Bankruptcy Law (1986). (Recall that the collective action problem is that the state-law "race of the diligent" regime virtually forces creditors to seize the debtor's property willy-nilly at the first hint of financial difficulty, thus destroying value.) The purpose of bankruptcy, per Professor Jackson and his frequent co-author, Professor Douglas Baird, is to provide a common, collective response to this problem that maximizes the value of the debtor's assets and efficiently distributes the proceeds to the creditors. The ideal bankruptcy law, in their worlds, would mirror the bargain that creditors hypothetically would have struck among themselves at the inception of lending relationships. Thus, it is often called the "creditors' bargain" theory. The role of the courts is to enforce the best interests of all the creditors by forcing each of them into the collective, orderly solution that is bankruptcy.

Often asserted as a corollary is the conclusion that bankruptcy law should not concern itself with redistribution; it should be limited to such procedural matters as blocking value-destructive creditor conduct. These scholars sometimes have called themselves "proceduralists," perhaps to emphasize they do not want bankruptcy law implementing any independent "substantive" policies. The proceduralists countenance the automatic stay, for example, because it blocks a rushing creditor from destroying going-concern sale value. Sections 1113 and 1114, which protect union employees, are by contrast madness in the proceduralists' eyes, as they evince a substantive pro-employment policy that has nothing to do with collective action problems. Proceduralists may demur that they are not necessarily against such policies, just that they should be relegated to employment statutes rather than the Bankruptcy Code. (They likely make such statements at dinner parties hosted by economists.)

The proceduralists are fundamentally concerned with the effect of bankruptcy law on market behavior. For them, one of the key mischiefs that substantive and redistributive policies wreak in bankruptcy is distorting business incentives. If bankruptcy offers a substantive goodie for Creditor X or Debtor Y unavailable at state commercial law, that actor will have an incentive to use bankruptcy for reasons beyond or unrelated to the financial distress of the company. Douglas Baird & Thomas H. Jackson, Corporate Reorganizations and the Treatment of Diverse Interests: A Comment on Adequate Protection of Secured Creditors in Bankruptcy, 51 U. Chi. L. Rev. 97, 101 (1984). The ultimate "proceduralist" goal of bankruptcy is to lower the cost of credit for debtors. Alan Schwartz, Bankruptcy Contracting Reviewed, 109 Yale L.J. 343 (1999) (opining that the more protective the bankruptcy system is for creditors—i.e., the harsher it is on debtors—the cheaper business debt capital will become by "maximizing the debt investors' insolvency state payoff"); see also Alan Schwartz, A Contract Theory Approach to Business Bankruptcy, 107 Yale L.J. 1807 (1998) (outlining foundation of his theory). There are limits to that approach. Cf. The Merchant of Venice. Of course, Professors Modigliani and Miller might opine that rising costs of debt capital should mean falling cost of equity capital, see Franco Modigliani & Merton H. Miller, The Cost of Capital, Corporate Finance, and the Theory of Investment, 48. Am. Econ. Rev. 261 (1958), but we don't think they turned their attention to chapter 11.

Another group of bankruptcy scholars (deemed "traditionalists" by the self-styled "proceduralists," although some of them might prefer the label "functionalists") has rejected these theories, believing that bankruptcy laws serve interests beyond those of maximizing value to creditors or producing the lowest cost for debt. Professor Elizabeth Warren is deeply skeptical that a single theory—and therefore a single-minded revision—will even capture all the interests that a bankruptcy system must serve. In a debate with Professor Baird, she wrote:

> I see bankruptcy as an attempt to reckon with a debtor's multiple defaults and to distribute the consequences among a number of different actors. Bankruptcy encompasses a number of competing—and sometimes conflicting—values in this distribution. As I see it, no one value dominates, so that bankruptcy policy becomes a composite of factors that bear on a better answer to the question, "How shall the losses be distributed?"

Elizabeth Warren, Bankruptcy Policy, 54 U. Chi. L. Rev. 775, 777 (1987). Indeed, Warren zestfully embraces the prospects for redistribution and other substantive issues through bankruptcy law that are the proceduralists' anathema. A few years later, she elucidated several normative goals that may be advanced through a business bankruptcy system, some shared by the proceduralists but others clearly not. We summarize them as follows:

> *Enhance Value.* By creating specialized collection rules to govern in the case of multiple default and by requiring collective rather than individual action, the value to be gleaned from the failing business can be increased while the expenses of collecting that value are decreased. Bankruptcy rules can also preserve going concern value while they can cabin many forms of strategic behavior that would otherwise waste collective resources.
>
> *Establish an Orderly Distribution Scheme.* By moving away from the race of the diligent at state law, there can be a considered judgment of who should receive preferences in the event that not all parties' expectations can be met. Distribution to parties with different legal rights can be settled in a legislative arena. Parties with no formal rights to the assets of the business, such as employees who will lose jobs and taxing authorities that will lose ratable property, may profit from a second chance at restructuring debt and giving the business a chance to survive *in situ.*
>
> *Internalize the Costs of Default.* A viable Chapter 11 system reduces the pressure on the government to bail out failing companies, thus forcing creditors to make market-based lending decisions and to monitor their debtors more closely.
>
> *Establish a Privately Monitored System.* The initiation decision in bankruptcy is one of the hardest. A system that provides sufficient incentives for debtors to choose it voluntarily or for creditors to force their debtors into it avoids the high costs that come with a publicly monitored system, both in terms of the costs of errors (decisions to place a company in bankruptcy that come too quickly or too slowly) and the costs of monitoring. Such a system also avoids the potential politicization of such decisions.

Elizabeth Warren, Bankruptcy Policymaking in an Imperfect World, 92 Mich. L. Rev. 336 (1993).

Although more recent writers have taken up the concern with "extra-creditor" interests in the publicly administered bankruptcy system, see, e.g., John R. Graham et al., Human Capital Loss in Corporate Bankruptcy (Center for Economic Studies, U.S. Census Bureau, Paper No. CES-WP 13-37, 2013) (quantifying the "human costs of bankruptcy" by estimating employee wage losses in the lead-up to and after filing), this strand of scholarship may be talking past the proceduralists. The debate really boils down to a fundamental question, on which reasonable scholars may simply disagree: is corporate bankruptcy just a form of civil litigation provided by society for sorting out disputes in a peaceful and orderly way or does it uniquely serve larger public interests? Indeed, after a few more go-rounds with Warren, Professor Baird threw up his hands, declaring an intellectual stalemate. Douglas G. Baird, Bankruptcy's Uncontested Axioms, 108 Yale L.J. 573, 574 (1998) ("In this Essay, I set out the two different sets of axioms now current among bankruptcy scholars, examine each, and suggest why people are drawn to one set or the other. I do not try to bridge the gap between the two camps, but rather to assess its implications, both for the future of scholarship and the dynamics of bankruptcy legislation.").

While couched as high theory, the academic debate also had a simmering policy undercurrent. Critics of the bankruptcy system that evolved in the decades after the Code complained that the law overshot the mark in empowering business debtors. Some went so far as to claim the system was vesting debtors with power to extort money from creditors by holding onto companies with negative value. Professor White calls it like he sees it:

> The incantation, "reorganization, yes, liquidation, no" echoed through the Commissions meetings and in the halls of Congress. Firms should be given every chance to save their goodwill; no one seems to have thought much of the firms with badwill that could be liquidated for a greater sum than they would command as going concerns, nor did anyone seem to believe that a large percentage of firms that would use chapter 11 might possess badwill, not good.

James J. White, Death and Resurrection of Secured Credit, 12 Am. Bankr. Inst. L. Rev. 139, 139-40 (2004).

For White, bootless attempts at reorganization when liquidation is clearly a superior option are wasteful and inefficient. Other scholars agree and upped their theoretical positions by intertwining policy proposals with their theorizing. For example, some proceduralists advocated radical changes to the chapter 11 process to align bankruptcy law better with what they saw as its theoretical foundation. An early such proposal was to "automate" reorganizations as a way to sidestep entirely the role of, in their minds, an inappropriately pro-debtor regime that involves negotiating with creditors. By allowing consensual plans of reorganization that may deviate from the absolute priority rule, the Code offers incentives for debtors to cajole (bully?) creditors into letting them keep some of their equity in the company. And the possession of inside information by management of the debtor's financial health sets the stage for lowball offers to scared creditors. Automation counsels stripping this discretion and mischief-permitting flexibility from the system through a type of forced auction. (You can now tell proponents of automation were ecstatic with the *203 North LaSalle* decision and its ode to auctions.)

Automated bankruptcy is inspired by the system used in some other countries but in fact derives from an academic article. Lucian A. Bebchuk, A New Approach to Corporate Reorganizations, 101 Harv. L. Rev. 775 (1988). Bebchuk's proposal has two central components. First, the courts should enforce absolute contractual priority in both liquidation and reorganization, and second, the control over the deployment of the assets of a business in general default should be determined by a sort of reverse credit bid by existing creditors or equity holders. Specifically, each class of equity or debt (predefined by contract) would either purchase at face value all the interests above it in priority or forfeit the class's interests. Any class that elected to purchase would own the company. If no lower class bought the debt above it, the highest class of debt would own the company outright. The new owner would then decide how to deploy the assets, whether through asset sale or continuing operation of the business. The idea here was to solve the valuation problem by making equity put its money where its mouth is and buy out the debt above it, unassisted by Code-facilitated leverage accorded the DIP. In other words, the "plan negotiation" process is automatic: either equity buys out the debt at face value or bows out and forfeits its stake—no need for a DIP, a plan, or anything. In Professor Bebchuk's original conception, the process would not require much court involvement and be completely controlled by creditors. In later proposals, the court would have some role to play. Barry E. Adler, A Theory of Corporate Insolvency, 72 N.Y.U. L. Rev. 343 (1997); Philippe Aghion, Oliver Hart & John Moore, Improving Bankruptcy Procedure, 72 Wash. U. L.Q. 849, 850 (1994). The chime-in by the future Nobel laureate was probably automation's peak of interest in the mid-1990s, but it soon fizzled out, in part because few real-world investors actually clamored for its implementation. Today, in a world of dominant secured parties with hog-tied control of many debtors, the idea of a theory premised upon the need to cabin the bullying power that DIPs have in bankruptcy over their creditors seems quaintly outdated.

B.   THE RISE AND FALL OF CONTRACTUALISM

After the first wave of Code scholarship trying to divine (some would say fruitlessly) the purpose of corporate bankruptcy law, a second wave—building upon the foundations of the proceduralists—started to explore the role of party autonomy. Borrowing from corporate law literature, these "contractualists" reasoned that if bankruptcy law is often inefficient by containing substantive, policy-based provisions unrelated to the collective resolution of debts, and if those inefficiencies are costly in the corporate debt markets, then parties should be allowed to opt out (by contract) from the mandatory scope of chapter 11. (The assumption of chapter 11 inefficiency is subject to robust empirical debate, see Elizabeth Warren & Jay L. Westbrook,

The Success of Chapter 11: A Challenge to the Critics, 107 Mich. L. Rev. 603 (2009), but for now our focus is on the basics of the contractualism theory.)

The contractualist approach starts with the beguiling premise that in a world of heterogeneous preferences, some debtors might prefer and be willing to pay for the automatic stay, DIP model of control, and other allegedly pro-debtor legal attributes of the current chapter 11 system, but other, presumably more risk-tolerant debtors, might not. If creditors charge more for a kinder, gentler bankruptcy system, then why not let the more confident debtors waive these mandatory protections and halt their cross-subsidization of the meek (or perhaps the prudent)?

Professor Robert Rasmussen deserves primary branding credit for this concept. His basic idea is of a "bankruptcy menu" from which a business chooses the bankruptcy provisions that would be best for it and its creditors. The choice would be made at the inception of the firm, included in its corporate charter, and unalterable without the agreement of all creditors (with exceptions for groups such as nonconsensual creditors, such as tort victims). Thus, each creditor would know from the start of the lending relationship the nature of the bankruptcy regime that would apply to the debtor and would extend credit priced on that basis. This excerpt summarizes his proposal, which adds the further suggestion to give debtors a "menu" of popular choices, including chapter 11, for governing law in the event of default:

> When a firm is formed, it would be required to select what courses of action it wishes to have available if it runs into financial difficulties down the road. The virtue of standardized options is that they reduce transactions costs and make communication to third parties easy. One can still allow parties to write their own contract if none of the options available suit their needs, though a well-crafted set of options should ensure that most firms prefer one of the options to the cost of creating a brand new bankruptcy procedure. The existence of a known menu of bankruptcy choices thus answers the transaction-cost argument for treating bankruptcy as a mandatory rule.
>
> A menu approach can handle the strategic-manipulation problem as well. An approach that limits the firm's ability to change its selection after it has incurred debt ensures that the threat of the firm amending its bankruptcy choice so as to transfer wealth from the creditors to the equity holders is eliminated. . . . [T]he important point is that these limitations ensure that a firm can publicly announce what bankruptcy option it would choose, and all future creditors would be able to rely on the option that the firm specifies.
>
> A menu approach to corporate bankruptcy law creates another benefit as well; it would aid the owners of a firm in deciding which option they should choose. By offering a discrete set of choices, the menu would enable banks and other creditors to anticipate the interest-rate adjustments that would be made for each option. They could then communicate to those establishing the firm the true cost of selecting one bankruptcy provision over another. The benefit of this communication is increased by the fact that . . . choosing the optimal bankruptcy term[s] may turn on the preferences of the firm's owners. Such owners, not Congress or the courts, are in the best position to assess these preferences, and the menu approach allows the owners to compare each option's benefits with its costs.

Robert K. Rasmussen, Debtor's Choice: A Menu Approach to Corporate Bankruptcy, 71 Tex. L. Rev. 51, 66-67 (1992).

Underlying the contractualist model is a belief shared with the proceduralists that bankruptcy law is too lenient on debtors and their managements. Contractualism seeks to solve this problem by allowing confident debtors to opt out of this decadent regime and make debtors who truly want it to pay for it. Professor Alan Schwartz takes the concern one step further. Rather than make debtor's management pay for the debtor-lenient regimes, such as (allegedly) chapter 11, that keep them employed for a few extra paychecks, we should just "bribe" the debtor's managers to accept a harsher outcome, such as liquidation, when doing so would be in the company's best interests. So long as the bribe is cheaper than the utility gain, welfare is increased. Fiduciary duties be darned! These bribes would naturally be specified by contract. Parting ways with Rasmussen, however, Schwartz recognizes that the circumstances of the debtor change over time such that the most efficient choice of bankruptcy regime (or bribe) at one moment may not be the most efficient at a later point. He proposes therefore that there be a rolling readjustment in the contracted regime to reflect these changes. Each new creditor would negotiate a bankruptcy bargain, including the management bribe price, with the debtor. If the bargain differed from the one made with the first creditor, the first creditor would automatically "upgrade" to the new bargain. Thus:

> My model assumed that two bankruptcy systems existed. One system, denoted L, resembled the current Chapter 7, and the other, denoted R, resembled the current Chapter 11. . . . [T]he parties in my model could write two types of bankruptcy contracts. The first would not deal explicitly with bankruptcy at all, leaving the insolvent firm free to choose the bankruptcy system it preferred ex post [L or R]. Since creditors are legally entitled to the full monetary return from a bankruptcy procedure, the firm would not consider this return in making its choice. Rather, the firm's owners/managers would choose the bankruptcy system that maximized their private benefits. The parties, however, could renegotiate after insolvency to induce the firm to choose the bankruptcy system that generated the highest monetary return when that system did not also maximize the firm's private benefits. The model assumed that a firm always gets greater private benefits in the reorganization system R because the managers get to run the firm for a longer time in that system and also have some chance of saving the business. Hence, the parties would renegotiate only when the liquidation system L turned out to generate a higher monetary return than the reorganization system R. The creditors then would pay the firm a sum to forgo the R system's greater private benefits and instead enter liquidation.
>
> The second contract I discussed—and the one Professor LoPucki considers—authorized the firm to keep a portion of the monetary return that would be generated by whatever bankruptcy system it chose. If this portion—the "bribe"—were set appropriately, the sum of the private benefits and cash payments the firm would get if it chose the optimal system always would exceed the firm's total payoff from choosing suboptimally. This contract was called renegotiation-proof because the parties would have no need to renegotiate later: The firm would choose the efficient bankruptcy system if the contract bribe was correctly specified.
>
> One or the other of these contracts would maximize the creditors' insolvency-state payoff and thereby minimize the firm's cost of capital, depending on the relevant economic parameters. . . .

A renegotiation-proof contract would have to be modified in those cases in which the creditors lent at different times because the optimal bribe could change with changes in the relevant economic parameters. The contract thus would need a conversion term, such that if the optimal bribe later changed, the bribes in all prior contracts would be updated to equal the newly optimal bribe: the portion of the bankruptcy return from whatever system the insolvent firm chose that would be sufficient to induce the firm to choose optimally. The initial creditor would sign a contract in which the bribe could change because the contractual bribe would not change in expectation.

Alan Schwartz, Bankruptcy Contracting Reviewed, 109 Yale L.J. 343, 346-48 (1999).

Note that the result that Professor Schwartz sought may be largely achieved in some hog-tied cases: secured creditors get control for their benefit while management is "bribed" with continued employment and perhaps stock options in the company that emerges from chapter 11. The greatest difference is that the arrangement is not embodied in an explicit contract as he suggests but dictated ad hoc by the lender.

Other scholars have offered incremental contractualist reforms by advocating for some party opt-out without endorsing whole-hog the ability of parties to write their own bankruptcy laws by contract. For example, Professor Steven Schwarcz argues debtors should be allowed to waive the automatic stay by contract—with careful policing. Waivers would not be permitted if they visited "a secondary material impact," which he defines as "unreasonable harm to the interests of creditors [generally]."

> Provisions of the Code sometimes should be viewed as default—not mandatory—rules. A prebankruptcy contract that is unlikely to result in a secondary material impact neither offends the bankruptcy policy of equality of distribution nor creates an externality that should be unenforceable under contract law. This determination can be made ex ante, at the time of contracting.
>
> A risk still remains that the prebankruptcy contract could impair the debtor's ability to rehabilitate. A court could assess that risk by observing ex post whether or not the debtor's ability to reorganize in bankruptcy has, in fact, been impaired by the prebankruptcy contract. If parties to a prebankruptcy contract cannot determine its enforceability until the debtor is in bankruptcy, however, creditors would be discouraged from offering valuable consideration for the contract, thereby making it more difficult for the debtor to reorganize outside of bankruptcy and impeding the policies of debtor rehabilitation and economical administration. Therefore, an ex ante solution to this problem is preferable. I have proposed as a solution that prebankruptcy contracts be enforceable only if the debtor receives value that is reasonably equivalent to the value of the contract. This requirement would promote debtor rehabilitation by providing the debtor with value that could help it reorganize and by permitting enforceability to be judged ex ante, at the time the prebankruptcy contract is formed. Therefore, a prebankruptcy contract for which the debtor receives reasonably equivalent value should be enforceable if, viewed ex ante, it is unlikely to result in a secondary material impact and does not manifestly impair a debtor's ability to be rehabilitated.
>
> As a corollary of this rule, however, if the debtor does not receive reasonably equivalent value, the policy of debtor rehabilitation may be implicated even if the prebankruptcy contract has no secondary material impact.

Therefore, a bankruptcy court should be able to consider the enforceability of such contracts ex post and, as appropriate, enforce them or not based on whether the contract has impaired the debtor's ability to reorganize in bankruptcy. By the same token, if the prebankruptcy contract, at the time of contracting, is likely to (and later does) cause a secondary material impact, it may be unenforceable even if the debtor receives reasonably equivalent value. Of course, if the prebankruptcy contract is likely to (and does) cause a secondary material impact, and the debtor does not receive reasonably equivalent value, the contract clearly violates bankruptcy policies and should not be enforced.

Steven L. Schwarcz, Rethinking Freedom of Contract: A Bankruptcy Paradigm, 77 Tex. L. Rev. 515, 584-85 (1999).

These theories have been criticized on various grounds; the first true skeptic was Professor Lynn LoPucki. He concludes one critique with this observation:

The case for freedom of contract rests squarely on the assumption that each party chooses the contract because the contract makes that party better off. Because each party is better off, all parties are better off in the aggregate. That aggregate then becomes a proxy for "social welfare." In the bankruptcy context, this theory holds that thousands of correct decisions by a debtor and each of its creditors and shareholders will generate one correct decision—the bankruptcy contract—in the aggregate. That decision will maximize social welfare.

The principal problem in attempting to apply this theory in the context of bankruptcy is that most creditors' interests are too small to warrant their active, knowledgeable participation. The task of bankruptcy-contract promoters is to find justifications for treating these creditors as if they had participated knowledgeably. Thus, Alan Schwartz would bind every earlier creditor to the contract made by the last, on the theory that the earlier one would have made the same decision; Steven Schwarcz would bind creditors to bankruptcy-procedure contracts on the basis of actual agreement by "representative members of a similarly situated class," on the theory that "distributional effects on other members of the class are likely to be small". . . . Only Robert Rasmussen seems to contemplate requiring the agreement of all creditors for the validity of a bankruptcy contract, and even he would imply it from the existence of the contract on the public record for a specified period before bankruptcy.

Relaxing the requirement for active, knowledgeable participation by all creditors in bankruptcy contracting reduces transaction costs. At the same time, however, it exposes the interests of nonparticipating creditors to the redistributional impulses of the active, knowledgeable participants. One cannot simply assume that if the redistributions thus achieved are small, the accompanying declines in efficiency will be small as well. William Whitford and I have shown that there is no necessary relationship between the two. The strength of the redistributional impulses evident in the current pattern of bankruptcy contracting, combined with the largely unexplored potential for even small redistributions to have large adverse effects on efficiency, should give pause to future bankruptcy-contracting theorists. Solutions that purport to take account of the preferences of all creditors without actually doing so may be both redistributional and inefficient.

Lynn LoPucki, Contract Bankruptcy: A Reply to Alan Schwartz, 109 Yale L.J. 317, 341-42 (1999).

Even the pro-contractualists worry about creditors who are "non-adjusting," that is, who could not negotiate even if they so preferred. Lucian Arye Bebchuk & Jesse M. Fried, The Uneasy Case for the Priority of Secured Claims in Bankruptcy, 105 Yale L.J. 857, 864, 881 (1996). These non-adjusting creditors include involuntary creditors (e.g., tort victims), quasi-involuntary creditors (e.g., hospitals, utilities), and "LoPuckian" creditors with contracts too small to be worth negotiating *ex ante* to protect against a risk of bankruptcy (e.g., a $5,000 supply contract). Recognizing the legitimacy of these creditors, some contractualists have proposed carving out a non-adjusting bypass for, e.g., tort victims, elevating them in priority above all other creditors who should be able to fend for themselves in the contractualist marketplace (demonstrating how normative theory frequently finds no outlet in the Code). Barry E. Adler, Bankruptcy Primitives, 12 Am. Bankr. Inst. L. Rev. 219, 242-43 (2004). A great summary of all these proposals is provided by Professor Susan Block-Lieb, who offers her own critiques as well. Susan Block-Lieb, The Logic and Limits of Contract Bankruptcy, 2001 U. Ill. L. Rev. 503.

Our own eight cents are to sidestep the theoretical fight due to the likely disqualifying empirical concerns. In a study testing some of the premises of contractualism, two of us concluded that such meaningful private ordering would not be worth the costly candle. Elizabeth Warren & Jay Lawrence Westbrook, Contracting Out of Bankruptcy: An Empirical Intervention, 118 Harv. L. Rev. 1197 (2005). The reported data are from a sample of business bankruptcy cases first filed in 1994 and followed for six years, along with additional data from cases filed in 2002. The data showed an average of 19 unsecured claimants per bankruptcy case, ignoring the large cases in which unsecured creditors number in the thousands. Given that these claimants are only the creditors still around on Bankruptcy Day, not those who were once creditors but were paid off and have now moved on, it is apparent that a good number of negotiations of bankruptcy contracts and changes in bankruptcy contracts would be required under any contractualist system.

Of course, because it is hard to know in advance which companies might eventually end up in bankruptcy, the contract negotiations would presumably be necessary for a much wider swath of loans than the universe of those ending up in general default, meaning many corporate parties would have to haggle over terms that might never apply. This sounds about as much fun as negotiating a prenuptial agreement, with the lender explaining that all borrowers are potential bankrupts so it must ask what bankruptcy terms might the debtor want when the business fails (or, worse, the screaming negative signal an entrepreneur would radiate turning the loan discussion to the topic: "OK, now let's talk about the terms that kick in once I go bust!"). As if that weren't bad enough, the data also show that Bebchuk and Fried's non-adjusting creditors probably make up a substantial percentage of the claimants in a typical bankruptcy case and they remain at the mercy of whatever contracts were drafted by the creditors in a position to negotiate. Instead of adjusting bankruptcy contract terms, these non-adjusters and weak-adjusters would probably have to set their prices on worst-case, lemon-flavored assumptions that would likely produce substantial efficiency losses. Indeed, the truly cynical will note that secured creditors can already "contract out" either by locking up all the debtor's property with a lien (the hog-tied debtor) or by allocating assets and liabilities in a corporate web of subsidiaries and affiliates, a method now referred to as "asset partitioning." See Henry B. Hansmann & Reinier H. Kraakman, The Essential Role of Organizational Law, 110 Yale L.J. 387, at 394-96 (2000) (defining asset partitioning); Lynn M. Lopucki, The Death of Liability, 106 Yale L.J. 1 (1996) (arguing asset partitioning and secured credit law undermines tort compensation system).

There is also a broader irony largely missed by the debate. If the purpose of bankruptcy under the hypothetical creditors' bargain is to provide a common, collective response to maximize the value of the debtor's assets, then the ideal bankruptcy law enacts the bargain that these creditors hypothetically would have struck among themselves at the inception of their lending relationships—presumably they would have asked for the most efficient system to bind themselves and others. Against the intuitive appeal of this collectivist analysis, the contractualist must construct a model that permits a number of creditors contracting with the debtor over time to achieve a contract-based result that increases welfare beyond this state-devised, majoritarian-targeted baseline in a cost-efficient manner. More damningly, even if these contracts could be negotiated cheaply, as soon as parties start to fight over the contracts' effects when things start to go south, a state-administered public court system is once again required.

Consider Federated Department Stores (owner of Bloomingdale's, Macy's, and other chains) and its 66 affiliates, who had 45,000 creditors who were divided into 77 separately identified classes of debt in the reorganization plan, including a large number of debt arrangements replete with contractual subordination agreements. One wonders how quickly and uncontestedly the losers under the contractual clauses—especially the management of the corporate debtors—would traipse to the bankruptcy slaughter per their contractual obligations; surely a lawsuit or two is imaginable "just to make sure" the contracts say what the winners contend. And if the parties do indeed start fighting amongst themselves, then perhaps we are back to the collective action problem that cried out for a compulsory state regime in the first place. This last point remains a central point of under-appreciated difference between the creditors' bargain school and the contractualists.

C.   BEYOND CONTRACTS: SELLING OUT

Contractualism debates petered out or at least sublimated into an even more provocative discussion that emerged as a new wave of scholarship about the prevalence and merits of prepacks and sales under § 363 eclipsing the traditional reorganization process. Indeed, Professors Baird and Rasmussen opine that § 363 sales and their close cousins, prepacks, have become so prominent that for traditional chapter 11s (that you spent so much time studying), it's the end of the world as we know it.

Corporate reorganizations have all but disappeared. Giant corporations make headlines when they file for Chapter 11, but they are no longer using it to rescue a firm from imminent failure. Many use Chapter 11 merely to sell their assets and divide up the proceeds. . . . Rarely is Chapter 11 a forum where the various stakeholders in a publicly held firm negotiate among each other over the firm's destiny. . . . To the extent we understand the law of corporate reorganizations as providing a collective forum in which creditors and their common debtor fashion a future for a firm that would otherwise be torn apart by financial distress, we may safely conclude that its era has come to an end. . . .

[F]irms in financial distress are unlikely to have a substantial going-concern surplus. Such a surplus comes from assets that are dedicated to a particular purpose. Current law is predicated on the belief that financially distressed firms hold such assets. . . . Railroads provide an especially vivid illustration. The left-hand rails are worth little apart from the right-hand rails. . . . [But] railroads were a special case. Most firms [now do] not depend upon assets that were custom-made for [their] operations and not of use elsewhere . . . [i]n a service-based economy. . . .

[E]ven when an economic enterprise depends on dedicated assets, rarely do the assets themselves need to remain in a particular firm. . . .

A viable firm requires Chapter 11 only if those who control it cannot collectively make coherent decisions outside the bankruptcy forum [or cannot write investment contracts that pre-specify those insolvency-state control rights]. . . . Even if control rights are not [contractually] allocated coherently, there is still no need for a collective forum that decides the fate of the firm if the firm can be sold in the marketplace as a going concern. The rise of such markets further undercuts the need for a traditional law of corporate reorganization. Indeed, the ability of modern bankruptcy judges to take advantage of these markets explains many of the Chapter 11 filings in recent years. . . .

When the number of creditors of a financially distressed firm is small enough, sales do proceed. When the number of investors is large, however, those in control of the firm (typically its senior creditors) are likely to use Chapter 11 to sell the assets of the firm as a going concern. . . . A firm in financial distress that seeks to sell itself may thus turn to Chapter 11 not to rehabilitate a failing enterprise but rather to dispose of it. . . .

Douglas G. Baird & Robert K. Rasmussen, The End of Bankruptcy, 55 Stan. L. Rev. 751, 751-55, 777-78, 787 (2002).

Some responded to this provocative knell-sounding by complaining it was armchair hypothesizing based on little more than casual anecdotal evidence. This emboldened Professors Baird and Rasmussen to double down with some data of their own. (Appreciate in the arc of business bankruptcy scholarship that what started in its most recent cycle as grand theoretical debates has now come full circle to empirical contests of what is actually going on in the system on the ground.)

The traditional account of corporate reorganizations assumes a financially distressed business faces three conditions simultaneously: (1) It has substantial value as a going concern; (2) its investors cannot sort out the financial distress through ordinary bargaining and instead require Chapter 11's collective forum; and (3) the business cannot be readily sold in the market as a going concern. . . . In The End of Bankruptcy, we showed that any one of these conditions is rarely found in a financially distressed business today. It is even less likely that all three of them will exist at the same time. . . . In his thoughtful Response, Lynn LoPucki urges us to provide a more rigorous empirical grounding for these ideas. Part I of this Reply provides such a foundation. It reviews all the large Chapter 11 cases that concluded in 2002. As we claimed in The End of Bankruptcy, traditional reorganizations have largely disappeared. Put concretely, in 84% of all large Chapter 11s from 2002, the investors entered bankruptcy with a deal in hand or used it to sell the assets of the business. In the remaining cases, going-concern value was small or nonexistent. . . .

In 2002, 93 large businesses completed their Chapter 11 proceedings. Of these, 52 (or 56% of the sample) were sales of one sort or another. In 45 of these cases, there was a sale of assets such that the business did not even emerge intact as an independent entity under a plan of reorganization. In addition to these clear cases of asset sales, seven other cases were in substance sales even though the business did emerge as a stand-alone enterprise under a plan of reorganization. . . . [For example,] Fruit of the Loom filed for Chapter 11 at the end of 1999. From the beginning, the senior creditors exercised control. They planned initially to take a controlling equity interest in the company, but when competing bidders appeared, they were content for the bankruptcy court to conduct a sale. Warren Buffett's Berkshire Hathaway proved to be the high bidder at $800 million in cash. . . . [Deans Baird and Rasmussen proceed to analyze the non-sales, finding many of them functional sales, prepacks, etc.—Eds.]

Douglas G. Baird & Robert K. Rasmussen, Chapter 11 at Twilight, 56 Stan. L. Rev. 673, 673-77 (2003).

While we are inclined to agree with the descriptive observation of Professors Baird and Rasmussen that a new model of corporate reorganization has emerged, we do not think it covers all types of debtor businesses. We believe plenty of SMEs go through traditional balance-sheet reorganizations. Moreover, we think the use (or "death") of traditional chapter 11 depends in significant part on control of the debtor. "Hog-tied" debtors are more susceptible to this pre-dictated restructuring with a single, strong voice calling the shots than are the rank-and-file SMEs. Recall that Professor Westbrook argues that functionally extra-judicial reorganization systems can work only if based on a system of dominant security interests tying up most if not all of a debtor's assets, a general-default system similar to that found in the United Kingdom. Some, but not all, lending relationships in this country exhibit this characteristic; we are loath to overgeneralize.

Moving beyond the descriptive to the normative, more recent scholarship looks at this sales-dominated culture and criticizes whether it is a welcome development for the field.

Bankruptcy reorganization provides a remedy for capital market inadequacy. It protects from dismemberment firms whose value cannot be realized through sale or preserved by soliciting investment in capital markets. Law and economics scholars—strong believers in the marketplace—are skeptical of the need for reorganization. They either deny the market's inadequacy or seek to design substitute markets. For decades, they have debated how best to end reorganization. . . .

[We] compared the prices for which thirty large public companies were sold with the values of thirty similar companies that were reorganized in the period 2000 through 2004. We found that companies sold for an average of 35% of book value but reorganized for an average fresh-start value of 80% of book value and an average market capitalization value—based on post-reorganization stock trading—of 91% of book value. Even controlling for the differences in the prefiling earnings of the two sets of companies, sale yielded less than half as much value as reorganization. . . .

In nearly every instance, the sales we examined were "market-tested" by public auction. But those auctions failed to prevent inadequate-price sales. In most cases, only a single bidder appeared. We interpret the data as showing that the high costs of evaluating companies, combined with the low probability of success for competing bidders, discourages competitive bids. . . .

Our data [also] suggest that [the presumption of 363 sales yielding quicker creditor payouts, championed by Professor James J. White] may be wrong. In the sale cases we studied, confirmation did not occur until an average of 611 days after the filing of the case, as compared with only 314 days for reorganization

Possible explanations for this market failure are not in short supply. The managers who decided to sell these companies rather than reorganize them frequently had conflicts of interest. So did the investment bankers who advised the managers and solicited bids. The stalking-horse bidders received protections in the form of breakup fees and substantial minimum bid increments that discouraged other bidders. The costs of participating in the bidding were high because the companies' situations were complex and changed rapidly. Bidders other than the stalking horse had little chance of winning. As a result, only a single bidder appeared at most bankruptcy auctions.

Lynn M. LoPucki & Joseph W. Doherty, Bankruptcy Fire Sales, 106 Mich. L. Rev. 1, 3-5, 9, 26-27, 31-32, 44-45 (2007).

One of the challenges muckrakers like Professor LoPucki face is relentless scrutiny. Professor White, in the best spirit of academic exchange, fought back.

[The data from Bankruptcy Fire Sales] are astounding numbers. If they are accurate, why would anyone, a creditor, a judge, or even the debtor or the debtor's lawyer, choose a 363 sale over reorganization? . . . If a typical company that is worth $91 million in reorganization is truly worth only $35 million in a 363 sale, either the auction market must be grossly inefficient or—contrary to all belief—the reorganization process is so efficient that it enhances the value of the companies reorganized.

In this paper I raise two other possibilities. First, I believe that Messrs. LoPucki and Doherty's enterprise numbers overstate the value that goes to the reorganized companies' creditors. Second, I believe there is a selection error in the samples of Messrs. LoPucki and Doherty. [White first re-runs the analyses using a different measure of firm value that excludes non-interest-bearing debt, which he contends is more consistent with finance theory. In doing so, he finds the "sales discount" vanishes. With telecoms removed, which he considers aberrant companies, the data even suggest a "sales premium"!—Eds.] . . . If our data are correct, the differences claimed by Messrs. LoPucki and Doherty do not exist. At least as measured by these sixty companies, the expected return for creditors from a section 363 sale is no different than the expected return from reorganization. . . .

To the extent that 363 sales return lower value than reorganizations might, I believe that Messrs. LoPucki and Doherty read the causation backwards. Section 363 sales do not cause low value, but low value might cause 363 sales. Put another way, the firms that find their way into 363 sales are weaker from the outset and that difference, not the process, explains lower returns. . . .

Messrs. LoPucki and Doherty [also] criticize the auction process. . . .

As Messrs. LoPucki and Doherty note, the selection of the stalking horse can be conceptualized as the "true sale." This is largely true, but not for the reasons they imply. Because of the advantages given to the stalking horse, interested buyers often submit competing bids during the selection process, in effect turning the selection of the stalking horse into a mini auction. Because interested buyers have already submitted their best bids in an attempt to be chosen as a stalking horse, they do not attend the "official" auction. In this situation the stalking horse price has been subject to competing bids and reflects the fair market value. . . .

James J. White, Bankruptcy Noir, 106 Mich. L. Rev. 691, 692, 701, 702, 708-10 (2008).

Professors LoPucki and White disagree over the numbers. Recent empirical evidence does indeed suggest that bankruptcy sales transfer value from debtors' creditors to buyers. See Jean-Marie Meier & Henri Servaes, The Bright Side of Fire Sales, 32 Rev. Fin. Stud. 4228, 4248-50 (2019) (analyzing dataset of 21,850 commercial transactions from 1982 to 2012 and finding higher average rate of return for buyers purchasing assets in bankruptcy sales than in traditional acquisitions). But wholly apart from the numbers, other scholars disagree on principle. They say sales should not be used, period, when they eclipse the policy-laden, publicly monitored system of business reorganization envisioned by the Code; we saw some of these same arguments back in Assignment 33 when considering the privatization intrinsic in the idea of a CRO in lieu of a publicly appointed trustee. A. Mechele Dickerson, Privatizing Ethics in Corporate Reorganizations, 93 Minn. L. Rev. 875 (2009). More broadly, we also saw a related concern in Assignment 31 when considering *sub rosa* plans of reorganization and the Supreme Court's exasperation in *Jevic* about parties trying to control the bankruptcy distribution process. Note that the contractualists/proceduralists discussed above might denigrate *Jevic* for getting matters entirely backward: more party control should be celebrated, not mulcted: after all, it's their money at stake. But others worry that there is an important difference between enabling party engagement and rewriting distribution rules passed by Congress. See Melissa B. Jacoby, Corporate Bankruptcy Hybridity, 166 U. Pa. L. Rev. 1715 (2018); Jonathan C. Lipson, Controlling Creditor Control: Jevic and the End (?) of LifeCare, 27 Norton J. Bankr. L. & Prac. 563 (2018). Even zealous free marketeers like Frank Easterbrook blanche at party hand-waving about "critical" vendors being enough to overcome statutory priority rules (recall his saltiness in the *Kmart* opinion back in Assignment 18).

The real rub is that with too much party control, especially over quick sales with minimal oversight, it becomes increasingly easier for the "haves" to squeeze out the "have nots." Consider the dramatic example of the auto bailouts—bailouts because the government provided the DIP financing when nobody else would and took equity stakes in the companies in return. Professors Roe and Skeel worry about speeding too quickly through the traditional reorganization process, with its procedural checks and, under *North LaSalle*, market tests of valuation. While heralded by some as rare moments of bipartisan political achievement, bankruptcy Professors Roe and Skeel did not like what they saw. Their critique includes a normative vision of how bankruptcy law is supposed to protect minority stakeholders and a concern with a government riding roughshod:

> Chrysler's operations entered and exited bankruptcy in forty-two days, making it one of the fastest major industrial bankruptcies in memory. It entered as a company widely thought to be ripe for liquidation if left on its own, obtained massive funding from the United States Treasury, and exited through a pseudo-sale of its main assets to a new government-funded entity. Most creditors were picked up by the purchasing entity, but some were not. The unevenness of the compensation to prior creditors raised considerable concerns in capital markets.
>
> Appellate courts had previously developed a strong set of standards for a § 363 sale: the sale must have a valid business justification, the sale cannot be a sub rosa plan of reorganization, and if the sale infringes on the protections afforded creditors under Chapter 11, the court can approve it only after fashioning appropriate protective measures.
>
> The Chrysler reorganization failed to comply with these requirements. . . . The plan surely was a sub rosa plan, in that it allocated billions of dollars—the core determination under § 1129—without the checks that a plan of reorganization requires. . . . [I]t's plausible to view the Chrysler bankruptcy as not having been a sale at all, but a reorganization. The New Chrysler balance sheet looks remarkably like the old one, sans a couple of big creditors. Courts will need to develop rules of thumb to distinguish true § 363 sales from bogus ones that are really reorganizations that squeeze out one or more creditor layers. We suggest a rough rule of thumb to start with: if the new balance sheet has creditors and owners who constituted more than half of the selling company's balance sheet, but with some creditors left behind, or if a majority of the new equity was drawn from the old capital structure, then the transaction should be presumed not to be a sale at all, but a reorganization. The Chrysler transaction would have failed that kind of a test.
>
> One might be tempted to dismiss the inquiry as needless worry over a few creditors. But we should resist that easy way out. Much corporate and commercial law has to do with the proper treatment of minority creditors and minority shareholders. For minority stockholders, there's an elaborate corporate-law machinery for freeze-outs when a majority stockholder seeks to engineer a transaction that squeezes out minority stockholders. For minority creditors, there's a century of bankruptcy and equity-receivership law designed to balance protection from the majority's potential to encroach on the minority and squeeze them out from their contractual priority against the minority's potential to hold out perniciously. These are neither small nor simply fairness-based considerations: capital markets depend on effective mechanisms that prevent financial majorities from ousting financial minorities from their ratable position in an enterprise. That's what's at stake.

Mark J. Roe & David Skeel, Assessing the Chrysler Bankruptcy, 108 Mich. L. Rev. 727, 767-68, 770-71 (2010).

Other bankruptcy professors disagreed, a response that you probably anticipated by this point:

> In both cases, the U.S. Treasury and the governments of Canada and Ontario agreed to provide the automakers with DIP financing on the condition that a sale of each debtor's assets occur on an expedited basis so as to preserve the value of the business, restore consumer confidence, and avoid the costs of a lengthy chapter 11 process. In both cases the purchaser of the assets

was a newly created entity, funded by the North American governments. In exchange for wage cuts that brought the automakers in line with their foreign competitors, and the union's promise not to strike for several years, the purchasers agreed to give equity stakes in the reorganized company to the UAW's retiree health care trust, called the Voluntary Employee Beneficiary Association (VEBA). . . .

In short, the basic structure used to reorganize both GM and Chrysler was not unprecedented. Indeed, it was entirely ordinary. In both cases the "good" assets were sold to new entities. The consideration for that sale goes to the "old" debtor, and will be distributed according to the absolute priority rule. None of this constitutes a covert reorganization plan or a corruption of the bankruptcy process. . . .

In his recent testimony before the House Subcommittee on Commercial and Administrative Law, Professor Baird advanced a neat argument that the bidding procedures approved in the automotive cases so "locked in" a particular deal that they amounted to a plan of reorganization, in violation of the caselaw discussed in the prior section of this paper.

In both automotive cases, the approved bidding procedures provided that to become a "Qualified Bidder" a bidder must agree to assume the same collective bargaining agreements that the initial bidder intended to assume. Because this requirement could have led a bidder to offer less cash for the debtors' assets—since it would have been forced to assume this additional liability Baird argues that the process became "both a sale and a *sub rosa* plan." . . .

The deterrence argument presumes that the procedures have more "stickiness" than they actually do. [C]aselaw is abundant and clear that bankruptcy courts have an obligation to consider the highest bid presented, even if it does not conform with previously approved bidding procedures. Any investor who contemplates buying a multi-billion dollar distressed corporation will be advised by experienced bankruptcy counsel who know this—the contrary presumption is not credible.

Irrespective of the potential effects of the bidding procedures, there are good independent reasons to think that there were no inhibited bidders who failed to appear. The automotive industry, both domestic and foreign, is presently heavily distressed. At the same time, the credit markets show no ability to provide the kind of financing that would be needed to purchase either GM or Chrysler. . . .

Stephen J. Lubben, No Big Deal: The GM and Chrysler Cases in Context, 83 Am. Bankr. L.J. 531, 536-42, 545-46 (2009).

Finally, a somewhat different (but ultimately related) tack of concern with bankruptcy sales is that the short-circuiting doesn't just have the potential to chill bidding and enable squeeze-outs by rushing the process, but that its necessary "reckoning" or "realization event" on Sale Day may artificially distort value allocation by accelerating its determination to a time that some or even many constituents find sub-optimal—particularly those lower down the food chain who may be out of the money. This problem is combined with the procedural discomfort of determining and allocating that value through the terms of the sale order (and, likely, provisions of the DIP loan) rather than through the plan that gets put to vote, arguably in tension with *Jevic*. Professors Melissa Jacoby and Edward Janger propose a solution to this timing problem by suggesting that courts should require the posting of an injunction bond, or retention of a disputed claims reserve, to preserve questions of valuation and value allocation for treatment pursuant to a confirmed plan subject to creditor vote without slowing down the actual § 363 sale that strikes while the iron is hot. Melissa B. Jacoby & Edward J. Janger, Ice Cube Bonds: Allocating the Price of Process in Chapter 11 Bankruptcy, 123 Yale L.J. 862 (2013).

Intrinsic in Jacoby and Janger's concerns is the concept of the "reorganization surplus"—the upside of preserving the business whose capture is enabled by the very process of chapter 11. A quick § 363 sale at low valuation cashes out the junior classes, who get allocated none of the proceeds that usually go to the secured creditor with a lien on the sold assets, and vests all the upside in the bargain-snatching purchaser (recall *Fisker* from Assignment 32). But it is far from clear that the upside belongs to the senior secured creditor (or the purchaser) because the surplus is in part the product of a public reorganization system. Indeed, Professor Ronald Mann has argued that it belongs to the state to allocate to whichever stakeholder it sees fit! Ronald Mann, Bankruptcy and the Entitlements of the Government: Whose Money Is It Anyway?, 70 N.Y.U. L. Rev. 993 (1995). These concerns about not just lost but "hoarded" value in the § 363 sale process are serious, and proposals to address them are not in short supply. (For a complicated attempt to implement this idea through "§ 363x" sales, see the ABI Commission to Study the Reform of Chapter 11, 23 Am. Bankr. Inst. L. Rev. 1 (2015).)

D.　WHITHER BANKRUPTCY THEORY?

Bankruptcy is becoming more international in an increasingly smaller global village. We have already mentioned the extensive comparative work in this country of Professor Jason Kilborn, who has fellow comparativists around the world. As countries reform their insolvency laws—led by organizations such as UNCITRAL, the World Bank, and the IMF—a strand of scholarship has developed (again, not without controversy) attempting to quantify the role of law reform, especially insolvency law, in economic development. See, e.g., José Garrido, The Role of Personal Insolvency Law in Economic Development, 5 World Bank Legal Rev. 111 (2014); John Armor, Simon Deakin, Priya Lele & Mathais Siems, How Do Legal Rules Evolve? Evidence from a Crosscountry Comparison of Shareholder, Creditor, and Worker Protection, 57 Am. J. Comp. L. 579 (2009) (questioning common "legal origins" assumption of common law versus civil law difference as explanation for differing shareholder rights).

One thing those international organizations are especially interested in is the role of MSMEs (micro, small, and medium enterprises). Increasing attention is focused on the special concerns these debtors raise, which include heightened cost-sensitivity and the difficulty in preserving going-concern human capital. Riz Mokal, Ronald Davis, Alberto Mazzoni, Irit Mevorach, Barbara Romaine, Janis Sarra & Ignacio Tirado, Micro, Small, and Medium Enterprise Insolvency: A Modular Approach (Oxford Univ. Press, 2018). In the United States, the SBRA is a logical outflow of the idea that one size may not fit all, perhaps demoralizing some theorists seeking a Grand Unification Theory but inspiring others who believe there is still much work to be done. Fellow travelers surely include those of the Environmental, Social, and Governance (or "ESG") school of corporate governance, who believe that the focus of management attention should not be restricted to the interests of creditors and stockholders but also should include employees, the public, and perhaps even the environment. See, e.g., Elizabeth Cooper & Hattice Uzun, Corporate Social Responsibility and Bankruptcy, 36 Stud. in Econ. & Fin. 130 (2019); K.C. Lin & Xiabo Dong, Corporate Social Responsibility Engagement of Financially Distressed Firms and Their Bankruptcy Likelihood, 43 Advances in Acct. 32 (2018); Martin Lipton, The New Paradigm: A Roadmap for an Implicit Corporate Governance Partnership Between Corporations and Investors to Achieve Sustainable Long-Term Investment and Growth, International Business Council of the World Economic Forum (Sept. 2, 2016). The ideas have taken root some places. See, e.g., § 166(2), Companies Act, No. 18 of 2013, India Code (2013) [India] (imposing duty upon directors of Indian companies to act "in the best interests of the company, its employees, the shareholders, the community and for the protection of environment"). This is an issue close to many of our hearts, both those who have been seduced by the Capitol and those still writing. See, e.g., Jay Lawrence Westbrook, Equity in Bankruptcy Courts: Public Priorities, 94 Am. Bankr. L.J. 203 (2020).

A final debate percolating is on the rise (some might say return) of relative priority: a rejection of the strict absolute priority that dictates lower classes must get zero if higher classes object in favor of a more flexible one saying that lower classes must simply get less if higher classes object. The European Union's new Restructuring Directive embraces relative priority, which may have much to commend in terms of pragmatics — although, since there is never a free lunch, may have costs in terms of valuation difficulties. Once again, opinion divides. Compare Douglas G. Baird, Priority Matters: Absolute Priority, Relative Priority, and the Costs of Bankruptcy, 164 U. Pa. L. Rev. 785, 792 (2017) (arguing that relative priority system, which looks at the present value of each claim and redistributes securities in the new firm according to that value, elegantly avoids bankruptcy's function as a reckoning day and its need for nonmarket valuations) with Jonathan Seymour & Steven L. Schwarcz, Corporate Restructuring Under Relative and Absolute Priority Default Rules: A Comparative Assessment. 1 U. Ill. L. Rev. (forthcoming, vol. 2021) (arguing that relative priority scheme would decrease likelihood of consensual reorganization, permit unfair outcomes, and not operate as an effective default rule).

E.   THE CLOSING WORD

We applaud these recent empirical studies and policy debates on the role of bankruptcy law, both here and around the world. And while we also commend the more purely theoretical work in the field, we conclude with the caution of one of our own:

> We must consider bankruptcy policies in light of their application to cases that arise in the real world. It is therefore critical to note that the markets bankruptcy affects are not perfect and that they contain substantial transaction costs, information asymmetries, and ambiguities about the property rights of the parties. While one might make this blanket warning to constrain any policy debate, it is a particularly pertinent limitation in the bankruptcy area for two reasons: bankruptcy policy is itself grounded in market imperfections, and critics have ignored market imperfections in constructing a hypothetical system that is superior to the current bankruptcy system.
>
> The basis for bankruptcy policy is so deeply rooted in market imperfections that any attempt to discuss such policy in a perfect market is a Zen-like exercise, much like imagining one hand clapping. Bankruptcy laws are created to deal with the problems of market imperfections. If, in fact, markets were perfect—if debtors and their creditors had perfect information about the market generally and each party's position within it; if debtors and creditors could costlessly monitor, renegotiate, and enforce their agreements; if the legal rights of parties were always unambiguous and clear to all actors—then bankruptcy laws undoubtedly would take a different form. Many features of the bankruptcy system, for example, are intended to deal with creditors' inadequate information and the high costs of gathering the information they need to make collection decisions. Debtors must disclose substantial information about their business operations so that all creditors will have low-cost, accurate information to inform their oversight and strategic decisionmaking during the bankruptcy process. If creditors had perfect, costless information, these provisions would be superfluous. Like other laws, bankruptcy laws take their shape from the problems with which they were created to cope. . . .
>
> Not surprisingly, to test the vitality of a number of economic principles, researchers often begin their analysis with the familiar incantation of a perfect market: a world without those transaction costs, information asymmetries, or ambiguous property rights to muddy the analytic waters. . . . It is interesting to imagine what kind of market would produce enough failure to stimulate an interest in a bankruptcy system but would be so perfect that a hypothetical bankruptcy system could operate without concern for market imperfections. While some tests of allocative efficiency may reasonably begin with the presumption of a perfectly functioning market, a policy discussion should not begin in such a state of grace. . . .
>
> We remain woefully short on reliable empirical data about the operation of the system, particularly with respect to the routine cases. Our theoretical grasp of the incentives at work for competing parties is primitive at best, and it certainly deserves elaboration. In short, there is much to learn. In learning, however, there is much known that we should not forget.

Elizabeth Warren, Bankruptcy Policymaking in an Imperfect World, 92 Mich. L. Rev. 336, 379-81, 387 (1993).

Problem Set 39

39.1. You have been invited to compete for an academic prize consisting of an opportunity to study bankruptcy law for a year, all expenses paid, in several very congenial venues, starting with Paris. The winner will be selected after a debate among students representing the various theoretical viewpoints discussed above. Choose a position advocating one of those views. Be prepared to discuss its strengths and weaknesses and to reference specific statutory provisions, cases, or scholarly articles you studied in this course to support your position. Think about whether any empirical data are available or might be developed to support your position or the position of others, but also be ready to make theoretical arguments. Focus on the fundamentals, such as (a) the market efficiencies available in the contract approaches as against the difficulty of negotiating among a number of creditors over time; and (b) the claim that bankruptcy should serve debtor and other interests in light of the Code provisions that seem to confirm that creditors have the overriding rights in bankruptcy.

39.2. The country of Freedonia has recently emerged from a dictatorial, quasi-socialist period and installed a democratic government committed to a regulated free-market system like that found in the United States. On the strength of your success in the theoretical competition described above, after your year of study, you have received a contract from USAID and the World Bank to advise the Freedonian government on a new bankruptcy system for business bankruptcy cases. (Another group is working on a consumer system.) Among the issues that concern the government are whether any bankruptcy system should include state-owned enterprises, which are being privatized slowly because of the harsh impact of the loss of the many jobs they supported. The country's prior bankruptcy law emphasized criminal penalties for officers and directors of failed companies and made no provision for discharge of individuals such as entrepreneurs. The government is now committed to encouraging a pro-business growth climate, but recognizes that a major cultural shift will be required. The country's government is unitary (i.e., not federal). What else do you need to know about Freedonia before making recommendations for a bankruptcy law? In particular, what else do you need to know about its legal system? Make a list of at least five questions, recognizing that if Freedonia had any bankruptcy experts it would not have sought your help. Sketch out your initial thoughts on what system you will propose and why.

DISCHARGED

SELECTED FEDERAL CONSUMER PROTECTION STATUTES

CONSUMER CREDIT PROTECTION ACT
15 U.S.C. § 1671 et seq.

§ 1674. Restriction on discharge from employment by reason of garnishment

(a) *Termination of employment.* No employer may discharge any employee by reason of the fact that his earnings have been subject to garnishment for any one indebtedness.

(b) *Penalties.* Whoever willfully violates subsection (a) of this section shall be fined not more than $1,000, or imprisoned not more than one year, or both.

FAIR CREDIT REPORTING ACT
15 U.S.C. § 1681 et seq.

§ 1681b. Permissible purposes of consumer reports

(a) *In general.* Subject to subsection (c), any consumer reporting agency may furnish a consumer report under the following circumstances and no other . . .

. . .

(3) To a person which it has reason to believe—

(A) intends to use the information in connection with a credit transaction involving the consumer on whom the information is to be furnished and involving the extension of credit to, or review or collection of an account of, the consumer; . . .

(b) *Conditions for furnishing and using consumer reports for employment purposes.*

(1) *Certification from user.* A consumer reporting agency may furnish a consumer report for employment purposes only if—

(A) the person who obtains such report from the agency certifies to the agency that—

(i) the person has complied with [relevant provisions of this law]; and

(ii) information from the consumer report will not be used in violation of any applicable Federal or State equal employment opportunity law or regulation; and

(B) the consumer reporting agency provides with the report, or has previously provided, a summary of the consumer's rights under this title, as prescribed by the Bureau under section 1681g(c)(3).

(2) *Disclosure to consumer.*

(A) *In general.* Except as provided in subparagraph (B), a person may not procure a consumer report, or cause a consumer report to be procured, for employment purposes with respect to any consumer, unless—

(i) a clear and conspicuous disclosure has been made in writing to the consumer at any time before the report is procured or caused to be procured, in a document that consists solely of the disclosure, that a consumer report may be obtained for employment purposes; and

(ii) the consumer has authorized in writing (which authorization may be made on the document referred to in clause (i)) the procurement of the report by that person. . . .

(3) *Conditions on use for adverse actions.*

(A) *In general.* Except as provided in subparagraph (B), in using a consumer report for employment purposes, before taking any adverse action based in whole or in part on the report, the person intending to take such adverse action shall provide to the consumer to whom the report relates—

(i) a copy of the report; and

(ii) a description in writing of the rights of the consumer under this title, as prescribed by the Bureau under section 609(c)(3). . . .

(c) *Furnishing reports in connection with credit or insurance transactions that are not initiated by the consumer.*

(1) *In general.* A consumer reporting agency may furnish a consumer report relating to any consumer pursuant to subparagraph (A) or (C) of subsection (a)(3) in connection with any credit or insurance transaction that is not initiated by the consumer only if—

(A) the consumer authorizes the agency to provide such report to such person; or

(B)

(i) the transaction consists of a firm offer of credit or insurance;

(ii) the consumer reporting agency has complied with subsection (e);

(iii) there is not in effect an election by the consumer, made in accordance with subsection (e), to have the consumer's name and address excluded from lists of names provided by the agency pursuant to this paragraph; . . .

. . .

(e) *Election of consumer to be excluded from lists.*

(1) *In general.* A consumer may elect to have the consumer's name and address excluded from any list provided by a consumer reporting agency under subsection (c)(1)(B) in connection with a credit or insurance transaction that is not initiated by the consumer by notifying the agency in accordance with paragraph (2) that the consumer does not consent to

any use of a consumer report relating to the consumer in connection with any credit or insurance transaction that is not initiated by the consumer.
. . .

§ 1681i. Procedure in case of disputed accuracy

(a) *Reinvestigations of disputed information.*

(1) *Reinvestigation required.*

(A) *In general.* Subject to subsection (f) and except as provided in subsection (g), if the completeness or accuracy of any item of information contained in a consumer's file at a consumer reporting agency is disputed by the consumer and the consumer notifies the agency . . . the agency shall, free of charge, conduct a reasonable reinvestigation to determine whether the disputed information is inaccurate and record the current status of the disputed information, or delete the item from the file in accordance with paragraph (5), before the end of the 30-day period beginning on the date on which the agency receives the notice. . . .
. . .

(2) *Prompt notice of dispute to furnisher of information.*

(A) *In general.* Before the expiration of the 5-business-day period beginning on the date on which a consumer reporting agency receives notice of a dispute from any consumer or a reseller in accordance with paragraph (1), the agency shall provide notification of the dispute to any person who provided any item of information in dispute. . . .
. . .

(5) *Treatment of inaccurate or unverifiable information.*

(A) *In general.* If, after any reinvestigation under paragraph (1) of any information disputed by a consumer, an item of the information is found to be inaccurate or incomplete or cannot be verified, the consumer reporting agency shall—

(i) promptly delete that item of information from the file of the consumer, or modify that item of information, as appropriate, based on the results of the reinvestigation. . . .
. . .

(C) *Procedures to prevent reappearance.* A consumer reporting agency shall maintain reasonable procedures designed to prevent the reappearance in a consumer's file, and in consumer reports on the consumer, of information that is deleted pursuant to this paragraph. . . .
. . .

(b) *Statement of dispute.* If the reinvestigation does not resolve the dispute, the consumer may file a brief statement setting forth the nature of the dispute. The consumer reporting agency may limit such statements to not more than one hundred words if it provides the consumer with assistance in writing a clear summary of the dispute.

(c) *Notification of consumer dispute in subsequent consumer reports.* Whenever a statement of a dispute is filed, unless there is reasonable grounds to believe that it is frivolous or irrelevant, the consumer reporting agency shall, in any subsequent consumer report containing the information in question, clearly note that it is disputed by the consumer and provide either the consumer's statement or a clear and accurate codification or summary thereof.

. . .

§ 1681j. Procedure in case of disputed accuracy charges for certain disclosures

(a) *Free annual disclosure.*

(1) *Nationwide consumer reporting agencies.*

(A) *In general.* All consumer reporting agencies described in subsections (p) and (w) of section 1681a of this title shall make all disclosures pursuant to section 1681g of this title once during any 12-month period upon request of the consumer and without charge to the consumer.

(B) *Centralized source.* Subparagraph (A) shall apply with respect to a consumer reporting agency described in section 1681a(p) of this title only if the request from the consumer is made using the centralized source established for such purpose in accordance with section 211(c) of the Fair and Accurate Credit Transactions Act of 2003.

. . .

§ 1681m. Requirements on users of consumer reports

(a) *Duties of users taking adverse actions on the basis of information contained in consumer reports.* If any person takes any adverse action with respect to any consumer that is based in whole or in part on any information contained in a consumer report, the person shall—

(1) provide oral, written, or electronic notice of the adverse action to the consumer;

(2) provide to the consumer written or electronic disclosure—

(A) of a numerical credit score as defined in section 1681g(f)(2)(A) used by such person in taking any adverse action based in whole or in part on any information in a consumer report; . . .

. . .

(e) *Red flag guidelines and regulations required.*

(1) *Guidelines.* The Federal banking agencies, the National Credit Union Administration, the Federal Trade Commission, the Commodity Futures Trading Commission, and the Securities and Exchange Commission shall jointly, with respect to the entities that are subject to their respective enforcement authority under section 1681s—

(A) establish and maintain guidelines for use by each financial institution and each creditor regarding identity theft with respect to account holders at, or customers of, such entities, and update such guidelines as often as necessary; . . .

. . .

§ 1681n. Civil liability for willful noncompliance

(a) *In general.* Any person who willfully fails to comply with any requirement imposed under this title with respect to any consumer is liable to that consumer in an amount equal to the sum of—

    (1)

        (A) any actual damages sustained by the consumer as a result of the failure or damages of not less than $100 and not more than $1,000; or

        (B) in the case of liability of a natural person for obtaining a consumer report under false pretenses or knowingly without a permissible purpose, actual damages sustained by the consumer as a result of the failure or $1,000, whichever is greater;

    (2) such amount of punitive damages as the court may allow; and

    (3) in the case of any successful action to enforce any liability under this section, the costs of the action together with reasonable attorney's fees as determined by the court.

. . .

§ 1681o. Civil liability for negligent noncompliance

(a) *In general.* Any person who is negligent in failing to comply with any requirement imposed under this title with respect to any consumer is liable to that consumer in an amount equal to the sum of—

    (1) any actual damages sustained by the consumer as a result of the failure; and

    (2) in the case of any successful action to enforce any liability under this section, the costs of the action together with reasonable attorney's fees as determined by the court.

(b) *Attorney's fees.* On a finding by the court that an unsuccessful pleading, motion, or other paper filed in connection with an action under this section was filed in bad faith or for purposes of harassment, the court shall award to the prevailing party attorney's fees reasonable in relation to the work expended in responding to the pleading, motion, or other paper.

§ 1681s. Administrative enforcement

(a) *Enforcement by Federal Trade Commission.*

. . .

    (2) *Penalties.*

        (A) *Knowing violations.* Except as otherwise provided by subtitle B of the Consumer Financial Protection Act of 2010, in the event of a knowing violation, which constitutes a pattern or practice of violations of this title [15 U.S.C.S. § 1681 et seq.], the Federal Trade Commission may commence a civil action to recover a civil penalty in a district court of the United States against any person that violates this title. In such action, such person shall be liable for a civil penalty of not more than $2,500 per violation.

. . .

EQUAL CREDIT OPPORTUNITY ACT
15 U.S.C. § 1691 et seq.

§ 1691d. Applicability of other laws

(a) *Requests for signature of husband and wife for creation of valid lien, etc.* A request for the signature of both parties to a marriage for the purpose of creating a valid lien, passing clear title, waiving inchoate rights to property, or assigning earnings, shall not constitute discrimination under this title: Provided, however, That this provision shall not be construed to permit a creditor to take sex or marital status into account in connection with the evaluation of creditworthiness of any applicant.

(b) *State property laws affecting creditworthiness.* Consideration or application of State property laws directly or indirectly affecting creditworthiness shall not constitute discrimination for purposes of this title.

(c) *State laws prohibiting separate extension of consumer credit to husband and wife.* Any provision of State law which prohibits the separate extension of consumer credit to each party to a marriage shall not apply in any case where each party to a marriage voluntarily applies for separate credit from the same creditor. . . .

FAIR DEBT COLLECTION PRACTICES ACT
15 U.S.C. § 1692 et seq.

§ 1692a. Definitions

As used in this title—

(1) The term "Bureau" means the Bureau of Consumer Financial Protection.

(2) The term "communication" means the conveying of information regarding a debt directly or indirectly to any person through any medium.

(3) The term "consumer" means any natural person obligated or allegedly obligated to pay any debt.

(4) The term "creditor" means any person who offers or extends credit creating a debt or to whom a debt is owed, but such term does not include any person to the extent that he receives an assignment or transfer of a debt in default solely for the purpose of facilitating collection of such debt for another.

(5) The term "debt" means any obligation or alleged obligation of a consumer to pay money arising out of a transaction in which the money, property, insurance, or services which are the subject of the transaction are primarily for personal, family, or household purposes, whether or not such obligation has been reduced to judgment.

(6) The term "debt collector" means any person who uses any instrumentality of interstate commerce or the mails in any business the principal purpose of which is the collection of any debts, or who regularly collects or attempts to collect, directly or indirectly, debts owed or due or asserted to be owed or due another. Notwithstanding

the exclusion provided by clause (F) of the last sentence of this paragraph, the term includes any creditor who, in the process of collecting his own debts, uses any name other than his own which would indicate that a third person is collecting or attempting to collect such debts. For the purpose of section 1692f(6), such term also includes any person who uses any instrumentality of interstate commerce or the mails in any business the principal purpose of which is the enforcement of security interests. The term does not include—

(A) any officer or employee of a creditor while, in the name of the creditor, collecting debts for such creditor;

(B) any person while acting as a debt collector for another person, both of whom are related by common ownership or affiliated by corporate control, if the person acting as a debt collector does so only for persons to whom it is so related or affiliated and if the principal business of such person is not the collection of debts;

(C) any officer or employee of the United States or any State to the extent that collecting or attempting to collect any debt is in the performance of his official duties;

(D) any person while serving or attempting to serve legal process on any other person in connection with the judicial enforcement of any debt;

(E) any nonprofit organization which, at the request of consumers, performs bona fide consumer credit counseling and assists consumers in the liquidation of their debts by receiving payments from such consumers and distributing such amounts to creditors; and

(F) any person collecting or attempting to collect any debt owed or due or asserted to be owed or due another to the extent such activity (i) is incidental to a bona fide fiduciary obligation or a bona fide escrow arrangement; (ii) concerns a debt which was originated by such person; (iii) concerns a debt which was not in default at the time it was obtained by such person; or (iv) concerns a debt obtained by such person as a secured party in a commercial credit transaction involving the creditor.

(7) The term "location information" means a consumer's place of abode and his telephone number at such place, or his place of employment.

(8) The term "State" means any State, territory, or possession of the United States, the District of Columbia, the Commonwealth of Puerto Rico, or any political subdivision of any of the foregoing.

§ 1692c. Communication in connection with debt collection

(a) *Communication with the consumer generally.* Without the prior consent of the consumer given directly to the debt collector or the express permission of a court of competent jurisdiction, a debt collector may not communicate with a consumer in connection with the collection of any debt—

(1) at any unusual time or place or a time or place known or which should be known to be inconvenient to the consumer. In the absence of knowledge of circumstances to the contrary, a debt collector shall

assume that the convenient time for communicating with a consumer is after 8 o'clock antimeridian and before 9 o'clock postmeridian, local time at the consumer's location;

(2) if the debt collector knows the consumer is represented by an attorney with respect to such debt and has knowledge of, or can readily ascertain, such attorney's name and address, unless the attorney fails to respond within a reasonable period of time to a communication from the debt collector or unless the attorney consents to direct communication with the consumer; or

(3) at the consumer's place of employment if the debt collector knows or has reason to know that the consumer's employer prohibits the consumer from receiving such communication.

(b) *Communication with third parties.* Except as provided in section 1692b, without the prior consent of the consumer given directly to the debt collector, or the express permission of a court of competent jurisdiction, or as reasonably necessary to effectuate a postjudgment judicial remedy, a debt collector may not communicate, in connection with the collection of any debt, with any person other than the consumer, his attorney, a consumer reporting agency if otherwise permitted by law, the creditor, the attorney of the creditor, or the attorney of the debt collector.

(c) *Ceasing communication.* If a consumer notifies a debt collector in writing that the consumer refuses to pay a debt or that the consumer wishes the debt collector to cease further communication with the consumer, the debt collector shall not communicate further with the consumer with respect to such debt, except—

(1) to advise the consumer that the debt collector's further efforts are being terminated;

(2) to notify the consumer that the debt collector or creditor may invoke specified remedies which are ordinarily invoked by such debt collector or creditor; or

(3) where applicable, to notify the consumer that the debt collector or creditor intends to invoke a specified remedy. If such notice from the consumer is made by mail, notification shall be complete upon receipt.

(d) "Consumer" defined. For the purpose of this section, the term "consumer" includes the consumer's spouse, parent (if the consumer is a minor), guardian, executor, or administrator.

§ 1692d. Harassment or abuse

A debt collector may not engage in any conduct the natural consequence of which is to harass, oppress, or abuse any person in connection with the collection of a debt. Without limiting the general application of the foregoing, the following conduct is a violation of this section:

(1) The use or threat of use of violence or other criminal means to harm the physical person, reputation, or property of any person.

(2) The use of obscene or profane language or language the natural consequence of which is to abuse the hearer or reader.

(3) The publication of a list of consumers who allegedly refuse to pay debts, except to a consumer reporting agency or to persons meeting the requirements of section 1681a(f) or 1681b(a)(3).

(4) The advertisement for sale of any debt to coerce payment of the debt.

(5) Causing a telephone to ring or engaging any person in telephone conversation repeatedly or continuously with intent to annoy, abuse, or harass any person at the called number.

(6) Except as provided in section1692b, the placement of telephone calls without meaningful disclosure of the caller's identity.

§ 1692e. False or misleading representations

A debt collector may not use any false, deceptive, or misleading representation or means in connection with the collection of any debt. Without limiting the general application of the foregoing, the following conduct is a violation of this section:

(1) The false representation or implication that the debt collector is vouched for, bonded by, or affiliated with the United States or any State, including the use of any badge, uniform, or facsimile thereof.

(2) The false representation of—

(A) the character, amount, or legal status of any debt; or

(B) any services rendered or compensation which may be lawfully received by any debt collector for the collection of a debt.

(3) The false representation or implication that any individual is an attorney or that any communication is from an attorney.

(4) The representation or implication that nonpayment of any debt will result in the arrest or imprisonment of any person or the seizure, garnishment, attachment, or sale of any property or wages of any person unless such action is lawful and the debt collector or creditor intends to take such action.

(5) The threat to take any action that cannot legally be taken or that is not intended to be taken.

(6) The false representation or implication that a sale, referral, or other transfer of any interest in a debt shall cause the consumer to—

(A) lose any claim or defense to payment of the debt; or

(B) become subject to any practice prohibited by this title.

(7) The false representation or implication that the consumer committed any crime or other conduct in order to disgrace the consumer.

(8) Communicating or threatening to communicate to any person credit information which is known or which should be known to be false, including the failure to communicate that a disputed debt is disputed.

(9) The use or distribution of any written communication which simulates or is falsely represented to be a document authorized, issued, or approved by any court, official, or agency of the United States or any State, or which creates a false impression as to its source, authorization, or approval.

(10) The use of any false representation or deceptive means to collect or attempt to collect any debt or to obtain information concerning a consumer.

(11) The failure to disclose in the initial written communication with the consumer and, in addition, if the initial communication with the consumer is oral, in that initial oral communication, that the

debt collector is attempting to collect a debt and that any information obtained will be used for that purpose, and the failure to disclose in subsequent communications that the communication is from a debt collector, except that this paragraph shall not apply to a formal pleading made in connection with a legal action.

(12) The false representation or implication that accounts have been turned over to innocent purchasers for value. . . .

(14) The use of any business, company, or organization name other than the true name of the debt collector's business, company, or organization. . . .

§ 1692f. Unfair practices

A debt collector may not use unfair or unconscionable means to collect or attempt to collect any debt. Without limiting the general application of the foregoing, the following conduct is a violation of this section:

(1) The collection of any amount (including any interest, fee, charge, or expense incidental to the principal obligation) unless such amount is expressly authorized by the agreement creating the debt or permitted by law.

(2) The acceptance by a debt collector from any person of a check or other payment instrument postdated by more than five days unless such person is notified in writing of the debt collector's intent to deposit such check or instrument not more than ten nor less than three business days prior to such deposit.

(3) The solicitation by a debt collector of any postdated check or other postdated payment instrument for the purpose of threatening or instituting criminal prosecution.

(4) Depositing or threatening to deposit any postdated check or other postdated payment instrument prior to the date on such check or instrument.

(5) Causing charges to be made to any person for communications by concealment of the true purpose of the communication. Such charges include, but are not limited to, collect telephone calls and telegram fees.

(6) Taking or threatening to take any nonjudicial action to effect dispossession or disablement of property if—

   (A) there is no present right to possession of the property claimed as collateral through an enforceable security interest;

   (B) there is no present intention to take possession of the property; or

   (C) the property is exempt by law from such dispossession or disablement.

(7) Communicating with a consumer regarding a debt by post card.

(8) Using any language or symbol, other than the debt collector's address, on any envelope when communicating with a consumer by use of the mails or by telegram, except that a debt collector may use his business name if such name does not indicate that he is in the debt collection business.

§ 1692k. Civil liability

(a) *Amount of damages.* Except as otherwise provided by this section, any debt collector who fails to comply with any provision of this title with respect to any person is liable to such person in an amount equal to the sum of—

(1) any actual damage sustained by such person as a result of such failure;

(2)

(A) in the case of any action by an individual, such additional damages as the court may allow, but not exceeding $1,000; or

(B) in the case of a class action, (i) such amount for each named plaintiff as could be recovered under subparagraph (A), and (ii) such amount as the court may allow for all other class members, without regard to a minimum individual recovery, not to exceed the lesser of $500,000 or 1 per centum of the net worth of the debt collector; and

(3) in the case of any successful action to enforce the foregoing liability, the costs of the action, together with a reasonable attorney's fee as determined by the court. On a finding by the court that an action under this section was brought in bad faith and for the purpose of harassment, the court may award to the defendant attorney's fees reasonable in relation to the work expended and costs.

(b) *Factors considered by court.* In determining the amount of liability in any action under subsection (a), the court shall consider, among other relevant factors—

(1) in any individual action under subsection (a)(2)(A), the frequency and persistence of noncompliance by the debt collector, the nature of such noncompliance, and the extent to which such noncompliance was intentional; or

(2) in any class action under subsection (a)(2)(B), the frequency and persistence of noncompliance by the debt collector, the nature of such noncompliance, the resources of the debt collector, the number of persons adversely affected, and the extent to which the debt collector's noncompliance was intentional.

(c) *Intent.* A debt collector may not be held liable in any action brought under this title if the debt collector shows by a preponderance of evidence that the violation was not intentional and resulted from a bona fide error notwithstanding the maintenance of procedures reasonably adapted to avoid any such error. . . .

(d) *Jurisdiction.* An action to enforce any liability created by this title may be brought in any appropriate United States district court without regard to the amount in controversy, or in any other court of competent jurisdiction, within one year from the date on which the violation occurs. . . .

SECURED CREDIT BASICS

As discussed in Assignment 2, an unpaid secured creditor can seize property of the debtor by a process called *repossession*—a tool hapless unsecured creditors lack. But what does it mean to be a "secured creditor"? A secured creditor is one who holds a *lien* on certain property pledged by the debtor that will serve as *collateral* to secure the debt. A lien is a type of property right, contingent upon default. The collateral is owned by the debtor, the lien on it is "owned" (one usually says "held") by the secured creditor. Liens come in various flavors. Some are granted as a matter of law by statute, whether the debtor consents or not, such as to a local municipality upon a failure to pay property taxes; others are offered by the debtor voluntarily, such as a mortgage granted to a bank to entice it to loan the debtor money to buy a house. The term "security interest" is usually reserved for the subset of *voluntary liens* on *personal property*, the car loan being the classic example. UCC §§ 1-201(35), 9-109(a). ("Personal" property, if your school did not have a first-year Property course, is roughly all property that cannot be plowed.) A voluntary security interest in *real* property (that which can be plowed) is called a mortgage.

It may help to keep the debt conceptually distinct from the security interest. If David Debtor signs an I.O.U. for $1,000 to Clarice Creditor, that is a debt (unsecured). If he also signs a document that says, "I, David Debtor, grant to Clarice Creditor a security interest in my MacBook Air to secure my indebtedness to her of $1,000," then that is a *security agreement*. UCC §§ 9-201, 9-203. The latter is largely meaningless without the former, but when paired with the former transforms Clarice from unsecured to secured.

Why do debtors offer security? Sometimes it is the only way the lender will agree to the loan. Offering collateral also tends to make the loan cheaper than borrowing on an unsecured basis, which is part of the reason that mortgage interest rates and car-loan rates are lower than credit card rates. Creditors without security are "general" or "unsecured" creditors.

A security interest in personal property, like the classic car loan, is created by complying with the state-law requirements derived from Article 9 of the Uniform Commercial Code and usually stems from execution of a *security agreement*. UCC § 9-203. Creation of liens on real property, which Article 9 excludes, UCC § 9-109(d)(11), is the subject of much less uniform state laws that are usually more formal than Article 9—perhaps requiring witnessing or notarization. (The laws governing security interests and mortgages are generally taught in Commercial Law classes and are intimately involved in both state-law judgment enforcement and bankruptcy.) When a lien is created, we say that it *attaches* onto the collateral. Under the UCC, attachment generally requires that three conditions be met: (1) the debtor have rights in the collateral (i.e., own it or own an interest in it); (2) the secured creditor advance value (most often through a loan that can be defaulted upon to trigger the collection right); and (3) the debtor execute a security agreement. UCC § 9-203(a), (b). A valid security agreement must describe the collateral and be authenticated by the debtor. UCC § 9-203(b)(3)(A).

Collateral can be encumbered by multiple liens. You may have heard of first and second mortgages. Those rankings generally refer to their *priority*. There is generally no happy sharing of the collateral among the various lienholders upon debtor default: strict priority rules dictate who gets paid first, and only when the first-priority creditor is paid in full may the second-priority creditor get paid anything from the collateral's value, and so on down the food chain. UCC § 9-301 et seq., § 9-608. Once all those creditors get paid, the residual of the collateral's value—the *equity*—reverts to the debtor. UCC § 9-615(d)(1). Much of a secured credit course will be devoted to issues of priority, which of course has major significance in bankruptcy when not everyone will be getting paid.

When the debtor defaults upon a secured loan, we have already discussed that the secured creditor can repossess, either through peaceable repossession, or, if the debtor sleeps on the collateral with a gun, through obtaining a writ of *replevin* to dispossess the debtor. UCC § 9-609. But divesting a debtor of possession does not divest ownership. After all, it's still the debtor who owns the collateral, notwithstanding its encumbrance by a lien—even a lien so large that we describe the collateral as being "underwater" (meaning the amount of the lien exceeds the value of the collateral). Article 9 also gives the secured creditor the right upon default to sell the collateral and transfer ownership to a new buyer, including the secured creditor itself under some circumstances, and thereby *foreclose* upon the debtor's continued ownership rights. UCC § 9-610. This is similar to an execution sale conducted by the sheriff after a levy, but Article 9 allows the secured creditor to conduct the sale itself. Just as privately run repossessions must be done without breaching the peace, privately run sales must be done in a *commercially reasonable manner*. Id. A sale that violates that requirement will result in liability for the secured creditor, but, importantly, not otherwise void the sale. UCC § 9-625. This contrasts with many states' real estate foreclosure rules, which require the sale to be *confirmed* by a court before being finalized. Repossession is thus often a first step to an Article 9 sale, although many lenders don't want to sell the collateral; they just want the debtor to get back on repayment track, which is why a repo'd car can be reclaimed upon getting current on the loan (with repossession fees tacked on, of course).

The proceeds of an Article 9 sale get paid first to the creditor running the sale, and then further down the priority waterfall. Importantly for someone buying property at such a sale (and disappointing to junior secured creditors), any junior liens are *discharged*. UCC § 9-617. But senior liens—say, a first-priority lien on a sale conducted upon debtor default by the second-priority secured creditor—stay on the collateral, and buyers should beware. After any and all junior liens are paid off, the excess *surplus* from the sale proceeds gets paid to the debtor. More likely, however, the proceeds are not enough to pay off the lienholders, and so a *deficiency judgment* can be entered against the debtor in favor of the foreclosing secured creditor, meaning the debtor still has to pay that amount (unsecured, of course). UCC § 9-608. A secured creditor can generally *credit bid* at its own sale, meaning that if it is owed $5,000 secured by a car on a defaulted loan, it can make the opening bid of $5,000 at the Article 9 sale on credit, and not have to pay cash to itself. If it wants to bid $6,000, however, it must pay the final $1,000 in real cash, because those proceeds must go to the junior lienholder or debtor.

An attached security interest may be a *purchase-money security interest—PMSI* in the trade—which is a lien that arises when funds are loaned to purchase the collateral itself, such as a car acquisition loan. UCC § 9-103. (A non-PMSI loan arises when the collateral is already owned by the debtor before borrowing, such as when homeowners tap their home equity for aptly named "home equity loans," or when a borrower offers a watch to a pawnbroker.) If there is a PMSI and non-PMSI encumbering the same piece of collateral, generally the PMSI will have priority. UCC § 9-324.

An attached lien can also be, and usually is, *perfected*. UCC § 9-301 et seq. This typically entails the creditor registering it in a public record in a state office, thereby giving notice of the lien to the world, much the same way mortgages are often perfected by being *recorded* at the real estate registry in the appropriate county office. For voluntary security interests, the UCC provides its own registration system, usually in some-place like a Secretary of State's office, and there are forms specified in the UCC called a "Financing Statement" or "UCC1" that provide for places to list the debtor's name, the secured party's name, the collateral encumbered by the lien, and so forth. UCC § 9-521. Perfection is a smart move because it cements a lien's power. For example, an unperfected lien can lose out to a subsequently perfected lien, reversing the general rule with liens that first in time is first in right. UCC § 9-322. Even more importantly, an unperfected lien of any sort is likely to be *avoided* (nullified) in a debtor's bankruptcy case, leaving the creditor unsecured. 11 U.S.C. § 544. Although registration is the most important method of perfection for personal property collateral, there are others as well. In particular, possession of tangible collateral perfects security interests, so a pawnbroker's lien both attaches and is simultaneously perfected when the borrower turns over the watch. UCC §§ 9-203(b)(3)(B), 9-313. And some liens have special perfection rules. For example, liens on motor vehicles are not usually perfected through the UCC system (unless inventory on a dealer's lot) but are done through notation on the motor vehicle's *certificate of title*. UCC § 9-311(a)(2).

Suffice it to say, secured credit gives leverage. Secured creditors rely on their collateral to improve the chances that they will be repaid. If the debtor defaults on the debt, the secured creditor may repossess the collateral. Seizing the debtor's property tends to have a focusing effect on the need to comply with payment obligations. For example, if the collateral is a car the debtor needs to get to work, that is a debt high on the debtor's list to be paid. In addition to priority, a lien may give a creditor a certain amount of control—or at least influence—over a debtor. The common comment, "Oh, the bank owns my house," is inaccurate legally but conveys a popular idea that someone with a mortgage has a powerful position vis-à-vis a debtor (and other creditors). In various ways, that power position will appear as an important factor in the real-world functioning of the law of debtors and creditors. It stands in contrast to the powerlessness inherent in the cost and delay of enforcing unsecured debt through the courts and in the low-return dividends on unsecured debt in bankruptcy, especially liquidation proceedings. But that is beyond the scope of this primer, so we will stop.

TABLE OF CASES

TABLE OF STATUTES
AND REGULATIONS

INDEX